D0635827

Encyclopedia
of
SOUTHERN BAPTISTS

Encyclopedia of SOUTHERN BAPTISTS

III

BROADMAN PRESS
Nashville, Tennessee

4265-11

ISBN: 0-8054-6511-1

Dewey Decimal classification number: 286.03
Library of Congress catalog card number 58-5417
Printed in the United States of America

IN MEMORIAM

DAVIS COLLIER WOOLLEY
1908–1971

EDITORIAL COMMITTEE

THE GENERAL COMMITTEE

I. Southern Baptist Convention Agencies

AMERICAN BAPTIST THEOLOGICAL SEMINARY
Burns, Herman Franklin, B.A.
Retired, former Manager, Art Department, Baptist Sunday School Board

ANNUITY BOARD
Bloskas, John D., B.A.
Director, Publications and Communications

BAPTIST JOINT COMMITTEE ON PUBLIC AFFAIRS
Garrett, Wilkins Barry, M.A., Th.M.
Director, Information Services

BAPTIST WORLD ALLIANCE
Bryant, Cyril Eric, Jr., A.B.
Director, Publications

BROTHERHOOD COMMISSION
Jennings, H. Roy, B.A.
Program Manager

CHRISTIAN LIFE COMMISSION
Craig, Floyd Allen, A.B., B.D.
Director, Public Relations

EDUCATION COMMISSION
Brantley, Rabun Lee, M.A., Ph.D.
Retired, former Executive Secretary

EXECUTIVE COMMITTEE
Fields, Wilmer Clemont, Th.M., Th.D.
Public Relations Secretary

FOREIGN MISSION BOARD
Fletcher, Jesse Conrad, Th.D.
Director, Mission Support Division

GOLDEN GATE BAPTIST THEOLOGICAL SEMINARY
Carleton, William Augustus, Th.M., Th.D.
Retired, former Dean and Professor of Church History

HISTORICAL COMMISSION
May, Lynn Edward, Jr., M.A., Th.D.
Research Director

HOME MISSION BOARD
Rutledge, Arthur Bristow, Th.D., D.D.
Executive Secretary-Treasurer

MIDWESTERN BAPTIST THEOLOGICAL SEMINARY
Wamble, Gaston Hugh, B.D., Th.D.
Professor of Church History

NEW ORLEANS BAPTIST THEOLOGICAL SEMINARY
Howe, Claude Leodis, Jr., M.S., Th.D.
Professor of Church History

RADIO AND TELEVISION COMMISSION
Duncan, Clarence Edgar, Jr., B.J.
Associate Executive Director

SEMINARY EXTENSION DEPARTMENT
Rigdon, Raymond May, Jr., B.D., Th.D.
Director

SOUTHERN BAPTIST FOUNDATION
Berry, Kendall, B.J.
Executive Secretary-Treasurer

SOUTHERN BAPTIST HOSPITALS, INC.
Blackmon, Charles Edmond, B.A., B.D.
Assistant Executive Secretary-Treasurer

SOUTHEASTERN BAPTIST THEOLOGICAL SEMINARY
Blackmore, James Herrall, B.D., Ph.D.
Director, Publications

SOUTHERN BAPTIST THEOLOGICAL SEMINARY
St. Amant, Clyde Penrose, Th.D., Ph.D., D.D., LL.D.
Professor of Church History

SOUTHWESTERN BAPTIST THEOLOGICAL SEMINARY
Baker, Robert Andrew, Th.D., Ph.D.
Professor of Church History

STEWARDSHIP COMMISSION
Allison, F. Paul, B.A.
Director, Communications

SUNDAY SCHOOL BOARD
Colson, Howard Paul, Th.M., Ph.D.
Editorial Secretary

II. Woman's Missionary Union

Hunt, Alma Fay, B.S., M.A.
Executive Secretary

III. State Conventions

ALABAMA
Allen, Lee Norcross, M.S., Ph.D.
Faculty/Administrator, Samford University

ALASKA
Miller, Richard Alvey, M.A., B.D.
Pastor, O'Malley Road Baptist Mission, Anchorage

ARIZONA
McKay, Charles Lloyd, Th.M., Th.D.
Pastor, First Southern Baptist Church, Scottsdale

ARKANSAS
Hinson, Thomas Alva, B.A., M.A.
Pastor, First Baptist Church, West Memphis

CALIFORNIA
Young, John Terry, B.D., Th.D.
Editor, *The California Southern Baptist*

COLORADO
Bayless, Ovid Luer, D.D.
Editor, *Rocky Mountain Baptist*

DISTRICT OF COLUMBIA
Langley, James Arthur, B.A., Th.D.
Executive Secretary, District of Columbia Baptist Convention

FLORIDA
Armour, Rollin Stely, S.T.M., Th.D.
Professor, Stetson University

GEORGIA
Webb, Lawrence Eugene, B.S., B.D.
Secretary, Public Relations, Baptist Convention of the State of Georgia

HAWAII
Walker, Edmond Richmond, Th.M., Th.D.
Executive Secretary, Hawaii Baptist Convention

INDIANA
Taylor, Kenneth Edwin, B.A.
Pastor, Pleasant Heights Baptist Church, Indianapolis

ILLINOIS
Dillow, Myron Delene, B.A., Th.M.
Pastor, First Baptist Church, Harrisburg

KANSAS
Westmoreland, Newton Jackson, B.A., D.D.
Former Executive Secretary, Kansas Convention of Southern Baptists

KENTUCKY
Crismon, Leo Taylor, M.S.L.S., Ph.D.
Librarian, Southern Baptist Theological Seminary

LOUISIANA
Alley, John Gallemore, B.A., B.D.
Pastor, First Baptist Church, Jonesboro

MARYLAND
Ryals, DeLane Marlin, A.B., B.D.
Pastor, West Monmouth Baptist Chapel, Freehold, New Jersey

MICHIGAN
Hubbs, Frederick David, B.A., D.D.
Former Executive Secretary, Baptist State Convention of Michigan, now Associate Executive Secretary, Missouri Baptist Convention

MISSISSIPPI
McLemore, Richard Aubrey, Ph.D., LL.D.
Director, Mississippi Department of Archives and History

MISSOURI
McCarty, Doran Chester, B.D., Th.D.
Associate Professor of Theology, Midwestern Baptist Theological Seminary

NEW MEXICO
Bergstrom, Herbert Eugene, B.D., Th.D.
Pastor, Parkland Baptist Church, Clovis

NEW YORK
James, Paul Spencer, B.A., Th.M.
Executive Secretary, Baptist Convention of New York

NORTH CAROLINA
Fisher, Benjamin Coleman, B.A., B.D., LL.D.
Executive Secretary, Education Commission of the Southern Baptist Convention, formerly Executive Secretary, Commission on Christian Higher Education, North Carolina Baptist State Convention

NORTHERN PLAINS (Montana, North Dakota, South Dakota, Wyoming)
Baker, John Pennington, B.A.
Executive Secretary-Treasurer, Northern Plains Baptist Convention

NORTHWEST (Oregon-Washington)
Grubbs, William Eugene, B.D., Th.D.
Former Executive Secretary, Baptist General Convention of Oregon-Washington, now Foreign Mission Board Consultant of Laymen Overseas

OHIO

Moore, Lamire Holden, B.A.
Editor, *Ohio Baptist Messenger*

OKLAHOMA

Gaskin, Jesse Marvin, A.B.
Pastor, First Baptist Church, Durant

SOUTH CAROLINA

Cloer, Daniel Webster, Th.M., Th.D.
Pastor, First Baptist Church, Lancaster

TENNESSEE

Kendall, William Frederick, Th.M., Ph.D.
Executive Secretary, Tennessee Baptist Convention

TEXAS

Baker, Robert Andrew, Th.D., Ph.D.
Professor of Church History, Southwestern Baptist Theological Seminary

UTAH-IDAHO

Welsh, Darwin Edward, B.A.
Executive Secretary, Utah-Idaho Southern Baptist Convention

VIRGINIA

Moore, John Sterling, B.A., Th.M.
Pastor, Manly Memorial Baptist Church, Lexington

WEST VIRGINIA

Tallant, Francis Rodman, B.A., Th.M.
Director, Christian Education, West Virginia Convention of Southern Baptists

IV. Special Areas

BIBLE

Brown, Raymond Bryan, S.T.M., Th.D.
Professor of New Testament Interpretation, Southeastern Baptist Theological Seminary

CHURCH ADMINISTRATION AND RELIGIOUS EDUCATION

Landry, Sabin P., Jr., J.D., Th.D.
Professor of Religious Education, Southern Baptist Theological Seminary

CHURCH MUSIC

Sims, Walter Hines, M.A., D.Mus.
Retired, former Secretary of Church Music Department, Baptist Sunday School Board of the Southern Baptist Convention

ETHICS AND SOCIAL CONCERN

Valentine, Foy Dan, Th.D., D.D.
Executive Secretary, Christian Life Commission of the Southern Baptist Convention

EVANGELISM

Havlik, John Franklin, B.D., Th.M.
Associate Director, Division of Evangelism, Home Mission Board of the Southern Baptist Convention

HISTORY

St. Amant, Clyde Penrose, M.A., Th.D., Ph.D., LL.D.
Professor of Church History, Southern Baptist Theological Seminary

MISSIONS

Falls, Helen Emery, M.A., M.R.E., Ed.D.
Professor of Missions, New Orleans Baptist Theological Seminary

OTHER BAPTIST BODIES

McBeth, Harry Leon, B.D., Th.D.
Associate Professor of Church History, Southwestern Baptist Theological Seminary

PASTORAL CARE

Segler, Franklin Morgan, Th.M., Th.D.
Professor of Pastoral Care, Southwestern Baptist Theological Seminary

PREACHING

Brown, Henry Clifton, Jr. (Cochairman) B.D., Th.D.
Professor of Preaching, Southwestern Baptist Theological Seminary

Cotey, Haddon Eugene (Cochairman) B.D., Th.D.
Pastor, First Baptist Church, Murfreesboro, Tennessee

Matthews, Charles DeWitt, Jr. (Cochairman) Th.M., Th.D.
Professor of Preaching, Midwestern Baptist Theological Seminary

SPECIAL ARTICLES

Patterson, William Morgan, B.A., Th.D.
Professor of Church History, Southern Baptist Theological Seminary

STATISTICS

Bradley, Martin Bird, B.S.
Secretary, Research and Statistics Department, Sunday School Board

STEWARDSHIP

Moore, Merrill Dennis, Jr., Th.M., D.D.
Retired, former Executive Director-Treasurer, Stewardship Commission of the Southern Baptist Convention

THEOLOGY

Tull, James E., M.A., Th.M., Ph.D.
Professor of Theology, Southeastern Baptist Theological Seminary

CONTRIBUTORS

Abernathy, John Arch
Abrams, Joseph Robert, Jr.
Acton, Hul-cee Marcus
Alexander, David Kay
Allen, Clifton Judson
Allen, Lee Norcross
Alley, John Gallemore
Alley, Reuben Edward, Sr.
Anderson, David Greene
Anderson, Park Harris, Jr.
Anderson, Wallace Edward
Appleton, Jon Gilbert
Archer, Cecil Edward
Armour, Rollin Stely
Armstrong, Ruth Martin
 (Mrs. Noel E.)
Atchison, Ray Morris
Atkins, Willie Clyde

Baggett, Hudson
Bagley, George Edwin
Bailey, Hugh Coleman
Bailey, Joe Weldon
Baker, John Wesley
Baker, Robert Andrew
Baker, William Lewis
Baldwin, Vanita M.
Ballenger, Isam Earl
Banks, Robert Thomas, Jr.
Barry, James Clinton
Basden, James
Batts, Henry Lewis
Baumgartner, Leslie
 Raymond
Bayless, Ovid Luer
Beckett, Charles Austin
Bee, Fanna Kees
Belew, Marion Wendell
Bell, Arthur Donald
Belote, James Dalby
Bennett, George Willis
Bennett, Hal Durward
Bennett, Harold Clark
Bennett, Howard Clifton
Bergstrom, Herbert Eugene
Berry, Kendall
Bethea, Ralph Chambers
Bidstrup, Mary O.
Bishop, Chester Lee
Bjorkman, Nadine Baker
Blackmon, Charles Edmond
Blackmon, George Truett
Blackmore, James Herrall
Bland, Thomas Albert
Blankenship, Harold Lewis
Blattner, Robert Eugene
Bloskas, John D.
Bowen, Olga
Bowling, Lura Springer
 (Mrs. Leslie Monroe)
Boyce, William Arthur
Boyd, Robert Melville
Boyd, William Edley
Bradley, James Curtis
Bradley, Martin Bird
Brady, Mrs. Otis Walter
Bragg, Eugene
Bramlette, William
 Howard, Jr.
Brantley, Mrs. Elizabeth
 Jones
Brantley, Rabun Lee
Brantley, Russell Harold, Jr.
Braswell, George Wilbur, Jr.
Braswell, Glen Edward
Brickle, Archie William
Brooks, Lamar Judson
Brooks, Richard Donoho
Brown, Archie Earl
Brown, Betty Jean
Brown, Ernest Emory, Sr.
Brown, Frances Elizabeth
Brown, Henry Clifton, Jr.
Brown, Raymond Bryan
Brown, S. Autry
Bruce, H. E.
Brumley, Chester Wilson, Sr.
Bryant, Cyril Eric, Jr.
Bryant, James Raleigh
Brymer, Jack Edward, Sr.
Bugg, Charles Basil
Bullard, George Woodrow
Bulson, George Leslie, Jr.
Burcham, Arthur
Burns, Herman Franklin

Cadwallader, Chester
 Samuel, Jr.
Caldwell, Maurice Laron
Callaway, Joseph Atlee
Cameron, Harold Edward
Camp, Berniece
Campbell, Robert Clinton
Canaday, James Alvin
Canafax, Jess Lee
Canning, Charlotte
 Dinsmore (Mrs. John R.)
Cantrell, James Clifton
Carleton, William Augustus
Carpenter, Kathryn Ellen
*Carroll, Cecil Benion
Carter, James Edward
Carter, John
Carter, S. Felton
Carter, Thomas Edwin
Cary, Mrs. Mabel Risse
Cathey, Wheeler Clifton
Caudill, Robert Paul
Causey, Joseph Newman
Cauthen, Baker James
Chenault, Bertie J.
Childress, Irving
Christian, John Richard
Clement, Alberic Samuel
Clendinning, Byron A., Jr.
Cloer, Daniel Webster
Coffey, Rufus
Cole, James Franklin
Coleman, Lucien Edwin, Jr.
Coleman, Robert Oliver
Collier, Earl Matthews
Collins, Lloyd Wesley
Colson, Howard Paul
Colson, William Henry
Compere, William Lowrey
Compton, Bobby Dale
Conger, Helen
Conner, Ray
Conway, Florrie Jewell
Cook, Donald Eugene
Cook, Melva
Cooper, Clifton Earl
Cooper, Roy E.
Corder, Benjamin Loyd
*Corum, Betty Jo
Cotey, Haddon Eugene
Cox, Ashley P., Jr.
Cox, Carey Edward
Cox, Ola Shipp (Mrs. Elmo)
Cox, Joseph Powhatan
Craig, Floyd Allen
Craig, Robert E.
Crane, Harold Elroy, Jr.

Crane, James Dreher
Crawley, James Winston
Crismon, Leo Taylor
Cromer, William Rush, Jr.
Croslin, Harrison C.
Cross, Irvie Keil
Crowe, John Marvin
Crow, Hilton Jones (Mrs. G. D.)
Crumpler, Earl Dean
Culpepper, Hugo Hurlston
Cummins, George Walton
Cuthbertson, William Welsh

Dalrymple, Guy H.
Daniel, James Harris
Davis, William Penn
Dawson, Irvin
Day, Kenneth
Dayringer, Richard Lee
Deusner, Charles Ford
DeVault, Doris
Dickson, Charles William
Dilday, Russell Hooper
Dillow, Don Eugene
Dillow, Myron Delene
Dixon, Robert Ernest
Dobbs, Hubert Lee
Dorsey, Luther Fred
Douglas, Ralph Lee
Douglass, Robert Satterfield
Draughon, Walter D., Jr.
Druin, Toby
DuBose, Francis Marquis
Duncan, Clarence Edgar, Jr.
Duncan, James O.

Eaves, James Franklin
Eddins, John William, Jr.
Edge, Findley Bartow
Edwards, Clarence Henry
Edwards, Walter Ross
Eklund, Ryan Bellman, Jr.
Elder, James Lyn
Elliff, James Thomas
Elliott, John Hackett, Jr.
Eskew, Harry Lee
Estep, William Roscoe, Jr.
Estes, Joseph Aubrey
Estes, Joseph Richard
Euting, George Lee
Evans, J. N., Jr.

Fallis, William Joseph
Falls, Helen Emery
Farmer, Arthur E.
Farmer, Darwin Ono
Fendley, Kenneth Claiborne
Ferguson, Leonard
Field, Aletha Taylor (Mrs. Harold Glen)
Fields, Marion Horace
Fields, Wilmer Clemont
Fincher, John Albert
Fisher, Benjamin Coleman
Fisher, James Wilson
Fletcher, Jesse Conrad
Flynn, Jean Martin
Flynt, James Wayne
Ford, Agnes Gibbs (Mrs. Arthur T.)
Ford, Leroy
Forman, Charles William
Fowler, Franklin Thomas
Fox, Baynard Francis
Fox, Clyde L.
Freeman, C. Wade
Fuller, Elizabeth Bates (Mrs. Ellis A.)
Fuson, Robert Cecil, Jr.
Fusselle, Warner Earle

Gabhart, Herbert Conway
Gardner, Robert Granville
Garrett, David
Garrett, James Leo, Jr.
Garrett, Wilkins Barry, Jr.
Gaskin, Jesse Marvin
Gaylor, Leon
Giddens, Howard Peterson
Gill, Rachel Truex (Mrs. Everett, Jr.)
Gilleland, Roy James, Jr.
Gillham, Moudy Frank
Ginn, Mrs. Douglas Jones
Glass, Victor Thomas
Goeller, Patricia Hiett (Mrs. Harry W., Jr.)
Goerner, Henry Cornell
Goff, Cecil Grant
Goldfinch, Sydney, Sr.
Goodson, Carl Edward
Groner, Frank Shelby
Gorton, Dan
Gray, Clarence Jones
Gray, Elmer Leslie
Gray, Lloyd Jack
Green, John Wesley
Green, Joseph Franklin, Jr.
Greer, Genevieve
Gregg, James Merryman
Gresham, Felix Morris
Griffith, Luther Orbra
Grigg, Wendell Randolph, Sr.
Grijalva, Joshua
Grizzard, Richard Stuart
Groves, Florence Belle
Gruver, Kate Ellen
Guffin, Gilbert Lee
Guston, Gustaf David

Hackley, Woodford Broadus
Hall, Dick Houston, Jr.
Hallock, Edgar Francis, Jr.
Hamilton, Mary Elizabeth Miller (Mrs. Lawrence E.)
Hamlet, Charles Buck III
Hamm, Glynn Paul
Hammett, Horace Greeley
Hansen, Keith Leyton
Harding, Earl O.
Harrell, Flynn Thomas
Harrell, William Asa
Harris, Robert Lawson
Harris, Thomas Lafayette
Harwell, Jack Upchurch
Hastings, Robert Jean
Hatfield, Lawson Gerald
Havlik, John Franklin
Hawkins, Aubrey Lamar
Hayes, Herman Paul
Hearnes, Betty Cooper (Mrs. Warren)
Heeren, Forrest Henry
Heilman, Earl Bruce
Helmbold, F Wilbur
Henderson, Eula Mae
Hendricks, William Lawrence
Hensley, John Clark
Herndon, George Collins
Herndon, Jesse Dee
Hess, Ruth Tucker
Hester, Harry Odell
Hester, Hubert Inman
Hewitt, Lawrence Purser
Hill, Eugene Lowell
Hill, Leonard Edmund
Hill, Louise Heirich (Mrs. Eugene L.)
Hinson, E. Glenn
Hixson, George Samuel
Hollis, Harry Newcombe, Jr.
Hollon, Ellis Wing, Jr.
Hook, James Don
Hopkins, Evelyn Elliott
Horne, Chevis Ferber
Hough, Raymond Franklin, Jr.
Householder, Lloyd Thomas
Howard, Henry Jacob
Howe, Claude Leodis, Jr.
Howse, William Lewis
Howse, William Lewis III
Hoyland, Mrs. Eunice
Hudgins, Ira Durwood
Hughey, John David, Jr.
Hunke, Edmund William, Jr.
Hunt, Joseph Franklin
Hunt, Thomas Webb
Hunt, William Boyd
Hurst, Harold Edward
Hurt, John Jeter, Jr.
Huss, John E.
Hutchens, Elizabeth Glenn
Hyatt, Cecil Maynard

Ingle, Clifford
Ingraham, Harold Edward
Irwin, Leonard Gayle

Jackson, Hermione Dannelly
Jackson, Robert Scott
James, Paul Spencer
Jeffers, John Henry
Jenkins, Glenn Allen

Jennings, Roy
Johns, Thomas Maxwell
Johnson, George Lee
Johnson, Gus
Johnson, Roy Lee
Johnston, Edwin
Joiner, Edward Earl
Jones, Jim Owen
Jones, Terry Lawrence

Keel, David
Keith, Edmond Dale
Kelly, Ernest Earl, Jr.
Kelm, George Leslie
Kendall, William Frederick
Kennedy, James Hardee
Kerr, David Eugene
Kidd, Gene
Kilgore, Robert H.
Kimbler, George Harvey
King, Bernard Dodson
King, Herman Leslie
King, Joe Madison
King, Spencer Bidwell, Jr.
King, Theron Hartis
Kirkland, Paul Gilbert
Knapton, Mary Therese (Mrs. Roger W.)
Kunkel, Martha White

Lambert, Paul M.
Lamm, Wilbur Clayton
Landers, William Houston
Lang, Thomas Freeman
Lannom, Eura Clemons (Mrs. George Ellis, Sr.)
Latta, Roderick Donald
Leeper, James Frederick
Leininger, Louis Lee
Lemons, Charles Chester
Lee, Dallas McInteer
Lemke, Mrs. Anita
Lester, James Adams
Levering, Rosalind Robinson (Mrs. Wilson K., Jr.)
Lindsay, Homer Gentry, Sr.
Looney, Floyd
Lott, Janie Mae
Lovell, Samuel George, Jr.
Luck, Joe Fred
Lumpkin, William Latane
Lycan, Gilbert Lester

Macon, Emily Bodden (Mrs. Leon Meertief)
Magruder, Eva Mae (Mrs. Charles E.)
Markham, O. C.
Martin, Buell Jean
Martin, Sara Hines (Mrs. David L.)
Mashburn, Sarah
Maston, Harold Eugene
Matthews, Charles DeWitt, Jr.
May, Lynn Edward, Jr.

McBeth, Harry Leon
McCall, Duke Kimbrough
McCall, Louis Edmund
McCartney, Mrs. Mable Holmes
McCarty, Doran Chester
McClain, Howard Gordon
McClellan, Albert Alfred
McConnell, Harry Cecil
McCullin, Charles
McCullough, Glendon
McDaniel, Arlie Leo, Sr.
McDonald, Edward Fredrick, Jr.
McDonald, Erwin Lawrence
McGahey, Bessie Spraggins (Mrs. Harold E.)
McGee, William Kay
McGinty, Hilary Herbert
McGowan, David Henry
McIlveene, Charles Steele
McKay, Charles Lloyd
McKinney, Raymond Andrew
McLaughlin, Charles Priddy
McLemore, Richard Aubrey
McReynolds, James Evans
McWilliams, Anne Washburn (Mrs. William D.)
Means, Frank Kester
Meigs, James Thomas
Mercer, Moses Eli
Merritt, Frances Lewis
Miller, Jones Ivey
Miller, Richard Alvey
Miller, Roscoe C., Jr.
Mills, Dottson Legrand
Mills, John Edwin
Monroe, Doris Driggers
Moody, Jesse Con
Moore, David Otto
Moore, John Allen
Moore, John Sterling
Moore, Lamire Holden
Moore, Merrill Dennis
Moore, Ralph Rutherford
Moore, Roy Lee, Jr.
Moratto, Marjorie Inez (Mrs. H. V.)
Morrison, Thomas Henry, Jr.
Moseley, Fred Baker
Mosteller, James Donovan
Moulton, Lynne Dianne
Murdoch, John Cochran
Murphy, Nicy Elizabeth
Myers, William Truett

Nash, Edwin Wycliffe, Jr.
Nees, Hugh
Nelson, Thomas Wheeler
Ness, Rowland McDowell
Newton, Joseph Allen
Nielsen, Richard Elmer
Nishikawa, Itsuko Sue (Mrs. Nobuo)
Noonkester, James Ralph
Norton, George Edgar
Norwood, Josephine Carroll
Nunnery, Paul Nash

Oates, Wayne Edward
Odle, Joe Taft
Oliver, Albert Benjamin
Oliver, Ellen Douglas
Overton, Carl McKinley

Page, Wendell Lee
Palmer, Gerald Burton
Parker, Hankins Fred
Parker, Lowell Bill
Parks, Robert Keith
Paschall, Henry Franklin
Patterson, Frank Willard
Patterson, I. N.
Patterson, Roberta Mae Turner
Patterson, William Morgan
Paulette, Richard Carrington
Perkins, John Wesley, Jr.
Peterson, Walfred Hugo
Pettus, Herschel Crockett
Phillips, J. Theodore
Pillow, Jerome Baird
Pinson, William Meredith, Jr.
Poerschke, Robert Ernst
Ponder, James Alton
Poole, William Augustus
Porter, Lee
Porter, Willis Hubert
Price, George Norman
Proctor, Robert Allen, Jr.
Pryor, Dorothy Marion
Puckett, Richard Gene
Pugh, Reuben Quinn
Purvis, George Elmo

Randolph, Grady Lonzo
Ray, Cecil Armstrong
Ray, Melba Little (Mrs. Walter A.)
Redford, Courts
Reid, Avery Hamilton
Reid, Ruby Vardamen (Mrs. Avery Hamilton)
Reynolds, William Jensen
Richardson, Charles Ray
Richardson, Darrell Coleman
Ricker, George E.
Riddle, George William
Rigdon, Raymond May, Jr.
Riggs, William Russell
Risenhoover, Carmel C.
Roberts, John Elgin
Roden, Charles P.
Rogers, Albert Nash
Rogers, Karleen Hill (Mrs. Glenn W.)
Rone, Wendell Holmes, Sr.

Roof, Mary Lou Menscer (Mrs. Colie W.)
Roselle, Charles M.
Rouse, John Edward
Royce, Philip Lee
Rust, Ray Pearce
Rutledge, Arthur Bristow
Ryals, DeLane Marlin
Ryland, Charles Hill

Sadler, George Washington
Sanders, Albert Neely
Sanders, Davis Milton
Sanders, Harold Glen
Sandlin, Bryce Neal
Sapp, James Morrison
Saunders, Marjorie
Scaggs, Paul A., Sr.
Scantlan, Samuel William
Scott, John Daniel
Scott, Quentin Lowell
Seelig, John Earl
Segler, Franklin Morgan
Selph, Bernes K.
Shackleton, Jack Shields
Shamburger, William Marsh
Sheehy, Linda Anne (Mrs. John E.)
Shelley, Bruce Leon
Shereda, Joseph Jerry
Shipman, Edward
Shirey, Robert Hobson
Shoemake, Howard Lee
Short, Mary Fulmer (Mrs. James Aubrey)
Sibley, J. Melburn, Jr.
Sims, Walter Hines
Sinclair, Helen
Skaggs, Jay Lynn
Sloan, Bluford M.
Smith, Budd Elmon
Smith, Harry Vaughn, Sr.
Smith, Ralph Lee
Smith, Robert Eugene
Smothers, Hubert Bon
Snead, William Roswell
Snedden, John Israel
Sneed, John Everett
Somerville, Wendell C.
South, Gilbert Eugene
Southerland, James Edward
Southern, John Albert
Spell, Howard Edgar
Spencer, Alvin Elbert, Jr.
Springer, Rudolph Arden
Stagg, Frank
Stainback, Arthur House
St. Amant, Clyde Penrose
Stanberry, James Phillip
Stephens, Mary Essie
Stephenson, Richard Murrell
Stewart, Jonas Lee
Stith, Milton Chandler
Stocksdale, Alan H.
Stokes, James Porter
Stone, Eugenia Wootton
Stowe, Darty F.
Stracener, William Guy
Strickland, Phil Dowell
Sutton, Roy F.
Swindall, Harold Wayne
Swope, Harold Lee

Tallant, Francis Rodman
Tanner, William Graydon
Taura, Arvin Katsuro
Taylor, Raymond Hargus
Taylor, Page
Tegenfeldt, Herman Gustaf
Tennison, Grayson C.
Thompson, James William
Thornton, Everett Whitfield
Tidsworth, Floyd, Jr.
Tippett, John T.
Todd, Wayne Edward
Tonks, Alfred Ronald
Torbett, Velma Rhea
Trentham, Charles Arthur
Tripp, Edgar Franklin
Trotter, Donald F.
Tucker, Robert Cinnamond
Tull, James E.
Turpin, Calvin Coolidge

Underwood, Cecil Talmadge

Valentine, Foy Dan
Vardeman, Ephraim Jeremiah
Vice, Cline Lowell
Vinzant, Carey Truett
Vinzant, Marion McGinty (Mrs. C. T.)
Virt, Eugene
Von Hagen, Keith Croswell

Wagner, William Lyle
Wagoner, Walter Raleigh
Waldrop, Homer
Waldrup, Rufus Earl
Walker, Arthur L.
Walker, Arthur Lonzo, Jr.
Walker, Charles Robert
Walker, Edmond Richmond
* Wallace, William D.
Walraven, Flora Irene
Wamble, Gaston Hugh
Wardin, Albert William, Jr.
Warren, Casper Carl
Washburn, Alphonso Victor, Jr.
Watson, Emerson Cleveland, Jr.
Watson, Harry Kern
Watson, William Joe
Watts, James Washington
Waud, Gilbert Burton
Wayland, John Terrill
Weaver, Oliver Cornelius
Weaver, William K.
Webb, Justine Truman
Webb, Lawrence Eugene
Weber, Paul, Jr.
West, Elmer Stone, Jr.
Westmoreland, Newton Jackson
Wheeler, George Edward
Wilkes, John Mannen
Wilkinson, Mike
Williams, Burton Eugene
Williams, Emmett Jackson
Williams, James D.
Williams, John Hayden
Williams, Philmore Eugene
Williams, Ted White
Willis, John Alfred
Wills, Keith Cameron
Wilson, Berner Freeman, Jr.
Wilson, Blodwen Jones (Mrs. G. R.)
Wilson, George Raymond, Sr.
Wilson, Robert Bruce
Winders, Ralph Bishop
Wise, Gene Hale
Wood, Levi Davis
Wood, Rudolph Malcolm
Woodward, Robert Franklin
Woofter, Edna Ruth
Woolf, Elbert Warren
* Woolley, Davis Collier
Wright, Charles I.

Yearby, Paul Vernon
Yelvington, Louise Durham (Mrs. Ramsey)
Young, Mrs. James Madderson, Jr.
Young, John Terry
Yount, Hubert Ray

* *Deceased*

INTRODUCTION
TO
VOLUME III

SINCE THE PUBLICATION of Volumes I and II in 1958, the ENCYCLOPEDIA OF SOUTHERN BAPTISTS has proven its validity and utility as a comprehensive, authentic source of information on Baptists in general and Southern Baptists in particular. The ENCYCLOPEDIA has provided Southern Baptists, as well as those interested in them, with historical insight, objective evaluation, and adequate information for a consistent understanding of Southern Baptists—their past and present life and their work. By the end of 1970 almost twelve thousand sets of the initial volumes were in circulation. The ENCYCLOPEDIA has been widely utilized as a basic resource on this second largest religious body in the United States.

Volume III of the ENCYCLOPEDIA is supplemental to the initial volumes. Incomplete in itself, this volume should always be used as a companion to Volumes I and II. The present volume expands and updates the content of the first two volumes by presenting significant developments in the life and work of Southern Baptists, 1956–70, and articles on some subjects inadvertently omitted in the initial volumes. Following the same format as its predecessors, Volume III was planned, supported, and produced by Southern Baptists themselves, working together through all their organized agencies and state Baptist bodies. Six hundred and forty-three writers contributed 1,151 articles, and a qualified editorial staff prepared the manuscript for publication. In the three volumes of the ENCYCLOPEDIA readers should find the facts that are essential for a genuine understanding of Southern Baptists in the context of their history, their theology, their methodology, and their present organization.

History.—The need for a fourth printing of the ENCYCLOPEDIA early in 1969 prompted officials of Broadman Press and the Historical Commission, SBC, to confer regarding the need for revising and updating Volumes I and II. The use of these volumes since publication had revealed that important subjects had been omitted. After considering this and other factors, such as the broad circulation of these initial volumes and the significant developments in Southern Baptist life and work in the decade following publication, these officials agreed to publish a third volume which would supplement and update the content of the first two volumes rather than to make a complete revision of Volumes I and II. By nature and content many of the articles in the ENCYCLOPEDIA were complete and needed no revision. It was determined that Volume III would therefore contain: (1) supplemental material to update the content of original articles needing revision, (2) articles on important subjects not included in Volumes I and II, and (3) monographs on new developments in the life and work of Southern Baptists since 1956.

Broadman Press requested that the Historical Commission develop and coordinate the project for producing a manuscript for Volume III, as it had done earlier in producing the initial volumes. Davis C. Woolley, executive secretary of the Historical Commission, devised a plan for publishing Volume III of the ENCYCLOPEDIA, following the basic format of the plan utilized in the production of the first two volumes. In April, 1969, the Historical Commission approved the plan and authorized Dr. Woolley to implement the project in cooperation with Broadman Press. He procured the commitment of each Southern Baptist Convention agency and state Baptist convention to cooperate in the preparation of Volume III, making it a cooperative venture as the production of the first two volumes had been.

In accord with this plan, the editorial committee was to be composed of representatives from the following agencies or groups: Sunday School Board, state executive secretaries, state editors. Historical Commission of the SBC, Executive Committee of the SBC, seminary historians, college and seminary librarians, state historians, and pastors. The editorial committee that was appointed consisted of Howard P. Colson, chairman, Harold G. Sanders, Erwin L. McDonald, W. Morgan Patterson, Porter W. Routh, Robert A. Baker, F Wilbur Helmbold, R. A. McLemore, and Gaye L. McGlothlen. William J. Fallis, chief editor of Broadman Press, and Davis C. Woolley and Lynn E. May, Jr., of the Historical Commission staff also participated in committee meetings. At its initial meeting in June, 1969, the committee elected Davis C. Woolley as managing editor. These men formulated all editorial policies, took an active part in planning the project, and in numerous other ways made a creative and indispensable contribution.

A general committee also was formed, composed of a representative of each Convention agency, each state Baptist convention, and the thirteen background areas to be included in Volume III. Designated as agency chairmen, state chairmen, and background area chairmen, these individuals were made responsible for determining subjects to be included, selecting writers, and assigning topics for monographs for their agency, state, or area. They also were responsible for content editing and verification. The seventy persons who served as chairmen played a vital role in planning and preparing the copy for this volume.

The content of Volume III was planned around the same basic categories of information formulated for the earlier volumes as well as material covering the history and work of each Baptist state convention and each Southern Baptist Convention agency since 1956. With guidance and correlation from the managing editor and his staff in Nashville, each chairman planned, procured, edited, and submitted monographs for Volume III. Through this systematic approach, the material procured for this volume presents a comprehensive picture of Southern Baptists, 1956–70.

Staff and writers.—More than six hundred and fifty people served on the committees, the editorial staff, and the writing staff which produced this work. These people are recognized leaders of the denomination who have contributed their time and talents because they realized the importance of the project. The articles for the ENCYCLOPEDIA were written and edited by persons qualified for the assignment by training and experience. Writers for Volume III are of the same high caliber as those chosen for Volumes I and II.

Editorial procedure.—The procedure employed in editing copy for Volume III was similar to that used in the production of the first two volumes. The ENCYCLOPEDIA chairman of each agency, state, and area was responsible for verifying, editing, and revising, as required, all monographs he assigned. He then forwarded the manuscripts to the managing editor. The editorial staff in the office of the Historical Commission accessioned, evaluated, checked, edited, styled, retyped, and arranged the monographs for submission to Broadman Press. A Broadman copy editor gave each monograph a final check before the manuscript was submitted to the printer. The editorial staff revised material as needed to eliminate needless detail and subjective evaluation, to correct omissions and duplications, and to make terminology consistent. The goal of the staff has been to make the content as complete, consistent, accurate, and objective as possible.

Pictures.—Photographs which illustrate many facets of Baptist life and work are included in this volume. Each Convention agency and state Baptist convention was given an opportunity to submit photographs illustrative of its work. The editorial staff made the final selection of pictures from those submitted. Most of them portray structures erected since 1956.

Acknowledgments.—Like its predecessors, Volume III of this ENCY-

CLOPEDIA is the product of a cooperative venture. It is not possible to mention here the hundreds of people, institutions, and agencies involved in this project; but we must acknowledge some who have made highly significant contributions. Gratitude is expressed to the sponsoring agencies: the thirty-two state conventions and the Executive Committee, boards, commissions, institutions, and auxiliaries of the Southern Baptist Convention which cooperated in the work. They contributed time, material, and financial support to help underwrite the costs of planning and preparing the manuscript for publication. Their subsidy has helped to make it possible for this volume to be sold at a far more reasonable price than would otherwise be possible.

Gratitude is due to members of the editorial committee and the general committee who contributed freely of their time and skill in planning, preparing, and processing the materials for this volume. Special appreciation is due Howard P. Colson, chairman of the editorial committee, for his counsel and assistance to the managing editor in planning Volume III and in implementing the project. To all writers whose names appear as contributors, appreciation is expressed for their dedicated research and for the writing of the monographs.

Acknowledgment should also be made of the contributions made by the employed staff. Terry Lawrence Jones, who has served ably as editorial assistant since January, 1970, shared in the editorial processes. Mrs. Walter A. Ray and her associates, Mrs. Harry W. Goeller and Mrs. Noel E. Armstrong, deftly handled the complex stenographic work and manuscript control so that each item was properly acknowledged, accessioned, processed, styled, retyped as needed, and filed. They also assisted in the editorial processes. Gratitude must also be expressed to Mrs. Reba McMahon and several part-time workers for assuming many of the routine duties normally performed by the staff members working on the ENCYCLOPEDIA. These workers constituted a capable team, without which this work could not have been accomplished.

Special appreciation is expressed for the work of Lynn E. May, Jr., associate to the managing editor. Dr. May shared in the development of plans and procedures, the evaluation of manuscripts, and the revision and rewriting of monographs. He then carried an overload of responsibility as he guided the project to completion during the illness of the managing editor. His conscientious and careful attention to the details of publishing Volume III freed the editor from anxiety during this period.

The ENCYCLOPEDIA staff worked closely with the staff of Broadman Press in the production of this volume. Chief editor of Broadman Press, William J. Fallis, and his associate, Mrs. Eugene J. Honea, shared in the editorial and publishing processes.

Content and usefulness.—The definitive statement on the purpose, content, viewpoint, and usefulness of the ENCYCLOPEDIA given in the introduction to Volume I (pages ix–xvi) is applicable to Volume III also. Since 1958 the ENCYCLOPEDIA has served a variety of persons and needs. It has been a source book for pastors, church program leaders, and members who have referred to it repeatedly for information relative to Baptist life and work. Students and others interested in Baptists have found in the initial volumes a compendium of information. Denominational leaders, editors, teachers, and other workers have utilized the ENCYCLOPEDIA as a basic reference source. Volume III supplements the content and extends the usefulness of Volumes I and II by portraying the major developments in the life and work of Southern Baptists from 1956 to 1970.

DAVIS C. WOOLLEY
Managing Editor

ACKNOWLEDGMENT

By means of this work the managing editor has placed his denomination, as well as the total Christian community, in his debt. Both directly and through his inspiration and guidance of others involved in the preparation of this volume, he has made a significant contribution to his denomination's history. The volume, in no small measure, reflects Davis C. Woolley's knowledge and love of Southern Baptists and his appreciation of the importance of their preserving a record of their life and work. In the task of directing the project he has manifested clarity of vision and balance of judgment. The book is the crowning achievement of his life—a worthy addition to the original two volumes so wisely planned and developed by his predecessor.

HOWARD P. COLSON
Chairman, Editorial Committee

HOW TO USE THIS VOLUME

Arrangement of Material.—The monographs are in alphabetical order, with the exception of those dealing with associations, which are alphabetically arranged under the name of the state. Alphabetizing of articles was done according to the main word in titles. For example:

Alabama Associations
Cox, Norman Wade
Historiography, Baptist
Mexico, Mission in
North Carolina, Baptist State Convention of
Sex Education
World Council of Churches

References.—An asterisk (*) by a title in this volume denotes that an article by that identical title appears in Volume I or II. A "cf." reference following a title refers the reader to an article in the earlier volumes on a similar subject but with a different title. Cross references are included to make all the material in this volume more accessible. "See" references at the end of monographs refer to supplementary information in related monographs. Bibliographies appearing with monographs refer to sources of additional information. A "(*q.v.*)," following an incidental reference to a person, refers the reader to a biographical sketch in Volume III. Biographical monographs in the previous volumes are referred to by "(*q.v.*, Vol. I)" and "(*q.v.*, Vol. II)."

Abbreviations.—The names of organizations are often abbreviated after their initial appearance in a monograph. Abbreviations most commonly used include FMB for Foreign Mission Board, HMB for Home Mission Board, SBC for Southern Baptist Convention, and WMU for Woman's Missionary Union.

Biographies.—This volume contains biographical sketches of 411 deceased Baptist leaders. Most of these are persons whose death occurred 1956–70. Also included are sketches of earlier Baptist leaders inadvertently omitted in Volumes I and II. Biographees were selected by special state and agency committees from among deceased leaders who rendered significant service as a pioneer, scholar, author, leader, preacher, missionary, editor, statesman, educator, or philanthropist.

Scope.—The breadth of subject matter in this volume will soon become evident to those who use it. Numerous definitive articles are included in the following areas: Biblical, Ethics and Social Concern, Evangelism, History, Missions, Music, Other Baptist Bodies, Pastoral Care, Preaching, Public Affairs, Religious Education, Stewardship, Study and Research, Theology, and miscellaneous general articles. Monographs on the Southern Baptist Convention, SBC agencies, agency programs, publications, etc., are included. An article may be found on each state convention, institution, publication, etc. Associational monographs are limited to new associations and changes in associations. Biographical articles provide basic information on the life and ministry of deceased leaders. Special monographs reflect the numerous changes in organization, programs, and publications of Southern Baptists, 1956–70.

Users should note that this volume contains numerous monographs related to the monographs on major organizations. For instance, the main article on the Foreign Mission Board is supplemented by separate articles on each mission and institution of the board plus special articles on related subjects such as Medical Missions, English-Language Churches Overseas, etc.

For Reference and Reading.—Like other encyclopedias, this volume was designed primarily as a reference work. Those who use it, however, will find its pages inviting them to explore its content further. Users will discover that this book is meant for reading, too.

ILLUSTRATIONS

A

ABORTION. Few, if any, societies during man's history have been without abortion. But societies have not allowed the practice of abortion to go uncontrolled. In almost all cultures —past and present—some limits and restrictions were advocated. The regulations dealt mainly with the time and the reason for the abortion. In most societies, abortion was to take place in the earliest possible stages of pregnancy, and certainly before the fetus became animate. The common allowable reasons for abortion in non-Christian cultures have included: protection of life and health of the mother; prevention of the birth of a child likely to be deformed; and limitation of the number of children so that parents could adequately care for their offspring.

Currently, abortion is widely practiced, yet it is considered in almost every nation a matter subject to law and state control. Some nations, such as Japan, Norway, Sweden, Denmark, and Finland, have permissive policies on abortion. Other nations, such as West Germany and Spain, have highly restrictive laws. In the United States, a trend is developing toward looser controls.

The United States has no federal laws governing abortion. Most states have laws dating to the middle of the 19th century which prohibit abortion except when the life, and sometimes the health, of the mother are threatened. Within the past two decades a strong sentiment for reform of these laws has developed. A number of states, including California, Colorado, Maryland, North Carolina, Georgia, New York, and Hawaii have liberalized their abortion laws. Generally, the new laws allow abortion under three conditions: (1) when there is substantial risk that the pregnancy will result in serious damage to the mental or physical well-being of the mother; (2) when the pregnancy is the result of incest, rape, or other "felonious intercourse"; and (3) when there is a substantial risk that the child will be born with serious mental or physical defects. In the states of New York and Hawaii, the law has been liberalized to the effect that the matter of abortion is basically between the patient and her doctor.

While few Protestant groups have any official position, most spokesmen seem to feel that abortion should be allowed to protect the health of the mother; few advocate abortion as a means of birth control.

As a Christian ponders the issue of abortion, three key issues must be considered. When does human life begin? Under what circumstances is it permissible to take human life? What does the Bible teach about abortion?

Southern Baptists have done little in exploring the moral implications of abortion. However, the Christian Life Commission prepared an eight-page pamphlet on the issue and set forth some answers. The commission also produced a resource paper on the subject. The Baptist student and church training departments of the Baptist Sunday School Board have focused upon the issue of abortion in their various publications. WILLIAM M. PINSON, JR.

ACADEMIC FREEDOM. Academic freedom is both a condition and an attitude. It is a condition provided by the board of trustees and the administration of an educational institution in which the teacher has the opportunity to consider genuine options, popular or not, in pursuit of truth in his discipline. Therefore, it is a condition in which there is no pressure to conform to a given cultural, theological, or political party line. When this condition prevails, a scholar's conclusions can be determined by his own judgment based upon relevant evidence rather than by external pressures coming from the society or from the institution.

Academic freedom, whether in a secular or religious school does not involve the absence of presuppositions, but rather their recognition. In theological seminaries which have a confessional basis, academic freedom is exercised within the context of theological guidelines. Such a condition does not infringe upon the professor's freedom provided he, in good conscience and good faith, accepts the guidelines.

Academic freedom is also an attitude on the part of the professor. It is possible even when the institution provides the condition for academic freedom that the teacher will permit extraneous pressures which have nothing to do with the pursuit of truth in his discipline to distort his findings.

Academic freedom is one of the most precious possessions of a democracy. Without it, propaganda and indoctrination take the place of free discussion and openness to new ideas. Academic freedom is, therefore, an essential element of an open society.

BIBLIOGRAPHY: R. M. McIver, *Academic Freedom in Our Time* (1955); P. F. Lazarsfeld, *The Academic Mind: Social Scientists in a Time of Crisis* (1958); T. Caplow and R. J. McGee, *The Academic Marketplace* (1958). PENROSE ST. AMANT

***ACADIA BAPTIST ACADEMY.** A standard, state accredited, coeducational, boarding high school, it is located on 71 acres of rural land near Eunice. The only school of its kind owned by the Louisiana Baptist Convention, its governing board consists of 15 trustees elected by the convention. Its purpose, reviewed and endorsed following a report by a special committee to the state convention in 1956, is to provide a complete general high school and college preparatory curriculum under distinctly Christian influence. The 1965–66 session dropped the eighth grade from the program of studies.

Since 1958 a completely new school plant has been built: administration and classroom building (1958), including the J. H. Strother Library, a gymnasium seating 900, and the Mary Lou Jenkins chapel seating 300 given by the Louisiana Woman's Missionary Union; W. J. Westberry dormitory for boys (1960); Hattie Elliott dormitory for girls (1961); cafeteria (1968); and faculty housing. Facilities are adequate for 250, of which 128 can be boarding students.

Stafford Rogers succeeded V. K. Fletcher as administrator in 1957. G. L. Higgins became the administrator and principal in 1965. Graduates number approximately 800. The 1969–70 school year began with a faculty of 11, enrolment of 230 coming from six states and six foreign countries, budget of $244,925, with Cooperative Program allocation of $95,000, net worth of $1,132,815.76, and indebtedness of $180,000.

CHARLES S. MCILVEENE

ACCENT. Since Oct., 1970, the monthly periodical for leaders and members of Acteens. Published by Woman's Missionary Union, the magazine contains features of interest to girls and basic resources for Acteens organization meetings and activities. *Accent,* leader edition, contains Highlights, the leadership section. Oneta Gentry is editor (1970). BETTY BROWN

ACHIEVEMENT GUIDES (cf. Standards of Excellence, Vol. II). Achievement Guides replaced Sunday School, Training Union, and Church Music Standards of Excellence and Woman's Missionary Union Aims for Advancement in Oct., 1967. Two major factors contributed to this development. For several years church leaders had expressed their need for new and more comprehensive evaluation instruments. Progress in programing from 1963 to 1966 had caused leaders of Southern Baptist Convention church program organizations to become aware of the need for improved instruments for churches to use in evaluating their total programs.

In order to coordinate the development and content of the guides, the Church Administration Department of the Sunday School Board was requested by the church program development group to design the Church Program Achievement Guide first. This was done and approved by the group in July, 1966. The following elements of the plan for programing became the major sections of the Church Program Achievement Guide: Program Plan, Relationships, Organization, Human Resources, Physical Resources, Financial Resources, and Administrative Controls.

The Sunday School, Church Music, Church Training, and Church Library Departments of the Sunday School Board, the WMU, and the Brotherhood Commission developed their guides in relationship to the Church Program Achievement Guide and to each other. All were evaluated by church and denominational leaders before they were released. The guides were considered experimental during their first year of use.

The guides were designed for suggested use by the church council and organization councils to evaluate and improve the work of the church and its organizations. In addition they were to be used by the national organizations in recognizing the quality of work in the churches. By combining evaluation and recognition in the same instruments, church leaders could evaluate and improve their work, knowing in advance the recognition they would receive.

All guides provided three levels of recognition: merit, advanced, and distinguished. These levels made the guides adaptable for use in all types and sizes of churches.

The Associational Sunday School Achievement Guide, which was experimental during the summer of 1968, was put into full use in 1969. On Oct. 1, 1968, the Sunday School Department of the Sunday School Board offered department and class achievement guides in addition to the general guide. Also in 1968 WMU age-level organizations changed from Aims for Advancement to Achievement Guides.

The initial response of the churches to the guides was positive but not widespread. Interest increased during 1968 and 1969. In 1969 all guides were updated and improved for use with the new programs and materials which became available Oct. 1, 1970. A new Vacation Bible School Achievement Guide appeared in 1969 for schools conducted in 1970. A guide for the Associational Training Union became available Jan. 1, 1970. W. L. HOWSE

ACTEENS. Since Oct., 1970, the missions organization for girls 12–17 (or school grades 7–12) in Woman's Missionary Union's graded program of missionary education. Through use of materials and plans provided in *Accent,* Acteens leads girls to engage in the basic WMU tasks of mission study, mission action, and mission support at their level of development and understanding. Evelyn Tully is director (1970). BETTY BROWN

ALABAMA, ASSOCIATION OF MISSIONARY BAPTIST CHURCHES OF. Sometimes titled the State Association of Alabama, this body of Landmark churches was constituted at least as early as 1927. In the 1952 session, the association projected the organization of a tri-state association consisting of Alabama, Mississippi, and West Florida. Further evidence regarding this organization seems to be unavailable. F.W. HELMBOLD

ALABAMA ASSEMBLIES (ASSOCIATIONAL). The associational assemblies provide facilities for individual church programs and association-wide camps and retreats.

Baldwin Baptist Camp, owned by the Baldwin Association, has two dormitories, a chapel and a dining hall on 22 acres of land fronting on the Gulf of Mexico.

Cooks Springs Baptist Camp is operated by the Birmingham Association on 1,600 acres leased from the American School of Evangelism. A home for senior citizens is also located on this property. It has a lake and accommodations for 300 campers.

Camp Morvin was given to Clarke County Association when the property ceased to be used as a school. Two buildings accommodating 100 campers are on five acres of land.

Colbert-Lauderdale Association owns and operates Spring Cove Baptist Assembly. Only day programs are conducted.

The 16 acres of lakefront land used for Lake Jackson Baptist Camp were given to Covington County Association in 1959. Four cabins provide facilities for 70 campers.

Fayette, Franklin, and Hale Associations have land for the development of assemblies.

The Limestone Baptist Camp site was donated to the Limestone Association in 1960. In addition to the buildings which house 64 campers, the home of the associational missionary is located on the grounds.

Marshall Association bought 11 acres on Guntersville Lake for a camp site in 1963. It is largely for day programs, except for an RA camp.

Citronelle Baptist Camp was purchased by the Mobile Association in 1946. It has six buildings and accommodates 200 campers.

Muscle Shoals Association has a camp site of 110 acres on which day programs are conducted.

Camp Tuscoba of the Tuscaloosa County Association includes 115 acres. Camps were first held there in 1959. ARTHUR L. WALKER, JR.

***ALABAMA BAPTIST.** Leon Macon died in Nov., 1965, after serving 15 years as editor. Hudson Baggett was elected editor, Apr., 1966. A native of Alabama, Baggett graduated from Howard College (now Samford University) and Southern Baptist Theological Seminary (Th.D.). He was pastor of the First Baptist Church, Florence, Ala., for several years and taught for nearly nine years in the religion department at Samford University.

Baggett became editor when some delicate social problems were coming to the fore in the nation. Racial conflict, which reached a peak in the sixties, affected the denomination and the *Alabama Baptist*. The strong reaction of public opinion is reflected in the paper during this time. Editorially, the stance of the paper is middle of the road. It strongly supports denominational causes, but it also allows dissenting opinions to be voiced. Editorials in the *Alabama Baptist* have dealt with some of the sensitive issues in recent years. The paper had a circulation of almost 150,000 in 1970, the highest in its history.

The early history of the paper, prepared by F. W. Helmbold, was published in the *Alabama Baptist Historian* (July, 1966). HUDSON BAGGETT

ALABAMA BAPTIST BIBLE SOCIETY. Founded in Oct. (?), 1836, with John L. Dagg (*q.v.*, Vol. I) elected president, and A. J. Holcombe secretary. James H. Devotie (*q.v.*, Vol. I) later became president and remained in office until 1856 when he removed to Georgia, and I. T. Tichenor (*q.v.*, Vol. II) was elected. Samuel Sterling Sherman (*q.v.*), president of Howard College, was secretary until about 1853, when P. H. Lundy succeeded him. By 1857 John Haralson had become secretary, and in 1858 A. B. Goodhue was elected. The chief agents (apparently colporteurs and solicitors) at various times included Solon Lindsley, Noah Haggard, Randolph Reddins, John D. Williams, F. M. Law, and Merritt Burns. In later years they were assisted by other agents. A depository was established in Selma in the early part of 1855. In 1856 the name was changed to the Alabama Baptist Bible and Colporteur Society. In Nov., 1860, a committee was appointed to liquidate the society. F. W. HELMBOLD

***ALABAMA BAPTIST CHILDREN'S HOME, THE.** The home serves about 350 children annually through (1) institutional care, (2) Mothers' Aid, (3) foster homes, and (4) assistance to students in college and/or special schools. Emphasis is placed on family rehabilitation. In 1963 a group home for 10 boys was established in Birmingham, and in 1969 another branch home to accommodate 60 children was opened in Decatur. With an annual budget of $550,000, the home depends on the Cooperative Program for about 10 per cent, a special offering in the churches for 75 per cent, and individual gifts for the remainder. R. HOBSON SHIREY

ALABAMA BAPTIST CREDIT UNION. The employees of the executive board of the Alabama Baptist State Convention organized a state chartered Credit Union in Montgomery, on Mar. 19, 1956. The first officers were: Leslie S. Wright, president; Miss Mary Essie Stephens, vice-president; and George E. Bagley, secretary-treasurer. There were 47 members at the beginning of the Credit Union. Total shares ($5.00 each) on Jan. 1, 1957, amounted to $6,682. On Dec. 31, 1969, these totaled $44,157. A total of 615 loans had been made to employees and their families through Dec., 1969. Amount of loans made from the Credit Union's beginning totaled $325,253. Savings of members have consistently earned 6 per cent interest.

The purposes of the Credit Union's organization were: "to promote thrift; to make loans to its members at reasonable rates of interest, for provident and productive purposes; to invest any surplus not required for loans to members in the way and manner by law provided; and, to exercise those functions described in the laws of the State of Alabama authorizing the organization of credit unions." Except for a very small payment to the secretary-treasurer, all officers and committees have served without remuneration. GEORGE E. BAGLEY

ALABAMA BAPTIST FOUNDATION, THE. The foundation administers endowment funds for local church and denominational causes. Presidents of the trustees have been Pat Roberson, Pell City, 1940–63, and N. J. Bell III, Montgomery, since 1964. A. H. Reid has been treasurer since 1940. Carl G. Campbell succeeded Leslie S. Wright as executive secretary in 1959. Vernon Yearby became executive secretary in 1966. Foundation assets were $2,250,000 in 1969. VERNON YEARBY

ALABAMA BAPTIST HISTORIAN. The semiannual publication of the Alabama Baptist Historical Society. The society voted at its annual meeting in 1963 to begin the publication, and the first issue was published in Nov., 1964. The editor was Arthur L. Walker, Jr., president of the Alabama Baptist Historical Society, 1962–66, and professor of religion at Samford University. With the Jan., 1967, issue F. Wilbur Helmbold, librarian at Samford University and curator of the society, became the editor.

ARTHUR L. WALKER, JR.

ALABAMA BAPTIST HISTORICAL COMMISSION. The organization of the Alabama Baptist Historical Commission was recommended by the special study committee of the Alabama Baptist State Convention in 1964. The organizational, financial, and program structure of the commission was adopted by the convention in 1965. Arthur L. Walker, Jr., was elected as the first chairman of the commission. Members are elected by the state convention for a three-year term.

The historical interests of the Alabama Convention had been fostered since 1936 by the Alabama Baptist Historical Society. The program structure of the commission called for it to maintain an historical collection, sponsor the Alabama Baptist Historical Society, and cooperate in the publication of *The Alabama Baptist Historian.* ARTHUR L. WALKER, JR.

***ALABAMA BAPTIST HISTORICAL SOCIETY.** The society came under the sponsorship of the Alabama Baptist Historical Commission in 1965. In structure and function it continued to serve in much the same way as in its original organization. The society began the publication of *The Alabama Baptist Historian* in 1964. The historical collection is housed at Samford University. F. Wilbur Helmbold became curator in 1957. Other officers are elected annually.

ARTHUR L. WALKER, JR.

***ALABAMA BAPTIST STATE CONVENTION.** In 1969 the 2,948 churches affiliated with the Alabama Baptist State Convention had 825,598 members. Giving rose to a record high: $4,993,809 to the Cooperative Program and $2,818,926 for designated offerings. In 1961 the convention voted to give a minimum of 35 per cent of all undesignated Cooperative Program gifts to the Southern Baptist Convention for support of worldwide missions. A reserve fund had grown to $708,864 toward a goal of one year's operating budget in reserve.

Membership.—The amended constitution allows one messenger to the annual convention from each cooperating church with a membership of 200 or less, and one additional messenger for each additional 200 members (limit of 25 messengers).

Executive Board.—Each association is allowed one member on the executive board. An additional member is allowed for each $50,000 given to the Cooperative Program (limit of 12 members). A proposal to be voted upon at the 1970 state convention calls for membership on the board to be based solely upon membership. The board meets twice annually.

After a two-year study of the board's organizational structure, the report by a committee of the board was adopted in 1969. The board set up three divisions: *Church Program Development Division,* including Sunday School, Training Union, Brotherhood and Royal Ambassadors, Church Music, Church Administration, Church Architecture, and Stewardship departments; *Church Ministries Division,* including evangelism, campus ministries, missions to special groups, ministers retirement, and associational missions; *Business Management Division,* including financial office, central services, Shocco Springs Baptist Assembly, state convention building supervision, and investments. The Public Relations Office was designated as a part of the administrative function of the executive secretary's office.

Public Relations.—In 1957 the executive board created the position of public relations director to promote the program of the convention through the communications media. Contacts with the press, radio, and television increased coverage of denominational affairs. In 1967 a paid advertising television program, called "Mainstream," projected the image of Alabama Baptists as Christians interested in people.

Special Groups.—A department, formerly working primarily with Negroes, was renamed in 1961 the Department of Missions to Special Groups. It ministered to Indians in southwest Alabama and to the deaf, while continuing work with the National (Negro) Baptist groups. This work received financial support from the SBC Home Mission Board.

Campus Ministries.—When the executive board was reorganized, the Student Department was renamed the Campus Ministry Department, and campus ministers became employees of the

ALABAMA BAPTIST CONVENTION (*q.v.*) BUILDING, Montgomery. Completed in 1963. Houses the offices of the convention and the state WMU.

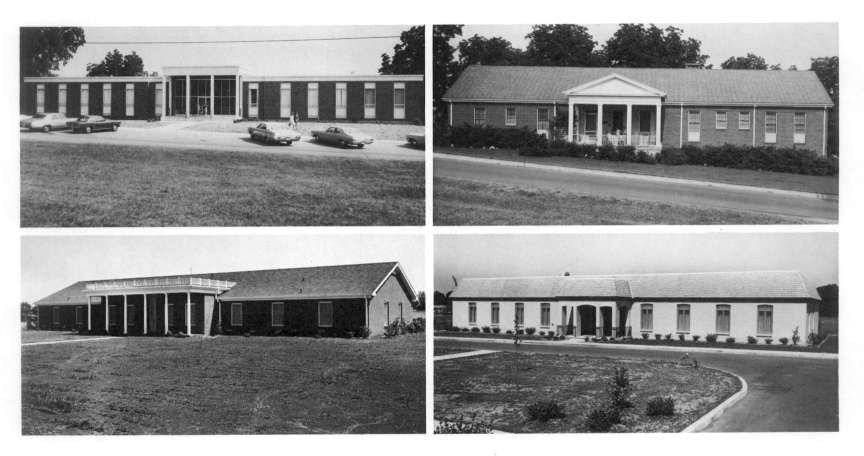

THE ALABAMA BAPTIST CHILDREN'S HOME, Incorporated (*q.v.*). *Top left:* Leo Bashinsky Administration Building, Troy. *Top right:* Samford Memorial Cottage for children, Troy. *Bottom left:* Cottage for children, Decatur. *Bottom right:* Charles Eyster Administration Building, Decatur. Decatur Branch dedicated July 12, 1970.

board. Alabama Baptists own student center buildings at the University of Alabama (Tuscaloosa), Florence State University, Troy State University, and a temporary facility at Jacksonville State University where property has been secured and plans are being developed for a building. A lot is owned in Mobile for future development.

Associational Missions.—The convention in 1970 allocated $36,000 for city missions programs in Birmingham, Mobile, Montgomery, Huntsville, Tri-Cities (Florence, Sheffield, and Tuscumbia), and Gadsden, and $77,850 for assistance on associational missionaries' salaries. The state convention and Home Mission Board, SBC, share evenly in the $19,800 budget for church-community weekday ministries, mission center, and juvenile rehabilitation programs in the Birmingham, Etowah, Madison, Mobile, Montgomery, and Russell associations.

Summer Assemblies.—Recent additions at Shocco Springs have included air-conditioned motel-type housing (private baths). One modern hotel was completed in 1966, costing $195,000, and another in 1970 at $300,000. Renovations and remodeling of existing buildings have made the assembly a year-round meeting place. Air conditioning was added to the dining room, auditorium, and classrooms.

An RA camp, completed in 1965 on a site adjoining Shocco Springs, accommodates 144 boys. In the same year the Woman's Missionary Union of Alabama completed a GA camp on the opposite side of Shocco Springs for a similar number of girls.

Office Building.—In May, 1963, a new Alabama Baptist State Office Building was occupied. The four-floor building, with 58,256 square feet of floor space, was constructed for $800,000, and is located at the corner of Narrow Lane Road and Southern Boulevard in Montgomery. It houses all offices of the executive board, the Baptist Foundation, and the Alabama WMU.

Education.—In 1965 a convention study committee recommended that Judson College become a coeducational institution. The proposal was defeated, but the Judson trustees were asked to report in 1968 on progress toward an enrolment goal of 600. The same convention voted to change the name of Howard College to Samford University. Messengers also voted to earmark 30 per cent of Cooperative Program funds for support of Baptist institutions of higher learning. Operating funds were to be distributed on the basis of credit hours taught, with capital funds distributed on the basis of need. In 1970 Judson, Samford, and Mobile received $1,081,000 in operating funds and $500,000 for capital needs. By action of the 1969 convention, trustees of the individual schools were permitted to allocate distribution of the total convention receipts between operating and capital funds.

Weekly Paper.—The *Alabama Baptist,* official weekly newspaper of the convention, had a

ALABAMA STATISTICAL SUMMARY

Year	Associations	Churches	Church Membership	Baptisms	S. S. Enrolment	V.B.S. Enrolment	T. U. Enrolment	W.M.U. Enrolment	Brotherhood Enrolment	Music Enrolment	Mission Gifts	Total Gifts	Value Church Property
1955	74	2,707	620,788	28,600	458,405	188,751	184,195	85,874	26,184		$3,190,067	$20,125,377	$ 78,775,526
1956	75	2,709	636,242	25,062	469,138	236,496	189,930	87,861	28,419		3,662,801	23,394,642	90,136,973
1957	76	2,737	657,530	26,368	478,360	233,714	195,310	92,945	34,684	35,886	4,038,565	24,850,884	101,852,823
1958	76	2,761	671,185	28,035	488,901	251,257	205,966	100,213	40,227	41,245	4,545,710	26,097,956	114,622,109
1959	77	2,794	692,877	30,413	504,528	254,832	217,374	104,243	43,432	47,185	4,677,784	28,846,186	125,244,868
1960	76	2,801	709,883	27,638	514,324	262,452	225,901	108,641	44,696	44,374	4,941,811	31,206,996	140,248,115
1961	76	2,824	727,124	28,937	522,623	266,760	232,698	110,391	44,750	49,829	5,316,851	32,460,257	151,285,155
1962	76	2,839	736,300	25,644	526,796	269,948	236,386	108,511	46,512	56,338	6,061,553	35,679,872	164,080,882
1963	76	2,856	749,632	25,757	529,471	260,736	240,063	111,382	47,261	63,622	6,022,309	36,657,587	179,292,481
1964	76	2,873	763,937	25,775	534,442	266,615	241,056	109,892	47,051	69,560	6,233,632	39,392,747	193,192,224
1965	76	2,904	774,627	24,941	535,007	264,452	233,859	106,725	39,494	65,821	6,757,342	43,316,167	202,831,592
1966	76	2,906	788,817	25,592	534,553	250,742	232,891	106,710	37,686	73,493	7,361,924	45,927,061	211,952,343
1967	76	2,919	803,561	27,789	533,593	257,705	236,964	106,205	38,059	82,707	7,648,632	48,941,152	236,855,981
1968	76	2,928	817,735	27,769	535,736	241,299	251,772	104,402	38,042	28,495	8,325,854	55,150,556	250,211,779

MRS. NOEL ARMSTRONG

circulation of 148,000 in 1970, second largest in the SBC. The paper received $42,500 from the 1970 Cooperative Program budget.

Baptist Foundation.—Total principal assets of the Baptist Foundation of Alabama at the end of 1969 were $2,292,538.

Temperance.—Continuing support for temperance work in Alabama was encouraged among Alabama Baptist churches with a special day of prayer and offering in the spring. In 1969 the Alabama Temperance Alliance changed its name to Alabama Council on Alcohol Problems (ALCAP) and enlarged its program to deal with the danger of drug abuse.

Crusade of the Americas.—Alabama Baptists in 1968 played a leading part in preparations for the Crusade of the Americas. In 1969 some 28,000 people were won to Christ, making it one of the best in recent years. In a statewide religious survey nearly 1,000,000 unsaved and unchurched prospects were discovered.

Growth Programs.—Alabama Baptists completed the third of three Five Year Advance Programs in 1966. Between 1951 and 1966 total membership increased from 552,543 to 788,817, and Cooperative Program gifts increased from $1,048,543 to $4,470,368.

A Seven Year Advance Program was adopted in 1966 to conclude in 1973, the 150th anniversary of establishment of the Alabama Baptist State Convention. Goals included: churches, 3,050; members, 895,000; baptisms, 37,300; Sunday School, 603,000; Training Union, 300,000; WMU, 150,000; Brotherhood and RA, 44,000; and Baptist Foundation endowment, $10,000,000.

GEORGE E. BAGLEY

ALABAMA BAPTIST MINISTERIAL BENEFIT SOCIETY, THE. Organized in 1902, with W. B. Crumpton as the leading spirit and president for 22 years, the society's purpose is to provide financial aid to the families of deceased members. When one member dies, each of the other members remits one dollar. Since organization 440 families have thus been helped. In 1969 the membership was 1,076. The 1969–70 officers were: S. J. Ezell, president; O. C. Kidd, vice-president; E. J. Williams, secretary-treasurer.

EMMETT J. WILLIAMS

ALABAMA BIBLE SOCIETY. The first Bible Society of Alabama was founded in 1824 with Israel Pickens as first President. A later society was founded in Tuscaloosa on Sunday evening, Dec. 8, 1844, as an auxiliary to the American Bible Society. The present organization bearing the same name was founded on Mar. 22, 1852, at the Court Street Methodist Episcopal Church in Montgomery. "A three-story building at No. 7 Dexter Avenue was donated by Abner McGehee to the society for a permanent Bible House." This organization has continued to the present day (1970).

F. W. HELMBOLD

ALABAMA CHRISTIAN LIFE AND PUBLIC AFFAIRS COMMISSION (cf. Social Service Commission, Alabama, Vol. II). The commission is the outgrowth of the convention's social concern, first expressed in random reports on temperance, labor, divorce, and similar subjects. It is composed of twelve members elected by the state convention for three-year terms. Its assigned purpose is to study the social, moral, economic, and political issues of the times as they may be related to Christianity in general and the denomination in particular, to inform the convention on such issues, and to recommend such actions as deemed appropriate.

JOHN H. JEFFERS

ALABAMA COUNCIL ON ALCOHOL PROBLEMS. Organized June 12, 1937, as Alabama Temperance Alliance, it received its present name on May 8, 1969. Alabama Baptists provide more than 90 per cent of its support through church budget gifts, associational offerings, and state mission funds. Its aim and program is to promote abstinence from alcoholic beverages through speaking in churches, schools, and rallies; writing in mailout bulletins, news articles, and tracts; producing visual aids; furnishing research on alcohol problems; organizing local units; assisting in wet-dry elections; and working on legislative measures. Similar work is being done increasingly relative to drugs and other moral problems. The council has consistently resisted the emphasis on moderation, maintaining that abstinence is the only ideal solution to the alcohol problem. Executive directors have been Earl Hotalen, 1937–46, James Swedenburg, 1946–67, and R. Elmer Nielsen, 1967–70. Offices are in the Birmingham Baptist Building, 807 So. 20th Street.

R. ELMER NIELSEN

ALABAMA NEGRO BAPTISTS. In 1962 the Alabama Baptist State Convention voted to appoint a committee of nine people to work with a like committee from the National Baptist Convention to find ways and means of working together in reaching Alabama for Christ. Since that time, the joint committee of Southern and National Baptists has met quarterly, alternating their meeting place between the Baptist Building, Montgomery, and Selma University. In 1968 this was made a convention committee. This committee sponsored a Joint Leadership Conference for both Southern and National Baptist leaders at Shocco Springs, Oct. 6–7, 1969. Interracial prayer groups, organized by the WMU (Southern Baptist), meet regularly in Birmingham and Montgomery. The Alabama Baptist Convention (National Baptist) and the Alabama Baptist Convention (Southern Baptist) send fraternal messengers to the annual meetings. In 1968 J. L. Ware, National Baptist leader in Birmingham, brought the keynote address to the Alabama Baptist Convention (Southern Baptist) meeting with the First Baptist Church of Huntsville. Negro students are studying in all the Baptist schools of Alabama, as well as in the

Extension Division of Samford University. Alabama Negroes, studying for the ministry and for social work, are enrolled in Southern Baptist seminaries. Integrated Vacation Bible Schools are well attended in Alabama. In 1969 a student center building was being erected adjacent to Alabama State University, Montgomery, and the first Negro student minister, John Cross, was working with students there. HARRY O. HESTER

ALASKA ASSOCIATIONS. CHUGACH BAPTIST ASSOCIATION. First association of Southern Baptists in Alaska, this body was formed by three churches in 1950, taking its name from the Chugach Mountains which lie to the east of Anchorage. A meeting to discuss the organization of an association in south central Alaska was held in Aug., 1950, and a committee appointed to write a constitution. On Sept. 10, 1950, the association was formally organized. Their stated purpose was to take care of the orphanage (Turnagain Children's Home) already established, to further mission work, and to work with the Home Mission Board. Felton Griffin was named the first moderator.

Through the cooperative work of the association, the Alaska convention, and the HMB, Southern Baptist churches grew rapidly in the area, and cooperating churches in the association included churches and missions in the Matanuska Valley, at Valdez on Prince William Sound, several towns on the Kenai Peninsula, and at Kodiak on Kodiak Island. In May, 1968, the churches on the Kenai Peninsula and at Kodiak withdrew to form the Tustamena Association. In the fall of 1969 there were 17 churches and three missions in the association.

The association operates a summer church camp near Wasilla in the Matanuska Valley north of Anchorage. From time to time they have directed a seminary extension program. They have contributed substantially to the continuing operation of the Turnagain Children's Home. In the great Alaska Good Friday earthquake of 1964 the church building at Valdez was destroyed and several other churches damaged slightly. For a short time in the early 1950's Miss Valeria Sherard served as an associational missionary. In 1968 the association, in cooperation with the Alaska Baptist Convention, selected E. C. Chron to be state mission director and Chugach Baptist Association missionary. Through the years the cooperating churches of this association have been the greatest strength of Southern Baptists in Alaska. RICHARD A. MILLER

TANANA VALLEY BAPTIST ASSOCIATION. Organized in 1954 by five churches and three missions in the "Interior" of Alaska cooperating with the Southern Baptist Convention. The name is taken from the Tanana River which drains a large portion of central Alaska. In 1969 the association included 10 churches and four missions located in Fairbanks, Delta Junction, Clear, College, North Pole, Salcha, Tok, and Fort Yukon. The total membership of the churches in 1969 was 2,624.

TONGASS BAPTIST ASSOCIATION. Organized in 1960 and reorganized in 1969, the association includes the cooperating Southern Baptist churches in southeastern Alaska, or the panhandle of Alaska. The name is taken from the Tongass National Forest covering almost the entire area. Since this section of Alaska consists of many islands and a narrow coastline with no interconnecting highways, making transportation a major problem, meetings of the association have usually consisted of the pastors of the cooperating churches. Churches in 1969 included First Baptist at Ketchikan and Sitka, and First and Glacier Valley in Juneau, and missions at Petersburg and Annette. Total membership in these cooperating churches in 1968 was 431.

TUSTAMENA BAPTIST ASSOCIATION. Organized in May, 1968, as a result of the increased population on the Kenai Peninsula due to the oil development. Pastors and state leaders who encouraged such an organization felt that more missions would be started if a new association was organized. Four churches and one mission, all formerly affiliated with the Chugach Association, voted to organize the association. These were the First Baptist churches of Kenai, Seward, and Soldatna, and the Frontier Southern Baptist Church of Kodiak, and Faith Mission, North Kenai. The first annual meeting was held May 24–25, 1968. Maurice Murdock was elected the first moderator.

RICHARD A. MILLER AND ROY MOORE

ALASKA BAPTIST CONVENTION (cf. Alaska, Baptists in, Vol. I).

I. The Beginnings of Baptists in Alaska. Baptist mission work in Alaska was begun by W. H. R. and Emily Corlies of Philadelphia, Pa., who came to Alaska in June, 1879, after having been challenged and encouraged by Sheldon Jackson, Presbyterian minister who was then eagerly promoting Alaskan missions and government. Emily Corlies was the daughter of Josiah and Eliza (Abbott) Goddard, missionaries of the Triennial convention, and was born in Siam while her parents were awaiting entrance into China. Before coming to Alaska, W. Corlies spent one year in medical training in order to be more useful. To support themselves in Alaska the Corlies sold their farm. For several years they labored with the Presbyterians in Wrangell before ministering to Indians and miners around the area of Juneau. Later they built a church building at Taku Harbor, south of Juneau, before returning to Pennsylvania in 1884.

In 1880, when there were only three Protestant churches in Alaska, Sheldon Jackson arranged a meeting of representatives of the Methodist, Presbyterian, Episcopalian, and Northern Baptist mission societies to facilitate the spread of the gospel in Alaska and to avoid duplication of effort. Each group took an area in which they would start mission work. Baptists accepted a region including Prince William Sound, Cook Inlet, and Kodiak Island.

Financial problems prevented a swift response

by Baptists to the needs of Alaska. After the passage of the Organic Act of 1884, Sheldon Jackson was named commissioner of education for Alaska. Until 1894 he cooperated with religious groups for the joint support of teacher-missionaries. In 1886 two Baptist couples, W. E. and Ida Roscoe of Eureka, Calif., and the James A. Wirths of Seattle, Wash., went to Kodiak and Afognak as teachers. Other Baptists came later. The difficulties of being both teacher and missionary soon became apparent. Mission efforts were not very successful.

The plight of the many orphans on Kodiak Island touched the hearts of the early Baptist teacher-missionaries. The Woman's American Baptist Home Mission Society responded to their pleas and began an orphanage in 1893 on Wood (Woody) Island at Kodiak. The workers at the home organized the Wood Island Baptist Church on July 26, 1896, the first Baptist church in Alaska.

With the discovery of gold in the Klondike, Alaska became a household word across America. The American Baptist Home Mission Society sent a missionary to Skagway during the height of the gold rush. A beautiful church building was erected and the North Star Baptist Church was organized. The decline of Skagway witnessed the death of this church. The missionary was transferred to the Valdez area, and for a number of years conducted work at Copper Center. When Baptists considered work in Valdez and Seward, both towns lying in the area originally assigned to Baptists, they found other church groups had preceded them. From time to time Baptists were urged to consider work in Nome and the Tanana Valley. It was never begun. Perhaps the need for money and workers prevented the expansion of the work. The only continuing Baptist work was the orphanage on Wood Island. Following a fire which destroyed its building, the orphanage moved to Kodiak in 1937. A church was organized in Kodiak in 1939.

II. Southern Baptists in the Territory of Alaska. While Baptists had labored in Alaska since 1879, there was only one Baptist church in all the vastness of Alaska when war suddenly rediscovered Alaska for the American people. Among the first American troops assigned to Alaska in World War II were National Guard units from the South. John Dodge, a Southern Baptist chaplain, in correspondence with the Home Mission Board, suggested areas where Baptist work in Alaska was needed.

On July 10, 1943, as American troops were completing the Aleutian campaign, Southern Baptist chaplain Aubrey Halsell left Seattle for Alaska. While a student at Ouachita University in Arkansas, he had vowed that if he were in a locality where there was no Baptist church, he would organize one. Arriving in Anchorage and finding no Baptist church, he wrote a friend, "By God's grace this shall not prevail another month." With the assistance of another Southern Baptist chaplain, Halsell conducted a revival and led in the organization of the First Baptist Church of Anchorage, with 17 charter members on Sept. 19, 1943. The church purchased two lots and a burned out residence on Sixth Ave., remodeled the building, and began worship services in the structure in Jan., 1944. Because of his efforts in establishing a Baptist church in Anchorage, Halsell was transferred by his superiors to the Aleutians.

The transfer of Halsell left the Anchorage church to depend on the individual members for leadership and emphasized the need for a civilian pastor. The Foreign Mission Board of the Southern Baptist Convention at first had encouraged the chaplain about help, but these hopes were short lived. However, Halsell contacted William Petty, a student at the Southern Baptist Theological Seminary, who accepted a call to the church in June, 1944.

In promoting the work in Anchorage, Halsell wrote an article, "Baptists in Alaska," which was published in the Southern Baptist Brotherhood *Journal* for the spring quarter of 1944. In Karnack, Tex., the article greatly impressed the pastor of the First Baptist Church, Felton H. Griffin. A few days later, after much prayer, Griffin wrote, "Dear Major: MOVE OVER I'M COMING IN. Anything I should bring with me? Felton H. Griffin." The chaplain was thrilled. On the bottom of the letter Halsell wrote, "How do you like this . . . they are coming and I don't mean maybe!!! God is so good to us. . . ."

In July, 1944, Griffin arrived in Anchorage, working as a house painter until he was called as pastor of the First Baptist Church after the resignation of Petty in 1945. In the summer of 1944, the Curtis O. Dunkins of Louisiana came to Fairbanks and began work in September. For several years two ladies in Juneau, Hilda Krause and Frances Black, had been operating a Baptist Good Will Center and Sunday School, and had tried to enlist the help of various Baptist groups to start a Baptist church. Through the Anchorage church they contacted J. T. Spurlin of Detroit who came to Juneau.

Under leadership of Felton Griffin, the First Baptist Church of Anchorage took on new life. While others may have considered some type of denominational organization, it was in the heart of Griffin that Alaska Baptist Convention was born. He saw the convention uniting all Baptists in Alaska into one convention, providing needed Christian fellowship, and as an organization meeting the needs of Alaska, which he believed one day would be a state with a large population. Messengers from the Juneau, Fairbanks, and Anchorage churches met in Anchorage and organized the Alaska Baptist Convention on Mar. 27, 1946. After the convention Griffin wrote: "Many wonderful things in this world have had a small beginning. The extent of work now, the amount of work we can do today, the funds that we can put in mission effort for Alaska are all limited as we begin our work. The beginning is not pretentious. The end of the work we cannot predict for this is a work of God. . . ."

The first annual session of the Alaska Baptist Convention met in Fairbanks in Aug., 1946. All churches reported growth and the Fairbanks church had a new pastor, Orland Cary (*q.v.*). The Northern Baptist Kodiak church sent the chairman of their deacons and the American Baptist Home Mission Society of New York sent Lincoln Wadsworth. These Northern Baptists were warmly welcomed and the convention expressed their deep pleasure at their presence in a long resolution in which they looked forward "to the day when all Baptist work in Alaska shall be knit together into a united bond of fellowship." The convention was caught between a desire to secure a united front in Alaska and a desire to cooperate with the Southern Baptist Convention.

After the convention meeting, tensions began to develop—the Fairbanks church united with a Baptist association in Texas; the convention was criticized as an "organizational monstrosity"; and native mission work was begun in Fairbanks with the support of a Texas church because the First Church did not wish to cooperate in the endeavor. But despite the difficulties the work grew, and substantial help was soon to come.

From the beginning the Home Mission Board, SBC, was aware of Alaska's needs, but the board was hesitant to begin work in Alaska without approval of the Executive Committee of the SBC, since Northern Baptists had work at Kodiak. The Executive Committee, SBC, in the spring of 1945, instructed the HMB to learn from the American Baptist Home Mission Society, of the Northern Baptist Convention, what the society would do to meet the needs of the new church in Anchorage which was asking the HMB for assistance. In September the society indicated they contemplated expanding their work to Anchorage and suggested that the HMB consider other fields. The society made an offer of assistance to the First Baptist Church, Anchorage, but this was rejected by the church. Meanwhile, at the urging of Griffin, many prominent Alaskans wrote the HMB urging the establishment of Southern Baptist mission work in Alaska.

In May, 1948, the SBC approved an investigation of the desirability and possibility of mission work in Alaska and authorized the HMB to proceed with such a program if the investigation was favorable. Following a visit by Courts Redford of the HMB, the board approved entry into Alaska and named the B. I. Carpenters of Ketchikan, who had been supported by the Baptist General Convention of New Mexico, to be the first Southern Baptist missionaries in Alaska. In 1949 the board's Department of Evangelism sponsored its first simultaneous crusade in Alaska and sent the first summer student missionaries.

The entry of the HMB into the mission field of Alaska brought help to the small convention at a time of substantial growth for the territory. Rapid military expansion in Alaska due to the cold and Korean wars was centered in Anchorage and Fairbanks where Southern Baptist mission work was to grow most rapidly.

In Sept., 1950, the Chugach Baptist Association, the first association in Alaska, was organized by three Anchorage churches, primarily to support a small children's home which had been started. In the fall of 1954, the Tanana Valley Association was organized by the churches in the Fairbanks area. In 1951 the SBC received the Alaska Baptist Convention as a cooperating constituency, and used the occasion to establish a policy for future action on the admittance of small new state conventions to the SBC.

Definite mission work by Southern Baptists for the natives of Alaska (Alaskans use the term native to refer to its aboriginal inhabitants—Eskimos, Indians, and Aleuts) was begun in Fairbanks in Jan., 1947. Other missions for natives begun prior to statehood were started in Anchorage (1953), the Eskimo village of Kotzebue (1953), and the Athabascan Indian village of Ft. Yukon (1955). From Kotzebue and Ft. Yukon other missions were started in surrounding villages. Both missions in Fairbanks and Anchorage began as segregated missions for natives, but now welcome all races, while trying to minister to the urban native population in a special way.

Many Negroes came to Alaska during the early fifties. While they were welcomed in the local churches, many desired congregations of their own. The Greater Friendship Baptist Church, organized in Anchorage in 1951, was the first Negro congregation of any denomination in Alaska and was the first Negro congregation to join the Alaska Baptist Convention. In 1953 a Negro congregation was organized in Fairbanks.

For five out of the first six annual meetings of the Alaska Baptist Convention, the Northern Baptist Church at Kodiak sent messengers. The Alaska convention met with the Kodiak church in 1951, but after this convention all fraternal cooperation by the Northern Baptists with the convention ceased.

In 1956 the Alaska convention, in cooperation with the HMB, began the establishment of a denominational organization. L. A. Watson of Denver, Colo., was elected as superintendent of missions and the first full-time executive secretary of the Alaska convention. The convention offices were in the basement of the Watson residence at 1037 16th Ave., Anchorage. The convention staff was enlarged in the next two years to include a bookkeeper-secretary, Bernice Gillespie; WMU secretary, Louise Yarborough; secretary of religious education, Roy Moore; and general missionary, Ben Hill. In the summer of 1958 the convention offices were moved to 419 W. 7th Ave., Anchorage, in a former residence. Also in 1956 the convention assumed support for the Turnagain Children's Home in Anchorage.

The growth of the convention during the years, 1946–58, was hampered by controversy which was present, sometimes on the surface but always beneath it. Part of the trouble was a conflict of personalities, but there were vital differences in other areas. This conflict reached a climax when the Tanana Valley Association withdrew fellowship from the First Baptist Church, Fairbanks, in Mar., 1958. For a short time the church withdrew from the state convention but returned in 1959. When Alaska became a state on Jan. 2, 1959, Alaska Baptists were more unified than at any period since the organization of the convention.

III. Southern Baptists in the State of Alaska, 1959–70. Alaska, whose population grew from 128,647 in 1950 to 226,167 in 1960, a growth of over 75.8 per cent, continued to grow during the decade of the sixties. (The population of Alaska in 1969 was estimated at 279,000). The growth of Southern Baptists continued and was centered in south central Alaska and the interior region around Fairbanks. The work in southeastern Alaska, the panhandle of the state, did not expand as rapidly as in the more populated sections of the state. The churches in this area did form the Tongass Baptist Association in 1960, but due to transportation difficulties were hampered in cooperative efforts. The association was reorganized in 1969. Following the discovery of oil on the Kenai Peninsula in 1960, churches in this area began to grow and they formed the Tustamena Baptist Association in 1969.

The Alaska Baptist Convention has had three executive secretaries since statehood. Following the resignation of L. A. Watson in Feb., 1963, William H. Hansen of Fairbanks accepted the position and served until May, 1966. E. W. Hunke, Jr., of Phoenix, Ariz., became executive secretary in Sept., 1966. In Nov., 1961, the convention abolished the position of general missionary. In May, 1968, E. C. Chron of Anchorage was elected state superintendent of missions. Allen Meeks became secretary of religious education in Nov., 1964, and Judy Rice was elected WMU secretary in Dec., 1968.

Since its organization the Alaska convention has published a monthly paper, the *Alaska Baptist Messenger,* edited by the executive secretary. In 1959 the convention established the Alaska Baptist Foundation. The convention owns a camping facility near Ketchikan on the Naha River. The property, known as Orton Ranch, was a gift to the convention from the Marion Dunhams of Ketchikan. The Chugach Association operates a summer camp near Wasilla. The convention supports one Baptist Student Union at the University of Alaska at College. From 1956 to 1964 the East Third Avenue Baptist Mission in Anchorage operated the Native Baptist Training School to provide missionary training for natives. Local churches have sponsored outstanding literacy and citizenship schools in Fairbanks and Anchorage.

During the first decade of statehood Alaska experienced two great natural disasters—the Good Friday earthquake of 1964 and the Fairbanks flood of Aug., 1967. The Mar. 27, 1964, earthquake, the strongest ever recorded in North America, caused extensive damage throughout south central Alaska. Churches in the Anchorage

ALASKA STATISTICAL SUMMARY

Year	Associations	Churches	Church Membership	Baptisms	S. S. Enrolment	V.B.S. Enrolment	T. U. Enrolment	W.M.U. Enrolment	Brotherhood Enrolment	Music Enrolment	Mission Gifts	Total Gifts	Value Church Property
1955	1	20	4,013	584	3,176		1,305	541	287		$ 39,165	$260,065	$1,503,725
1956	2	19	4,111	252	3,253	2,130	1,360	537	235		38,351	291,608	1,892,925
1957	2	21	4,901	403	3,769	2,134	1,583	762	245	373	40,868	324,417	1,834,700
1958	2	21	4,935	498	3,643	2,401	1,615	804	401	411	57,721	328,145	1,983,200
1959	2	23	5,724	489	4,141	2,715	1,873	754	372	431	50,691	402,392	2,426,599
1960	3	25	6,258	585	4,699	3,193	1,997	835	594	416	56,992	450,900	3,301,300
1961	4	27	6,698	662	5,187	4,014	2,298	1,041	408	683	60,180	470,158	3,135,060
1962	4	30	7,210	501	5,780	3,858	2,583	952	471	757	59,944	462,268	3,161,271
1963	4	30	7,398	535	5,672	3,934	2,663	1,126	568	705	58,549	512,977	3,319,086
1964	3	33	7,808	427	5,357	3,524	2,384	968	469	691	61,972	531,020	3,395,801
1965	3	34	7,584	507	5,877	4,084	2,142	967	474	582	95,444	669,048	3,250,286
1966	3	34	8,162	650	5,573	4,082	2,390	1,001	383	651	92,583	810,943	3,766,487
1967	3	35	8,459	675	6,090	5,024	2,823	1,111	333	791	109,786	640,659	5,134,615
1968	3	37	9,547	741	6,466	3,815	3,041	1,125	254	847	119,227	937,951	5,314,915

E. W. HUNKE and TERRY L. JONES

area and the Seward church suffered minor damage. The building at Valdez was damaged beyond repair and this structure was reconstructed in the new town of Valdez built after the quake.

Alaska celebrated the centennial of its purchase from Russia in 1967. The Alaska Baptist Convention sponsored a booth at the official Alaska Centennial Exposition in Fairbanks and had scheduled its convention for this city in mid-August. The worst flood in Alaska's history hit Fairbanks the day before the convention was to begin, causing extensive damage to nine churches and four parsonages. Once the water receded, the churches faced the task of preparing for the severe northern winter which was only six weeks away. Under the leadership of the HMB and the SBC Brotherhood Commission, Southern Baptists with the cooperation of many airlines, sent 102 men to Fairbanks, who with 20 Alaskans, repaired the damage before winter. The reconstruction job was a remarkable example of denominational cooperation.

As the city of Anchorage continued its remarkable growth in the late sixties, the First Baptist Church, in July, 1965, sold its downtown church building and property to a large department store. They relocated at 10th and L Street, along Anchorage's Park Strip, and erected Southern Baptist's first million-dollar church structure in Alaska.

In 1969, 37 churches and 17 missions were cooperating with the Alaska convention. Of this number three churches were predominantly Negro, one church and five missions were predominantly in Eskimo villages, three missions were in predominantly Indian villages, and two missions primarily served natives in urban areas. The Chugach Association included 18 churches and three missions; Tanana Valley Association 10 churches and four missions; Tongass Association four churches and two missions; and Tustamena Association four churches and one mission. One church and seven missions, all located in native villages in western and northern Alaska, were not affiliated with any association.

The 1970 Alaska Baptist Convention budget called for a total of $224,189, including $120,338 from the HMB and $10,200 from the Sunday School Board. The convention will send 29 per cent of Alaska Cooperative Program receipts to SBC causes.

In addition to Southern Baptists, the following Baptist groups have churches in Alaska: American Baptists, Conservative Baptists, Free-Will Baptists, Baptist General Conference, Bible Baptists, General Association of Regular Baptists, Baptist Mid-Missions, and independent Baptist churches.

The growth of Southern Baptists in Alaska can be attributed to a number of factors. First, the timing was exactly right. In the early forties when Southern Baptists began churches in Alaska, the territory was on the verge of a remarkable boom. Second, the early leaders had remarkable abilities. Their vision and aggressiveness cannot be minimized. Third, the contributions of the HMB were most influential. The thousands of dollars expended speak loudly, but perhaps more vital was the assistance given through the numerous simultaneous revival campaigns and the summer mission programs in cooperation with the Baptist Student Union. Fourth, Alaska Baptists did not expend their energies on institutions but concentrated on establishing churches and missions. Fifth, and most important, the evident blessings of God were present.

The discovery in 1968 of perhaps the largest oil field in North America on Alaska's barren Arctic coast and the subsequent Sept. 10, 1969, oil and gas lease sale which brought the state of Alaska over $900,000,000 indicate a continuance of rapid growth for Alaska and hopefully for Alaska Baptists. RICHARD A. MILLER

***ALEXANDRIA BAPTIST HOSPITAL.** See LOUISIANA BAPTIST CONVENTION.

***ALIEN IMMERSION.** Alien immersion was an issue which troubled many Southern Baptists during the period, 1956–70. In general, Southern Baptist churches in the southeastern states continued to recognize the validity of alien immersion, while many Southern Baptist churches in the other states in the Convention, particularly the Southwest, did not. While the constitution of the Southern Baptist Convention does not mention alien immersion, thereby leaving room for differences of opinion on the subject, at least two state Baptist conventions affiliated with the SBC, Kansas and California, have constitutional provisions denying membership to Baptist churches which accept alien immersion and open communion.

Alien immersion was a point of tension as recently as 1969 in the state convention sessions of California, Arkansas, New Mexico, and Texas. While discussion of the subject in these and other areas appeared to have subsided shortly after the convention meetings, the thorny problems posed by alien immersions will more than likely continue to be debated among Southern Baptists. J. E. TULL

ALL-UNION COUNCIL OF EVANGELICAL CHRISTIANS-BAPTISTS AND COUNCIL OF CHURCHES OF THE EVANGELICAL CHRISTIANS AND BAPTISTS (cf. All-Soviet Council of Evangelical Christians-Baptists, Vol. I). Efforts to unite the Baptists and the Evangelical Christians in Russia were unsuccessful until Oct., 1944, when the All-Union Council of Evangelical Christians-Baptists (AUCECB), composed of 10 individuals, was formed with Jacob Zhidkov as president. Baptists and Evangelical Christians, spread throughout the vast area of the U.S.S.R., were organized into 70 districts, each of which was led by a senior or chief presbyter who supervised the presbyters leading the local congregations. In 1945 Pentecostals were invited to unite with the AUCECB;

many did so, but the majority soon withdrew. In 1946 the AUCECB began to publish *Bratskii Vestnik* ("Brotherly Leader"). In 1963 Brethren Mennonites united with the AUCECB.

During the sixties a separation occurred within the fellowship of Baptists and Evangelical Christians. Following stricter enforcement of government measures against religious bodies and augmented by the Evangelical Free Christians and the Pure Baptists, neither of whom had entered the union of 1944, and by the other groups, a group protesting the policies of the AUCECB emerged in 1961 under the leadership of Alexei F. Prokofiev and Gennadi K. Kryuchkov. Called *Prokofievtsy* ("Prokofievites") and *Initsiativniki* ("Initiative-group" or "Action-Group"), the group became the Council of Churches of the Evangelical Christians and Baptists (CCECB) in 1965. Its protest against the AUCECB was threefold: too great conformity to governmental control (especially in registration), too centralized and unrepresentative church polity (especially the 10-member council and the senior presbyters), and too little aggressive evangelization. National congresses called by the AUCECB in 1963 and 1966 adopted constitutional changes designed to meet objections raised by the *Initsiativniki,* and some of the latter reunited with the AUCECB at its 1969 congress.

Forbidden to establish Sunday Schools, youth organizations, extensive benevolent institutions, or theological seminaries, Baptists and Evangelical Christians in the U.S.S.R. have held to the central Christian affirmations and despite great obstacles have transmitted the gospel through preaching and music in their worship services and through the personal testimony and the exemplary lives of their members. Their relations with the Russian Orthodox Church, which prior to 1905 had actively collaborated with the imperial government in the persecution of dissenters, have ameliorated in recent years. Baptists and Evangelical Christians have been described as "a synthesis of Western Protestantism with Russian-Ukrainian piety" (Kolarz). The AUCECB holds membership in the Baptist World Alliance.

BIBLIOGRAPHY: Michael Bourdeaux, *Opium of the People: The Christian Religion in the U.S.S.R.* (1966). Michael Bourdeaux and Peter Reddaway, "Soviet Baptists Today," *Survey* (Jan., 1968), 48–66. Michael Bourdeaux, *Religions Ferment in Russia: Protestant Opposition to Soviet Religious Policy* (1968). Walter Kolarz, *Religion in the Soviet Union* (1961). J. C. Pollock, *The Faith of the Russian Evangelicals* (1964).

JAMES LEO GARRETT, JR.

ALLEN, ANDREW QUINCY (b. Petersburg, Tex., Jan. 9, 1904; d. Dallas, Tex., Jan. 14, 1960). Sunday school state secretary and denominational leader. After attending West Texas State Teachers' College, Allen graduated from the University of Texas (B.B.A., 1926) and Southwestern Baptist Theological Seminary (M.R.E., 1929). He married Martha Pipkin on June 18, 1930, and had one child, Caylor Drew. He served as associate pastor, First Baptist Church, St. Joseph, Mo., and educational director, East Grand Baptist Church, Dallas, Tex. Allen was superintendent of the Sunday School and Brotherhood Department, Tennessee Baptist Convention, children's leader for the Sunday School Board, Nashville, and assistant administrator of Baylor Hospital, Dallas, before assuming his principal work as secretary of the Sunday School Department, Baptist General Convention of Texas, 1949–60. He was president of the Southwestern Baptist Religious Education Association, 1953, and was used by the Foreign Mission Board to help organize Sunday School work in South America. Allen was buried in Dallas, Tex.

R. HOOPER DILDAY

ALLEN, WILLIAM SIMS (b. near Hico, Tex., Oct. 27, 1888; d. San Antonio, Tex., June 1, 1951). Teacher, educator, writer, college president. Graduate of Baylor University (A.B., 1912), and Columbia University (A.M., 1915; Ph.D., 1923), he was awarded the LL.D. by Simmons University, Abilene, Tex., 1932; and the L.H.D. by Stetson University, 1944. He married Gertrude Eudaly, June 22, 1914; they had no children.

From 1912 to 1916 he served as public-school teacher and principal in Italy and Waco, Tex. He joined the faculty of Baylor University in 1916 as instructor in Latin and in 1924 was named dean of the College of Arts and Sciences. Named Baylor's acting president, 1931–32, he was dean and chairman of the School of Education, 1932–34. He served as president of Stetson University, 1934–47.

Allen was president of the Florida Baptist Convention (1940, 1941) and Florida Association of Colleges (1945). He was active in the Southern Association of Colleges and Schools, the DeLand Chamber of Commerce, the National Association of School Principals, and many other organizations. He was a member of Phi Kappa Delta, Kappa Delta Pi, and Kiwanis. Author of numerous magazine articles, he also wrote *Study in Latin Prognosis* (1923). During World War I Allen served in the U. S. Army at Fort Sheridan, Ill., and at Baylor where he taught military history.

As president of Stetson, Allen strengthened Stetson's academic life, improved relations with the Florida Baptist Convention, and led an important building program. In recognition of his contribution to Stetson and Baptists, the Florida Baptist Convention in 1950 named the new Baptist Student Union Building on Stetson's campus Allen Hall.

Allen is buried in Hico, Tex.

OLGA BOWEN

AMBASSADOR LEADER. A quarterly publication for leaders and counselors published by the Brotherhood Commission, (1959–70). Subscriptions exceeded 5,000 before the first issue

(Feb., 1959) was off the press. Circulation increased from 15,555 in 1960 to 21,062 in 1962. Two years later it jumped to 27,000 copies. Circulation increased to 27,976 in 1967 and reached a peak of 29,389 in 1968. It dropped to 28,448 in 1969.

The last copy of the *Leader* was the July–Sept., 1970, issue. At this time the magazine was absorbed by two other magazines: *Crusader Counselor* and *Probe (Leadership Edition)*. DARRELL C. RICHARDSON

***AMBASSADOR LIFE.** A monthly mission magazine for boys published by the Brotherhood Commission. On Oct. 1, 1957, the magazine was transferred from the Woman's Missionary Union to the Commission. During 1956, under the sponsorship of the WMU, monthly circulation average was 67,000 copies. At the close of 1957, average monthly circulation had risen to 77,000 copies. Monthly circulation grew to 90,739 in 1960. The following year it increased to 95,101, a gain of 4,362. Circulation in 1962 reached 101,959. The average monthly circulation in 1964 was 113,000 (over 1,500,000 copies were produced during the year). During 1965 the circulation grew to 114,989. It increased to 123,787 in 1967 and reached a high of 126,986 in 1969.

The last issue was dated Sept., 1970. At this point two publications (*Crusader* and *Probe*) replaced *Ambassador Life.*

DARRELL C. RICHARDSON

***AMERICAN BAPTIST ASSOCIATION.** The annual national meetings of the association are composed of three messengers from each cooperating church. Interests of the churches in the fields of missions and publications are served between annual sessions by a 25-member missionary committee and a 16-member literature committee. Committees and officers are elected annually.

Educational institutions supported by these churches are the Missionary Baptist Seminary and Institute, Little Rock, Ark.; Texas Baptist Institute, Henderson, Tex.; Oklahoma Missionary Baptist Institute, Marlow, Okla.; Florida Baptist Institute, Lakeland, Fla.; Eastern Baptist Institute, Hamilton, Ohio; Carolina Missionary Baptist Institute, Greenville, S. C.; California Missionary Baptist Institute, Bellflower, Calif.; Louisiana Missionary Baptist Institute, Minden, La.; Seminario Bautista Missionero De Mexico, Monterrey, N. E. Mexico; Mexican Baptist Institute, Pharr, Tex.; Illinois Missionary Baptist Institute, Washington, Ill.; Baptist Christian College, Shreveport, La.; Missionary Baptist College, Sacramento, Calif.; and Bogalusa Bible School, Bogalusa, La.

Nine of the schools publish periodicals. They are *The Missionary Baptist Searchlight,* Little Rock, Ark.; *The Baptist Monitor,* Henderson, Tex.; *The Baptist Sentinel,* Bellflower, Calif.; *The Baptist Anchor,* Lakeland, Fla.; *The Missionary Baptist News,* Minden, La.; *The Soul-Winner,* Shreveport, La.; *The Baptist Review,* Marlow, Okla.; and *Missionary Baptist Herald,* Sacramento, Calif. The Illinois Baptist Association publishes the *Illinois Missionary Baptist.* Two independently owned publications, *The Missionary,* Nashville, Tenn., and the *Baptist World,* Little Rock, Ark., also serve the interests of these churches.

Statistics show 2,105 churches for the association in 1951 with a total membership of 286,691. By 1968 the total number of churches had grown to 3,247, with an inclusive membership of 731,000. For the same period the organization's Sunday Schools increased from 1,147, with an enrolment of 146,000, to 3,247 schools, with an enrolment of 271,500. In 1958 there were 2,100 ordained ministers in the association, increasing over the next decade to 3,175. Only six periodicals were listed in 1956, with 12 listed in 1968. From 1959 to 1968 the number of schools sponsored by these churches increased from 8 to 14. For the same period their missionary force increased from 39 to 72. I. K. CROSS

***AMERICAN BAPTIST CONVENTION.** A chief executive officer, the general secretary, associate general secretaries, and chief executives of national program agencies (American Baptist Home Mission Societies, American Baptist Foreign Mission Society, American Baptist Board of Education and Publication, and Ministers and Missionaries Benefit Board) serve as administrators for the convention. The General Council, an elective body of 46 persons, functions as the policy-making and long-range planning body of the convention. Cooperative programs are conducted through national, state, and city organizations.

A headline event for the convention was the gathering of all national denominational agencies under one roof in a beautiful new office building at the Valley Forge Interchange of the Pennsylvania Turnpike.

A significant achievement in Christian education was the creation of the Christian Faith and Work Plan, an all-church curriculum designed by the American Baptist Board of Education and Publication in the conviction that

> The objective of the church's educational ministry is that all persons be aware of God through his self-disclosure, especially his redeeming love as revealed in Jesus Christ; and, enabled by the Holy Spirit, respond in faith and love, that as new persons in Christ they may know who they are and what their human situation means; grow as sons of God, rooted in the Christian community; live in obedience to the will of God in every relationship; fulfill their common vocation in the world; and abide in the Christian hope.

Teaching materials, in line with the above objective, were based on foundations for curriculum that were worked out cooperatively by Christian education specialists of 16 denominations, including both the American Baptist Convention and the Southern Baptist Convention. The materials developed on this basis were created in close cooperation with the Church of the Brethren, the Church of God in Anderson, Ind., and the Disciples of Christ, and were introduced into general use in Sept., 1969.

Denominational agencies at all levels have focused attention on planning for "Mission in Reconciling Action in the 70's."

Pursuant to the commitment made in 1950 in connection with the change of name, an "Affirmation of Welcome" was adopted in 1958, emphasizing the fact that it was not a document of recruitment but a friendly assurance of readiness "to confer with any group of Christians of like faith and mind in the United States of America, without regard to geographical location, cultural, social, racial, or national background who desire to bear witness to the historic Baptist convictions in a framework of cooperative Protestantism." In response, a growing number of churches in the South, especially in the black community, are affiliating with the convention and are served by a staff headed by J. C. Herrin, assistant general secretary for work in the South.

The creation of the Baptist Council on Cooperation in World Mission was a significant development in the area of mission policy. The council grew out of the Overseas Planning Consultation in 1957 and the Hong Kong Consultation on World Mission in Dec., 1963, and Jan., 1964, conducted by the American Baptist Foreign Mission Societies. The council serves as an instrument through which indigenous leaders on overseas fields take a meaningful part in policy making and long-range planning for the fuller implementation of the Great Commission. Consistent with the historic policy of developing native leadership, the American Baptist Foreign Mission Society is in the process of transferring mission property ownership and management to Christian nationals on several fields.

Reorganization.—Several steps were taken in order to achieve a more effective organization. In 1961 the denomination approved a structure under which the separately incorporated national missionary and educational agencies function explicitly in their respective areas of responsibility as program boards of the denomination; and the central corporate body functions through divisions of Archives and History, American Baptist Men, American Baptist Women, Christian Social Concern, Communication, Cooperative Christianity, Management and Organization, Program Planning, and World Mission Support. The American Baptist Publication Society and the Board of Education were merged in 1964 to form the American Baptist Board of Education and Publication; and the two foreign mission societies were consolidated into a single entity in 1968. The home mission societies reorganized in 1969. Further steps in basic reorganization are under active consideration by the Study Commission on Denominational Structure. An ongoing study of administrative areas and relationships is developing regional organizational structures designed to enable the churches to participate more faithfully and more effectively in the fulfilment of Christ's mission and to manifest more clearly the true marks of the church.

Overseas Missions.—The American Baptist Foreign Mission Society, the direct descendant of the Triennial Convention, the oldest Baptist mission organization on the national level in the United States, currently supports mission work in Burma, Europe, Hong Kong, India, Japan, Maylasia, Okinawa, Philippines, Republic of Congo, and Singapore. As of Jan. 1, 1969, the society had 317 missionaries and 9,540 national workers serving with overseas churches having a membership of 811,615. The society maintains a total of 576 schools, colleges, seminaries, and Bible schools, 23 hospitals, and 37 dispensaries.

Education and Publication.—The American Baptist Board of Education and Publication coordinates a program of Christian higher education through 43 denominationally related schools and colleges and theological seminaries. It carries on a major program of Christian education at the American Baptist Assembly, Green Lake, Wis., where approximately 30,000 participants receive training in a variety of educational and missionary conferences each year. The board shares with several other denominations in United Ministries in Higher Education, an ecumenical approach to witness on college and university campuses.

Home Missions.—The American Baptist Home Mission Societies support mission work in all 50 states as well as in Puerto Rico, Haiti, El Salvador, Nicaragua, and Mexico. The Division of Parish Development provides counsel and services to local congregations and helps in establishing new churches. The Division of Social Action supports Christian centers, small group homes, nursing homes, hospitals, and retirement centers. The Department of Chaplaincy Services ministers through 168 military chaplains and 209 institutional chaplains and through Selective Service counseling. Both personal and social emphases are continued in the evangelistic program which seeks to extend the kingdom of God through personal commitment of individuals and the renewal of the structures of society. In inner-city ministries the paternalistic attitudes and practices which were an acceptable style in former days were discarded in favor of partnership with the people where they are in developing a sense of their own dignity and integrity. The emphasis is on helping people do things for themselves.

Professional skills are exercised in a variety of specialized ministries through newly created corporations. Through the American Baptist Service Corporation and the American Baptist Management Corporation, the societies have become the largest private, nonprofit owner and operator of low- and medium-income housing in the United States. Through the American Baptist Extension Corporation, local congregations are provided a loan service for construction, capital fund raising counsel, and program studies.

Ministerial Support.—In the New England

states and New York, the Ministers and Missionaries Benefit Board and the Commission on the Ministry conducted a successful pilot project in a salary-support program designed to bring all ministerial salaries to or above an agreed upon minimum. The development of personnel support systems for ministers, missionaries, and lay employees include expanded pension and health benefits, as well as the establishment of the Center for the Ministry where professional counseling is available in the areas of career development, continuing education, and placement.

Some Marks of American Baptists.—Some meaningful marks of the American Baptist Convention pertain to policies and practices with respect to open communion, race relations, and interdenominational cooperation. An open communion policy prevails in all areas of the convention, on the ground that the Lord himself is the host at the table and his disciples are the invited guests. Concerning race relations, the convention has worked for equal rights and equal opportunity for Negroes and other minority groups in church membership, employment, housing, education, voting, and the use of public accommodations. It has repudiated all forms of segregation, based on race, color, or ethnic origin, as contrary to the gospel of Christ and as incompatible both with the Christian doctrine of man and with the nature of the church. The convention's first black president, Thomas Kilgore, Jr., was elected in 1969. The convention is a charter member of the Baptist World Alliance, the National Council of the Churches of Christ in the U. S. A., and the World Council of churches, and has always been ecumenical in outlook and relationships. With respect to ecclesiology, the convention tends to emphasize the basic nature of the church as being the general order of all who have been incorporated by the Holy Spirit into the Body of Christ; and the churches are looked upon as particular local expressions of the universal church. This view is held to be consistent with the emphasis made in most of the historic Baptist confessions of faith as over against the local church concept which gained wide acceptance in some areas on the basis of the New Hampshire Confession. The churchly nature of the convention as a "body of Christians seeking to order its life in accordance with the Scriptures under the guidance of the Holy Spirit" was emphasized in an enlarged statement of purpose which was adopted in 1969, identifying the convention "as a manifestation of the church universal."

In line with the ecumenical commitment of the convention, a Commission on Christian Unity was established in 1966 to engage American Baptists in a wider and deeper understanding of the meaning of Christian unity and to enter such conversations as may be authorized with respect to closer relations with other bodies. Conversations with the Church of the Brethren, concerning the possibility of merger, have progressed to the point where "Principles for a Plan of Union" were formulated for study and response by the churches. Conversations looking toward closer working relationships are in process with the Seventh Day Baptist General Conference and the Progressive National Baptist Convention. Mutually enlightening conversations are proceeding with the Bishops' Committee for Ecumenical and Interreligious Affairs of the Roman Catholic Church, which requested the opportunity of dialogue in the interest of a better understanding between Roman Catholics and American Baptists.

In the persons of W. Hubert Porter and Robert G. Torbet, the convention has been in an observer-consultant relationship with the Consultation on Church Union since 1963, but the convention decided by action of the General Council not to become an official participant.

Mission Support.—The World Mission Campaign for capital funds for home and overseas missions provided one of the success stories of the decade. Pledges amounting to $17,932,566 were received on a goal of $10,000,000 for cash contributions. Including campaign contributions and institutional support, a new record for missionary giving in a single year was set in 1968 when contributions totaling $19,756,021 were received, a 10.4 per cent increase over the previous year. During the decade, the amount of money given in support of the missionary program increased by approximately 85 per cent. The 1969 budget for the basic mission program was $13,331,500. Annually the basic budget is supplemented by several million dollars of nondonation income from investments, legacies, matured annuities, and other sources.

Throughout the decade, the membership statistics have been on a plateau, with little change from year to year in the total of approximately 6,000 churches with about 1,500,000 members. A recent annual report listed 6,039 churches with 1,491,186 members and a church school enrolment of 767,239. Contributions for all local expenses amount to approximately $110,000,000 per year. W. HUBERT PORTER

AMERICAN BAPTIST FOREIGN MISSION BOARDS (cf. American Baptist Foreign Mission Society, Vol. I; and Woman's American Baptist Foreign Mission Society, Vol. II). In 1955 the American Baptist Foreign Mission Society and the Woman's American Baptist Foreign Mission Society were integrated into one organization called the American Baptist Foreign Mission Boards. Presently (1967) missionaries are distributed thus: Bengal-Orissa-Bihar, 12; North East India, 21; South India, 38; Hong Kong, 7; Japan, 34; Malaysia-Singapore, 4 in special service; Okinawa, 6; Philippines, 27; Thailand, 42; Congo, 100; and Europe, 7 working with autonomous Baptist organizations. Due to government regulations, the last missionaries were withdrawn from Burma in 1966, but word from there indicates the work continues to move forward.

A survey team completed an objective study of the various national conventions in 1968 and recommended that over a 15-year period the national churches assume full responsibility for the financing of the programs of local churches, associations, and national conventions. This will apply to the long-established fields, but in the newer ones, such as Thailand, Congo, Hong Kong, and Okinawa, it is expected that the Mission Society will need to carry considerable financial responsibility for some years to come. The 1968 operating budget for the boards was $3,594,000. HELEN E. FALLS

***AMERICAN BAPTIST FOREIGN MISSION SOCIETY.** See AMERICAN BAPTIST FOREIGN MISSION BOARDS.

***AMERICAN BAPTIST HOME MISSION SOCIETY.** In 1968 this society reported in its Division of Latin America a total of 22 missionaries assigned to El Salvador, Haiti, Mexico, and Nicaragua. In addition, there were 10 nationals who were fully supported by the society and 91 who were partially supported. The overseas work budget of $157,359 helped to support two hospitals, six schools, and three seminaries. In addition to the work in Latin America, $70,217 was spent on work in North America.

HELEN E. FALLS

***AMERICAN BAPTIST THEOLOGICAL SEMINARY.** Victor Thomas Glass, named acting president June 1, 1956, served until July, 1957. Maynard P. Turner, Jr., served as president from Aug. 5, 1957, to July, 1963. Charles E. Boddie took office as president Aug. 1, 1963.

L. S. Sedberry (*q.v.*) retired as executive secretary of the Southern Baptist Commission on the American Baptist Theological Seminary, Dec. 31, 1961, after 12 years on the campus. Rabun L. Brantley, executive secretary of the Education Commission, SBC, was asked to serve also as secretary-treasurer of the commission on the seminary in Jan., 1962. In 1966, the Education Commission was asked to become the receiving and disbursing agent of the commission. Full management of budgeted funds was delegated to the officers and trustees of the seminary in Jan., 1966.

J. C. Miles, professor of Bible, died Aug. 2, 1957, after association with the seminary from 1930 until his death. Joining the seminary faculty when the only other teacher was J. H. Garnett, he taught Bible, church history, sociology, church doctrine, and was professor of Old Testament Greek and Hebrew at the time of his death. He was founder and director of the Department of Seminary Extension. Interest from memorial funds of the J. C. Miles Chair of Bible helps pay salaries of those teaching Bible.

Robert W. Hailey, son of O. L. Hailey (*q.v.*, Vol. I), died Oct. 13, 1963, having served as recording secretary of the commission. He was assistant to E. P. Alldredge (*q.v.*, Vol. I), former executive secretary of the commission.

About 85 students per year study for the A.B. degree in religion. Enrolment was 91 in 1969, when nine degrees were awarded. Scholarships are awarded to several students each year for advanced study in prominent colleges and seminaries. HERMAN F. BURNS

***ANABAPTISTS.** The years 1955–70 witnessed a new recognition of and widened interest in Anabaptist research. It has been established as a legitimate field of historical investigation, shed its "stepchild" status, and attracted leading church historians and researchers. Thus, an historical task begun in an earlier generation by Mennonites and the Baptist historian Albert Henry Newman (*q.v.*, Vol. II) has been taken up by many others.

An impressive number of monographs has been published on the leaders, doctrines, and practices of Anabaptism as well as on its significance for modern church history. A work of encyclopedic proportions is George H. Williams' *The Radical Reformation* (1962).

BIBLIOGRAPHY: R. Armour, *Anabaptist Baptism* (1966). W. R. Estep, *The Anabaptist Story* (1963). R. Friedmann, *Hutterite Studies* (1961). E. W. Gritsch, *Reformer Without a Church: Thomas Muentzer* (1967). G. F. Hershberger, ed., *The Recovery of the Anabaptist Vision* (1957). H. J. Hillerbrand, *A Bibliography of Anabaptism 1520–1630* (1962). G. H. Williams, ed., *Spiritual and Anabaptist Writers*, in "The Library of Christian Classics," vol. XXV (1957). J. K. Zeman, *The Anabaptists and the Czech Brethren in Moravia 1526–1628* (1969).

W. MORGAN PATTERSON

***ANDERSON COLLEGE.** In Oct., 1957, John E. Rouse became the seventh president of this South Carolina institution. Rouse came to this position from the pastorate of the First Baptist Church in Laurens, S. C. At this time a general study of Baptist colleges resulted in what was known as the Cornett Report. A committee from the South Carolina Baptist Convention, in consultation with the committee of the Education Commission of the Southern Baptist Convention, made the following recommendations concerning Anderson College: (1) that the trustees and administration see to it that there be no deficit in current operations; (2) that the matter of attaining accreditation be given immediate priority; (3) that no new buildings be constructed during the current capital needs program, except those already under construction; (4) that Anderson College's capital needs appropriations be held in escrow until final decision is made regarding the future of the college.

These stipulations recommended by the Cornett Report were promptly met, and the future of Anderson College has grown steadily brighter to this date, 1970. The college became completely coeducational with dormitories for men as well as women. The following buildings were added under the direction of Rouse: infirmary, three men's dormitories, student center building, gymnasium, music chapel, and the Watkins Teaching Center. In addition to these new buildings, extensive renovations, improvements, and enlargements have been made. The newly acquired home for the president was enlarged and refurbished, and the former one was converted into a music department and air conditioned. The college also installed modern operational equipment, improved facilities for the music and language departments, and provided adequate faculty offices.

Additional properties were obtained. Approximately 15 acres, adjacent to the original 32 acres, were purchased. Several nearby dwellings necessary for college personnel were purchased. A 650-acre farm five miles from the college was donated to the college. A corporation known as the Anderson College Investment Corporation was formed to purchase and operate Bailey Court, a 100-unit apartment complex. This is an eleemosynary corporation operating for the benefit of the college.

Physical improvements made on the campus include paving roads and parking lots, placing all electrical and telephone wires underground, and improving overall beautification through care of trees, shrubbery, and grassed lawns.

Some improvement was realized by increased endowment and receipt of trust funds. The Living Endowment for Anderson College (LEAC) made a noteworthy contribution to upgrade all the faculty. Two local major financial campaigns met with good response and the standing of the college in the eyes of the citizens of Anderson is gratifying. The property value stood at $5,000,000 in 1970 and the annual operating budget was $1,000,000. The enrolment of the college has steadily increased from less than 200 to more than 900 during the administration of Rouse. JOHN E. ROUSE

ANGOLA, MISSION IN. Southern Baptists were preceded in Angola by British, Canadian, and Portuguese Baptists. In 1929 missionaries of the Portuguese Baptist Convention began a mission near Nova Lisboa. From this beginning eight churches developed and in 1966 formed the Baptist Convention of Angola, with approximately 400 members. On invitation of Angola and Portuguese conventions, the Foreign Mission Board sent Harrison and June (Summers) Pike as fraternal representatives in 1968. Pike became pastor of the church in Luanda and also served an English-language group there. A radio ministry was begun in 1970, and plans were projected for training pastors and lay leaders for Angolan churches. H. CORNELL GOERNER

***ANN HASSELTINE YOUNG WOMAN'S AUXILIARY.** In 1963 the WMU executive board appointed a special committee to study Ann Hasseltine and Grace McBride YWA's. The committee brought the following recommendation in 1965: "that WMU provide a plan for college YWA in the church to be effective not later than Oct., 1966; that where the plan for the college YWA on the campus seems more appropriate, it be followed."

The name Ann Hasseltine was not used after 1966. The 1969 report listed 186 church-centered college YWA groups with a membership of 2,007; and 83 campus YWA's with 2,817 in membership. DORIS DE VAULT

ANNUITY BOARD (cf. Relief and Annuity Board, Vol. II). SBC agency located in Dallas, Tex., known as Relief and Annuity Board from 1918 until 1960, when the Convention authorized the change in name. The board administers two programs: the Program of Management of Retirement Annuities and the Program of Ministers' Relief Administration.

As of Dec. 31, 1954, the board held assets totaling $35,091,515 and had paid out during that year benefits of $1,763,467 and relief grants of $321,060.

When R. Alton Reed became executive secretary in 1955, the board was offering the Southern Baptist Protection Plan, the first plan which provided coverage attractive to the young minister during his active service as well as retirement.

All previous plans had provided coverage primarily for retirement. Some older plans even allowed age benefit credits for years of service rendered in which no dues were paid. Giving prior service credits in those plans created an actuarial liability for the various state conventions. The extent of the liability was not known, so the first act of Reed's administration was to determine the total liability for all states.

In the spring of 1958 the actuary reported that liabilities for all plans—state and agency—exceeded $25,000,000; even so, no member at any time ever failed to receive the benefits he was promised.

Reed proposed a four-point solution which in less than a decade wiped out all liabilities. His proposal included:

1. Write all members in the Ministers' Retirement Plan who had not paid dues since 1955 asking them to resume participation or surrender their certificates for refund.

2. Increase participation of churches from 11,000 to 20,000, and encourage them to pay dues whether or not they had a pastor.

3. Pool reserves of all states to improve administrative and actuarial liability.

4. Start a promotional campaign to increase membership from 37 to 75 per cent of eligible members.

During 1958 a record of 1,548 new applicants joined the Protection Plan. Each year thereafter, through 1964, that record was exceeded.

In 1960 the board became the first denominational pension agency to offer a variable plan built around common stocks. A term insurance plan, the Life Benefit Plan, followed in 1964. A year later, the Health Benefit Plan, providing hospital-surgical-major medical benefits, was inaugurated.

As the work grew, more staff members were employed. Additional space was necessary, so a 15-story building was constructed. In 1959 the board moved into its new quarters, occupying less than three floors and leasing the others.

The growth also demanded organizational expansion. In 1963 after extensive studies, four divisions and seven departments were created. The four divisions were: Development, Member Records, Investment, and Finance and Accounting. The departments were: Actuarial, Building Management and Leasing, Electronic Data Processing, Member Accounts, Personnel, Publications and Communications, and Relief and Annuitants Service. In 1964 the Life and Health Benefits Department was created.

Wallace Bassett retired in 1965 after serving as a trustee from the Board's beginning and as president for 45 years. E. Hermond Westmoreland of Houston succeeded him.

In 1965 Reed reported that enlistment in some state plans was sufficient to eliminate their liabilities. Projections indicated that by 1970 all states would be in the black.

By late 1966, the actuarial liabilities had been eliminated almost four years earlier than predicted. This achievement allowed the board to begin a program of liberalizing benefits. In Feb., 1967, the trustees approved recommendations to liberalize coverage which included:

Put all members in either the Southern Baptist Protection Program or the Southern Baptist Benefit Program, depending on the plan they were in formerly;

Combine the basic and two supplemental plans offered separately into the above mentioned programs;

Increase some existing benefits such as disability;

Add new benefits for child, education, and dependent parent;

Make all benefits retroactive to Nov. 22, 1966, the date the last state convention approved them;

Issue, henceforth, one certificate, eliminating the need for another when a member transfers from one state to another;

Pool all state and agency plans to improve administrative and actuarial handling;

Fund completely the (old) Annuity Fund which had been a burden from the beginning;

Direct promotion to the church;

Encourage the church to pay 10 per cent of total salary toward greater retirement benefits;

Fund each benefit when entered upon;

Allow a member to pay on $4,000 a year salary, even though he may receive less;

Liberalize the permissible service rule pertaining to retired ministers serving churches;

Give a dividend check out of interest earnings in excess of assumed rate used when funding the benefits to persons receiving benefits.

The dividend check called the "13th Check" has been paid each year since 1966. The first check represented an eight per cent dividend and equaled the amount of one monthly check; the others have been for 12 per cent.

For years the Relief Program had incurred deficits. But a dramatic reversal started in 1957 due to efforts to certify actual need of recipients. Through 1969 relief needs continued to decrease as more people retired with age benefits than ever before.

The annual report of the board to the SBC in June, 1969, indicated 23,714 persons participating in Plan A of the Southern Baptist Protection Program, 9,362 in Plan B, and 2,424 in Plan C. Another 840 members were in the Southern Baptist Benefit Program, currently closed to new members. Of the 174 agencies, 145 have state- and Convention-wide programs for their employees. The Life Benefit Plan had 11,341 members; the Health Benefit Plan, 15,521; and the Group Life Insurance Plan, inaugurated in 1967, had 3,147. Assets (funds held for participants in the plans) reached

	RELIEF AND ANNUITY BENEFITS BY YEARS			TOTAL ASSETS AND INVESTMENT EARNINGS BY YEARS	
	Relief Benefits	Annuity Benefits	Totals	Total Assets	Investment Earnings
1919–55	$5,622,129.40	$16,872,314.58	$22,494,443.98	$ 42,031,744.01	$13,083,347.08
1956	320,443.24	1,626,211.59	1,946,654.83	49,106,570.01	1,805,318.09
1957	331,979.64	1,913,881.54	2,245,861.18	55,798,566.34	2,133,537.14
1958	321,846.03	2,092,921.87	2,414,767.90	63,580,338.27	2,424,377.92
1959	310,303.21	2,267,455.85	2,577,759.06	72,202,524.38	2,810,064.28
1960	287,809.53	2,457,804.07	2,745,613.60	82,036,033.31	3,420,883.98
1961	225,593.77	2,654,222.44	2,879,816.21	93,269,312.90	4,072,023.53
1962	212,870.26	2,878,602.68	3,091,472.94	105,400,192.31	4,621,363.70
1963	201,421.07	3,052,212.90	3,253,633.97	119,546,778.80	5,347,941.69
1964	182,558.41	3,267,912.28	3,450,470.69	135,354,421.15	5,873,903.02
1965	172,815.24	3,561,296.72	3,734,111.96	152,406,442.02	6,795,350.45
1966	171,242.23	4,085,002.32	4,256,244.55	169,350,234.95	7,644,015.98
1967	175,145.25	4,644,252.76	4,819,398.01	188,016,599.60	8,757,316.78
1968	173,863.46	6,369,307.15	6,543,170.61	208,218,706.31	9,042,104.70
	$8,710,020.74	$57,743,398.75	$66,453,419.49		$77,831,548.34

B. J. CHENAULT

511 NORTH AKARD BUILDING, Dallas, Tex. The Annuity Board, SBC (*q.v.*), occupies six of the 15 floors of this building. Opened in 1959, it is part of the Board's investment program.

THE ARIZONA SOUTHERN BAPTIST CONVENTION (*q.v.*), purchased this building in Phoenix in 1967; utilizes the third floor for its offices and leases the first and second floors.

FLEMING LIBRARY BUILDING, Grand Canyon College (*q.v.*), Phoenix, Ariz. Constructed in 1957; houses classrooms on the second floor.

$208,218,707. Benefits in the amount of $6,543, 169 were paid to annuitants.

In July, 1968, a Long-Range Committee was appointed by the trustees to study needs of Baptist ministers and lay employees and to see if the board met those needs. Every area of the board's ministry was studied including the need for reorganizational structure. Recommendations from personnel, programs, and services were to be implemented in 1970.

Darold Morgan of Dallas was elected president, succeeding E. Hermond Westmoreland.

In Oct., 1969, a new Group Insurance Program was inaugurated to replace the previously offered Life Benefit Plan. JOHN D. BLOSKAS

ANSWER, THE. A syndicated television film series which came into being in 1956 under the original title of *This Is The Answer.* Paul M. Stevens, director of the Radio and Television Commission, SBC, started working on the series idea in 1954. Professional television writers developed scripts for the first dozen episodes based on the parables of the New Testament. With the assistance of Family Films of Hollywood, Calif., filming on the series began there in 1955. In Apr., 1956, a premier press screening was held at the Normandy Theater on West 57th Street in New York City. Immediately thereafter the series was released for television distribution.

From the start, all episodes of *The Answer* were filmed in color even though no commercial color telecasting was to begin for several years. The series enjoyed a popular replay when colorcasting became a reality in the early sixties.

After the first series, episodes branched out in story form to include modern stories with moral, ethical, and spiritual emphases all based on biblical teachings, and human interest documentaries related to missionary endeavor.

In 1959 a major evangelistic thrust was planned for *The Answer.* Called *Televangelism,* it was an attempt to enlist Baptist viewers to visit and witness in connection with the telecasts in January, February, and March of that year. Although many problems of scheduling and promotion were encountered, mail response reflected that the special emphasis went far in achieving its goal.

The series name was changed with the 1960 series to *The Answer.* Through 1969 production, a total of 102 subjects have been released in the series. The average number of stations carrying the series annually has been about 120, while mail response runs about 500 letters a week.

Production costs per program have averaged $20,000, with the resulting film remaining in the telecast schedule at least four years.

W. TRUETT MYERS

ARCADIA BAPTIST HOME. Louisiana Baptists began a new ministry in 1960 with the opening of a home to provide comfort and safety in a Christian environment for ambulatory aged people. Four women were admitted the first day. The single building is located on 115 acres near Arcadia in Bienville Parish. The home has a capacity for 55 residents in 36 bedrooms.

First recorded investigation of a home for the aged was by a committee appointed by the executive board of the Louisiana Baptist Convention in 1955. After a report to the state convention in 1957, the convention approved the resolution to create a benevolent ministry for the elderly, accepted the offer of the Arcadia First Baptist Church for the land, authorized construction of a facility which cost approximately $300,000, voted $25,000 a year in Cooperative Program funds to amortize the capital outlay and initiate the program, and elected a 12-member governing board of trustees.

Mrs. Florence Norris, first administrator, was succeeded by Raymond W. Gaudet in 1966. The home added complete nursing care for elderly residents in 1968.

In 1969 residents of the home numbered 51. Net value of property and equipment was $221,243. The 1970 operating budget was $179,423. Income from residents is the primary source of operating revenue.

CHARLES S. MCILVEENE

***ARCHITECTURE, CHURCH.** European architecture and other foreign designs influenced the early church architecture of Southern Baptists. From Europe came the Gothic, Romanesque, Renaissance, and Georgian styles. The influence of Sir Christopher Wren and the New England meetinghouse perpetuated the use of Colonial and Georgian architecture for two centuries.

After World War II, there developed in the United States and among Southern Baptists a desire to use more modern and contemporary styling in architecture. Contributing factors, along with the desire to break away from foreign influences, were the cost of such structures, zoning requirements in cities and counties, the cost of materials available, and the construction methods employed. Such influences have produced almost every possible geometric shape for church buildings since World War II. Some configurations have proved to be expensive and undesirable, even though they create curiosity and call attention to the building.

As yet no distinctly American style of church architecture seems to be arising. There is a growing awareness that the most successful design of a church building must come from the theology, the environmental influences, and the ideals adopted for worship, teaching, training, and other organized activities of the church itself. Fortunately, every kind of needed building material is available and accepted today as new buildings are designed.

The three most significant architectural emphases of Southern Baptists during recent decades are master planning, unit building, and the multiple use of space. Experienced architects and thoughtful church survey and planning committees make every possible effort to secure a master plan for using all property wisely and providing for all phases of church life in the design of a building, even though the full plan will not be realized until a later date. Churches have discovered that buildings may be designed by units and constructed as needs arise and as finances are available. Methods of framing and the materials used in buildings for educational and activities purposes make it possible for these buildings to be constructed in such a manner that they may be rearranged in minimum time at minimum cost.

During recent years Baptist churches have become more conscious of the contribution a building environment can make to creating a better atmosphere for worship. Also, there has been a desire for greater participation in worship by the congregation, together with a desire for a closer contact between the minister and the congregation. These desires and a period of general prosperity have led to improvements in the space provided for pulpit platforms and choir areas. More comfort has been provided through a widespread application of air conditioning and the use of carpeting and upholstered seating.

Southern Baptists' entire educational program has been undergoing changes and improvements. These include new grouping-grading, organizational plans, and curriculum. All of these have called for a careful study of existing church-building floor space as well as a careful planning of all floor space to be used in the future.

In 1956 the value of Southern Baptist Church property was reported as $1,491,385,336. In 1969 the value was reported as $3,656,597,050. Most of the increase came about in new property and buildings acquired by the churches. Many of the churches have been organized since 1956.

The Church Architecture Department of the Sunday School Board, serving the churches in the Southern Baptist Convention, in 1969 received an average of 185 requests per week for services and consultation. The department consulted with nearly 5,000 churches during that year.

BIBLIOGRAPHY: C. Harry Atkinson, *How To Get Your Church Built* (1964). William A. Harrell, *Providing Adequate Church Property and Buildings* (1969). Albert Christ-Janer and Mary Mix Foley, *Modern Church Architecture* (1962). John E. Morse, *To Build A Church* (1969). Joseph Stiles, *Acquiring and Developing Church Real Estate* (1965).

W. A. HARRELL

***ARGENTINA, MISSION IN.** In 1957 the Argentine Baptist Convention adopted a cooperative plan of finances. A coordinating council, composed of representatives from both the convention and the mission, was created. The national encampment at Thea was first used in 1960. In 1964 Argentine Baptists entered a "Decade of Advance," hoping to double the number of churches and church members. They participated effectively in the Crusade of the Americas. In 1969, 86 missionaries cooperated with 18,000 members in 241 churches, of which about four fifths were self-supporting. FRANK K. MEANS

ARIZONA, BAPTIST CHILDREN'S HOME OF. Located at 3101 West Missouri, Phoenix, Ariz. Interest in having a children's home in Arizona was present from the beginning of the convention. Gifts for needy and dependent children were channeled through the New Mexico convention in those early days. The movement gained momentum in 1956 when Mr. and Mrs. J. B. Carnes of Yuma gave $20,000 to be used for the building of a home for needy and dependent children in Arizona. Others added to this fund from time to time. Charles L. McKay led out in seeking advice and counsel from all of the children's homes of the Southern Baptist Convention.

On May 9, 1958, the Arizona Corporation Commission granted a certificate of incorporation for Baptist Children's Home of Arizona. On Mar. 3, 1959, the executive board of Arizona Southern Baptist Convention voted to transfer funds held in trust by the board to the elected trustees of the proposed home. On Feb. 29, 1960, the trustees of the home elected George R. Wilson, Sr., who was then pastor of Central Baptist Church, Phoenix, and serving as the chairman of the executive board, to be the superintendent-treasurer of the new institution. Five acres of land were purchased from the convention with the aid of a gift from the L. E. Jennings family. The cottage for 12 children was built in 1960 at a cost of $29,000. Mr. and Mrs. Otis Dickson were employed as houseparents in 1961, and the first child was received shortly afterwards. By 1970, 58 children had been received and cared for. In 1970 all land and equipment were paid for, and some $15,000 were in savings for a new cottage.

GEORGE R. WILSON, SR.

***ARIZONA ASSOCIATIONS.**

I. New Associations. APACHE. From its organization in 1961 to 1970, there were over 2,000 baptisms. In 1969, 24 churches and two missions reported 5,255 members, $175,000 mission gifts, and $2,201,027 property value.

LAKE MEAD. Organized in 1956 by churches in Clark County, Nev., formerly affiliated with Mohave Association. In 1969, 24 churches and five missions reported 4,936 members, $28,532 mission gifts, and $1,937,069 property value.

RIVER VALLEY. Organized at the First Baptist Church, Needles, Calif., in 1964, by messengers from Chloride, Kingman, Needles, Parker, Bullhead City, and River Valley Chapel. In 1969 nine churches and two missions reported 1,465 members, $10,550 mission gifts, and $756,500 property value.

TROY BROOKS. Organized under the name of Hassayampa Baptist Association on Nov. 3, 1957, by the Wickenburg, Yarnell, First Southern, Prescott, Bagdad, Miller Valley, and Prescott churches, from the Estrella and Grand Canyon associations. In 1958 the name was changed to Troy Brooks in honor of missionary Troy Brooks. In 1969 the association reported 1,246 members, 106 baptisms, $7,469 mission gifts, and $408,700 property value.

WHITE MOUNTAIN. Organized on Mar. 24, 1964, by the McNary, Showlow, Lakeside, Springerville, Whiteriver, Overgaard, Pinetop, Alpine, and Burton churches from Little Colorado Association. In 1969, 10 churches reported 1,246 members, 109 baptisms, $7,469 mission gifts, and $353,500 property value.

II. Changes in Associations. HASSAYAMPA. Organized Nov. 3, 1957. Its name was changed in 1958 to Troy Brooks Association.

ROY F. SUTTON

ARIZONA SOUTHERN BAPTIST CONVENTION (cf. Arizona, Baptist General Convention of, Vol. I).

I. History. In Sept., 1956, Charles L. McKay became executive-secretary-treasurer, a post he retains in 1970. McKay came from the Baptist Sunday School Board where he had served as secretary of evangelism and enlargement for five years.

In 1960 the name was changed from Baptist General Convention of Arizona to Arizona Southern Baptist Convention, which met with wide approval.

The convention purchased an office building at 316 West McDowell, Phoenix, and moved into it in 1956. The downtown building which was occupied by the convention was sold to the Sunday School Board for the use of the Baptist Book Store.

Early in 1967 the convention offices were again moved. The "400 Building" at 400 West Camelback, appraised at $450,000, was purchased by the convention's executive board, and the third floor of the building serves as offices for the convention. The first two floors are leased to retire the indebtedness on the building. Future plans call for a home office building to be erected to meet the needs of the Arizona convention.

In addition to the 80 churches given up by the Arizona convention to constitute the Colorado Baptist Convention, 50 churches and missions were given up in 1965 to constitute the Utah-Idaho Convention. Most of these churches in the Utah-Idaho area still have their loans for building and expansion with the Arizona convention. In 1970 several of these loans were seriously in arrears, which greatly handicapped the Arizona convention's loan fund.

In spite of the churches lost to the Colorado and Utah-Idaho conventions, the number of churches increased from 154 with 25 missions in 1956, to 228 churches and 58 missions in 1969. The total membership increased from 29,041 in 1956 to 68,168 in 1969. There were 48,728 people baptized into these churches during this period.

Grand Canyon College.—This institution was given full accreditation into the North Central Association of Colleges and Universities in 1968. The budget in 1970 was in excess of $1,000,000 with more than $2,500,000 in assets. Presidents during this period were Loyed Simmons, Eugene Patterson, and Arthur Tyson. Acting presidents were Glenn Eason and Charles L. McKay.

Baptist Children's Home.—The home received its charter in 1960 and George R. Wilson, Sr., pastor of Central Baptist Church, Phoenix, became its first superintendent. He has served in this post since 1960.

Hospitals.—The Arizona convention entered the hospital ministry on Feb. 1, 1961, when the Parkview Hospital in Yuma was acquired by the newly formed Baptist Hospital Association of Arizona. Within the next two years the convention purchased what is now Baptist Hospital of Scottsdale and Baptist Hospital of Phoenix. The total patient capacity of the three hospitals in 1969 was 518. A full-time chaplain serves in each hospital. All three of these hospitals before purchase were having serious financial difficulty. The three had reached an operating deficit of approximately $1,000,000. The Arizona convention has operated these successfully and in 1969 they had a net worth of more than $8,000,000. All three hospitals have achieved national accreditation.

Foundation.—The convention's foundation was incorporated in 1950 but it was not until 1962 that the trustees elected a full-time director, Glen Crotts, then pastor of First Southern Baptist Church, Tucson. He still serves in this position. The foundation had difficulty serving all the people who sought its services.

Church Loans Division.—For years it was difficult to finance new church buildings in a pioneer area. The Arizona convention has operated a revolving loan fund, the Trust and Memorial Fund, to help churches purchase land and build first units. In addition, the convention issued $5,000,000 in convention bonds and made them available to churches for building and expansion. In 1970 the loans totaled $688,217. This church loans division is operated by the executive board. The division was directed by Roy F. Sutton, J. Dee Cates, and Bill Parker.

The Assembly.—The camps and assemblies at Paradise Valley Baptist Ranch serve as one of the most unifying forces in the convention. Some 1,500 to 2,000 people enjoy some time each summer at the ranch. Ten weeks of convention-sponsored activities are conducted each summer, with many church groups also sponsoring retreats. The Cooperative Program provides 1 per cent for camp indebtedness. From 1957 to 1969 the following construction was completed at the ranch: a chapel, dining hall, hotel, WMU building, fellowship hall, children's building, caretaker's home, 16 family cottages, 6 church-constructed cabins, winterized dormitories, a fully equipped kitchen, and a swimming pool. Ernie and June Myers managed the assembly for about six years. Several permanent buildings were built during that time. The past several years Mr. and Mrs. Roy F. Sutton and Bill Parker have managed it.

The Baptist Beacon became a weekly newspaper in 1946. Editors were Barry Garrett, Kelly Simmons, James Staples, J. Dee Cates, Frank Gillham, and James Staples who again assumed this duty in Apr., 1970. The circulation of the *Baptist Beacon* was approximately 11,000 in 1970.

The combined budgets of the convention and its institutions in 1956 totaled $600,404. The combined budget for 1970 was $20,853,595.

II. Program of Work. *Executive board.*—The board has charge and control, except when ordered by the convention of all the work of the convention in the interim of its sessions. This board consists of 31 members, equitably distributed, including the president of the convention, who is also chairman of the executive board. The executive board, as the convention ad interim, presents to the convention annually for its adoption a comprehensive budget. It is instructed and commissioned by the convention to study the affairs of the boards and institutions of the convention, to make recommendations to them concerning needed adjustments, and to make whatever other recommendations concerning them it deems advisable.

Associate and assistant executive secretaries contributed to the growth of the work in the Arizona convention. From 1956 to 1970 these were Howard Halsell, E. W. Hunke, Roy F. Sutton, and Dan C. Stringer, Jr. In 1970 Sutton was the associate executive secretary of the convention, as well as director of the division of missions. Stringer was assistant executive secretary and institutional and financial coordinator for the convention.

Evangelism.—In Jan., 1966, W. D. Lawes resigned as state secretary of the department of evangelism to become an associate in the Home Mission Board's division of evangelism. Charles McKay served as interim until May, 1966, when Irving Childress became state secretary. In 1967 the first area-wide crusade in Arizona was conducted in Flagstaff, with others following. From 1958 to 1969, 43,209 baptisms were reported.

Sunday School.—In 1962 Mel C. Craft succeeded Ernie Myers as secretary of the Sunday School department. In 1966 Craft was succeeded by Jess L. Canafax. Harvey Kimbler assumed these duties in 1968. Between 1956 and 1969 enrolment in Sunday School increased from 29,342 to 46,831. Myers and Craft also served as church building consultants, and Myers managed the ranch in the summer during camps and assemblies. Vacation Bible School enrolment increased from 16,879 in 1956 to 22,339 in 1969.

Training Union.—C. E. Archer served as secretary of the Training Union department, 1956–69. Enrolment grew from 11,239 in 1956 to 20,525 in 1969. Archer also worked with music, BSU, Brotherhood, and church recreation. When Archer left the department to serve as pastor of the First Baptist Church, Buckeye, Robert Warren, pastor of the First Southern Baptist Church, Glendale, succeeded him. Warren leads the Training Union, Brotherhood, and music work of the convention.

Missions.—The mission division works through 15 district associations. E. W. Hunke and Roy F. Sutton served as directors of the division, 1956–70. Hunke resigned to become executive secretary-treasurer of the Alaska Convention in 1966, at which time Sutton was elected as director. In 1960 the convention entered a cooperative agreement with the Home Mission Board to coordinate associational and language missions. Irwin Dawson was the first director of language missions under this new agreement, with Dan C. Stringer as associate. The convention employed in 1970, four Chinese, 15 Indian, 23 Spanish, and 2 Mission Center missionaries.

WMU.—Almarine Brown served almost the entire period as executive secretary of Woman's Missionary Union for the Arizona convention. The WMU enrolment increased from 4,340 to 7,450, and during this time the work with Royal Ambassadors was transferred to the Brotherhood. After serving 12 years, Miss Brown retired from this position. She was succeeded by Mary Jo Stewart in 1969.

Stewardship.—Due to lack of funds, the work of the stewardship department was of necessity distributed to the various department heads. Those assisting with this were E. W. Hunke, Roy F. Sutton, Dan C. Stringer, Jr., J. L. Canafax, Irving Childress, and Charles L. McKay. In 1956 mission gifts through the Cooperative Program totaled $292,488. In 1969 the total was $507,502.

Brotherhood.—W. D. Lawes and C. E. Archer were the two secretaries of the department, 1956–69. The men's organizations increased from 1,887 to 2,457. Churches with Royal Ambassadors organizations increased from 80 to 200.

Church Building.—Church building consultants from 1956 to 1969 were Ernie Myers, Mel Craft, and Bill Parker. These three men assisted more than half of the Arizona churches and, in addition, most of the Utah-Idaho churches and those in southern Nevada in their space problems. They cooperate with the Church Architecture Department of the Baptist Sunday School Board in Nashville, Tenn.

BSU.—In 1968 Irving Childress succeeded Paul Barnes as state BSU secretary. The number of campuses served by the convention reached 15, where over 100,000 students were enrolled. In 1970 active BSU organizations numbered eight. Six of the directors were volunteers and two received partial support.

Music.—The music ministry has perhaps developed in Arizona faster than most other facets of the convention's work. In 1957 the record reveals only 450 people officially enrolled in the music ministry. In 1970 the enrolment was 5,875. Men serving the music ministry in the

ARIZONA STATISTICAL SUMMARY

Year	Associa-tions	Churches	Church Member-ship	Baptisms	S. S. Enrol-ment	V.B.S. Enrol-ment	T. U. Enrol-ment	W.M.U. Enrol-ment	Brother-hood En-rolment	Music Enrol-ment	Mission Gifts	Total Gifts	Value Church Property
1956	15	154	29,041	2,696	29,342	16,879	11,239	4,340	1,887		$292,488	$1,670,272	$ 6,347,200
1957	15	163	33,015	2,823	30,476	17,235	13,186	5,847	2,934	450	289,457	1,986,931	8,901,441
1958	18	184	37,018	3,310	35,766	19,498	14,940	6,866	2,265	485	317,331	2,217,730	8,925,690
1959	20	185	38,487	3,217	35,504	18,859	14,895	6,648	3,151	570	318,127	2,308,390	10,088,070
1960	19	200	44,800	3,148	40,178	20,788	16,953	7,984	2,580	2,350	324,954	2,845,713	12,811,536
1961	19	205	49,893	3,688	43,278	22,211	18,804	8,616	2,628	4,255	362,538	2,890,085	15,132,611
1962	20	217	54,487	3,977	46,401	23,813	19,360	8,550	2,713	5,425	386,704	3,385,211	17,495,183
1963	20	226	58,619	3,735	48,944	26,153	20,715	8,766	2,801	3,793	405,206	3,609,892	18,983,695
1964	22	251	62,229	3,900	52,086	27,963	21,470	8,983	4,691	4,295	416,607	3,885,095	21,301,923
1965	15	212	58,050	3,606	46,196	25,278	18,610	7,704	2,819		442,461	3,796,601	20,343,165
1966	15	216	59,582	3,528	47,583	27,103	19,264	8,072	3,497		424,571	3,942,756	17,395,199
1967	15	222	63,101	3,828	47,052	27,825	19,122	7,945	3,057		446,198	4,152,395	24,262,857
1968	15	226	65,523	3,881	47,370	25,825	19,599	7,758	2,859	5,239	487,608	4,715,997	24,680,000
1969	15	228	68,168	3,391	46,831	22,339	20,525	7,450	2,457	5,534	507,502	4,948,019	25,948,011

MRS. GEORGE R. WILSON, SR.

state were C. E. Archer, Paul Barnes, and Robert Warren, who is now (1970) serving.

C. E. ARCHER, JOE CAUSEY, IRVING CHILDRESS, HARVEY KIMBLER, CHARLES L. MCKAY, BILL PARKER, EUGENE VIRT

***ARKANSAS ASSOCIATIONS.**

I. New Associations. BOONE-NEWTON. Formed by the merger of the two associations, Oct. 20, 1961. In 1968, 28 churches reported 4,244 members and $1,105,400 property value.

CALVARY. Formed by the merger of White County and Woodruff County Associations, Oct. 23, 1961. In 1968, 39 churches reported 8,178 members and $1,830,500 property value.

NORTH PULASKI. Organized Oct. 17, 1961, by 30 churches from Pulaski Association. In 1968, 34 churches reported 1,289 members and $7,721,657 property value.

VAN BUREN COUNTY. Organized by 12 churches from Stone-Van Buren-Searcy Association and 1 church from Faulkner County Association, Nov., 1967. In 1968, 13 churches reported 1,143 members and $128,902 property value. J. T. ELLIFF

II. Changes in Associations. BOONE COUNTY. Was merged into Boone-Newton in 1961.

NEWTON COUNTY. Was merged into Boone-Newton in 1961.

WHITE COUNTY. Was merged into Calvary in 1961.

WOODRUFF COUNTY. Was merged into Calvary in 1961. J. T. ELLIFF

***ARKANSAS BAPTIST ASSEMBLY.** An assembly located near Siloam Springs, which accommodates summer meetings held to promote various phases of the program of the state convention. Three men have directed the assembly program since 1956: Edgar Williamson, 1957–59; J. T. Elliff, 1961–65; and Lawson Hatfield, 1965– . In 1968 the registration reached 2,115 compared with 1,559 in 1955. Property, buildings, and equipment were valued at $150,000 in 1968. RALPH DOUGLAS

***ARKANSAS BAPTIST FOUNDATION.** Following W. A. Jackson's resignation as executive secretary in Jan., 1956, came several years without full-time leadership. Benjamin L. Bridges (*q.v.*) having retired as executive secretary of the state convention, gave much of his time to the foundation from Nov., 1956, to Feb., 1959, when failing health forced him to terminate his service. On July 1, 1961, Ed F. McDonald, Jr., accepted the position of executive secretary. During the first eight years of his administration, the assets of the foundation increased from $82,000 to over $250,000. Work with wills and estate planning is slow and harvest comes later.

Emphasis is being placed on a strong and active board of directors, which met four times in 1969. The board has produced an investment policy, a revision of the Bylaws, subject to convention approval, and a project to develop a job description for the executive secretary. A program of work has been outlined for the secretary in 1970 that promises to be productive. Payments to agencies and institutions reached an all time high in 1969. ED F. MC DONALD, JR.

ARKANSAS BAPTIST HISTORY COMMISSION. Arkansas Baptists organized a state convention in 1848, but the convention did not appoint a committee on statistics until 1871. Other actions antecedent to a history commission included annual listing of ministers and obituaries of ministers. Early statistical secretaries include: J. K. Pace, W. A. Clark, O. L. Hailey, and E. J. A. McKinney. P. S. G. Watson privately collected data and began a history of Baptists in Arkansas, but his materials were lost during the Civil War.

In 1906 the convention constituted its first history commission "to collect data." By 1912 chairman J. B. Searcy had prepared a history for publication, but neither "advance subscriptions" nor convention appropriations produced sufficient funds. The last note on that manuscript states that a copy was loaned to Baptist Bible Institute, New Orleans, to be copied. In 1935 the convention instructed its executive board "to make arrangements with E. J. A. McKinney to finish the History of Arkansas Baptists." McKinney's death stymied the project until 1944, when the convention again elected a history commission. Comprised of J. S. Rogers, Thomas L. Harris, and B. L. Bridges, the commission led the convention to elect a history committee to work with Rogers in producing a history. The convention published Rogers' *History of Arkansas Baptists* in 1948. That same year, the convention authorized the organization of The Arkansas Baptist Historical Society which existed until dissolved by the convention in 1960.

The History Commission, Arkansas Baptist State Convention, replaced the historical society. The commission is composed of nine members —one from each of the eight districts and one member-at-large as chairman—elected to three-year rotating terms. In 1965 the convention elected George T. Blackmon as executive secretary for an indefinite term. The original commissioners were J. T. Midkiff, E. Harold Elmore, George E. Pirtle, Margaret Smith Rose, Bernes K. Selph, James H. Dean, H. S. Coleman, Walter Johnson, Harlan A. Abel, and George T. Blackmon, chairman. The commission is the convention's agency in the field of history. It has led in locating, collecting, preserving, and using documents of the eleven Baptist denominations in Arkansas. Its greatest achievements have been in locating and preserving on microfilm minutes of local churches, associations, and state organizations. It now (1970) holds 264 reels of microfilm containing over 12,000 items of such documents. GEORGE T. BLACKMON

ARKANSAS BAPTIST HOME FOR CHILDREN (cf. Bottoms Baptist Orphanage, Vol. I). An agency of the Arkansas Baptist State Convention, located at Monticello, Ark., operated under the direction of a board composed of 18 ministers and laymen who represent the eight districts within the state. Established in 1894, the institution assumed its present name in 1961. The care of children and the relation of children to their natural home or the Arkansas Baptist Home for Children is the heartbeat of this institution. The child care program of the home is an organization of services to meet the spiritual, physical, mental, emotional, and social needs of children for whom Arkansas Baptists are responsible. The home has changed from a long-term program to a short-term rehabilitative process because of cultural changes and the changing needs of children today.

In 1966 the board employed a trained social worker as its administrator and began to concentrate on helping children learn how to live in society through their own homes or substitute homes. A foster home program was established along with group homes to meet this growing need. The board of trustees sold the farming operation and focused complete attention on child care. Also, in cooperation with this effort, the eating facility was changed to each cottage. In 1968 the board voted to do away with the two-story dormitories and build two new cottages.

From 1957 to 1967 the annual budget has increased approximately $100,000. Along with the increase in expenditures the home has experienced an increase in receipts through the Cooperative Program and the annual Thanksgiving Offering.

The home has opened two offices located in areas of strategic population within the state and these are directed by trained social workers who have experience in child care. These offices are jointly sponsored and supervised by the Home Mission Board of the Southern Baptist Convention, the State Mission Department of the Arkansas Baptist State Convention and local associations in cooperation with the home. The offices give services to children in their own homes, as well as foster homes and group homes. With the addition of these offices in the state, the home has tripled the number of children served.

The children who are received into the Institutional Program receive care from social workers, psychologists, psychiatrists, and other trained personnel. The staff attends regular weekly staff development conferences that are sponsored by the home to train them to work with adolescents. The home offers supportive, supplementary, and substitute services. Supportive services include personal contacts, such as home visits by the social work staff in order to help the family better communicate with and understand each other, and to mobilize and help the family take advantage of community resources. Supplementary services help a child or family to alleviate temporary financial problems. The substitute services fall into three categories: foster homes, group homes, and institutional care. Since 1956 the following men have served as superintendent of the home: H. C. Seefeldt, 1956–61, John R. Price, 1962–66, and Maurice Caldwell, 1966– MAURICE CALDWELL

ARKANSAS BAPTIST MEDICAL CENTER (cf. Arkansas Baptist Hospital, Vol. I). Known today as the Arkansas Baptist Medical Center, the hospital was established by the Arkansas Baptist State Convention in 1920. Through an elected board of trustees, the convention controlled and operated the center until 1966.

In 1966 the trustees reported to the convention that the cost formula of Medicare had precipitated a financial crisis and they felt that they could no longer operate a first-rate medical institution with their anticipated income. Through the years the administration had tried successfully to net approximately seven per cent of the gross receipts. This net, plus Cooperative Program money and special gifts, constituted the only capital needs income. But Medicare proposed to pay only the actual cost of patient care plus two per cent.

However, the federal government offered funds from Hill-Burton and Hill-Harris Acts for capital needs. Consistently forbidden by the convention to accept federal grants, the trustees and the executive board of the convention brought a recommendation that the medical center be given to a private nonprofit association which would be composed of past and present trustees (1966). This association would be self-perpetuating, would appoint trustees to operate the center, and would at its discretion apply for and receive public funds. Each member of the association and each trustee would be a member of a church cooperating with the Arkansas Baptist State Convention. Any violation of this stipulation would give the convention cause to reclaim the center if it so desired.

The debate on the recommendation was lengthy and sharp. Opponents charged that the convention would be giving away $15,000,000 to $20,000,000 of property bought with mission money. Proponents answered that, percentagewise, income from the convention had been negligible through the entire existence of the center and that the property had been accumulated and sustained with private gifts and by wise and effective administration. Opponents expressed a fear that accepting federal funds would give the government complete control of the center. Proponents answered that "the denomination has lost its ability to maintain separation of control even though it has not accepted federal grants."

A substitute motion that the convention keep the center "and permit the trustees to apply for, and receive, public funds for use by the Arkansas Baptist Medical Center" failed by a vote of 516 to 431. Most of the night of Nov. 7th was used for debate and parliamentary maneuvering. Several substitute motions, including one to sell the center and give the proceeds to Ouachita Baptist University, were defeated. Finally the convention voted 488 to 327 to accept the recommendation. Each subsequent day of the convention's sessions, motions to reconsider, to rescind, and to recount all the ballots were defeated. Thus the Arkansas Baptist Medical Center, though retaining its name, became the property of a private, nonprofit association.

The convention's actions were challenged in court, but both the lower and the Supreme Courts sustained the convention. DON HOOK

ARKANSAS BAPTIST NEWSMAGAZINE (cf. Arkansas Baptist, Vol. I). Official organ of the Arkansas Baptist State Convention, published each Thursday, except the weeks of July 4 and December 25. Editor B. H. Duncan retired Jan. 1, 1957, due to terminal illness of leukemia and died a few weeks later, on March 19.

Erwin Lawrence McDonald, a native of London, Pope County, Ark., and a graduate of Ouachita Baptist College (now Ouachita Baptist University) and Southern Baptist Theological Seminary, was elected editor effective Mar. 1, 1957. McDonald, a former Arkansas newspaperman, returned to Arkansas from Louisville, Ky., where he was serving as coordinator of the Kentucky Baptist Schools and Colleges. Beginning with the March 7 issue of the paper, the page size was changed from 9 inches by 12 inches to 8½ inches by 10 inches and the number of pages per issue increased from 16 to 24. Other changes included a new emphasis on news coverage, a policy of dealing editorially with controversial issues, and establishment of a letters-to-the-editor section open to the constituency of the paper for discussion of matters of general concern.

The new and descriptive word "newsmagazine" was added to the name of the publication beginning with the issue of Jan. 21, 1960, in an effort to eliminate confusion of mail between the paper and Arkansas Baptist Hospital (now Arkansas Baptist Medical Center), frequently addressed as "Arkansas Baptist." The paper had a circulation of approximately 48,000 as of Jan., 1957. As of Oct., 1969, the circulation totaled 58,750, with 777 churches of the state convention having the paper in their budgets to go to all of their active members. Besides Editor McDonald, the paper staff in 1970 included Mrs. E. F. Stokes, associate editor; Mrs. William L. Kennedy, managing editor; Mrs. Harry Giberson, secretary to the editor; and Mrs. Weldon Taylor, mailing clerk. ERWIN L. MCDONALD

***ARKANSAS BAPTIST STATE CONVENTION.** When Benjamin Lafayette Bridges (*q.v.*) relinquished the office of secretary of the Arkansas Baptist State Convention, Aug. 1, 1957, after 29 years leadership, it was but normal that evaluation be made and new procedures studied. Bridges had struggled with debts practically all his years in office. His faith and wise counsel had guided his people through the maze of despair to victory, and his strong arm had supported many of the denominational agencies from infancy to adolescence. Changing conditions demanded time now for definition and development. To understand Baptist history of Arkansas during the past 12 years it is essential to remember that this history grows out of a general background of secularism and dialectic philosophy, plus racial disturbances, an effort to establish a two-party political system, an agricultural-industrial revolution, and the liberalizing tendencies of a growing welfare society.

In this religio-political, as well as the economic atmosphere, S. A. Whitlow assumed the duties of secretary of the Arkansas Baptist State Convention, Jan. 1, 1958. This native son graduate of Ouachita Baptist College and Southern Baptist Theological Seminary, brought to the office the mature experience of three Arkansas pastorates, plus service on numerous denominational committees and boards. Preceding his coming the executive board had adopted a budget formula for Ouachita and Southern colleges and invited professional managerial consultants to analyze the program and set the organizational house in order. Whitlow asked that the latter item be deferred for a year to give him time to study the situation. The results of a self-analysis conducted during the year under his direction were: better coordination in the staff and departments; reorganization of the executive board; all bookkeeping put in one accounting department; camps and assemblies placed under the executive board; job descriptions written; salary scales set up; and fringe benefits provided for the employees of the convention. Lawson Hatfield succeeded Edgar Williamson as Sunday School secretary; T. K. Rucker took the new position as field representative for the Annuity Board; and group hospital insurance for all church-related workers was made available.

A vote by the convention in 1959 to borrow $200,000 to purchase and improve camps and assembly sites evidenced expansion. This was further seen (1960) in an experiment known as the Pilot Plan, which called for an educational director in a district to test a plan for promoting the total educational program of the churches. Southern Baptist College requested the convention to assume control of the institution during this session. This independent school, controlled by its own board, had been treated as a mission project by the state convention. A committee was appointed to study the offer. After studying this matter nearly a decade, the convention assumed ownership and control of the institution in 1968. Establishing a historical commission that year, and strengthening racial relations by institutions for teaching, counseling, and studying finances showed interest in the past and present.

By 1960 sociological factors demanded a new ministry among children and resulted in changing the name of Bottoms Baptist Orphanage to Arkansas Baptist Home for Children. The convention granted Ouachita Baptist College permission to launch a fund raising campaign to bring her endowment to $2,000,000. The coming of J. T. Elliff as director of religious education finalized the second phase of the organizational plan adopted when Whitlow became secretary. This division included the Sunday School, Brotherhood, Church Music, and Training Union departments. Jesse Reed's selection as secretary of evangelism, the purchase of a new campsite (220 acres) at Paron, and a summer Bible conference for preachers on Ouachita College campus, sponsored jointly by the school and convention, evidenced further progress. The executive board endorsed a preaching mission to Scotland that year led by a pastor of the state.

Arkansas Baptists worked closely with the Home Mission Board of the Southern Baptist Convention during these years, especially in the field of race relations. The Convention-wide Student Department assisted state BSU director Tom Logue, who promoted student work in college centers by securing sites for buildings and increasing personnel. The church development ministry for the purpose of strengthening smaller churches proved beneficial; an assistant in the missions department was added to direct this work.

By 1963 the winds of change began blowing strongly. Organizational work felt this, interest lagged in some areas, and the call to devise new and better ways to proclaim the gospel intensified. The Pilot Program, still being studied, provided a listening post for the churches. The convention gave use of the RA camp, near Ferncliff, to the Negroes to augment their work. The missions department established a ministry to the deaf that year and directed the work with associational missionaries in an effort to undergird the associations' ministry. Study revealed the need of long-range planning and budget programing to build a program of work based on the needs realized by the churches and the allocation of money to accomplish these goals. This led to the adoption of a budget formula; namely, that each year's budget would be "based on and governed by the percentage increase (or decrease) for the first six months of the current year as compared to the corresponding period of the preceding year." Secretary Whitlow thought this to be the most far-reaching strategy in budget procedure. Though financial receipts continued to increase and total gifts to the Cooperative Program almost doubled during this period, the percentage of total receipts of churches given to the Cooperative Program dropped from 11.45 per cent to 10.60 per cent. Such gifts resulted in sound investment; many baptisms came through the effort of the missions department.

Though an auxiliary to the state convention, the WMU carried its load in the field of missions, teaching, giving, praying, and supporting the total work. The WMU commemorated the 75th anniversary of its work in Arkansas, Apr., 1964, with a historical pageant in the First

Baptist Church, Little Rock, its birthplace. Other departments within the convention balanced out the work load as they wrestled with the growing problems of modern man.

Arkansas Baptists did not confine their work strictly to denominational lines. They co-operated with other religious bodies in the state to combat social and moral problems through the medium of the "Christian Civic Foundation." This body helped defeat casino gambling in the state in 1964.

The first doctrinal question to face the convention in almost two decades arose in the 1965 session when messengers from the First Baptist Church, Russellville, were refused seats, due to the church's view on "alien immersion." A committee had been appointed in 1959 to study the doctrine of ordination, though it did not report until 1963, and then without any controversial recommendations.

To help meet the growing demand for expansion, the Arkansas Baptist Hospital purchased 52 acres of land on North University Avenue, Little Rock, 1965, at a cost of $1,050,000. The next year the convention voted to permit the hospital to sever its relationship with Arkansas Baptist State Convention, to be an independent corporate body solely under the control of its board of trustees, so that it might accept federal aid, unencumbered by any concept of separation of church and state. A suit brought against the convention to prevent this action failed.

Next, the problem of federal aid loomed up in the educational field. Leaders discussed the question in a special meeting in Little Rock, Aug., 1965, and in many unofficial meetings across the state during the next two years. Arkansas Baptists did not receive aid in the full sense of the term, though there were areas where its colleges were receiving governmental help, such as: aid to students, contractural agreements for special services, building loans at comparable rates, acceptance of surplus property, and special scholarships and fellowships. A committee, appointed in 1966 to see if such aid was in violation of separation of church and state, reported that the aid being received violated no principle of separation. In almost every session of the convention during these years some project of Christian education was given consideration. Due to these, and other needs, the convention appointed a committee (1965) to survey this work on a 10-year projection.

Mounting tensions stimulated by educational and doctrinal problems brought heated discussions in the annual session of 1968. In an effort to heal broken fellowship, a reconciliatory committee was appointed to serve in dealing with current frictional situations. The appointment of a rotating nominating committee set the stage for fair and equitable representation on boards and committees.

Arkansas Baptists engaged in expanded ministries in 1968. They assisted the sister conventions of Michigan, Colorado, and Idaho-Utah, in missions and evangelistic efforts. The convention

ARKANSAS STATISTICAL SUMMARY

Year	Associations	Churches	Church Membership	Baptisms	S. S. Enrolment	V.B.S. Enrolment	T. U. Enrolment	W.M.U. Enrolment	Brotherhood Enrolment	Music Enrolment	Mission Gifts	Total Gifts	Value Church Property
1955	45	1,146	283,820	15,037	206,455	75,543	94,452	36,574	11,942		$1,872,565	$10,696,915	$ 41,438,545
1956	45	1,169	285,402	13,452	209,864	75,869	94,406	36,420	12,105		2,074,569	11,848,752	46,103,573
1957	44	1,143	289,981	12,232	204,840	78,201	92,093	36,263	12,061		2,166,205	11,585,421	48,452,202
1958	44	1,152	294,056	12,919	207,526	81,669	91,337	37,069	10,522		2,227,910	11,663,200	53,726,171
1959	44	1,155	296,945	12,681	208,411	77,556	93,656	37,250	11,561		2,322,344	13,034,828	57,887,934
1960	44	1,158	301,435	11,838	210,733	82,725	93,911	36,583	11,285		2,420,481	13,702,776	61,056,837
1961	44	1,164	309,931	12,771	215,158	82,539	95,711	36,697	11,998	19,549	2,505,362	14,210,331	64,909,872
1962	43	1,177	313,806	11,248	215,507	84,103	95,319	36,177	9,925	21,396	2,757,803	15,568,888	70,517,141
1963	43	1,178	318,378	10,226	215,501	85,289	95,845	36,017	9,436	21,509	2,854,565	16,086,452	76,278,640
1964	43	1,184	321,664	10,413	215,969	86,464	93,605	34,373	8,586	22,909	3,024,896	16,917,823	81,309,653
1965	43	1,188	326,354	10,401	215,049	84,145	94,032	35,534	9,259	23,472	3,128,603	17,889,465	84,024,094
1966	43	1,190	332,198	10,411	213,261	82,580	91,781	33,971	8,741	25,530	3,401,770	18,906,315	92,180,559
1967	43	1,191	338,471	11,598	212,961	86,088	92,459	34,555	9,263	28,483	3,594,676	20,602,971	97,933,807
1968	44	1,189	343,336	11,386	213,496	85,978	100,476	34,957	9,049	29,021	3,901,588	23,111,680	101,418,714

NADINE B. BJORKMAN

elected Rivos Dorris, pastor in North Little Rock, director of chaplains, Jan. 1, 1968. Along with these expansion steps must be listed the "special ministries" that were taking hold upon the mind of Baptists: juvenile rehabilitation, resort areas, weekday ministry, and Hope House. The state joined the Home Mission Board, SBC, and Central Association in establishing a missionary in Hot Springs to help meet the multiple need of a resort area. Transients, followers of the race track, and vacationers need a particular ministry.

For years, the Arkansas convention had sought a more commodious building site to house its offices. In 1967 it purchased the property of the Coca-Cola Company, 525 W. Capitol Avenue, Little Rock, for $471,000. Located in the very heart of downtown Little Rock, it was easily accessible from every direction. The building and parking lot were renovated at a cost of $859,027.77. The convention employees occupied this modernly designed and equipped building, Jan. 1, 1969, with the formal dedication, June 3.

After serving eleven and a half years as executive secretary, S. A. Whitlow resigned, effective June 30, 1969. The executive board elected Charles H. Ashcraft as the new secretary. Ashcraft, reared and educated in Arkansas, at the time of his election was serving as secretary of the Idaho-Utah convention. He assumed his duties, Sept. 1. BERNES K. SELPH

ARKANSAS BAPTIST STATE CONVENTION, FELLOWSHIP PROBLEMS OF THE. Fellowship problems in the Arkansas Baptist State Convention during the period from 1956 through 1969 fall into two categories: those which brought disharmony and disturbance and those which created a breach of fellowship.

The first of these categories includes issues which were openly, and often hotly, debated in public. Others were never brought to public debate but affected the relationship between pastor and people and also disturbed the harmony of the convention.

Needs of the educational institutions of the convention brought the issues of administration, finance, and Federal Aid to the fore. Some of these matters were debated in the annual sessions of the convention (e.g., the acceptance of Southern Baptist College as an institution of the convention in 1968).

A dominant issue during the 1966 convention was the release of the Arkansas Baptist Medical Center to a self-perpetuating board of trustees.

The integration-segregation question was never before the convention for debate but created an undercurrent of murmuring in the churches of the state.

The matters which brought about an open break in the fellowship of the convention were open communion and alien immersion. A review of the convention's actions related to these issues in earlier years will provide helpful background for understanding the controversy that emerged in the sixties.

In Dec., 1937, the convention authorized its secretary "to notify the President of the Southern Baptist Theological Seminary that the teaching of alien immersion and open communion is objectionable to the Arkansas Baptist State Convention. The secretary of the convention received a reply from John R. Sampey (*q.v.*, Vol. II), president of the seminary, in a letter dated Dec. 20, 1937, stating that "the teaching of open communion . . . would be contrary to the Abstract of Principles signed by each professor" though alien immersion is not made "a test of fellowship."

Here the matter rested until 1949, when a resolution was offered to interpret the terms "regular Baptist churches" in Article III, Section I, of the constitution "to mean that if any church shall practice open communion, accept alien immersion, or shall affiliate with any organization connected with the Federal Council of Churches, the World Council of Churches, or any organization similar to, or growing out of either of them, such church shall be considered unsound in faith and practice and shall not have messengers seated in this Convention." The convention referred this matter to a special constitution committee to report in 1950.

Later in the 1949 meeting a resolution was offered concerning the action previously taken. It reaffirmed the "position on these Baptist distinctives." The resolutions committee brought this resolution back to the convention in the following form: "Be it resolved: That this Convention refuse to seat any messenger from any church that accepts alien immersion; practices open communion; or affiliates with any branch of the Federal Council of Churches; World Council of Churches; or any other organization similar to, or growing out of such."

The constitution committee reported in 1950: "since the Convention adopted the report of the committee on resolutions last year . . . it is our conviction that no further action by the Convention is necessary."

A search of the records of the convention reveals no further actions with regard to these questions until 1965. That year the First Church, Russellville, adopted a "Statement of Faith" which made the validity of baptism and participation in the observance of the Lord's Supper a matter of subjective determination on the part of the individual. When the convention met, the question of seating messengers from First Church, Russellville, was raised and was referred to the credentials committee. Before the committee reported, a resolution referring to the 1937 convention's action was offered and adopted putting the 1965 convention "on record as objecting to the reception of alien immersion and the practice of open communion." Subsequently the convention rejected the credentials committee's recommendation that messengers from the Russellville church be seated.

In the 1966 convention meeting, a resolution

inviting the First Baptist Church of Russellville to attend any remaining sessions of this convention and/or future conventions was offered. Along with a resolution interpreting the words "regular Baptist churches" of the constitution, it was referred to the credentials committee who later reported they were "powerless to act since the Russellville church has not sought to be received." The other resolution was returned to the floor since it was "for all practical purposes the same in content as the amendment presented by Don Hook last year." The resolution inviting the Russellville church to attend the sessions of the convention was again offered and after discussion the body adopted a motion that the matter be tabled indefinitely.

In the meeting of the convention in 1968, a resolution was offered citing previous convention actions relative to the questions of "open communion" and "alien immersion" and calling for the withdrawal of fellowship from First Church, Russellville; First Church, Malvern (for voting to practice open communion); University Church, Little Rock (for receiving members not only by alien immersion but also on sprinkling for baptism). By amendment, the Lake Village church was also included (for adopting the practice of open communion). Following a lengthy discussion, the resolution was adopted by a vote of 491 to 312. Later a reconciliation committee was authorized by the 1968 convention.

The actions of the convention in these matters came because, as one reflected on the 1949 action, "Deep concern was being expressed by many over the state," and "it was felt that the Convention should redefine 'Regular Baptist Churches' and . . . declare its position."

CARL OVERTON

***ART, RELIGIOUS.** Traditionally Baptists have avoided religious art symbolism in the architecture of their churches and in connection with their worship. Even the cross, the most universally acceptable Christian symbol, has been viewed with misgiving.

Myriad publications of various Southern Baptist agencies employ contemporary art, design, and photographic skills of today for teaching and inspirational purposes. Artist-designers and editors collaborate to produce church literature and promotional items that aid in teaching and training and in promoting causes widely to millions of Baptists. The necessary components of message, printed words, designs, and illustrations must be organized into attractive and efficient relationships to appeal and communicate to the reader, requiring the art functions of design and layout. A growing number of Baptist agencies, such as Woman's Missionary Union, Foreign Mission Board, Home Mission Board, Brotherhood Commission, Radio and Television Commission, and some state conventions, include competent art personnel within their staffs, while many obtain such services on a free-lance basis. These agencies offer talented and trained young Baptists attractive opportunities for employment and Christian life investment in art and photographic positions.

Because of the scope of its many programs, the Sunday School Board, SBC, maintains a large Art Department of several sections organized to service advertising, editorial, merchandising, and promotional needs of its many components. The curriculum materials published by the board use a great many designs and illustrations and among them are many teaching picture sets. The art for these is done by illustrators specializing in biblical and children's illustration, and the free-lance artists employed live in many parts of the nation.

HERMAN F. BURNS

ASHLAND AVENUE BAPTIST. See WALKER, CLARENCE O'NEILL.

ASPLUND, JOHN (b. Central Sweden, *c.* 1752; d. Fishing Creek, Va., 1807). Itinerant preacher, historian. Trained as a clerk in Sweden, he came to America by way of England. Converted about 1782, he joined the Ballard's Bridge Baptist Church, Chowan Co., N. C., which soon licensed him to preach. Later, Southampton Co., Va., became his residence for many years, and he may have been ordained there.

In 1790, after a trip to Europe, he determined to engage in an itinerant ministry to gather data on the Baptist churches of North America with a view to publishing his findings. In this venture his purpose was to promote the unity of the denomination and provide materials for future Baptist historians. John Rippon, Isaac Backus (*q.v.*, Vol. I), and Morgan Edwards encouraged and assisted his labors. In 18 months, 1790–91, he traveled 7,000 miles, visiting 25 associations and 250 churches.

His *Register of the Baptist Denomination in North America, to the First of November, 1790,* was published in Richmond, Va., in April, 1792, a first of its kind. A second printing appeared in Philadelphia in September, 1792. Asplund made another tour in 1792–94, traveling 10,000 miles, visiting 24 associations, 550 churches, and enlarging his circle of acquaintance to include 700 ministers. In 1794 he published in Boston a new edition of the *Register* to cover the period from 1790 through a part of 1794. After studying for a time at Dartmouth College, he prepared a third edition of the *Register* which was published in Hanover, N. H., in 1796. Asplund's last place of residence was on the Eastern Shore of Maryland. He was drowned in 1807 when attempting to swim Fishing Creek in Virginia.

WILLIAM L. LUMPKIN

***ASSAM AND MANIPUR, COUNCIL OF BAPTIST CHURCHES OF.** See INDIA, COUNCIL OF BAPTIST CHURCHES IN NORTH EAST.

ASSEMBLY OPERATION. The objective of the Sunday School Board's Program of Assembly Operation is to provide facilities to operate the assemblies at Ridgecrest and Glorieta as a service to other agencies and programs of the Southern Baptist Convention and the Woman's Missionary Union (for their use in conducting their assembly programs) and to provide facilities and conduct summer camps (such as Camp Ridgecrest and Camp Crestridge) with a spiritual emphasis for boys and girls.

The program leaders are entirely responsible for the structure, content, and conduct of their programs. There is a cooperative obligation between the Sunday School Board and the other agencies of the Convention to utilize the assemblies.

Ridgecrest and Glorieta are owned and operated by the Sunday School Board. The division directors of the board responsible to the administration for the operation of Glorieta and Ridgecrest have been R. L. Middleton, H. E. Ingraham (both retired), and Hubert B. Smothers.

The Sunday School offerings received at the assemblies during the summer conferences are divided among the cooperating state conventions. HUBERT B. SMOTHERS and H. E. INGRAHAM

ASSOCIATIONAL ADMINISTRATION SERVICE, PROGRAM OF. While the Home Mission Board has assisted associations in their administration since its beginning, its program of associational administration dates from 1966. The objective is "to work with and assist associations, state conventions, and Southern Baptist Convention agencies toward achieving effective administration in the associations." Loyd Corder, associate director, Division of Missions, is staff leader, sharing responsibility for the program with the Departments of Pioneer, Metropolitan, and Rural-Urban Missions. In Oct., 1966, E. C. Watson became consultant in associational administration and a member of the program team.

Associational Administration Service does basic research in associational administration; participates in training events; and consults and coordinates with leaders of the associations, state conventions, and the Convention. It produces *The Associational Planning Guide* annually, *Associational Administration* (a bulletin) monthly, tracts on the duties of associational leaders, and has published a book, *Superintendent of Missions for an Association* (1969) by E. C. Watson.

E. C. WATSON

ATLANTA BAPTIST COLLEGE. A four-year coeducational liberal arts college located in Atlanta, Ga., sponsored by the Atlanta Baptist Association. In 1950 the association appointed a committee composed of E. G. Kilpatrick, chairman, Paul S. James, Dick H. Hall, Jr., and Monroe F. Swilley, Jr., to "study the advisability and possibility of establishing a junior college in Atlanta." In 1954 the committee, with Swilley as chairman, recommended that the association approve the establishment of a college. The Atlanta area was surveyed for possible sites. R. Orin Cornett, then secretary of the Southern Baptist Convention's Education Commission, was consulted concerning the proposed college. In 1958 the Georgia Baptist Convention approved a recommendation of its Education Commission for a campaign by the Atlanta association to raise $3 million for use in establishing the college as an agency of the convention. Also that year, a 464 acre site was purchased.

Full responsibility for the college was assumed by the Atlanta association, Oct. 22, 1963. In 1964 the charter was signed, and the first board of trustees was selected with 36 members. Officers were Monroe F. Swilley, Jr., chairman, O. Ray Moore, vice-chairman, and J. J. Wooten, secretary.

Ground was broken Aug. 28, 1966, and the school opened Sept. 18, 1968. Enrolment the first year was 284. Swilley became the college's first president, Jan. 1, 1969. In 1969 the college had a total of 562 acres and four buildings. The cost of land and buildings totaled $3,638,000.

The college, as stated in its charter, is dedicated "to the search for God's Truth as revealed to mankind . . . established and maintained by the Baptist Denomination to impart to students, against a background of Christian faith, a knowledge of man, the universe in which they live, and the relationship of both to the Creator and our Redeemer, Jesus Christ."

BIFF F. WILSON

AUSTRALIAN BAPTIST MISSIONARY SOCIETY, INC. (cf. Australian Baptist Foreign Mission Society, Vol. I). The name of the Australian Baptist Foreign Mission Society was changed to its present form in 1959. Telefomin, in the western corner of New Guinea, was opened to missionaries in 1951 and has become a center for work in four other valleys. The society began pioneer work at Oksapmin, the center of another valley system near Telefomin, in 1963. As well as churches and dispensaries, there are primary schools and Bible schools for the training of pastors and leaders. There are approximately 9,500 church members on these New Guinea fields. In 1958 missionaries entered West Irian and settled among the Dani people in the North Baliem Valley. The church is firmly established with some 5,500 members. The R. S. Pickup Hospital at Pit River is the center of the medical work. The most recent advance was in 1969 when three nursing sisters were sent to Zambia. They are working among the Lamba people at Fiwale Hill and Kafulafuta in cooperation with the South African Baptist Missionary Society. The first evangelist joined them in 1970 and others are in training to go.

There are 125 missionaries in service with the mission which is administered by a board whose executive is located in Melbourne. Two regional committees are responsible for detailed field administration. The mission's annual budget is about $270,000. C. H. EDWARDS

AUSTRIA, MISSION IN. The Foreign Mission Board, SBC, first entered Austria in Oct., 1965, with the arrival of William L. and Sally (Crook) Wagner as fraternal representatives. Prior to 1963 work in Austria was supported by the Forest Park Association in Chicago. They withdrew support and the Austrian Baptist Missions Committee was formed with members from various American and European Baptist groups. A youth center, started in 1968, works in conjunction with the Baptist church of Salzburg. There are eight churches in Austria and six preaching points in the Baptist Union.
WILLIAM L. WAGNER

***AVERETT COLLEGE.** A new four-year program, leading to the bachelor's degree has been initiated, with the first senior class graduating in 1971. The projected enrolment for the 1970–71 session is 800 with a faculty of 48. The Bachelor of Arts degree in church ministry is offered to those who have been unable to secure seminary training; it is also designed to train young women to assist in churches. The curriculum includes a major in religion and philosophy. Male students are now admitted. A new dormitory for women opened in 1970, and a new library building designed to house 100,000 volumes was scheduled for completion in 1971. The college has recently renovated the dormitories, purchased a new infirmary, and secured the Ayres House, east of the campus, for the music department. Vice-president C. Wendell Smith has devised a 10-year master plan for development and construction. On Sept. 1, 1966, Conwell A. Anderson succeeded Curtis V. Bishop as president.
R. STUART GRIZZARD

AWARE. Since Oct., 1970, the quarterly periodical for leaders of Girls in Action. Published by Woman's Missionary Union, the magazine contains basic resources for GA organization meetings and activities, features of interest to GA leaders, and Vistas, the leadership section. Mrs. Jesse Tucker is editor (1970).
BETTY BROWN

B

BABB, EARL VANDORN (b. Laurens County, S. C., Apr. 30, 1884; d. Seneca, S. C., July 5, 1960). Minister. He was a man of deep humility and sincerity. Son of C. A. and Dora (Woods) Babb, he was educated at local county schools, Furman University (graduated in 1909), and attended Colgate Seminary until 1912. He received the D.D. degree from Newberry College, a Lutheran liberal arts school. Babb was ordained by Rabun Creek Baptist Church, Laurens, S. C., Sept. 19, 1909. His pastorates included four churches: First, Easley, S. C., 1912–15; First, Newberry, S. C., 1916–25; First, Laurinburg, N. C., 1926–30; and Seneca, Seneca, S. C., 1930–50. In 1914 Babb married Agnes Chandler of New York State. They had one son, Winston Chandler Babb (*q.v.*). In 1937 E. V. Babb married Ruth Adams of Seneca, S. C. He was active in associational work, serving on the education, temperance, executive, missions, and other committees. He served as moderator of the Beaverdam Baptist Association, 1942–44. The South Carolina Baptist Convention elected him to serve on the board of education, 1917–21. Babb served two years on the general board of the convention, 1921–22, and as a trustee of the *Baptist Courier,* 1921–24. He is best remembered for his "main street ministry." JAMES P. STOKES

BABB, WINSTON CHANDLER (b. Easley, S. C., May 29, 1913; d. Greenville, S. C., Jan. 21, 1968). Historian, teacher, and Baptist layman. Son of a Baptist minister, Earl V. Babb (*q.v.*), and Agnes (Chandler) Babb, he was educated at Furman University (B.A., 1934) and the University of Virginia (M.A., 1936; Ph.D., 1954). He married Mary Elizabeth Davis of Barfield, Tenn., on July 6, 1938, and they had one daughter, Judith Chandler (Mrs. Joe G. Neuwirth). In World War II, he rose from private to captain in the Corps of Engineers. Joining the history faculty of Furman University in 1946, he became chairman of the department in 1960. He was faculty representative of the university to the Southern Conference Athletic Association and was president of that organization for two terms. Active on various committees at Furman, he was chairman of the faculty at the time of his death. Babb was a master teacher, a valued colleague, and a sincere friend and counselor of students. He held memberships in the American Historical Association and South Carolina Historical Association, of which he was vice-president at the time of his death. An outstanding Baptist layman, he was a dedicated deacon and long-time Sunday School teacher of the First Baptist Church, Greenville,

S. C. He is buried in Springwood Cemetery, Greenville, S. C. ALBERT N. SANDERS

***BACONE COLLEGE.** Bacone College is Oklahoma's oldest institution of higher learning. It is American Baptist related and has 22 denominations represented in its student body. The school offers liberal arts education at the junior college level, but is moving toward a baccalaureate degree curriculum. Its 36-member board is self-perpetuating, with 16 elected from the Muskogee area. In 1969 the school had 700 students, 40 faculty members, a budget of $985,000, and a property value of $2,000,000, with only $85,000 indebtedness. In the student body four distinct racial backgrounds are represented, including 50 per cent American Indians from 50 tribes in 34 states. Caucasians account for 40 per cent, Negroes near 10 per cent, and there are a few Orientals. Bacone is financed through tuition, endowment, private foundation gifts, individual gifts, auxiliary agencies, and federal aid. Garold D. Holstine has been president since 1967. J. M. GASKIN

BAGBY, TAYLOR CRAWFORD (b. Rio de Janeiro, Brazil, May 29, 1885; d. Corinth, Miss., Nov. 7, 1959). Son of W. B. and Anne Luther Bagby, he was educated at Mackenzie College, Sao Paulo, Brazil, Baylor University (A.B., 1907), and Southern Baptist Theological Seminary (Th.M., 1912). Bagby returned to Brazil in 1914 as an independent missionary, but was appointed by the Foreign Mission Board in 1918. He served in Sao Paulo 36 years and in Goias, eight years. "Pastor Têcê," as he was lovingly called by all who knew him, was preeminently a preacher, pastor, founder and builder of churches, musician, author, and friend and counselor of young preachers. He married Frances Adams, Jan. 1, 1913. JESSE C. FLETCHER

BAHÁ' Í WORLD FAITH. Bahá' í World Faith was born out of Islam and nurtured by the major world religions into a dialectic of "the best" of each. This world faith holds that God has revealed his word to every generation of the past through men such as Abraham, Moses, Krishna, Buddha, Christ, Muhammad, and Zoroaster. But no single manifestation was complete. The faith began in Persia in 1844 with a man who called himself the Báb or "gate." He pointed toward a modern manifestation who would come in the future. In 1863 Bahá'u'lláh declared himself to be the chosen manifestation of God. He claimed to be the revelation of God to man come of age. He emphasized certain principles to help accomplish this unity: the oneness of mankind, independent investigation of truth, common foundation of all religions, essential harmony of science and religion, equality of men and women, elimination of all prejudice, universal compulsory education, spiritual solution of the economic problem, universal auxiliary language, and universal peace upheld by a world government.

That which the Lord hath ordained as sovereign remedy and the mightiest instrument for the healing of all the world is the union of all its peoples in one Universal Cause, one Common Faith. —Bahá'u'lláh

The national Bahai headquarters are located at 536 Sheridan Road, Willmette, Ill.

EDWARD W. NASH, JR.

***BAHAMAS, MISSION IN.** Since 1956, 16 career missionaries, six associates, and nine short-term personnel continued the work. Prince Williams High School was founded in 1962, and Bahamas Baptist High School in 1965, but in June, 1972, all educational efforts are to be in theological training. The mission works with all Baptist groups to evangelize and to develop, train, and strengthen churches on 20 islands.

ERNEST E. BROWN, SR.

BAILES, PORTER MARCELLUS (b. Mar. 28, 1888, Ft. Mill community, S. C.; d. Jan. 25, 1963, Tyler, Tex.). Pastor and denominational leader. Son of Ellen Hill and Z. T. Bailes, he attended Mars Hill, Furman University (B.A. and D.D.), and Southern Baptist Theological Seminary (Th.M.). Bailes was pastor at First Baptist churches in LaGrange, Ky., 1916–17; Greer, S. C., 1917–26; Lakeland, Fla., 1926–28; and Tyler, Tex. 1928–55. He married Sarah Button on June 24, 1914. They had two children: Porter, Jr., and Joe Dean. The latter was killed in action in the Korean War. Active in denominational work, he served as vice-president of the Southern Baptist Convention and chairman of its committee on committees; chairman, executive board of Baptist General Convention of Texas; trustee of East Texas Baptist College for over 25 years. He was author of three books: *Revival Sermons* (1938), *Lift Your Skyline* (1940), and *In Quest of the Best* (1942). He was buried at Tyler, Tex.

W. M. SHAMBURGER

BAILIE MEMORIAL BOYS' RANCH. A home for boys, located in eastern Washington, near Mesa, operated under direction of a board elected by Baptist General Convention of Oregon-Washington. It began as a project gift by Mr. and Mrs. Loen Bailie on the homestead site of his parents. A gift by William Fleming of Texas provided half the cost of the first cottage for twelve boys in 1963. The remainder came from a bond issue by the Oregon-Washington convention. Many financial difficulties caused the ranch board in 1967 to recommend that the convention cut its ties with the project, but the convention's executive board, to which the matter was referred, voted to extend the trial period of the project. A new ranch board launched a campaign for funds, assisted by "Missionary Millionaires" of Amarillo, Tex., and another gift from Bailie. A second cottage for 12 boys was erected in 1969, along with a home and office combination building for the superintendent. Boys are given home and supervision, chiefly from fees paid by the agency under whose supervision they come to the ranch. Capacity of the ranch in 1969 was 24 boys plus a staff of five to seven. Most of the farm-ranch operation was being conducted by others on a lease agreement for benefit of the ranch boy-care program. An item in the Baptist budget also provided additional income, along with gifts directly from the churches and friends.

ROY L. JOHNSON

***BAPTISM.** The years 1955–70 saw a tremendous upsurge of interest in the doctrine of baptism. Many books on the subject, produced by Baptist scholars at home and abroad, flowed from the new interest in biblical theology, ecumenical dialogue, and practical considerations related to the baptism of small children and to the vitality of church membership.

Some years ago a group of scholars commissioned to study baptism reported: "It is beyond dispute that in no church body does baptism have the decisive significance which the witness of the New Testament ascribes to it." Baptist scholars are discovering the accuracy of this statement for themselves. Among them are George R. Beasley-Murray, Warren Carr, Neville Clark, A. Gilmore, Dale Moody, and R. E. O. White.

For many years Baptists spent so much time in polemics about the mode (immersion) and the subject (an accountable believer) that they were apt to overlook the deeper spiritual truths connected with it. In fear of sacramentalism they have declared baptism a "mere" symbol. The scholars named above agree in general that New Testament baptism was much more than mere symbol. For example, a study of Romans 6:1–11 will reveal that the writer's chief interest was a call to a high plane of Christlike living.

Beasley-Murray, in his *Baptism in the New Testament* (1962), makes a very definite effort at discovering just what the New Testament teaches about baptism. He reports that in the effort he experienced spiritual renewal not only with reference to baptism but also with reference to his whole view of Christ, gospel, and the church. He rejects sacramentalism with 1 Peter 3:21 and I Cor. 10:1 ff, but emphasizes the gracious action of God himself in baptism as seen in Rom. 6:1–11 and Col. 2:12 and in many other passages. For him God, the Holy Spirit, and Jesus Christ have a great deal more to do with baptism than most Baptists have realized.

A second very important development is the proposal on the part of leading Baptist scholars that baptism could become a means of Christian understanding and Christian unity. Carr, Gilmore, and Moody have written books on the subject. The other men named above, and Stephen Winward, have made major contributions on the matter. At the heart of the issue is the relation of baptism to Christ and to his church. Johannes Schneider, the Baptist professor of New Testament in the University of Berlin, bases his whole argument on the unbreakable relationship of baptism and the church.

A third important development is the problem of the baptism of young children. It enters into ecumenical discussions but becomes a very personal problem when a child of six or seven makes a profession of faith in Christ and asks for baptism. Southern Baptist churches have been deeply disturbed by the increasing number of younger children being baptized. They find themselves coming closer and closer to infant baptism. In 1969 Southern Baptists baptized 1,422 children under six years of age, 35,168 were aged 6 to 8, and 136,705 were 9 to 12. These three groups made up almost half of the total baptisms for that year.

The main problem is that Southern Baptists have no theology of childhood. The relation of the child to the church has not been thought through. Carr points out the mistreatment of children in a revivalistic situation. Gilmore in his *Baptism and Christian Unity* (1966), has a chapter on "Baptism and the Child." Clark endeavors to deal with the problem with a new theology of childhood. Among Southern Baptists Clifford Ingle made a special effort to develop such a theology. A volume edited by him and to which he contributes considerably is a worthy step in this direction. Without such a theology Baptist churches have floundered in a variety of ways in serving their children, not knowing why they were doing what they were doing—including baptizing very young children.

Perhaps a conclusion taken from R.E.O. White will serve to illustrate the new importance being given to baptism: "The ultimate issue in every question of church practice, order or doctrine must lie in the spiritual result which each may be expected to achieve in the full redemption of sinful men. The recall to the biblical doctrine and practice of initiation is a recall to confessional Christianity, to an ethical gospel, and to a Spirit-conscious and Spirit-endowed church; to a quality of Christian character and a depth of Christian life that draw all their meaning and power from *baptism into Christ*."

JOHN T. WAYLAND

***BAPTIST AND REFLECTOR.** In 1959 the Tennessee Baptist Press was dissolved and the administrative committee of the executive board of the Tennessee Baptist Convention was charged with the functions performed by the Tennessee Baptist Press, Inc., serving as the board of directors of said press. A three-man committee serves as liaison between the editor and the administrative committee. On Sept. 1, 1961, David Keel came to the paper as circulation manager. In Oct., 1968, James A. Lester became editor, succeeding retiring editor Richard N. Owen. The editorial offices were moved in Aug., 1969, to the executive board building of the Tennessee Baptist Convention in Brentwood, Tenn.

The present circulation of the paper is 71,000, representing 622 churches which engage in the paper's Every Family Plan. The remainder of subscribers are made up of Club accounts and individual subscriptions. DAVID KEEL

BAPTIST BIBLE INSTITUTE, GRACEVILLE, FLORIDA (cf. Bible Institute, Florida Baptist, Vol. I). In 1957 this institution became an agency of Florida Baptist Convention, which elects all trustees. James E. Southerland became president, Dec., 1957. The purpose of the school is to offer three or more years of theological studies to adult students preparing to serve churches affiliated with the Southern Baptist Convention. A faculty of 14 holds 39 earned degrees from accredited colleges, universities, and SBC seminaries. Nine have their earned doctorates from one of the Southern Baptist theological seminaries. The school year, 1969–70, showed 315 enrolled. Buildings built, 1958–69, included 26 brick houses and eight permanently installed mobile homes; all 34 are three-bedroom student homes. Six new buildings include the chapel, classroom building, administration building, library, student center (with 400-seat dining room), and the president's home. The 1969–70 budget was $386,103. In 1969–70 students from 26 states and two foreign countries worked toward the Baptist Bible Institute Diploma, with special emphasis in pastoral training, sacred music, or religious education. Courses are for 98 semester hours, paralleling seminary courses except for the languages. Several fully accredited senior colleges accept up to 65 semester hours of transfer credit toward a baccalaureate degree without requiring an entrance examination. Students must be over 21, not college graduates, members of Southern Baptist churches, and meet strict character requirements both for admission and to remain in school. JAMES E. SOUTHERLAND

BAPTIST BUILDING FEDERAL CREDIT UNION. Organized in Oklahoma City, Okla., in 1958, its purpose is to encourage thrift and to provide loans to members at a modest rate of interest. With assets as of Jan. 1, 1970, of approximately $100,000, its management is voluntary. All loans carry loan cancellation insurance with an extra charge to the borrower. Also, life insurance is carried on each member in relation to his investment in the Credit Union. In the first 12 years of operation, only one loan was charged off. Federal Credit Union officials evaluate this as an enviable record. Oklahoma Baptist Building employees and their families are eligible for membership. J. M. GASKIN

BAPTIST BULLETIN SERVICE. The Executive Committee of the Southern Baptist Convention has editorial responsibility for the Baptist Bulletin Service. The service makes available to local churches a Sunday bulletin with a full-color front cover and a back cover of appropriate text, with the inside pages blank for local use. As many as 1,250,000 are used weekly. Since Nov., 1948, the Baptist Sunday School Board has had responsibility for printing, promoting, and distributing the bulletins. Albert McClellan was editor of the Bulletin Service from 1949 to 1959 when he was succeeded by W. C. Fields.
LEONARD E. HILL

BAPTIST CENTER, SWITZERLAND. Established in 1963 to correlate various mission activities located on the campus of European Baptist Theological Seminary in Ruschlikon (Zurich), Switzerland. An administrative committee was formed in the beginning but discontinued in 1969. The press service was established in 1961 as the news agency of the European Baptist Federation. A seminary professor served as director on a half-time basis until 1966 when a missionary associate, who is a professional journalist, became full-time director. In 1969 the press service sent out 328 news reports and features to 175 addresses, mostly editors of Baptist papers and some others in Europe and elsewhere. A photo service to editors was also maintained. The recording studio was set up in 1963. Programs were prepared first in Hungarian, later in Spanish, Portuguese, Italian, French, Russian, and Polish. Most of the programs were broadcast by Trans World Radio in Monaco. The studio served as training center for radio and television work and sponsored regional conferences in other parts of Europe. The seminary, during its 1969–70 session, had 50 students from 21 countries. JOHN ALLEN MOORE

BAPTIST CHILDREN'S AID SOCIETY (cf. Children's Aid Society, Maryland Baptist, Vol. I). Formerly known as the Baptist Children's Home of Maryland, incorporated in 1920. The society is operating today for the purpose of serving needy children in Maryland Baptist families. It is required that the children be enrolled and attending Sunday School and church. The program of ministry covers a wide area of services including emergency family allowances, budget planning, counseling, housing, medical and dental assistance, clothing, and opportunity for Christian camp experience. The society works closely with various social agencies, hospital doctors, psychologists, psychiatrists, school counselors, and the social services workers. Boys and girls are encouraged to complete high school, and in certain situations the society is paying for board and instruction in private schools. In 1968 the society rendered service to 157 children representing 40 families. The children are in their own homes or in foster homes. Through Christian concern and love, the society endeavors to reach out to these children with the message of God's love for them that they may come to acknowledge Christ's saving power in their lives. The work is supported by the Baptists of Maryland through contributions, sponsoring groups, investment income, and the Cooperative Program. The woman's advisory board, representing 45 churches, is effective in promoting the work. The board of trustees, numbering 16 members is responsible for the work of the society. Mrs. Thelma Culbreth has been executive secretary since 1965.

See also MARYLAND BAPTIST UNION ASSOCIATION, VOL. II. ROWLAND MC D. NESS

BAPTIST CHILDREN'S HOMES OF NORTH CAROLINA, INC. On Jan. 1, 1958, the name of the Baptist Orphanage of North Carolina was changed to the Baptist Children's Homes of North Carolina, Inc., to more adequately describe its multi-service ministry. Home offices are in Thomasville, on the Mills Home campus, where they have been since the agency's beginning in 1885. W. R. Wagoner succeeded W. C. Reed as chief executive in 1958, and now carries the title of president of the homes.

Group care is provided children at the following homes: Mills, Thomasville; Kennedy, Kinston; Odum, Pembroke; Greer, Chapel Hill; and Wall, Wallburg; with work in progress on the Broyhill Home for Children, near Waynesville, and a Home for Unwed Mothers in Asheville. A statewide foster home program is maintained to serve preschool children and others, who need the close relationships which can be formed in the small family setting. Family services are rendered by professionally trained and experienced social workers out of centers in Asheville, Charlotte, Thomasville, Raleigh, Kinston, and Fayetteville.

A demonstration child development center is maintained on the Mills Home Campus where services are provided local preschool children in day care, nursery school, and kindergarten services. Professionally trained leadership is available to help churches desiring to start similar programs. Children who have been in the care of the homes through graduation from high school are assisted in higher education and various types of specialized training. More than 1,200 children are served annually by the children's homes. Financial support is provided through the Cooperative Program, the Thanksgiving Offering, special gifts, and estate planning. W. R. WAGONER

BAPTIST CHILDREN'S VILLAGE, THE (cf. Mississippi Baptist Orphanage, Vol. II). Paul N. Nunnery succeeded W. G. Mize as superintendent on Oct. 15, 1960. In 1961 the agency instituted changes in program and facilities, with emphasis upon progressive social services to meet changing needs of children and families from homes which are broken or in a state of crisis. By amendment to its charter in 1961, the corporate title of the agency was changed to The Baptist Children's Village, in recognition of emotional damage occasioned by the terms "orphan" and "orphanage." In 1961 the special county school district operated on campus for enrolled children was abandoned and the children were enrolled in public schools. A department of music as therapy was organized. A department of activities was instituted which includes recreational and athletic organizations, a remedial reading program, therapeutic sewing classes, and vocational workshop instruction. A department of social case works, assisted by a child psychologist, directs intake and dismissal processes, counsels children, and supervises a system of foster homes. Normally, fifty children are afforded private care in these homes.

In 1965 the agency campus was relocated on 147 acres of land on Flag Chapel Drive in Jackson. The new facility, representing a $2,000,000 investment was financed by the sale of the former site. The 20 new buildings are of single-story, brick construction, fully air-conditioned, and designed to project the image of a community of homes. Forty young people have been afforded a college education in the period 1961–69. The annual case load includes 262 boys and girls. PAUL N. NUNNERY

BAPTIST CHURCH EXTENSION SOCIETY OF MARYLAND (cf. Church Extension Society, Baltimore Baptist, Vol. I). In 1958 the present name was adopted to indicate statewide service. The society makes both gifts and loans to new works and churches in need of assistance. The loans are at a low interest rate and on a long-term basis. The society is also the guarantor of Broadway Plan Bonds issued by Baptist churches in Maryland under a duly approved plan. A separate guarantee fund is maintained and each bond is endorsed with the society guarantee. A further work of the society has been the actual ownership of church buildings in newly created cities in the state and the holding of same until such time as a congregation is prepared to assume the work.

ALAN H. STOCKDALE

BAPTIST CHURCH MANUALS. Baptist church manuals are treatises on church order which concisely discuss the nature of the church, its membership, ministry, and worship. They seek to provide a better understanding of Baptist polity and practice and to lead the churches in orderly conduct. They reflect the Baptist thought of their day and challenge churches to relate to contemporary issues.

Since the Philadelphia Association adopted Benjamin Griffith's *A Short Treatise of Church Discipline* in 1743, more than 40 different manuals have been used by Baptists in America. The most popular have been J. M. Pendleton's *Church Manual* and the various works by Edward T. Hiscox.

Recent publications, including revised editions of old standard manuals, are: Edward T. Hiscox, *The Hiscox Standard Baptist Manual* (1964); William R. McNutt, *Polity and Practice in Baptist Churches* (1959); Norman H. Maring and Winthrop S. Hudson, *A Baptist Manual of Polity and Practice* (1963); J. M. Pendleton, *Bap-*

tist Church Manual (1966); and Bobby Dale Compton, *Baptist Church Manuals in America: A Study in Baptist Polity and Practice* (1967).

BOBBY DALE COMPTON

BAPTIST COLLEGE AT CHARLESTON. An institution of higher learning of the South Carolina Baptist Convention. Founded in 1964 after reaching basic requirements for funds and land site to the approval of the convention. The first committee organized for investigation of the possibility of a Baptist College in the Charleston area began work in 1952. In 1958 in Greenville, South Carolina Baptists in their state convention agreed to "look with favor on the creation of an education fund by the Charleston Association and the City of Charleston, with the cooperation and assistance of other associations in the Southern part of the state and when this fund reaches $500,000 and a site suitable to the Convention will, at its next session, give serious consideration to the establishment of a college. . . ."

On Feb. 5, 1960, a written declaration of the Charter of the Baptist College of Lower South Carolina was filed with the Secretary of State. The ceremony for the signing of the charter took place in the sanctuary of the First Baptist Church of Charleston, mother church of Southern Baptists.

In 1964 the convention voted overwhelmingly to accept the new Baptist College at Charleston as an institution of South Carolina Baptists. The report stated that the basic requirements had been met, that funds and a 500-acre site were in hand. The land, purchased from the city of Charleston, is located in Charleston County, at the intersection of South Carolina Highway 78 and Interstate 26. It is within commuting distance of one-half million people. Landscaping artists and architects were engaged to prepare proposals for the immediate and long-range plans for the construction of the new college.

John Asa Hamrick, who had been named chairman of the first board of trustees elected by the convention, was chosen by the members of the board to be the first president, Dec., 1964. Having then become an institution of the South Carolina Baptist Convention, and with $1,000,000 in assets, permission to borrow $1,500,000 more, and a president at the helm, the project moved rapidly toward actuality.

Baptist College enrolled its first students in Jan., 1965, opening in late September with a student body of 588. There were 419 freshmen, 24 sophomores, and 154 students in evening classes.

First Baptist Church of North Charleston, under the leadership of Paul M. Pridgen, pastor, made major adjustments in its busy life to provide room for the college which was emerging. The education buildings, the chapel, and the sanctuary of North Charleston's First Church became the college's birthplace. Fifteen full-time professors and eight part-time instructors made up the faculty. Resident students were housed in a downtown hotel and commuted daily across the city to attend classes.

In Sept., 1966, classes met on the campus for the first time. In 1967 a total of 1,435 students registered. A dormitory complex was completed in time for the opening of school and campus buildings numbered six. The academic complex is designed to accomodate from 2,000 to 2,500 students, but can be expanded to four times that number.

Students are now able to choose a major in any one of 15 disciplines of study. The Bachelor of Arts degree may be earned with a major in economics, elementary education, English, history, foreign language, music, or religion. Minors may be obtained in these majors, plus art, sociology, political science, library science, philosophy, speech, and dramatic arts. The Bachelor of Science degree may be earned with a major in biology, business administration, chemistry, health and physical education, mathematics, physics, or psychology. Teacher certification may be secured with a major in business, elementary education, mathematics, natural science, or social science. Pre-professional courses are offered in medicine, ministry, law, medical technology, and dentistry. A nursing education program leading to the Associate in Arts degree in Science may be completed in two years and one summer session. A well-rounded offering in musical studies is well staffed. The athletic department is headed by a faculty of seven, and equipped with modern facilities.

Progress toward accreditation has been made. The status of "Candidacy" was granted upon the first application in 1968 and a team from the Southern Association of Colleges and Schools visited the campus in May, 1969, with reference to full accreditation.

The Department of Health, Education, and Welfare issued Baptist College institutional certification in 1967 and secured participation for the school in student aid programs. In early 1967 the director of the office of the South Carolina Teacher Education and Certification Department notified Baptist College its 1968 graduates were certified to teach in South Carolina schools. All undergraduate courses which applied to the program had also been approved.

In June, 1968, the college graduated 41 men and women, 30 with the B.S. degree and 11 with the B.A. degree.

Late 1969 found the college with an enrolment of 2,145, completing a $1,000,000 library building, to be named for L. Mendel Rivers, Congressman from South Carolina. Also nearing completion is a second dormitory complex. The first phase of the library building will house 150,000 volumes.

The college has a healthy student activities department. There are seven social clubs, four for men and three for women. Academic clubs and sciences have departmental clubs in each major area. Gamma Beta Phi, National Honor Society, has 20 charter members. Church affiliated organizations are encouraged. The Ministerial Alliance and the Baptist Student Union programs are coordinated by the office of the dean of student services.

The development of a strong academic program has been undergirded by the selection of a fine faculty, of whom more than 40 per cent hold the Ph.D. or terminal degree.

The Baptist College states as its purpose: to provide in a Christian environment, training for qualified men and women. Its philosophy is: to provide opportunities, within available resources, and education that will help the student realize his full potential as an individual and his responsibility as a citizen; to maintain a joint quest for truth by faculty and students; to promote and maintain professional competency in all instruction and research involved in programs leading to the authorized degrees; to help the students to find and prepare for the vocations for which they are best suited; to develop and sustain organizations and services which are needed to insure a healthy, cultural, social, religious, and intellectual life; to contribute scholarly, cultural, and spiritual resources to contemporary society; to exemplify the finest concepts of the Baptist Convention of South Carolina for higher education. RYAN B. EKLUND

BAPTIST CONGRESSES, 1882–1912. First held in 1882, the Baptist Congress met each year through 1912 with the exception of 1891. The purpose was to provide a forum for discussion on important and relevant matters. Issues such as "Race and Religion on the American Continent," "Man's Fall and Redemption in the Light of Evolution," and "The Rural Church" were among the many topics discussed. Participation was open to any member of a Baptist church.

The initial meeting was held in Brooklyn, primarily at the instigation of Baptist pastors in that area, but the succeeding meetings were held in different locales, ranging from Chicago to Augusta, Ga. Although the congresses attracted a number of notable Baptist scholars, including Shailer Matthews, A. H. Newman (*q.v.*, Vol. II), Walter Rauschenbusch (*q.v.*, Vol. II), and A. H. Strong (*q.v.*, Vol. II), they were discontinued in 1912 because of failing attendance and the fact that their function was being superseded by other groups such as the Northern Baptist Convention.

BIBLIOGRAPHY: A. H. Newman, *A Century of Baptist Achievement* (1901). Davis Woolley (ed.), *Baptist Advance* (1964). CHARLES B. BUGG

***BAPTIST COURIER, THE.** On Mar. 1, 1966, John Elgin Roberts became editor, succeeding Samuel Hovey Jones who retired. An office building was erected at Manly and Pettigru streets in Greenville, S. C., and occupied in May, 1968. The one-story building contains 3,000 square feet. With land and furnishings, it is valued at $120,000. It houses a staff of 10. Circulation on Jan. 1, 1970, was 102,000, with 870 churches subscribing for every family. The paper is published weekly except for one week in summer and the last week in December.

JOHN E. ROBERTS

BAPTIST EDUCATION STUDY TASK. A comprehensive study of Southern Baptist higher education, the Baptist Education Study Task (BEST) was sponsored by the Education Commission, Southern Baptist Convention, in 1966–67. The Executive Committee of the Convention supported the study with an appropriation of $50,000, most of which was used. Rabun L. Brantley, executive secretary of the Education Commission, was general chairman, and Albert McClellan, program planning secretary, Executive Committee, SBC, was chairman of the steering committee.

The purposes of the study were stated as follows:

> to identify and study the issues, problems, and opportunities facing Southern Baptist higher education.
>
> to explore these issues and problems in the context of current American higher education and of the needs and objectives of the denomination.
>
> to consolidate findings and suggest a reasonable basis on which Southern Baptist higher education may advance.

Twenty-four seminars of 20 persons each were set up in the 17 states having Baptist colleges, or planning one. The seminars met six times in the spring of 1966 and 1967, totaling about 18 hours of study for each. The First National Conference of 300 persons was held in Nashville on June 13–16, 1966, and the Second National Conference of 300 persons met in Nashville June 12–15, 1967. More than 8,000 persons participated in one or more areas of the study. Four regional accrediting agencies participated in the study by sending representatives to speak on accreditation.

On Sept. 15, 1967, a printed report of 113 pages was published. The study was the most extensive one on higher education ever made by the Convention. RABUN L. BRANTLEY

BAPTIST EXAMINER, THE. A weekly paper, edited by John R. Gilpin. It seems to have begun early in 1932, with editorial office at Russell, Ky., but printed and mailed at Benton, Ark. With the issue of May 17, 1941, it was both edited and printed at Russell, Ky., until May 10, 1961, when both operations were transferred to Ashland, Ky. It carries above its masthead "Missionary, Premillennial, Biblical, Baptistic."

LEO T. CRISMON

BAPTIST FAITH AND MESSAGE, THE (1963). Against the background of theological controversy created by Broadman Press's publication of *The Message of Genesis* by Professor Ralph Elliott of Midwestern Baptist Theological Seminary, the Executive Committee of the Southern Baptist Convention recommended to the Convention in San Francisco in 1962 that a special committee, to be composed of state convention presidents (23), be designated to draft a doctrinal statement, similar to the 1925 Statement of Baptist Faith and Message, to serve as "information to the churches" and "guidelines to the various agencies" of the SBC. The chairman of the committee was Herschel H. Hobbs, president of the SBC, 1961–63, and pastor of the First Baptist Church, Oklahoma City, Okla.

The new statement was submitted to the SBC in Kansas City in 1963, and the following introduction and text were approved:

The 1962 session of the Southern Baptist Convention, meeting in San Francisco, California, adopted the following motion:

"Since the report of the Committee on Statement of Baptist Faith and Message was adopted in 1925, there have been various statements from time to time which have been made, but no over-all statement which might be helpful at this time as suggested in Section 2 of that report, or introductory statement which might be used as an interpretation of the 1925 Statement.

"We recommend, therefore, that the president of this Convention be requested to call a meeting of the men now serving as presidents of the various state conventions that would qualify as a member of the Southern Baptist Convention committee under Bylaw 18 to present to the Convention in Kansas City some similar statement which shall serve as information to the churches, and which may serve as guidelines to the various agencies of the Southern Baptist Convention. It is understood that any group or individuals may approach this committee to be of service. The expenses of this committee shall be borne by the Convention Operating Budget."

Your committee thus constituted begs leave to present its report as follows:

Throughout its work your committee has been conscious of the contribution made by the statement of "The Baptist Faith And Message" adopted by the Southern Baptist Convention in 1925. It quotes with approval its affirmation that "Christianity is supernatural in its origin and history. We repudiate every theory of religion which denies the supernatural elements in our faith."

Furthermore, it concurs in the introductory "statement of the historic Baptist conception of the nature and function of confessions of faith in our religious and denominational life. . . ." It is, therefore, quoted in full as a part of this report to the Convention:

"(1) That they constitute a consensus of opinion of some Baptist body, large or small, for the general instruction and guidance of our own people and others concerning those articles of the Christian faith which are most surely held among us. They are not intended to add anything to the simple conditions of salvation revealed in the New Testament, viz., repentance towards God and faith in Jesus Christ as Saviour and Lord.

"(2) That we do not regard them as complete statements of our faith, having any quality of finality or infallibility. As in the past so in the future, Baptists should hold themselves free to revise their statements of faith as may seem to them wise and expedient at any time.

"(3) That any group of Baptists, large or small, have the inherent right to draw up for themselves and publish to the world a confession of their faith whenever they may think it advisable to do so.

"(4) That the sole authority for faith and practice among Baptists is the Scriptures of the Old and New Testaments. Confessions are only guides in interpretation, having no authority over the conscience.

"(5) That they are statements of religious convictions, drawn from the Scriptures, and are not to be used to hamper freedom of thought or investigation in other realms of life."

The 1925 Statement recommended "the New Hampshire Confession of Faith, revised at certain points, and with some additional articles growing out of certain needs. . . ." Your present committee has adopted the same pattern. It has sought to build upon the structure of the 1925 Statement, keeping in mind the "certain needs" of our generation. At times it has reproduced sections of that Statement without change. In other instances it has substituted words for clarity or added sentences for emphasis. At certain points it has combined articles, with minor changes in wording, to endeavor to relate certain doctrines to each other. In still others—e.g., "God" and "Salvation"—it has sought to bring together certain truths contained throughout the 1925 Statement in order to relate them more clearly and concisely. In no case has it sought to delete from or to add to the basic contents of the 1925 Statement.

Baptists are a people who profess a living faith. This faith is rooted and grounded in Jesus Christ who is "the same yesterday, and to-day, and for ever." Therefore, the sole authority for faith and practice among Baptists is Jesus Christ whose will is revealed in the Holy Scriptures.

A living faith must experience a growing understanding of truth and must be continually interpreted and related to the needs of each new generation. Throughout their history Baptist bodies, both large and small, have issued statements of faith which comprise a consensus of their beliefs. Such statements have never been regarded as complete, infallible statements of faith, nor as official creeds carrying mandatory authority. Thus this generation of Southern Baptists is in historic succession of intent and purpose as it endeavors to state for its time and theological climate those articles of the Christian faith which are most surely held among us.

Baptists emphasize the soul's competency before God, freedom in religion, and the priesthood of the believer. However, this emphasis should not be interpreted to mean that there is an absence of certain definite doctrines that Baptists believe, cherish, and with which they have been and are now closely identified.

It is the purpose of this statement of faith and message to set forth certain teachings which we believe.

1963 STATEMENT

I. THE SCRIPTURES

The Holy Bible was written by men divinely inspired and is the record of God's revelation of Himself to man. It is a perfect treasure of divine instruction. It has God for its author, salvation for its end, and truth, without any mixture of error, for its matter. It reveals the principles by which God judges us; and therefore is, and will remain to the end of the world, the true center of Christian union, and the supreme standard by which all human conduct, creeds, and religious opinions should be tried. The criterion by which the Bible is to be interpreted is Jesus Christ.

Ex. 24:4; Deut. 4:1–2; 17:19; Josh. 8:34; Psalms 19:7–10; 119:11,89,105,140; Isa. 34:16; 40:8; Jer. 15:16; 36; Matt. 5:17–18; 22:29; Luke 21:33; 24:

44–46; John 5:39; 16:13–15; 17:17; Acts 2:16 ff.; 17:11; Rom. 15:4; 16:25–26; 2 Tim. 3:15–17; Heb. 1:1–2; 4:12; 1 Peter 1:25; 2 Peter 1:19–21.

II. GOD

There is one and only one living and true God. He is an intelligent, spiritual, and personal Being, the Creator, Redeemer, Preserver, and Ruler of the universe. God is infinite in holiness and all other perfections. To him we owe the highest love, reverence, and obedience. The eternal God reveals Himself to us as Father, Son, and Holy Spirit, with distinct personal attributes, but without division of nature, essence, or being.

1. God the Father

God as Father reigns with providential care over His universe, His creatures, and the flow of the stream of human history according to the purposes of His grace. He is all powerful, all loving, and all wise. God is Father in truth to those who become children of God through faith in Jesus Christ. He is fatherly in His attitude toward all men.

Gen. 1:1; 2:7; Ex. 3:14; 6:2–3; 15:11 ff.; 20:1 ff.; Levit. 22:2; Deut. 6:4; 32:6; 1 Chron. 29:10; Psalm 19:1–3; Isa. 43:3,15; 64:8; Jer. 10:10; 17:13; Matt. 6:9 ff.; 7:11; 23:9; 28:19; Mark 1:9–11; John 4:24; 5:26; 14:6–13; 17:1–8; Acts 1:7; Rom. 8:14–15; 1 Cor. 8:6; Gal. 4:6; Eph. 4:6; Col. 1:15; 1 Tim. 1:17; Heb. 11:6; 12:9; 1 Peter 1:17; 1 John 5:7.

2. God the Son

Christ is the eternal Son of God. In His incarnation as Jesus Christ He was conceived of the Holy Spirit and born of the virgin Mary. Jesus perfectly revealed and did the will of God, taking upon Himself the demands and necessities of human nature and identifying Himself completely with mankind yet without sin. He honored the divine law by His personal obedience, and in His death on the cross He made provision for the redemption of men from sin. He was raised from the dead with a glorified body and appeared to His disciples as the person who was with them before His crucifixion. He ascended into heaven and is now exalted at the right hand of God where He is the One Mediator, partaking of the nature of God and of man, and in whose Person is effected the reconciliation between God and man. He will return in power and glory to judge the world and to consummate His redemptive mission. He now dwells in all believers as the living and ever present Lord.

Gen. 18:1 ff.; Psalms 2:7 ff.; 110:1 ff.; Isa. 7:14; 53; Matt. 1:18–23; 3:17; 8:29; 11:27; 14:33; 16:16,27; 17:5; 27; 28:1–6, 19; Mark 1:1; 3:11; Luke 1:35; 4:41; 22:70; 24:46; John 1:1–18,29; 10:30,38; 11:25–27; 12:44–50; 14:7–11; 16:15–16,28; 17:1–5, 21–22; 20:1–20,28; Acts 1:9; 2:22–24; 7:55–56; 9:4–5,20; Rom. 1:3–4; 3:23–26; 5:6–21; 8:1–3,34; 10:4; 1 Cor. 1:30; 2:2; 8:6; 15:1–8,24–28; 2 Cor. 5:19–21; 8:9; Gal. 4:4–5; Eph. 1:20; 3:11; 4:7–10; Phil. 2:5–11; Col. 1:13–22; 2:9; 1 Thess. 4:14–18; 1 Tim. 2:5–6; 3:16; Titus 2:13–14; Heb. 1:1–3; 4:14–15; 7:14–28; 9:12–15,24–28; 12:2; 13:8; 1 Peter 2:21–25; 3:22; 1 John 1:7–9; 3:2; 4:14–15; 5:9; 2 John 7–9; Rev. 1:13–16; 5:9–14; 12:10–11; 13:8; 19:16.

3. God the Holy Spirit

The Holy Spirit is the Spirit of God. He inspired holy men of old to write the Scriptures. Through illumination He enables men to understand truth. He exalts Christ. He convicts of sin, of righteousness and of judgment. He calls men to the Saviour, and effects regeneration. He cultivates Christian character, comforts believers, and bestows the spiritual gifts by which they serve God through His church. He seals the believer unto the day of final redemption. His presence in the Christian is the assurance of God to bring the believer into the fulness of the stature of Christ. He enlightens and empowers the believer and the church in worship, evangelism, and service.

Gen. 1:2; Judg. 14:6; Job 26:13; Psalms 51:11; 139:7 ff.; Isa. 61:1–3; Joel 2:28–32; Matt. 1:18; 3:16; 4:1; 12:28–32; 28:19; Mark 1:10,12; Luke 1:35; 4:1,18–19; 11:13; 12:12; 24:49; John 4:24; 14:16–17,26; 15:26; 16:7–14; Acts 1:8; 2:1–4,38; 4:31; 5:3; 6:3; 7:55; 8:17,39; 10:44; 13:2; 15:28; 16:6; 19:1–6; Rom. 8:9–11,14–16,26–27; 1 Cor. 2:10–14; 3:16; 12:3–11; Gal. 4:6; Eph. 1:13–14; 4:30; 5:18; 1 Thess. 5:19; 1 Tim. 3:16; 4:1; 2 Tim. 1:14; 3:16; Heb. 9:8,14; 2 Peter 1:21; 1 John 4:13; 5:6–7; Rev. 1:10; 22:17.

III. MAN

Man was created by the special act of God, in His own image, and is the crowning work of His creation. In the beginning man was innocent of sin and was endowed by his Creator with freedom of choice. By his free choice man sinned against God and brought sin into the human race. Through the temptation of Satan man transgressed the command of God, and fell from his original innocence; whereby his posterity inherit a nature and an environment inclined toward sin, and as soon as they are capable of moral action become transgressors and are under condemnation. Only the grace of God can bring man into His holy fellowship and enable man to fulfill the creative purpose of God. The sacredness of human personality is evident in that God created man in His own image, and in that Christ died for man; therefore every man possesses dignity and is worthy of respect and Christian love.

Gen. 1:26–30; 2:5,7,18–22; 3; 9:6; Psalms 1; 8:3–6; 32:1–5; 51:5; Isa. 6:5; Jer. 17:5; Matt. 16:26; Acts 17:26–31; Rom. 1:19–32; 3:10–18,23; 5:6,12,19; 6:6; 7:14–25; 8:14–18,29; 1 Cor. 1:21–31; 15:19,21–22; Eph. 2:1–22; Col. 1:21–22; 3:9–11.

IV. SALVATION

Salvation involves the redemption of the whole man, and is offered freely to all who accept Jesus Christ as Lord and Saviour, who by His own blood obtained eternal redemption for the believer. In its broadest sense salvation includes regeneration, sanctification, and glorification.

1. Regeneration, or the new birth, is a work of God's grace whereby believers become new creatures in Christ Jesus. It is a change of heart wrought by the Holy Spirit through conviction of sin, to which the sinner responds in repentance toward God and faith in the Lord Jesus Christ.

Repentance and faith are inseparable experiences of grace. Repentance is a genuine turning from sin toward God. Faith is the acceptance of Jesus Christ and commitment of the entire personality to Him as Lord and Saviour. Justification is God's gracious and full acquittal upon principles of His righteousness of all sinners who repent and believe in Christ. Justification brings the believer into a relationship of peace and favor with God.

2. Santification is the experience, beginning in regeneration, by which the believer is set apart to God's purposes, and is enabled to progress toward moral and spiritual perfection through the presence and power of the Holy Spirit dwelling in him. Growth in grace should continue throughout the regenerate person's life.

3. Glorification is the culmination of salvation and is the final blessed and abiding state of the redeemed.

Gen. 3:15; Ex. 3:14–17; 6:2–8; Matt. 1:21; 4:17;

16:21–26; 27:22–28:6; Luke 1:68–69; 2:28–32; John 1:11–14,29; 3:3–21;36; 5:24; 10:9,28–29; 15:1–16; 17:17; Acts 2:21; 4:12; 15:11; 16:30–31; 17:30–31; 20:32; Rom. 1:16–18; 2:4; 3:23–25; 4:3 ff.; 5:8–10; 6:1–23; 8:1–18,29–39; 10:9–10,13; 13:11–14; 1 Cor. 1:18,30; 6:19–20; 15:10; 2 Cor. 5:17–20; Gal. 2:20; 3:13; 5:22–25; 6:15; Eph. 1:7; 2:8–22; 4:11–16; Phil. 2:12–13; Col. 1:9–22; 3:1 ff.; 1 Thess. 5:23–24; 2 Tim. 1:12; Titus 2:11–14; Heb. 2:1–3; 5:8–9; 9:24–28; 11:1–12:8,14; James 2:14–26; 1 Peter 1:2–23; 1 John 1:6–2:11; Rev. 3:20; 21:1–22:5.

V. GOD'S PURPOSE OF GRACE

Election is the gracious purpose of God, according to which He regenerates, sanctifies, and glorifies sinners. It is consistent with the free agency of man and comprehends all the means in connection with the end. It is a glorious display of God's sovereign goodness, and is infinitely wise, holy, and unchangeable. It excludes boasting and promotes humility.

All true believers endure to the end. Those whom God has accepted in Christ, and sanctified by His Spirit, will never fall away from the state of grace, but shall persevere to the end. Believers may fall into sin through neglect and temptation, whereby they grieve the Spirit, impair their graces and comforts, bring reproach on the cause of Christ, and temporal judgments on themselves, yet they shall be kept by the power of God through faith unto salvation.

Gen. 12:1–3; Ex. 19:5–8; 1 Sam. 8:4–7,19–22; Isa. 5:1–7; Jer. 31:31 ff.; Matt. 16:18–19; 21:28–45; 24:22,31; 25:34; Luke 1:68–79; 2:29–32; 19:41–44; 24:44–48; John 1:12–14; 3:16; 5:24; 6:44–45,65; 10:27–29; 15:16; 17:6,12,17–18; Acts 20:32; Rom. 5:9–10; 8:28–39; 10:12–15; 11:5–7,26–36; 1 Cor. 1:1–2; 15:24–28; Eph. 1:4–23; 2:1–10; 3:1–11; Col. 1:12–14; 2 Thess. 2:13–14; 2 Tim. 1:12; 2:10,19; Heb. 11:39–12:2; 1 Peter 1:2–5,13; 2:4–10; 1 John 1:7–9; 2:19; 3:2.

VI. THE CHURCH

A New Testament church of the Lord Jesus Christ is a local body of baptized believers who are associated by covenant in the faith and fellowship of the gospel, observing the two ordinances of Christ, committed to His teachings, exercising the gifts, rights, and privileges invested in them by His Word, and seeking to extend the gospel to the ends of the earth.

This church is an autonomous body, operating through democratic processes under the Lordship of Jesus Christ. In such a congregation, members are equally responsible. Its Scriptural officers are pastors and deacons.

The New Testament speaks also of the church as the body of Christ which includes all of the redeemed of all the ages.

Matt. 16:15–19; 18:15–20; Acts 2:41–42,47; 5:11–14; 6:3–6; 13:1–3; 14:23,27; 15:1–30; 16:5; 20:28; Rom. 1:7; 1 Cor. 1:2; 3:16; 5:4–5; 7:17; 9:13–14; 12; Eph. 1:22–23; 2:19–22; 3:8–11,21; 5:22–32; Phil. 1:1; Col. 1:18; 1 Tim. 3:1–15; 4:14; 1 Peter 5:1–4; Rev. 2–3; 21:2–3.

VII. BAPTISM AND THE LORD'S SUPPER

Christian baptism is the immersion of a believer in water in the name of the Father, the Son, and the Holy Spirit. It is an act of obedience symbolizing the believer's faith in a crucified, buried, and risen Saviour, the believer's death to sin, the burial of the old life, and the resurrection to walk in newness of life in Christ Jesus. It is a testimony to his faith in the final resurrection of the dead. Being a church ordinance, it is prerequisite to the privileges of church membership and to the Lord's Supper.

The Lord's Supper is a symbolic act of obedience whereby members of the church, through partaking of the bread and the fruit of the vine, memorialize the death of the Redeemer and anticipate His second coming.

Matt. 3:13–17; 26:26–30; 28:19–20; Mark 1:9–11; 14:22–26; Luke 3:21–22; 22:19–20; John 3:23; Acts 2:41–42; 8:35–39; 16:30–33; Acts 20;7; Rom. 6:3–5; 1 Cor. 10:16,21; 11:23–29; Col. 2:12.

VIII. THE LORD'S DAY

The first day of the week is the Lord's Day. It is a Christian institution for regular observance. It commemorates the resurrection of Christ from the dead and should be employed in exercises of worship and spiritual devotion, both public and private, and by refraining from worldly amusements, and resting from secular employments, work of necessity and mercy only being excepted.

Ex. 20:8–11; Matt. 12:1–12; 28:1 ff.; Mark 2:27–28; 16:1–7; Luke 24:1–3,33–36; John 4:21–24; 20:1,19–28; Acts 20:7; 1 Cor. 16:1–2; Col. 2:16; 3:16; Rev. 1:10.

IX. THE KINGDOM

The kingdom of God includes both His general sovereignty over the universe and his particular kingship over men who willfully acknowledge Him as King. Particularly the kingdom is the realm of salvation into which men enter by trustful, childlike commitment to Jesus Christ. Christians ought to pray and to labor that the kingdom may come and God's will be done on earth. The full consummation of the kingdom awaits the return of Jesus Christ and the end of this age.

Gen. 1:1; Isa. 9:6–7; Jer. 23:5–6; Matt. 3:2; 4:8–10,23; 12:25–28; 13:1–52; 25:31–46; 26:29; Mark 1:14–15; 9:1; Luke 4:43; 8:1; 9:2; 12:31–32; 17:20–21; 23:42; John 3:3; 18:36; Acts 1:6–7; 17:22–31; Rom. 5:17; 8:19; 1 Cor. 15:24–28; Col. 1:13; Heb. 11:10,16; 12:28; 1 Peter 2:4–10; 4:13; Rev. 1:6,9; 5:10; 11:15; 21–22.

X. LAST THINGS

God, in His own time and in His own way, will bring the world to its appropriate end. According to His promise, Jesus Christ will return personally and visibly in glory to the earth; the dead will be raised; and Christ will judge all men in righteousness. The unrighteous will be consigned to hell, the place of everlasting punishment. The righteous in their resurrected and glorified bodies will receive their reward and will dwell forever in heaven with the Lord.

Isa. 2:4; 11:9; Matt. 16:27; 18:8–9; 19:28; 24:27,30,36,44; 25:31–46; 26:64; Mark 8:38; 9:43–48; Luke 12:40,48; 16:19–26; 17:22–37; 21:27–28; John 14:1–3; Acts 1:11; 17:31; Rom. 14:10; 1 Cor. 4:5; 15:24–28,35–58; 2 Cor. 5:10; Phil. 3:20–21; Col. 1:5; 3:4; 1 Thess. 4:14–18; 5:1 ff.; 2 Thess. 1:7 ff.; 2; 1 Tim. 6:14; 2 Tim. 4:1,8; Titus 2:13; Heb. 9:27–28; James 5:8; 2 Peter 3:7 ff.; 1 John 2:28; 3:2; Jude 14; Rev. 1:18; 3:11; 20:1–22:13.

XI. EVANGELISM AND MISSIONS

It is the duty and privilege of every follower of Christ and of every church of the Lord Jesus Christ to endeavor to make disciples of all nations. The new birth of man's spirit by God's Holy Spirit means the birth of love for others. Missionary effort on the part of all rests thus upon a spiritual necessity of the regenerate life, and is expressly and repeatedly commanded in the teachings of Christ. It is the duty of every child of God to seek constantly to win the lost to Christ by personal effort and by all other methods in harmony with the gospel of Christ.

Gen. 12:1–3; Ex. 19:5–6; Isa. 6:1–8; Matt. 9:37–38; 10:5–15; 13:18–30,37–43; 16:19; 22:9–10; 24:14; 28:18–20; Luke 10:1–18; 24:46–53; John 14:11–12; 15:7–8,16; 17:15; 20:21; Acts 1:8; 2; 8:26–40; 10:42–48; 13:2–3; Rom. 10:13–15; Eph. 3:1–11; 1 Thess. 1:8; 2 Tim. 4:5; Heb. 2:1–3; 11:39–12:2; 1 Peter 2:4–10; Rev. 22:17.

XII. EDUCATION

The cause of education in the kingdom of Christ is co-ordinate with the causes of missions and general benevolence and should receive along with these the liberal support of the churches. An adequate system of Christian schools is necessary to a complete spiritual program for Christ's people.

In Christian education there should be a proper balance between academic freedom and academic responsibility. Freedom in any orderly relationship of human life is always limited and never absolute. The freedom of a teacher in a Christian school, college, or seminary is limited by the pre-eminence of Jesus Christ, by the authoritative nature of the Scriptures, and by the distinct purpose for which the school exists.

Deut. 4:1,5,9,14; 6:1–10; 31:12–13; Neh. 8:1–8; Job. 28:28; Psalms 19:7 ff.; 119:11; Prov. 3:13 ff.; 4:1–10; 8:1–7,11; 15:14; Eccl. 7:19; Matt. 5:2; 7:24 ff.; 28:19–20; Luke 2:40; 1 Cor. 1:18–31; Eph. 4:11–16; Phil. 4:8; Col. 2:3,8–9; 1 Tim. 1:3–7; 2 Tim. 2:15; 3:14–17; Heb. 5:12–6:3; James 1:5; 3:17.

XIII. STEWARDSHIP

God is the source of all blessings, temporal and spiritual; all that we have and are we owe to Him. Christians have a spiritual debtorship to the whole world, a holy trusteeship in the gospel, and a binding stewardship in their possessions. They are therefore under obligation to serve Him with their time, talents, and material possessions; and should recognize all these as entrusted to them to use for the glory of God and for helping others. According to the Scriptures, Christians should contribute of their means cheerfully, regularly, systematically, proportionately, and liberally for the advancement of the Redeemer's cause on earth.

Gen 14:20; Lev. 27:30–32; Deut. 8:18; Mal. 3:8–12; Matt. 6:1–4,19–21; 19:21; 23:23; 25:14–29; Luke 12:16–21,42; 16:1–13; Acts 2:44–47; 5:1–11; 17:24–25; 20:35; Rom. 6:6–22; 12:1–2; 1 Cor. 4:1–2; 6:19–20; 12; 16:1–4; 2 Cor. 8–9; 12:15; Phil. 4:10–19; 1 Peter 1:18–19.

XIV. CO-OPERATION

Christ's people should, as occasion requires, organize such associations and conventions as may best secure co-operation for the great objects of the kingdom of God. Such organizations have no authority over one another or over the churches. They are voluntary and advisory bodies designed to elicit, combine, and direct the energies of our people in the most effective manner. Members of New Testament churches should co-operate with one another in carrying forward the missionary, educational and benevolent ministries for the extension of Christ's kingdom. Christian unity in the New Testament sense is spiritual harmony and voluntary co-operation for common ends by various groups of Christ's people. Co-operation is desirable between the various Christian denominations, when the end to be attained is itself justified, and when such co-operation involves no violation of conscience or compromise of loyalty to Christ and his Word as revealed in the New Testament.

Ex. 17:12; 18:17 ff.; Judg. 7:21; Ezra 1:3–4; 2:68–69; 5:14–15; Neh. 4; 8:1–5; Matt. 10:5–15; 20:1–16; 22:1–10; 28:19–20; Mark 2:3; Luke 10:1 ff.; Acts 1:13–14; 2:1 ff.; 4:31–37; 13:2–3; 15:1–35; 1 Cor. 1:10–17; 3:5–15; 12; 2 Cor. 8–9; Gal. 1:6–10; Eph. 4:1–16; Phil. 1:15–18.

XV. THE CHRISTIAN AND THE SOCIAL ORDER

Every Christian is under obligation to seek to make the will of Christ supreme in his own life and in human society. Means and methods used for the improvement of society and the establishment of righteousness among men can be truly and permanently helpful only when they are rooted in the regeneration of the individual by the saving grace of God in Christ Jesus. The Christian should oppose in the spirit of Christ every form of greed, selfishness, and vice. He should work to provide for the orphaned, the needy, the aged, the helpless, and the sick. Every Christian should seek to bring industry, government, and society as a whole under the sway of the principles of righteousness, truth, and brotherly love. In order to promote these ends Christians should be ready to work with all men of good will in any good cause, always being careful to act in the spirit of love without compromising their loyalty to Christ and his truth.

Ex. 20:3–17; Lev. 6:2–5; Deut. 10:12; 27:17; Psalm 101:5; Micah 6:8; Zech. 8:16; Matt. 5:13–16,43–48; 22:36–40; 25:35; Mark 1:29–34; 2:3 ff.; 10:21; Luke 4:18–21; 10:27–37; 20:25; John 15:12; 17:15; Rom. 12–14; 1 Cor. 5:9–10; 6:1–7; 7:20–24; 10:23–11:1; Gal. 3:26–28; Eph. 6:5–9; Col. 3:12–17; 1 Thess. 3:12; Philemon; James 1:27; 2:8.

XVI. PEACE AND WAR

It is the duty of Christians to seek peace with all men on principles of righteousness. In accordance with the spirit and teachings of Christ they should do all in their power to put an end to war.

The true remedy for the war spirit is the gospel of our Lord. The supreme need of the world is the acceptance of His teachings in all the affairs of men and nations, and the practical application of His law of love.

Isa. 2:4; Matt. 5:9,38–48; 6:33; 26:52; Luke 22:36,38; Rom. 12:18–19; 13:1–7; 14:19; Heb. 12:14; James 4:1–2.

XVII. RELIGIOUS LIBERTY

God alone is Lord of the conscience, and He has left it free from the doctrines and commandments of men which are contrary to His Word or not contained in it. Church and state should be separate. The state owes to every church protection and full freedom in the pursuit of its spiritual ends. In providing for such freedom no ecclesiastical group or denomination should be favored by the state more than others. Civil government being ordained of God, it is the duty of Christians to render loyal obedience thereto in all things not contrary to the revealed will of God. The church should not resort to the civil power to carry on its work. The gospel of Christ contemplates spiritual means alone for the pursuit of its ends. The state has no right to impose penalties for religious opinions of any kind. The state has no right to impose taxes for the support of any form of religion. A free church in a free state is the Christian ideal, and this implies the right of free and unhindered access to God on the part of all men and the right to form and propagate opinions in the sphere of religion without interference by the civil power.

Gen. 1:27; 2:7; Matt. 6:6–7; 24:16:26; 22:21; John

8:36; Acts 4:19–20; Rom. 6:1–2; 13:1–7; Gal. 5:1,13; Phil. 3:20; 1 Tim. 2:1–2; James 4:12; 1 Peter 2:12–17; 3:11–17; 4:12–19.

HERSCHEL H. HOBBS, Oklahoma City, Oklahoma (President of the Southern Baptist Convention), *Chairman*
HOWARD M. REAVES, Mobile, Alabama
ED. J. PACKWOOD, Phoenix, Arizona
C. Z. HOLLAND, Jonesboro, Arkansas
W. B. TIMBERLAKE, Pomona, California
C. V. KOONS, Washington, District of Columbia
MALCOLM B. KNIGHT, Jacksonville, Florida
DICK H. HALL, JR., Decatur, Georgia, *Secretary*
CHARLES R. WALKER, Marion, Illinois
WALTER R. DAVIS, Hammond, Indiana
GARTH PYBAS, Topeka, Kansas
V. C. KRUSCHWITZ, Elizabethtown, Kentucky
LUTHER B. HALL, Farmerville, Louisiana
ROBERT WOODWARD, Frederick, Maryland
DOUGLAS HUDGINS, Jackson, Mississippi, *Vice-Chairman*
PAUL WEBER, JR., Springfield, Missouri
R. A. LONG, Roswell, New Mexico
NANE STARNES, Asheville, North Carolina
C. HOGUE HOCKENSMITH, Columbus, Ohio,
HUGH R. BUMPAS, Oklahoma City, Oklahoma
DAVID G. ANDERSON, North Charleston, South Carolina
E. WARREN RUST, Cleveland, Tennessee
JAMES H. LANDES, Wichita Falls, Texas
R. P. DOWNEY, Salem, Virginia

W. MORGAN PATTERSON

BAPTIST FEDERATION OF CANADA, CANADIAN BAPTIST FOREIGN MISSION BOARD. In 1968 Orville E. Daniel was serving as general secretary of this board. At the same time the board spent $252,551 for overseas work and $451,191 on personnel support. There were a total of 110 missionaries in three countries, distributed as follows: Bolivia, 27; Congo, 15; and India, 63. There were 6 hospitals, 5 clinics, 22 schools, and 3 seminaries supported in these countries. The total income from North America was $849,582.

See also CANADIAN BAPTIST FOREIGN MISSION BOARD.

HELEN E. FALLS

BAPTIST HISTORIOGRAPHY. See HISTORIOGRAPHY, BAPTIST.

BAPTIST HISTORY AND HERITAGE. A journal published semiannually by the Historical Commission, SBC, 1965–69, and quarterly since 1970. It is designed to help Baptists understand their history and appreciate their heritage.

LYNN E. MAY, JR.

BAPTIST HOME FOR CHILDREN, JACKSONVILLE (cf. Florida, Baptist Home for Children, Vol. I). The home is owned and operated by three associations: Jacksonville, Northeast Florida, and Black Creek, which came into an active role in 1967. In 1961 Superintendent Silas M. Bishop died and was succeeded by George E. Norton, who continues (1970) to serve in that capacity. In 1965 a fifth cottage was added to the campus to take care of older girls. The campus is very attractive with large oaks, a swimming pool, and gym, even though located in the city. It also has a lake recently named Lake John Henry in honor of a long-time trustee, John Henry Mitchell. In 1960 a full-time case worker was added. Mrs. Norton also takes an active part in managing the home. In 1968 the home admitted 35, discharged 35, and cared for a total of 100 children. Total assets of the home increased from $264,935 in 1956 to approximately $1,000,000 in 1970.

GEORGE E. NORTON

BAPTIST HOME OF THE DISTRICT OF COLUMBIA (cf. District of Columbia Baptist Home [for aged], Vol. I). Plans for the construction of the new home were completed in early 1960. On August 12 construction was begun at the new site located at 3700 Nebraska Avenue, N. W., Washington, D. C. The cornerstone for the new edifice was laid Sept. 17, 1961. Residents were moved from the former home in Georgetown, into the new home Mar. 27, 1962. The cost of the home was $1,231,800. The rated capacity for guests was 63. Plans are now under way for an addition, with eight floors and 144 guest units. The estimated cost for the addition is $2,200,000.

The president of the board of trustees is John M. Firmin. Administrator for the home is William P. Harris. The home has a staff of about 30. Applicants for residency in the home are required to have been members of one of the convention churches for at least five years. The $312,700 annual budget for operation and maintenance of the home is jointly shared by the residents, endowment funds, the board of trustees, contributions from the District of Columbia convention, and general contributions.

M. CHANDLER STITH

***BAPTIST HOSPITAL, INC. (Mid-State).** The two block complex of 10 buildings and surrounding property has an asset value of $30,000,000 and makes Baptist Hospital one of the largest general hospitals in Nashville. Total capacity in 1970 was 625 beds and 80 bassinets. Physical and specialized areas include 17 operating rooms, expanded pathology laboratories, treatment rooms, service areas, full service data processing and central supply system, a cardiac pavilion, an intensive care unit, an emergency pavilion, a heart station, inhalation therapy, physical therapy, and an isotope unit. In 1970 expansion was made in pediatrics, obstetrics, X-ray, and areas in the East and South buildings.

Students receive training in medical technology, X-ray, licensed practical nursing, operating technician, radiology technician, inhalation therapy, and cardiac nursing. The medical staff consists of 430 physicians, and rotating internships of 12 months duration cover 16 medical fields and hospital chaplaincy. Baptist Hospital is approved and accredited by the Joint Commission on Accreditation of Hospitals, American Medical Association, American Hospital Association, Tennessee Hospital Association, Southeastern Hospital Conference, and Middle Tennessee Hospital Council. GENE KIDD

BAPTIST HOSPITALS, INC. (cf. Hospital Commission of Kentucky Baptists, Vol. I). The governing body for all hospitals affiliated with the Kentucky Baptist Convention. Organized in 1968 with a 24-member board of directors, in 1969 it owned and controlled all the property of the three Kentucky Baptist hospitals. It replaces the Hospital Commission of Kentucky Baptists which had been incorporated in 1960 and given legal authority over the three hospitals. In 1965, H. L. Dobbs was appointed full-time executive director of the commission. He is now president of the new organization. The former administrators of the three hospitals, Homer D. Coggins, of Kentucky Baptist Hospital, Louisville, Ben R. Brewer, of Central Baptist Hospital, Lexington, and James V. Dorsett, of Western Baptist Hospital, Paducah, now serve as executive vice-presidents. Total property value is $13,566,807, with a total indebtedness of $1,190,000. The total number of beds is 863, with 81 bassinets. The medical staff of 894 is assisted by 1,977 other employees. Admissions in 1969 were 42,109. H. L. DOBBS

***BAPTIST HOUR.** See RADIO AND TELEVISION COMMISSION, THE.

BAPTIST JOINT COMMITTEE ON PUBLIC AFFAIRS. See PUBLIC AFFAIRS COMMITTEE, BAPTIST JOINT.

BAPTIST JUBILEE ADVANCE. In 1951 Porter Routh, executive secretary, Executive Committee of the Southern Baptist Convention, suggested the possibility of a worthy celebration of the 150th anniversary of Baptist beginnings on the national level in America. In Jan., 1955, a group of Southern Baptists and American Baptists met in Washington, D. C., and voted to encourage the leaders of both conventions "to consider the adoption of some common goals and long-range objectives such as might relate to stewardship, evangelism, Christian education, and the celebration of the sesquicentennial of the Triennial Convention."

C. C. Warren, having been elected President of the Southern Baptist Convention in May, 1955, upon instruction from the Convention, presented the matter to the American Baptist Convention then in session at Atlantic City. The idea of the celebration was enthusiastically approved.

Each of the Baptist bodies in America was invited to send representatives to a meeting in Chicago, Dec. 8, 1955, to consider the matter. About 40 persons came, representing approximately 20,000,000 of the 22,000,000 Baptists in America. Canadian Baptists joined shortly thereafter. Though the group was characterized by a rather wide variance in backgrounds, opinions, etc., a spirit of gratitude for a common heritage was evident. The Baptist Joint Committee on the Baptist Jubilee was formed and the basic principles of cooperation on the part of the participating bodies were published in Apr., 1956.

The purpose of the Baptist Jubilee was "to work cooperatively, to witness effectively, and to celebrate worthily" in a program focusing the efforts of Baptists on common goals or objectives which each participating body could achieve within the framework of its own organization. A dream on the part of Baptists throughout the land was to bring about in the third Jubilee year, 1964, the greatest achievements of any single year in Baptist history. The intention was to give the world a dramatic presentation of what Baptists stand for, what they have achieved, and "to gain a mighty impetus for greater achievements for God's glory in the years ahead."

The joint efforts for the years 1959–64 were planned and executed under the name Baptist Jubilee Advance. The Baptist Joint Committee on the Jubilee Advance met twice annually for about eight years, giving direction to the preparation for the significant five-year program, 1959–64. Annual emphases were observed. Each participating body determined its own methods, programs of procedure, slogans, and symbols. Each, however, conformed to the general guidelines leading to the Baptist Jubilee Celebration in Atlantic City in 1964.

During 1959 the Baptist Jubilee Advance emphasis was on "Cooperative Christianity." The theme was "New Life for You." In 1960 the emphasis was on "Bible Teaching and Training"; the theme: "Unto a Full-Grown Christian." During 1961 the emphasis was on "Stewardship and Enlistment"; the theme: "I Will Be Faithful." In 1962 the emphasis was on "Church Extension"; the theme: "My Church Reading Out." In 1963 the emphasis was on "World Missions"; the theme: "Sharing Christ with the Whole World." In 1964 the Third Jubilee Celebration marked 150 years of organized Baptist life in America; the theme: "For Liberty and Light." C. C. WARREN

BAPTIST JUBILEE CELEBRATION. Held in Atlantic City, May 22–24, 1964, this celebration commemorated 150 years of organized Baptist life in America. The event marked the sesquicentennial of the establishment of "the General Missionary Convention of the Baptist Denomination in the United States of America for Foreign Missions," commonly called the Triennial Convention. Atlantic City was chosen in preference to Philadelphia, the birthplace of the Triennial Convention, because of its 40,000 seat convention hall which could accommodate the anticipated crowd. Approximately 35,000 attended one or more sessions of the six-day event, which began with simultaneous annual meetings of the American Baptist and the Southern Baptist Conventions.

Registrants received a copy of *Baptist Ad-*

vance, a 512-page history of the achievements of Baptists in North America for a century and a half. The book, a cooperative project of the conventions participating in the Baptist Jubilee Advance, involved 63 contributors.

The presiding officer for the Celebration was Theodore F. Adams, of Richmond, Va., past president of the Baptist World Alliance. The opening devotion at each session was conducted by those who had served as annual chairmen of the Baptist Jubilee Advance (1959–64).

The program had been planned by representatives of all the participating bodies with Edwin F. Tuller, general secretary of the American Baptist Convention as chairman. The main features of the program were: (1) keynote address by John C. Diefenbaker, former Prime Minister of Canada, (2) address by Lyndon B. Johnson, President of the United States, (3) historical glimpses of Baptists by historian Kenneth Scott Latourette (*q.v.*), Yale University, (4) dramatic presentation, "The Quest of All People for Freedom," and (5) a worship service led by Joao Soren of Brazil, president of the Baptist World Alliance. A high hour was reached on Saturday evening with a 45-minute oratorio, *What Is Man?,* by Samuel Miller, Harvard University, with music by Ron Nelson, Brown University. The oratorio was performed by the Singing City Chorus of Philadelphia under the direction of Thor Johnson of Northwestern University, accompanied by the 60-member Baltimore Symphony Orchestra.

The celebration was brought to a climactic ending on Sunday afternoon, May 24th, with a message by evangelist Billy Graham.

C. C. WARREN

BAPTIST LAYMEN'S CORPORATION (Oklahoma). Formed by 27 Baptist laymen from churches in the greater Oklahoma City, Okla., area, the Baptist Laymen's Corporation was chartered Feb. 12, 1960. Its purpose is to develop, encourage, promote, and finance religious, educational, charitable, benevolent, and scientific work of any kind, particularly those activities performed by the Baptist General Convention of Oklahoma. Its first project in 1963, was to finance and construct the Doctors' Medical Building. The next project was financing, construction, and operation of the Oklahoma City Baptist Golden Age Homes in 1965. Both projects were financed by sale of bonds in the sum of $950,000. Assets in 1969 totaled about $1,500,000 with capital indebtedness of $882,836.

J. M. GASKIN

BAPTIST MEDICAL CENTER, BIRMINGHAM (cf. Birmingham Baptist Hospitals, Vol. I). A 250-bed addition to Birmingham Baptist Hospital which became the main hospital of the 430-bed institution, was opened in Feb., 1966. The 500-bed Baptist Medical Center on Montclair Road replaced the Highland Avenue Baptist Hospital in Dec., 1966. Expansion included construction of the Charles J. Donald Professional Office building adjacent to Birmingham Baptist Hospital, and on the Montclair site a professional office building, parking deck, and John H. Buchanan Hall to house the Ida V. Moffett School of Nursing. The first open-heart surgery performed in a community hospital in Alabama took place at Baptist Medical Center in Oct., 1968. The name of the hospital system was changed on July 1, 1969, to The Baptist Medical Center. The Baptist Hospitals Foundation of Birmingham, Inc., was set up in 1967 to receive gifts to the hospitals. Programs in health education include a school of anesthesia for nurses, and residencies in hospital administration and surgery.

JANIE LOTT

BAPTIST MEMORIAL HOSPITAL. See MEMORIAL HOSPITAL, BAPTIST, MEMPHIS.

***BAPTIST MEMORIAL HOSPITAL (Jacksonville, Fla.).** Owned and operated by the Southern Baptist Convention, this institution became a subsidiary to Southern Baptist hospitals in 1965. Lawrence Payne, administrator of the hospital, 1954–65, was named director of development and expansion. George A. Mathews succeeded him as administrator.

A 60-bed addition to the Wolfson Memorial Children's Hospital (operated in connection with Memorial Hospital) was opened in 1959. In 1964 an 84-bed expansion program was initiated to meet a critical community bed shortage and the Executive Committee, SBC, approved the hospital's plans for a $20,000,000 expansion program. The hospital completed a new powerhouse in 1968. The following year a new heart catheterization laboratory was completed and construction was begun on an 800-car parking facility.

The hospital operates five educational programs: School of Medical Technology, School of Radiology, Physical Therapy Training Program, an intern and resident training program, and an administrative residency program.

In 1968 the hospital treated 20,894 inpatients and 49,869 outpatients and recorded 2,472 births. The institution contributed medical service valued at $459,880 for persons unable to pay. The hospital received $16,500 from the Cooperative Program and $78,057 from designated local gifts. The operating expenses for 1968 were $7,611,279.

Medical services are provided for Foreign Mission Board personnel. In 1969 the hospital reported a bed capacity of 415 and a plant valued at $11,254,599.

GEORGE A. MATHEWS

BAPTIST MEN'S JOURNAL (cf. Brotherhood Journal, Vol. I). A quarterly publication containing information and program materials for Baptist men, published by the Brotherhood Commission. This publication originated as *The Southern Baptist Brotherhood Annual.* It became *The Southern Baptist Brotherhood Quarterly* in 1937, the *Southern Baptist Brotherhood Journal* in 1944, and *The Brotherhood*

THE BAPTIST MEDICAL CENTER — MONTCLAIR (*q.v.*), Birmingham, Ala.

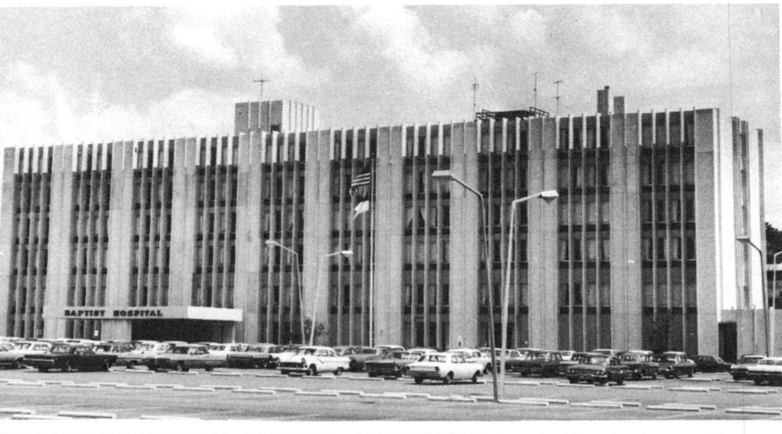

THE BAPTIST MEDICAL CENTER—PRINCETON (*q.v.*), Birmingham, Ala.

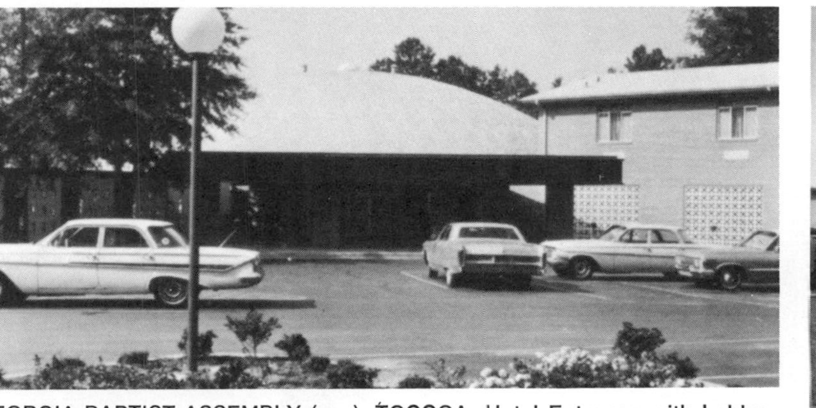

GEORGIA BAPTIST ASSEMBLY (*q.v.*), TOCCOA: Hotel Entrance with Lobby Dome and Hotel Wing.

GEORGIA ASSEMBLY (*q.v.*): Hotel Wing and Chapel, Toccoa.

RIDGECREST BAPTIST ASSEMBLY (*q.v.*), North Carolina, Pritchell Hall. Main hotel and administration building, completed in 1965 at cost of $1,000,000. Replaced the original Pritchell Hall (1914).

GLORIETA BAPTIST ASSEMBLY (*q.v.*), New Mexico, Holcomb Auditorium. Named for T. L. Holcomb, executive secretary of Sunday School Board, 1935–53. Dedicated, June 20, 1966. Contains 25 conference rooms and 2,600-seat auditorium. Cost $1,230,000.

Journal in 1952. Throughout its history this periodical was 5 x 8 inches in size. In Oct., 1966, the commission increased the size of the magazine to 8½ x 11 inches and changed the title to *Baptist Men's Journal.*

The first editor of this major Brotherhood publication was Lawson H. Cooke who served in this capacity until his retirement, Dec. 31, 1951. George W. Schroeder, the new executive secretary of the commission, became editor in 1952. In 1959 Roy Jennings, newly elected editorial secretary, became editor. The *Journal* won the Associated Church Press Award of Merit in 1961. With the July–Sept., 1964, issue Kenneth Everett became the editor. The commission named Roddy Stinson editor in 1966. At this time the magazine was expanded to provide mission curriculum materials for Baptist men and young men.

Baptist Public Relations Awards of "Exceptional Merit" have been received for several articles published in the *Journal.* The Apr.–June, 1968, issue of the *Journal* was given the same "Exceptional Merit" award for the outstanding single issue of a Baptist publication during the year.

The circulation of a single issue went over 100,000 for the first time in 1955, climbing to 110,000 copies distributed. Average circulation per quarter reached its peak in 1958 with 114,000.

Circulation dropped to a low of 84,000 in 1964. It rose to 96,540 in 1967, but dropped to 90,067 in 1968. DARRELL C. RICHARDSON

***BAPTIST MESSAGE.** The official newspaper of the Louisiana Baptist Convention. After 37 years, Finley W. Tinnin (*q.v.*) retired as editor, Jan. 1, 1958. He was succeeded by James F. Cole. An in-depth study and an extensive survey conducted by a consulting firm employed by the convention revealed that the readership of the paper desired a change in format (from a tabloid to magazine) and newsprint. To achieve the changes, the convention voted the establishment of a printing plant due to inadequate printing sources in the state of Louisiana. By 1960 a new high in circulation (72,000) had been achieved. However, rising costs in printing necessitated increases in subscription rates, the first in 32 years, and a substantial drop in circulation was experienced. Three years later, additional increases became mandatory; once again, a decline in circulation followed. A need to incorporate the *Baptist Message* with a separate board of trustees became apparent to the executive board of the Louisiana Baptist Convention and was approved by the convention in 1963. Annually, issues of the *Baptist Message* are microfilmed by the Historical Commission, SBC.

JAMES F. COLE

***BAPTIST MESSENGER.** Published at 1141 North Robinson, Oklahoma City, with a circulation of 82,715 in 1969. Value of the press and equipment was $157,369.98. The operating budget of $220,509.40 was received from these sources: Cooperative Program, $36,509.40; subscriptions and special pages, $170,000; advertising and miscellaneous sources, $14,000. The 16-page weekly is devoted to news reporting of Baptist churches and institutions in Oklahoma and the Baptist denomination at large. The advertising policy requires that companies must be licensed to do business in Oklahoma, must be helpful to the churches and their members, and must not attempt to defraud the readers. Jack Gritz completed 20 years as editor in Aug., 1969.

J. M. GASKIN

BAPTIST MISSIONARY ASSOCIATION OF AMERICA (cf. North American Baptist Association, Vol. II). In theology the churches are evangelical, missionary, fundamentalistic, and premillennial. In associational capacity they respect the equality of churches as constituent units and the equal rights and privileges of ministers of the gospel after their understanding of the New Testament order. The name of the body was changed in Apr., 1969, to the Baptist Missionary Association of America because the term "North" in the original name was misleading and misunderstood by many, especially in the southern part of the United States.

There are 1,517 Baptist Missionary Association of America churches located in 25 states. The association headquarters are at 716 Main St., Little Rock, Ark. Craig Branham is the general secretary of missions.

In a 10-year period (1959–68), the number of Baptist Missionary Association of America churches reporting statistics increased from 1,169 to 1,290 with a membership increase from 134,067 to 173,337. Church contributions for missionary purposes for the same period increased from $723,799 to $1,549,578, with the total gifts for local and missionary purposes increasing from $5,288,388 to $11,065,794. This represents an increase in church contributions of more than 100 per cent.

Serving Baptist Missionary Association of America mission fields are 117 missionaries: four in Australia, six in Bolivia, 11 in Brazil, two in Canada, two in Costa Rica, two in France, two in Guatemala, six in Japan, 20 in Mexico, eight in Nicaragua, eight in the Republic of China, two in Uruguay, two in Italy, two in Angola, 14 in Portugal, two in Cape Verde, four working with Latin Americans in Texas and New Mexico, two with American Indians in Montana, and 18 working in the United States.

Fifteen state associations and 80 local and district associations that support the Baptist Missionary Association of America have 65 missionaries working on the local and state mission fields. These supporting associations also own and operate three orphanages, three junior colleges, two Bible schools, 13 state Baptist papers, one book store, and other mission projects.

North American Theological Seminary, Jacksonville, Tex.; John W. Gregson, president; Harvest Gleaner Hour (radio and television ministry), Conway, Ark., Harold Morris, director; Daniel Springs Memorial Encampment, Gary, Tex., Eugene Gauntt, director; Baptist News Service (research and public relations), Jacksonville, Tex., Leon Gaylor, director; Baptist Bible and Book House, Little Rock, Ark., T. O. Tollett, manager; and Baptist Building Savings, Inc., Little Rock, Charles W. McKamy, director, are all owned and operated by the Baptist Missionary Association of America.

The Baptist publications committee with business offices in Little Rock and editorial offices in Texarkana, Ark.-Tex., owned and operated by the Baptist Missionary Association of America, publishes a full graded series of Sunday School, Training Service, and study course literature. D. O. Silvey is editor of publications.

The National Women's Missionary Auxiliary and the Baptist Missionary Association of America Brotherhood are affiliated organizations supporting the mission projects of the parent organization. The Baptist Missionary Association of America publishes several periodicals including its mission magazine, *The Gleaner.* LEON GAYLOR

***BAPTIST MISSIONARY SOCIETY (of Great Britain).** In 1961 Portuguese reprisals to a nationalist revolt in Angola and consequent guerilla warfare led to the enforced departure of missionaries and to the exile in the Congo Republic of over 400,000 Angolan Christians. A tightening of restrictions on new missionaries entering India since 1967 has meant a diminution in the number in that country. Since 1955 the work in Parana State, Brazil, has rapidly developed involving a total of 25 missionaries in 1969. Also the society has become a participant in the United Mission to Nepal. In 1969 the total number of missionaries was 270, and the income for the year £502,014.

A. S. CLEMENT

***BAPTIST PRESS.** The news service of the Southern Baptist Convention, serving the 31 Baptist state papers, the religious, and secular press. In 1958 a Washington, D. C., regional office was opened with W. Barry Garrett as editor. Later that same year a Dallas regional office was opened with Leonard Holloway as editor. In 1959 W. C. Fields succeeded Albert McClellan as Baptist Press director. Another regional office was opened in Atlanta with Walker L. Knight as editor in 1959. That year the Baptist Press logotype—BP—became registered U. S. Trademark. In 1960, largely to meet the needs of the news media for the fast transmission of news copy, the SBC teletype network was established with 25 stations in 19 cities in 13 states in the Eastern half of the nation. It was discontinued in 1965 because of rising costs of the equipment. In 1961 Baptist Press became one of three denominational news services accredited at the White House, as well as the press galleries of the U. S. Senate and House of Representatives. In 1965 Theo Sommerkamp completed 10 years as assistant director of the news service and moved to Zurich, Switzerland, to become the director of the European Baptist News Service. He was succeeded by James A. Newton of Dallas. That same year TWX high speed teletypewriter equipment was installed for use among the regional offices. On Dec. 1, 1965, separate mailings of Baptist Press stories by the regional offices ceased and all (BP) copy was done in a central daily mailing from the main office in the Southern Baptist Convention Building, Nashville. On Nov. 1, 1966, the Baptist Press Bureau at the Sunday School Board, Nashville, opened with Lynn M. Davis, Jr., as bureau chief. Terminology was changed from "regional offices" to Baptist Press "bureaus." On Jan. 1, 1970, the Baptist Press bureau at the Foreign Mission Board opened in Richmond with Jesse C. Fletcher as acting chief. By 1970 the press service was going daily to about 350 news media offices—Baptist state papers, daily newspapers, wire services, national magazines, radio and television stations and networks, and other publications of both religious and secular press—mainly in the United States. W. C. FIELDS

***BAPTIST PROGRAM, THE.** The magazine is the general program journal for the staff leadership of the churches and related organizations of the Southern Baptist Convention, including state Baptist conventions and associations. Its purpose is to aid these church, agency, and organization staff workers to participate effectively in planning and supporting the overall program of the denomination.

The Baptist Program's objectives, as approved by the SBC Executive Committee in 1969, are to equip its readers with comprehensive information on Southern Baptist programs and objectives; to gain support for the Cooperative Program and the SBC causes it makes possible; to strengthen the work fostered by the denomination; to help church and denominational workers in their leadership roles to relate their efforts to the total program of Southern Baptists; and to communicate information on current trends, attitudes, actions, and developments which affect the general work of Southern Baptists. W. C. Fields succeeded Albert McClellan as editor in 1959. The circulation in 1970 was 58,000. LEONARD E. HILL

BAPTIST PUBLIC RELATIONS ASSOCIATION. An organization established in 1954 by Southern Baptist professional personnel working in the related areas of public relations, journalism, audiovisuals, radio and television, promotion, fund-raising, and development. Meetings include an annual three-day workshop early in the year and a fellowship breakfast during the annual meeting of the Southern Baptist Convention. A monthly newsletter keeps the approximately 200 members in contact with each other. In 1964 an awards program was instituted. Some years entries have totaled nearly 300. Officers are elected for one-year terms. Meeting places vary, but occur mainly in the

Eastern half of the nation. Purposes of the organization are: (1) to share promotional ideas among individuals engaged in public relations and related work for Southern Baptist organizations; (2) to assist Baptist agencies, institutions, and state conventions in the establishment and development of effective public relations programs; and (3) to provide a medium for understanding and fellowship for those engaged in this distinctive channel of Christian service.

W. C. FIELDS

***BAPTIST RECORD.** Published continuously since 1877, this publication has been the official journal of the Mississippi Baptist Convention since 1919.

W. C. Fields, editor from 1956 to 1959, made several innovations in style and features, and especially in an increased use of photographs. When Fields resigned to become director of public relations for the Southern Baptist Executive Committee, he was succeeded, in July, 1959, by Joe T. Odle, who had served as associate executive secretary of the convention board since 1956.

Under Odle's leadership the paper saw a steady circulation growth from 91,000 in 1959 to 109,000 in 1969. Almost 1,400 of the more than 1,870 churches in the state use the Every Family Plan of sending the paper to their families, and paying for it monthly from the church budget.

In 1962 the paper changed to offset printing, and in 1965 moved the mailing from the Baptist Building to the printing office. Maintenance of lists and preparation of mailing strips still is done in the publication offices. In early 1970 the paper went to computerized mailing.

On Jan. 1, 1969, the *Baptist Record* changed its format to six columns, and its page size to the standard size used by most modern newspapers.

Since 1924 the *Record* has not received a subsidy from the Cooperative Program, but has met its budget through income from circulation and advertising. In 1969 the paper had a staff of 10 persons.

JOE T. ODLE

BAPTIST SPANISH PUBLISHING HOUSE (cf. Spanish Baptist Publishing House, Vol. II). Highlights of the 1960's included enlargement of production area, establishment of wholesale deposits, 60th anniversary celebration, marked New Testaments produced, and creation of advisory committee. A staff of 82, including 22 missionaries, publishes literature used in 41 countries. In 1970 the net worth, including buildings, was $2,000,000. Production reported in 1969 was 3,416,509 copies of 31 periodicals; 567,773 copies of 57 book titles; 5,600,000 tracts; and 2,000,000 booklets and miscellaneous pieces. Twenty-eight Crusade of the Americas items were produced in 1967–69.

FRANK W. PATTERSON

***BAPTIST STANDARD.** David M. Gardner retired as editor in 1954 after a 10-year tenure during which the *Standard* enjoyed its greatest growth in circulation. His administration also gave stability to the paper, with assets totaling approximately $1,000,000 when he left office. Gardner was succeeded by E. S. James, whose 12-year editorship lifted the circulation to 368,000. Among his innovations were a "letters page," in which readers voiced their views, and the addition of an artist to the staff.

James retired Nov. 1, 1966, and was succeeded by John J. Hurt, Jr., who for almost 20 years had been editor of *The Christian Index* in Georgia. New offset printing equipment installed two years later introduced color to the *Standard* pages and expedited production. Circulation at the close of 1969 was 370,000. *Prophets With Pens,* a 158-page history of the *Standard* by Presnall H. Wood and Floyd W. Thatcher, was published in 1969.

JOHN J. HURT

***BAPTIST STUDENT UNION.** The name applied to most Baptist programs conducted on colleges and university campuses. Specifically, it is used to define the student organization, but generally, to represent the total ministries conducted on campuses by Southern Baptists. BSU now (1970) includes not only regular students, but internationals, faculty, and others in the academic community. The work has expanded to approximately 750 campuses with a large number of professional directors of Baptist student work. Thirty-two state conventions have departments of student work.

Nationally, leadership of BSU is assigned to the Student Department of the Sunday School Board. In 1961 David K. Alexander succeeded G. Kearnie Keegan (*q. v.*) as department head and served until 1968. He was succeeded by Charles M. Roselle in 1969.

In 1962 the philosophy and objectives were restated. The last paragraph of the statement of philosophy reads: "The unique nature of the university situation demands specialized ministry by our denomination to the individuals in the campus community with their need for redemption and Christian nurture."

The 11 objectives are: "to lead students and faculty members to commitment to Jesus Christ as Saviour and Lord; to involve them in responsible church membership and in denominational understanding and participation; to guide them in worship and devotional experiences; to involve them in Christian social life and recreation; to lead them to participate in Christian world missions; to lead them to accept and practice the principles of Christian stewardship; to lead them to examine academic discipline from a Christian perspective; to enlist and train them for a life of Christian service."

The Student and *Collage,* official periodicals for students and leaders respectively, are augmented by a Campus Ministry Curriculum for on-campus study. Growth in colleges and enrolments with accompanying demands on BSU brought questions about the program. This led the Sunday School Board in 1968 to request the

Executive Committee of the SBC to conduct a study of the program of student work. The Executive Committee conducted a nationwide, two-year study through a 39-member committee. The recommendations of the committee were adopted by the SBC, June 2, 1970.

In summary, that action approved continued assignment of the student program to the Sunday School Board with requested changes in organizational structure and relationships and increased financial support. It requested all other Convention agencies to coordinate their student work projects through the national program assigned to the Sunday School Board.

CHARLES M. ROSELLE

BAPTIST THEOLOGIANS. See THEOLOGIANS, BAPTIST.

***BAPTIST TRAINING UNION.** The years 1956–59 marked the close of an era in the history of Baptist Training Union work. During those years the program and curriculum that had been developed earlier were refined and expanded. Editors at the Sunday School Board were selected for each age group and materials were prepared for all age groups in a church.

In 1959 J. E. Lambdin (*q.v.*) retired after 30 years as secretary of the Training Union Department.

On Dec. 28, 1959, over 7,000 Southern Baptists gathered in Atlanta, Ga., where 64 years earlier the BYPU of the South had come into being. This meeting provided a thrilling climax to Lambdin's ministry. On Jan. 24, 1960, just a few days after his retirement, he suffered a fatal heart attack.

On Jan. 1, 1960, Philip B. Harris became secretary of the Training Union Department. He came to this position from Southwestern Baptist Theological Seminary, where for 10 years he had served as professor of religious education.

Early in 1960 the Training Union Department joined other departments of the Sunday School Board in beginning a critical study of its objectives, methods, activities, and purposes. Out of this study developed a new statement of purpose: "The objective of the Program of Training Union Work is to discover, develop, and promote principles and methods for the establishment, enlargement, and improvement of Training Union in the churches." This basic program is implemented through comprehensive subprograms of research (discovery), program design (development), and field services (interpretation).

Specific objectives regarding the ministry of the Training Union Department were formulated. The department determined to discover the requirements of churches and to develop suggested objectives for the training program of the churches in their tasks of:

(1) Interpreting systematic theology and ethics, Christian history, and church polity and organization.
(2) Giving orientation to new church members.
(3) Training church members in the performance of responsibilities as church members.
(4) Discovering, recruiting, and giving special training to potential leaders for the church.
(5) Providing organization and leadership for special projects of the church.
(6) Providing and interpreting information regarding the work of the church and denomination.

During the sixties the Training Union Department began to provide materials for two vital areas in Southern Baptist church life: church leader training and new church member orientation.

In 1961 the department joined with the Church Administration Department of the Sunday School Board in sponsoring associational clinics to train church officers and committees. Other leadership training materials were consequently added as part of the Church Study Course.

In 1965 the department released a full line of materials for training new church members. Those products included a general manual, *New Church Member Orientation Manual,* by Earl Waldrup, and teacher and pupil materials for Adults, Young People, Intermediates, and Juniors.

In the sixties the department also moved to provide undated materials which churches could use at the time of their need. The first products of this nature were a series of resource units on evangelism and witnessing. These were followed by a series on family living. In response to requests for flexibility of organization, the Training Union Department introduced alternate organization plans for Junior, Intermediate, Young People, and Adult unions.

During this period of transition and newness, the department strengthened its work in research by adding a full-time specialist in the area of research and program design. This enabled the department thoroughly to field-test innovations before introducing them to churches.

In the sixties the work of the department developed closely in relation to other programs of the Sunday School Board and other agencies of the Southern Baptist Convention. These developments, along with continued increase in products and services of the department, led in 1967 to a reorganization of the department to provide opportunity for appropriate outside contacts and adequate internal administration. Philip B. Harris continued in his role as department secretary, giving increased attention to external relations. Lloyd T. Householder, Jr., was named department manager and made responsible for the internal operation of the department. At the same time, editorial and field service personnel were brought together in organizational units of related work.

In 1968 and 1969 the resources of the department were mobilized to complete the most comprehensive redesign of all facets of the Training Union program in its history. The redesign work resulted in marked changes in the age-group unit and departmental organization. It also resulted in new administration books for the total program and for each age division.

The new program, introduced in 1970, stresses the need for churches to determine their training needs and choose curriculum materials from the vast supply, to meet these needs. The program for the seventies is characterized by flexibility but seeks to maintain a constant emphasis on the three types of training which have emerged as the distinctive responsibility of Training Union: new church member orientation, church member training, and church leader training. DONALD TROTTER

BAPTIST VILLAGE (cf. Georgia Baptist Village for the Aged, Vol. I). Georgia Baptists' home for retired people was opened for residents Apr. 2, 1958, at Waycross, Ga., as buildings were dedicated. Following two years of study by committees of the Georgia Baptist Convention's executive committee, the convention in 1955 established a 24-member board of trustees. Under the leadership of Executive Secretary-Treasurer Searcy S. Garrison, the convention also accepted the committee recommendation that 348.8 acres of land be accepted as a gift from citizens of Waycross and Ware County, Ga. Arrangements were also made to purchase approximately 200 adjoining acres. Harvey R. Mitchell was named administrator of the home. The original study committee appointed by the executive committee was composed of Dick H. Hall, Jr., A. Judson Burrell, and T. Hiram Stanley. On their recommendation, nine additional members were added to the committee.

In 1955 a charter for Georgia Baptist Home for the Aged, Inc., was granted by the state of Georgia. The name, Baptist Village, Inc., was adopted and the charter amended in 1957. After visits to and studies of other retirement homes, a master plan was developed for facilities to care for 300 residents. Construction began Jan. 10, 1957. By 1969 Baptist Village had three units of 28 apartments each, a dormitory housing 66 as part of the administration building, and an infirmary with capacity for 84 persons, providing for a total of 234 residents. In 1969 plans called for three additional units, which would add 84 private rooms in the section for ambulatory residents, completing the original projection of housing for 300 residents. Plans were also in process for a chapel near the infirmary, enabling residents in wheel chairs to attend services. The chapel building will also be used for general activities for residents.

Applicants are not turned away because of lack of finances. Some residents pay their complete maintenance. Others are aided through Baptist Village Day offerings from Georgia Baptist churches. Assets totalled $3,577,270 in 1969. DICK H. HALL, JR.

BAPTIST WOMEN. Since Oct., 1970, the missions organization for women age 30-up in Woman's Missionary Union's graded program of missionary education. Through materials and plans provided in *Royal Service,* Baptist Women leads members to engage in the basic WMU tasks of mission study, mission action, and mission support. Margaret Bruce is director (1970). BETTY BROWN

***BAPTIST WORLD ALLIANCE.** The membership of Baptist churches in the world grew by 50 per cent in the 15 years, 1955–70. Baptist World Alliance (BWA) statistics in Feb., 1970, showed a total of 31,023,937 Baptists in 125 countries, as compared with 20,693,358 in 95 countries in 1955. Eighty-seven Baptist conventions and unions in 69 countries are now affiliated with the Alliance, and the membership of these cooperating bodies is 26,499,346.

Great progress in Alliance activity was noted during the presidency of Theodore F. Adams, 1955–60. Robert Stanley Denny moved to the Washington, D. C., office as associate secretary in Jan., 1956, with primary responsibility in youth work but serving also as a generalist under General Secretary Arnold T. Ohrn. A year later, Jan., 1957, Cyril E. Bryant was added to the staff as director of publications, serving as editor of an expanded Baptist World magazine and director of the newly established BWA News Service. In 1958 Erik Ruden, former secretary of the Baptist Union of Sweden, moved to London as associate secretary of the Alliance, with primary responsibilities in Europe. The quinquennial was marked with an increase in world travel, with Adams, Ohrn, and Denny visiting Baptist work on every continent.

The Fifth Baptist Youth World Conference met in Toronto, Canada, in July, 1958, with a registration of 8,022 young people from 67 countries. W. G. Wickramasinghe of Ceylon, who had served as chairman of the youth committee since the retirement of Joel Sorenson of Sweden in 1955, was reelected.

Ohrn and Adams led a revitalization of the study commission concept, and in 1957 named representative international personnel to four study groups: evangelism, missions, religious liberty, and Bible study. A year later, discussions were begun on doctrine, membership training, and world peace. These commissions afforded opportunity at annual meetings of the executive committee for leaders from many nations to share their views on important subjects.

The half-decade also opened up new contacts with Baptists in the Soviet Union. At the close of the London Congress in 1965, Ohrn, Adams, Joseph H. Jackson, and V. Carney Hargroves, of the United States, were privileged to make a two-week tour of Baptist churches in Russia. In the following year, 1956, five Russian Baptists spent a month in the United States. These trips, and many others to and from Eastern Europe, were arranged through the Alliance as a recognition of our international fellowship.

Violations of the principle of religious liberty were noted in two predominantly Catholic countries. Churches were closed in Spain, and discriminations were being shown also in Colombia. Ruden and Adams visited government officials in Spain, and Adams visited those in Colombia. As representatives of an international fellowship, they were successful in bringing about an easing of tension.

Rio de Janeiro, Brazil, was selected as a meeting place for the Tenth Congress, June 26–July 3, 1960. It was the first time a Congress had been held outside North America or Europe. It was also the first time a Congress had been held in a nominally Roman Catholic country. The Brazilian Baptist Convention and mission groups in Brazil joined hands to host the meeting.

"Jesus Chirst is Lord" was chosen as theme of the Congress, using the text from Philippians 2:10–11. An official registration of 12,688 from 60 countries was significant for a meeting so far removed from previous centers of alliance activity. Even more significant was the impact of the Congress on the country in which it met; the world meeting gave status to Baptists who previously had been regarded as little more than a sect. Adams presided with marvelous poise that added dignity to the meeting. Visitors to the Congress continued their travel to mission fields throughout Latin America. A 1,000-voice Brazilian choir joined 2,000 other singers in an international choir directed by William J. Reynolds.

Weekday sessions were held in a 30,000 seat coliseum, Maracaozinha, but the climactic service was held on Sunday afternoon in the huge Maracana Stadium. A crowd estimated by police at 185,000 overflowed the stadium (largest crowd in the stadium's history) to hear evangelist Billy Graham, with interpretation by Joao F. Soren, pastor of Rio's First Baptist Church. The service was telecast throughout Brazil for an unprecedented evangelistic outreach.

Soren, a Brazilian Baptist leader, was elected president of the Alliance—again the Alliance reaching for the first time outside the boundaries of North Amercia and Europe. Josef Nordenhaug (*q.v.*) of Norway was elected general secretary, to succeed Ohrn who was retiring.

Nordenhaug sought to present the Alliance purpose and functions in an understanding manner. Likening Alliance functions to "the five fingers of the Baptist hand of fellowship," he listed them as:

1. An agency of communication between Baptists through publications, dissemination of news, film and radio, personal visits, and correspondence.
2. A forum for study and fraternal discussion of doctrines, practice, and ways of witness to the world.
3. A channel of cooperation in extending help to each other and those in need.
4. A vigilant force for safeguarding religious liberty and other God-given rights.
5. A sponsor of regional and religious and worldwide gatherings for the furtherance of the gospel.

All programs previously initiated came to fuller bloom. Adolfs Klaupiks, who has been retained on a temporary basis as coordinator of relief since 1948, was given permanent status, and a new and stronger emphasis was given to international cooperation for relief and human suffering. R. Dean Goodwin was named chairman of a reorganized relief committee. The Women's Department and the Youth Committee continued their activity, and a Men's Department was organized with John A. Dawson of Chicago as chairman. The study commissions were reorganized under the four main topics: doctrine, religious liberty and human rights, evangelism and missions, and Christian teaching and training.

The Sixth Baptist Youth World Conference met in Beirut, Lebanon, July 15–21, 1963, with a registration of 3,000 from 50 countries. Gunnar Hoglund of Chicago, representing the Baptist General Conference, was elected chairman of the Youth Committee, succeeding Wickramasinghe.

The Eleventh Baptist World Congress met in Miami Beach, Fla., June 25–30, 1965, drawing a registration of 19,598 from 79 countries. Attendances of more than 50,000 were counted in evening meetings at the Orange Bowl statium in Mami. The Congress theme was "The Truth That Makes Men Free," from John 8:32.

Dialogue perhaps came to the fore at this meeting more than in previous sessions. A panel discussion each morning, moderated by Theodore F. Adams, brought Baptists from various countries to the platform for free discussion between themselves with the assembled crowd observing and listening. The first period was given to a discussion of the Baptist World Alliance. The four other periods talked of "witnessing to the truth" in each of four general areas: (1) the predominantly Christian community, (2) where Baptists are in the minority and other Christian faiths predominate, (3) in a secular society, and (4) where other religions are dominant.

Afternoons during the Congress were given to sectional meetings. The four study commissions met to hear prepared papers and discuss them quite frankly, each participant speaking in the light of Christian opportunity in his part of the world. More than 250 persons, representing most if not all the 79 countries in attendance, participated in one way or another on the Congress program. Herschel H. Hobbs, of Oklahoma City, delivered the keynote address, and J. Ithel Jones of Cardiff, Wales, preached the Congress sermon.

The Congress at Miami Beach again reached beyond North America and Europe for its leader. William B. Tolbert, Jr., a black man from Monrovia, Liberia, was nominated and enthusiasticallly elected. Tolbert was pastor of two churches in Liberia, president of the Convention of Liberian Baptists, and vice-president of the Republic of Liberia.

Tolbert's leadership in the role of president brought to dramatic focus the international nature of the Alliance. Baptists particularly in Africa and Asia cited his election as a refutal of the pagan propaganda that Christianity is a white man's religion. His high position in the

Liberian government opened many doors for him in travel to visit Baptists in remote parts of the world.

An action of the Miami Beach Congress amended bylaws to provide that every member organization should be represented on the Executive Committee of the Alliance, and that the member groups would nominate their own representative. This change placed initiative for selection on the member bodies in their scattered parts of the world rather than on a nominating committee at the quinquennial congresses.

The Seventh Youth World Conference met in Berne, Switzerland, July 22–28, 1968, drawing together 6,000 young people from 58 countries. In addition to an array of distinguished speakers including Paul Tournier of Switzerland, Annie Vallotton of France, and Samuel Proctor of the United States, the program majored on group discussions. The full assemblage divided into 200 groups, each with wide geographic distribution, to discuss contemporary topics.

Contemplating a growing consciousness of Baptist relationships with other church groups, Nordenhaug initiated a fifth study commission to deal with cooperative Christianity. James Leo Garrett of Louisville, Ky., was named chairman, with Rudolf Thaut of Hamburg, Germany, cochairman. The commission had its first meeting at Baden bei Wien, Austria, in Aug., 1969.

Adolfs Klaupiks, who had worked with the Alliance as coordinator on relief since 1948, retired in 1968. Frank H. Woyke, for 22 years the executive secretary of the North American Baptist General Conference, was named secretary and charged with responsibilities in relief and rehabilitation, the North American Baptist Fellowship, and the study commissions.

Nordenhaug asked in 1968 that he be permitted to retire at the close of the Baptist World Congress in 1970, and a committee consisting of all past presidents and current vice-presidents of the Alliance was named to recommend a successor. The committee, with Adams as chairman, recommended to the Executive Committee, meeting at Baden in Aug., 1969, that Denny be elected to take office as general secretary in July, 1970. He was so elected.

Following the Baden meeting and a conference of the European Baptist Federation in Vienna, Nordenhaug, Tolbert, and Goulding visited Baptists in Romania—the first delegation of Baptists permitted to enter that country since World War II. Nordenhaug became ill in Romania of a heart ailment but was able to return to his home outside Washington, D. C. He died Sept. 18, 1969. Members of the Executive Committee asked Denny to assume the role of general secretary as of Nov. 1, 1969.

The Twelfth Baptist World Congress met in Tokyo, Japan, July 12–18, 1970—another exclamation point to its international outreach.

In 1970 Baptists were known to live and witness in all the 125 countries listed. Where no figure is given, the number was not then available. In some reports there is a certain amount of overlapping because some churches affiliated with more than one convention.

AFRICA	
Algeria	
Angola	3,085
Basutoland	
Botswana	
Burundi*	2,776
Cameroon*	48,185
Cape Verde Islands	
Central African Republic	18,589
Chad	
Congo Republic	2,221
Dahomey	
Democratic Republic of the Congo	450,000
Egypt	164
Ethiopia*	140
Ghana*	4,992
Guinea	
Ivory Coast	2,402
Kenya	4,184
Liberia*	21,200
Libya	550
Malawi	9,005
Morocco	50
Mozambique	2,250
Nigeria*	80,016
Rhodesia	6,187
Rwanda	7,255
St. Helena	80
Senegal	
Sierra Leone	368
South Africa*	46,154
South-West Africa	52
Tanzania	5,182
Togo*	310
Uganda	1,889
Zambia	4,025
TOTAL FOR AFRICA	721,311

ASIA	
Burma*	249,474
Ceylon*	1,758
China (Mainland) †	123,000
China (Taiwan) *	10,920
Hong Kong*	25,216
India*	633,349
Japan*	31,952
Korea*	10,421
Macao	362
Malaysia*	3,791
Nepal	
Okinawa	3,328
Pakistan*	21,227
Singapore	1,940
South Vietnam	917
Thailand	5,205
TOTAL FOR ASIA	1,122,860

CENTRAL AMERICA	
Bahamas	30,456
Bermuda	226
British Honduras	117
Costa Rica*	971

Cuba*	16,235
Dominican Republic	368
El Salvador*	2,436
French West Indies	40
Guatemala*	3,099
Haiti*	103,637
Honduras*	743
Jamaica*	36,298
Leeward Islands	162
Nicaragua*	4,182
Panama and Canal Zone*	5,144
Puerto Rico*	9,501
St. Lucia	150
St. Vincent	150
Trinidad and Tobago*	1,755
TOTAL FOR CENTRAL AMERICA	215,670
EUROPE	
Austria*	760
Belgium*	354
Bulgaria*	300
Czechoslovakia*	4,163
Denmark*	7,022
England*	180,185
Finland*	2,870
France*	2,468
Germany, DDR*	25,130
Germany, West*	74,580
Greece	
Hungary*	19,600
Iceland	56
North Ireland and Erie*	6,922
Italy*	5,414
Luxembourg	20
Netherlands*	10,329
Norway*	6,563
Poland*	2,500
Portugal*	3,329
Romania*	120,000
Scotland*	17,895
Spain*	5,500
Sweden*	49,717
Switzerland*	1,500
U. S. S. R.*	550,000
Wales*	77,270
Yugoslavia*	3,595
TOTAL FOR EUROPE	1,178,042
MIDDLE EAST	
Cyprus	
Gaza	39
Israel*	190
Jordan*	200
Lebanon*	450
Turkey	70
Yemen	
TOTAL FOR MIDDLE EAST	949
SOUTH AMERICA	
Argentina*	19,132
Bolivia*	2,005
Brazil*	342,195
Chile*	11,885
Colombia*	5,546
Ecuador	1,149
Guyana	895
Paraguay*	1,471
Peru	1,306
Surinam	42
Uruguay*	1,754
Venezuela*	2,175
TOTAL FOR SOUTH AMERICA	389,555
SOUTHWEST PACIFIC	
Australia*	48,520
Guam	936
Indonesia	18,024
New Guinea	13,500
New Zealand*	17,306
Philippines*	47,126
TOTAL FOR SOUTHWEST PACIFIC	145,412
NORTH AMERICA	
Canada*	175,022
Mexico*	42,374
United States*	27,032,742
TOTAL FOR NORTH AMERICA	27,250,138
GRAND TOTAL	31,023,937

* One or more Baptist groups in each country marked by an asterisk are members of the Baptist World Alliance. The full Baptist population may include groups not affiliated with the Alliance.

† Estimate.

C. E. BRYANT

BAPTIST WORLD ALLIANCE, THE WOMEN'S DEPARTMENT OF THE. The Women's Department with its six continental unions is an integral part of the Baptist World Alliance, working toward the fulfilment of the BWA purpose stated in the preamble to its constitution.

In harmony with the spirit and content of the BWA purpose, the women have pursued the purposes of their organization: to promote fellowship, deeper sympathy, and understanding among Baptist women of the world; to encourage women to bind themselves together in national and continental women's unions; to exchange information concerning activities and methods of work; and to promote the Baptist Women's Day of Prayer.

The Women's Department, like the BWA, is not an administrative body, but is essentially fraternal and inspirational. Membership is extended to all Baptist women in countries holding membership in the BWA.

The Women's Department is best understood in relationship to the parent body. At the first BWA Congress in London, 1905, no women's session was held, although 219 women from beyond British shores registered. Two women, Nannie Burroughs, Washington, D. C., and Mrs. Norman Mather Waterbury, Boston, addressed the London Congress.

For the second BWA Congress, in Philadelphia, 1911, the Alliance leaders, J. N. Prestridge and J. H. Shakespeare, planned an afternoon meeting for women. Mrs. A. G. Lester, Chicago, presided over this first women's session. Encouraged by Fannie E. S. Heck, president of Woman's Missionary Union, SBC, Baptist women organized their first women's committee in 1911, with Mrs. Andrew MacLeish, Chicago, chairman, and Edith Campbell Crane (*q.v.*), corresponding secretary of WMU, secretary. A circular letter was instituted.

In the absence of both the chairman and secretary, Mrs. W. C. James, president of WMU, presided over the women's meeting at the 1923 BWA Congress. Mrs. F. C. Spurr, England, was elected chairman.

During the fourth Congress of BWA, in Toronto, 1928, Mrs. Albert Matthews, Canada, presided over the women's session. The women's committee was dissolved by the women themselves when the BWA voted to place two women on the executive committee of the Alliance. Mrs. W. J. Cox, president of WMU, and Frau Bertha Gieselbusch, Germany, were the two women elected to the BWA executive committee.

In the next Congress, in Berlin in 1934, it became apparent that the new plan was unsatisfactory. J. H. Rushbrooke, general secretary of the Alliance, had planned a sectional meeting for the women and asked Mrs. F. W. Armstrong, president of WMU, to preside. Nineteen women from 16 different nations answered roll call. Rushbrooke, aware of the desire of the women to do more and better work, stated that perhaps this could be done if there were a standing committee to lead the women. To pave the way for such a committee, the constitution of the Alliance was amended to include a minimum of five women on the executive committee. Frau Baresel-Kobner of Germany had succeeded Frau Gieselbusch on this committee, and Mrs. F. W. Armstrong had succeeded Mrs. W. J. Cox. The three added by election were Mrs. Ernest Brown, England; Mrs. S. W. Layten, Pennsylvania; and Mrs. John Nuveen, Illinois.

Reorganization of the women's committee came at the sixth BWA Congress in Atlanta, 1939. Mrs. Albert Matthews, Canada, presided over the women's session planned by Rushbrooke. The executive committee of the Alliance recommended that the women members of the executive committee constitute a women's committee and be given power to appoint an equal number of women. The ravages of World War II curtailed the work of this committee.

A woman's meeting was held at the Copenhagen Congress in 1947, but no officers were elected. In Aug., 1948, the executive committee of the Alliance enlarged the women's committee to include two representatives each from the continents of Africa, Asia, Australia, Europe, and South America; and four representatives from North America. Mrs. George R. Martin, president of WMU, was appointed chairman of this enlarged committee. Prior to this meeting of the executive committee, W. O. Lewis, general secretary of BWA, invited representative women from Great Britain, Italy, Germany, France, Switzerland, Denmark, and Holland to attend the meeting. These women, working closely with Mrs. Brown and Mrs. Martin, organized the European Baptist Women's Union. Prompted by this action, the Alliance executive committee instructed the women's committee to organize the women on every continent.

Preceding the 1950 BWA Congress in Cleveland, Ohio, women from Brazil, Cuba, Canada, Denmark, Norway, Finland, Great Britain, Germany, Hawaii, Italy, and from Baptist conventions in the United States formulated the purposes and plans of the women's committee. A plan of work was adopted and the following officers were elected: chairman, Mrs. George R. Martin; secretary, Lois Chapple, England; and co-chairmen: for Europe, Fru Johannes Norgaard, Denmark; for Australia, Mrs. A. C. Church; for Latin America, Mrs. Esther Silva Diaz, Brazil; for Africa, Mrs. J. T. Ayorinde, Nigeria; and for North America, Mrs. Edgar Bates, Canada. Mrs. Frank Wigginton, United States, was elected to the Alliance executive committee and thus became identified with the women's committee. Mrs. Ernest Brown was reelected to the executive committee. These women, along with 27 other committee members from 21 countries, made up the women's committee. This committee made plans for a quarterly exchange of news to be circulated by the secretary, agreed to promote a Baptist Women's Day of Prayer, and discussed organization of other continental unions.

In the afterglow of the Cleveland Congress Baptist women throughout the world moved forward in their promotion of the aims and ideals of the BWA. Before the next Congress the North American Baptist Women's Union and the Latin American Baptist Women's Union had been organized, in 1951 and 1953 respectively. The Jubilee Congress in London, 1955, was marked by continued advance in the women's work. The name and status of the organization was changed from Women's Committee to Women's Department. Mrs. Martin was reelected chairman. Mrs. Edgar Bates became the first treasurer. The organization adopted as its official emblem a shield with an open Bible and the motto "Workers Together."

In the next year the Women's Department led in the organization of the Asian Baptist Women's Union, the Australia–New Zealand Baptist Women's Union (name changed in 1968 to Baptist Women's Union of the South-West Pacific), and the Baptist Women's Union of Africa.

The quarterly newsletter started in Jan., 1951, was discontinued in Nov., 1957, when space for women's news was provided in *The Baptist World*. Since 1962, the Women's Department has issued a quarterly bulletin called "Together."

The Baptist Women's Day of Prayer, sponsored by the Women's Department since 1950, has been a great unifying and strengthening force among Baptist women around the world. The offering taken on the Day of Prayer is used for promotion of the Women's Department work.

Mrs. George R. Martin served as chairman of the Women's Department from its reconstitution by the executive committee in 1948 through the BWA Congress in Rio de Janeiro in 1960. She was influential in organizing the unions in Europe, North America, Latin America, Africa, Asia, and Australia. Mrs. Edgar Bates succeeded Mrs. Martin in 1960. Mrs. R. L. Mathis, president of WMU, was elected treasurer; and Mrs. M. B. Hodge, United States, succeeded Miss Chapple as secretary.

At the BWA Congress in Miami, 1965, Mrs. Bates was reelected president. (A 1965 recommendation changed the title "chairman" to "president" and the continental union co-chairmen became known as vice-presidents.) Mrs. Mathis was reelected treasurer, and Mrs. Olivia de Lerin, Mexico, was elected secretary.

The Women's Department and its executive committee meet regularly in connection with the BWA Congress. The administrative committee of the executive committee meets each year. Continental union meetings are held every five years. DORIS DEVAULT

BAPTIST YOUNG WOMEN. Since Oct., 1970, the missions organization for young adult women ages 18 (or high school graduation) through 29, married or single, in Woman's Missionary Union's graded program of missionary education. Through use of materials and plans provided in *Contempo,* Baptist Young Women leads members to engage in the basic WMU tasks of mission study, mission action, and mission support. Aline Fuselier is director (1970). BETTY BROWN

BAPTISTS AND ECUMENISM. Baptists are related to various aspects of the Ecumenical Movement in different ways. Baptist bodies comprising approximately one third of the world's total Baptist population are directly related to the World Council of Churches. A few other national Baptist communions belong to various national councils but do not yet hold membership in the World Council. Some Baptists, while rejecting membership in both the National and World Councils do, engage in functions, conferences, and cooperative projects sponsored by these ecumenical organizations. Yet, there are other Baptist groups that even refuse membership in the Baptist World Alliance. Some Baptist churches and individuals do belong to the National Association of Evangelicals and others to the American Council of Christian Churches and their international counterparts. Obviously, Baptist response to ecumenical Christianity is uneven.

What is the explanation for such a wide variation in attitude and ecumenical relationship on the part of Baptists? Possibly, the answer to this question lies in Baptist theological orientation and ecclesiological development. While some Baptists are doubtless "liberal" and others "fundamentalist" in their theological complexion, the overwhelming majority consider themselves conservative Evangelicals. In their eyes Protestant ecumenical leadership is definitely "modernist" if not apostate. Thus, they fear their own doctrinal integrity would be compromised by belonging to the various councils. Traditionally, Baptists have refused to give their denominational structures the authority or functions of a church. Their strong local church emphasis makes Baptists suspicious of organizations which they cannot control and which in turn may threaten the autonomy of either denominational structures or that of the churches. Even Baptists who have a long record of interdenominational cooperation and ecumenical involvement have refused to take part in merger schemes which attempt to obliterate denominational lines in creating various "United Churches." Doubtless, Baptist sense of mission, love of religious liberty, and insistence upon believer's baptism provide a distinctive Baptist ethos that continues to demand a separate witness in spite of the undeniable appeal of contemporary ecumenism.

While Baptist action toward a greater involvement with the ecumenical movement has not been very apparent, it would be a mistake to assume that Baptist thinking and attitudes are totally negative in this respect. Since Vatican Council II, Baptists have participated in numerous ecumenical conferences with Roman Catholics. If anything, conferences involving Roman Catholics and Baptists in ecumenical dialogue have been more numerous in Latin America than similar meetings in the United States. Even in Spain Baptists have participated in such conferences. A few Baptist scholars attended some of the sessions of Vatican Council II in spite of a lack of status as official observers. In 1969 the Baptist World Alliance established a Commission on Cooperative Christianity, which in its first meeting included Roman Catholic and Mennonite participants as well as Baptists. Wake Forest University has established an Ecumenical Institute which actively sponsors dialogue between Southern Baptists and Roman Catholics. While all of this activity does not indicate a desire to unite with Rome on the part of Baptists, it does seem to demonstrate that their attitude toward Roman Catholicism is in the process of change. In numerous instances Baptists are discovering a common ground of faith that makes for a closer fraternal relationship to Roman Catholic participants in such meetings than to their Protestant counterparts.

This current ecumenical thrust among Baptists is a result, in part, of a Baptist affirmation that the Body of Christ includes all who have committed themselves to Jesus Christ in faith. It is entirely feasible that more Baptist bodies will find a way to relate themselves positively to various organizational aspects of the ecumenical movement as that movement seeks new avenues of cooperation which respect the peculiar attributes of Baptist denominational life.

BIBLIOGRAPHY: W. R. Estep, Jr., *Baptists and Christian Unity* (1966). W. R. ESTEP, JR.

BAPTISTS TODAY, ANALYSIS OF. Discernible trends and developments in Baptist life are here set forth, largely without interpretation and with no order of priority.

Denominational structures are fairly stable. The past decade has not seen much merging of existing structures, nor the rapid formation of new ones. Such new Baptist groups as have originated have been small and isolated, and none presently shows signs of winning many adherents.

Practically all Baptist groups face a sharp decline in growth rate, and some face actual declines in membership. The Southern Baptist Convention is an example of the first. While still growing, the *rate* of growth is down. This has produced questions, insecurity, and a sense of bafflement at how to penetrate modern culture, particularly in urban centers.

Probably, Baptists have greater theological and doctrinal polarity now than at any time in this century. Always, Baptists have had theological differences, but sharp polarization is more intense now. Most major Baptist bodies have their own examples of this problem, with tension points either in schools, denominational publishing boards, or denominational executive positions. The problem is illustrated in Southern Baptist life by the publication of controversial books by Broadman Press and attacks upon those books (written primarily by professors). Calls by the Convention president for dissidents to leave the Convention also illustrate this polarization.

There is more interest in social and ethical issues, especially since mid-century. Such groups as the American Baptist Convention have long been committed to social action but in this era have intensified their efforts, interpreting evangelism largely in social dimensions. Others, like the SBC, have been slower to emphasize social issues but are doing so now. The "Crisis Statement" of the SBC in 1968, the election of a Negro as president of the ABC in 1969, new courses in Black Studies at Baptist schools, new books from denominational presses, conference and assembly programs indicate an increased emphasis and openness on race.

The educational level of Baptist ministers continues to rise. Most Baptist groups have not experienced the minister shortages which have plagued other denominations. Baptists are also branching out into several less traditional forms of ministry.

The North American Baptist Fellowship, a cooperative group involving several Baptist groups in America, was formed in 1966 as a committee of the Baptist World Alliance. This fellowship, which resulted partly from efforts to conserve benefits of the Baptist Jubilee Advance, sought to promote further cooperation among Baptists in America. One of its earliest tasks was to correlate plans for the Crusade of the Americas. The NABF works through a steering committee made up of representatives of member groups. By 1970 these included the American Baptist Convention, the Baptist Federation of Canada, the General Association of General Baptists, the National Baptist Convention of America, the National Baptist Convention of Mexico, the Progressive National Baptist Convention, the Seventh Day Baptist General Conference, and the Southern Baptist Convention.

Baptists continue to be involved, both formally and informally, in Protestant ecumenism. Several groups participate in the National Council of Churches. Others, like the SBC, do not, but seem more willing to talk with others, if nothing more. The American Baptist Convention declined to be a full participant in COCU (Consultation On Church Union) but has an observer-consultant relationship. There are tentative merger talks, or talks leading to closer working relationships, between various Negro Baptist bodies, between the Progressive National Baptist Convention and ABC, between ABC and the Church of the Brethren, between ABC and the Seventh Day Baptist General Conference, and others. In addition, many Negro Baptist congregations are effecting dual or multiple alignment with black and white groups. An increasing number of congregations in the South, both black and white, are seeking affiliation with the ABC, which historically has had its greater numerical concentration in the North.

Despite efforts at cooperation, there is now probably greater estrangement between the two largest white Baptist groups, ABC and SBC, than at any time in this century. Resentment at SBC "invasion" of the North, increasing ABC affiliations in the South, the ABC refusal to participate in the Crusade of the Americas, and increasingly divergent interpretations of overall Christian mission contribute to this estrangement.

There appears to be a trend for some Baptist groups to use periodical literature produced by other groups. The American Baptist Publication Society supplies some periodical material for Seventh Day Baptists and Canadian Baptists. Selected curriculum materials produced by the Sunday School Board of the SBC are used by non-Southern Baptist groups. There seems also to be a trend for some SBC churches to select some of their literature from non-SBC and non-Baptist sources.

Baptists face new areas of controversy and new intensity in old areas. Criteria for local church affiliation with denominational bodies is increasingly troublesome among the more conservative bodies. Local churches with divergent practices on baptism, the Lord's Supper, and divergent interpretation on doctrine no longer find it easy to affiliate with associations and conventions on purely functional grounds. The question of government aid to church schools also has become more crucial for Baptists. A vigorous debate rages presently (1970) over whether Baptist schools should accept such aid if available. This is part of a larger crisis of Baptist colleges, in which many Baptist leaders openly question the validity of such schools in modern American culture.

In general, Baptists continue to enjoy financial health. While per capita giving has declined sharply among Protestants, Baptist giving continues to rise. However, some observers predict a leveling off in the 1970's. LEON MCBETH

BARNES, FREDERICK MORGAN (b. Plantersville, Ala., Dec. 5, 1885; d. Montgomery, Ala. Dec. 10, 1946). Pastor and denominational leader. Son of Michael Harrison and Sarah (Friday) Barnes, he married Marie Griffin, Dec. 29, 1920. He was educated at the Dallas County High School, Howard College (A.B. and honorary D.D.), and Southern Baptist Theological Seminary (Th.B.). Pastor of several churches while in school, he served as pastor of the First Church, Guntersville, Ala., 1913–22, and Clayton Street Church, Montgomery, Ala., 1923–35. He served as executive secretary-treasurer of the Alabama Baptist State Convention from 1935 until Dec. 31, 1944, when he retired because of ill health. Barnes served as moderator of the Marshall and Montgomery County Associations in Alabama, president of the Alabama Baptist State Convention, chairman of the executive board of the Alabama Baptist State Convention, and trustee of the Baptist Foundation of Alabama. A. HAMILTON REID

BARNES, WILLIAM WRIGHT (b. Elm City, Wilson County, N. C., Feb. 28, 1883; d. Ft. Worth, Tex., Apr. 6, 1960). Preacher, seminary professor, and church historian. Educated at Wake Forest College (A.B., A.M., 1904) and Southern Baptist Theological Seminary (Th.M., 1909; Th.D., 1913), he received an honorary D.D. from Wake Forest College, 1934, and L.H.D. from Hardin-Simmons University, Abilene, Tex., 1952.

In 1904–05 he was tutor of children of American families in Santiago, Cuba. From Feb., 1909, to May, 1912, Barnes was principal of El Colegio Cubano-Americano in Havana, Cuba, under the Home Mission Board. In 1913 he became Professor of Church History, Southwestern Baptist Theological Seminary, Ft. Worth, where he served until his retirement in 1953. He married Ethel Dalrymple, Oct. 20, 1909, and they had two sons, William Wright and Arch Dalrymple Barnes.

He was moderator of Tarrant County Baptist Association (Texas), 1914–24, and ministered as *ad interim* pastor of several churches in Ft. Worth and other Texas cities. He served on commissions and committees of the Baptist General Convention of Texas and the Southern Baptist Convention. He wrote numerous articles for the Baptist state papers of the South, for the *Review and Expositor,* the *Southwestern Journal of Theology,* and *The Chronicle.* He translated into English *Ebenezer,* the story of the first fifty years (1840–1890) of Baptist work in Saxony, Germany. Lectures on the history of Baptists outside the United States were mimeographed for class use. In 1923 the booklet, *The Southern Baptist Convention, A Study in the Development of Ecclesiology,* was published and went through several printings. In 1954 Broadman Press published his history, *The Southern Baptist Convention, 1845–1953,* the official centennial story of Southern Baptists. Barnes is buried in Greenwood Cemetery, Ft. Worth.

ROBERT A. BAKER

BARNETT, FRANK WILLIS (b. Barbour County, Ala., Oct. 23, 1865; d. Birmingham, Ala., June 29, 1941). Son of Methodist minister Augustus William and Celeste (Treutlen) Willis Barnett, he was educated at a primary school in St. Louis, Mo., a private school in Paris, France, the University of Alabama, and Vanderbilt University. He traveled widely in Europe, studying briefly at the Sorbonne, the University of Vienna, and the University of Berlin. He also studied at the New York Law School, and Southern Baptist Theological Seminary. He entered the Baptist ministry in 1895, serving churches in Johnson City and Nashville, Tenn., and Forsyth, Ga. Barnett married Maude Proctor, June 21, 1899. In 1901 he purchased the privately owned *Alabama Baptist* and moved it to Birmingham. He sold it in 1919 to the Alabama Baptist Convention and became an associate editor of the Birmingham *Age-Herald,* where he worked until the time of his death. J. WAYNE FLYNT

BARNETTE, JASPER NEWTON (b. Mitchell County, N. C., Oct. 3, 1887; d. Nashville, Tenn., May 27, 1965). Layman, author, and religious educator. Son of James D. and Sarah (Jones) Barnette, he was converted and united with Double Springs Baptist Church in July, 1900. He was educated in public schools of North Carolina and Shenandoah Collegiate Institute, Dayton, Va. Hardin-Simmons University conferred an honorary doctorate on him in 1952. Barnette taught at Round Hill Academy and later became a farmer in Double Springs community, N. C. He married Edna Hawkins. They had two children: Jasper N., Jr., and Mary Sue (Mrs. Roupen M. Gulbenk).

Barnette gave his life to Southern Baptist Sunday School work. As superintendent of the Sunday School at Second Baptist Church, Shelby, N. C., and later at Double Springs Baptist Church, he was successful in discovering and applying basic principles of Sunday School work. As a result he was called to be associate in the Sunday School Department of the North Carolina Baptist State Convention, 1921. His effective leadership in Sunday School work in North Carolina, particularly in rural churches and associational work, gained Convention-wide recognition.

In 1927 he became an associate of Arthur Flake (*q.v.,* Vol. I) in the Sunday School Administration Department of the Sunday School Board, SBC, giving special attention to Sunday School organization and associational work. In

1936, T. L. Holcomb, then secretary of the Sunday School Board, named him as Sunday School promotional chairman of the five-year program, which was an emphasis on the associational organization as a channel to make every method and resource of the Sunday School Board available "to the last church."

In 1943 he was elected secretary of the Sunday School Department, made up of the former departments of Administration, Young People's and Adult, Intermediate, Elementary, Education (Teacher Training), and Vacation Bible School work. Between 1943 and Barnette's retirement, Dec. 31, 1957, Southern Baptist Sunday School work experienced its most pronounced growth. A great forward thrust in enrolling people in Sunday School was projected, climaxing in the Convention-wide drive for "A Million More in 1954." This emphasis resulted in a net Sunday School enrolment gain of 596,000 in 1954. The net gain in Sunday School enrolment for the 15-year period was 3,639,372.

Barnette's personal dedication, drive, and leadership ability were demonstrated in the response of the people with whom he worked. He wrote *Associational Sunday School Work* (1933), *A Church Using Its Sunday School* (1937), *The Place of the Sunday School in Evangelism* (1958), *One to Eight* (1954), *The Pull of the People* (1956), and *The Sunday School and the Church Budget* (1960). These books had a combined circulation of more than a million copies.

A. V. WASHBURN

BARTON, LEVI ELDER (b. Jonesboro, Ark., Apr. 25, 1870; d. Montgomery, Ala., May 31, 1965). Pastor and denominational leader. Son of farmer William Henderson and Elizabeth (Morgan) Barton, he married Rosa Belle Hurt, Nov. 9, 1899. They had four children. Barton was educated at Union University, Jackson, Tenn. (A.B., 1898; honorary D.D., 1911). He was pastor of the following Baptist churches: Hope, Hope, Ark., 1899–1900; Suffolk, Suffolk, Va., 1900–04; Quitman, Quitman, Ga., 1904–08; West Point, West Point, Miss., 1908–13; Jackson Hill, Atlanta, Ga., 1913–16; Fayetteville, Fayetteville, Ark., 1917–20; Larchmont, Norfolk, Va., 1921–24; First, Andalusia, Ala., 1924–29; and First, Jasper, Ala., 1935–42. Barton wrote *Helps for Soul-Winners* (1945), *Three Dimensions of Love* (1942), *Take Heed* (1942), *Amazing Grace* (1954), and many magazine and newspaper articles. He served as executive secretary of both the Arkansas (1919–21) and the Alabama (1930–34) Baptist state conventions. He was vice-president of the Southern Baptist Convention and the Alabama convention; member of the Foreign Mission Board, SBC; and other Baptist committees, boards, and commissions. He was director of the Alabama Temperance Alliance and member of the Rotary Club.

A. HAMILTON REID

BARTON, MARY ANN (MAMIE) (b. Chick Springs, Greenville County, S. C., Nov. 11, 1868; d. Simpsonville, S. C., Feb. 12, 1963). Daughter of Hugh Montgomery and Maria Louise (Shockley) Barton, she attended school at Taylors until she was 17. Getting a teacher's certificate by passing the state test, she taught school for three years. In 1889–90, she attended the Greenville public schools. She taught again until she went to Winthrop College at Rock Hill in 1899 for a two-year course. She was a teacher until she was appointed state missionary. She worked under the South Carolina State Mission Board, 1907–15, as pastor's assistant in the first church and Tabernacle church in Pelzer, S. C. She organized mission societies and bands, established Sunday Schools, taught adult night school, and cared for the poor suffering from pellagra. When World War I came, women missionaries were laid off and the money spent for army chaplains. Mary Ann Barton returned to the public schools of Greenville and Anderson counties until her retirement in 1930. She was a charter member of the Taylors Missionary Society organized in June, 1890, and an active member for 65 years, serving as president, 1917–22. She was mission study chairman of the North Greenville Association for over 20 years. She is buried in the cemetery of the First Baptist Church, Taylors, S. C. JEAN MARTIN FLYNN

BASDEN, HAROLD GILLESPIE (b. Memphis, Tenn., Nov. 1, 1917; d. Richmond, Va., May 16, 1969). Graduate of Mississippi College (B.A.) and Southwestern Baptist Theological Seminary (Th.M., Th.D.), Basden taught in Mississippi College and was pastor of churches in Mississippi and Texas. He was associate secretary for promotion for the Foreign Mission Board from Jan., 1964, until his death. In Texas he was member of various boards and committees, among them the committee on separation of church and state ("Basden Report"). He was on the national board of trustees of Protestants and Other Americans United for Separation of Church and State. He married Marjorie Abbott in 1944. G. NORMAN PRICE

BASS MEMORIAL BAPTIST HOSPITAL (cf. Enid General Hospital, Vol. I). The Enid General Hospital at Enid, Okla., opened in a nine-room rented house, Oct. 5, 1910. In 1914, the institution was incorporated, and after numerous expansion programs at periodic intervals, the Enid General Hospital Foundation gave the institution to the Baptist General Convention of Oklahoma, Oct. 12, 1953. It was then a 110-bed facility, valued at $1,000,000. In 1967 the name was changed to Bass Memorial Baptist Hospital upon receipt of a $200,000 gift from Harry Bass to spearhead a $1,000,000 fund-raising campaign for expansion purposes. In 1969 property value was $1,603,379, with a debt of $267,758. Capacity was 104 beds, and there were 253 employees. Joe Baker completed 16 years as administrator Oct. 12, 1969. J. M. GASKIN

BASSETT, WALLACE (b. Middle Grove, Mo., Dec. 31, 1884; d. Dallas, Tex., Oct. 8,

1968). Pastor and denominational leader. Son of a Missouri farmer, he attended school at William Jewel Academy, Newton Theological Seminary, and Kansas City Theological Seminary. Degrees were conferred by La Grange College, Ph.B., 1909; D.D., 1916; and Baylor University, D.D., 1920. He married Lottie Bounds in Dec., 1906, and had four children: Margaret (Travis) Johnson, Elaine (William) Mayfield, Verona (John) Olson, and Wallace H. Bassett. Bassett was pastor of two First Baptist Churches in Texas, Sulphur Springs and Amarillo. In 1918 he went to Cliff Temple Baptist Church, Dallas, Tex. His first wife died in 1938, and in 1940 he married Hassie Mayfield. He spent 48 years at Cliff Temple, served 44 years as president of the Annuity Board of the SBC, 39 years on the Texas Baptist Executive Board, and 41 years on the Baylor University board. He was president of the Baptist General Convention of Texas, 1947–48.

He published two books, *Beatific Verities* (1917) and *A Star at Midnight* (1940).

JAY L. SKAGGS

***BATON ROUGE GENERAL HOSPITAL.** See LOUISIANA BAPTIST CONVENTION.

BATSON, PAUL OTIS (b. Taylors, S. C., Nov. 20, 1896; d. Sumter, S. C., Dec. 12, 1962). Pastor and denominational officer. Son of Joe and Hattie Loftis Batson, he was ordained, Mar. 6, 1921. He attended North Greenville Academy and graduated from Furman University in 1921. He was pastor of South Greenwood, Jordan Street, and Mt. Moriah in Greenwood; Second, Ninety-Six; Clarendon, Alcolu, 1932–53; Graham, Sumter County, 1925–59; and Providence, High Hills, and Long Branch Baptist churches of South Carolina.

He served as a trustee for the South Carolina Baptist Hospital, vice-president of the South Carolina Baptist Convention, 1954, and moderator of the Santee Association. Furman University gave him a D.D. in 1951. He married Eva Lyons on Sept. 19, 1921. They had six sons: Paul O., Jr., Lloyd Ellis, Joseph Ray, Francis Marion, Joel Chandler, and David Neal.

DANIEL W. CLOER

BAXTER, GEORGE SIMPSON (b. Alpha, Ark., Jan. 19, 1879; d. Shawnee, Okla., Oct. 29, 1955). Physician, civic leader, and Baptist layman. After receiving his M.D. degree in 1905 at Memphis Hospital Medical College, he did his internship at Patterson, N. J., practiced medicine at Casa, Ark., 1907–09; then moved to Shawnee, Okla., where he practiced until his death. Baxter was 28 years a trustee of Oklahoma Baptist University, and the school's physician 30 years. Baxter Hall at the University's Brotherhood dormitory and Baxter Parlor at the student union are named for him. J. M. GASKIN

BAYLOR, WILLIAM HENRY (b. Princess Anne County, Va., Oct. 25, 1865; d. Baltimore, Md., Jan. 8, 1964). One of nine children of Richard and Annie E. Baylor, he was baptized into the fellowship of Sandy Creek Baptist Church, Amelia Co., Va., Sept., 1874. Graduating from Richmond College in 1888, he entered Rochester Theological Seminary in the fall. Due to the death of his father, a practicing physician, he returned to Virginia after a year to care for his mother. Ordained in Jan., 1890, he served as pastor of Calvary Church, Portsmouth, Va., 1890–94. In Feb., 1890, he married Lula S. Gills, who died Sept., 1892. Called to pastorate of First Baptist Church, New Albany, Ind., he married Julia Phillips (church organist) Jan., 1896. During this pastorate, he completed his seminary training, graduating from Southern Baptist Theological Seminary in 1898. Called to Grace Baptist Church, Baltimore, Md., May, 1898, he remained pastor for 17 years during which time 850 members were added. From 1915 to 1926, he served as executive secretary of the Maryland Baptist Union Association, now known as the Baptist Convention of Maryland. After 12 years service he accepted a call to Park View Baptist Church, Portsmouth, Va., where he served for nearly 15 years. On retirement in June, 1941, he became pastor emeritus, and moved to Baltimore, Md. For 30 years he was a trustee of the University of Richmond which conferred a D.D. degree on him in 1917. Baylor was listed in *Who's Who in America* in 1917. In retirement he continued to be active, preaching in 76 churches as supply or interim pastor. He is author of a brochure, "Better Not or Some Don'ts for Young Preachers" (1947). Twenty thousand copies of this brochure were distributed to colleges, seminaries, and individuals in 40 states. LESLIE M. BOWLING

***BAYLOR UNIVERSITY.** Celebrating its 125th anniversary in 1969–70 as the largest Baptist educational institution in the world, Baylor attributes much of its growth to the emphasis that was placed on expansion of program and facilities in the past 15 years. The list of new buildings constructed since 1955 was climaxed by the $3,800,000 Moody Memorial Library that was completed in the fall of 1968. Some of the other buildings constructed since then are Morrison-Constitution Hall, which houses the law schools; Marrs-McLean and Sid Richardson Science buildings; the Hankamer School of Business building; and most recently the Hankamer Student Financial Aid and Placement Center.

Between 1955 and 1969, enrolment increased from 3,500 to more than 6,500 students. Five new dormitories were constructed to provide adequate housing. Annual gifts increased from less than $1,000,000 to a high of $6,000,000 in 1968. Endowment rose from less than $13,000,000 (1962) to more than $23,000,000 (1970), while financial aid to the students via loans, salaries, and scholarships climbed to $3,000,000 annually, an increase of $2,000,000 annually since 1955.

Baylor's administration also was reorganized.

SAMFORD UNIVERSITY (*q.v.*), chartered in 1841, long known as Howard College, redesignated as a university in 1965, Birmingham, Ala.

MOBILE COLLEGE (*q.v.*), founded 1961, is located on a 400-acre campus twelve miles north of Mobile, Ala.

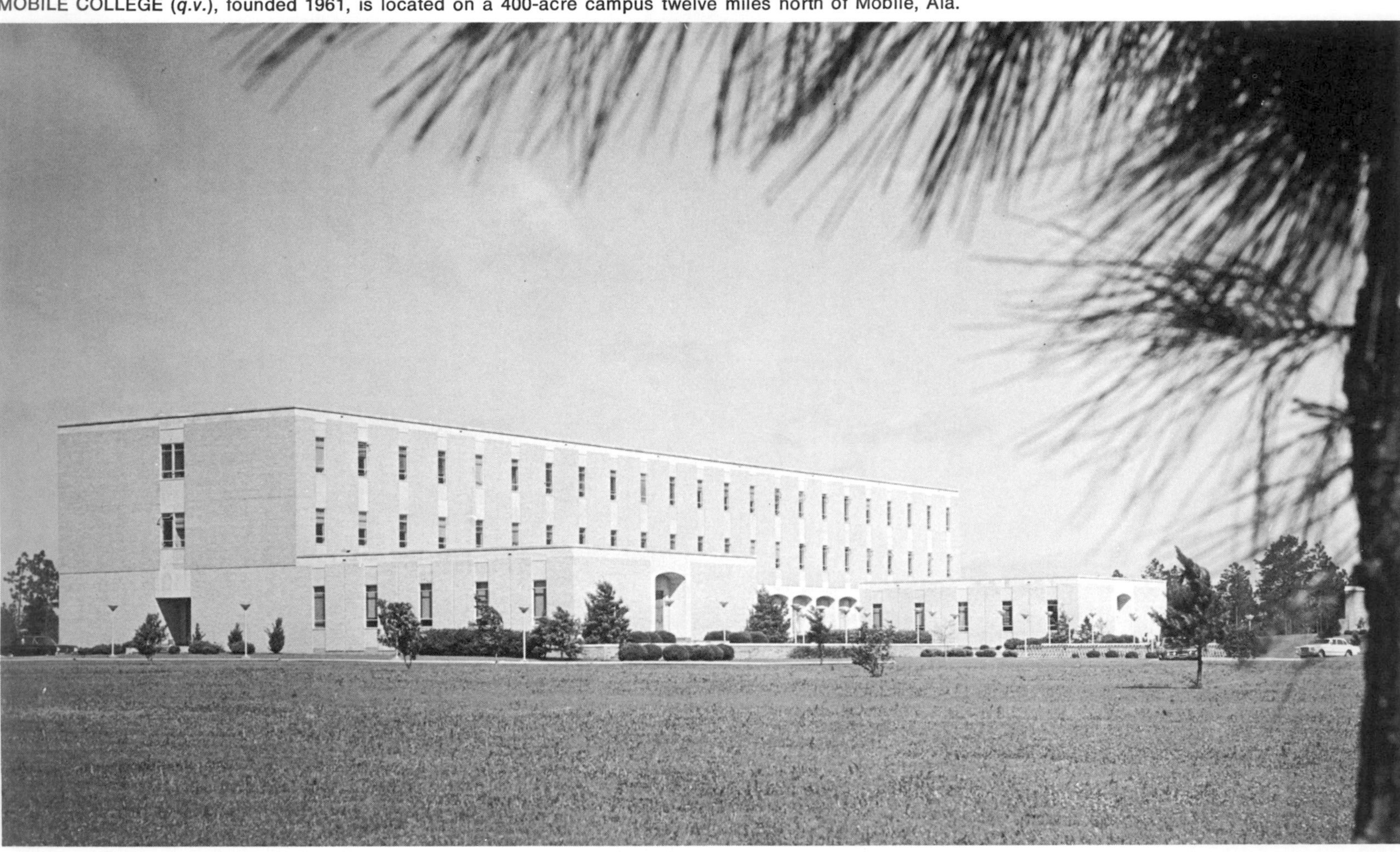

On Apr. 18, 1961, Abner V. McCall became the tenth president of the university, succeeding W. R. White, who now is president-emeritus. Vice-presidents also were elected to serve in the areas of student affairs, student financial aid and placement, development and administration, and research. C. C. RISENHOOVER

***BAYLOR UNIVERSITY HOSPITAL.** This medical center has shown continuing progress since 1954. From 1909 to 1969, 1,200,000 patients have been admitted to the hospital. Treatment and free hospitalization have been provided to thousands of charity patients at an annual cost of more than $1,100,000. The seven-floor, $5,500,000 Karl and Ester Hoblitzelle Women and Children's Hospital was dedicated on Oct. 22, 1959. Two new additions for the medical center under construction in 1969 were the Erik and Margaret Jonsson Medical and Surgical Hospital and the Carr P. Collins Center for Continuing Care. Net value of the hospital's properties exceeds $50,000,000.

MARJORIE SAUNDERS

BEALL, NOBLE YOUNG (b. Dallas County, Ga., Mar. 8, 1900; d. Marianna, Fla., Oct. 7, 1947). Pastor, missionary, educator. His parents, Thomas Newnan and Adelaide (Fuller) Beall, moved the family to Geneva County, Ala., in 1902. He was educated in public schools, Newton Junior College, Howard College, now Samford University (A.B.), Southern Baptist Theological Seminary, and Emory University (M.A.). From Selma University, Selma, Ala., he received the D.D. degree in 1940. On July 29, 1925, he married Jewell Chancy. Their children were Helen, Charles, and Judson. During 1924–34, Beall served on BYPU staff of Alabama Baptist Convention, pastor of First Baptist Church, Ozark, and of Twelfth Street Baptist Church, Gasden, Ala. He was director of work with Negroes for the Home Mission Board, 1934–45. He was professor of religion at Stetson University, 1945–47. At his death, Beall had served one month as president of Chipola Junior College, Marianna, Fla. He was author of *The Preacher and His Task* (1939). WENDELL R. GRIGG

BEAM INTERNATIONAL. *The Baptist Radio Beam* was initiated in 1949 as a quarterly newsletter, 8½ x 11, by the late S. F. Lowe (*q.v.*, Vol. II), first director of the Radio Commission. The periodical was designed as an information and promotion vehicle and aimed at Southern Baptists. Paul M. Stevens, commission director, merged the newsletter with another quarterly publication which carried reprints of sermons preached on *The Baptist Hour* radio program. *The Beam* portion of the newsletter title was retained, and it became a 5½ x 8½ monthly with 24 pages. The first issue, Jan., 1954, was Volume 5, Number 1. During the first several years of the new format, *The Beam* was directed at the denomination and utilized primarily in securing recognition for the agency as an evangelistic and missionary force. The magazine also gave the printed sermons an enlarged ministry and conserved them for further individual study.

The Beam began to reflect the progress of electronic communications and the place of religious broadcasting within the industry. Circulation grew slowly until it passed the 10,000 mark in Mar., 1956. Clarence E. Duncan, director of promotion, started *The Beam* in 1954 and served as editor until Oct., 1957. Alvin Shackleford became the first full-time editor in Nov., 1957. In Oct., 1960, *The Beam* felt the hand of a professional layout artist for the first time, Rachel Joy Colvin. The new look, coupled with an increase in pages, enabled the magazine to gather momentum and circulation.

Virgil W. Hensley was editor from Nov., 1961, to Oct., 1963. James T. Johns succeeded him. A journalism graduate steeped in the workings of the commission, Johns brought *The Beam* to a new level of prestige and influence. With the advent of the Jan., 1967, issue, the size of the magazine was again changed to 8½ x 11, four-color covers became standard, and the name was changed to *Beam International.*

The larger format was kept for 13 issues under the guidance of Charles Roden, who became editor in July, 1967. At this point, the commission recognized that, even with an all-time high circulation of 40,000 subscribers, the cost was too great and the audience too small to justify the publication. Thus, at the peak of its popularity, *Beam International* was phased out as a magazine.

The commission then placed the elements of the magazine—the editorial, feature items, and news of religious broadcasting—in a four-page newsletter which retained the name *Beam International,* and was distributed free to all United States broadcasting outlets—a controlled circulation of 8,000. *The Baptist Hour* sermons were printed quarterly and offered by subscription. All the remaining material was placed in an advertising format and space purchased in state Baptist newspapers as often as financially feasible. In its new format, *Beam International* continues its stewardship of communication and aids the commission in fulfilling its responsibility to the denomination. CLARENCE DUNCAN

***BEAUREGARD BAPTIST MEMORIAL HOSPITAL.** See LOUISIANA BAPTIST CONVENTION.

BELGIUM, MISSION IN. Southern Baptist missionaries entered Belgium in Oct., 1967, when Rudolph and Helen (Siner) Wood moved from Luxembourg, where they had served an English-language congregation begun by American businessmen. Although Belgian Baptists—less than 400 in number—had received financial support previously, missionary placement resulted from an English-language church being establshed by military families involved in the removal of NATO headquarters from France. In 1969 George and Della (Singleton) Poulos began helping this church with 14 nations in its potential outreach. Wood assumed leadership of a work in Brussels, national capital and European Common Market center.

RUDOLPH M. WOOD

BELIEVERS' CHURCH, CONFERENCE ON THE CONCEPT OF THE. This interdenominational conference, held at the Southern Baptist Theological Seminary, Lousville, Ky., June 26–30, 1967, sought to clarify the meaning, assess the validity, and investigate the relevance of the concept of the committed and disciplined church which is thought to be common to the Anabaptist, radical Puritan, Pietist, Wesleyan, Restorationist, and Pentecostal traditions. Planned by an interdenominational committee of church historians and theologians, convoked by Southern Seminary, and attended by 150 participants—theological professors, pastors, editors, denominational executives, and laymen—the conference featured 13 addresses pertaining to the people of God as a believing people, a people in community, a people under the Word, and a people in the world. A second Believers' Church Conference was held at Chicago Theological Seminary, June 29—July 2, 1970.

BIBLIOGRAPHY: Donald F. Durnbaugh, *The Believers' Church: The History and Character of Radical Protestantism* (1968); James Leo Garrett, Jr., ed., *The Concept of the Believers' Church* (1970).

JAMES LEO GARRETT, JR.

BELL, MARTHA E. McINTOSH (b. Society Hill, S. C., Sept. 29, 1848; d. Ridgecrest, N. C., Oct. 14, 1922). First president of Woman's Missionary Union, SBC. Born into a Christian home, Miss McIntosh was converted at an early age and grew up in a church known for its missionary spirit. Educated at St. David's Academy in her home community and in a boarding school for girls in Charleston, she was fitted by background and experience for the presidency of WMU. She had worked in her church missionary society and later served as chairman of the state central committee of woman's mission societies of South Carolina (first central committee in the South, organized in her own church at Society Hill). Elected president of WMU in the 1888 organizational meeting, she served for four years, guiding the young missionary organization with quiet dignity and patient efficiency.

In 1895 Miss McIntosh married T. P. Bell (*q.v.*, Vol. I), corresponding secretary of the Baptist Sunday School Board and later editor of *The Christian Index* in Atlanta. She devoted her married life to making a home for her husband and his three children by a former marriage. She is buried in Society Hill, S. C. DORIS DEVAULT

***BELMONT COLLEGE.** The 1969–70 fall enrolment numbered 1,000 students, not including a summer school of 459, under a faculty of 65 members. Four buildings have been added since 1959: Williams Library, Massey Auditorium, physical education, and a women's dormitory. In 1969 total property value was $5,997,711, and the 1969–70 operating budget was $1,500,000. Present (1969) endowment was approximately $1,000,000 with much stress being placed on expanding this fund. The college is operated under the direction of a 27-member board of trustees, elected by the Tennessee Baptist Convention, one third of whom are chosen annually.

Belmont was fully accredited by the Southern Association of Colleges and Schools in 1959. Major programs of study are offered in 15 areas of concentration. The Bachelor of Arts and Bachelor of Science degrees are granted, with 1,300 having received degrees since the first graduating class in 1955.

In 1959 Herbert C. Gabhart succeeded R. Kelly White as president. The college emphasizes high academic standards with a wholesome Christian atmosphere permeating every aspect of its life. HERBERT C. GABHART

BENEDICT, DAVID (b. Norwalk, Conn., Oct. 10, 1779; d. Pawtucket, R. I., Dec. 5, 1874). Baptist minister and historian. Son of Thomas and Martha (Scudder) Benedict, he became a shoemaker's apprentice at age 14, serving in this position for seven years before becoming a journeyman in a New York City shoe business for a year. Having decided for the ministry, in 1802 he entered the academy of Stephen S. Nelson at Mount Pleasant, N. Y., where he paid his expenses by tutoring younger pupils. He entered Brown University as a junior in 1804 and graduated in 1806, delivering an address on "Ecclesiastical History" which attracted much attention.

After graduation he accepted his only pastorate, the newly organized First Baptist Church, Pawtucket, R. I., which had been gathered through his labors while he was at Brown. He served his congregation for 23 years. On May 5, 1808, he married Margaret Hubbel Gano, daughter of Stephen Gano. Married for 60 years, they had 12 children.

In the early years of his ministry, Benedict began to collect materials for a history of the Baptists in America. Because of his deep interest in Baptist history, he finally gave up his pastorate. In his historical inquiries he carried on a large correspondence and traveled some 7,000 miles in the 17 states of the United States. He was said to have had a wider knowledge of Baptist men and affairs than anyone during his lifetime. For 10 years he was postmaster at Pawtucket, and for 56 years a trustee of Brown University.

Benedict's initial major work was *A General History of the Baptist Denomination in America and Other Parts of the World* (2 vols., 1813). This was the first general history of the Baptist denomination around the world, though most of the material deals with American Baptists. An abridgment of this work was published in 1820. Other publications were: *Abridgment of Robinson's History of Baptism* (1817), *History of All Religions* (1824), *A General History of the Baptist Denomination in America and Other*

Parts of the World (1848), a different work from the first bearing the same title, and *Fifty Years Among the Baptists* (1860), his last publication. At the time of his death he was working on a *History of the Donatists,* which was published posthumously in 1875.

Benedict used the material of Morgan Edwards (*q.v.*), Isaac Backus (*q.v.,* Vol. I), and John Asplund (*q.v.*) and also employed their method of gathering facts. His work is marred in part by a desire to prove an unbroken succession of Baptists from the first century. In spite of certain deficiencies in his material, he provides an important early source on American Baptists.

JOHN S. MOORE AND WILLIAM L. LUMPKIN

***BENGAL-ORISSA: THE CHRISTIAN SERVICE SOCIETY.** This organization continues the mission work begun in 1836, and now includes the states of Bengal, Orissa, and Bihar. Increasing Communist strength has affected mission work by rejection of visas, scrutiny of activities, and vocal criticism of foreigners and the church. Fewer American Baptist missionaries are serving on this field than during the last 100 years. In accordance with the general policy of the American Baptist Foreign Mission Society, funds for projects have been turned over to the Christian Service Society, and staff responsibility for properties and programs has been transferred to Indian personnel.

Plans for expansion of Nekursini Hospital, opened in 1965, are progressing. The medical program of the society also includes dispensaries and a leprosy treatment program. Through an agricultural extension program, Baptists in Bengal-Orissa-Bihar are trying to reach all the rural churches and surrounding villages with information, seed, and equipment. Promising young people are being encouraged with scholarship aid and training programs.

Statistics (1969): missionaries, 12; national workers, 221; churches, 56; baptisms, 173; church members, 4,638; schools and colleges, 31; enrolled, 3,341; hospitals and dispensaries, eight; patients, 39,080.

JAMES D. MOSTELLER

BERMUDA, MISSION IN. The Foreign Mission Board, SBC, sent Robert and Mary (Culpepper) Harris to Bermuda in Feb., 1966, after the First Baptist Church, ten years old, requested a pastor. Most members of the small but active church were American military personnel. Savings, plus a loan, made possible a new church building, dedicated Sept. 3, 1967. The church then reached out to local families until Bermudians formed half the membership. Other missionary personnel have included John Virkler, missionary journeyman, and E. Jackson and Helen (Elliott) Whitley. During the Crusade of the Americas, a deep revival was experienced.

ROBERT L. HARRIS

BERRY, EVA (b. Bellfactory, Madison County, Ala., Jan. 6, 1905; d. Greenfield, Iowa, June 2, 1957.) WMU leader. A graduate of Howard College (A.B., 1930), Birmingham, Ala., and WMU Training School, Louisville, Ky., she served as church secretary in two churches. She was WMU Young People's Secretary for Alabama for nine years; WMU Young People's worker in the Birmingham Baptist Association for one year; WMU field worker in Missouri, four years; and WMU executive secretary in Missouri for six years. Following a period of employment by the Broadway Plan of Church Finance, agency of the Southern Baptist General Convention of California, Fresno, she became executive secretary of the WMU of Kansas, the position held at the time of her death in an automobile accident.

N. J. WESTMORELAND

BETHEA, PERCY ANDREW (b. Marion County, S. C., July 22, 1875; d. Darlington, S. C., May 31, 1961). Philanthropist. Son of Andrew and Annie (Allen) Bethea, he was educated at Wake Forest College, Winston-Salem, N. C., and Atlanta Dental School (D.D.S.). He married Estelle Guest, June 10, 1908; they had no children. He practiced dentistry and conducted vast farming interests. Bethea made substantial gifts to Southeastern Baptist Theological Seminary to aid ministerial students and to Wake Forest College, which named Bethea Chapel for him. He gave to the South Carolina Baptist Convention $100,000 and 100 acres of land near Darlington, Ga., to be used as a home for the aged. The institution was named for him. Subsequent gifts of approximately $150,000 were given to the home.

DAVIS M. SANDERS

***BETHEA BAPTIST HOME.** Joe Burnett became superintendent-treasurer of this South Carolina institution in 1961 and served for two years. A. W. Brickle became superintendent in 1964. A 42-bed infirmary was opened in 1967. The home operates at a full capacity of 120 residents.

A. W. BRICKLE

***BETHEL COLLEGE (Hopkinsville, Ky.).** Closed for classroom operation, May 31, 1964, after 110 years successively as a Baptist related school.

Presidents included William E. Richardson (1951–60), William E. Burton (1960–61), acting president Mark Lowry (1961–62), and Park Harris Anderson, Jr. (1962–64). According to the charter, assets reverted to the Kentucky Baptist Convention for the benefit of its Baptist colleges. Trustee chairman H. Curtis Erwin led in the liquidation process, turning over to the convention $98,895, including $4,867 of endowment funds. This was set up as the "Bethel College Memorial Endowment Fund," with the Kentucky Baptist Foundation to provide endowment funds for Georgetown, Cumberland, and Campbellsville colleges. President Anderson attributed the demise of the college to (1) substandard equipment and antiquated buildings, in spite of a courageous effort by the Kentucky convention in raising $250,000 in a special campaign; (2) almost total lack of endowment; and (3) announcement of a proposed state Community College in Hopkinsville.

Campbellsville College was designated as the permanent depository of the Students' Personal Records and the National Defense Student Loan Records. The convention is the custodian of all legal documents. The charter of the college is being maintained, with the executive secretary-treasurer of the convention as process agent.

HAROLD GLEN SANDERS

***BIBLE INSTITUTE, THE.** An educational institution supported by a Baptist state convention which seeks to provide a broad curriculum of Bible, theological, and other pastoral training, religious education, and church music studies. The Bible institute differs from the Bible college in that the college usually offers regular college courses with three years biblical studies, while the institute specializes in theology, religious education, and other church related studies. Baptist Bible colleges, institutes, and schools not supported by or affiliated with state conventions are not included in the scope of this article.

The four Bible institutes operated by Southern Baptists are: Baptist Bible Institute, Graceville, Fla.; Clear Creek Baptist School, Pineville, Ky.; Fruitland Baptist Bible Institute, Hendersonville, N. C.; and Mexican Baptist Bible Institute, San Antonio, Tex. All are supported by their respective state conventions. These institutions exist to train men and women who choose that route for their own reasons. For many, if not most, the reason is a late start in the ministry. A typical Bible institute student might be about 32, with a wife and children. Such men come from almost every vocation not requiring a college education. Most are high school graduates. Many have left high-paying jobs, skilled trades, or their own businesses. In some of the schools, and in some years, more than half were ordained deacons when they entered the ministry. As Southern Baptists have become increasingly urbanized, greater numbers of enrollees have come from city jobs and addresses to seek out Bible institute training. Also, after two decades of almost continuous war, and large numbers in the military service, many retired servicemen enrol in these schools.

Mature, noncollege graduates such as these usually know what they want—immediate training in the Bible and other subjects that will prepare them for service to the churches. The curriculum is designed for their needs. They also choose a Bible institute because there they study with others of their own approximate age. Also, as they seek pastorates or other church staff ministries in the area while in school, they compete only with fellow institute students who have similar backgrounds.

There appears to be no foreseeable time when Baptists will not need their Bible institutes. While more people than ever graduate from college, there are other and larger groups of the population who—for many reasons—will not. Bible institutes do not compete with either colleges or seminaries. This is because the institutes major upon theological training for the mature, noncollege graduates. The October, 1969, fall enrolment showed 626 attending the four Bible institutes named; 98 had graduated in May.

WALTER D. DRAUGHTON, JR.
HAL D. BENNETT
JAMES E. SOUTHERLAND

***BIBLE READERS' COURSES.** While the Training Union Bible Readers' Course continued, several church program organizations carried different daily Bible reading references in their periodicals. For example, the Sunday School daily Bible reading plan was correlated with the uniform Sunday School lessons. In Jan., 1968, however, all church program organizations printing daily Bible reading references in their periodicals began to carry a single set of readings. Most listed only the Bible references. *Open Windows* carried the references with comments for use in private worship. *Home Life* carried the references with comments for use in family worship.

ELMER L. GRAY

***BIBLICAL RECORDER.** The decade of the sixties was a period of growth and change for this North Carolina Baptist journal. J. Marse Grant, a layman, became editor of the weekly paper in Jan., 1960, succeeding Levy L. Carpenter (*q.v.*) who had been editor since 1943. Cyrus W. Bazemore, associate editor under Carpenter, became director of circulation and field promotion in 1963, when a third member of the editorial staff, Roger Branch, was added as an associate. Branch left the staff in 1966 to return to school and was replaced by Toby Druin as associate editor. Bazemore retired Dec. 31, 1968, after 17 years with the *Recorder*.

Under Grant's direction the *Recorder* expanded its news and photo coverage of events of the Baptist state convention and its affiliated churches, and adopted a strong editorial policy. These editorials covered the total spectrum of issues confronting Christians, uging them to deal more effectively with the spiritual and social issues of the day. Heavy emphasis was placed on Christian involvement in such social areas as improved care for the elderly, church programs to benefit the alcoholic, and better race relations. The *Recorder* was very active in the 1967 and 1969 sessions of the North Carolina General Assembly in successfully combatting efforts to liberalize the state's liquor laws.

Baptists of North Carolina responded by increasing the circulation of the journal from 62,000 to 89,000, for an increase of nearly 50 per cent, by the close of the decade.

TOBY DRUIN

BINNS, WALTER POPE (b. Washington, Ga., Sept. 18, 1895; d. Falls Church, Va., Dec. 3, 1966). Preacher and educator. A graduate of Boy's High School, Atlanta, Ga., he earned the

A.B. degree from Mercer University which later awarded him the honorary D.D. and LL.D. degrees. In 1918 he married Blanche (Mallory) of Macon, Ga. They had four children: Mallory, Walter, Emma, and Blanche.

Binns served as army chaplain in World War I. His pastorates were: Laurenceville, Ky.; Moultrie, Ga.; La Grange, Ga.; Roanoke, Va. He served as president of William Jewell College, Liberty, Mo., 1943–62. Binns also served as a trustee of Mercer University, member of the executive committee of the Southern Baptist Convention, Baptist World Alliance, chairman of the Baptist Joint Committee on Public Affairs, and was active in P.O.A.U. He wrote *Behold the Man!* (1960). He was buried in Macon, Ga. H. I. HESTER

BITTING, CHARLES CARROLL (b. Philadelphia, Pa., Mar., 1830; d. Philadelphia, Pa., Dec. 24, 1898.) Pastor and denominational leader. He served pastorates in Hanover County, Va., Alexandria, Lynchburg, and Richmond, Va.; and Baltimore, Md. From 1866–69 Bitting was corresponding secretary of the first Sunday School Board of the Southern Baptist Convention, then located at Greenville, S. C. For one year (1872–73) he served the American Baptist Publication Society as district secretary for the southern states. From 1883 until 1897, he was Bible secretary for the American Baptist Publication Society. HOWARD P. COLSON

BLACKWELL, REECE CROXTON (b. Jefferson, S. C., Jan. 3, 1903; d. Greenville, S. C., Dec. 17, 1968). College professor and mathematician. Son of James Wellington and Minnie (Horton) Blackwell, he was educated in the public schools of Jefferson, S. C., Wingate Junior College (N. C.), Furman University (B.A., 1924), and the University of North Carolina at Chapel Hill (M.A., 1927; Ph.D., 1939). Blackwell married Lillie Alice Dill of Taylors, S. C., on Sept. 6, 1928. They had four children: Dill Broadus, Elsie Alice, Nancy Rose, and Reece Croxton, Jr. Blackwell was dean of boys and professor of mathematics, Wingate Junior College, 1924–26, instructor of mathematics, University of North Carolina, 1927–29, assistant professor of mathematics, Furman University, 1929–31, and junior instructor, Johns Hopkins University, 1931–33. In 1934 he returned to Furman University and served as assistant professor of mathematics, 1934–39, associate professor, 1939–49, and professor, 1949–68. From 1958–68, he was chairman of the department of mathematics, and from 1952–54, he served as chairman of the faculty. He was chairman of the Greenville County Democratic Party, 1967–68. Blackwell was an active Baptist layman. During his residence in Greenville, as a member of Pendleton Street Baptist Church, he served as Sunday School teacher, chairman of the deacons, and chairman of the building committee. In 1965, he was first vice-president of the South Carolina Baptist Convention, and in 1943–47, 1947–52, and 1956–66, he was a member (chairman, 1957–60, 1964–66) of the board of trustees of the *Baptist Courier.* ROBERT C. TUCKER

***BLUE MOUNTAIN COLLEGE.** A senior college for women, located at Blue Mountain, Miss. Established in 1873, it became the property of the Mississippi Baptist Convention in 1919. Lawrence T. Lowery (*q.v.*) was president 1925–60. Wilfred C. Tyler (*q.v.*), served as president 1960–65. Harold Fisher has been president since 1965. During the sixties the enrolment increased from 314 to 596; the assets of the college from $2,005,083 to $3,390,594; and the endowment from $626,372 to $1,209,178. A plant development program increased the value of the physical properties from $1,316,318 to $1,856,534. R. A. MCLEMORE

***BLUEFIELD COLLEGE.** Since 1956 several new buildings have been added: a girl's dormitory (1959); a chapel and fine arts building (1966); and a gymnasium (1968). In 1962 the alumni established a scholarship fund. The Southern Association of Colleges and Schools renewed its accreditation after regular periodic study in 1964.

The trustees of Bluefield continue to reject use of federal funds. In the school year 1968–69 Bluefield received $136,406 for operating expenses and $44,713 for capital needs from denominational sources. In 1968 the endowment was $118,458 and the value of buildings and grounds was approximately $1,974,316.

A faculty of 30 instructed 396 students at the junior college level in the 1969–70 session. Thirty students were preparing for church-related vocations. Baptists accounted for 70 percent of the total enrolment in 1969. CARRINGTON PAULETTE

BOLT, WILLIAM JESSE. (b. Anderson County, S. C., Sept. 29, 1885; d. Greenville, S. C., July 3, 1960). Graduate of Furman University (B.A., 1916) and Southern Baptist Theological Seminary (Th.M., 1919), he served as pastor of six churches in South Carolina, Indiana, and Kentucky over a 44-year period. His longest pastorate was 19 years at First Baptist Church, Harlan, Ky. He was a trustee of Georgetown College, Ky. He preached the annual sermon, Kentucky Baptist Convention, 1935. Bolt married Hattie Boroughs of Pickens County, S. C., 1917. JOHN E. ROBERTS

***BOOK STORES, BAPTIST.** A group of 51 stores owned by the Sunday School Board of the Southern Baptist Convention and operated by the Book Store Division as a service to the denomination. Exclusively retail, the stores major in selling religious books, Bibles, and supplies for all church organizations. Audiovisual equipment is also sold. Eleven of the stores operate religious-film libraries. A special service for church libraries is also offered. Church music, songbooks, and hymnals are distributed along with educational furniture and other special items.

Policies and procedures are set by the Sunday School Board, but each manager has considerable freedom to manage the store under the authority delegated to him. Central financial accounting is done at the board, including charge accounts with customers. Each store is a separate operation, yet part of the whole. Cooperative purchasing of goods for resale, combined advertising, and other standard procedures are maintained, resulting in more efficient operations and ultimate benefit to the denomination. Income from store operations becomes a part of the board's earnings budgeted for programs supported by the board.

Effective Oct. 1, 1969, a Campus Stores Department was established in the Book Store Division. Beginning with six stores located on Southern Baptist seminary campuses, it seeks to own and operate stores on Southern Baptist college campuses.

The Book Store Division also operates Broadman Readers Plan, a reading club for adults. The division organization includes four stores-departments (Eastern, Central, Western, and Campus), the Retail Advertising and Sales Promotion Department, and special clerical services.

Operating from coast to coast, the book stores' motto "Service with a Christian Distinction," is an incentive for each employee to be the best Christian in business he knows how to be, sympathetic to the demands of every customer.

KEITH C. VON HAGEN

BOONE, WILLIAM COOKE (b. Bowling Green, Ky., Feb. 8, 1892; d. Jackson, Tenn., July 9, 1970). Son of Arthur Upshaw and Eddie Belle Cooke Boone, he represented the fifth generation from Squire Boone (1744–1815), pioneer Kentucky Baptist preacher. He was educated at William Jewell College (A.B., 1912; A.M., 1913), Southern Baptist Theological Seminary (1912–14), and Columbia University (summer, 1923). Georgetown College conferred a D.D. degree on him in 1928. He was ordained at Memphis, Tenn., on Mar. 24, 1914.

Boone's Baptist pastorates were First, Hernando, Miss., 1914–16; Marianna, Ark., 1917–18; First, Owensboro, Ky., 1918–27; First, Roanoke, Va., 1927–30; First, Jackson, Tenn.; and Crescent Hill, Louisville, Ky., 1940–45. He was president of Oklahoma Baptist University, 1930–32. He became executive secretary of the executive board of the General Association of Baptists in Kentucky (now Kentucky Baptist Convention) on Jan. 1, 1946, where he served until his retirement in the summer of 1961. He then moved to Jackson, Tenn., where he organized the Woodland Baptist Church (1965) and served as its pastor through 1967.

He published two books: *What God Hath Joined Together* (1935) and *What We Believe* (1936). He conducted tours through Europe and the Near East from 1925 until after his retirement.

Boone married Ruth Trotter on Sept. 1, 1915. They had five children: Mrs. Ruth Fusselle, Mrs. Martha Foust, Mrs. Nan Arendall, Arthur U. Boone, II, and William C. Boone, Jr.

LEO T. CRISMON

BOTSWANA, MISSION IN. Marvin and Elizabeth (Haley) Reynolds, appointed by the Foreign Mission Board in 1967, established residence in Francistown, Botswana, early in 1968. After language study, they began Bible classes and religious services, resulting in the first converts in 1969. They were joined in 1970 by Charles and Jane (Powers) Bellenger. Bellenger, first resident dentist in the new republic, began a dental practice based in Francistown, with mobile clinics projected into nearby villages as an aid to the evangelistic outreach.

H. CORNELL GOERNER

BOYD, JESSE LANEY, SR. (b. Bogue Chitto, Pike County, Miss., June 23, 1881; d. Clinton, Miss., June 24, 1967). He was educated in the public schools and received degrees from Mississippi College (1908), and Southern Baptist Seminary (1914). He married Clara D. Reeves of McComb, Miss., in 1908, and they had two children, Alice Katharine Boyd and Jesse Laney Boyd, Jr. After her death he married Ada Brister (1962).

Boyd served as pastor of the following Mississippi churches: Coldwater; First, Gloster; First, Biloxi; First, Magee; Pickens; Bomar Avenue, Vicksburg; Calvary, Meridian; and Union. He served as a chaplain in France, 1917–19.

Early in his career Boyd taught in the public schools; he served as president of Clarke College 1943–45; and after 1947 was a part-time member of the faculty of Mississippi College.

Boyd helped organize a program for the preservation of Mississippi Baptist historical materials in 1926 and was the leader in this work for more than 40 years. In 1956 he led in the organization of the Mississippi Baptist Historical Commission, and was its executive secretary-treasurer until his death.

Among Boyd's writings were *A Popular History of the Baptists in Mississippi* (1930), and a *History of Baptists in America, Prior to 1845* (1957). He was a contributor to the *Encyclopedia of Southern Baptists* (1958), and the director of "Operation Baptist Biography" in Mississippi. He was a charter member of the Southern Baptist Historical Society. He served as a member of the Historical Commission, SBC, 1951–53.

Bibliography: "Jesse Laney Boyd Papers," Mississippi Baptist Historical Commission, Library, Clinton.

R. A. MC LEMORE

***BOYS RANCH TOWN, OKLAHOMA.** Located on 160 acres of land northeast of Oklahoma City, Boys Ranch Town had 50 boys under care in 1970. Charles T. Boldin, superintendent, had 16 employees. Buildings consist of three cottages, administration, superintendent's residence, and trades and educational building.

Total property value was $700,000 in 1970, with no debt. J. M. GASKIN

BRADLEY, EARL LOCA (b. Asheville, N. C., Sept. 23, 1902; d. Raleigh, N. C., Oct. 5, 1962). Minister and denominational leader. Son of Franklin Ellis and Maggie Dalton Bradley, he married Frances Elease Lingerfeldt on Aug. 1, 1925. They had two children, a son and a daughter. Bradley was educated at Mars Hill Junior College (1928) and Wake Forest College (B.A., 1930). He also did graduate work at Duke Divinity School. Ordained in 1921, Bradley held pastorates in several churches in western North Carolina, and was pastor of Calvary Baptist Church, Wilmington, 1938–45. In 1945 he was called as field secretary for the Baptist State Convention. In 1954 Bradley became secretary of stewardship promotion, and in 1959 was named director of the Division of Stewardship Promotion and Editorial Services. TOBY DRUIN

BRADLEY, SAM ED (b. Van Buren, Ark., June 11, 1909; d. Little Rock, Ark., Sept. 3, 1963). Pastor and child care executive. After attending public schools in Van Buren and Ft. Smith, Ark., Bradley graduated from Ouachita College (A.B., 1931), Arkadelphia, Ark., and Southern Baptist Theological Seminary (Th.M., 1937), Louisville, Ky. He married Fairie Burton of Benton, Ark., on Jan. 9, 1932. They reared two children. Bradley served as pastor of Glasgow Baptist Church, Glasgow, Ky., and First church, Fulton, Ky. In the summer of 1947 he left the pastorate and entered upon his career as a child care executive. First elected superintendent of the Louisville Baptist Orphans Home (now Spring Meadows Children's Home), he later (1959) was chosen by the Kentucky Baptist Board of Child Care to be its first general superintendent. During his years at the children's home, and later in the central office, many progressive changes were effected in the child care program of Kentucky Baptists. He served as president of child care executives of Southern Baptists in 1956. Due to failing health he retired in Jan., 1963. C. FORD DEUSNER

BRANCH, DOUGLAS McKINLEY (b. Wake County, N. C., Nov. 8, 1908; d. Ahoskie, N. C., Feb. 1, 1963). Pastor and denominational leader. Son of Atlas M. and Nora Branch, he married Jessie Walker of Windsor. They had one son and two daughters. In 1937 Branch graduated with honors from Wake Forest College which later awarded him an honorary D.D. Ordained at Mt. Moriah Church in the Raleigh Association in 1935, he served as pastor of several rural churches while a student and in 1938 became pastor of First Baptist Church, Cary. In 1941 he joined the state mission board as a field worker and general missionary. Branch returned to school for a bachelor of divinity degree at Southern Baptist Theological Seminary. He served as pastor of churches at Scotland Neck, Kannapolis, and Rocky Mount before being elected unanimously in May, 1959, as general secretary-treasurer of the Baptist state convention. The year before he had served as chairman of the committee of 25, whose report resulted in a complete restructuring of the convention. Branch also served as a member of the Executive Committee of the Southern Baptist Convention and was chairman of the committee to study total Southern Baptist Convention Program. He was killed in an automobile wreck following an address at Chowan College. TOBY DRUIN

BRANHAM, LEON EDWARD (b. Richland County, S. C., May 20, 1910; d. Greenville, S. C., Aug. 11, 1958). Deacon, Sunday School superintendent, and denominational worker. Educated in Columbia High School and the University of South Carolina, he married Ethel Rabon in 1934. They had one daughter, Debora Arlene. He served in the United States Army overseas during World War II. Beginning in Jan., 1946, he worked with the Baptist Sunday School Board in the Baptist Book Store, Columbia, S. C. Promoted to visual aids consultant, he was appointed manager of the Baptist Book Store, Greenville, S. C., in June, 1955. An example of his work is reflected in the growth of this store during his term of service. MRS. COLIE W. ROOF

BRANNON, J. D. (b. Spartanburg, S. C., Mar. 2, 1900; d. Fort Worth, Tex., Dec. 24, 1965). Pastor and district missionary. He was educated at Furman University, Texas Christian University, University of South Carolina, and Southwestern Baptist Theological Seminary (Th.M., 1930). Following his pastorate at Rotan, Tex., he moved to Abilene, serving as missionary for District Seventeen (six associations), 1935–37. From Houston he served the four associations of District Four, 1937–41. He was missionary of District Twelve, composed of Cooke, Denton, Erath, Jack, Johnson, Montague, Palo Pinto, Paluxy, Parker, Tarrant, and Wise Associations, 1941–65. He edited the *Gulf Coast Baptist* and wrote a column, "This Is a Good Old World" for the *Baptist Standard*.

CHARLES P. MC LAUGHLIN

***BRAZIL, MISSION IN.** The Brazilian Baptist Convention, with full encouragement from the missions, has its own cooperative plan of financing, a new headquarters building, and a national executive secretary for its executive board. It hosted the Baptist World Alliance Congress in 1960. The Brazilian evangelistic crusade in 1965 provided inspiration, leadership, and procedures for the Crusade of the Americas. Special approaches initiated during recent years include agricultural projects, social work, lay-leadership training, student ministries, and the Everett Gill Memorial Hospital. A theological institute in Belem was taken over by the convention in 1965 and upgraded to seminary status. In 1969 almost 300 missionaries and more than 1,400 Brazilian pastors and workers labored in Brazil. FRANK K. MEANS

***BREWTON-PARKER JUNIOR COLLEGE.** Continued progress is attributed to three things: geographical location in southeast Georgia more than 50 miles from any other institution of higher learning, financial policy of remaining debt free while additional buildings are being erected, and growth in enrolment since 1955 from approximately 200 students to 720 in 1969.

Following the resignation of President M. A. Murray in 1957, J. Theodore Phillips was elected. The college was admitted to the Southern Association of Colleges and Schools in 1962. An intercollegiate athletic program has continued. In 1960 a radio program, "On Campus," was developed and carried on 42 Georgia stations. The program continued in 1969 as a 15-minute digest of campus activities, produced by students, and was heard over several hundred different radio and TV stations by tape.

Chief financial benefactors since 1955 have been J. E. Parker, the Maria W. Cook family, H. Terry Parker, and Mr. and Mrs. R. T. Gilder, Sr. Buildings have increased from 9 to 16, land area from 132 to 3,310 acres, endowment from $203,000 to $475,000, and property value from $500,000 to $2,100,000. J. THEODORE PHILLIPS

BRIDGES, BENJAMIN LAFAYETTE (b. Double Wells, Jefferson County, Ark., Aug. 9, 1888; d. Little Rock, Pulaski County, Ark., Apr. 8, 1965). Pastor and denominational leader. Son of William Nathan and Julia (Caldwell) Bridges, he married Lucile Moore, Sept. 4, 1917. They had one child, James William. After the death of his first wife, Bridges married Vivian Stone, Oct. 29, 1934. Converted in 1906, he was ordained by Fellowship Baptist Church, Witcherville, Ark., Feb. 9, 1908. He was educated at Friendship Baptist Academy, Star City, Ark.; Ouachita Baptist College (now University), Arkadelphia, Ark. (A.B., 1914; D.D., 1932). He also took a correspondence course from Southwestern Baptist Theological Seminary, Fort Worth, Tex. Bridges was pastor of the following Arkansas churches: Tyro and Pleasant Hill, Tyro, 1909–10; Hickory Grove, Rest; Palmyra, 1909–10; Hazel Street (Immanuel), Pine Bluff, 1913–14; First, Crossett, 1915–18; First, Paragould, 1918–29; First, Little Rock, 1930–31. He was interim pastor of Tabernacle, Little Rock; Natural Steps, Holly Springs, and Vimy Ridge, Pulaski County; and Cedar Heights, North Little Rock, Ark. He served as recording secretary, Arkansas Baptist State Convention, 1920–25, was on the state mission board, 1922–26, and was a trustee of Ouachita Baptist College, 1919–22. In 1929 he served as state superintendent of evangelism. Bridges was executive secretary-treasurer of the Arkansas Baptist State Convention, 1931–58. As state director of the Baptist Honor Club, 1943–52, Secretary Bridges led Arkansas Baptists to redeem their longstanding indebtedness. Through budget and club receipts, 65 per cent of principal on notes and bonds of $1,381,324.69, settled in 1937 at 35 per cent, was paid in ten annual payments. From 1958 to 1959, he was secretary of the Arkansas Baptist Foundation. He was a first lieutenant, United States Army Reserve. Bridges was a director of Arkansas Power and Light Company, 1942–65.

GEORGE T. BLACKMON AND T. L. HARRIS

BRIGGS, JOHN E. (Eddie) (b. Person County, N. C., July 12, 1873; d. Washington, D. C., Nov. 19, 1960). Baptist pastor and church building pioneer. Converted at 15, he was educated at Bethel College, Mercer University (A.B., 1898), and the Southern Baptist Theological Seminary (Th.M., 1901). He received the honorary D.D. from the University of Richmond, 1917, and Mercer University, 1936. Briggs was pastor at Siloam Baptist Church, Greensboro, Ga., 1901–04; Capitol Avenue Church, Atlanta, Ga., 1905–09; Fifth Baptist Church, Washington, D. C., 1909–43; and Temple Baptist Church, Washington, 1943–49. He also served as a missionary of the state mission board of Georgia, 1904–05. He married Marion Threadcraft Law of Portsmouth, Va., 1902. She died in 1926. He married Daisy K. Hasbrouck in 1935. Throughout his pastorates he enlarged the membership through door to door visitation. Records show 1,100 additions during his five years at Capitol Avenue, Atlanta, and more than 5,000 (2,500 by baptism) during his 34 years at Fifth, Washington. He was instrumental in founding nine new churches in the Washington area. Though he never earned any large salary he contributed generously to new church building projects through his earnings in real estate and stock market investments. He was a member of the Home Mission Board, SBC, trustee of Southern Baptist Theological Seminary, a founder and trustee of Eastern Baptist Theological Seminary, moderator of Columbia Associaton of Baptist Churches, and a founder of the District of Columbia Baptist Foundation. He is memorialized in name by Briggs Memorial Baptist Church, Washington. C. E. BRYANT

BRISTER, RAYMOND GUY (b. west Mississippi, Nov. 6, 1882; d. Long Beach, Calif., June 16, 1955). One of 11 children born to Charles Franklin and Frances Vasti (Guest) Brister, he was led to profess faith in Christ at age 10 by a preacher cousin, Robert Brister. He often read a Bible given him, incurring the displeasure of his Hardshell Baptist family. Constant harrassment at home prompted him to leave at 13 and go to live with his grandparents. When 17, he went to Grandfield, Okla., as a farm hand, and the next year he married Ola May Prichard. They had eight children. At 29 Brister, then a deacon, entered the ministry and Oklahoma Baptist University. During the following 13 years he served pastorates in Oklahoma and Texas. In 1942 he moved to California where he organized the First Southern Baptist Church in Long Beach, which he served until his death.

Brister's strong convictions and his fearless stand on matters of public morals and civic righteousness made him friends and enemies.

During his early ministry he was twice beaten almost to death by opponents, and on another occasion was knifed; however, he won one of his assailants to Christ, who became a faithful preacher. He also won a Hardshell Baptist brother to Christ, who became pastor of churches in Texas and New Mexico.

When Brister arrived in Long Beach, Calif., he was met by the wartime housing shortage. However, he rented an old store building, got a job at a defense plant, and sent for his family. Before the end of the year, the store building home was also the meeting place of First Southern Baptist Church, which had been constituted with 16 members. The family soon moved out, but the church continued to meet there until the war was over when buildings could be constructed. Through the years that followed, Brister led in the establishment of many other churches in the area. He was one of the founders of California Baptist College, served on the state convention's board of directors, and was at the time of his death a member of the Foreign Mission Board, SBC. FLOYD LOONEY

BRISTOW, LOUIS JUDSON, SR. (b. Timmonsville, Sumpter County, S. C., Jan. 19, 1876; d. New Orleans, La., Nov. 15, 1957). Son of James Tazewell and Elizabeth (Blackwell) Bristow, he became a printer, newspaper correspondent, and editor. As soldier and correspondent in Cuba during the Spanish American War, his stories had wide circulation. He studied for the ministry at Southern Baptist Theological Seminary. In 1902 he married Caroline Cornelius Winkler and they had three children: Gwen (Mrs. Bruce Manning), Louis J., Jr., and Caroline (Mrs. P. J. Riley).

He held pastorates in South Carolina. Through newspaper stories and in the state Baptist convention, he led a movement resulting in establishment of the Baptist Hospital at Columbia, S. C., 1913–18.

He built and was superintendent of Alabama Baptist Hospital in Selma, Ala., 1922–24, and established a hospital for Negroes there. He was on the committee to plan, build, and establish Southern Baptist Hospital in New Orleans, which he served as superintendent, 1924–47. He designed the nurse's pin of the New Orleans hospital. The hospital's motto, "Healing Humanity's Hurt," was taken from the title of a book he wrote in 1927.

Bristow retired in 1947. He served one term as vice-president of the Southern Baptist Convention. Even in difficult times he kept the hospital financially stable and gave himself to the relief of human suffering. JOHN G. ALLEY

***BRISTOW MEMORIAL HOSPITAL.** Since 1954 when the Baptist General Convention of Oklahoma acquired the Bristow Memorial Hospital at Bristow, Okla., by a lease agreement, property value of the facility has increased to $373,000. Capacity is 39 beds and 6 bassinettes. Percentage of daily occupancy in 1969 was 39.60. The institution has 45 employees. It is debt free. J. M. GASKIN

BROADCASTING NETWORKS AND SOUTHERN BAPTISTS. Southern Baptist program appearances on the three television networks in the United States has been a slow but rewarding development. The networks, in the early days of television, decided to apportion the public service time and broadcast budgets which they would allot to religion to the three major faith groups—the Roman Catholics, represented by the National Council of Catholic Men (since changed to the National Catholic Office of Radio and Television), the Jews, represented by the Jewish Theological Seminary of America, and the Protestant Christian churches, represented by the National Council of Churches of Christ in America. Since Southern Baptists did not hold membership in any of these organizations, the prospects for network television time being made available to the denomination seemed dim.

The sheer size of the denomination in the fifties (nearing 10,000,000 members) caused some networks to give occasional programs to Southern Baptists on special occasions—usually worship services or direct preaching programs.

In 1953 Paul M. Stevens, newly elected director of the Radio and Television Commission, SBC, made it a project of priority to secure for Southern Baptists television time on the networks. Persistent efforts and a desire to produce unusual and provocative programs gradually opened the way to the networks.

Since 1957 Southern Baptists have had programs allotted to them each year by ABC, CBS, and NBC. In 1969 a total of 16 half-hour programs were sponsored by the commission on the networks.

For the most part, programs on the networks are given—both time and production costs—with no strings attached. In special instances and for special programs, costs have been shared by the denomination. Subsequently, full ownership of the films made for the telecast have passed to Southern Baptists once shown on the network. In this way the denomination had the opportunity to present some unusual program materials on national television and then to own rights to all subsequent use of these materials both on television and for religious education classes. Other than these special projects, all production costs and time costs are borne by the networks and given to Southern Baptists gratis. The Convention, through the commission, is responsible for script content (the message) which is usually worked out in cooperation with production personnel at the networks.

Production facilities and time valued in excess of $200,000 per network hour have been made available to Southern Baptists for a single special program. Audiences of 12,000,000 to 20,000,000 viewers tune in these prime time programs. At the present time (1969) the Convention is averaging 16 regular 30-minute network programs per year and two to three hour-long specials. W. TRUETT MYERS

BROADMAN BIBLE COMMENTARY, THE. A 12-volume work published by Broadman Press. Volumes 1 and 8 were released in Oct., 1969; the concluding volumes (7 and 12) were scheduled for release in Apr., 1972.

In 1959 the Sunday School Board invited representative seminary and college Bible professors, with pastors and denominational leaders, to consider potential interest in a multivolume commentary, the concept and possible format. In July, 1961, the elected board committed itself "to provide the financial resources necessary to the production, publication, and promotion of a commentary that will reflect credit on Broadman Press and take its place along with other recognized works in this field."

Definite planning was delayed until early 1966. The executive secretary, James L. Sullivan, requested Clifton J. Allen to serve as general editor. William J. Fallis and Joseph F. Green of the Broadman Books Department were named associate editors. Four consulting editors were asked to assist in selecting writers, evaluating materials, and advising on matters of biblical scholarship. These were John I Durham and Roy L. Honeycutt, Jr., for the Old Testament; and Jack W. MacGorman and Frank Stagg for the New Testament.

In Sept., 1966, the editors presented to an advisory board a statement approved by the executive secretary dealing with basic concept, editorial process, and a partial list of prospective writers. This board of 26 persons included seminary personnel, Baptist college Bible teachers, pastors, and denominational leaders, together with eight staff members of the Sunday School Board. It explored fully various questions of concept, qualifications of writers, and ways of handling critical issues. Eventually, 58 persons were enlisted as writers. Fifty of these were Southern Baptists, four were from the American Baptist Convention, and four were from Great Britain.

The Commentary is directed toward ministers and serious lay students of the Bible. It seeks to draw fully upon the fruits of critical research and theological study, always conceiving the Bible to be God's authoritative revelation.

CLIFTON J. ALLEN

***BROADMAN PRESS.** Trade name used by the Sunday School Board, SBC, to designate production and distribution of books, audiovisuals and audio aids, music and recordings, and church supplies which are offered for sale through both trade accounts and Baptist Book Stores. Broadman Press functions through four programs: program of Broadman Book Publishing, program of Broadman Film Production, program of Broadman Music Publishing, and program of Broadman Supplies Production. It produces under four distinct imprints: Broadman Books, Broadman Films, Broadman Music, and Broadman Supplies. The delineation of programs, the use of distinctive imprints, and a clear-cut definition of each product line, along with objectives and goals, have all set the stage for better communication among the several producing departments and a more aggressive effort in product development and sales for all lines under the Broadman Press imprint.

Broadman Books.—Since 1956 the Broadman books product line has expanded both in the number of books published annually and in its marketing approach. The largest annual list has been 60 titles in the fiscal year 1966–67, and the average for five years ending Sept., 1969, was 54 titles. The total number of Broadman books in print in 1969 was 454. The juvenile book publishing that was initiated in 1946, and reactivated in 1956, had its peak production years in 1960 and 1961, with eight new titles each year. Juvenile books in print in 1969 were 76, with some in two bindings.

Major publishing ventures since 1956 include *Encyclopedia of Southern Baptists,* two volumes totaling 1,580 double-columned pages; *The Bible Story Book,* 672 pages with 130 illustrations mostly in color; Broadman Readers Plan, a book club which began in 1964 for distributing each year 12 specially prepared new books to a current membership of 15,000; and *The Broadman Bible Commentary,* a 12-volume work which began publication, Oct., 1969, and will be complete in Apr., 1972.

Major policy innovations were long-range planning and product development based on market research and strengthened management and editorial resources.

Broadman Films.—Broadman Films Production is the program which produces and sells audiovisual materials and leases/sells equipment. Motion pictures, filmstrips, slides, overhead transparencies, recordings, and tapes are produced under Broadman Films label. These materials are sold through the Church Audiovisual Education (CAVE) Plan directly to the churches, to Baptist Book Stores, and to trade dealers. Tapes and tape recorders are sold directly to members of the Minister's Tape Plan. Audiovisual equipment is leased/sold to churches through the CAVE Plan. Most audiovisuals, except motion pictures, are produced by Broadman Films staff. A major change in film production policy in 1966 resulted in securing most Broadman motion pictures through outside professional channels.

Approximately 300 films and filmstrips are in release under the Broadman label. Representatives of these products are: the films, *Magnificent Heritage* and *I Don't Want to Get Involved;* the filmstrip, *How to Study the Bible;* and a set of overhead Bible Map Transparencies.

Broadman Music.—Broadman Music Publishing Program edits, produces, and distributes music products to meet the needs of the music program of churches. These products include hymnals, songbooks, vocal and instrumental ensemble and solo books and music, as well as choir music and materials and recordings for individuals and groups in various age divisions. Three of the hymnals—*Broadman Hymnal, Christian Praise,* and *Junior Hymnal*—have together sold well over 10,000,000 copies. (*Baptist Hymnal,* which is a Convention Press publication, has alone sold over 5,750,000 copies.) Most Broadman records have been prepared to support the ministry of music among children both at home and in the church. Choral music includes various collections, anthems, cantatas, oratorios, music dramas, and sacred folk musicals. *Good News,* the first of these folk musicals, was published in 1967 and has sold more than 90,000 copies. Instrumental music includes music for piano, organ, handbells, and for various instrumental ensembles. In 1966 Broadman's first full-time music sales specialist was employed.

Broadman Supplies.—Supplies of various kinds for the churches have been produced by the Sunday School Board since its beginning. The present Program of Broadman Supplies Production has as its objective "to design, produce, and distribute a variety of church supplies, equipment, and educational aids which will contribute to the efficiency of the churches and to individual spiritual development." Well over 800 items include: record systems for church organizations, materials for church finance, certificates of promotion, absentee cards, maps, offering envelopes, baptismal robes, novelties, and many others. Outstanding Broadman Supply items developed recently have been Silver Sheen communion ware, Best Board chalkboards, Church Finance Record System, Bible maps, and outdoor bulletin boards.

While Broadman Press functions through several departments and divisions of the Sunday School Board, most of the work—planning, editing, designing, advertising, promoting, selling, and distributing—is done within the Publishing Division. Broadman Press products are available through book stores and other outlets in all the states and several foreign countries.

See also SUNDAY SCHOOL BOARD and CONVENTION PRESS.

BIBLIOGRAPHY: Robert E. Baker, *The Story of the Sunday School Board* (1966).

HERMAN L. KING and WILLIAM J. FALLIS

***BROTHERHOOD, BAPTIST.** The history of Brotherhood work since 1956 reflects influences of change similar to the period 1907–55.

Enrolment in Brotherhood.—At the end of 1955 Brotherhood enrolment had grown to 289,307 in 10,142 church Brotherhoods, up 5.8 per cent over the previous year. The 1955 report included 1,410 new Brotherhoods. By 1959 church records indicated 425,000 men were enrolled in more than 15,000 church Brotherhoods, an all-time high. Enrolment fluctuated up and down for the next four years, but reflected a gradual decline. Records for 1968 showed 261,132 men in 11,120 churches.

Enrolment in Royal Ambassadors.—The Southern Baptist Convention adopted the proposal of the Woman's Missionary Union in 1954 to transfer sponsorship of the Royal Ambassador movement from the WMU to the Baptist Brotherhood Commission. At that time enrolment was 114,974 boys in 8,346 Royal Ambassador chapters. The transfer was completed over a three-year period with a joint committee directing the work. On Oct. 1, 1957, the transfer of Royal Ambassador materials, including *Ambassador Life,* was moved from the WMU in Birmingham, Ala., to the Brotherhood Commission in Memphis, Tenn.

Royal Ambassador enrolment continued to climb the next few years, hitting its highest peak with 244,656 boys in 14,933 chapters in 1963. After four years of declining enrolment the number of RAs climbed to 187,606 in 1968, with 11,096 churches reporting chapters.

Brotherhood Program Changes.—Enrolment of men and boys weren't the only things which changed in Brotherhood work. In designating program responsibilities the charter of the Brotherhood Commission approved in 1956 stated that the commission exists "for the purpose of promoting the work of the Convention among the men and boys who are members of the Southern Baptist churches affiliated with it."

The major duties of the commission were defined as: "To seek and discover the talents of the men and boys in Southern Baptist churches, challenge them to action, and utilize their talents for Christ." To achieve these ends the commission was instructed to (1) develop and project a program of work directed toward the enlistment of men and boys in the life and work of their churches, (2) produce necessary publications, tracts, and other materials through which they will become acquainted with the work of their denomination, and (3) seek to promote and conduct such meetings as may be necessary to build concern among the men and boys in the matter of spreading the Christian message to the farthest reaches of the world.

In 1960 Brotherhood leaders offered a new Brotherhood program to the churches. Men were encouraged to study and work in the areas of Royal Ambassadors, Christian witnessing, personal stewardship, and world missions. As a part of the new program, the commission began publishing an annual *Brotherhood Handbook* which provided a year's program of activities for church Brotherhoods.

The Commission introduced a new Royal Ambassador program to the churches in 1961. It initiated new techniques aimed at attracting and holding the interest of boys in a deeper study and involvement in missions.

The commission defined world missions as the active effort of sharing Christ with all peoples in every part of the world with the purpose of leading them to personal faith in Christ. Leaders defined missionary education as the sum of the efforts of a Baptist Brotherhood to develop in boys a Christlike concern for all peoples, an intimate knowledge of how Christian fellowship is being extended at home and abroad, and a hearty participation in all efforts to enlarge this fellowship of Christian faith until it covers the earth.

As part of a plan to identify more clearly the responsibilities of all agencies, the SBC adopted a new program statement of the Brotherhood Commission in 1965. The objective of the commission was defined as the support of the Convention's task in bringing men to God through Christ by fostering programs that will assist the churches in their tasks of leading men, young men, and boys to a deeper commitment to missions, to a more meaningful prayer life for missions, to a larger stewardship on behalf of missions, and to a personal involvement in missions. The Convention assigned to the commission three programs to reach these objectives: Brotherhood promotion, Royal Ambassador promotion, and supporting services.

In 1967 to better align its work with the newly approved program assignments, the commission adopted a major change in the names and terminology used in the units within the church Brotherhood organization. Under the new concept the word "Brotherhood" described the total missionary education and missions involvement tasks of the church relating to men, young men, and boys. The three divisions were Royal Ambassadors, Baptist Young Men, and Baptist Men.

In keeping with the commission's new program assignment in the area of missionary education and missions promotion, the curriculum materials for the Brotherhood program changed considerably 1965–66. The commission designed the curriculum content of all publications to have missions at its core, and added suggestions for practical mission activities.

In 1970 to meet more adequately the need for guidance during the times of change, the Brotherhood Commission revised three books for leaders. Their new titles were *Brotherhood Program of a Baptist Church, Associational Brotherhood Program,* and *Baptist Men in Missions.* A new quarterly magazine for administering a Brotherhood program in churches and associations, *Brotherhood Builder,* appeared in 1970, replacing the annual *Brotherhood Handbook.*

The first major changes in Royal Ambassador work were reflected in 1959 when the commission announced plans for an enlarged RA program. The main intention of the commission was to keep missionary education at the heart of the movement, at the same time surrounding the program with elements which attract boys to the organization.

On Oct. 1, 1961, the commission released to the churches this enlarged RA program. To inaugurate the new program several books, manuals, and other aids to service the new program were developed. Leaders were trained in the states, associations, and churches. Magazines for boys' work, *Ambassador Life* and *Ambassador Leader,* were redesigned to provide a curriculum plan for the three age groups—Crusaders (ages 9–11), Pioneers (ages 12–14), and Ambassadors (ages 15–17). These publications carried out this purpose until 1970.

In 1967 the commission accepted the responsibility for developing patterns of organization and literature for churches to provide missionary education for boys in school grades 1–3 (ages 6–8) starting in 1970.

The decision to bring boys in grades 1–3 into the RA program grew out of a new grouping-grading plan the Baptist Sunday School Board, Brotherhood Commission, and WMU agreed to support. This plan called for four divisions—preschool, children, youth, and adult, with opportunities for churches to exercise great flexibility in each.

To bring about a curriculum plan for boys in the children's division, the commission agreed to begin providing mission guidance for all boys in the range, effective Oct. 1, 1970. The commission launched two new magazines containing the curriculum for this age group: *Crusader,* a monthly reading magazine for boys, and *Crusader Leader,* a quarterly publication for counselors.

To fulfil its new responsibility among boys of this important age group, the commission offered the churches not only new curriculum materials but also suggestions covering a practical leadership approach. Among these suggestions was the use of both men and women and husband and wife teams in leading the younger boys in their learning experiences in the area of missions education.

New books were published in 1970 which dealt with this age group. *Lad 1* was developed as a manual of requirements for boys 6 years of age and in the first grade. *Lad 2* was developed for boys in the second grade, age 7. *Lad 3* was prepared for 8-year-old boys in the third grade. *Page, Squire,* and *Knight* books were also revised and reissued in 1970. These manuals were for boys 9–11 in the fourth, fifth, and sixth grades. The commission published a revised book, *Crusader Counselor's Guide,* to help the leaders of boys in these age groups.

The book, *Pioneer Counselor's Guide,* for leaders of boys in grades 7–12 (ages 12–17), was revised in 1970 to reflect concept refinements for boys in the youth division. The commission also introduced two advancement manuals: *Pioneer Adventure* for boys in grades 7–9, and *Ambassador Service* for boys in grades 10–12.

Curriculum magazines inaugurated in 1970 for the youth division were *Probe,* a monthly reading magazine for boys, and *Probe* (*Leadership Edition*), for Pioneer boy officers and counselors.

Variety of Mission Experiences.—In the development of new programs for men and boys, a variety of unusual opportunities emerged for men and boys to increase their understanding of missions.

In 1955 the commission began sponsoring a young men's missions conference at Glorieta Baptist Assembly. The next year it was held at Ridgecrest Baptist Assembly. In following years the conference alternated its location between the two assemblies. This type of activity developed into a world missions conference in the summer of 1967, under the sponsorship of the Brotherhood Commission and the WMU, with the cooperation of the Home and Foreign Mission Boards. The first conference attracted 2,276 young men, with 134 decisions for life commitment to world missions. Similar conferences were held at Glorieta in 1968, Ridgecrest in 1969, and Glorieta in 1970.

Mission tours were added in 1955 when the commission sent a team of eight men to view Baptist mission fields in South America. During the same year a team of Brotherhood leaders were sent on a speaking tour of Cuba. Since 1956, the commission has sponsored twelve mission tours to mission fields in Mexico with the cooperation of the FMB.

The First National Conference of Southern Baptist Men sponsored by the Brotherhood Commission convened in the Municipal Auditorium of Oklahoma City in 1957, and attracted 6,282 men. Theme for the conference was "Free Men Through the Ages." The Second National Conference of Baptist Men was held in Memphis Sept. 13–15, 1961, with 4,300 men from 38 states in attendance.

As added emphasis to Layman's Day, Sunday, Oct. 12, 1958, the commission inaugurated a new plan called Layman's Day Soul-Winning Crusade. The idea was to encourage men to visit lost people the week before Layman's Day so that there could be a great gathering of lost souls for Christ on Layman's Sunday. Another purpose of this plan was to prepare and train men for their part in the 1959 simultaneous evangelistic crusades throughout the convention.

In cooperation with the HMB, the Brotherhood Commission promoted a tour of laymen to Alaska to participate in Denominational Week in the churches of that state during 1959.

During 1960 the commission recruited approximately 550 men to serve from four to eight days in pioneer areas in mission work. They served in Colorado, Montana, New York, Ohio, Oregon, Washington, and Wyoming during 1961 under the supervision of pioneer area missionaries. When the final count was in, 822 men had participated in pioneer mission work during 1961. Visible results included 800 professions of faith, 290 joining the church by letter, and 145 rededications.

In 1961 the commission, in cooperation with the HMB, recruited 892 men to assist 575 churches in lay-led revivals on the West Coast. Measurable results of the witnessing men included 29,411 visits on the field, 623 decisions while visiting, 3,004 messages delivered in churches, 582 professions of faith in church services, 428 decisions by letter, 4,347 rededications, 129 decisions for special service, 185 addresses to civic groups and men's breakfasts, and 64 radio and television appearances. Total attendance at services in churches was 161,481.

The commission enlisted 194 men to take part in a simultaneous evangelistic crusade in 96 churches on the Florida Gold Coast in 1967. A similar project in the Northeast involved 285 men. That same year earthquakes and floods in Alaska brought the Brotherhood Commission and HMB together in a recruiting effort to restore churches there. A total of 104 skilled men went on short notice at their own expense to engage in a great rebuilding effort.

The commission developed and correlated plans which involved men in planning for the Crusade of the Americas held in the spring of 1969. The commission helped arrange for the Laymen's Hemispheric Evangelistic Conference held in Rio de Janeiro, July 15–21, 1968.

Activities for boys were just as varied. The second Convention-wide RA Congress held Aug. 12–14, 1957, brought 8,500 boys to Fort Worth, Tex. The program was built around the theme, "Christ in Me, the Hope of the World." The third National RA Congress in Washington, D. C., on Aug. 13–15, 1963 was restricted to boys 12–17. It drew 4,400. The fourth National RA Congress was held Aug. 13–15, 1968, in Oklahoma City, and attracted 10,326 boys 9–17. The theme was world missions.

To meet an interest in camping and relate the activity to missionary education, the commission conducted the first Convention-wide campcraft training course in 1959. Its object was to train leaders to guide boys of RA chapters into vivid outdoor experiences with God.

The next year the Brotherhood Commission published the book, *Royal Ambassador Campcraft,* as an aid in this endeavor.

In cooperation with the FMB, the commission conducted a work camp for older RAs in Mexico during the summer of 1964. Twenty-two boys spent two weeks building elements of a new church at Torreon.

The following year the commission sponsored a service project involving older RAs in Guatemala. This three-week work-and-education tour also included visits to several mission stations in Mexico.

Correlation and Coordination.—In another effort to assist churches, the Brotherhood Commission turned to correlation and coordination with other Southern Baptist boards and agencies. Through conferences with the heads of other boards and agencies, the commission shaped its program and promotional efforts so that the men in the churches would become more thoroughly acquainted with what the entire denomination was seeking to do.

In the area of program servicing the commission arranged with the Sunday School Board in 1960 to begin selling all Brotherhood merchandise through Baptist Book Stores with the exception of magazines. In 1965 the commission joined the Sunday School Board and WMU in a plan to channel to churches through magazines and field services information about denominational emphases.

In the area of curriculum planning, the commission, Sunday School Board, and WMU developed the Life and Work Curriculum used by Southern Baptist churches in 1966–69. This pioneering effort led to more joint efforts in curriculum planning for churches.

Coordination also extended to training. In 1967 the commission's training program was merged into the Church Study Course program. The commission's study books were included as part of Category 21, dealing with Brotherhood principles and methods.

Brotherhood Commission staff members meet regularly with representatives of other Baptist agencies to develop plans and coordinate programs to help the churches carry out Convention-wide emphases.

Building Progress at Brotherhood Commission.—The need for office space at the Brotherhood Commission paralleled program development endeavors. In 1956 the commission completed its first step in a four-stage long range building program by erecting a new office wing. The moving of the Royal Ambassador work from Birmingham to Memphis increased the need for space. In 1957 a $30,000 unit was added to the office building. In Feb., 1959, ground was broken for the erection of the third unit of the long-range building program. The unit, costing more than $170,000 equipped, was occupied in Sept., 1959. It provided space for the promotion and program servicing divisions of the commission. Construction was completed Feb. 1, 1961, for the fourth unit of the commission's long-range building program. This three-story structure contained 11,000 square feet. The cost of this new unit was approximately $135,000, with the third floor left unfinished. This floor was finished four years later at a cost of $70,000.

Early in 1964 the commission purchased a 75 x 168 foot parcel of property (a medical clinic) immediately to the west of its building for $40,000. The commission increased its real estate holdings in 1967 through the purchase of property immediately east and adjoining its present facilities at a cost of $35,183. The next year it bought a residence and lot 50 x 162 feet adjoining commission property on the north and the east for $14,044.

In May, 1969, ground was broken for a new operations building adjoining the main commission building on the east. This two-story, 12,000-square-foot structure, completed Jan. 1, 1970, houses the commission's business, shipping, and storage operations.

Goals for 1970–71.—Facing the immediate future the Brotherhood Commission set a goal of reaching 16,000 churches with a Brotherhood program and increasing to 510,000 the number of men and boys enrolled in Brotherhood, with 300,000 in Baptist Men, and 210,000 in Royal Ambassadors. A goal also was set to increase the total number of credits awarded in the Brotherhood area of the Church Study Course to 10,000 annually. Plans were made to increase the number of associations reporting organized Brotherhood work to 1,000. DARRELL C. RICHARDSON

BROTHERHOOD BUILDER. A quarterly periodical, published by the Brotherhood Commission, first issue dated Oct.–Dec., 1970. The purpose of this publication is to help general Brotherhood officers, pastors, and staff members in churches and associations to plan, coordinate, and evaluate Brotherhood work on a month-to-month and annual basis. Subjects generally are administrative, with suggestions and articles designed to help Brotherhood officers establish and organize units, then sustain their work.

DARRELL C. RICHARDSON

BROTHERHOOD HANDBOOK. An annual paperbound book published by the Brotherhood Commission (1959–69) to give church Brotherhood leadership additional help in making the organizations they lead more effective. *Handbook* sales were 20,721 in 1960. Distribution increased to 26,000 copies in 1964 and reached a peak of 29,367 in 1967. Circulation dropped sharply to 20,590 in 1968, but rose to 21,215 in 1969. This was the last issue of the *Brotherhood Handbook.* It merged with *Brotherhood Builder,* a quarterly magazine.

DARRELL C. RICHARDSON

BROUGHTON, LEONARD GASTON (b. Wake County, N. C., 1864; d. Atlanta, Ga., Feb. 22, 1936). Son of Gaston H. and Louisa Hawkins (Franks) Broughton, he studied at Wake Forest College, N. C., and later graduated from Kentucky School of Medicine, University of Kentucky. While practicing medicine at Reedsville, N. C., he entered the ministry, and was ordained in 1893.

Broughton's first pastorate was the Calvary Baptist Church, Roanoke, Va. In Mar., 1897, he came to Atlanta, Ga., to be pastor of the Third Baptist Church located on Jones Avenue. During his first year he led about 200 members to secure a site near the center of the city and established Tabernacle Baptist Church. While in Atlanta Broughton founded the Tabernacle Baptist Infirmary (1903), which became the Georgia Baptist Hospital (1913), and also established the Tabernacle Dormitory for young women.

Known in Britain and America for his fiery zeal for righteousness, Broughton accepted the pastorate of Christ's Church, London, in 1913, serving until 1918. Returning to America, he served as pastor of the following churches: First, Knoxville, Tenn., 1918–21; Grove Avenue, Richmond, Va., 1921–26; First, Jacksonville, Fla., 1926–29; and Baptist Tabernacle, Atlanta, which he served until declining health forced his retirement in 1931. The remaining years of his ministry were given to evangelism. In addition he was a frequent lecturer on temperance

and a strong advocate of prohibition. He published many pamphlets, articles, and 10 books.
GEORGE EUTING

BROUSSARD, MINNIE KAY (b. DeSoto Parish, La., Mar. 14, 1892; d. Lafayette, La., Oct. 4, 1962). She taught school in Leesville, La., where in 1920 she met and married Moise Broussard. They moved to Lafayette, their home for the rest of their lives, and Mrs. Broussard taught there.

Becoming a Christian after their marriage and, having no formal education, Mr. Broussard attended Acadia Academy for two years to learn to read the Bible. He attended Delgado Trade School in New Orleans, learned the furniture business, and opened a furniture store in Lafayette.

The Broussards led in organizing Northside Baptist Church in Lafayette and were among the 34 charter members. Intensely interested in missions in south Louisiana, they dedicated themselves and much of their money to winning the French to Christ. They gave money for Bibles, church buildings, French radio ministry, missionary salaries, and willed over $100,000 to Acadia Academy and the SBC Home Mission Board.

In unofficial capacities they served their church and others. He enclosed evangelistic tracts in business letters. They maintained a missionary room in their home for visiting preachers and missionaries. They gave baskets of food and other help to the needy without telling anyone. Their many gifts of money were quietly made so that few knew of their philanthropy. They had no children. JOHN G. ALLEY

BROWN, FRED FERNANDO (b. Glenville, Jackson County, N. C., Nov. 27, 1882; d. Knoxville, Tenn., Aug. 9, 1960). Pastor and denominational leader. Son of Horatio Alonzo and Dorcas Elizabeth (Woodard) Brown, he earned the B.A. (1908) and M.A. (1909) from Wake Forest College; Th.M. (1912) and Th.D. (1913) from Southern Baptist Theological Seminary. He married Nona Lee Dover, Apr. 12, 1914. Their children are Nona Lee (Mrs. John A. Kaserman), Ailene (Mrs. W. J. Card), Imogene (Mrs. Hugh Ed Kaserman), Fred F., Jr., and Mary Elizabeth (Mrs. Christian Goedbloed). Ordained in 1913, his pastorates were in Harrodsburg and Frankfort, Ky.; First Baptist Church, Sherman, Tex., 1916–21; and First Baptist Church, Knoxville, Tenn., 1921–1946. He served as special chaplain with American Expeditionary Force and Army of Occupation, World War I, at request of President Woodrow Wilson. He led the devotional service for dedication of Smoky Mountain National Park at request of President Franklin Roosevelt, 1930. He authored the book, *This Is My Church,* in 1929. He was executive secretary of the promotion committee of the Southern Baptist Convention, 1931–33; was a leader in SBC debt-paying campaigns, including the Crucible Service Campaign, 1932–33; and was president of the Convention, 1933. He served as trustee for Carson-Newman College, Southeastern Baptist Theological Seminary, and East Tennessee Baptist Hospital; was director of Tennessee Baptist Orphanage; and member of executive board, Tennessee Baptist Convention. He was awarded the D.D. degree, Wake Forest College, 1925; the LL.D. degree, Carson-Newman College, 1951, and the H.H.D. degree, Lincoln Memorial University, 1951. He was listed in *Who's Who in America,* 1954–55. He was buried in Highland Memorial Cemetery, Knoxville. CHARLES A. TRENTHAM

BROWN, JUNIUS CALVIN (b. Apex, N. C., Dec. 2, 1886; d. Madison, N. C., Dec. 30, 1968). Lawyer. Son of James Gaston and Cornelia Hunter (Brown), Brown received the B.A. and LL.B. from Wake Forest College and began the practice of law in Madison in 1913. He did graduate work in law and letters at the University of Grenoble, France, in 1918. Brown married Eliza Ray Pratt of Madison on Feb. 9, 1921. He served in the North Carolina State Senate in 1923–24. He was attorney for Rockingham County, 1929–59, and for the City of Madison, 1913–63. Brown was a trustee and chairman of the deacons for the First Baptist Church of Madison, and was Sunday School superintendent for 20 years. He established an undergraduate scholarship fund at Wake Forest in 1958 in honor of his wife. The fund, to assist needy and deserving students from North Carolina, is the third largest undergraduate scholarship fund at the university. The Junius Calvin Brown Fellowships in the Wake Forest School of Law were established in 1969 in honor of Brown, who bequeathed half of his estate to the university.
ELIZABETH BRANTLEY

BROWN, THOMAS DANIEL (b. Madison Station, Madison County, Miss., Jan. 29, 1881; d. Anderson, S. C., May 6, 1967). Pastor and teacher. Son of Thomas Daniel and Josephine (Barnes) Brown, he married Mary Eva Rhoades Oct. 9, 1911. They had five children: Thomas Rhoades, twins Mary and Martha, Carolyn, and Ruth. Converted in his teen-age years, he was ordained by First Baptist Church, Canton, Miss., July 25, 1908. He was educated at Mississippi College (B.A., 1908) and Southern Baptist Theological Seminary (Th.M., 1911). He received the D.D. from Ouachita Baptist College, Arkadelphia, Ark., 1915. He served the following Baptist churches as pastor: First, Monroe City, Mo., 1911–12; First, Hope, Ark., 1913–17; First, Little Rock, Ark., 1917–19; First, El Dorado, Ark., 1919–26; St. Charles Ave., New Orleans, La., 1931–34; Highland, Louisville, Ky., 1934–42; First, Hattiesburg, Miss., 1942–46; and First, Macon, Miss., 1947. As an educator he served as teacher and head of the Bible Department, Ouachita Baptist College, 1926–29; and teacher at Clear Creek Mountain School, Pinesville, Ky., 1947–57. Brown also served as executive secretary of the Arkansas Baptist State Convention,

1929–30; editor of the *Baptist Advance,* 1930; trustee of Ouachita College 1915–26; member of the Arkansas State Mission Board, 1922–28; member of the Foreign Mission Board, SBC, 1917–18; and president of the Kentucky General Association, 1941. GEORGE T. BLACKMON

BRUNER, JAMES WILLIAM (b. Hancock County, Ky., Jan. 24, 1881; d. Dallas, Tex., Feb. 13, 1959). Pastor, denominational leader, and founder of Texas Baptist Endowment Department. One of eight children reared in a Catholic home, he was converted and joined a Baptist church at age 19. He graduated from Clinton College, Kentucky, and received the honorary LL.D. degree from Oklahoma Baptist University, 1936. Bruner married Bertha A. McDonald in 1908. They reared six children. Ordained in 1904 by First Baptist Church, Clinton, Ky., he held six student pastorates before accepting Second Baptist Church, Paducah, in 1908. Other pastorates included the First Baptist Churches of Hartford, Ky.; Center, Tex.; Quanah, Tex.; Roswell, N. Mex.; and Chickasha, Okla. He served as state secretary of New Mexico Baptist Convention, led the $75,000,000 Campaign in New Mexico and the $100,000 Club in Oklahoma, was assistant to the president at Southwestern Baptist Theological Seminary, and was secretary of the Endowment Department of Baptist General Convention of Texas from 1940 to 1952. CECIL A. RAY

BRUNER, WESTON (b. Clarkson, Ky., Jan. 21, 1867; d. Richmond, Va., Apr. 2, 1950). Pastor, author, and evangelist. Educated at Bethel College, Kentucky (B.A., 1890; M.A., 1891), and Southern Baptist Theological Seminary (Th.M., 1894; Th.D., 1895), he received an honorary D.D. from Bethel in 1898. He married Mary Kirkpatrick in 1892. After her death in 1900, he married Maria Gwathmey in 1902. He was pastor of churches in Maryland, Virginia, Washington, D. C., Georgia, and Texas. From 1910 to 1917 Bruner was superintendent of evangelism for the Home Mission Board, directing the work of several evangelists. Work was supported by revival offerings. He retired in 1941. Bruner served as trustee, Baptist Bible Institute (New Orleans); member, Sunday School Board; and member, Southern Baptist Hospital Commission. He was a member of Phi Gamma Delta. He wrote: *The Coming Revival, The Soul Winner, Second Coming of Our Lord, The Magic of Making a Man,* and *The Lure of Love.*

JOHN F. HAVLIK

BRYAN, DANIEL BUNYUN (b. Chatham County, N. C., Dec. 23, 1886; d. Wake Forest, N. C., Dec. 9, 1963). Educator. Son of Atlas and Suzanna Bryan, Bryan received his first education at a one-teacher school near Pittsboro. He took an examination and taught in a one-teacher school before going to study at Buies Creek Academy. Later he was principal of the high school at Rich Square for two years. He received the B.A. from the University of North Carolina (1911), the M.A. from Columbia University (1914), and the Ph.D. from New York University (1915). He taught at the University of Richmond (then Richmond College) from 1915–21.

Bryan joined the Wake Forest College faculty in 1921 as professor of education and became dean of the college in 1923. He was dean and professor for 34 years and taught thousands of future teachers before his retirement in 1957. He was a Sunday School teacher and chairman of the board of deacons at Wake Forest Baptist Church. Bryan married Affie Griffin on May 15, 1912. They had five children: D. B., Jr., Euphemia Stone (Mrs. E. H. Platte), Helen (Mrs. W. B. Owen), Mary Griffin (Mrs. G. M. Holt), and Elizabeth (Mrs. Heywood Smith).

ELIZABETH BRANTLEY

BRYAN, NELSON AUGUSTUS (b. Lebanon, Tenn., Nov. 7, 1889; d. San Angelo, Tex., May 21, 1967). Educated at Cumberland University (B.A., 1912) and Vanderbilt University (M.D., 1917), he served as a medical officer, U. S. Navy, 1917–20. He was appointed missionary to China, June 10, 1920. He was superintendent of Warren Memorial Hospital, Hwanghsien, Shantung, 1920–42, and of Yangchow Baptist Hospital, Kiangsu Province, 1946–49. Bryan was interned by the Japanese Army, 1941–42, and repatriated in 1942. He went to Korea in 1951 to do medical relief work. With a Korean doctor, two nurses, and an old Army tent, medical work began, which later developed into the Wallace Memorial Hospital, Pusan. He married Frances Allison, Aug. 14, 1917. They had three children: John Nelson, Ann, and Sarah Frances.

JOHN A. ABERNATHY

BUCKNER, WILLIAMS VORE (b. Eufaula, I. T., now Okla., Dec. 18, 1881; d. Long Beach, Calif., Dec. 16, 1964). The youngest of five children of Henry Frieland Buckner (*q.v.,* Vol. I) and Mollie (Vandivere) Buckner, pioneer missionaries to the Creek Indians, he was baptized at age 12 by his uncle, Robert Cook Buckner (*q.v.,* Vol. I), who also participated in his ordination in 1903.

Buckner attended government schools with the Indians before studying at Bacone College, Muskogee, I. T., and Ouachita College, Arkadelphia, Ark. A soldier in the Spanish-American War, he later taught school, became active in politics, and when Oklahoma achieved statehood he served in both branches of the state legislature. He also served as public lands appraiser, mine inspector, and in various other offices while serving as pastor of small churches.

He "retired" in 1942 and went to California, where he assisted in the organization of no less than 20 churches and served as interim pastor of at least 10 churches, most of which were plagued by financial or fellowship problems. Many of them were strong and thriving churches due to his wise leadership.

Buckner married Ida Ervin in 1904. They had three children: Ruby, Ruth, and Wilson. Mrs. Buckner died in 1956 and the following year he married Zulieka Alexander. FLOYD LOONEY

***BUCKNER BAPTIST BENEVOLENCES.** Buckner Benevolences now compromises nine units of work, operating in five regional centers. Those located in Dallas are Buckner Baptist Children's Home (formerly Buckner Orphans Home) with space for 420 dependent, neglected children; Buckner Baptist Trew Home for the Aging, a custodial care unit opened in 1954, with space for 101, Buckner Baptist Ryburn Home, added in 1966, and providing skilled nursing care for 104 residents, and 22 cottages with 44 occupants; Buckner Baptist Maternity Home for unwed mothers, opened in 1966, with a capacity of 42; and Buckner Baptist Marriage and Family Counseling Center, added in 1963, and located in the Family Services building on the Children's Home campus. In Houston the Buckner Baptist Haven for Aging, opened in 1955, cares for 114 persons. In San Antonio, Buckner Baptist Maternity Home has a capacity of 35, and in Lubbock, Buckner Baptist Children's Home (formerly Buckner Home for Girls, opened in 1955) has a capacity of 96. In Burnet, Buckner Baptist Boys Ranch has a capacity of 72.

The total property value of all Buckner's units as of Aug. 31, 1969, was $7,611,726. The total budget for all units in 1968–69 was $2,705,336. Buckner is supported through the Cooperative Program of Texas Baptists; endowment, held by the Baptist Foundation of Texas; income from wills, trusts, and bequests; resident support; and individual and church contributions. The total income for 1968–69 was $2,706,118.

In addition to its resident-care services, Buckner also provides mother's aid, a program designed to help a widowed or deserted mother keep her children in her own home; private home foster care; church-sponsored foster group homes; and a work-oriented camp program, to help boys who are unable to adjust to a structured, well-ordered society. R. C. CAMPBELL

***BUDGET OF THE CONVENTION.** Since 1959 the Executive Committee, SBC, has worked out the Convention budget in the following manner: (1) The agencies are requested to submit comprehensive descriptions of their budget and financial needs on a program basis. (2) This material is carefully reviewed by all the members of the Executive Committee. (3) The agencies are asked to present publicly their needs orally to the members of the Executive Committee. (4) The program committee, carefully considering the work to be accomplished, makes proposals to the Executive Committee on the distribution of funds. (5) The Executive Committee recommends the Cooperative Program budget to the Convention. Beginning in 1971 the Convention fiscal year will run from Oct. 1 to Sept. 30. Most agencies will operate on the same schedule. The Convention does not approve agency budgets. In addition to the Cooperative Program Budget the Executive Committee develops for Convention approval an SBC Operating Budget which covers the cost of the annual meeting, the *Annual,* special committees, and the Executive Committee. All agencies are required to report to the Convention on the use of all funds.

ALBERT MC CLELLAN

BURKHALTER, FRANK ELISHA (b. Cotton Gin, Freestone County, Tex., Apr. 19, 1880; d. Waco, Tex., May 23, 1963). Newspaperman, publicity director, and professor of journalism. Son of P. H. and Sallie (McMillan) Burkhalter, he was educated at Baylor University (Ph.B., 1907) and Columbia University (A.B., 1908). After newspaper work in Fort Worth, San Antonio, and Waco, Tex., he became editor-in-chief of Waco (Tex.) *Morning News,* 1915–16. He served as publicity director of Texas A & M College, 1918–19; publicity director of the 75 Million Campaign, 1919–25; and continued as publicity director of the Cooperative Program, 1925–29. He contributed significantly to the success of these programs. He was a deacon, First Baptist Church, Nashville, Tenn., and First Baptist Church, Waco. In Nashville, he served as Sunday School superintendent and teacher of 16-year-old Intermediate boys. He was active leader of Boys Club work in Waco, 1911–16, and 1930–63. He taught journalism at Baylor University, 1929–45, and in Biarritz (France) American University, 1945. Burkhalter never married. He wrote nine books, including *Winning the Adolescent Boy* (1935), *Living Abundantly* (1942), and *Men Following the Master* (1959). He also contributed to the *Centennial History of Texas Baptists* (1936) and *Encyclopedia of Southern Baptists* (1958).

MERRILL D. MOORE

***BURMA BAPTIST CONVENTION.** Representing nearly 250,000 Baptists in Burma, this body is composed of representatives from 17 tribal groups, each with a different language, which in turn promote their work through associations.

In Mar., 1966, the Burma government canceled the stay permits of all Protestant missionaries and about two-thirds of the Catholic missionaries. Most of the missionaries had to be out of the country by the end of May. A period of active transfer of responsibilities and property followed. Fortunately for the Baptists, all churches had long had their own pastors. Thus the church program continued uninterrupted, as did the administration of the Burma Baptist Convention, the Baptist Board of Publication, and the language group Baptist conventions and associations.

The state took over the responsibilities for schools and hospitals. National Christians in turn took over the work carried on by the missionaries. Nineteen seminaries and Bible Schools are training new leaders for the churches of Burma. The Publication Society is preparing concordances to Judson's Burmese Bible and the Sgaw Karen Bible, and Judson Aung has been appointed editor and translator of a one-volume Bible commentary to be produced in Burmese.

With a membership now of over 241,000, Baptists in Burma outnumber Roman Catholics two to one, and all other Protestants 20 to one. In 1967 there were 2,135 national workers, 2,546 churches, 9,169 baptisms, 241,052 church members, and 866 Sunday Schools, with 34,846 pupils. Burma Baptists are cooperative interdenominationally. They are affiliated with the Burma Christian Council, the East Asia Christian Conference, the Baptist World Alliance, and the World Council of Churches.

Burma is still closed to outsiders except for tourists who may stay only 24 hours and those on government business. Likewise, Burma Baptists are unable to attend conferences outside the country because of restrictions on all Burma citizens. The Baptists there are then grateful for the brief visits and letters. In 1969 word comes from the field that "Baptists in Burma are stronger than ever numerically, in commitment to God, and in determination to 'Arise and Build' for Christ." JAMES D. MOSTELLER

BURNETT, GEORGE JACKSON (b. Auburn, Ky., Dec. 26, 1874; d. Waco, Tex., Feb. 7, 1959). Son of Joseph Herndon and Laura (Duff) Burnett, he was educated at Bethel College (B.A., M.A.). He taught in private schools and was assistant principal of the Loudon Seminary (Tennessee), 1894–96. He also was instructor in Latin and mathematics at Liberty College, Glasgow, Ky., 1897–98. He married Laura Taylor Yates in 1903. They had four daughters.

In 1899 Burnett became vice-president and acting head of Liberty College, of which his father was president. When his father resigned, he became president. In 1907 he was asked by Tennessee Baptists to set up the proposed Tennessee College for Women. He served as its president until 1924. From 1924 until his death Burnett spent his efforts in refinancing denominational colleges. He was a member of the Association of Colleges and Secondary Schools, president of the Tennessee Baptist Convention, 1915–17, and president of the Tennessee College Association, 1921–22. MRS. AGNES G. FORD

BURNEY, SARAH JOE HURST (b. Waynesboro, Ga., May 11, 1882; d. Covington, Ga., Aug. 21, 1963). Denominational and Woman's Missionary Union leader. Wife of Frank S. Burney, a lawyer, she lived in Waynesboro, Ga., where she was active throughout her life in First Baptist Church. Thirteen years as Georgia WMU Margaret Fund chairman, she was also WMU, SBC, chairman, 1922–38. Burney Gifts to Margaret Fund students were named in her honor.

As Georgia WMU president and vice-president, WMU, SBC, 1937–42, she led Georgia to reach WMU, SBC, 50th anniversary goals, which were to begin interracial meetings (now annual Baptist women's institutes) as follow-up to 1939 Baptist World Alliance; commemorate Lottie Moon's Cartersville residence by placing a marker at First Baptist Church; and magnify its support of the Cooperative Program.

She represented Georgia on the Convention's Committee on Boards in 1942, nominating the first woman ever elected to the Home Mission Board. One of first women to address the chair from the Convention's floor, she was a member of the Executive Committee, 1946–51, and camp chairman when the state WMU-owned Camp Pinnacle was established at Clayton, Ga. Her lifelong concern for youth and love for WMU were expressed in family gifts to the camps and a generous personal bequest to Georgia WMU. She was prayer chairman on the state WMU executive board, 1956–60, writing its 75th anniversary history, *Wrought of God* (1960).

DOROTHY PRYOR

BURNEY GIFTS. Personal gift checks sent three times during the regular academic year to all Margaret Fund students. The Burney Gifts plan was inaugurated in 1938 in honor of Mrs. Frank S. Burney (*q.v.*), Georgia, Margaret Fund chairman, 1922–38. Woman's Missionary Union members contribute to the Burney Gifts Fund according to their state plans. The money is channeled through WMU, SBC, and the three checks are sent in the name of all members. Interest from WMU endowment funds also provides resources.

Former Margaret Fund students appointed as regular missionaries of the Home or Foreign Mission Board receive a special gift of $100 from the Burney Fund. Those appointed as missionary associates, missionary journeymen, or US-2 missionaries receive $50 from the fund.

DORIS DEVAULT

BURNS, PERCY PRATT (b. Jemison, Ala., June 7, 1884; d. Birmingham, Ala., June 4, 1957). Educator. Son of Baptist minister Amaziah Erasmus and Ella Isadora (Deramus) Burns, he was educated in the public schools of Alabama, Howard College (B.A., *summa cum laude,* 1904), and Harvard University (M.A., 1920). Mercer University bestowed on him the Litt.D., 1928. On June 26, 1912, he married Effie Salena Sheppard of Edgefield, S. C. He returned to Howard in 1911, served briefly as registrar and dean of students, then became head of the English department, 1912–57, and academic dean, 1924–57. Burns was chairman of the board of directors of the *Alabama Baptist,* 1945–57. He was buried in Elmwood Cemetery, Birmingham.

RAY M. ATCHISON

BURRIS, CRAVEN CULLOM (b. Stanly County, N. C., Mar. 6, 1891; d. Monroe, N. C., Jan. 24, 1969). Son of James Taylor and Frances

(Allen) Burris, he attended Wingate School and graduated from Wake Forest College (B.A., 1917; M.A., 1928). He married Virginia Currie of Raeford, N. C., on July 11, 1921. They had six children: James C., Mary (Mrs. Harry H. Hall), Craven Allen, William C., Frances (Mrs. Thomas Crooke), and Robert N.

Ordained to the ministry in 1917, he served as pastor of rural churches in North Carolina, 1917–68, including King Street, Waxhaw (25 years), and Hopewell in Union County (30 years). For 50 years he was associated with Wingate Junior College, Wingate, N. C., where he taught Latin and English, served as dean, 1927–37, and as president, 1937–54. During his administration, Wingate College was accepted by the Baptist State Convention of North Carolina as one of the family of Baptist colleges in North Carolina (1947), and in 1951 the college was accredited by the Southern Association of Colleges and Schools. Upon his retirement as president, he was elected president-emeritus and taught English until 1962. For many years he was chairman of the Union County Board of Education. He is buried at Wingate, N. C.

JAMES H. BLACKMORE

BUTLER, CLARENCE ANDREW (b. Cherryville, Mo., Sept. 23, 1896; d. Bolivar, Mo., Nov. 23, 1963). Son of Thomas A. and Mattie Garrison Butler, he married Alma Dye in Arnett, Okla., in 1915. They had four children. Butler graduated from Oklahoma Baptist University (B.S., 1925) and Oklahoma University (M.A., 1929). In 1953 he joined the sociology faculty at California Baptist College, and in 1954 became registrar. He retired in 1961 and moved to Missouri, but ended retirement to teach at Southwest Baptist College until his death.

CECIL M. HYATT

BUTLER, JOSEPH REUBEN (b. Sligo, Mo., May 2, 1897; d. Riverside, Calif., Aug. 12, 1966). Son of Thomas A. and Mattie Garrison Butler, he studied at Oklahoma Baptist University, but interspersed his study with periods of teaching in public schools, until his graduation with the B.A. degree in 1929. Later he earned the M.A. from the University of Missouri. He married Lena Grayson in Fargo, Okla. Experienced in public schools as a teacher, coach, principal, and superintendent, he moved to Escondido, Calif., to teach math in 1946 and brought recognition to himself as author of *Short Cuts in Mathematics* and as coach of winning math teams. He came to California Baptist College in 1954 to assist in developing the teacher training program.

CECIL M. HYATT

C

***CALIFORNIA, BAPTIST FOUNDATION OF.** Julian L. Stenstrom resigned as executive secretary-treasurer of the foundation in July, 1960. During his tenure, operation of the Broadway Plan of Church Finance was assumed, a building purchased, a staff acquired, and a printing plant established. Arlie McDaniel, chairman of the foundation's board of directors and former president of the Southern Baptist General Convention of California, served as executive secretary from Sept. 1, 1960, until Dec. 1, 1962. During this period, the foundation operation was stabilized, as an operational gain was achieved, the press showed a small profit for the first time (in 1962), and plans were laid to revitalize the Broadway Plan. Carol Nichols, pastor of the First Southern Baptist Church of Salinas, was elected to succeed McDaniel, Apr. 18, 1963.

In Feb., 1966, David C. Oglesby, business manager of the convention, became assistant executive secretary-treasurer of the foundation, and became acting executive secretary-treasurer upon Nichols' resignation, Mar. 12, 1966. Oglesby instituted a program of administrative and fiscal reforms. Cecil J. Pearson became executive secretary-treasurer, Nov. 1, 1966. Pearson studied law before entering the ministry and was an avid student of business and finance. Stringent cost controls, further changes in administrative procedure, and staff reductions began to improve a bleak financial picture.

In Nov., 1966, the state convention described the proper function of the foundation as "the securing and managing of endowment funds." The foundation was forbidden to buy and sell for a profit. Action as a lending or collection agency was discouraged. The administrative expenses of the foundation were to be borne by the convention, and the same fiscal procedures observed as the other convention agencies sharing Cooperative Program money. Ownership and operation of the printing press was conveyed to the convention. A Division of Church Finance (California Plan of Church Finance) was established, with separate bookkeeping and direction, separating the church financing function from the foundation.

R. Bates Ivey was selected to head the finance division in Mar., 1967. Oglesby returned to the position of convention business manager. An operating gain was shown for 1967, as compared with losses in the $40,000 bracket for the years 1964–66. The foundation, now housed in the new Baptist building, granted a 10-year lease on its old quarters. A third annual substantial operating gain was achieved in 1969. California Plan of Church Finance had issued almost $1,000,000 in church debentures during the year. The church loan portfolio was in good condition. Several strong new trusts had been written, and nonprofitable trusts eliminated. Although church financing had in the past overshadowed estate planning and endowment fund management (for which the foundation primarily exists), an incalculable contribution had been made to the proliferation of Southern Baptist churches in California and to evangelistic outreach. While the history of the foundation had been dominated by a series of fiscal and administrative crises, the total assets of the foundation grew to almost $2,400,000 in 17 years. PAUL HAMM

***CALIFORNIA, THE SOUTHERN BAPTIST GENERAL CONVENTION OF.** The latter half of the fifties saw continuing gains for Southern Baptists in California, but growth rates slowed during the sixties. The initial surge of growth which, in a 20-year period, produced more than 700 new churches and a new state convention with three agencies, gave way to internal development and reorganization as problems arose.

Internal problems in the convention's agencies, Sunny Crest Children's Home, California Baptist College, and California Baptist Foundation, prompted the convention's board of directors to seek the right to review and approve the budgets, bylaws, and the composition of the boards of the convention's auxiliaries.

In 1957 the convention approved a recommendation from its board of directors that a committee be appointed to conduct a long-range study of the financial need and administrative structure of all programs and agencies of the convention. This committee was composed of Robert D. Hughes, chairman, Robert Wells, B. LaVern Lewis, Harold E. Dye, Dale Hufft, Mrs. Carol Nichols, Charles Kendrick, Arlie L. McDaniel, Sr., V. B. Breazeale, and John Watson, who later resigned when employed by Sunny Crest Children's Home. The committee employed the management consultant firm of Booz, Allen, and Hamilton, which had studied several Southern Baptist organizations.

The convention was called into special session, May 9–11, 1960, to act on the extensive report of its special committee. The result was a sweeping reorganization as the convention spelled out the relation of the auxiliary agencies and institutions to the executive board and to the convention itself. It settled the question of the composition and selection of boards, providing 32 members for the executive board, 16 for the California Southern Baptist Board of Christian Higher Education (trustees for California Baptist College and other educational institutions if any are created), 16 for the board of directors of the California Baptist Foundation, and 20 for the California Southern Baptist Board of Child Care. Members serve a four-year term and may not be reelected until a lapse of one year.

Eight committees were made responsible for other convention business. Members serve a three-year term and may not be reelected to a committee until a lapse of one year. One committee, the committee on committees, is appointed by the convention president and the two vice-presidents. The following committees are elected by the convention: committee on convention arrangements, committee on credentials, committee on order of business, committee on resolutions, committee on memorials, committee on Southern Baptist history in California, and the committee on board nominations.

The special convention of 1960 clearly stated that each convention agency is subject to the convention itself. It gave a committee of the executive board the responsibility of acting as a continuing overall long-range planning committee. The executive board has responsibility of reviewing the budgets, audits, and annual reports of the agencies as well as considering their requests for convention support through the annual Cooperative Program budget. A comprehensive business and financial plan restricts the agencies from creating indebtedness beyond a certain point without the approval of the convention. New programs may not be inaugurated without convention approval.

The major portion of the report adopted in 1960 related to the structure and programs assigned to the executive board, previously called the board of directors. A total reorganization was made. The executive secretary, formerly elected by the convention, was made the executive secretary-treasurer of the executive board, elected by the board. He is the chief program planning and administrative officer of the board, and has the added responsibility of serving as the secretary-treasurer of the convention itself. Three assistant executive secretaries are authorized in the program structure. Each is the head of one of the three divisions, which are the church services division, the cooperative missions division, and the stewardship and public relations division. This latter division has not yet been implemented. A business manager, on an organizational level with the assistant executive secretaries but without the title, is the chief financial and business services assistant to the executive secretary. Other professional assistants, notably a program analyst, in offices not yet implemented, are suggested to assist the executive secretary in planning the convention's overall program.

The California Southern Baptist is recognized as a separate auxiliary agency of the convention but under the supervision of the executive board with the editor directly responsible to the board, as is the executive secretary.

The years since 1960 have been years of implementation of the changes ordered. While the greatest changes were made in the structure of the executive board, and in the overall convention structure, a process was instituted whereby continuing studies would be conducted by the executive board. These special studies have resulted in a complete change of program in 1964 for Sunny Crest Children's Home from a program of institutional child care to one of foster home placement, with a major emphasis on family services and the possibility of further development of a broad range of social ministries. In 1966 sweeping changes were ordered for the California Baptist Foundation. In 1967 the convention adopted an extensive study of California Baptist College, making many recommendations for academic, financial, and administrative development.

Within the executive board, the major change was in giving the executive secretary a clearer administrative responsibility over the staff and programs and in defining program responsibilities and relationships. A church services division was created, grouping the departments of Sunday School, church training, Brotherhood, Woman's Missionary Union (which was made a department under the executive board instead of an auxiliary to the convention), student work, church music, and evangelism into a single division to aid in developing a balanced and correlated program. Stewardship education and promotion was made a department within the church services division, pending further study of the advisability of making it a division as voted in 1960.

Shelton Gambrell Posey retired as executive secretary, Dec. 31, 1960, and was given the title of executive secretary-treasurer emeritus. Grady C. Cothen was elected to succeed him on Feb. 10, 1961. He led in the first major steps of reorganization, resigning June 10, 1966, to become president of Oklahoma Baptist University. Robert D. Hughes, who had previously served as state convention president, chairman of the executive board, and chairman of the special long-range planning committee, became executive scretary-treasurer, Dec. 1, 1966.

Edmond R. Walker became the first assistant executive secretary of the executive board, Jan. 1, 1957, directing the missions program. Under the new organization following 1960, Richard Kay was elected the assistant executive secretary in charge of the church services division, Nov. 27, 1961. When Edmond Walker resigned in Aug., 1963, to become executive secretary of the Hawaii Baptist Convention, Ralph E. Longshore was elected to succeed him on Sept. 9, as assistant executive secretary and director of the cooperative missions division. David C. Oglesby was elected business manager Sept. 9, 1963, holding the post continuously except for several months he served as acting executive secretary of the California Baptist Foundation during a pe-

CALIFORNIA STATISTICAL SUMMARY

Year	Associations	Churches	Church Membership	Baptisms	S. S. Enrolment	V.B.S. Enrolment	T. U. Enrolment	W.M.U. Enrolment	Brotherhood Enrolment	Music Enrolment	Mission Gifts	Total Gifts	Value Church Property
1955	31	515	97,169	10,381	106,488	39,687	39,510	15,724	7,367		$ 372,627	$ 5,082,712	
1956	37	563	104,532	11,033	115,023	40,154	45,065	17,297	7,767		871,994	6,812,120	$22,721,898
1957	36	627	117,142	10,772	121,366	49,503	50,721	21,022	6,746	8,252	948,043	6,869,967	26,787,965
1958	37	664	134,028	14,010	130,892	52,317	57,730	22,713	9,470	9,341	1,033,345	8,519,724	39,369,489
1959	38	710	143,978	12,046	134,698	59,780	59,142	23,402	9,705	9,944	1,126,931	8,193,266	32,146,911
1960	39	728	156,176	11,503	145,097	66,336	58,399	23,952	8,241	10,440	1,217,460	11,369,210	42,229,027
1961	38	748	165,544	12,006	150,930	69,918	65,471	24,978	9,875	11,706	1,296,391	11,175,879	45,823,210
1962	41	750	178,265	11,876	157,984	76,576	68,784	25,127	8,296	13,490	1,486,189	12,518,868	55,369,783
1963	40	767	178,524	11,491	162,663	78,213	69,839	25,283	8,471	14,992	1,573,411	13,408,562	74,229,976
1964	40	799	196,670	13,179	168,500	84,211	69,743	24,874	8,407	16,477	1,748,649	14,385,920	72,094,616
1965	40	829	201,905	12,650	177,750	90,921	71,219	26,172	7,694	14,174	1,815,052	15,585,216	81,456,252
1966	38	851	221,187	12,182	175,449	98,688	70,944	26,814	8,669	17,369	1,910,517	16,020,198	88,244,069
1967	38	855	230,182	13,490	177,678	102,989	71,452	27,033	9,054	18,508	1,959,262	17,433,721	97,373,264
1968	36	251	237,819	13,809	176,061	85,973	75,830	25,186	8,503	18,707	2,072,541	18,557,076	99,795,026

J. TERRY YOUNG

riod of internal crisis in that agency. He replaced Dale Brister.

The Sunday School Department is led by R. L. Pattillo, Jr., who became department director, Sept. 8, 1959, succeeding W. Alvis Strickland, after having served previously as an associate in the department and as a general missionary in California.

The Church Training Department is directed by Valton Prince who was elected Nov. 9, 1964, to succeed James Frost who had held the post since Aug., 1956. Frost, who had succeeded Russell Noel, resigned May 31, 1962, to accept a pastorate but was reelected to the convention post July 10, 1962, feeling he should remain in denominational work.

The Brotherhood Department is presently combined with the Church Music Department, directed by Duane Barrett who assumed the dual responsibility, Jan. 1, 1969, after having served as an associate in church training and music since Feb., 1965. James C. Graves was elected Brotherhood director, Apr. 16, 1962, succeeding Walter Bisbee who had resigned Dec. 31, 1961. Graves assumed half-time responsibility for stewardship education and promotion, Feb. 1, 1965.

The stewardship education and promotion program became a full-time department under Graves' direction, Jan. 1, 1969.

The WMU Department is directed by Miss Eula Stotts who was elected Sept. 1, 1964. Having been an associate in the department since Oct. 1, 1957, she replaced Miss Clara Lane who had resigned Dec. 31, 1963.

The Department of Evangelism is directed by Harry D. Williams, Jr., who assumed his duties Dec. 1, 1969, succeeding William Eugene Grubbs, who had resigned in Nov., 1968, to become executive secretary of the Oregon-Washington convention. Grubbs, elected Jan. 28, 1965, had followed D. Wade Armstrong who served from Feb. 1, 1957, until Aug. 31, 1964. Armstrong succeeded Hurschel H. Stagg, who became an associational missionary and soon retired.

The Student Department director is Wendell J. Foss, who on Oct. 1, 1969, succeeded Edward S. Rollins who had held the post since Nov. 1, 1956. Foss had served as an associate in the Sunday School department since Apr., 1962.

The language missions department is directed by E. Jack Combs. He served in this capacity under the Home Mission Board from May 1, 1955, and on Jan. 1, 1960, his work was transferred to the executive board of the California convention in keeping with a change in HMB policies.

The Department of Work with National Baptists is led by Jack O'Neal who was elected director, Nov. 27, 1961.

In 1962, four and one-half acres of land in the northeast section of Fresno was purchased for a future building site. In 1963 the convention was unexpectedly faced with major renovations of its old downtown building, to bring it up to existing building codes. Since it was not feasible to make expensive modifications to an aged building which was badly overcrowded, the convention voted to build a new three-story office building containing 30,000 square feet, costing $587,000. It was occupied in Oct., 1965.

Through the convention's history there has been a strong emphasis on starting new missions and churches and upon evangelism. Churches in the convention once established 110 new missions on a single day, July 29, 1956. Statewide evangelistic campaigns have been held frequently, the most notable being an attempt to baptize 50,000 converts in 1958, the Encounter-California Crusade in 1968, and the Crusade of the Americas in 1969. In recent years there has been a growing interest in Christian social ministries as evidenced by the redirection of the child care program in 1964, inauguration of several programs under the cooperative missions division in cooperation with the Home Mission Board, adoption in 1968 of the Southern Baptist Convention's Statement Concerning the Crisis in the Nation as the sentiment of the California convention, and intensive studies of a Christian approach to social problems by the convention's executive board staff.

The Cooperative Program has been heavily emphasized as the basic means of supporting all Baptist work outside the local church. Special offerings for state causes have had only limited success. Financial needs have grown much faster than income for the state convention and the present convention staff is approximately the same size as in 1956. J. TERRY YOUNG

*CALIFORNIA ASSOCIATIONS.

I. New Associations. BETHEL. Organized as Tri-County, in 1955, with eight churches having 899 members. In 1958 name was changed to South Tulare County. In 1966 name was again changed to Bethel.

CALVARY-ARROWHEAD. Organized Nov. 7, 1961, as a merger of Calvary and Arrowhead, with 54 churches and 12,014 members.

CRESCENT BAY-WEST LOS ANGELES. Organized Oct. 20, 1959, with 18 churches reporting 4,184 members, formerly with San Fernando Valley and Los Angeles.

EAST BAY. Organized Oct. 12, 1956, as a merger of Golden Gate and West Contra Costa, with 42 churches and 7,968 members.

HIGH DESERT. Organized Oct. 10, 1968, by a merger of Antelope Valley, Eastern Sierra, and Mojave Desert associations, with 26 churches and 5,109 members.

KERN COUNTY. On Oct. 14, 1963, San Joaquin Valley changed its name to Kern County.

LIVERMORE-AMADOR. Organized in 1968 with four churches from South Bay Association with 1,010 members.

LONG BEACH-HARBOR. Organized Oct. 21, 1955, with eight churches and 2,810 members, formerly in Los Angeles Association.

MID-VALLEY. Organized Oct. 14, 1965, from merger of Fresno and Fresno-Madera associa-

CALIFORNIA SOUTHERN BAPTIST GENERAL CONVENTION (*q.v.*) OFFICE BUILDING, Fresno. Built in 1965 at a cost of $587,000. Provides offices for convention and Baptist Book Store.

CALIFORNIA BAPTIST COLLEGE (*q.v.*), Administration Building, Riverside. One of nine buildings of Spanish-style architecture on a 75-acre campus. Enrolment 690 in 1970.

FIRST BAPTIST CHURCH, Gulfport, Miss. A colonial structure representative of many church buildings completed within the decade 1960–70.

MACEDONIA BAPTIST CHURCH, Brookhaven, Miss., one of the largest rural churches in Mississippi.

FIRST BAPTIST CHURCH, Vicksburg, Miss. Auditorium.

tions, including 39 churches with 8,829 members.

MOTHER LODE. Organized in Oct., 1958, with three churches and 122 members.

SACRAMENTO. On Oct. 14, 1955, name changed from Sacramento-Sierra when Sierra Foothills was organized.

SANTA CRUZ. Organized Oct. 17, 1955, with four churches and 288 members, from Monterey Association.

SHASTA. Organized July 4, 1955, with six churches and 492 members.

SIERRA FOOTHILLS. Organized Oct. 24, 1954, with seven churches and 896 members, formerly in Sacramento-Sierra Association.

TRINITY. Organized May 25, 1956, with eight churches and 918 members, formerly with Calvary Association.

II. Changes in Associations. ANTELOPE VALLEY. Organized June 5, 1962, with eight churches and 1,658 members. On Oct. 10, 1968, it merged with Eastern Sierra and Mojave Desert to form High Desert Association.

ARROWHEAD. Organized Oct. 25, 1956, with 10 churches and 1,571 members. Merged with Calvary Association to form Calvary-Arrowhead on Nov. 7, 1961.

CALVARY. Merged with Arrowhead, Nov. 7, 1961, to form Calvary-Arrowhead.

EASTERN SIERRA. Organized in 1962 with four churches having 704 members formerly of Mojave Desert Association. On Oct. 10, 1968, it merged with Antelope Valley and Mojave Desert to form High Desert Association.

FRESNO. Merged with Fresno-Madera to form Mid-Valley, Oct. 14, 1965.

FRESNO-MADERA. Merged with Fresno to form Mid-Valley, Oct. 14, 1965.

GOLDEN GATE. In 1956 merged with West Contra Costa to form East Bay.

METROPOLITAN LOS ANGELES. Organized in 1961, voted to join the San Fernando Valley Association, Oct. 12, 1967.

MID-WAY. Disbanded Oct. 1, 1960, with churches affiliating with adjacent associations.

MOJAVE. Merged with Antelope Valley and Eastern Sierra, Oct. 10, 1968, forming High Desert.

NEW HOPE. Organized in 1957 with nine churches having 861 members from Mid-Way and Central Valley. On May 1, 1963, it joined with Central Valley.

SACRAMENTO-SIERRA. On Oct. 14, 1955, it shortened its name to Sacramento.

SAN GABRIEL VALLEY. Merged with Los Angeles Association Oct. 18, 1965.

SAN JOAQUIN VALLEY SOUTHERN MISSIONARY. Changed name to Kern County Oct. 14, 1963.

SOUTH BAY. Organized Oct. 9, 1961, with 23 churches and 4,714 members from a division of East Bay. Merged with East Bay again in 1967.

SOUTH TULARE COUNTY. Organized in 1955 as Tri-County, changed name in 1958. Name changed again in 1966 to Bethel.

TRI-COUNTY. Organized Oct. 20, 1955, with eight churches having 899 members from Fresno-Madera Association. Name changed in 1958 to South Tulare County. Name changed to Bethel in 1966.

WEST CONTRA COSTA. Merged with Golden Gate, 1956, to form East Bay. J. TERRY YOUNG

***CALIFORNIA BAPTIST COLLEGE.** In 1955 the leadership of the college initiated a program of advance to secure academic accreditation and to enlarge and improve its faculty and facilities. The college made a new approach to financing with the employment of Dewey Squyres, who took a year's leave of absence from his pastorate to raise funds for the institution. Two prior ventures for raising money—the operation of a rest home for elderly people and the operation of a farm—had proved to be economically inadequate. In 1957 the college employed J. L. Harden as business manager.

During the years prior to receiving accreditation, an arrangement with La Sierra College made it possible for a student to meet the requirements for a teaching credential. Furthermore, all Southern Baptist seminaries accepted graduates of the college without academic reservations.

P. Boyd Smith, first president of the college, resigned in the school year of 1957–58, and T. W. Medearis, chairman of the California Southern Baptist Board of Christian Higher Education, served as acting president until the election of Loyed R. Simmons, as president in July, 1958. On Oct. 20, 1958, Simmons was inaugurated as president, Robert E. Craig was installed as academic dean, and Olie T. Brown became dean of students.

The Western Association of Schools and Colleges made its initial visit to the campus on Nov. 20, 1959, investigated the school, and made recommendations for improvements before requesting an examination for accreditation. Part of their recommendation involved financial support. A special fund raising campaign by the Southern Baptist General Convention of California provided the funds needed. On Oct. 23, 1961, the Western Association granted the college a two-year preliminary accreditation.

When the school moved to Riverside in 1955, the library contained 4,000 volumes. Sibyl C. Brown, librarian, promoted a book-of-the-month plan through the Training Unions of Southern Baptist churches over the state, which increased the holdings substantially. Contributors of major gifts include Judge and Mrs. J. S. Bracewell, Mr. and Mrs. William Fleming, Edith Boyington, and Annie Gabriel (*q.v.*), for whom the library is named because of a gift of her life's savings of 180 shares of stock in American Telephone and Telegraph Company. A unique collection within the library is the D. E. Wallace Library on Evangelism and Psychology. At the time of accreditation, the library contained 27,000 volumes. By 1969 the holdings reached 77,000 volumes.

Other affiliations and developments concurrent with the program for accreditation include the school's membership in the Council for the Advancement of Small Colleges; a memorial gift of rental property valued at $100,000 by the A. A. Wallace family in memory of their deceased son and former faculty member, D. E. Wallace (*q.v.*) ; the election of Floy S. Wise as academic dean upon the resignation of Robert E. Craig; the purchase of five acres of adjoining land and the erection of two apartment buildings for married student housing; and acceptance of a plan to erect the Book of Life Building conceived by L. E. Nelson, chairman of the Division of Humanities. Dewey H. Jones became dean of the college following the retirement of Floy S. Wise in 1965.

A. A. Wallace, enamoured by the Book of Life concept, issued a challenge to the college by a gift of additional income property valued at $112,000, contingent upon matching contributions. This would finance the first unit to house a chapel in a building designed to illustrate the vast and varied influence of the Bible in the lives of men and in society.

In 1965 the college adopted a new master plan for better use of the campus site, featuring a module pattern, and the college constructed a women's residence hall (housing 274) , a men's residence hall (housing 162) , and a gymnasium. The construction of the residence halls released valuable space in the administrative buildings which could be used for administrative and instructional purposes and for library expansion.

Accreditation by the Western Association of Schools and Colleges opened the doors of professional societies to the faculty and graduates. In 1969 a chapter of the Alpha Chi national honor society was installed on the campus.

The teacher training program at the college is highly regarded among professional educational groups in southern California. The department is fully recognized by the California State Department of Education and Riverside and adjoining school districts have invited participation in a program of intern teaching and student teaching. It is noteworthy that upon completion of this program of work, without exception, every student has been offered a contract with the district for employment as a teacher.

Guidelines for future growth and development of the college were adopted by the Southern Baptist General Convention of California in 1967. The primary objective is quality education.

Among those who made a singular contribution in the establishment and development of the college are C. A. Butler (*q.v.*) , J. R. Butler, (*q.v.*) , Annie Gabriel, Maurice H. Martin (*q.v.*) , and D. E. Wallace.

The college began in 1950 with eight volunteer faculty members and 74 students. There were no college owned buildings and the operating budget was $12,680.00. In 1969 there were 46 faculty members and 677 students with an operating budget of $1,257,846.00. In 1954 the first class of eight was graduated, while 110 were graduated in 1969. In 1969 there were a total of 897 graduates located in almost every part of the world.

Loyed R. Simmons, president of the school since 1958, submitted his resignation to the trustees on Nov. 8, 1969. In compliance with his request he was released from all responsibilities as of Nov. 30, 1969, although his resignation did not become effective until May 31, 1970.

CECIL M. HYATT

***CALIFORNIA SOUTHERN BAPTIST, THE.** Floyd Looney, editor since 1944, resigned on Feb. 15, 1961, to become western field secretary for the Annuity Board, SBC. J. Kelly Simmons (*q.v.*) , elected to succeed him, April 7, 1961, died on Feb. 1, 1963. J. Terry Young became editor on July 1, 1963. Young, a graduate of Baylor University and Southwestern Baptist Theological Seminary, had served as pastor in California since 1957 and was vice-chairman of the executive board of the state convention at the time of his election. Polly McNabb has served as associate editor since Aug., 1949. Circulation at the end of 1969 was 27,000.

J. TERRY YOUNG

CALIFORNIA SOUTHERN BAPTIST CHILD CARE AND FAMILY SERVICES. The first cottage for children at Sunny Crest Baptist Children's Home was completed in Oct., 1955. From that date through 1956 there were delays in further building due to lack of money and some consideration of relocating. On Jan. 30, 1957, 12 acres of land were sold to the Bakersfield City school system, providing financing for a second cottage, the superintendent's home, and furnishings.

On Mar. 1, 1957, the Sunny Crest Children's Home was officially opened. Sunny Crest continued operating for several years with two cottages. Most of the time fewer than 10 children were housed in each cottage. The feeling grew that a better service could be rendered by a changed program.

In 1960 the Southern Baptist General Convention of California met in a special session on May 9–11. A new direction and organization was adopted for the child care program, with the title of the board of trustees being changed to California Southern Baptist Board of Child Care. At this same session the convention also authorized the total program committee of the executive board to make a periodic study of the entire human welfare program.

Under this provision the total program committee of the executive board appointed a fact finding and study committee in Feb., 1963. Members of the committee were Gaines S. Dobbins, Elmer Austin, James Hatley, Grady C. Cothen, and Arlie L. McDaniel, chairman. During the ensuing year the committee held several meetings. Walter Delamarter of Southern Baptist Theological Seminary, Louisville, Ky., served as a special consultant.

The committee made its recommendations to the total program committee of the executive board in Apr., 1964. In Aug., 1964, a hearing session was held in Fresno to permit interested persons from all areas of the state to hear the recommendations and express their views.

At the annual meeting of the state convention in Long Beach, Nov. 10–12, 1964, a recommended reorganization of the entire child care program was adopted. Essentially this program called for closing Sunny Crest Children's Home, sale of the property, and establishment of an office in the Baptist Building in Fresno with the primary purpose of providing child care through a foster home program as approved and licensed by the Welfare Department of the State of California.

The new program required a director with a Master of Social Work degree to comply with California requirements for licensing. The board employed Robert A. Williams, social worker in the state of Washington, as executive director to begin his work May 1, 1965. During the year, under the direction of Williams, all the property in Bakersfield was sold and the program of Sunny Crest Children's Home terminated.

In 1966 E. K. Huddleston was employed as director for the Fresno area and plans were made toward opening of area offices in San Francisco and Los Angeles. In 1967 Williams opened an office in Los Angeles and spent part of each week in that area. In 1968 David G. Anderson was employed as director for the Los Angeles office and Williams assumed the responsibilities of the Fresno area in addition to his duties as executive director, since E. K. Huddleston had resigned during the year. The child care program began to expand its services to other areas of family need, and added the new name, Board of Child Care and Family Services. ARLIE L. MCDANIEL, SR.

***CALIFORNIA SOUTHERN BAPTIST STATE ASSEMBLY.** Development of Jenness Park, a summer assembly site in the high Sierras of central California, has been slow due to lack of funds. In 1961 the programming at the assembly was changed from a family type program offering general leadership training to a youth assembly because facilities were not suitable for families.

In 1969 the executive board of the state convention recommended that statewide assemblies be dropped in favor of emphasizing regional and associational assemblies to reach more people, and that the controversial assembly site be sold, but the proposal was rejected by a two-vote margin. J. TERRY YOUNG

CALLAWAY, TIMOTHY FURLOW (b. Americus, Ga., Mar. 30, 1882; d. Gadsden, Ala., Aug. 25, 1966). Pastor, denominational worker. Converted and joined First Baptist Church, Americus, Ga., Mar. 1, 1896, he was ordained by the same church, Dec. 26, 1906. He graduated from Mercer Law School (1902) and practiced law in Americus for four years. He married Lula Brown, Dec. 26, 1906. They had four children: Mary Hinton Hoffman, Edwin Brown, Catherine Furlow Stringer, and Timothy F., Jr. He served the following Baptist churches as pastor: First, Orlando, Fla., 1907–11; Second, Macon, Ga., 1912–13; Tabernacle, Macon, 1916–18; and First, Thomasville, Ga., 1927–51. Evangelist of the Georgia Baptist Convention, 1917–26, he was a member of the Georgia Baptist Foundation, Georgia Baptist history committee, public affairs committee, and executive committee of the Georgia Baptist Convention. He also served as president of the Georgia Baptist Convention, Georgia Baptist Sunday School Convention, and Georgia Temperance League. Callaway was elected senior citizen of Thomas County, 1961, was a charter member of Protestants and Other Americans United for Separation of Church and State, and a trustee of Mercer University. HOWARD P. GIDDENS

CAMERON, EVAN DHU (b. Rockingham, N. C., Feb. 26, 1862; d. Tahlequah, Okla., July 29, 1963). Minister and educator. After graduation with honors from the Rockingham Academy in 1878, he taught school a short time, entered Trinity College (now Duke University), and in 1881 graduated from Kick and Dillard Law School, Greensboro, N. C. He practiced law seven years, then was licensed to the ministry in the Methodist Church, South, in 1888. In 1889 he moved to Texas, and to Indian Territory (now Oklahoma) in 1891, to become pastor of St. Luke's Methodist Church, Oklahoma City. Cameron was superintendent of instruction in Oklahoma Territory, 1894–97, and was elected to the same office for the new state of Oklahoma, 1907–11.

In 1901 he became impressed with Baptist doctrines and united with that faith at Chickasha, Okla. His first Baptist pastorate followed at McAlester, and other pastorates included Muskogee, Guthrie, Claremore, Checotah, Okmulgee, Henryetta, and Tahlequah, Okla. In 1915 he was recipient of the D.D. degree, the first conferred by Oklahoma Baptist University.

J. M. GASKIN

***CAMP CARSON AND CAMP LINDEN.** Two Tennessee Baptist assemblies. Since 1956 the convention has its camp program to include these departments: evangelism, missions, and church music. The camp program receives $30,000 annually from the WMU and support through the Cooperative Program. Camp attendance was estimated at over 100,000 with 17,144 decisions for Christ. GLENN JENKINS

CAMP HUDGENS. Located 10 miles northwest of McAlester, Okla., Camp Hudgens for boys was purchased from the Rainbow Order and given to the Baptist General Convention of Oklahoma, Mar. 10, 1959. As a memorial to her late husband, Mrs. J. E. Hudgens gave the facility as a camp for Royal Ambassadors. It was formally dedicated Feb. 27, 1960. The first RA camps were held in 1960 with 426 attending. Through 1969 a total of 6,883 boys and leaders had attended, with 1,240 recorded decisions.

Facilities include caretaker's home, swimming pool, dining hall, five winterized cabins, unit lodge, outdoor chapel, and recreation facilities. The land area has doubled. The summer program includes missions, worship, group work, recreation, and outdoor living skills. The camp has pioneered among RA camps in the SBC, including a travel camp, canoe trip, and day camp in its program. During the six weeks' season in 1969, 718 boys and 83 staff campers registered. Bob Banks has been director since the camp was founded. BOB BANKS

***CAMP LINDEN.** See CAMP CARSON AND CAMP LINDEN.

CAMP PARON. A Baptist encampment near Paron, Ark., owned and operated by the Arkansas Baptist Convention. Authorized by the convention in 1959 to locate a site for Royal Ambassador and Girls Auxiliary camps, the executive board chose a site of 271 acres at Paron, 42 miles west of Little Rock in Maumelle Mountains. Melvin C. Thrash, business manager of the executive board, led in the construction of the camp, 1963–64.

Facilities include 12 brick dormitories that will accommodate 204 people, a dining room that will care for 300 people, an activity building, a tabernacle that will seat 250 people, and class pavilions.

The camp is used almost every week of the year (buildings are winterized) by church, associational, and denominational groups. Business managers for the camp and assembly have been: Melvin C. Thrash, 1961–64; John Cutsinger, 1964–66; Ralph Douglas, since 1966.

RALPH DOUGLAS

CAMPBELL, DUNCAN ROBERTSON (b. Perthshire, Scotland, Aug. 13, 1814; d. Covington, Ky., Aug. 11, 1865). Educated for the Presbyterian ministry at the University of Edinburgh, he later served as a Presbyterian pastor in Nottingham, England, and as a missionary in London. Dissatisfied with the practice of infant baptism, he came to America in May, 1842, and was immersed into the fellowship of First Baptist Church, Richmond, Va., at the earliest opportunity. "He publicly stated, in a convincing and impressive manner, his reasons for changing his ecclesiastical relations. He was soon licensed to preach, and entered on a bright career of usefulness, which unfortunately proved to be short." After a brief stay in Richmond, during which he served Leigh Street Church, he went to the pastorate of two Mississippi churches. In Aug., 1845, he came to Kentucky and accepted the pastoral care of Georgetown Church, 1845–49. Then he became a professor at the Western Baptist Theological Institute, serving as pastor of the Newport Church also. Elected president of Georgetown College in 1853, he also became pastor of Great Crossings Church that same year. The college progressed materially and spiritually under Campbell's leadership until the war broke out in 1861. He died suddenly on his way home from New York.

LEO T. CRISMON

***CAMPBELL COLLEGE.** Located midway between Raleigh and Fayetteville, the college is one of North Carolina's largest fully accredited senior colleges. The library has a capacity of 140,000 volumes and reading space for 2,500 students. It was a junior college from 1926 to 1961, when the first year of senior college work was added. The college received full accreditation by the Southern Association of Colleges and Schools in Dec., 1965, as a four-year liberal arts senior college. This institution awards the B.A. and B.S. degrees, with an occasional Associate of Arts diploma. Majors are available in the following departments: Biology, Business, Chemistry, French, Geology, History, Home Economics, Health and Physical Education, Mathematics, Music, Psychology, Religion, and Social Science. The distribution of degrees awarded is concentrated in teacher certification, business administration, social science, and elementary education.

Norman Adrian Wiggins succeeded Leslie Hartwell Campbell, son of the founder, as president on June 6, 1967. In 1968–69 the college had 124 faculty members, a staff of 300, and a plant with 30 major buildings on a 64-acre campus. The 1968–69 student body of 2,402 represented 25 states and nine foreign countries. Total assets for 1969–70 were $10,259,000, with annual expenditures at $4,930,000, and endowments at $852,000. QUENTIN L. SCOTT

***CAMPBELLSVILLE COLLEGE.** A senior, coeducational liberal arts college located at Campbellsville, Ky. President John Maurice Carter (1911–), by personal appeal to the messengers of the state Baptist general association in 1957, persuaded the association to authorize Campbellsville and Cumberland colleges to become senior colleges. Officially Campbellsville College became a senior college in 1959, when it was tentatively accredited by the state Board of Education. In 1964 it received full accreditation from the Southern Association of Colleges and Schools.

Under the presidency of Carter (1948–67), the college enlarged its physical plant and increased its student body to 1,000 students. Carter devoted his first efforts to finance and student assistance. When federal student loan funds were available for students, the self-help Campbellsville College Student Industries program was discontinued (1968).

Before Carter retired in 1967, the following buildings were constructed: Druien Hall, Carter Hall, and North Hall (dormitories); Science Building, Library, and Music Building (academic buildings); and Alumni Chapel and a Student Union Building.

Julius Kemper Powell, executive vice-president since 1962, succeeded him as president in 1967. In recognition of his distinguished service to the college, the trustees named the new health and physical education building the J. K. Powell Athletic Center in his honor. A large residence hall, Stapp Hall, was erected. The library was increased to 60,000 volumes. Powell retired in July, 1969.

William Randolph Davenport (1925–) became president on Aug. 1, 1969, coming from the University of Michigan. The net worth of the college in 1969 was $4,550,000. The operating budget was $1,435,000, coming from tuition of $708,361, $180,000 from the Kentucky convention, and $68,000 in gifts from friends. The endowment is $434,000. The student body for 1968–69 was 985. The faculty numbered 57. Trustees are elected by the Kentucky Baptist Convention. It has an active student program and in-service training for student pastors.

HAROLD GLEN SANDERS

CANADIAN BAPTIST COOPERATION, COMMITTEE ON. A special committee authorized by the Southern Baptist Convention in 1957 to deal with emerging tensions with Canadian Baptists. The appearance in western Canada of churches in cooperation with the Baptist General Convention of Oregon-Washington was the chief cause of these tensions. During most years the committee met annually or more often with Canadian Baptist representatives, thus forming a joint committee. In 1968 the convention discontinued the committee and assigned its responsibilities to its representatives on the North American Baptist Fellowship. W. Bertram King, under Home Mission Board appointment from 1957 as Southern Baptist liaison representative to Canadian Baptists, assisted the committee throughout its existence. ARTHUR B. RUTLEDGE

CANADIAN SOUTHERN BAPTISTS. In 1953 the Emmanuel Baptist Church of Vancouver, B. C., asked for affiliation with the Baptist General Convention of Oregon-Washington after a study of Southern Baptist literature revealed doctrines and practices acceptable to them. The church name was then changed to Kingcrest Southern Baptist Church. Although not accepted by the Southern Baptist Convention, this church was the first of over two dozen congregations which affiliated with Oregon-Washington Baptists during the next 15 years. They organized a Canadian Southern Baptist Conference which meets yearly; aided pastors from the United States to work among them; were assisted financially by the Fleming Foundation of Texas; and became regular contributors to the work of Southern Baptists through the Oregon-Washington Convention, which held its annual session in Vancouver, B. C., in 1963—the first state or regional body of Southern Baptists ever to hold an official annual convention outside the United States. Southern Baptists in Canada maintain an office in Vancouver, with a superintendent of Church Ministries who helps coordinate their mission work. They reported approximately 1,500 members in 26 congregations in three western provinces of Canada in 1968. ROY L. JOHNSON

CANNADA, WILLIAM HENRY (b. Chick Springs, Greenville County, S. C., Sept. 16, 1872; d. Pickens, S. C., Jan. 27, 1968). Son of Elisha Davis and Thursa Jane (Taylor) Cannada, he was educated at Furman University (B.A., 1898) and Southern Baptist Theological Seminary (Th.M., 1902). While at Furman, Cannada was ordained by the Taylors First Baptist Church, Nov. 6, 1898, and preached at Forestville and Reedy Fork Baptist churches in the Greenville Baptist Association. He married Norma Jenkins of West Point, Ky., Sept. 16, 1902. They were appointed missionaries to Brazil in Oct., 1902. From 1902 to 1910 they were at Pernambuco, Brazil, where Cannada founded and directed Gilreath Baptist College and Seminary. Struck in the eye by steel fragments from a hammer he was using to open crates for chairs for the school, he returned to New York for treatment. He lost the eye. From 1912–15, he taught and operated the school farm at North Greenville High School (now North Greenville Junior College), Tigerville, S. C. Cannada was principal of Edisto Baptist Academy, Seivern, Aiken County, S. C., 1915–29. He was pastor of two Charleston, S. C., Baptist churches: Hampstead Square, 1931–43, and Mount Pleasant, 1934–35. He was also supply pastor of Calvary Baptist Church, 1944. The Cannadas had three children: Edith Rosalind (Mrs. J. Oscar Miller), William Henry, Jr., and Nellie Winterton (Mrs. Jack Hearn). Cannada is buried in the cemetery of the First Baptist Church, Taylors, S. C. JEAN MARTIN FLYNN

CANNING, JOHN ROSS (b. Hale, Mo., Aug. 28, 1911; d. Tacoma, Wash., Feb. 3, 1966). Pastor and denominational leader. Son of Thomas and Stella Canning, he was born and reared in the small farm community of Hale, Mo. Ordained by Hale Baptist Church in 1935, he became pastor at Bosworth, Mo., and married Charlotte Dinsmore. They had five children: Alyce Jane, Elva Ruth, Ross Lyle, Eugene Ray, and Glen David. While serving churches in north central Missouri he attended William Jewell College, graduating in 1941. He served as an Air Force Chaplain, 1943–46. Canning was pastor in Norborne, Mo., while attending Central Baptist Seminary, graduating with the B.D. and M.R.E. degrees in 1948. Pastor in Harrisonville, Mo., 1949–54, he accepted a missionary challenge in the Pacific Northwest, becoming pastor of the Trinity Baptist Church, Springfield, Ore. In May, 1958, he became Sunday School secretary for the Oregon-Washington Convention, serving for three years. After a short pastorate in Longview, Wash., he served as pastor of the Calvary Baptist Church, Anchorage,

Alaska, from 1961 until his death. He was a respected leader in the Oregon-Washington and Alaska conventions, serving as president of both bodies. He is buried in Avalon, Mo.

RICHARD A. MILLER and ROY L. JOHNSON

CARD, GEORGE WALDO (b. Hantsport, Nova Scotia, Jan. 1, 1882; d. Nashville, Tenn., July 29, 1961). A graduate of Burdette Business College, Boston, Mass., he married Mary Buford Twyman of Louisville, Ky., in 1914. They had two sons: William Judson and Philip Twyman, state Training Union secretary of Colorado. After engaging in business in Louisville, Card served Walnut Street Baptist Church there as director of music and education, 1922–23. He was manager of the advertising department of the Sunday School Board, 1924–30; then secretary of the sales and advertising department until 1952. Card compiled *Songs of Faith* (1933) and *Abiding Songs* (1936), and enthusiastically promoted good books through special publications of his department. He served several Nashville churches as minister of music and was widely used as an evangelistic song leader.

HOWARD P. COLSON

CARLSON, ERNEST LESLIE (b. Chicago, Cook County, Ill., Oct. 14, 1893; d. Fort Worth, Tex., Dec. 12, 1967). Professor and clergyman. Son of Swedish immigrants Patrick Edward and Emma (Bengtson) Carlson, he was reared on a farm in Pinckneyville, Ill. Educated at Southern Illinois Normal University, Moody Bible Institute (Dip. Rel. Ed., 1915; Dip. Mus., 1916), Texas Christian University (A.B., 1921; M.A., 1928), and Southwestern Baptist Theological Seminary (Th.M., 1920; Th.D., 1936), he was a public school teacher in 1912, and was a gospel singer, 1914–17 being ordained to the ministry in 1917. He joined the faculty of Southwestern Baptist Theological Seminary in 1921, and served as professor of biblical backgrounds, archaeology, Old Testament, and Semitic languages until retirement Aug. 1, 1964. He served several pastorates in Texas, primarily at Azle, Lillian, and Rio Vista.

His books were *Confirming the Scriptures* (1941), *Introductory Hebrew* (1945, rev. 1956), and *A Study of the Prophet Micah* (1950) in joint authorship with Benjamin A. Copass (*q.v.*, Vol. I). In 1956 he collaborated with Ovid R. Sellers in a revision of *Monuments and the Old Testament* by Ira M. Price. He wrote the commentary on the book of Micah for *Wycliffe Bible Commentary* (1962), and served as consulting editor of *Baker's Bible Atlas* (1961). He was a frequent contributor to Southern Baptist publications. *Studies in Exegesis of Micah and Hebrew Syntax* (1950), written in collaboration with Copass, was a mimeographed textbook used in his Hebrew classes.

On Sept. 16, 1917, he married Edna S. Massey. She died Jan. 22, 1956. They had four children: Ernest Leslie, Jr., John Edward, Edna Louise, and Benjamin Eugene. He married Marjorie Smyth, Feb. 7, 1957. She died Aug. 21, 1969. He was a Mason and a member of the American Schools of Oriental Research, American Oriental Society, National Association of Biblical Instructors, and Society of Old Testament Study. He is buried at Laurel Land Memorial Park in Fort Worth, Tex.

ROBERT O. COLEMAN

CARPENTER, ALFRED ANDREAS (b. Sussex, N. J., June 29, 1893; d. Atlanta, Ga., Oct. 4, 1963). Pastor and home missions leader. Son of George Thomson and Lizzie (Andreas) Carpenter, he married Minnie Bryant, Jan. 7, 1917. Ordained on Sept. 5, 1923, he graduated from Oklahoma Baptist University (1926) and Southwestern Baptist Theological Seminary (M.R.E. and Th.B., 1929).

Carpenter was pastor of churches in Cement, Okla., Dallas, Tex., and Blytheville, Ark. In Arkansas he also was on the board of Jonesboro Baptist College and the Baptist state convention and was superintendent of evangelism. He served as superintendent of missions, pastor of Balboa Heights Church, and on the staff of the governor in Panama. He also served as director of church loans for the Home Mission Board, SBC.

At the start of World War II, Carpenter organized and directed the chaplain's commission under the HMB's auspices. In 1946 he became secretary of direct missions for the HMB. In 1949 Carpenter resumed his chaplaincy leadership. Before retiring in 1960, he expanded the ministry to include hospitals, industry, and institutions. He received a Presidential Citation, Medal of Merit, appreciations from the Bureau of Naval Personnel and War and Navy departments, and a citation from the National Military Chaplains Association.

COURTS REDFORD

CARPENTER, LEVY LEONIDAS (b. Wake County, N. C., Nov. 29, 1891; d. Greenville, S. C., Aug. 22, 1966). Son of Rufus J. and Bettie (Rogers) Carpenter, he was educated at Wake Forest College (B.A., 1913), Southern Baptist Theological Seminary (Th.M., 1916; Th.D., 1918), and Yale University (Ph.D., 1927). He married Lucille O'Brien of Oxford, N. C., on Sept. 2, 1919. They had two sons: Robert O'Brien and William L. Carpenter. Carpenter was instructor at Southern Seminary, 1916–18; a Chaplain in the United States Army, 1918; pastor of Forest Avenue (now College Park) Baptist Church in Greensboro, N. C., 1919–21; Chaplain and Bible Professor at University of South Carolina, 1921–26; associate professor of Religious Education at Furman University, 1926–27; professor of Religion (1927–30) and head of the department of Religion (1930–36) at Limestone College; associate professor of Bible at Baylor University (1936–42); and editor of the *Biblical Recorder,* journal of North Carolina Baptists, 1942–59. He wrote the following books: *Primitive Christian Application of the Doctrine of the Servant* (1929); *The Quest* *for God through Understanding* (1937); *A Program of Religious Education* (1937); and *A Survey of Religious Education* (1940); was coauthor of *Introduction to Religious Education* (1932), and *The Upward Look* (1936). He is buried in Oakwood Cemetery, Raleigh, N. C.

JAMES H. BLACKMORE

CARROLL, MOYES BROOKS (b. North Augusta, Aiken County, S. C., July 5, 1916; d. Dallas, Tex., Dec. 30, 1966). Pastor and denominational leader. A graduate of Furman University (B.A., 1937), Southwestern Baptist Theological Seminary, (Th.M., 1941), he received a D.D. from East Texas Baptist College in 1955. Married Dec. 27, 1938, to Josephine Ray, he had six children: Ann (Al) Mayton, Ted R., Kay (Basil) Clark, Sue, Joy, and Sid. Carroll was ordained by First Baptist Church, North Augusta, S. C. His pastorates, all in Texas, were Red Springs; Meridian; First, Matador; First, Brady; First, Henderson; and East Grand, Dallas. He was trustee of several institutions and the *Baptist Standard;* president of the Baptist General Convention of Texas, 1959–60; vice-president of Southern Baptist Convention, 1965.

B. J. MARTIN

***CARSON-NEWMAN COLLEGE.** From 1956 to 1969, Carson-Newman College continued its growth, academic and physical. The enrolment increased from 1,184 to 1,697 full-time students (1969) and 95 part-time students. The full-time faculty has increased from 65 to 119. The addition of philosophy increases to 16 the number of departments of instruction. Curriculum innovations include an honors program of independent study, pass-fail option junior and senior years, separate accreditation by the National Association of Schools of Music and the National Council for Accreditation of Teacher Education. The library has increased from 47,700 to 95,000 volumes. Chapters of 11 general and departmental honor societies were added.

Campus development was marked by the construction of six major buildings: Holt Field House (1959), Manley Infirmary (1962), Stokely Memorial Dining Hall-Classroom Building (1963), Men's Residence Hall (1964, 1967) Fite Administration Building (1967), and the library (1970). The college also erected a 4,000 seat stadium (1966) and a president's home (1969), twice expanded Butler and Burnett residence halls, and extensively remodeled Sarah Swann Hall and Henderson Hall Auditorium. The campaign for funds for an 82,000-square-foot science center was nearing completion with construction beginning in 1970. The value of the physical plant increased from $3,100,000 to $13,000,000.

After 20 years of leadership in the college, D. Harley Fite retired in Sept., 1968, and was succeeded by John Albert Fincher, who was inaugurated in Apr., 1969.

JOHN A. FINCHER

CARSWELL, GUY THOMAS (b. Morganton, N. C., Sept. 29, 1894; d. Charlotte, N. C., Oct. 11, 1966). Lawyer. Son of Abel H. and Mary (Huffman) Carswell, he served overseas with the Army for two years during World War II. He was married to Clara (Horn) on Oct. 13, 1917. Carswell received the B.A. and LL.B. degrees from Wake Forest College in 1922, and practiced law in Charlotte from 1922 until his death. He was elected a fellow in the American College of Trial Lawyers in 1955. He received an honorary degree from Wake Forest in 1962.

Carswell was one of the organizers of the Myers Park Baptist Church, Charlotte, in 1943. He taught a Sunday School class at First Baptist Church for 40 years, and later taught at Myers Park. He served as chairman of the deacons for both churches.

Carswell was a member of the Wake Forest board of trustees for 25 years. He also served as a trustee for Gardner Webb College, and as a member of the board of visitors for Wingate College. One of the activities he enjoyed most, and one which he never mentioned, was financing the college education of deserving and needy students. The Guy T. Carswell Scholarships, the top scholarships at Wake Forest University, were established in 1968 in honor of Carswell and his wife, and are based on a bequest of more than $2,200,000 left to the university by Carswell.

ELIZABETH BRANTLEY

***CARVER SCHOOL OF MISSIONS AND SOCIAL WORK.** With the opening of the regular session on Sept. 17, 1956, Carver began its 50th Anniversary celebration, highlights of which included the publication of a school history, written by past president Carrie U. Littlejohn, and a drive to raise $15,000 to be added to the Carver Memorial Fund.

During the commemorative year, technical details and legal matters were worked out for the transfer of the school to the control and ownership of the Southern Baptist Convention; and in their respective annual meetings in Chicago in May, 1957, Woman's Missionary Union and the SBC gave final approval to the transfer.

The Good Will Center property, purchased in part with trust funds from the estate of Ellen T. Rider, was not a part of the transfer. In order to carry out better the provisions of the Rider will, that the funds be used for evangelistic work, the executive board of WMU in Feb., 1958, voted to transfer the center to the Home Mission Board, SBC. The board agreed to accept the property and to carry on the work of the center.

In June, 1957, the new board of trustees (elected at the 1957 Convention) held its organizational meeting and chose as chairman John Sandidge, a Louisville attorney. At the meeting Emily K. Lansdell submitted her resignation as president of the school.

The new board quickly undertook a reappraisal of the need of the denomination for the school, and of the school's objectives, programs, organization, and administration. It also considered the desirability and feasibility of merging

Carver School with Southern Baptist Theological Seminary or another institution. To assist in this appraisal, the trustees employed a firm of consultants to make a planning survey, which was completed in Apr., 1958. The consultants recommended, and the trustees concurred, that the school continue as a separate institution and improve and expand its programs. They felt that merger would hinder or make impossible the attainment of regional accreditation necessary for the continued successful operation of the school.

The Committee to Study the Total Southern Baptist Program, authorized by the 1956 Convention, studied the report of the consultants and trustees. In its report to the 1959 Convention, the committee recommended that Carver be continued as a separate institution and that the school include in its annual report to the Convention for the next five years a special report of progress made toward accreditation. The Convention adopted both recommendations.

By 1962 it became apparent that accreditation was not going to be attainable, and in June, John Sandidge read to the Convention in San Francisco a recommendation that Carver School be merged as soon as possible with Southern Baptist Theological Seminary. The Convention adopted the recommendation, setting into motion steps that led to merger on Aug. 1, 1963.

In spite of the problems faced during the period 1957–63, Carver School of Missions and Social Work made considerable progress: the faculty was strengthened, the curriculum was revised, and extensive gains were made in physical assets. Much of this progress was due to the efforts of Nathan C. Brooks, Jr., who became president of Carver on June 18, 1958. Born in Bridgeton, N. C., Dr. Brooks received the A.B. degree from Wake Forest College and the Th.M. degree from Southern Baptist Theological Seminary. In 1957 Wake Forest conferred on him the D.D. degree. He pursued further graduate studies at Columbia University and Union Theological Seminary. Before coming to Louisville as president of Carver School, he had served as pastor of a number of churches in several states and was a Carver School trustee.

Total assets of the school at the time of merger were $1,635,007.59, including land, buildings, equipment, investments, endowment funds, and cash.

BIBLIOGRAPHY: Carrie U. Littlejohn, *History of Carver School* (1956). BETTY BROWN

CARY, ORLAND R. (b. Snyder, Tex., Apr. 6, 1906; d. Fairbanks, Alaska, Nov. 19, 1961). Pioneer Baptist pastor in Alaska. Son of Caswell M. and Fannie G. Cary, he was the third oldest son in a family of 10 children. During his early years the family lived near Knapp, Tex. He was converted at the age of nine in a brush arbor meeting. Cary left public school and attended an automotive and electrical trade school. While working for various pipeline and electrical companies he completed his high school work in 1930 at the Academy of West Texas State Teacher's College. He attended Texas A. & M., 1930–32, then transferred to Baylor University, from which he was graduated in 1934. In 1936 he was ordained by a small rural church in Texas. For several years he was pastor of several quarter and half time rural churches, supporting himself in part by additional secular work, usually teaching school. Cary took additional college work at Simmons University, Abilene, Tex., Texas Tech University, Lubbock, Tex., and attended Southwestern Baptist Theological Seminary, 1940–41.

While pastor of the First Baptist Church, Peaster, Tex., and teaching at the Caddo High School, he was inducted into military service in June, 1943. He served in the European Theatre as an X-ray technician. After induction Cary applied for the chaplaincy, but it was not until he returned from overseas and was eligible for separation that the Army was ready to commission him. While in the Army he met and married an Army nurse, Mabel Risse from Wisconsin, on Jan. 3, 1945. They had nine children.

Following his discharge Cary was called as pastor of a mission of the First Baptist Church, Brownfield, Tex., a church which had become very interested in the new Southern Baptist mission work in Alaska. In May, 1946, the newly organized First Baptist Church, Fairbanks, Alaska called him as pastor. He served this church until Nov., 1958. During his ministry the church received 1,589 members by baptism and transfer of membership, and was instrumental in the organization of four Alaskan churches: First Baptist, North Pole, First Baptist, Big Delta, St. John's Baptist, Fairbanks, and Native Baptist, Fairbanks. For two years before his death, he served as pastor of the Airport Road Baptist Church, Fairbanks.

In addition to his work as a pioneer pastor, he was a leader and president of the Alaska Baptist Convention and one of the organizers of the Tanana Valley Baptist Association.

MABEL R. CARY

CASH, WARREN (b. Apr. 4, 1760, Albemarle County, Va.; d. Sept. 15, 1849, Hardin County, Ky.) He was born to Nancy Cash and Francis Fidler, who were married by a Presbyterian or Baptist dissenter preacher in 1757 or 1758, when Virginia law forbade dissenter preachers from performing marriages. Children born of these marriages were considered illegitimate and the law required that they bear the names of their mothers. Young Warren went by the name of Warren Fidler, however, until he had a violent quarrel with his father over wages due Warren and left home in anger, around 1773, and later (about 1776) joined the Revolutionary Army, taking the name of his mother to spite his father. He served in the army until 1780. On Nov. 24, 1782, in Fluvanna County, Va., he married Susannah Baskett, a daughter of William Baskett, a Baptist preacher. They had 12 children. "All biographical material concerning Warren and Susannah discloses unmistakably that Warren was an 'illiterate, rough soldier of the Revolution, and a bold sinner' when he reached Kentucky in 1784; that Susannah was a well educated daughter of a prosperous Virginia planter; that she taught her husband to the point where he became an effective, popular, though not brilliant preacher."

Cash, his wife, and child spent the winter of 1784–85 in Grubb's Fort in Madison County, Ky. In the spring of 1785 they moved to the present site of Mortonsville, in Woodford County, where "he and Susannah joined the Clear Creek Baptist Church, then under the ministry of John Taylor [*q.v.*, Vol. II], and in 1799, he was ordained to preach by elders John Penney and William Hickman [*q.v.*, Vol. I]." Kentucky churches Cash served were as follows: Clear Creek, 1786, Beech Creek, 1796, Fox Run, 1799, Simpson's Creek, 1802–06, New Salem, 1802–06, Bethel (Hardin County), 1806–24, Gilead, 1824–49, Union (Hardin County), 1804–49, and Otter Creek, 1806–49. LEO T. CRISMON

CASTON, JOSEPH BARNWELL (b. Lancaster County, S. C., Jan. 9, 1882; d. Columbia, S. C., Sept. 6, 1968). Pastor, educator, and state convention officer. Son of William T. and Jane (Ingram) Caston, he was educated at Furman University, Mercer (A.B., Th.G.), Southern Baptist Theological Seminary, Louisville, Ky., Southwestern Baptist Theological Seminary, Fort Worth, Tex., and Columbia Presbyterian Seminary, Columbia, S. C. He was awarded an honorary Doctor of Laws degree by the Atlanta Law School. He was pastor of churches at Gray and Irvington, Ga., and at Bethune, Lynchburg, Bamberg, and Camden, S. C.

Active in the state convention, Caston served on the Baptist general board of South Carolina and on its executive committee as well as on a subcommittee to set up the South Carolina Ministers' Retirement Plan in 1938. He was also a trustee of the South Carolina Baptist Foundation and vice-president of the South Carolina Baptist Convention, 1944. Interested in education, he served as trustee of Coker and Anderson Colleges, and was superintendent of the Pageland schools before entering the ministry. He married Cora Gardner of Lancaster County, and they had two children: W. Frank, and Mrs. H. D. Anderson. DANIEL W. CLOER

CAYLOR, JOHN (b. Opp, Ala., Mar. 23, 1894; d. Little Rock, Ark., Dec. 20, 1966). Pastor, educator, editor, home mission leader, and author. The second of three sons and two daughters born to Major General and Julia Frances Caylor, he married Floriene Mabel Finney Aug. 26, 1920. They had three children: Julia Katherine (Mrs. Crawford Reid), Patty Lou (Mrs. J. B. Jones), and John, Jr. He studied at Howard College (now Samford University), Oklahoma Baptist University (B.A., 1920), University of Alabama (M.A., 1923), and both Southern and Southwestern Baptist Theological Seminaries. He received an honorary D.D. from Louisiana College. Caylor taught Bible at the University of Texas, 1923–24, and was president of Burleson College, Greenville, Tex., 1927–30. He served as student secretary, and as pastor and associate pastor in Alabama, Texas, and Louisiana. From 1946 until his retirement, Dec. 31, 1959, Caylor was secretary of the Department of Education for the Home Mission Board.

A member of Pi Kappa Alpha, Masons, Kiwanis, and Rotary International, Caylor served as trustee of Acadia Baptist Academy, Louisiana, and Southern Seminary; and as a member of the executive board of the Louisiana convention, 1938–45. During his retirement he served on the staff of First Baptist Church, Little Rock.

KATE ELLEN GRUVER

***CEDARMORE KENTUCKY BAPTIST ASSEMBLY.** Since 1955 Cedarmore increased its acreage by 962 acres on two sides of Six Mile Creek which forms Dragon Lake. The resident manager, Marvin M. Byrdwell, has served since the beginning in 1951. A master plan was developed in 1962. Improvements include a complete water and sewage system (1963–64); Boone Lodge (1964), named for former general secretary W. C. Boone; bathhouse (1965) near the olympic pool (1960); new cedar-wall boys and girls camps begun on adjacent mountains (1965), along with 15 Conestoga wagons for boys; and Ferguson-Jaegle air-conditioned conference center (1968), in honor of Mrs. George R. Ferguson, executive secretary-treasurer, and Mrs. W. H. Jaegle, treasurer, of Kentucky WMU.

During the early years, it was used mainly as a summer camp for missionary education. With the construction of the dining room and the motels in 1951, WMU conference building in 1955, and the air-conditioned Boone Lodge and Ferguson-Jaegle conference center, it has become a year-round conference center for youth and leadership, serving approximately 19,000 during 1969. Popular for retreats, conferences, clinics, and assemblies, it is used widely by Kentucky Baptist churches, associations, state groups; and it is becoming a popular national conference center for Southern Baptists and others. Current value of property is $1,800,000, and future expansion in the Master Plan should double that figure. Direction of the work is given by the executive board's assembly and camps committee. Kentucky WMU has been a strong support in finances and use.

HAROLD GLEN SANDERS

***CENTRAL BAPTIST HOSPITAL.** Located at Lexington, Ky. In 1965 the hospital completed the first phase of its long-range building program, which increased the number of beds from 173 to 235. The hospital is affiliated with the University of Kentucky in a nursing degree program, and with Midway Junior College in an associate degree program for nurses. It is also affiliated with the Appalachian School for practical nurses. It has a school for X-ray and laboratory technology. Since 1965 Ben R. Brewer has been the administrator, now called executive vice-president, in the relationship with Baptist Hospitals, Inc. H. L. DOBBS

CENTRAL BAPTIST THEOLOGICAL SEMINARY. Central Baptist Theological Seminary is located in Kansas City, Kans. Option on first property was secured Aug. 21, 1901, and the first session was begun on Oct. 21, 1902, in a 30-room home, known as Lovelace Hall, situated on two acres of land. First called Kansas City Baptist Theological Seminary, the name was changed to Central Baptist Theological Seminary, May 1, 1941.

Original board members were: Franklin L. Streeter, W. C. Stiver, F. C. Bingham, James F. Wells, Z. Nasen, B. W. Wizman, E. F. Neal, and E. B. Meredith, all of Kansas City, Kans.; Charles Lovelace, Turner, Kans.; and S. M. Brown (*q.v.*, Vol. I), I. N. Clark, and S. A. Northrup of Kansas City, Mo.

Six people comprised the original faculty: Phillip Wendell Crannell, president and professor of homiletics and pastoral theology; J. F. Wells, English Scripture and church history; Alexander C. Rafferty, systematic theology; F. L. Streeter, New Testament Greek; H. T. Morton, professor of Hebrew; and Preston J. Dillenbeck, acting professor of public speaking.

The seminary was founded independent of convention control and the board was self-perpetuating. Early emphasis was on missions. Degrees offered were B.D. for regular course work and a B.Th. for nondegree, nonlanguage studies. In 1920 the seminary began offering the Th.D. degree.

A woman's missionary training school was created in 1913, two blocks from the main seminary campus. It operated as a separate school until 1938, when its identity was subsumed by the seminary proper. From its inception the average enrolment of students has been 75 each year. In 1970 approximately 50 persons were enrolled.

Presidents of the school and their tenures are: Phillip W. Crannell, 1902–26; L. M. Dentonn, 1927–35; J. I. Crawford (acting) 1936; Harvey E. Dana (*q.v.*, Vol. I), 1938–45; W. W. Adams, 1954–56; and Paul T. Losh 1956– .

Central Seminary experienced a major adjustment difficulty following the time when the Missouri Baptist churches largely became cooperative with the Southern Baptist Convention. The seminary had been supported jointly by Kansas and Missouri Baptist churches. Whether the seminary could continue dually aligned and drawing support from these churches of two separate conventions was the issue. This was attempted until the SBC founded Midwestern Baptist Theological Seminary in Kansas City, Mo., in 1957. This action drained support formerly given to Central Seminary by the Missouri and Kansas Southern Baptist churches.

DAVID O. MOORE

CHAMBLEE, AQUILA (b. Canton, Ga., Dec. 3, 1869; d. Fort Valley, Ga., Jan. 30, 1963). Pastor and college president. Graduated from Etowah Institute, Mercer University, and the Southern Baptist Theological Seminary, he received an honorary D.D. from Mercer. Ordained, Dec. 28, 1892, his pastorates, all in Georgia, included Butler, Island Creek, Sandersville, Warthen, Sisters, Forsyth, Cartersville, Hawkinsville, Finleyson, Pineview, Byromville, Wadley, Bryon, and Bartow churches. He married Mamie Louise Beck of Tennille, Ga., Sept. 6, 1898. While living in Forsyth, Chamblee taught Bible courses at Bessie Tift College. In 1922 he became president of the college, where he served until 1938. An economic depression clouded his presidency. During this period, he skillfully guided the institution without incurring any debt. Upon retirement in 1938, he established his home in Fort Valley, Ga. Recognized by his denomination, he served as president of the Georgia Baptist Convention, 1936–39, and vice-president of the Southern Baptist Convention, 1939–40.

J. POWHATAN COX

CHAPLAINCY MINISTRIES, HOME MISSION BOARD PROGRAM OF (cf. Chaplain, Vol. I). The objective of the Program of Chaplaincy Ministries is to bring Southern Baptist ministers into contact with chaplaincy opportunities and to work with and assist churches, associations, and state conventions in providing a spiritual ministry to military personnel and their families and to persons in hospitals, in penal and other institutions, and in business and industry. The Division of Chaplaincy of the Home Mission Board functions as the Chaplains' Commission of the Southern Baptist Convention and promotes the chaplaincy program. Between 1955 and 1970 this program expanded in a number of areas, particularly in hospital, institutional, and industrial chaplaincy ministries.

Southern Baptists have had a sufficient number of ministers interested in this program to meet the demands of the military chaplaincy and of the opportunities provided in the hospital, institutional, and industrial chaplaincy. At the beginning of 1970, this program reported 1,005 Southern Baptist chaplains actively engaged in service as compared with 700 in 1955. Of these, 691 were military, 217 hospital, 81 institutional, and 16 industrial. In addition, there were 489 army, navy, and air force reserve chaplains, 93 national guard chaplains and 89 civil air patrol chaplains working with various units throughout the nation. This brought the total number of Southern Baptist ministers serving in some area of the chaplaincy to 1,676.

Two Southern Baptist chaplains served as chief of chaplains during the 1955–70 period:

Robert P. Taylor, Air Force (1962–66), and James W. Kelly, Navy (1965–).

Alfred Carpenter (*q.v.*), the first director of the division, retired at the close of 1960 and died in 1963. He was succeeded in 1961 by Geo. W. Cummins, the former associate director. In the board's reorganization in 1959, the Chaplains Commission became one of five divisions, and the work of military personnel ministries was transferred from the Cooperative Missions Department to the Division of Chaplaincy. E. L. Ackiss, who had served as secretary of this work since 1954, remained in this position until his death in 1961.

With the development of the institutional and industrial chaplaincy, James C. Peck became secretary of this work in 1959, serving in this capacity until his death by accident in 1961. In 1966 the work of institutional and industrial chaplaincy was divided into two separate areas of responsibility.

In 1962 Willis A. Brown became secretary of Military Personnel Ministries and in 1970 became associate director of the division. Others who have served on the staff of the division are: Cecil D. Etheredge, institutional and industrial chaplaincy, 1963–65; L. L. McGee, hospital chaplaincy, 1962–64; Gerald E. Marsh, hospital chaplaincy, 1965–69; T. E. Carter, institutional chaplaincy, 1965–68; Lowell E. Sodeman, industrial chaplaincy, 1966– ; Richard W. McKay, institutional and hospital chaplaincy, 1969– ; William L. Clark, military personnel ministries, 1970– ; and Alfred Carl Hart, institutional chaplaincy, 1970– . GEO. W. CUMMINS

CHAPLAINCY PROGRAMS IN NON-BAPTIST INSTITUTIONS (TEXAS). Through the Human Welfare Commission, the Baptist General Convention of Texas sponsors chaplaincy programs in several non-Baptist institutions.

University of Texas Medical Branch, Galveston.—J. R. Breland, first chaplain, served from Apr. 15, 1962, until his death in 1964. A. C. Turner was interim chaplain for seven months. S. Denton Bassett, present chaplain (1969) has served since June 1, 1965. This program is fully supported through Cooperative Program.

Southern Baptist Convention Chaplaincy Services, Rochester, Minn.—This program was initiated July 1, 1964. B. J. Williamson, first chaplain, continues in service (1969). The Baptist General Convention of Texas and the Home Mission Board, SBC, jointly sponsor the program.

Texas Department of Corrections.—A chaplaincy program has operated in the maximum Security Unit, since July 1, 1964, with Avery Timmons serving as chaplain. The Pre-Release Center program has been conducted since Sept. 15, 1966, with Hylon Vickers as chaplain. Both programs were supported fully by the Baptist General Convention of Texas until Oct. 1, 1969, when the Texas Department of Corrections began to provide full support. JAMES BASDEN

CHAPMAN, JAMES HORTON (b. Grove Hill, Ala., Nov. 5, 1881; d. Birmingham, Ala., Oct. 28, 1969). Educator and denominational leader. Son of Gross Scruggs (M.D.) and Eugenie Horton (Woodard) Chapman, he graduated from the University of Alabama (M.A., 1905) and Southern Baptist Theological Seminary (Th.M., 1908). He was ordained in Nov., 1908. Chapman was pastor of First Church, Florence, Ala., 1913–17; assistant secretary of the Alabama State Mission Board, 1912–13; and director of the state summer assemblies and "preacher schools," 1913–22. After additional study at Boston University, 1917–18, he joined the faculty of Howard College (now Samford University) and established the Department of Religious Education there in 1918. He retired in 1958.

In 1933 Chapman was chairman of the committee which led in the establishment of the Alabama Baptist Historical Society and served as curator of the society, 1936–58. He also served in 1936 on the committee which eventually led to the establishment of the Historical Commission of the Southern Baptist Convention. He was a founder and the first president (1928–29) of the Association of Southern Baptist Teachers of Bible and Religious Education (now Association of Baptist Professors of Religion). He was a contributing author of *Introduction to Religious Education* (1932) and *A Survey of Religious Education.*

On Dec. 23, 1924, he married Fanny L. Sheppard of Edgefield, S. C. They had no children.

ARTHUR L. WALKER, JR.

CHILDREN'S MUSIC LEADER. A music quarterly for leaders of Beginner, Primary, and Junior age groups in the music program published by the Church Music Department of the Baptist Sunday School Board, beginning with the fourth quarter, 1966, and concluding with the third quarter, 1970. It was replaced in Oct., 1970, by *The Music Leader.* W. HINES SIMS

CHILDREN'S WORK. The period 1955–70 in Southern Baptist churches witnessed the church taking children and their presence in the congregation much more seriously than before. As a result, not only is more provision now being made for children during the regularly scheduled activities for adults at the churches, but in response to the cultural emphasis on the importance of early childhood, Southern Baptists have risen to the challenge of providing literature for parents and teachers that is based on the best that is now known in mental hygiene, child development, current theology, and learning theory.

Leadership, however, remains a serious problem. It is apparent that adults, serving as teachers and leaders for children, have not kept pace educationally with the kind of information and learning patterns that are behind the development of the printed curriculum for children.

Nor have they kept informed of the changes that have affected most aspects of family living.

Moreover, no children's work can achieve a high degree of success without the undergirding support of parents in the home, and this support is not always apparent. What is sorely needed is a greater emphasis upon a preventive ministry through premarital counseling, prenatal education for parents-to-be, and continuing support, care, and education for parents as children grow. As yet, Southern Baptists have not developed curriculum or suggested specific structures for implementing these needs. The only formal approaches which have been made have been educational approaches that have depended on the interest of individual parents plus whatever informal ministry pastor and educational staff might activate for a congregation.

Only a very small proportion of Southern Baptist churches have either full or part-time professional supervision for work among children in the churches. Supervisors of work with children give the majority of their time to making schedules, enlisting workers, and buying equipment and materials. The majority of these workers with children have no formal training for their tasks beyond the occasional denominational seminars and study groups conducted for their benefit. For the most part, the ministry to children in Southern Baptist churches remains under the supervision of the pastors of the local churches.

Churches have moved into weekday education for very young children in increasing numbers. Most programs for three, four, and five year olds are designed to meet the educational needs of children in the particular congregation. An increasing number of day-care programs also are supervised by churches. These serve mainly the people who are able to pay for this service. The dedication to ministry on the part of teachers in these programs is high, for in relation to public-school teachers' salaries, salaries for the church school teachers remain at a lower level. A very few churches have weekday education through the grammar or high school level, with the quality of these varying greatly. Inner-city churches and missions are beginning to offer supplemental Weekday Bible Study as well as remedial programs to improve academic skills. It seems, however, that the cutting-edge for the future in work with children will be ministry to the children through the family with better understanding of today's dynamics of family life. ELIZABETH G. HUTCHINS

***CHILE, MISSION IN.** The land has suffered several physical disasters during recent years. The mission and Foreign Mission Board have met these crises with heroic efforts, as well as financial gifts, under difficult circumstances. Student groups meet regularly; radio ministries, begun in 1950, have expanded; television ministries were added; and evangelism was magnified through a nation-wide effort in 1967. A clinic for prenatal and child care began functioning in Antofagasta in 1965. By 1969, 53 missionaries served in 7 cities. FRANK K. MEANS

***CHINA, MISSION IN.** Through two decades of Communist control, severe pressures against Christians occurred periodically, culminating during the Cultural Revolution (1966–67) in the closing of most churches. Small groups of believers still meet quietly for Bible study and prayer. Official government warnings attested to the continued existence of an embattled yet viable Christian movement in China at the close of the sixties. Former China missionaries now serve in 11 other countries. JAMES D. BELOTE

***CHINESE, HOME MISSIONS TO.** See LANGUAGE MISSIONS, PROGRAM OF.

***CHOWAN COLLEGE.** In 1957 President Bruce Whitaker succeeded F. Orion Mixon (*q.v.*), under whose administration the junior college had witnessed the addition of its first residence hall for men, a science building, a student union, a structure to house the department of graphic arts, and a gymnasium-classroom facility. The college was accredited by the Southern Association of Colleges and Secondary Schools under Mixon's administration. Under Whitaker, the college experienced phenomenal growth in physical and fiscal assets, in prestige as an academic institution, and in enrolment. A carefully wrought "master plan," adopted by the board of trustees, saw the addition of five residence halls, a cafeteria-student union building, a classroom facility, a library-fine arts structure, a maintenance building, and athletic facilities for intercollegiate football, baseball, and track. Evaluation of the physical plant amounted to over $6,000,000 in 1969, as compared to $660,000 in 1956.

Increased emphasis has been placed upon the liberal arts and the preprofessional curricula, with approximately 80 per cent of the college's annual graduates pursuing further education in senior colleges or universities. The department of graphic arts, unique for the private junior college, has received wide acclaim, both for the quality of its training program and for its publications. The number of full-time faculty members increased from 22 in 1956, to 69 in 1969–70. With an enrolment of 1,316 in 1969–70, the college operated on a budget of $2,265,000.
HARGUS TAYLOR

CHRISTIAN. The name assigned the followers of the gospel of Jesus Christ and mentioned in only three places in the New Testament, Acts 11:26; 26:28; and I Peter 4:16. According to Acts 11:26, "in Antioch the disciples were for the first time called Christians." The name "Christian" appears to be a designation given Christians originally by others rather than by themselves. Members of the church seemed to have preferred to call themselves "brothers" (Acts 1:16), "disciples" (Acts 11:26), and "believers" (Acts 2:44).

According to Tacitus (*Annals,* XV, 44, 3), the name was in use at the time of Nero's persecution of the Christians (A.D. 64). Pliny, governor of Bithynia, in a famous letter written *c.* 112 to the Roman emperor Trajan, inquired of the emperor whether Christians should be punished because of the name "Christian" or because of specific crimes only. He spoke of their outstanding character, though he had put some of them to death.

The early Christians were often called upon to die "for the name" as martyrs of their faith in Christ (I Peter 4:16). By the middle of the second century they began to use the designation themselves. The Romans used it as a designation of members of the church.

The word "Christian" is derived from the word noun, *Christos,* which means "Christ." However, the word is often spelled *Chrestian (os)*, which points to an origin in the adjective *chrestos,* which means "good" or "kindly." Patristic writers used both spellings, with an "i" and with an "e." Tertullian (*c.* 160–*c.* 220) insisted that the confusion of Christus with Chrestus helped to demonstrate that Christians did not deserve persecution.

RAYMOND BRYAN BROWN

***CHRISTIAN INDEX, THE.** The weekly newsmagazine of the Georgia Baptist Convention has continued since 1956 to serve the same purposes for which it was founded in 1822 by Luther Rice and James Davis Knowles. Under the leadership of editor John Jeter Hurt, Jr., elected in 1947, circulation continued to grow. It had reached 133,000 when Hurt resigned in Sept., 1966, to become editor of the *Baptist Standard,* weekly newsmagazine of the Baptist General Convention of Texas. A former public newsman, Hurt gave the paper a heavy emphasis on current religious news and application of the Christian faith to social concerns in such areas as race relations and separation of church and state. Jack U. Harwell succeeded Hurt in Nov., 1966. A trained journalist and public relations specialist, Harwell had served as associate editor under Hurt for nine years.

The *Index* functions under a 10-member board of directors, elected by and answerable to the executive committee of the Georgia Baptist Convention. The 1969 operating budget was $325,000. In 1969, the staff set a goal of securing 150,000 subscribers by the paper's 150th anniversary in 1972. Other sesquicentennial observances were planned, including publication of a book by Harwell on the history of the *Index.*

JACK U. HARWELL

***CHRISTIAN LIFE COMMISSION.** See also articles on state CHRISTIAN LIFE COMMISSIONS under names of states.

CHRISTIAN LIFE COMMISSION (Texas). Established in 1950 to challenge Texas Baptists to fulfil the moral responsibilities of the new life in Christ even as they continue to emphasize faithfully the necessity of the new birth. A. C. Miller was named secretary of the commission and served until 1953. Foy Valentine then served until 1960, when he was succeeded by Jimmy Allen, 1960–68. The present secretary is James M. Dunn. Two associates serve as director of citizenship education and director of research and organization. The commission is presently composed of eight pastors, three lawyers, two doctors, and two professors. It also serves as the Public Affairs Committee of the denomination.

PHIL STRICKLAND

***CHRISTIAN LIFE COMMISSION, THE.** The Christian social concerns emphasis agency of the Southern Baptist Convention located at 460 James Robertson Parkway in Nashville, Tenn. 37219. Its purpose and objectives are stated in the two programs of work adopted by the Convention in 1961 and reaffirmed in 1968.

The commission's program of Christian Morality Development has the following objectives: (1) to assist the churches by helping them understand the moral demands of the gospel, and (2) to help Southern Baptists apply Christian principles to moral and social problems. This program represents the commission's primary reason for being, and into it are poured most of the agency's resources.

The program of Specialized Service and Coordination has the following objectives: (1) to study world peace, counseling and guidance, and human welfare as these relate to Southern Baptists, (2) to provide information and counsel to interested individuals and organizations desiring help regarding these matters, and (3) to provide special assistance for coordination of Southern Baptist interests and efforts in the areas of world peace, counseling and guidance, and human welfare.

Since 1955 the commission has experienced substantial growth under the leadership of Acker C. Miller until Jan. 1, 1960, and Foy D. Valentine since June 1, 1960. The Cooperative Program support for the commission's programs of work for 1955 was $17,000; in 1970 it had risen to $173,400, with the total budget including sale of literature and designated gifts amounting to $227,400.

The professional staff of the commission grew from one to five during the decade of the sixties. Ross C. Coggins served as the commission's first director of communications, beginning in 1961; and William M. Dyal, Jr., served as director of organization, beginning in 1964. Floyd A. Craig, of Oklahoma, was elected as director of public relations in 1967. W. L. Howse III of Texas succeeded Dyal as director of organization, Jan. 1, 1968, and Elmer S. West, Jr., of North Carolina became the commission's director of program development, June 1, 1968, succeeding Coggins. On Aug. 1, 1969, Harry N. Hollis, Jr., of Kentucky, was named the commission's director of special moral concerns. By 1970 the commission had a total of 11 permanent employees.

The recent expansion of the commission's staff and work was grounded in the strong leadership of Jesse Burton Weatherspoon (*q.v.*), who was the guiding light in the commission's early days of struggle for identity and a place of usefulness in the life of the Convention. Weatherspoon (1886–1964) was chairman of the commission, 1943–55. Two executive secretaries served the commission during Weatherspoon's chairmanship, Hugh Alexander Brimm and Acker C. Miller.

During the years 1956–59, under the leadership of Miller and in spite of severe budget limitations, the commission worked at producing printed materials, conducting conferences, and addressing the Convention on such issues as family life, peace, race relations, beverage alcohol, aging, labor relations, economic life, and salacious literature. One of the many significant statements brought before the Convention from year to year was made in Chicago, Ill., on May 30, 1959, when the appeal was made to Baptists, white and Negro, and to other Christian friends, to give careful consideration to a statement of principles that emphasized: (1) that God created man in his own image and, therefore, every man possesses infinite worth and should be treated with respect as a person; (2) that Christ died for all men and that the Christian view of every man must reflect the spirit of the cross; (3) that God is no respecter of persons and that prejudice against persons or mistreatment of persons on the grounds of race is contrary to the will of God; (4) that Christ said, "Thou shalt love thy neighbor as thy self" and, therefore, Christians are obligated to manifest goodwill toward all people and help them to achieve their fullest potentialities as persons; (5) that Christian love, as exemplified by Christ, is the supreme law for all human relations and, therefore, Christians have the assurance that such love, conscientiously practiced, will resolve tensions and bring harmony and goodwill in race relations; (6) that all true Christians are brothers in Christ and children of God and, therefore, are obligated to cultivate prayerful concern for one another and to show confidence in one another; and (7) that every person is accountable to God and, therefore, the right of an individual opinion, tested by the teachings of Christ, along with freedom to express it, always in the spirit of Christian love, should be granted to all and respected by all.

The statement expressed how to apply the principles:

> In accordance with these principles of our Christian faith, and as free citizens, this Commission protests the violence in all its ugly forms that is being used against the Negro people in the current segregation struggle issue or at any other time. In recognition of the Negro's right as a citizen of these United States, we call upon the law enforcement agencies of local, state, and national governments to protect him, irrespective of his position or culture, from lawless attacks on his person or property; and to protect any other individual or group who seeks to live in a chosen community as free citizens engaged in peaceful pursuits according to their own convictions and conscience.

The commission's statement on world peace called the churches to project their influence for world peace:

> (1) By making better men by hastening the spread of the gospel and its teachings among all peoples throughout the world. . . . (2) By the disarmament of ideas favorable to war. . . . (3) By working toward the general acceptance of law and order over the world. . . . (4) By making one's influence felt for world peace by the cultivation and direction of a Christian intelligence in social and economic relations. . . .

The 1959 Convention, at its conclusion, adopted three recommendations relative to the earlier statements:

> (1) That the Christian Life Commission accelerate its program of study, activity, and education in the interest of world peace. (2) That the Christian Life Commission seek ways of co-operation with similar agencies of other Baptist bodies in the United States in the interest of World Peace. (3) That the Christian Life Commission provide a Non-Governmental Organizations observer at the United Nations within budget limitations.

The commission moved promptly in the implementation of this mandate, sponsoring in New York during the early sixties, several seminars related to peace and the United Nations in cooperation with the American Baptist Convention's Division of Christian Social Concerns.

The decade of the sixties saw the commission move with greatly accelerated pace to assist Southern Baptists in the application of the gospel.

Foy D. Valentine came to the commission from the position as director of the Christian Life Commission of the Baptist General Convention of Texas, where he had served for seven years. A graduate of Baylor University, Waco, Tex., Valentine received his Th.M. and Th.D. degrees from Southwestern Baptist Theological Seminary in Forth Worth, Tex., where his major field of study was Christian social ethics.

During the first year of Valentine's leadership, he served as a consultant for the religion section of the program of the White House Conference on Aging, expanded the commission's literature ministry by increasing the commission's inventory of literature, became the Southern Baptist Non-Governmental Organizations observer to the United Nations, and made plans for the first special study seminar for Southern Baptist leaders, which became one of the commission's most useful instruments in emphasizing applied Christianity.

In Atlantic City, N. J., at the 1964 Convention, the Christian Life Commission opened its report with these words:

> In 1963 the Christian Life Commission experienced by far the most useful, exciting, and effective year

in its history. With a widely diversified approach, the Commission emphasized the application of Christian principles to the great moral and social problems with which Southern Baptists are grappling.

In spite of this optimistic beginning, when the commission's report was presented with recommendations on gambling, race relations, poverty, and capital punishment, two paragraphs from the capital punishment recommendation were deleted, and the recommendation concerning race relations was substituted entirely. Following a night called meeting composed primarily of individuals from Alabama, Louisiana, and Mississippi to plan a strategy to defeat the commission's recommendation on race relations, a substitute for the recommendation was offered from the floor of the Convention by James Middleton, pastor of Shreveport's First Baptist Church. By a standing vote, the substitute motion was declared lost by the presiding officer, K. Owen White. Since the vote was close, a motion to vote again, this time by ballot, was adopted. That afternoon it was announced that the substitute motion was carried by a very narrow margin.

The work of the commission was brought to the attention of Southern Baptists at the Atlantic City Convention as had seldom, if ever, been done before. The commission's growth in the next five years was unprecedented in spite of occasional attempts to mute the commission's voice and weaken its work.

The Convention, meeting in Dallas in 1965, not only voted to adopt the commission's recommendations but also overwhelmingly rejected a move to abolish the commission. That year the commission reported that its written materials had a circulation during the previous year of 29,613,413 pieces, and in 1966 that figure was reported to have climbed to more than 70,000,000. During these two years the commission was responsible for the production of book manuscripts on such varied subjects as Christian citizenship, gambling, alcohol and alcoholism, and Christian living.

At the Convention in 1967, held in Miami Beach, the commission presented a statement on peace which concluded with this challenge:

We call upon all of the churches not to be blinded by distorted appeals to false patriotism so that they lose sight of the personal tragedy, the great sorrow, and the fantastic cost attached to the present conflict. A spirit of solemn penitence is in order.

We urge all Southern Baptist churches and our fellow believers everywhere to unite in earnest prayer for peace and for renewed vision among God's people for the task of declaring and demonstrating his love to the suffering peoples of the earth.

Senator Mark Hatfield from Oregon then spoke to the commission's report. The Convention again voted by a larger majority to reject a motion to abolish the commission.

A significant action on the part of the commission during 1968 was the free distribution of more than 50,000 copies of the 275-page *Resource Guide to Current Social Issues.* The guide was prepared especially for this purpose by William M. Pinson, Jr., of the Southwestern Baptist Theological Seminary Christian ethics department to provide practical help to Southern Baptist pastors, ministers of education, and denominational workers on the most important moral issues of the day.

The commission-sponsored conferences for Baptist leaders both at the Southern Baptist summer assemblies and in cities such as Washington, New York, Chicago, and Atlanta enabled the agency to reach hundreds of key people directly and millions indirectly. The proceedings of these conferences were generally printed and made available, numerous articles about the conferences and the specific content of the messages delivered were carried in the state Baptist papers as well as in the secular press, and many of the messages became feature articles in such publications as *The Baptist Program* and *Home Missions* magazine. The National Broadcasting Company's Faith in Action radio series also carried a number of the programs from these conferences. Churches also made wide use of the taped programs for church training activities of various kinds.

In 1965 the commission presented its first "Distinguished Service Award for Leadership in Christian Social Ethics" to Brooks Hays "in recognition of unique and outstanding contributions to Southern Baptists, the nation, and mankind in the interest of world peace, racial justice, and Christian citizenship." The 1966 award went to T. B. Maston for his outstanding contributions "through inspired teaching, insightful writing, and prophetic proclamation of the ethical imperatives of the Christian gospel." In 1967 the award was given to Acker C. Miller for his "exemplary Christian character, undauntable spirit, prophetic denominational leadership, and faithful proclamation of the ethical imperatives of the Christian gospel."

The commission's emphasis on applied Christianity was greatly strengthened by the establishment of equivalent offices of work in several of the strong state Baptist conventions. Texas had begun such work under A. C. Miller's leadership in the late 1940's; Mississippi inaugurated such a program in 1966 with J. Clark Hensley as its first executive secretary; Virginia inaugurated such work in 1970 with Gene Williams as director; and North Carolina authorized the establishment of such work in 1970. In addition, most of the other state Baptist conventions had active standing committees to work in the area of Christian social concerns.

The report to the 1970 Convention declared:

The year 1969 climaxed a decade when the Christian Life Commission's emphasis on applied Christianity came of age among Southern Baptists. Throughout the churches, associations, state conventions, and various agencies there has been a strong upsurge of involvement in matters related to Christian social ethics. The Commission has sought to serve God and Southern Baptists in encouraging that upsurge, cultivating the developing interest, and providing general leadership for the denomination in the area of Christian social concern.

The commission's main objective has been to develop among Southern Baptists the kind of Christian morality, private and public, which will strongly undergird the total Southern Baptist witness for Jesus Christ.

FLOYD A. CRAIG and FOY D. VALENTINE

CHRISTIAN SERVICE CORPS. See SPECIAL MINISTRIES, HOME MISSION BOARD DEPARTMENT OF.

CHRISTIAN SOCIAL MINISTRIES, HOME MISSION BOARD PROGRAM OF. The Home Mission Board established the Department of Christian Social Ministries in 1966. Its two-fold objective, "to express Christian love and to provide a Christian witness through special missions actions," gathered together in one department the varied services to the disadvantaged previously assigned to several departments. It recognizes the social, moral, and religious forces in the United States and seeks to develop effective ways of sharing the gospel, using social work and clinical pastoral education techniques in ministering to human needs in Christ's name. Paul R. Adkins, the first secretary of the department, 1966–68, was succeeded by T. E. Carter, who had served in the Division of Chaplaincy since 1965.

In 1957, Clovis A. Brantley assumed staff responsibility for good will center work, after 17 years as a home missionary in New Orleans, La., and Memphis, Tenn. Assisting was Mrs. Noble Y. Beall, now consultant for center work. In 1967 "Baptist centers" came into use to describe the variety of ministries that had evolved and now included church community weekday ministries. Many churches were revitalized by utilizing existing church facilities while identifying with their local community needs. In 1968 William E. Amos, Jr., was added as consultant, having served previously as missionary in Louisville, Ky. He served until the end of Oct., 1969.

In 1960 Robert R. Harvey was elected the first director of migrant missions. The itinerant missionary was gradually eliminated and churches were enlisted to minister to the migrants in their areas, using such activities as day care centers, Bible classes, Vacation Bible Schools, religious films, and worship services. Harvey was succeeded in 1966 by J. Edward Taylor who, with his wife, had been missionaries to the migrants since 1957.

Responding to a 1954 resolution of the Southern Baptist Convention, the board began an approach to juvenile rehabilitation. J. V. James led this ministry from 1957 to 1962, followed by L. William Crews. In 1968 over 125 associations were participating in this ministry.

The board's active involvement in literacy techniques began in 1960, with Anne Grove as the first literacy worker during an experimental two-year period. In 1962 Mildred Blankenship assumed leadership of this ministry. The board's approach provides instructional opportunities for training volunteer teachers rather than employing field missionaries. Woman's Missionary Union and Home Mission Weeks at Glorieta and Ridgecrest assemblies provide annual workshop opportunities. Missionaries find literacy missions an effective means of Christian service and witness.

In 1966 the Convention's Executive Committee requested the board to provide for disaster relief in the United States. The responsibility was assigned to this program and a reserve fund was established for relief purposes. Material help in on-the-scene assistance has been provided in numerous situations, sometimes in collaboration with the Brotherhood Commission, state, and local Baptist leaders.

A new staff position was created 1968 with primary responsibilities for communication between the board and Baptist child-care agencies. Travis B. Lipscomb assumed (1968–) the leadership in this ministry, with other department responsibilities.

In 1969 board-approved organizational changes in the department's administrative structure eliminated overlapping of responsibilities.

T. E. CARTER

CHRISTIAN UNITY BAPTIST ASSOCIATION. A small Baptist group, which began in 1935, composed of churches which had been members of the Macedonia Baptist Association (formed in 1910 by two churches which had separated from the Mountain Union Baptist Association of Regular Baptists) and of churches which left the Mountain Union Association in the thirties. The churches in the first separation from the Mountain Union Association withdrew because of their acceptance of open communion. The churches in the second separation left largely because of their acceptance of the preaching of women.

Advocating the "unity, liberty and equality" of Christian believers, this body is Arminian in theology, holds that those who have been regenerated "and endure to the end" will be saved, and practices foot washing. Some churches conduct Sunday Schools.

A district association, the only general body maintained by this group, reported 11 churches and approximately 650 members in the mid-sixties. Following a recent division, only five churches with 227 members sent messengers to the 1969 meeting. The congregations are located in the Blue Ridge Mountains of northwestern North Carolina and southwestern Virginia. The association maintains fraternal relations with the Separate Baptists. ALBERT W. WARDIN, JR.

***CHRISTIANITY, HISTORY OF.** Christianity in its institutional, theological, and cultural expressions has undergone significant changes since 1958. These years actuate a curious sense of bewilderment and hope. The chief characteristic of this period was the rapidity of change within and without the church. Our situation, Robert Adolfs wrote, is "characterized by a hitherto unknown acceleration in the course of events by a growing estrangement from the traditional patterns of life and thought." He speaks of "rapidation" as a "complex and comprehensive phenomenon of our present age in which an acceleration of historical developments takes place in all spheres of human society in increasing discontinuity with the past." The "religious revival" of the fifties was followed by "religious renewal" in the early sixties, which in turn was followed quickly by the "religious revolution" that erupted in the mid sixties.

Major changes in both Roman Catholicism and Protestantism are quite evident. In 1958 the biblical realism of Karl Barth in Europe and Reinhold Niebuhr in America dominated the theological scene. The major institutional concern in Protestantism (besides constructing ever more ornate church buildings) was the ecumenical movement. There was then little evidence in the Roman Catholic Church of the ferment which produced and characterized the Second Vatican Council and the subsequent vigorous debate within Catholicism concerning theological, ethical, and institutional issues.

The decade 1960–70 witnessed a reevaluation of the 19th century Protestant theological tradition associated with Frederich Schleiermacher and Albrecht Ritschl in Europe and Horace Bushnell in America. Paul Tillich, who began his career in Germany and completed it in America, sought to blend theological realism with a philosophical, particularly existential, approach. His *Systematic Theology* moves in a world of discriminating appreciation for the 19th-century theological development and was an important stimulus in shaping the new situation.

Tillich's theology is an ingenious reinterpretation of biblical faith as a response to questions which reason can raise but cannot solve. The relativism of Tillich was tempered by the "revelatory situation" on the objective side and what he called "ultimate concern" on the subjective side. He developed a conception of "idolatry" and the "demonic" which provided both theologians and preachers with an imaginative and daring category for interpreting the contemporary scene. The relativism of Tillich was carried to its final point by the "death of God" theologians like Thomas Altizer, Paul van Buren, and William Hamilton. These "secular theologians," skeptical of philosophical theism and divine revelation alike, talked glibly about the "death of God." This theological fad lasted a short time and soon "died."

This radical theology, drawing upon the critical dimensions of Tillich's approach, "expelled" God and put upon man alone the unbearable burden of history. However, the constructive elements in Tillich's thought—a positive attitude toward revelation and an openness to mystical and philosophical theism—was an important factor in the theological scene in 1970. Eclecticism characterizes the current situation in Protestant theology, with a growing interest in eschatology. Jürgen Moltmann's "theology of hope" is the most clearly discernible element of continuity. Moltmann wants Christians to face the future, not the past. "The Church lives on memories," he writes in *Religion, Revolution, and the Future,* "the world on hope." But the world's hope rests on fragile foundations. Viable hope lies not in evolutionary progress inherent in man but in Christ's cross and resurrection. The resurrection is "the sign of future hope" and the cross means "hope to the hopeless."

The ecumenical movement was at center stage in 1958 and now has been pushed into the wings. The effort of the Consultation on Church Union, organized in 1960, to create a church "truly catholic, truly evangelical, and truly reformed" continues; but war and the threat of war, the pollution of the environment, and the search by the young for a more meaningful life overshadowed ecumenical interests. The situation in the world in 1970 was too critical for churchmen to expend enormous time and energy debating the theological and ecclesiological issues which keep organized Christianity apart. Ecumenical concerns, of course, continue particularly informal ecumenicity where Christian folk of various heritages work together on common purposes. The paradox of the situation today is that at a time when professional ecumenicity is at a low ebb actual ecumenicity is more widespread than ever before.

Particularly in Europe, the Christian-Marxist dialogue has displaced ecumenicity as the major concern of churchmen. The polarization of the world between the communist East and the democratic West has become such a monumental threat to humanity that better understanding must be sought not only among Christian communions but also between a Christian perspective and a Marxist one. The escalation of American involvement in Vietnam, in 1964, and the Russian invasion of Czechoslovakia, in 1968, made this effort more difficult but even more crucial.

In America the concern of the church for such crucial issues as poverty, pollution of the atmosphere, racism, and the generation gap resulted in less theological debate and ecclesiastical tinkering and more dialogue on matters of common concern. This concern precipitated strong support and considerable opposition. The church, alive to the burning issues of the seventies, exposed itself to the danger of absorption in current issues to the neglect of historical perspective and theological depth. However, the danger of too much attention to secular society is not greater than the danger of shirking responsibility for the plight of humanity in a time when hope struggles against despair with an uncertain outcome and the stakes are life or death on a terrestrial scale.

Vatican II, of course, marked a significant

turning point for the Roman Catholic Church. Until that time the Roman Catholic Church officially looked backward and tended to reaffirm the past, particularly the Middle Ages. There is significant continuity in perspective from the medieval period through the Council of Trent, Vatican I, the Papal Encyclical against modernism in 1903, to the dogma of the Assumption of Mary in 1950. The posture of the Roman Catholic Church was that of an enclave of truth in a world which was losing its way by pursuing the values of modernity.

Those who say that the Catholic Church was completely changed by Vatican II and those who contend that it was not changed at all occupy extreme and untenable positions. Everything did not change but some things did as a result of this historic meeting. The effort to "update" the church was a serious and sincere one.

The most serious theological problem in post-Vatican II Roman Catholicism is the meaning of dogma. Historically dogma has been an unchangeable declaration because it was a belief identified with Christian truth on the basis of the authority of the Roman Catholic Church, particularly the Pope. This concept of finality was strengthened tremendously by the declaration of the dogma of papal infallibility in 1870. Another effect of this preoccupation with finality was the tendency to regard nondogmatic but widely held beliefs and practices as also unchangeable. Vatican II precipitated a debate concerning this entire matter.

Hans Küng is an example of a progressive Roman Catholic theologian who is disturbed by the traditional understanding of dogma. He seeks to soften its intransigence by making a distinction between the kernel of dogma, which comes from revelation, and the historical form of a dogma, which comes from the cultural situation in which the dogma is forged.

Another problem which Vatican II opened up involves widely held beliefs, such as clerical celibacy and birth control, which are still officially insisted upon as if they were dogmatic. Though widely held doctrines which are not officially dogmatic do not theoretically have the force of dogma, their force is equal to dogma as long as the Pope insists upon their finality, even though this may be temporary. It is also quite clear in contemporary discussion that though there is a good deal of resistance to the "infallibility" of the Pope, particularly among Dutch Catholics, that such finality is probably an essential feature of Roman Catholicism.

In 1948 Kenneth Scott Latourette wrote that "the Roman Catholic Church is handicapped, probably permanently and increasingly, by being too closely bound to a particular cultural tradition and by being based primarily upon a small section of the globe." This is probably as true now (1970) as it was when he wrote it. However, the population explosion means any prediction about the "growth" of any human institution is quite tenuous. Also, the effort of Roman Catholicism to update itself in Vatican II could result in its penetration of cultures which would have been impervious to its strategies prior to Pope John XXIII. Another possibility is that the confusion and division within Catholicism which the effort to modernize it has elicited in the immediate post-Vatican II period will permanently impair the growth of the Catholic church.

The future of the Roman Catholic Church is thus not clear. What seems clear is that the present profile of Roman Catholicism is not notably appealing, especially to the young. The historical intransigence of the Roman Catholic Church appears here and there, especially in assertions by the Pope of his undiminished authority and of his adamant opposition to any relaxation of regulations concerning clerical celibacy and birth control.

What lies ahead for Protestantism is equally problematical. Extreme forms of secular Christianity espoused by *avant-garde* churchmen, actuated by serious concern for the relevancy of religion but corroded by relativism and skepticism, made less impact upon the late sixties than was supposed at the time. Harvey Cox's *Secular City* and Malcolm Boyd's *Are You Running With Me Jesus?* shocked some out of dreary stereotypes which passed for Christianity but the positive contribution to clarifying the role of the Christian and providing morale for the despair and confusion in the church is less evident.

The mood of America in 1970 was a curious mixture of the so-called "silent majority," longing for the simplicities of "prerevolutionary" America, and the "voluble minority," especially the young, searching for new styles of life and militantly in pursuit of a new world without the idiocy of war and with clean air. A "dead" God held little interest in a time of experimentation with everything from LSD to spiritualism. Young people especially were much more interested in being "turned on" by drugs or religion or sex than "turned off" by the metaphysical skepticism of the new theology. A generation in search of its "soul," a widely used word in the sixties, looked askance upon the institutional church but was quite open to a "religious" view of the world and did not gag on the word "God."

In 1970 larger horizons, whether man in outer space or man's inner life (expanded consciousness), beckoned thoughtful folk in and out of the church. What lies ahead in religion is probably continued experiments to synthesize Christianity and secular concerns, social and psychological, in the context of the history of religions.

Bibliography: Paul Tillich, *Systematic Theology,* 3 vols (1953, 1956, 1963). Jürgen Moltmann, *Theology of Hope,* translated by James W. Leitch (1965). Harvey Cox, *The Secular City* (1965). Hans Küng, *The Church,* translated by Ray and Rosalen Ockenden (1967). Walter M. Abbott, ed., *The Documents of Vatican II* (1966). PENROSE ST. AMANT

***CHRISTOLOGY.** Christology is serious reflection on the meaning and implications of the affirmation that Jesus is the Christ. The Christological task involves an attempt to express the mystery of the revelation of God through Jesus in language and perspectives which are most understandable to Christians. This perennial intellectual quest is that of *fides quaerens intellectum,* faith in search of understanding.

At its best Christology has drawn upon existential, historical, and philosophical insights in its formulation. Such a comprehensive approach is obvious in the New Testament and should be normative in every contemporary exposition. The present dilemma in Christological studies arises, in part, from the failure of some scholars to give adequate attention to one or more of the existential, historical, or philosophical components. There are several complicating factors, e.g., the radical skepticism concerning the validity of all philosophical endeavor, which hinder the correlation of the three perspectives essential to Christology. Outstanding scholars, both Protestant and Roman Catholic, realizing this desperate situation, are probing for ways of formulating a more meaningful Christology.

A radical reaction to Christology based on experience or history came in the writings of Karl Barth. Barth and a host of other theologians, e.g., Emil Brunner, D. M. Baillie, and Paul Tillich, emphasized revelation as the mysterious, divine-human encounter which is paradoxical or dialectical in nature. They warned against the inherent limitations of all doctrinal expressions. Søren Kierkegaard's writings were the primary source for dialectical Christology which found lucid expression in D. M. Baillie's book, *God Was In Christ.* Baillie stresses that in the experience of the mystery of revelation the dichotomy between the Jesus of History and the Christ of Faith is transcended in the paradox of grace. Contemporary Christology is indebted to the dialectical theologians for a new interpretation of revelation. A helpful Christology in this secular age will make explicit the understanding of revelation with which it is oriented.

Almost 60 years before Karl Barth's presentation of a dynamic concept of revelation from above, the thought of Charles Darwin (*The Origin of Species,* 1859) was preparing the way for the presentation of an interpretation of revelation and Christology from below. The church looked with distrust upon the process philosophy of A. N. Whitehead and its modification by Charles Hartshorne. This insight, which is in part Hebraic, has been refined in the writings of D. D. Williams, Paul Tillich, Karl Rahmer, Teilhard de Chardin, and John Macquarrie. Taken alone, a Christology from below is likely to be inadequate. A contemporary Christology, however, which neglects this emphasis will prove to be even more unacceptable. A dynamic Christology from below will do much to correlate the concepts of creation and redemption and, furthermore, to insure the Chalcedonian affirmation, *vere homo.*

While the dialectical theologians were approaching Christology from above and the metaphysical realists from below, the emphasis by the existentialists, i.e. Rudolf Bultmann, was on a Christology from within. Bultmann's valuable work on the problem of myth should not be allowed to overshadow the key to his Christology which is an ontology of faith. The significance of this approach to Christology is constructively appropriated by John Macquarrie. Some linguistic analysts have recklessly ignored this insight into revelation and Christology. Although the existential component alone is insufficient for the formulation of Christology, it can no longer be neglected.

The attempts to handle the problem of supernaturalism, or the transcendent, from above, below, or within have not been entirely successful. They have been, however, more constructive than the attempts by the positivists and their successors who have either denied, ignored, or treated superficially the reality of mystery in the universe in general and man in particular. The emphasis on a Christology judged by the principle of verification and a revelation without mystery is being subjected to careful scrutiny by Professors William Horden and James A. Martin, Jr. Contemporary Christology is indebted to the analytical philosophers for their reminders about epistemology and language usage.

The most recent efforts in Christology are seen in the "Death of God" theologians such as T. J. J. Altizer and Paul van Buren. It is appropriate to note, however, that these writers are raising a question which is crucial in the New Testament, "What are the implications of the death of the Son of God for God Himself?" The church, however, has always contended for a Christological interpretation of God, but it has never accepted a reduction of theology to Christology or Jesusology.

BIBLIOGRAPHY: John Macquarrie, *Principles of Christian Theology* (1966). John McIntyre, *The Shape of Christology* (1966).

JOHN W. EDDINS, JR.

***CHURCH ADMINISTRATION.** See LEADERSHIP.

CHURCH LOANS, HOME MISSION BOARD PROGRAM OF. This HMB program is assigned to the Division of Church Loans to "assist churches, associations and state conventions to provide financing for purchase of church sites and for construction of church buildings." Four funds provide resources from which to extend loans:

(1) **The Church Building Loan Fund.*—It grew to over $4,000,000 from 1959 to 1969. These funds were received from individuals through gifts, wills, annuities, and other special sources.

(2) **The Church Extension Loan Fund.*—By 1970 it had increased its assets to over $19,000,000. These funds were derived from three basic sources: special appropriations from the Cooperative Program, special appropriations

from the board's budgets, and designated budget items from the Annie Armstrong Easter Offering for Home Missions.

(3) *The Site Fund.*—It has derived its resources from the same sources as the Church Extension Loan Fund. Its objective is to obtain property to hold for future church use. Loans are interest free for two and one half years and require only token payments on principal during the initial interest-free period. Assets at the close of 1969 were over $4,500,000.

(4) *Borrowing.*—In 1953 the board was authorized to borrow $500,000 to enlarge its loan assistance to the churches. In 1961 the board was authorized by the Southern Baptist Convention to enlarge its borrowing to an amount equal to 50 per cent of the total of the Church Extension Loan Fund and the Site Fund. In 1967 this authority was enlarged to an amount equal to the total of these two funds, conditioned upon the board limiting its liability to the collateral to secure the loan plus not less than a 10 per cent funded reserve. At the close of 1969 the board had outstanding borrowing of $6,000,000.

At the close of 1969 seven staff men assisted with the administration of funds and assisted the churches with their building and loan requirements. They were J. C. (Pat) McDaniel, William C. Dudley, Billy T. Hargrove, William T. Updike, Thomas V. Haynes, and Thomas F. Thrailkill. Robert H. Kilgore, division director, succeeded G. Frank Garrison who retired as director in 1965 after 11 years of service. Also retiring then was Berner F. Wilson, assistant to the division director, after 11 years of service. Roy F. Lewis, a staff member since 1961, resigned Nov., 1969, to return to the pastorate, and in Feb., 1970, McDaniel resigned to become executive secretary of the Kansas Baptist Convention. Early in 1970 B. Olin Cox and Bob Stidham were elected to fill these vacancies.

ROBERT H. KILGORE

CHURCH MEMBER ORIENTATION. The reception, care, and development of new church members has emerged as a significant concern in many Southern Baptist churches since 1956. This concern had its roots both in theological and practical considerations. From the theological perspective, questions increasingly emerged relative to the historic Baptist doctrine of a regenerate church membership. From the practical perspective, there was a growing concern over the large number of individuals who unite with a church but who fail to become related in any way to the life, study, and ministry of the church. Leader's saw a close relationship between spiritual vitality and a truly regenerate church.

The basic purpose and approach of new member orientation is to lead the individual to reflect upon his experience, to see it more clearly, and to become more deeply committed to the way he has chosen.

By 1969, 55 per cent of Southern Baptist churches were making some effort to provide counsel and instruction for the new member. Two major factors that have contributed to the rather phenomenal development in this area were the addition of a consultant in charge of new member orientation in the Training Union Department of the Sunday School Board in Oct., 1961, and the publication of *New Church Member Orientation Manual* (1965), by Earl Waldrup, who was the first consultant assigned to this area of work.

Of the 55 per cent of the churches that are doing something to provide orientation, approximately 75 per cent offer this only to new converts; only 25 per cent offer classes for those who unite with the church by transfer of letter. The pastors lead the study in the large majority of cases.

The basic pattern that seemed to emerge was a four-week course of study taught on Sunday night during the Training Union hour. The four emphases were usually as follows: (1) the salvation experience, (2) Baptist doctrines, (3) the work of the denomination (or Baptist history), and (4) the work of the local church.

The Training Union Department, in an effort to help the churches improve new member orientation, devised graded curriculum for children, youth, and adults. This curriculum provides a 13-week course of study. "In Covenant" is for adults, "Belonging" is for youth, and "Promises to Keep" is for older children.

There is wide variety in what individual churches are doing. Some are undertaking a much more serious and ambitious approach than that suggested by the Sunday School Board. By far the large majority, however, are undertaking much less than that suggested. Some receive persons into membership immediately when they present themselves. Others suggest that the individual complete the course of study before being received into membership. A few require completion of the study as a prerequisite to membership. After the course of study, some churches let the individual indicate again whether he still desires to unite with the church. Some have a service of celebration on Wednesday evening when new members are received into the church fellowship.

FINDLEY B. EDGE

CHURCH STUDY COURSE (cf. Study Courses, Vol. II). A study group of the curriculum committee of the Sunday School Board was appointed in Dec., 1956, to make an objective study of existing study courses and to determine if there were ways to improve them. After more than two years of research and careful consideration, the study group recommended that the existing Sunday School Training Course, Graded Training Union Study Course, and Church Music Training Course be merged into one unified study course system to be named the Church Study Course. The board authorized the merger effective Oct. 1, 1959. Woman's Missionary Union principles and methods were added Oct. 1, 1961, and Brotherhood Commission principles and methods were added Jan. 1, 1967.

The course was fully graded. It provided a system of awards consisting of a series of five diplomas of 20 books each for Adults and Young People, two diplomas of five books each for Intermediates, and two diplomas of five books each for Juniors. The Young People and Adult diplomas were called Christian Training Diploma, Approved Workman Diploma, Master Workman Diploma, Distinguished Workman Diploma, and Special Citation Diploma.

The purpose of the course was "to help Christians to grow in knowledge and conviction, to help them to grow toward maturity in Christian character and competence for service, to encourage them to participate worthily as workers in their churches, and to develop leaders for all phases of church life and work."

The course was comprehensive. The books were groups in 21 categories as follows: Survey Courses, Bible, Christian Home, Christian Life, Church Membership, Doctrine, Evangelism, History, Leadership, Missions, Special Studies, Stewardship, The Christian in the Social Order, The Denomination, Understanding the Individual, Church Administration, Sunday School Principles and Methods, Training Union Principles and Methods, Music Ministry Principles and Methods, Woman's Missionary Union Principles and Methods, and Brotherhood Principles and Methods.

The Church Study Course was promoted by the Sunday School Board through its Sunday School, Church Training, Church Music, and Church Administration departments; by the WMU; by the Brotherhood Commision; and by the respective departments in the states affiliated with the SBC.

The total number of book awards earned between the launching of the course Oct. 1, 1959, and its complete revision Dec. 31, 1969, was 10,729,447.

Organization, program, and curriculum plans developed for use by the churches in the seventies seemed to require many changes in the Church Study Course. These changes were incorporated in a plan called the New Church Study Course, which became effective Jan. 1, 1970.

The New Church Study Course offers increased flexibility. It provides courses of varying length and difficulty, varied format and types of course materials, additional types of credit, and improved organization of courses.

The New Church Study Course consists of two types of courses: the Christian development courses for all church members and the Christian leadership courses for church leaders.

The purpose of the Christian Development Course is to provide courses of study which will help church members grow toward maturity in Christian living and competence in Christian service. These courses offer more comprehensive, advanced, and varied learning experiences than can be provided through curriculum periodicals. Tests, exercises, credits, and diplomas of achievement are offered to help church members measure their progress in developing needed knowledge, understanding, and skills. The Christian development courses are organized into subject areas as follows: The Church, Christian Growth and Service, Biblical Revelation, Christian Theology, Christian Ethics, Christian History, Missions, and Church Music.

Diplomas offered to Youth and Adults are as follows: Diploma in Christian Development, Advanced Diploma in Christian Development, Distinguished Diploma in Christian Development, and Master Diploma in Christian Development.

The Christian leadership courses provide a comprehensive series of courses organized into the following subject areas: Introductory Courses in Church Leadership, Understanding Work with Age Level and Special Groups in a Church, Developing General Leadership Skills, Bible Teaching Program, Training Program, Church Missions Program—Woman's Missionary Union, Church Missions Program—Brotherhood, Church Music Program, Pastoral Ministries, and Program and Administration Services. Tests, exercises, credits, and diplomas are offered to help leaders measure their growth in leadership ability. Diplomas are awarded to Youth and Adults as follows: Diploma in (a Program or Service) Leadership, Diploma in Christian Leadership, Advanced Diploma in Christian Leadership, and Distinguished Diploma in Christian Leadership.

Both Christian development courses and Christian leadership courses are designed to be effective for individual and class study. Learning aids, study guides, and teaching guides are available for some courses. Credits are granted to Youth and Adults for reading, individual study, and class study. J. M. CROWE

CHURCH TRAINING DEPARTMENT. See BAPTIST TRAINING UNION.

CHURCHES, NEW MINISTRIES OF THE. Beginning in the sixties local congregations, denominations, and inter-faith groups have been accelerating the search for new forms of ministry. They have attempted to reexamine the ministry of the church in the light of the ministry of Jesus and his instruction to the church. Spurred on by renewal efforts, the church has seen its ministry as an extension of the ministry of Christ in the world.

In this respect the church's ministry in the world takes the form of servant. In recent years it has moved more and more toward a functional design where the ministries enable the church to relate to men where they are living out the deep concerns of their lives and to minister unto them in the context of that need. These ministries are designed in the recognition of changing social conditions and attempt to reflect sociological awareness, psychological insight, and theological understanding of contemporary life.

New patterns of church ministries may be

found today at almost every level of church involvement. Individual congregations have introduced the use of art forms in worship, modern techniques in religious education, and social work methods into weekday activities. They have entered into cooperative ministry with secular agencies in efforts to combat poverty, to minister to the needs of youth, and to become more involved with family services. They have enlarged their staffs to include professional persons in related fields among the helping professions. They have placed a new stress on the use of the laity and have seen the laity as the reference group for mission and ministry. Nowhere have these stresses been more obvious than in the new emphasis upon church and community weekday ministries, such as those that fall in the general areas of education, day care, clubs, mobile ministries, Bible study, welfare, visitation and evangelism, recreation, coffee houses, music, and other special projects.

Another approach of particular interest to Southern Baptists is the "Mission Action" program promoted through the use of prepared guidebooks. In 1970 guidebooks projected specific activities which churches might attempt in providing ministries to the aged, physically handicapped, migrants, illiterates, the military, prisoners, alcoholics, unwed mothers, the sick, the economically disadvantaged, internationals, and to several other special groups. Each guidebook contains from 10 to 60 or more separate actions which might be pursued. Included among them are the ministries that are oriented toward worship and religious education where the stress is upon verbalization, and other ministries that are service and deed oriented.

Responsible leadership has insisted upon a design for church ministry that is flexible and that serves in areas of human need. Cooperation with other helping groups wherever possible is encouraged. Many churchmen have concluded that both the deification of the status quo and of innovation must be avoided as the church searches for the "new wineskins" for the gospel.

BIBLIOGRAPHY: "New Patterns of Ministry," *Review and Expositor,* LXVI:2 (Spring, 1969).

G. WILLIS BENNETT

CHURCHES AND CHURCH-TYPE MISSIONS, PROGRAM OF ESTABLISHING NEW. Established in 1966, the objective of this program is to work with and assist churches, associations, and state conventions in establishing and bringing to self-support new churches and missions (that may become churches). It is implemented through the programs of metropolitan, rural-urban, pioneer, and language missions. It develops and suggests techniques and procedures for discovering and analyzing new church opportunities. In cooperation with leaders of related Southern Baptist Convention programs, it defines objectives, responsibilities, organization, and relationships of the church missions committee and the associational missions committee. It discovers and communicates effective techniques and procedures for use by churches, associations, and state conventions in establishing new churches and missions, and for bringing them to self-support with adequate programs and organizations.

LOYD CORDER

CHURCHES AND PUBLIC PROGRAMS. According to the Constitution, the United States of America was established by "we the people" to achieve goals which the founders felt could best be achieved by uniting and working together. The three branches of government on the national level and their counterparts on the state and local levels undertake public programs to achieve these goals. At the time the Constitution was written many programs which were oriented toward people and their welfare were financed and administered by the churches and other private associations. Today most of these private programs have been augmented or supplanted by public programs at the local, state, and national levels. The other powers which governments have traditionally held have expanded in breadth and in depth. In both types of programs the churches have had varying degrees of concern and influence. They have been particularly involved in public programs since World War II.

Though most Baptists in the United States have traditionally thought in terms of a constitutional separation of church and state, since the mid-fifties many have become more aware of at least five concepts that relate to churches and public programs. (1) The principle of religious liberty is scriptural and must not be compromised for political, social, or sectarian expediency. (2) There are religious functions which must be performed only by the churches; there are secular functions which are exclusively state functions; and there are public functions in which both the churches and the government need to cooperate. (3) Baptists can cooperate with government in policy areas where Christians have biblical responsibilities without violating their beliefs on religious liberty. (4) Public programs, when they are being shaped by legislative, administrative, or judicial action, can—and must—have the input of Christian ideals and witness. A failure to do so leaves the input to those either opposed or neutral to Christianity and its values. (5) The churches and their members have a responsibility to be vigilant in holding officials accountable for their stewardship of responsibility.

These developing insights have been evidenced in a number of major policy decisions since 1955. The programs in which the churches have been most active include such broad areas of activity as health, welfare, education, poverty, taxation, social security, civil rights, and moral issues involving control of pornography, gambling, sex education, etc. In each of these the various religious groups have played a role.

There are a number of problems in the involvement of the churches in public programs. Some of them are listed below:

(1) Representation: who speaks for Southern Baptists? A church, an association, a convention, or an agency speaks for itself only and does not speak for all Baptists. They try to make this clear, and governmental officials realize this fact. This limits the impact of Baptist witness to government except on those few issues on which we are united. This is perhaps a price Southern Baptists are willing to pay for the religious freedom they enjoy within their own denomination.

(2) Information: how can Baptists know the facts? Communication is a problem in spite of an excellent system of state denominational papers and the cooperation of those agencies who publish materials for churches and special groups. But public affairs is a dynamic arena which does not gear itself to deadlines. Secular sources and civil liberties groups often have a neutral or even antichurch bias. Action on church-state public issues without adequate information from responsible denominational sources can lead to embarrassment, conflict in testimony, and a neutralizing of Baptist witness.

(3) Decision: how can decisions be made by Southern Baptists? An annual meeting in a convention with thousands of messengers has difficulty in meeting the needs of rapidly changing times. The decision-making process of Southern Baptists relating to the developing public programs has left much to be desired. Both competence and consensus should be sought in the future as Baptists decide their role in public programs.

(4) Influence: are Southern Baptists to be effective stewards of influence? Southern Baptists are confronted with the problem of exercising an influence in public affairs commensurate with their size and the validity of their insights. JOHN W. BAKER

***CITY MISSIONS.** See METROPOLITAN MISSIONS, HOME MISSION BOARD PROGRAM OF.

CLAPP, JOSEPH CAROLOS, JR. (b. Fulton, Ky., Dec. 18, 1916; d. Corpus Christi, Tex., Jan. 10, 1968). President, University of Corpus Christi. Ordained as a minister in 1936, he was educated at Union University (B.A.), and New Orleans Baptist Theological Seminary (B.D., Th.M., and Th.D.), with additional graduate study at Tulane University and Vanderbilt University. Clapp married Brownie M. West of Jackson, Tenn., in 1939. They had one child, Carol (Mrs. Richard Capp). He served as director of public relations at New Orleans Seminary, 1954–55; professor of religion at Furman University, 1955–57; and professor of religion, 1948–53, and public relations director and development vice-president at William Jewell College, 1961–64. He was pastor of First Baptist Church, Greer, S. C., 1956–61. Vice-president for development at University of Corpus Christi, 1964–65, he served as president of the school, Dec., 1965, until his death. Under his leadership the university became fully accredited.

MARY HAMILTON and OLAN H. RUNNELS

CLARKE, WILLIAM NEWTON b. Cazenovia, N. Y., Dec. 2, 1841; d. DeLand, Fla., Jan. 14, 1912). Pastor, theological professor, author. He was the third child of William Clarke, a Baptist minister and descendant of Jeremiah Clarke, the second president of Rhode Island Plantations under the charter of 1644, and Urania Miner Clarke, the descendant of Miners who came to Massachusetts c. 1630 and became Baptists. Clarke graduated from Oneida Conference Seminary, a Methodist preparatory school in Cazenovia; Madison (later Colgate) University, 1861; and Hamilton Theological Seminary, 1863. He served as pastor of Baptist churches in Keene, N. H., 1863–69; Newton Center, Mass., 1869–80; Montreal, Canada, 1880–83; Hamilton, N. Y., 1887–90. He was professor of New Testament interpretation, Toronto Baptist College, Toronto, Canada, 1883–87; professor of theology, 1890–1908, and lecturer in Christian ethics, 1908–12, at Hamilton Theological Seminary.

Clarke delivered numerous series of lectures to universities and schools of theology. He was awarded honorary doctorates by Yale University of Chicago and Columbia University. His published works include the following: *Commentary on the Gospel of Mark,* "American Commentary on the New Testament" (1881); *Centennial Anniversary of the Baptist Church at Newton Center* [Mass.], Nov. 14, 1880 (1881); *An Outline of Christian Theology* (1894); *Mystery in Religion* (1897); *The Circle of Theology: An Introduction to Theological Study* (1897); *Can I Believe in God the Father?* (1899); *What Shall We Think of Christianity?* (1899); *A Study of Christian Missions* (1900); *Huxley and Phillips Brooks* (1903); *The Use of the Scriptures in Theology* (1905); *The Christian Doctrine of God* (1909); *The Ideal of Jesus* (1911); *Sixty Years with the Bible: A Record of Experience* (1912); and *Immortality, A Study of Belief,* and *Earlier Addresses* (1920).

Clarke married Emily Smith of Waverly, Pa., in 1869. They spent the winters from 1906 to his death in DeLand, Fla., where he used the library of Stetson University.

BIBLIOGRAPHY: Emily Smith Clarke, ed., *W. N. C.: A Biography, with Additional Sketches by His Friends and Colleagues* (1916); Claude L. Howe, Jr., "The Theology of W. N. C." (unpublished Th.D. thesis, New Orleans Baptist Theological Seminary, 1959). JAMES LEO GARRETT, JR.

***CLARKE MEMORIAL COLLEGE.** President W. Lowery Compere assumed administrative leadership of this Mississippi Baptist junior college, Jan., 1955, following 10-year presidency of William Earle Green. That year the school received $140,000 bequest as residuary legatee, estate of Mrs. Bessie Eastland Kent, Forest, Miss.

Sanders Memorial Library, built 1956, was named in memory Mr. and Mrs. Wiley Sanders, recognizing $25,000 gift by their son, H. B. Sanders, Aberdeen. Cockrell Gymnasium was named for Earl Cockrell, Tupelo, in appreciation of his contributions to the college. Women's residence hall was erected 1957. A dormitory that burned in 1960 was rebuilt and named Huddleston Hall in appreciation of $80,000 gift by Mrs. A. O. Huddleston, Leland. A bequest of $60,000 was received in 1960 from the estate of Jennie Stevens, Canton.

An expansion program, approved by Mississippi Baptist Convention in 1960, added $650,000 to plant and endowment. A science hall was erected in 1962. Lott Fine Arts Building was constructed 1967, named in honor of Mr. and Mrs. Reuben Lott, Laurel, recognizing $100,000 contribution. A property bequest valued at $60,000 was received in 1969 from the estate of W. P. Bridges, Jackson.

Total assets, 1969: plant, $1,522,268, and endowment, $551,894. Number graduates 1956–1969: approximately 1,100. W. LOWREY COMPERE

***CLEAR CREEK BAPTIST SCHOOL.** Located in Pineville, Ky. Dennis Merrill Aldridge has served as president since 1954. Improvements include (1) rebuilding of a new modern Student Industries Building (1958) to replace one which burned in 1956; (2) 12 units of student apartments (1968–69); (3) remodeling of Kelly Hall providing additional classrooms; and (4) improvement of roads and grounds. The library has 10,000 volumes. Currently it has 155 students enrolled and a faculty-staff of 17. It operates a recording studio and sends a radio program entitled "Clear Creek Chimes" over 49 stations in Kentucky and adjoining states. In cooperation with the Kentucky Baptist Convention and the Home Mission Board, it has added a department of in-service training for its ministerial students. Assets in 1968 were $1,039,573.

HAROLD GLEN SANDERS

CLEGG, JAMES LOYD (b. Walton County, Ga., Sept. 22, 1897; d. Macon, Ga., Dec. 26, 1962). Pastor and denominational leader. Active in the Georgia Baptist Convention, he served as recording secretary, 1944–60, having been assistant secretary from 1936. He also served as a member of the executive committee. Clegg earned the Th.B. from Mercer University in 1924. Mercer conferred on him the honorary D.D. degree (1948). His pastorates extended over a period of 36 years from 1923 to 1959. The longest was First Baptist Church, Dalton, Ga., 1936–53, when illness forced an inactive period until 1956. Other Georgia pastorates included Locust Grove, Hampton, Norwood, Mt. Beulah, Sweetwater, and Warrenton. He married Mary Phillips. They had three children: James L., Jr., Charles C., and Mary Ann. BERNARD D. KING

CLONINGER, VERNON FRANKLIN (b. Walla Walla, Wash., Dec. 21, 1888; d. Chetopa, Kans., June 28, 1968). Pastor, evangelist, and radio preacher. Converted in 1907 at Timber Hill Evangelical Church, near Dennis, Kans., he was ordained into the ministry on Apr. 21, 1921, by the First Baptist Church, Cherryvale, Kans. Lacking formal education, he attended Central Baptist Theological Seminary, Kansas City, Kans., 1922–23. While pastor of the First Baptist Church, Oswego, Kans., he also preached at a nearby church or in a schoolhouse Sunday afternoons and week nights. He was a pioneer in radio preaching. Beginning on radio station KGGF, Picher, Okla., in 1926, he continued after it was moved to Coffeyville, Kans., for 21 years. For 19 years in full-time and part-time relationships, he ministered to 10 or more churches in southeast Kansas. Cloninger sought ties with Southern Baptists in Missouri without success. In 1939 he accepted the call to the Virginia Avenue Baptist Church, Bartlesville, Okla., where he served for nine years and became permanently identified with Southern Baptist churches. He married Mattie Pilkington on Jan. 2, 1910. They had three children: Lawrence, Alonzo, and Orpha.

N. J. WESTMORELAND

***COLLEGE, THE DENOMINATIONAL.** The denominational colleges have been subject to all of the many changes which have marked higher education in the sixties. Curricula have been updated, calendars have been altered, audiovisuals are more frequently used, faculty-trustee-student relationships have been explored, the question of governance of the colleges has been challenged, and the spirit of academic revolution is on every hand.

Though considerably shocked by some of the new ideas, some clear-thinking educators have been willing to admit that perhaps the academic establishment as it has been known during the first half of the 20th century is overdue for some drastic changes. Apparently many of the proposed reforms would not have normally taken place for years to come. Student pressures particularly have prodded administrations into making relatively quick adjustments. No doubt much good will come from these changes even though something may also be lost.

The availability of federal funds for higher education has tempted the church-related colleges to accept tax-fund aid even though against their former practices. The sharp rise in the cost of operating colleges has driven all of them to seeking new sources of income with which to operate.

In the middle sixties the government was rather free in providing funds, especially in research. As the decade moved toward its end, escalating Vietnam war costs and inflation brought about some reduction in areas of federal aid. After depending on tax aid for a while, colleges experienced a financial pinch when these funds were reduced. Undoubtedly these educational funds will be restored when conditions improve. The church-related colleges which had used less public money naturally had less adjusting to do when the funds were reduced.

Some church-related colleges, notably those operated by Southern Baptists, steered away from accepting outright grants from government. Whether such colleges can continue this policy and continue operating remains to be seen. The churches could supply the needs, but history tends to show that they are not likely to do so.

Federal loan funds for students have been generally approved because the money goes to the student before going finally to the colleges. Pending court cases could go far toward solving the problem of accepting or not accepting federal funds.

Though people hesitate to speak of competition between colleges, the fact remains that students often make their choices of colleges on the basis of tuition costs. The proliferation of state-supported community colleges with small fee charges have recently presented enrolment problems for church-related colleges which have had to continue to raise their tuition charges.

The church-supported colleges find it necessary to continue to sell their constituency on the peculiar values to be found in their schools and apparently have succeeded since enrolments have grown steadily. However, on account of housing shortages the church colleges have not increased enrolments in the same ratio as have the tax-supported colleges.

As the denominational college enters the decade of the seventies no trend of phasing out the schools has developed. Here and there some denominational college has closed or merged. Where mergers are effected some real strengths may be gained.

Certainly in the case of Southern Baptist colleges, the beginning of the decade of the seventies finds the schools in the best situation in their history so far as condition of the plants, qualifications of the faculties, and being accredited are concerned. The prospects of having enough funds to continue in this favorable position will depend on the discovery of additional sources of support. RABUN L. BRANTLEY

COLLEGE AND CAREER. In 1961 this publication succeeded *Career News,* which was established in 1956 by the Education Commission. It is published 10 times a year. The purpose of the eight-page three-column paper is to be a medium for articles on planning for college and making career choices, suitable primarily for sophomores, juniors, and seniors in high school and freshmen in college. The paper has been largely used in the churches as a part of their annual emphases on Christian education and Baptist schools. Bulk subscriptions are often taken by churches for their young people. Conventions in 16 states send subscriptions to all high school libraries requesting the paper. The February number is a special one, carrying information on Baptist schools.

RABUN L. BRANTLEY

COLLINS, BENJAMIN FRANK (b. Grainger County, Tenn., Feb. 7, 1893; d. New Market, Tenn.; Nov. 12, 1967). Son of Jim and Susan Collins, he was educated at Carson-Newman College (A.B.) and Southwestern Baptist Theological Seminary (Th.M., 1925). He married Nancy Elizabeth Jones on June 7, 1938. They had two children: Benjamin F., Jr., and James Harris. He served pastorates in Mississippi, and in Brainerd, Chattanooga (10 years), and Goodlettsville (15 years), Tenn. He served as a trustee of Carson-Newman College for 15 years, and a member of the executive board of the Tennessee Baptist Convention for 12 years.

JOHN R. CHRISTIAN

***COLOMBIA, MISSION IN.** The Barranquilla hospital's outpatient department treats thousands of patients every year and has a training program for practical nurses. Clinics are conducted in nearby towns. "Cultural centers" have helped overcome ingrained prejudices against evangelical churches. Schools are maintained in connection with most churches. Radio and television work is somewhat limited. Students in the International Seminary in Cali have assisted in establishing missions and organizing churches in the Cauca Valley. In 1969, 58 Southern Baptist missionaries were serving in seven cities. FRANK K. MEANS

COLORADO, BAPTIST FOUNDATION OF. Organized June 15, 1956, with an original corpus of $51,750. Of this amount $50,500 was given by Mr. and Mrs. William Fleming of Fort Worth, Tex. In 1969 the corpus totaled $240,544.27. Chester Ramsay, first president of the foundation, became executive director in Oct., 1965. W. H. Landers was elected executive director Jan. 1, 1969, succeeding Ramsay who died Oct. 25, 1967. O. L. BAYLESS

COLORADO, BAPTIST GENERAL CONVENTION OF (cf. Colorado Baptist General Convention, History of, Vol. I).

I. Baptist Beginnings. A group of Southern Baptists, belonging to the Mount Tabor Baptist Church near Hot Springs, Ark., moved to Colorado and settled near Byers. A Baptist church was organized in 1930, but there were no other Southern Baptist churches with which to affiliate. After a checkered history of affiliation, Mount Tabor Baptist Church of Byers, Colo., affiliated with the Denver Association of Southern Baptists in 1954.

Alamosa is the site of the first definite Southern Baptist Church in Colorado. This work began in the spring of 1934, under the sponsorship of the Northeastern Association of the Baptist Convention of New Mexico. L. W. Rieschel was the first pastor. After some years of activity, this church disbanded. College Heights, the present Southern Baptist church in Alamosa, was constituted in 1954. Rieschel was instrumental in beginning Southern Baptist work in Cortez, the oldest continuing Southern

Baptist Church in Colorado. This church was organized in Aug. 1938, in the home of B. D. Wood. In 1939 this church affiliated with the Baptist Convention of New Mexico.

All other Southern Baptist churches organized in Colorado through 1950 affiliated with the Baptist Convention of New Mexico. These included First Southern, Pagosa Springs, First, Mancos, Friendship, Dove Creek, First, Nucla, and First Southern, Grand Junction.

New life and strength characterized church efforts and expansion in Colorado following the 1951 meeting of the Southern Baptist Convention in San Francisco. The Baptist convention of New Mexico was contacted about the possibility of their assuming responsibility for the work in Colorado. The state leadership of New Mexico, in agreement with leaders of the Home Mission Board, SBC, and the Baptist General Convention of Arizona, felt the work should be under the auspices of the Arizona convention.

Organized Southern Baptist work on the eastern slope of the state was begun when Denver Temple Baptist Church was constituted, Aug. 19, 1951. This work grew more rapidly than did that on the western slope. Financial assistance from individuals, churches, associations and state conventions outside the area, was channeled to the missions and churches being organized primarily through the Arizona convention.

The first regional convention of more than two states in the history of the SBC was organized at the Denver Temple Baptist Church, May 5, 1954. Representatives from churches in five states were present: Colorado, Wyoming, Montana, North Dakota, and South Dakota. The second meeting of this regional convention was Nov. 22–23, 1954 at the same church. The third meeting was held at First Southern Baptist Church, Casper, Wyo., Apr. 25–26, 1955. At the latter meeting, the regional body was dissolved, looking forward to the organization of the Colorado Baptist General Convention.

II. History of General Convention. The Colorado Baptist General Convention was organized Nov. 21, 1955, at Colorado Springs, Colo., with 90 churches, (77 from the Arizona Convention and 13 from the New Mexico Convention) with a total membership of 9,815. The convention began operation Jan. 1, 1956.

Paul W. Davis, president of the Arizona convention, presided at the organizational meeting of the new convention. W. C. Bryant, then pastor of First Southern Baptist Church, Colorado Springs, was elected as the first president of the Colorado Baptist General Convention.

Willis J. Ray, executive secretary-treasurer of the Arizona convention was elected executive secretary-treasurer of the new Colorado convention. Ray served in this capacity until retirement Sept., 1962. Glen E. Braswell, pastor of South Denver Baptist Church, succeeded Ray.

Southern Baptist churches often began by meeting in Seventh Day Adventist buildings, labor temples, Masonic halls, rented buildings, and even in mortuaries. Pastors worked at secular occupations to provide a living for their families.

A five-year advance program adopted by the convention in 1956 set goals for a Baptist building in 1957, an assembly site in 1958, a Baptist college in 1959, and formation of a new convention made up of the four northern states, Wyoming, Montana, North and South Dakota in 1960.

At the 1956 convention, meeting with First Southern Baptist Church, Colorado Springs, reports revealed $51,491.15 given through the Cooperative Program in nine months, 1,501 baptisms, and a total of 105 churches working with the convention.

In the years preceding formal organization of the Colorado Baptist General Convention, many Baptists in the Southern Baptist Association of Colorado (an association of churches affiliated with the Baptist General Convention of Arizona) began to think and talk about establishment of a Southern Baptist college in their midst. At a workers' conference of the association held in Wheatland, Wyo., Aug. 5, 1952, action was taken to start an educational institution in Colorado. A college board of trustees was elected. Plans for the college did not materialize. In 1954 the trustees reported to the convention that no attempt would be made to open the school until the Southern Baptists of Colorado were able to afford it.

During the first annual session of the Southern Baptist Association of Colorado, Oct. 14, 1952, a proposal by missionary L. A. Watson was adopted to begin publication of an associational paper under the name *Rocky Mountain Baptist.* The first issue, Nov., 1952, was dedicated to the interest of the proposed Colorado Baptist College.

On June 15, 1956, six months after the Convention began operation, the Baptist Foundation of Colorado was organized. Funding of building programs was difficult for new churches in the new convention. Seeking a solution to the problem, the convention meeting in special session in Denver Temple Baptist Church, Feb. 11, 1957, formed the Southern Baptist Security Bond Corporation.

In June, 1960, purchase of the 1,433 acre H. H. Hoopingarner ranch near Monument, Colo., was consummated. This property was and is used in the development of a Colorado Southern Baptist Assembly.

As an alternative to establishing a college, the Colorado convention entered upon a program of chairs of Bible adjacent to state college campuses. The first, a pilot project, began operation at the University of Wyoming, Laramie, in the fall of 1966. Launching of this new effort was made possible by Guy Rutland, Jr., of Decatur, Ga., giving $25,000 for purchasing a Baptist Student Union center at the university and underwriting of operating costs for two years by the Baptist Foundation of Colorado. Carrol Smith, a graduate of Hardin-Simmons University and Southwestern Baptist Theological Seminary, and approved by the Wyoming University, became the BSU director and professor.

The goal set in 1956 to organize a new convention of the four northern states in 1960 did not become a reality until 1967. During the 1966 meeting of the Colorado convention in Rapid City, S. Dak., Oct. 25–27, David Bunch, pastor of the Sioux Valley Baptist Church, Sioux Falls, S. Dak., moved that a committee of two each from the states of Wyoming, Montana, North Dakota, and South Dakota, be named by the Colorado convention president Lewis Adkison to form a constitution for the new convention. This committee consisted of Lewis Dawson and Cecil Osborne, Montana; W. J. Hughes and Bob Richardson, North Dakota; E. J. Speegle and Ralph Ehren, Wyoming; Harold Weatherly and Dan Ward, South Dakota. Lewis Adkison served as chairman of the committee. The report was given to the organizational meeting of the new Northern Plains Baptist Convention, Nov. 7–9, 1967, in Rapid City, S. Dak.

Churches in western Nebraska which had been cooperating with the Colorado convention since its beginning withdrew from the Colorado body and affiliated with the Kansas-Nebraska Convention effective Jan. 1, 1967.

In 1967 there were 189 churches in the Colorado convention with a membership of 42,819 located as follows: Colorado, 114 churches and 32,390 members; Wyoming, 22 churches and 4,086 members; Montana, 33 churches and 3,096 members; North Dakota, 12 churches and 1,399 members; South Dakota, 11 churches and 1,848 members. Membership in the churches during the first 12 years of the convention's existence had increased from 9,815 to 42,819.

AUTRY BROWN

III. Program of work. "The purpose of the convention is to provide a channel through which autonomous churches can work together in promoting all enterprises which they collectively deem necessary in carrying out Christ's Great Commission." The convention meets in an annual session at the time and place determined by messengers to the convention. This session is composed of elected messengers from churches on the following basis: "Each cooperating church is entitled to two (2) messengers if the membership is fifty (50) members or major fraction thereof; no church having more than eight (8) messengers."

The convention performs its functions through an executive board, agencies and various committees. Members of the executive board and agencies are elected for a specified period of time on a rotating basis by convention messengers upon recommendation of the convention nominating committee. The executive board is composed of ministers and laity from associational areas in the state of Colorado on the following bases: 1. One (1) board member from each associational area that has a minimum of five (5) cooperating churches and four hundred (400) members. 2. Each associational

COLORADO STATISTICAL SUMMARY

Year	Associations	Churches	Church Membership	Baptisms	S. S. Enrolment	V.B.S. Enrolment	T. U. Enrolment	W.M.U. Enrolment	Brotherhood Enrolment	Music Enrolment	Mission Gifts	Total Gifts	Value Church Property
1956	8	101	11,113	1,511	13,259	7,133	5,928	2,418	1,125		$ 56,032	$ 819,392	$ 3,355,713
1957	10	115	14,027	1,840	15,608	8,667	7,260	3,165	1,480	800	109,057	1,103,751	3,965,851
1958	14	130	16,686	1,987	18,302	10,188	8,324	3,844	1,169	1,118	144,299	1,389,603	5,675,358
1959	15	140	19,516	2,192	21,099	11,801	9,603	4,018	1,033	1,216	156,881	1,494,111	6,569,214
1960	16	152	24,556	2,312	23,838	12,369	11,048	4,557	1,215	1,507	167,000	1,689,999	8,332,760
1961	17	162	26,269	2,596	27,622	14,928	12,607	4,987	1,457	1,750	197,395	1,974,912	9,165,357
1962	18	167	29,446	2,496	29,781	16,155	13,853	5,484	2,385	2,189	253,784	2,229,236	10,604,425
1963	20	178	31,781	2,767	31,051	17,688	14,183	5,616	2,776	2,859	311,730	2,484,786	11,406,426
1964	21	186	35,076	2,815	33,223	17,817	14,696	5,581	2,213	3,319	302,920	2,626,331	13,200,365
1965	22	196	38,658	2,967	33,643	18,232	15,011	5,971	1,404	2,835	364,855	2,980,533	14,293,757
1966	23	188	40,614	2,937	33,981	19,604	14,587	6,503	1,949	3,283	415,811	3,225,614	15,762,881
1967	22	189	42,819	2,724	33,667	18,640	14,762	6,340	1,790	3,997	420,651	3,189,304	15,797,591
1968	10	117	34,941	2,126	25,570	11,730	13,152	4,368	1,669	3,700	332,294	2,717,668	12,448,861

ALETHA FIELD

area will have an additional board member for every additional nine hundred (900) members in the cooperating churches as reported at the annual session of the association. 3. No more than six (6) members shall be elected from an associational area. Board members are elected to represent the total interests and programs of the convention, and not as associational representatives.

According to the constitution the executive board employs all convention personnel, except the executive secretary-treasurer, as is necessary to achieve the purpose of the convention. The board is charged with the responsibility of directing the business of the convention in the interim session. To carry out the functions of the convention, an executive secretary-treasurer is employed by the convention to serve as the chief executive officer for the executive board, the chief administrator, and program officer for the executive board staff.

The *Rocky Mountain Baptist* is the official news media of the convention. The eight-page publication is financially supported by subscriptions, advertising, and a substantial amount from the convention budget.

The Colorado Southern Baptist Church Loan Corporation is an agency of the convention which has been providing building assistance to churches since 1958. The Baptist Foundation of Colorado was established for the purpose of handling wills and trusts, and to receive and invest gifts and bequests made to the convention and its interests.

Ponderosa Southern Baptist Assembly is owned and operated by the convention. Many and varied assembly programs are provided at Ponderosa. Summer programs are directed by staff members. A committee of the executive board is responsible for assembly operations through a resident supervisor.

Programs of work have been assigned on the following basis: Missions-Stewardship, Evangelism-Brotherhood, Sunday School-Music, Training Union-Baptist Student Union, and Woman's Missionary Union. All of these programs are classified as departments except Missions-Stewardship which is classified as a division. The director of the division of missions supervises the mission ministries of area missionaries, language missionaries, special-type mission services, and the financial assistance provided churches through church pastoral aid.

All department directors provide assistance to churches on a year-around basis through leadership conferences and clinics. There is a continuing effort to work with and assist associational leaders in their program responsibilities.

GLENN BRASWELL

COLORADO ASSOCIATIONS.

I. New Associations. ARKANSAS VALLEY. Organized Nov. 16, 1953, by messengers from six churches which withdrew from the Southern Baptist Association of Colorado "for convenience and fellowship." Articles of faith were adopted. Affiliated with Arizona Baptist General Convention until 1956, it was a charter association in affiliation with the Colorado Baptist General Convention. In 1969 eight churches reported 76 baptisms, 1,363 members, $78,765 total gifts, $9,388 mission gifts, and $443,600 church property.

CONTINENTAL DIVIDE. Organized Apr. 17, 1958, at Temple Baptist Church, Salida, Colo., by messengers from six churches which withdrew from Pikes Peak Association. In 1969 nine churches reported 99 baptisms, 1,398 church members, $99,310 total gifts, $10,424 mission gifts, and $426,000 church property.

DENVER. Came into existence Sept. 28, 1954, when messengers from 12 churches remaining in the Southern Baptist Association of Colorado, after fourteen churches had withdrawn to form two new associations (Pikes Peak and Arkansas Valley), voted to change the name to Denver Association. The association is served by an area superintendent of missions, director of Christian Social Ministries, and a director of Community Week-day Program. In 1969, 34 churches reported 748 baptisms, 15,982 church members, $1,332,527 total gifts, $162,744 mission gifts, and $6,406,818 church property. Three of the 34 churches are Negro congregations.

GRAND VALLEY. Organized Dec. 18, 1956, by messengers from five churches which withdrew from San Juan Association of Colorado. In 1969, nine churches reported 72 baptisms, 1,594 church members, $98,097 total gifts, $14,785 mission gifts, and $529,000 church property.

LONG'S PEAK. Organized Jan. 5, 1958, by messengers from four churches which withdrew from Platte Valley Association. Referred to as the "academic association," within its geographic area are Colorado's three largest educational institutions, Colorado University, Colorado State University, and Colorado State College. In 1969 13 churches reported 136 baptisms, 2,534 church members, total receipts of $258,970, mission gifts of $47,550, and $965,413 in church property.

MESA VERDE. On Sept. 11, 1958, by a vote of the messengers present the name San Juan Association of Colorado was changed to Mesa Verde. The San Juan Baptist Association of Colorado was organized Aug. 15–16, 1955, during the annual meeting of the San Juan Association of New Mexico, at First Baptist Church, Aztec, N. Mex. Ten churches formed the new association. These churches and the association cooperated with the New Mexico Convention until Jan., 1956, when the Colorado Baptist General Convention began operation. In 1969 nine churches reported 56 baptisms, 1,634 church members, $83,520 total gifts, $10,606 mission gifts, and $316,800 church property.

PLATT VALLEY. Organized Sept. 7, 1954, by messengers from 11 churches, eight of which withdrew from Denver Association of Southern Baptists to organize. The organizational meeting was held at First Southern Baptist Church, Ft. Morgan, Colo., presided over by Roy F. Sutton, moderator of Denver association. In 1969 five churches reported 36 baptisms, 786 church members, $70,411 total gifts, $8,315 mission gifts, and $391,000 church property.

PIKES PEAK. Organized Sept. 7, 1954, by messengers from 11 churches, eight of which withdrew from the Southern Baptist Association of Colorado. In 1969 17 churches reported 552 baptisms, 8,658 church members, $681,918 total gifts, $78,297 in mission gifts, and $2,865,950 church property.

ROYAL GORGE. Organized in Sept. 1962, by messengers from seven churches in Pikes Peak Association and one church in Continental Divide Association, which withdrew from their respective associations to form the new association. In 1969, 12 churches reported 166 baptisms, 2,483 church members, $173,155 total gifts, $20,881 mission gifts, and $830,781 church property.

UNCOMPAHGRE. Organized Sept. 3, 1966, at First Baptist Church, Telluride, Colo., by messengers from six churches which withdrew from Grand Valley Baptist Association. In 1969 seven churches reported 47 baptisms, 485 church members, $42,074 total gifts, $2,907 mission gifts, and $211,800 church property.

II. Changes in Associations. EAST RIVER ASSOCIATION OF SOUTHERN BAPTISTS. Organized Nov. 2, 1964, by messengers from four churches east of the Missouri who withdrew from the South Dakota Association of Southern Baptists. It became a part of Northern Plains Baptist Convention, organized in Nov., 1967.

FRONTIER BAPTIST ASSOCIATION, WYOMING. Organized Jan. 6, 1958, in order to provide for a more effective program on an associational basis, by messengers from five churches which withdrew from Old Faithful Association. Became a part of Northern Plains Baptist Convention, organized in Nov., 1967.

GREEN RIVER BAPTIST ASSOCIATION. Organized May 11, 1964, by messengers from four churches in Old Faithful Association who withdrew to organize this association, it became a part of Northern Plains Baptist Convention, organized in 1967.

HI-LINE ASSOCIATION. Organized Sept. 20, 1959, by messengers from three churches in Montana Eastern Association which withdrew, plus messengers from Calvary Baptist Church, Glasgow, to form this association. It became a part of the Northern Plains Baptist Convention, organized in Nov., 1967.

MONTANA EASTERN SOUTHERN BAPTIST ASSOCIATION. Organized Nov. 12, 1957, by churches which remained in Montana Association when Montana Western Association was organized. The name changed to Yellowstone Association of Southern Baptists (Montana), Sept. 8, 1961.

MONTANA-NORTH DAKOTA SOUTHERN BAPTIST ASSOCIATION. Organized at Billings, Mont., Sept. 24, 1953, by messengers from five churches in Montana and one church in North Dakota, which by mutual consent with messengers from churches in Wyoming dissolved the Wyoming-Montana Southern Baptist Association for the purpose of organizing two new associations, Montana-North Dakota and Old Faithful, Wyoming. Montana-North Dakota Southern Baptist Association dissolved Dec. 14, 1954, when North Dakota churches withdrew to form North Dakota Southern Baptist Association. Montana churches organized Montana Southern Baptist Association on the same day.

MONTANA SOUTHERN BAPTIST ASSOCIATION. Name adopted by churches left in Montana after organization of North Dakota Southern Baptist Association Dec. 14, 1954, by North Dakota churches which withdrew from Montana-North Dakota Southern Baptist Association.

MONTANA WESTERN SOUTHERN BAPTIST ASSOCIATION. Organized Nov. 12, 1957, by messengers from five churches in west Montana, which withdrew from the Montana Southern Baptist Association. The name changed to Triangle Association in 1958.

MONTANA YELLOWSTONE ASSOCIATION OF SOUTHERN BAPTISTS. Name adopted by Montana Eastern Southern Baptist Association at their annual meeting Sept. 8, 1961, at Trinity Baptist Church, Billings, Mont. It became a part of Northern Plains Baptist Convention, organized in Nov., 1967.

NORTH DAKOTA EASTERN SOUTHERN BAPTIST ASSOCIATION. Created Sept., 1962, when North Dakota Southern Baptist Association was divided. The new association took this name, and the remaining association was named North Dakota Western Southern Baptist Association. It became a part of Northern Plains Baptist Convention, organized in Nov., 1967.

NORTH DAKOTA SOUTHERN BAPTIST ASSOCIATION. Organized Dec. 14, 1954, at Williston, N. Dak., by messengers from five churches in North Dakota which withdrew from the Montana-North Dakota Southern Baptist Association. It dissolved in Sept., 1962, when North Dakota Western and North Dakota Eastern Associations were formed.

NORTH DAKOTA WESTERN SOUTHERN BAPTIST ASSOCIATION. Created in Sept., 1962, when North Dakota Southern Baptist Association was divided into two associations designated North Dakota Eastern and North Dakota Western. It became a part of Northern Plains Baptist Convention organized in Nov., 1967.

OLD FAITHFUL. Organized at Billings, Mont., Sept. 24, 1953, by messengers from seven churches in Wyoming, which by mutual consent with messengers from churches in Montana and Williston, N. Dak., dissolved the Wyoming-Montana Southern Baptist Association for the purpose of organizing two new associations, (Old Faithful and Montana-North Dakota Southern Baptist Association). The association became a part of the Northern Plains Baptist Convention, organized in Nov., 1967.

SAN JUAN BAPTIST ASSOCIATION OF COLORADO. Organized Aug. 15–16, 1955, during the annual meeting of the San Juan Association of New Mexico, at First Baptist Church, Aztec, N. Mex. Ten churches formed the new association. These churches, and the association, cooperated with the New Mexico convention until Jan., 1956, when the Colorado Baptist General Convention began operation. Name changed to Mesa Verde Association, Sept. 11, 1958.

SOUTH DAKOTA ASSOCIATION OF SOUTHERN BAPTISTS. The name dates from Sept., 1963. West River Association changed its name to South Dakota Association with the organization of churches in Eastern South Dakota. It ceased to exist Nov. 2, 1964, when name West River was again adopted for area west of Missouri River. The area east of Missouri River became East River Association.

SOUTHERN BAPTIST ASSOCIATION OF COLORADO. Organized at Denver, July 7, 1952, in the chapel of Grove Junior High School, by messengers from four churches in Colorado and two in Wyoming. The first association of Southern Baptist churches in the states of Wyoming, North Dakota, South Dakota, Montana, and Colorado. In 1954 this association was divided into three associations known as Denver, Pikes Peak, and Arkansas Valley.

SOUTHWEST MONTANA SOUTHERN BAPTIST ASSOCIATION. Organized June 27, 1958, at Deer Lodge, Mont., by messengers from four churches in Montana Western Association, which withdrew to form this association. The name changed to Treasurer State Association of Southern Baptists at the 1958 annual meeting.

TREASURER STATE ASSOCIATION OF SOUTHERN BAPTISTS. Name adopted by Southwest Montana Association at 1958 annual meeting, it became a part of the Northern Plains Baptist Convention, organized in Nov., 1967.

TRIANGLE ASSOCIATION. Formerly Western Southern Baptist Association, its name changed to Triangle during the 1958 annual meeting of the Montana Western Association. It became a part of the Northern Plains Baptist Convention, organized in Nov., 1967.

WEST RIVER ASSOCIATION OF SOUTHERN BAPTISTS. Organized Nov. 15, 1956, by messengers from four churches in Old Faithful Southern Baptist Association, Wyoming, who withdrew from the Wyoming Association to form West River. With establishment of missions in eastern South Dakota, the association changed its name to South Dakota Association of Southern Baptists, Sept., 1963. When East River Association was formed, Nov. 2, 1964, churches in area west of the Missouri River again adopted the name West River. It became a part of Northern Plains Baptist Convention, organized in 1967.

WESTERN NEBRASKA SOUTHERN BAPTIST ASSOCIATION. Organized Sept. 6, 1960, by messengers from five churches in Platte Valley Association which withdrew for the purpose of organizing a Nebraska Association. In a meeting held at Oak Street Baptist Church, Kimball, Nebr., the churches in this association voted to affiliate with the Kansas-Nebraska convention beginning Jan. 1, 1967.

WYOMING-MONTANA SOUTHERN BAPTIST ASSOCIATION. Organized Feb. 17, 1953, at Casper, Wyo., by messengers from three Wyoming churches and one from Montana (the Wyoming churches had affiliated with the Southern Baptist Association of Colorado). Articles of faith were adopted. On Sept. 24, 1953, at a special meeting of the association held in Billings, Mont., the Wyoming churches formed Old Faithful Association, the churches of Montana formed the Montana-North Dakota Southern Baptist Association.

YELLOWSTONE BAPTIST ASSOCIATION, WYOMING. Organized Aug. 28, 1961, by messengers from six churches in Old Faithful Association who felt they could more adequately and effectively carry on their work through a new association. It became a part of Northern Plains Baptist Convention, organized in Nov., 1967. O. L. BAYLESS

COLORADO SOUTHERN BAPTIST CHURCH LOAN CORPORATION. An agency established as a result of a special meeting of the Colorado Baptist General Convention, Feb. 11, 1957, called to study a proposal for providing financing for new churches, without proven financial responsibility and resources. The convention authorized a $1,000,000 bond issue, designated "Southern Baptist Security Bonds." Willis J. Ray, executive secretary of the Colorado convention served as administrator until July 1, 1958. The first bond purchased was for $500 by Elvie S. Taylor, pastor Highland Park Baptist Church, San Antonio, Tex. The first loan made by the corporation was in May, 1957, to the First Baptist Church, Manitou Springs, Colo. W. H. Landers of McKinney, Tex., became president and administrator of the corporation July 1, 1958. The name Colorado Southern Baptist Church Loan Corporation was adopted in 1963. A total of 125 loans have been made to 75 churches in the Colorado area. As of Aug. 31, 1969, bonds outstanding totaled $3,283,249. The corporation does not issue bonds for individual churches or conduct church bond campaigns. The bonds are issued by the corporation and moneys received from bond sales are loaned to the churches and related institutions in Colorado, Wyoming, Montana, North Dakota, South Dakota, and western Nebraska. The Aug. 31, 1969, audit shows a reserve of $202,331 to protect against anticipated losses. W. H. LANDERS

COMMUNICATION, HOME MISSION BOARD DIVISION OF. One of six divisions of HMB staff, formed as Division of Education and Promotion in 1959, renamed in 1967. It is comprised of four departments: editorial services, missionary education, audiovisuals, and art services, plus picture service and circulation service offices.

The division developed from a department of education, led by Joe W. Burton, 1942–45, and John L. Caylor (*q.v.*), 1946–59; a department of schools of missions, formed in 1943 with Lewis W. Martin as secretary; and a department of promotion begun in 1951 with L. O. Griffith as secretary, absorbing the audiovisuals field services performed by R. G. Van Royen, 1945–51.

With the formation of the division, two of the three departments received new names: the Department of Education became the Department of Editorial Services, with Caylor as secretary; and the Department of Schools of Missions became the Department of Missionary Education, with Martin as secretary. The Department of Promotion, with J. C. Durham, Jr., as secretary, was renamed the Department of Audio-Visuals in 1966. The Department of Art Services was added in 1966, with Thomas H. Baker becoming secretary after four years as staff artist. Walker L. Knight became secretary of the Department of Editorial Services, including editorship of *Home Missions,* in 1959, following Caylor's retirement; and Kenneth E. Day became secretary of Missionary Education in 1966, following Martin's retirement. The division was enlarged by the addition of a book editor, Kate Ellen Gruver, 1960; an assistant secretary, Department of Editorial Services, Dallas M. Lee 1966; and a photographer, Donald O. Rutledge, 1966.

In 1959 the Editorial Services department became a regional office for the Baptist Press. In 1968 "world missions conferences" replaced "schools of missions." The sixties witnessed a growing cooperation with Woman's Missionary Union, the Brotherhood Commission, and the Foreign Mission Board in missionary education and promotion.

The title, Division of Communication, underlines the division's objective of "providing plans, materials, and information to churches, associations, state conventions, and other Southern Baptist Convention agencies in the support of and involvement in missions in the homeland." The division's services include production of a magazine, mission study books, slides, filmstrips, motion pictures, recordings, news stories, exhibits; provision of speakers for conferences, camps, churches, and other groups; maintenance of a resource library; and assistance in production and distribution of various printed materials.

The staff at the close of 1969 consisted of L. O. Griffith, director, Walker L. Knight, secretary, and Dallas M. Lee, assistant secretary, Editorial Services Department; Kate Ellen Gruver, book editor; J. C. Durham, Jr., secretary, Audio-Visuals Department; Donald O. Rutledge, photographer; Kenneth E. Day, secretary, Missionary Education Department; and Thomas H. Baker, secretary, Art Services Department.

L. O. GRIFFITH

COMMUNICATION CONFERENCE, SBC. A meeting of Southern Baptist leadership each fall in connection with the September meeting of the SBC Executive Committee. The conference is conducted under the auspices of the public relations committee of the Executive Committee and is planned by the public relations secretary. The one or two-day conference is designed to aid SBC leaders to increase their understanding and skills in communication and public relations. A secondary purpose is to put into practice effective communication by dealing with subjects that are of vital interest to the participants. Regular participants include members of the SBC Executive Committee, the heads of SBC agencies and their principal associates, the state executive secretaries and their principal associates, the state editors, and other members of the Baptist Public Relations Association. The conference grew out of the Promotion Conference which met at the same time of the year and with virtually the same participants. The Promotion Conference began in 1927–28 and dealt largely with stewardship and Cooperative Program promotion. When the Stewardship Commission was established in 1960 these needs were met through other gatherings of SBC leaders and the Promotion Conference gradually shifted to an emphasis on communication. The name was changed to SBC Communication Conference in 1963.

See also PROMOTION CONFERENCE, Vol. II.

W. C. FIELDS

COMMUNICATIONS AWARDS. See DISTINGUISHED COMMUNICATIONS MEDAL AWARD AND SCHOLARSHIP.

CONNECTICUT, SOUTHERN BAPTISTS IN. See MARYLAND, BAPTIST CONVENTION OF, and NEW YORK, BAPTIST CONVENTION OF.

CONNELL, GEORGE BOYCE (b. Douglasville, Ga., Feb. 1, 1905; d. Macon, Ga., Apr. 21, 1959). Educator. He married Doris Collier, Dec. 28, 1929, and they had one son, Hewlette C. He was educated at Mercer University (A.B., 1924; A.M., 1930), and received the LL.D. from Howard College (1954). Connell was a teacher of history and coach at A. and M. School, Barnesville, Ga., 1925–26, and Piedmont (Baptist) Institute, Waycross, Ga., 1926–28. He served as vice-president, dean, and head of the English Department of Gordon Military College, Barnesville, 1928–46; vice-president and associate professor of English, Mercer University, 1946–53. In 1953 he became president of Mercer, serving until his death. During his administration he strengthened the faculty and improved the physical plant by adding a student center and several academic buildings. Connell was also president of the following: Georgia Association of Colleges, Association of Southern Baptist Colleges and Secondary Schools, Georgia Foundation of Independent Colleges, Inc., and Dixie Athletic Conference. Chairman of the Georgia Committee of the Rhodes Scholarship Trust, he was also national director of the National Conference of Christians and Jews. EDWIN T. JOHNSTON

***CONNIE MAXWELL CHILDREN'S HOME.** Child-care agency of South Carolina Baptist Convention located at Greenwood, S. C. The agency consists of an institutional program centered in Greenwood, foster homes, mother's aid families, casework assistance to children in their own homes, group homes, aid to children in specialized education and training service, and a limited adoption service. A total of 366 children were cared for in all services during 1969. Superintendent Sam M. Smith has served in this capacity since July 1, 1946, and has been a member of the staff since 1930. The home has had only three superintendents during its 78-year history.

The campus facilities consist of more than 800 acres of land and 41 permanent buildings. New church, administration, and activities buildings and nine new cottages have been constructed since 1954. A program of replacement of old buildings and facilities begun in 1948 is being continued. Special services were held in May, 1967, commemorating the 75th anniversary of the arrival of the first child at Connie Maxwell, May 22, 1892. More than 5,000 children have been served by the agency.

In 1970 total assets were $6,000,000, including land, buildings, equipment, invested contingent funds, and a permanent endowment of $1,400,000. The budget for the fiscal year 1968–69 was $659,000, with 53 per cent of the current income derived from direct offerings from the churches and Sunday Schools, and 19 per cent from the Cooperative Program. The remaining 28 per cent came from personal gifts, receipts from relatives of children under care, endowment, and income from productive enterprises. The agency employs a staff of 92 people.

The Connie Maxwell Alumni Association, organized in 1932, has contributed more than $50,000 for improving the physical facilities of the home. The latest project of the alumni is the raising of $30,000 to furnish the newest building on campus—the Sam M. Smith Activities Building, completed in 1970 and named for the superintendent who is an alumnus of the home.

In 1969 a development program was set up with a full-time director, to enlarge the basis of current and capital support of the agency.

JOHN C. MURDOCH

***CONSCIENTIOUS OBJECTORS.** During recent years, especially since the involvement of the United States in the Vietnam War, there has been a growing number of conscientious objectors throughout the nation. Many of these have registered with their draft boards, have been recognized as conscientious objectors, and have been assigned alternate service. An increasing number of young men find themselves conscientiously opposed to the particular war in Vietnam. Since the government does not grant exemptions to those who object to a particular war, these men must be willing to accept applicable civil or criminal penalties for their action. Many of them, rather than face jail sentences, have left their native land and have been granted asylum in other countries, in most cases Canada or Sweden.

In the spring of 1970 a total of 60 conscientious objectors had registered with the Executive Committee of the Southern Baptist Convention. All of these were related to the draft procedures brought about by the Vietnam War.

At its annual meeting in 1969, the SBC heard a resolution which reaffirmed its action in support of conscientious objectors taken in 1940; however, the resolution was defeated. It was understood that this did not nullify the 1940 action.

ELMER S. WEST, JR.

***CONSERVATIVE BAPTIST FOREIGN MISSION SOCIETY, THE.** On Jan. 1, 1969, Conservative Baptists had 481 missionaries serving in 20 mission fields, compared to 320 in 1954. Of these, 182 were actively engaged in Asia and the Far East (Hong Kong, India, Indonesia, Japan, Pakistan, Philippines, and Taiwan), 150 were in Africa (Congo, Ivory Coast, Madagascar, Senegal, and Uganda), 98 were in South America (Argentina, North and South Brazil), and 51 in Europe (Austria, France, Italy, Jordan, and Portugal). In addition, there were 32 short-term workers in the Missionary Assistants Corps. These are appointed for two-year terms. On their overseas mission work Conservative Baptists spent $3,199,058.72 in 1968. The society uses radio, literature, linguistics, translation work, education, and medicine in its endeavor to establish self-sustaining churches in the 20 countries it serves. In Jan., 1969, there were 227 organized churches, 404 chapels, and 555 preaching points which provided the base for work overseas.

GEORGE L. KELM

CONSERVATIVE BAPTISTS. A loosely allied family of churches, chiefly across the northern states, combining conservative theology with missionary zeal. The Conservative Baptist "movement" reflects both traditional Baptist denominational features and characteristics of voluntary (or "independent") missionary societies.

Three national organizations are the major means of cooperation. The Conservative Baptist Association of America is the association of churches. It approves military chaplains, stimulates local churches in Christian education, and encourages church planting.

The Conservative Baptist Home Mission Society, founded in 1950, supports missionaries in North and Central America. In 1969 the society had 123 missionaries. In 1968 the Conservative Baptist Foreign Mission Society was sponsoring 481 missionaries on 20 foreign fields. Each of these national agencies publishes a magazine: the *Builder,* the *Challenge,* and the *Impact,* respectively.

In addition to these agencies, Conservative Baptists support four schools: Judson Baptist College, a junior college in Portland, Ore.; Southwestern College in Phoenix, Ariz.; Western Conservative Baptist Seminary in Portland, Ore.; and Conservative Baptist Theological Seminary in Denver, Colo. Without a denominational unified budget, each of these schools, as well as the three national agencies, makes direct appeals for support to the congregations.

While the denominational character of the "movement" is reflected in the Conservative Association and its related state associations, the missionary commitment of the group is revealed in the statistics of the agencies. In 1969 the Association reported 1,130 affiliated churches and an income of only $83,000. The foreign society, on the other hand, received $3,200,000 from 1,724 churches. The home society accounted for another $1,015,000. Obviously, the mission societies were assisted by a number of independent churches.

In the early sixties two points of view within the "movement" were clearly discernible. A minority fundamentalist party called for stricter denominational standards. In particular, cooperation with Billy Graham Crusades and other evangelical endeavors was challenged. The vast majority of Conservative Baptists, however, reflected a confidence in their national agencies and a desire to cooperate with other evangelicals. In 1965, when the fundamentalists failed to gain a large following, 28 churches, chiefly from the Midwest, organized the New Testament Association of Independent Baptist Churches.

At the 1968 annual meetings of the Association and the two mission societies held in Chicago, a standing commission known as the Inter-Society Commission was created. This commission, composed of the three presidents and three other executive officers from each of the national agencies, was formed to study means of closer cooperation of the three organizations and to make recommendations to the boards and constituencies of the agencies.

The same year (1968) saw the formation of the Stewardship Ministries Commission, which was designed to offer financial counsel to Conservative Baptists for the benefit of the cooperating national agencies.

See also: Conservative Baptist Association of America, Vol. I; Conservative Baptist Foreign Mission Society, The, Vol. I; and Fundamental Baptist Fellowship (Northern Baptist), Vol. III.

Bibliography: B. L. Shelley, *Conservative Baptists: A Story of Twentieth-Century Dissent* (1962).

BRUCE L. SHELLEY

CONSERVATIVE BAPTISTS. See also Fundamental Baptist Fellowship (Northern Baptist).

CONTEMPO. Since Oct., 1970, the monthly periodical for officers and members of Baptist Young Women. Published by Woman's Missionary Union, the magazine contains features of interest to young adults, basic resources for organization meetings and activities, and Laser, the leadership section. Laurella Owens is editor (1970).

BETTY BROWN

CONVENTION PRESS. Publishing medium of the Sunday School Board of the Southern Baptist Convention since Feb. 10, 1965, for books and booklets prepared particularly for use in Southern Baptist churches. Included are books in the Church Study Course, the Foreign Missions Graded Series, Vacation Bible School teacher and pupil books, *Baptist Hymnal,* and general titles dealing with denominational history and programs. Most titles are edited in the Education Division of the Sunday School Board. Distribution is generally restricted to sales through Baptist Book Stores. Sales at the publishing level totalled $1,795,000 for 1968–69.

J. M. CROWE

COOPER, ALLEN BRITTEN (b. Izard County, Ark., July 19, 1898; d. Houston, Tex., Feb. 19, 1965). Pastor and church builder. Cooper was converted at 16 and entered the ministry at 19. Attending Mt. Home College, he received the A.B. from Ouachita Baptist College, Arkadelphia, Ark. He served as pastor of Baptist churches in Nashville, Tenn., Kingsland and Brinkley, Ark., before going to Missouri, where he served churches in Charleston, Gravel Ridge, New Bethel, and Wyatt. Cooper built 14 church buildings: Wolf Island, Barnes Ridge, Bement, Dorena, Gravel Ridge, New Bethel, Unity, Wyatt, Alfalfa Center, Deventer, Hinson, and in three Negro communities. Cooper was a pioneer in Baptist work among Negroes. He was a leader in the establishment of the Chair of Bible in Southwest Missouri State College, and was its first field secretary. Cooper married Janie May (Laurence) in 1917. They had six daughters and two sons.

BETTY HEARNES

COOPERATIVE COLLEGE REGISTRY, THE. The Education Commission has been a sponsor of the Cooperative College Registry for six years. It now shares this sponsorship with nine other evangelical communions; in addition, a few schools participate on an annual fee basis.

The Registry is a nonprofit organization which introduces new college teachers as well as experienced faculty and administrators to over 300 regionally accredited liberal arts colleges and universities, for positions ranging from instructor to college president. The major denominational colleges in the United States are in this group. More than 12,000 persons, available for employment, register each year; many are suitable for Baptist schools. All disciplines are represented.

The central office of the Registry is in the headquarters of the American Council on Education, at One Dupont Circle, Washington, D. C., a building which informally serves as a national center for higher education.

The Education Commission pays a percentage of the total operation of the Registry as a service to all Baptist colleges and universities. It also is involved in the governance of the organization. Since the Registry is financed by member denominations in the interest of higher education, it offers free service to registrants.

A facet of this ministry is the maintenance of a duplicate set of files in the Atlanta office of the United Board for College Development, located at 159 Forest Avenue, Northwest, Suite 514. This arrangement makes possible the serving of approximately 60 historically church-related Negro colleges in the South, 15 of which are Baptist. The Atlanta file involves visitation service only. W. HOWARD BRAMLETTE

***COOPERATIVE PROGRAM.** The Cooperative Program has remained unchanged in its basic concepts since its inaugural in 1925. Basically, it is a partnership between state conventions and the Southern Baptist Convention, with both having equal responsibility and equal privileges. In the early years expenses for promotion were equally shared and the principle of 50–50 distribution promoted. Over the years, this principle suffered some erosion, but in 1970 a series of meetings were held to secure a clearer understanding of relationships. The Cooperative Program includes only undesignated gifts. (The article in Volume I of the *Encyclopedia* erroneously states that it includes special offerings. In one state this interpretation has been given at times, but in the SBC, and in all other states, the Cooperative Program includes only undesignated offerings.) In 1958 the total SBC Cooperative Program was $42,929,283. This was divided $27,390,095 or 63.80 per cent to state causes and $15,539,188 or 36.20 per cent to SBC causes. In 1969 it totalled $78,220,474, a gain of 82.21 per cent over 1958. This was divided $50,787,034 (64.93 per cent) to state causes and $27,433,440 (35.07 per cent) to SBC causes.

ALBERT MCCLELLAN

CORDELL MEMORIAL HOSPITAL (Cordell, Okla.). The city of Cordell, Okla., voted a $175,000 bond issue July 12, 1955, and launched a fund-raising drive the following September to build and equip a 30-bed facility, which in 1956 was leased to the Baptist General Convention of Oklahoma. The hospital was dedicated Dec. 1, 1957, and opened for patients the next day. In 1969 the property value was $409,862, with no debt. Capacity had increased to 35 beds, and a 60 percent occupancy was reported. There were 66 employees. J. M. GASKIN

CORUM, BETTY JO (b. Knoxville, Tenn., Feb. 11, 1927; d. Birmingham, Ala., Sept. 15, 1970). Daughter of W. W. and Mary Elizabeth (Brewer) Corum, she graduated from Carson-Newman College in 1949 and became educational director at Robertsville Baptist Church, Oak Ridge, Tenn. In 1954 she received the MRE from Southwestern Baptist Theological Seminary, Fort Worth, Tex. From 1954–60 Miss Corum was director of Junior-Intermediate work for the Training Union Department of the Tennessee Baptist State Convention. She was editor of Intermediate Training Union materials for the Sunday School Board, SBC, 1960–65. In 1965 she moved to Birmingham to become director of the Editorial Services Department of WMU, SBC, which position she held at the time of her death. Miss Corum wrote numerous lesson materials, articles, and poems for Baptist publications; was author of a book of poetry, *A Corner of Today* (1969); and was co-author of "Hello World," a youth musical which premiered in Dec., 1969. She is buried in Woodlawn Cemetery, Knoxville, Tenn.

DORIS DEVAULT

***COSTA RICA, MISSION IN.** In 1969 there were 20 churches and seven mission congregations with a membership of 1,028, and Sunday School enrolment of 2,048. The Costa Rica Convention has departments for missions, Brotherhood, WMU, youth, Christian education, and medical work. The three mission centers—San Jose, San Ramon, and Turrialba—are manned by six couples under appointment by the Foreign Mission Board. SYDNEY GOLDFINCH, SR.

COUNSELING. See PASTORAL CARE.

COUNTRY CROSSROADS. See RADIO AND TELEVISION COMMISSION, THE.

COWSERT, JACK JIMMERSON (b. Goodman, Miss., Sept. 16, 1890; d. Wingate, N. C., June 15, 1966). Missionary to Brazil, 1920–60. Cowsert graduated from Mississippi College, and was pastor of churches in Texas while studying at Southwestern Bapist Theological Seminary (Th.M., 1919; M.R.E. 1928). He served in Rio de Janeiro, where from 1928 until retirement he was connected with the Baptist Publishing House in various positions. He was a founder and director of Bible Press of Brazil, organized in 1940. His work also included local pastorates, city director of evangelism, mission treasurer, and membership on denominational boards. He married Grace Bagby, Sept. 18, 1918. They had three children: Helen, Esther, and George.

EDGAR F. HALLOCK

COX, ERNEST EUGENE (b. Boaz, Ala., Oct. 3, 1892; d. Birmingham, Ala., Apr. 24, 1961). Superintendent, Alabama Baptist Children's Home. The second of 11 children of Luther Offie and Claudia Viola (Creel) Cox, he attended public school in Albertville, earned the A.B. (1922) at Howard College, and did graduate work at the University of Alabama. On Nov. 25, 1914, he married Mary Gordon Gamble. Cox was a teacher and principal in the Guntersville schools for 30 years. He was active in Red Cross, Boy Scouts, Rotary, Civitan, and denominational activities. In Mar., 1950, he became superintendent of the children's home. Cox was president of the Alabama Conference of Child Care Institutes and Agencies, and of the Alabama Conference of Social Work. He retired as superintendent of the children's home, Oct. 31, 1960, and moved to Birmingham where he lived until his death. JACK BRYMER

COX, ETHLENE BOONE (b. Lucy, Tenn., July 22, 1890; d. Memphis, Tenn., Aug. 3, 1965). Seventh president of Woman's Missionary Union, SBC, and treasurer of WMU, 1934–52. Her father, Daniel Matthias Boone, a direct descendant of "frontiersman Daniel," died when she was three years old. Her mother, Jessie (Bradshaw) Boone, married Judge George Shannon of Saltillo, (Hardin Co.,) Tenn., when Ethlene was eight.

When she was 12, Ethlene professed her faith in Christ and joined the nearby Methodist church. Special studies in elocution and training at the college near Saltillo were followed by employment in Memphis, where she met Wiley Jones Cox, a pharmacist. They were married on June 18, 1913, in the First Baptist Church, Memphis, where Cox was a deacon. Ethlene was soon baptized into the fellowship and remained a member there until her death 52 years later.

Immediately after joining First Baptist Church, she began working in Sunday School, BYPU, and WMU. Her work in Shelby County brought her to the attention of Tennessee women, and in 1923 she was elected president of the state WMU. When the WMU annual meeting met in Memphis in 1925, she was elected president of WMU, SBC, which office she held for eight years, declining reelection in 1933 because of her husband's health. At that time there was set up in the Lottie Moon Christmas Offering the Mrs. W. J. Cox Fund for WMU Work on foreign fields in commemoration of her service as president.

In 1934 just prior to her husband's death, Ethlene Cox consented to election as treasurer of WMU. Assisted by Mattie Morgan, she served as treasurer for nineteen years. Administration of the Margaret Fund was her most rewarding responsibility as treasurer.

Widely acclaimed for her ability as a speaker, she addressed the sectional meeting for women at the Baptist World Alliance Congress in Toronto in 1928. That year she was appointed as one of the first two women on the BWA executive committee and served until 1934. In 1929 in Memphis, she became the first woman to address the annual meeting of the SBC. She was a major speaker on the Sunday evening program of the BWA Congress in Atlanta in 1939.

A member of the League of American Pen Women, she is the author of two books: *Star Trails* (1926), a series of vesper messages delivered at YWA conferences at Ridgecrest; and *Following in His Train* (1938), a Golden Jubilee history of WMU. In addition, she wrote the feature "On My Window Seat" for the first three years it was published in *The Window of YWA* (1929–32), and for many years contributed articles to *Royal Service* and *The Window of YWA*. She is buried in Memorial Park, Memphis, Tenn.

DORIS DEVAULT

COX, NORMAN WADE (b. Climax, Ga., Oct. 28, 1888; d. Mobile, Ala., Feb. 9, 1968). Son of Barkley Wade and Alice Louise (Brock) Cox, he was educated at Mercer University (A.B., 1914) and Southern Baptist Theological Seminary (Th.M., 1918). He married Osye Lee Mathews in 1910. They had two children: Graham Wade and Sara Margaret (Mrs. Jarman Thigpen). Ordained as a minister in 1910 by his home church at Climax, he served student pastorates in Georgia and Kentucky. After seminary he served First, Barnesville, Ga., 1918–20; Court Street, Portsmouth, Va., 1920–22; First, Savannah, Ga., 1922–27; First, Meridian, Miss., 1927–31, 1939–51; First, Mobile, Ala., 1931–32; and Fifth Avenue, Huntington, W. Va., 1932–39. A popular speaker, he was in demand for revival meetings and assemblies.

On Feb. 15, 1951, Cox became the first executive secretary of the Historical Commission, SBC. Under his guidance the collection of the Southern Baptist Historical Society, auxiliary of the commission, was moved from Louisville, Ky., to Nashville, Tenn., and the Dargan-Carver Library, a jointly operated research library, was established at the Baptist Sunday School Board.

The most outstanding contribution of Cox to the historiography of Baptists was the publication of the two-volume *Encyclopedia of Southern Baptists* in 1958. This project was an example of Southern Baptist cooperation. In 1954 he had completed the project to publish a history of the Southern Baptist Convention which had been in production 10 years with W. W. Barnes (*q.v.*) as writer. Another outstanding contribution in the area of Baptist history was the use of microfilm for preserving historical records. Six and a half million pages of rare Baptist books, periodicals, and church records were microfilmed in seven years. These materials from all over the world were made available to libraries, particularly those in Baptist seminaries and colleges.

While a pastor, Cox edited a Baptist paper in West Virginia, and wrote a column in the daily papers where he lived. He wrote *Youth's Return to Faith* (1938), *God Did It* (1942), *Dreams, Dungeons, and Diadems* (1954), *God and Ourselves* (1960), and *We Southern Baptists* (1961). He served as associate editor of *The Quarterly Review*, 1951–59. He was active in denominational work serving as president of the Mississippi convention; moderator of the Lauderdale (Miss.) Association; member of the Committee on Business Efficiency, Correlating Committee, and Executive Committee of the Southern Baptist Convention; and was a trustee of Southern and Southwestern Baptist Theological seminaries. Cox, more than any other man in his generation, inspired Southern Baptists to conserve and use their history. He believed that Southern Baptists could not understand themselves without knowing their history.

DAVIS C. WOOLLEY

CRABTREE, ASA ROUTH (b. Russell County, Va., Aug. 11, 1889; d. Roanoke, Va., Apr. 15, 1965). Missionary to Brazil. He graduated from Richmond College (B.A.), Union Theological Seminary (B.D.), and Southern Baptist Theological Seminary (Th.D.). Appointed missionary June 9, 1921, he served as professor and director of Rio Baptist College, later as professor and president of South Brazil Baptist Theological Seminary, pastor of Tijuca Church in Rio, director of book department of Baptist Publishing House in Rio, and counselor. He served in Portugal for one year (1958–59) as fraternal representative of the Foreign Mission Board. Crabtree wrote *Baptists in Brazil* (1953). He married Mabel Henderson, June 12, 1918. JESSE C. FLETCHER

CRANE, EDITH CAMPBELL. See LANHAM, EDITH CAMPBELL CRANE.

CRISIS IN OUR NATION, STATEMENT CONCERNING THE. The prevalence of civil disorder, racism, poverty, and social injustice caused a crisis in the United States in the sixties. Unrest and disturbances triggered by the murder of Martin Luther King, Jr., in Memphis, Tenn., Apr. 4, 1968, prompted Southern Baptist leaders to prepare a statement calling for action dealing with the crisis in the nation. Denominational leaders representing several Convention agencies drafted the statement. Initially endorsed by 79 leaders, including executives of SBC agencies and most of the executives and editors of state Baptist conventions, the statement was modified by the Executive Committee, SBC, immediately prior to the Convention's annual meeting in 1968. On recommendation of the committee, the Convention adopted the statement, including proposals for its implementation, by a majority vote of approximately 73 per cent. While recognizing that no individual or organization can speak for all Baptists, the Convention approved the statement as representative of "the concern, confession, commitment, and appeal by the majority of the messengers meeting in Houston, Texas, June 5, 1968." Subsequently SBC agencies, some state conventions, and other groups took measures to implement the intent of the statement. The text of the statement is given below.

LYNN E. MAY, JR.

WE FACE A CRISIS. Our nation is enveloped in a social and cultural revolution. We are shocked by the potential for anarchy in a land dedicated to democracy and freedom. There are ominous sounds of hate and violence among men and of unbelief and rebellion toward God. These compel Christians to face the social situation and to examine themselves under the judgment of God.

We are an affluent society, abounding in wealth and luxury. Yet far too many of our people suffer from poverty. Many are hurt by circumstances from which they find it most difficult to escape, injustice which they find most difficult to correct, or heartless exploitation which they find most difficult to resist. Many live in slum housing or ghettos of race or poverty or ignorance or bitterness that often generate both despair and defiance.

We are a nation that declares the sovereignty of law and the necessity of civil order. Yet we have had riots and have tolerated conditions that breed riots, spread violence, foster disrespect for the law, and undermine the democratic process.

We are a nation that declares the equality and rights of persons irrespective of race. Yet, as a nation, we have allowed cultural patterns to persist that have deprived millions of black Americans, and other racial groups as well, of equality of recognition and opportunity in the areas of education, employment, citizenship, housing, and worship. Worse still, as a nation, we have condoned prejudices that have damaged the personhood of blacks and whites alike. We have seen a climate of racism and reactionism develop resulting in hostility, injustice, suspicion, faction, strife, and alarming potential for bitterness, division, destruction, and death.

WE REVIEW OUR EFFORTS. In the face of national shortcomings, we must nevertheless express appreciation for men of goodwill of all races and classes who have worked tirelessly and faithfully to create a Christian climate in our nation.

From the beginning of the Southern Baptist Convention, and indeed in organized Baptist life, we have affirmed God's love for all men of all continents and colors, of all regions and races. We have continued to proclaim that the death of Jesus on Calvary's cross is the instrument of God's miraculous redemption for every individual.

Inadequately but sincerely, we have sought in our nation and around the world both to proclaim the gospel to the lost and to minister to human need in Christ's name. Individually and collectively, we are trying to serve, but we have yet to use our full resources to proclaim the gospel whereby all things are made new in Christ.

WE VOICE OUR CONFESSION. "If my people, which are called by my name, shall humble themselves, and pray, and seek my face, and turn from their wicked ways; then will I hear from heaven, and will forgive their sin, and will heal their land" (2 Chron. 7:14).

The current crisis arouses the Christian conscience. Judgment begins at the house of God. Christians are inescapably involved in the life of the nation. Along with all other citizens we recognize our share of responsibility for creating in our land conditions in which justice, order, and righteousness can prevail. May God forgive us wherein we have failed him and our fellowman.

As Southern Baptists, representative of one of the largest bodies of Christians in our nation and claiming special ties of spiritual unity with the large conventions of Negro Baptists in our land, we have come far short of our privilege in Christian brotherhood.

Humbling ourselves before God, we implore him to create in us a right spirit of repentance and to make us instruments of his redemption, his righteousness, his peace, and his love toward all men.

WE DECLARE OUR COMMITMENT. The Christ we serve, the opportunity we face, and the crisis we confront compel us to action. We therefore declare our commitment, believing this to be right in the sight of God and our duty under the lordship of Christ.

We will respect every individual as a person possessing inherent dignity and worth growing out of his creation in the image of God.

We will strive to obtain and secure for every person equality of human and legal rights. We will undertake to secure opportunities in matters of citizenship, public services, education, employment, and personal habitation that every man may achieve his highest potential as a person.

We will accept and exercise our civic responsibility as Christians to defend people against injustice. We will strive to insure for all persons the full opportunity for achievement according to the endowments given by God.

We will refuse to be a party to any movement that fosters racism or violence or mob action.

We will personally accept every Christian as a brother beloved in the Lord and welcome to the fellowship of faith and worship every person irrespective of race or class.

We will strive by personal initiative and every appropriate means of communication to bridge divisive barriers, to work for reconciliation, and to open channels of fellowship and cooperation.

We will strive to become well informed about public issues, social ills, and divisive movements that are damaging to human relationships. We will strive to resist prejudice and to combat forces that breed distrust and hostility.

We will recognize our involvement with other Christians and with all others of goodwill in the obligation to work for righteousness in public life and justice for all persons. We will strive to promote Christian brotherhood as a witness to the gospel of Christ.

WE MAKE AN APPEAL. Our nation is at the crossroads. We must decide whether we shall be united in goodwill, freedom, and justice under God to serve mankind or be destroyed by covetousness, passion, hate, and strife.

We urge all leaders and supporters of minority groups to encourage their followers to exercise Christian concern and respect for the person and property of others and to manifest the responsible action commensurate with individual dignity and Christian citizenship.

We appeal to our fellow Southern Baptists to join us in self-examination under the Spirit of God and to accept the present crisis as a challenge from God to strive for reconciliation by love.

We appeal to our fellow Southern Baptists to engage in Christian ventures in human relationships, and to take courageous actions for justice and peace.

We believe that a vigorous Christian response to this national crisis is imperative for an effective witness on our part at home and abroad.

Words will not suffice. The time has come for action. Our hope for healing and renewal is in the redemption of the whole of life. Let us call men to faith in Christ. Let us dare to accept the full demands of the love and lordship of Christ in human relationships and urgent ministry. Let us be identified with Christ in the reproach and suffering of the cross.

We therefore recommend to the messengers of the Southern Baptist Convention that:

1. We approve this statement on the national crisis.
2. We rededicate ourselves to the proclamation of the gospel, which includes redemption of the individual and his involvement in the social issues of our day.
3. We request the Home Mission Board to take the leadership in working with the Convention agencies concerned with the problems related to this crisis in the most effective manner possible and in keeping with their program assignments.
4. We call upon individuals, the churches, the associations, and the state conventions to join the Southern Baptist Convention in a renewal of Christian effort to meet the national crisis.

CROUCH, AUSTIN (b. Carrolton, Mo., July 13, 1870; d. Nashville, Tenn., Aug. 28, 1957). Pastor and denominational leader. Son of Elbert Hildebrande and Adelaide (Newell) Crouch, he was educated at Baylor University (A.B., 1898), Howard College (M.A., 1906), and Southern Baptist Theological Seminary (1899–1900). He received honorary degrees from Union University and Carson-Newman College. Ordained as pastor at McKinney, Tex., in 1893, he served churches in Whitesboro, Allen, Waco, and Dallas, Tex.; Corinth, Miss.; Birmingham, Ala.; Jonesboro, Ark.; and Murfreesboro, Tenn. He also served as superintendent of church extension for the Home Mission Board, SBC.

He was elected as the first executive secretary-treasurer of the Executive Committee of the Southern Baptist Convention in 1927 and served until his retirement in 1946. Crouch made five notable contributions to the denomination: (1) At the 1925 Convention in Memphis he called for a Business Efficiency Committee to bring order out of the chaos of Southern Baptist finances. Appointed as chairman, he led the committee to revamp the Executive Committee and to instal a Business and Financial Plan. (2) Following the approval of the Cooperative Program in 1925 many states were slow to cooperate. Crouch succeeded in leading these states one by one into cooperation. (3) During the early years of the reorganized Executive Committee its life was in jeopardy, being resisted by many of the pastors who thought it represented the beginnings of a super church and by some agency executives who saw it as a threat to their direct responsibility to the Convention. His firmness and fairness in administration soon dispelled opposition to the committee. (4) The period up to about 1945 was one beset by depression, war, debt, and near bankruptcy. Crouch's business acumen and integrity not only helped stabilize the Convention, it won the confidence and friendship of bankers, whose help the denomination greatly needed. (5) His sense of mission gave Southern Baptists spiritual leadership hand in hand with business leadership when both were necessary for survival. The day of his death he was seeking a publisher for a book he was writing on the atonement. His other books included *The Plan of Salvation* (1924), *The Bright Side of Death* (1951), *How Southern Baptists Do Their Work* (1951), *The Progress of the Christian Life* (1949), and *Is Baptism Essential to Salvation?* (1953). Even in his denominational role, Crouch was a preacher and evangelist.

Norman W. Cox (*q.v.*), a longtime friend, once said of him: "He did not talk unless he had something to say. . . . He patiently listened, studied much, found and examined the facts, weighed all the elements involved, meekly let others expose their ignorance or disclose their inadequate ideas in a torrent of words. Finally in such a situation he got the floor and in a few words presented the relevant facts. He then drew a clear conclusion that could not be controverted. . . . His timing was the fruit of exceptional insight. . . . This method required time but was accurate and effective."

Crouch was instantly killed when struck by a car on Aug. 28, 1957, within sight of the church where he had held membership for 30 years, though he could not see the church for he had been almost blind for the last 12 years of his life. He left no survivors, having been preceded in death by the first Mrs. Crouch (Arianna Hill) in 1900 and the second Mrs. Crouch (Myrtle Oldham) in 1946. His children were his friends, especially young men in whom he invested his confidence and his time.

ALBERT MCCLELLAN

CRUSADE OF THE AMERICAS. A Baptist evangelistic crusade, Jan., 1968, through Dec., 1969, involving 20,000,000 Baptists in North, South, and Central America. Fifty thousand churches responded to the challenge of Rubens Lopes of Brazil, given to the Southern Baptist Convention and the Baptist World Alliance in 1965.

The first planning meeting at Cali, Colombia, resulted in the Cali Declaration setting forth Crusade objectives as: (1) the deepening of the spiritual life within the churches, homes, and individual Christians; (2) the evangelizing of the American continents; (3) the establishing of true moral and spiritual bases for the betterment of mankind's economic, social, and physical welfare.

The declaration, drafted by a committee including C. E. Autrey and H. H. Hobbs of the SBC, said: "This is an invitation to all Baptist conventions in the Americas to join hearts and hands in the crusade. Let us go forth to confront lost souls with the good news of the gospel of salvation."

The Home Mission Board's Evangelism Division led Southern Baptist participation. An SBC steering committee for planning and coordination included Wayne Dehoney, chairman; Ray Roberts; J. Conally Evans; H. H. Hobbs; Owen Cooper; and M. B. Carroll.

The Foreign Mission Board, working through missionaries and national conventions in South and Central America, undergirded the work outside the United States and Canada. Rubens Lopes of Brazil was general chairman of the Crusade, and Henry Earl Peacock of Brazil was general coordinator.

Reports from 25 of the 50 groups indicated a total of 494,018 decisions for Christ during 1969; 368,225 represented baptisms in the SBC. Results not measured in a statistical way included: (1) a new openness of Baptists of many races and many denominations toward one another; (2) a rediscovery of the role of the laity in evangelism; (3) the establishing of many Baptist churches; and (4) a new commitment to evangelism. Crusade leadership expressed hope that the spirit expressed in the crusade would "produce a blessed world explosion of evangelistic zeal."

JOHN F. HAVLIK

CRUSADER. A monthly reading magazine for boys in grades 1–6, published by the Brotherhood Commission since Oct., 1970. The purpose of the magazine is to provide mission information and to stimulate participation in mission activities by boys enrolled in the Crusader portion of the Royal Ambassador program. "Crusader Parent" (A Family Mission Guide) is an insert which is included in *Crusader* the first month of each quarter, containing suggestions for parent involvement at parent-son meetings, orientation on their son's units of study, and possible family mission activities.

DARRELL C. RICHARDSON

CRUSADER COUNSELOR. A quarterly magazine published by the Brotherhood Commission for men and women who lead Royal Ambassadors in grades 1–6. Begun in Oct., 1970, this publication contains weekly program plans, plus articles designed to make men and women more effective counselors.

DARRELL C. RICHARDSON

CUBA, MISSIONS IN (cf. Cuba, Baptists in, Vol. I). The Baptist Convention of Western Cuba developed encouragingly through 1958 when dark days came upon the country. As the Batista regime became more oppressive, many longed for freedom of worship. Fidel Castro was greeted as a liberator and freedom was enjoyed for a time. Religious activities were not abruptly terminated but decrees progressively closed freedom's doors. Churches and ministers were registered, school properties taken, and Bibles confiscated. After visiting the island early in 1961, Home Mission Board officials reported that work flourished despite uncertainties. A crusade in Havana Province resulted in 2,192 professions of faith. Late in 1961, one board official found Cuba a changed country. Several missionaries left, and many seemingly sincere Christians embraced Communism.

In Apr., 1965, Herbert Caudill, David Fite, and 53 other leaders were imprisoned. These included all convention officers. In Nov., 1966, Caudill was placed under house arrest to seek medical attention, and two specialists went from the United States to perform eye surgery. In Dec., 1968, Fite was released, and in Feb., 1969, the Caudill and Fite families returned to the United States.

In 1968 the convention reported 90 churches, 6,667 members, and 161 baptisms. New work was almost impossible. All services were limited to church buildings. Denominational meetings required government approval. The home for the aged, the assembly, the seminary, and the *Voz Bautista* enjoyed limited freedom. With these limitations the work in 1970 continued.

L. D. WOOD

CULLOM, WILLIS RICHARD (b. Halifax County, N. C., Jan. 15, 1867; d. Wake Forest, N. C., Oct. 20, 1963). Son of Joel John and Mary Eliza (Johnson) Cullom, he was a graduate of Wake Forest College (M.A., 1892), and Southern Baptist Theological Seminary (Th.M., 1895; Th.D., 1904). He did graduate work at the University of Chicago and Union Theological Seminary in New York City. In 1915 he received a D.D. degree from Richmond College. He made three trips to Europe and the Near East. On June 2, 1897, he married Frances Farmer of Louisville, Ky. They had four children: Elizabeth (Mrs. Fant Kelly), Edward F., Nancy (Mrs. Lawrence Harris), and Sarah (Mrs. C. C. Pearson). In 1896 the trustees of Wake Forest College invited him "to inaugurate the study of the Bible" as a part of the curriculum of the college. For 42 years he taught Bible at Wake Forest. He also pioneered in other efforts to train ministers, including organizing the ministerial conference at Wake Forest, 1896, and the North Carolina Baptist Pastors' Conference, 1907. In 1908 he initiated a Ministers' Assurance Association. In 1907 he had become director of the North Carolina Million-Dollar campaign for Baptist colleges, which merged (1919) into the Southern Baptists' 75-million campaign, which he also directed in North Carolina. For several years he served as chairman of the Southern Baptist Education Commission. Ordained an "elder" by his home church, Quankie, in 1888, he served as pastor of neighboring churches through his student years and while he taught at Wake Forest. After his retirement from the college in 1938, and from the pastorate in 1941, he served as supply preacher and adviser to pastors and churches for more than 20 years. He is buried in Wake Forest Cemetery.

BIBLIOGRAPHY: J. H. Blackmore, *The Cullom Lantern: A Biography of W. R. C.* (1963).

JAMES H. BLACKMORE

***CUMBERLAND COLLEGE.** A Kentucky Baptist senior college since 1961, located at Williamsburg, Ky. In 1957 the state Baptist general association authorized Cumberland College to move to senior college status. The third year was added in 1959–60, and the first graduating class was in 1961.

President James Malcolm Boswell (1906–) led in a program of development. Since 1954 nine major building units have been added to the college facilities: a classroom, chapel, administration building, two dormitories for women, two dormitory housing units for men, a biology building, a chemistry building, a combination cafeteria and kitchen, and a library. The value of the property and endowment was in excess of $5,500,000, as of July, 1969. The library contains 55,000 volumes.

As of the academic year 1968–69, the enrolment of full-time students was 1,705, with 54 part-time students. The academic staff numbered 101. The college has 5,200 graduates, more than half of whom have graduated since 1960.

The 1968–69 operating budget of the college was $2,503,000, with $155,000 coming from the Kentucky Baptist Convention for operations, plus $63,000 for capital needs from this sponsoring group. Cumberland College shares in the receipts from the Christian education advance campaign of the convention.

The trustees of this fully accredited college are elected by the Kentucky Baptist Convention. Cumberland has a liberal arts program and is coeducational. An active Baptist Student Union program and an in-service program for student pastors are promoted cooperatively with the convention.

HAROLD GLEN SANDERS

CUNNINGHAM, COLLIS (b. Forsyth, Ga., Aug. 31, 1890; d. Montgomery, Ala. May 5, 1962). Pastor and missionary. Son of Alfred Benjamin and Cenie (White) Cunningham, he married Hester Gertrude Faulkner. Cunningham was a graduate of Howard College, A.B., and Southern Baptist Theological Seminary, Th.M. He received the D.D. from Selma University. He served as student pastor at Dixiana, Ashville, Pell City, and Leeds, Ala., and Cecilia, Ky. He was a missionary to Japan under the Foreign Mission Board, SBC, 1922–26. Cunningham was pastor of the First Baptist Church, Tallassee, Ala., 1926–44. In 1944 he became a missionary in the Salem-Troy Association in Alabama. In 1945 his field of work was enlarged to a district consisting of the southeastern part of the state. In 1951 the Alabama Baptist Convention established a department of work with National Baptists (Negro) and chose Cunningham to lead in this work. He filled this position until he retired in 1961.

A. HAMILTON REID

CURB, DAN NAPOLEON (b. Marion, Ala., June 3, 1872; d. Oklahoma City, Okla., Apr. 3, 1957). Minister, missionary, and denominational leader. Son of A. M. and Fannie J. Curb, he was ordained at Leon, Okla., in May, 1903, by Newport Church. His Oklahoma pastorates included Ryan, Nash, Fairview, Shattuck, and Ardmore. He served on the board of directors of the state convention and Oklahoma Baptist University trustees prior to entering denominational service. Curb was field representative for Oklahoma Baptist Children's Home, 1930–46. He married Etta Woolridge on Aug. 12, 1896. They had five children: Charles Hayes, Elizabeth (Mrs. J. W. Read), Dallas G., Velma (Mrs. R. N. Matthews), and Dan N., Jr.

J. M. GASKIN

CURRICULUM, SOUTHERN BAPTIST CHURCH. Until the sixties, curriculum designs for Sunday School, Training Union, church music, WMU, and Brotherhood had each been independently planned. But in the early sixties, mainly under the leadership of W. L. Howse, director of the Education Division of the Sunday School Board, a movement got under way to correlate these various curriculums. Representatives of the five organizations began holding monthly meetings for study and planning, both with respect to church program as a whole and with respect to church curriculum.

One of the decisions reached had to do with the assignment of "curriculum areas" to each of the organizations. Sunday School should teach the biblical revelation; Training Union, systematic theology, Christian ethics, Christian history, church polity and organization, and skills for the performance of church functions; church music, music and hymnody; and WMU and Brotherhood, missions.

In the planning process, editorial workers collaborated to develop a suitable curriculum philosophy and design. This eventuated first in the Life and Work Curriculum, a correlated plan for adults and young people, involving all five organizations, which began its appearance in the churches in Oct., 1966. Later this same approach was used in the formulation of the new curriculum for the seventies, which was launched in Oct., 1970. In this latter plan, all age groups were involved. The following paragraphs indicate each organization's part in the total curriculum plan for Southern Baptist churches. HOWARD P. COLSON

Brotherhood.—A curriculum plan for Brotherhood units has been in existence since 1910, but only since Oct., 1966, on a correlated basis with the other church program organizations. The original plan of 1910 emphasized missionary education. During the next 55 years, however, the emphasis shifted to a variety of other subjects. In 1965 Brotherhood returned to its first love—missions.

The first curriculum plan for Royal Ambassadors was developed in 1946. Its development became the responsibility of the Brotherhood Commission in 1956. From the beginning the emphasis in this curriculum plan was missions. The two plans merged into a single plan when the program emphasis for Baptist Men was changed to missions in 1965.

The Brotherhood curriculum plan for 1966–69 was correlated with corresponding divisions of adults and young people in the other church programs. A major influence in this plan was the Sunday School Life and Work Curriculum plan for the same period. Brotherhood curriculum planners used the Sunday School plan to prepare a similar plan with a missions emphasis.

In the plans for 1969–73, one of the major correlating factors for youth and adults was critical issues isolated in the denomination's 70 Onward research project into needs of churches. ROY JENNINGS

Church Music.—The course of study offered by the Sunday School Board for the church music program has been less structured than other curriculums. Music leaders have had suggestions for building study programs suited to the needs and proficiencies of individual churches. Since its beginning, the Church Music Department produced periodicals, books, music, and recordings in increasing number and variety. A promotional program generated educational efforts by church music correlated with the curriculums of the other educational programs. This included the planned use of study course texts, vocal and instrumental music, and hymns, and the investigation of specific musical content areas by age groups at times when such study related to other educative experiences.

In 1955 the first graded activity suggestions appeared in *The Church Musician.* They were succeeded in 1956 by printed lesson materials (units) for Beginners, Primaries, and Juniors. A structured curriculum framework built on identifiable correlating factors subsequently was developed for the younger age groups.

A music study program for young people and adults was a part of the Life and Work Curriculum beginning in 1966. In 1970 the curriculum of Church Music was carried in the dated plan in study courses, 13 new periodicals, and a multitude of additional resources.

J. WILLIAM THOMPSON

Sunday School.—The introduction of the Life and Work Curriculum for young people and adults, which was introduced in 1966, may be identified as one of the most significant Southern Baptist Sunday School curriculum developments. This series is a Bible-based, church-oriented, and action-inducing curriculum. Whereas Uniform lessons are planned in cycles to cover as much Bible content as possible, Life and Work lessons are selected for intensive study related to specific tasks and functions of the church. Life and Work is a correlated curriculum providing the biblical base for other church program organization curriculums.

A new curriculum for Weekday Bible Study was completed in 1969. It consists of eight pupil texts with a teacher's guide for each. The curriculum consists chiefly of Bible content selected for children and youth 9 through 16 years of age.

The revised program designs introduced by Southern Baptists in Oct., 1970, called for new Sunday School curriculum designs. To meet this need the Sunday School Board introduced four new curriculum series. Each contains Sunday School materials to supplement the offerings in Uniform and Life and Work. These are (1) Forefront, (2) Foundation (for preschoolers and children), (3) Support, and (4) Program Helps. With the availability of six curriculum series, the Sunday School Board established for the first time in its history curriculum distinctives designed to meet the variety of Bible-study needs that exist in Southern Baptist churches.

Two other major developments completed the new Sunday School curriculum design for the 70's. The new Bible Survey Series of books in the study course consists of eight texts with teaching guides. These provide a comprehensive survey of the Bible. A new dated Vacation Bible School curriculum provides for church and mission Vacation Bible Schools.

EARL WALDRUP

Training Union.—The curriculum materials for use in Training Union continued to change and grow as the organization and needs in churches developed. In 1963 an easy-to-read version of *Baptist Adults* was launched, entitled *Training Union Quarterly Simplified.* A Spanish language edition of the same material, *La Fe Bautista,* was released in 1964.

Major changes in Adult and Young People's materials were completed in Oct., 1966. These changes were in connection with the Sunday School Board's development of the Life and Work Curriculum. Changes included the addition of leadership periodicals, known as group training guides. The periodicals for Married Young People and Young Adults were dropped at that time.

The existing Training Union curriculum for Young People and Adults was continued under the heading of Christian Training Curriculum. Periodicals in this curriculum included a personal training guide for Young People, a training guide for leaders of Young People, a personal training guide for Adults, and a training guide for Adult union leaders. A corresponding set of personal training guides and guides for leaders of unions was developed for the Life and Work Curriculum.

A complete new curriculum for use in Training Union was introduced in Oct., 1970. This curriculum was developed over a period of three years and was designed to meet a wide variety of church and individual needs, and to conform to the grouping-grading plan introduced by all Southern Baptist educational programs. A total of 24 periodicals are included in the new curriculum. DONALD F. TROTTER

WMU.—WMU participated with other church program organizations in designing a correlated curriculum which began in 1966. WMU defined its scope in three areas: the missionary message of the Bible, the progress of Christian missions, and the contemporary missions work of Southern Baptists and others. In 1968 WMU introduced a flexible organization plan for adults which allowed members to choose an area of study and a study group based on their interests.

Beginning in Oct., 1970, content and study procedures for Bible study and current missions groups appeared in *Royal Service* for Baptist Women and *Contempo* for Baptist Young Women. Mission books and Round Table groups use group guides for their study of current missions books and missions background books. Study suggestions for general meetings are in these adult magazines.

Other age-level organizations have study materials in the member or leader magazine for each age level: *Accent* for Acteens and *Accent,* Leader Edition; *Discovery* for Girls in Action and *Aware* for GA leaders; *Start* for Mission Friends leaders. These magazines also carry resources and supplementary materials for mission study, mission support, and mission action. *Dimension* is the magazine for WMU officers.

See also SUNDAY SCHOOL BOARD, WOMEN'S MISSIONARY UNION, and BROTHERHOOD.

BETTY JO CORUM

CURTIS, OMAR CLAY (b. Cisco, Tex., Nov. 13, 1900; d. Amarillo, Tex., Oct. 4, 1961). Pastor and district Missionary. Before his conversion he was in business in Big Spring, Tex. Ordained in 1935, he served as pastor of churches in Andrews, Seminole, Perryton, and Pampa, Tex. From 1953 to 1961 he served as a Texas missionary for district ten comprised of Amarillo, Canadian, North Fork, Palo Duro, Panhandle, and Trans-Canadian Associations, where he made an outstanding record. He also served as a trustee of Wayland Baptist College.

CHARLES P. MCLAUGHLIN

CURTIS, THOMAS FENNER (b. England, 1815; d. Boston, Mass., 1872). Pastor, educator, and denominational executive. He came to Augusta, Me., with his parents (Thomas Curtis and Susan Reynoldson) in 1833. He served pastorates in Georgia, *c.* 1838–43. In Mar., 1843, he became pastor of First Baptist Church, Tuscaloosa, Ala., serving until 1848. With fourteen others he represented Alabama at the organizational meeting of the Southern Baptist Convention in Augusta, Ga., and was elected a member of the first Board of Domestic Missions (now Home Mission Board). In 1849 he became professor of theology at Howard College, Marion, Ala., and recording secretary of both the board and the Alabama Baptist State Convention, serving in the latter capacity for only one year. Two years later he was elected corresponding secretary for the board, from which he was removed in 1853. He moved to Lewisburg, Pa., *c.* 1853, where he taught theology at the University of Lewisburg (later Bucknell) until *c.* 1867. He authored three books: *Communion* (1850), *The Progress of Baptist Principles* (1855; 2nd ed. 1857), and *The Human Element in the Inspiration of the Sacred Scriptures* (1867), as well as numerous articles. A. RONALD TONKS

***CZECHOSLOVAK BAPTIST CONVENTION OF NORTH AMERICA.** The 1969 convention met in Union City, Pa., for its 58th annual session with about 150 in attendance. It adopted a missionary budget of $7,770. Haiti received the greater amount, being a substitute for Czechoslovakia, now closed to its ministry. Ten native workers in Haiti receive financial support, and of these, three are supported by the Woman's Missionary Union. Special ministries, such as relief work, literature, etc., are cared for from special gifts. One gift of $2,031 to the American Bible Society enabled the printing of 1,000 Czechoslovak Bibles. Another gift of $11,000 went to Haiti for a church building, a memorial to the Czechoslovak Baptist work in that country.

A monthly publication, *Pravda a Slavna Nadeje* (Truth and Glorious Hope), edited in Chicago by Mr. and Mrs. J. P. Piroch, reaches into 25 countries. Free copies are sent to families who cannot subscribe. A radio ministry is carried on from Windsor, Canada, by J. Zajicek. A recent influx of refugees into Canada has given the Canadian churches many opportunities to serve them, some hearing the gospel for the first time. Current officers are: president, J. Karenko, vice-president, R. Karhan, executive secretary, A. Kmetko, and assistant secretary, J. Novak. JOSEPH J. SHEREDA

D

DAHOMEY, MISSION IN. Small Baptist groups, composed largely of Yoruba settlers from Nigeria, appeared in Dahomey during the first half of the 20th century. Repeated appeals for assistance were addressed to the Nigerian Baptist Convention and the Foreign Mission Board, SBC. In 1969, Neville and Emma (Osborne) Claxon, who had served in Nigeria, were assigned to Dahomey and went to France for language study in preparation for their service. H. CORNELL GOERNER

DALLAS BAPTIST COLLEGE. A Christian senior college cooperating with the Baptist General Convention of Texas and controlled by a board of trustees elected by the convention. In 1950 the idea of establishing a Baptist senior college in the Dallas area was presented to the administrators of Decatur Baptist College, a junior college established at Decatur, Texas in 1891. In 1965 after much planning, the college was moved to a 200-acre site overlooking Mountain Creek Lake in southwest Dallas. Dallas Baptist College maintained its status as a junior college with an enrolment of 900 students through 1967.

The school began its transition to a senior college in 1968 by adding the junior class. In 1969 the senior class enrolled with the first baccalaureate degrees conferred in the spring of 1970. In the $2,500,000 Learning Center, students view course material at the learning carrel, a booth equipped with audio headsets, a television monitor, and a touchtone dial for selecting 15-minute video-taped presentations. The building is designed with capacity for a 150,000-volume library, 1,200 learning carrels, 35 seminar rooms, and faculty offices. Under the leadership of president Charles P. Pitts, the curriculum emphasizes a developmental studies program, freeing the student from scheduled classes, thus allowing individual progress. See also DECATUR COLLEGE, Vol. I. LYNN MOULTON

DANIEL, JOHN TOURJEE (b. Dublin, Tex., Sept. 23, 1891; d. Oklahoma City, Okla. Nov. 14, 1967). Minister and denominational leader, he was recording secretary for Baptist General Convention of Oklahoma, 1932–67. He graduated from Bible Institute of Los Angeles, Calif., B.D., 1915, and Oklahoma Baptist University, A.B., 1924. He was awarded a D.D. by the latter in 1948. He was distinguished as a builder of church buildings, a conservative preacher in his theology, and a member of many convention boards and committees. Death came while he was on the platform for an evening session of the state convention. He is buried at Oklahoma City. SAM W. SCANTLAN

DANIEL, ROBERT THOMAS (b. Washington County, Ga., Jan. 18, 1904; d. Wake Forest, N. C., May 16, 1959). Pastor, seminary professor, and author. Son of Thomas S. and Ada Francis (Little) Daniel, he was a graduate of Mercer University, A.B., 1927, Southwestern Baptist Theological Seminary Th.M., 1937 and Th.D., 1942, and Texas Christian University, M.A., 1941. He did graduate studies at Furman University, University of South Carolina, and Garrett Biblical Institute. He married Alberta Carl of Greenwood, Miss., May 21, 1937. They had two sons, Carl R. and Lee B. Daniel. While teaching in the public high schools of North Carolina, 1925–33, he served as pastor of several small churches. He was pastor of Central Baptist Church, Italy, Tex., 1934–38; instructor and professor of Old Testament at Southwestern Baptist Theological Seminary, 1935–52; and professor of Old Testament at Southeastern Baptist Theological Seminary, 1952–59. In 1950 he was elected president of the Southwestern Section of the National Association of Biblical instructors, and for many years was a member of several learned societies. He is the author of *How to Study the Psalms* (1953) and numerous articles in scholarly journals. Dying after a prolonged

DARGAN-CARVER LIBRARY (*q.v.*), Baptist Research Center in Nashville, Tenn. Occupied in 1965. Volume capacity of 101,340 and seating capacity of 87. Reading room, museum, and archival areas shown above.

BAPTIST MUSEUM area in Dargan-Carver Library (*q.v.*), Nashville, Tenn. Offices of the Historical Commission, SBC, are adjacent to the library which is jointly operated by the Commission and Sunday School Board.

CHOWAN COLLEGE (*q.v.*), Murfreesboro, N. C. *Top:* McDowell Columns, familiar landmark at Chowan College, was opened in 1851. Contains auditorium and provides offices for the administration. *Bottom:* Whitaker Library seats 400; has shelves for 100,000 books.

illness, he was buried in the Seminary Cemetery at Wake Forest, N. C. JAMES H. BLACKMORE

***DANISH BAPTIST FOREIGN MISSION SOCIETY.** Ruanda-Urundi, mission field of Danish Baptists in east-central Africa, gained independence in 1962 as the Republic of Rwanda and the Kingdom of Burundi (which also became a republic in 1966). The Baptist Union of Rwanda-Burundi was established in 1960, with mission and church property being turned over to the union. After independence this became two separate Baptist unions.

Baptists in Rwanda experienced very rapid growth, with membership of the churches increasing from about 500 in 1962 to approximately 10,000 in 1969. Baptisms in 1968 totaled 2,756 and, at the beginning of 1969, 4,589 were preparing for baptism. Problems in rapid church growth were intensified by a very serious shortage of trained leaders. There was only one ordained national pastor. Ninety-nine evangelist-teachers, most with minimum training, taught and conducted worship services in 138 primary schools. Baptists operated one vocational school, one secondary school, and two clinics. Nine young men were enrolled in the pastors' school in Nyantanga.

In Burundi Baptists experienced more moderate growth. They recorded 249 baptisms in 1968. At the end of 1969 they reported approximately 3,000 members, 8 ordained pastors, and 43 evangelist-teachers serving 49 schools. There were three students in pastoral training at Mweya and two in the Congo.

In 1969, 10 missionaries served in Rwanda and 12 in Burundi, including one in each country supported by Swedish-language Baptist churches of Finland. The 20 supported by Danish Baptists represented one missionary for each 350 members of churches in Denmark. Danish Baptist gifts to foreign missions increased from 134,100 kroner in 1955 to 316,647 in 1965, and the budget for 1970 was 583,000 kroner ($77,733). JOHN ALLEN MOORE

***DARGAN-CARVER LIBRARY.** The library continues to be a research center. Its services are available to researchers from the Sunday School Board, other denominational agencies, seminaries, colleges, and universities, for bibliographies, abstracts, literature searches for articles, books, periodicals, theses, and dissertations.

The library is directed by Hubert B. Smothers, who succeeded Harold E. Ingraham in 1966 as director of the Sunday School Board's Service Division, and Davis C. Woolley, who followed Norman Wade Cox (*q.v.*) in 1959 as executive-secretary of the Historical Commission. Helen Conger is the librarian.

In July, 1965, the library moved from the fourth floor into new quarters on the first floor of the Sunday School Board Tower Building with three times as much floor space. Holdings at present include approximately 48,800 books, 72,000 associational minutes, 8,600,000 pages of microfilm, 14,200 periodicals, and much invaluable archival material.

In 1964 a revised plan of operating the library was inaugurated whereby the Historical Commission pays for library space utilized and services rendered by the library staff.

A unit of the library is the Baptist Historical Museum. One of the largest collections in the museum is Bibles. There are many rare and unusual editions, including a 1955 replica of the Gutenberg Bible (1455) with its illuminated pages.

The audiovisual section was transferred from the Church Library Department to the library in 1967. HELEN CONGER

DAVIS, FRANCIS ASBURY, SR. (b. Baltimore, Md., July 25, 1893; d. Baltimore, Aug. 5, 1966). Civic, business, and denominational leader. Eldest son of E. Asbury and Jennie (Conradt) Davis, he graduated from Johns Hopkins University with a major in Greek. He married Antoinette Biggs, daughter of Francis S. Biggs (*q.v.*, Vol. I). They had four children. Davis was a member of McCormick Memorial Baptist Church (formerly North Avenue Baptist Church) until its dissolution in 1934. Uniting with University Baptist Church, he served as a deacon, Bible teacher, and member of the finance committee. Davis served the Baptist Convention of Maryland as president, 1927–28; executive committee chairman; investment committee chairman; Church Extension Society president. For about 40 years he was a member of the state mission board, treasurer of the Baptist Children's Aid Society of Maryland, and unpaid editor and contributor to *The Maryland Baptist*. He helped build the chapel at Camp Wo-Me-To near Jarrettsville, Md. which is owned and operated by the WMU of Maryland. Davis was on the first board of coordination and promotion of the SBC and was the first Maryland member of the SBC Executive Committee. He was a member of the FMB, and trustee of the Southern Baptist Foundation, and of Southern, New Orleans, and Midwestern seminaries. Davis was president, F. A. Davis and Sons, Inc., a wholesale tobacco firm established by his grandfather; also, director, United States Fidelity and Guarantee Co., Provident Savings Bank, and Baltimore Transit Co; trustee, University of Richmond, Roland Park Country School, and Goucher College; president, Y.M.C.A. and Baltimore Council of Social Agencies. As chairman of the advisory committee of the Baltimore Department of Public Welfare, he helped upgrade the city hospitals. He was a sensitive Christian man of keen wit.

MRS. WILSON K. LEVERING, JR.

DAWSON, JOHN CHARLES (b. Huntsville, Ala., Aug. 10, 1876; d. Alexandria, Va., Apr. 9, 1966). Educator. Son of Granville Joseph and Alice (Roberts) Dawson, he married Fletcher Stinson in 1906. They had one child, Dorothy (Mrs. Whitney P. McCoy). After the death of his wife, he married Avis Marshall, 1933, who died in 1938. He was educated at Georgetown College (A.B., 1901), Howard College (M.A., 1910), and Columbia University (Ph.D., 1921). He received the LL.D. from Howard College, 1917, and Georgetown College, 1927. He served as professor of modern languages, 1903–31, acting dean, 1919–21, and president, 1921–31, of Howard College. He was also head professor of romance languages, University of Alabama, 1931–47. As dean of the A.E.F. students, Toulouse, France, the "Floral Games" bestowed on him the *Médaille d'Argent* (1919). The French government conferred on him the *Palmes Académiques,* with rank of *Officer d'Académie* (1943). Dawson wrote *Toulouse in the Renaissance* (1923), and *Étienne Dolet, A French Regicide in Alabama* (1923). HUL-CEE M. ACTON

DAWSON, WILLIE EVELYN TURNER (b. San Antonio, Bexar County, Tex., Sept. 9, 1888; d. Austin, Tex., Apr. 18, 1963). Teacher, lecturer, pastor's wife. The death of accountant Donald Turner sent Willie and her mother, Alice, to relatives in Dallas. Finishing Bryan High School, Willie taught kindergarten. Baptized by George W. Truett (*q.v.,* Vol. II), she attended First Baptist Church until her June 3, 1908, marriage to Joseph Martin Dawson made her a pastor's wife at Hillsboro, Tex., 1908–12, Temple, 1912–15, and Waco, 1915–46. A gifted speaker, she lectured to thousands. Though serving as Young Woman's Auxiliary superintendent, 1913–18, for Baptist Women Mission Workers, she maintained a large Bible class and raised funds for Memorial Dormitory, Baylor University, and Woman's Building, Southwestern Seminary, Ft. Worth. Her challenge precipitated the mercurial rise in Lottie Moon offering gifts, 1930. In 1953 Baylor honored her with an LL.D. degree, naming a dormitory for her. Washington, D. C., days, 1946–53, were busy with Dawson Bible Class, social occasions, and endless addresses (unscheduled at Baptist World Alliance, 1947, programmed at Baptist World Congress, 1950). Following retirement in Austin, Tex. (1954), illness curtailed her activities. After Mrs. Dawson's burial in Oakwood Cemetery, Waco, Alice Cheavens accepted from Southern Baptist Pastor's Wives her mother's award as Ideal Preacher's Wife, 1963. Three sons and two daughters are distinguished in law, business, writing, and teaching.

ROBERTA TURNER PATTERSON

***DEBT AND SOUTHERN BAPTISTS.** The Convention's Business and Financial Plan specifically states that: "It is understood that an agency may borrow money for seasonable needs, provided, however, that such borrowing shall not exceed the amount of its budget allowance remaining at the time of borrowing, and provided further that if an emergency should arise additional money may be borrowed on the approval of the Executive Committee of the Convention," and "Capital Investments, an agency or institution shall not create any liability or indebtedness except such as can and will be repaid out of its anticipated receipts for current operations within a period of three (3) years, without the consent of the Convention or the Executive Committee. In order to obtain such approval, the agency must file a statement showing the source of such anticipated receipts." The Convention also requires that each agency have some reserve as a precaution against operations debt. In Feb., 1970, nine of the 20 agencies reported debt of $7,431,861. In addition, Southern Baptist Hospital reported a debt of $9,800,000. In 1969 local church debt stood at $870,000,000. This compared with a 1967 figure of $830,000,000. The Convention is not responsible for state convention, associational, or local church debt. ALBERT MC CLELLAN

DEERE, DERWARD WILLIAM (b. Rolla, Ark., Feb. 6, 1914; d. Greenbrae, Calif., Nov. 11, 1968). Seminary professor and Christian mystic. Son of Elijah Bithon and Frances (Overton) Deere, he graduated from Malvern (Arkansas) High School (1930) and Magnolia A. and M. (now Southern) College (L.I., 1934) where he managed the college book store. Assistant manager of J. C. Penny Company in Malvern (1935–38), he married Reba Beryl Council on Feb. 5, 1938. A graduate of Ouachita Baptist College (now University) (A.B., 1942), Southern Baptist Theological Seminary (Th.M., 1945; Th.D., 1948), he did additional study at Pacific School of Religion (1951, 1953, 1959), the University of California and San Francisco Theological Seminary (1953); and Stanford University (1954). He spent a year (1965–66) in the study of prophecy and worship as set forth in the Old Testament at Regents Park College, Oxford, and additional study in Scotland at the universities of Edinburgh, Glasgow, and St. Andrew's. He was a teaching fellow in the Old Testament Department (1945–48) and a teaching assistant (1948–50) at Southern Seminary.

Deere became associate professor of Old Testament at Golden Gate Baptist Theological Seminary in May, 1950. He was professor of Old Testament interpretation at the seminary from 1958 until his death. He was a visiting professor of Old Testament at Southern Seminary, 1954–55. His Baptist pastorates included Perla, Ark., 1940–41; Mountain View Church, Benton, Ark., 1940–41; Westport, Ky., 1943–45; Buffalo Lick Church, Shelbyville, Ky., 1943–50; and interim pastorates in Kentucky and California.

In 1955 he traveled extensively in 22 countries in Europe and Israel. He was the author of *The Twelve Speak* (Vol. I, 1958; II, 1961); translator of Jeremiah, Zephaniah, Habakkuk, and Psalms 116–134 of *The Berkeley Version of the Bible* (1959); and contributor to *The Wycliffe Bible Commentary* (1962). At the time of his death, he had completed a manuscript on Ezekiel (*The Watchmen of Israel*), and Ruth, and had manuscripts in progress on Isaiah and the Psalms. He had a reading proficiency in Hebrew, Greek,

Latin, French, and German, and a working acquaintance of Aramaic and Babylonian Cuneiform.

Deere was a Christian mystic whose theology defied the application of labels such as conservative or liberal. A capable linguist and Bible critic, he believed the interpretation of the Scriptures is received from Yahweh himself, who reveals the spirit of the message not found in the letter alone. Students sometimes facetiously accused him of "spiritualizing" the Old Testament. His remarkable regard for the Old Testament and its truths was revealed in the semijocular expression, "The New Testament is just a postscript to the Old." Deere's special interest and expertise was Old Testament prophecy and its present-day application. He maintained a vibrant, dynamic, supportive relationship with an untold number of students, former students, pastors, and church members —many of whose addresses he knew by memory —through handwritten notes, gifts, and personal contacts. He left handwritten notes to approximately 50 of these friends, written on the day he died. G. PAUL HAMM

DEJARNETTE, BYRON CLINTON SHELTON (b. Breckinridge County, Ky., Nov. 5, 1900; d. Louisville, Ky., May 19, 1964). Son of Letitia Adkisson and Samuel DeJarnette, he graduated from Georgetown College (A.B., 1923) and attended the Southern Baptist Theological Seminary, 1930–33. He was secretary of the Training Union Department, General Association of Baptists in Kentucky (now Kentucky Baptist Convention) 1934–53. Because of failing health he became office administrator from 1954 until Oct. 31, 1956, when it became necessary for him to retire.

He married Emma Middleton on Dec. 26, 1938. She was an approved worker in the Training Union Department and traveled over the state with her husband. LEO T. CRISMON

DELAWARE, SOUTHERN BAPTISTS IN. See MARYLAND, BAPTIST CONVENTION OF.

DEMYTHOLOGIZING. Rudolf Bultmann first began his efforts to demythologize (*entmythologisieren*) the language of the New Testament in 1941. This language, he held, was inappropriate, inadequate, and indeed incomprehensible as a vehicle of thought in the modern world. Recognizing what he calls "mythological" elements in the New Testament gospels which derive from the concrete, supernaturalistic world view of the first century (Jewish apocalypticism, Hellenistic gnosticism), Bultmann has sought not to eliminate these elements, but to *interpret* them.

By means of existentialist philosophy (Heidegger) Bultmann has attempted to communicate the intention of the first-century writers of Scripture to the scientifically oriented man of the 20th century. In seeking to determine the existential significance of the so-called mythological concepts of the gospels (*e.g.*, the cross, resurrection), he endeavors to uncover a common ground of understanding upon which men of the first and the 20th centuries can stand. This common ground can be expressed best in terms of *meaning*, the meaning of the language of Scripture for and about human existence. Thus demythologizing is a hermeneutical effort to solve the problem of New Testament language.

BIBLIOGRAPHY: R. C. Briggs, *Interpreting the Gospels* (1969). Rudolf Bultmann, *Jesus Christ and Mythology* (1958). DONALD E. COOK

DEVOTIE, NOBLE LESLIE (b. Tuscaloosa, Ala., Jan. 24, 1838; d. Fort Morgan near Mobile, Ala., Feb. 12, 1861). Pastor and chaplain in the Confederate Army. Oldest son of James Harvey (*q.v.*, Vol. I) and Christian (Noble) DeVotie. He attended Howard College (now Samford University) and was graduated from the University of Alabama in 1856. While at the University of Alabama he was a founder of the Sigma Alpha Epsilon national social fraternity. After being graduated from the Presbyterian Theological Seminary in Princeton, N. J., in 1859, he returned to his native state to become pastor of the Baptist Church of Selma. He was ordained by that church on Nov. 20, 1859.

When a call was issued in late 1860 by the governor of Alabama, A. B. Moore, for troops to occupy Forts Morgan and Gaines, DeVotie became the chaplain of one of the Selma companies which was assigned to Fort Morgan. Upon arrival at Fort Morgan he was appointed chaplain to the garrison.

On the night of Feb. 12, 1861, he fell into the bay and was drowned. The *Columbus Times*, Columbus, Ga., called him, "The first martyr to the Southern cause." He was buried in Columbus, Ga., where his father was pastor.

ARTHUR L. WALKER, JR.

DICKINSON, ALFRED JAMES (b. "East View," Louisa County, Va., Dec. 25, 1864; d. Birmingham, Ala., Aug. 6, 1923). Pastor and denominational leader. Son of Charles Richard and Bettie (Valentine) Dickinson, he graduated from Richmond College, Va. (M.A.), and attended Southern Baptist Theological Seminary, 1886–88. Ordained by Walnut Street Church, Louisville, Ky., in 1888, he served as pastor of Lee Street Church, Baltimore, Md., 1886; Central Church, Memphis, Tenn., 1887, 1888–1889; First Church, Selma, Ala., 1890–1901; and First Church, Birmingham, Ala., 1901–18. During World War I he worked with YMCA and after that he was engaged in reform and welfare work until his death.

The D.D. degree was conferred on him in 1893 by the University of Alabama. He served on the board of trustees of Alabama Girls' Technical Institute and College for Women, Montevallo, Judson College, Howard College (now Samford University), and Marion Institute. He also served as a member of the Alabama State Board of Missions. In 1894 he made the motion that an annual ministers' conference be held in connection with the annual meeting of the Alabama Baptist State Convention. Much of his writing and work emphasized the need for the local church to be involved in social concerns.

He married Lucy Broadus Stone of Culpeper, Va., Aug. 13, 1888. Their children were Alfred J., Jr., Lucy Broadus (Mrs. Raymond G. Marks), Elizabeth Valentine (Mrs. Samuel B. McDowell), and Charles Richard.

ARTHUR L. WALKER, JR.

DIMENSION. Since Oct., 1970, the quarterly periodical for WMU officers in a church. Published by Woman's Missionary Union, the magazine contains materials to help WMU officers plan, coordinate, and evaluate WMU work on a regular basis. The editor is Ethalee Hamric (1970).

BETTY BROWN

DISCOVERY. Since Oct., 1970, the monthly periodical for members of Girls in Action. Published by Woman's Missionary Union, the magazine contains curriculum-related materials such as stories, feature articles, poems, and other items of interest to girls. Mrs. Jesse Tucker is editor (1970).

BETTY BROWN

DISNEY ASSEMBLY. Located near Disney, Okla., on a 45-acre plot is the Disney Baptist Assembly, owned by the Craig-Mayes and Rogers associations. The first session was Aug. 10–15, 1953, held at Grand Lake, and the first encampment on the present site was July 12–16, 1954. Equipped with complete camping facilities, property value in 1969 was $7,500. Support comes from church budgets and a state convention appropriation.

J. M. GASKIN

DISTINGUISHED COMMUNICATIONS MEDAL AWARD AND SCHOLARSHIP. At the Southern Baptist Convention, Atlantic City, N. J., in 1964, the first presentation of the Distinguished Communications Medal was made to Robert W. Sarnoff, then president of the National Broadcasting Company. The medal design is from Michelangelo's "The Creation of Man" and utilizes the hand of God reaching out to touch the hand of Adam, giving life to the man. The award was designed and is offered by the Radio and Television Commission, SBC, to honor individuals who have made an unusual and lasting contribution to a facet of communications. The award is made available annually, but only presented to uniquely qualified candidates. The two other DCM recipients, for 1966 and 1967, respectively, are Bill D. Moyers, press secretary to former President Lyndon Johnson; and the late Walt Disney, who made history as a film producer and cartoonist.

Communications Scholarships.—An integral part of the Distinguished Communications award is an annual $500 scholarship, bearing the name of the DCM recipient, and made available to a young person planning a career in electronic communications—radio, television, or film. Each scholarship recipient is eligible to apply for the scholarship for a second year. The purpose of the scholarships is to interest Southern Baptist young people in communications careers.

CLARENCE DUNCAN

***DISTRICT OF COLUMBIA BAPTIST CONVENTION.** By the end of 1968, 16 additional churches had been added to the convention membership: Clinton, Greenbelt, and Northside, 1957; Camp Springs, 1958; Twinbrook and Fort Foote, 1959; Whitehall, 1961; Wheaton Woods, 1962; Upper Marlboro, Shiloh, and Park View, 1963; Fort Washington, Seat Pleasant, and Upper Room, 1965; Cresthill, 1966; Korean of Washington, 1967.

A few of the churches have made some changes in name structure. Churches that merged are: Bethel and Luther Rice Memorial into Luther Rice Memorial; and University and Second into University. Churches changing names are: Fifth to Riverside and Anacostia to First Friendly. Withdrawing from fellowship in the convention were: Riverdale, Temple Hill, and Suitland. Churches that closed are: Christ (Minnesota Avenue), and Congress Heights.

The membership of the convention for 1969 was 59 churches and three chapels. The chapels are: Fairland, sponsored by Takoma Park Church; Ritchie Chapel, sponsored by Forestville, Upper Marlboro, and Parkway; and Johenning Chapel, sponsored by the Anna B. Johenning Baptist Center. In 1968 these churches and chapels reported a membership of 38,937, total contributions, $4,803,019, mission contributions, $686,490; total property value, $27,345,750, with outstanding indebtedness of $6,698,463.

Program of Work of District of Columbia Baptists. On Tuesday, Nov. 18, 1958, in business session, the convention approved a resolution to establish a Survey Committee of Fifteen, whose duties were to review, survey, and analyze the present and future projects of the convention, presenting such facts and recommendations to the convention through its executive committee, executive board, or at the annual meeting, as conditions may warrant. The purpose of the committee was to try to anticipate the needed progress and development of our denomination in this area, and to endeavor to balance this progress with the mission, best interest, and resources of the convention. Membership of this committee was selected by the nominating committee and presented to the executive board for approval, Jan., 1959. Henry R. Osgood was elected chairman. A progress report was made to the convention's annual session in Nov., 1959. A further report was made in 1960.

In 1961 three recommendations were made to the executive board and approved by the board: (1) The establishment of a mandatory retirement age of 65 for employees of the convention. It was also provided that an employee might be retained on annual invitation of the executive committee to age 70. (2) Additional Christian centers, church related, and community ministry, were encouraged. (3) It was recommended that a Joint Committee of Maryland and District of Columbia representatives be established to coordinate the activities of both conventions in the metropolitan area.

In 1962 the committee reported that an intensive survey and analysis was under way with professional assistance. No recommendations were offered. In 1963 the committee reported to the executive board on programs for the future organization of the District of Columbia Baptist Convention and consideration of programs. In 1964 the final report was presented to the convention, resulting in the adoption of a resolution that the work of the convention should be carried on through 12 programs:

1. A program of child care, consisting of work of the Baptist Home for Children of the District of Columbia (including such work outside the home as may be undertaken with regard to foster parents and other areas of child care).

2. A program of care for the aged, consisting of the work of the Baptist Home of the District of Columbia (including such work outside the home as may be undertaken by the institution's board).

3. A program of capital and endowment giving, consisting of the work of the District of Columbia Baptist Convention Foundation, Inc., offering to those desiring to make gifts or leave bequests to Baptist causes the opportunity to have such gifts and bequests safely invested and the income used in keeping with the purposes of the donor and the objectives of the convention.

4. A program of support for ministers' retirement, consisting of the financial provision for participation of the professional staff of the convention and ministers of the churches, in the pension and annuity plans of the denomination.

5. A program of convention operations, consisting of the administration and leadership of the convention and its staff, general program operations, and headquarters maintenance and equipment.

6. A program of promotion and public relations, consisting of the general promotion of understanding of the convention and all of its programs (including national and international missions as well as the local work of the convention), the editing and publication of the convention periodical, the provision of news about the convention and its work to the press, radio, and television, and assistance to the churches in the promotion of proper goals and techniques of administration and stewardship.

7. A program of Christian education, consisting of assistance to the local churches with respect to educational programs and methods, including the work of the Sunday School, the Training Union and evening fellowship, the ministry of music, and the Brotherhood and Men's Fellowship. This program shall also include cooperation with the Christian life witness committee on matters of moral and spiritual concerns of the churches with regard to public problems (including the separation of church and state). This program shall include such cooperation with the work of the Woman's Missionary Organization as to assure a coordinated approach to the Christian education of women, young women, girls, and primary, beginner, and nursery children in the local churches.

8. A program of local missions and church extension, consisting of the encouragement of chapels, missions, and mission churches, the operation of one or more Good Will centers, and the assistance to local churches as they seek to find and use appropriate opportunities for extension of their work into new locations. The program shall include both administrative services and guidance, and interim financial aid where appropriate until a mission or newly established church reaches self-support. These ministries and services have been instituted:

Missions Investors Plan.—A plan to provide the funds to assist the churches in obtaining property and for construction, was approved by the executive board, June, 1959. A maximum of two calls per year, at $10 per call, has resulted in contributions of approximately $80,000 to assist in 17 approved projects. The plan was amended in 1969 to include contributions for services not directly related to land purchase or construction.

An Experimental Urban Ministry.—Begun in June, 1967, to discover ways of ministering to the unchurched in high-rise apartment areas, the ministry was a joint venture of the convention and the American Baptist Home Mission Societies, under the leadership of Robert D. Caldwell.

The executive board approved plans for the establishment of a Baptist committee on wider cooperation, June, 1968. Other participating bodies cooperating in this committee include the Baptist Convention of Washington, D. C., and vicinity, Mount Vernon Baptist Association, Montgomery County Baptist Association, Severn Baptist Association and Northern Virginia Baptist Association. The purpose of this committee is the aggressive endeavor to draw together all associational Baptist bodies in the greater Washington area in cooperative effort, to provide an effective channel of communication and vehicle of action to the bodies involved, and to promote growing fellowship and understanding among all participating groups as people of God to bear witness to the world of our oneness in Christ as we address ourselves to human need in urban and suburban life.

H. Wesley Wiley, became full-time director of Metropolitan Ministries Program, including the staff leadership of the Baptist committee on wider cooperation, Jan. 1, 1969. This ministry is a cooperative effort with the Home Mission Board of the Southern Baptist Convention.

Anna B. Johenning Baptist Center.—The cen-

DISTRICT OF COLUMBIA STATISTICAL SUMMARY

Year	Churches	Church Member-Ship	Baptisms	S. S. Enrol-ment	V.B.S. Enrol-ment	T. U. Enrol-ment	W.M.U. Enrol-ment	Brother-hood En-rolment	Music Enrol-ment	Mission Gifts	Total Gifts	Value Church Property
1955	50	34,203	2,060	29,074	9,268	3,705	4,303	1,515		$461,125	$2,326,569	$12,589,339
1956	52	35,091	1,727	28,769	6,646	5,875	4,261	1,590		488,570	2,912,997	14,209,537
1957	53	34,326	1,694	28,413	9,381	5,605	3,941	1,345		468,574	2,943,625	14,888,545
1958	54	32,299	1,562	26,816	8,570	5,593	4,272	1,393		467,971	2,773,250	15,525,982
1959	56	34,604	1,550	26,373	8,198	5,464	4,278	1,020	3,405	549,132	3,102,466	16,615,198
1960	55	35,216	1,510	26,983	4,050	5,888	5,057	1,224	3,364	549,141	3,308,515	17,837,592
1961	54	35,066	1,536	26,219	8,083	5,437	4,676	1,275	3,302	585,029	3,306,000	18,898,572
1962	55	34,745	1,423	27,637	9,132	6,095	4,577	827	3,914	616,225	3,520,702	19,122,051
1963	55	34,229	1,089	27,283	9,446	5,908	4,661	700	3,412	636,305	3,833,058	20,730,577
1964	57	37,306	1,211	28,096	9,126	5,738	4,720	750	3,667	618,003	3,979,907	22,609,914
1965	60	39,183	1,281	28,507	8,933	5,710	5,026	723	3,966	612,288	3,992,778	24,116,296
1966	61	39,044	1,333	27,530	9,106	4,756	4,605	663	3,908	629,379	4,267,150	25,341,168
1967	62	39,396	1,170	26,598	8,902	4,432	4,914	491	3,964	623,956	4,660,218	25,793,528
1968	62	38,937	1,129	25,480	7,820	3,944	4,598	494	3,580	686,490	4,803,019	27,345,750

M. CHANDLER STITH

ter building was dedicated on Jan. 31, 1960. The building was erected by the HMB, SBC, upon land purchased and given by the District of Columbia Baptist Convention. This convention also furnished and equipped the center and agreed to pay its cost of operation. Edna Woofter has directed the activities of the center since 1959.

9. A program of evangelism and institutional witness, consisting of assistance to local churches on programs and methods of evangelistic outreach, and such work as is appropriate in a ministry to persons in institutions (hospitals, rest homes, home for the aging, home for delinquents, and jails). Chaplain T. O. Jones is in charge of institutional ministries.

10. A program of work with college students, consisting of a ministry to students in local universities and colleges, both those coming from the United States and from foreign countries, and a ministry to students in our churches who are enrolled in colleges and universities elsewhere. Howard Rees directs this program.

11. A program of work with the Woman's Missionary Organization, consisting of the organized work for the women of our churches, and the sponsorship of such organizations for young women, girls, and primary, beginner, and nursery children of the churches as may be undertaken from time to time. Mrs. Harold B. Tillman directs this program. The purpose of Woman's Missionary Organization is to promote missions through Women's Missionary Organizations in the churches and chapels of the District of Columbia convention, cooperating with the program of the District of Columbia convention, the Woman's Missionary Union, auxiliary to the Southern Baptist Convention, and the American Baptist Women of the American Baptist Convention.

12. A program of national and international missions, consisting of the financial support of the Cooperative Program of the Southern Baptist Convention and the World Mission Budget of the American Baptist Convention, and the stimulation of interest and understanding in our churches pertaining to the work of these conventions. M. CHANDLER STITH

DOCUMENTARY HYPOTHESIS. The theory that there are four primary literary sources in the Pentateuch, designated J, E, D, P. J stands for the Jehovist or Yahwist and is believed to have been written in approximately 850 B.C. E represents the Elohist and is dated about 750 B.C. D is used for the Deuteronomist, and emerges from about 621 B.C. P document is held to have been compiled around 500–450 B.C. J is said to extend at least through Genesis, Exodus, and Numbers. E generally parallels and supplements J. D is represented mainly by the book of Deuteronomy. P runs from Genesis through Numbers (Leviticus is P).

The documentary hypothesis has been subjected to rigorous criticism in recent years. Some scholars find sources in addition to J, E, D, and

P, and others, for instance, deny the existence of E or P as sources. In its broader form, however, the documentary hypothesis is widely accepted by Old Testament scholars. The whole problem of literary sources in the Pentateuch and in the Old Testament may be studied profitably in Otto Eissfeldt's *The Old Testament: An Introduction* (1965). RAYMOND BRYAN BROWN

DODSON, FLORA ELIZABETH (b. Monticello, Ky., Feb. 23, 1888; d. Winston-Salem, N. C., May 22, 1965). Missionary to China and Hong Kong, 1917–58. Educated at Eastern Kentucky State Normal, WMU Training School, Peabody (B.A.), and Columbia University (M.A.), she taught in Pooi To Middle School, Canton, and was principal of their demonstration school before becoming principal of Pooi In Bible School. During World War II she spent nine months in Japanese prison camps. In 1950 she went to Hong Kong, where she taught in Henrietta Shuck Memorial and Pooi To Schools and helped start publication work.
MRS. EUGENE HILL

DOMINICAN REPUBLIC, MISSION IN. After a survey in early 1962, Howard and Dorothy (Moore) Shoemake arrived in the capital city of Santo Domingo in August to begin Southern Baptist work. After many months of very slow progress, the first services were conducted in the Templo Bautista Central on Jan. 12, 1964, in the heart of the city. Billy W. and Ann (Fuller) Coffman arrived in mid-1964 (resigned 1968). The Ozama work, started by the Coffmans only days before civil war broke out in 1965, was organized Feb. 5, 1967, as the first church associated with Southern Baptist work. Medical work was started in the Ozama mission by Agustin Cornelio, Dominican physician. He was the first Dominican baptized and first president of the Dominican Baptist Convention, organized in Oct., 1968. Paul and Nancy (Roper) Potter arrived Sept., 1966, and Thomas and Josie (Slaughter) Ratcliff came two months later. A church organized in Santiago Mar. 3, 1968, has two missions and outpatient clinic. The English-language First Baptist Church of Santo Domingo was organized in Apr., 1967, and Templo Bautista Central, Santo Domingo, on Oct. 27, 1967. This church sponsors three missions, three medical centers, and a primary school. Work was begun in the Mata Hambre section of the capital in Jan., 1968.
HOWARD LEE SHOEMAKE

DOWELL, SPRIGHT (b. Cary, Wake County, N. C., Jan. 2, 1878; d. Macon, Ga., Feb. 24, 1963). Baptist educator and layman. Son of George James and Trannia Avery (Yates) Dowell, he was baptized by his father at age 12. He was educated at Wake Forest College (A.B., 1896) and Columbia University (A.M., 1911). He received the LL.D. from University of Alabama, Howard College, Baylor University, Wake Forest College, and Mercer University. Dowell taught school in North Carolina and Alabama. He was supervising principal of Birmingham, Ala., public schools and state superintendent of education and director of teacher-training for Alabama. Dowell studied law and was admitted to the Alabama Bar. He was president of Alabama Polytechnic Institute (now Auburn University), Auburn; and served as president of Mercer University, Macon, Ga., 1928–53; and interim president of Mercer, 1959–60. President of Georgia Baptist Convention (1949–50), he wrote two books: *Columbus Roberts: Christian Steward Extraordinary* (1951) and *A History of Mercer University, 1833–1953* (1958). He married Camille Early, Dec. 28, 1898. They had five children: William, Camille, Edwin, Mary, and Spright. P. HARRIS ANDERSON

DOZIER, EDWIN BURKE (b. Nagasaki, Japan, Apr. 16, 1908; d. Fukuoka, Japan, May 10, 1969). Missionary to Japan. He graduated from Wake Forest College (awarded D.D., 1955) and Southern Baptist Theological Seminary (Th.M.). He married Mary Ellen Wiley, Apr. 30, 1932, and returned to Japan. They were appointed missionaries in 1933. Dozier served on the faculty of Seinan Gakuin, first as professor and later as chancellor. He spent World War II years working with Japanese-speaking people in Hawaii. First missionary to return to Japan after the war, he reestablished contact with Japanese Baptists, assisted in organizing the Japan Baptist Convention, helped develop publication work, and established new churches. He wrote several books, including *Japan's New Day* (1949).
JESSE C. FLETCHER

DRY, MARCUS BAXTER (b. Union County, N. C., Oct. 23, 1871; d. Cary, N. C., Jan. 27, 1946). First principal of Wingate School, Wingate, N. C., now Wingate Junior College. The Dry Meditation Chapel, adjacent to the Webb-Austin Auditorium of Wingate College, was dedicated to his memory in 1963. He was educated at Wake Forest College (M.A., 1896), where he was valedictorian of his class, and he did postgraduate work in North Carolina, and at Columbia University, New York. He was principal of Wingate School, 1896–1908, and in conjunction with this work he purchased *The Baptist Messenger* and edited this monthly newspaper, May, 1905—Mar., 1908. He married Wilma Perry, Dec. 28, 1904. They had three children: Helen (Dry) King, William Henry, and Hallie Virginia Dry. He was principal of Cary High School, Cary, N. C., 1908–42. Formerly a private academy with local Baptist sponsorship, this school became the first public high school in North Carolina under the High School Law of 1907. Dry was active in the development of public school education, was a member of the first North Carolina Textbook Commission, conducted teachers' institutes for the North Carolina Department of Education, and pioneered in vocational training for handicapped children. LAMAR BROOKS

DUDLEY, JOHN GRANT (b. Crawford County, Ark., July 24, 1909; d. Arkansas County, Tex., Sept. 15, 1963). Hospital administrator. Educated in public schools of Ft. Smith, Ark., he attended University of Arkansas, Fayettville, Ark. Dudley was administrator of Arkansas Baptist Hospital, Jan., 1942—Nov. 15, 1946; administrator, Memorial Baptist Hospital, Houston, Tex., Nov., 1946—Dec., 1957, and executive director, from Dec., 1957, until his death. Married to Melba Bibb, Nov. 30, 1930, his children are: John Richard Dudley, Mrs. Joe E. Yeary, Mrs. John R. Culver, and Mrs. C. E. Dickson. Dudley was president, American Protestant Hospital Association in 1953, and president, Texas Hospital Association in 1957. JOE F. LUCK

DU LANEY, ARTHUR AINSLEE (b. Ben Lomond, Ark., Dec. 16, 1893; d. Albuquerque, N. Mex., Oct. 15, 1966). Pastor, professor, and Christian statesman. Ordained Apr. 16, 1915, by Ben Lomond Church, he was educated at Hardin-Simmons University (A.B. *magnum cum laude,* 1917) and University of Texas (M.A., 1919). He married Irene Duncan, Jan. 5, 1918. They had three children. He taught at Mountain Home College (Mountain Mission School), Mountain Home, Ark.; Central College, Conway, Ark.; and Montezuma Baptist College, Las Vegas, N. Mex. He was pastor in Carthage, Mo., Roswell, N. Mex. (14 years), and Los Alamos, N. Mex. While in Missouri he served on the state mission board and was president of the executive committee of this board. In New Mexico he was moderator of the Pecos Valley Association, president of the Baptist Convention of New Mexico in 1955 and 1956, delivered the annual sermon at the convention in 1952, and was president of the state mission board. He also served as New Mexico's representative on the following Southern Baptist Convention boards, commissions, and committees: Foreign Mission Board, Radio and Television Commission, Education Commission, program committee, and calendar committee. He served as member of New Mexico Department of Public Welfare for 14 years as secretary, vice-chairman, and chairman. HERBERT E. BERGSTROM

DUNN, GENEVA MILDRED OLDHAM (b. Duff, Grayson County, Ky., Feb. 1, 1911; d. Memphis, Tenn. Sept. 27, 1969). Denominational editor and writer. Daughter of Jessie Artimus and Alda Mae Oldham, she lived in Kentucky and Illinois until age six when she moved to Clayton, N. Mex. She was converted at age nine. After graduation from high school in Haltville, Calif., she attended New Mexico Normal University and Oklahoma Baptist University where she received the A.B. degree in 1936. She also did graduate study at Southwestern Baptist Theological Seminary. Mrs. Dunn was author of articles and special features in *Baptist Training Union Magazine, Window of YWA, Royal Service, Home Life, Brotherhood Journal,* and many other Baptist periodicals, 1949–68. She wrote program materials for *Baptist Young People's Union Quarterly* and *Baptist Adult Union Quarterly,* and was author of *Courage to Win,* Broadman Press, 1967. She worked as newspaper reporter for papers in California, New Mexico, and Missouri; also worked as a bank clerk, proofreader for Oklahoma Baptist University Press, and as church secretary, First Baptist Church, Mexico, Mo. On June 7, 1937, she married Cloyd Vern Dunn at Shawnee, Okla. He died in Nov., 1947, after a long illness. After her husband's death she served as an associate editor for Home Mission Board, 1948–57. The Brotherhood Commission employed her as associate editor in 1957. She was the only woman ever to serve as editor at the Brotherhood Commission. She was editor of *Ambassador Life* and *Ambassador Leader* when her distinguished career in religious journalism was closed by death. DARRELL C. RICHARDSON

E

***EAGLE EYRIE ASSEMBLY.** Since 1956 the land area has been increased to 363 acres. In 1969 the assembly included 34 lodges, a 48-room hotel, a dining hall with a capacity of 1,000, an auditorium seating 800, 29 classrooms, a children's building, a staff house, a mansion house used for offices and staff quarters, a prayer chapel, a picnic pavilion, two swimming pools, and a gate house snack shop. Eagle Eyrie has all modern conveniences to provide for year-round use. There are 985 beds available to guests in the hotel and lodges. During 1968, 14,319 Baptists participated in the state-wide assembly programs. The total estimated value of the assembly grounds was $2,500,000 in 1969. Malcolm H. Burgess was named acting manager in 1959 and has been manager since 1960. JOHN S. MOORE

EAST AFRICA, MISSION IN. The first Southern Baptist missionaries arrived in East

Africa in Dec., 1956. What was then known as British East Africa developed into three completely independent nations—Kenya, Tanzania, and Uganda—in the early sixties. One Baptist mission organization was formed. Pioneer missionaries had all served previously in Nigeria: W. O. "Wimpy" Haper (*q.v.*) and Juanita (Taylor) Harper settled at Dar es Salaam, Tanganyika; Jack and Sarah (Cook) Walker went to Mbeya, Tanganyika; Davis and Mary (Hogg) Saunders established a station at Nairobi, Kenya. Within a short time community centers were developed at Nairobi and Dar es Salaam, and a tuberculosis hospital was opened at Mbeya. With newly appointed couples strengthening the staff, new stations were opened in Kenya at Mombasa, Nyeri, Kisumu, and Kitale. In Tanzania, work was begun at Tanga, Tukuyu, Arusha, and Kigoma. Later expansion resulted in stations at Nakuru, Kenya and at Lindi, Tanzania. Work was begun in Uganda in 1962, but the Uganda Mission was organized as a separate work in 1967.

The East Africa Baptist Theological Seminary, with instruction in Swahili, was opened at Arusha in 1962. Baptist high schools were opened at Mombasa and Nyeri, Kenya. A Bible school opened at Tukuyu in 1966 was designed to prepare pastors and lay leaders unable to meet qualifications for seminary work. In 1963 the Brackenhurst Baptist Assembly was opened at Limuru, Kenya. Publication work, begun at Mombasa, was later transferred to Nairobi, where a modern building was provided. Literature was published in Swahili, Kikuyu, Kinyakusa, and English. In 1969 a radio recording studio was opened on a plot adjacent to the publishing house in Nairobi.

From the beginning, Baptist missionaries met with good response both in the population centers and rural villages. Special evangelistic campaigns in 1967 stimulated church growth. By the end of 1969, over 240 Baptist churches in East Africa reported a combined membership of about 10,000. The missionary staff numbered 140. H. CORNELL GOERNER

EAST OREGON BAPTIST CONVENTION. Organized in Aug., 1892, by a group of Baptists, largely from the South, for the purpose of seeking affiliation with the Southern Baptist Convention and separating from churches in the Northwest which accepted "alien immersion" and practiced "open communion." The name was changed in 1893 to Baptist Convention of the North Pacific Coast. ROY L. JOHNSON

***EAST TENNESSEE BAPTIST HOSPITAL.** The original plans for the hospital included a doctor's building, but it was not until Dec., 1956, that the Blount Professional Building was opened. It houses 39 suites of offices and a 300-space parking lot. In 1958 four additional floors were added to the hospital plant providing additional patient beds, a new radiology department, elevator, and an enlarged obstetrical suite. The Graves-Wyatt Chapel was opened in 1961, which has a prayer room, family room, and the department of pastoral care. A six-bed intensive care unit and family surgical lounge opened in 1962. The first installation in Tennessee of the Brewer system, an automated system of storing, dispensing, and accounting for drugs, was installed in 1963. This assures the availability of an adequate supply of most commonly used drugs at each nurses' station at all times.

Construction was completed in 1964 on a $177,000 cancer therapy unit. In 1967 a $5,000,000 addition brought bed capacity to 350. Housed here also are new laundry and dietary departments, pediatrics and radiology departments, intensive, coronary, and intermediate care units with a new surgical family lounge. In 1969 the most modern obstretical floor was completed. Presently under construction is another doctors' building, a $1,000,000 six-story structure which will provide space for 50 more physicians, thus helping the hospital to enhance its position as a leading health care facility in the community. The School of Nursing has continued to grow over the years and now has 85 students and annually graduated approximately 25 nurses. WILLIAM WALLACE

***EAST TEXAS BAPTIST COLLEGE.** Since 1954 the school has made large strides. Harvey D. Bruce was succeeded as president by Howard Clifton Bennett in 1960. During 1968–69 the enrolment increased to a total of 917, endowment rose to $2,044,614, and property value reached $4,046,210. The operating budget of 1969–70 was $1,406,725. Major buildings added in recent years include Warren F. Keys Gymnasium, 1959, and Evelyn Linebery Hall, 1961. A major emphasis in the curriculum is the In-Service Guidance Program which provides direction for over 200 students committed to church-related vocations. HOWARD C. BENNETT

EASTERN ORTHODOXY. Eastern Orthodoxy, a family of self-governing churches, representing the Eastern tradition in Christendom, officially recognized by the Patriarch of Constantinople, united not by centralized organization but by a bond of unity in faith and worship, claims eminence as the canonical and traditional heir of the early church, thereby distinguishing it from Roman Catholicism (Western). "Eastern" designates its origin in the Near East (Greek) and Eastern Europe. "Orthodox," defining its affinity to the doctrine of the first seven ecumenical councils, means "right belief" and "right worship." Essential features include: (1) preserving the traditional early doctrines; and (2) the Liturgy as the heart of worship.

BIBLIOGRAPHY: E. Benz, *The Eastern Orthodox Church* (1963); S. Runciman, *The Eastern Schism* (1955); T. Ware, *The Orthodox Church* (1963); N. Zernov, *Eastern Christendom* (1961); *The Church of the Eastern Christians* (1942). J. THOMAS MEIGS

EASTHAM, FRED CHEESMAN (b. Beaumont, Tex., Dec. 11, 1899; d. Dallas Co., Mo., Dec. 14, 1959). Son of Alfred and Gertrude Eastham, he attended Baylor University, Simmons University (Hardin-Simmons), and Baptist Bible Institute (New Orleans Baptist Theological Seminary). He received the honorary D.D. from Hardin-Simmons and William Jewell. He married Wanda Howard McCormick, Sept. 5, 1922. They had one daughter, who died in infancy. Licensed and ordained by First Baptist Church, Beaumont, Tex., Eastham was pastor of the following churches: First Baptist of Capps, Tex.; Tye, Tex.; Silsbee, Tex.; Roseland, La.; McKinney Ave., Dallas, Tex.; First Baptist, Eastland, Tex.; Wichita Falls, Tex.; and Springfield, Mo. He also served as Secretary of Evangelism of the Home Mission Board and planned the first Southern Baptist simultaneous evangelistic campaign. He was president of the Missouri Baptist Convention. Eastham served on the following boards: Hardin-Simmons, Southwest Baptist College, William Jewell College, Sunday School Board, Home Mission Board, Southern Baptist Hospital, Radio and Television Commission, and executive boards of Texas and Missouri conventions. Twice he was the preacher for the "Columbia Church of the Air" (C.B.S.). For 23 years his Sunday services were on radio and they were on television at Springfield as soon as mobile units were available. He is buried in Dallas, Tex. DORAN C. MCCARTY

***ECUADOR, MISSION IN.** Missions advance was attributed largely to a theological institute opened in Guayaquil in 1961, book stores in Guayaquil and Quito, wide use of mass communications media, an elementary school in Quito, and associational work. At Chone, an agricultural project was developed as a unique approach to Christian witnessing and to help the people improve their living conditions. In 1969, 28 missionaries served in six cities.

FRANK K. MEANS

***ECUMENICAL MOVEMENT, THE.** Since 1954 the ecumenical movement has undergone a number of changes. The World Council of Churches (WCC), chief organizational expression of the movement, was directly and indirectly responsible for many of these developments.

The third assembly of the WCC, meeting at New Delhi (1961), involved a number of historic events. Twenty-three new communions were added to the WCC. The enlarged membership necessitated the adding of two official languages, Russian and Spanish. A new confessional basis for WCC membership was adopted. The new confession reads:

> The World Council of Churches is a fellowship of churches which confess the Lord Jesus Christ as God and Savior according to the Scriptures and therefore seek to fulfill together their common calling to the glory of the one God, Father, Son and Holy Spirit.

The new trinitarian "creed" changed to some extent the denominational and theological complexion of the WCC since it helped to facilitate the admission of several Eastern Orthodox Churches. At New Delhi, the International Missionary Council, after having given birth to the modern ecumenical movement in 1910 and having maintained a separate existence for a half-century, finally became an integral part of the WCC. The statement on religious liberty adopted in 1961 was a most forthright declaration.

The fourth assembly of the WCC was held at Uppsala in 1968. Obviously, Uppsala strengthened ties with Rome which were first apparent at New Delhi. While New Delhi had five official Roman Catholic observers, this number had increased in 1968 to 14. Too, at Uppsala, the Roman Church for the first time became represented in the membership of the Faith and Order Commission. It was also evident that while the WCC had largely dispensed some years before with the "Life and Work" aspects of the Council, it could not escape them at Uppsala. To a considerable extent the fourth assembly was preoccupied with the international issues of Biafra, the Middle East, and Vietnam. The more burning social issues of racism, poverty, secularism, and technology also proved inescapable. Two other aspects of Uppsala were obvious: its size (largest Assembly of WCC yet held), and increasing Eastern Orthodox influence within the ecumenical movement.

Doubtless the modern ecumenical movement, along with other factors, called forth the new Roman Catholic venture in ecumenism. Under the leadership of John XXIII plans were laid for the first council since Vatican I (1870). Vatican II actually convened 1962–65. Of 16 *schemata,* the decrees "On the Church," "Revelation," "Ecumenism," "Non-Christians," and "Religious Freedom" have made an unprecedented impact upon Protestants and Catholics alike. Even though Vatican II was characterized by the papacy as a "pastoral council," its dogmatic implications are inescapable. However, its greatest success may have been in the realm of changing attitudes. As a result, there is, doubtless, a greater fraternal feeling between Catholics and Protestants than has existed heretofore.

Among Protestants in the United States, the Consultation on Church Union (COCU), is currently (1970) generating the most interest in things ecumenical. Under its auspices nine denominations, the African Methodist Episcopal and African Methodist Episcopal Zion Churches, Christian Church (Disciples of Christ), Christian Methodist Episcopal Church, Episcopal Church, Presbyterian Church (U. S.), United Church of Christ, United Methodist Church, and United Presbyterian Church (U. S. A.), are in the process of forming the "Church of Christ, Uniting," with a total constituency of some 26,000,000.

In the meantime, the National Council of Churches (NCC) is attempting to broaden its base of support. Three factors force the issue: the emerging new (COCU) church, decreasing revenues, and the realities of a persistent denominationalism outside of the National Council. Therefore, conciliar leadership is looking toward a more inclusive organization such as a "general ecumenical council" to include Roman Catholics, Pentecostals, Baptists, and others who do not now belong to the NCC.

A fourth front, often neglected in ecumenical studies, is that comprised by Evangelicals. There is some indication that the exponents of the National Association of Evangelicals and similar organizations are more socially oriented now (1970) than previously. In several respects these Evangelicals seem to represent a position not nearly as far removed from the mainstream of Protestant ecumenism as once they did.

While the ecumenical movement seems to be in the process of restructuring its institutional expressions with some degree of hesitancy and certainty, there is little doubt that the spirit of ecumenicity is penetrating the whole of Christendom in an unprecedented fashion.

BIBLIOGRAPHY: W. M. Abbott, *The Documents of Vatican II* (1966). W. R. Estep, Jr., *Baptists and Christian Unity* (1966). WCC, *The New Delhi Report* (1961). WCC, *The Uppsala Report* (1968).

W. R. ESTEP, JR.

***EDUCATION, SOUTHERN BAPTIST.** In 1970 Southern Baptists were operating 73 seminaries, colleges, and schools. There were six seminaries, one seminary jointly operated by Southern Baptists and the National Baptist Convention, U.S.A., Inc., 43 senior colleges, 12 junior colleges, seven academies, and four Bible schools.

Midwestern Baptist Theological Seminary was opened in 1957, Kentucky Southern College in 1960, Mobile College in 1961, Houston Baptist College in 1960, Baptist College at Charleston, 1964, Missouri Baptist College in St. Louis, (also operates the Hannibal-LaGrange campus in Hannibal, Mo.) 1963, Atlanta Baptist College, 1968, and Palm Beach Atlantic College in 1968.

Howard College in Birmingham changed its name to Samford University in 1965. Shorter College became officially coeducational, with dormitory facilities for men, in 1957.

During the sixties the trend was for Baptist junior colleges to become senior institutions. There were only 12 two-year colleges remaining in 1970, where 10 years before there were 21. The presence in their vicinity of newly created two-year community colleges made it necessary for Baptist junior colleges to become senior colleges in order to be different enough to attract students willing to pay higher tuition charges. The following have become senior colleges: Southwest Baptist College, 1964; Gardner-Webb College, 1969; Mars Hill College, 1962; Averett College, 1970; Campbell College, 1961; Cumberland College, 1959; and Campbellsville College, 1959.

After 110 years Bethel College, Hopkinsville, Ky., closed in 1964. Kentucky Southern College was founded in 1960 and merged with the University of Louisville in 1969. Decatur Baptist Junior College was merged with the new Dallas Baptist College in 1965. Magoffin Baptist Institute closed in 1960.

In 1958 the Southern Baptist Convention gave the five seminaries through the Cooperative Program $3,568,427, and in 1970 the Convention gave the six seminaries (Midwestern opened in 1959) a total of $4,934,489.

The 16 states having colleges and schools gave them through the Cooperative Program in 1957–58, $5,319,100 for current operations, and $3,970,475 for capital needs. In 1969–70 the states gave their schools $11,116,375 for current operation and $3,876,909 for capital needs.

By the year 1969–70 the total enrolment of Baptist seminaries, colleges, and schools had reached 110,143, up from 59,371 in 1957–58.

RABUN L. BRANTLEY

***EDUCATION COMMISSION OF THE SOUTHERN BAPTIST CONVENTION.** The staff of the Education Commission has occasionally been asked by the states having Baptist schools to conduct studies related to the future directions of their schools, and especially to help determine whether new colleges should be undertaken. The commission has made several such studies, but always upon request. It is a policy of the commission not to initiate the idea of starting a new school.

The commission's publication for teen-agers, *Career News,* had a name change to *College and Career* in Oct., 1961; and *The Southern Baptist Campus Directory* now (1970) is published every two years instead of every four years.

In Mar., 1961, the administration of the Dorothea Van Deusen Opdyke Fund was passed from the Executive Committee of the Southern Baptist Convention to the Education Commission. The corpus of the fund is now $250,000, and the annual income is awarded in scholarships to needy mountain students for college expenses. About 250 scholarships a year go to Baptist students enrolled largely in Baptist schools.

A loan fund for doctoral degree candidates was inaugurated in 1962, funded with income from funds held by the Southern Baptist Foundation which came from the estates of M. May Robertson and Joseph L. Sheppard. In 1964 the J. W. Farmer Loan Fund was similarly set up. The loans may be repaid through service at a Baptist school.

The third Sunday in February is listed on the denominational calendar as Baptist College, Seminary, and School Day. The churches are encouraged to hold an annual emphasis on Baptist schools and Christian education either on the special day or later. The commission prepares guidelines and materials for the churches to use in observing the emphasis. The special Sunday was formerly observed in April.

The most extensive study of higher education by Southern Baptists, the Baptist Education Study Task (BEST), was sponsored by the Education Commission in 1966–67. Three years later some of the states and colleges were conducting follow-up meetings having to do with the areas of the study.

The second full-time executive secretary-treasurer, Rabun L. Brantley, came to the commission in Sept., 1959, succeeding R. Orin Cornett, who resigned after eight years of service. Brantley retired on Aug. 31, 1970. Ben C. Fisher was named to succeed Brantley.

In 1962 the Southern Baptist Convention adopted a program for the Education Commission with four areas of emphasis: (1) A program of Christian education, promotion, and information; (2) a program of school and college studies and surveys; (3) a program of teacher recruitment and placement; (4) a program of assistance in college recruitment. Since Feb., 1962, the commission offices have been located in the Convention Building, 460 James Robertson Parkway, Nashville, Tenn.

RABUN L. BRANTLEY

EDUCATIONAL PSYCHOLOGY. Educational psychology is the systematic study of learning processes. Through scientific investigation, the educational psychologist attempts to explain learning behavior in order that it may be understood and controlled more effectively.

For nearly a century after Robert Raikes began the first Sunday School in 1780, educational psychology was more nearly a philosophy than a science, for American psychologists did not begin to study human learning experimentally until about the beginning of the 20th century. In fact, it was because of his work in this field, that Edward L. Thorndike of Columbia University (1874–1949) received recognition as the leading pioneer in the scientific investigation of learning. Other educational psychologists followed with significant contributions in the field and, by the beginning of the seventies, a vast amount of experimental data had been accumulated. However, even by that time, educational psychologists had not yet attained success in their efforts to develop a comprehensive, universally acceptable theory of learning.

Perhaps more than any other science, educational psychology has been divided into competing schools. "Stimulus-response" theories of learning, such as "behaviorism," explained learning on the basis of cause-effect connections between the behavior of an individual and his environment. "Cognitive" theorists, on the other hand, looked upon learning as the restructuring of experience as perceived by the learner.

While Christian teachers have become increasingly aware of the contribution of educational psychology to their understanding of the learning process, learning theory has yet to be applied systematically on a large scale to the practice of religious education. One limiting factor has been the uncertain state of learning theory itself. Another problem has been the difficulty of relating strictly scientific interpretations of the learner to the Christian's theological understandings of man. But educational psychology has caused the religious educator to "think psychologically" about the learner, and thus to become more sensitive to individual differences, patterns of growth and development, and factors related to motivation in learning.

Psychological research has also contributed directly to the development of methodology in religious education. A notable example has been programmed instruction, which has evolved as an application of laboratory findings to instructional problems.

Religious education has profited from the work of behavioral scientists in the area of group dynamics, also. Research in this field has provided insights into the ways in which group structures affect individual participation, motivation, emotional tone, and problem-solving activities.

LUCIEN E. COLEMAN, JR.

EDWARDS, MORGAN (b. Trevethin Parish, Monmouthshire, Wales, May 9, 1722; d. Pencader, Del., Jan. 28, 1795). Baptist minister and historian. At 16 he adopted Baptist views and began to preach. For seven years he supplied a church at Boston, Lincolnshire, while he studied at Bristol College. Though not ordained until June 1, 1757, he was pastor at Cork, Ireland, 1750–59. Here he married Mary Nun, daughter of Joshua Nun, by whom he had eight children, one son being an officer in the British army. After preaching at Rye, Sussex, for one year, he came to America on May 23, 1761, and soon thereafter became pastor of the Baptist church in Philadelphia, Pa., serving there until July 8, 1771. During this pastorate he was a moving force in the establishment of Rhode Island College, now Brown University.

Edwards was active in the work of the Philadelphia Association from the time of his arrival in America, and was clerk of that body, 1769–71, 1773. He began to gather materials for a history of the Baptists in America in 1770, with the intention of visiting the provinces from New Hampshire to Georgia. On Oct. 16, 1771, the Philadelphia Association appointed Edwards its evangelist at large. Following this appointment he spent one year traveling through the southern colonies gathering detailed information for his history. Edwards meticulously assembled facts in separate notebooks for each province visited. Later he expanded each notebook into a volume which deleted some of the notebook material, but also added new data.

Of a 12-volume work which he planned, five parts of *Materials Towards a History of the American Baptists* have been printed: Pennsylvania (1770), New Jersey (1792), Rhode Island (1867), Delaware (1885), and North Carolina (1930). Manuscript notebooks treating Delaware, Virginia, North Carolina, South Carolina, and Georgia are in the Bucknell Library, Crozer Theological Seminary, Chester, Pa. Expanded manuscript volumes on Maryland, Virginia, North Carolina, South Carolina, and Georgia are in the Furman University Library, Greenville, S. C. Both the Crozer and Furman manuscripts are available on microfilm.

His detailed material is remarkably accurate. He used primary sources when available, also interviewed Baptist leaders and aged people. In addition to his histories he published *The Customs of Primitive Churches* (1768), 42 volumes of sermons, and a number of scholarly addresses between 1761 and 1788.

Edwards was approaching 40 years of age when he came to the colonies and found it difficult to adopt the aims of the American Revolution. Because of his loyalist views he lost favor with many Baptists. This may account in part for a habit of intoxication which led to his exclusion from the church for several years. At the close of his services with the Philadelphia church, he moved to Newark, Del. He never again served as pastor but supplied pulpits, traveled extensively, and lectured on religious subjects. His second wife, a Mrs. Singleton of Delaware, predeceased him. He is buried in Mt. Moriah Cemetery, Philadelphia, Pa.

JOHN S. MOORE

EISENBERG MUSEUM. The Eisenberg Museum was established at Southern Baptist Theological Seminary, Louisville, Ky., in June, 1961. Jerome Eisenberg, a New York Jewish businessman (antiquarian) and the primary donor of the collection of materials, named the museum in honor of his parents, Gertrude and Samuel Eisenberg of Miami Beach, Fla. Other donations in the original collection came from friends of Jerome Eisenberg.

The museum centers primarily on the acquisition of materials relating to the New Testament period and is particularly fortunate to possess an extensive collection of Jewish coins (including a collection of choice specimens given by Denberg). The materials from Machaerus (excavated by E. J. Vardaman in 1968 with funds supplied by Mr. and Mrs. Cully Cobb) and Caesarea (excavated by Vardaman in 1962 with funds supplied by encouragement of J. Eisenberg) are of special interest. An inscription referring to Nazareth resulted from the Caesarea excavations.

BIBLIOGRAPHY: E. J. Vardaman and J. Leo Garrett, eds., *The Teacher's Yoke* (1964). E. J. VARDAMAN

ELAM, GEORGE FRANKLIN (b. Parker County, Tex., Sept. 7, 1884; d. Albuquerque, N. Mex., Jan. 24, 1962). Public-school teacher, principal, pastor, and Training Union secretary. The sixth of 13 children born to James Franklin Elam, he was educated at North Texas State Normal School (A.B.). He married Ethel Lorine Robertson on Sept. 17, 1922. Their children were George F., Jr., Dorothy, Jimmy, and Jerry. While working as a shoe salesman in Weatherford, Tex., Elam became interested in BYPU work. He went to Dallas, Tex., to see T. C. Gardner, Texas BYPU secretary, to learn more about young people's work. Elam soon became the first president of Parker County Association BYPU. He entered Southwestern Baptist Theological Seminary, Fort Worth, in 1920 and received the B.R.E. degree in 1923.

Elam served as BYPU secretary for New Mexico from 1923 to 1952. Under his leadership the BYPU Convention of New Mexico was organized (Nov., 1923). BYPU work was expanded to other age groups, and New Mexico became one of the first states to make the change to Baptist Training Union (June, 1934). Elam traveled over one million miles in the state carrying out his duties.

HERBERT E. BERGSTROM

ELLIOTT, LESLIE ROBINSON (b. Rozetta, Henderson County, Ill., Sept. 30, 1886; d. Fort Worth, Tex., May 2, 1965). Theological librarian and denominational leader. Oldest son of Judson Andrew and Minnie Hortense (Robinson) Elliott, he was converted at 16. Elliott was baptized by his father, then pastor of First Baptist Church, Phoenix, Ariz. He graduated from William Jewell College (B.A., 1910; D.D., 1957), attended Southern Baptist Seminary, 1910–12, until illness compelled withdrawal, and completed seminary training at Southwestern Baptist Seminary (Th.M., 1921; Th.D., 1925). He married Mary Ethelyne Shearer of Unionville, Mo., May 31, 1911. Ordained by the Immanuel Baptist Church of Louisville, Ky., July, 1911, Elliott served churches in Butler, Mo., 1912–15, Arvada, Colo., 1915–17, and Del Rey, Calif., 1917–19.

After serving as a student assistant since 1919, Elliott was appointed librarian at Southwestern Baptist Seminary in 1922, and developed one of the world's foremost theological libraries before his retirement in 1957. He also taught New Testament Greek, 1925–42. He led in the establishment of the American Theological Library Association, 1947, served as president for the first two terms, 1947–49, and represented ATLA in formation of the International Association of Theological Libraries in 1955. After retirement he was Acting Librarian for Midwestern Baptist Seminary, 1957–58.

Elliott contributed much to the preservation of Baptist history as executive secretary and curator of the Texas Baptist Historical Committee, 1931–57; member of the SBC Historical Commission, 1950–56; director of the Southern Baptist Historical Society; and as leader in projects to microfilm early British and American Baptist historical materials.

Elliott's published writings include *A Comparative Lexicon of New Testament Greek* (1945), *The Efficiency Filing System* (1951, 1959), *God and Business* (1936), and *Syntax in Diagram* (1950). He edited *Centennial Story of Texas Baptists* (1936) and Texas monographs in the *Encyclopedia of Southern Baptists* (1958).

Elliott is buried in Greenwood Memorial Park, Fort Worth. KEITH C. WILLS

ELLIOTT, PHILIP LOVIN (b. Swain County, N. C., Sept. 22, 1891; d. Boiling Springs, N. C., Apr. 14, 1961). Minister and educator. Son of Isaac Bartley and Rachel Diana (Jenkins) Elliott, he was educated at Wake Forest College (B.A., 1919), and the University of North Carolina (M.A., 1925). He later did graduate study at Johns Hopkins and Duke universities. He was awarded honorary doctor's degrees from Carson-Newman College and Wake Forest College.

Elliott was ordained at Mars Hill in 1915 and served several student pastorates. He began his career as an educator as principal of Mitchell Collegiate Institute in 1919. He served as enlistment secretary for the Baptist state convention, 1920–22, and was dean and head of the English Department at Mars Hill College, 1923–25. From 1925–30 he was also vice-president at Mars Hill, resigning in 1930 to begin a 13-year tenure as head of the English Department at Western Carolina College. Elliott served as president of Gardner-Webb College from 1943 until his death. He married Etta Maurine Carringer of Robbinsville in Aug., 1918. They had four children: Ruth Eleanor (Mrs. L. Taylor Oakes), Diana Jayne (Mrs. Ed Grady), Philip L., Jr., and Rachael Elizabeth. TOBY DRUIN

ELLIOTT CONTROVERSY. See MIDWESTERN BAPTIST THEOLOGICAL SEMINARY.

ELLIS, DAVID ALVIN (b. Shelby County, Tenn., Nov. 30, 1878; d. Memphis, Tenn., Dec. 29, 1958). Pastor, denominational leader. Son of Tennie Carter and J. E. Ellis of Cordova, Tenn., he was educated at Union University (A.B., D.D.). He married Ora Wilson of Moscow, Tenn., Dec. 25, 1900. They had two children, Evelyn (Mrs. M. B. Wallace) and Judson. His Tennessee pastorates included: Dyersburg, Jackson; LaBelle, Memphis (16 years); McLean, Memphis (22 years). He also served in Corinth, Miss. He was moderator of the Shelby County Association for 13 years. For many years he was chairman of the board of trustees of Union University. He also served on the executive committees of the Baptist Memorial Hospital, Tennessee Baptist Convention, and Southern Baptist Convention. His entire estate was given to Baptist Institutions and agencies at his death. RALPH R. MOORE

ELSEY, CHARLES WILLIAM (b. Laurel County, Ky., June 10, 1880; d. Shelbyville, Ky., Sept. 2, 1964). He was educated in the public schools of Fayette County, Ky., Georgetown College (A.B., 1905), and the Southern Baptist Theological Seminary (Th.G., 1907). On Nov. 26, 1912, he was married to Birdie Gibson Young of Lexington, Ky. Ordained on June 29, 1902, Elsey served three Kentucky pastorates in 55 years: Fifth Street Church, Lexington, 1902–08, First Baptist, Cynthiana, 1908–21, and First Baptist, Shelbyville, 1926 until his retirement in 1957. He was president of Cumberland College, Williamsburg, Ky., 1921–25. He was a trustee of Georgetown College and of the Kentucky Baptist Children's Home. He was on the Board of Managers of the *Western Recorder,* 1919–41, and a member of the Baptist Education Society of Kentucky. Elsey was moderator of the General Association of Baptists in Kentucky for two sessions, 1939–40. As a presiding officer or as a participant in discussion, he possessed a sense of humor which, with a calm and steadying hand, made it possible for him to relieve tension and to keep matters moving orderly. LEO T. CRISMON

ELSOM, ANNA LOUISA SHEPHERD (b. Nelson County, Va., Nov. 29, 1834; d. Nelson County, Va., Oct. 13, 1915). Leader of the first Sunbeam Band. Eldest of six children born to Garland A. and Elizabeth Ligon Shepherd, Anna was baptized Nov. 2, 1849. On that same day the Fairmount Baptist Church was constituted with 25 members. She married Robert W. Elsom Sept. 25, 1856. They had three children: Percy G., Ernest L. and James C.

For years Mrs. Elsom taught the children's "Sunbeam" class at Fairmount Church. In 1886 George Braxton Taylor (*q.v.*), the pastor, organized these children into a Sunbeam Missionary Society with Mrs. Elsom as leader. Mrs. Elsom is affectionately called "the Mother of Sunbeams." DORIS DE VAULT

ENGLISH-LANGUAGE CHURCHES OVERSEAS. Since World War II increasing numbers of Americans have lived overseas. Military bases, oil developments, and other business enterprises have produced sizable communities of Americans. Spiritual concerns of Baptist people in such centers led to spontaneous development of Sunday Schools and worship groups in various lands. These grew into English-language Baptist churches. In many cities the ministry of such churches extends beyond the American residents to the international community in general and to English-speaking nationals.

In some countries where English is the medium of instruction for the school system, there are English-language congregations composed primarily of local people. References to English-language churches overseas generally focus, however, on churches ministering mainly to displaced Americans or the international English-speaking community.

Because of the large number of American armed service personnel and dependents overseas, the Home Mission Board, through its chaplaincy division, in the middle fifties studied the possibility of promoting servicemen's centers in areas of American military concentration. The report from the study encouraged the developing of English-language churches instead. Soon afterward the survey committee of the Southern

Baptist Convention recommended and the Convention adopted (at Houston in 1958) a proposal that "the Foreign Mission Board should continue and expand its efforts to establish churches for English-speaking people in major cities in countries served by the Foreign Mission Board." The effect of that action was to confirm the assignment to the FMB of responsibility for this aspect of Southern Baptist work.

The FMB in Sept., 1958, and in Apr., 1960, adopted policy guidelines for the continuing promotion of English-language churches. Some of the earliest churches developed in the middle fifties in Venezuela, Germany, Thailand, and Japan. The FMB began appointing missionaries to give pastoral leadership to such churches (a process strengthened when the missionary associate category of missionary personnel was added in 1961).

As early as 1958 churches in Germany formed the Association of Baptists in Continental Europe, and in 1964 this became the European Baptist Convention (English-Language).

By the end of the sixties the FMB was associated with English-language congregations in 37 lands in all parts of the world. The list of such congregations numbered approximately 100.

WINSTON CRAWLEY

ESTES, EMMETT FLOYD (b. DeKalb County, Mo., Oct. 22, 1878; d. Louisville, Ky., Nov. 23, 1961). Son of Alfred Estes, he was ordained at Maysville, Mo., June 17, 1914, and graduated from William Jewell College (B.A., 1918), Liberty, Mo. He was pastor at Albany, Mo., 1919–22, and of West Broadway Church, Louisville, Ky., 1923 until his retirement in 1957. He attended the Southern Baptist Theological Seminary for three sessions, 1924–27. Estes was moderator of the Long Run Association, 1934 and 1950, and was preacher of the annual sermon in 1928. He preached the annual sermon before the General Association of Baptists in Kentucky in 1944. He was a member of the board of directors of the *Western Recorder*, 1942–56, and much of the time chairman of the board. He was succeeded on the board by his son Joseph Richard Estes, who served until 1960. E. F. Estes married Anna Grace Harman on Feb. 26, 1910, and they had four children: Marie Harman (Mrs. Joseph Stopher), James Tyler, Jack Floyd, and Joseph Richard. Mrs. Estes died Sept. 21, 1961, at age 72.

LEO T. CRISMON

ETHIOPIA, MISSION IN. Two couples sent by the Foreign Mission Board, SBC, took up residence at Addis Abeba, capital of Ethiopia, in the summer of 1967. William and Nina (Allen) Lewis had previously served in Tanzania, while John and Marie (Golson) Cheyne had missionary experience in Rhodesia. After language study, they secured government permission to begin a community development project in the Menz District, about 150 miles north of Addis Abeba. In 1969 Samuel and Virginia (Currey) Cannata moved to Mehal Meda. Cannata supervised community health centers there and in nearby Tsai Tsina. In 1970 a handcraft school was opened at Tsai Tsina, and an agricultural project was begun in the Menz District. The mission program included literacy courses and Bible classes. English-language services were conducted in Addis Abeba, in addition to work in the native Amharic language.

H. CORNELL GOERNER

EVANGELISM, LAY. The fact that traditional methods of evangelism have become less effective, especially in the cities, has caused the church to look again at the potentials of lay evangelism. As the world comes less and less to the church, the church seeks more and more ways to go to the world. Lay evangelism is the patent and biblical answer. It is difficult, however, for the church to break out of established molds and return to the "lay church" of the New Testament. "Every Christian a witness," may be a good slogan, but it is not accomplished without meeting certain prerequisites.

The fellowship that gives rise to lay involvement in evangelism is one of joyous commitment. The infectious enthusiasm of the New Testament church has been pointed out by many scholars as one of the sources of their dynamic witness. Lay people are not inclined to be enthusiastic about an institutional church or a cultural religion. They are enthusiastic about an authentic fellowship and a personal Savior. The element of "mission into danger" calls for a commitment that results in spiritual joy.

The lay person in the church must possess a faith that is authentic if it is to communicate. The person out of the church must come to see the Christian as a fellow sinner who has discovered forgiveness in Jesus Christ. If the laity is to possess such a faith, the church must have pastors and teachers who are capable of communicating such faith. The action-oriented laity has difficulty understanding the faith from pastors who are trained in the terms of Greek philosophy and medieval theology rather than in the biblical "mighty acts of God." The faith must be related to the problems of daily life and their solutions.

For lay evangelism to be effective there must be genuine contact with persons in the world. The church cannot be a religious "ghetto." The laity must be trained to have sufficient vitality and discipline to become involved in the world without the compromise of their faith. The church becomes the training center for this kind of layman. He will discover that the streets, shops, and offices are his places of ministry. The services of the church are for worship, training, and sharing "the mighty acts of God" in the streets, shops, and offices.

The church must have a strategy and materials for involving the laity in evangelism. The strategy and the materials should be freed from organizational structures within the church which tend to have abstract objectives. The strategy must be kept to the person-to-person concept. The materials should include helps for laying spiritual foundations for lay evangelism. They must be adaptable to all age groups and educational levels. Local meetings of groups of lay evangelism persons must be assisted in making plans to evangelize key persons in key social structures. Materials for lay witnessing must be designed in such a way as to require an open Bible. The studies should magnify the lordship of Christ, the work of the Holy Spirit, and nature of Christian commitment. JOHN F. HAVLIK

EVANGELISM, THE NEW. The new evangelism has been profoundly affected by the rediscovery of the Christian doctrine of man in the church and the emphasis upon social justice in society within the last two decades. A new theology of evangelism has emerged that finds its focus in the individual. This new focus is in part a reaction to the depersonalization of man in modern society. Certain characteristics have emerged that may intensify within the next few decades.

The congregation is the base of operation rather than the center of Christian activity. Ministry, including evangelism, is conceived as activity in the world. The meetings of the congregation are conceived as a center of worship, celebration, and reporting what God has done in the streets.

The laity is the human resource for evangelism. There is less stress on buildings and programs as methods to evangelize. The personal witness of the laity becomes the major thrust of the church. The role of the minister is seen as the teacher-trainer of the congregation. Less stress is laid upon the pastor as an administrator.

The gospel is the divine resource for evangelism. With all the conceptual changes, there is little evidence to support a wide rejection of the gospel. There appears to be more evidence that the church accepts the relevance of the gospel for the needs of modern man.

Ministry with compassion and witness with hope are the authenticators of the church. The church is more involved with the needs of humanity. The mission of the church in part is conceived as the meeting of those needs. No conflict is seen in the cry for personal repentance and the cry for social justice. Evangelism has not succumbed to the pessimism of society. There is hope for man and society in the gospel. The apostolic note of joy is recovered.

"The whole church applying the whole gospel to the whole man," is verbalized in many ways. This statement has become the slogan of the evangelistic church. Evangelism is seen as the task of every believer. It is not something that one can pay to have done for him. The old cliche "If you can't go, send a missionary" is rejected. The social thrust of the "gospel of the kingdom of God" and the personal demands of the "gospel of your salvation" are proclaimed with equal authority. The social, physical, and mental needs of the person demand ministry just as his spiritual need. Racism is rejected because it divides humanity made in God's image. Saving souls without regard to the total man is also rejected because it dissects a man made in God's image. There are no barriers of race, sex, or class for the new evangelism. Every Christian is a witness. Every man is the object of our love and evangelism. The universe, the world, society, the race, and the individual are all objects of redemption. JOHN F. HAVLIK

EVANGELISM AND SOCIAL MINISTRY. There has been within modern evangelical thought a sharp division between those who emphasize evangelistic action and those who emphasize social action. The words of Christ in his conversation with the teacher of the Law and the consequent parable of the good Samaritan made clear the need for personal regeneration and social reconciliation. Christ, who cared enough to die for the sins of man, cared also when they were sick, hungry, insane, or lame. He ministered to the whole man. Some basic guidelines help us to keep the relationship between evangelism and social ministry clear.

First, it must be clear from the New Testament that Christian conversion is necessary to Christian community and that morality is a consequence, not a cause, of salvation. New Testament evangelism centers in the gospel, the good news of the forgiveness of sins on the basis of personal repentance because Christ died and rose again. The gospel is the good news of God's love for persons. Salvation is first a personal matter between an individual and God. It is at this point that the gospel has particular relevance for a society that is in a process of depersonalization.

Second, it must be equally clear that the gospel has deep social meanings. It is not by chance that some of the great social activists of the 18th and 19th centuries were the revivalists. Social ministry is impossible without a deep sense of social justice and an involvement in social action. Christ realized more deeply than any man that the disease was sin; but he knew also that the symptoms of hunger, poverty, and sickness needed his ministry. Regeneration is the true solution to social questions, but there is an infinite work of patience and compassion to be done by the Christian brotherhood to pervade all of life's relationships with a spirit of justice and compassion.

The third understanding is that evangelism must challenge what Emil Brunner called the "axioms of contemporary culture." The evangelist must not be blind to what is good in contemporary culture, nor dumb about what is evil and false in that same culture. Because people matter to God, they will matter to the evangelist. The evils of war, poverty, racism, and our ecological crimes will be cried out against because they hurt persons made in God's image. The great evangelists of the 18th and 19th centuries saw no conflict in preaching the gospel and challenging social evils. The evangelist who raises his voice as a champion of the poor or the challenger of social evil is in the good company of the Hebrew prophets, Jesus Christ, and the great evangelists.

The fourth of these guidelines is that evangelism is interested and involved in the growth of the believer as a part of "the new race of men," the body of Christ, the church. Within the body of Christ, the disinherited of the earth are regarded as the children of God and as of infinite worth. The church exists as an illustration in the world of "the kingdom of God," that ultimate society. This kingdom is God's social order, and the church is constantly picturing it and calling men to it in preaching "the gospel of the kingdom of God."

BIBLIOGRAPHY: Merrill R. Abbey, *Preaching to the Contemporary Mind* (1963). Timothy L. Smith, *Revivalism and Social Reform* (1957). Sherwood Eliot Wirt, *The Social Conscience of the Evangelical* (1968). JOHN F. HAVLIK

EVANGELISM DEVELOPMENT, HOME MISSION BOARD PROGRAM OF (cf. Evangelism, Home Mission Board Program of, Vol. I). The objective of the program, which centers in the Division of Evangelism, is "to work with and assist churches, associations, and state conventions in interpreting, promoting, and properly relating the message, methods, motivation, and spirit of New Testament evangelism." The importance of this program, approved by the Southern Baptist Convention in 1966, in the work of the board is revealed in the first of 14 guidelines for determining board objectives and goals. It states: "Evangelism, which aims at making men disciples of Jesus Christ, shall continue to be the heart of our home mission program." The same guideline indicates the broad scope of this program by stating: "evangelism includes commitment and involvement; and, therefore, attention shall be given to conversion, baptism, church membership, and spiritual growth."

The work of the program is structured as study and research, program design, consultative and advisory services, and field services. Staff expertise includes personal evangelism, revival evangelism, student evangelism, programing, and associational evangelism. The staff includes a director and six associates. C. E. Autrey, director, retired in Aug., 1969. At the beginning of 1970 the associates were Eual F. Lawson, Jack Stanton, John F. Havlik, Harold E. Lindsey, William D. Lawes, and Nathan Porter. Kenneth L. Chafin was named director in Dec., 1969.

Evangelism development is an emphasis program since it supports an emphasis (evangelism) in the church. It channels information and interpretation through curriculum and guidance materials of the church program organizations. Correlation and coordination with other denominational programs are achieved through the coordinating committee of the Inter-Agency Council and its sub-committees. In years when evangelism is designated as the denomination's central thrust, the church program organizations carry a large portion of the emphasis, e.g., the Crusade of the Americas, 1968–69. That year the division's annual *Evangelism Plan Book* became the major correlating instrument for many other denominational programs with special stress on the church program organizations. Through the annual *Plan Book* assistance is given to pastors and church councils in planning evangelism projects and emphases for the year.

This program is supported by a promotional plan that includes annual conferences in every state convention and clinics in every association. These meetings provide inspiration and guidance for pastors and other church leaders. Thirty-four state secretaries and about 1,000 associational chairmen of evangelism provide field services for the churches. Two annual meetings of the division's staff and the state secretaries are held for planning evangelism emphases and projects. Associational chairmen have annual planning conferences at Ridgecrest and Glorieta assemblies.

State conventions and associations are assisted by the production of guidance materials in personal evangelism, lay witnessing, and revival evangelism. In pioneer areas and new state conventions financial assistance is given toward salaries of state evangelism secretaries and in special revival evangelism secretaries and in special revival evangelism projects such as area crusades. Staff assistance is provided other Baptist bodies, upon their invitation, in planning and conducting special crusades. Such crusades have been conducted in Canada, Jamaica, New Zealand, and Latin America. This work is in cooperation with the Foreign Mission Board in places where it has missionaries. Assistance is provided associations for personal-evangelism training of church leaders. In some places area evangelistic crusades have been conducted involving Christian people from many denominations.

In 1967 the division initiated work with the academic community. The program is interpreted to seminary students and faculties in annual seminary evangelism workshops. Pastors with large numbers of students in their constituency are brought together for special assistance in area meetings. New approaches to campus evangelism are constantly explored and initiated. Lay witnessing revivals in pioneer areas and other needy places are conducted in cooperation with the Brotherhood Commission.

The evangelism emphasis carried by the church program organizations' curriculum and guidance materials rely upon the expertise of the division's staff. (Staff personnel serve as writers, consultants, and resource persons for writers and editorial staff of the church program organizations.)

Student summer missionary appointees with special evangelistic assignments receive special evangelistic training. In keeping with the special assignment given the board regarding the Crisis Statement, the division has studied the effect of racism on evangelism and has related to the social problems of today's world in its guidance materials and *Plan Book*. JOHN F. HAVLIK

EXCEPTIONAL PERSONS, MATERIALS FOR USE WITH. Publication of *The Braille Baptist* was begun by the Sunday School Board in 1946. In 1960 *The Intermediate Braille Baptist* was launched, the name being changed to *The Youth Braille Baptist* in 1970.

In 1965 the Board's Training Union Department was assigned the responsibility of designing a program and curriculum materials for work with the mentally retarded.

Formed in 1966 to explore the needs of the deaf, the blind, the gifted, and the mentally retarded, a committee for work with exceptional persons issued a brochure on "Your Church and the Gifted." The first curriculum material prepared especially for use with the mentally retarded was published in 1966. "Adventures in Christian Living and Learning," a two-part graded series of curriculum resources for use with trainable children and youth, was released in 1969. A two-part graded series of curriculum resources for use with educable children and youth became available in 1970.

Publication of *Sunday School Quarterly for the Deaf* (Uniform lessons) was begun in 1957. *The Training Union Quarterly for the Deaf* followed in 1958. In 1963 these titles were changed to *Sunday School Lessons Simplified* and *The Training Union Quarterly Simplified*. Thus they could serve not only the deaf but other persons with reading difficulties. The latter periodical was replaced by *Source Digest* in 1970. At the same time, *Simplified Bible Study* was launched to carry the Life and Work lessons for adults in simplified form. DORIS D. MONROE

***EXECUTIVE COMMITTEE OF THE SOUTHERN BAPTIST CONVENTION.** The Executive Committee of the SBC has changed some of its structures and procedures since 1956, but these have not altered the basic purpose or organization.

Reorganization, 1959.—One of the recommendations of the Convention's Committee to Study Total Program in 1958 and 1959 was that the Executive Committee be divested of certain program responsibilities and that it be reorganized to accomplish basic executive and administrative functions from a neutral stance. As a result the committee surrendered its stewardship promotion responsibilities, although it retains editorial control over the Baptist Bulletin Service and the SBC Mat and Stencil Service. These materials are sold by the Sunday School Board. It then reorganized with four basic committees, administrative, program, finance, and public relations. The membership of the Executive Committee was made responsible for the staff work of all committees. Other staff members are assigned to help them in accordance with their job description and reporting responsibilities. In 1968 the public relations committee was reduced in size and became a subcommittee of the administrative committee.

Headquarters Building.—The Committee to Study Total Program also proposed that the Executive Committee be provided a building which would also be used to house other Nashville-based Convention agencies. Ground was broken for the SBC Building, 460 James Robertson Parkway, Nashville, Tenn., late in 1961. The agencies occupied the building early in 1963. It cost about $1,000,000 and was paid for by the Baptist Sunday School Board, in keeping with Convention instructions. Besides the Executive Committee, the building houses the Stewardship Commission, SBC Foundation, Christian Life Commission, Education Commission, and Seminary Extension Department. It also contains five conference rooms, a parlor, and an assembly room that seats 225. The foundation of the building was developed to carry two additional floors or to be extended in three different directions.

Staff Changes.—With the reorganization of the Executive Committee in 1959, two new staff members were appointed: W. C. Fields, employed as public relations secretary, and John H. Williams as financial planning secretary. Albert McClellan was moved from the place of director of publications to program planning secretary. The staff, including professional and clerical, is (1970) around 18 people, unchanged from 1959. Porter W. Routh has served as executive secretary since 1951.

Increased Budget.—The budget of the Executive Committee for 1960 was $222,000. In 1970 it was $369,700, an increase of 66.53 per cent. The committee budget is derived from the Convention operating budget which is made up of funds both from the Baptist Sunday School Board and the Cooperative Program. In 1960 the Cooperative Program part of the Convention operating budget was $200,000 or 1.14 per cent of the total. In 1970 it was $200,000 or .74 per cent of the total.

Press Relations.—The Executive Committee also staffs the annual meeting of the Southern Baptist Convention. One significant development of this responsibility has been the growth of the Convention press relations. In 1970 at the 125th anniversary session of the Southern Baptist Convention, Denver, 199 registered in the Convention newsroom. The press room produced 500 items of press material, provided 59 news photos, gave 709 daily news feeds to radio stations, and provided 269 filmclips to television stations.

Administration.—The administrative structure of the Executive Committee provides for three committees, each composed of 18 or more members. The administrative committee is responsible for the administrative affairs of the Convention assigned to the Executive Committee as well as for the committee's own administrative affairs. It is responsible for (1) studying and recommending improvements in the organization and procedures of the Convention and its committees; (2) recommending the annual Convention operating budget including the budget of the Executive Committee; (3) making preliminary plans for future Convention sessions; (4) making arrangements for the annual Convention session; (5) approving the organization, personnel, and allied policies governing the staff of the Executive Committee; and (6) approving the policies and evaluating the Executive Committee public relations and press service. The administrative committee is organized with subcommittees dealing with personnel, Convention arrangements, bylaws, public relations, and such other subcommittees as may be needed from time to time.

The program committee is responsible for considering and recommending action concerning: (1) broad program objectives and policies; (2) assignments of programs to agencies of the Convention; (3) availability of resources, including financial resources, to carry out programs; (4) allocation or appropriations of undesignated financial resources; and (5) appraisal of program coordination and achievements. The program committee is organized with subcommittees dealing with board, institutions, commissions, and such other subcommittees as may be needed from time to time.

The finance committee is responsible for considering and recommending action concerning: (1) broad financial objectives and policies; (2) the operational effect of approved financial policies; (3) the appropriateness of general financial policies and practices, including auditing, followed by agencies of the Convention; and (4) any evidence of undesirable financial conditions shown in audit or other reports. The finance committee is organized with subcommittees dealing with business and financial plan, audits, long-range financial projections, and such other subcommittees as may be needed from time to time.

Program Planning.—The Committee to Study Total Program introduced concepts that led to the planning of program budgeting systems conducted under the supervision of the executive secretary on the advice of the program committee. Planning is the definition or discovery of long-range program objectives. Programming is the relating of these objectives to planned activities. Budgeting is the relating of cost to programs and plans. "Systems" is information feedback and evaluation. Among the new procedures adopted to make this possible is the Organization Manual which describes the program base, the budget and financial data query form, the budget and financial data book, and the evaluation process which was still under development in 1970.

Financial Planning.—The financial planning secretary provides professional staff assistance to the finance committee and other committees as needed. He also serves in the following areas: (1) principal financial planning assistant to the executive secretary-treasurer; (2) chief accountant of the Executive Committee staff; (3) reviews and appraises the financial policies and practices of agencies of the SBC to the extent the Executive Committee is concerned with these matters; (4) works with program planning secretary in projecting undesignated revenues for such periods as may be appropriate; (5) supervises the accounting personnel of Executive Committee; (6) serves as principal budget assistant to the executive secretary-treasurer; and (7) serves as principal assistant to the executive secretary-treasurer in planning for the annual sessions of the SBC by (a) maintaining information on potential cities; (b) coordinating invitations from cities, checking accuracy of the invitations as to facilities; (c) working with local committees on Convention arrangements; and (d) serving as Convention manager as it pertains to physical arrangements, equipment, exhibits, etc.

Public Relations.—The Executive Committee provides a public relations service for the Convention, its agencies, and constituency. The service of the public relations office is conducted under policies and procedures approved by the Executive Committee through its administrative committee. The public relations secretary is responsible to the executive secretary for working with the various subcommittees of the Executive Committee, the agencies, and organizations of the Convention in his assigned area of public relations and communications. He maintains liaison with appropriate news media on behalf of the Executive Committee and the SBC. As approved by the Executive Committee, he stimulates improvement in the public relations and communications efforts of the agencies, institutions, and organizations of the SBC.

The public relations secretary is the principal public relations assistant to the executive secretary-treasurer. He formulates, for the approval of the executive secretary-treasurer and the Executive Committee, overall public relations policies, practices, and procedures in line with the responsibilities of the Executive Committee. He assists in the general SBC work of promotion and publicity, furnishing a central information service, preparing articles, supplying data, arranging interviews, answering correspondence referred to him, and facilitating the free flow of information within the denomination. He and his staff assist denominational leadership in keeping up with news of activities and developments of importance to the general work of Southern Baptists.

The public relations secretary is editor of *The Baptist Program,* the general program journal for the professional leaders of the denomination. He directs Baptist Press, the denominational news service, and provides a channel of news of, about, and for Southern Baptists. As press representative of the Convention he cooperates with news media in furnishing intelligent, accurate, and creditable reports of the work and life of Southern Baptists. He directs the Baptist Bulletin Service, the SBC Mat and Stencil Service, and supervises the development and production of calendars and calendar information for the denomination. The public relations office develops printed materials, audiovisuals, exhibits, and other materials for public presentations. The public relations secretary gives staff assistance, when appropriate and as requested, to various SBC organizations and groups. He is expected to participate in organizations and activities outside the SBC to increase understanding and support for Southern Baptists and their work.

With the approval of the executive secretary-treasurer and the Executive Committee, the public relations secretary and his staff stimulate research and study of opinions and attitudes which affect the work of the SBC and work to gain improvement in problem areas. He takes initiative in the development of worthy goals and high standards of professional skill in the practice of public relations in the SBC. He and the public relations office give assistance in organizing and conducting of seminars, clinics, and conferences on public relations, communications, journalism, and related areas of special value to Southern Baptist personnel working in these areas.

Committee of 10.—In Feb., 1970, the Executive Committee appointed a committee of 10 to study the result of the recommendation of the Committee to Study Total Program as adopted by the Convention and to make recommendation for basic revisions.

See also PROGRAM PLANNING, SOUTHERN BAPTIST CONVENTION and BUDGET OF THE CONVENTION.

W. C. FIELDS, ALBERT MC CLELLAN, and JOHN H. WILLIAMS

EXTENSION CENTERS, BAPTIST COLLEGES. Carson-Newman continues to operate an off-campus program for adults with some special centers offering college credit courses.

The Howard College Extension Division program was the first extension program of this nature to operate in our Baptist colleges. In 1970 this program operated 30 to 50 centers annually, and had enrolled approximately 20,000 adults, 1947–69.

Since 1956 the Mercer Extension Program of Christian Education has offered only extension credit. Three certificates are offered after required hours and required courses have been completed. A total of 419 received these certificates, 1956–69. The enrolment (1956–69) was 12,190, with 1,504 of these being ministers. The total enrolment since the beginning of the program is about 18,000, with some 2,200 of these being ministers. The primary purpose of the program is to help those involved in the church work to be better prepared.

In 1958 Stetson University inaugurated "The Extension Division of Christian Education." From 1958–62, Stetson served more than 1,000 adults through its extension program. In 1962 Stetson began to offer college credit courses in addition to diploma courses through its Extension work for college credit.

The University of Richmond extension program carries the title, School of Christian Education. Since 1956 this program has averaged 433 enrolled each year, and has served 54 churches and/or communities. This program operates for college credit and Certificate of Achievement credit. Total enrolled for Certificate of Achievement credit since 1956, 887, and for college credit, 2,049.

See also HOWARD COLLEGE EXTENSION DIVISION, Vol. III.

J. AUBREY ESTES

EXTREMISM. Extremists of all types have made their presence felt throughout history. Today's extremism is rooted, at least in part, in the rapid political, economic, and social changes of our day. This extremism has seriously affected the nation in general and Southern Baptists in particular.

Extremists sow hate, spread distrust, foment strife, and generally disrupt American society today. Some groups, with million-dollar budgets, extensive membership lists, and persuasive propaganda, pose serious threats to our society.

Extremism has been discussed by Southern Baptist Theological Seminary professor Wayne Oates, in his book on *Pastoral Counseling in Social Problems.* He says: "Extremism is an individual or group reaction against threat. The sense of threat is out of keeping with reality. Extremism is an over-response to the stimulus of the threatening agent. Therefore, extremism represents symbolically the distorted and infected personal needs of the extremist."

The extremist has several characteristics that he uses to his advantage. Some of these characteristics are: he is suspicious of change, he oversimplifies problems and solutions, he displays little regard for the need to understand complex issues, he sees issues as either right or wrong, and he has no place for compromise. A person with one or two of these characteristics would not necessarily be an extremist, but a person marked by a number of these traits may properly be considered an extremist.

At the 1969 Southern Baptist Convention meeting in New Orleans, the Christian Life Commission presented a statement on extremism along with the following recommendations:

(1) That by careful study we seek to become alert to the extremist forces, left and right, in church and society, which if allowed to go unchallenged will divide us and ultimately take us down the dreadful road to ruin;

(2) That we become adequately informed about the major extremist groups with focused concern on their tactics, their goals, their use of the mass media, and their financial support;

(3) That in confronting extremism we re-examine our basic beliefs in order that we may be able clearly to communicate to our fellow Baptists and

to others the Christian convictions by which we seek to live;

(4) That we involve ourselves in helping to solve the complex moral, economic, political, and social problems which continue to plague multitudes of our citizens; working actively with those who support the reform and the renewal of our basic institutions of society; that they may more nearly serve the purposes of God and the needs of men;

(5) That we here affirm our deep conviction that extremism of whatever variety and wherever found does not communicate the spirit of Christ and that we stand fast against any man or group who would subvert truth and corrupt justice through fear, suspicion, divisiveness, and violence;

(6) That, remembering the attitude of our Lord toward the extremists of his day, we strive to develop the strength to love as he loved, neither giving in to the pressures of men bent on evil destruction nor yielding to the temptation to hate those who despitefully use us;

(7) That we take care, lest in our concern to avoid the excesses of extremism we become lukewarm in our commitment to Christ as Lord and thereby are found neutral on vital moral issues and astraddle every important fence;

(8) That we seek to remedy those conditions which foster extremism and breed violence by doing justly, loving mercy, and walking humbly with God (Micah 6:8);

(9) That we seek in all kinds of situations and between all kinds of people to be peacemakers, accepting the risk of being misunderstood, maligned, and finally done in by extremists on both sides of the struggle to serve truth, preserve freedom, and extend human dignity;

(10) That in Christian concern for the victims of extremism we "bear one another's burdens" (Gal. 6:2) when those who are "persecuted for righteousness sake" (Matt. 5:10) fall on hard times with no means of support;

(11) That we here affirm our unreserved Christian compassion not only for the victims of extremism but also for the extremists themselves whose reconciliation to God and to man, created in God's image, we also seek;

(12) Finally, that we acknowledge the grace of God to be adequate for every sin, including that of extremism, which besets man and that we seek to declare his whole gospel as the ultimately adequate answer for our current crisis.

Although the recommendations were not formally adopted, the entire report, including these recommendations, was received as information by the Convention.

In 1969 the Christian Life Commission produced and widely distributed a pamphlet entitled "Issues and Answers: Extremism" as well as a resource paper on the subject.

In 1969 at the Glorieta and Ridgecrest Baptist assemblies, the Christian Life Commission sponsored conferences on "Extremism, Left and Right." These addresses were delivered by all the Southern Baptist seminary professors of Christian social ethics:

"The Anatomy of Extremism, Left and Right"; "Common Features in Extremism's Ugly Faces"; "Who's Who Among the Extremists"; "Sources of Extremism"; "Psychological Dimensions of Extremism"; "Tactics of Extremists"; "Extremists and the Mass Media"; "The Gospel and Extremism"; and "Christians Coping with Extremism."

The addresses from the conferences were reported widely through Baptist Press. Three of them were carried in the Nov., 1969, issue of the *Baptist Program.* The addresses were also edited and accepted for publication in book form.

Extremists are a threat to democracy, national security, and the Christian movement. Many Americans are unaware of the nature and extent of extremist activity. Others support extremist organizations without being fully aware of the harm they do. Every Christian should be knowledgeable concerning the dangers of extremism.

W. L. HOWSE, III

F

***FALLS CREEK ASSEMBLY.** Beginning in 1967, four one-week encampments were held in Oklahoma Baptists' only statewide assembly at Falls Creek in the Arbuckle Mountains. Samuel W. Scantlan served two lengthy periods as business manager, Jan. 1, 1944—Dec. 8, 1950, and Sept. 19, 1956—Dec. 31, 1966. Johnson Roberts suceeded him, Jan. 1, 1967. The B. B. McKinney (*q.v.,* Vol. II) Chapel and the Westmoreland Chapel were dedicated during the 1965 encampment season. Tangible assets of convention-owned property include 195 acres of land, 39 buildings, 41 class pavilions, a huge swimming pool, and a 5,000-seat tabernacle worth about $100,000. Total property value is near $600,000 not including privately owned facilities.

Since it was founded in 1917, total registrations recorded through 1969 were 573,262. The record attendance was 28,233 in 1969. There have been 49,874 life commitments recorded.

SAM W. SCANTLAN

***FALLS CREEK INDIAN ASSEMBLY.** Using the facilities of Falls Creek Baptist Assembly near Davis, Okla., this encampment has met annually since 1947. Registration in 1969 totaled 1,022, with 80 recorded decisions. Director from 1954 until his death in 1966 was Bailey O. Sewell (*q.v.*), who was succeeded by Laddie Adams. Indian leaders from 25 tribes provide the programs and do camp work. The 20th encampment in 1966 was named for Sewell.

J. M. GASKIN

FAMILY MINISTRY. A Southern Baptist Convention program assigned to the Sunday School Board. In 1959 the Convention approved the following program statement: "The objective of the Program of Family Ministry is to interpret and promote the standards and values of Christian family life and to provide assistance to churches in their ministry to families."

The responsibility for the program was originally given to the Family Life Department, with Joe W. Burton as program leader. As a result of a reorganization of work at the Sunday School Board in 1966, the Program of Family Ministry was assigned to the Church Training Department and B. A. Clendinning, Jr., became program leader. The responsibility for *Home Life* magazine, with Burton continuing as editor, was assigned to the Sunday School Department. The method of operation in regard to the channeling principle remained as it had been; the emphasis on family ministry is channeled through all program organizations, no one having a dominant role.

In the local church the distribution of responsibility for family ministry is the same. The church's total effort is planned and coordinated by the church council, and each organization carries that part of family ministry which is logical and in line with program assignments.

A church's emphasis on family ministry centers in three areas: (1) education for marriage and family living, (2) ministry to the needs of families, and (3) encouragement and training for family members in worship, witness, learning, ministering, and applying Christian truths daily in and through the home.

A balanced emphasis is based on a concern for the total development of individuals in every relationship of life. It recognizes the home as the most significant force in early maturity and a strong, continuing force affecting all areas of growth throughout life. The goal of a well-planned family ministry emphasis in a church is a person better equipped for living and learning within the family, and a wholesome family unit characterized by mutual love, concern, and upbuilding.

B. A. CLENDINNING, JR.

FARMER, THADDEUS HOWARD (b. Brownwood, Tex., Sept. 1, 1891; d. Oklahoma City, Okla., Jan. 20, 1965). Leader in Baptist Young People's Union, Sunday School, and BSU work in Oklahoma. Educated in Texas at Decatur Baptist College and Southwestern Baptist Theological Seminary, he moved to Oklahoma as BYPU secretary, Jan. 1, 1924. He served as manager of Falls Creek Assembly, 1925–36. He became Sunday School and BTU secretary, Dec. 6, 1933. He was made the first BSU secretary in Oklahoma in 1934. In 1936 he resigned due to pressures brought on by the great depression and personal disagreements in denominational administration. He then entered the life insurance industry.

J. M. GASKIN

FLEMING, WILLIAM (b. Fannin County, Tex., May 18, 1881; d. Fort Worth, Tex., May 4, 1963). Oil man, philanthropist. Son of James Reed and Sarah Eudora (Gillespie) Fleming, he attended Grayson College. On Jan. 3, 1900, he married Anna Maud Lewis who died in 1941. On Jan. 30, 1948, he married Bessie Massey. He had one daughter, Mary D. (Mrs. F. Howard) Walsh. Fleming was active in Baptist denominational life. He became a director of the Baptist Foundation of Texas in 1932. Fleming served on the board of trustees of Southwestern Baptist Theological Seminary, 1950–63, and as chairman of that board, 1958–63. He also worked with the Boy Scouts. In 1952 Baylor University conferred the D.H. degree and Hardin-Simmons University the H.L.D. in 1958. He was buried in Whitewright, Tex.

W. R. ESTEP, JR.

***FLORIDA ASSOCIATIONS.**

I. New Associations. BIG LAKE ASSOCIATION, Organized in 1955 of churches from Palm Lake, Indian River, and Peace River associations. In 1969, 16 churches reported 297 baptisms, 4,592 members, $356,456 total gifts, $46,003 mission gifts, and $1,315,500 property value.

CHOCTAW ASSOCIATION. Organized in 1959 with eight churches (seven from Okaloosa Association and one new church). In 1968, 12 churches reported 353 baptisms, 7,097 members, $560,704 total gifts, $95,995 mission gifts, and $1,842,615 property value.

HALIFAX ASSOCIATION. Organized in 1958 by 14 churches from Seminole Association and two new churches. In 1968, 22 churches reported 328 baptisms, 10,899 members, $790,915 total gifts, $86,654 mission gifts, and $4,172,312 property value.

RIDGE ASSOCIATION. Organized in 1954 with 20 churches and four missions from five Florida associations. In 1969, 39 churches reported 530 baptisms, 15,937 members, $1,047,525 total gifts, $120,601 mission gifts, and $4,836,178 property value.

ROYAL PALM BAPTIST ASSOCIATION. Organized in 1958 by nine churches from Peace River Association. In 1968, 19 churches reported 470 baptisms, 9,031 members, $750,364 total gifts, $107,948 mission gifts, and $3,789,285 property value.

TAYLOR ASSOCIATION. Organized in 1958 with 11 churches from middle Florida Association. In 1969, 14 churches reported 110 baptisms, 3,813 members, $268,753 total gifts, $45,255 mission gifts, and $1,143,000 property value.

II. Changes in Associations. APALACHEE ASSOCIATION. Organized in 1951 as Gadsden Association with six churches, the name was changed to Apalachee in 1955. In 1968, 12 churches reported 29 baptisms, 1,015 members, $57,474 total gifts, $4,785 mission gifts, and $227,500 property value. EARL JOINER

***FLORIDA BAPTIST CHILDREN'S HOME, LAKELAND.** The home opened a Branch Home in Miami in 1957 to serve the metropolitan area of the lower east coast of Florida. Mr. and Mrs. Joseph Johnson served as managers there until their resignation in 1964 when Roger Dorsett succeeded them. The Lakeland home has a capacity of 108 children and has 3 caseworkers on the staff; the Branch Home with a capacity of 36 has 1 caseworker. Dr. and Mrs. T. M. Johns retired as superintendent and assistant superintendent of the home on June 30, 1969, after 37 years of service. Dorsett has been superintendent since then, and Lloyd K. Godwin, Jr., assistant superintendent. Graham Shaw, III is now (1970) manager of the Branch House. T. M. JOHNS

***FLORIDA BAPTIST FOUNDATION, THE.** On Jan. 1, 1962, Gould A. Leichliter retired as executive secretary of the foundation. Gus Johnson was elected executive secretary-treasurer to take office on that date, and the office was moved from Plant City, Fla., to Jacksonville, Fla. As of Sept. 30, 1968, the foundation held on behalf of various objects and agencies the amount of $771,015.88. GUS JOHNSON

***FLORIDA BAPTIST HISTORICAL SOCIETY.** The first curator of the society, Harry C. Garwood (*q.v.*), died in 1960 and was succeeded by Edward A. Holmes, Jr., who served until 1962. In that year the society published Garwood's book, *Stetson University and Florida Baptists,* with Holmes as editor. The society's book and archival collection was moved into the new DuPont-Ball Library at Stetson University in 1968 and named the Harry C. Garwood Library in memory of Garwood's service to Florida Baptists. James A. Sawyer served as president of the society most of this time, and Rollin S. Armour as curator since 1962.
ROLLIN S. ARMOUR

FLORIDA BAPTIST RETIREMENT CENTERS. The Florida Baptist Retirement Centers came into being by state convention actions in 1957 and 1958. By 1959 J. Perry Carter had been named general director and 25 acres of land acquired at Vero Beach. Construction was begun on the first unit in 1960 and by 1961 the center was open. In 1962 Carter retired and was succeeded by Leo B. Roberts. In 1970 the centers had a three-phase program including nursing care, custodial care, and duplex apartments. On Sept. 1, 1969, the center had nine buildings valued at $650,435 and 62 residents with ages ranging from 66 to 96 years. E. EARL JOINER

***FLORIDA BAPTIST STATE CONVENTION.**

I. History of the Convention, 1955–69. In the decade, 1950–59, Florida Baptists faced some of the greatest crises and challenges in their mission and educational programs in the rapid increase in state population (from 2,771,305 to 4,951,560), and in the number of Baptists students enrolled in college. The convention was sensitive to the needs and responded to the challenge by greatly enlarging its Cooperative Missions Department (1953), and beginning a program of special aid to churches in college centers.

Also during this decade the Florida Baptist Convention celebrated its centennial with a historical pageant written by Mrs. John H. Maguire and presented by 150 Stetson students at at the 1954 convention.

The convention expressed its sense of social and spiritual mission in several forms. First, it was expressed in the first International Student Retreat sponsored jointly by the Department of Student Work in Nashville, the State Baptist Student Union, and the Woman's Missionary Union. This became an annual event. Second, the first camp for Negro boys and girls was sponsored by the state WMU. Third, in 1955 the WMU built a house for missionaries to the migrants in Immokalee, where they were employed under a joint arrangement between the Florida Baptist Convention and the Home Mission Board, SBC. Finally, keen interest developed in establishing a retirement home.

In 1957 the convention approved a recommendation by which Baptist Bible Institute, which had operated as a local Baptist school for several years, became an agency of the convention.

Florida Baptists finished the fifties with a record of 28,626 baptisms in 1959, a record never matched in the sixties despite the continued rapid increase in state population.

In the decade, 1960–69, Florida Baptists continued their numerical growth while the fairly steady increase in the annual number of baptisms came to a halt and declined slightly with 24,732 baptisms reported in 1968. However, the convention made significant progress in several ways calculated to strengthen and broaden its base for better service and witness in the future.

First, the convention authorized in 1960 the purchase of land in the south section of Jacksonville for the construction of a new Baptist building to accommodate a current growth in the administrative staff and to anticipate future needs. The new building was constructed and occupied in 1959. Second, land was bought in 1962 for the purpose of developing a State Assembly Camp at Lake Yale, near Eustis, Fla. Construction of buildings began almost immediately, and by the end of the decade there were 14 buildings on 200 acres of land and numerous assembly programs were being conducted there with a resident secretary of camps and assemblies, Paul Glore, who was appointed in 1965.

Third, a new combination executive office was created with the appointment in 1962 of Paul Meigs as secretary of evangelism and vocational guidance. In addition to promoting evangelism, a significant part of his work is given to discovering, guiding, and encouraging young people considering a church related vocation. Fourth, in 1967 the state board of missions created a committee for the purpose of making a thorough study of the total program of Florida Baptists.

Before the work and suggestions of this study committee were executed, John H. Maguire retired as executive secretary-treasurer on Dec. 31, 1967. Between 1945 and 1966, under his leadership, church membership increased from 184,140 to 581,956, the number of churches from 826 to 1,400, and total gifts to world missions from $346,359 to $3,527,886.

Harold C. Bennett was elected executive secretary-treasurer and assumed office on Oct. 15, 1967. Since the beginning of his administration several events have occurred. First, the state convention began a process of reorganization of the local mission programs by placing the main responsibility for associational missions on the local association, rather than on the state administrative offices. Second, the Florida WMU became an integral part of the state convention organization in 1968, by assuming the new status of a regular department of the convention. Third, the administrative structure of the convention staff was reorganized into a division type structure in which most of the departments were placed under one of the two major divisions: education and missions. The Education Division included the Church Music, Student, Sunday School, and Training Union departments. L. Keener Pharr was elected director of this division and assumed office on July 5, 1969. The Missions Division includes the Brotherhood, Evangelism and Vocational Guidance, and WMU departments. J. Woodrow Fuller was elected director of this division and assumed office on Aug. 1, 1969. Fourth, on Sept. 5, 1969, the state board changed the name of the Training Union Department to the Church Training Department, effective Oct. 1, 1969. Finally, facing the challenge of growing urbanization of the people of Florida, the convention decided to participate in the Crusade of the Americas, hoping to regain the degree of momentum in growth enjoyed earlier. From the standpoint of statistics, however, the crusade was a failure, for despite special promotional efforts, the total number of baptisms reported for the year 1969 was 225 less than the previous year.

II. **Program of Work.** The Florida Baptist Convention meets annually and is composed of messengers from Baptist churches in the state of Florida which are in friendly cooperation with the convention and sympathetic with its purposes and work. Between sessions the work of the convention is conducted by the State Board of Missions.

The object of the convention as stated in the constitution is to facilitate the union and operation of Florida Baptists in the work of upbuilding the kingdom of Christ in the state and throughout the world. Its more specific objects are to promote spiritual religion by all scriptural means, to foster the spirit of worldwide missions, to support Christian and theological education, to encourage the spirit and practice of liberal and systematic benevolence, and to direct all contributed funds according to the wish of the individual or organization making the contribution, if such wish is expressed. The convention officers responsible for presiding over the annual meetings, recording the action, and implementing the decisions of the convention include a president, first and second vice-presidents, and a recording secretary.

The State Board of Missions includes not only members from each of the 47 associations but also three ex officio members, namely: the president, the recording secretary, and the executive secretary-treasurer of the convention. The recording secretary and the executive secretary-treasurer are without vote. The board elects its own chairman and vice-chairman, and the executive secretary-treasurer and his assistant serve as general secretary and assistant general secretary respectively. The board meets quarterly and performs its work through the employment of an executive secretary-treasurer and other employees, and through organizing itself to carry out the work of the convention as directed in its annual sessions, and in its Constitution and By-Laws.

The executive secretary-treasurer, Harold C. Bennett, has the responsibility of recommending employees and generally supervising all areas of work. In addition he holds and directs the use of funds for carrying out the work of state missions, makes an annual estimate of the needs, and formulates state objectives for all causes.

The duties of the assistant executive secretary-treasurer, S. O. Bean, include supervision of the department of camps and assemblies which is directed by Paul Glore. This department provides housing, meals, and recreation facilities to departments of the convention, associations, churches, institutions, agencies, and other groups, including those outside the denomination. At present the convention has two assembly camps, the West Florida Assembly with 14 buildings on 38 acres of land, and Lake Yale Assembly with 38 buildings on approximately 200 acres of land.

The director of business services, Frank C. Richardson, has the responsibility of accounting for money handled by the state offices, supervising mail services and printing. The director of promotion, Charles E. Peterson, is responsible for publicizing the work of the convention and promoting a regular program of stewardship in the churches.

The Education Division, directed by L. Keener Pharr, consists of the Church Music, Student, Sunday School, and Church Training departments. All the programs of the Sunday School Board, SBC, are the responsibility of this division also when those programs relate to Florida. Finally, this division is responsible for promotion of church administration services. Other work directed by this division is described below in connection with the work of the departments.

Church Music.—This department, headed by Paul Bobbitt, seeks to promote a fully organized and functioning music ministry in every church. This objective is pursued in the local churches, the association, and throughout the state by means of promotion, training schools and clinics, associatonal, regional, and state music festivals, and a three-weeks summer camp held annually at West Florida Baptist Assembly.

Student Work.—Headed by Joe Webb, the Department of Student Work seeks to bridge the gap between the students' family context and the less personal environment of college. It seeks also to aid the students' personal growth and encourages attendance and involvement in the life of the church. This department is further concerned with the promotion of mission activity among college students and the means of engaging them thus include international student retreats, youth-led revival teams, and special summer mission efforts in which students are sent to assist in mission fields around the world. As of 1969 Florida Baptists had six Baptist Student Union buildings on major college campuses, including the University of Florida, Florida State University, Stetson University, the University of South Florida, Jacksonville University, and the University of Miami. Campus directors include Peggy Ott Hackler in the Jacksonville area, Alton Harpe, Jr., at Florida State University, Thomas E. Lilly in the Tampa area, J. H. Mabry, Jr., at Stetson University, Frank W. McCollough in the Miami area, and Robert L. Smith at the University of Florida.

Sunday School.—Headed by James E. Frost, this department is charged with the responsibility of strengthening the Sunday School work of the churches. Working with J. E. Frost are associates Frank Delrose, Herbert W. McGlamery, and Richard E. Roberts. This department majors on training sessions for Sunday School teachers and officers at every level of convention life and the distribution of instructional and promotional materials. In addition, this department cooperates with the Church Architecture Department of the Sunday School Board, SBC, in counseling with local churches on building needs.

Church Training.—This department, headed by Robert S. Cook, seeks to assist the churches in providing a training program which promotes the growth and training of church members. To supplement the regular training program of the churches, this department also promotes a program of church recreation, family life ministry, and the development of church libraries. Charles Ragland serves as associate in this department.

The Missions Division, directed by J. Woodrow Fuller, consists of the Brotherhood, Evange-

FLORIDA STATISTICAL SUMMARY

Year	Associations	Churches	Church Membership	Baptisms	S. S. Enrolment	V.B.S. Enrolment	T. U. Enrolment	W.M.U. Enrolment	Brotherhood Enrolment	Music Enrolment	Mission Gifts	Total Gifts	Value Church Property
1955	41	1066	371,807	22,463	319,533	115,479	105,945	53,472	17,753		$2,302,857	$17,282,924	$ 60,380,961
1956	41	1101	388,487	21,930	333,684	120,690	111,165	55,359	20,049		2,495,126	20,158,928	71,230,194
1957	41	1148	411,145	22,431	353,078	126,143	119,888	57,082	21,898		2,837,126	21,496,715	79,079,097
1958	44	1180	429,871	25,588	365,084	135,534	125,704	65,982	25,943		3,114,856	22,716,150	91,210,122
1959	46	1219	455,175	28,626	382,224	139,849	134,410	62,509	26,837		3,525,129	25,931,907	106,177,697
1960	46	1257	480,407	25,621	397,771	145,562	140,510	72,696	28,547	37,592	3,887,390	28,778,183	121,570,059
1961	46	1292	507,881	28,123	412,460	148,902	149,029	72,274	29,710	42,741	3,980,688	29,168,051	130,525,505
1962	47	1327	528,885	25,962	418,088	155,259	151,498	82,698	28,417	49,619	4,334,199	31,887,199	149,110,145
1963	47	1353	543,676	23,720	421,074	156,590	153,493	74,856	29,354	51,284	4,325,465	32,374,844	158,870,661
1964	47	1382	557,031	25,028	426,800	154,556	154,037	77,516	27,309	56,172	4,657,406	35,264,809	167,216,507
1965	47	1384	570,614	24,160	431,667	158,509	152,157	76,476	26,945	58,374	4,994,598	37,813,846	178,230,339
1966	46	1404	581,956	24,402	426,817	153,990	149,482	87,670	26,622	59,866	5,429,052	39,285,537	190,616,739
1967	46	1416	600,836	24,985	430,419	162,169	152,971	75,264	26,665	62,503	5,541,612	41,884,919	203,193,988
1968	46	1433	614,900	24,732	424,385	154,258	145,441	74,133	26,124	65,776	5,715,838	45,394,886	214,105,070

FRANK C. RICHARDSON

lism and Vocational Guidance, and WMU departments. This division correlates its work with the mission programs of work of the SBC. A unique new venture now in process in this division is a cooperative arrangement with the Home Mission Board, SBC, in developing language missions, work with National Baptists, weekday and Christian social ministries, migrant work, and other programs.

Brotherhood.—The purpose of the Brotherhood Department is to enlist every man in a job in the church and deepen his commitment to missions. It seeks to accomplish this objective by working with associations and churches, training them in enlisting men and boys in the work of missions. The Brotherhood Department also holds annual workshops for Brotherhood and Royal Ambassador officers, who direct the Brotherhood program for boys. This work is headed by G. A. Ratterree, who is assisted by R. W. Galbraith, Sr.

Evangelism and Vocational Guidance.—This department, headed by Paul Meigs, promotes evangelism at all levels of convention life throughout the year but climaxing in an annual Evangelistic Conference each January. It also encourages and guides young people who are considering a church related vocation, and those who have already surrendered their lives to serve in such a vocation. In addition to cooperating with the Foreign Mission Board, SBC, and the Sunday School Board, SBC, in guiding these young people, this department sponsors an annual Church-Related Vocations Conference.

WMU.—This department is headed by Miss Carolyn Weatherford. Assisting her are Mary Copes, Young Woman's Auxiliary director, Ruth Bagwell, Girls' Auxiliary director, and Elizabeth Painter, Sunbeam director. Having served the convention for many years as an auxiliary, the WMU became a regular department in 1969. Its purpose and methods, however, have not changed. They include the promotion of missions through local church organizations such as Sunbeams, GA organization, YWA organization, and Woman's Missionary Societies. These organizations promote missions by study, prayer, and participation through financial support for missions, and witnessing to the lost in local communities. Summer camps and house parties are also a major part of the work. Finally, the Florida WMU gives regular scholarship assistance to young women preparing for mission service.

E. EARL JOINER

***FLORIDA BAPTIST WITNESS.** This state paper continues to be published weekly except the weeks of July 4th and Christmas by the five-member, convention-elected *Florida Baptist Witness* Commission. William Guy Stracener has been editor and manager since Aug. 15, 1949, during which time circulation has increased from 23,000 to 66,006 as of Jan. 1, 1970. At that time a total of 960 Florida churches were using one or the other of the paper's group subscription plans.

W. G. STRACENER

***FOREIGN MISSION BOARD.** Baker J. Cauthen, executive secretary since Jan. 1, 1954, has led the FMB in all its work and programs. During its 125 years of history, the board has appointed 4,427 missionaries—2,355 since Jan. 1, 1956. These missionaries have been appointed for service in the following 79 countries: Angola, Argentina, Austria, Bahamas, Belgium, Bermuda, Botswana, Brazil, Chile, China, Colombia, Costa Rica, Dahomey, Dominican Republic, Ecuador, Ethiopia, Egypt (U.A.R.), Guinea, France, French West Indies, Gaza, Germany, Ghana, Guam, Guatemala, Guyana, Honduras, Hong Kong, Hungary, Iceland, India, Indonesia, Iran, Israel, Italy, Ivory Coast, Jamaica, Japan, Jordan, Kenya, Korea, Lebanon, Leeward Islands, Liberia, Libya, Luxembourg, Macao, Malawi, Malaysia, Manchukoa, Mèxico, Morocco, Nigeria, Okinawa, Pakistan, Paraguay, Peru, Philippines, Portugal, Rhodesia, Romania, Senegal, Singapore, South West Africa, Spain, Switzerland, Taiwan, Tanzania, Thailand, Togo, Trinidad, Turkey, Uganda, Uruguay, Venezuela, Vietnam, Yemen, Yugoslavia, and Zambia.

In order to provide adequate home office space for the personnel and facilities necessary to administer a rapidly expanding overseas operation, the FMB voted, Apr., 1955, to construct a new headquarters building, and selected a committee responsible for planning and building this new structure. The entire 3800 block of Monument Avenue was purchased, and a two-story building of 55,000 square feet, begun in Sept., 1957, and costing (building and grounds) $1,445,887.02, was dedicated in Apr., 1959, just three months after its occupation by the board's home office staff.

The first area missions conference sponsored by the board for the fixing of mission strategy was held in Brazil in 1956. In succeeding years, similar conferences have been conducted in the other areas, some of which have included both nationals and missionaries.

Rogers M. Smith was named to the newly created position of administrative associate to the executive secretary in Oct., 1958.

In 1960 the FMB authorized the field representative plan for Latin America, setting up four fields: (1) North Field (Baptist Spanish Publishing House in El Paso, Tex., Mexico, Guatemala, Honduras, and Costa Rica), (2) Central Field (Ecuador, Colombia, Venezuela, Peru, and the Caribbean), (3) South Field (Paraguay, Uruguay, Argentina, and Chile), and (4) Brazil.

Recognizing the need for medical counsel at many points in its total program, the board created in 1961 the position of medical consultant and elected Franklin Fowler, M.D., missionary since 1947, to this position.

In order to meet urgent and immediate needs which English-speaking missionaries could fill, the board in 1961 set up a new category of

FOREIGN MISSION BOARD (*q.v.*) CHAPEL, with the appointment of new missionaries. Between January 1, 1956, and January 1, 1970, 2,355 missionaries were set apart by the Foreign Mission Board for overseas service.

FOREIGN MISSION BOARD (*q.v.*) HEADQUARTERS. Erected in 1958 on famous Monument Avenue, Richmond, Va., this building houses the administrative, professional, and clerical staff who were administering Southern Baptist Foreign Missions in 71 countries, January, 1970.

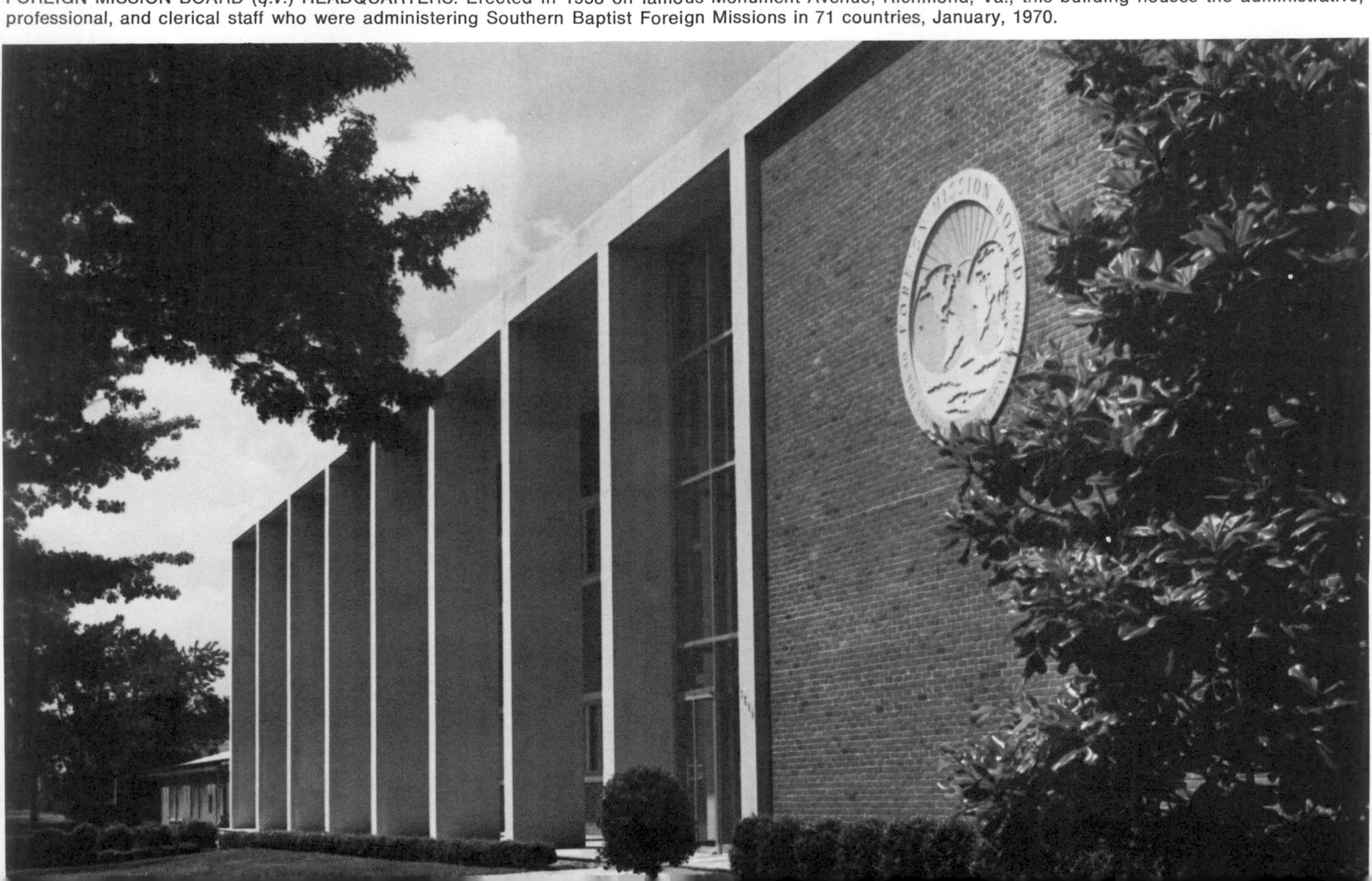

missionary service, the missionary associate, and began the employment of older persons as missionary associates. Since that date, 185 have been employed as missionary associates.

In 1963 the board divided the area then termed Africa, Europe, and the Near East into two areas: (1) Africa (south of the Sahara), which at that time included Ghana, Kenya, Liberia, Malawi, Nigeria, Rhodesia, Tanzania, Uganda, and Zambia, and (2) Europe and the Middle East, which at that time included France, Germany (West), Italy, Portugal, Spain, Switzerland, Gaza, Israel, Jordan, and Lebanon. H. Cornell Goerner, area secretary for Africa, Europe, and the Near East since 1958, became area secretary for Africa. John D. Hughey, missionary since 1943 and president of the European Baptist Theological Seminary since 1960, was elected area secretary for Europe and the Middle East.

The position of consultant in evangelism and church development was created early in 1963 and Joseph B. Underwood was elected to this post. Special projects in evangelism and church development, with simultaneous evangelistic campaigns involving churches in the same city or country, or even in a much broader area, have been increasingly promoted. The FMB has made special advance funds available for projects in mass evangelism and church development. Such projects have utilized Southern Baptists with outstanding experience in evangelism and church development to contribute greatly to these efforts overseas.

In Apr., 1964, the FMB, after long and careful study by its staff and committees, adopted a new program of advance calling for (1) 5,000 missionaries at the earliest possible date, (2) geographical and programs of work expansion, and (3) an annual budget in excess of $65,000,000 to underwrite this advance program.

At the same time, the board created another category of missionary service, the missionary journeyman. Since that date 280 missionary journeymen have been sent out to reinforce the work of missions around the world.

As a further advance step in working with missionary candidates, the board in May, 1965, adopted a regional personnel representative plan which authorized the election of missionaries unable to return to their field to serve as regional personnel representatives under supervision of the board's personnel department.

A comprehensive Consultation on Foreign Missions was held at Miami Beach, Fla., June 30—July 3, 1965. In order to secure the dialog, suggestions, and free discussion essential to a productive consultation, the board invited 350 persons to participate. Of these, 281 responded —59 national Baptist leaders and 61 missionaries from 41 countries, 101 denominational leaders, 41 board members, and 19 of the board's administrative staff.

Advance preparation for the consultation's work included papers, written by assignment, on relevant subjects such as relationships in missions, types and methods of work, and mobilization of resources. These were read in plenary sessions and formed the basis of discussion by small work groups. A findings committee distilled the discussions and summarized the recommendations, which were not mandates to the FMB, but constituted very valuable resource material to which the board has given much consideration and implementation in its plans, projects, and programs toward missions advance.

In the light of a long-felt need for a more extensive orientation of missionary appointees and as a result of a strong recommendation of the Consultation on Foreign Missions, the FMB in Oct., 1965, approved a plan for an extended orientation period. Therefore, after detailed planning and selection of a director—David Lockard, missionary in Rhodesia since 1952—extensive orientation for appointees was begun at Ridgecrest Baptist Assembly in Sept., 1967. Four 16-week sessions, covering a period of two years, were conducted there, with every appointee doing one session. The orientation site was moved to Callaway Gardens, Pine Mountain, Ga., in Sept., 1969, and a 16-week session has been completed there. Since its inauguration in 1967, 405 missionaries have received this long-term orientation.

The six programs of work defined by the FMB and approved by the Southern Baptist Convention in 1966 are as follows: support for foreign missionaries, evangelism and church development in foreign lands, publication work in foreign lands, schools and student work in foreign lands, hospital and medical care in foreign lands, and benevolent ministries in foreign lands. Through these programs, the board endeavors to achieve its general objective of doing everything possible to bring all men in other lands around the world to a saving knowledge of Jesus Christ and to involve them in Christian growth and service as members of indigenous churches. Specific objectives to implement this were also outlined by the board.

In 1966 the board inaugurated an information processing systems and elected William K. Dawson manager. The board created a position of consultant in church music and mass communications and elected Claude Rhea to this post in 1967.

In a step to strengthen its administrative process, the board in 1968 created the overseas division and the position of division director. It elected Winston Crawley, missionary, 1947–54, and secretary for the Orient since 1954, to this post.

Also in 1968 the board divided the area of Latin America into two areas, namely: (1) South America, which at that time included Argentina, Brazil, Chile, Colombia, Ecuador, Paraguay, Peru, Uruguay, and Venezuela, and (2) Middle America and the Caribbean, which at that time included the Baptist Spanish Publishing House in El Paso, Tex., Bahamas, Bermuda, Costa Rica, French West Indies, Guatemala, Honduras, Jamaica, Mexico, and Trinidad and Tobago. Frank K. Means, secretary for Latin America since 1954, became area secretary for South America. Charles Bryan, missionary since 1950 and field representative for Central Field since 1961, was elected secretary for Middle America and the Caribbean.

The Orient was also divided in 1968 into two areas: (1) East Asia—Hong Kong, Japan, Korea (South), Macao, Okinawa, and Taiwan (Republic of China), and (2) Southeast Asia—Guam, Indonesia, Malaysia, Philippines, Singapore, Thailand, and Vietnam (South). India and Pakistan, formerly part of the Orient area, were added to the Europe and Middle East area in 1968. R. Keith Parks, missionary to Indonesia since 1954, was elected secretary for Southeast Asia. James D. Belote, missionary to Hawaii, China, and Hong Kong since 1940, was named secretary for East Asia.

For many years, the board's missionaries and national Baptists used the radio as a means of communicating the gospel and the board has made substantial appropriations for radio (and later for TV) on its mission fields. But in 1960, the FMB, upon a specific request from the Chile Mission, appointed its first missionary (Alan W. Compton) for the expressed assignment of a radio-TV ministry overseas. In 1965 the board named Compton as radio-TV representative for all Latin America. In 1967 Wesley Miller, director of the Baptist Radio Recording Studio in Ruschlikon, Switzerland, since 1963, was named radio-TV representative for Europe and the Middle East. Milton E. Cunningham, missionary to Africa since 1957 and director of the Baptist radio-TV ministry in Zambia since 1963, was named radio-TV representative for Africa. The board also has plans to name radio-TV representatives for the remainder of its mission areas. The board appropriated more than $70,000 for radio-TV work in 15 fields in 1960, and in 1966, $350,000 for radio-TV ministries in 40 countries.

Continuing its strides in advance, the board at its Oct., 1968, meeting created two divisions: mission support and management services. At the same meeting, Jesse C. Fletcher, missionary personnel secretary, 1960–63, and secretary of the department of missionary personnel since 1963, was named director of the mission support division. In May, 1969, Sidney C. Reber, missionary associate in Singapore since 1963, was elected director of management services.

In Feb., 1969, the board inaugurated the field representative plan for Africa and for Europe and the Middle East. The next month, the following field representatives were named: Davis L. Saunders, East and Central Africa; John E. Mills, West Africa; John Allen Moore, Europe; and William W. Marshall, Middle East.

Since 1956, when the number of missionaries was 1,020, the FMB has appointed 2,355 missionaries, classified as follows: career, 1,877; short-term, 13; missionary associates, 185; and missionary journeymen, 280.

At the beginning of 1970, 2,490 missionaries were under appointment to 71 countries or separate political entities. The following fields have been entered since Jan. 1, 1956: Angola, Austria, Belgium, Bermuda, Botswana, Dahomey,* Dominican Republic, Ethiopia, Egypt (U.A.R.),* France, French West Indies, Germany, Guam, Guyana, India, Iran, Ivory Coast, Jamaica, Kenya, Leeward Islands, Liberia, Libya, Malawi, Morocco, Okinawa, Pakistan, Portugal, Senegal, South West Africa, Tanzania, Togo, Trinidad and Tobago, Turkey, Uganda, Vietnam, Yemen, and Zambia. (*Missionaries have been named for service in this country, pending official government permission for residence and work there.)

Receipts for Southern Baptist foreign missions since 1956 have totaled $313,345,637. These receipts have come from the following sources: (1) Cooperative Program, $134,724,130; (2) Lottie Moon Christmas Offering, $138,425,886; (3) special gifts, $26,143,330; and (4) earnings on investments, etc., $14,052, 291. EUGENE L. HILL

***FOREIGN MISSIONARIES, SOUTHERN BAPTIST CONVENTION, 1956–69.** A total of 2,355 new missionaries were appointed from 1956 through 1969. The total since the beginning of the Foreign Mission Board in 1845 is 4,421. The figure includes career missionaries, missionary associates, special project personnel, and missionary journeymen, but does not include reappointments. The peak year for appointments was 1969, with 261.

Included with each name are: native state, year of appointment, and country of service. Symbols used are as follows: Missionary Journeyman (J), Missionary Associate (A), and Special Project (P).

Ables, Raymond Edgar; Ala.; 1968, Ecuador.

Ables, Linda Wood (Mrs. R. E.); Kan.; 1968, Ecuador.

Acree, Irvin Hugh; Va.; 1966, Uruguay.

Acree, Annette Moore (Mrs. I. H.); Va.; 1966, Uruguay.

Adams, Bobby Ell; Okla.; 1959, Chile and Colombia.

Adams, LaVerne James (Mrs. B. E.); Okla.; 1959, Chile and Colombia.

Adams, Carroll H. (J); Ky.; 1965, Guyana.

Adams, John Truett; Tex.; 1965, Tanzania.

Adams, Martha Scharbauer (Mrs. J. T.); Tex.; 1965, Tanzania.

Adams, Judith Gray (J); Va.; 1969, Gaza.

Adian, Virginia (J); Tex.; 1965, Liberia.

Adkins, Thomas Spencer; Okla.; 1958, Hong Kong.

Adkins, Ellen Cobbs (Mrs. T. S.); Tex.; 1958, Hong Kong.

Akin, Cordell, Jr.; Ind.; 1968, Tanzania.

Akin, Martha Smith (Mrs. C., Jr.); Calif.; 1968, Tanzania.

Akins, Luther Bynum; Tex.; 1956, Taiwan.

Akins, Sybil Means (Mrs. L. B.); Tex.; 1956, Taiwan.

Akins, Wade (J); La.; 1968, Vietnam.

Albright, LeRoy; Ky.; 1958, Rhodesia and Zambia.
Albright, Jean Flowers (Mrs. L.); Ga.; 1958, Rhodesia and Zambia.
Alexander, Charles Leroy; Okla.; 1966, Chile.
Alexander, Betty Nabors (Mrs. C. L.); Okla.; 1966, Chile.
Alexander, James Mitchell (J); N.C.; 1966, Japan.
Alexander, Mark Midgett, Jr.; Va.; 1956, Argentina.
Alexander, Cecile Price (Mrs. M. M., Jr.); Miss.; 1956, Argentina.
Alexander, Max Nolan; Ark.; 1961, Tailand.
Alexander, Betty Nickell (Mrs. M. N.); Ark.; 1961, Thailand.
Allard, Joseph Charles; N. C.; 1966, Brazil.
Allard, Gloria Little (Mrs. J. C.); N. C.; 1966, Brazil.
Allen, Bobby Eugene; Ark.; 1965, Indonesia.
Allen, Barbara Fleeman (Mrs. B. E.); Ark.; 1965, Indonesia.
Allen, Charles Aubrey, Jr.; N. C.; 1958, Guatemala.
Allen, Jean Short (Mrs. C. A., Jr.); N.C.; 1958, Guatemala.
Allen, Jica Junior (J); Ky.; 1969, Liberia.
Allen, Walter Eugene; Tex.; 1960, Tanzania and Kenya.
Allen, Billie Metcalf (Mrs. W. E.); Tex.; 1960, Tanzania and Kenya.
Allison, Clarence Alvin; Ark.; 1960, Tanzania and Kenya.
Allison, Alta Brasell (Mrs. C. A.); La.; 1960, Tanzania and Kenya.
Allison, George Arnold; Okla.; 1965, Italy.
Allison, Mary Gene King (Mrs. G. A.); Ala.; 1965, Italy.
Allmon, Susan (J); Ga.; 1969, Japan.
Amis, Robert Edward; Ky.; 1965, Nigeria.
Amis, Joan Skaggs (Mrs. R. E.); Ky.; 1965, Nigeria.
Anaya, Jose Antonio; N. M.; 1969, Spain.
Anaya, Alice Contreras (Mrs. J. A.); N.M.; 1969, Spain.
Anderson, Carolyn (J); Mo.; 1968, Vietnam.
Anderson, James Winfred; Ky.; 1966, Philippines.
Anderson, Yvonne Rae Williams (Mrs. J. W.); Mo.; 1966, Philippines.
Anderson, Jim (J); Ark.; 1968, Kenya.
Anderson, Justice Conrad; Tex.; 1957, Argentina.
Anderson, Mary Ann Elmore (Mrs. J. C.); La.; 1957, Argentina.
Anderson, Mary Lynn (J); Tex.; 1969, Japan.
Anderson, Phillip Marion; Ala.; 1964, Philippines.
Anderson, Martha Brandon (Mrs. P. M.); Ala.; 1964, Philippines.
Anderson, Rita Sue (J); Ky.; 1969, Liberia.
Anderton, Frederick Hurst; Ala.; 1964, Italy.
Anderton, Mollie Stephens (Mrs. F. H.); Ala.; 1964, Italy.
Andrews, Muriel Kay (J); Miss.; 1966, Brazil.
Annis, James Blanton; Fla.; 1964, Ghana.
Annis, Dorothy Williams (Mrs. J. B.); Tenn.; 1964, Ghana.
Arnold, Madeline (J); Ind.; 1968, Paraguay.
Arnold, William Edward; Ky.; 1956, Ghana.
Arnold, Georgia LaVerne Hutchens (Mrs. W. E.); Ky.; 1956, Ghana.
Arthur, George Edward; Calif.; 1967, Indonesia.
Arthur, Gwendolyn Barrett (Mrs. G. E.); Tex.; 1967, Indonesia.
Askew, Thomas (J); Ga.; 1968, Hong Kong.
Atchison, Bill Campbell; Tex.; 1961, Brazil.
Atchison, Carol Ann Eden (Mrs. B. C.); Tex.; 1961, Brazil.
Atnip, Logan Cloyce; Ark.; 1956, Rhodesia.
Atnip, Virginia Hill (Mrs. L. C.); Ga.; 1956, Rhodesia.
Aultman, Larry Louis (J); Miss.; 1969, Malawi.
Austin, Naomi Ruth; Tex.; 1965, Philippines and Indonesia.
Autry, Joe Gene (J); Tex.; 1967, Korea.

Bailey, Bettie Joyce (J); S. C.; 1969, Tanzania.
Bailey, Chester Roy; Tex.; 1965, Colombia.
Bailey, Ruby Rives (Mrs. C. R.); Tex.; 1965, Colombia.
Bailey, Doyle Leon; La.; 1965, Argentina.
Bailey, Barbara Parsons (Mrs. D. L.); La.; 1965, Argentina.
Baker, Charles Berry; Okla.; 1968, Korea.
Baker, Marsha Ruth (Mrs. C. B.); Kan.; 1968, Korea.
Baker, Frank Jackson (A); Fla.; 1964, Korea.
Baker, Margaret Reaves (Mrs. F. J.) (A); Tex.; 1964, Korea.
Baker, Robert Erin; Tenn.; 1960, Brazil.
Baker, Barbara Sue Sewell (Mrs. R. E.); Tenn.; 1960, Brazil.
Ballard, James Harold; N. C.; 1965, Brazil.
Ballard, Shirley Munn (Mrs. J. H.); S. C.; 1965, Brazil.
Ballenger, Isam Earl; Fla.; 1965, Germany.
Ballenger, Katherine Thomason (Mrs. I. E.); S. C., 1965, Germany.
Balyeat, Kent Windsor; La.; 1961, Argentina.
Balyeat, Lloydene Umstot (Mrs. K. W.); Kan.; 1961, Argentina.
Banks, James Allison (A); Fla.; 1968, Israel.
Banks, Sue Bradley (Mrs. J. A.) (A); Ark.; 1968, Israel.
Barker, Herbert Ward; Mo.; 1959, Taiwan.
Barker, Emma Jean Archer (Mrs. H. W.); Mo.; 1959, Taiwan.
Barnes, Emmett Albert; Mo.; 1966, Lebanon.
Barnes, LaNell Taylor (Mrs. E. A.); Ark.; 1966, Lebanon.
Barnes, Joseph Alger (A); N. C.; 1966, Nigeria.
Barnes, Irene Flowers (Mrs. J. A.) (A); N. C.; 1966, Nigeria.
Barron, James Roland; Ala.; 1968, Ghana.
Barron, Linda Rierson (Mrs. J. R.); N. C.; 1968, Ghana.
Barron, Thomas Olon; La.; 1967, Indonesia.
Barron, Hazel Clark (Mrs. T. O.); Miss.; 1967, Indonesia.
Bass, Jerry (J); Tex.; 1968, Colombia.
Bassett, Perry (J); Tex.; 1968, Austria.
Bateman, Dallas Lane; La.; 1965, Kenya.
Bateman, Marjorie Crowe (Mrs. D. L.); La.; 1965, Kenya.
Baugh, Joseph Franklin, Jr.; Ky.; 1959, Pakistan and Tanzania.
Baugh, Jean Amis (Mrs. J. F., Jr.); Ky.; 1959, Pakistan and Tanzania.
Beard, Charles Robert (A); Tenn.; 1967, Taiwan.
Beard, Saranell Head (Mrs. C. R.) (A); Ala.; 1967, Taiwan.
Beaty, Robert Edward; Tenn.; 1958, Rhodesia.
Beaty, Thelma Osborne (Mrs. R. E.); Ind.; 1958, Rhodesia.
Beck, George Frederick; Fla.; 1969, Indonesia.
Beck, Linda Rountree (Mrs. G. F.); Tex.; 1969, Indonesia.
Beckett, Charles Austin; N. C.; 1961, Pakistan.
Beckett, Jeanne Plunkett (Mrs. C. A.); Va.; 1961, Pakistan.
Beckham, Norman Ray; Calif.; 1965, Venezuela.
Beckham, Donna Matthews (Mrs. N. R.); Tenn.; 1965, Venezuela.
Bedenbaugh, Charles Wrenn; S. C.; 1959, Tanzania.
Bedenbaugh, Betty Marshall (Mrs. C. W.); Ill.; 1959, Tanzania.
Bedsole, Jerry Paul; Ala.; 1969, Ethiopia.
Beevers, Ernest Bryant; Miss.; 1967, Indonesia.
Beevers, Barbara Tetlow (Mrs. E. B.); Pa.; 1967, Indonesia.
Bell, Ray Edward (A); Ark.; 1966, Rhodesia.
Bell, Billie Davis (Mrs. R. E.) (A); La.; 1966, Rhodesia.
Bell, Sarah Martha; Miss.; 1957, Indonesia.

Bellenger, Charles Lewis (A); Ala.; 1969, Botswana.
Bellenger, Jane Powers (Mrs. C. L.) (A); Ala.; 1969, Botswana.
Bellinger, Robert Nugent; La.; 1963, Liberia.
Bellinger, Patty Hooppaw (Mrs. R. N.); Ill.; 1963, Liberia.
Bellington, Robert Paul; Mo.; 1959, Brazil.
Bellington, Doris Gibson (Mrs. R. P.); Mo.; 1959, Brazil.
Benedict, Paul Winfield, Jr. (A); N. C.; 1969, Japan.
Benedict, Sue Suddath (Mrs. P. W., Jr.) (A); Ga.; 1969, Japan.
Benefield, Leroy; Okla.; 1958, Philippines.
Benefield, Nina Lou Mason (Mrs. L.); Okla.; 1958, Philippines.
Bengs, Harold Earl, Jr.; Okla.; 1967, Vietnam.
Bengs, Sheridan Derrick (Mrs. H. E., Jr.); La.; 1967, Vietnam.
Bennett, Charleeda (J); Fla.; 1968, Korea.
Bennett, Elvis Preston; Tex.; 1961, Japan.
Bennett, Audie Ercanbrack (Mrs. E. P.); Tex.; 1961, Japan.
Bennett, Troy Carson; N. C.; 1956, Pakistan.
Bennett, Marjorie Trippeer (Mrs. T. C.); Ohio; 1956, Pakistan.
Berrey, Mrs. Ruth (A); Ala.; 1963, Nigeria.
Berry, Travis Sisler; Ala.; 1956, Brazil.
Berry, Bernice Hayles (Mrs. T. S.); Ala.; 1956, Brazil.
Berry, Willie Mae; S. C.; 1965, Ghana.
Bethea, Ralph Chambers; Miss.; 1959, Indonesia, Tanzania, and India.
Bethea, Lizette McCall (Mrs. R. C.); Tenn.; 1959, Indonesia, Tanzania, and India.
Bible, Mattie Lou; La.; 1956, Brazil.
Bickers, Howard Benard, Jr.; Tex.; 1965, Malawi.
Bickers, Arleen Phillips (Mrs. H. B.); Tex.; 1965, Malawi.
Bickers, William Jesse; La.; 1968, Paraguay.
Bickers, Annette Clark (Mrs. W. J.); La.; 1968, Paraguay.
Bickerstaff, Nona Kay; Tex.; 1965, Bahamas.
Bilbary, Clay Don (A); Tex.; 1968, Guyana.
Bilbary, Carolyn Boyce (Mrs. C. D.) (A); Tenn.; 1968, Guyana.
Billings, Herbert Dale; Tex.; 1963, Guatemala.
Billings, Hazel Geraldine Rosier (Mrs. H. D.); Tex.; 1963, Guatemala.
Bishop, Edwina (J); N. C.; 1966, Thailand.
Bivins, Roy Lee; Ga.; 1961, Israel.
Bivins, Sarah Kolb (Mrs. R. L.); S. C.; 1961, Israel.
Blackwood, George Dale (A); Okla.; 1968, Costa Rica.
Blackwood, Sue Lakey (Mrs. G. D.) (A); Ark.; 1968, Costa Rica.
Blakely, Vestal Nelson; Okla.; 1969, Kenya.
Blakely, Carol Jean Faulkner (Mrs. V. N.); Calif.; 1969, Kenya.
Blankenship, Harold Lewis (A); Tenn.; 1965, Libya.
Blankenship, Dorothy Amos (Mrs. H. L.) (A); Ala.; 1965, Libya.
Blanton, Herbert Theodore (A); N. C.; 1968, Bahamas.
Blanton, Betty Steely (Mrs. H. T.) (A); Ark.; 1968, Bahamas.
Blattner, Doris Mildred; Mo.; 1963, Philippines and Indonesia.
Blount, Martha Ann; Tex.; 1966, Brazil.
Blundell, Claude Ray; Tex.; 1965, Uganda.
Blundell, Martha Darlington (Mrs. C. R.); Ga.; 1965, Uganda.
Boatwright, Claude Sawyer; Ga.; 1958, Japan.
Boatwright, Betty Williams (Mrs. C. S.); Ga.; 1958, Japan.
Bobo, James (J); Tex.; 1967, Vietnam.
Bockstruck, Lloyd Dewitt (J); Ill.; 1969, Kenya.
Boles, Olin Douglas; Tex.; 1966, Brazil.
Boles, Marilyn Miller (Mrs. O. D.); Tex.; 1966, Brazil.
Bond, Gerald Clayton; La.; 1958, Ghana and Togo.
Bond, Helen Terry (Mrs. G. C.); Ky.; 1958, Ghana and Togo.
Bond, Marvin Thomas; Miss.; 1961, Hong Kong.
Bond, Billie Jean Faulkner (Mrs. M. T.); Miss.; 1961, Hong Kong.
Bonnell, Dutton Aaron, Jr.; Fla.; 1961, Zambia.
Bonnell, Marilyn Richards (Mrs. D. A.); Fla.; 1961, Zambia.
Bonnette, Elmer Ordel; S. C.; 1961, Pakistan.
Bonnette, Hazel Knight (Mrs. E. O.); Ga.; 1961, Pakistan.
Boone, Hal Buckner; Tex.; 1958, Tanzania and Uganda.
Boone, Patricia Held (Mrs. H. B.); Ky.; 1958, Tanzania and Uganda.
Boothe, Dwain Holt; Okla.; 1968, Thailand.
Boothe, Sylvia DeHart (Mrs. D. H.); Okla.; 1968, Thailand.
Borland, Hazel (J); Ark.; 1965, Hong Kong.
Boss, Sally Ann (J); Va.; 1966, Kenya.
Boswell, James Beryl; Va.; 1968, Peru.
Boswell, Linda Lester (Mrs. J. B.); W. Va., 1968, Peru.
Boswell, Ronald Neal; Tex.; 1964, Brazil.
Boswell, Marlene Drumgold (Mrs. R. N.); Tex.; 1964, Brazil.
Bowers, Connie Mack; Ga.; 1966, Nigeria.
Bowers, Martha Vassar (Mrs. C. M.); Ga.; 1966, Nigeria.
Box, Paul; Okla.; 1959, Malaysia.
Box, Pattye Norwood (Mrs. P.); Okla.; 1959, Malaysia.
Bozeman, Oscar Kondert, Jr.; La.; 1958, Korea.
Bozeman, Marie Walser (Mrs. O. K., Jr.); Mo.; 1958, Korea.
Bradford, L. Galen (A); Tex.; 1962, Japan.
Bradford, Arline Younger (Mrs. L. G.) (A); Tex.; 1962, Japan.
Bradley, Rolla Merle; Kan.; 1963, Korea.
Bradley, Genevieve Wellborn (Mrs. R. M.); Tex.; 1963, Korea.
Brady, Otis Walter; S. C.; 1956, Bahamas and Guyana.
Brady, Martha Yates (Mrs. O. W.); N. C.; 1956, Bahamas and Guyana.
Bragg, Kenneth Raymond; Ga.; 1967, Japan.
Bragg, Faye Helms (Mrs. K. R.); N. C.; 1967, Japan.
Braly, Byron Duke; Tex.; 1966, Yemen.
Braly, Anne Bagby (Mrs. B. D.); Brazil; 1966, Yemen.
Brandon, James Oscar; Tex.; 1968, Brazil.
Brandon, Barbara Williams (Mrs. J. O.); Okla.; 1968, Brazil.
Brantley, Peggy Diane (J); Tex.; 1969, Mexico.
Brasuell, Johnnie Mae; Okla.; 1967, Yemen.
Braswell, George Wilbur, Jr.; Va.; 1967, Iran.
Braswell, Joan Owen (Mrs. G. W., Jr.); N. C.; 1967, Iran.
Braughton, Charles Thurman; Okla.; 1967, Malaysia and Pakistan.
Braughton Kathleen Blount (Mrs. C. T.); Ark.; 1967, Malaysia and Pakistan.
Bray, Albert Leroy; Calif.; 1969, Colombia.
Bray, Ina Venable (Mrs. A. L.); Okla.; 1969, Colombia.
Breeden, Lemuel Glynn; Tex.; 1956, Colombia.
Breeden, Ila Hayworth (Mrs. L. G.); Tex.; 1956, Colombia.
Breland, Murray Neil; S. C.; 1968, Thailand.
Breland, Barbara Mears (Mrs. M. N.); S. C.; 1968, Thailand.
Brian, Thomas (J); Tex.; 1967, Bahamas.
Brice, George Bealor; S. C.; 1965, Brazil.
Brice, Judith Hutton (Mrs. G. B.); Va.; 1965, Brazil.
Bridges, Julian Curtis; Fla.; 1959, Mexico.
Bridges, Charlotte Martin (Mrs. J. C.); Ga.; 1959, Mexico.
Bridges, Nancy Lee; Okla.; 1966, Philippines.
Brincefield, Clara Mae; N. C.; 1963, Chile.

Brizendine, John Wesley; Mo.; 1967, Liberia.
Brizendine, Genevieve Billings (Mrs. J. W.); Mo.; 1967, Liberia.
Brown, Aquilla (J); S. C.; 1965, Guatemala.
Brown, Bradley Davis; Ga.; 1963, Liberia.
Brown, Carolyn Folsom (Mrs. B. D.); Ga.; 1963, Liberia.
Brown, Ernest Emory, Sr.; Ga.; 1963, Bahamas.
Brown, Marian Smith (Mrs. E. E., Sr.); Ky.; 1963, Bahamas.
Brown, James Curtis, Jr.; Miss.; 1963, Costa Rica.
Brown, Myrtis Rogers (Mrs. J. C., Jr.); La.; 1963, Costa Rica.
Brown, James Edsel (A); Ky.; 1963, Nigeria.
Brown, Mayme Joseph (Mrs. J. E.) (A); Ky.; 1963, Nigeria.
Brown, Nobel Dale; Ky.; 1962, Nigeria.
Brown, Theo (J); Tex.; 1968, Ghana.
Brubeck, Roger William; Mo.; 1968, Uganda.
Brubeck, Carol Wallace (Mrs. R. W.); Kan.; 1968, Uganda.
Bruce, Joe Wayne (J); Mo.; 1966, Chile.
Bruce, Robert Carrol; Ky.; 1961, Japan.
Bruce, Frances Kirkpatrick (Mrs. R. C.); Ky.; 1961, Japan.
Brunson, Julian Ralph; S. C.; 1958, Malaysia.
Brunson, Charlotte Hicks (Mrs. J. R.); Tenn.; 1958, Malaysia.
Bryan, Jesse Dwain; La.; 1965, Spain.
Bryan, Beverly Bailey (Mrs. J. D.); La.; 1965, Spain.
Bryant, Thurmon Earl; Okla.; 1958, Brazil.
Bryant, Doris Morris (Mrs. T. E.); Tex.; 1958, Brazil.
Buckley, R T; Miss.; 1967, Belgium and Pakistan.
Buckley, Frances Goynes (Mrs. R T); Miss.; 1967, Belgium and Pakistan.
Buckner, Charles Edward; N. C.; 1967, Indonesia.
Buckner, Mary Ann Moore (Mrs. C. E.); Tenn.; 1967, Indonesia.
Buie, James Wesley; Miss.; 1965, Spain.
Buie, Christine Griffith (Mrs. J. W.); Ala.; 1965, Spain.
Bullington, Billy Lee; Ark.; 1966, Togo.
Bullington, Evelyn Robinson (Mrs. B. L.); Tex.; 1966, Togo.
Bundy, Mary Frances (J); S. C.; 1967, Hong Kong.
Burgin, Robert Duaine; Tex.; 1966, Korea.
Burgin, Sylvia Beth Lester (Mrs. R. D.); Tex.; 1966, Korea.
Burkwall, Paul A. (J); Mo.; 1965, Nigeria.
Burnett, Cherri (J); Okla.; 1966, Liberia.
Burnett, Johnny Nathaniel; Tex.; 1966, Brazil.
Burnett, Barbara Ann Evans (Mrs. J. N.); Ark.; 1966, Brazil.
Burnett, Ralph Willard; Okla.; 1961, Argentina.
Burnett, Patricia Hawk (Mrs. R. W.); Kan.; 1961, Argentina.
Burney, Robert Shafter; Fla.; 1967, Nigeria.
Burney, Edith Bleckley (Mrs. R. S.); Ga.; 1967, Nigeria.
Burnham, James Leonard; Ga.; 1969, Israel.
Burnham, Mary Anne Coffey (Mrs. J. L.); Tenn.; 1969, Israel.
Burrell, Jimmie Lou (J); Miss.; 1969, Thailand.
Burriss, Walter Mack; S. C.; 1965, Malaysia.
Burriss, Carolyn Thrasher (Mrs. W. M.); S. C.; 1965, Malaysia.
Burt, Daniel Hix, Jr.; Tex.; 1957, Brazil.
Burt, Mary Smith (Mrs. D. H., Jr.); Tex.; 1957, Brazil.
Burtis, John Robert; Tex.; 1967, Argentina.
Burtis, Betty Allen (Mrs. J. R.); Okla.; 1967, Argentina.
Bushey, Saundra (J); Okla.; 1967, Argentina.
Butcher, Orby Lee, Jr.; Okla.; 1960, Thailand.
Butcher, Elizabeth Luellen (Mrs. O. L., Jr.); Kan.; 1960, Thailand.
Butler, Franklin Jerome (J); Ga.; 1967, Philippines.
Byrd, Harry Emerson; N. C.; 1966, Guatemala.
Byrd, Jean Farrell (Mrs. H. E.); N. C.; 1966, Guatemala.
Byrd, Juanita (J); Ky.; 1967, Switzerland.

Cain, William Henry; Ala.; 1961, French West Indies.
Cain, Violet Sharpe (Mrs. W. H.); N. C.; 1961, French West Indies.
Calhoun, John Caldwell, Jr.; Conn.; 1963, Malaysia and Thailand.
Calhoun, Lois Valetos (Mrs. J. C.); N. C.; 1963, Malaysia and Thailand.
Callaway, Arlene Jensen (Mrs. M. P.) (A); Iowa; 1966, Morocco and Yemen.
Campbell, Charles George (A); Tenn.; 1969, Thailand.
Campbell, Eleanore Ayers (Mrs. C. G.) (A); Tenn.; 1969, Thailand.
Campbell, Mary (J); Tex.; 1968, Philippines.
Cannata, Samuel R. J., Jr.; Tex.; 1957, Rhodesia and Ethiopia.
Cannata, Virginia Currey (Mrs. S. R. J., Jr.); Miss.; 1957, Rhodesia and Ethiopia.
Cannon, Mary Dunning; N. C.; 1959, Japan.
Canzoneri, George Arden; Miss.; 1959, Brazil.
Canzoneri, Lillian Ray (Mrs. G. A.); Miss.; 1959, Brazil.
Carlin, Cecil Gerald; Mo.; 1963, Ghana.
Carlin, Mary Lou Williamson (Mrs. C. G.); Okla.; 1963, Ghana.
Carlin, Louis Elbert (A); Okla.; 1967, Ghana.
Carlin, Billie Martin (Mrs. L. E.) (A); Okla.; 1967, Ghana.
Carney, J W; Miss.; 1962, Pakistan.
Carney, Mary V. Holt (Mrs. J W); Ark.; 1962, Pakistan.
Carpenter, Jimmie Harold; La.; 1961, Indonesia.
Carpenter, Joyce C. Strother (Mrs. J. H.); China; 1961, Indonesia.
Carpenter, John Mark; Ga.; 1961, Liberia.
Carpenter, Betty Hawkins (Mrs. J. M.); Ga.; 1961, Liberia.
Carpenter, Wanda Jean (J); Ky.; 1967, Ghana.
Carrington, Lou Ann (J); Tex.; 1968, Nigeria.
Carroll, George Webster; W. Va.; 1956, Tanzania and Uganda.
Carroll, Betty Lou Wilt (Mrs. G. W.); Fla.; 1956, Tanzania and Uganda.
Carson, Mary Ann (J); Tex.; 1969, Hong Kong.
Carswell, Sidney Graves; Ga.; 1963, Brazil.
Carswell, Ruth Holland (Mrs. S. G.); Ark.; 1963, Brazil.
Carter, Jack Lee; Tex.; 1969, Thailand.
Carter, Geneva Reeves (Mrs. J. L.); Tex.; 1969, Thailand.
Carter, Jimmie Dale; Tex.; 1957, Brazil.
Carter, Sue Worthington (Mrs. J. D.); Tex.; 1957, Brazil.
Carter, Joan; Ga.; 1961, Tanzania and Kenya.
Carter, Pat Harold; Tex.; 1958, Mexico.
Carter, Evelyn Winham (Mrs. P. H.); La.; 1958, Mexico.
Caskey, Philip N. (J); Okla.; 1965, Philippines.
Cave, John David; S. C.; 1961, Argentina.
Cave, Laura Carden (Mrs. J. D.); Tenn.; 1961, Argentina.
Cecil, James Winfred (A); Ark.; 1967, Hong Kong.
Cecil, Katharine Gardner (Mrs. J. W.) (A); Ky.; 1967, Hong Kong.
Chambers, Glynda Darlene (J); Ill.; 1969, Gaza.
Chambless, Sylvia (J); Ala.; 1965, Chile.
Chambless, Virgil Walton, Jr.; Ga.; 1961, Mexico.
Chambless, Lorena Thomas (Mrs. V. W., Jr.); Fla.; 1961, Mexico.
Chechovsky, Susan Kay (J); Okla.; 1966, Liberia.
Chilton, Charles Ashby; Va.; 1969, Philippines.

Chilton, Fay White (Mrs. C. A.); Md.; 1969, Philippines.

Chong, Coleman (J); Miss.; 1967, Thailand.

Choy, Samuel (A); Hawaii; 1967, Korea.

Choy, Elsie Toyama (Mrs. S.) (A); Hawaii; 1967, Korea.

Chrisman, Joyce Ann (J); Kan.; 1969, Brazil.

Christian, Carle Ernest; Ohio; 1965, Mexico and Costa Rica.

Christian, Grace Henck (Mrs. C. E.); Pa.; 1965, Mexico and Costa Rica.

Christilles, Carol (J); Tex.; 1968, Korea.

Clark, Dwight Clifford; Mo.; 1969, Bahamas.

Clark, Ann Salter (Mrs. D. C.); Ark.; 1969, Bahamas.

Clark, Eric Herschel; England; 1959, Kenya.

Clark, Phyllis Hope (Mrs. E. H.); England; 1959, Kenya.

Clark, Gene Austin; N. C.; 1956, Japan.

Clark, Dorothy Lawhon (Mrs. G. A.); Fla.; 1956, Japan.

Clark, Mary Louise; N. C.; 1964, Rhodesia.

Clark, Stanley Dale; La.; 1962, Argentina.

Clark, Kathleen Hyde (Mrs. S. D.); La.; 1962, Argentina.

Clarke, Linda (J); Okla.; 1967, Nigeria.

Clarke, Sheila (J); Fla.; 1968, Nigeria.

Clement, Richard Davis; Ky.; 1965, Ecuador.

Clement, Barbara Hargrave (Mrs. R. D.); Hawaii; 1965, Ecuador.

Clemmons, William Preston; Tenn.; 1959, Italy.

Clemmons, Betty Owens (Mrs. W. P.); S. C.; 1959, Italy.

Clendinning, Byron Arthur, Jr.; Miss.; 1958, Switzerland.

Clendinning, Monte Lee McMahan (Mrs. B. A., Jr.); Miss.; 1958, Switzerland.

Clift, Annie Sue; Tenn.; 1961, Japan and Yemen.

Cline, Paul Francis (J); La.; 1966, Kenya.

Cobb, Patricia Gayle (J); Ala.; 1969, Peru.

Coffey, Lou Ellyn (J); Tex.; 1965, Gaza.

Coffman, Billy Wayne; Tex.; 1962, Dominican Republic.

Coffman, Beulah A. Fuller (Mrs. B. W.); Tenn.; 1962, Dominican Republic.

Cole, Charles William; Okla.; 1968, Indonesia.

Cole, Barbara Norwood (Mrs. C. W.); Okla.; 1968, Indonesia.

Cole, John Phillip (A); Ill.; 1969, Liberia.

Cole, Lotella Wesley (Mrs. J. P.) (A); Ill.; 1969, Liberia.

Cole, Roger Williamson; N. C.; 1966, Brazil.

Cole, Elizabeth Hamner (Mrs. R. W.); Ala.; 1966, Brazil.

Coleman, Adrian Wayne; Tex.; 1961, Liberia.

Coleman, Norma E. Tinsley (Mrs. A. W.); Tex.; 1961, Liberia.

Coleman, David Michael; Tenn.; 1968, Nigeria and Rhodesia.

Coleman, Linda Gholdston (Mrs. D. M.); Ky.; 1968, Nigeria and Rhodesia.

Coleman, Wilma Anita; Tenn.; 1962, Japan.

Collins, Joan Marie; Pa.; 1959, Tanzania.

Colston, Billy Gene; Miss.; 1967, Korea.

Colston, Geraldine Rutland (Mrs. B. G.); La.; 1967, Korea.

Colvin, James Robert (J); N. C.; 1966, Kenya.

Combs, Anita (J); Tex.; 1967, Japan.

Compere, William Arthur; Miss.; 1965, Nigeria.

Compere, Doris Meek (Mrs. W. A.); Miss.; 1965, Nigeria.

Compher, Robert Reid; Md.; 1963, Vietnam.

Compher, Priscilla Weeks (Mrs. R. R.); Ala.; 1963, Vietnam.

Compton, Alan Wesley; N. C.; 1960, Chile.

Compton, Jane Luther (Mrs. A. W.); N. C.; 1960, Chile.

Compton, Bobby Dale; N. C.; 1966, Colombia.

Compton, Peggy Lowe (Mrs. B. D.); S. C.; 1966, Colombia.

Conley, Jackie Gene; Tex.; 1964, Tanzania and Kenya.

Conley, Sally Lucas (Mrs. J. G.); Tex.; 1964, Tanzania and Kenya.

Conyers, Myrtle Marie; Mo.; 1959, Hong Kong.

Cook, Katherine Sue (J); Mo.; 1969, Hong Kong.

Cooke, Emma Ellen (A); N. C.; 1969, Lebanon.

Cooper, Jackie Bernard; S. C.; 1968, Argentina.

Cooper, Arlene Harrison (Mrs. J. B.); S. C.; 1968, Argentina.

Cooper, Nell June; N. C.; 1956, Japan.

Cooper, Sally (J); Va.; 1965, Argentina.

Corley, Barbara (J); Tex.; 1968, Thailand.

Corley, Marion Lee; Ala.; 1962, Colombia.

Corley, Evelyn Allen (Mrs. M. L.); Tex.; 1962, Colombia.

Cornwell, Phyllis Jane (J); Tenn.; 1969, Indonesia.

Corwin, William Earnest; Pa.; 1967, Indonesia.

Corwin, Elizabeth Hudman (Mrs. W. E.); Okla.; 1967, Indonesia.

Couch, John Richard; Mo.; 1958, Jordan.

Couch, Nellie J. Brooks (Mrs. J. R.); Tenn.; 1958, Jordan.

Coursey, George Claylan; Tex.; 1968, Kenya.

Coursey, Patricia Davis (Mrs. G. C.); Tex.; 1968, Kenya.

Covington, Robert Cooper; Ala.; 1960, Malaysia.

Covington, Gerry D. Smith (Mrs. R. C.); Ala.; 1960, Malaysia.

Cox, George Fountain; S. C.; 1966, Japan.

Cox, Annette Young (Mrs. G. F.); S. C.; 1966, Japan.

Cox, Theodore Olan; Ind.; 1959, Japan.

Cox, Patricia Roberts (Mrs. T. O.); Ind.; 1959, Japan.

Coy, Richard Frank; Okla.; 1960, Chile.

Coy, Betty Burleson (Mrs. R. F.); Okla.; 1960, Chile.

Crabb, Stanley, Jr.; Ky.; 1958, Italy.

Crabb, Patricia Maddux (Mrs. S., Jr.); Ky.; 1958, Italy.

Craig, Betty Jo; Tex.; 1964, Nigeria.

Craigmyle, James Phillip; Ind.; 1969, Lebanon.

Craigmyle, Doris Rogers (Mrs. J. P.); Me.; 1969, Lebanon.

Crawford, James Leroy; Okla.; 1969, Nigeria.

Crawford, Sammye Henson (Mrs. J. L.); Okla.; 1969, Nigeria.

Crider, Robert Franklin; Ala.; 1969, Spain.

Crider, Barbara Whatley (Mrs. R. F.); Ala.; 1969, Spain.

Crisp, Latithia (J); Tenn.; 1968, Switzerland.

Cromer, Ted Eugene; Okla.; 1964, Liberia.

Cromer, Dorothy Lewis (Mrs. T. E.); Ind.; 1964, Liberia.

Cruce, Billy Francis; Fla.; 1968, Uganda.

Cruce, Janice Goode (Mrs. B. F.); Ala.; 1968, Uganda.

Cruse, Darrell Dale; Ky.; 1965, Brazil.

Cruse, Elizabeth L. Brame (Mrs. D. D.); Ky.; 1965, Brazil.

Cullen, Robert Lee; Tex.; 1968, Thailand.

Cullen, Joy Souther (Mrs. R. L.); La.; 1968, Thailand.

Cumbee, Gloria (J); Mo.; 1968, Ghana.

Cummins, Alonzo Addison, Jr.; Tex.; 1965, Kenya.

Cummins, Peggy O'Bryant (Mrs. A. A., Jr.); Tex.; 1965, Kenya.

Cummins, Harold Thomas; Ark.; 1959, Pakistan and Kenya.

Cummins, Betty Noe (Mrs. H. T.); Mo.; 1959, Pakistan and Kenya.

Cunningham, Milton Emery, Jr.; Tex.; 1957, Rhodesia, Switzerland, and Zambia.

Cunningham, Barbara Schultz (Mrs. M. E., Jr.); Tex.; 1957, Rhodesia, Switzerland, and Zambia.

Dabney, C. Alexander, Jr. (J); Ill.; 1967, Brazil.
Dalton, Nancy Ellen (J); Tex.; 1966, Hong Kong.
Damon, William Jesse; Tex.; 1965, Brazil.
Damon, Roberta McBride (Mrs. W. J.); Okla.; 1965, Brazil.
Daniel, Lola Mae (A); Tex.; 1962, Taiwan.
Daniell, David Preston; Tex.; 1966, Mexico.
Daniell, Lorna Chilton (Mrs. D. P.); Okla.; 1966, Mexico.
Darnell, James Hugh; Okla.; 1969, Ivory Coast.
Darnell, Jerlene Clark (Mrs. J. H.); Ga.; 1969, Ivory Coast.
Davenport, Billy Joe; Tex.; 1963, Brazil.
Davenport, Martha Ann Reid (Mrs. B. J.); Tex.; 1963, Brazil.
Davenport, Stephen Walker; Ga.; 1963, Argentina.
Davenport, Bonnie Pearce (Mrs. S. W.); N. C.; 1963, Argentina.
Davidson, Roy Guy, Jr.; Tenn.; 1965, Malawi.
Davidson, Patsy Dodds (Mrs. R. G.); Tex.; 1965, Malawi.
Davis, Alfred Lee, Jr.; Ga.; 1958, Hong Kong.
Davis, Ellen Martin (Mrs. A. L., Jr.); Ga.; 1958, Hong Kong.
Davis, Charles Wynn; Ala.; 1957, Venezuela.
Davis, Frances E. Hughen (Mrs. C. W.); Fla.; 1957, Venezuela.
Davis, Gamaila Ann (J); Okla.; 1969, Venezuela.
Davis, Larry (J); Kan.; 1968, Nigeria.
Davis, Marva (J); Miss.; 1965, Chile.
Dawdy, M. Lucille (A); Ill.; 1964, Taiwan.
Dawson, Robert (J); Tex.; 1967, Israel.
Deakins, Sherry (J); Tenn.; 1968, Nigeria.
Deal, John Lee; Ala.; 1966, Malaysia.
Deal, Revonda Moncrief (Mrs. J. L.); Ala.; 1966, Malaysia.
Dean, Clark Earl (A); Mich.; 1967, Hong Kong.
Dean, Marjorie Perkins (Mrs. C. E.) (A); Va.; 1967, Hong Kong.
Dean, Pratt Judson; Ala.; 1966, Japan.
DeBord, Samuel Alexander; Ohio; 1956, Tanzania.
DeBord, Marthena Lindsay (Mrs. S. A.); Ky.; 1956, Tanzania.
Denmark, Iler Dean; Ga.; 1967, Nigeria.
Denmark, Mary Ann McGrady (Mrs. I. D.); Ga.; 1967, Nigeria.
Dewey, Charlotte Gay (J); Ark.; 1969, Korea.
Dickerson, Ruth; Ky.; 1963, Pakistan.
Dickman, Jean Francetta; Fla.; 1957, Gaza.
Dietrich, Vernon Lee; Tex.; 1962, Thailand.
Dietrich, Dorothy Rolen (Mrs. V. L.); Ala.; 1962, Thailand.
Dillard, Jim Claude; Ark.; 1969, Nigeria (J—1965).
Dillard, Janet Davis (Mrs. J. C.); Ky.; 1969, Nigeria (J—1965).
Ditmore, Louis Steve; Tex.; 1964, Peru.
Ditmore, Shirley Tibbs (Mrs. L. S.); Tex.; 1964, Peru.
Ditsworth, Mary Alice; Miss.; 1956, Indonesia.
Divers, John Daniel; Va.; 1965, Argentina.
Divers, Mary Evelyn Hensley (Mrs. J. D.); N. C.; 1965, Argentina.
Dixon, Curtis Leon; Okla.; 1966, Brazil.
Dixon, Bettye McCown (Mrs. C. L.); Okla.; 1966, Brazil.
Dixon, John Pedrick (A); Fla.; 1966, Guyana.
Dixon, Marjorie Floyd (Mrs. J. P.) (A); Tex.; 1966, Guyana.
Dixon, John Rodolph; S. C.; 1967, Peru.
Dixon, May Bailey (Mrs. J. R.); S. C.; 1967, Peru.
Dodson, Joyce Ann (J); Ariz.; 1969, Kenya.
Dodson, Maurice Erwin; Tex.; 1963, Mexico.
Dodson, C. LaNelle Thompson (Mrs. M. E.); Tex.; 1963, Mexico.
Dolifka, Donald Ray; Colo.; 1968, Tanzania.
Dolifka, Mary Alice Dorsey (Mrs. D. R.); Tex.; 1968, Tanzania.
Donaldson, Buck, Jr.; La.; 1959, Tanzania and Nigeria.
Donaldson, Barbara Hasty (Mrs. B., Jr.); Minn.; 1959, Tanzania and Nigeria.
Donalson, S. Dianne (J); Ga.; 1965, Jordan.
Donehoo, William Wilson; Ga.; 1959, Colombia.
Donehoo, Martha Statham (Mrs. W. W.); Ga.; 1959, Colombia.
Donley, Donald Eugene; Ill.; 1966, Ghana.
Donley, Esther Lindley (Mrs. D. E.); Ill.; 1966, Ghana.
Dorr, David Clarence; Md.; 1958, Gaza and Yemen.
Dorr, Roberta Kells (Mrs. D. C.); Minn.; 1958, Gaza and Yemen.
Dosher, Edward Price; Tex.; 1956, Nigeria.
Dosher, Mayrene Jackson (Mrs. E. P.); Tex.; 1956, Nigeria.
Dossett, M. Ellen (J); Ala.; 1965, Kenya.
Dotson, Ebbie Kilgo (Mrs. C. J.); Ala.; 1957, Rhodesia.
Dotson, Anneli Valtonen (Mrs. C. J.); Finland; 1963, Rhodesia.
Dotson, James (A); Tenn.; 1962, Okinawa.
Dotson, Gladys Longley (Mrs. J., (A); Tenn.; 1962, Okinawa.
Dotson, Lolete Marie; Ala.; 1956, Nigeria.
Douglass, Richard Bary; Okla.; 1968, Brazil.
Douglass, Marilyn Lacy (Mrs. R. B.); Okla.; 1968, Brazil.
Douthit, Thomas Eugene, Jr.; Okla.; 1963, Korea.
Douthit, Doris Watters (Mrs. T. E., Jr.); Okla.; 1963, Korea.
Doyle, Charles Donald; Tex.; 1964, Costa Rica.
Doyle, Patricia Slone (Mrs. C. D.); N. M.; 1964, Costa Rica.
Doyle, Gerald Wayne; Tex.; 1959, Ecuador.
Doyle, Mauriece Patterson (Mrs. G. W.); Tex.; 1959, Ecuador.
Dreessen, Richard Smith; Okla.; 1966, Kenya.
Dreessen, Betty Jo Covington (Mrs. R. S.); Okla.; 1966, Kenya.
Dubberly, Thomas Eugene; Fla.; 1960, Uruguay.
Dubberly, Carolyn Finch (Mrs. T. E.); Ga.; 1960, Uruguay.
Duck, Roger Glenn; Tex.; 1957, Venezuela and Colombia.
Duck, Lavonia G. Redden (Mrs. R. G.); Tex.; 1957, Venezuela and Colombia.
Dudley, Dwight Norfleet; Fla.; 1960, Japan and Okinawa.
Dudley, Anne Vinson (Mrs. D. N.); Tex.; 1960, Japan and Okinawa.
Duke, Harold Dean; Mo.; 1960, Chile and Colombia.
Duke, Barbara Cordray (Mrs. H. D.); Ga.; 1960, Chile and Columbia.
Duke, Jesse Carlton; Ga.; 1963, Lebanon.
Duke, Annie R. Cohran (Mrs. J. C.); Ga.; 1963, Lebanon.
Duke, Rita Joyce; Ala.; 1962, Taiwan.
Duncan, Marshall Gaines; Tenn.; 1964, Kenya.
Duncan, Margie Rains (Mrs. M. G.); Tenn.; 1964, Kenya.
Dunn, William Terry; Ala.; 1968, Lebanon.
Dunn, Patricia Berger (Mrs. W. T.); Md.; 1968, Lebanon.
DuPriest, Milton Eugene; Tex.; 1959, Japan.
DuPriest, Julia LaVaughn (Mrs. M. E.); Tex.; 1959, Japan.
DuVall, Wallace Larkin; Ga.; 1956, Nigeria.
DuVall, Pearl Holmes (Mrs. W. L.); La.; 1956, Nigeria.
Dyer, Audrey (A); Minn.; 1961, Nigeria.

Easton, Betty (J); Ill.; 1965, Bahamas.
Eaton, Paul Douglas; N. M.; 1969, Uganda.
Eaton, Kay Loomis (Mrs. P. D.); Fla.; 1969, Uganda.
Edgemon, Leroy Talley, Jr.; Tex.; 1968, Okinawa.
Edgemon, Anna Marie Wilson

(Mrs. L. T., Jr.); Tex.; 1968, Okinawa.
Edminster, Herbert Clyde; Tex.; 1968, Rhodesia.
Edminster, Wanda Standley (Mrs. H. C.); Tex.; 1968, Rhodesia.
Edwards, Tilman Keith; S. C.; 1957, Nigeria.
Edwards, Alice Blankenship (Mrs. T. K.); N. C.; 1957, Nigeria.
Elliott, Dennis Edward; Ala.; 1963, Thailand.
Elliott, Katherine Adcock (Mrs. D. E.); Tenn.; 1963, Thailand.
Ellis, Richard Perry; Tex.; 1969, Brazil.
Ellis, Roberta Johnson (Mrs. R. P.); Mo.; 1969, Brazil.
Ellison, Kenneth Zed; Va.; 1967, Indonesia.
Ellison, Mary Gordon (Mrs. K. Z.); Ga.; 1967, Indonesia.
Elmore, Lanny Monroe; N. C.; 1968, Uganda.
Elmore, Brenda Clay (Mrs. L. M.); N. C.; 1968, Uganda.
Emanuel, Wayne Eugene; Okla.; 1958, Japan.
Emerson, June Elizabeth (J); Ohio; 1966, Hong Kong.
Emmons, Dorothy Elizabeth; Miss.; 1959, Kenya and Tanzania.
Enge, Siegfried Gerhard; Germany; 1966, Argentina.
Enge, Donna Winch (Mrs. S. G.); Okla.; 1966, Argentina.
Engstrom, George Edwin (A); Ark.; 1967, Philippines.
Engstrom, Jeannette Faus (Mrs. G. E.) (A); Colo.; 1967, Philippines.
Erwin, Robert S. (J); Ala.; 1965, Brazil.
Erwin, Thomas (J); Tenn.; 1968, Kenya.
Estes, Joseph Richard; Ky.; 1960, Switzerland.
Estes, Helen F. Trout (Mrs. J. R.); Tenn.; 1960, Switzerland.
Eubank, Ocie Jacqueline; Ga.; 1968, Nigeria (P—1965).
Eubanks, Narbert Brannan; Tex.; 1967, Nigeria.
Eubanks, Barbara Perkins (Mrs. N. B.); Ala.; 1967, Nigeria.
Evans, Bobby Dale; Ga.; 1965, Malaysia.
Evans, Dorothy Bausum (Mrs. B. D.); China; 1965, Malaysia.
Evans, Charles Elmer; Ga.; 1958, Tanzania and Kenya.
Evans, Elizabeth Young (Mrs. C. E.); Ky.; 1958, Tanzania and Kenya.
Evans, Pat (J); S. C.; 1968, Columbia.
Evatt, Nancy Lee (J); S. C.; 1967, Ghana.
Evenson, Ronald Kenneth; Okla.; 1957, Uruguay and Spanish Publishing House.
Evenson, Mary Ann Van'tKerkhoff (Mrs. R. K.); Mich.; 1957, Uruguay and Spanish Publishing House.

Fairburn, Margaret Laurine; Miss.; 1963, Liberia.
Fallin, Margo (J); Ala.; 1968, Rhodesia.
Fanoni, Roy Henry; Ohio; 1960, Nigeria.
Fanoni, Dorothy Wittjen (Mrs. R. H.); Tex.; 1960, Nigeria.
Faris, Alvin Kent; Ohio; 1966, Brazil.
Faris, Sarah Bullock (Mrs. A. K.); N. C.; 1966, Brazil.
Farris, Theron Vernelle; Tex.; 1957, Japan.
Farris, Ruth J. Peacock (Mrs. T. V.); Tex.; 1957, Japan.
Farthing, Earl Davis; N. C.; 1960, Japan.
Farthing, Lovie C. Cashwell (Mrs. E. D.); N. C.; 1960, Japan.
Favell, Clay Hudson; N. C.; 1958, Ghana.
Favell, Jean M. Christy (Mrs. C. H.); Ark.; 1958, Ghana.
Faw, Wiley B.; Ky.; 1962, Nigeria.
Faw, Geneva Willis (Mrs. W. B.); N. C.; 1962, Nigeria.
Fenner, Charlie Worden; Tex.; 1959, Japan.
Fenner, Joy Lynn Phillips (Mrs. C. W.); Tex.; 1967, Japan.
Fields, Robert William; Ky.; 1962, Israel.
Fields, Edwina Wehrmeyer (Mrs. R. W.); Ky.; 1962, Israel.
Finley, Robert Naylor (A); Ohio; 1966, Singapore.
Finley, Portia Crothers (Mrs. R. N.) (A); Ind.; 1966, Singapore.
Fisher, Maury Jones; Ga.; 1968, Thailand.
Fisher, Ann Andrews (Mrs. M. J.); Ga.; 1968, Thailand.
Fitch, Virginia (J); Tenn.; 1968, Brazil.
Fite, M. Jo Anne (J); Calif.; 1968, Brazil.
Fitts, Marvin Eugene; Miss.; 1959, Peru.
Fitzgerald, Dean Turner, Jr.; Mo.; 1966, Jordan.
Fitzgerald, Dona Walls (Mrs. D. T.); Okla.; 1966, Jordan.
Flaugher, Shirley Ruth (J); Calif.; 1966, Hong Kong.
Fleet, Ray Thomas; Tenn.; 1964, Brazil.
Fleet, Ruby Edson (Mrs. R. T.); Ark.; 1964, Brazil.
Flewellen, Sidney Ray; La.; 1958, Ghana and Nigeria.
Flewellen, Della Guillory (Mrs. S. R.); La.; 1958, Ghana and Nigeria.
Flournoy, Houston Marshall; Ala.; 1963, Brazil.
Flournoy, La Verne Kirkland (Mrs. H. M.); Fla.; 1963, Brazil.
Floyd, John David; Ark.; 1965, Philippines.
Floyd, Helen Nutt (Mrs. J. D.); Ark.; 1965, Philippines.
Ford, Marvin Ross; N. Y.; 1964, Ecuador.
Ford, Anna Newton (Mrs. M. R.); Pa.; 1964, Ecuador.
Forehand, Mary Anne; Tex.; 1969, Spain.
Forrester, Richard Arthur; Ga.; 1963, Venezuela.
Forrester, Joan Turner (Mrs. R. A.); Ga.; 1963, Venezuela.
Foster, James Edward; Fla.; 1962, Ghana.
Foster, Sylvia Crawford (Mrs. J. E.); Okla.; 1962, Ghana.
Fowler, Roy Allen; Ga.; 1960, Brazil.
Fowler, Patricia Ross (Mrs. R. A.); Ky.; 1960, Brazil.
Fox, Calvin Leon; Ark.; 1967, Philippines.
Fox, Margaret Cotton (Mrs. C. L.); Ark.; 1967, Philippines.
Fox, Hubert Alonzo; Mo.; 1963, Thailand.
Fox, Ann Robinson (Mrs. H. A.); Mo.; 1963, Thailand.
Fox, Mary Pauline; Tex.; 1964, Nigeria.
Franks, Robert Stephenson; Okla.; 1961, Mexico.
Franks, Sallie F. Dollins (Mrs. R. S.); Ark.; 1961, Mexico.
Fray, Marion Gerome, Jr.; Mo.; 1957, Rhodesia.
Fray, Jane Dawley (Mrs. M. G., Jr.); Tex.; 1957, Rhodesia.
Frazier, Billy Ray; Tex.; 1962, Brazil.
Frazier, Annita Sibley (Mrs. B. R.); Tex.; 1962, Brazil.
Frazier, William Donaldson; Tenn.; 1956, Nigeria.
Frazier, Ina Sandidge (Mrs. W. D.); Tenn.; 1956, Nigeria.
Frederick, Lewis Wayne; Miss.; 1969, French West Indies.
Frederick, Florence Blush (Mrs. L. W.); La.; 1969, French West Indies.
Freeman, John Dungan; Tex.; 1969, Thailand.
Freeman, Nancy Davis (Mrs. J. D.); Tenn.; 1969, Thailand.
Fricke, Robert Carl; Tex.; 1965, Mexico.
Fricke, Anne Chambers (Mrs. R. C.); Ala.; 1965, Mexico.
Fried, David Daniel (P); Ark.; 1966, Nigeria.
Fried, Elsie E. Moreau (Mrs. D. D.) (P); Tex.; 1966, Nigeria.
Frierson, Leon Roy (A); Ga.; 1968, Japan.
Frierson, E. Jeanine Mays (Mrs. L. R.) (A); Ga.; 1968, Japan.
Frost, Jimmy (J); Tex.; 1967, Philippines.
Frye, Charles Ray; N. C.; 1966, Malaysia.
Frye, Katherine Bradley (Mrs. C. R.; N. C.; 1966, Malaysia.

Fuller, James Wayne; Minn.; 1963, Jordan.
Fuller, Frances Anderson (Mrs. J. W.); Ark.; 1963, Jordan.
Furr, Max Taylor; N. C.; 1967, Peru.
Furr, Joan Fisher (Mrs. M. T.); Va.; 1967, Peru.

Gaines, Jane Ellen; Ala.; 1967, Nigeria.
Gammage, Albert Walter, Jr.; Fla.; 1957, Korea.
Gammage, Nettie Oldham (Mrs. A. W., Jr.); Tenn.; 1957, Korea.
Gann, Marvin Dale; Mo.; 1964, Kenya and Tanzania.
Gann, Nelda Plank (Mrs. M. D.); Mo.; 1964, Kenya and Tanzania.
Gardner, Vera Mae; Kan.; 1962, Thailand.
Garner, Darrel Eugene; Okla.; 1969, Malawi.
Garner, Judy Brown (Mrs. D. E.); Ark.; 1969, Malawi.
Garrett, Harold Dean; Mo.; 1966, Philippines.
Garrett, Marilyn Schwenneker (Mrs. H. D.); Neb.; 1966, Philippines.
Garrett, Robert Henry; Okla.; 1964, Rhodesia.
Garrett, Eloise Sharp (Mrs. R. H.); N. M.; 1964, Rhodesia.
Garvin, Harry Burton; Tex.; 1969, Uganda.
Garvin, Doris Shott (Mrs. H. B.); Tex.; 1969, Uganda.
Gateley, Harold Grant; Ark.; 1964, Korea.
Gateley, Audrey Temple (Mrs. H. G.); Ariz.; 1964, Korea.
Gatlin, Joseph Almon, Sr.; Ga.; 1963, Tanzania.
Gatlin, Dorothea Holland (Mrs. J. A., Sr.); Ga.; 1963, Tanzania.
Gayle, James Merrill; Tex.; 1965, Vietnam.
Gayle, Margaret McMahon (Mrs. J. M.); Tex.; 1965, Vietnam.
Gayle, John Harris; D. C.; 1969, Indonesia.
Gayle, Sharon Walker (Mrs. J. H.); S. D.; 1969, Indonesia.
Geiger, James William, Jr.; Fla.; 1966, Chile.
Geiger, Mary Jo Shelton (Mrs. J. W., Jr.); Tenn.; 1966, Chile.
Gentry, Jack Leonard; N. C.; 1964, Taiwan.
Gentry, Ruby Hickman (Mrs. J. L.); N. C.; 1964, Taiwan.
Gentry, Melvin Gene; Fla.; 1964, Indonesia.
Gentry, Mary Lou Godwin (Mrs. M. G.); Fla.; 1964, Indonesia.
Gerloff, John (A); Mo.; 1964, Liberia.
Gerloff, Mary E. Hooks (Mrs. J.) (A); Miss.; 1964, Liberia.
Geron, Cary Ann (J); Tex.; 1965, Switzerland.
Giannetta, Adolfo Amelio; Italy; 1960, Brazil.
Giannetta, Lidia Acacia (Mrs. A.); Italy; 1960, Brazil.
Gibson, James Edward; Tenn.; 1969, East Africa.
Gibson, Harriett Dianne Dyer; Tenn.; 1969, East Africa.
Gilbert, Charles Herman; Neb.; 1963, Mexico.
Gilbert, Ruth Holman (Mrs. C. H.); Okla.; 1963, Mexico.
Gilbert, James Pascal; Miss.; 1957, Ecuador.
Gilbert, Dorothy Smith (Mrs. J. P.); Tenn.; 1957, Ecuador.
Giles, James Edwin; Tex.; 1957, Colombia.
Giles, Mary Nell Morrison (Mrs. J. E.); Tex.; 1957, Colombia.
Gillham, Moudy Frank; Tex.; 1957, Pakistan and Japan.
Gillham, Hazel Holmes (Mrs. M. F.); Tex.; 1957, Pakistan and Japan.
Gilliland, Oliver Earl, Jr.; Okla.; 1964, Indonesia.
Gilliland, Peggy Workman (Mrs. O. E., Jr.); S. C.; 1964, Indonesia.
Gilmore, Billy Owen; Tex.; 1962, Brazil.
Gilmore, Lee Ann Cole (Mrs. B. O.); Ark.; 1962, Brazil.
Gilmore, Helen Elizabeth; Tenn.; 1963, Tanzania and Kenya.
Gilstrap, Robert Edward, Sr.; Ga.; 1961, Guatemala.
Gilstrap, Hazel E. Ditsworth (Mrs. R. E., Sr.); Miss.; 1961, Guatemala.
Givens, Sistie Virginia; Okla.; 1958, Brazil.
Gladen, Van; Tex.; 1956, Mexico.
Gladen, Alma Ruth Franks (Mrs. V.); Ark.; 1956, Mexico.
Glass, Ernest Wilson; N. C.; 1956, Malaysia.
Glass, Charlotte M. Magruder (Mrs. E. W.); Mo.; 1956, Malaysia.
Glenn, Doris Lee (J); Tex.; 1969, Kenya.
Goatcher, Earl Gene; Ark.; 1962, Thailand.
Goatcher, Joann Horton (Mrs. E. G.); Tex.; 1962, Thailand.
Goble, Harry Anderson; N. C.; 1960, Guam.
Goble, Doris Anne Cash (Mrs. H. A.); N. C.; 1960, Guam.
Godwin, Colon Leo; N. C.; 1958, Ghana.
Godwin, Carolyn Smith (Mrs. C. L.); N. C.; 1958, Ghana.
Golden, Cecil Hayman; Ala.; 1957, Honduras.
Golden, Ina Claire Mabry (Mrs. C. H.); Ala.; 1957, Honduras.
Golston, Jerold Evan; Ohio; 1968, Brazil.
Golston, Verla Roark (Mrs. J. E.); Mo.; 1968, Brazil.
Goodwin, James Garland, Jr.; N. C.; 1956, Korea.
Goodwin, June Batson (Mrs. J. G., Jr.); S. C.; 1956, Korea.
Goodyear, Nancy Lee (J); N. M.; 1969, Bahamas.
Graham, Hillery Clifford (A); La.; 1969, Guyana.
Graham, Helen Ashford (Mrs. H. C.) (A); La.; 1969, Guyana.
Graham, Joe Billy; Tenn.; 1962, Taiwan.
Graham, Elizabeth White (Mrs. J. B.); Tenn.; 1962, Taiwan.
Graham, Thomas Wayne; Fla.; 1967, Japan.
Graham, Dot Easterlin (Mrs. T. W.); S. C.; 1967, Japan.
Grant, Richard Blanchard; Tex.; 1968, Brazil.
Grant, Leo Merle Ryden (Mrs. R. B.); Tex.; 1968, Brazil.
Graves, Sally Kate (J); Tex; 1967, Paraguay.
Gray, John Robert; Ala.; 1959, Nigeria.
Gray, Grace Denney (Mrs. J. R.); Ky.; 1959, Nigeria.
Gray, William Hawthorne, Jr.; Tex.; 1960, Mexico.
Gray, Nadine Sikes (Mrs. W. H., Jr.); Tex.; 1960, Mexico.
Green, Addison Jack; La.; 1965, Brazil.
Green, Gypsy Williams (Mrs. A. J.); La.; 1965, Brazil.
Green, James Henry; La.; 1964, Mexico.
Green, Barbara Hanscom (Mrs. J. H.); Ill.; 1964, Mexico.
Green, Thomas Stuart; Tex.; 1958, Paraguay and Argentina.
Green, Anita Newell (Mrs. T. S.); Tex.; 1958, Paraguay and Argentina.
Green, Trina Gay (J); Tex.; 1966, Chile.
Green, Urban Luther; Okla.; 1963, Nigeria.
Green, Loretta Rust (Mrs. U. L.); Okla.; 1963, Nigeria.
Greene, James Young; N. C.; 1961, Korea.
Greene, Judith Church (Mrs. J. Y.); N. C.; 1961, Korea.
Greene, Robert Francis; N. C.; 1969, Taiwan.
Greene, Mary Bear (Mrs. R. F.); Ohio; 1969, Taiwan.
Greene, Victor Adair; Tenn.; 1962, Philippines.
Greene, Mariella Miller (Mrs. V. A.); S. C.; 1962, Philippines.
Greenway, Zora Frances; Tex.; 1959, Rhodesia and Nigeria.
Greenwood, Richard Ray; Mo.; 1962, Guatemala.
Greenwood, Lahoma Mason (Mrs. R. R.); Tex.; 1962, Guatemala.
Greer, William Bryan (A); Tex.; 1966, Nigeria.
Greer, Margaret Hamilton (Mrs. W. B.) (A); Tenn.; 1966, Nigeria.
Gregory, Lester Laverne; Mo.; 1958, Costa Rica.
Gregory, Betty Good (Mrs. L. L.); Mo.; 1958, Costa Rica.

Griffin, Clarence O'Neal; S. C.; 1960, Philippines and Indonesia.
Griffin, Ruth Putnam (Mrs. C. O.); N. C.; 1960, Philippines and Indonesia.
Griffin, Harry Dee; Okla.; 1962, Japan.
Griffin, Barbara Jo Terry (Mrs. H. D.); Okla.; 1962, Japan.
Griggs, John Paul; Tex.; 1962, Rhodesia.
Griggs, Florence Sanders (Mrs. J. P.); Ky.; 1962, Rhodesia.
Grindstaff, Wilmer Ernest (A); Mo.; 1968, Israel.
Grindstaff, Maxine Carnett (Mrs. W. E.) (A); Mo.; 1968, Israel.
Grisham, Reva Jeanine (J); Tex.; 1969, Jordan.
Groce, Verl Lynn; Mo.; 1969, Ethiopia (J—1966, Tanzania).
Groce, Suzanne Knapp (Mrs. V. L.); Fla.; 1969, Ethiopia.
Groseclose, Leslie David (J); W. Va.; 1969, Israel.
Grossman, Paul Henry; Ind.; 1965, Liberia.
Grossman, Peggy Chamberlin (Mrs. P. H.); Ky.; 1965, Liberia.
Grubbs, William Eugene; Ala.; 1958; Indonesia and Philippines.
Grubbs, Phyllis Coffman (Mrs. W. E.); Kan.; 1958; Indonesia and Philippines.
Guerry, Judy (J); S. C.; 1968, Honduras.
Guess, William Jackson (A); Fla.; 1964, Germany.
Guess, Barbara Cross (Mrs. W. J.) (A); Fla.; 1964, Germany.
Guynes, Judith Lorrain (J); Tex.; 1966, Chile.
Gwynn, Orman Wayne; Tex.; 1964, Brazil.
Gwynn, Elizabeth Folkes (Mrs. O. W.); Tex.; 1964, Brazil.

Hagstrom, Annie Olivia; Finland; 1956, Jordan and Ghana.
Haile, Patricia Ann (P); S. C.; 1968, Gaza.
Hailey, William Morgan, Sr.; Tex.; 1967, Indonesia.
Hailey, Christine Wilson (Mrs. W. M., Sr.); Va.; 1967, Indonesia.
Hale, Broadus David; Okla.; 1967, Brazil.
Hale, Margaret Owens (Mrs. B. D.); La.; 1967, Brazil.
Hale, Sandra Fern (J); Mo.; 1967, Chile.
Hale, Signard Dennis; Ga.; 1965, Spain.
Hale, Judith Greene (Mrs. S. D.); Tenn.; 1965, Spain.
Hall, Adrian (J); Ga.; 1968, Ghana.
Hall, Diane (J); Va.; 1968, Vietnam.
Hall, Laqueta Joy; Ky.; 1963, Nigeria.
Hall, Robert Jean; Calif.; 1963, Nigeria.
Hall, Martha Weber (Mrs. R. J.); Mo.; 1963, Nigeria.
Hall, Ruth Ann; Tenn.; 1967, Nigeria.
Hamilton, Todd Condell (A); Ohio; 1964, Philippines.
Hamilton, Doris Winn (Mrs. T. C.) (A); Tex.; 1964, Philippines.
Hammett, John Hunter; Tex.; 1959, Taiwan.
Hammett, Patsy Price (Mrs. J. H.); Tex.; 1959, Taiwan.
Hampton, James Edward; Ark.; 1956, Kenya and Tanzania.
Hampton, Gena Ledbetter (Mrs. J. E.); Ark.; 1956, Kenya and Tanzania.
Hampton, Robert Alba; Mo.; 1965, Brazil.
Hampton, Wilma Rodenberg (Mrs. R. A.); Mo.; 1965, Brazil.
Hamrick, Howard; Miss.; 1957, Indonesia.
Hamrick, Betty J. Spiers (Mrs. H.); Miss.; 1957, Indonesia.
Hancock, Glenda Sue (J); Mo.; 1969, Ecuador.
Hancock, Ruth Elaine; Va.; 1959, Hong Kong.
Hancox, Jack Donald; Tenn.; 1959, France and Ivory Coast.
Hancox, Doris White (Mrs. J. D.); Tenn.; 1959, France and Ivory Coast.
Harbin, Lonnie Byron; Ala.; 1969, Brazil.
Harbin, Dora Dunkley (Mrs. L. B.); Miss.; 1969, Brazil.
Harbuck, George Clifton, Jr.; Ga.; 1969, Paraguay.
Harbuck, Patricia Barbour (Mrs. G. C., Jr.); Va.; 1969, Paraguay.
Hardison, Wesley Aurel; Ky.; 1960, Philippines.
Hardison, Francis L. Leathers (Mrs. W. A.); Ky.; 1960, Philippines.
Hardister, Graydon Bridges; Ark.; 1965, Jordan.
Hardister, Betty Williams (Mrs. G. B.); Ark.; 1965, Jordan.
Hardwick, Ellis Britt; Ga.; 1969, Nigeria.
Hardwick, Marilee Ridley (Mrs. E. B.); Ga.; 1969, Nigeria.
Hardy, Lawrence Parker (A); Ga.; 1967, Liberia.
Hardy, Alice Boaen (Mrs. L. P.) (A); Ga.; 1967, Liberia.
Hardy, Robert Dean; Ky.; 1958, Japan.
Hargrove, Vivian Gail (J); Mo.; 1969, Ghana.
Harkins, Thomas Franklin; Ala.; 1967, Korea.
Harkins, Janie Meador (Mrs. T. F.); S. C.; 1967, Korea.
Harlan, Ronald Dean; Ind.; 1964, Venezuela.
Harlan, Katie McMahan (Mrs. R. D.); N. C.; 1964, Venezuela.
Harper, Eleanor (J); Ky.; 1965, Nigeria.
Harper, Harry Julian, Jr.; Md.; 1968, Colombia.
Harper, Donna Compton (Mrs. H. J., Jr.); Ohio; 1968, Colombia.
Harper, Hilda (J); Miss.; 1968, Peru.
Harrell, Ralph Webster; N. C.; 1958, Tanzania and Kenya.
Harrell, Rosaline Knott (Mrs. R. W.); N. C.; 1958, Tanzania and Kenya.
Harris, Mary Emogene; Miss.; 1960, Nigeria.
Harrison, Sharon (J); Tex.; 1968, Tanzania.
Harrod, J D; Ky.; 1966, Brazil.
Harrod, Donice McCormick (Mrs. J D); S. C.; 1966, Brazil.
Hart, Betty Louise; La.; 1964, Chile.
Hart, D. Carolyn (J); N. C.; 1967, Gaza.
Hart, Sherman Clifton, Jr. (A); Ala.; 1967, Nigeria.
Hart, Joyce Hurst (Mrs. S. C., Jr.) (A); Fla.; 1967, Nigeria.
Hartfield, Jimmy Jack; Miss., 1960, Mexico.
Hartfield, Susie Armstrong (Mrs. J. J.); Miss.; 1960, Mexico.
Harvey, Charles Ernest; Fla.; 1961, Brazil.
Harvey, Janice Thompson (Mrs. C. E.); Fla.; 1961, Brazil.
Harvey, Charlotte Roena (J); Calif.; 1969, Thailand.
Harvey, Muerner Strasmore (A); Tex.; 1968, Hong Kong.
Harvey, Billy Bonifield (Mrs. M. S.) (A); Okla.; 1968, Hong Kong.
Harvill, James Thomas; Ark.; 1961, Mexico.
Harvill, Marie C. Crum (Mrs. J. T.); Ark.; 1961, Mexico.
Hashman, William Lewis; Calif.; 1964, Japan.
Hashman, Jeani M. Jackson (Mrs. W. L.); Wash.; 1964, Japan.
Hawkins, E. Henry (J); Ala.; 1965, Venezuela.
Hawkins, Franklin Dean; S. C.; 1966, Brazil.
Hawkins, Patricia McCormick (Mrs. F. D.); S. C.; 1966, Brazil.
Hawkins, James Washburn (A); Ga.; 1968, Brazil.
Hawkins, Frances Cone (Mrs. J. W.) (A); Ga.; 1968, Brazil.
Hayes, Charles Kenneth; Ky.; 1964, Japan.
Hayes, June C. Snider (Mrs. C. K.); Ky.; 1964, Japan.
Hayes, Herman Paul; La.; 1959, Vietnam.
Hayes, Dottie Primeaux (Mrs. H. P.); La.; 1959, Vietnam.
Haylock, Arthur Ray; Fla.; 1960, Honduras.
Haylock, Martha G. Higdon (Mrs. A. R.); Ala.; 1960, Honduras.
Haynes, Henry Powell III; Okla.; 1962, Venezuela.

Haynes, Betty Bankston (Mrs. H. P. III); Okla.; 1962, Venezuela.
Haynes, Pat (J); Tenn.; 1968, Tanzania.
Heiss, Donald Raymond; Ohio; 1957, Japan.
Heiss, Joyce Sheckler (Mrs. D. R.); Ohio; 1957, Japan.
Hellinger, Richard Harris (A); Fla.; 1968, India.
Hellinger, Frances Syfrett (Mrs. R. H.) (A); Fla.; 1968, India.
Helm, Charles W. (J); Mo.; 1965, Peru.
Helton, Yvonne Erma (J); Kan.; 1969, Dominican Republic.
Henderson, Richard Charles; Wash.; 1963, Ghana and Philippines.
Henderson, Katherine V. Stough (Mrs. R. C.); Ill.; 1963, Ghana and Philippines.
Henderson, William Glenn (A); Ky.; 1967, Liberia.
Henderson, Margery Mathis (Mrs. W. G.) (A); Ky.; 1967, Liberia.
Henderson, William Griffin (A); Tenn.; 1969, Hong Kong.
Henderson, Clarice Logan (Mrs. W. G.) (A); Va.; 1969, Hong Kong.
Henderson, Willie Guy; Miss.; 1958, Korea.
Henderson, Lois Robertson (Mrs. W. G.); Tex.; 1958, Korea.
Hendrick, Robert Mack; W. Va.; 1968, Argentina.
Hendrick, Joanne Tyre (Mrs. R. M.); Fla.; 1968, Argentina.
Hensley, Robert Carroll; N. C.; 1963, Bahamas.
Hensley, Betty Jo Carroll (Mrs. R. C.); N. C.; 1963, Bahamas.
Hensley, Robert Lee; Tex.; 1964, Brazil.
Hensley, Farolyn Taylor (Mrs. R. L.); N. Y.; 1964, Brazil.
Hensley, Verlene Marie (J); Mo.; 1966, Philippines.
Henson, Carol June; Tenn.; 1960, Chile.
Henson, Louie Gene; S. C.; 1963, Brazil.
Henson, Exie Vee Wilde (Mrs. L. G.); N. C.; 1963, Brazil.
Herndon, Glenn Elmer; Ga.; 1968, Colombia.
Herndon, Patricia Vaughters (Mrs. G. E.); Ga.; 1968, Colombia.
Herndon, John Melvin; Ala.; 1964, Portugal.
Herndon, Norma Headrick (Mrs. J. M.); Ala.; 1964, Portugal.
Herrell, Sharon Leverna (J); Tenn.; 1967, Japan.
Herrin, Manget (A); Ga.; 1969, Guyana.
Herrin, Elaine Jones (Mrs. M.) (A); Calif.; 1969, Guyana.
Herrington, Glen Dale; La.; 1963, Malaysia.
Herrington, Mary Ann Johnson (Mrs. G. D.); Tex.; 1963, Malaysia.
Hersey, Ramona (J); D. C.; 1968, Bahamas.
Hester, James Edward; Tex., 1962, Italy.
Hester, Ethel Tackett (Mrs. J. E.); Tex.; 1962, Italy.
Hibbard, Hazeldean; Ky.; 1956, Nigeria.
Hickey, Glenn Elliot; Ark.; 1964, Brazil.
Hickey, Dorothy Thomerson (Mrs. G. E.); Ark.; 1964, Brazil.
Hickman, L. Diane (J); Tex.; 1967, Japan.
Hicks, Terry Allen; Tex.; 1963, Nigeria.
Hicks, Wanda L. Gatlin (Mrs. T. A.); Ala.; 1963, Nigeria.
Hill, J. Allen (J); Ala.; 1968, Philippines.
Hill, Betty Jean (J); Fla.; 1967, Liberia.
Hill, David Leslie; Kan.; 1963, Philippines.
Hill, Janet Nabors (Mrs. D. L.); Neb.; 1963, Philippines.
Hill, James McDonald (A); Tenn.; 1968, Kenya.
Hill, Elinor Easley (Mrs. J. M.) (A); Ark.; 1968, Kenya.
Hill, Regional Adolphus; S. C.; 1966, Trinidad.
Hill, Mary Ellen Kemp (Mrs. R. A.); S. C.; 1966, Trinidad.
Hill, Thomas Willard; S. C.; 1956, Costa Rica and Spanish Publishing House.
Hill, Cornice Winter (Mrs. T. W.); Miss.; 1956, Costa Rica and Spanish Publishing House.
Hill, William Dennis (J); N. C.; 1967, Philippines.
Hilliard, Russell Boston; Ga.; 1957, Spain.
Hilliard, Edith Bassett (Mrs. R. B.); Ga.; 1957, Spain.
Hilton, Sandra Karen (J); Tex.; 1969, Guyana.
Hinkle, John (J); Tenn.; 1968, Malawi.
Hinton, Anna Jean; Ky.; 1956, Brazil.
Hintze, William Robert; Tex.; 1960, Ecuador.
Hintze, Barbara R. Laughman (Mrs. W. R.); Tex.; 1960, Ecuador.
Hix, Glenn Luther; N. C.; 1957, Taiwan.
Hix, Mabel Green (Mrs. G. L.); Ala.; 1957, Taiwan.
Hobart, Mary Louise; Mo.; 1959, Tanzania.
Hobbs, Jerry; Okla.; 1957, Thailand.
Hobbs, Darline Anderson (Mrs. J.); Okla.; 1957, Thailand.
Hobson, Charles Milton; Tex.; 1963, Colombia and Paraguay.
Hobson, Wanda Nave (Mrs. C. M.); Ky.; 1963, Colombia and Paraguay.
Hocum, Merna Jean; Iowa; 1956, Brazil and Guyana.
Hodges, Betty Claudine; Miss.; 1957, Chile.
Hodges, Ruford Burton, Jr.; S. C.; 1967, Korea.
Hodges, Jo Morris (Mrs. R. B.); Ala.; 1967, Korea.
Hodges, Rufus Dean, Jr.; Ga.; 1958, Nigeria.
Hodges, Irene Chavous (Mrs. R. D.); Ga.; 1958, Nigeria.
Hogg, Gayle Alonzo (A); Tex.; 1969, Trinidad.
Hogg, Sylvia Dickey (Mrs. G. A.) (A); Tex.; 1969, Trinidad.
Hoglen, Wilburn Cordell; N. C.; 1969, Venezuela.
Hoglen, Betty Miller (Mrs. W. C.); Tenn.; 1969, Venezuela.
Hogue, LeRoy Benjamin; Okla.; 1966, Taiwan.
Hogue, Janell Ohagan (Mrs. L. B.); Okla.; 1966, Taiwan.
Holcomb, Sari Powell (Mrs. Omer) (A); Okla.; 1964, Tanzania.
Holder, Vivian Dell; La.; 1968, Switzerland.
Holifield, Robert Ames; Miss., 1962, Italy.
Holifield, Flora Cole (Mrs. R. A.); Miss.; 1962, Italy.
Holland, Robert Miller; Ky.; 1969, Japan.
Holland, Kathleen Thompson (Mrs. R. M.); Ky.; 1969, Japan.
Holley, Herbert Howard; Ala.; 1956, Malaysia.
Holley, Frances Sayers (Mrs. H. H.); Ala.; 1956, Malaysia.
Holloway, Billy Wayne; La.; 1963, Uganda and Kenya.
Holloway, Jane Strauss (Mrs. B. W.); N. C.; 1963, Uganda and Kenya.
Holmes, Robert Eugene (J); Miss.; 1966, Argentina.
Honjo, Ralph Satoshi; Hawaii; 1966, Japan.
Honjo, Irene Harada (Mrs. R. S.); Hawaii; 1966, Japan.
Hood, Alton Lee; N. C.; 1964, Thailand.
Hood, Olga McLean (Mrs. A. L.); Canada; 1964, Thailand.
Hooper, Dale Grey; N. C.; 1959, Kenya.
Hooper, Beulah Johnson (Mrs. D. G.); Va.; 1959, Kenya
Hooper, Frank Arthur III; Ga.; 1957, Israel.
Hooper, Marjorie Foster (Mrs. F. A. III); Tex.; 1957, Israel.
Hooten, Jimmie Dee; Tex.; 1961. Kenya and Uganda.
Hooten, Peggy Ratcliff (Mrs. J. D.); Tex.; 1961 Kenya and Uganda
Hope, Benjamin Edgar; Ark.; 1967, Brazil.
Hope, Berdie Lou Moose (Mrs. B. E.); Okla.; 1967, Brazil.
Hopkins, Charles Turner; Ark.; 1962, Nigeria.
Hopkins, Carlene Densford (Mrs. C. T.); Tenn.; 1962, Nigeria.

Hopper, John David; La.; 1965, Switzerland.
Hopper, Jo Ann Wells (Mrs. J. D.); Okla.; 1965, Switzerland.
Hornbuckle, Linda Ellen (J); Tex.; 1966, Switzerland.
Horton, Anita Jane (J); Ala.; 1968, Brazil.
Houser, James Lawrence; Pa.; 1964, Kenya.
Houser, Molly Rogers (Mrs. J. L.); Tex.; 1964, Kenya.
Hovde, John Howard (A); Wis.; 1966, Liberia.
Hovde, Carole J. Shelton (Mrs. J. H.) (A); Okla.; 1966, Liberia.
Howle, David Blake; Ala.; 1963, Korea.
Howle, Carole Moore (Mrs. D. B.); Ala.; 1963, Korea.
Hubbard, Kenneth Cordell; Tenn.; 1969, Kenya.
Hubbard, Faye Walker (Mrs. K. C.); Tenn; 1969, Kenya.
Hubbard, Mary Anna (J); Okla.; 1968, Rhodesia.
Huckaby, Samuel Eugene; Ga.; 1969, Chile.
Huckaby, Janice Adams (Mrs. S. E.); Ga.; 1969, Chile.
Hudson, James Vassar, Jr.; Miss.; 1967, Korea.
Hudson, Linda Pickett (Mrs. J. V., Jr.); La.; 1967, Korea.
Huey, F B, Jr.; Tex.; 1960, Brazil.
Huey, Nonna L. Turner (Mrs. F B, Jr.); Tex.; 1960, Brazil.
Hughes, Mary Fran (J); D. C.; 1968, Hong Kong.
Hughes, Royce Brown; Tenn.; 1963, Brazil and Leeward Islands.
Hughes, Bobbie Stephens (Mrs. R. B.); Tenn.; 1963, Brazil and Leeward Islands.
Hull, Wendell Ray; Tex.; 1959, Kenya.
Hull, Dorothy Edwards (Mrs. W. R.); Mo.; 1959, Kenya.
Humphries, James Fagg (A); Ga.; 1966, Vietnam.
Humphries, Mary Lookingbill (Mrs. J. F.) (A); Ark.; 1966, Vietnam.
Hunt, Betty Jane; Ala.; 1957, Korea.
Hunt, Bob Wright; Ala.; 1961, Taiwan.
Hunt, Rosalie Hall (Mrs. B. W.); Hawaii; 1961, Taiwan.
Hurst, Hawthorne Hampton; Tenn.; 1965, Nigeria.
Hurst, Ramona Smith (Mrs. H. H.); Tenn.; 1965, Nigeria.
Huskison, Edna (J); Miss.; 1968, Kenya.
Hutcherson, Sylvia Lee (J); Tex.; 1969, Indonesia.
Hutson, Barney Rhodes; Tex.; 1966, Argentina.
Hutson, Clara Massey (Mrs. B. R.); Tex.; 1966, Argentina.
Hutto, Diane Lindsey (J); S. C.; 1969, Kenya.

Ichter, William Harold; Pa.; 1956, Brazil.
Ichter, Jerry Catron (Mrs. W. H.); La.; 1956, Brazil.
Ingouf, John Edward; La.; 1960, Indonesia.
Ingouf, Glenn Green (Mrs. J. E.); Ala.; 1960, Indonesia.
Ingram, Lawrence David; Ohio; 1969, Hong Kong.
Ingram, Shirley Campbell (Mrs. L. D.); Fla.; 1969, Hong Kong.
Irby, Rodney Ray; Tex.; 1969, Chile.
Irby, Virginia Caraway (Mrs. R. R.); Tex.; 1969, Chile.

Jacks, Hal Kenneth; S. C.; 1965, Indonesia.
Jacks, Carol Arnett (Mrs. H. K.); Ala.; 1965, Indonesia.
Jackson, Shirley Louise; Ark.; 1956, Brazil.
Jacobs, John Irvin (A); Ohio; 1969, Guyana.
Jacobs, Jean Holley (Mrs. J. I.) (A); Miss.; 1969, Guyana.
James, Lynda Faye (J); Mo.; 1969, Ghana.
James, Samuel McFall; N. C.; 1962, Hong Kong and Vietnam.
James, Rachel Kerr (Mrs. S. M.); N. C.; 1962, Hong Kong and Vietnam.
Janes, Isaac Grundy, Jr.; Ky.; 1966, Chile.
Janes, Jean Bell (Mrs. I. G., Jr.); Ky.; 1966, Chile.
Jarrett, Wilma Catherine (J); Ga.; 1967, Ecuador.
Jester, David Linville; Tanzania; 1957, Nigeria.
Jester, Marie Hans (Mrs. D. L.); Ind.; 1957, Nigeria.
Jimmerson, Joseph Andrew; Ga.; 1959, Indonesia and Hong Kong.
Jimmerson, Iris Salter (Mrs. J. A.); Ga.; 1959, Indonesia and Hong Kong.
Johnson, Charles (J); Ark.; 1968, Tanzania.
Johnson, Daniel Calhoun; N. C.; 1958, Chile.
Johnson, Sarah Kennedy (Mrs. D. C.); N. C.; 1958, Chile.
Johnson, Glen Lavern; Mo.; 1964, Argentina.
Johnson, Rayella Bounds (Mrs. G. L.); Mo., 1964, Argentina.
Johnson, Margaret Anita; Tex.; 1969, Brazil.
Johnson, Mary Kay (J); Tex.; 1967, Vietnam.
Johnson, Patterson Smith; S. C.; 1959, Pakistan.
Johnson, Betty Oglesby (Mrs. P. S.); S. C.; 1959, Pakistan.
Johnson, Paul Burke; Miss.; 1968, Philippines.
Johnson, Vera Rose (Mrs. P. B.); N. C.; 1968, Philippines.
Johnson, Robert Elton, Jr.; Ala.; 1965, Brazil.
Johnson, Joy Emery (Mrs. R. E., Jr.); Mo.; 1965, Brazil.
Johnson, Sharon Elaine (J); Tex.; 1966, Japan.
Johnston, James David; Ky.; 1958, Nigeria.
Johnston, Marie Havens (Mrs. J. D.); La.; 1958, Nigeria.
Johnston, Juanita; Ala.; 1956, Thailand.
Jolley, Earl Edwin; La.; 1959, Argentina.
Jolley, Veta Cook (Mrs. E. E.); Tex.; 1959, Argentina.
Jones, Alyce (J); Ark.; 1968, Liberia.
Jones, Archie Valejo; N. C.; 1959, Ecuador.
Jones, Julia Hough (Mrs. A. V.); N. C.; 1959, Ecuador.
Jones, Bobby Leland; Okla.; 1967, Indonesia.
Jones, Mary Jo Carriker (Mrs. B. L.); Okla.; 1967, Indonesia.
Jones, Delilah Elaine; Ill.; 1960, Nigeria.
Jones, Don Cleo; Tex.; 1956, Korea.
Jones, Juanita Wheelock (Mrs. D. C.); Okla.; 1956, Korea.
Jones, Donald William; Ohio; 1968, Pakistan.
Jones, Helen Brandon (Mrs. D. W.); Ky.; 1968, Pakistan.
Jones, Kay Frances (J); Miss.; 1967, Chile.
Jones, Kenneth Earl (J); N. M.; 1969, Brazil.
Jones, Mack Prentiss; Miss.; 1963, Paraguay and Uruguay.
Jones, Marie Martin (Mrs. M. P.); Miss.; 1963, Paraguay and Uruguay.
Jones, Thomas Arthur, Sr.; Ga.; 1968, Kenya.
Jones, Nancy Kirk (Mrs. T. A., Sr.); Ga.; 1968, Kenya.
Jones. William Herschel, Jr.; Ky.; 1964, Zambia.
Jones, Dorothy Jean Aly (Mrs. W. H.); Ga.; 1964, Zambia.
Juergens, Jerry Edward; Okla.; 1969, Hong Kong.
Juergens, Mary Lester (Mrs. J. E.); Okla.; 1969, Hong Kong.

Kammerdiener, Donald Ralph; Okla.; 1962, Colombia.
Kammerdiener, Meredith Ruch (Mrs. D. R.); Mo.; 1962, Colombia.
Keaton, Larry N. (J); Ohio; 1965, Israel.
Keith, Billy Phagan; Okla.; 1961, Japan.
Keith, Mona Lou Pigg (Mrs. B. P.); Tex.; 1961, Japan.
Kelley, Pam (J); S. C.; 1968, Rhodesia.
Kelley, Sandra (J); N. C.; 1968, Liberia.
Key, Jerry Stanley; Okla.; 1959, Brazil.
Key, Johnnie Johnson (Mrs. J. S.); Tex.; 1959, Brazil.

Keyes, Leslie Gordon; La.; 1958, Honduras.
Keyes, Naomi Lucas (Mrs. L. G.); Mo.; 1958, Honduras.
Kidd, Jesse Lee (A); Ark.; 1969, Brazil.
Kidd, Wilma Gemmell (Mrs. J. L.) (A); Neb.; 1963, Brazil.
Kidd, Wheeler; Ala.; 1965, Malaysia.
Kidd, Marie Lansdell (Mrs. W.); Ala.; 1965, Malaysia.
Kilpatrick, Franklin Arnold; Tex.; 1969, Zambia.
Kilpatrick, Paula Smith (Mrs. F. A.); Tex.; 1969, Zambia.
Kimbrough, Clint; Fla.; 1967, Brazil.
Kimbrough, Dolores Hancock (Mrs. C.); S. C.; 1967, Brazil.
Kimler, Eugene Brownie, Jr.; Mexico; 1958, Venezuela.
Kimler, Eugene Brownie, Jr.; Mexico; 1958, Venezuela.
Kimler, Eva Nell Turner (Mrs. E. B., Jr.); Tex.; 1958, Venezuela.
King, David Warren; Mich.; 1959, Lebanon.
King, Maxine Steele (Mrs. D. W.); Tex.; 1959, Lebanon.
King, Ernest Lawrence, Jr.; Va.; 1959, Indonesia.
King, Dorothea DeWitt (Mrs. E. L., Jr.); Iowa; 1959, Indonesia.
King, Eunice Wyona; Ky.; 1959, Nigeria.
King, Julian Franklin; Tenn.; 1969, Brazil.
King, Janice Hixon (Mrs. J. F.); Calif.; 1969, Brazil.
Kingsley, Gene Eulgar; Ala.; 1960, Malawi.
Kingsley, Beverly Geisendorff (Mrs. G. E.); Tex.; 1960, Malawi.
Kinney, Richard Howard (A); Pa.; 1967, Switzerland.
Kinney, Daisy Davis (Mrs. R. H.) (A); S. C.; 1967, Switzerland.
Kirby, Donna Kay; Ga.; 1966, Hong Kong.
Kirk, Sally Sue; Okla.; 1969, Yemen.
Kirkendall, James Finch; Mo.; 1962, Lebanon.
Kirkendall, Elizabeth Pittman (Mrs. J. F.); Okla.; 1962, Lebanon.
Kirkland, Donald; Fla.; 1968, Ghana.
Kirkland, Shirley McQuinn (Mrs. D.); Ga.; 1968, Ghana.
Kirksey, Marilois; Tex.; 1963, Brazil.
Kite, Billy O'Neal; Ala.; 1968, Zambia.
Kite, Thelma Olney (Mrs. B. O.); Iowa; 1968, Zambia.
Knapp, Douglas M.; Fla.; 1963, Tanzania.
Knapp, Evelyn J. Brizzi (Mrs. D. M.); Fla.; 1963, Tanzania.
Kneisel, Harvey John, Jr.; Okla.; 1963, Jamaica and Guyana.
Kneisel, Charlene Lewis (Mrs. H. J., Jr.); Okla.; 1963, Jamaica and Guyana.
Knight, Frances Carol; Tex.; 1961, Nigeria.
Knight, Howard Carsie; N. C.; 1959, Argentina.
Knight, Joyce Wheeler (Mrs. H. C.); Fla.; 1959, Argentina.
Kortkamp, Paula Suzanne; Ill.; 1962, Mexico.
Krause, Lewis Marvin; Okla.; 1962, Germany.
Krause, Adeline Pitney (Mrs. L. M.); Mo.; 1962, Germany.
Kruschwitz, Billy (J); Ky.; 1968, Nigeria.
Kube, Ruth Peyton; Va.; 1957, Nigeria.

Lacey, Robert Hiram; N. M.; 1967, Kenya.
Lacey, Evelyn Trammell (Mrs. R. H.); Tex.; 1967, Kenya.
Laffoon, Robert Glenn; Mo.; 1965, Tanzania.
Laffoon, Hannah Baker (Mrs. R. G.); Mo., 1965, Tanzania.
LaGrone, Charles Edwin; Tex.; 1967, Argentina.
LaGrone, Cynthia Ivey (Mrs. C. E.); Tex.; 1967, Argentina.
Laing, Donald Kersey; Okla.; 1967, Brazil.
Laing, Barbara Clark (Mrs. D. K.); Tex.; 1967, Brazil.
Laird, Roy (A); Miss., 1962, Philippines.
Laird, Anna E. Lewis (Mrs. R.) (A); Miss.; 1962, Philippines.
Lambert, Rebekah Dance; Tenn.; 1957, Korea.
Lambright, Robert Lamar; Ky.; 1957, Indonesia.
Lambright, Ann Patrick (Mrs. R. L.); Miss.; 1957, Indonesia.
Langford, Charles Donald; Tenn.; 1963, Hong Kong.
Langford, Mary McCrary (Mrs. C. D.); Tex.; 1963, Hong Kong.
Langley, Earl Edward (A); Tex.; 1969, Taiwan.
Langley, Lois Henson (Mrs. E. E.) (A); Tex.; 1969, Taiwan.
Lanier, Donald Lee; Okla.; 1966, Hong Kong.
Lanier, Margaret Barrett (Mrs. D. L.); Ill.; 1966, Hong Kong.
Lanier, William Chandler; Ga.; 1960, Israel.
Lanier, Sallie May Cook (Mrs. W. C.); Tenn.; 1960, Israel.
Larimer, Betty Ruth (P); Fla.; 1968, Nigeria.
Latham, Dorothy Jean; Miss.; 1959, Brazil.
Laughridge, Edward Harrell (A); S. C.; 1968, Trinidad.
Laughridge, Frances Morton (Mrs. E. H.) (A); S. C.; 1968, Trinidad.
Law, Jean Hugh; Okla.; 1962, Kenya.
Law, Maxine Guin (Mrs. J. H.); Tex.; 1962, Kenya.
Law, Thomas Lee, Jr.; Tex.; 1962, Spain.
Law, Betty Freeman (Mrs. T. L., Jr.); Tex.; 1962, Spain.
Lawhon, Charles Henry, Sr.; Fla.; 1960, Philippines.
Lawhon, Elizabeth Timmons (Mrs. C. H., Sr.); Fla.; 1960, Philippines.
Lay, Diana Floretta; Ohio; 1961, Ghana.
Leavell, James B., Jr. (J); Miss.; 1967, Japan.
Leavell, Judith Bowman (Mrs. J. B., Jr.) (J); Tex.; 1967, Japan.
Ledbetter, Michael J; N. C.; 1962, Guatemala and Mexico.
Ledbetter, Ethel Trivette (Mrs. M. J); N. C.; 1962, Guatemala and Mexico.
Lee, Carl Glenn; Tex.; 1967, Indonesia.
Lee, Twila Turner (Mrs. C. G.); Ark.; 1967, Indonesia.
Lee, Hal Burnham, Jr.; La.; 1962, France.
Lee, Lou Ann Green (Mrs. H. B., Jr.); La.; 1962, France.
Lee, Lewis Earl; Tex.; 1960, Peru.
Lee, Jo Rutherford (Mrs. L. E.); Tex.; 1960, Peru.
Leech, John Marvin; Tex.; 1969, Indonesia.
Leech, Linda Lowe (Mrs. J. M.); Calif.; 1969, Indonesia.
Leeper, James Frederick; Tex.; 1965, Turkey.
Leeper, Jean Davis (Mrs. J. F.); Mich.; 1965, Turkey.
Leftwich, Eugene Leon; Kan.; 1964, Nigeria.
Leftwich, Marian Kammler (Mrs. E. L.); Ill.; 1964, Nigeria.
Legg, Lloyd Gene; Tex.; 1956, Nigeria.
Legg, Mary Leigh Anderson (Mrs. L. G.); Tex.; 1956, Nigeria.
Lemonds, Patricia Mae (J); Mo.; 1966, Rhodesia.
LeRoy, Julian Ray; S. C.; 1962, Brazil.
LeRoy, Jeanelle Davis (Mrs. J. R.); Ga.; 1962, Brazil.
Levinson, Carol (J); N. C.; 1965, Nigeria.
Levrets, Fred Leon; Tex.; 1964, Nigeria.
Levrets, Mary Lou Knight (Mrs. F. L.); Okla.; 1964, Nigeria.
Lewis, Francis Lamar; Okla.; 1958, Indonesia.
Lewis, Beverly Johnson (Mrs. F. L.); Okla.; 1958, Indonesia.
Lewis, Harold Wayne; Ohio; 1965, Trinidad.
Lewis, Martha Teague (Mrs. H. W.); S. C.; 1965, Trinidad.
Lewis, Thomas Leighton; Ga.; 1966, Brazil.
Lewis, Dorothy Cutrell (Mrs. T. L.); N. C.; 1966, Brazil.

Lewis, Wilbur Curtis; Okla.; 1959, Paraguay.
Lewis, Gladys Sherman (Mrs. W. C.); Okla.; 1959, Paraguay.
Lewis, William Estal, Jr.; Fla.; 1958, Tanzania and Ethiopia.
Lewis, Nina Allen (Mrs. W. E., Jr.); Fla.; 1958, Tanzania and Ethiopia.
Ligon, William Theophilus; Ala.; 1965, Spain.
Ligon, Dorothy Jean Reeves (Mrs. W. T.); Fla.; 1965, Spain.
Lincoln, Clyde Roy III (J); N. C.; 1966, Germany.
Lindholm, Raymond Victor; Calif.; 1965, Nigeria and Ethiopia.
Lindholm, Lauralee Horner (Mrs. R. V.); Calif.; 1965, Nigeria and Ethiopia.
Lindsay, Eleanor Maxine; Ky.; 1959, Gaza and Jordan.
Lindstrom, Dale Clifton; Colo.; 1969, Venezuela.
Lindstrom, Janet Atkins (Mrs. D. C.); Colo.; 1969, Venezuela.
Lindwall, Hubert Neal; Mo.; 1960, Guatemala.
Lindwall, Sue Francis (Mrs. H. N.); Ark.; 1960, Guatemala.
Lineberger, Marion Thomas, Sr.; N. C.; 1964, Argentina.
Lineberger, Polly Wood (Mrs. M. T., Sr.); S. C.; 1964, Argentina.
Linkenhoker, Fred D. (J); Va.; 1965, Vietnam.
Lites, Milton Allan; Ark.; 1969, Taiwan.
Lites, Nannette Webb (Mrs. M. A.); Ark.; 1969, Taiwan.
Litsey, Velna Faye (J); Ky.; 1967, Liberia.
Little, John (J); Ark.; 1967, Costa Rica.
Livingston, George Fitzhugh, Jr.; Ala.; 1967, Colombia.
Livingston, Karen Wingham (Mrs. G. F., Jr.); Ind.; 1967, Colombia.
Lloyd, Robert Hougland; Ky.; 1956, Argentina.
Lloyd, Charlotte A. Green (Mrs. R. H.); Tex.; 1956, Argentina.
Lochridge, James Thaddeaus; Ga.; 1958, Philippines.
Lochridge, Mary Frances Manuel (Mrs. J. T.); N. C.; 1958, Philippines.
Lofland, Wilson Leon; Tex.; 1963, Pakistan.
Lofland, Teddy A. Smith (Mrs. W. L.); Tex.; 1963, Pakistan.
Lofland, Dora Howard (Mrs. W. L.); Ind.; 1965, Thailand and Pakistan.
Long, David Clifton (J); N. C.; 1969, Uganda.
Long, Valda Eloise; Fla.; 1956, Nigeria and Tanzania.
Lott, Dorotha Del; Miss.; 1964, Brazil.
Lovan, Nadine; Ky.; 1958, Ghana.
Love, Billy Hershel; Okla.; 1966, Malaysia.
Love, Thelma Hayes (Mrs. B. H.); Ark.; 1966, Malaysia.
Love, Charles Peyton; Ky.; 1965, Guyana.
Love, Mary Leech (Mrs. C. P.); Tex.; 1965, Guyana.
Love, Max Henry; Ga.; 1964, Japan.
Love, Flora Gardner (Mrs. M. H.); Ga.; 1964, Japan.
Lovelace, Beryle (A); Tex.; 1965, Japan.
Lovelace, Elouise Roberts (Mrs. B.) (A); Tex.; 1965, Japan.
Low, Jon (J); Tex.; 1968, Nigeria.
Lozuk, George Sylvester; Tex.; 1956, Venezuela.
Lozuk, Veda Tyson (Mrs. G. S.); Tex.; 1956, Venezuela.
Lusk, Richard Lee; S. C.; 1961, Hong Kong and Macao.
Lusk, Ida Bennett (Mrs. R. L.); Tenn.; 1961, Hong Kong and Macao.
Lutz, Beverly Irene; Tenn.; 1962, Paraguay.
Lynch, Bobby Layton; Ark.; 1962, Taiwan.
Lynch, Margie Lackey (Mrs. B. L.); Okla.; 1962, Taiwan.
Lyons, Nancy (J); S. C.; 1965, Nigeria.
Lytle, Norman Frederick; Ohio; 1964, Israel.
Lytle, Martha Yocum (Mrs. N. F.); Ky.; 1964, Israel.

McAden, Nancy Carol (J); Va.; 1969, Ghana.
McAlister, Martha Anne (J); N. C.; 1967, Ghana.
McAuley, Martha Jane (J); Ala.; 1966, Japan.
McCalman, Carol Glynn; Ark.; 1959, Brazil.
McCalman, Sarah Allen (Mrs. C. G.); Ark.; 1959, Brazil.
McClain, Kathryn Ann (J); Tex.; 1966, Tanzania.
McClellan, Carolyn; Tex.; 1966, Yemen.
McClelland, Charles Winfred (A); Fla.; 1969, Rhodesia.
McClelland, Vertie Pitts (Mrs. C. W.) (A); Fla.; 1969, Rhodesia.
McDonald, Sarah Sue; Ark.; 1959, Malaysia.
McElrath, William Nold; Ky.; 1964, Indonesia.
McElrath, Elizabeth Hendricks (Mrs. W. N.); N. C.; 1964, Indonesia.
McGuckin, John Newell; Okla.; 1968, Argentina.
McGuckin, Mary Lou Barringer (Mrs. J. N.); Ala.; 1968, Argentina.
McKinley, Hugh Thomas; Ala.; 1957, Rhodesia.
McKinley, Rebecca Knott (Mrs. H. T.); N. C.; 1957, Rhodesia.
McKinley, James Frank, Jr.; Ky.; 1958, Pakistan.
McKinley, Betty Cecil (Mrs. J. F., Jr.); Ky.; 1958, Pakistan.
McKinney, Landrum Guy, Jr.; Tex.; 1956, Hong Kong.
McKinney, Florence Fielder (Mrs. L. G., Jr.); China; 1956, Hong Kong.
McMillan, Tom Weaver; Tex.; 1959, Kenya and Tanzania.
McMillan, Marilyn Jones (Mrs. T. W.); Ky.; 1959, Kenya and Tanzania.
McMinn, Don Jackson; Ga.; 1966, Korea.
McMinn, Virginia Turner (Mrs. D. J.); Tenn.; 1966, Korea.
McNeall, Donald William; Mo.; 1966, Brazil.
McNeall, Wanda Smith (Mrs. D. W.); Mo.; 1966, Brazil.
McNeely, Gerald Albert; Ky.; 1957, Spain.
McNeely, June Hall (Mrs. G. A.); Ky.; 1957, Spain.
McPhail, Jasper Lewis; Miss.; 1961, India.
McPhail, Dorothy Binford (Mrs. J. L.); Ark.; 1961, India.
McQueen, Bettye Ann; Tex.; 1964, Nigeria.
McTyre, John Holland; Ga.; 1957, Chile.
McTyre, Maurine Robles (Mrs. J. H.); Ill.; 1957, Chile.
McWhorter, Ava Nell; La.; 1967, Gaza (P-1964).
Maddox, Charles C. (A); Ala.; 1967, Ghana.
Maddox, Grace Henry (Mrs. C. C.) (A); Ga.; 1967, Ghana.
Maddox, Wayne Render (A); Va.; 1969, Okinawa.
Maddox, Dorothy Rogers (Mrs. W. R.) (A); Tenn.; 1969, Okinawa.
Magyar, John George; Mo.; 1969, Colombia.
Magyar, Joyce Rauls (Mrs. J. G.); Mo.; 1969, Colombia.
Mahaffey, Jack Edward; S. C.; 1965, Thailand.
Mahaffey, Oneida Dodson (Mrs. J. E.); S. C.; 1965, Thailand.
Maher, Herbert (A); Ga.; 1964, Guam and Philippines.
Maher, Helen Wright (Mrs. H.) (A); Tex.; 1964, Guam and Philippines.
Maiden, Mrs. Jamie (A); Va.; 1963, Nigeria.
Maiden, Joanna Cranston; Va.; 1958, Nigeria.
Mallory, Lowry, Jr. (A); Ala.; 1967, Kenya.
Mallory, Ruth Baker (Mrs. L., Jr.) (A); Tex.; 1967, Kenya.
Mallow, Jeannie (J); Tex.; 1965, Jordan.
Malone, William Patton, Jr.; Tex.; 1958, Argentina.
Malone, Janis Metcalf (Mrs. W. P., Jr.); Tex.; 1958, Argentina.
Mann, Lloyd W. (J); Okla.; 1965, Costa Rica.

Maroney, Jimmy K. (J); Tex.; 1967, Ghana.
Maroney, Kay Farmer (Mrs. J. K.) (J); Tex.; 1967, Ghana.
Marrow, Milburn Maurice; Tex.; 1967, Tanzania.
Marrow, Lois Venable (Mrs. M. M.); Okla.; 1967, Tanzania.
Marshall, Bertha Jane; Ind.; 1957, Japan and Gaza.
Marshall, Jesse Ralph, Jr.; Miss.; 1958, Thailand.
Marshall, Betty Lou Jackson (Mrs. J. R., Jr.); Miss.; 1958, Thailand.
Marshall, William Walter; Ky.; 1969, Cyprus.
Marshall, Alice Gardner (Mrs. W. W.); Ky.; 1969, Cyprus.
Martin, Charles L., Jr.; Ala.; 1956, Japan.
Martin, Anne Crittendon (Mrs. C. L., Jr.); Tex.; 1956, Japan.
Martin, David Lee; Mo.; 1967, Trinidad.
Martin, Sara Hines (Mrs. D. L.); Va.; 1967, Trinidad.
Martin, Earl Richard; Pa.; 1956, Kenya and Tanzania.
Martin, Jane Winchester (Mrs. E. R.); D. C.; 1956, Kenya and Tanzania.
Martin, Garvin Carter; Va.; 1962, Philippines.
Martin, Charlotte Britt (Mrs. G. C.); Va.; 1962, Philippines.
Martin, Glen Ray; Ill.; 1956, Malaysia.
Martin, Betty N. Davis (Mrs. G. R.); Ill.; 1956, Malaysia.
Martin, Jack Leland; Mo.; 1965, Thailand.
Martin, Gladys Way (Mrs. J. L.); La.; 1965, Thailand.
Martin, Marilyn (J); Tex.; 1968, Guatemala.
Martin, Oscar D, Jr.; Tex.; 1961, Brazil.
Martin, Barbara Cheek (Mrs. O. D, Jr.); Ga.; 1961, Brazil.
Martin, William Frank, Jr.; Tex.; 1968, Ecuador.
Martin, Vivian Peterson (Mrs. W. F., Jr.); Minn.; 1968, Ecuador.
Masaki, Tomoki; Hawaii; 1956, Japan.
Masaki, Betty Takahashi (Mrs. T.); Hawaii; 1956, Japan.
Mason, James Donald; Ala.; 1967, Zambia.
Mason, Cassandra Wornal (Mrs. J. D.); W. Va.; 1967, Zambia.
Matheny, William Edward; Ill.; 1964, Peru.
Matheny, Mirle Mathews (Mrs. W. E.); Miss.; 1964, Peru.
Mathieson, Elihu Price; Tex.; 1968, Japan.
Mathieson, Mary Darden (Mrs. E. P.); Tex.; 1968, Japan.
Matthews, William Harold; Ky.; 1957, Philippines.
Matthews, Clara Lee (Mrs. W. H.); Ky.; 1957, Philippines.
May, Ernest Victor, Jr. (A); Ky.; 1969, Dominican Republic.
May, Frances Burke (Mrs. E. V., Jr.) (A); Ga.; 1969, Dominican Republic.
May, William Porter; Fla.; 1965, Ecuador.
May, Marilyn Crane (Mrs. W. P.); Kan.; 1965, Ecuador.
Mayberry, Floyd Irwin (A); Mo.; 1968, Japan.
Mayberry, Lela Cantrell (Mrs. F. I.) (A); Mo.; 1968, Japan.
Mays, Everett Truman; Ky.; 1966, Nigeria.
Mays, Wanda Wolfe (Mrs. E. T.); W. Va.; 1966, Nigeria.
Mayse, Marilyn (J); Mo.; 1968, Nigeria.
Meador, Patricia Lane (J); Tenn.; 1966, Japan.
Medaris, Edward Gene; Okla.; 1964, Trinidad.
Medaris, Martha J. Hawkins (Mrs. E. G.); Tex.; 1964, Trinidad.
Medcalf, Winfred Louis; Okla.; 1959, Thailand.
Medcalf, Patricia Hensley (Mrs. W. L.); Okla.; 1959, Thailand.
Meeks, Jerry James (J); S. C.; 1967, Brazil.
Merrell, Rondal D.; Okla.; 1964, Vietnam.
Merrell, Betty Caughron (Mrs. R. D.); Okla.; 1964, Vietnam.
Merritt, Dewey Elwyn; Miss.; 1956, Nigeria.
Merritt, Sarah Elizabeth Cooper (Mrs. D. E.); Ky.; 1956, Nigeria.
Merritt, John Wesley; Miss.; 1964, Italy.
Merritt, Elizabeth Pope (Mrs. J. W.); Ala.; 1964, Italy.
Metts, Brooks, Jr. (J); Miss.; 1967, Nigeria.
Middleton, Charles Raymond; La.; 1968, Malawi.
Middleton, Glenda Evans (Mrs. C. R.); La.; 1968, Malawi.
Mikolaski, Samuel (A); Yugoslavia; 1965, Switzerland.
Mikolaski, Jessie C. Bain (Mrs. S.) (A); Canada; 1965, Switzerland.
Milam, Kenneth Baker; Ind.; 1969, Indonesia.
Milam, Judith Morehead (Mrs. K. B.); Ill.; 1969, Indonesia.
Milburn, Gary (J); Tex.; 1968, Tanzania and Ghana.
Milby, Franklin Eugene; Ky.; 1963, Rhodesia.
Milby, Reva Morris (Mrs. F. E.); Ky.; 1963, Rhodesia.
Miller, Charles Leland; Fla.; 1960, Philippines.
Miller, Roberta Ely (Mrs. C. L.); Wis.; 1960, Philippines.
Miller, David Lee; Pa.; 1961, Brazil.
Miller, Glenda McCauley (Mrs. D. L.); Calif.; 1961, Brazil.
Miller, E. Wesley (A); Ill.; 1963, Switzerland.
Miller, Jean Minter (Mrs. E. W.) (A); Okla.; 1963, Switzerland.
Miller, Lewis Alfred (A); Ind.; 1969, Taiwan.
Miller, Joanna Pratt (Mrs. L. A.) (A); Tex.; 1969, Taiwan.
Miller, Linda Gail (J); Va.; 1967, Kenya.
Miller, Paul Henderson; N. C.; 1964, Nigeria.
Miller, Eveline Farmer (Mrs. P. H.); Canada; 1964, Nigeria.
Milligan, Alfred Ray; Tex.; 1958, Kenya.
Milligan, Ellen I. Maxwell (Mrs. A. R.); Tex.; 1958, Kenya.
Mills, Dottson Legrand; Ala.; 1956, Argentina and Jamaica.
Mills, Betty Frink (Mrs. D. L.); Fla.; 1956, Argentina and Jamaica.
Mills, John Corbin; Okla.; 1965, Liberia.
Mills, Virginia Land (Mrs. J. C.); D. C.; 1965, Liberia.
Mines, Donald Eugene; Fla.; 1964, Argentina.
Mines, Margie DeLoach (Mrs. D. E.); Tex.; 1964, Argentina.
Misner, Mariam Lou; Mo.; 1956, Indonesia.
Mitchell, Dewey Leon; N. M.; 1957, Indonesia.
Mitchell, Anne Moore (Mrs. D. L.); Tex.; 1957, Indonesia.
Mobley, Harris Witsel; Ga.; 1959, Ghana.
Mobley, Vivian Anderson (Mrs. H. W.); Ga.; 1959, Ghana.
Mobley, Marion Alonzo; Ga.; 1959, Japan.
Mobley, Carolyn Ham (Mrs. M. A.); Ga.; 1959, Japan.
Mock, Darrell Alexander (A); Okla.; 1967, Japan.
Mock, Norma Lea Thomas (Mrs. D. A.) (A); Okla.; 1967, Japan.
Montgomery, E. Gail (J); Miss.; 1968, Philippines.
Montgomery, Ira Edward, Jr.; Tex.; 1964, Rhodesia and Kenya.
Montgomery, Mary Gail Couch (Mrs. I. E., Jr.); Tex.; 1964, Rhodesia and Kenya.
Moody, Paul Samuel; Ga.; 1959, Thailand.
Moody, Virginia Ashe (Mrs. P. S.); Ga.; 1959, Thailand.
Moore, Billy Bob; Ark.; 1966, Kenya.
Moore, Aletha Lane (Mrs. B. B.); Tex.; 1966, Kenya.
Moore, Charles Beatty, IV; Ark.; 1967, Peru.
Moore, Judy F. Sandusky (Mrs. C. B., IV); Tex.; 1967, Peru.
Moore, Dono William (A); Tex.; 1969, Ghana.
Moore, Betty Jo Fry (Mrs. D. W.) (A); Okla.; 1969, Ghana.
Moore, Dorothy Marie (J); Wash.; 1969, Dominican Republic.
Moore, Eucled Doyle; Tex.; 1967, Tanzania.

Moore, Janelle Williams (Mrs. E. D.); N. M.; 1967, Tanzania.
Moore, Marylu; D. C.; 1963, Italy.
Moore, Merrill Dennis, Jr.; Ala.; 1964, Gaza.
Moore, Patricia Pitchford (Mrs. M. D., Jr.); Okla.; 1964, Gaza.
Moore, Peyton Matterson; Miss.; 1964, Vietnam.
Moore, Celia Torres (Mrs. P. M.); N. Y.; 1964, Vietnam.
Moore, Vernon Lee (A); Ky.; 1968, Malaysia.
Moore, Marion Poor (Mrs. V. L.) (A); N. J.; 1968, Malaysia.
Moore, Willis Trueman; Ark.; 1957, Pakistan.
Moore, Jane Bassett (Mrs. W. T.); Ark.; 1957, Pakistan.
Moorefield, Virgil Hisgen, Jr.; Ky.; 1958, Italy and Switzerland.
Moorefield, Jane Richardson (Mrs. V. H., Jr.); Ky.; 1958, Italy and Switzerland.
Moorhead, Walter James; S. C.; 1962, Philippines.
Moorhead, Emma R. Northern (Mrs. W. J.); Tenn.; 1962, Philippines.
Morgan, David Welborn; La.; 1963, Hong Kong.
Morgan, Zeddie C. McGee (Mrs. D. W.); Miss.; 1963, Hong Kong.
Morgan, Janet (J); Okla.; 1967, Hong Kong.
Morgan, William LeRoy; Miss.; 1964, Brazil.
Morgan, Noreta Smith (Mrs. W. L.); Tenn.; 1964, Brazil.
Morphis, Luther (A); N. C.; 1963, Germany.
Morris, Cecelia (J); Tex.; 1968, Vietnam.
Morris, Charles Herbert; Ariz.; 1957, Malaysia.
Morris, Erica Hofmann (Mrs. C. H.); Germany; 1957, Malaysia.
Morris, Richard Edward; Tenn.; 1958, Taiwan.
Morris, Christena Simmons (Mrs. R. E.); Tenn.; 1958, Taiwan.
Morris, Russell Allen; Okla.; 1965, Singapore.
Morris, May Phillips (Mrs. R. A.); Okla.; 1965, Singapore.
Morris, Russell Ralph; Colo.; 1957, Jordan, Tanzania and Kenya.
Morris, Betty Lane (Mrs. R. R.); Tex.; 1957, Jordan, Tanzania and Kenya.
Morse, James Otto; Okla.; 1958, Colombia.
Morse, Esther R. Cowsert (Mrs. J. O.); Brazil; 1958, Colombia.
Moseley, James Rennie; Ala.; 1962, Nigeria.
Moseley, Myra Barnett (Mrs. J. R.); Ala.; 1962, Nigeria.
Moseley, Maxine; Ala.; 1969, Ghana.
Moses, Edmond Boxley, Jr.; Fla.; 1969, Nigeria.
Moses, Mary Ann Pugh (Mrs. E. B., Jr.); Miss.; 1969, Nigeria.
Mosley, Ben Doyle, Jr. (A); Okla.; 1969, Liberia.
Mosley, Donna Lovelace (Mrs. B. D., Jr.) (A); Okla.; 1969, Liberia.
Moss, Zebedee Vance; N. C.; 1959, Zambia.
Moss, Evelyn Krause (Mrs. Z. V.); N. C.; 1959, Zambia.
Mosteller, Paul Clifford; Fla.; 1956, Thailand.
Mosteller, Dorothy Brizendine (Mrs. P. C.); Tenn.; 1956, Thailand.
Mueller, Emil William; Mo.; 1960, Liberia.
Mueller, Agnes Southern (Mrs. E. W.), R. N.; Tex.; 1960, Liberia.
Mullins, Lawrence Darrell; Va.; 1966, Indonesia.
Mullins, Juanita Parks (Mrs. L. D.); Tenn.; 1966, Indonesia.
Murphey, John Warford; Ky.; 1969, Italy.
Murphey, Alta Mae Johnston (Mrs. J. W.); Tex.; 1969, Italy.
Murray, Ben Ronald; Okla.; 1966, Peru.
Murray, Dean Carpenter (Mrs. B. R.); Okla.; 1966, Peru.
Muse, James Carl, Jr.; Okla.; 1961, Ecuador.
Muse, Patsy Slabaugh (Mrs. J. C., Jr.); Okla.; 1961, Ecuador.
Musen, James Donald; Ky.; 1968, Kenya.
Musen, Jenny Rossetter (Mrs. J. D.); Ky.; 1968, Kenya.
Myers, Charles D. (J); N. C.; 1965, Ghana.
Myers, Lewis Isham, Jr.; Miss.; 1960, Vietnam.
Myers, Antoinette Alexander (Mrs. L. I., Jr.); Miss.; 1960, Vietnam.
Myers, Robert Vernon (A); D. C.; 1968, Bahamas.
Myers, Jeane Christie (Mrs. R. V.) (A); D. C.; 1968, Bahamas.
Myers, Shelby Payton; Miss.; 1963, Nigeria.
Myers, Helen Green (Mrs. S. P.); Miss.; 1963, Nigeria.
Myrick, Mary Ann (J); Miss.; 1967, Zambia.

Nance, John Irvin; Okla.; 1962, Indonesia.
Nance, Mary Moore (Mrs. J. I.); Okla.; 1962, Indonesia.
Nash, Robert Norman; Ga.; 1964, Philippines.
Nash, Janet Carpenter (Mrs. R. N.); Ga.; 1964, Philippines.
Nations, Archie Lee; La.; 1960, Japan.
Nations, Lois Sheffield (Mrs. A. L.); N. C.; 1960, Japan.
Neal, Lillie Joy (J); Miss.; 1969, Zambia.
Neely, Alan Preston; Ark.; 1963, Colombia.
Neely, Virginia Garrett (Mrs. A. P.); Tex.; 1963, Colombia.
Neely, Herbert Willingham; S. C.; 1960, Rhodesia.
Neely, Jacqulyn Sloan (Mrs. H. W.); S. C.; 1960, Rhodesia.
Nelson, Betty Vivian (J); Tex.; 1966, Liberia.
Nelson, Edward Warren; Iowa; 1957, Chile and Spanish Publishing House.
Nelson, Gladys Samp (Mrs. E. W.); S. D.; 1957, Chile and Spanish Publishing House.
Nelson, George Barry; Mo.; 1969, Indonesia.
Nelson, Judith Ray (Mrs. G. B.); Mo.; 1969, Indonesia.
Nelson, Glynis (J); Tex.; 1968, Japan.
Newton, Joseph Allen; Fla.; 1965, Spain and Morocco.
Newton, Nancy Walker (Mrs. J. A.); Tenn.; 1965, Spain and Morocco.
Nicholas, Roy Edward; Mich.; 1956, Gaza.
Nicholas, Anne Youngblood (Mrs. R. E.); Ky.; 1956, Gaza.
Nichols, David Walker (J); Tenn.; 1966, Nigeria and Liberia.
Nichols, Gilbert Athol; Ark.; 1958, Paraguay.
Nichols, Deane Marshall (Mrs. G. A.); Ark.; 1958, Paraguay.
Nichols, Lee Holloway; Ala.; 1966, Korea.
Nichols, Norma Hiers (Mrs. L. H.); S. C.; 1966, Korea.
Nicholson, Kenneth Royce; N. M.; 1967, Liberia.
Nicholson, Joyce Roof (Mrs. K. R.); N. J.; 1967, Liberia.
Nickell, John Ambrose, Jr.; Okla.; 1967, Nigeria.
Nickell, Carolyn Williams (Mrs. J. A.); Okla.; 1967, Nigeria.
Nickell, Linda (J); Okla.; 1968, Korea.
Noble, J. Thomas, Jr. (J); Va.; 1967, Italy.
Noland, Paul Wayne; La.; 1962, Brazil.
Noland, Betty Branch (Mrs. P. W.); La.; 1962, Brazil.
Norman, John Thomas; Tex.; 1962, Colombia.
Norman, Joan Watson (Mrs. J. T.); Tex.; 1962, Colombia.
Northcutt, Irvin Lanier; Ala.; 1959, Peru.
Northcutt, Mildred Meadows (Mrs. I. L.); Ga.; 1959, Peru.
Northcutt, Mary Jo (J); Tex.; 1965, Taiwan.
Norwood, Charles Gayle; La.; 1968, Philippines.
Norwood, Lillian Mayes (Mrs. C. G.); La.; 1968, Philippines.
Nowell, Charles Grady; N. C.; 1966, Honduras.
Nowell, Barbara Short (Mrs. C. G.); N. C.; 1966, Honduras.
Nowland, Harvey Louis, Jr.; Wis.; 1966, Peru.

Nowland, Roberta Jordan (Mrs. H. L., Jr.); Wis.; 1966, Peru.
Nuckles, Arnold (J); N. C.; 1968, Ivory Coast and Liberia.
Nunnelley, Edith Gates (Mrs. Newman F.) (A); Tex.; 1967, Nigeria.

Oakes, George (A); England; 1965, Brazil.
Oates, Alma Elizabeth; Tenn.; 1957, Brazil.
O'Brien, William Robert; Tex.; 1962, Indonesia.
O'Brien, Dellanna West (Mrs. W. R.); Tex.; 1962, Indonesia.
O'Conner, Louis, Jr.; Ala.; 1956, Korea and Hong Kong.
O'Conner, Barbara Crumbley (Mrs. L., Jr.); Ohio; 1956, Korea and Hong Kong.
Odom, Rebecca (J); Fla.; 1968, Japan.
Oertli, Virginia Ernestine (J); Tex.; 1966, Korea.
Ogden, Lane Gordon, Sr.; Okla.; 1964, Zambia.
Ogden, Louise Wood (Mrs. L. G., Sr.); Tex.; 1964, Zambia.
Oliphint, Keith Lamar; Tex.; 1965, Tanzania.
Oliphint, Peggy Howell (Mrs. K. L.); Tex.; 1965, Tanzania.
Oliver, Arthur Bruce; Tex.; 1959, Brazil.
Oliver, Margaret Stripling (Mrs. A. B.); Tex.; 1959, Brazil.
Oliver, Bennie May; Tex.; 1957, Brazil.
Oliver, Charles William; Tex.; 1967, Italy.
Oliver, Sandra Darr (Mrs. C. W.); Mo.; 1967, Italy.
Oliver, DeVellyn; Ark.; 1958, Philippines.
Oliver, James Claude, Jr.; Ala.; 1966, Colombia.
Oliver, Marilyn White (Mrs. J. C., Jr.); Okla.; 1966, Colombia.
Olson, Carole (J); Tex.; 1968, Japan.
Oody, T. Eugene (A); Tenn.; 1963, Liberia.
Oody, Betty White (Mrs. T. E.) (A); Tenn.; 1963, Liberia.
O'Reagan, Daniel Wayne; Tex.; 1964, Japan.
O'Reagan, Beverly Broussard (Mrs. D. W.); La.; 1964, Japan.
Orr, R. Allen (J); Ala.; 1965, Philippines.
Oue, Takahiro; Japan; 1969, Japan.
Oue, Lana O'Banion (Mrs. T.); Ky.; 1969, Japan.
Owen, Evelyn Wood; Ala.; 1956, Japan.
Owen, Richard Allen; S. C.; 1965, Brazil.
Owen, Barbara Stroud (Mrs. R. A.); Ga.; 1965, Brazil.
Owens, Carlos Richard; Tenn.; 1957, Tanzania and Kenya.
Owens, Myrtice Taylor (Mrs. C. R.); Fla.; 1957, Tanzania and Kenya.
Owens, James Thomas; Fla.; 1963, Mexico.
Owens, Charlotte Judge (Mrs. J. T.); Fla.; 1963, Mexico.
Owens, Nannie Belle; Ark.; 1957, Nigeria.
Owens, Raymond Eugene; Va.; 1966, Switzerland.
Owens, Margaret Bradsher (Mrs. R. E.); N. C.; 1966, Switzerland.
Owensby, Ronell Lester; N. C.; 1966, Venezuela.
Owensby, Annie Laura Pack (Mrs. R. L.); N. C.; 1966, Venezuela.

Page, Wendell Lee; Mo.; 1965, French West Indies.
Page, Margaret Andrews (Mrs. W. L.); Mo.; 1965, French West Indies.
Palmer, Harry Jerold, Jr.; Tenn.; 1963, Nigeria.
Palmer, Grace Powell (Mrs. H. J., Jr.); N. C.; 1963, Nigeria.
Paris, Charlotte Anne (J); Ill.; 1969, Taiwan.
Park, James Kenneth; Ky.; 1964, Chile.
Park, Divina Key (Mrs. J. K.); Ky.; 1964, Chile.
Parker, Gerald Keith; N. C.; 1969, Switzerland.
Parker, Jonlyn Truesdail (Mrs. G. K.); Va.; 1969, Switzerland.
Parker, Robert Raymond, Jr.; S. C.; 1968, Rhodesia.
Parker, Mary Stroup (Mrs. R. R., Jr.); S. C.; 1968, Rhodesia.
Parker, Wendall Carter; N. M.; 1967, Guatemala.
Parker, Jane Averitt (Mrs. W. C.); Ala.; 1967, Guatemala.
Parker, Wyatt Mortimer; Tenn.; 1958, Brazil.
Parker, Cosette Carter (Mrs. W. M.); Tenn.; 1958, Brazil.
Parkman, William Hugo; Ala.; 1958, Philippines.
Parkman, Doris McKoy (Mrs. W. H.); Ala.; 1958, Philippines.
Parsons, Everett Lee, Jr.; W. Va.; 1967, Ecuador.
Parsons, Carolyn Baird (Mrs. E. L., Jr.); Tenn.; 1967, Ecuador.
Partain, Jackie Gene; Tex.; 1962, Tanzania and Kenya.
Partain, Ruth Lloyd (Mrs. J. G.); Tex.; 1962, Tanzania and Kenya.
Pate, Mavis Orisca; La.; 1964, Pakistan and Gaza.
Patrick, Russell Allen; Mo.; 1965, Colombia.
Patrick, Nancy Lemoins (Mrs. R. A.); Mo.; 1965, Colombia.
Patten, John Evans; Ga.; 1960, Thailand.
Patten, Nanette Davis (Mrs. J. E.); Ga.; 1960, Thailand.
Patterson, John Wellington; Ariz.; 1956, Colombia.
Patterson, Patricia Wilson (Mrs. J. W.); Mo.; 1956, Colombia.
Patton, Glenn; Tenn.; 1966, Lebanon.
Patton, Georgia Stockton (Mrs. G.); Tenn.; 1966, Lebanon.
Payne, James Bolling; Va.; 1959, Nigeria.
Peach, Jarrell Dorman; Tex.; 1969, Gaza.
Peach, Shirley Nowlin (Mrs. J. D.); Mo.; 1969, Gaza.
Peacock, Billy Ray; La.; 1968, Korea.
Peacock, Teressa Mazzara (Mrs. B. R.); La.; 1968, Korea.
Peacock, Henry Earl; Ga.; 1957, Brazil.
Peacock, Margaret Dorminey (Mrs. H. E.); Ga.; 1957, Brazil.
Pearce, William Boyd; Tex.; 1958. Kenya.
Pearce, Sydney Brewer (Mrs. W. B.); Tex.; 1958, Kenya.
Pearson, Flossie Faye; Miss.; 1968, Taiwan.
Peden, Homer, Jr.; Tex.; 1965, Philippines.
Peden, Jean Kensing (Mrs. H., Jr.); Okla.; 1965, Philippines.
Peebles, Mary Carla (J); Fla.; 1969, Malawi.
Penkert, Doris Louise; Tex.; 1960, Brazil.
Pennell, Wayne Arthur; N. C.; 1961, Indonesia.
Pennell, Elinor Hasty (Mrs. W. A.); Ga.; 1961, Indonesia.
Perkins, Ira Samuel; Miss.; 1961, Brazil.
Perkins, Betteye Williams (Mrs. I. S.); Miss.; 1961, Brazil.
Perryman, Maurine Tate; N. C.; 1958, Jordan.
Phillips, Gene Dillard; S. C.; 1956, Rhodesia.
Phillips, Eugenia Jarvis (Mrs. G. D.); N. C.; 1956, Rhodesia.
Phillips, Linda, (J); Calif.; 1965, Liberia.
Phillips, Marian Hazel; N. C.; 1960, Nigeria.
Phillips, Marshall Eugene; Ky.; 1961, Kenya.
Phillips, Dorsie Murphy (Mrs. M. E.); Ky.; 1961, Kenya.
Philpot, James Morgan; Ark.; 1967, Mexico.
Philpot, Rosalind Sheffield (Mrs. J. M.); Tex.; 1967, Mexico.
Phlegar, Donald Vaughn; Va.; 1967, Thailand.
Phlegar, Barbara Anne Carley (Mrs. D. V.); Miss.; 1967, Thailand.
Pickle, George (J); Tex.; 1968, Vietnam.
Pike, Harrison Hayes; Tex.; 1956, Brazil and Angola.
Pike, June Summers (Mrs. H. H.); Ark.; 1956, Brazil and Angola.
Pinder, Robert Henry; Fla.; 1963, Argentina.

Pinder, Jane Hagood (Mrs. R. H.); Fla.; 1963, Argentina.
Pinkston, Dallas Edwin; Ark.; 1966, Ivory Coast.
Pinkston, Greta McFerrin (Mrs. D. E.); Ark.; 1966, Ivory Coast.
Pinkston, Gerald Wayne; Tex.; 1957, Indonesia.
Pinkston, Florence Goldston (Mrs. G. W.); Tex.; 1957, Indonesia.
Pinson, Merilyn (J); W. Va.; 1968, Liberia.
Pippin, Ernest Carson; Va.; 1960, Argentina.
Pippin, Martha Smith (Mrs. E. C.); Tenn.; 1960, Argentina.
Pitman, Gerald Gene; Tex.; 1960, Nigeria.
Pitman, Ann Dodson (Mrs. G. G.); Tex.; 1960, Nigeria.
Plampin, Richard Thomas; Ga.; 1957, Brazil.
Plampin, Carolyn Goodman (Mrs. R. T.); Ga.; 1957, Brazil.
Plumlee, Shirley Swan (J); Ark.; 1966, Ghana.
Plunk, Mell Ren; Tex.; 1963, Jamaica and Argentina.
Plunk, Sue Briggs (Mrs. M. R.); Tex.; 1963, Jamaica and Argentina.
Poe, Joe Tom; Tex.; 1956, Chile and Spanish Publishing House.
Poe, Eleanor Ostwalt (Mrs. J. T.); N. C.; 1956, Chile and Spanish Publishing House.
Poe, John Alexander; N. C.; 1956, Brazil.
Poe, Jean Howard (Mrs. J. A.); Tenn.; 1956, Brazil.
Poe, Thomas Franklin (J); W. Va.; 1969, Ghana.
Poor, James Wallace; Mo.; 1968, Uruguay.
Poor, Elizabeth Magee (Mrs. J. W.); Mo.; 1968, Uruguay.
Poovey, Harry Emmett; N. C.; 1963, Taiwan.
Poovey, Vivian Dyer (Mrs. H. E.); Ga.; 1963, Taiwan.
Pople, Ray (J); Tenn.; 1968, Argentina.
Porter, Linda Joy; Tenn.; 1966, Nigeria.
Posey, Jesse Earl, Jr.; Ala.; 1956, Philippines.
Posey, Mamie Lou Eubanks (Mrs. J. E., Jr.); Miss.; 1956, Philippines.
Potter, Paul Edwin; Mo.; 1965, Dominican Republic.
Potter, Nancy Roper (Mrs. P. E.); Mo.; 1965, Dominican Republic.
Potter, Rebecca Jean (P); Tenn.; 1965, Yemen.
Pou, Joseph Cornilous (A); S. C.; 1965, Liberia.
Pou, Frances Edwards (Mrs. J. C.) (A); S. C.; 1965, Liberia.
Poulos, George William; Mo.; 1966, Greece, Germany, and Belgium.
Poulos, Della Singleton (Mrs. G. W.); Tex.; 1966, Greece, Germany, and Belgium.
Powell, Amaryllis Gwen; Miss.; 1969, Jordan.
Powell, Arthur James; Fla.; 1962, Lebanon.
Powell, Harriett Stones (Mrs. A. J.); Fla.; 1962, Lebanon.
Pratt, Genevieve Jeanne (J); Ky.; 1969, Lebanon.
Price, Harold Lee; Tex.; 1962, Japan.
Price, Victoria Hardegree (Mrs. H. L.); Ga.; 1962, Japan.
Price, Kathryn Herring (J); Ark.; 1969, Lebanon.
Privett, Areta (J); Tex.; 1967, Nigeria.
Pruit, Morris Glen; N. M.; 1967, Togo.
Pruit, Carol Anne Hester (Mrs. M. G.); Tex.; 1967, Togo.

Raborn, John Clifford; Tex.; 1957, Hong Kong.
Raborn, Nelwyn Martin (Mrs. J. C.); Tex.; 1957, Hong Kong.
Rader, Dick Allen; Okla.; 1967, Zambia.
Rader, Sue Harris (Mrs. D. A.); Okla.; 1967, Zambia.
Rader, Janyce Etta (P); Tenn.; 1965, Nigeria.
Rader, Joyce Edna (P); Tenn.; 1965, Nigeria.
Ragan, Jarrett (A); Ga.; 1963, Malaysia.
Ragan, Charlotte Bruner (Mrs. J.) (A); Ky.; 1963, Malaysia.
Railey, David Earl; Ark.; 1966, Hong Kong.
Railey, Joy Kersh (Mrs. D. E.); Ark.; 1966, Hong Kong.
Ramsey, Lois Mae (J); Ill.; 1966, Nigeria.
Ranager, C. Alfreda (J); La.; 1967, Philippines.
Randall, Mary Josephine; Ala.; 1958, Japan.
Rascon, Rose Linda (J); Tex.; 1969, Ecuador.
Ratcliff, Thomas Edward; Tex.; 1965, Dominican Republic.
Ratcliff, Josie Slaughter (Mrs. T. E.); Tex.; 1965, Dominican Republic.
Reber, Sidney (A); Miss.; 1962, Malaysia.
Reber, Alwilda Montgomery (Mrs. S.) (A); Mo.; 1962, Malaysia.
Redding, James Claiborne; Tenn.; 1964, Peru.
Redding, Marilyn Moore (Mrs. J. C.); Ga.; 1964, Peru.
Redmon, Donald Hugh; Fla.; 1963, Costa Rica.
Redmon, Jo Eubanks (Mrs. D. H.); Miss.; 1963, Costa Rica.
Reece, Zemery Don; N. C.; 1959, Nigeria.
Reece, Gwendolyn Downes (Mrs. Z. D.); Ala.; 1959, Nigeria.
Reed, Marcus Carthron; Tenn.; 1960, Israel.
Reed, Ruth Caldwell (Mrs. M. C.); Tenn.; 1960, Israel.
Reeder, James Lendon; Ala.; 1961, Philippines.
Reeder, Mary L. Willis (Mrs. J. L.); Ala.; 1961, Philippines.
Reese, Gordon Benjamin; Mo.; 1969, Chile.
Reese, Donna Dunkin (Mrs. G. B.); Mo.; 1969, Chile.
Reeves, Samuel Dwain; La.; 1967, Argentina.
Reeves, Elizabeth Baker (Mrs. S. D.); Fla.; 1967, Argentina.
Register, Ray Gustava, Jr.; S. C.; 1964, Israel.
Register, Rose Mary Rich (Mrs. R. G., Jr.); Ind.; 1964, Israel.
Reynolds, Forest Donald (J); Mo.; 1966, Ghana.
Reynolds, Marvin Robert; Ark.; 1967, Botswana.
Reynolds, Elizabeth Haley (Mrs. M. R.); Ark.; 1967, Botswana.
Rice, Herbert Warren; N. C.; 1968, Indonesia.
Rice, Bette Gordon Kelley (Mrs. H. W.); Va.; 1968, Indonesia.
Rice, Lawrence Elliott; D. C.; 1969, Venezuela.
Rice, Karene Mary Tant (Mrs. L. E.); S. C.; 1969, Venezuela.
Richards, Donald Joe; Tex.; 1958, Brazil.
Richards, Shari Sherman (Mrs. D. J.); Tex.; 1958, Brazil.
Richards, Jimmie Larue; Ala.; 1969, Dominican Republic.
Richards, Pamela Barker (Mrs. J. L.); Va.; 1969, Dominican Republic.
Richardson, William Donald; Mo.; 1961, Ghana.
Richardson, Irma Gowan (Mrs. W. D.); Ill.; 1961, Ghana.
Richardson, William Leonard Carlton; Okla.; 1964, Brazil.
Richardson, Kathryn Mallory (Mrs. W. L. C.); Mo.; 1964, Brazil.
Ricketson, Samuel Abernethy; China; 1966, Taiwan.
Ricketson, Corella Bounds (Mrs. S. A.); Okla.; 1966, Taiwan.
Riddle, Joyce Faye (P); N. C.; 1968, Gaza.
Riemenschneider, J W; Tex.; 1969, E. Africa.
Riemenschneider, Paula Fletcher (Mrs. J W); Tex.; 1969, E. Africa.
Riley, Charles Duane; Okla.; 1965, Brazil.
Riley, Mattie Lou Davis (Mrs. C. D.); Okla.; 1965, Brazil.
Rinker, James M. (J); Ark.; 1965, Ecuador.
Rippeto, Jimmie Fred (A); Mo.; 1969, Hong Kong.
Rippeto, Judy Graves (Mrs. J. F.) (A); Mo.; 1969, Hong Kong.
Ritchie, Judy Elaine (J); N. C.; 1969, Brazil.
Rivenbark, Edward Harl (J); N. C.; 1967, Kenya.
Roberson, William Thomas; N. C.; 1959, Vietnam.

Roberson, Audrey Hanes (Mrs. W. T.); N. C.; 1959, Vietnam.
Roberts, Hoyt Mason; N. C.; 1962, Honduras.
Roberts, Louise Poole (Mrs. H. M.); Ga.; 1962, Honduras.
Roberts, M. Emily (J); Ga.; 1965, Liberia.
Roberts, Will J; Okla.; 1962, Kenya.
Roberts, Marie Morgan (Mrs. W. J); Okla.; 1962, Kenya.
Robinson, Arthur C. (A); Ore.; 1964, Taiwan.
Robinson, Ruth McIntosh (Mrs. A. C.) (A); Calif.; 1964, Taiwan.
Robinson, Frank Lee, Jr.; Ga.; 1965, Taiwan.
Robinson, Dorris Fuson (Mrs. F. L., Jr.); Tenn.; 1965, Taiwan.
Robinson, D. Gene (J); Calif.; 1967, Philippines.
Robinson, P. Janice (J); Miss.; 1965, Nigeria.
Robinson, Jerry Lynn; Tex.; 1968, Brazil.
Robinson, Shermie Vickers (Mrs. J. L.); Tex.; 1968, Brazil.
Rodgers, Wilma Leona; Mo.; 1968, Ivory Coast.
Roediger, Connie (J); Ohio; 1967, Rhodesia.
Rogers, Carol Ray; N. C.; 1963, Malaysia and Indonesia.
Rogers, Joyce Campbell (Mrs. C. R.); S. C.; 1963, Malaysia and Indonesia.
Rogers, Helen Arlene; Calif.; 1956, Colombia.
Rollins, Linda (J); Ky.; 1966, Philippines.
Romoser, Bruce Allen; Calif.; 1968, Argentina.
Romoser, Auburn Spencer (Mrs. B. A.); Tex.; 1968, Argentina.
Rose, Donald (A); Mont.; 1963, Germany.
Rose, Gertrude Du Bois (Mrs. D.) (A); Mich.; 1963, Germany.
Rose, Thomas Andrew (A); Okla.; 1968, Liberia.
Rose, Ruby Wright (Mrs. T. A.) (A); Tex.; 1968, Liberia.
Ross, Frank Gilbert; Tex.; 1958, Mexico.
Ross, Carolyn O'Brien (Mrs. F. G.); Tex.; 1958, Mexico.
Routh, Walter Andrew, Jr.; Fla.; 1963, Vietnam.
Routh, Pauline Hays (Mrs. W. A., Jr.); Ky.; 1963, Vietnam.
Rowland, Wade Russell; N. C.; 1969, Tanzania.
Rowland, Betty Ausborn (Mrs. W. R.); Ala.; 1969, Tanzania.
Ruchti, William Charles, Jr.; Tex.; 1960, Italy.
Ruchti, Helen Holmes (Mrs. W. C., Jr.); La.; 1960, Italy.
Rummage, Ralph Lee; Okla.; 1959, Rhodesia.
Rummage, Laverne Russell (Mrs. R. L.); Tex.; 1959, Rhodesia.
Russell, Phillip Kay (J); N. C.; 1969, Hong Kong.
Russey, Karen Sue (J); Colo.; 1969, Vietnam.
Ryther, Carl Felix; S. D.; 1962, Pakistan.
Ryther, Jean Kelley (Mrs. C. F.); Tex.; 1962, Pakistan.

Sanders, Edward Owen; Okla.; 1959, Indonesia.
Sanders, Jaletta Davis (Mrs. E. O.); Okla.; 1959, Indonesia.
Sanders, Lynda Kay (J); Miss.; 1967, Zambia.
Sanderson, John Cavender; Mich.; 1968, Trinidad.
Sanderson, Hannah Trigg (Mrs. J. C.); Ky.; 1968, Trinidad.
Sanderson, Rennie Vee; Miss.; 1960, Japan.
Saunkeah, Jasper, Jr.; Okla.; 1963, Argentina.
Saunkeah, Dorothy Reed (Mrs. J., Jr.); Okla.; 1963, Argentina.
Savage, Teddy Edward; Okla.; 1960, Zambia.
Savage, Verna Zinn (Mrs. T. E.); Okla.; 1960, Zambia.
Scaggs, Billie Vertrice; Ky.; 1969, Nigeria.
Scales, Louie Tarlton; Tex.; 1969, E. Africa.
Scales, Jo Long (Mrs. L. T.); Tex.; 1969, E. Africa.
Scarborough, William Murray (A); Ark.; 1966, Yemen.
Scarborough, Muriel Green (Mrs. W. M.) (A); Ark.; 1966, Yemen.
Schleiff, Gerald Eugene; Ark.; 1967, Rhodesia.
Schleiff, Barbara Robertson (Mrs. G. E.); Ark.; 1967, Rhodesia.
Schmidt, Sidney Philip; N. D.; 1961, Malaysia.
Schmidt, Darleen Wilson (Mrs. S. P.); Neb.; 1961, Malaysia.
Schnick, Homer Lee (A); Okla.; 1968, Hong Kong.
Schnick, Peggy Davis (Mrs. H. L.) (A); Okla.; 1968, Hong Kong.
Schochler, Lowell Carmen; Tex.; 1962, Brazil.
Schochler, Melba Gatlin (Mrs. L. C.); Tex.; 1962, Brazil.
Schoolar, John Earl; Miss.; 1968, Okinawa.
Schoolar, Clara Huckaby (Mrs. J. E.); Tex.; 1968, Okinawa.
Schweer, George William; Mo.; 1957, Indonesia.
Schweer, Wanda Beckham (Mrs. G. W.); Okla.; 1957, Indonesia.
Scott, Bobbie Rue; Tex.; 1967, Malawi.
Scott, Gwendolyne Matlock (Mrs. B. R.); Okla.; 1967, Malawi.
Scott, Dorothy Ruth (P); Ala.; 1964, Tanzania.
Scott, Freddie Rae; Tex.; 1963, Philippines.
Scott, Mary Fenton (Mrs. F. R.); Okla.; 1963, Philippines.
Scott, Howard Edwards (A); Tex.; 1969, Philippines.
Scott, Frances Billingslea (Mrs. H. E.) (A); Kan.; 1969, Philippines.
Seaborn, Miles Lafayette, Jr.; Okla.; 1958, Philippines.
Seaborn, Inda Hammons (Mrs. M. L., Jr.); Okla.; 1958, Philippines.
Seat, Leroy Kay; Mo.; 1966, Japan.
Seat, June Tinsley (Mrs. L. K.); Mo.; 1966, Japan.
Segars, Jacqueline Maner (J); Ala.; 1969, Japan.
Seitz, Berta (J); Ark.; 1965, Nigeria.
Self, Janice Irene (J); Fla.; 1967, Rhodesia.
Sellers, Robert (J); Fla.; 1968, Indonesia.
Senter, Arville Earl; Tex.; 1963, Tanzania.
Senter, Pauline McMahon (Mrs. A. E.); Tex.; 1963, Tanzania.
Shamburger, Sue Renee (J); Tex.; 1969, Bahamas.
Shaw, Carroll Wayne; Tex.; 1959, Rhodesia.
Shaw, Jacqulyn Hall (Mrs. C. W.); Tex.; 1959, Rhodesia.
Sheaffer, Marilyn Kay; Kan.; 1966, Gaza.
Shelby, Jack Murle; Ill.; 1968, Malaysia.
Shelby, Avah Phillips (Mrs. J. M.); Ill.; 1968, Malaysia.
Shelton, Keith Delano; Okla.; 1965, Peru.
Shelton, Anna Lee Painton (Mrs. K. D.); N. M.; 1965, Peru.
Shelton, Raymond Lee; Ill.; 1962, Thailand.
Shelton, Margie Phillips (Mrs. R. L.); Ill.; 1962, Thailand.
Shirley, Charles William; Tenn.; 1958, Argentina.
Shirley, Betty Parsons (Mrs. C. W.); Tenn.; 1958, Argentina.
Shoemake, Robert Edward (J); Tex.; 1967, Japan.
Short, Arthur Bert, Jr. (J); Miss.; 1969, Hong Kong.
Short, Katherine Smith (Mrs. A. B., Jr.) (J); Tenn.; 1969, Hong Kong.
Short, James Mabry, Jr.; Tex.; 1956, Mexico.
Short, Sarah Bradshaw (Mrs. J. M., Jr.); Tex.; 1956, Mexico.
Shults, Newell Mack; Tenn.; 1966, Brazil.
Shults, Audrey Minor (Mrs. N. M.); Va.; 1966, Brazil.
Simms, Donald McVay; Ala.; 1965, Guatemala.
Simms, Barbara Prestwood (Mrs. D. M.); Tex.; 1965, Guatemala.
Simoneaux, Michel Saville; La.; 1969, Japan.
Simoneaux, Bonnie Rushing (Mrs. M. S.); Miss.; 1969, Japan.
Simpson, Samuel Lipford; Miss.; 1964, Ecuador.

Simpson, Sue Kelley (Mrs. S. L.); Miss.; 1964, Ecuador.
Sinclair, Hobson Lewis; Ky.; 1960, Hong Kong.
Sinclair, June Garrott (Mrs. H. L.); Ky.; 1960, Hong Kong.
Singleton, Ira Porter, Jr.; Tenn.; 1960, Rhodesia.
Singleton, Georgia Lowrance (Mrs. I. P., Jr.); Tenn.; 1960, Rhodesia.
Skinner, Rebecca; Miss.; 1968, Tanzania.
Slack, James Byron; La.; 1964, Philippines.
Slack, Mary Prestridge (Mrs. J. B.); Miss.; 1964, Philippines.
Sledd, Maxwell Duaine; Ky.; 1961, Nigeria.
Sledd, Betty Sanders (Mrs. M. D.); Mich.; 1961, Nigeria.
Smith, Betty Marie; Tex.; 1964, Brazil.
Smith, Clarence Rolland; Okla.; 1965, Venezuela.
Smith, Ila Mae Duncan (Mrs. C. R.); Tex.; 1965, Venezuela.
Smith, Donald Edward; Ill.; 1960, Nigeria.
Smith, Betty Baker (Mrs. D. E.); Mo.; 1960, Nigeria.
Smith, Donald Lee; Okla.; 1969, Kenya.
Smith, Ruth Ann Posey (Mrs. D. L.); Okla.; 1969, Kenya.
Smith, Donald Royce; Tex.; 1956, Venezuela.
Smith, Doris Stull (Mrs. D. R.); Tex.; 1956, Venezuela.
Smith, Ebbie Cullen; Tex.; 1960, Indonesia.
Smith, Donna Rodman (Mrs. E. C.); Okla.; 1960, Indonesia.
Smith, Howard Lee; Miss.; 1957, Nigeria and Ghana.
Smith, Ada Blanton (Mrs. H. L.); Tex.; 1957, Nigeria and Ghana.
Smith, Hugh Greene; Ky.; 1963, Malaysia.
Smith, Kathryn Greenfield (Mrs. H. G.); Mo.; 1963, Malaysia.
Smith, Jack Arthur (A); Ill.; 1962, Japan.
Smith, Velma McLaughlin (Mrs. J. A.) (A); Tex.; 1962, Japan.
Smith, James Edward, Jr.; Okla.; 1969, Japan.
Smith, Sharon Craig (Mrs. J. E., Jr.); Okla.; 1969, Japan.
Smith, James Leslie; Tex.; 1958, Indonesia.
Smith, Edna Broadley (Mrs. J. L.); Ky.; 1958, Indonesia.
Smith, Jesse Allen; S. C.; 1959, Philippines.
Smith, Frances Barnette (Mrs. J. A.); S. C.; 1959, Philippines.
Smith, John Decatur; Miss.; 1963, Vietnam and Indonesia.
Smith, Nellie Brock (Mrs. J. D.); Miss.; 1963, Vietnam and Indonesia.
Smith, Joseph Wendell; Ky.; 1967, Indonesia.
Smith, Betty Woodring (Mrs. J. W.); Ky.; 1967, Indonesia.
Smith, Larry E. (J); Ark.; 1965, Thailand.
Smith, Lewis Ruil; Ga.; 1959, Hong Kong.
Smith, Shirley Gibbs (Mrs. L. R.); Fla.; 1959, Hong Kong.
Smith, Linda (J); Ga.; 1968, Peru.
Smith, Loy Connell; N. C.; 1958, Nigeria.
Smith, Eunice Andrews (Mrs. L. C.); N. C.; 1958, Nigeria.
Smith, Marilyn Rose (J); Okla.; 1969, Indonesia.
Smith, Maurice; Tex.; 1959, Ghana.
Smith Evelyn Rickman (Mrs. M.); Tex.; 1959, Ghana.
Smith, Murray C; La.; 1961, Uruguay.
Smith, Dixie Sills (Mrs. M. C); La.; 1961, Uruguay.
Smith, Paul Saint Clair; Miss.; 1961, Jordan.
Smith, Virginia Walker (Mrs. P. S. C.); Mo.; 1961, Jordan.
Smith, Robert Eugene; Okla.; 1960, Brazil.
Smith, Eulene Smith (Mrs. R. E.); Mo.; 1960, Brazil.
Smith, Robert Lee; Fla.; 1963, Indonesia.
Smith, Barbara Richards (Mrs. R. L.); Fla.; 1963, Indonesia.
Smith, Roderick William; S. C.; 1960, Uruguay.
Smith, Ruth Gettys (Mrs. R. W.); S. C.; 1960, Uruguay.
Smith, Sarah Jean (J); D. C.; 1967, Indonesia.
Smith, Shelby Andrew; Ala.; 1958, Ecuador and Trinidad.
Smith, Eleanor Westover (Mrs. S. A.); Pa.; 1958, Ecuador and Trinidad.
Smith, Frances Ann Higdon (Mrs. S. A.); La.; 1968, Trinidad.
Smith, Wade Hamil; Ala.; 1962, Brazil.
Smith, Shirley Cook (Mrs. W. H.); Ala.; 1962, Brazil.
Smith, William Louis; Miss.; 1963, Brazil.
Smith, Carolyn Brand (Mrs. W. L.); Fla.; 1963, Brazil.
Smith, Winifred Lee; Tex.; 1957, Argentina.
Smith, Beverly J. Hefley (Mrs. W. L.); Ark.; 1957, Argentina.
Snell, Roy Edgar; N. C.; 1963, Korea.
Snell, Sarah Brooks (Mrs. R. E.); N. C.; 1963, Korea.
Snider, Sue Evelyn; Tex.; 1961, Ghana.
Snyder, Freddie Joe; Tex.; 1962, Lebanon and Kenya.
Snyder, Hazel Smirl (Mrs. F. J.); Tex.; 1962, Lebanon and Kenya.
Sodergren, Kenneth (J); Md.; 1966, Nigeria.
Sommerkamp, Theo Enoch, Jr. (A); Fla.; 1965, Switzerland.
Sommerkamp, Jean Childers (Mrs. T. E., Jr.) (A); Okla.; 1965, Switzerland.
Sorrells, Wayne Everett; N. C.; 1969, Brazil.
Sorrells, Virgie Kirby (Mrs. W. E.); N. C.; 1969, Brazil.
Southerland, Lawrence Monroe, Jr.; S. C.; 1961, Japan.
Southerland, Marcella Brown (Mrs. L. M., Jr.); S. C.; 1961, Japan.
Spain, Sarah Frances (J); Ala.; 1966, Colombia.
Spann, James Frederick; Ark.; 1962, Brazil.
Spann, Bettye Brawner (Mrs. J. F.); Ark.; 1962, Brazil.
Spann, Jimmie Durr; Tex.; 1957, Uruguay.
Spann, Norma Sparks (Mrs. J. D.); Tex.; 1957, Uruguay.
Sparkman, Rosa Louise; Fla.; 1960, Nigeria.
Spaulding, James Edwin (A); Ky.; 1968, Bahamas.
Spaulding, Barbara Bogie (Mrs. J. E.) (A); Ky.; 1968, Bahamas.
Spencer, Harold Edwin; Ill.; 1963, Philippines.
Spencer, Evelyn Reichmann (Mrs. H. E.); Ill.; 1963, Philippines.
Spessard, Rosemary Jean; Ill.; 1961, Thailand.
Spiegel, Donald James; Mo.; 1958, Brazil.
Spiegel, Betty Wooton (Mrs. D. J.); Ohio; 1958, Brazil.
Sprowls, Lillie (J); N. M.; 1968, Hong Kong.
Spurgeon, Harlan Elsworth; Mo.; 1957, Taiwan.
Spurgeon, Joann Long (Mrs. H. E.); Ind.; 1957, Taiwan.
Squyres, Jerry Willie (J); La.; 1966, Taiwan.
Stahl, Dana (J); Okla.; 1967, Nigeria.
Stalcup, Carol (J); Calif.; 1965, Ghana.
Stampley, Mary Dann; Miss.; 1961, Ghana.
Stamps, Stanley Duthiel; Miss.; 1962, Ecuador.
Stamps, Glenna Morgan (Mrs. S. D.); Tex.; 1962, Ecuador.
Stan, Elaine (J); Ind.; 1965, Japan.
Stanley, James Ira; Ga.; 1965, Philippines.
Stanley, Rosalyn Reavis (Mrs. J. I.); Tex.; 1965, Philippines.
Stanley, Robert Lynn; Tex.; 1966, Philippines.
Stanley, Nora Blan (Mrs. R. L.); Okla.; 1966, Philippines.
Stark, Doris (J); Ark.; 1967, Hong Kong.
Starnes, Howard Cloyes; N. C.; 1960, Korea.
Starnes, Mary Jo Bumgarner (Mrs. H. C.); N. C.; 1960, Korea.
Staton, Dora Jane (P); Ill.; 1966, Jordan.
Steel, Emil Richard; Tex.; 1969, Mexico.

Steel, Betty Woods (Mrs. E. R.); Tex.; 1969, Mexico.
Stella, Anthony, Jr.; Fla.; 1964, Korea.
Stella, Mary V. Sommerkamp (Mrs. A., Jr.); Fla.; 1964, Korea.
Stennett, William Whitfield; Va.; 1963, Guatemala.
Stennett, Elizabeth Graeff (Mrs. W. W.); D. C.; 1963, Guatemala.
Stephens, Charles Thomas, Jr.; N. C.; 1966, Indonesia.
Stephens, Yvonne Yoder (Mrs. C. T., Jr.); N. C.; 1966, Indonesia.
Stephenson, Carol Ann (J); Ill.; 1969, Nigeria.
Stepp, John B., Jr.; S. C.; 1960, Brazil.
Stepp, Pearl Riveland (Mrs. J. B., Jr.); N. D.; 1960, Brazil.
Stertz, James Gail; Mo.; 1961, Germany.
Stertz, Eda Klarer (Mrs. J. G.); Fla.; 1961, Germany.
Stevens, Howard Lamar; Ga.; 1960, Mexico.
Stevens, Norma Young (Mrs. H. L.); Ga.; 1960, Mexico.
Stewart, Riley Jay Elliott; Va.; 1964, Kenya.
Stewart, Laura Lee Gray (Mrs. R. J. E.); W. Va.; 1964, Kenya.
Stewart, Robert Ralph; Neb.; 1958, Thailand.
Stewart, Maxine Ashburn (Mrs. R. R.); Ala.; 1958, Thailand.
Stiles, Donna Louise; Neb.; 1962, Rhodesia.
Stiles, James Harland, Jr.; Ark.; 1967, Colombia.
Stiles, Oneida Milford (Mrs. J. H., Jr.); Tex.; 1967, Colombia.
Stocks, Rozier Lee, Jr.; N. C.; 1965, Zambia.
Stocks, Doris Childers (Mrs. R. L., Jr.); Okla.; 1965, Zambia.
Stone, Faye Irene (J); Va.; 1966, Nigeria.
Stone, Mary Evelyn; Ga.; 1959, Ghana.
Stouffer, Paul Weagley; Pa.; 1960, Brazil.
Stouffer, Peggy Saturday (Mrs. P. W.); Ga.; 1960, Brazil.
Stringer, Linda Ann (J); Tex.; 1966, Rhodesia.
Struble, Raymond Harlan, Jr. (J); Fla.; 1966, Nigeria.
Stuckey, Robert Homer; Ill.; 1962, Indonesia.
Stuckey, Suzanne Knight (Mrs. R. H.); Ill.; 1962, Indonesia.
Stull, Fred David; Peru; 1960, Peru and Chile.
Stull, Bettye Deen (Mrs. F. D.); Ky.; 1960, Peru and Chile.
Sturgeon, Howard Eldon; Ky.; 1957, Mexico.
Sturgeon, Jo Ann Ferguson (Mrs. H. E.); Ky.; 1957, Mexico.
Sullivan, Brenda Jaye (J); Miss.; 1966, France.
Sullivan, John Hartmon; Tenn.; 1958, Nigeria.
Sullivan, Rose Pollard (Mrs. J. H.); La.; 1958, Nigeria.
Summers, Mimosa (J); Ohio; 1965, Hong Kong.
Summers, Ramona (J); Ill.; 1965, Taiwan.
Sutton, Horace Thomas (A); Ala.; 1969, Guatemala.
Sutton, Peggy Barlow (Mrs. H. T.) (A); Ala.; 1969, Guatemala.
Sutton, John Boyd; Va.; 1959, Brazil.
Sutton, Joan Johnson (Mrs. J. B.); Ky.; 1959, Brazil.
Swafford, Gary Kenneth; Ala.; 1968, Malawi.
Swafford, Carolyn Hatchett (Mrs. G. K.); Ala.; 1968, Malawi.
Swann, Roger (J); Tenn.; 1968, Kenya.
Swedenburg, James Reece, Jr.; Ala.; 1969, Korea.
Swedenburg, Joyce Hawk (Mrs. J. R., Jr.); Ark.; 1969, Korea.
Swedenburg, Mary Savannah; Ala.; 1969, Japan.
Swenson, Ann Marie; Argentina; 1962, Spanish Publishing House.
Swicegood, Glen Meredith; Ga.; 1963, Brazil.
Swicegood, Audrey Price (Mrs. G. M.); Fla.; 1963, Brazil.
Sydow, Vernon Emil, Jr.; Tex.; 1963, Brazil and Leeward Islands.
Sydow, Carolyn Peters (Mrs. V. E., Jr.); Tex.; 1963, Brazil and Leeward Islands.

Tabor, Charles Gordon; N. C.; 1957, Korea.
Tabor, Ellen Dennis (Mrs. C. G.); S. C.; 1957, Korea.
Tankersley, Annette (J); Ga.; 1965, Hong Kong.
Tarry, Joe Ellis; N. M.; 1964, Brazil.
Tarry, Leona Isbell (Mrs. J. E.); N. N.; 1964, Brazil.
Taylor, Delbert Leroy; Okla.; 1968, Colombia
Taylor, Lois Constant (Mrs. D. L.); Okla.; 1968, Colombia.
Taylor, Jack Eligia; Tex.; 1962, Mexico.
Taylor, Mimie Anderson (Mrs. J. E.); Tex.; 1962, Mexico.
Taylor, Lora (J); Tex.; 1968, Rhodesia.
Taylor, Preston Alford; Ark.; 1960, Argentina.
Taylor, Dovie Bowers (Mrs. P. A.); Tex.; 1960, Argentina.
Tcherneshoff, Peter John; Fla.; 1962, Brazil.
Tcherneshoff, Rheta Thrasher (Mrs. P. J.); Ala.; 1962, Brazil.
Teel, James Howard; Ala.; 1963, Pakistan.
Teel, Maxine Yeager (Mrs. J. H.); Ala.; 1963, Pakistan.
Teel, James Oscar, Jr.; Tex.; 1956, Ecuador and Argentina.
Teel, Georgia Williams (Mrs. J. O., Jr.); Tex.; 1956, Ecuador and Argentina.
Teems, Bob Aaron; N. C.; 1968, French West Indies.
Teems, Mary Ann Yoder (Mrs. B. A.); S. C.; 1968, French West Indies.
Templeton, James Logan, Jr.; Tex.; 1962, Hong Kong.
Templeton, Lounette Glover (Mrs. J. L., Jr.); Tex.; 1962, Hong Kong.
Terry, James Oliver, Jr.; La.; 1968, Philippines.
Terry, Mabelee Worthen (Mrs. J. O., Jr.); Ark.; 1968, Philippines.
Terry, R W; Tex.; 1960, Ghana, Iceland, and Germany.
Terry, Dale Fields (Mrs. R W); Tex.; 1960, Ghana, Iceland, and Germany.
Thetford, Randall Lee; Tex.; 1965, Philippines and Guam.
Thetford, Priscella Keel (Mrs. R. L.); Tex.; 1965, Philippines and Guam.
Thomas, Bill Clark; Ky.; 1963, Malaysia.
Thomas, Ruth Douglas (Mrs. B. C.); Ky.; 1963, Malaysia.
Thomas, Clifford Eugene; Okla.; 1961, Malawi.
Thomas, Betty Lou Lynn (Mrs. C. E.); Okla.; 1961, Malawi.
Thomas, Phyllis (J); N. C.; 1968, French West Indies.
Thompson, Cecil Lavon; N. C.; 1956, Argentina.
Thompson, Jean Ward (Mrs. C. L.); Tenn.; 1956, Argentina.
Thompson, Davis Henry; Ala.; 1958, Argentina.
Thompson, Thelma Huffman (Mrs. D. H.); Tenn.; 1958, Argentina.
Thompson, James Ross; Mo.; 1968, Colombia.
Thompson, Laveta Jones (Mrs. J. R.); Mo.; 1968, Colombia.
Thompson, Kenneth Ralph; La.; 1958, Korea.
Thompson, Mary Smith (Mrs. K. R.); Ark.; 1958, Korea.
Thompson, Mary Sue; Mo.; 1967, Nigeria.
Thorne, Dale Grant; Okla.; 1965, Israel.
Thorne, Anita White (Mrs. D. G.); Okla.; 1965, Israel.
Thorpe, Bennett Terry; Ky.; 1958, Rhodesia and Malawi.
Thorpe, Wilma Waldin (Mrs. B. T.); Fla.; 1958, Rhodesia and Malawi.
Threlkeld, Garland Marcellus (A); Mo.; 1968, Ethiopia.
Threlkeld, Sally Murphy (Mrs. G. M.) (A); Tex.; 1968, Ethiopia.
Thresher, M. Sue (J); Ark.; 1965, Nigeria.
Thrower, Jack Elwyn; Okla.; 1959, Brazil.
Thrower, Barbra Burke (Mrs. J. E.); Okla.; 1959, Brazil.

Thurman, Clarence, Jr.; Ky.; 1959, Malaysia.
Thurman, Eddie Tilden (Mrs. C., Jr.); Ky.; 1959, Malaysia.
Thurman, Thomas Edward; Miss.; 1964, Pakistan.
Thurman, Gloria Philpot (Mrs. T. E.); Ala.; 1964, Pakistan.
Tidenberg, James Garland; N. M.; 1962, Tanzania and Kenya.
Tidenberg, Parilee Nelson (Mrs. J. G.); Tex.; 1962, Tanzania and Kenya.
Tipton, Shirley Thomas; Ky.; 1959, Tanzania, Kenya, and Uganda.
Tipton, Virginia Dixon (Mrs. S. T.); Ky.; 1959, Tanzania, Kenya, and Uganda.
Tischer, Robert Glen (J); Calif.; 1969, Philippines.
Titus, Jill (J); Tex.; 1965, Hong Kong.
Todd, Chester Lee; La.; 1968, Tanzania.
Todd, Alice Exley (Mrs. C. L.); Calif.; 1968, Tanzania.
Tolar, Jack Eldon, Jr.; Tex.; 1962, Nigeria.
Tolar, Barbara Corrington (Mrs. J. E., Jr.); Ark.; 1964, Nigeria.
Tomita, C. Louise (J); Hawaii; 1968, Japan.
Tomlinson, Ben Wallace; Ga.; 1965, Taiwan.
Tomlinson, Betty Adair (Mrs. B. W.); Tex.; 1965, Taiwan.
Tope, Charles Alvin; Mo.; 1959, Tanzania, Kenya, and Uganda.
Tope, LaVerne Warnecke (Mrs. C. A.); Mo.; 1959, Tanzania, Kenya, and Uganda.
Towery, Britt Edward, Jr.; Tex.; 1956, Taiwan and Hong Kong.
Towery, Joan Long (Mrs. B. E., Jr.); Tex.; 1956, Taiwan and Hong Kong.
Travis, Robert Felts; N. C.; 1964, Kenya.
Travis, Ruth McFarland (Mrs. R. F.); Ind.; 1964, Kenya.
Treadway, James Allan; Tex.; 1963, Taiwan.
Treadway, Ann Harty (Mrs. J. A.); Tex.; 1963, Taiwan.
Treat, Carl Dennis; Okla.; 1967, Uruguay.
Treat, Marlene Seaton (Mrs. C. D.); Okla.; 1967, Uruguay.
Tribble, Clifford Lamar; Tenn.; 1963, Chile.
Tribble, Elizabeth Watkins (Mrs. C. L.); N. C.; 1963, Chile.
Trimble, James William; La.; 1961, Lebanon.
Trimble, Vivian C Paulk (Mrs. J. W.); La.; 1961, Lebanon.
Troop, Joseph Eugene; Mo.; 1959, Brazil.
Troop, Leona Walker (Mrs. J. E.); Mo.; 1959, Brazil.
Trott, Edward Bruce; Tex.; 1957, Brazil.
Trott, Freda Porter (Mrs. E. B.); Miss.; 1957, Brazil.
Trotter, George Richmond; Va.; 1964, Indonesia.
Trotter, Martha Wilson (Mrs. G. R.); Va.; 1964, Indonesia.
Trubenbach, Sandra (J); Tex.; 1967, Peru.
Tucker, Harold Robert, Jr.; Tex.; 1963, Venezuela.
Tucker, Margaret Roberts (Mrs. H. R., Jr.); Tex.; 1963, Venezuela.
Tumblin, John Addison, Jr.; Brazil; 1956, Brazil.
Tumblin, Alice Puryear (Mrs. J. A., Jr.); D. C.; 1956, Brazil.
Tunmire, Faye Virginia; N. C.; 1956, Philippines.
Turman, Joe Garner; Tex.; 1968, Vietnam.
Turman, Gloria Reece (Mrs. J. G.); Tenn.; 1968, Vietnam.
Turnage, Loren Cleland; Mo.; 1959, Colombia.
Turnage, Cherry Kincheloe (Mrs. L. C.); Okla.; 1959, Colombia.
Turner, Alpha L. Belvin (Mrs. W. M.) (A); La.; 1967, Gaza.
Turner, Donald Edwin; Mich.; 1965, Brazil.
Turner, Donna Fletcher (Mrs. D. E.); Ohio; 1965, Brazil.
Turner, Gwin Terrell; Miss.; 1959, Argentina.
Turner, Norma Brasher (Mrs. G. T.); Miss.; 1959, Argentina.
Turner, Milton Ray (A); Tex.; 1969, Ecuador.
Turner, Betty Dozier (Mrs. M. R.) (A); Tex.; 1969, Ecuador.
Tyler, Janie Day (J); Okla.; 1969, Colombia.
Tyner, Grover Francis, Jr.; Ga.; 1963, Philippines.
Tyner, Libby Alexander (Mrs. G. F., Jr.); N. C.; 1963, Philippines.

Valerius, Erling Clifford; Fla.; 1963, Brazil.
Valerius, Carrie McLean (Mrs. E. C.); Ala.; 1963, Brazil.
Van Cleef, Lois (J); N. Y.; 1969, Nigeria.
Vanderburg, Ruth Jane; Ark.; 1956, Indonesia.
Vandiver, Roy (J); Tex.; 1968, Nigeria.
Varner, George Kenneth; S. C.; 1969, Taiwan.
Varner, Patricia Arthur (Mrs. G. K.); S. C.; 1969, Taiwan.
Varner, Victor Nelson; Tex.; 1965, Brazil.
Varner, Joan Criswell (Mrs. V. N.); Okla.; 1965, Brazil.
Veatch, Carol Allen, Sr.; Ga.; 1964, Bahamas.
Veatch, Helen Hubbard (Mrs. C. A., Sr.); Ga.; 1964, Bahamas.
Verner, Walter Eugene; Tex.; 1958, Ghana.
Verner, Marjorie Rieben (Mrs. W. E.); Ala.; 1958, Ghana.
Vestal, James Gordon; Tex.; 1963, Chile.
Vestal, Ella Reeves (Mrs. J. G.); Tex.; 1963, Chile.
Viertel, Weldon Ernest; Tex.; 1959, Bahamas.
Viertel, Joyce Garrett (Mrs. W. E.); Tex.; 1959, Bahamas.
Virkler, John (J); Va.; 1968, Bermuda.

Wagner, William Lyle; N. M.; 1965, Austria.
Wagner, Sally Crook (Mrs. W. L.); Colo.; 1965, Austria.
Wakefield, Robert Earl; Mo.; 1961, Malaysia.
Wakefield, Margarita Adkison (Mrs. R. E.); Mo.; 1961, Malaysia.
Wakefield, William Ray; Mo.; 1960, Philippines.
Wakefield, Delcie Musgrave (Mrs. W. R.); N. Y.; 1960, Philippines.
Waldron, Samuel Milton; Ga.; 1966, Philippines.
Waldron, Mary Thomas (Mrs. S. M.); Ga.; 1966, Philippines.
Waldrop, Leo Eugene (J); Tex.; 1966, Guyana.
Walker, Elbert Henry; Colo.; 1957, Philippines.
Walker, Dorothy Mathews (Mrs. E. H.); Ga.; 1957, Philippines.
Walker, Freddie; Ill.; 1968, Kenya.
Walker, Betty Akery (Mrs. F.); Ga.; 1968, Kenya.
Walker, Graham Brown (A); Ky.; 1969, Singapore.
Walker, Jeanne Francisco (Mrs. G. B.) (A); Fla.; 1969, Singapore.
Walker, James Charles; Ala.; 1962, Malawi and Rhodesia.
Walker, Charlotte Fulton (Mrs. J. C.); Ala.; 1962, Malawi and Rhodesia.
Walker, Laurence Allen; Tenn.; 1968, Brazil.
Walker, Nancy Applewhite (Mrs. L. A.); Tenn.; 1968, Brazil.
Walker, Richard Edward; Tex.; 1964, Brazil.
Walker, Beatrice Rodgers (Mrs. R. E.); Ark.; 1964, Brazil.
Wall, Nancy Lee (J); S. C.; 1967, Ghana.
Walsh, Billy Joe; Okla.; 1961, Mexico.
Walsh, Ruby Dugger (Mrs. B. J.); Ark.; 1961, Mexico.
Walters, Doris Lavonne; N. C.; 1966, Japan.
Ward, Emily (J); Ala.; 1969, Brazil.
Ware, James Cullen; La.; 1958, Mexico.
Ware, Susan Goodwin (Mrs. J. C.); La.; 1958, Mexico.
Warmath, William Carman; Miss.; 1959, Japan.
Warmath, Mary Cox (Mrs. W. C.); Ark.; 1959, Japan.
Warren, Charles Edward, Jr. (J); Va.; 1969, Zambia.
Warren, William Harley; Tex.; 1958, Brazil.

Warren, Lola Robinson (Mrs. W. H.); Tex.; 1958, Brazil.
Watanabe, George Hideo; Hawaii; 1967, Japan.
Watanabe, Amy Konishi (Mrs. G. H.); Hawaii; 1967, Japan.
Watkins, Kenneth Hughen; Ala.; 1967, Paraguay.
Watkins, Linda Claville (Mrs. K. H.); Fla.; 1967, Paraguay.
Watson, Harold Ray; Miss.; 1964, Philippines.
Watson, Joyce Daniel (Mrs. H. R.); Tex.; 1964, Philippines.
Watson, James Maurice; Okla.; 1962, Spain.
Watson, Ruth Vineyard (Mrs. J. M.); Ark.; 1962, Spain.
Watson, Thomas Laird; Tex.; 1959, Uruguay and Peru.
Watson, Joan Smith (Mrs. T. L.); N. M.; 1959, Uruguay and Peru.
Watters, James Lee; Okla.; 1962, Japan.
Watters, Darleene Ryburn (Mrs. J. L.); Okla.; 1962, Japan.
Watts, James Dale; Miss.; 1967, Italy.
Watts, Charlotte Lowe (Mrs. J. D.); Miss.; 1967, Italy.
Weatherford, Rosalie Wooding (P); Va.; 1969, Paraguay.
Webb, Janet Eloise (J); Okla.; 1966, Nigeria.
Weber, Roberta Jeanne (J); Mo.; 1969, Hong Kong.
Welch, Norvel Wayne; Tex.; 1963, Brazil.
Welch, Hattie Leach (Mrs. N. W.); Tex.; 1963, Brazil.
Weldon, Katharine Kay; Tex.; 1963, Mexico.
Weller, Jac Summers (A); Ohio; 1969, Singapore.
Weller, Jane Vanoy (Mrs. J. S.) (A); Ala.; 1969, Singapore.
Wells, Frank Sidney; Ala.; 1961, Korea and Indonesia.
Wells, Jo Ann Fossett (Mrs. F. S.); Ala.; 1961, Korea and Indonesia.
Wells, Melvin Albert (A); Kan.; 1968, Zambia.
Wells, Carrie Rooker (Mrs. M. A.) (A); Okla.; 1968, Zambia.
Wensel, Barbara Lee; D. C.; 1956, Mexico.
West, James Raymond; Tex.; 1969, Venezuela.
West, Bobbie Gilbert (Mrs. J. R.); Tex.; 1969, Venezuela.
Westbrook, Charley Erwin; Okla.; 1963, Argentina.
Westbrook, Darlene Gurskey (Mrs. C. E.); Okla.; 1963, Argentina.
Western, Blake Weatherford; Okla.; 1966, Japan.
Westmoreland, James Newton; Tenn.; 1960, Rhodesia.
Westmoreland, Wynema J. Mayo (Mrs. J. N.); Okla.; 1960, Rhodesia.
Whatley, Annice (J); Ga.; 1965, Jordan.
Wheeler, John Paul; Fla.; 1963, Switzerland.
Wheeler, Kay Hooper (Mrs. J. P.); Fla.; 1963, Switzerland.
Wheeler, Samuel Wayne; Ga.; 1966, Honduras.
Wheeler, Annette Montgomery (Mrs. S. W.); Fla.; 1966, Honduras.
Wheeler, Veronica Mae (J); Miss.; 1966, Nigeria.
Whelan, Willie Earl; Ky.; 1959, Korea.
Whelan, Elaine Power (Mrs. W. E.); N. Y.; 1959, Korea.
White, Betty (J); Miss.; 1968, Hong Kong.
White, Daniel Raburn; Tex.; 1960, Spain.
White, Frieda Bryson (Mrs. D. R.); Okla.; 1960, Spain.
White, J. Wayne; Okla.; 1963, Mexico.
White, Winnie Dudley (Mrs. J. W.); Tex.; 1963, Mexico.
White, Kathryn Fern; Okla.; 1958, Hong Kong.
White, Rufus King (J); Ga.; 1969, Guatemala.
Whitley, Elijah Jackson, Jr.; Ala.; 1963, Venezuela and Bahamas.
Whitley, Helen Elliott (Mrs. E. J., Jr.); Ala.; 1963, Venezuela and Bahamas.
Whitlow, Henry Stephen; La.; 1965, Hong Kong.
Whitlow, Betty Krudwig (Mrs. H. S.); Ark.; 1965, Hong Kong.
Whitson, Charlton Davis (A); Ala.; 1967, South West Africa.
Whitson, Betty Huckaby (Mrs. C. D.) (A); Ala.; 1967, South West Africa.
Whitson, David Hudson; Ala.; 1962, Tanzania.
Whitson, Betty Ann Clark (Mrs. D. H.); Tex.; 1962, Tanzania.
Whitten, Bonna Fay (J); Miss.; 1965, Paraguay.
Wicks, Harold David; Ala.; 1967, Nigeria.
Wicks, Rebecca Branum (Mrs. H. D.); Ala.; 1967, Nigeria.
Wigger, Larry David; Mo.; 1968, Vietnam.
Wigger, Barbara Jett (Mrs. L. D.); Mo.; 1968, Vietnam.
Wiggs, Charles William; N. C.; 1960, Korea.
Wiggs, Bonnie Johnson (Mrs. C. W.); N. C.; 1960, Korea.
Wiginton, Travis Eugene; Okla.; 1960, Korea.
Wiginton, Gaynell Harris (Mrs. T. E.); Okla.; 1960, Korea.
Wikman, John Harry, Jr.; Mich.; 1967, India and Gaza.
Wikman, Barbara Biggers (Mrs. J. H., Jr.); Ark.; 1967, India and Gaza.
Wilkes, John Mannen; Okla.; 1965, France and Switzerland.
Wilkes, Doylene (Mrs. J. M.); Okla.; 1965, France and Switzerland.
Williams, Allen Gregory, Sr., (A); Tex.; 1969, Tanzania.
Williams, Helen Phelps (Mrs. A. G., Sr.) (A); Tenn.; 1969, Tanzania.
Williams, Charles Benton; Tenn.; 1959, Thailand.
Williams, Elizabeth Rogers (Mrs. C. B.); Tenn.; 1959, Thailand.
Williams, Clara Lynn; Tenn.; 1965, Brazil.
Williams, Diane Patricia (J); Miss.; 1969, Philippines.
Williams, Donald Lawrence (J); Calif.; 1966, Nigeria.
Williams, Irvin Earl; La.; 1967, Liberia.
Williams, Jane Williams (Mrs. I. E.); Tenn.; 1967, Liberia.
Williams, James Austin, Jr. (A); Tex.; 1967, Mexico.
Williams, Faye Mathews (Mrs. J. A., Jr.) (A); Okla.; 1967, Mexico.
Williams, Juanita (J); Kan.; 1968, Switzerland.
Williams, Pamela Jean (J); Okla.; 1969, Vietnam.
Williams, Robert Dee; Tex.; 1964, Nigeria.
Williams, Ruby Williamson (Mrs. R. D.); Miss.; 1964, Nigeria.
Williamson, Guy Smith; Ga.; 1960, Mexico.
Williamson, Julia Heaton (Mrs. G. S.); Ga.; 1960, Mexico.
Willis, Avery Thomas, Jr.; Ark.; 1964, Indonesia.
Willis, Shirley Morris (Mrs. A. T., Jr.); Okla.; 1964, Indonesia.
Willis, Harlan Leigh; Tex.; 1960, Thailand.
Willis, Fannie Joe Hester (Mrs. H. L.); Tex.; 1960, Thailand.
Willmon, Jesse Conrad; Ala.; 1963, Lebanon.
Willmon, Jeannine Richardson (Mrs. J. C.); Ala.; 1963, Lebanon.
Willocks, Robert Max; Tenn.; 1956, Korea.
Willocks, Neysa Ferguson (Mrs. R. M.); Tenn.; 1956, Korea.
Wilson, Barbara Joan; Okla.; 1968, Tanzania.
Wilson, Ernest Clay, Jr.; Tex.; 1959, Brazil.
Wilson, Billie Haynie (Mrs. E. C., Jr.); Tex.; 1959, Brazil.
Wilson, Gene O'Neil; S. C.; 1963, Brazil.
Wilson, Angelle Kenney (Mrs. G. O.); Ga.; 1963, Brazil.
Wilson, George Raymond, Jr.; Okla.; 1956, Hong Kong.
Wilson, Elizabeth Schreiber (Mrs. G. R., Jr.); Fla.; 1956, Hong Kong.
Wilson, James Monroe; Ark.; 1963, Brazil.
Wilson, Betty Miller (Mrs. J. M.); N. D.; 1963, Brazil.

Wilson, Joe Leon; Ark.; 1963, Thailand.
Wilson, Alice Gardner (Mrs. J. L.); Va.; 1963, Thailand.
Wilson, Michael Henry; Ohio; 1960, Taiwan.
Wilson, Catherine Spillman (Mrs. M. H.); Ky.; 1960, Taiwan.
Wilson, Ralph Augustus; Tex.; 1966, Honduras.
Wilson, Sue Austin (Mrs. R. A.); Okla.; 1966, Honduras.
Wilson, Sarah Georgia; N. C.; 1957, Argentina.
Wiltshire, Ashley Turman, Jr. (J); Va.; 1967, Thailand.
Wine, Mary Ellen (J); Va.; 1965, Korea.
Winfield, Mary Louise (J); Tenn.; 1966, Korea.
Wingo, Nancie Jane; Tex.; 1963, Lebanon.
Winham, John Terrance (J); Tex.; 1966, Germany.
Wisdom, Charles Joseph; La.; 1967, Mexico.
Wisdom, Lilly Faye McKinney (Mrs. C. J.); Tex.; 1967, Mexico.
Wisener, Sandra (J); Ala.; 1968, Nigeria.
Witt, Mary Magdalene; Tenn.; 1963, Brazil.
Wolf, Robert Henry; Okla.; 1956, Mexico.
Wolf, Kathleen Kay (Mrs. R. H.); Okla.; 1956, Mexico.
Wolfe, Cheryl (J); Calif.; 1967, Ghana.
Wolfe, Kenneth Roy; Kan.; 1961, Brazil.
Wolfe, Glenda Burk (Mrs. K. R.); Mo.; 1961, Brazil.
Womack, Jack; Ala.; 1969, Uruguay.
Womack, Nancy Neighbors (Mrs. J.); Ala.; 1969, Uruguay.
Wood, Darrell Wayne; Okla.; 1968, Hong Kong.
Wood, Priscilla Kelly (Mrs. D. W.); Mo.; 1968, Hong Kong.
Wood, Norman Wayne; Okla.; 1962, Zambia.
Wood, Jean Powell (Mrs. N. W.); Okla.; 1962, Zambia.
Wood, Rudolph Malcolm; Va.; 1964, Luxembourg and Belgium.
Wood, Helen Siner (Mrs. R. M.); Va.; 1964, Luxembourg and Belgium.
Wood, Sydney Kenneth; Pa.; 1960, Japan.
Wood, Audrey Ell Richmond (Mrs. S. K.); La.; 1960, Japan.
Woodfin, Yandall Clark III; Tex.; 1966, Switzerland.
Woodfin, Leta Beene (Mrs. Y. C.); Tex.; 1966, Switzerland.
Worley, Robert Donald; N. M.; 1968, Spain.
Worley, Jerry Fletcher (Mrs. R. D.); Tex.; 1968, Spain.
Worten, Harry Von; Okla.; 1964, Indonesia.
Worten, Marjorie Jones (Mrs. H. V.); Tex.; 1964, Indonesia.
Worthy, Charles Clyde; Ala.; 1968, Israel.
Worthy, Carolyn (Mrs. C. C.); Ala.; 1968, Israel.
Wright, Elizabeth Jean (J); D. C.; 1966, Rhodesia.
Wyatt, Dale Parks (J); Va.; 1967, Switzerland.
Wyatt, Laura Ann (J); Tex.; 1968, Ghana.
Wyatt, William Emerson; S. C.; 1960, Nigeria.
Wyatt, Winnie Dowden (Mrs. W. E.); La.; 1960, Nigeria.
Wyman, David Gregory; N. M.; 1969, Mexico.
Wyman, Barbara Walker (Mrs. D. G.); N. M.; 1969, Mexico.
Wynn, Norma (J); Okla.; 1965, Tanzania.

Yarbrough, Bobby Ray; Ga.; 1966, Uruguay.
Yarbrough, Sharon Russell (Mrs. B. R.); Ind.; 1966, Uruguay.
Yarbrough, James Archie; Ga.; 1959, Nigeria.
Yarbrough, Nancy Smith (Mrs. J. A.); Fla.; 1959, Nigeria.
Yates, Jane (J); Ariz.; 1968, Gaza.
Yates, Remona Jo; Tex.; 1969, Paraguay.
Yoars, Ralph Arnold; La.; 1969, Hong Kong.
Yoars, Betty Alexander (Mrs. R. A.); N. C.; 1969, Hong Kong.
Young, Anita (J); Miss.; 1967, Argentina.
Young, Dwight Leroy (J); N. M.; 1966, Hong Kong.
Young, Fred Douglas (J); La.; 1969, Kenya.
Young, Karin Hooper (Mrs. F. D.) (J); La.; 1969, Kenya.
Young, Glenn Raymond (J); Ariz.; 1966, Philippines.
Young, Hugh Howland; Ga.; 1968, Japan.
Young, Norma Lucas (Mrs. H. H.); Ky.; 1968, Japan.
Young, Jack Newberry; Mo.; 1961, Brazil.
Young, Jean DeVore (Mrs. J. N.); Tex.; 1961, Brazil.
Young, James Edward; Miss.; 1969, Yemen.
Young, Guinevere Jenkins (Mrs. J. E.); Miss.; 1969, Yemen.

ANNIE BELLE SELLERS
GENEVIEVE GREER

***FORK UNION MILITARY ACADEMY.** In recent years Fork Union has resisted pressure to enlarge its enrolment, and in the 1968–69 session had 662 regular session cadets with a faculty of 60. College preparatory work is offered for fifth through twelfth grades plus one year of postgraduate study. Summer school sessions were resumed in 1969. Fork Union enjoys full accreditation by the state and the Southern Association of Colleges and Schools.

Fork Union has an endowment of $1,466,000. The total income for the fiscal year ending June 30, 1968, was $1,613,664. No government funds are accepted. The R.O.T.C. unit was discontinued in 1965 and was replaced with nongovernment military training. Kenneth T. Whitescarver succeeded J. Caldwell Wicker as president on July 1, 1968. A new science building which includes a planetarium was erected in 1970.

CARRINGTON PAULETTE

FORM CRITICISM. A method of research developed by Martin Dibelius and Rudolf Bultmann (1919–21) for the purpose of studying and understanding synoptic gospel materials at a depth beyond that proposed by source criticism. Although the methodology had been used earlier in the Old Testament (Gunkel) and is now applied in other parts of the New Testament, it has been in the area of gospel research that the most significant and controversial achievements have been made.

The basic assumption of form criticism is that behind the gospel narratives as we now possess them lie folk or oral traditions which developed within the church in the time span between the events of the incarnation and the writing about these events in documents. Form criticism attempts to classify the various units of oral tradition (pericopes) now extant in the gospel narratives according to general categories or forms [*e.g.*, paradigm, *Novelle,* legend, parenesis, myth (Dibelius)] and postulates the life-situation within the church which affected the form, or created it entirely, and caused it to be preserved and handed on.

The geographical and chronological sequence of a given gospel (cf. Mark with Luke) is considered to be the work of the author of the gospel as a framework or setting for the pericopes and therefore has no biographical value.

See also REDACTION CRITICISM.

BIBLIOGRAPHY: R. C. Briggs, *Interpreting the Gospels* (1969). Rudolf Bultmann and Karl Kundsin, *Form Criticism* translated by F. C. Grant (1962). Edgar V. McKnight, *What Is Form Criticism?* (1969).

DONALD E. COOK

FOSTER, LIDA CHILES (b. Knox County, Tenn., Mar. 13, 1882; d. Columbia, S. C., Sept. 1, 1969). Educator and philanthropist. Daughter of Noah Hampton and Cordelia (Tarver) Chiles, she was educated at Carson-Newman College, Jefferson City, Tenn., and Woman's Missionary Union Training School, Southern Baptist Theological Seminary, Louisville, Ky. She married A. J. Foster of Clinton, Tenn., in 1903. She served as approved state Intermediate worker, South Carolina Baptist Convention, 1924–42. She contributed over $500,000 to Baptist institutions. She is buried in Knoxville, Tenn. S. GEORGE LOVELL, JR.

FOUNDATIONS. A quarterly published since 1958 by the American Baptist Historical Society, it succeeded *The Chronicle* (1938–57). It has usually carried editorials, articles on historical and theological subjects, book reviews, and, frequently, notes from religious journals. Editors have been George D. Younger (1958–68) and John E. Skoglund (1969–). For an analysis of its first six years of publication, see W. Morgan Patterson, *Foundations,* VII (Apr., 1964), 202–208. W. MORGAN PATTERSON

FRANCE, MISSION IN. Southern Baptist missionaries entered France in 1960 at the joint invitation of the French Baptist Federation (formed Feb. 18, 1911) and an English-language Baptist congregation composed mainly of allied military personnel. Jack D. and Doris (White) Hancox initially went to Orleans to serve this church and establish liaison with the federation. Five other English-language churches were constituted later. In 1967 when non-French military personnel were reassigned, all but one church disbanded. Emmanuel Church, Paris, maintained a ministry to English-speaking civilians in the capital area while authorizing its members transferring to Belgium to form a mission there. The France Mission aids fellow Baptists primarily in evangelism, church building construction, Christian education, and broadcasting. A five-year plan to locate places of worship in new areas extended from 1965 to 1969. The federation's 95 churches and preaching points report 2,500 members. At the beginning of 1970 four Southern Baptist missionaries were assigned to France: Hal and Lou Ann (Green) Lee and John and Doylene (Currin) Wilkes. Through work with language church groups situated in France, the mission is able to assist with evangelism, church development, and Scripture distribution for certain areas within eastern Europe.

JOHN M. WILKES

FRANKLIN, JAMES HENRY (b. Pamplin, Va., May 13, 1872; d. Richmond, Va., Mar. 23, 1961). Pastor, educator, humanitarian. The son of Samuel R. and Mary (Burruss) Franklin, he was educated at Richmond College and Southern Baptist Theological Seminary (Th.M., 1898). He married Augusta Terry, Nov. 15, 1900, and was the father of one daughter, Caroline.

Franklin held pastorates in Colorado from 1898 to 1912. He served as executive secretary of the American Baptist Foreign Mission Society, 1912–34. From 1934 until his retirement in 1943 he was president of Crozer Theological Seminary, Chester, Pa. In his retirement he taught in the Department of Religion at the University of Richmond.

He was president of the Northern Baptist Convention, 1934–36; and a member of the International Missionary Council, 1921–34. The French government awarded him the Legion of Honor for his service during the reconstruction of Europe after World War I. His published works include: *The Never Failing Light* (1933), *In the Track of the Storm* (1919), and *Ministers of Mercy* (1919). Franklin was awarded honorary degrees by the University of Denver, Brown University, and the University of Richmond. He was buried in Hollywood Cemetery, Richmond, Va. IRA D. HUDGINS

FRAZIER, CHARLES FRANKLIN (b. Callis, Collin County, Tex., Sept. 8, 1888; d. Coolidge, Ariz., Dec. 25, 1964). Missionary to the Pima Indians in Arizona. Converted at 14, he was a veteran of World War I. He preached and sang in Texas, New Mexico, and Arizona. He married Elsie Pendleton of Gainesville, Tex., in 1933. He served as pastor of the following First Baptist churches in Arizona: Willcox, Coolidge, and Pima of Sacaton. He was licensed by Sycamore Heights Baptist Church, Fort Worth, Tex., and ordained by Calvary Baptist Church, Casa Grande, Ariz. From 1939 until retirement in 1953, he and his wife served under appointment of the Home Mission Board, SBC, as missionaries to the Pima Indians. Following retirement he served at Florence and Sacaton as pastor and at the same time was chaplain at the Florence Federal Prison. J. TRUMAN WEBB

***FREE WILL BAPTISTS, NATIONAL ASSOCIATION OF.** The Free Will Baptist denomination is a fellowship of evangelical believers united in extending the witness of Christ throughout the world. In 1969 the national association had 2,142 churches, with a membership of 184,869. The denomination had 3,395 ordained clergy.

In 1961 about half of the Free Will Baptist churches of North Carolina split from the main body when they publicly avowed a connectional form of church government rather than the accepted congregational form. The other North Carolina churches immediately filled the void left by the split and increased North Carolina's financial and membership support in all phases of Free Will Baptist ministries.

The national offices were relocated in Nashville, Tenn., in 1965 in a new building. The Sunday School Department built its own plant on the national offices' site in 1967. Two years later, the department began a complete Free Will Baptist Sunday School curriculum for all ages. The Church Training Service Department, formed in 1962, within the first seven years of operation developed its own curriculum, national youth program, and a national campsite located near Nashville. Free Will Baptist Bible College, begun in 1942 as a denominational ministry, expanded its campus in a $3,000,000 building program. Two other colleges, begun by state associations, were established between 1960 and 1969: Oklahoma Bible College at Moore, Okla., and California Christian College at Fresno, Calif. Numerous Free Will Baptist church-operated Christian day schools were organized in several states during the mid-sixties. In 1970 foreign missionaries numbered 70, working in 8 foreign countries. Home missionaries numbered 32 and worked in 11 states, Canada, Mexico, Puerto Rico, and the Virgin Islands.

Denominational publications include *Contact* magazine, the official voice of the denomination; *Mission-grams,* a bimonthly home missions publication; *Heartbeat,* the foreign missions magazine; and the *Free Will Baptist College Bulletin.*

The national offices are located at 1134 Murfreesboro Road, Nashville, Tenn. National departments operating here include the executive office, Church Training Service, Foreign Missions, Home Missions and Church Extension, Master's Men, Retirement and Insurance, Sunday School, and Woman's National Auxiliary Convention. The mailing address is P. O. Box 1088, Nashville, Tenn. 37202. Free Will Baptist Bible College is located at 3606 West End Avenue, Nashville, Tenn. 37205.

RUFUS COFFEY AND JIM JONES

FRENCH WEST INDIES, MISSION IN. In 1964 the first Southern Baptist missionaries entered the French West Indies, composed of three islands—Guadeloupe, Martinique, and St. Martin—and their dependencies. Five years later two couples were serving on Guadeloupe, where they and only one other evangelical mission sought to witness to people whose predominant religion is Catholicism. Roman Catholic tradition strongly binds the mixture of African and French cultures. Beginnings were slow as the people struggled to break the bonds of tradition upon hearing the gospel message. Two churches, two missions, and four national pastors were reported in 1969. WENDELL L. PAGE

FREY, LEIBERT GARLAND (b. Spottsville, Henderson County, Ky., June 12, 1893; d. Nashville, Tenn., Sept. 3, 1961) . Frey was educated at LaRue College, Owensboro, Ky., Kentucky State Normal School, Bowling Green, (Ky.) Business University, Union University, Jackson, Tenn., and Pace and Pace Institute, New York City. He taught in public schools in Memphis, Tenn., and Henderson County, Ky., and in private schools in Jackson and Humboldt for 17 years. Frey organized West Tennessee Business College at Jackson and operated it for 12 years.

Ordained at West Jackson Baptist Church, Jackson, Tenn., in 1933, he served the following West Tennessee churches as pastor: Maple Springs, Ararat, Westover, Poplar Heights, Bells, and Alamo. He was moderator of Madison-Chester Association 16 years. In 1956 he initiated the Rural Church Development Program, which was designed to strengthen rural Baptist churches. Frey wrote *The Romance of Rural Churches* (1948) , a number of tracts and pamphlets, and a manual for associational missionaries. He also served as secretary and business manager of executive board, Tennessee Baptist Convention, 1942–47, secretary, State Missions Department, 1948–60, and recording secretary, Tennessee Baptist Convention, 1939–60.

He married Ruby Marguerite Bevill, on Sept. 22, 1915. They had four children: Robert Charles, Bryan Leibert, William Bevill, and Sarah Louise (Mrs. Robert B. Baker) . He is buried in Woodlawn Memorial Park, Nashville, Tenn. WALLACE ANDERSON

FROST, MARGARET. See RODEN, MARGARET FROST.

FUNDAMENTAL BAPTIST FELLOWSHIP (NORTHERN BAPTIST). A group of fundamentalist Baptists, organized in 1920 as a protest movement against theological liberalism within the Northern Baptist Convention. Adopting the name, Fundamentalist Fellowship of the Northern Baptist Convention, the Fellowship met before the annual sessions of the Northern convention and also acted as a conservative pressure group within the convention. In the beginning premillennialism was not a test of fellowship nor did this group favor separation from the convention.

In the forties the Fundamentalist Fellowship became more militant and led in the formation of the Conservative Baptist Foreign Mission Society in 1943, the Conservative Baptist Association of America in 1947, and the Conservative Baptist Home Mission Society in 1948. Renamed Conservative Baptist Fellowship in 1946, the fellowship cooperated with other national Conservative Baptist bodies (independent organizations) . Growing differences regarding cooperative evangelism and other matters led the fellowship to cease such cooperation in 1955 and to sponsor the formation of the World Conservative Baptist Mission (now called the Baptist World Mission) , a new home and foreign mission society to serve Conservative Baptists. But the mainstream of the Conservative Baptist movement refused to accept the new society. At the 1965 session of the Conservative Baptist Fellowship, individuals who favored separation from the Conservative Baptist movement approved the formation of the New Testament Association of Independent Baptist Churches of America, whose churches would be entirely separate from any other national Baptist body. This new association has not received wide endorsement.

In 1965 the fellowship changed its name to Fundamental Baptist Fellowship and in 1968 transferred its national offices from Chicago to Denver. A self-perpetuating board controls its affairs, and its annual meetings are primarily preaching sessions with a minimum of business. The fellowship receives funds from its members, individuals who sign its doctrinal statement (including belief in the premillennial return of Christ and the pretribulation rapture of the church) and contribute annually, and from independent Baptist churches. In 1970 G. Archer Weniger of Oakland, Calif., was president of the fellowship, and M. James Hollowood served as editor of its paper, the *Information Bulletin*.

See also CONSERVATIVE BAPTISTS.

ALBERT W. WARDIN, JR.

***FURMAN UNIVERSITY.** In 1948 the trustees decided to consolidate all operations of the university on a new 1,200-acre site five miles north of the city. Since the coordination of Furman and the Greenville Woman's College in the thirties, the university had operated on two campuses separated by the business district of Greenville, S. C. With the post-World War II growth of both university and city, interchange of students and faculty became more difficult. The city preempted part of both properties for arterial streets, and space for development was limited. Financed by combining accumulated building funds, money raised by a special drive, a $3,500,000 capital needs grant from the Baptist state convention, and federal loans, building began in 1954. By 1958 enough buildings were finished to make possible the closing of the century-old downtown campus of the men's college, and all men and senior women registered for the 1958–59 session on the new campus. In 1961 the remaining women students moved into newly completed residence halls, and Furman University operated as a single unit on the sixth campus in its history. The present campus occupies 590 acres, with an adjacent 155-acre golf course, of the 1,200-acre tract.

Under John Laney Plyler's (*q.v.*) quarter-century administration, Jan. 1, 1939, to Aug. 31, 1964, the university passed from the depression years, through the difficult adjustments of World War II and its aftermath, the building of the new campus, and the changes necessitated by consolidated operations. University assets grew from $3,375,000 to well over $29,000,000, and the endowment from $1,000,000 to $7,000,000. Enrolment increased by nearly 600 students and tremendous strides were made in upgrading academic standards. When Plyler retired, Dean Francis Wesley Bonner served as executive head of the university until Gordon Williams Blackwell assumed the duties of president on Feb. 1, 1965.

Under Blackwell's administration, the university has liberalized its admission policy, improved communications within the university, strengthened religious activities programs, made innovative curricular change, and stimulated its development program. Since Jan., 1965, all qualified students are admitted. Modifications of social regulations, faculty and student participation in university governance, and free interchange of ideas among administration, faculty, and students have resulted from improved communications. A well-staffed chaplaincy seeks to meet religious needs of today's students. With the adoption of a new curriculum in 1968, the student has more flexibility in personal program development and opportunities not only for individual directed study but also for non-Western studies and studies abroad in the university's Fall-in-England and other programs. Increased use of visiting scholars and lectures stimulate intellectual curiosity. The building of new facilities continues with the completion of the science center, the computer center, three residence halls, and a playhouse. Funding for continuing development and enrichment resulted from the meeting of a Ford Foundation challenge grant in 1969 and the success of a campaign for $10,000,000 by May 31, 1971.

Enrolment for the fall term of 1969–70 was 2,011, of whom 1,066 were men and 945 women. In addition, 218 were enrolled in the Evening Division. To teach these students there was a faculty of 144 supported by a library of 175,000 volumes. The university offers the B.A., B.S., B.Mus., M.Ed., M.A. in education, and M.S. in chemistry. The total assets of the university in 1969 were $40,795,000. The $8,773,000 endowment includes participation in the Duke Endowment. For operations in 1968–69 the Baptist state convention allotted $234,206 to the total budget of $6,146,506. ALBERT N. SANDERS

G

GABRIEL, ANNIE (b. Boonville, Mo., Feb. 20, 1886; d. San Bernardino, Calif., July 4, 1968). The third of ten children born to James B. and Delilah Gabriel, she was well acquainted with poverty, poor health, and adversity, but was determined to gain an education. She enrolled in the University of Texas, later studied in the University of Cincinnati, Merril-Palmer of Detroit, and the University of Iowa. By 1935 she earned the B.A. and M.A. degrees, in addition to being trained as a nurse. Her years in study had been interrupted by ill health, service as a public-school teacher, and various fields of nursing. Through frugality she accumulated 180 shares of stock in American Telephone and Telegraph Company. She gave this stock, in a life income trust, to the library of California Baptist College which was named after her.

CECIL M. HYATT

GAINES, ROBERT EDWIN (b. Abbeville Co., S. C., Dec. 7, 1860; d. Richmond, Va., June 19, 1959). College professor, lecturer, Baptist leader. His parents were William A. and Mary Elizabeth (Gaines) Gaines. Educated at Furman University (A.M., 1886), Johns Hopkins and Harvard, he taught country schools, S. C., 1878–80; Furman University, 1882–87; Wright's University School, Md., 1888–89. He was professor of mathematics, University of Richmond, 1890–1948 and professor emeritus, 1948–59. He served as Dean, Richmond College, 1919–22; Director, University of Richmond Graduate School, 1929–38.

Gaines delivered the Gay Lectures, Southern Baptist Theological Seminary; Holland Lectures, Southwestern Baptist Theological Seminary; also he lectured in 25 states, D. C., and Canada. He was president, Baptist General Association of Virginia, 1922–23; president, Virginia Baptist Board of Missions and Education; president, Foreign Mission Board, SBC; Field Secretary, Interdenominational Layman's Missionary Movement (1913–14); camp director, Army Y.M.C.A., Camp Hancock (1918); actuary, Life Insurance Co. of Virginia; member, A.M.S. and A.A.A.S., Phi Beta Kappa. He received the following honorary degrees: Litt. D., Furman University (1908); Sc.D., University of Richmond (1958). On June 11, 1896, he married Janet M. Harris and had one daughter, Elizabeth Pendleton (Mrs. William J. Gaines). He was buried in Hollywood Cemetery, Richmond, Va.

WOODFORD B. HACKLEY

GALLOWAY, JOHN L. (b. Glasgow, Scotland, Mar. 21, 1877; d. Macao, Apr. 7, 1968). Missionary to China and Macao. Galloway graduated from Technological School (1898) and Bible Training School (1901), Glasgow, Scotland. He went to China under the Bible Missionary Society and began work in Macao in 1908. After appointment by Foreign Mission Board in 1910, he and his wife, the former Lillian Todd, continued working in Macao and on numerous nearby islands. He led in developing strong Baptist work on Macao, including a minsitry to thousands of boat people living in the harbor and to Portuguese soldiers recruited from Portuguese African colonies.

EUGENE L. HILL

GARCIA, MATIAS CASTAÑEDA (b. Zacatecas, Mex., Feb. 24, 1872; d. San Antonio, Tex., July 26, 1958). Missionary to Spanish-speaking people in Texas. Garcia was educated in the University of Zacatecas and graduated as a teacher. He became politically involved with Pancho Villa during the Mexican Revolution of 1910. The death of Villa forced him to flee to the United States. Garcia was converted under the preaching of ex-priest Felix Buldain in San Antonio and served as pastor of El Calvario Church, 1924–52. He married Adelina Villarreal in 1927. Garcia's evangelistic preaching earned him the name of "the Mexican George W. Truett." He was instrumental in the organization of the Mexican Children's Home and the Mexican Baptist Bible Institute and served as president of the Mexican Baptist Convention of Texas.

JOSHUA GRIJALVA

GARDNER, EUGENE NORFLEET (b. Franklin, Va., Nov. 12, 1894; d. Henderson, N. C., May 12, 1968). Son of Abraham L. and Lelia J. (Norfleet) Gardner, he was a graduate of University of Richmond (B.A., 1914, M.A., 1915), Southern Baptist Theological Seminary (Th.M., 1918), and the University of Chicago (B.D., 1920). In 1952 the University of Richmond conferred the D.D. upon him. He married Ruth Carver of Louisville, Ky., on Dec. 20, 1920. They had two children: Lelia Norfleet (Mrs. Robert M. Hathaway) and Alice Ruth (Mrs. Joe L. Wilson). After the death of his wife in 1941, he married Mattie Macon (Norman) White on July 16, 1944. Ordained by the Franklin Baptist Church, Virginia, on Oct. 15, 1915, his pastorates included the following Baptist churches: Mills Home, Thomasville, N. C.,

1925–29; First, Dunn, N. C., 1929–39; First, Henderson, N. C., 1939–52; and First, Laurinburg, N. C., 1953–60. He served as president of the general board of the Baptist State Convention of North Carolina, trustee of Wingate College, recording secretary for the state convention, 11 years, a member of the Foreign Mission Board, SBC, Radio Commission, and the Relief and Annuity Board. In 1951 he went on a preaching mission to Japan and visited mission fields in many parts of the world. He also wrote: *Old Testament Characters* (1932), *Lamp unto My Feet* (1939), *Magnifying the Church* (1949), *Journey to Japan* (1952), *Always the Ten Commandments* (1958), and *Changing Patterns in Christian Programs* (1964). He is buried in Poplar Spring Cemetery, Franklin, Va.

JAMES H. BLACKMORE

GARDNER, HELEN (b. Gardner, Tenn., Mar. 4, 1903; d. Mt. Pleasant, Miss., Dec. 29, 1966). Daughter of J. G. and Alice Cate Gardner of Gardner, Tenn., she grew up in Jackson, Tenn., where she attended grade and high school and Union University. She worked with her brother, T. C. Gardner (*q.v.*) in the Training Union Department of the Texas Baptist Convention. She became increasingly active in religious education. She served as director of activities for these Baptist churches: Bellevue, Memphis, Tenn., 1944–59; First, Decatur, Ga., 1959–62; Highland Heights, Memphis, Tenn., Aug. 15, 1962, until her death. She was named to *Who's Who in Texas* for achievements in religious education.

VELMA RHEA TORBETT

GARDNER, THURMAN CLEVELAND (b. in 1888, near Martin, Tenn.; d. May 6, 1968, San Angelo, Tex.). State Training Union leader. Son of Alice Cate and James Grizzard Gardner, he married Lucile Blake, June 4, 1917. They had one child, Thurman C., Jr. Gardner served as president of the College of Marshall, Marshall, Tex., 1913–16. His principal work was that of secretary, Training Union Department, Baptist General Convention of Texas, 1916–56. Under his leadership the enrolment of the Training Union in Texas increased from 15,841 in 1916 to over 400,000 in 1956. He developed the Eight-Point Record System, which was widely adopted, and authored many publications on Training Union material, including *Grading the Training Union for Efficient Work, Advanced Training Union Methods* (1924), *Training Union Programs—Fifty-two Varieties* (1927), and *Modern Training Union Methods* (1931). He was president of the Southwestern Baptist Religious Education Association in 1940. After his retirement in 1956 he served as vice-president of East Texas Baptist College, Marshall. He was buried in Dallas.

R. HOOPER DILDAY

***GARDNER-WEBB COLLEGE.** A liberal arts college, located in Boiling Springs, N. C. While continuing its program of community service through ministering to the local churches in its area, the college fulfils its purpose. The enrolment for 1969–70 was 1,460. Strong additions have been made to the curriculum in the fields of data processing, nursing education, and business, while still retaining a strong emphasis on the liberal arts. The former junior college now is a four-year institution, with the third year added in 1969, and the fourth in 1970.

E. Eugene Poston succeeded Phillip L. Elliott as president in 1961. The college is accredited by the North Carolina Association of Colleges and Universities, the North Carolina Board of Higher Education, and the Federal Immigration Service.

WILLIAM EDLEY BOYD

GARROTT, ERNEST PERRY JACKSON (b. Christian County, Ky., July 3, 1882; d. Batesville, Ark., June 8, 1962). Pastor and denominational leader. A graduate of Bethel College, Russellville, Ky., and Southern Baptist Theological Seminary, Garrott moved to Arkansas in 1905 to become assistant editor of *Baptist Advance*. He served as pastor of the First Baptist Church in the following Arkansas towns and cities: Newport, 1906–07; Batesville, 1907–10; Forrest City, 1910–12; Heber Springs, 1914–19; Conway, 1919–39; Prescott, 1939–42; Batesville, 1942–48. From 1912 to 1914 he was pastor of Pulaski Heights Church in Little Rock. During most of this period he was active as a member of the executive board of the Arkansas Baptist State Convention. He was a trustee of Ouachita Baptist College, which conferred upon him a D.D. in 1923. The Arkansas Baptist State Convention elected him recording secretary, 1912–17, and president, 1931–32. Active in Southern Baptist affairs, he served on the Home Mission Board, Foreign Mission Board, and was a trustee of Baptist Bible Institute and Southern Seminary. Garrott preached the annual Convention sermon in 1939. He was at his best as a Bible teacher and pastor. On July 24, 1907, he married Eula Maxfield. Their son, W. Maxfield Garrott, became a missionary to Japan.

J. EVERETT SNEED

GARWOOD, HARRY CRAWFORD (b. Champaign County, Ill., Oct. 8, 1884; d. Melbourne, Fla., Apr. 22, 1960). Pastor, educator, editor, author. Graduate of Stetson University (A.B., 1913) and Southern Baptist Theological Seminary (Th.M., 1917), studied at Peabody College (at intervals), 1924–30, and Yale University (Ph.D., 1934). He married Grace Leone Smith, Sept. 19, 1914. They had no children. He taught in public schools, Clay County, Fla., 1903–05. He was pastor of Carlyle Avenue Church, Louisville, Ky., 1915–17, and Stanton Memorial Church, Miami, Fla., 1917–21. Garwood served at the Chaplain's Training School, Camp Taylor, Louisville, Ky., 1918.

Professor of Religion, Stetson University, 1921–60, he also served as dean of the university, 1941–47; acting president, 1947–48; dean of College of Liberal Arts, Stetson, 1950–52; and Dean Emeritus until 1960. Curator of the Florida Baptist Historical Collection, he was secretary-treasurer of the Florida Baptist Historical Society, 1954–60, and was a member of the Historical Commission, SBC, 1954–60. Garwood was a member of the American Academy of Political and Social Sciences, Southern Baptist Teachers of Bible and Religious Education, Florida Association of Colleges, Athenian Club (DeLand), and Rotary. He wrote numerous articles, edited *The Gospel Herald* (Weekly), 1907–08, and wrote *Stetson University and Florida Baptists* (1962). In 1968 the Florida Baptist Historical Collection at Stetson was named for him. Garwood is buried in Oakdale Cemetery, DeLand, Fla. GILBERT L. LYCAN

GAYER, THEODORE WILMOT (b. Enon, Washington Parish, La., Oct. 12, 1880; d. Franklinton, La., Feb. 4, 1963). As a boy he moved to Franklinton and graduated from Central Institute in 1899. In 1902 he graduated from what is now Northwestern State College, Natchitoches, La. While there he was licensed to preach. He taught school, then went to Southern Baptist Theological Seminary (Th.M., 1911).

On Dec. 26, 1906, he married Alice Johnson. They were married 50 years and had two sons: Theodore Sampey and Delos Andrew. After her death he moved to Pineville, La., and married Mrs. Ollie Beall Tudor, Apr. 24, 1958.

He held pastorates in Maryland, Mississippi, Oklahoma, Tennessee, Louisiana, and Texas. Denominational responsibilities included state evangelist in Florida, stewardship secretary in Tennessee, and superintendent of Louisiana Baptist Children's Home in Monroe (1941–46), president of Louisiana Baptist Convention (1948) and interim secretary of the convention, member of SBC Education Commission, trustee of Southern Seminary, and director of public relations for Baptist Hospital in Alexandria, La. He was also chairman of the Louisiana Baptist history committee. He was active in civic as well as religious activities wherever he lived. He served as chaplain during World War I.

Following his retirement from the Baptist Children's Home he was given the sobriquet of Bishop of Washington Parish, where he was moderator for five years, while serving in all sections of Louisiana as supply pastor.

JOHN G. ALLEY

***GAZA, MISSION IN.** War between Jews and Arabs in 1967 and exchange of Egyptian for Israeli authority did not end the ministry of the Gaza Baptist Hospital to refugees. The nursing school grew, and better qualified students sought admission, partly because they could not leave Gaza to attend Arab universities. In 1969 the Baptist church had 25 members. A library and study center was also opened. JOHN D. HUGHEY

GENERAL ASSOCIATION OF BAPTISTS. Constituted in 1939 of members and delegates from primitive associations in Tennessee (Duck River, Mt. Zion and [New] Liberty), Alabama (Mt. Pleasant), and Georgia (True Vine). Other associations, including one from Kentucky, were later affiliated.

F. WILBUR HELMBOLD

***GENERAL CONFERENCE OF AMERICA, BAPTIST.** The headquarters of the conference in 1970 was located at 5750 North Ashland Avenue, Chicago, Ill. 60626. The general structure consisted of a general secretary, secretary of foreign missions, secretary of home missions, and secretary of publications.

The conference grew from 481 churches with 65,507 members in 1958 to 668 churches with 101,226 members in 1968. During the same period the ordained clergy increased from 406 to 850. The total gifts increased from $8,254,924 to $21,106,754.

The conference owns and operates three schools: Bethel College, St. Paul, Minn., a liberal arts college with a student body of about 1,000; Bethel Theological Seminary, St. Paul, Minn.; and Vancouver Bible Institute, Surrey, British Columbia, Canada. The official organ of the conference is *The Standard,* edited in 1970 by Donald Anderson. G. DAVID GUSTON

***GENERAL CONFERENCE OF AMERICA, BAPTIST, FOREIGN MISSION BOARD.** Missionaries serving under the conference in 1970 number 145. No new countries were entered from 1955 to 1970, but the work was enlarged in each one previously claimed. In Japan the Osaka Biblical Seminary was jointly supported with North American Baptists and Mennonite Brethren. In the Philippines the Baptist Theological College at Ran Remigio developed. Special emphases on medical and educational work were significant in Ethiopia. In Argentina evangelistic work was carried on in three northwestern provinces. In Brazil missionaries served in close cooperation with the Brazilian Baptist Convention. Income of the board for 1969 totaled $994,818.86. In 1969 the executive secretary was Franklin O. Nelson, 5750 North Ashland Avenue, Chicago, Ill. 60626. H. G. TEGENFELDT

***GEORGETOWN COLLEGE.** A four-year liberal arts college. In 1956 the college launched a program to build dormitories. A campaign for a boys' dormitory netted $150,000. In 1958 another campaign was successful in locating funds for a new woman's dormitory. Knight Hall for women was completed in 1960, with space for 270 women, at a cost of $700,000.

As a result of a survey by the Kentucky Baptist Convention in 1958, there were unsuccessful efforts to relocate the school in Louisville. Having faced other periods of tension during its history, the college continued to thrive. In Feb., 1959, President H. Leo Eddleman was named president of the New Orleans Baptist Theological Seminary.

In May, 1959, Robert Lee Mills (1916–) became Georgetown's 20th (and second lay) president. His initial concerns were for an environment of academic quality. The average annual pay for a full-time professor was $4,890 and an instructor received $3,200. Mills gave serious attention to upgrading faculty pay and benefits.

Mills's first years were devoted to long-range planning. Properties adjacent to the campus were purchased for expansion and beautification. Many of the older buildings were pointed up. A major addition to Anderson Hall for men was finished in 1962. Capital needs were determined and a development program was begun. Attention was given to acquiring a student center, science center, and fine arts center estimated to cost $4,000,000.

In 1961 the Kentucky convention voted to launch the Christian education advance campaign to help meet capital needs of its colleges and schools, student centers, and state assembly. Georgetown shared in this campaign for $9,000,000 in the state. It received more than $400,000 directly, and was allocated $77,000 annually for 20 years by the convention.

In Nov., 1963, Louisville businessman Lee E. Cralle and his wife announced their intention to give the college a student center. His initial gift of $650,000 was the largest gift ever received by the college. In 1965 they made an additional gift sufficient to construct the center known as the Lee E. Cralle Student Center. The cost was $1,100,000. It was dedicated on Oct. 16, 1965.

The college erected four 86-bed dormitory units on the commons surrounding Rucker Hall at a cost of $300,000 each. The park-like development was opened in the winter of 1966.

Construction on a science center began in Mar., 1967. The 52,000 square foot center was completed in the summer of 1968, and dedicated on Oct. 12, 1968. It is Georgetown's largest academic facility. The center contains a planetarium along with many other interest centers.

Two major issues within the denomination have claimed attention in recent years. There was divided sentiment from pastors over Georgetown's decision to borrow money from the Federal Government for construction of buildings. The college made two points in support of its position. (1) Building dormitories with conventional loans would make the cost to the student prohibitive. (2) The Kentucky convention on three occasions had confirmed its faith in the college's board of trustees to operate the school. To question each trustee board's action was to place Georgetown in jeopardy of losing its valued accreditation.

The second issue that touched off criticism was the college's determination to permit social dancing on campus. The student government association presented a position paper on dancing to the trustees at the 1968 fall meeting. The trustees concurred in the findings of the students and agreed to break the 140-year-old no-dancing policy. Attempts to reverse the decision at the 1968 and 1969 conventions failed to change the policy.

In 1969–70 the college received $225,000 for operations and nearly $100,000 for capital needs from the Kentucky convention. Alumni contributed an additional $120,000. Bequests accounted for more than $400,000 in new money. The college's operating budget was $3,300,000—a three-fold increase in 10 years. The value of buildings and grounds exceeded $8,000,000. Endowment was slightly under $2,000,000. The library contained 95,000 volumes. The college in 1970 had a student body of 1,485, with a faculty and staff of 112.

The college is a member of the Southern Association of Colleges, the Southern Baptist Education Association, Association of American Colleges, the National Conference of Church-Related Boards, the Association of Kentucky Colleges and Universities, and the Kentucky Independent College Foundation. It is sponsored by the Kentucky Baptist Convention which elects its trustees. KENNETH FENDLEY

***GEORGIA, BAPTIST CONVENTION OF THE STATE OF.** On Jan. 1, 1955, Searcy S. Garrison succeeded James W. Merritt as executive secretary-treasurer of the Georgia Baptist Convention's executive committee. For more than 11 years, Garrison had been pastor of Bull Street Baptist Church in Savannah. Earlier he was pastor at Barnesville, Norman Park, and other Georgia cities. He also taught Bible at Norman College.

Capital Improvements and Endowment Programs of the convention, begun in 1955, provided more than $10,563,034 on a matching basis. The first program, 1955–60, provided $2,781,484.50 for endowment of colleges, and $2,781,484.50 as matching funds by colleges to apply on building renovations and new buildings. The second program, 1960–65, provided $3,030,000 from the Cooperative Program on a goal of $5,710,000 for new buildings and endowment of Georgia Baptist institutions. By 1970 the third program had produced $4,751,550 through the Cooperative Program on a goal of $5,475,000 for new buildings and endowment for the institutions.

In 1955 the executive committee acquired property near Waycross, Ga., for a home for the aged. In 1970 Baptist Village, with Harvey R. Mitchell, administrator, was nearing final development of plans for a residency of 300, with an investment in buildings, grounds, and equipment as of July 31, 1969, of $2,435,230. Baptist Village is operated by a board of trustees elected by the convention. The executive committee, through a special committee, approved all preliminary negotiations and planning for this institution.

A major reorganization of department secretaries of the executive committee into a staff was undertaken in 1955, with reglar monthly meetings to correlate work of the executive committee, and provide a voice for all programs and ministries to the executive committee through the executive secretary and the administration committee.

The Baptist Professional Building, adjacent to Georgia Baptist Hospital in Atlanta, constructed at a cost of $1,650,327, was paid for in 1969. A nursing education building, costing $2,500,000, was completed and occupied in 1963, with living accommodations for 500 student nurses, and classroom facilities for the hospital's school of nursing education.

In 1956 a detailed study of the associational missionary was approved.

In 1956 the convention accepted title to the Pine Mountain Children's Home, Meansville, making it a branch of the Georgia Baptist Children's Home, upon recommendation of the executive committee.

The executive committee in 1957 accepted a proposal of Shorter College trustees to turn the Baptist-related college at Rome over to the convention. This was done in 1959.

In 1957 the executive committee, through its administration committee, created an office of promotion and public relations, with services in the area of stewardship promotion, general promotion, and public relations. This office, a part of the office of the executive secretary, functioned until late 1968 when a full-time public relations secretary was secured. Stewardship and the Baptist Protection Program administration responsibilities were combined in Jan., 1970.

A program of area mission work was approved by the executive committee in 1957. This ministry provided for a cooperative work in several associations with salary and travel allowance provided jointly by the associations and state mission funds, with the missionary serving as a state mission worker. Purpose of the program was to provide a plan for three or more associations to cooperate in associational mission work.

In 1959 the convention, upon recommendation of the executive committee, accepted title to Norman College, Norman Park, making the Baptist-sponsored junior college a member of the convention family. Norman, begun in 1900, had been owned and operated by 16 associations in Southwest Georgia prior to 1959.

Following negotiations by the executive secretary, the administration committee, and the executive committee, the convention in Nov., 1963, approved the purchase of the Lake Louise Bible Conference grounds from R. G. LeTourneau, and began projection of a full-scale Baptist assembly. The assembly, a phase of the state missions program of the convention, has undergone major renovations, and construction in excess of $1,519,596 (audit June 30, 1969) was completed by the convention. Situated near Toccoa, Ga., the assembly provides a year-round meeting place for Georgia Baptist agencies, institutions, and programs. Capacity in 1970 was approximately 385.

A major expansion of the Baptist student work program, including development of student centers at state-owned colleges, occurred during the sixties. Through special state mission offerings and allocations from the Cooperative Program and the Capital Improvements and Endowment Program, funds were provided for construction of centers at the University of Georgia, Athens; Georgia Southern College, Statesboro; and Georgia Institute of Technology, Atlanta. Buildings in Valdosta and Milledgeville were purchased and renovated to be used as Baptist Student Centers serving colleges in those cities.

Major renovations of the Baptist Building in Atlanta were made in 1956, 1959, and 1966, costing more than $125,000. During 1955–69 additional property, along Baker Street in Atlanta, behind the Baptist Building, was acquired by the executive committee for parking.

Also of importance to the work of the executive committee was preparation of a manual of operations for agencies and institutions and programs, completed in 1961. A policy manual for state mission employees also was prepared.

In 1956 a program of work with National Baptists was begun as a part of state missions, sponsored jointly by the Georgia convention and the Home Mission Board, SBC.

In 1965 Camp Glynn, owned and operated by Woman's Missionary Union, auxiliary to the Georgia Baptist Convention, was given to the executive committee and is operated currently as a phase of the state missions program under the direction of the manager of the Georgia Baptist Assembly.

Beginning in 1963, a Denominational Emphasis Program was promoted through the office of the executive secretary as a part of the executive committee's program of promotion of the Cooperative Program. This denominational emphasis provides for denominational workers to participate in presenting cooperative Baptist work on one day to churches in several associations. This program took the place of regional conferences, a feature of executive committee promotion since the early thirties.

In 1966 the convention received an Atlanta hotel as a gift from the Beazley Foundation of Norfolk, Va. The remodeled Peachtree On Peachtree Inn is a benevolent ministry to the elderly. It was approved and chartered as a Georgia Baptist institution through efforts led by the convention's executive secretary-treasurer. William L. Rainwater was the first administrator. Cecil T. Underwood succeeded him in Nov., 1967.

Provision was made by the executive committee in 1966 for an administrative assistant to the executive secretary. This assistant serves as a leader in cooperative missions work within the state as well as to provide staff assistance to the executive secretary in administration.

Several cooperative mission ministries were developed during the sixties and assigned to an assistant to the executive secretary. Ministries include chaplain programs at Reidsville, Battey State Hospital, Talmadge Memorial Hospital, and Jekyll Island. Coordination is given to the 6 area and 42 associational missionaries of the state and consultation to those ministers serving under the pastoral aid program.

GEORGIA BAPTIST BENEVOLENT INSTITUTIONS

Top: BAPTIST VILLAGE (*q.v.*), Waycross retirement home, founded 1955. *Center:* PEACHTREE-ON-PEACHTREE INN, Inc. (*q.v.*), Atlanta retirement home, founded 1967. *Bottom:* PALMETTO BRANCH, Georgia Baptist Children's Home. New campus occupied 1968.

NEW
BAPTIST
STUDENT
CENTERS
IN
GEORGIA

Top: UNIVERSITY OF GEORGIA, Athens, Ga. *Center:* GEORGIA SOUTHERN COLLEGE, Statesboro, Ga. *Bottom:* GEORGIA TECH, Atlanta, Ga.

There are several state ministries done in cooperation with the HMB, SBC, associations, and churches. Coordination of these ministries is assigned to the assistant to the executive secretary. These ministries include language ministries to Spanish-speaking groups and the deaf of the state; Baptist centers and weekday ministries in Atlanta, Columbus, Macon, Savannah, Athens, and Gainesville. Each summer a student mission program is coordinated throughout the state.

In 1966 a *Book of Charters* of Georgia Baptist institutions and agencies was published. In 1967 the executive committee elected Jack Harwell editor of *The Christian Index* following John J. Hurt who became editor of *The Baptist Standard* published by the Baptist General Convention of Texas.

Georgia Baptist leaders in the Georgia seminar of the Baptist Education Study Task (BEST), promoted by the Southern Baptist Education Commission, 1965–67, observed that while Georgia Baptists had supported colleges for a long time, no effort had ever been made to set forth a definite statement of purpose for supporting the colleges. Following the BEST studies, the Georgia convention's education commission led in an effort to draft such a statement. State, associational, and local church leadership were involved in the study.

In 1969 the Georgia convention approved a "Statement of Purpose of Georgia Baptists in Giving Support to Baptist Colleges." It said in part: "1. Faithfulness to the commission of Christ requires involvement in education." (Reference is made to Matt. 28:19–20.) "2. Baptists support colleges in an effort to provide for their young people and others of like spirit and purpose institutions of higher learning with a Christian philosophy, perspective and commitment. 3. Baptists support colleges in the conviction that Christian education is essential to providing adequate leadership for the churches and denomination. 4. Baptists support colleges in the conviction that they are contributing to the welfare of the state and nation in the operation of these institutions. 5. Georgia Baptists support colleges through the state convention organization in order to provide a broad basis of support, and in order to enlist the largest number of churches and individual Baptists possible in the support of these institutions."

Growth of the work of the executive committee is expressed statistically in the growth of the churches, and the increases each year in the scope of convention ministries. In 1954 gifts through the executive committee for the Cooperative Program were $1,791,040; in 1969, gifts were $5,851,118, reflecting an increase of 226 per cent for this period.

At the 1969 session of the convention numerous changes in the constitution were voted to effect organizational changes and to adopt current nomenclature. The convention was planning the celebration of its sesquicentennial in

GEORGIA STATISTICAL SUMMARY

Year	Associations	Churches	Church Membership	Baptisms	S. S. Enrolment	V.B.S. Enrolment	T. U. Enrolment	W.M.U. Enrolment	Brotherhood Enrolment	Music Enrolment	Mission Gifts	Total Gifts	Value Church Property
1955	93	2,763	784,265	34,597	573,934	203,055	177,013	116,130	42,842		$ 4,368,108	$26,349,252	$102,870,159
1956	94	2,805	804,634	33,023	588,708	228,030	184,798	121,149	48,375		4,917,074	29,536,068	117,810,425
1957	94	2,833	824,351	33,075	595,923	231,176	193,676	124,242	54,282	49,456	5,448,255	31,737,665	135,716,269
1958	94	2,861	843,253	34,603	603,968	233,390	200,471	132,923	59,264	55,214	5,950,735	33,422,382	152,164,978
1959	94	2,890	865,611	36,752	614,965	237,424	210,989	137,793	61,133	59,780	6,021,915	36,318,778	168,786,243
1960	94	2,923	887,385	33,329	624,040	254,947	215,778	140,335	61,619	56,469	6,510,562	39,051,877	188,308,534
1961	94	2,937	901,914	34,139	634,638	259,919	220,514	138,545	62,260	63,641	6,702,714	40,742,008	204,834,110
1962	94	2,964	918,483	32,056	639,453	269,351	224,801	138,902	63,758	71,390	7,266,625	43,738,914	219,016,731
1963	94	2,976	935,120	28,472	642,392	271,560	227,216	141,185	67,418	77,430	7,921,511	45,733,982	232,109,610
1964	94	2,997	955,274	30,135	645,746	273,850	224,321	140,222	62,666	71,376	8,358,819	49,089,402	252,627,453
1965	94	3,010	966,831	29,207	641,854	283,907	212,859	135,926	53,069	75,779	8,970,896	53,382,700	264,641,120
1966	94	3,008	980,446	30,721	639,687	281,909	208,803	138,511	50,879	82,813	10,406,168	57,082,508	278,521,548
1967	94	3,011	995,670	30,108	636,453	286,622	208,882	138,866	51,388	90,593	10,388,824	60,642,159	302,306,823
1968	94	3,017	1,007,194	29,018	634,818	285,535	220,995	132,908	49,764	92,276	11,123,051	68,346,683	324,531,394

MRS. NOEL ARMSTRONG

1972. The observance, marking the formal organization of the convention in 1822, will include special events throughout the year, a special convention program in November, and the scheduled publication of a history of the convention.

Following retirement of T. W. Tippett (*q.v.*) as Sunday School secretary in 1956, Julian T. Pipkin was elected secretary. Gainer E. Bryan, Sr., Training Union secretary, retired in 1963. He was succeeded by Garnie A. Brand, who resigned in 1969. Brand was succeeded by Waldo A. Woodcock.

Durward V. Cason, Sr., was elected first secretary of the then Program of Negro Work (now the Program of Work with National Baptists) in 1957. He retired in 1966 and was succeeded by Earle F. Stirewalt. In 1957 James A. Lester was named secretary of promotion and public relations. He resigned in 1968 to become editor of the *Baptist and Reflector,* published by the Tennessee Baptist Convention. Lawrence E. Webb became first full-time public relations secretary in 1968. A. Judson Burrell was named stewardship and Baptist protection secretary in 1969, succeeding Arthur Hinson, who retired. Reginald T. Russell retired as secretary of evangelism in 1963 and was succeeded by O. M. Cates.

W. L. Rainwater was named in 1966 as administrative assistant to the executive secretary. Resigning to become first administrator of Peachtree On Peachtree Inn in 1967, Rainwater was succeeded by Ernest J. Kelley. In 1963 Miss Janice Singleton retired as executive secretary-treasurer of the Georgia WMU, and was succeeded by Miss Dorothy Pryor.

In 1963 Clifton A. Forrester was elected as the first manager for the Georgia Baptist Assembly.

JAMES ADAMS LESTER

***GEORGIA ASSOCIATIONS.**

I. New Associations. MURRAY COUNTY. Organized Sept. 13, 1968, at Spring Place Church by 11 churches located in Murray County and formerly a part of the North Georgia Association. In 1969, 13 churches reported 107 baptisms, 3,698 members, $202,378 total receipts, $16, 069.17 mission gifts, and $1,124,000 property value.

PIEDMONT-OKEFENOKEE. Organized Oct. 17, 1969, by the combining of the Piedmont Association (organized 1817) and Okefenokee Association (organized in 1936). The 57 churches located mainly in Pierce, Ware, and Brantley counties in Southeast Georgia in 1969 reported 555 baptisms, 14,111 members, $838,529 total receipts, $105,844 mission gifts, and $4,025,255 property value.

II. Changes in Associations. GOOD SAMARITAN. Composed of nine churches located in Carroll and Douglas counties. Voted in its annual session Oct. 18, 1969, to withdraw from the Georgia Baptist Convention because of policy differences between the two. Some of the churches did not vote to withdraw. In 1968 this association reported nine churches, 53 baptisms, 931 members, $24,649 total receipts, $1,050 mission gifts, and $94,000 property value.

OKEFENOKEE. United with the Piedmont Association to form the Piedmont-Okefenokee Association on Oct. 17, 1969.

PIEDMONT. United with the Okefenokee Association to form the Piedmont-Okefenokee Association on Oct. 17, 1969.

LAWRENCE WEBB

GEORGIA BAPTIST ASSEMBLY. Established in 1963 as a phase of the state mission program of the Georgia Baptist Convention. The 1,000-acre site in northeast Georgia near Toccoa is used virtually every week of the year by the convention's state mission departments, churches, and associations. Inspiration and training are provided each summer through a family Bible conference, and weeks sponsored by Sunday School, Church Training, and Church Music departments of the convention. Throughout the year, other activities are scheduled by the Brotherhood and Student Work departments, the executive committee, and Georgia Baptist Foundation, Inc.

Under the leadership of Executive Secretary-Treasurer Searcy S. Garrison, a 500-acre tract was purchased in 1963 for $195,000 from the LeTourneau Foundation. Industrialist R. G. LeTourneau had operated a laymen's retreat at that location, known as Lake Louise Conference Grounds. Two adjoining tracts, totalling 198 acres, were bought at the same time for $29,857. By 1965 additional properties had been purchased for a total of approximately 1,000 acres. The convention's executive committee named Bernard D. King, secretary of the Brotherhood Department, as an assistant to the executive secretary for the purpose of organizing the new ministry, elected as interim manager Channing P. Hayes, who had been manager of Lake Louise, and launched plans for immediate renovation and long-range development. Clifton A. Forrester was elected manager of the assembly in 1964 and continues to the present (1970).

The facilities were put into use soon after the purchase, even while extensive remodeling was beginning. In 1964, $250,000 was spent in renovations, including reconstruction and furnishing of an existing building as a chapel. A camping area was also begun. Remodeling began on the central building which contains bedroom wings, dining room, class and conference rooms, offices, and living quarters for the staff. Money for continued building and improvement is provided in the convention's Capital Improvements and Endowment Program established in 1965, and through the annual State Mission Offerings in Sunday Schools and Woman's Missionary Union organizations.

Work began in 1965 on a boys' camp, Camp Tugalo, on the assembly property. The same year, Georgia Baptist WMU gave the convention Camp Glynn, a 269-acre site in coastal Georgia near Brunswick, valued at $222,000. State Royal Ambassador camps were held for the first time at Camp Tugalo in 1966 and at Camp Glynn in 1967. RA camps previously were held at the WMU Camp Pinnacle near Clayton, Ga. By 1969, Camp Tugalo had six cottages, a central bathhouse, dining room and kitchen facilities for 100, and a family camping area.

Latest building additions at the assembly are two lodges housing approximately 40 persons each, designed for youth groups. In 1969 the assembly could accommodate approximately 385 guests. Long-range projections call for facilities for 1,200 persons. By Nov., 1969, the total investment in the assembly was $1,562,786.

LAWRENCE E. WEBB

***GEORGIA BAPTIST CHILDREN'S HOME.** A multiple-services agency which ministers to more than 700 dependent boys and girls each year. The primary service is residential care on the home's three campuses, although a foster home program has been in operation since 1960. In recent years, a social service program has been set up and expanded on three campuses. A special program of "reeducation" for mildly disturbed children was started in 1969.

Owned and operated by the Georgia Baptist Convention, which elects 30 trustees to administer agency affairs, the campuses are located at Baxley, Meansville, and Palmetto, with a central office at 291 Peachtree Street, Atlanta. The Pine Mountain campus, located near Meansville, was accepted as a gift in 1957. The property in Hapeville, which the home had owned since 1899, was sold to the city of Atlanta for airport expansion, and that campus was relocated in Aug., 1968, on a 400-acre tract of land in South Fulton County, near Palmetto. Combined campus acreage is approximately 4,000 acres.

John Carey Warr (*q.v.*) served as general manager from Jan. 1, 1950, until his death on June 9, 1969. Clarence F. Sessions, who joined the staff in 1968 as chaplain and assistant general manager, was named acting general manager. Resident superintendents are: A. W. Coleman, Odum Branch, Walter H. Logan, Pine Mountain, and David H. McGowan, Palmetto.

ASHLEY P. COX, JR.

***GEORGIA BAPTIST FOUNDATION.** From Jan. 1, 1956, to Sept. 30, 1969, permanent assets of the foundation increased from $2,147,515 to $10,110,752. The Georgia Baptist Convention through the Cooperative Program contributed more than $3,500,000 to this total through the Capital Improvements and Endowment Program, whereby the six Georgia Baptist colleges raised a "matching dollar" to qualify for the corresponding endowment dollar. Gary Vinson of Waynesboro, Ga., who had made substantial gifts for benefit of the Georgia Baptist Children's Home, gave $50,000 endowment for a home for the aged, furnishing added stimulus for opening Baptist Village in 1957.

In 1958 the Durward V. Cason, Jr., Memorial Fund was established with annual income to be used for education of Negro youths, in memory of the son of the convention's former secretary for work with National Baptists who drowned in 1957. More than 1,000 gifts to the fund have been made by individuals and churches, with about 40 per cent of the gifts coming from Negroes. In 1969 the corpus had reached $42,192, and more than $7,000 income had been earned, with 32 young people assisted.

The foundation provides permanent benefit for every institution and cause of Georgia and Southern Baptists. Gifts have ranged from the $7.21 estate of Mrs. Susan Seymour, invested for benefit of the Children's Home, to a "life-income" trust of $400,000, with ultimate benefit to Norman and Shorter Colleges, made in 1969 by Jud B. Roberts. In July, 1967, Charles C. Duncan became assistant secretary to serve with Executive Secretary Harry V. Smith, Sr.

HARRY V. SMITH, SR.

GEORGIA BAPTIST HISTORICAL SOCIETY. Efforts to organize a Georgia Baptist historical society began in 1878 and continued sporadically, with an active society in existence at various times. The present society was organized in 1964, with Arthur Jackson as president, followed by J. Emmett Henderson and Edmond D. Keith, 1968– . The purpose of the society is to collect, preserve, and make available for study items of historical interest to Georgia Baptists, including histories, memoirs, letters, church histories, files of *The Christian Index*, associational minutes, and hymnals. The collection is housed in Stetson Memorial Library at Mercer University, supervised by Mrs. Mary Overby, curator. In 1968 the society issued the first volume of *Viewpoints*, a collection of papers read at annual meetings. The society plans to publish an issue of *Viewpoints* every two years.

See also GEORGIA BAPTIST HISTORY, COMMITTEE ON THE PRESERVATION OF, VOL. I.

EDMOND D. KEITH

GEREN, PAUL FRANCIS (b. El Dorado, Ark., Dec. 5, 1913; d. near London, Ky., June 22, 1969). Author, soldier, educator, diplomat, and college president. The son of Baptist minister Hiram Marion and Julia Goodwin Geren, he was educated at Baylor University (B.A., 1936), Louisiana State University (M.A., 1937), Harvard University (M.A., 1940; Ph.D., 1941). St. Mary's University awarded him an LL.D., in 1962. He married Elizabeth Powers in 1946. They had three daughters: Natasha, Juliana, and Nancy. He was a candidate for the U. S. Congress in 1946. For almost 20 years he was a Foreign Service officer with the Department of State and served in India, Syria, Jordan, Libya, and the Federation of Rhodesia and Nyasaland, as well as in administrative posts in Washington and New York. He attained the rank of minister. He was the first deputy director of the Peace Corps, 1961–62.

He taught at Judson College of the University of Rangoon, Burma, in 1941 as a missionary professor under the American Baptist Foreign

Mission Society; and at Forman Christian College, Lahore, Pakistan (at that time India). He also taught at Louisiana State University, Berea College, and Southern Methodist University. He was executive vice-president of Baylor University, 1956–58, where he founded the J. M. Dawson studies in church and state; and president of Stetson University, 1967–69. He died in an automobile accident the day before his resignation from the latter post was to be effective. From 1959 to 1961 he was executive director of the Dallas Council on World Affairs. The business school at Nyatsime College in Rhodesia is named for him in recognition of his assistance in its establishment.

Upon the outbreak of war in Burma in 1941 he volunteered as a Red Cross ambulance driver for Gordon Seagrave, the "Burma Surgeon," and later escaped from Burma in the famous march with General Stilwell. His *Burma Diary* recounts episodes from that experience. He later served with Merrill's Marauders with whom he earned a direct commission and the Bronze Star.

Geren was a frequent contributor to professional and academic journals and newspapers. His other books are: *The Pilgrimage of Peter Strong (an autobiography,* 1948), *New Voices, Old Worlds* (1958), and *Christians Confront Communism* (1962). A popular speaker, he was awarded the Distinguished Alumni Award (Golden Anniversary) by Pi Kappa Delta, a national forensic society, in recognition of his ability in this area. He was also a Fellow of the Society for Religion in Higher Education. His life was well summarized by Irvin Northcutt who said at the Geren memorial service at Stetson, "he recognized the duty of man 'to do justice, to love mercy, and to walk humbly with God.'" ROLLIN S. ARMOUR

GERMANY, WEST, MISSION IN. A dual opportunity has existed for missionaries in Germany since the first missionary family arrived in 1961. Coinciding with the call for missionaries to serve in English-language work was the German Baptist Union's invitation to the Foreign Mission Board for a fraternal representative. Most of the mission personnel were connected directly with English-language churches. In cities such as West Berlin and Munich, churches served their military and civilian membership under the guidance of a missionary pastor. From its beginning, a church in Hamm ministering primarily to American employees of a large company was served by a missionary pastor.

Essential to the 26 English-language churches of Germany is a missionary adviser who serves as general secretary to the European Baptist Convention (English-Language). The mission seeks to relate these churches to the German Baptist Union and other European Baptist bodies. A fraternal representative, working directly with German Baptists, is available to serve and assist German churches when needed. For instance, assistance was provided one year during Baptist-sponsored evangelistic crusades. The mission anticipates a strengthening of bonds with the German Union, between English and German-speaking Christians. ISAM E. BALLENGER

GETTYS, ALBERT C. (b. near Shelby, Cleveland County, N. C., Nov. 27, 1886; d. Mar. 27, 1959). Author, minister, and educator. His parents were Mary Elizabeth (Hord) and Martin Gettys, farmer. He was educated at Decatur Baptist Junior College, Baylor University (B.A., 1912), and Southwestern Baptist Theological Seminary (Th.M., 1918, Th.D., 1921). Mary Hardin-Baylor College conferred on him its first honorary doctorate (L.H.D., 1954). He married Lydia I. Dickson, June 22, 1916. Gettys was pastor at Crowell, 1912–16, Palacios, 1916–17, Lewisville, 1917–18, Georgetown, 1925–27, and Bryan, 1945–46, all in Texas. He was teacher of Bible, Mary Hardin-Baylor College, Belton, 1921–51. After retirement in 1951, he was called back as acting president of the school, 1952–54. Gettys wrote *A Program of Religious Education* and was co-author of *Evangelism and Stewardship in Religious Education.* He is buried in Vernon, Tex. WILLIAM G. TANNER

GHANA, MISSION IN (cf. Gold Coast, Mission in, Vol. I). The British colony and protectorate known as Gold Coast won independence in 1957 and resumed the ancient African name of Ghana. Ghana Baptist Mission was formed in 1957. Baptist churches continued cooperating with the Nigeria Convention until the Ghana Baptist Convention was organized in 1964. Advance includes hospital established in 1957, settlement for lepers, WMU camp, community center, and hostel for missionary children. In 1969 the mission reported 41 missionaries, 36 churches (29 self-supporting) with 3,760 members, and 33 African pastors. H. CORNELL GOERNER

GHEENS, CHARLES EDWIN (b. Louisville, Ky., July 4, 1878; d. Louisville, Ky., Nov. 11, 1961). Member of the board of trustees of the Southern Baptist Theological Seminary, 1921–61. His father, C. W. Gheens, was a member of the board, 1880–1920. The younger Gheens was vice-chairman of the board, 1950–56, and a member of the executive committee of the board, 1957–61. He was a member of the financial board of the seminary, 1921–61, and chairman of the financial board, 1932–61. In 1927 he married Mary Jo Lazarus.

Gheens was an influential member of the larger community of Louisville and Kentucky, as well as a part of the plantation community of Gheens, La., where he raised sugarcane for the support of his candy manufacturing business in Louisville. Gheens was an instrumental member of the financial planning leadership of the seminary during several crises, particularly the depression of the thirties. He also exercised intellectual and cultural leadership in the life of the seminary through his generous contributions to the library, through his and Mrs. Gheens' interest in the Faculty Guest Center, and most especially through the establishment of the Gheens Lectureships. The Gheens Lecture Hall in the library is a continuing testimony to his generosity to quality education among Southern Baptist ministers. WAYNE E. OATES

***GIBSON BAPTIST ASSEMBLY.** The 1969 value of 20 acres and 13 cabins, tabernacle, book store, concession stand, and recreation facilities was $250,000. The annual budget is *c.* $6,000, provided from state convention funds, Panhandle Association, and registration fees. Total registration in 1969 was 568. J. M. GASKIN

GILFOY, KARENZA DAVIS (b. Houston, Chickasaw County, Miss., Nov. 8, 1888; d. Jackson, Miss., Feb. 4, 1967). Daughter of Joe C. and Ella (Lowry) Davis, she attended Mississippi A. & M. College (Mississippi State University) and taught in public schools of northeast Mississippi. She married Hiller Gilfoy in 1909. They had one son, James Robert (d. 1964). On the death of her husband in 1916, Mrs. Gilfoy entered the business world. In 1928 she was named bookkeeper and assistant manager of the Baptist Hospital in Jackson. In 1935 the board named her superintendent, a post she held until her retirement in 1954. Under her administration the hospital increased from 85-bed capacity to 325. The Gilfoy School of Nursing was named in her honor in 1965.

Mrs. Gilfoy held numerous civic leadership responsibilities. In recognition of her civic activities, she received the Golden Deeds Award of the Jackson Exchange Club in 1962. Mrs. Gilfoy is buried in Woodland, near Houston, Miss. R. A. MCLEMORE

GILL, EVERETT, SR. (b. Huntsville, Mo., Nov. 4, 1869; d. Raleigh, N. C., Feb. 5, 1958). Educated at William Jewell College (A.B., 1890) and Southern Baptist Theological Seminary (Th.M., 1894; Th.D., 1895), he also received the D.D. from Georgetown College, 1910, and William Jewell College, 1937. Gill married Emma G. Williams, Oct. 10, 1895. They had five children: Harrison Williams, Charles Fairchild, Everett, Jr., Geraldine, and Mary Elizabeth (Mrs. J. B. Sims). He served as pastor of churches in Missouri and Kentucky. He was captain of the American Red Cross, Italian front, 1918. Gill served on the American Relief Administration in Russia, 1921–22. Appointed missionary to Italy, 1904, he was superintendent of the North Italian Mission, 1905–07, 1910–16, and Southern Baptist representative for Euope, 1921–39. He retired in 1939. He wrote *La Scuola della Chiesa* (The School of the Church, 1913), *Iglesias del Nuevo Testamento* (New Testament Churches, n.d.), *Europe and the Gospel* (1931), *Europe: Christ or Chaos* (1937), and *A. T. Robertson—A Biography* (1943). MRS. EVERETT GILL, JR.

GILLHAM, TROY MOUDY (b. Greenville, Hunt County, Tex., July 24, 1907; d. Phoenix, Ariz., May 13, 1966). Son of James Verner and Etta V. (Chapman) Gillham, he was educated at Baylor University (B.A., 1944) and did graduate work at Texas Technological College, University of Arizona, and Arizona State University. On Aug. 10, 1928, he married Lillie G. Bankston. They had two children, Maudy Frank and Marian Sue (Mrs. Bobby Pennington). Gillham was a banker, 1927–39, prior to entering the ministry. He was pastor of the following Baptist churches, 1939–66: Crosbyton, Tex.; Santa Anna, Tex.; Post, Tex.; Barstow, Calif.; and Phoenix, Ariz. From 1951 to 1954 he served as area missionary of the Arizona Southern Baptist Convention for the Tucson area. Gillham was metropolitan missions superintendent in Phoenix, Ariz., 1954–57, and area missionary for the Estrella and Troy Brooks associations, 1961–66. He assisted in the organization of 51 of the churches and missions that in 1970 made up a part of more than 300 churches and missions in the Arizona convention. M. FRANK GILLHAM

GILLIAM, NORRIS (b. Ladonia, Tex., Oct. 7, 1903; d. Nashville, Tenn., Feb. 15, 1957). Pastor, administrator, and promoter of stewardship. Educated at Union University (B.A., 1923; D.D., 1937) and Southwestern Baptist Theological Seminary (Th.M., 1927), he married Mary Ballard of Horn Lake, Miss., in 1923. They had two sons: Norris, Jr., and Robert McCargo. He was pastor of Houston Community Baptist Church, Dallas, Tex., 1924–27; Merit Baptist Church, Merit, Tex., 1925–27; First Church, Idabel, Okla., 1927–30; First Church, Kenova, W. Va., 1930–36; First Church, Springfield, Tenn., 1936–41; and Lockeland Church, Nashville, Tenn., 1942–45. He served as executive secretary-treasurer, Tennessee Baptist Foundation, 1946–54; contracts and investment counselor, Sunday School Board, 1954–57; and on a number of denominational boards and committees. HOWARD P. COLSON

***GIRLS' AUXILIARY.** Girls' Auxiliary organizations increased from 21,930 in 1955 to 34,999 in 1968; membership increased from 222,151 to 331,571. Evidence of the organization's widespread popularity with girls came in 1963, when its 50th Anniversary was observed. Highlight of the observance was the first national GA Convention, held in Memphis, Tenn. Plans called for one three-day meeting, but the number of registrants necessitated three conventions of three days each. Attendance for the three conventions totaled 21,533.

At the national level, the following persons provided leadership between 1955–70: Margaret Bruce, secretary, department of youth, 1955–57; Betty Brewer, GA secretary, 1955–57, and director of the GA Department, 1957–64; Dorothy Weeks, editorial associate, 1954–64, and editor of GA materials, 1964–68; Katharine Bryan, promotion associate, 1961–65; Marjorie Jones, GA director, 1964–69; Oneta Gentry, editor of GA materials, 1969–70; and Evelyn Tully, GA director, Dec., 1969–Sept., 1970.

In 1970, when the new grouping-grading plan became effective, members of Girls' Auxiliary were absorbed into organizations designed to correspond to the new age groups. Younger girls became members of Girls in Action and older girls, members of Acteens. BETTY BROWN

GIRLS IN ACTION. Since Oct., 1970, the missions organization for girls ages 6–11 (or school grades 1–6) in Woman's Missionary Union's graded program of missionary education. Through materials and plans provided in *Aware* and *Discovery,* Girls in Action leads members to engage in the basic WMU tasks at their own level of development and understanding. Bobbie Sorrell is director (1970). BETTY BROWN

GLASS, WILEY BLOUNT (b. Gray Rock, Franklin County, Tex., Sept. 4, 1874; d. Richmond, Va., Nov. 14, 1967). Southern Baptist missionary to China. Educated at Baylor University (A.B., 1901) and Southern Baptist Theological Seminary (Th.M., 1903), he received an honorary D.D. from Baylor University in 1919. Ordained by Goolesboro (now Talco) Baptist Church, Talco, Tex., Aug., 1897, he was pastor of the Mart Baptist Church, Mart, Tex., 1900–01. In 1903 the Foreign Mission Board appointed him to China where he served for 42 years as teacher, pastor, and evangelist. He also assisted with famine relief work during the 1907, 1920, and 1921 famines in China. He retired from his missionary career in 1942. By marriage July 22, 1903, to Eunice Irene Taylor, three children survived infancy. H. Bentley and two daughters who served as missionaries: Mrs. Baker James (Eloise) Cauthen in China, and Lois Glass, presently (1969) in Taiwan. On Mar. 13, 1916, he married Jessie Ligen Pettigrew. Their children were Gertrude and Byron Pettigrew. L. JACK GRAY

***GLEN DALE CHILDREN'S HOME.** Two new cottages for children were opened in 1958, and in 1960 two additional cottages and a new administration building were occupied. The old Lynnland College building and the dormitories which had served the home so long were razed. This completed the building program begun in 1947. A department of social service was established in 1960. C. Ford Deusner resigned as superintendent of Glen Dale in Apr., 1963, to become general superintendent of the Kentucky Baptist Board of Child Care. He was succeeded by Ralph T. McConnell. In June, 1965, the home celebrated the 50th anniversary of its opening. Its alumni at that time numbered approximately 2,000. C. FORD DEUSNER

GLENN, VIVIAN CECIL (b. Stamford, Jones County, Tex., July 28, 1908; d. John, Stanton County, Kans., Oct. 15, 1966). The 11th child of William C. Glenn, he attended Texas Technological College at Lubbock, Tex. In the early thirties, he became a farmer in southwest Kansas, paying for a farm during the "dust bowl" years. The peril of the dust storms brought financial disaster to most farmers and a sharp decline in land values, but Glenn was able to expand at a large personal profit. On July 15, 1939, he married Rozella Maxine Welch. They had one daughter, Maxine. He was an ardent church worker for 25 years. He was active in Southern Baptist work in Colorado and Kansas.

In 1963 he paid his own way to participate in the Japan Baptist New Life Crusade and visited mission fields in Egypt, the Holy Land, and Russia. He was a director of the Kansas Southern Baptist Foundation, 1961–66; president of the Kansas Baptist Brotherhood, 1962–63; and was the Kansas member of the Brotherhood Commission, SBC, at the time of his death. N. J. WESTMORELAND

***GLORIETA BAPTIST ASSEMBLY.** Since 1956 Glorietta has hosted thousands of people attending 17 different conferences each year during its summer operation. the staff grew from 200 in 1956 to a 1969 inventory of 450 jobs, including 125 adult staffers.

Facilities added 1956–66 include: a three-story addition to Oklahoma Hall (1956); Cactus Lodge, a staff dormitory for boys (1957); Yucca Lodge, staff building for girls, and the Children's Building (1958); a Garden Apartment unit and three Pine Lodge units (1959); a 40 room addition to Oklahoma Hall, a new wing on New Mexico Hall containing five additional conference rooms, the book store, gift shop, chuck wagon, clinic, and offices (1960); a Texas Hall addition and the Garden Apartments (1961); a second wing of New Mexico Hall (1962); Thunderbird Plaza with 76 units (1963); and 18 Western Town Apartments (1965); and the new Holcomb Auditorium, dedicated July 20, 1966. Named in honor of T. L. Holcomb, former executive secretary-treasurer of the Sunday School Board, this four-story building, containing 25 conference rooms as well as a 2,600 seat auditorium, was built at a cost of $1,233,030. In 1966 an additional 1,200 acres were added to the assembly complex to bring the total to 2,500 acres and more than 150 buildings.

On Nov. 1, 1966, Mark Short, Jr., succeeded E. A. Herron who had served as manager since 1950. In 1967 the mall in front of New Mexico Hall was rebuilt, four bathhouses were completed in the Camp Shelter area, and winter operation was inaugurated with approximately 10,000 people using the facilities during the first two years. On Apr. 15, 1968, three Thunderbird units were completed (46 rooms with private baths). These units also furnish provisions for winter use. Chaparral Inn, a heated lodge containing 62 rooms with private baths, was completed in 1969. That same year a high capacity well pump was installed.

The summer registrations increased from 10,574 in 1956, to 27,131 in 1969. The beautiful Glorieta Gardens continue to be an attraction not only for the registered guests but for hundreds of other visitors during the year.

HUBERT B. SMOTHERS AND H. E. INGRAHAM

GNOSTICISM. The name given an interpretation of human existence that emerges clearly in the second century with an emphasis on salvation by means of mystical knowledge given through revelation. The word "Gnosticism" is derived from the Greek word, *gnosis,* which means knowledge. Gnosticism is syncretistic and exists in various forms or systems that manifest different degrees of indebtedness to Zoroastrianism, Babylonian religion, Judaism, Hellenistic philosophy and religion, and Christianity.

Clement of Alexandria (c. 150–c. 215), a critic of the Gnostics, gave information concerning some Gnostic groups who considered themselves Christian. Among the most important Christian sources for knowledge about gnosticism are the writings of Justin of Rome (c. 100–c. 165), Irenaeus of Lyons (c. 130–c. 200), and Hippolytus (c. 170–c. 236).

Among the most important primary sources are Gnostic writings such as the Gospel of Mary, the Apocryphon of John, the Sophia of Jesus Christ, the Gospel of Truth, the Gospel of Thomas, the Gospel of Philip, and more than 40 other Gnostic treatises, many not yet published, contained in leather-bound books discovered in 1945, near Nag-Hammadi in Egypt.

The central concern of gnosticism is salvation, which is gained through self-knowledge that is revealed, rather than through faith. Evil in the world is explained by holding that the world is created and ruled by the evil Demiurge, or "creator god," who is a different god from the supreme Divine Being. Therefore, man lives in an evil material environment. But some men possess a spark or seed of divine spiritual substance which may be rescued from the evil material world and assured of a return to the home in the Divine Being by means of the secret knowledge given through revelation. Self-knowledge is the key to salvation, which gives freedom. Some Gnostics used their freedom to become ascetics, others to become libertines. Men who gain salvation are called "spiritual," while other men are called "fleshly" or "material."

Christ, the emissary who enters the evil world with the saving "gnosis" (knowledge) from the supreme Divine Being, did not really become incarnate, however, nor did he really die; he only *seemed* to have a human appearance, or he only *temporarily* inhabited the man Jesus.

Gnosticism probably existed in a limited form prior to the first century. But it is not clear that the Gnostic redeemer motif existed prior to that century.

Christianity recognized the grave peril posed by the various forms of gnosticism in reference to the Christian understanding of God, Christ, creation, salvation, and history and rejected it. Some New Testament scholars believe that some of the writings of the New Testament reflect an interaction with gnosticism, among them 1 John, 1 Corinthians, Colossians, and several others.

BIBLIOGRAPHY: Robert M. Grant, *Gnosticism* (1961); *Gnosticism and Early Christianity* (1966). Hans Jonas, *The Gnostic Religion* (1958). R. M. Wilson, *Gnosis and the New Testament* (1968).

RAYMOND BRYAN BROWN

GOD IS DEAD THEOLOGY. See RADICAL THEOLOGY.

GOLDEN GATE BAPTIST SEMINARY, URBAN PROGRAM OF. From the beginning of his presidency, Harold K. Graves dreamed of making Golden Gate Baptist Theological Seminary especially meaningful in relation to its vital urban setting. He wrote in the *Gateway* in 1966:

> We are faced with the problem of communicating the changeless Gospel to men in a changing society. My call to go to Golden Gate Seminary as president fourteen years ago seemed to offer a place where I might be involved in this quest. Here in the urban cosmopolitan setting of the San Francisco Bay Area live 4,000,000 people. Southern Baptists have no other comparable laboratory with a seminary in its midst.

Dreams and plans reached a climactic stage on the occasion of an address to the seminary trustees, faculty, and staff by Grady Cothen, then executive secretary of the California convention. He issued the following challenge: "Why not make Golden Gate Seminary a center for a study in depth of urban life and a laboratory to learn how to present Christ effectively to the cities?" The challenge came at the right moment. The response was positive. Immediately, procedures were set in motion for an in-depth study by the faculty looking toward the implementation of a special urban emphasis at Golden Gate. Early in 1965, Distinguished Professor Gaines S. Dobbins was asked to spearhead this project. He responded by proposing a fivefold study program involving the faculty in a year of investigation and research on the subject.

As an outcome of this investigation the faculty concluded that a professor should be added to the faculty who was a specialist in this area of concern. They voted unanimously to recommend to the trustees the establishment of a Chair of Missions and Evangelism with the specific responsibility for this new urban emphasis. They requested that a professor be employed immediately and that the chair be financed by interested friends until a minimum endowment of $300,000 could be raised. The faculty also invisioned the development of an Urban Church Institute which would offer special urban training opportunities in addition to the urban emphasis which would be given in the regular resident degree programs.

At the trustee meeting held in connection with the SBC in Detroit in 1966, the trustees elected to this new position Francis M. DuBose, then superintendent of missions in Detroit. Employed jointly by the Home Mission Board and the Baptist State Convention of Michigan, DuBose had been vitally involved both in urban research and ministry.

Immediately upon the arrival of the new professor, steps were taken to implement the plans for this new urban program. The emphasis upon the emerging urban context of witness and mission became a major aspect of the content of the introductory courses in evangelism and missions. In addition, the new chair introduced an undergraduate elective and a graduate seminar on urban missions. Along with these courses came a new emphasis upon field work, with individual and group field projects becoming a part of the learning experience of each course of study. This new emphasis on field work led the faculty to investigate its value in terms of the total seminary program. This has led to a broader concept of field education, one which integrates field experience into the total experience of seminary training.

The first year of the operation of the program of the new chair, plans were projected for the first annual Urban Church Institute to be held in May, 1968. The department of metropolitan missions of the HMB agreed to sponsor the Institute jointly with the Chair of Missions and Evangelism. J. N. Evans, secretary of the department, and his staff agreed to share in the expenses of the Institute and to cooperate in planning the program. The basic purpose of the Institute is to make an intensive investigation of the problems and prospects of the church's mission in an urban society—approaching the subject from a different perspective each year. The Institute proper is held each summer, but preparations for it and research resulting from it continue throughout the year and relate to the total emphasis of the Chair of Missions and Evangelism. The working philosophy of the Institute is to combine the theoretical and practical. Lectures by leading scholars and urban specialists, general and group discussions, and field trips constitute the format of the Institute program. The Institute leadership has felt strongly about participants coming with some theoretical orientation to the urban problem. It is therefore required of all prospective participants that they agree to a preparatory reading assignment and the preparation of a book review to be a part of the findings of the Institute. The normal length of the Institute is two weeks; and for those who meet all requirements, two hours of credit are given.

The theme for the first year was "The Mission of the Church in an Urban Society: Sources of Understanding." Featured guest lecturers were: William Alonso, professor of city and regional planning and chairman of the Center for Planning and Development Research, University of California, Berkeley; Robert Lee, professor of social ethics and director of the Institute of Church and Society, San Francisco Theological Seminary; and George W. Webber, then director of MUST (Metropolitan Urban Service Training), a professor at Union Theological Seminary, and former director of the famed East Harlem Protestant Parish. These men, widely acknowledged scholars and authors and themselves related to urban life in some special way, brought an excellent background understanding to the Institute. This laid the foundation for lectures by Southern Baptist churchmen and scholars who sought to interpret the facts and relate the insights to the practical situations of church life.

The theme of the second Institute was "The Strategy of the Christian Mission in Urban America." Featured guest lecturers were Ivan Vallier, research sociologist and associate director of the Institute of International Studies, University of California, Berkeley; E. V. Hill, prominent leader in the National Baptist Convention, pastor of Mt. Zion Missionary Baptist Church, Watts area, chairman of the Housing Authority, chairman of the subcommittee on equal employment opportunities, Los Angeles; and Robert Lee who was also featured lecturer at the first Institute. As in the first Institute, Southern Baptist state and national leaders and seminary professors contributed significantly as lecturers and resource persons.

The total findings of each Institute are averaging some 500 pages of resource material. In addition to the group summaries, the findings include such items as lectures, book reviews, congregational case studies, bibliographies, evaluations, and pertinent information on program personnel and participants. The findings have attracted wide attention and have been requested by such groups as the *Urban Affairs Quarterly,* the Urban Institute of L.S.U., and MUST.

The Institute has attracted people interested in the urban problem from over the nation including Alaska and Hawaii. The participants usually constitute a balanced group of churchmen involved in representative ministries in urban settings: Anglo, ethnic, and black pastors; city mission administrators; persons in various types of Christian social ministries; and other urban ministers. The Institute has inspired participants to lead in the development of urban conferences in their local urban areas.

A significant development of the Chair of Missions and Evangelism has been a series of Tuesday evening experimental classes on the general theme of "The Mission of the Church in the Racially Changing Community." Soon after the coming of the new professor, he began conversations with Jack O'Neal, director of the department of work with National Baptists for the California convention, out of a concern to relate the emphasis of the new chair to the work of the state convention in the area of race relations. These dialogues led to prayer groups and to more heart-searching discussions on the part of Bay area church leaders concerned with race relations.

The result was the decision to offer at Golden

Gate an experimental course focusing upon the ministry of the church in the racially changing community. The state convention's department of work with National Baptists agreed to underwrite the cost of the guest lectures. C. Arthur Insko, professor of Christian ethics, agreed to work with the Chair of Missions and Evangelism in this new venture. Some 40 pastors and metropolitan missionaries were invited to take the course. An effort was made to bring to the class men of varying racial and ethnic backgrounds who were either facing a racially changing neighborhood as pastors or who were seeking to relate to such communities as urban mission administrators. The class was made up of whites, blacks, and representatives of various minority groups: American Indian, Chinese, Mexican, and other Latin Americans. Five guest lecturers were invited for a total of 11 two-hour class periods. Raymond Harvey, pastor of the Greenwood Missionary Baptist Church of Tuskegee, Ala., dealt with "Man Made in the Image of God as He Relates to His Family and Church." Victor Glass, secretary of the department of work with National Baptists of the HMB, dealt with "The Christian and the Social Ethics of Human Relations in the Changing Community." Paul Gillespie, pastor of the racially integrated Tacoma Park Baptist Church of Washington, D. C., dealt with "The Integrated Church Serving Effectively in the Racially Changing Community." John Nichol, pastor of the racially integrated Oakhurst Baptist Church of Decatur, Ga., dealt with "Using Christian Social Ministries to Reach and Serve the Multiracial Community." Foy Valentine, secretary of the Christian Life Commission, SBC, dealt with "Moral and Social Problems Encountered by the Church in the Racially Changing Community." Professors DuBose and Insko gave guidance to the course and directed study groups which prepared papers on 10 areas pertinent to the subject. The materials of the course—lectures, discussion, and group reports—were published in a limited paperback edition of 208 pages by the state's Department of Work with National Baptists, under the title *The Mission of the Church in the Racially Changing Community*.

As a sequel to the first course, the chair cooperated with the Department of Work with National Baptists in offering a course on *The Mission of the Negro Church in America*. The first year, S. M. Lockridge, pastor of the Calvary Baptist Church, San Diego, served as guest teacher under the director of the professor of the chair. The purpose of this course is to study the development of National Baptist churches and their role in the expansion of Christianity in the United States. Insights into the leadership role of the Negro minister in the black community, the therapeutic value of the church to the suffering membership, and the Christian influence of the Negro church and its leadership in the midst of the civil and religious revolution in America are studied in an effort better to understand and meet the mission challenge of a changing America. Special attention is given to evaluating the effectiveness of the urban Negro congregation in light of the general decline of Protestant churches in the American central city.

In seeking to understand the background of the problems facing the church in the racially changing community during the first experimental course, it seemed evident that there needed to be a more in-depth look into this area. Consequently, another course was created: "Social Issues Confronting the Church in the Racially Changing Community." The format for this course has been to employ specialists to speak to some social issue, and then to follow each lecture or lecture series with lectures and discussions which deal first with "Implications for the Thought and Life of the Church" and then with "Implications for the Mission and Ministry of the Church." Professor Insko also shared with the chair of missions and evangelism in the development of this course in cooperation with the state's Department of Work with National Baptists.

Thus three distinct courses have developed from this effort. After the first course, these have been open to all. In every course both students and nonstudents have enrolled for credit, and visitors from the community have been in regular attendance.

The urban emphasis inspired in part by the Chair of Missions and Evangelism has projected itself into other vital areas of seminary life. Each year the Student World Mission Conference, which attracts several hundred students from colleges in western states, gives a major emphasis to some aspect of the urban context of the Christian mission. Various conferences sponsored by the HMB on the Golden Gate campus relate in a special way to the chair's urban emphasis. The professor of the chair cooperates with the Foreign Mission Board in studying the special needs in urban centers of the board's overseas fields. Lecture-study tours have been sponsored in a number of countries.

Thus through regular and experimental courses, through the Urban Church Institute, through an expanding concept of field education, through an urban emphasis which relates to the total life of the seminary—the Chair of Missions and Evangelism is seeking to play a meaningful role in the fulfilment of the seminary's dream to make Golden Gate a vital source for Christian training in terms of its own vital urban context. FRANCIS M. DUBOSE

***GOLDEN GATE BAPTIST THEOLOGICAL SEMINARY.** Golden Gate Baptist Theological Seminary has continued to progress. The removal in 1959 to the Marin County campus accelerated other important areas of expansion. The buildings, landscaping, and campus installation have attracted the admiration of thousands of visitors. The unusual location on a small peninsula in lovely San Francisco Bay affords a mountain view in one direction and the city of San Francisco across the water in the other. Harold Graves is president.

The library, which in 1956 contained 16,000 volumes, now includes more than 71,000 items. The seminary is a contributing member of the Graduate Theological Union Library in Berkeley. This gives Golden Gate students and faculty access to one of the greatest theological collections in the world.

The location of the seminary on the west coast in the most populous state of the union has given a cosmopolitan character to its student body. In 1970 the students came from 44 states, the District of Columbia, and 27 foreign countries.

The institution was accredited by the American Association of Theological Schools in 1960. In 1968 it was given a preliminary visit by the executive secretary and the chairman of the accrediting commission of the Western Association of Schools and Colleges. The commission then placed the seminary on its list of Approved Candidates for Accreditation. Final inspection for complete accreditation was scheduled for the spring of 1971. WILLIAM A. CARLETON

GOLDEN, WILLIAM CORNELIUS (b. Graves County, Ky., Sept. 27, 1858; d. Orlando, Fla., May 27, 1939). Converted at 17, he soon felt called to preach. He reentered public school, worked his way through Clinton College, and entered Southern Baptist Theological Seminary in 1883. During his seminary years, he was pastor of nearby churches. After graduation he served churches in Bellefountaine, Ohio, and Pine Bluff, Ark. He was pastor of Third Church, Nashville, Tenn., for 10 years. Golden married Mildred E. Bennett, Mar. 4, 1898. They had one son, W. C., Jr. From 1902 to 1910 he served as state mission secretary for Tennessee, where his chief concern was to promote the building of rural churches. He also did much to promote the work of the children's homes. In 1943 the Tennessee State Mission Offering was named for the Goldens. Golden entered the field of evangelism under the Home Mission Board in 1910. He spent much time in Florida, serving the Palm Avenue Church in Tampa for five years. Golden was buried in Nashville, Tenn.

MRS. DOUGLAS GINN

GOOD SAMARITAN HOME. Begun in New Orleans in 1953 by the New Orleans Baptist Association, the Home Mission Board shared in its support from 1960 until it was closed in 1969. The home ministered to women with acute problems produced by alcoholism, dope addiction, prostitution, and imprisonment. Shelter, meals, and used clothing were provided for women stranded without money or job.

CHARLES MCCULLIN

GOODRICH, ARTHUR LEON (b. Kenly, N. C., Sept. 12, 1891; d. Clinton, Miss., Mar. 14, 1956). Editor, minister, and civic leader. Son of J. L. Goodrich of Benson, N. C., he earned degrees at Wake Forest College and the Southern Baptist Seminary, and did advanced study at Vanderbilt University. In 1946 he received the honorary D.D. degree from Mississippi College. He married Lillie Barbour and to this union were born Launa and Thyra. After the death of his first wife, Goodrich married Rose Mann, and to this union were born John Wright, Roseleen, and Jean. On the decease of his second wife, Goodrich married Evie Landrum on Aug. 31, 1937.

Goodrich served pastorates at Porter Memorial Church, Lexington, Ky., and the First Baptist Church, Pontotoc, Miss. He was named circulation manager of the *Baptist Record,* Jan. 1, 1935, and became editor in 1941. He held this post until his death. He promoted a program of circulation development that resulted in an increase of circulation from 4,001 to 89,227. One reason for his success was the "Every Family Plan," under which the churches included in their budget subscriptions for every family in the membership. He was a member of the Evangelical Press Association, the Associated Church Press (once vice-president), and the Southern Baptist Press Association (three times president, twice vice-president, and twice secretary-treasurer).

Goodrich was active in the Kiwanis Club (nine year perfect attendance), and a world traveler. R. A. MC LEMORE

***GRACE McBRIDE YOUNG WOMAN'S AUXILIARY.** The special committee for study of college and Grace McBride YWA organization appointed in 1963 by the WMU executive board, was dismissed in 1967 with no definite recommendations for Grace McBride YWA. In 1969 there were 63 Grace McBride YWA organizations with a membership of 903.

DORIS DEVAULT

GRAHAM, BILLY, CHAIR OF EVANGELISM. In 1965 a conjunction of circumstances opened the way for the trustees of the Southern Baptist Theological Seminary to establish the Billy Graham Chair of Evangelism and request the Southern Seminary Foundation to begin a campaign to seek $500,000 in endowment for the new chair. Expressions from the students requesting a department of evangelism, conferences between President Duke K. McCall and Billy Graham in an effort to persuade the evangelist to lend his name to the chair, and increased emphasis upon evangelism in the curriculum of the seminary were part of the beginnings. With the assurance of support from the Billy Graham Evangelistic Association toward the expense of the chair while funds for endowment were being sought, the faculty nominated and the trustees elected Kenneth L. Chafin as the first Billy Graham professor of evangelism in 1965. Southern Seminary Foundation announced in June, 1969, that through the cooperation of faculty, staff, trustees, alumni, and friends $625,000 had been received in cash and pledges for the endowment of the chair.

PAUL G. KIRKLAND

GRAHAM, BILLY, COLLECTION. The Billy Graham Collection at the James P. Boyce Centennial Library of the Southern Baptist Theological Seminary, Louisville, Ky., is contained in the Billy Graham Room and Billy Graham Research Room. These areas were provided and furnished by a $50,000 gift from the J. Boone Aiken Foundation, Florence, S. C., to house and preserve the records and other valuable documents of the ministry of Billy Graham. On Monday evening, May 9, 1960, the Room was dedicated in connection with a Baccalaureate Sermon at the Seminary by Billy Graham. Materials contributed by Billy Graham and others are books, tape recordings, etc. All the books published by Billy Graham and their translations into modern languages and all available books about him and his ministry are contained in the collection. On Feb. 22, 1962, a portrait of Billy Graham was unveiled at a Missionary Day service at the Seminary at which he was the speaker. The portrait was painted by Mrs. Aileen Ortlip Shea, of Wellsville, N. Y. She is the wife of a brother of George Beverly Shea. The painting was made possible by a gift of Mrs. Carl Haemsch of Henderson, Tenn. Each year about 2,500 persons visit the Billy Graham Room. Many research students use the collection of materials.

LEO T. CRISMON

***GRAND LAKE BAPTIST ASSEMBLY.** In 1969 property consisted of 26 cabins, a caretaker's home, a tabernacle, swimming pool, and kitchen and dining hall. Estimated value of property was $200,000, with a $7,000 debt. Total registration in 1969 was 741.

J. M. GASKIN

***GRAND VALLEY HOSPITAL (Pryor, Okla.).** Since the Baptist General Convention of Oklahoma acquired the Grand Valley Hospital by lease agreement in 1954, property value of the facility has grown to $629,790. In 1969 there was a debt of $56,996. Capacity is 57 beds, and the daily occupancy is 68 per cent. There are 104 employees.

J. M. GASKIN

GREEN, DENT F. (b. Jackson Gap, Ala., Dec. 5, 1868; d. Decatur, Ala., Jan. 5, 1945). Lawyer, banker, and Baptist leader. Son of John Berry and Levia Ann (Henderson) Green, he married Annie Plaster. Green was educated at Childersburg High School; Marion Military Institute, Marion, Ala., B.S.; and Howard College, honorary LL.D. Admitted to the bar in 1897, he was a member of the Alabama legislature, 1898–1900; register in chancery, Morgan County, 1900–08; solicitor, Morgan County, 1908–09; vice-president of the Tennessee Valley National Bank, Decatur, Ala., 1909–18; state superintendent of banks, 1918–20, 1929–32; and elected state senator, 1916. In 1920 he became executive secretary-treasurer of the Alabama Baptist State Convention, later serving as president of the convention. Green also served as vice-president, Alabama National Bank, Montgomery, 1932–33; chairman of the board of trustees, Tennessee Valley Bank, Decatur, Ala., 1934–45; and trustee of Judson College. He was on various Southern Baptist Convention committees. He was also a member of the Masons, Rotary Club, and Kiwanis Club.

A. HAMILTON REID

GREEN, GEORGE (b. London, England, July 26, 1872; d. Danville, Va., Nov. 26, 1962). Southern Baptists' first medical missionary to Africa, 1906–45. Graduated from Ontario's Woodstock College and Medical College of Virginia (M.D., 1905), he later studied at Southern Baptist Theological Seminary and Royal College of Physicians and Surgeons, Edinburgh, Scotland. He married Lydia Williams, Jan., 1907, and arrived in Ogbomosho three months later. Green helped to plan and build a hospital in Ogbomosho and, except for furlough years, continued to serve there until retirement. He also held administrative responsibilities in the mission and the Nigeria Convention. He received the Jubilee Medal from the British Government in 1935. Shoun (king of Ogbomosho) made him "Chief of the Medicine Men" in 1944.

I. N. PATTERSON

GREENE, A. ROY, SR. (b. Clarksville, Tenn., Feb. 11, 1903; d. Nashville, Tenn., Jan. 12, 1962). Founder of the Greene Double-Cola Company and prominent layman. He married Jessie Lee Nolen, Nov. 28, 1920. They had six children: Roy, Jr., O'Brien, Charles, Bobby, Joe, and Dorothy (Mrs. Robert Parrish). He served as president of Tennessee Businessmen's Association. Greene helped organize the first Tennessee Brotherhood Convention, served as president of the Tennessee Brotherhood for five years, Tennessee's representative on the Brotherhood Commission, SBC, for 10 years, and chairman of the commission in 1956. He helped organize Woodmont and Forrest Hills churches in Nashville. A deacon at Woodmont and Shelby Avenue, Nashville, he served as interim pastor at North Edgefield and Shelby Avenue. Greene was vice-president of the board of trustees for Baptist Hospital, Inc., and chairman of its business and finance committee. He became the second layman to serve as president of the Tennessee Baptist Convention in 1953.

ROY J. GILLELAND

GRESHAM CHAPEL, THE VIRGINIA. The chapel in the new Baptist Building at Lutherville, Md., is named in memory of Virginia Jones Gresham (1916–64), wife of Roy D. Gresham, executive secretary-treasurer of the Baptist Convention of Maryland.

DELANE MARLIN RYALS

GROSS, ARTHUR LEE, SR. (b. Great Falls, S. C., Nov. 20, 1907; d. Belvidere, Ill., Aug. 4, 1969). Baptist layman. Educated at Furman University (A.B., 1929), he taught school and coached six years before entering the life insurance business. He married Betty Propst in 1936. Gross became director of South Carolina Baptist Retirement Plans, Oct. 1, 1938, serving in this capacity for 16 years. In 1954 he became the first superintendent of the Bethea Baptist Home for Aging, Darlington, S. C., which he helped design and open, Oct. 1, 1960. In 1961 he was elected secretary-treasurer, then president, of Southern Mutual Church Insurance Company. He served as moderator of the Fairfield Baptist Association, and vice-president, South Carolina Baptist Convention, 1964. At the time of his death he was serving on: board of directors, Radio and Television Commission, SBC; board of trustees, Bethea Baptist Home; chairman of finance and deacon in Rosewood Baptist Church, Columbia (where he was licensed to preach). A. W. BRICKLE

GROUP LIFE INSURANCE PROGRAM. See LIFE AND HEALTH BENEFITS DEPARTMENT.

GROVE GENERAL HOSPITAL (Grove, Okla.). Opened as a 25-bed facility in 1960 by physician Norman A. Cotner, partially by community funds, but mostly financed by the founder, the Baptist General Convention of Oklahoma acquired this institution and opened it, Nov. 11, 1963, as a "satellite" institution under the auspices of the Miami Baptist Hospital. It is the first hospital to operate in this manner in Oklahoma. When it was acquired the value was $199,175.23, and the capacity was 25 beds. In 1969 the value had increased to $371,239.46, with a debt of $139,174.35, and bed capacity of 36 with 63 per cent occupancy. There were 48 employees in 1969. J. M. GASKIN

***GROWTH OF SOUTHERN BAPTISTS.** Southern Baptists grew from a membership of 351,951 in 1845 to 11,489,613 in 1969. The number of churches increased from 4,126 in 1845 to 34,335 in 1969. From 1955 to 1969 their number increased by 3,014,872 members and 3,958 churches. In 1970 Southern Baptists were the largest Protestant group in the United States, having surpassed the United Methodist Church in membership.

Sunday School enrolment increased from 6,641,715 in 1955 to 7,418,067 in 1969. Training Union ongoing enrolment stood at 2,343,595 in 1969, compared to 2,223,502 in 1955. Woman's Missionary Union enrolment grew from 1,245,358 in 1955 to 1,291,221 in 1969; and Brotherhood enrolment increased from 404,281 to 430,339 during the same period. Vacation Bible School enrolment went from 2,652,788 in 1955 to 3,648,255 in 1969. In 1969, 14,140 churches reported having a church library; 18,074 churches reported having a music ministry, with 1,062,494 enrolled.

Another indication of the growth of Southern Baptists was the increase in total gifts and mission gifts through the churches. Total gifts in 1955 were $334,836,283, of which $58,360,247 was reported as mission gifts. In 1969 total gifts were $809,608,812, including $133,224,335 in mission gifts. Total per capita gifts increased from $39.51 in 1955 to $70.46 in 1969.

Cooperative Program receipts in 1969 were $78,220,474, an increase from $35,717,008 in 1955. Of these receipts, $27,443,440 was distributed to Convention-wide causes, compared to $13,588,160 in 1955.

The home and foreign mission programs experienced tremendous growth in recent years. Foreign missionary personnel increased from 1,020 in 1955 to 2,490 in 1969. The Lottie Moon Offering increased from $3,951,000 in 1955 to $15,297,558 in 1969. The number of home missionaries increased from 1,105 in 1955 to 2,235 in 1969.

The Sunday School Board is responsible for 25 programs of work, including the operation of 52 Book Stores and two Convention-wide assemblies at Ridgecrest and Glorieta. Approximately 97,000,000 periodicals were published in 1969, compared to 65,000,000 in 1955.

Southern Baptist seminaries reported a total enrolment of 5,853 in 1969, plus 6,188 enrolled through seminary extension centers, and property valued at $48,147,260. In 1955, enrolment was 5,885, and property was valued at $21,353,809.

Forty-three Southern Baptist senior colleges and universities reported a total enrolment of 83,699 in 1969, compared with 43,945 enrolled in 30 schools in 1955. Property value increased from $96,968,766 in 1955 to $403,351,213 in 1969.

Twenty-three Baptist junior colleges, academies, and Bible schools reported a total enrolment of 14,403 in 1969, with property valued at $39,099,047. In 1955, 11,574 were enrolled in 33 schools with property valued at $25,370,000.

Forty-three Southern Baptist hospitals reported a total bed capacity of 14,920 and property valued at $333,546,830 in 1969. In 1955, 37 hospitals had a total bed capacity of 8,836, with property valued at $97,817,000.

Sixteen Southern Baptist homes for aged reported a total of 1,863 residents in 1969, and 27 Baptist children's homes reported 3,889 residents plus 2,276 children living off campus. In 1955, Southern Baptists had 10 homes for aged with 450 residents, and 23 children's homes.

Southern Baptists had 30 state conventions in 1969, an increase from 24 in 1955. Two additional state conventions are being organized in 1970. Southern Baptists have churches in all 50 states and in Canada. KARLEEN ROGERS

GUAM, MISSION IN. Freedom is fast becoming a reality on Guam, America's Micronesian possession. From 1521 to 1898 it was under the firm rule of the Spanish; then the United States Navy took control. The Organic Act of 1950 made the island an unincorporated territory and extended citizenship to its people. It also established executive, legislative, and judicial branches of the local government in civilian hands. The 21-member legislature is elected every year. In 1970 the governor, formerly appointed by the president of the United States, will be elected by the people.

Baptists have been in Guam since 1911. However, Southern Baptists sent their first missionaries to Guam in 1961 at the request of a group of military and civil service families who had organized the Ardmore Baptist Mission. In 1961 that first couple, Harry and Doris (Cash) Goble, led in organizing Calvary Baptist Church. The next year the Marianas Baptist Mission came into existence, and in 1966 Tamuning Baptist Mission near the capital city of Agana was organized. In 1969 three missionary couples served on this island. Another couple was expected to begin student work among more than 1,700 students from all Micronesia, an area including more than 2,000 islands and atolls. Many lay Christians find a unique opportunity of service through civil service and public school teaching, usually on a two-year contract.

LOUIS E. MCCALL

GUARANTEED INCOME. In recent years, many proposals have been made regarding the possibility that the federal government might guarantee an income for the poor as a partial answer to the growing menace of poverty in America. There is no one answer to the problem of poverty because the poor have many different needs. They need more than money. They need hope, a sense of dignity, and purpose.

Three basic proposals have been offered to provide a minimum income to the poor. The *negative income tax* would provide for payment to the poor by the Internal Revenue Service. The amount would depend on the difference between the amount earned by the family and the government-established minimum income level. The *social dividend* proposal would allow the government to pay a basic "dividend" to everyone, rich and poor alike. This dividend would then be included in taxable income: the poor would keep most of the dividend while the well-to-do would return most or all of theirs in the form of taxes. *Family allowances* provide that every family in the United States, rich or poor, would receive a certain amount of money for each child. Amounts received per child would vary depending upon the age of the child and the actual plan adopted.

A guaranteed income is no cure-all; it is, however, an effort to cope with one of America's greatest social issues—the plight of the poor. As far as this issue is concerned, little has been done to lead Southern Baptists to support any particular proposal. The Christian Life Commission has published a pamphlet entitled "Issues and Answers: Guaranteed Income" and prepared a research paper on the subject for study by the serious student. FLOYD A. CRAIG

GUATEMALA, MISSION IN (cf. Guatemala-Honduras, Mission in, Vol. I). At the beginning of 1970 the Guatemala Baptist Convention was made up of 34 churches, with 44 missions reporting 3,099 members. Two Bible institutes offered different levels of training: (1) for men with six years or more of schooling and (2) for rural pastors and lay leaders. The convention also helped support a religious education promoter and sponsored radio-TV programs. The Baptist Book Store served the entire convention. In 1969 the mission included 22 missionaries (career and short-term).

CHESTER S. CADWALLADER, JR.

GUIDE. A mission leadership magazine published by the Brotherhood Commission for officers of Baptist Men and Baptist Young Men since Oct. 1, 1966. It was a 32-page quarterly magazine. Circulation started at 10,000 copies with the first issue and climbed sharply to 20,500 with the second. The average circulation per issue climbed to 29,389 in 1968, but dropped to 28,448 in 1969. DARRELL C. RICHARDSON

GULFSHORE AND KITTIWAKE ASSEMBLIES. In public auction the Mississippi Baptist Convention Board purchased the United States Maritime Academy property on Henderson Point at Pass Christian, Miss., in 1959 for $455,000. Mississippi Baptists remodeled and furnished the buildings and renamed the property Gulfshore.

The assembly officially opened Apr. 25, 1960, with a pastors' and missionaries' retreat. It was formally dedicated July 22, 1960. Registration for the first summer was 3,814. In Mar., 1965, W. T. Douglas became the first full-time resident manager, succeeding the first two managers of assemblies, W. R. Roberts and A. L. Nelson.

When hurricane Betsy struck on Sept. 9, 1965, she left an estimated $250,000 damage at Gulfshore. However, the damage was repaired, and the assemblies program continued.

In 1955 the board had purchased Kittiwake Assembly. Also at Pass Christian, Kittiwake faces the Gulf Coast shore line for 487 feet, and contains 14 acres. Its first summer of operation began in 1956, with 12 weeks of camps and assemblies, and an attendance of 1,979. After Gulfshore opened, Kittiwake was used chiefly for Royal Ambassador camps and individual church retreats. Attendance at Gulfshore and Kittiwake in 1969 totaled 13,000, even though two planned conferences were not held.

On Aug. 17, 1969, hurricane Camille completely destroyed all buildings at Kittiwake. Reported to be the strongest storm ever to hit the continental United States, Camille totally demolished ten buildings at Gulfshore Assembly, leaving four still standing, though seriously damaged.

BIBLIOGRAPHY: Anne W. McWilliams, *Beside the Point, The Gulfshore Story* (1967).

ANNE WASHBURN MCWILLIAMS

GUNN, WILLIAM FREDERICK (b. Crawfordsville, Ga., June 27, 1885; d. Clayton, Ga., Aug. 11, 1964). Educator. He married Hettie Barton, Sept. 6, 1917. They had two sons: Fred Allyn and William Barton. From Mercer University he received his A.B. (1915) and M.A. (1917) degrees and an honorary LL.D. He did further graduate study at Columbia University. Gunn taught in public schools, 1906–20; was a superintendent of schools, 1920–33; served as dean, registrar, and head of department of education at West Georgia College, 1933–46; and was president of Bessie Tift College, 1947–52. He held membership in various educational associations and accrediting commissions, and founded the group which was the forerunner of Future Teachers of America. He is buried in Christ Church Cemetery, St. Simons, Ga.

FLORA WALRAVEN

GUNTER, RICHMOND BAKER (b. Leake County, Miss., Sept. 3, 1880; d. Jackson, Miss., Mar. 17, 1964) . Corresponding secretary of Mississippi Baptist Convention board during the depression. Son of George Aaron Gunter and Mary Ellen Phillips, he graduated from Mississippi Central Normal School, Walnut Grove (1904) , Mississippi College (1907) , and Southern Baptist Theological Seminary (Th.M., 1912) . He married Tyna Amelia Pate of Coffeeville, Miss., Oct. 1. 1912, and after her death married Katie South. Gunter taught three years in the public schools. Ordained by the Standing Pine Baptist Church, Leake County, Nov. 23, 1908, he served as pastor of the Lena, Walnut Grove, Carthage, Leakesville, Laurel, and Louisville, Miss., churches. In 1915 he led the First Church of Louisville to be the first church in Mississippi to use the percentage division of gifts. He was a member of the future program commission which recommended to the Southern Baptist Convention in Memphis in 1925 the adoption of the Cooperative Program. As secretary of the Mississippi Baptist education commission, 1917–19, and publicity director for Mississippi of the 75 Million Campaign, 1919–24, he earned the reputation of a brilliant fund raiser.

He served as corresponding secretary of the convention board from Jan. 1, 1922, to Feb. 1, 1939. During the depression he reduced his salary and sold his home owned by the denomination, and applied the proceeds toward the state convention debts. The first state Baptist building was purchased under his leadership. He was president of the Mississippi Baptist convention, 1940–42. Mississippi College awarded him a D.D. (1921) , named a women's residence hall in his honor, and named him "Alumnus of the year" (1963) . His last pastorates were Florence, Pickens, and Briar Hill. He was buried in Florence, Miss. C. B. HAMLET, III

GUYANA, MISSION IN. On Aug. 1, 1962, Otis and Martha (Yates) Brady arrived in Guyana (then British Guiana) to initiate Southern Baptist missionary work. Central Baptist Church was organized in Nov., 1963, with 35 charter members. Consistent growth the first seven years produced seven churches, 19 missions, 757 members, and 2,497 enrolled in Sunday School, with beginnings in Training Union, WMU, and Brotherhood. In 1969, 16 missionaries (career and short-term) were assigned to Guyana. The Guyana Baptist Theological Institute begun in 1963 offers intensive multilevel training for laymen and pastors. Radio broadcasting provides training for Guyanese who help meet the demand for locally produced programs. Secular newspapers are used to promote the work, and in Dec., 1969, a Guyanese Baptist paper was published.

Two annual events, the evangelism conference and camp, provide additional training, inspiration, and unity. Special projects in evangelism, religious education, stewardship, music, and dentistry were significant in developing the work. Missionaries work with Guyanese in various capacities, but the developing strategy, growing out of primary concern for evangelism and church development, points to service as advisers to churches and in leadership training. The Crusade of the Americas gave a sense of urgency in total evangelism and Baptist fellowship. MRS. OTIS W. BRADY

H

HALL, ALDIS NORTON (b. Hannibal, Mo., Nov. 11, 1865; d. Muskogee, Okla., Dec. 23, 1940) . He was converted and baptized at Fifth St. Baptist Church, Hannibal, Mo., in 1886. Ordained by Washington Avenue Baptist Church (now Gaston Ave.) , Dallas, Tex., Nov. 5, 1898, he served as pastor and evangelist in Texas, and twice pastor of First Church, Muskogee, Okla., for a total of 28 years. Although Hall completed only about the eighth grade in school, he was distinguished as a pastor and denominational leader. Twice he preached the state convention annual sermon in Oklahoma (1907, 1924) , and was its president, 1924–28. He was moderator of associations in Dallas and Muskogee counties, and led in establishing Oklahoma Baptist Hospital.

ROBERT S. JACKSON

ATLANTIC CITY'S CONVENTION HALL, just off the famed Boardwalk, was the meeting place for the Baptist Jubilee Celebration, the Southern Baptist Convention, and the American Baptist Convention, May 19–24, 1964.

GOLDEN GATE BAPTIST THEOLOGICAL SEMINARY (*q.v.*), Mill Valley, Calif. ***Top:*** Student Center (*right*) and housing villages under the slopes of Mt. Tamalpais. *Center:* Platt Village for faculty housing in foreground, with academic buildings on the crest of the hill. ***Bottom:*** Administration Building.

HAM, MORDECAI FOWLER (b. Allen County, Ky., Apr. 2, 1877; d. Louisville, Ky., Nov. 1, 1961). Son of Lady Oliver McElray and Tobias James Ham, he was "descended from eight generations of Baptist ministers . . . from Roger Williams, pioneer Baptist preacher of America." Educated at Ogden College, Bowling Green, Ky., he received a D. D. degree from Bob Jones College, Cleveland, Tenn. His ministry began at Bowling Green in 1900 and he was ordained at Greenwood, Ky., on Oct. 11, 1901. He entered evangelistic work, in Kentucky and other southern states, and continued until 1927 when he accepted the pastorate of the First Baptist Church, Oklahoma City, Okla., for two years. He then returned to evangelism.

On June 3, 1905, he married Annie Laurie Smith of Eminence, Ky. At his death he was survived by his wife, three children, four grandchildren, and four great-grandchildren.

In the thirties Ham preached in a gospel tent on Broadway in Louisville and later in a tabernacle. He also did extensive radio preaching in Louisville and other southern cities. His publications include *Battle Front Messages, Sermons that Brought Revival* (1950), and about a dozen others. He numbered his converts at over 300,000 in 1950 and at 1,000,000 at the end of his ministry. Among them were evangelists Billy Graham and Grady Wilson.

BIBLIOGRAPHY: Ham, E. E., *Fifty Years on the Battle Front with Christ; a Biography of Mordecai F. Ham* (1950).

LEO T. CRISMON

HAMILTON, WILLIAM WISTAR, SR. (b. Hopkinsville, Ky., Dec. 9, 1868; d. New Orleans, La., Nov. 19, 1960). Minister, evangelist, educator, and denominational leader. Son of William Perry and Catherine Price (Roach) Hamilton, he married Zula Belle Doyle of Oxford, Miss. They had four children: William Wistar, Jr., Perry Elwood, Doyle Roach, and Virginia Belle.

Ordained in 1893, his pastorates were as follows: Vinton and Bonsack Baptist churches near Roanoke, Va., 1893–96; East Radford, Va., 1896–98; Bluefield, W. Va., 1898–1900; McFerran Memorial Church (later Fourth Avenue), Louisville, Ky., 1900–06; First Baptist Church, Lynchburg, Va., 1909–18; St. Charles Avenue Baptist Church, New Orleans, La., 1922–28; and Gentilly Baptist Church, New Orleans, 1942–46. He also served as secretary of the department of evangelism, Home Mission Board, SBC, 1906–09, president of the Baptist Bible Institute (now New Orleans Baptist Theological Seminary), New Orleans, 1928–42, and as chaplain of the Southern Baptist Hospital, New Orleans, 1947–57. He was president of the Southern Baptist Convention, 1940–42; also, president of the Southern Baptist Young People's Union in earlier years.

He held earned degrees from King College, Bristol, Tenn. (B.A., 1890), and the Southern Baptist Theological Seminary, Louisville, Ky. (Th.M., 1893, Th.D., 1904). He received honoary degrees from Georgetown College, Georgetown, Ky. (D.D., 1904), and from Bristol College, Bristol, Tenn. (LL.D., 1932). Hamilton was a member of the Masonic Order, the Knights of Pythias, and the United Order of American Mechanics. His grandson, Todd Condell Hamilton, appraised his leadership in a D.R.E. thesis at New Orleans Baptist Theological Seminary, 1965.

Hamilton contributed widely and constantly to denominational papers and periodicals. His authorship included the following books: *The Helping Hand* (1908), *Worldly Amusements—How to Decide, Sane Evangelism* (1909), *Bible Evangelism* (1921), *Wisdom in Soul Winning* (1929), *The Fine Art of Soul Winning* (1935), and *A Bible Revival* (1940). There were also five expository treatments of the books of the Bible, giving the teaching of each in simple form.

One of the most remarkable achievements of his life was the payment of the indebtedness which threatened the life of the Baptist Bible Institute when $353,000 worth of bonds went into default in 1932. But bankers still trusted his integrity and influence. With the faculty cut down to five, including himself, he held the school together. Facing payments every six months that had to be made unless foreclosure was accepted, his appeals to faculty, students, and friends all over the Convention met those payments. Sometimes the needed amount did not come in until the very hour the payment was due. Near the end of his life the love, prayers, and determination of those days asserted themselves again as he drew upon his limited funds to furnish the Prayer Room in the seminary chapel of today.

Frank Tripp, who knew him intimately through these years of struggle, asserted that "few men have made the contribution to the growth and development of Southern Baptist churches and agencies as William Wistar Hamilton."

JAMES WASHINGTON WATTS

HANCOCK, AARON WILLIAM (b. Red Oak, I.T., Feb. 7, 1894; d. McAlester, Okla., Feb. 5, 1965). Choctaw Indian minister and missionary to the Choctaw, Chickasaw, Seminole, and Creek Indians in Oklahoma. Son of Willis and Jeney Hancock, he married Hilda Sulterska, Aug. 18, 1917. He was educated at Oklahoma Baptist University (A.B., 1936). In 1961 he retired after 27 years of active mission service with the Home Mission Board, SBC, but continued working in mission schools and conferences until his last illness three months before his death. He is buried in Hill Side Cemetery, McAlester, Okla.

SAM W. SCANTLAN

HANEY, GEORGE GRANVILLE (b. Cannel City, Ky., Jan. 18, 1907; d. Dayton, Ohio, Jan. 4, 1967). Pioneer Ohio Southern Baptist pastor. Son of Verias Preston Haney, he married Lucille Bales, May 4, 1934. They had three sons: George Gale, David P., and Vernon Lee. Haney was ordained to the ministry in 1946. He served as pastor of three Ohio Baptist churches: First, South Lebanon, 1946–48, where he was the first pastor of the mission in Town Hall, and he built the first unit; First, Miamisburg, 1948–52; Urbancrest, Lebanon, 1952–55, where he was first pastor of the mission in the YMCA, and he built the first two units. His denominational service consisted of serving on the state executive board and associational capacities. He is buried in Dayton, Ohio. A plaque in his memory is placed in the Baptist Building of the State Convention of Baptists in Ohio reading: "George G. Haney, 1907–1967, Pioneer Ohio Southern Baptist Pastor. He loved the church and gave himself for it." JOSEPH F. HUNT

HANSEN, THOMAS (b. Aabenraa, Denmark, Mar. 4, 1897; d. Gainesville, Fla., June 22, 1964). Pastor, evangelist, denominational leader. Graduate of Des Moines University Academy (1917) and Danish Baptist Theological Seminary of Des Moines University (1920), he was a student at University of Florida (1920–25) and was awarded the D. D. by Stetson University in 1935. He married Edna Grace Petersen, June 27, 1923; they had two children, Keith L. and Kenneth L.

Ordained by the First Baptist Church, Elk Horn, Iowa, July, 1920, Hansen served the following Florida Baptist churches as pastor: First, Newberry, 1920–25; First, Starke, 1925–26; Main Street, Jacksonville, 1929–50; and First, Fort Lauderdale, 1928–29, and 1950–62. He served as president of the Florida Baptist Convention, 1945 and 1946; member, state board of missions, 1940–42, 1948–53, and president, 1940–41; member Foreign Mission Board, SBC, 1936–42; trustee, New Orleans Baptist Theological Seminary, 1947–57; and trustee, Stetson University, 1948–64. Hansen was active in establishing Baptist Memorial Hospital, Jacksonville. He served as the first president of United Florida Drys. In 1964 he assisted Stetson in its development program with Florida Baptist churches.

During his 41 years as a pastor, he was responsible for 4,400 converts, and organized and helped build 5 Baptist churches: Lake Forest, Jacksonville (1946); Wilton Manors (1955), Southwest (1956), Lauderdale Manors (1957), and Parkway (1961), all in Fort Lauderdale. He is buried in Lauderdale Memorial Gardens Cemetery, Fort Lauderdale. KEITH L. HANSEN

***HARDIN-SIMMONS UNIVERSITY.** Since 1954 the leadership changed three times. President E. A. Reiff (*q.v.*) resigned due to ill health in 1962. He was succeeded by James H. Landes, who served until Feb. 24, 1966, when Elwin L. Skiles became president. The enrolment increased to 2,713 resident students in 1968, with 123 faculty and administration members. Total endowment and annuity funds in 1968 were $4,473,732. Total plant value was $10,650,010. The school became a member of the American Association of University Women in 1961 and of the American Association of Colleges for Teacher Education in 1962. Provisional accreditation was granted by the National Council for Accreditation of Teacher Education.
CHARLES R. RICHARDSON

HARGIS, CHARLES PARKER (b. White Lily, Pulaski County, Ky., Feb. 22, 1882; d. Louisville, Ky., Jan. 20, 1960). Son of Rachel Ping and William Hargis, he was educated at White Lily grade school, and attended Baptist Bible Institute, New Orleans, La. (now New Orleans Baptist Theological Seminary). He became a field worker for the Sunday School Department of the General Association of Baptists in Kentucky (now Kentucky Baptist Convention) in the summer of 1923 while living at Somerset. For a few years he worked out of Lexington, and from 1940 to the end of Feb., 1950, when he retired, he lived in Louisville.

Hargis married Sarah Ann Boyd of Providence, Ky. One daughter, Pauline (Mrs. Badgett Dillard), the first woman teacher elected to the faculty of Southern Baptist Theological Seminary, Louisville, was the instructor in Elementary Education (1953) and Assistant Professor, 1954–58. After the death of Mrs. Hargis (Aug. 28, 1937), at Lexington, Mr. Hargis married Miss Flossie Dalton of Askins, Breckinridge County, Ky., who survived him.
LEO T. CRISMON

***HARGRAVE MILITARY ACADEMY.** Academic and military training for grades 8 through 12 plus one year of postgraduate study is offered. The regular session in 1968–69 had an enrolment of 585 with 379 in summer school. Full accreditation is accorded by the state and the Southern Association of Colleges and Schools. Hargrave was designated one of 10 pilot schools in the Superior, Talented, Students Program of S.A.C.S. in 1961. However, the emphasis is on training the average boy. Help is provided for slow readers. In 1968 denominational contributions to Hargrave were $85,775; the value of building, and grounds was estimated at $3,082,674; Joseph H. Cosby was president.
CARRINGTON PAULETTE

HARPER, WINFRED OZELL (b. Gorman, Tex., Dec. 30, 1920; d. Dar es Salaam, Tanganyika, Sept. 4, 1958). Pioneer missionary to East Africa. Educated at Hardin-Simmons University and Southwestern Baptist Theological Seminary, he was pastor of several Texas churches and served in the Navy. Harper and his wife, the former Juanita Taylor, were appointed to Nigeria in 1950. He taught in high school at Abeokuta, did field evangelism in Okeho and Oyo, and directed language and orientation school for new missionaries. One of three missionaries selected to explore mission work in East Africa, he led in establishing work there. He drowned in Azanian Sea during an outing celebrating the arrival of additional missionaries. JESSE C. FLETCHER

HARRIS, MARK HINES (b. Carroll County, Tenn., Mar. 2, 1898; d. Shelby County, Tenn., June 17, 1969). Son of Maude Hillsman and Rutledge Mitchell Harris, Harris was educated at Union University (A.B., D.D.), and Southwestern Baptist Theological Seminary (Th.M.). He married Dorothea Frances Furr of Wesson, Miss., Dec. 23, 1925. They had three children, Mark Alexander, Yvonne (Mrs. Bill Justis), and Sylvia (Mrs. Joe Guasco). His pastorates included Ridgely, Tenn., and Speedway Terrace, Memphis (28 years). He served as a member of executive board of Tennessee Baptist Convention. Harris was a trustee of Baptist Memorial Hospital, children's homes, and Union University. He served as moderator of Shelby County Baptist Association, and as president of Tennessee Baptist Convention (1946).

RALPH R. MOORE

HARRISON, LUTHER A. (b. Copiah County, Miss., Dec. 15, 1899; d. Monroe, La., Mar. 6, 1948). Son of J. H. and Emma (Beaseley) Harrison, he was educated at county schools, Mississippi State University, and Southwestern Baptist Theological Seminary (B.M.). He married Myrtle Brent of Sumit, Miss., on June 6, 1929. They had two children: Wanda Jean (Mrs. Walter Holland) and Charles. Harrison served as minister of education, and music at Turner Memorial, Fort Worth, Tex., 1929–32; minister of music at First Baptist, Suffolk, Va., 1932–35; Grace Memorial, Richmond, Va., 1935–37; and associate pastor and education director at Immanuel, Little Rock, Ark., 1937–41; and First, Oklahoma City, Okla. 1941–45. He was music secretary of the Mississippi Baptist Convention from Sept., 1945, until his death. He was killed in a one-car accident on a return trip from Southwestern Seminary. He is buried in Lakewood Cemetery, Jackson, Miss. Harrison was the coauthor of *Practical Music Lessons* (1950) and several unpublished hymns.

R. A. MCLEMORE

***HARRISON-CHILHOWEE BAPTIST ACADEMY.** The decade of 1960–70 was one of growth and progress at Harrison-Chilhowee Baptist Academy. Eight new buildings were added during this period, and the older facilities were either razed or remodeled. A master plan for the campus and physical facilities was adopted, which resulted in an orderly and satisfactory system of services for the operation of the school.

The endowment of the school increased from $10,000 to $160,000 during this time, and the gift of a farm in 1969 added approximately $100,000 more to the total. Plans for a campaign for permanent endowment culminated in the approval by the Tennessee Baptist Convention for a campaign to begin in 1970 to add $500,000 to the present amount. Also approved by Chilhowee's trustees was a plan to upgrade and enlarge the academic offerings of the school to provide the best possible preparation for college.

CHARLES C. LEMONS

HART, JOSEPH LANCASTER (b. Essex County, Va., Nov. 26, 1877; d. Dallas, Tex., Sept. 8, 1966). Pioneer missionary in Argentina (1903–21) and Chile (1921–47). While in Richmond College (B.A., 1900) and Southern Baptist Theological Seminary (B.D., 1903), he was pastor of Virginia and Kentucky churches. An evangelist, he organized 10 churches in Rosario and Santa Fe Province. After transferring to Chile, he did general work. In the final decade before his retirement, Hart began Baptist work in northern Chile. Author of *Gospel Triumphs in Argentina and Chile* (1925), he married Tennessee Hamilton in 1904. Their daughter, Lois, is a missionary nurse in Antofagasta, Chile.

H. CECIL MCCONNELL

***HAWAII, MISSION IN.** Statehood for Hawaii in 1959 hastened the process by which full responsibility for Baptist work in the islands passed to the Baptist churches and Hawaii Baptist Convention. At the end of 1960 the Hawaii Mission of the Foreign Mission Board ceased to exist. Continuing financial aid has been provided by the Foreign Mission Board on a diminishing basis during the transition period, and several missionaries of the board have remained on loan to the work of the Hawaii Baptist Convention.

See also HAWAII BAPTIST CONVENTION.

WINSTON CRAWLEY

HAWAII ASSOCIATIONS. BIG ISLAND. Organized Jan. 17, 1960, at Kaumana Drive Baptist Church, by two churches on the island of Hawaii. In 1969, 3 churches and missions reported 24 baptisms, 429 members, $46,157 total gifts, $9,973 mission gifts, $350,000 property value, and $45,436 church debt.

CENTRAL LEEWARD OAHU BAPTIST. Organized Oct. 16, 1961, at First Baptist Church, Waipahu, by six churches located on the leeward side of Oahu. In 1969, 15 churches and missions reported 287 baptisms, 4,188 members, $298,428 total gifts, $44,267 mission gifts, $1,903,112 property value, and $548,287 church debt.

GARDEN ISLE. Organized Sept. 19, 1960, by two churches on the island of Kauai, at Niimalu, Kauai. In 1969 four churches and missions reported 12 baptisms, 261 members, $25,292 total gifts, $3,618 mission gifts, $217,425 property value, and $20,975 church debt.

HONOLULU. Organized Aug. 8, 1961, at University Avenue Baptist Church, by eight churches in the city of Honolulu. In 1969, 10 churches and missions reported 127 baptisms, 3,294 members, $396,470 total gifts, $50,515 mission gifts, $2,929,277 property value, and $744,964 church debt.

MAUI COUNTY. Organized Feb., 1961, by four churches and one mission on the islands of Maui, Molokai, and Lanai. In 1969 eight churches and missions reported 34 baptisms, 375 members, $39,388 total gifts, $6,409 mission gifts, $470,769 property value, and $71,030 church debt.

WINDWARD. Organized Jan. 18, 1963, at Pali View Baptist Church, by two churches and two missions located on the windward side of the island of Oahu. In 1969, 5 churches and missions reported 25 baptisms, 944 members, $83,148 total gifts, $13,063 mission gifts, $670,000 property value, and $122,590 church debt.

KATSURO TAURA

HAWAII BAPTIST CONVENTION. Early in 1960, the Mission, begun by the Foreign Mission Board, SBC, in 1940, changed its charter name to the Hawaii Baptist Convention. The Mission officially went out of existence and the Foreign Mission Board worked through the convention. All assets of the Mission and the responsibility for operations and management were transferred to the convention.

Stanton Nash, educational director of the First Baptist Church of Oklahoma City, Okla., was elected executive secretary-treasurer of the convention, July 21, 1959. He succeeded Victor Koon who served as field secretary of the mission and executive-secretary of the convention, 1949–58. Under the leadership of Nash, a convention budget, program, and staff began to function as a unit.

Weston Ware was elected director of Baptist student work in Apr., 1961. Nash resigned as secretary of the convention, Apr., 1963. The executive board elected Edmond Walker, assistant executive secretary-treasurer of Southern Baptist General Convention of California, as executive secretary-treasurer of the convention, July, 1963. Walker assumed the duties as secretary on Sept. 1, 1963.

In the annual meeting, Nov. 7, 1963, the convention decided to study the administrative structure and functioning relationship of all committees of the convention and executive board (including the agencies and auxiliaries) and develop a long-range projection of financial needs both operational and capital. The committee consisted of Ernest E. Mosley, chairman; Shirley Lynch; Stanley K. Togikawa, secretary; Moriyashi Hiratani; Mrs. Edgar Jackson; Carl Kinoshita; Hubert Tatum; Richard S. Uejo; Charles Watkins; and Mrs. Andy Chaffin. A revised structure for the convention and executive board committees was adopted in Nov., 1964.

In Nov., 1965, the convention adopted the long-range committee report setting up administrative services and three program divisions. The administrative services include management service in church loans, procurement of wills and endowment, annuity plans, insurance, property management, assembly operations, and book store operations. Informational services include publications, denominational relations, and public relations.

The programs of the convention are organized into three divisions: cooperative missions, church development, and Christian education. In 1970 Malcolm Stuart, a foreign missionary appointee, was director of the missions division. Katsuro Taura, elected in May, 1966, was director of the church development division. Taura gives general directions to Sunday School, Training Union, and related work. Mrs. Sue Nishikawa, elected Oct., 1954, was director of Woman's Missionary Union and music in the church division. Larry Thomas, elected Aug., 1969, was director of student work in the church division. Stanley Sagert, elected May, 1970, was the director of the Christian education division and superintendent of Hawaii Baptist Academy.

The Baptist Book Store is owned and operated by the convention under an agreement of service with the Baptist Sunday School Board, SBC. The Book Store was started by the Mission in 1944 in the Olivet Baptist Church. The store was turned over to the convention in Jan., 1960. Managers of the book store under convention operations include Mrs. Lila (Dyer) Alhman, 1960–63, Bill Butts, 1964–68, and Danny and Carol Smith, 1969– . In June, 1967, the Book Store moved from downtown to 1225 Nehoa Street where the convention offices and academy are located.

Puu Kahea Baptist Assembly.—The assembly, a campsite owned and operated by the convention, is located in Waianae, 35 miles from Honolulu. Puu Kahea (echoing hills) was purchased by the Mission in Oct., 1949. The campsite consisted of 16 acres of land and several buildings which dated back to the Waianae Sugar Plantation Company days. The main building which was the plantation managers residence was remodeled for camp use. Sleeping arrangements for 100 people were made possible by using the second floor lanai and inside rooms. The dining hall, located on the first floor, seated 200. Other buildings were added to accommodate around 200 people at the assembly. The grounds are beautifully landscaped with royal palm trees, shrubs, and vines from many parts of the world.

The Waianae Baptist Church shares the same site as Puu Kahea. By agreement, the church auditorium is in use during convention activities at the assembly. The assembly site is located near the Makaha beach where the international surfing championships are held. Mr. and Mrs. Rudolph Peterson have been the resident managers at Puu Kahea since its beginning in 1949.

Baptist Student Centers.—Through its cooperative church development division, the convention administers student ministries through two Baptist student centers. The first and largest is located adjacent to the Manoa campus of the University of Hawaii which had a student enrolment of 20,000 in 1970. The student center building was made possible by the Lottie Moon Offering and other gifts. The center located near the campus offers a chapel, library, prayer room, recreation facilities, kitchen, and lounge. The lounge was furnished through an allocation of the Annie Armstrong Offering in 1963. The building was constructed in 1959 and dedicated in the fall of 1960. Leadership in student ministry at this location began as early as 1941, but was not undertaken as Baptist Student Union work until 1946 when Josephine Harris was appointed by the Foreign Mission Board for that assignment. Until the construction of the new center in 1959–60, the student ministry centered in the dormitory located immediately behind the new building. This center has a dormitory which houses outer-island students and many international students.

After Hawaii became a state, the convention was reorganized and student work was placed in the church development division. Miss Harris moved to the "Big Island" of Hawaii to help with the student ministry on the University of Hawaii, Hilo campus. This student center now ministers to a campus of 1,000 students.

Henry Webb came as a summer missionary in 1964, and was elected director of the student work and served until Oct., 1968, when he accepted the pastorate of Kalihi Baptist Church in Honolulu. In cooperation with the women's missionary department, the student department launched the S-M-I-T-H (Sustained Ministry to Internationals Through the Home) Program under Webb's direction. There are from 1,500 to 2,000 international students in attendance at the Manoa campus each year, many of whom are related to the East-West Center, an institute for cultural and technical interchange between East and West, a projection of the federal government.

Larry Thomas was elected as director in July, 1969. Hawaii is a new state and its population is relatively young with median age 24, therefore student work takes on great importance in this new and growing state.

The Hawaii Baptist Paper.—The Hawaii Baptist was started in Aug., 1947, by the Mission with Joe W. Bailey serving as the first editor. Many missionaries have served as editors: Lindell O. Harris, 1947–49; Chester R. Young, 1949–52; and Miss Hannah Plowden, 1957–61. Others who have served as editors are: David Petherbridge, 1953–57 (associate editor, 1966–69); Stanton Nash, 1961–63; Edmond Walker, 1963– . Marilyn Bennet Hillyer was appointed associate editor in 1969. The paper is sent to every Baptist family in Hawaii Baptist churches. Hawaii Baptists increased from 18 churches with 3,539 members in 1955 to 30 churches and 17 missions with 9,554 members in 1969.

The convention offices moved from the Olivet Baptist Church to 1225 Nehoa Street adjacent to Hawaii Baptist Academy in June, 1967.

BIBLIOGRAPHY: *Chester R. Young, A History of Hawaii Baptist Convention* (1959).

EDMOND WALKER

HAWAII STATISTICAL SUMMARY

Year	Associations	Churches	Church Membership	Baptisms	S. S. Enrolment	V.B.S. Enrolment	T. U. Enrolment	W.M.U. Enrolment	Brotherhood Enrolment	Music Enrolment	Mission Gifts	Total Gifts	Value Church Property
1958	1	21	4,553	413	7,977	4,009	2,348	1,795	472	618	$ 42,129	$ 305,484	$1,750,827
1959	1	21	5,123	355	8,432	3,724	2,578	1,792	506	503	54,125	370,172	2,118,785
1960	1	24	5,686	414	8,907	3,946	2,677	1,784	551	592	60,135	427,757	2,379,050
1961	5	24	6,080	464	9,391	3,921	2,734	1,622	482	678	69,674	461,471	2,674,049
1962	6	24	6,767	575	9,696	4,273	3,054	1,654	482	744	81,601	553,640	3,926,549
1963	6	26	7,489	591	10,208	4,623	3,097	1,764	546	635	88,098	550,995	3,852,947
1964	6	27	7,468	472	10,028	4,777	2,850	1,629	537	640	91,863	1,624,028	4,863,934
1965	6	27	7,709	487	10,191	4,493	2,928	1,607	453	578	101,107	743,689	4,867,066
1966	6	27	8,106	478	10,256	4,932	2,507	1,556	356	589	113,703	778,806	6,113,621
1967	6	27	8,703	431	10,202	3,583	2,493	1,426	468	672	111,437	720,881	6,236,234
1968	6	29	8,953	516	9,367	3,365	2,204	1,140	590	932	117,467	1,067,773	6,793,000
1969	6	29	9,554	521	9,184	2,978	2,006	1,096	522	878	123,860	1,125,309	6,712,083

LYNETTE YAMASHITA

***HAWAII BAPTIST ACADEMY.** Hawaii Baptist Academy, a college preparatory school, was founded in 1949 jointly by the Hawaii Baptist Convention and the Hawaiian Baptist Mission of the Foreign Mission Board, SBC, with Hugh P. McCormick principal, 8 teachers, and 36 students in grades 7 and 8. Four of the nine-member board of trustees were elected from the mission and five from the convention. Purchase and erection of temporary buildings were financed by a gift of $125,000, given over a period of five years from the Woman's Missionary Union of Virginia. Adding one grade annually, the academy completed its junior-senior high section, grades 2–12, by the fall of 1953.

McCormick retired as principal Jan. 1, 1960. His successors, 1960–64, were: Harold C. Diggs, 1960; Carl H. Rambo, 1960–63; and Byron F. Todd, 1964.

New structuring for the administration of the academy was implemented in 1965 when the executive board of the Hawaii Baptist Convention created the Division of Cooperative Christian Education of the Baptist state convention. Todd was elevated to the position of director of this new division. His work included being superintendent of the academy and assisting church-related private schools. At this time the academy was brought under the direct control of the executive board of the Hawaii convention. Structure of responsibility was established to be from the faculty and staff through the principals to the superintendent, to the executive secretary, then to the school programs committee (a subcommittee of the executive board), to the board, and to the Baptist state convention. While Todd was superintendent of the academy, Wayne King served as principal of the high school (1964–65 and 1965–66). Following the resignations of Todd and King in 1966, Travis Ellis was elected high school principal. He also performed many of the duties of superintendent. Luther F. Dorsey, present (1970) director of the Division of Cooperative Christian Education, assumed his duties as superintendent of the academy in 1967. Mrs. Barbara Nelson, English teacher (1964–67), and assistant to the superintendent (1967–69), became high school principal in 1969. Hubert R. Tatum, foreign missionary, was director of development of the academy from 1965 to Dec., 1969.

The academy's elementary school began in 1950 with the transfer of grades one, two, and three from the Olivet Baptist Church School. At the same time grade four was added. Grades five and six were begun in 1951 and 1952 respectively. In 1952 the first floor of the elementary building was completed and Miss Laura Cromwell became elementary principal. A kindergarten was added in 1963, completing the elementary grades. Subsequent elementary principals have been Miss Marie Cunningham (1961–63), Mrs. Ruth Blackwood (1965 to Jan., 1968), Miss LaFerne Daugherty (teaching principal, spring of 1968), and Miss Patricia Simmons (lead teacher, 1968–69, and principal, 1969).

Sources of initial financial support were the FMB, state WMU, convention funds, P.T.A., territorial mission offerings, and tuition. Current support is from Hawaii Baptist Convention, personal gifts, and tuition. Tuition charges in 1949 were $110 per student as compared with $350 (1–6), $450 (7–8), and $500 (9–12) for 1969–70. Current (1970) charges are less than half the costs of most private schools in Hawaii.

Dedicated to the principle that education involves the entire person—mind, body, and soul —the academy endeavors to create within each student social competence, vocational awareness, concern for mental and physical growth, desire for wise use of leisure time, and love of God through personal faith in Jesus Christ. Bible study, Christian ethics, worship assemblies, daily devotions, and evangelistic emphases are integral parts of the school's program. The 1969–70 student body came from nine ethnic groups, 29 religious denominations, and 49 local churches, with 70 students of no religious preference. An average of 50 students profess faith in Christ each year, and many experience a deepening of their Christian faith.

Plans for developing the physical facilities of the academy have moved through various stages. The "temporary" buildings of 1949 are still in use. The elementary building, constructed of concrete blocks, had one floor built in 1952 and the second floor in 1954. Adjacent "Mitchell property" was acquired in 1959 for the use of both the academy and of the Academy Baptist Church (now Central Baptist Church). Further property purchases doubled the size of the Heulu Street campus. Work was begun, Sept., 1969, on the first building of a three-phase master plan for developing the school plant. In 1970 a three-story building which will house a cafetorium, eight classrooms, and a chapel was under construction. This building was to be financed and used jointly by the academy and Central Baptist Church. Plans to employ a person to work full time in fund-raising and public relations for the Academy were adopted.

Accreditation by the Western Association for Schools and Colleges was accorded the Academy under Todd's leadership in 1965. A two-year extension under Dorsey's administration was granted in 1968. Preparation for a five-year accreditation is being finalized, Feb., 1970. Enrolment in the academy reached a peak of 485 students in 1968–69. Records since 1963 reveal that 96 per cent of the academy's graduates were accepted by schools of higher learning. The academy's certified and classified staff numbers 31 adults from divergent backgrounds, including four different races. LUTHER F. DORSEY

HAWAIIAN BAPTIST MISSION. Following World War II, former mission fields began to reopen and the Hawaii missionaries of the Foreign Mission Board were given a choice of transferring to other fields of the board or to remain in Hawaii "on loan" for an indefinite period. There were 38 missionaries assigned to Hawaii in 1959, 15 couples and 8 single women. At the end of 1969 all but three couples and two single women had transferred to other fields or retired.

Hawaii Statehood.—The agitation for statehood for Hawaii gained momentum after World War II, and on Mar. 12, 1959, Congress passed the statehood bill. The first statehood decade, 1959–69, was one of great economic growth and prosperity. It was a period of great population increase and social change. Hawaii Baptists were faced with the necessity of expanding and improving their outreach at a time when the FMB took steps to phase out its work in Hawaii. Missionaries of the board stationed in Hawaii initiated steps to transfer funds and administrative responsibility to the Hawaii Baptist Convention in the late fifties.

Transition from Foreign Mission Board to the Hawaii Baptist Convention.—Victor Koon, field secretary for the Hawaiian Baptist Mission, was executive secretary for the Hawaii Baptist Convention from 1949 to Dec., 1958. The first step in this transition was taken at a meeting of the executive board of the Hawaii Baptist Convention on June 19, 1958, when the Hawaiian Mission of the FMB requested that each convention institution and each church submit their requests for financial aid and that the convention's executive board appoint a committee of lay church members to work with the mission in preparing the 1959 estimates for local workers' salaries.

Ten-Year Program.—The most significant action in 1959 was the agreement between the mission and the Hawaii Baptist Convention churches on a Ten-Year Program. According to this plan, the FMB would decrease annually the amount of appropriation granted to churches for workers' salaries in order that the churches might be self-supporting in 10 years. The amount the church was receiving on Jan. 1, 1959, would be the basis on which the 10 per cent annual reduction would be computed. The ceiling for any church would be $800.

The FMB further agreed with the convention that it would appropriate a lump sum amount for the convention's administration, beginning with the amount it was appropriating at the end of 1959, and decrease the amount over a period of approximately 15 years at the rate of 8 per cent for the first five years, 7 per cent for the next five years, and 5 per cent for the last five years. This beginning sum was $210,000.

In the Nov., 1959, annual meeting of the Hawaii convention, the convention accepted from the Hawaiian Mission of the FMB the ownership and administration of the following, to be effective Jan. 1, 1960: the Hawaii Baptist Academy, the Baptist Student Center, the Building and Loan Fund, and the assets in the Hawaii Baptist Mission (the Corporation).

Mrs. Sue (Saito) Nishikawa, secretary since Oct., 1954, for the Woman's Missionary Union Department, continued on in that position as an employee of the executive board. Stanton Nash was elected as the executive secretary-treasurer of the convention in Sept., 1959, and served through May, 1963.

Sam Choy, pastor of Kahului Baptist Church, was elected as director of the Education Division, Jan., 1962, and served through June, 1966, when he was appointed as a missionary to Korea.

The Home Mission Board and the Hawaii Convention.—On Apr. 21, 1961, the executive board of the Hawaii convention voted to ask the HMB for financial assistance for associational missionaries. On Oct. 13, 1961, the board voted to enter into a cooperative missions program with the HMB and accepted the following statement: "The Home Mission Board of the Southern Baptist Convention and the Hawaii Baptist Convention shall cooperate in the support and direction of mission personnel to serve within the Hawaii Baptist Convention territory in State and Associational work, beginning January 1, 1962." The agreement outlined the general principles, personnel policies, conferences, literature and new types of work. The agreement and working relationship between the two boards is reviewed in an annual conference.

SUE (SAITO) NISHIKAWA

HAYCRAFT, SAMUEL (b. Va., Sept. 11, 1752; d. Hardin County, Elizabethtown, Ky., Oct. 15, 1823). A layman, lawyer, and judge, he served as a Revolutionary War soldier. He married Margaret Van Meter at Pittsburgh, Pa., and came to Kentucky in 1779 or 1780. He was one of the founders of the Severns Valley Baptist Church, June 18, 1781. He was one of the first to build a house in Elizabethtown after living in a fort. In addition to being a farmer he served as sheriff. He had a distinguished son, Samuel Haycraft, Jr. (1795–1878) who published a *History of Elizabethtown* (1869).

LEO T. CRISMON

HEAD, ELDRED DOUGLAS (b. Sparta, Bienville County, La., Nov. 15, 1892; d. San Angelo, Tex., Apr. 13, 1964). Pastor, teacher, writer, and seminary president. Son of James Douglas and Lucy Venetia (Hardy) Head, he was educated at Baylor University (B.A., 1916; M.A., 1927), and Southwestern Baptist Theological Seminary (Th.M., 1920; Th.D., 1930). He was licensed to preach at Arcadia, La., in 1911, and ordained by the First Church, Waco, Tex., in 1914. In 1942 Baylor University conferred on him the D.D., and in 1949 Georgetown College the LL.D. His marriage in 1916 to Gladys Thornton ended with her sudden death in 1921. In 1924 he married Effie McDaniel. Their only child, E. D. Head, Jr., was born in 1925.

Head was preeminently a preacher. His pastorates, all in Texas, included those at Dyersville, Union Hill, Fowler, Kopperl, Searsville, Fairview, Speegleville, Chalk Bluff, Mertens, Valley Mills, Whitney, and First Church, Houston, 1932–42. He held frequent revivals and served widely as a conference preacher.

Head taught at Baylor Academy, 1914–16, Baylor University, 1920–32, and Southwestern Baptist Theological Seminary, 1942–50. He served as president of Southwestern Seminary, 1942–53.

His books include *Why All This Suffering?* (1941), *Burning Hearts* (1947, translated into Portuguese), and *New Testament Life and Literature as Reflected in the Papyri* (1952). In 1952 he revised L. R. Scarborough's (*q.v.*, Vol. II), *With Christ After the Lost.* Mimeographed texts entitled *Evangelism in Acts* and *Revivals in the Bible* were prepared for seminary use. For more than 16 years he prepared the weekly Sunday School lesson for the Texas *Baptist Standard.* His denominational service involved activity on boards of various agencies, a three-year presidency of the Baptist General Convention of Texas, moderating an association, membership on the executive committee of the Baptist World Alliance, and preaching tours in Europe and Japan. He is buried at Forth Worth, Texas. BOYD HUNT

HEALTH BENEFIT PLAN. See LIFE AND HEALTH BENEFITS DEPARTMENT.

HENDERSON, SAMUEL (b. Jefferson County, Tenn., Mar. 4, 1817; d. Troy, Ala., Feb. 16, 1890). Minister and editor. Son of John F. and Nancy (Mohler) Henderson, he married Eliza W. McGee in 1840. Ordained to the ministry, he assumed his first pastorate at Alpine Baptist Church, Talladega County, Ala. During his pastorate at the First Baptist Church, Tuskegee, Ala., 1846–67, he was instrumental in establishing the East Alabama Female College, editor of *South Western Baptist,* 1853–65, delegate to Alabama Secession Convention, voting for immediate secession, trustee of Southern Baptist Theological Seminary, Greenville, S. C., and editor of the "Alabama Department" of the Georgia *Christian Index,* 1866. He served as president of the Alabama Baptist Convention, 1868–74. The convention created "The Henderson Colportage Fund" to assist in distribution of books and circulation of the *Alabama Baptist,* and elected Henderson a "life member," in 1883. Following pastorates in several central Alabama churches, he retired in 1889 to a farm in Shelby County.

BIBLIOGRAPHY: Jon Appleton, "Samuel Henderson: Southern Minister, Editor, and Crusader, 1853–66," unpublished M.A. Thesis, Auburn University, 1968.

JON APPLETON

***HENDRICK MEMORIAL HOSPITAL.** Located at Abilene, Tex., this nonprofit general hospital serves patients without regard to race, creed, or color. It is fully approved by the Joint Commission on Accreditation of Hospitals. In 1968–69 the hospital reported 345 beds, 15,737 patients, free service of $549,965, patient income of $5,709,194, operating expense of $5,514,389, and donations from the Baptist General Convention of Texas of $104,000. Total asset value is over $12,000,000. Recent benefactors include George S. Anderson, who built the $1,500,000 Anderson Building as a memorial to his wife; and Malcom and Mary Meek who gave an $800,000 children's hospital, school of nursing, and blood bank named in their honor.

E. M. COLLIER

HEREFORD, CARL EUGENE (b. Apple Grove, W. Va., May 10, 1901; d. Lubbock, Tex., Dec. 9, 1968). Pastor and denominational leader. He graduated from Marshall University, Huntington, W. Va., 1923; Southwestern Baptist Theological Seminary (Th.M.) in 1934; also received a D.D. from Howard Payne College, 1939. He married Eula Cook in 1921. They had one daughter, Mrs. Ben Lewis. Baptized in 1914, Hereford was ordained at Huntington, W. Va., in 1921. He was pastor of First Baptist churches, Malden, W. Va., Handley, Lubbock, and Corpus Christi, Tex. He also served Seventh Avenue, Huntington, W. Va., Fort Worth Baptist, Fort Worth, and Columbus Avenue, Waco, Tex. Hereford was vice-president of the Baptist General Convention of Texas in 1957. He served on the state executive board, Foreign Mission Board, and Home Mission Board; was a trustee of Wayland, Howard Payne, and Mary Hardin-Baylor colleges, Hillcrest Memorial Hospital, Waco, and Valley Baptist Hospital, Harlingen, Tex. Hereford was instrumental in founding the University of Corpus Christi. After retirement in 1961, he served the Kingdom Building Foundation until 1964. W. H. COLSON

HERMENEUTICS; HERMENEUTIC. The word "hermeneutics" is generally understood as referring to the science of interpretation and explanation. The term may be used in reference to the interpretation of any literary piece, but in Christian theology "hermeneutics" has had to do particularly with the process of interpretation related to the exegesis of a given biblical text or texts.

The word "hermeneutic" or the phrase "the new hermeneutic" (German: *Hermeneutik*) is associated with the work of Gerhard Ebeling and Ernst Fuchs and that of their followers, e.g. John B. Cobb, Robert W. Funk, and James M. Robinson.

Influenced by the existentialist philosophy of Martin Heidegger and the New Testament interpretation of Rudolf Bultmann, Fuchs and Ebeling sought to go beyond "demythologizing" in an effort to communicate the Christian revelation. The new hermeneutic is concerned with the interpretation of the text, but it moves beyond the text to raise questions and to seek answers about the self and the meaning of human existence. Thus the hermeneutical process is more than historical (objective) criticism and exegesis; it is a new approach to theology. The language of the text is viewed as an "event" which "happens" in the present of the interpreter—linked to the past, but illuminating the present and the future through faith.

BIBLIOGRAPHY: Paul J. Achtemeier, *An Introduction to the New Hermeneutic* (1969).

DONALD E. COOK

HEWITT, WILLIAM ALLEN (b. Amite County, Miss., Jan. 4, 1876; d. Jackson, Miss., June 18, 1961). Pastor in Mississippi and Texas. Son of Emily Jane (Lofton) and Thomas Jefferson Hewitt, he was reared on a farm. He was educated at Mars Hill School, Mississippi College (A.B., 1898), Southern Baptist Theological Seminary (B.D., 1901), University of Chicago Divinity School (Th.M., 1906). Converted at age 15, he was ordained by Mars Hill Church five years later. Student pastorates include Byram, Hinds County, Miss., and Bowmar Ave., Vicksburg, Miss. Hewitt was pastor of First Baptist Church, Columbia, Miss., 1901–04; Columbus, Miss., First Church, 1905–11. In 1912 he united two small churches in Dallas, Tex., into Cliff Temple Baptist Church which he served as pastor for five years. In Dec., 1917, he accepted a call to First Church, Jackson, Miss., where he served from Dec. 29, 1917, to Apr. 6, 1946. Hewitt was a member of the Home Mission Board, Southern Baptist Convention, 1923–39. The Convention elected him as second vice-president in 1928. He married Olive Aline Haley at McComb, Miss., Jan. 22, 1902; children: Thomas Jefferson Hewitt, Spartanburg, S. C.; William Haley Hewitt, Clinton, Miss.; Mrs. Sarah Aline Robinson, Bloomington, Indiana; Mrs. Ruth Bonita Doty, Jackson, Miss.; Lawrence Purser Hewitt, Jackson, Miss. Hewitt was buried in Lakewood Memorial Park, Jackson.

LAWRENCE PURSER HEWITT

HICKERSON, JULIUS RHAT, SR. (b. Tullahoma, Tenn., July 16, 1890; d. Brownwood, Tex., Apr. 8, 1956). Pastor and district missionary. Educated at William Jewell College and Southwestern Baptist Theological Seminary, he was pastor of rural churches while serving as professor of history at Sioux Falls College, 1914–15, and as an employee of Tennessee Department of Agriculture, 1917–20. Pastorates included Bridgeport, Ala., Big Springs and Farmers Branch in Dallas County, Tex., Mercedes and Commerce, Tex., where he served for 15 years. He was missionary of District Sixteen encompassing Brady, Brown, Coleman, Comanche, Concho Valley, Hamilton, Mills, Runnels, San Saba associations of Tex., 1942–53, until ill health forced him to retire.

CHARLES P. MCLAUGHLIN

HIGH PLAINS BAPTIST HOSPITAL. A Texas Baptist hospital located in Amarillo Medical Center. The hospital opened Feb. 20, 1968. Its building and 25 acres were donated by Amarillo Area foundation, Inc. In Nov., 1962, the Foundation and Baptist General Convention of Texas agreed that the foundation would build a hospital, and that the convention would own and operate it. Almost $6,000,000 for construction came from contributions from people of the High Plains area. Initial capacity was 241 beds, with design for expansion to 440 beds. Subsequent gifts made possible the opening of a coronary care unit and addition of 38-bed Bivins Center for Rehabilitation and Chronic Diseases. High Plains admitted 8,955 patients during its first 19 months. It provides clinical experience in a Christian atmosphere for paramedical students, and offers a full-time department of pastoral care. The hospital is a member of Texas, American, and Protestant Hospital Associations and is accredited by the Joint Commission on Accreditation of Hospitals. Emmett R. Johnson, Fellow, American College of Hospital Administrators, is the administrator.

RUTH TUCKER HESS

HIGHER CRITICISM. A term used to designate the critical, literary, and historical study of the Bible.

See BIBLICAL CRITICISM.

RAYMOND BRYAN BROWN

HILL, JOHN LEONARD (b. Owen County, Ky., Sept. 15, 1878; d. Nashville, Tenn., Nov. 13, 1964). He received A.M. degrees from Georgetown College, Georgetown, Ky., and Columbia University, New York, N. Y.; the Litt.D. and LL.D. from Union University, Jackson, Tenn.; and the L.H.D., Hardin-Simmons University, Abilene, Tex. He married Emma Wilson of Williamstown, Ky., in 1907; there were no children. Mrs. Hill died in 1959. Hill taught in Kentucky high schools, 1900–09. He served as professor of history and political science at Georgetown College, Ky., 1902–22, and dean, 1913–22.

He was book editor of the Sunday School Board, 1922–49, director of promotion for Ridgecrest and Glorieta Baptist assemblies, 1949–53, and editor, *Home and Foreign Fields* magazine, 1932–37. Hill wrote *Blackboard Outlines in the Life of Jesus* (1925), *Some Learning Processes,* with L. P. Leavell (*q.v.,* Vol. II) (1932), *From Joshua to David* (1934), *Purely Personal* (1937), *Outline Studies in Luke* (1937), *Outline Studies in Mark* (1945), and *Studies in John's Gospel* (1948).

Hill was in wide demand as a lecturer and speaker in churches, conventions, and assemblies throughout the South. He was active in the temperance and prohibition cause. For 36 years he taught the Fidelis Bible Class of women in First Baptist Church, Nashville, Tenn., averaging over 300 in weekly attendance. The lesson was broadcast regularly over radio station WSM, Nashville. He also served as deacon and chairman of deacons in his church for many years.

HOWARD P. COLSON

HILLCREST BAPTIST HOSPITAL (cf. Hillcrest Memorial Hospital, Vol. I). In Dec., 1963, the name of the hospital was officially changed to Hillcrest Baptist Hospital. It is located in Waco, Tex. In 1969 the bed capacity was 300 in five buildings; its land, equipment, and other assets were valued at $6,871,567.82. The hospital's mortgage indebtedness in 1969 was $705,522.24. To aid the hospital in carrying out its program, the Baptist General Convention of Texas assists financially through the Cooperative Program, and friends of the hospital also give substantial help through their gifts to the hospital. Hillcrest is accredited by the Joint Commission on Accreditation of Hospitals. Administrator Julian H. Pace has guided Hillcrest since 1943. ROY E. COOPER

HILLMAN, WALTER (b. Martha's Vineyard, Mass., Jan. 9, 1829; d. Clinton, Mass., Apr. 9, 1894). Educator, pastor, college president. He was the son of Captain Walter Hillman. Hillman married Adelia M. Thompson, Sept. 18, 1855. He attended Connecticut Literary Institute, Suffield, Worchester Academy, Mass. (1849), where he served as sub-principal in 1851, and received the M.A. degree from Brown University, 1854. An article in the *Brown Alumni Monthly* states that "on his graduation in 1854 he was recommended by Dr. Wayland to the Chair of Mathematics and Natural Science in Mississippi College in Clinton." Hillman became principal of Central Baptist Female Institute in 1853. At the close of the war between the states the title of the property passed to Hillman to satisfy debts due him, and in 1891 its name was changed to Hillman College. During the crisis years following the war, he jointly served both Central Female Institute and Mississippi College as president. Hillman is credited with saving the Mississippi College Chapel as a result of an interview with U. S. Grant when the general was en route from Jackson to Vicksburg. The Clinton Baptist Church ordained Hillman in 1855, and he served the church as pastor, 1862–64. EARL KELLY

HINTON, ISAAC TAYLOR (b. Oxford, England, July 4, 1799; d. New Orleans, La., Aug. 28, 1847). Youngest son of James Hinton, a Baptist minister, he migrated to America in 1832, settling in Philadelphia. First Baptist Church, Richmond, Va., called and ordained him as pastor in 1833. Later pastorates were in Chicago and St. Louis. In 1844, while serving as an appointee of the American Home Mission Society, he was also pastor of First Baptist Church, New Orleans, La. Transferring his ties to the Southern Baptist Convention, he was appointed as the Home Mission Board's first missionary to New Orleans. He died of yellow fever in 1847. J. N. EVANS

HIPPS, JOHN BURDER (b. Madison County, N. C., Feb. 12, 1884; d. Wake Forest, N. C., Dec. 30, 1967). Missionary, educator, and author. Son of mountain preacher Robert H. and Sarah Malinda (Cogdill) Hipps, he was a graduate of Mars Hill College, Wake Forest College (B.A., *Magna Cum Laude,* 1907), Southern Baptist Theological Seminary (Th.M., 1913), Union Theological Seminary in New York City (S.T.M., 1921), and Columbia University (M.A., 1926). He received an honorary D.D. from Wake Forest College in 1935. On June 29, 1921, he married Lydia B. Brown of Ames, Iowa. They had one son, Robert Owen. After her death in 1924, he married Margaret Faith Stroh of Wheaton, Ill., July 29, 1926. They had one son, Jackson Stroh. He began his career as teacher of a small school at Lusk Baptist Chapel on Spring Creek in North Carolina, 1902–05; later he served as principal of the Lee Baptist Institute, a mountain mission school of the Southern Baptist Home Mission Board, at Pennington Gap, Va., 1907–10. Ordained on Sept. 18, 1910, he became pastor of the Deep Springs Baptist Church near Pennington Gap. He was appointed missionary to China by the Foreign Mission Board, SBC, July 8, 1913, and arrived in Shanghai, Nov. 4, 1913. For 34 years, 1915–49, he served at the University of Shanghai (both the Shanghai Baptist College and the Baptist Seminary) as instructor, professor, dean, board of founders representative, and chairman of the Division of Religious Studies. During an extended furlough, 1941–43, made necessary because of the Japanese occupation of Shanghai, he visited 36 colleges and universities in the United States on behalf of foreign missions. In Apr., 1944, he returned to China, going first to Chungking in west China where the University of Shanghai had opened. Later (1945–46), he aided in the rehabilitation of the university on its own campus in Shanghai. After the fall of Shanghai to the Communists, May 27, 1949, it became increasingly difficult to stay in China. On Sept. 25, 1949, he and his wife sailed for America. He was engaged in a speaking tour across the country until in May, 1951, when he was elected professor of missions at Southeastern Baptist Theological Seminary. He served there until his retirement on May 10, 1957. He wrote two books: *A History of the University of Shanghai* (1964) and *Fifty Years in Christian Missions, An Autobiography* (1966). He is buried in the Seminary Cemetery at Wake Forest, N. C. JAMES H. BLACKMORE

***HISTORICAL COMMISSION OF THE SOUTHERN BAPTIST CONVENTION.** Norman Wade Cox (*q.v.*), first executive secretary, led the Historical Commission forward in its ministry to Southern Baptists until retirement, Aug. 31, 1959. On that date he was succeeded by Davis Collier Woolley (*q.v.*), then director of the Howard College Extension Division. Lynn E. May, Jr., has served as research director since 1956.

By Convention assignment the commission conducts: (1) a program of recording, procurement, and preservation of Baptist historical materials, and (2) a program of utilization of historical materials in serving the history interests of Southern Baptists.

Through promotional materials, conferences, periodical articles, and continued cooperation with state Baptist historical agencies, the commission has led churches, associations, state conventions and agencies, and Southern Baptist agencies to engage in a systematic effort to improve the recording of history as it is made and to preserve the materials of Baptist history. The commission has continued to add to Dargan-Carver Library a wealth of books, theses, periodicals, pamphlets, vital records, manuscripts, photographs, films, tape recordings, and other historical and archival materials pertaining to Baptist life and work. This library has become a Baptist research center second to none in the nation. By means of microfilm alone, the commission has acquired over 8,500,000 pages of Baptistiana. Through the commission's microfilm service, churches, associations, and conventions are preserving their records and making them available for research.

Under Woolley's administration the commission has given increasing attention to its program of utilization. The commission encourages and assists churches, associations, conventions, and agencies in writing and publishing their history. Conferences conducted by the commission on writing history, interpreting Christian history, and utilizing historical records have stimulated a growing interest in the heritage of Baptists. The commission further promoted this interest by issuing a quarterly *Newsletter,* 1960–69, contributing historical articles to the *Quarterly Review* and other periodicals, and publishing its own journal, *Baptist History and Heritage.* Issued semimonthly, 1965–69, the latter became a quarterly in 1970. Encouraged by the commission, the Sunday School Board published a series of study course books on Baptist history in 1964. Woolley served as managing editor of *Baptist Advance,* the historical volume published in cooperation with other Baptist bodies as a part of the Baptist Jubilee Advance observance held in Atlantic City, N. J., in 1964. The commission initiated and sponsored the work of creating Volume III of the *Encyclopedia of Southern Baptists.*

The commission performed a vital research service for the program committee of the Executive Committee, SBC, 1959–63, by preparing a résumé of the historical development of each SBC agency for use in the development of program statements for the agencies. Research projects have also been conducted to assist other denominational leaders and organizations, including churches seeking to write their history.

The commission has conducted numerous projects to help implement its programs. Through Operation Baptist Biography, launched in 1958, data has been gathered on more than 8,500 living and deceased Baptist leaders. A Baptist Union Catalog offers researchers a guide to the resources of numerous Baptist collections in America. The commission worked with artist Erwin Hearne in his portrayal of eight "Great Moments in Baptist History" in a series of oil paintings. An oral history project has yielded an invaluable collection of tape recordings. Assistance was given in the production of a two-record album, "Baptist Voices of Yesterday." Encouraging states and agencies to index their publications, the commission has published an *Index to Annuals* of the SBC, an *Index of Graduate Theses in Baptist Theological Seminaries,* and, since 1965, an annual *Southern Baptist Periodical Index.*

Dargan-Carver Library and the commission staff moved into new quarters on the first floor of the Sunday School Board Administrative Tower in 1965. Hundreds of writers, editors, and research personnel utilize the resources of this research center each year. The commission helped lead Southern Baptists to conduct a meaningful observance of the Convention's 125th Anniversary in 1970. LYNN E. MAY, JR.

***HISTORIOGRAPHY, BAPTIST.** In the years 1955–70 there has been a noticeable increase in the number of Baptist historical writings. Many are well done, readably written, documented, and based on adequate research and scientific methodology. A large group includes histories of Baptist colleges, state Baptist bodies, associations, and individual churches. Some treatises take the form of unpublished doctoral and master's theses, while others are published as articles in *Foundations, Baptist History and Heritage, Review and Expositor, The Quarterly Review,* and *The Baptist Quarterly* (England).

Also, an increase in Baptist historical materials for use in churches is to be seen. Books, guides, and pamphlets have been published to provide a resource for the churches to use in their study of the Baptist heritage. Furthermore, in its literature the Sunday School Board of the SBC has frequently explored the historical theme.

In 1963 the comprehensive, widely used volume of Robert G. Torbet, *A History of the Baptists,* was revised and updated. Of special interest to Southern Baptists might be: William A. Mueller, *A History of Southern Baptist Theological Seminary* (1959); William L. Lumpkin, *Baptist Foundations in the South* (1961); Robert A. Baker, *A Baptist Source Book, With Particular Reference to Southern Baptists* (1966), *The Story of the Sunday School Board* (1966), and *The Thirteenth Check: The Jubilee History of the Annuity Board of the S.B.C., 1918–68* (1968); William A. Mueller, *The School of Providence and Prayer* (1969); Arthur B. Rutledge, *Mission to America: A Century and a Quarter of Southern Baptist Home Missions* (1969); Baker J. Cauthen, *et al., Advance: A History of Southern Baptist Foreign Missions* (1970); and *Review and Expositor* issue (Spring, 1970) devoted to "The 125th Anniversary of the Southern Baptist Convention."

Two bibliographical articles giving extensive compilations of recent Baptist historical writings in America are to be found in *Founda-*

tions (Oct., 1965), 375–81, and *Baptist History and Heritage* (July, 1967), 117–26. The bibliographical aids compiled by the Historical Commission, SBC, have greatly assisted the historical researcher: *Index of Graduate Theses in Baptist Theological Seminaries; Index to Annuals, Southern Baptist Convention;* and *Southern Baptist Periodical Index.* Edward C. Starr continues the publication of *A Baptist Bibliography* with volume XIV treating Section Lea-McGuire. W. MORGAN PATTERSON

HOBSON, WILLIAM ANDREW (b. Bibb County, Ala., June 5, 1862; d. St. Petersburg, Fla., Sept. 22, 1960). Pastor, teacher, editor, denominational servant. Son of Francis Marion and Mary Catherine Shows Hobson, he was a graduate of the University of Alabama, Howard College, and Southern Baptist Theological Seminary. He was awarded the D. D. by Howard. He married Lou Alma Cheek of Birmingham on Oct. 2, 1887. They had two children: Mary Kate and Tolbert Francis.

Hobson was pastor of several churches in Alabama and Kentucky including Ruhama Church, Birmingham. He also taught Bible at Howard College. In Florida he was pastor of First Church, Jacksonville, 1900–23; and Grace Temple, 1924–27, and Hobson Memorial Church (earlier named Russell Park, then Disston Ave.), 1932–60, both in St. Petersburg. In Jacksonville he organized the School of the Prophets. Once part owner and editor (1904) of the *Southern Baptist Witness,* he helped merge that paper with the *Florida Baptist Witness.*

He served as a member of the Florida Baptist State Board of Missions, 1900–26, and its president, 1912–24; trustee of Stetson University, 1903–60, and its Goodwill Ambassador, 1928–31; and a charter trustee (1900) of the Florida Baptist Orphanage. He was a member of the Sunday School Board, 1910–23, and the Executive Committee of the Southern Baptist Convention, 1927–36. He is buried in Evergreen Cemetery, Jacksonville, Fla. HOMER G. LINDSAY, SR.

HODGES, ISAM BRADLEY (b. Fulton County, Ark., Jan. 18, 1895; d. San Leandro, Calif., Mar. 3, 1967). Pioneer leader of Southern Baptist work in California, founder and first president of Golden Gate Baptist Theological Seminary, Mill Valley, Calif. Born to farming people in northern Arkansas, Hodges married his childhood sweetheart, Minnie Nibblett, Sept. 18, 1916. He was educated at Ouachita Baptist University (B.A., 1923), Southwestern Baptist Theological Seminary (Th.M., 1926), and Berkeley Baptist Divinity School (M.A., 1937). Following a pastorate in Pine Bluff, Ark., he fulfilled a lifelong dream in 1935 of moving to California. In June, 1937, he was called as pastor to the Golden Gate Baptist Church, Oakland, Calif. Under his leadership the church changed its affiliation from the Northern Baptist Convention to the Southern Baptist Convention. It was in this church the Golden Gate Baptist Theological Seminary began operation Sept. 4, 1944. Hodges served as president, 1944–46. After he was succeeded as president by O. B. Herring, Hodges returned to the pastorate. He served the University Baptist Church, Berkeley, Calif., and First Southern Baptist Church, San Lorenzo, Calif., where a stroke forced his retirement in 1962. Hodges aided in the formative years of the Southern Baptist General Convention of California, serving as president in 1943. He was on the Executive Committee, SBC, for eight years. His pioneer vision of building a center of theological training on the west coast encouraged Southern Baptists to establish a witness beyond the area prescribed by comity agreements with Northern Baptists. H. W. SWINDALL

HOLMAN, RUSSELL (b. Warwick, Franklin County, Mass., Aug. 14, 1812; d. Marshall, Mo., Dec. 2, 1879). Pastor, missionary, and denominational leader. Converted and called to Christian service at age 17, he entered Brown University *c.* 1837. In 1838 he went to Kentucky as an agent for a publication house. He then became pastor of Pitman Creek Church, Green County, Ky., which ordained him on July 29, 1840. In somewhat poor health, he went to New Orleans as a missionary with the American Baptist Home Mission Society (*c.* 1843) and founded the first Baptist church in that city. Holman became corresponding secretary of the Domestic (Home) Mission Board of the SBC on Dec. 1, 1845, serving until July 15, 1851. Between 1851 and 1856 he assumed a professorship of mathematics at Howard College and several pastorates in Alabama. On Jan. 1, 1857, he again became corresponding secretary of the board, serving until Jan., 1862, although because of a continuing eye problem Martin T. Sumner (*q.v.*) assumed most of his responsibilities.

Between 1862 and 1865 Holman served as an evangelist in the Confederate Army. In 1865 he was financial agent for the board in Missouri. The following year, he was asked by the board to assume the delicate task of reestablishing the Coliseum Place Church in New Orleans as a part of the Southern Baptist Convention. After completing this task, he remained at home for about a year during his wife's illness to care for his children. In 1867 the Baptist church in Chillicothe, Ill., called him as their pastor.

In 1870 Holman suffered a stroke and, hoping for a more favorable climate, moved to Saline County, Mo. Between 1870 and 1876 he served as pastor of the Bethel and Rehoboth churches in that county. In 1876 he suffered a second stroke which incapacitated him, forcing him to retire permanently from the pastorate.

A. RONALD TONKS

HOLMES, AGNES KENNEDY (b. Cameron, N.C., July 25, 1881; d. Eufaula, Ala., May 13, 1964). She served from 1924–46, first as an Intermediate worker, later as children's editor and Southern Baptist Sunday School Board librarian.

From 1935–47 she edited materials for the Story Hour. She also served as editor of *Storytime* and *The Cradle Roll Home*.

HOWARD P. COLSON

HOLT, ARCHIE JUDSON (b. Pittsburg, Camp County, Tex., Dec. 15, 1889; d. Waco, Tex., Mar. 3, 1969). Pastor and denominational leader. Son of William P. and Sallie (Malone) Holt, he married Runa Brown, Sept. 3, 1918, and they had three children: Archie Judson, Jr., Edward Harold, and Margaret (Mrs. Jack W. Gunn). Baylor University awarded him the A.B., 1916, and the D.D., 1953. He received the Th.M. in 1920 from Southwestern Baptist Theological Seminary. Later he served these institutions many years as a trustee; and served 40 years as a trustee of Hillcrest Baptist Hospital. From 1912 to 1958, Holt served as pastor to various Texas churches, including Lamar Avenue, Wichita Falls; First Baptist, Mart; and 30 years at Calvary, Waco.

HUBERT YOUNT

***HOME MISSION BOARD OF THE SOUTHERN BAPTIST CONVENTION.** Samuel Courts Redford served for 11 years as executive secretary-treasurer, beginning Jan. 1, 1954. "During the next decade financial receipts almost tripled, the missionary force more than doubled, and the supporting staff showed a corresponding enlargement." Important expansion took place during this administration in program areas of work. The "Big Cities Program," a Long-Range Rural Church Committee, language missions work, new work in literacy missions, organization of a survey department, and greater emphasis on chaplaincy ministries and migrant missions are examples. The board led the denomination in the 30,000 Movement, 1956–64, seeking to establish 30,000 new missions and churches.

In 1959 the Southern Baptist Convention took action which gave specific directives to the board that were to have long-range significance. Plans were made to implement the Convention's request to develop a unified, coordinated missions program for the nation. Between 1959 and 1961, Arthur B. Rutledge, then director of the Division of Missions, led in establishing state agreements with 26 of the existing 28 state conventions, providing for cooperative planning of mission work, selection and appointing of missionaries, and budgeting on the basis of percentage sharing in one budget. Work was administered through state offices.

Redford was assisted during his administration by G. Frank Garrison, a businessman who had been recording secretary (1931–44) and president of the board (1944–53). Garrison served as assistant executive secretary-treasurer (1954–65) with responsibility for finances and church loans.

Rutledge succeeded Redford as executive secretary-treasurer upon the latter's retirement Jan. 1, 1965. He had served as a pastor in Texas, as secretary of stewardship and direct missions for two years with the Texas convention, and since Mar. 1, 1959, as the first director of the missions division. There were urgent matters which demanded immediate attention: formulation of the board's program statement, related staff adjustments, and selection of goals and objectives.

The Convention's action of 1959 had directed all its agencies to define the basic, continuing areas of responsibilities in order to avoid overlapping and to achieve coordination. The board appointed a committee in 1962 to begin working with the staff in formulating a program statement. R. Houston Smith of Louisiana served as chairman.

Fred B. Moseley became assistant to the executive secretary-treasurer (later becoming assistant executive secretary-treasurer) Jan. 1, 1965, with major responsibility for leading the staff in program development and coordination. He had been secretary of City Missions for the board (1959–61), and executive secretary-treasurer of the Oregon-Washington convention for three years.

The committee and staff completed the program statement in 1965. Approval was given by the Convention in 1966.

At the suggestion of the executive secretary-treasurer-elect the board appointed a committee in Dec., 1964, in annual meeting to develop long-range objectives and goals. Lewis E. Rhodes, of Tennessee, served as chairman. In the fall of 1966, the committee presented a report setting forth 14 basic guidelines which were approved. These were to be of major significance in setting the tone of the agency's work during this administration. In the spring of 1967 the second part of the committee's report, entitled "Direction '77," stated goals to be achieved by 1977.

The responsibilities to be of assistance to churches, associations, and state conventions led to increased emphasis on research, surveys, planning of programs, writing, consultation, and pilot projects. Flexibility and experimentation in strategy, tactics, and techniques marked the work of the board during the sixties. While outstanding progress has been made in all quantitative considerations for expansion, the major impact of this agency in the Convention's life during the last half of the decade was with reference to the qualitative thrust of the church on mission in the 20th century.

Without the dramatic increase in financial income between 1955 and 1969, the growth of this agency's work would not have been possible. Cash receipts in 1955 were $3,544,856. By 1964 these had risen to $8,316,717. In 1970 the total income for the current budget was expected to be $14,440,000. Of this amount $5,083,680 was expected from the Cooperative Program and $5,500,000 from the Annie Armstrong Easter Offering. These two sources of income constitute the lifeline of the board's work.

Types of work done by the board are expressed as programs. The statement approved by the Convention in 1966 defined the board's areas of continuing responsibility in terms of 12 programs: evangelism development, chaplaincy ministries, church loans, establishing new churches and church-type missions, associational administration service, pioneer missions, rural-urban missions, metropolitan missions, work with National Baptists, Christian social ministries, and work related to nonevangelicals. The last two were begun in 1966 as separate programs, although most of the work had been carried on earlier related to other activities.

By 1959 the staff's work load had become heavy enough to necessitate a new pattern of organization of staff personnel. Until then much of the work was structured in departments that were responsible directly to the executive secretary. At this time these departments were grouped under five divisions, which correlated the work of the departments assigned to them and in turn were responsible directly to the executive secretary. The divisions related to evangelism, church loans, chaplaincy, missions, and education and promotion (later called communication). In 1966 a sixth division composed of the business activities was added.

In 1954 there were 954 home missionaries. As of Dec. 31, 1969, the number had increased to 2,235. In addition to these, 921 college students served as student summer missionaries in 1969.

Leonard Sanderson succeeded Charles E. Mathews as secretary of evangelism in 1956, becoming the first director of the newly formed Division of Evangelism in 1959. Later that year he was succeeded by C. E. Autrey, who had been professor of evangelism at Southwestern Baptist Theological Seminary, Fort Worth, Tex. The evangelism offices were transferred from Dallas, Tex., to Atlanta, Ga., in 1965. By 1968 the division had enlarged to seven staff positions including Eual F. Lawson, Jack Stanton, John F. Havlik, Harold E. Lindsey, William D. Lawes, and Nathan Porter. C. E. Wilbanks, C. Y. Dossey, Newman McLarry, and Gray Allison also served during the sixties, the first two leaving the staff by retirement and the others by resignation. Autrey retired Sept. 1, 1969, after serving longer than any other board evangelism program leader. He was succeeded by Kenneth L. Chafin, who had been professor of evangelism at Southwestern Baptist Theological Seminary and had served about three years as the Billy Graham associate professor of evangelism at Southern Baptist Theological Seminary.

This program of work has stressed both personal and mass evangelism through the years. In more recent times staff associates have been assigned to give specific emphasis to metropolitan evangelism and to academic evangelism. Increasing attention has been given to writing, promoting associational clinics and state evangelistic conferences, homeland and overseas crusades, personal witnessing, and a Correspondence Bible Course. A broadening of the evangelism base is taking place. The Crusade of the Americas in 1969 had three objectives:

1. A deepening of the spiritual life within the churches, home, and individual Christians;

2. The evangelizing of the American continent;

3. The establishing of true moral and spiritual bases for the betterment of mankind's economic, social, and physical welfare.

Alfred A. Carpenter (*q.v.*) was elected in 1941 as the first full-time director of chaplaincy ministries, serving until his retirement in 1960. In 1955 Geo. W. Cummins became associate director, succeeding Carpenter as director in 1961. The Division of Chaplaincy was established in 1959. This ministry became one of the board's twelve programs in 1966, and has grown to include military, hospital, institutional, and industrial ministries. Ernest L. Ackiss, Willis A. Brown, James C. Peck, Cecil D. Etheridge, Thomas E. Carter, Lowell F. Sodeman, L. L. McGee, Gerald E. Marsh, Richard W. McKay, William L. Clark, and Alfred C. Hart have served on the chaplaincy staff. At the close of 1969 Brown was associate division director, Sodeman served in industrial chaplaincy, Hart in institutional chaplaincy and Brown also in ministries to military personnel.

G. Frank Garrison directed church loans operations from 1954 until his retirement at the end of 1965. Under his direction the corpus of loan funds increased fourfold. Berner F. Wilson, Thomas V. Haynes, and Roy F. Lewis had joined the staff. On Jan. 1, 1966, Robert H. Kilgore became director of the Division of Church Loans, coming from seven years' experience in banking and service as mortgage loan secretary of the Baptist Foundation of the Texas state convention. At the close of 1969 the staff consisted of Haynes, Shamar F. Shraikill, J. C. McDaniel, Billy T. Hargrove, W. C. Dudley, and W. T. Updike. Wilson had retired and Lewis had resigned. McDaniel resigned early in 1970 to become executive secretary of the Kansas convention. He was replaced by Olin Cox. By the end of 1969 the board's total net loan assets totaled over $20,000,000.

Nine of the 12 programs of work approved by the Convention in 1966 were assigned to the Division of Missions. Hugo H. Culpepper was director of this division, 1965–70. He and his wife had served as foreign missionaries for 19 years in the Orient and South America. From 1959 through 1964 he had served as professor of missions at the Southern Baptist Theological Seminary where he was the first incumbent of the W. O. Carver ((*q.v.*, Vol. I) chair of Christian missions and world religions. Loyd Corder became associate director of the missions division Jan. 1, 1966, with specific assignment for correlating staff teams charged with the responsibility of the programs of establishing new churches and of associational administration service. E. C. Watson became staff consultant for this latter service in 1966. In relation to establishing new churches, Project 500 was a special

1967–69 project to establish 500 strategically located new churches.

Between 1955 and 1969 the following six new state conventions were organized: Colorado, Michigan, Indiana, Utah-Idaho, Northern Plains, and New York. The pioneer missions department had worked closely with all of these areas to bring them to the point of organizing. A. B. Cash, department secretary from 1959 and until his retirement at the end of 1967, was succeeded by M. Wendell Belew. Two staff associates were added as the work grew, F. J. Redford and Quentin Lockwood. This department works in about 25 of the 50 states of this nation. Largely through its leadership, the board carries out the 1959 Convention's instructions to "continue to increase its emphasis on work in areas where there is no state convention or where the state convention is not well established."

Until 1959 both rural-urban and metropolitan missions work were included in the Department of Cooperative Missions under Solomon F. Dowis (*q.v.*). In the 1959 reorganization, Moseley became secretary of a new Department of City Missions, succeeded in 1962 by Harold C. Bennett. On Jan. 1, 1964, the name was changed to Department of Metropolitan Missions. J. N. Evans, Jr., became department secretary in mid-1966, and two associates were added the following year, F. Russell Bennett, Jr., and George A. Torney III. Lewis W. Newman served as department secretary of rural-urban missions for two years, succeeded in 1966 by C. Wilson Brumley. Two associates were added to this staff during the next two years, John B. McBride and Roy W. Owen.

Until 1959 most language missions work was done in the direct missions department, with Loyd Corder as secretary until 1959 when he became secretary of the new language missions department. His associate, Gerald B. Palmer, became department secretary in 1966. Elias L. Golonka, Oscar I. Romo, L. D. Wood and Irvin Dawson became staff associates between 1963 and 1967. This is the largest department of the missions division in terms of missionary personnel and budget.

Guy Bellamy was secretary of Negro work until the end of 1964. Victor T. Glass became his associate in 1957. The work was placed in the missions division in 1959 as the Department of Work with National Baptists. Glass became secretary Jan. 1, 1965, and later added two associates, W. R. Grigg and Emmanuel L. McCall. Historically the board has worked "with" Negroes to strengthen their churches. Increasing attention also has been given to the changing racial patterns in the nation.

The Department of Christian Social Ministries was organized in 1966 to implement one of the new programs. Paul R. Adkins, department secretary from 1966 until 1968, was succeeded by T. E. Carter. The work was restructured with emphasis on Baptist centers, youth and family services, migrant missions, and literacy missions. Disaster relief and child care agency liaison ministries were later added. Clovis A. Brantley, Mrs. Noble Y. Beall, L. W. Crews, J. Edward Taylor, Mildred Blankenship, Travis B. Lipscomb, Charles McCullin, and Warren Rawles are the staff in this department.

The second new department organized in 1966 was for Work Related to Nonevangelicals. Joseph R. Estes became department secretary that year. Historically Jewish work and Catholic information service had been carried on as ministries. Two new areas were added, Christian sects and non-Christian world religions. W. B. Mitchell, William E. Burke, and M. Thomas Starkes have served as staff associates. The nature of this department's work is research, writing of materials, and promotion of volunteer field ministries.

The Department of Special Mission Ministries is not a program outlet but is structured in the missions division as a supporting ministry, including student summer missions, the Christian Service Corps, and US-2. The department secretary, E. Warren Woolf, assumed the responsibilities of Beverly Hammack who had directed summer missions, 1961–67. Mrs. George W. Adams had assisted the executive secretary in this work until 1961. Until his retirement in 1960, Fred A. McCaulley led the tentmakers ministry, the forerunner to the Christian Service Corps. R. Donald Hammonds came to the staff in 1967 and Elbert E. Smith in 1970.

In the category of supporting ministries are two departments related to the administration of the board and two divisions. Glendon McCullough is secretary of the Department of Missionary Personnel, charged with the work involved in missionary appointments, with Cecil D. Etheredge, P. Edward Rickenbaker, and Edward E. Seabough as associates.

In 1962 Billy T. Hargrove was succeeded by Leonard G. Irwin as secretary of the Department of Survey and Special Studies. His associates are W. A. Powell, O. D. Morris, D. F. Mabry, and T. R. Coy.

Work in the area of business services was directed by G. Frank Garrison until his retirement in 1965, assisted through the years by Curtis L. Johnston, B. M. Crain, Ransome W. Swords, and Mrs. Jeanette B. Williams. Lewis W. Newman, director of this division, 1966–68, was succeeded by Dan C. McQueen, a certified public accountant, in 1968. New staff members in recent years are Meeler Markham, William B. Ard, and Harry A. Steele, who succeeded B. M. Crain.

L. O. Griffith came to the board in 1951, from the position of associate executive secretary of the Kentucky Baptist Convention. Secretary of the Department of Promotion, in 1959 he was named director of the new Division of Education and Promotion, changed in 1967 to Division of Communication. In this division the staff and their primary responsibilities have been: Lewis W. Martin, schools of missions until 1965, succeeded by Kenneth Day, with area of work renamed in 1968 world missions conferences;

Walker L. Knight, editor of *Home Missions* magazine, assisted by Dallas M. Lee, news editor; Kate Ellen Gruver, book editor and in charge of resource library since 1960; J. C. Durham, Jr., audiovisuals, assisted by Donald O. Rutledge, photographer; and Thomas H. Baker, art and printing.

Until 1968 the board was located at 161 Spring Street, N. W., in Atlanta, Ga. Because of the need for more space, in 1968 the board moved to its new seven-story building at 1350 Spring Street, N. W., Atlanta, Ga. 30309, with 90,000 square feet of floor space and adequate parking space. The board has a 10-year lease with an option to buy in 1972.

See also CHAPLAINCY MINISTRIES, PROGRAM OF; CHRISTIAN SOCIAL MINISTRIES, PROGRAM OF; CHURCH LOANS, PROGRAM OF; COMMUNICATION, DIVISION OF; MISSIONARY PERSONNEL, DEPARTMENT OF; PIONEER MISSIONS, PROGRAMS OF; SPECIAL MISSION MINISTRIES; SURVEY AND SPECIAL STUDIES, DEPARTMENT OF; NONEVANGELICALS, PROGRAM OF WORK RELATED TO PROJECT 500, NATIONAL BAPTISTS, PROGRAM OF WORK WITH; BUSINESS SERVICES, DEPARTMENT OF.

HUGO H. CULPEPPER

***HOMER MEMORIAL HOSPITAL.** See LOUISIANA BAPTIST CONVENTION.

HONDURAS, MISSION IN (cf. Guatemala-Honduras, Mission in, Vol. I). The first resident mssionaries to Honduras were appointed in 1952 but did not arrive on the field until 1954. Fifteen years later, the staff had grown to 13 career missionaries. Honduras and Guatemala became separate missions in 1958. That same year the Association of Honduran Baptist Churches was organized. Work includes theological institute in Tegucigalpa and medical clinic in El Porvenir. In 1969, 10 churches and 12 missions reported 437 members. HAROLD E. HURST

***HONG KONG-MACAO, MISSION IN.** Hong Kong Baptist College, sponsored by Hong Kong Baptist Association, was established in 1956 with 152 students and five departments. It moved to its own campus in 1966, and three years later, offered courses in 12 departments to 2,800 students. Hong Kong Baptist Hospital's new building was completed in 1963. Continued growth resulted in 50 churches and mission chapels in 1969, with 20,000 members. The missionary staff of 79 served with national leaders in a program of evangelism and varied social ministries.

JAMES D. BELOTE

HOPE. Theologically, hope is the confidence given by God to those who have faith in him. The ground of man's hope is God's character and activity (Jer. 14:8). In the Bible hope is not grounded in man or his work but in the creative and sustaining power of God and above all in what God has done and will do in Jesus Christ. In the Old Testament hope in God gives trust, confidence, and patience to men as they commit themselves to the God who secures their future (Ps. 13:5; 42:5; Isa. 51:5).

In the New Testament hope is the expectation given those who accept God in Christ as the source and goal of hope. In I Timothy 1:1 it is stated simply: "Christ Jesus our hope" (cf. Rom. 4:17–21; 15:3). Paul, who develops the meaning of hope, makes it clear that hope derives from the indwelling Christ (Col. 1:27). And the Holy Spirit conveys hope to the believer and sustains and nurtures it (Rom. 5:5; I Cor. 2:9–16; Rom. 15:4). Consequently, it is sometimes said that the Holy Spirit is the present tense of hope. The resurrection of Christ is the ground of hope, because it is the mighty act of God who makes believers confident of their future (I Thess. 4:13–18; I Cor. 15:1–58). Hope is extended to all men who respond to God's saving work in Jesus Christ (Eph. 2:12; Rom. 5–8).

The author of Hebrews declares, "Let us hold fast the confession of our hope without wavering, for he who promised is faithful" (Heb. 10:23). Characteristically, he writes of *the* hope, and thus emphasizes the objective character of Christian hope. He speaks of hope as the "anchor of the soul" (6:19). In I Peter we read, "Blessed be the God and Father of our Lord Jesus Christ! By his great mercy we have been born anew to a living hope through the resurrection of Jesus Christ from the dead" (1:3; 1:21). Hope points to the second advent of Christ (1:13). First John 3:3 sets forth hope as a motive for purity. In many passages hope is understood as waiting for the eschatological future (cf. Col. 1:5; Titus 2:13; Heb. 7:19).

The entire ministry of Jesus is meant to bring hope to all men (Matt. 12:21). In a genuine sense, according to the New Testament, Jesus does not merely bring hope to men, he is hope itself. RAYMOND BRYAN BROWN

HOPKINS, HAMPTON COLVARD (b. Ashe County, N. C., July 27, 1903; d. Gadsden, Ala., Dec. 29, 1956). Preacher and educator. Hopkins received the A.B. degree, Wake Forest College, 1928, B.D., Southern Baptist Theological Seminary, 1941, and D.D., Howard College, 1948. Ordained to preach, May 25, 1932, he married Eva Elliott on June 14, 1933. They had three daughters. Three churches in Elizabethton, Tenn. (East Side, Oak Street, and Big Springs), were constituted under his leadership. Other Tennessee pastorates were Siam Church, Elizabethton, 1934–42; Calvary, Erwin, 1942–43; and First Baptist, Lenoir City, 1948. He was pastor of the South Highland Church, Bessemer, Ala., 1943–48. He became associate director of the Extension Division for Christian Training at Howard College and was director, 1950–52. He was chairman of the executive board of the Alabama Baptist Convention, 1953–56. In 1952 he returned to the pastorate and served Twelfth Street Church, Gadsden, until his death. He was buried in Elizabethton, Tenn.

BIBLIOGRAPHY: E. E. Hopkins, *He Had to Preach* (1959). EVA E. HOPKINS

HOUSTON BAPTIST COLLEGE. Founded by the Baptist General Convention of Texas in 1960, Houston Baptist College in less than 10 years has achieved a reputation of academic excellence. Its orderly growth and remarkable success in such short time are testimony to the dedication and foresight of its founders and to the need for an outstanding four-year, coeducational, liberal arts college. Under its first president, William H. Hinton, the college opened with a freshman class of 196 students in Sept., 1963, on a 200-acre campus 12 miles from downtown Houston. Six contemporary, air-conditioned buildings comprised the original campus. The college moved forward rapidly. Between 1963 and 1969 it constructed the Atwood Theology Building, the Sharp Gymnasium, and the Moody Library; gained full accreditation (1968) ; graduated three classes totaling 267 students; added teacher education and degree granting nursing programs to the curriculum; and with membership in the N.C.A.A., the college fields intercollegiate teams in four sports. Enrolment for 1968 was 1,118; faculty strength was 67 with approximately 50 per cent holding the earned doctorate. The campus is valued at $15,000,000. DAN GORTON

HOWARD COLLEGE EXTENSION DIVISION (cf. Extension Centers, Baptist Colleges, Vol. I) . Inaugurated formally in Jan., 1947, the division grew out of and was patterned on a program begun earlier by Gilbert L. Guffin at Walker College, Jasper, Ala. The division, now part of Samford University, has enrolled (1947–69) approximately 20,000 in 30 to 50 centers annually operated in Alabama. Formerly known as the Howard Plan, the program of the division became a pattern for formation of similar extension services by other colleges, such as Mercer University, Carson-Newman College, the University of Richmond, and Stetson, as well as the Extension Departments of Southern Baptist seminaries. Directors have been Gilbert L. Guffin, 1947–49; Hampton C. Hopkins (*q.v.*) , 1950–53; Davis C. Woolley, 1953–59; Hudson Baggett (interim director) , 1959–61; and R. Lee Gallman, 1960–65. In Feb., 1967, the division was restructured. Dean of Religion Gilbert L. Guffin was named, in addition to his other duties, as chairman. Directors serving under him have been: T. Harold Benson, 1967–69, and George H. Jackson, 1969–

GILBERT L. GUFFIN

***HOWARD PAYNE COLLEGE.** In 1955 the college completed a four-story dormitory for girls, redecorated Mims Auditorium, the Student Center, and the book store. The Coggin Chapel was renovated in 1956 to accommodate the speech and drama department. A former church was improved to house Fleming Religion Center in 1958. In 1962–63 the Winebrenner Science Hall and J. W. Jennings Hall were completed. Jennings Hall was converted to house freshman girls in 1969, and boys were moved to a 12-story dormitory. Remodeling and extension of the administration building on the former Daniel Baker campus was begun in 1964 as the Douglas MacArthur Academy of Freedom to accommodate the Social Science honors program. By May, 1969, the total endowment had increased to $3,106,467 not including large gifts for funded scholarships and trusts.

FRANCES L. MERRITT

HOWELL, SUE O. (b. Morgantown, W. Va., June 19, 1866; d. Herrington, Kan., Aug. 5, 1956) . Teacher, missionary, and denominational worker. She moved in childhood with her parents to Illinois where she later taught school. Following graduation from a Baptist training school in Chicago, she came to Oklahoma City, Okla. In 1908 she became the first employed executive secretary for Woman's Missionary Union of Oklahoma, serving until 1919. She aided in founding Falls Creek Baptist Assembly in 1917, and raised funds to build "Howell Hall," a dormitory for girls on the assembly grounds. Through her leadership the Good Will Center in Oklahoma City was founded, mission study courses and the Standard of Excellence were introduced to WMU in Oklahoma, and women were inspired at the local church level to increase their giving to missions. J. M. GASKIN

HUDSON, CLAY IRBY (b. Auburn, Ala., Jan. 21, 1884; d. Nashville, Tenn., Sept. 10, 1953) . Pastor and SBC Sunday School Board worker. Educated at Howard College, Birmingham, Ala., and Union University, Jackson, Tenn., he married Colice Corbitt of Nashville, Tenn., 1910. After her death in 1927, he married Mary Bowers of Wake Forest, N. C., 1929. He served the following Baptist churches as pastor: First, Athens, Ala.; First, Decatur, Ala.; North Edgefield and Shelby Avenue, Nashville, Tenn.; and Pritchard Memorial, Charlotte, N. C. He came to the Sunday School Board to assist Prince E. Burroughs (*q.v.*, Vol. I) in the Department of Church Administration. He did such excellent work in promoting the study of church administration books that when Baptist Adult Union work took form, he was asked to join the Training Union Department in 1936, to promote Adult work. He pioneered in helping to carry forward one of the most far-reaching educational movements that Southern Baptists ever launched. HOWARD P. COLSON

HUEY, HENRY JEREMIAH (b. Carlisle County, Ky., Feb. 9, 1901; d. Albuquerque, N. Mex., Feb. 9, 1968) . Pastor and denominational leader. He was educated at Union University, Jackson, Tenn. (A.B., M.A.) , and Southwestern Baptist Theological Seminary (Th.M.) . Union University conferred upon him the D.D. degree. He married Johnnie Brooks on Oct. 4, 1925. They had three sons: Henry Jeremiah, Jr., Brooks, and Edwin. Pastorates he served include First Baptist churches in: Newbern, Tenn., Bolivar, Tenn., and Milan, Tenn. The latter pastorate was for 26 years. In Nov., 1954, he became executive secretary of the Tennessee Baptist Foundation, which he held until his death. He served on numerous boards and committees of the Tennessee Baptist Convention including: Union University board of trustees, 1927–54; executive board, Tennessee Baptist Convention, 1928–54 (president 1946–54); and member of and first president of Belmont College board of trustees, 1950–51. Huey was president of West Tennessee Baptist Pastor's Conference, 1938–39; moderator of Gibson Baptist Association, 1939, 1940, and 1947; and president of the Tennessee Baptist Convention, 1951. He was a member of the Masonic Lodge and the A.T.O. college fraternity. Huey died of a coronary deficiency while in Albuquerque to attend a meeting of Southern Baptist foundation executives. He is buried at Milan, Tenn.

JONAS STEWART

HUGHES, JOHN GILLIAM (b. Cedar Bluff, Tenn., Sept. 30, 1892; d. Memphis, Tenn., May 26, 1956). Educated at Union University (B.A., 1917; D.D., 1931), he married Beulah Brown, June 28, 1916. They had two sons, John G., Jr., and Brown. His pastorates included: Central Baptist Church, Memphis, Tenn., 1914–15; Spring Creek, Eddyville, Ky., 1915–17; Clinton, Ky., 1918–21; First, Lebanon, Tenn., 1923–28; First, Union City, Tenn., 1928–33; First, Kingsport, Tenn., 1933–41; and Union Avenue Church, Memphis, Tenn., 1941–56. He served as trustee of Union University, 1928–33, vice-president of Tennessee Baptist Convention, 1929–31, and president of the Tennessee convention, 1937–39. He wrote *Son of Consolation* (1941). He is buried in Memorial Park, Memphis, Tenn.

JAMES F. EAVES

HUGO GOLDEN AGE HOME (Hugo, Okla.). The Baptist Foundation of Oklahoma received title to a 68-acre tract of land at Hugo, Okla., Sept. 12, 1956, as a gift from the Will and Lee Baskett families. The state convention put $35,000 in the project and southeastern Oklahoma citizens entered a drive to raise $65,000 for buildings. The first wing was dedicated May 9–10, 1959, and one year later a second wing was added, increasing the capacity to 33, and the property value to $220,000. The original wing was named the Will Baskett wing. A third addition in 1963 increased the capacity to 61, and was named the J. F. Murrell (*q.v.*) wing in honor of the home's first administrator. In 1969 property value was $361,983, plus a $30,000 administrator's home. Debt was $137,105.

J. M. GASKIN

HUMPHREYS, ROBERT EDWARD (b. Morristown, Tenn., June 10, 1893; d. Owensboro, Ky., July 16, 1968). Son of Margaret E. Hutton and Nathaniel K. Humphreys, he was educated at Carson-Newman College (A.B., 1916) and Southern Baptist Theological Seminary (Th.G., 1919). He received a D.D. degree from Bethel Woman's College, Hopkinsville, Ky., and from Georgetown College, 1947.

Ordained in 1915, he served rural churches during college and seminary days. He was pastor of Central Baptist Church, Bearden, Tenn., 1919–27. On Oct. 19, 1927, he became pastor of the First Baptist Church, Owensboro, Ky., which he served until Oct. 16, 1955.

Denominational experiences were: director, Baptist Education Society of Kentucky, and of Christian Education Department of General Association of Baptists in Kentucky; trustee of Georgetown College; member, Baptist State Board of Missions, Board of Ministers Aid Society of Kentucky, Relief and Annuity Board, and Foreign Mission Board, SBC; and moderator, General Association of Baptists in Kentucky, 1948–49.

On May 11, 1918, he married Willie Eola Renfro of Spring City, Tenn. They had three children, Martha Jane, Margaret E., and Robert, Jr.

LEO T. CRISMON

HURT, JOHN JETER (b. Bollsville, Va., Mar. 1, 1873; d. Atlanta, Ga., Dec. 26, 1961). Minister, college president, author, and editor. Son of George S. and Laura (Drake) Hunt, he graduated from Bryant and Stratton Business College at age 17. Ordained in 1901, he edited the *Arkansas Baptist Advance,* 1900–03. Hurt was educated at Richmond College and Southern Baptist Theological Seminary (Th.G., 1903). His honorary degrees included the D.D. from Union in 1914, Wake Forest in 1921, and LL.D. from Georgetown in 1933.

On June 30, 1908, he married Ethelyn Lovell of Ft. Smith, Ark. They had five children: J. J., Jr., George T., Harrison H., James L., and Mrs. Mary Lee Bennett. Hurt served as president of the board of trustees of Central College, Arkansas, 1906–12, the North Carolina State Baptist Convention, 1914–22, and the Alumni Association of the Southern Baptist Theological Seminary. He was vice-president of the Tennessee Baptist Convention, 1927, and of the Southern Baptist Convention, 1935.

His pastorates included First Baptist churches in Durham, N. C., 1912–16, Wilmington, 1916–23, and Jackson, Tenn., 1923–32. He was president of Union University, Jackson, Tenn., 1932–45. In 1946 he was elected acting president of New Orleans Baptist Theological Seminary.

Hurt was the author of: *Struggles for Religious Liberty in Virginia* (1912), *A Handbook for Every-Member Canvass* (1931), *My Fifty Favorite Stories* (1960), *Sermons: Short-Medium-Long* (1959), and *This is My Story* (1957).

ROBERT E. CRAIG

HUTCHISON, MARGARET (b. Little Rock, Ark., Sept. 12, 1899; d. Oklahoma City, Okla., Feb. 6, 1967). She attended Little Rock public schools and Louisiana State Normal College, 1917–19, graduating from Louisiana College (B.A., 1925), and Baptist Bible Institute at New Orleans, La., with the BCT degree. Active in denominational work as a Woman's Missionary Union leader, she was Young People's secretary in Arkansas, 1929–46, an associate in the schools of mission department of the Home Mission Board, 1946–48, and was executive secretary-treasurer of Oklahoma WMU, 1948–63. Her written works include *Strawberry Road* (1947). She is buried at Shreveport, La. J. M. GASKIN

HYATT, ALEXANDER JAMISON (b. Monticello, Drew County, Ark., Mar. 27, 1910; d. Mill Valley, Calif., Nov. 7, 1967). Seminary librarian, pastor, and army chaplain. His father, Robert Fee Hyatt, was a druggist and his mother was active in church and civic affairs. After finishing Monticello High School as salutatorian of his class, he attended Monticello A. & M. College, University of Arkansas and Baylor University (B.A., 1931). He received his theological training in Southern Baptist Theological Seminary (Th.M., 1934), Southwestern Baptist Theological Seminary, 1946, and Golden Gate Theological Seminary (Th.D. 1950). He also earned the master's degree in Library Science at the University of California. He married Alice Nelson June 30, 1932. They had four children: Alice Eloise (Bryan), Alexander J., Jr., Lewis Nelson, and Hazel Ruth (Kuykendall). After laboring as associational missionary and pastor in his native state, he spent three years (1942–45) as a chaplain in the army and then located in California where he was pastor at Napa, Chico, and Richmond. He was elected moderator of two associations, member of the Home Mission Board, member of California convention executive board, and trustee of California Baptist College. Hyatt did an outstanding work in building the library at Golden Gate where he served from 1956 to 1967. During his tenure, the holdings were increased and upgraded to conform to accreditation standards as well as to provide for many areas of specialization. He looked upon the library as not merely a collection of books but as a means of service, and did everything possible to make its contents available to all who needed its resources. He is buried in Sutter, Calif. WILLIAM A. CARLETON

***HYMN WRITERS, BAPTIST.** Interest in new hymn texts and hymn tunes increased among Southern Baptists during the sixties. This growing concern for contemporary contribution to the everbroadening stream of Christian song may be attributed to several possible factors. Not the least of these is the hymn-writing competitions sponsored by the Church Music Department of the Baptist Sunday School Board.

The listing given here includes names of authors and composers whose writings have appeared since 1956. Also, names of writers are included which were inadvertently omitted in Volume II, or whose earlier songs have only recently come into wider use. One title is given for each author and one tune name for each composer.

Authors.—Sybil Leonard Armes, "How Gracious Are Thy Mercies, Lord"; Betty P. Barrett, "Increase in Knowledge of Thy God"; Gene Bartlett, "Set My Soul Afire"; E. M. Bartlett, Sr. (*q.v.*, Vol. I), "Victory in Jesus"; James T. Bolding, "Lord, We Give Ourselves to Thee"; Robert E. Brickhouse, "Lord, Light My Soul with Holy Flame"; Justin G. Burt, "Thy Will Be Done in Me"; Ross Coggins, "Send Me, O Lord, Send Me"; Roy H. Corley, "Walk Ye in Him"; Ragan Courtney, "His Gentle Look"; Alta C. Faircloth, "Sing Hosannas"; Virginia Figh, "Faith for Thy Service"; Barbara Gaultney, "My Lord Is Near Me All the Time"; Jeana Graham, "Teach Us"; Joseph H. Green, "Thy Supper, Lord, Before Us Spread"; Mary E. Hall, "I See the Christ Among the Crowd"; L. T. Hastings, "Lead Me, Savior"; Erwin C. Johnson, "O Gracious Lord, Accept Our Praise"; Diane O. Jordan, "Arise Now, Fellow Christians of the Nations"; G. Kearnie Keegan (*q.v.*), "Teach Me, O Lord, I Pray"; Lillian Y. Leavell, "We Lift Our Hearts in Songs of Praise"; LeRoy McClard, "Jesus Is Lord of All"; Albert McClellan, "What Is It, Lord"; Hugh D. McElrath, "We Praise Thee with Our Minds, O Lord"; William N. McElrath, "O Son of Man, Who Walked Man's Way"; Betty Beauchamp Moody, "O Lord, My Lips Can Never Speak"; Jess Moody, "Send Thy Power Again"; Roger L. Oldham, "Almighty God, Increase Our Faith"; James T. Owens, "Come to Jesus Now"; George L. Payne, "Rejoice, and Let Us Go"; Novella D. Preston, "My Singing Is a Prayer"; R. Maines Rawls, "Take My Life, Lead Me, Lord"; Delma B. Reno, "Praise the Lord, the King of Glory"; Mary Lou Reynolds, "Praise Him, O Praise Him"; Sam W. Scantlan, "The Holy Spirit Speaks"; Ed Seabough, "One World, One Lord, One Witness"; W. Hines Sims, "Christ the Only Hope"; G. Temp Sparkman, "Where's the Promise of the City"; Bernice M. Staples, "O Let Thy Heart Be Moved by Compassion"; Mrs. Fernan F. Stump, "Give to Your God"; Joan Sutton, "It Is No Sacrifice to Follow Jesus"; Broadman Ware, "Teach Me, O Lord, to Care"; Kate Wilkins Woolley, "Free to Be Me."

Composers.—Gene Bartlett, "Tabor"; E. M. Bartlett, "Victory"; Charles F. Brown, "Little Creek"; Charles F. Bryan, "McMinnville"; Justin G. Burt, "Thy Will"; A. L. Butler, "Redeemed"; James D. Cram, "Hunters Glen"; Talmage W. Dean, "Cowden"; Alta C. Faircloth, "Dunwody"; Barbara Gaultney, "My Lord Is Near Me"; Robert Graham, "Teach Us"; L. T. Hastings, "Lead Me"; Raymond H. Herbek, "Adams"; William L. Hooper, "Chislehurst"; Donald P. Hustad, "Harvey"; Bill H. Ichter, "Campanha"; Phillip Landgrave, "Tabernacle"; LeRoy McClard, "Jesus Is Lord of All"; William N. McElrath, "Springbook"; George A. Minor, "Harvest"; Roger L. Oldham, "Almighty God"; James T. Owens, "Come to Him Now"; George L. Payne, "Rejoice"; R. Maines Rawls, "Take My Life"; Elwyn C. Raymer, "Kimbel"; Buryl Red, "Generic"; William J. Reynolds, "Paschall"; W. Hines Sims, "Charles"; Roger Sneed, "Keys"; Bernice M. Staples, "Compassion"; Joan Sutton, "No Sacrifice"; Beryl Vick, Jr., "Mark"; Johann Y. Yang, "Celestial Calm"; Philip M. Young, "Acclamation."

A new hymn and tune from Scotland: George B. Hossack, "God of Our Fathers, by Whose Grace"; Alistair Stewart, "Ceud Bliadna."

In England the *Baptist Hymn Book* (1962) includes a number of new texts and tunes from contemporary English Baptist authors and composers which should be included.

Authors.—Robert David Brown, "Thou, Lord, Hast Given Thyself"; John Philip Giles, "Here, in This Water, I Do Vow to Thee"; Terrot Reaveley Glover, "Jesus and Joseph Day After Day"; Richard Birch Hoyle, "Thine Be the Glory" (tr.); Frederick Arthur Jackson, "Master, We Thy Footsteps Follow"; Hugh Martin, "Lord Jesus, in Thy Footsteps"; Leslie Holliss Moore, "Jesus, We Love to Meet Thee"; Ernest A. Payne, "Our Father God" (tr); Alice M. Pullen, "At Work Beside His Father's Bench"; H. Wheeler Robertson, "O Thou Whose Love Has Brought Us Here."

Composers.—David Baker, "Thanksgiving"; Reginald Baker, "Mansfield Road"; Gertrude Bedford, "Bletchley"; Henry Ford Benson, "Aurora"; Carey Bonner, "Tilak"; Francis Eric Dawes, "Kilantringan"; John Hughes (Dongelley), "Dinas Bethlehem"; John Hughes (Pontypridd), "Cwm Rhondda"; David de Lloyd, "Richmond Hill"; Arthur Ewart Rusbridge, "Horfield"; Jehu Shepherd, "Avondale"; C. Stanley Smallman, "Dear Love"; John Harries Thomas, "Hemel"; Gilbert Charles Thorn, "Branksome"; Harry Webster, "Nil Nisi Labore."

BIBLIOGRAPHY: Hugh Martin, ed., *The Baptist Hymn Book Companion* (1962, rev. 1967). William J. Reynolds, *Hymns of Our Faith* (1964).

WILLIAM J. REYNOLDS

***HYMNALS, BAPTIST.** The abundance of hymn collections published in America by or for Baptists speaks forcefully of the practice of congregational song among Baptists. No extensive identification of these collections had been attempted prior to the *Encyclopedia of Southern Baptists* (1956).

The Newport collection of 1766 is recognized as the first Baptist hymn collection compiled and published in the colonies. However, a reprint of the English publication *Evangelical Hymns and Songs,* by Benjamin Wallin, had appeared in 1762. There followed many American reprints of Baptist hymnals which appeared first in England: Richard Burnham's *Hymns,* Boston, 1796; John Dobell's *New Selection,* Morristown, N. J., 1810; John Rippon's *Psalms and Hymns of Dr. Watts, with Rippon's Selection,* Philadelphia, 1820; Sommers and Dagg's *Psalms and Hymns of Dr. Watts, with Rippon's Selection,* Philadelphia, 1827.

Following the Newport collection, American compilers were more numerous and their collections appeared more frequently. Philip Hughes collection (title unknown), Wilmington, Delaware, 1782; Benjamin Cleaveland, *Hymns on Different Spiritual Subjects,* Norwich, Conn., 1786; an anonymous collection, *Baptismal Hymns,* Boston, 1791; John Stanford, *A Collection of Evangelical Hymns,* New York, 1792; Andrew Harpending, *Hymns,* Mount-Holly, N. J., 1799; Samuel Holyoke, *The Christian Harmonist,* Salem, Mass., 1804 (provided tunes for Watts, Rippon, and Joshua Smith); William Staughton (*q.v.*, Vol. II), *A Selection of Evangelical Hymns,* Burlington, N. J., 1807; Lewis Baldwin, *Original Hymns and Spiritual Songs,* Philadelphia, 1808; James Fenn, *Hymns and Poems,* Schenectady, N. Y., 1808; anonymous, *The Boston Collection,* Boston, 1808; Ebenezer Jayne, *Hymns and Spiritual Songs,* Morristown, N. J., 1809; William Collier, *A New Selection of Hymns,* Boston, 1812; Archibald Maclay, *A Selection of Hymns,* New York, 1816; Himes and Wilson, *A Selection of Hymns,* Greenfield, Mass., 1817; David Benedict (*q.v.*), *The Pawtucket Collection,* Providence, R. I., 1817; Samuel Dyer, *Dyer's New Selection of Sacred Music,* Baltimore, 1817 (tunebook); James Winchell, *An Arrangement of . . . Watts,* Boston, 1819; James Winchell, *Sacred Harmony,* Boston, 1819 (tunebook); Thomas B. Ripley, *A Selection of Hymns,* Portland, Me., 1821; Gustavus F. Davis, *The Young Christian's Companion,* Boston, 1826; Samuel Dyer, *Philadelphia Collection of Sacred Music,* New York, 1828 (tunebook); Daniel Greene, *Conference Hymns,* Providence, R. I., 1828; E. W. Freeman, *A Selection of Hymns,* Exeter, N. H., 1829; R. Winchell, *The Baptist Songster,* Wethersfield, Conn., 1829; J. A. Burke, *A Selection of Favorite Conference Hymns,* Albany, N. Y., 1829; Jonathan Howe, *Choice Hymns,* Boston, 1829; P. M. Davis, *The Baptist Conference and Prayer Meeting Hymn Book,* Binghamton, N. Y., 1830; C. M. Fuller, *A Selection of Hymns,* Auburn, N. Y., 1830; Luke Barker, *A Collection of Psalms, Hymns, and Spiritual Songs,* New York, 1831; B. M. Hill, *Hymns of Zion,* New Haven, 1832; Babcock and Mason, *Union Hymns,* Boston, 1834; Cummings and Worth, *The Conference Manual,* Concord, N. H., 1835; Linsley and Davis, *Select Hymns,* Hartford, Conn., 1836; John B. Hague, *Hymns,* (n.p.) 1842; A. D. Gillette, *Hymns for Social Meetings,* Philadelphia, 1843; Jacob Knapp, *The Evangelical Harp,* Utica, N. Y., 1845; Richard Knight, *A Choice Selection,* Providence, R. I., 1847; Stow and Smith, *The Social Psalmist,* Boston, 1848; J. H. Hanaford, *Ocean Melodies,* Boston, 1848; John Dowling, *Conference Hymns,* New York, 1849; Joseph Banvard, *The Christian Melodist,* Boston, 1849; Fuller and Jeter, *Supplement to the Psalmist,* Philadelphia, 1850; Lemuel Burkitt, *A Collection of . . . Hymns,* Philadelphia, 1850; and Committee of the Second Baptist Church, *Select Hymns,* Philadelphia, c. 1850.

The first hymnal published by the American

Baptist Publication Society, Philadelphia, was George B. Ide and Edgar M. Levy's *The Baptist Harp,* 1849.

A number of hymn collections by Baptist compilers were specifically designed for use in revivals: John Butler, *Revival Hymns,* Boston, 1839; Edwin Burnham, *Revival Hymns,* Boston, 1867; A. B. Earle, *Revival Hymns,* Boston, 1865; John Dowling, *Conference and Revival Hymns,* New York, 1868; Emerson Andrews, *Revival Songs,* Boston, 1870.

In the 19th century there were numerous "Baptist editions" of hymnals prepared for other congregations: Rufus Babcock, *A Manual of Christian Psalmody,* Boston, 1832 (a Baptist edition of Mason and Greene's Church Psalmody, 1831); John S. Holme, *The Baptist Hymn and Tune Book,* New York, 1857 (a Baptist edition of *The Plymouth Collection,* 1855); Francis Wayland, *A Baptist Edition of The Sabbath Hymn Book,* New York, 1858; T. S. Griffiths, *Songs for the Sanctuary,* New York, 1869 (a Baptist edition of C. S. Robinson's *Songs for the Sanctuary,* 1865); Robinson and MacArthur, *The Calvary Selection,* New York, 1878 (a Baptist edition of Robinson's *Psalms, Hymns, and Spiritual Songs,* 1875); Sanders and Lorimer, *People's Praise Book,* New York, 1889 (a Baptist edition of *Carmina Sanctorum*); Robinson and Judson, *The New Laudes Domini,* New York, 1892; and R. S. MacArthur, *In Excelsis* (Calvary Edition), New York, 1897.

Mention should be made of Baptist compilers of oblong shaped-note tune books which were exceedingly popular in the South: William Walker, *The Southern Harmony,* 1835, *Southern and Western Harmonist,* 1846, and *The Christian Harmony,* 1866; B. F. White (*q.v.,* Vol. II) and E. J. King, *The Sacred Harp,* 1844; and John G. McCurry, *The Social Harp,* 1855.

Hymn collections which appeared in the South and Midwest were: Jesse Mercer (*q.v.,* Vol. II), *The Cluster of Spiritual Songs,* Augusta, Georgia, 1813; Silas M. Noel, *Selection of Hymns,* Frankfort, Ky., 1814; John Purify, *A Selection of Hymns,* Raleigh, N. C., 1823; William P. Biddle and William J. Newborn, *The Baptist Hymn Book,* Washington, D. C., 1825; Absalom Graves, *Hymns, Psalms and Spiritual Songs,* Cincinnati, 1825; John Courtney, Sr., *A Selection of Hymns,* Richmond, 1831; H. Miller, *A New Selection,* Cincinnati, 1835; S. P. Hill, *Christian Melodies,* Baltimore, 1836; J. M. Peck, *Dupuy's Hymns and Spiritual Songs,* Louisville, 1843; A. A. Guernsey, *A Collection of Hymns,* Strongsville, Ohio, 1843; J. M. D. Cates, *The Baptist Companion,* Nashville, 1846; Eli Ball, *The Manual of the Sacred Choir,* Richmond, 1849; Sidney Dyer, *The Southwestern Psalmist,* Louisville, 1851; I. B. Woodbury, *The Casket,* Charleston, S. C., 1855; and G. E. Leonard, *The Harp of Glory,* Lexington, N. C., 1898.

Baptist compilers contributed to the great output of Sunday School song collections. Among these were Joseph A. Warne, *Baptist Sabbath School Hymn Book,* 1844; *The Little Sunday School Hymn Book,* Charleston, S. C., 1863; *The Confederate Sunday School Hymn Book,* Charleston, S. C., 1893; Charles J. Elford, *The Sunday School Hymn Book,* Greenville, S. C., 1865; *Kind Words in Melody,* Greenville, S. C., 1871; J. R. Graves, *The Little Seraph for Churches and Sunday Schools,* Memphis, 1873; E. H. Johnson, *Songs of Praise for Sunday Schools,* Philadelphia, 1882; E. H. Johnson, *Select Sunday School Songs,* Philadelphia, 1885; and MacArthur and Chittenden, *The Calvary Hymnal for Sunday School, Prayer Meeting and Church Service,* Boston, 1891.

Of widespread use were the collections of Bradbury, Lowry, Doane, Sherwin. Among these were W. B. Bradbury, *The Devotional Hymn and Tune Book,* Philadelphia, 1864 (the only new Baptist hymn book to be published during the Civil War); Robert Lowry and W. H. Doane, *Gospel Music,* New York, 1876; Lowry and Vail, *Chapel Melodies,* New York, 1868; Doane, *Songs of Devotion,* New York, 1870; Lowry, Doane, and Sherwin, *Chautauqua Carols,* New York, 1878; Lowry and Doane, *Select Gems,* Philadelphia, 1899; and Doane, *Song Evangel,* Louisville, 1906.

Baptist collections appeared in the Southwest late in the 19th century. Most influential of these was W. E. Penn (*q.v.,* Vol. II) whose *Harvest Bells No. 1,* 1881, *No. 2,* 1884, *No. 3,* 1886, were used in revivals, camp meetings, and church services. Other collections which followed are Marion S. Kerby, *The Song Gem,* Temple, Tex., 1888; George R. Cairns, *Gathered Gems of Gospel Song,* Dallas, 1889; Daniel P. Airhart, R. S. Coward, J. A. Brown, and J. P. Lane, *Soul Songs,* Waco, Tex., 1892; J. C. R. Kyger, *Bells of Heaven,* Waco, Tex., 1895; M. S. Kerby, *Awakening Melodies,* Dallas, 1895; J. C. F. Kyger, *The Revival Harp, No. 1,* Waco, Tex., *No. 2,* 1899; J. C. F. Kyger, *Happy Voices,* Waco, Tex., 1898; J. C. F. Kyger, and A. Bunyan Little, *Sacred Chimes,* Waco, Tex., 1900; and J. A. Brown, F. J. Harrell and J. T. Franklin, *Heart Praise,* Fort Worth, 1910.

Other 20th-century compilations include: Shepard and Lawrence, *The New Baptist Praise Book,* Philadelphia, 1914; W. Plunkett Martin (*q.v.*) and J. W. Jelks, *Songs of Redemption,* Atlanta, Ga., 1920; *Victorious Praise,* Nashville, 1921; I. E. Reynolds and Robert H. Coleman, *Kingdom Songs,* Nashville, 1921; *Living Hymns,* Philadelphia, 1923; I. E. Reynolds and B. B. McKinney, *Jehovah's Praise,* Fort Worth, Tex., 1925; S. W. Beazley, *Service Hymnal,* Chicago, 1925; *Hymns for Creative Living,* Philadelphia, 1935; *Christian Worship,* Philadelphia, 1941; and *Christian Praise,* Nashville, 1964.

WILLIAM J. REYNOLDS

***HYMNS, THEOLOGICAL IMPLICATIONS OF.** The history of hymnody revolves around a few great creative outbursts. At other times, change is slow, almost unnoticeable. The publication of *Baptist Hymnal* in 1956 brought some identifiable changes to the hymn-singing practices of Southern Baptists, but no substantial change of more recent date can be seen.

Baptist Hymnal was carefully edited for theological content, and it thus has reinforced the use of hymns that teach orthodox theology. All of the great distinctive doctrines of Christian faith, such as the Trinity, incarnation, and atonement, are clearly and forcefully presented. In the selection of hymns, it has enriched the available store of hymns of praise. Two hymns of this type, "To God Be the Glory" and "God of Grace and God of Glory," have gained wide use following their appearance in *Baptist Hymnal.* Perhaps a trend toward hymns of this kind is also evident in the fact that the only other hymn to become widely popular in this period, "How Great Thou Art," is also a hymn of praise.

While hymns for congregational use, therefore, are showing little change, another major change in church music deserves attention. In 1967, *Good News,* a Christian folk musical for young people, was published. It gained wide popularity almost immediately and was followed in short order by several other works of similar style and content. The music is lively, reflecting the rhythmic, melodic, and harmonic characteristics of recent popular music. The texts emphasize Christian decision and service in daily life. These texts go beyond most conventional hymns in calling for Christians to live out the doctrines they profess. It is now too early to say whether or not this new form will make a lasting impact on Christian hymnody. It points, however, to the possibility of a new hymnic style that will express current emphases and needs in Christian faith and life. JOSEPH F. GREEN

I

IDAHO, BAPTISTS IN. See UTAH-IDAHO SOUTHERN BAPTIST CONVENTION.

IGLESIAS, ALCIBIADES (LONNIE) (b. Nargana, San Blas, Panama, Sept. 4, 1904; d. Colon, Panama, Sept. 14, 1964). Translator and missionary. Converted as a young boy, he studied in Panama, Venezuela, and the United States. Iglesias returned to San Blas Islands as an independent missionary, with his bride, Marvel Ilya of Detroit, Mich. Beginning a school on Ailigandi in 1933, he reduced the Cuna language to writing and began translating the Scriptures. When the Home Mission Board assumed support in 1955, this work served five islands with three schools and a paid staff of 18. Under Iglesias' leadership Baptist churches, schools, and a medical clinic were established on the islands. At his death, most of the New Testament had been translated into the Cuna language. LOYD CORDER

IHLEY, HERMAN (b. Furman, S. C., June 29, 1914; d. Hampton, Ga., Apr. 15, 1970). Preacher and denominational worker. The son of Sidney Albert and Sarah Mixon Ihley, he was converted at age nine and baptized into Calvary Baptist Church, Savannah, Ga., and was ordained by that church in 1935. Graduated from high school in Savannah, he attended Mercer University, 1932–36, active in deputation service preaching and in teaching clinics. He married Bernice Juhan, Aug. 24, 1937, at First Baptist Church, Adel, Ga. He received Th.M. degree (1939) and Th.D. (1942) from Southern Baptist Theological Seminary, Louisville, Ky. During seminary training, he was pastor of Mt. Horeb Baptist Church near Orleans, Ind., and Hopewell Baptist Church in Henry County, Ky. His ministry included the following Baptist pastorates: Central, Americus, Ga., 1942–43; and First, Elberton, Ga., 1943–56. He served in the Navy during World War II, 1943–46. In the National Guard during his college days, and again after Naval career until retirement, he then transferred to the Army Reserve, attaining rank of Lt. Colonel. He was state Sunday School Secretary, North Carolina Baptist State Convention, 1957–67, and secretary, Department of Interracial Cooperation, Kentucky Baptist Convention, Mar. 1, 1967, until death. He had an unusually creative ministry of "building bridges of understanding, love, and cooperation" between white and black Baptists, churches, and agencies. HAROLD GLEN SANDERS

ILLINOIS, BAPTIST FOUNDATION OF. The roots of the Baptist Foundation of Illinois go back to 1954 when $10,412 was made available from the William Huddleston estate. United Income Fund Certificates were purchased and an endowment committee was named to encourage other gifts and bequests and to manage funds that were given. The original gift was to provide dividend and capital gains income to be used as a higher education fund. The endowment committee promoted gift annuities for a brief time and eventually began to major on encouraging individuals to make their wills remembering the

Baptist cause in Illinois. When H. C. Croslin became secretary of the department of Stewardship and Promotion on Dec. 1, 1961, he was asked to give special attention to the promotion of wills. This promotion succeeded with hundreds of new wills being written, naming various Baptist causes as beneficiary.

By 1964, it became evident to the endowment committee that Illinois Baptists needed an expanded program of endowment and capital giving, and they proposed that a Baptist Foundation be established to receive and manage such funds. On Nov. 4, 1965, the Baptist Foundation of Illinois was formally established by the Illinois Baptist State Association, and the endowment committee became its first board of trustees. H. C. Croslin was named executive director. Assets and acquisitions continued to increase and totaled $86,963 on Sept. 30, 1969. Endowment funds produced $32,625 in interest, dividends, and capital gains which were distributed to various Baptist causes during the period 1954–69. H. C. CROSLIN

***ILLINOIS ASSOCIATIONS. New Associations.** ALTON INDUSTRIAL. Organized July, 1959, by 16 churches formerly affiliated with Madison County Association. Since Jan. 1, 1960, it has been served by a superintendent of missions. In 1969, 16 churches reported 6,016 members, 184 baptisms, $400,122 total receipts, $58,445 total mission gifts, $2,834,000 property value, and $864,086 church debt.

BLACKHAWK. Organized May, 1958, by five churches formerly affiliated with Great Lakes Association. In 1969, 12 churches reported 2,549 members, 179 baptisms, $269,554 total receipts, $32,337 mission gifts, and $1,213,700 property value.

CAPITAL CITY. Organized in 1955 by seven churches in Springfield and surrounding area. In 1969, 14 churches reported 2,637 members, 104 baptisms, $262,823 total receipts, $31,271 mission gifts, and $1,446,500 property value.

EAST CENTRAL. Formerly known as Illini Association, changed its name in 1955. In 1969, 21 churches reported 4,286 members, 233 baptisms, $377,598 total receipts, $48,973 mission gifts, and $1,775,500 property value.

FOX VALLEY. Organized Oct., 1959, by 11 churches which had been affiliated with Great Lakes Association. In 1969, 16 churches reported 3,103 members, 324 baptisms, $457,599 total receipts, $36,424 mission gifts, and $1,622,600 property value.

LAKE COUNTY. Organized Sept., 1959, by seven churches formerly part of Great Lakes Association. In 1969, 15 churches reported 2,986 members, 503 baptisms, $275,414 total receipts, $21,992 mission gifts, and $1,389,500 property value.

METROPOLITAN CHICAGO. Organized as Greater Chicago Association Sept., 1957, by 11 churches. Since Jan. 1, 1958, the association has employed a superintendent of city missions. Name was changed to Chicago Southern Association in 1958 and to Metropolitan Chicago Association in 1968. In 1969, 76 churches and 8 church-type chapels reported 12,076 members, 919 baptisms, $1,417,193 total receipts, $145,546 mission gifts, and $4,934,970 property value.

METROPOLITAN PEORIA. Organized as Mid-State Association, May, 1961, by six churches. The name was changed to Greater Peoria Association in 1962 and to Metropolitan Peoria Association in 1968. In 1969, 21 churches reported 3,961 members, 226 baptisms, $420,987 total receipts, $49,283 mission gifts, and $1,627,992 property value.

SINNISSIPPI. Organized 1960 by five churches formerly affiliated with Blackhawk and Fox Valley associations. In 1969, 15 churches reported 2,165 members, 97 baptisms, $183,121 total receipts, $14,664 mission gifts, and $1,070,000 property value.

THREE RIVERS. Organized Oct., 1959, by 12 churches in northeast Illinois. In 1969, 29 churches reported 5,123 members, 417 baptisms, $615,450 total receipts, $71,706 mission gifts, and $1,863,685 property value.

WISCONSIN-MINNESOTA. Organized Oct., 1956, at Kenosha, Wis., by seven churches. Illinois transferred sponsorship to the Baptist General Convention of Texas.

Changes in Associations. GREAT LAKES. Disbanded in 1959 with formation of Fox Valley, Lake County, and Three Rivers associations.

GREATER CHICAGO. Organized in Sept., 1957, by 11 churches. In 1958 changed its name to Chicago Southern Association, and in 1968 it became the Metropolitan Chicago Association.

ILLINI. In 1955 it changed its name to East Central Association.

MID-STATE. Organized in May, 1961, by six churches, the name was changed to Greater Peoria Association in 1962 and to Metropolitan Peoria Association in 1968.

WABASH VALLEY. Disbanded in 1967. Churches affiliated with Mt. Erie Association.

HAROLD E. CAMERON

***ILLINOIS BAPTIST, THE.** Until Jan. 1, 1968, the paper was distributed by individual subscriptions and the church budget plan, much like that of similar Baptist papers in other states. But starting on that date the Illinois Baptist State Association included the paper in the state Cooperative Program budget, with all members of Illinois churches eligible for subscriptions without further payment. This step more than doubled the circulation in one year.

In 1969 an office of communications was established to broaden the publicity, promotion, and public relations of Baptists in Illinois. The editor of *The Illinois Baptist,* Robert J. Hastings, was named first director of the office, and John M. Whitman was named associate editor, with responsibilities for public relations and publicity through secular media, such as daily and weekly newspapers, radio, and TV.

When the Illinois Baptist State Association adopted a new constitution in 1969, it again reaffirmed *The Illinois Baptist* as the official publication of the association, and requested all departments and agencies to utilize the paper for basic promotion.

L. H. Moore succeeded B. J. Murrie as editor in 1956. Moore resigned in 1966, and Robert J. Hastings became editor in 1967. Circulation increased from 14,200 in 1956 to 52,603 in 1969. The paper is published at Carbondale, Ill.

ROBERT J. HASTINGS

***ILLINOIS BAPTIST CHILDREN'S HOME.** An institution owned by the Illinois Baptist State Association and located near Carmi. A total of 839 children have lived in care of the home as of Feb., 1970, with 404 being cared for since 1955.

The home is licensed by the Department of Children and Family Services of the state of Illinois. Five cottages provide accommodations for 62 children. Buildings on campus include the renovated school for an administration building, staff apartments, and homes for the resident director and director of child care (superintendent). The land has increased from 450 acres in 1956 to 850 in 1970, and the estimated value of all property, including farm buildings, is above $750,000.

An enlarged social work staff enables the home to offer other than residential care. The home has a growing foster care program and is now (1970) engaged in some adoptive services. In 1969, 117 children were serviced, 29 lived in foster homes, and three adoptions were completed.

Superintendents of the home since 1955 are Wade B. East, 1951–59, S. Otho Williams, 1959–62, and Theron H. King, 1963– . The 1970 staff include superintendent, assistant to the superintendent, resident director, business manager, director of social services, secretary, food manager, houseparents, seamstress, farm manager, and assistant farm manager.

THERON H. KING

ILLINOIS BAPTIST HISTORICAL COMMITTEE. The committee (society) was constituted in 1922, to procure and preserve historical materials. Minutes of the state, district associations, local churches, and state paper are sources. Microfilm is used. The repository is Illinois Baptist State Association Historical Library, Baptist Headquarters, Springfield, Ill.

The history, *Southern Baptists in Illinois,* by Lamire H. Moore, was printed in 1957. The Oak Hill Baptist Church records, the last church home of John Mason Peck (*q.v.,* Vol. II), containing minutes recorded by Peck were duplicated for storage at the Illinois Baptist Historical Library, and Southern Baptist Theological Seminary.

A bronze plaque was placed at the First Baptist Church, Pinckneyville, where the Illinois state association was organized in 1907; another was placed at First Baptist Church, Elizabethtown, to commemorate the organization of Big Creek Church in 1806; and a large granite marker was placed at Grassy Creek Cemetery where Grassy Creek Church of 1800 stood, about five miles southeast of Carterville, Ill.

In 1967 the restoration of the New Design Baptist Church Cemetery (Monroe County) was started. The 2.69-acre tract is where the "Meeting House" of the New Design Church (of 1796) was built in 1832.

Baptist pioneers buried there include Daniel Hilton (1779–1840), pastor and founder of Fountain Creek Church in 1821; James Lemen, Sr. (*q.v.,* Vol. II) (1760–1823), soldier, preacher, and statesman; and descendants of these and other pioneers.

Ten rows containing 259 graves of named persons and 76 others unnamed are plotted by measurement with recorded information. Duplicate records are placed with Monroe County Clerk, Waterloo, Ill., Southern Baptist Theological Seminary, and Illinois Baptist State Association Historical Library. The Illinois Baptist State Association received title to the property, Sept. 8, 1969.

L. L. LEININGER

ILLINOIS BAPTIST RETREATS, ASSEMBLIES, AND CAMPSITES. Lake Sallateeska is 10 miles north of Pinckneyville. It has 80 acres, 24 cabins, a dining hall, tabernacle, and superintendent's home. In 1960 a long-range planning committee recommended that one state camp be developed to provide for both assembly and camp-type programs. Voting in 1964 to relocate the camp in an area accessible to the entire state, the state convention purchased 150 acres of land near Effingham. Many Illinois Baptists were dissatisfied with this location and did not desire a large assembly program. Department secretaries had also decided to use BSU centers in which to conduct leadership conferences. The convention voted to sell the Effingham site, purchase another site in the northern part of the state, and upgrade Sallateeska. In 1968 the convention purchased 430 acres of land near Streator. An investment of $80,000 of Church Bond Guaranty Funds was made in 200 acres of tillable land, and $55,000 was paid from the state camp fund for the remaining 230 acres. The 1968 convention also voted to sell Sallateeska and purchase a site near Salem. It was discovered later that the Salem site was not available. In Sept., 1969, the state camp committee was negotiating for the purchase of 80 acres adjacent to Sallateeska. This would provide for 160 acres at this site. The Streator and Sallateeska sites will provide for year-round camping and conference facilities. Funds for the development of the two sites were expected from the sale of other state properties.

ARCHIE E. BROWN

***ILLINOIS BAPTIST STATE ASSOCIATION.**

I. History. Southern Baptists in Illinois have experienced rapid growth since World War II, especially in the northern half of the state

Prior to that time, Southern Baptist work was centralized in southern Illinois (south of Springfield). Postwar population movements into the industrial cities of the north precipitated the need for Southern Baptist work in northern Illinois. The 1968 "Report of the Committee on Relocation of the Baptist State Offices" showed the spread of Southern Baptist churches over the state. In 1950 there were 568 churches south of Springfield and only 27 in that city and north, a ratio of 1 to 20 churches. In 1958 there were 757 churches in the state; 127 were located north of Springfield and 630 south, a ratio of about 1 to 5. In 1967 there were 885 churches; of these 242 were located in the northern section and 643 in the southern, a ratio of 3 to 8. In 1968 there were some 907 churches with a membership of 183,226.

Broadway Bond Plan.—In Apr., 1956, the Illinois Baptist State Association board of directors entered into contract with the Broadway Plan, Inc., Houston, Tex., to provide finances for new churches. The bond plan was underwritten by the state association. The plan provided for the issuing of bonds by local churches with the state setting the guidelines and Broadway Plan, Inc., preparing the bond issues. From 1956 to 1970, the plan made over $15,500,000 available to Illinois churches for buildings and grounds. Over 500 bond issues were completed for 266 churches. The success of the plan contributed to the growth of Baptists in Illinois during the past 20 years.

Indiana Convention.—In 1958 the Baptist churches of Indiana formed the State Convention of Baptists of Indiana. Several churches affiliated with the Illinois Baptist State Association and located in Indiana became a part of this new convention. E. Harmon Moore, associate executive secretary of Illinois state association, was called as executive secretary, assuming his duties in Jan., 1959.

Executive Secretary Resigns.—Noel M. Taylor resigned as executive secretary of the state association effective Oct. 31, 1965, and became executive vice-president of the Broadway Plan, Inc., of Houston, Tex. H. C. Croslin was elected interim executive secretary. On Jan. 16, 1967, James H. Smith, pastor of First Baptist Church of Fergeson, Mo., and a former assistant to the executive secretary of Missouri Baptist Convention, was called as executive secretary of Illinois Baptist State Association. He assumed his duties on Feb. 1, 1967.

Relocation of Offices.—In 1967 the state association voted to relocate the state headquarters building in a more central city. In Nov., 1968, the state convention approved the report of the relocation committee to move the offices to Springfield, Ill., and to build a new state headquarters building. On Nov. 19, 1969, ground was broken for this building. ARTHUR E. FARMER

Organizational Structure.—A committee for the study of the organizational structure and salary schedule for the state association was appointed in Feb., 1966, as a subcommittee of the executive committee of the board of directors. The committee was enlarged from 5 to 10 members in Nov., 1967, and made a committee of the board of directors.

Assistance of the Department of Business Research of Southern Illinois University was secured. Following the first phase of the study, it was apparent that assistance was needed on a continuing basis to help with drafting and implementing recommendations. John J. McCarty of Herrin was employed as professional consultant.

A study of the constitution of the state association revealed that the *assumed* organizational structure was quite different from the extant. Instead of one executive system, there were a multitude of executive systems, with each having its own executive or manager. The constitution provided for no organic relationship between departments of work and/or the prescribed duties of the executive secretary.

After the adoption of the new constitution in Oct., 1969, a three-day orientation was held in Springfield, Ill., in Nov., 1969, to explain to board members and staff the new organizational structure, to consider the adoption of a policy document and role specifications for committees of the board and staff employees. This document was adopted without amendments.

C. R. WALKER

I. *The New Constitution.*—The constitution of the state association is a document of fundamental principles by which Baptists secure guidance in accomplishing specifically stated objectives.

The orginal constitution for the state association grew out of a controversy in relationship to doctrine and polity of the Illinois Baptist State Convention. Therefore, the Illinois Baptist State Association was organized in the First Baptist Church, Pinckneyville, Ill., on Jan. 31, 1907. The association adopted the "New Hampshire Declaration of Faith" as its articles of faith, and in May, 1910, became aligned with the Southern Baptist Convention.

Radical renovation of the constitution was not initiated until C. R. Walker gave the report of the committee on restructure at the annual meeting, Oct. 31, 1968. This committee concluded that the board of directors of the state association should manage the work of the association in the interim of annual sessions. The board was asked to structure an executive system and deploy resources allocated toward its objectives.

The committee on restructure urged the 1968 annual meeting of the state association "to request its Constitution Committee to study the constitutional involvements and either draft a proposed new constitution or make recommended amendments to the present constitution in keeping with this committee's report and recommendations."

The president, W. T. Branon, called a special

"Constitutional Convention" for May 16–17, 1969, which received the constitutional committee's report. The new constitution was officially adopted on Oct. 28, 1969. Significant changes in the constitution were:

II. *Doctrine.*—The convention adopted as its expression of faith, "The Baptist Faith and Message" as adopted by the Southern Baptist Convention, May 9, 1963.

III. *Membership.*—The requirement for membership magnified the autonomy of each Baptist body.

Churches of the state association are no longer limited to a maximum number of messengers. Each cooperating church is granted two messengers for the first 100 resident members or fractional part thereof and one additional messenger for each additional 100 resident members.

Parliamentary ruling is to be governed by *Roberts' Revised Rules of Order* rather than *Kerfoot's Parliamentary Law.*

IV. *Officers.*—The basic change in the officers was in the name or title of the clerk and assistant clerk to read: recording secretary and assistant recording secretary. Officers shall not serve more than two consecutive years.

V. *Board, Committees, and Corporation.*—Article VII was almost completely changed to comply with the resultant study of the committee on organizational structure's recommendations. The primary criteria for selection of members of the board of directors is: a person's ability to make maximum contribution to the objectives of the association; equitable representation; a minimum of one-third and a maximum of one-half of the board members shall be lay persons; nominations were made to specific committees of the board; and absenteeism from two consecutive board meetings automatically eliminates membership.

The board is divided into four equal committees and each is responsible for establishing objectives: church extension, church development, special ministries, and administrative. The board employs one executive system to do the assigned work of the association and establish policy limits and provide resources within which the executive system functions.

The board develops and maintains a policy document, including structure, employment and dismissal procedures, general responsibilities, prescribed and discretionary role content for all committees of the association, committees of the board, and all managerial and supervisory personnel within the executive system.

DON E. DILLOW

II. **Program of Work.** *Sunday School.*—A Sunday School Department is operated as a part of the state association's program of assistance to churches. In addition to the Sunday School program this department was charged with responsibility for Vacation Bible School, weekday Bible Study, church kindergarten, and church building consultation.

In 1955 the total Sunday School enrolment for the state was 113,616. Final tabulation of statistics taken from church letters in 1969 showed an enrolment of 139,014. A more careful evaluation of these statistics shows that much of the growth can be attributed to new work. During the same period Sunday School enrolment in the more established areas actually showed a decline.

Vacation Bible Schools increased from 526 in 1955 to 635 in 1969. Enrolment for this period grew from 42,782 to 70,549. Interest in continuing weekday programs is growing. A few churches established weekday nursery and church kindergarten programs.

During this period several changes were made in personnel. Wheeler L. Thompson retired in Sept., 1964. Ernest R. Adams succeeded Thompson and served until Sept. 1, 1968. During these years the work load of the department increased and the position of associate Sunday School secretary was added in July, 1966. In 1970 the department was under the leadership of John W. Perkins, Jr., director, and Donald E. Herman, associate. JOHN W. PERKINS, JR.

Missions.—In 1970 the state mission program included two city mission programs; a rural-urban program; two area mission programs, one of which is language culture; a Baptist center program in East St. Louis; and pastoral missionary programs in Macomb and Rock Island.

In 1969 there were 30 superintendents serving 34 associations. Thirteen associations received financial assistance toward the support of their missionaries. Pastoral aid and rental assistance were available to assist new work. In 1959 the Home Mission Board, SBC, entered into a cooperative agreement with the state missions department to supply funds on a percentage basis with Illinois.

From 1954 to 1970, 354 new churches were constituted. Several of these were language culture congregations.

During 1968 a statewide radio program known as Tuesday Night Bible Study was initiated with James H. Smith, executive secretary of the state association, serving as Bible teacher.

HAROLD E. CAMERON

Brotherhood and Annuity.—In 1955 the Woman's Missionary Union relinquished sponsorship of Royal Ambassadors to the Brotherhood Department. This was done in keeping with similar action taken by the SBC.

In 1956 George E. Wheeler, state Brotherhood secretary, and six other laymen from Illinois, completed a mission tour of Mexico. The tour was under the direction of the Brotherhood Commission, SBC. The same year 60 men from Illinois attended the National Conference of Southern Baptist Men in Oklahoma City, Okla.

The 1958 state Brotherhood Convention was attended by 1,003 men, the highest in the convention's history. The same year 220 boys from Illinois attended the Convention-wide Royal Ambassador Congress in Fort Worth, Tex.

In 1960 leadership in the departments of Brotherhood and stewardship teamed up to promote the Annuity Board program. Meetings to present the program were held in each of the 35 associations in the state. A total of more than 1,500 laymen attended the meetings. As a result, more than 100 pastors and churches were enlisted in the program. On Jan. 1, 1961, the Brotherhood Department assumed responsibility for promoting the Annuity program. On that date 35 per cent of Illinois pastors and churches were participating. By 1969, 58 per cent were participating.

In 1968 George Wheeler attended the Hemispheric-wide Evangelistic Congress in Brazil, held in connection with the Crusade of the Americas. This same year 43 laymen from central and southern Illinois made a "Look-See Trip" to metropolitan Chicago. The purpose was to enable the men to observe firsthand the great mission potential of the area. The record-breaking 1968 state mission offering reflected, in part, the result of the tour. In 1968 a Convention-wide Royal Ambassador Congress was held in Oklahoma City, Okla. A total of 320 Royal Ambassadors and their counselors attended.

In lieu of a state Brotherhood convention in 1969 the Brotherhood and evangelism departments jointly sponsored and promoted six regional evangelism conferences to promote the Crusade of the Americas. More than 3,600 persons attended the six conferences.

GEORGE E. WHEELER

Stewardship Department.—Stewardship and missions were jointly promoted from 1952 through 1956, preceding the establishment of a stewardship department. On Jan. 21, 1957, the board of directors established the Department of Stewardship and Promotion, and A. C. Queen was named secretary. This department was charged with the following responsibilities: the initiation of the Forward Program of Church Finance of Southern Baptists; the encouraging of the making of wills in which the Illinois Baptist State Association is remembered; and the promotion of contracts by churches and pastors with the Relief and Annuity Board. Promotion of the Cooperative Program became a responsibility of this department in 1958.

On Aug. 10, 1961, Queen became the secretary of the newly created Department of Higher Education, and on Nov. 1, 1961, H. C. Croslin was named secretary of the department. The responsibility for promotion of the Annuity Board's programs was transferred to the Brotherhood Department on Jan. 1, 1962, and additional emphasis was placed on the area of wills procurement. In 1968 the name of the department was changed to Stewardship Department.

H. C. CROSLIN

Evangelism.—The Evangelism Department was given effective leadership by James Baldwin, until his resignation in 1959. In 1960 H. Lee Swope was elected to serve as secretary of evangelism and to guide Illinois Baptists to increase their evangelistic opportunities in the metropolitan north. Of special significance was the preparation and promotion of the Lake Michigan "Operation Penetration" that joined Illinois with the states bordering Lake Michigan in a great evangelistic crusade during the late sixties.

In the fall of 1967 James A. Ponder was elected secretary. The Department of Evangelism planned and coordinated the promotion of the Baptist Crusade of the Americas in Illinois, 1968–69, served as coordinating liaison between nine major Baptist conventions located within the state that were cooperating in the Crusade of the Americas. JAMES A. PONDER

Church Training.—Illinois Baptist churches enrolled 31,405 in Training Union during 1954–55. In 1955 all 27 associations conducted "M" Night with a total attendance of 7,352. Primary attention was given to increasing numerical records. Very little was done to increase effectiveness of the curriculum or to improving the style and effectiveness of the programing. The state Training Union Convention registered 611 in 1955, 583 in 1956, and 900 in 1957. Four district conventions were conducted in 1958, with 927 in attendance. In 1959 only 628 were in attendance. Conventions were becoming less effective in reaching large numbers of people. There has not been a Training Union Convention since 1963, when the attendance was 375.

In 1963 the department launched an effort to share the "study programs" assigned to Training Union: interpreting systematic theology, Christian ethics, Christian history, and church polity and organization. Interpretation clinics were held over the state, which were attended by 1,793 persons in 1965.

The largest number of churches having Training Union in a single year was 616 churches in 1962. A peak enrolment of 44,000 was reached that same year. Since 1962 there has been a small but consistent decline both in ongoing training enrolment and in number of churches with Training Unions. In 1968 a total of 48,000 persons were registered in Training Union. This number included both ongoing and short-term courses. BLUFORD M. SLOAN

Church Music—In 1955 First Baptist Church, Eldorado, became the first Illinois church to attain the Standard of Excellence for church music, followed in 1956 by First Baptist, Energy. State choir and hymn-playing festivals were initiated in 1956, with one at DuQuoin and the other at Decatur. Approved music workers were first used in 1956.

In 1957 Earl Wayne Morris became state music secretary. From 1961 to 1964 Bluford Sloan was interim music secretary. LeRoy McClard was secretary, 1964–65. In June, 1967, Rod Latta became music secretary.

In 1963 a training conference for associational music officers was held, and 651 churches reported an elected music director. The task of the music program is to teach music; train people to lead, sing, and play music; provide music in the church and community; and provide and interpret information regarding the work of the church and denomination. Various means are used to implement these goals. ROD LATTA

ILLINOIS STATISTICAL SUMMARY

Year	Associations	Churches	Church Membership	Baptisms	S. S. Enrolment	V.B.S. Enrolment	T. U. Enrolment	W.M.U. Enrolment	Brotherhood Enrolment	Music Enrolment	Mission Gifts	Total Gifts
1955	29	716	131,114	8,531	113,516	42,782	31,405	16,784	6,078		$ 830,042	$ 5,089,153
1956	30	756	136,259	7,420	119,019	45,623	34,051	18,446	6,364		928,984	5,712,950
1957	32	822	143,321	7,932	123,767	47,507	36,551	20,064	5,447		1,063,619	6,285,682
1958	30	856	150,798	8,589	130,048	50,853	40,130	21,916	6,347		1,117,117	6,739,261
1959	33	785	147,615	7,882	123,905	46,886	38,857	21,506	9,412		1,100,780	6,770,393
1960	34	815	152,047	7,339	124,497	50,232	40,665	22,065	9,158		1,134,440	7,228,678
1961	35	840	156,509	7,352	128,640	50,147	42,683	22,729	9,500		1,148,939	7,573,373
1962	35	862	161,622	8,082	135,391	54,327	44,228	23,550	10,101		1,579,450	8,086,519
1963	35	880	165,333	7,188	134,702	54,096	45,005	23,959	10,471		1,300,370	8,626,872
1964	35	905	170,386	8,193	135,762	55,574	44,191	23,965	10,137		1,407,252	8,990,998
1965	35	913	172,962	6,926	136,464	64,946	42,306	23,468	7,558	10,661	1,511,281	9,761,393
1966	35	897	174,919	7,109	136,440	60,099	42,470	22,807	7,896	10,346	1,649,212	10,949,701
1967	34	903	178,792	6,884	136,997	66,323	42,294	23,761	7,303	12,495	1,771,554	12,521,327
1968	34	907	183,226	7,334	133,449	64,764	45,555	23,288	7,644	12,731	1,942,492	13,032,598

ARTHUR E. FARMER

ILLINOIS BAPTIST STUDENT CENTER, CARBONDALE. The center began in Dec., 1938, as an educational venture adjacent to the campus of Southern Illinois University. Its courses in Bible, Greek, religious education, and music were of college calibre, some of which the university accepted for credit toward a liberal arts degree.

Originally called the Baptist Foundation, the name was changed in 1955 to Southern Illinois College of the Bible. In 1966 the name was again changed to its present designation: Baptist Student Center. In 1966 property consisting of a men's dormitory, a women's dormitory, administration building, and chapel was sold to the university and construction began on new facilities. Completed at a cost of $1,134,000, the new complex was occupied in the fall of 1967.

The facility accommodates 296 students, with dormitories for men and women, cafeteria, classroom space, library, and recreational area.

In 1967 the university authorized its own department of religion, at which time credit for study at the Baptist Student Center was suspended. Courses now offered are extracurricular in nature and are mainly survey courses in Bible and church history.

A staff of two resident counselors and eight resident fellows seeks to maintain a Christian influence in the living areas. A center director, Bible instructor, Christian activities counselor, and music director combine to offer a varied program of Christian activities for interested college students.

The center is owned and operated by the Illinois Baptist State Association.

ROBERT C. FUSON

ILLINOIS BAPTIST STUDENT CENTER, CHAMPAIGN. In 1955 plans for a new student center in Champaign, Ill., were begun. A dormitory for men, cafeteria, classrooms, chapel, and necessary space for work with students was provided. On Aug. 9, 1960, ground was broken and construction of the building begun.

On Sept. 1, 1959, Gilbert B. Waud became the first full-time teacher of the religion courses accredited by the University of Illinois. During the previous eight years the courses had been taught by V. W. Entrekin, state BSU secretary, and local pastors. When the building was completed in Nov., 1961, Waud was also made center director. Miss Lucile Peak served as BSU campus director until June, 1963. Waud assumed the added responsibility of the student work until Dec., 1964, when Larry Allison became BSU campus director, serving until Aug., 1966. In Aug., 1964, George Baker became business manager and dormitory director, remaining until June, 1966.

The University of Illinois faculty began a movement in 1963 to provide religious instruction in the University curriculum, which reduced the enrolment in courses taught at the center. During the spring semester of 1966 it was decided to discontinue a full-time teaching program because the enrolment had decreased from an average of 20 each semester to five. Waud remained as part-time teacher and center director until Maurice Willis succeeded him in Mar., 1967.

The board of directors of the Illinois Baptist State Association voted in Apr., 1968, to close the dormitory, discontinue cafeteria operation, and to sell the student center property, and, when sold, to provide only for work with students. The student work would continue in the present building until the sale was consummated. Miss Eleanor Harper became BSU campus director in Aug., 1969. GILBERT B. WAUD

ILLINOIS BAPTIST STUDENT MINISTRIES. V. W. Entrekin continued to serve as Illinois Baptist student union secretary (since 1949), and as BSU secretary at the University of Illinois. In 1955 BSU work was reported at Southern Illinois University (SIU), University of Illinois, and Wheaton College.

During 1957 Eugene Maston, a graduate student at the University of Chicago, began working with students in the Chicago area. Work was also established at Northwestern University. BSU work was reported on the following campuses in 1961: Chicago area, Eastern Illinois University, Illinois State University, Mt. Vernon Junior College, Northern Illinois University, Northwestern University, Southeastern Illinois College, SIU Alton, SIU Carbondale, SIU East St. Louis, and University of Illinois.

Edwardsville churches contributed $8,026 in 1961–62 for a Baptist Student Center near the site of the proposed SIU campus. Over 800 attended the annual BSU Convention in 1961.

On July 17, 1962, the board of directors of the state association voted to discontinue the departments of higher education and Baptist Student Union, and that their programs be combined in one Department of Student Ministries, with A. C. Queen as secretary and V. W. Entrekin as associate secretary. Lee Swope, state secretary of evangelism, became student ministries secretary in 1967. During 1969 Bob Blattner was elected as BSU secretary for Illinois.

The BSU continues to encourage students in responsible churchmanship. Baptist students are currently engaged in a variety of activities on eight campuses. These include chapel services, Bible and discussion groups, campus evangelistic efforts, choral and drama groups, international teas and banquets, student summer missions, and missions to rest homes and prisons.

The following individuals were employed as campus BSU directors: Lucille Steele, Southern Illinois University, 1955–64; Nell Magee, University of Illinois, 1957–60; Lucile Peak, University of Illinois, 1961–63; Larry Allison, University of Illinois 1963–66; Charles Gray, Southern Illinois University, 1963–66; Maurice Willis, University of Illinois, 1967–68; Bob Blattner, Southern Illinois University, 1967–69; and Eleanor Harper, University of Illinois, 1969– . BOB BLATTNER

INDIA, COUNCIL OF BAPTIST CHURCHES IN NORTH EAST (cf. Assam and Manipur, Council of Baptist Churches of, Vol. I). The Council of Baptist Churches in North East India (CBCNEI), formerly the Council of Baptist Churches in Assam and Manipur, is the result of the American Baptist Mission in Assam which began in 1836. Some 276 missionaries have served a total of 4,493 years in this area. Although the number of missionaries has been decreasing, Indian leadership is assuming responsibility effectively. A recent tragedy was the assassination of Edward Singha, former head of the council since 1956, the first Indian minister to hold the post.

There has been steady growth in the membership of the churches of North East India. The centennial of the beginning of work in the Garo Hills and the establishment of the first church was celebrated in 1967. There are now Christians in 1,000 villages with 46,000 members in the Garo churches, in a total population of 300,000.

There are three schools of high quality operated by Baptists. Many communities wish to have Christian schools for general education. The council has a policy of providing financial aid for establishing a school if the community bears operating costs. Eastern Theological College reports its highest enrolment in history. Progress of the medical program has been slower because of insufficient funds to raise the six hospitals to desired standards. Relief work continues to be an important focus.

Statistics (1969): Missionaries, 21; national workers, 1,830; organized churches, 2,981; baptisms, 10,999; church members, 197,881; seminaries and Bible schools, 12; students, 350; schools and colleges, 166; students, 12,781; hospitals and dispensaries, 13; patients, 43,362.

JAMES D. MOSTELLER

INDIA, MISSION IN. American (Northern) Baptists preceded Southern Baptists in mission work in India, serving in the north. Several Southern Baptists served under the other board before the Foreign Mission Board, SBC, was able to secure entrance for missionaries.

The first missionaries appointed to India by Southern Baptists were Jasper and Dorothy (Binford) McPhail. Arriving in 1962, they served at the Vellore Christian Medical College and Hospital, interdenominational teaching center. An Indian pastor, Mollela Joshua, joined the missionaries in 1966 to lead in evangelistic work. Five churches were organized and several other preaching centers formed within three years. Lay preachers have carried the load. Three Indian students are in seminary training. Hinduism is the predominant religion.

Ralph and Lizette (McCall) Bethea, John and Barbara (Biggers) Wikman, and Richard and Frances (Syfrett) Hellinger conduct mobile medical clinics while hospital buildings are under construction in Bangalore, in central South India. A Bible correspondence course, literacy classes, poultry and gardening projects, and sewing classes were a part of the work in late 1969. RALPH C. BETHEA

INDIANA, STATE CONVENTION OF BAPTISTS IN.

I. Southern Baptist Beginnings. Southern Baptist work began in Indiana from the influence of the neighboring conventions in Illinois and Kentucky. Most of the early Southern Baptist churches were originally composed of Southern Baptists who had moved into Indiana. When the Second Baptist Church of Hymera was constituted in 1914 and affiliated with the Palestine Association of the Illinois Baptist State Association it became the first Southern Baptist church in Indiana. In the intervening years before the convention was established, Southern Baptists, independently of one another, began Southern Baptist work in at least four different sections of the state.

In the area of Evansville, Ind., in 1920, the Rosedale Baptist Church (later Walnut Street, now First Southern, Evansville) was established and joined itself to the Fairfield Association in Illinois, transferring in 1928 to the Ohio Valley Association affiliated with the General Association of Baptists in Kentucky. Within a year another established church in the Evansville area, Calvary Baptist Church, withdrew from the Northern Baptist Convention and affiliated with the Southern Baptist Convention through the Fairfield Association of Illinois, also later transferring to the Ohio Valley Association of Kentucky. There were other older Baptist churches in this area which were aligned with different Baptist bodies and did not affiliate with the SBC until much later. In 1948 the Indiana churches of the Ohio Valley Association along with some churches in Kentucky established the West Kentuckiana Baptist Association and affiliated with the General Association of Baptists in Kentucky.

The second area of Southern Baptist work was in the southeastern segment of the state. A number of Kentucky Baptists who had moved into the area near Brookville and Metamora, Ind., in the late twenties and early thirties established Old Liberty Baptist Church near Brookville in 1931. These small churches joined the Laurel River Baptist Association in Kentucky in 1934 contributing regularly to that body until 1939. The Old Liberty Church was disbanded but several other churches, like the McKindrie Baptist Church (now First Baptist Church of Blooming Grove) and Smyrna, New Trenton, in this same area assisted with the establishment of the Whitewater Association of Kentucky for churches in both Ohio and Eastern Indiana. The missionary of this association was V. B. Castleberry who served until 1951 when most of the Indiana churches in the Whitewater Association decided to establish a separate association. This new association, called the Indiana Association of Missionary Baptists, sought affiliation with Kentucky Baptists but its request was refused when the general association in Kentucky decided that only individual churches outside Kentucky could be admitted but that associational boundaries would remain in Kentucky. The Indiana Association of Missionary Baptists maintained an independent existence until 1954 when it affiliated with the Illinois Baptist State Association. During this interval a newspaper, the *Indiana Southern Baptist Herald,* was published.

The third area of nascence occurred in 1934 in the northwestern corner of Indiana when a few Southern Baptists established a church in East Chicago, Ind. The church outgrew its rented quarters and a new building was built in Hammond known as the First Southern Baptist Church of Hammond. This church sought fellowship with the Macoupin Association of Illinois. In 1943 this church and five other Southern Baptist churches in the Chicago area organized the Great Lakes Baptist Association, but in 1955 the Southern Baptist churches in northern Indiana formed the Lake Michigan Baptist Association affiliated with the Illinois Baptist State Association.

The fourth area of growth in Indiana was in the southern portion of the state across the Ohio River from Louisville, Ky. The First Southern Baptist Church of Clarksville was established in 1948 joining the Long Run Association of Kentucky.

II. Organization of State Convention. Each of the separate areas was apparently oblivious of the others as no real effort was made to correlate the work until the Illinois Baptist State Association set aside money in 1954 to employ a pioneer missionary in Indiana. Some of the churches, largely those affiliated with Kentucky, were not initially interested in this overture, although shortly afterward they joined in with enthusiasm. Between 1953 and 1958 great strides were made by Southern Baptists in Indiana. The first work was established in Indianapolis, several new associations were formed, but most significantly plans were laid for statewide work.

In early 1955 a meeting sponsored by the Home Mission Board, SBC, was held in Evansville to correlate the different branches of Southern Baptist work in Indiana. As a direct result plans were laid for a fellowship meeting of all Southern Baptists in Indiana in September under the direction of Eldred M. Taylor, secretary of missions of Kentucky Baptists and E. Harmon Moore, secretary of stewardship and missions of the Illinois Baptist State Association. The first fellowship meeting was held Sept. 29 and 30, 1955, at the First Southern Baptist Church, Indianapolis, then renting a building at the corner of New York and New Jersey streets in downtown Indianapolis. The purpose of the meeting was solely for fellowship and inspiration and "all members from a Baptist church in good standing were considered messengers." A total of 98 people registered for the meeting, officers were elected, and plans were made for the following year.

ILLINOIS BAPTIST STATE ASSOCIATION (*q.v.*). This $1.5 million building houses offices of the association, plus rental suites. State headquarters moved to Springfield from Carbondale in 1971.

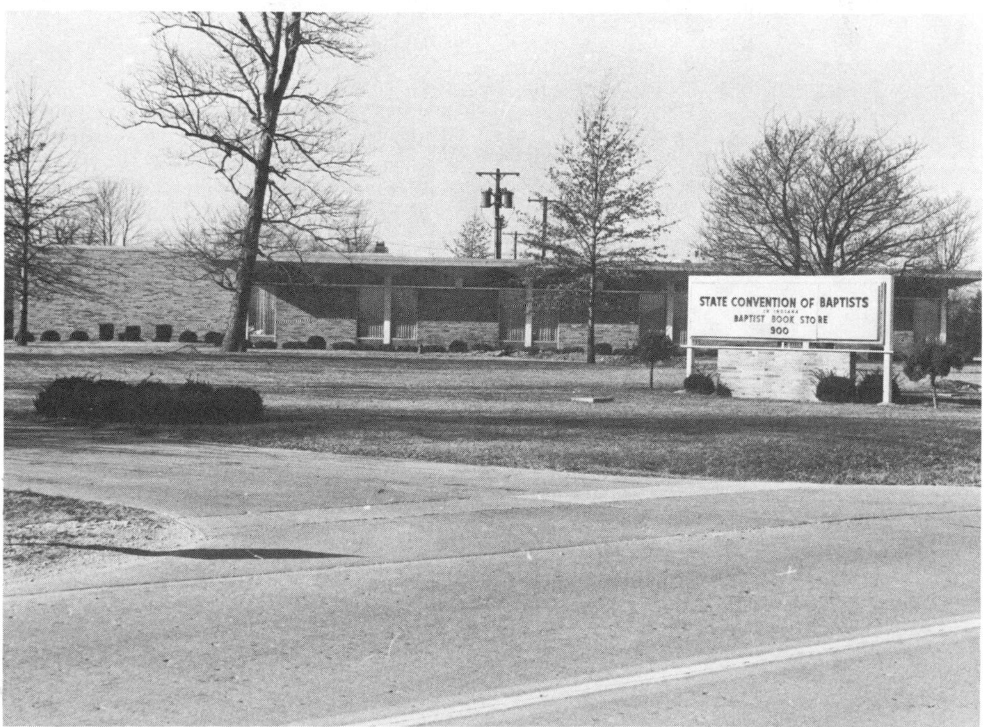

INDIANA BAPTIST STATE CONVENTION (*q.v.*). State headquarters. Located on Interstate 465 in west Indianapolis. Cost $251,000. Occupied February 3, 1964.

MISSISSIPPI BAPTIST HOSPITAL (*q.v.*), Jackson, Miss. Architect's drawing of the $25,000,000 structure which will contain 600 beds. To be completed in 1974.

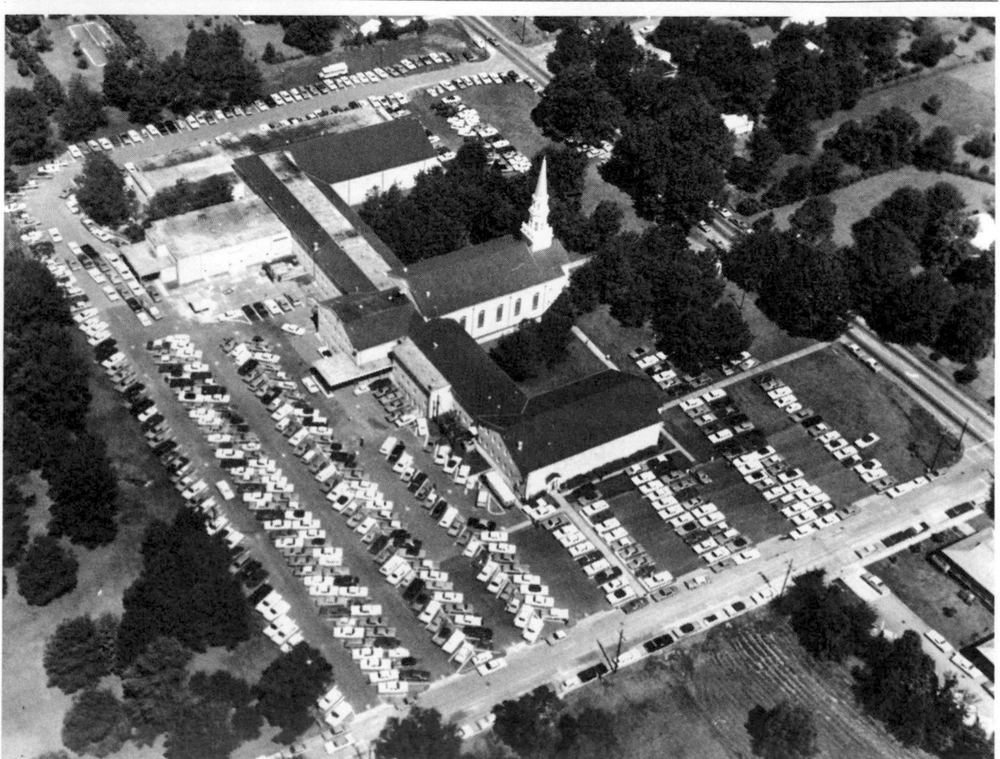

BROADMOOR BAPTIST CHURCH, Jackson, Miss. An aerial view shows the spacious educational plant.

Prior to a statewide simultaneous revival, a second fellowship meeting was held in the new First Southern Baptist Church in Indianapolis, Sept. 28 and 29, 1956. It was at this meeting that definite plans for a state convention were formulated. Each church was requested to send three to five messengers to the fellowship meeting in 1957 to look toward the organization of a convention in 1958.

The third meeting convened in the First Southern Baptist Church, Indianapolis, in late Sept., 1957. Special committees were appointed to prepare a program, prepare a budget, and suggest a constitution and bylaws for a new convention, while the participating churches were requested to send three to five messengers each on Oct. 3 and 4, 1958, to form a new state convention in Indiana for Southern Baptists.

The State Convention of Baptists in Indiana, which organized on Oct. 3, 1958, had 384 messengers present representing 99 churches in Indiana, although there were actually 111 churches cooperating with the convention. The officers elected by the first convention were Stephen H. Cobb, president; W. R. Davis, vice-president; O. R. Gregg, recording secretary; and V. B. Castleberry, historical secretary. An executive board of 24 members met during the first day of the convention to prepare a budget and organize other business activities. With W. W. Rhody as chairman, the executive board proposed a budget of $100,750 to be adopted for the year 1959. On Dec. 5, 1958, the board elected E. Harmon Moore, associate executive secretary of the Illinois Baptist State Association for an indefinite term as the executive secretary-treasurer of the State Convention of Baptists in Indiana as well as secretary of evangelism.

Moore began his work on Jan. 1, 1959, establishing the convention offices in Plainfield, Ind. The business of the convention under the direction of Moore was carefully planned. The state conventions in Illinois and Kentucky had agreed after the 1957 regional fellowship meeting to retain 10 per cent of the Cooperative Program receipts in a special account to be turned over to the new Indiana convention when it was established. This procedure enabled the new convention to receive $3,806.22 from Illinois and $3,364.84 from Kentucky.

The new executive board selected the following personnel to serve the convention during its first year: W. W. Rhody, pastor of Fairview Baptist Church, Richmond, Ind., became religious education secretary, Apr. 1, 1959; George M. Slayton, pastor of the University Baptist Church, Carbondale, Ill., secretary of missions, church finance, and Brotherhood, June 1, 1959; and Louise Berge, Knoxville, Tenn., WMU secretary, Aug. 5, 1959. The board also selected area missionaries Leonard Whitlock, C. E. Wiley, H. J. Conger, L. L. Daye, and, for three months, Charles Everitt to serve in different areas of the state.

The most significant enterprise undertaken by the convention in 1959 was the establishment of the *Indiana Baptist* in July to be published monthly. The executive secretary, E. Harmon Moore, served as editor.

The executive board of the convention carefully set forth the requirements for each of its employees. It also clearly enunciated the relationship between the missionaries and mission churches with the convention.

After the first year of operation the convention reported 124 cooperating churches with 23,365 members. In the convention area there were six associations: Eastern Indiana, Lake Michigan (the northwestern section of Indiana), Northern Indiana, Southeastern, Southwestern, and West Central.

III. Program of Work. *Departments.*—In its first year the convention established four major departments of work: evangelism; missions, church finance, and brotherhood; religious education; and Woman's Missionary Union. The work of these departments grew steadily and was reorganized as the needs of the convention changed. The departments and secretaries are as follows: evangelism, E. Harmon Moore, 1959–65; evangelism and brotherhood, William H. Slagle, 1965–67, L. E. Lawson, 1968; missions, church finance, and brotherhood, George M. Slayton, 1959–61, F. J. Redford, 1962–67; missions and church finance, James H. Currin, 1967–69, R. V. Haygood, 1969– ; religious education, W. W. Rhody, 1959–63; Sunday School and church music, James H. Currin, 1963–64; Sunday School and church building, James H. Currin, 1964–67, Lew Reynolds, 1967– ; Training Union, student work, church building, W. W. Rhody, 1963–64; Training Union, student work, church music, Robert Wayne, 1964–69, Eldon Boone, 1969–70; WMU, Louis Berge, 1959–65, Mrs. Otha Winningham, 1966, Martha Fellows, 1967, Margaret Gillaspie, 1968– ; editor, E. Harmon Moore, 1959–65, Alvin C. Shackleford, 1965–

Growth and Significant Enterprises.—The convention office was first established in the Plainfield Southern Baptist Church but soon moved to a large separate building in Plainfield. A committee of the executive board, appointed in 1960 to secure a suitable permanent office site, investigated several locations and made offers to purchase. At least three offers were rejected due in part to price and, in one instance, because the convention refused to pledge in writing to remain silent regarding future alcoholic beverage license in the area of the property. In Aug., 1962, the convention purchased a 3.67 acre plot at 10th Street and Interstate Highway 465 in Indianapolis and by Jan. 1, 1964, had moved into the new building. The total cost of the site, building, and equipment was $268,271.07. The Baptist Sunday School Board, SBC, paid $65,000 in advance rent which assisted materially with the building for a portion of the office space in order to establish a Baptist Book Store in Indianapolis.

The convention, believing that its first responsibility was to build strong self-supporting churches, established very few institutions. Baptist Student Union Centers were started in 1960 at Indiana and Purdue Universities. By 1969 there were Baptist Student Union Centers on seven campuses in Indiana.

The program of church missions was fostered with vigor largely through the following area missionaries. In 1959 they were: Northeast, H. J. Conger; East Central, L. L. Daye; Northwest, Leonard Whitlock; and Southwest, C. E. Wiley. This group increased steadily through the years until by 1969 the state was divided into nine areas with nine area missionaries: Central Area, Charles E. Smith; East Central Area, Thomas Sykes; Northeast Area, Lowell Wright; Northwest Area, Lyndon W. Collings; Southeast Area, Presley Morris; Southwest Area, C. E. Wiley; Wabash Valley Area, Jess Dittmar; West Central Area, Gene Lake; and White River Area, Virgil Clark.

The convention established a regular system of financial loan support for new churches and missions. The Broadway Bond Plan was used, but the convention was always careful to be sure it did not become overextended financially. At the first annual convention it was decided to establish a Long Range Planning Program Committee to study and meet the needs for 25 years. While the convention always acted in faith, the leadership wisely directed the work toward realistic goals.

The first WMU Convention was organized, Apr. 9–10, 1959, at Washington Avenue Baptist Church, Evansville, with 2,995 members in 77 organizations. Mrs. T. B. Rollins of Gary was elected as the first president. In 1960 the WMU began a small promotional quarterly entitled *Hoosier Helper*.

In 1960 the convention also launched its first camping program at a rented site. In 1966 a permanent camp was secured in Morgan County near Monrovia, Ind. Additional land was obtained in 1967, bringing the total area of the property to 342 acres.

The first Evangelistic Conference, Training Union Convention, and BSU Convention were held during the first year of the convention's life.

Consideration was given to providing a regular child care program within the convention, but although funds were given for this purpose it was decided that a formal institution should not be undertaken until the convention was larger.

By 1962 the convention reached a membership of 25,000 which entitled it to be recognized by the SBC with representation on SBC agencies. The growth of Indiana Southern Baptists was evidenced by the rise in the number of new churches and missions as well as by the increasing frequency of publication of the *Indiana Baptist* from monthly to semimonthly in 1964 and to weekly in 1966. The number of associations increased from 6 in 1959 to 14 in 1969.

The year 1964 marked several important milestones. A Baptist Book Store was opened, a new

INDIANA STATISTICAL SUMMARY

Year	Associations	Churches	Church Membership	Baptisms	S. S. Enrolment	V.B.S. Enrolment	T. U. Enrolment	W.M.U. Enrolment	Brotherhood Enrolment	Music Enrolment	Mission Gifts	Total Gifts	Value Church Property
1958	6	111	20,119	1875	22,546	9,000		2829	1023			$1,070,744	$ 4,241,656
1959	6	118	22,533	2066	25,226	10,000	8,299	3352	1280	1,142	$132,046	1,250,467	4,963,823
1960	6	129	25,189	2240	27,334	12,000	9,858	4291	1526	1,243	157,089	1,416,348	5,612,394
1961	6	144	28,712	2325	30,635	14,000	11,504	5214	1716	1,489	173,318	1,631,435	7,508,877
1962	7	165	30,654	2370	32,642	13,000	12,569	5440	1768	1,895	203,125	1,897,023	8,182,880
1963	9	181	33,474	2235	34,008	15,000	12,366	5905	1555	2,379	233,715	1,950,947	8,942,579
1964	11	189	36,561	2812	36,361	18,000	13,687	6331	1645	2,758	267,874	2,271,578	10,128,564
1965	11	198	40,311	3002	40,563	19,376	13,853	6794	1596	2,680	298,766	2,863,146	11,062,343
1966	11	208	44,419	3256	43,138	22,438	14,043	7031	1726	2,861	342,237	2,975,596	12,322,851
1967	11	211	46,892	3491	44,892	23,445	14,118	6860	1399	3,658	376,671	3,251,165	13,912,951
1968	13	223	49,394	3051	44,597	22,349	15,753	6718	1178	4,012	404,887	3,886,215	15,471,000
1969	14	225	50,511	3109	43,393	22,419	13,963	6084	1058	3,964	430,365	4,112,700	17,221,000

A. RONALD TONKS

state office building was completed, and the Gary Baptist Center was established. The following year the functions of the convention were increased through a Christian life committee and the expansion of the executive board from 24 to 30 members.

The convention also purchased property for a BSU Center at Purdue University in West Lafayette, Ind. The establishment of a Baptist Foundation in 1967 enabled the convention to secure endowment funds for future institutions. The outreach of the convention in 1967 and 1968 is noteworthy. A new Indianapolis Baptist Center under the direction of Mr. and Mrs. John Tranthem was established. Both language mission and migrant mission work were undertaken.

By the end of the decade the State Convention of Baptists in Indiana had been firmly established. Through wise leadership a solid financial foundation was constructed on which future plans and programs could be built.

A. RONALD TONKS

INDIANA ASSOCIATIONS.

I. Extant. CENTRAL. Organized in 1957 with eight churches in First Southern Baptist Church, Lafayette. In 1969, 41 churches reported 471 baptisms, 7,792 members, $773,386 total gifts, $76,176 mission gifts, $3,234,000 property value, and $1,590,166 church debt.

EAST CENTRAL. Organized in 1964 with 13 churches in the Anderson Muncie area, formerly in Eastern Indiana Association. In 1969, 10 churches reported 111 baptisms, 1,385 members, $135,891 total gifts, $11,928 mission gifts, $492,000 property value, and $130 779 church debt.

EASTERN INDIANA. Organized in 1951 with seven churches (four of which were formerly in Whitewater Association, Ohio-Kentucky) as Indiana Association of Missionary Baptists. In 1954 it became Eastern Indiana Association, affiliated with Illinois Baptist State Association. In 1958 it affiliated with State Convention of Baptists in Indiana. In 1969, 15 churches reported 176 baptisms, 2,288 members, $134,383 total gifts, $11,963 mission gifts, $617,000 property value, and $331,728 church debt.

LAKE MICHIGAN. Organized in 1955 with churches from the Great Lakes Association affiliated with Illinois Baptist State Association. In 1958 it affiliated with State Convention of Baptists in Indiana. In 1969, 25 churches reported 422 baptisms, 7,916 members, $583,977 total gifts, $78,678 mission gifts, $2,807,000 property value, and $1,093,016 church debt.

MIAMI. Organized in 1967 with six churches from East Central Association. In 1969, seven churches reported 68 baptisms, 1,041 members, $102,049 total gifts, $9,800 mission gifts, $416,000 property value, and $184,626 church debt.

NORTH CENTRAL. Organized in 1968 with two churches from Northeastern Association. In 1969 two churches reported 18 baptisms, 270 members, $33,379 total gifts, $3,570 mission gifts, $190,000 property value, and $123,360 church debt.

NORTHEASTERN. Organized in 1963 with four churches from Northern Indiana Association. In 1969 four churches reported 33 baptisms, 489 members, $83,771 total gifts, $8,369 mission gifts, $327,000 property value, and $121,633 church debt.

NORTHERN INDIANA. Organized in 1958 with nine churches from Lake Michigan Association. In 1969, 18 churches reported 167 baptisms, 3,257 members, $221,266 total gifts, $28,956 mission gifts, $921,000 property value, and $431,095 church debt.

SOUTH CENTRAL. Organized in 1964 with 11 churches from Southeastern Association. In 1969 eight churches reported 129 baptisms, 1,058 members, $105,351 total gifts, $10,526 mission gifts, $349,000 property value, and $188,072 church debt.

SOUTHEASTERN. Organized in 1958 with six Indiana churches from Long Run Association of Kentucky. In 1969, 24 churches reported 402 baptisms, 5,695 members, $518,401 total gifts, $42,330 mission gifts, $1,825,000 property value, and $724,799 church debt.

SOUTHWESTERN. Organized in 1958 with 28 Indiana churches from West Kentuckiana Association of Kentucky. In 1969, 40 churches reported 786 baptisms, 15,181 members, $1,102,825 total gifts, $118,307 mission gifts, $4,798,000 property value, and $1,399,222 church debt.

WABASH VALLEY. Organized in 1962 with six churches from West Central Association. In 1969, 10 churches reported 185 baptisms, 1,750 members, $172,015 total gifts, $13,138 mission gifts, $592,000 property value, and $224,317 church debt.

WHITE RIVER. Organized in 1967 with eight churches from Southwestern Association. In 1969 nine churches reported 40 baptisms, 809 members, $74,166 total gifts, $7,840 mission gifts, $299,000 property value, and $99,719 church debt.

WHITEWATER. Organized in 1962 with four churches, two from Eastern Indiana Association. In 1969, 12 churches reported 111 baptisms, 1,580 members, $71,840 total gifts, $6,451 mission gifts, $354,000 property value, and $84,092 church debt. This association is in the same general area of Indiana as Whitewater Association of (Ohio) Kentucky.

II. Extinct. INDIANA ASSOCIATION OF MISSIONARY BAPTISTS. Organized in 1951, it changed its name in 1954 to Eastern Indiana Association.

WEST CENTRAL. Organized in 1957, it changed its name in 1966 to Central Association.

A. RONALD TONKS

INDIANA BAPTIST. Official newspaper of the State Convention of Baptists in Indiana, established July 1, 1959, with a circulation of 6,319. E. Harmon Moore, executive secretary of the convention, served as editor from 1959 until Sept. 30, 1965. Alvin C. Shackleford, the present

(1970) editor, assumed that position on Oct. 1, 1965. The circulation in 1969 was 5,909.

A. RONALD TONKS

***INDIANS, HOME MISSIONS TO.** See LANGUAGE MISSIONS, HOME MISSION BOARD PROGRAM OF.

***INDONESIA, MISSION IN.** Since 1952, many outstanding events have affected the mission work. Growing Communist pressure, economic chaos, anti-American propaganda, and slowing down of response to the gospel characterize the years 1960–65. However, the trend reversed and Indonesia became one of the most responsive mission fields. By 1969 seminary enrolment reached 130, student work and the radio-TV ministry were growing, and indigenous cultural forms were utilized to express the gospel. Church membership numbered 9,717 in 26 churches and 127 chapels, and 111 missionaries served in 15 cities in Java and Sumatra.

R. KEITH PARKS

***INLOW YOUTH CAMP.** Purchased in 1940 by Woman's Missionary Union and held in trust by the Baptist Convention of New Mexico, the camp is located 60 miles southeast of Albuquerque on Highway 10 in the Manzano Mountains. The property is valued at $104,899.17, including land, buildings, and equipment. The camp has a capacity of 300. There are camps for members of WMU (GA camps, YWA retreats, and Sunbeam Band day camps) held in the summer. Other camps held in the summer are: Indian, Spanish, junior music, youth music, church retreats, and family reunions. Activities include recreational as well as inspirational ones. The camp is directed by the manager who is the executive secretary of New Mexico WMU, with the caretaker living on the property the year round. A board of trustees plans and supervises the activities of the camp.

From 1964 to 1969, five permanent cabins were built, each in memory of a New Mexico Baptist. The persons memorialized are: Mrs. Rhea Cottle (1964), Mrs. Jane Quesenberry (1965), H. C. Reavis (1966), Harry P. Stagg (1967), and L. M. Walker (1969). In 1969 the ground breaking ceremony for the sixth cabin was held. This cabin was named in honor of Mr. and Mrs. F. A. Green.

VANITA M. BALDWIN

INSURANCE SERVICE, DEPARTMENT OF. See LIFE AND HEALTH BENEFITS DEPARTMENT.

*** INTER-AGENCY COUNCIL.** This consultative group was reorganized and enlarged in 1958 when the Southern Baptist Convention directed all of its agencies to coordinate their work through the Inter-Agency Council (IAC). Membership was expanded to include the executive, his chief assistant, and the chairman or president of each Convention agency (some agencies by preference do not have full membership); also included are representatives of Woman's Missionary Union, state secretaries, editors, and public relations people. To accomplish its purpose to coordinate all Convention programs and emphases, the council was restructured by the formation of various committees and subcommittees. The council itself is responsible for general coordination and approval of special projects. The administrative, coordinating, agenda, and calendar committees of the council handle the details of project assignments. Membership in the coordinating committee is based primarily on programs conducted by the agencies. This pivotal committee is organized into six subcommittees: church program and services, academic education, missions, emphasis programs, procedures, and coordination program planning. Each subcommittee handles projects in its respective area. The coordinating committee and its six subcommittees are assisted by four work groups which carry out assignments in their particular areas: program design, study and research, editorial work, and field services. Through this comprehensive organizational structure, the IAC carries out its responsibility of consultation, communication, and cooperation among the agencies in coordinating their programs for the benefit of the churches, associations, and state conventions. The council does not launch or execute programs.

The following principles are basic to the work of the Inter-Agency Council and its committees, subcommittees, and work groups: IAC is not a council of the Convention, has no authority over the SBC agencies, and bears a purely advisory relationship to the agencies. The council makes no formal reports to the Convention or Executive Committee; receives no matter of reference from the Convention; may receive for consideration problems from the SBC Executive Committee; may report on problems to the Executive Committee, but is not required to take formal action on problems referred to it by the Executive Committee.

The IAC coordinating committee, its subcommittees, and work groups comprise the main working forces of the council. The following accomplishments reflect the vital role played by the IAC in the life and work of the denomination. The council developed an *Orientation Manual* for the use of the employed staff and elected members of all Convention agencies. Program leaders of all agencies utilize the *Manual* as they work together in accomplishing related projects and in promoting emphases shared through curriculum materials, promotion materials, and field services on behalf of the churches. Since 1962 the council has assisted in planning the annual emphases of the Convention. Through its committees the council has coordinated the work of the agencies and their approach to the churches, associations, and state conventions in promoting the annual emphases. Coordinated Promotion Planning is the process developed by the council for bringing its coordinated plans to the attention of the state conventions and then to the churches. Through this process state convention and SBC program leaders combine their efforts to achieve the basic denominational thrust for a given period.

In keeping with the functions assigned by the Convention in 1958, the IAC has considered program problems of importance to SBC agencies and planned ways to overcome them through cooperative effort. Through the council, agencies have resolved problems regarding program content and relationships. They have eliminated duplication of effort, improved the effectiveness of existing programs, and devised ways of cooperating in carrying on programs authorized by the Convention. By request the council prepares a denominational calendar for consideration by the Convention's Committee on Denominational Calendar. On recommendation of the council, SBC agencies have implemented measures to correlate and strengthen their programs so that they contribute more effectively to the total Convention effort.

DAVIS C. WOOLLEY

INTERSTATE BAPTIST MISSION. A body of Baptist church representatives formed to promote the organization of new churches to meet war-time expanding population needs on the Pacific Coast, particularly in the Northwest. Affiliated churches were not expected to sever their connection with existing associations. It was organized as Coastal Area Mission, Dec. 14–15, 1942, in the YMCA Building, Portland, Ore. C. C. Brown was the first president. The name was changed the next year. Leonard B. Sigle was missionary of the body, and *Pacific Coast Baptist* was its official paper. Affiliated churches were located in Washington, Oregon, and California. Its Oregon-Washington churches helped organize Northwest Baptist Association, and this led to the organization of the Baptist General Convention of Oregon which sought and obtained affiliation with the Southern Baptist Convention. ROY L. JOHNSON

INZER, JOHN WASHINGTON (b. Hico, Tex., Jan. 6, 1890; d. Dallas, Tex., July 29, 1957). Pastor and denominational leader. Educated at Southwest Texas Normal School, Simmons College, Abilene, Tex., and Southwestern Baptist Theological Seminary, he was ordained in 1909. He served as pastor of the following Baptist churches in Alabama: South Avondale, Birmingham, 1913–17; Dauphin Way, Mobile, 1917; and First, Montgomery, 1930–38. Inzer also served the First Baptist churches of Chattanooga, Tenn., 1919–29, and Asheville, N. C., 1938–43. On Dec. 31, 1918, he married Marie Smith, in whose memory the president's home at Samford University is named. Inzer served as a chaplain during World War I, later working as a national organizer for the American Legion, and served as national chaplain of that body. He served as a member of the Baptist Home Mission Board, SBC, the state executive boards of Tennessee and Alabama, Sons of Confederate Veterans, and Society of the Founders of American Legion. An active Rotarian for many years, he served as district governor, 1945–46. On Nov. 6, 1954, he married Mrs. Pearl Truett Johnson. WILLIAM K. WEAVER

IRAN, MISSION IN. George and Joan (Owen) Braswell, under appointment for student work in the Middle East, entered Iran in Feb., 1968, as the Foreign Mission Board's first representatives. Braswell became a member of the staff of Armaghan Institute, a university ministry arm of the Presbyterian Church, U.S.A., which guaranteed his legal status in the country while he explored patterns of ministry for which Baptists might be responsible. In Teheran, Braswell began teaching English to university students at Armaghan, became a professor at the Muslim Faculty of Theology of the University of Teheran, and established friendly relations with the Zoroastrian Society.

GEORGE W. BRASWELL, JR.

***ISRAEL, MISSION IN.** By Dec. 1969, 33 missionaries were under assignment to Israel—largest number in any country of Europe and the Middle East. Response to the gospel was still slow among Jews and Arabs, but Baptists were widely respected and were laying good foundations for the future. They were operating two book stores, an art gallery, two schools, a farm, camps and conferences, and a Christian service training center. A new translation into Hebrew of the Gospel of Mark by Robert Lindsey was published. JOHN D. HUGHEY

***ITALY, MISSION IN.** At the end of 1969, 25 missionaries were engaged in publications, teaching (seminary, training school for girls, and linguistic school), broadcasting, social work (orphanage, old people's home, and child care centers), mobile evangelism, and church development. In 1967 five churches of the English-supported La Spezia Mission joined the Italian Baptist Union with the consent of their mission society. Membership of Italian Baptist churches was slightly above 5,000 in 1970.

JOHN D. HUGHEY

IVORY COAST, MISSION IN. Southern Baptists' first missionaries, John and Virginia (Miller) Mills arrived in Abidjan, the capital city, on July 5, 1966, having transferred from service in Nigeria. Prompted by correspondence with and fragmentary reports about Yoruba Baptist traders from Nigeria, who had established 20 congregations in the major centers, a survey was made in 1964 which resulted in this new work for Southern Baptists. Sunday School and worship services were begun in French for the *Ivoiriens* (Ivory Coast citizens) in rented quarters while a site was being secured for the construction of a permanent building. The first French-speaking converts were baptized in June, 1968. In addition, advice and help were given to Yoruba churches.

By 1969 two additional missionary couples and two single ladies (one still in language study in France) had been assigned for service in the Ivory Coast. Attendance in the one indigenous congregation averaged 75. One of the first young men to be baptized was attending a seminary in neighboring Ghana in preparation for the ministry. Yoruba congregations fluctuated greatly due to the constant coming from and going to Nigeria, but they averaged perhaps 2,000 attendance in the 18 active congregations.

JOHN E. MILLS

J

JACKSON, ARTHUR (b. Mansfield, Ga., Jan. 31, 1886; d. Atlanta, Ga., Aug. 13, 1966). Preacher, foundation and endowment executive, denominational leader. He was educated at Locust Grove Institute (Baptist), 1909–10, Mercer University (A.B., 1915), and Southern Baptist Theological Seminary (Th.M., 1918). He received the honorary D.D. from Mercer University, 1935. Jackson married Eulaine Adams of Royston, Ga. They had two daughters: Mrs. E. M. Cary and Mrs. John G. Johnson, III.

Ordained Dec. 8, 1908, he was pastor of First Baptist churches of Royston, Barnesville, and Savannah, Ga.; Hendersonville, N. C.; and Morningside Baptist Church, Atlanta, Ga. Three times vice-president, Georgia Baptist Convention; twice president, Georgia Baptist Sunday School Convention; trustee to numerous Baptist institutions and agencies in Georgia and North Carolina and the Southern Baptist Theological Seminary, he also helped lead Georgia Baptists to inaugurate an endowment program. Largely through his efforts, the Georgia Baptist Foundation was chartered in 1941. An original trustee of the foundation, he became its first executive secretary-treasurer in 1943, serving until his retirement Jan. 1, 1956. He saw resources of the foundation grow from the original $7,000 to over $2,000,000. Numerous wills providing valuable bequests to Baptist causes were written under his leadership. After retirement, he served interim pastorates in Georgia and Alabama.

LAWRENCE E. WEBB

***JAMAICA, MISSION IN.** Dottson and Betty (Frink) Mills transferred from Argentina in 1963 to serve as representatives to the Jamaica Baptist Union. A five-year program of advance was undertaken for 1964–69: stewardship, Christian education, evangelism, expansion, and missions. Azariah McKenzie became general secretary, the first full-time employee of the union. Daniel and Betty Alice (Cowan) Carroll transferred to Jamaica in 1969.

DOTTSON MILLS

JAMES, MINNIE LOU KENNEDY (b. Palestine, Tex., Feb. 1, 1874; d. Richmond, Va., Jan. 10, 1963). Sixth president of Woman's Missionary Union, SBC. After preparation in Houston Teacher's College, she taught school in Rockford, Tex., where she met William Carey James, also in the education field. They were married in 1894. In 1902, when W. C. James decided to enter the ministry, the family, which now included a small daughter, Margaret, moved to Louisville, Ky., where he entered Southern Baptist Theological Seminary. Mrs. James again taught school. In 1907 W. C. James became pastor of Grove Avenue Baptist Church in Richmond, Va. That same year Mrs. James was elected to the executive board of the Virginia WMU. Two years later she became president of Virginia WMU, serving two periods of two years each: 1909–11 and 1914–16. In the interim she served as chairman of the Jubilate Committee which planned the WMU 25th anniversary celebration. In 1916 she was elected president of WMU, SBC, which office she held for nine years. During these years Mrs. James led WMU to successfully complete its part of the 75-Million Campaign; to strengthen its partnership with SBC; to launch *World Comrades,* a quarterly magazine for young people; to employ a young people's secretary and a field secretary, and to begin a YWA camp at Ridgecrest. She also supported resolutions which later brought women to membership on SBC boards and committees.

Mrs. James represented WMU at the third congress of the Baptist World Alliance in Stockholm in 1923, and was elected to preside over the women's meeting. Her trip to Europe aroused her interest in training European young women for missionary work. In 1930, after her retirement from WMU, a training school for girls was established in Bucharest, Romania, and in her honor was named the James Memorial Training School.

For many years Mrs. James contributed the feature "Current Events" to *Royal Service;* from Oct., 1928, to Dec., 1930, she wrote the WMS programs. She also wrote two books: *Fannie E. S. Heck* (1939), a biography of her predecessor; and *History of Bethlehem Baptist Church, Ches-*

terfield County, Virginia (1940). She is buried in Richmond, Va. DORIS DEVAULT

***JAPAN, MISSION IN.** From 1955 to 1969, all phases of Baptist work continued to grow. By the end of 1969, statistics showed 141 churches with 21,000 members, 200 national pastors, over 700 other national workers serving in Baptist schools, hospital, and publication work, and 148 missionaries. Significant projects in the sixties included the New Life Movement (1963), nationwide evangelistic crusade involving large numbers of American and Japanese leaders and missionaries, and Asia-wide Sunday School and stewardship campaigns. JAMES D. BELOTE

JENNESS PARK. See CALIFORNIA SOUTHERN BAPTIST STATE ASSEMBLY.

JESTER, JOHN ROBERTS (b. Clay County, Ga., June 8, 1875; d. Columbia, S. C., May 14, 1965). Youngest son of Thomas P. Jester, a schoolteacher and planter, and Martha Frances Roberts, he was educated at Mercer University (B.S., 1899), and Southern Baptist Theological Seminary (1904–05), and received an honorary D.D. from Oklahoma Baptist University in 1926. He married Annie Allen Perry in 1900. They had five sons: John R., Jr., Perry Northen, Dana Edward, Harold Thomas, and Arthur Mannering. Jester was instrumental in constituting the First Baptist Church of West Palm Beach, Fla., and the First Baptist Church, Miami, Fla., in 1896. His pastorates include First, Montesuma, West Point, and Bainbridge, Ga., 1899–1904; First, Shawnee, Okla., 1911; Broadway, Fort Worth, Tex., 1912–15; First, Greenwood, S. C., 1918–22; First, Winston Salem, N. C., 1922–35; and First, Winchester, Ky., 1939–47. He was corresponding secretary of the Georgia Baptist Education Board, 1905–07, and field secretary of the endowment fund of the University of Richmond, 1916–17. Elected president of Oklahoma State Baptist College at Blackwell, Okla., on Sept. 4, 1908, serving until 1910. He was an evangelist, 1935–39, and 1947–61. Denominational offices which he held are as follows: vice-president, Oklahoma State Convention, 1909–10; board of trustees, Southwestern Baptist Theological Seminary, 1924–27; vice-president of North Carolina Baptist State Convention, 1930; president of the general board, North Carolina Baptist State Convention, 1924–25; Executive Committee, Southern Baptist Convention, 1927–30, 1942–47; and vice-president, Southern Baptist Convention, 1932. EARL D. CRUMPLER

JETER, MARY CATHERINE WILLIAMS (b. Petersburg, Va., 1824; d. Richmond, Va., Sept. 24, 1887). Woman's Missionary Union leader. She was the daughter of Henry and Armintia (Thurston) Williams. She married Christopher Jennett in 1850, and in 1857 she was married to Josiah Dabbs. Her third husband (1863) was Jeremiah Bell Jeter (*q.v.*, Vol. I) who became senior editor of *The Religious Herald*. Mrs. Jeter assisted her husband in editing this publication.

Mrs. Jeter led in the formation of two missionary societies and two institutions, all of which are functioning today, and over all of these bodies she presided from their origin until her death. They are: WMU, Auxiliary to the Richmond Association (1872); WMU, Auxiliary to the Baptist General Association of Virginia (1874); Richmond Home for Unwed Mothers (1874); and Richmond Baptist Home for Ladies (1883). She was buried in Hollywood Cemetery, Richmond, Va.

MRS. H. EDWARD MCGAHEY

JEWETT, MILO PARKER (b. St. Johnsbury, Vt., Apr. 27, 1808; d. Milwaukee Wis., June 9, 1882). Educator and Baptist minister. Son of Calvin and Sally (Parker) Jewett, he married Jane Augusta Russell, of Plymouth, N. H., Sept. 16, 1833. Jewett studied at the Bradford, Vt., Academy, Dartmouth College (B. A., 1828), the law office of Josiah Quincy, Rumney, N. H., Andover Theological Seminary, 1830–33, and was awarded the LL.D. degree by the University of Rochester, 1861. Jewett was principal of Holmes Academy, Plymouth, N. H., 1829–30; taught at Marietta Collegiate Institute (Marietta College) in Ohio, 1834–38; was president, Judson Female Institute (Judson College) Marion, Ala., 1838–55; purchased Cottage Hill Seminary, Poughkeepsie, N. Y., from Matthew Vassar, 1856, and founded Vassar College, 1861, serving as president until 1867. Commissioner of public schools, Milwaukee, Wis., he was chairman of the board of visitors of the state university, and trustee of the Milwaukee Female College (later Milwaukee-Downer College). Jewett Halls at Judson and Vassar perpetuate his name. CALVIN C. TURPIN

JOHENNING BAPTIST CENTER, THE. Located at 4025 Ninth Street, S. E., Washington, D. C., the center was built in 1959 by the Home Mission Board of the Southern Baptist Convention at a cost of $87,500. The District of Columbia Baptist Convention purchased the building site of more than half a city block for $23,600 and furnished the building at an additional cost of $17,000. The local convention also has the responsibility of financing the operation of the program. In 1965 a $144,000 addition was built by the HMB.

The need for a Christian influence in a densely populated, fast growing section of the city was brought to the attention of a Baptist pastor who was serving on the Southeast's Area U Board of the Commissioners' Youth Council. Over 4,000 families lived within an eight-square-block area. Many lived in low income housing and were there as a result of slum clearance and urban renewal in southwest Washington. There were no churches and few educational, recreational, or commercial facilities in the immediate area. The area was predominately white during the early years of the center's ministry. However, it was a cosmopolitan area where people from Germany, Austria, Cuba, Puerto Rico, Italy, Japan, and India resided. These people actively participated in center activities. There has been a gradual transition and in 1969 a totally black community evolved. This apartment-populated area is continually in a state of transition; however, this evolution has given a degree of stability which has brought to the fore a desire on the part of the community for a greater role in the responsibility for and leadership of this community center.

The center provides weekday club activities—educational, recreational, and spiritual—for more than 500 children and young people. Besides Sunday School and worship services, there are opportunities for adults to participate in interest groups, adult education, and in family centered activities.

The building is named in honor of Mrs. Anna B. Johenning, who served as a city missionary for many years under the sponsorship of the Woman's Missionary Organization of the District of Columbia convention. The professional staff is appointed and paid by the HMB. Edna R. Woofter is director of the center. The volunteer staff comes from various churches in the District of Columbia, nearby Virginia and Maryland, and from the immediate community.

EDNA R. WOOFTER

JOHNSON, CHARLES OSCAR (b. Coal Creek, Tenn., Sept. 23, 1886; d. Oakland, Calif., Nov. 24, 1965). Educated at Carson-Newman College (A.B., 1910) and Southern Baptist Theological Seminary (Th.M., 1920), he received the following honorary degrees: D.D., Linfield, Franklin, and Carson-Newman colleges; and LL.D., William Jewell College. He married Rose Lee Long, Sept. 6, 1910. They had three children: Ralph Milton, Frank Clifton, and Ruther.

Ordained in 1909, he served as pastor of the following Baptist churches: Newport Beach, Calif.; South Park, Los Angeles; First, Campbellsburg, Ky.; First, Tacoma, Wash.; and for 27 years the Third, St. Louis, Mo. During his pastorate at Third Baptist, there were more than 11,000 additions to the church.

Johnson served as president of the Northern Baptist Convention (now American Baptist Convention) and first vice-president of the Southern Baptist Convention. He was president of the Baptist World Alliance, 1947–50.

In St. Louis he was active in both religious and civic affairs, serving as president of the Metropolitan Church Federation in 1936, and was a member of the St. Louis Public School Board for six years, serving part of that time as president. After retirement from Third Church in 1958, he served as Distinguished Professor at Berkeley Baptist Divinity School until his death.

ROBERT SMITH

JOHNSON, CHARLES PRICE (b. LaGrange, Lewis County, Mo., Oct. 1, 1914; d. Fort Worth, Tex., May 22, 1965). Theological librarian and denominational leader. Son of Walter Henry and Margaret E. (Stephenson) Johnson, he married Lillias Nell Stewart, May 26, 1937. They had one daughter, Maredith Nell, 1952, and one son, Stewart Charles, 1955. He was educated at Friends University, Wichita, Kan., 1933–34, Ottawa (Kan.) University (A.B., 1936), Southwestern Baptist Theological Seminary (Th.M., 1940, M.R.E., 1940, Th.D., 1948), and North Texas State University (Library Service), 1953–54.

Ordained by the West Side Baptist Church of Wichita in 1937, Johnson's Texas pastorates included Smithfield Baptist Church, Smithfield, 1937–40, Central Baptist Church, Italy, 1940–41, and he was interim pastor for numerous churches in Texas, Oklahoma, and Louisiana, 1947–64. He also served as minister of education for First Baptist Church, Ottawa, 1941–42, student secretary, 1943–44, and director of Christian education, 1944–47, for the Kansas Baptist Convention. He was curator for the Texas Baptist Historical Society and member of the Oklahoma Baptist Historical Society.

Most widely known for his contributions to theological librarianship, Johnson succeeded L. R. Elliott (*q.v.*) as director of libraries at Southwestern Baptist Seminary in 1957, after serving as reference librarian, 1947–57. He supervised publication of *Union List of Baptist Serials* (1960), was joint editor of *J. Howard Williams, Prophet of God and Friend of Man* (1963), and *Chapel Messages* (1966). He was president of the Texas Baptist Library Convention, 1959–60, the American Theological Library Association, 1964–65, and member of the Fort Worth Public Library Board, American Library Association, and Texas Library Association. In 1964 Johnson was representing the Theological Education Fund of London and New York in India as a library consultant seeking to improve the library facilities of theological schools when his final illness compelled his return home. Johnson is buried in Highland Cemetery, Ottawa, Kan.

KEITH C. WILLS

JOHNSON, GEORGE LANNING, JR. (b. Clifton Hills, Mo., Aug. 26, 1896; d. Moberly, Mo., Nov. 20, 1965). Pastor and Baptist educator. Son of farmer George Lanning and Elizabeth (Ficklin) Johnson, he was educated at William Jewel College (A.B., 1919) and Southwestern Baptist Theological Seminary (Th.M., 1926; Th.D., 1933). He married Roma Lucille Fullington on Feb. 22, 1920. They had two daughters, Betty Jane (Mrs. Eugene W. Daily) and Elizabeth Lucille (Mrs. Darold H. Morgan). Both daughters married Baptist ministers.

Johnson was converted at the age of 17 and surrendered to preach during a revival. During seminary days he held student pastorates in Texas and Oklahoma. He served as pastor of First Baptist churches in LaGrange, 1926–28, and Fayette, Mo., 1928–36; and in Marion, Ill., 1936–38. His major contribution was in the field of Christian education. He was dean and later president of the Southern Illinois College of Bible (first known as the "Baptist Foundation"), Carbondale, Ill., 1938–61. During his tenure of service in this position it is estimated that 3,500 students studied Bible in his classrooms. Among his students are men and women serving as pastors, missionaries, and leaders in the state and Southern Baptist Convention. He served his denomination as Illinois representative on the Christian Education Commission, SBC, 1945–61. Following his retirement in 1961, the Johnsons moved to Moberly, Mo. He is buried in the Oakland Cemetery, Moberly.

MYRON D. DILLOW

JOHNSON, HANSFORD DUNCAN (b. Aiken County, S. C., June 13, 1887; d. Macon, Ga., Mar. 2, 1965). Pastor and educator. He was educated at Mercer University (A.B., 1913) and Newton Theological Institution, Mass. (B.D., 1916). Ordained in 1910, he served churches in Woburn, Mass., 1916–18; Georgia churches in Eastman, 1919–20, Sylvania, 1920–21, and Valdosta, 1921–28; and in Louisville, Ky., Broadway Church, 1928–39. Johnson became Roberts Professor of Christianity at Mercer in 1939. He led in the development of an interdepartmental program of ministerial education, which was designated in 1945 as the Roberts School of Christianity. He served as dean of this program until his retirement in 1957. He was also dean of the Mercer Chapel, 1945–58. Johnson was trustee of Mercer, 1923–28, and of the Southern Baptist Theological Seminary, 1929–39. He was president of the Baptist Education Association of Kentucky, 1930–39. He received honorary degrees of D.D. from Mercer in 1928, and LL.D. from Georgetown College in 1934. He married Maudelle Williams in 1909. Their children were Fred and Nelloise (Mabry).

H. LEWIS BATTS

JOHNSON, JOHN LIPSCOMB, SR. (b. Spotsylvania, Va., Aug. 12, 1835; d. Clinton, Miss., Mar. 2, 1915). Educator, pastor, chaplain, editor, and author. Son of Lewis and Jane Dabney Johnson, he received the B.A. degree from the University of Virginia in 1859. Although appointed as a missionary to Japan, poor health and the war prevented Johnson from fulfilling the appointment. Johnson was awarded the LL.D. degree by Southwestern Baptist University and the University of Mississippi, and the D.D. degree by both Mississippi College and the University of Georgia. He married Julia Anna Toy, sister of Crawford H. Toy (*q.v.*, Vol. II), on July 12, 1861. Six children were born to this union. During the war years he served as chaplain to the 17th Virginia Infantry, and to the hospitals at Lynchburg. Johnson served the African Church, Lynchburg, as pastor for several months following the war.

A distinguished educational career included: teacher at Hollins Institute; president of Roanoke Female Institute (Rollins College), Danville, Va., 1870–73; professor of English at the University of Mississippi, 1873–89; president of Mary Sharp College, Winchester, Tenn., 1889–91; and president of Hillman College, Clinton, Miss., 1901–05. While serving as head of the English Department at the University, he developed a curriculum which was copied by many universities. Johnson's pastorates included several Virginia churches—Enon, Mt. Herman, Court Street Church, Portsmouth; and Free Mason Street Church, Norfolk. His pastorates also included the following Mississippi churches: Grenada; Mt. Moriah and Waterford, Marshall County; Mid-Way, Abbeyville, and Clear Creek, Lafayette County; Duck Hill; Coffeeville, 1874, and First Baptist, Columbus, 1891–98. He was editor of *The Baptist Layman* published in Winona and was author of *Occasional Sermons* (1889) and *Autobiographical Notes* (1958). His denominational labors included service as vice-president of the Mississippi Baptist Convention, 1876; president of the Mississippi Baptist State Mission Board, Oxford, 1877–81; and trustee of Southern Baptist Theological Seminary, Louisville, Ky., 1884.

EARL KELLY

JOHNSON, ROY (b. Marshall County, Ky., Dec. 12, 1889; d. Kansas City, Mo., Apr. 6, 1964). Pastor in the Blue River Association for 35 years, he served the following churches: Hume, Besonia, Grain Valley, and Lone Jack. Successful in business (land development, monument company, savings and loan), he is a graduate of William Jewell College, Liberty, Mo., 1913. Johnson served as board member of the Baptist Memorial Hospital, Kansas City, and the Missouri Baptist Foundation. The foundation received his entire estate in trust at his death with earnings going to his wife until her death. Since her death (1966), income from the trust funds have been distributed to the Blue River Association; First Baptist Church, Independence; William Jewell College; Home for Aged Baptists; Baptist Children's Home; and the School of the Ozarks. The family home was given to Blue River Association. Among his gifts before his death were the Marguerite Apartments at William Jewell. He married Marguerite Lowe in Independence, Mo., in 1915. EARL O. HARDING

JOHNSTON, OLIN DEWITT (b. near Honea Path, Anderson County, S. C., Nov. 18, 1886; d. Columbia, S. C., Apr. 18, 1965). Son of Edward A. and Lelia (Webb) Johnston, he was converted at Barkens Creek Baptist Church, Aug., 1906. He was educated at Spartanburg Junior College (1915), Wofford College (A.B., 1921), and the University of South Carolina (M.A., 1923; LL.B., 1924). Johnston served in the United States Army for two years during World War I, receiving a citation of merit for bravery. He married Gladys Atkinson of Spartanburg, S. C., on Dec. 27, 1924. They had three children: Olin D., Jr., Sallie Leigh (Mrs. Vernon W. Scott), and Gladys Elizabeth (Mrs. Dwight Patterson).

A lawyer with the firm of Johnston and Williams, his public career began with election to the State House of Representatives from Anderson County, 1923–24. He was elected to the same body from Spartanburg, 1927–30. Defeated in a race for the governorship of South Carolina in Nov., 1930, he was elected governor Sept. 11, 1934. On Aug. 25, 1942, he won a second term as governor. In July, 1944, he was elected to the United States Senate, a position he held until his death. Important committee assignments received during his term in the Senate included chairmanship of the Post Office and Civil Service committees for the 84th through 88th Congresses.

An active Baptist layman, he served as a deacon in both the Southside Baptist Church, Spartanburg, S. C., and the Kensington Baptist Church, Kensington, Md. Johnston also was a Shriner, Optimist, Veteran of Foreign Wars, and member of other civic and fraternal organizations.

BIBLIOGRAPHY: J. E. Huss, *Senator From the South* (1961). JOHN E. HUSS

JONES, CHARLES PAUL (b. Hamilton, Mo., Jan. 9, 1878; d. Kansas City, Mo., Dec. 20, 1955). Baptist minister. Ordained at the age of 17 by the First Baptist Church, McFall, Mo., he graduated from William Jewell College, Liberty, Mo., in 1908, and was awarded the D.D. degree by his alma mater in 1941. He married Myrtle Moling, Feb. 2, 1898, and they had three children: Paul Dwight, Jeanetta, and Charles Truman. After his wife's death in Mar., 1945, he married Clara B. McConnell, Apr. 24, 1946. He pastored churches in Missouri prior to serving the Blue River Association, 1914–25, and the Kansas City Baptist Association, 1925–45. He retired in Oct., 1945. PAUL M. LAMBERT

JONES, MINETRY LEIGH, SR. (b. Carolina County, Va., June 4, 1855; d. St. Joseph, Mo., Apr. 24, 1932). Son of Thomas Sellers and Mary Elizabeth (Pollard) Jones, he attended public schools and Richmond Institute in Richmond, Va. Moving to St. Joseph, Mo., Dec. 31, 1882, he worked in tobacco sales. Jones organized Jones-Payne Hat Company in 1901. He married Cornelia A. Garnett, daughter of Daniel Garnett, a Baptist minister, Nov. 1, 1887. They had three children: Richard Turner, Elizabeth, and Minetry Leigh, Jr.

Jones was active as a member of First Baptist Church, St. Joseph, Mo. He also served as moderator of St. Joseph Baptist Association for 26 years, moderator of Missouri Baptist General Association, 1924–26, and trustee of William Jewell College, 1920–32. He is buried in St. Joseph. DAVID O. MOORE

JONES, ORABELLE CROSS (b. Laurel, Miss., May 13, 1903; d. Nashville, Tenn., Jan. 20, 1957). Daughter of Samuel Curtis and Lea (Beasley) Cross, she studied kindergarten work at Mary Hardin-Baylor College and received the M.R.E. from Southwestern Baptist Theological Seminary. She was professor of elementary education, School of Religious Education, Southwestern Seminary, 1925–31. On July 18, 1928, she married Harold R. Jones of Fort Worth, Tex. They had one daughter, Ann (Mrs. Larry Link). Mrs. Jones was superintendent of Cradle Roll work, 1944–46, superintendent of Nursery work, 1947–55, and editor of Nursery materials, 1956–57, in the Sunday School Department of the Sunday School Board. She was the author of *The Nursery Department of the Sunday School* (1946; rev., 1954). The confidence of Sunday School Board personnel in Mrs. Jones's knowledge, experience, and objectivity was the greatest factor in bringing about the unification of Nursery work in the Sunday School and Church Training departments. She was editor of *Living with Children* at the time of her death. W. L. HOWSE

JORDAN, CLARENCE LEONARD (b. Talbotton, Ga., July 29, 1912; d. Sumter County, Ga., Oct. 29, 1969). Founder of Koinonia Farm and Bible translator. He graduated from the University of Georgia in agriculture, 1933, Southern Baptist Theological Seminary, B.D., 1936, and Ph.D., in 1939. He married Florence Kroeger in 1936. They had four children.

After four years as a city missionary in Louisville, Ky., Jordan established Koinonia Farm near Americus, Ga., in 1942. His purpose was to share agricultural expertise with poor rural farmers and to demonstrate brotherhood, peace, and sharing through community. An integrated community developed that included up to 60 people, many of whom shared Jordan's outspoken pacifism. The community, which experimented with formal membership, still shares a common treasury.

Violence flared against Koinonia Farm in 1956 after Jordan sought to help two Negroes enrol in a segregated state college. Gunfire, bombs, and fires were directed at the community periodically through 1956. In 1957 a Sumter County grand jury charged Koinonia Farm with Communist party connections, but after investigation, returned a no-bill.

When a boycott forced Koinonia out of poultry, cattle, and hog operations, Jordan moved to a direct-mail pecan products business.

In 1963 Jordan began work on the cotton patch versions to help "strip away the fancy language, the artificial piety, and the barriers of time and distance" in Scripture. He translated all of the New Testament except Mark, Revelation, and one-half of John's Gospel.

He published the *Cotton Patch Version of Paul's Epistles* in 1968, and *The Cotton Patch Version of Luke and Acts* in 1969.

In 1968 Jordan shifted Koinonia from community to a nation-wide program of proclamation, discipleship schools, and a Fund for

Humanity that provides jobs and housing for the rural poor. Koinonia Partners, Inc., was formed as a nonprofit corporation to administer the new concept. Jordan was not an officer.

Through the Fund for Humanity, houses are sold at cost, through no-interest loans; land is freed for families to farm in partnership, theirs by virtue of usership; and jobs are provided through industries such as the pecan product business.

Jordan died on the farm, a victim of pneumonia and a heart attack. DALLAS M. LEE

***JORDAN, MISSION IN.** The Ajloun hospital undergirds the country's whole mission program; nursing school graduates go all over Jordan and to other Arab countries. Baptist schools also exert a good influence. In 1969 the book store in Amman sold or gave away 2,000 Bibles, 2,000 New Testaments, 10,000 Gospels, and 2,000 Christian books. At that time the five churches had 173 members. The 17 missionaries there were handicapped by troubled conditions in the Middle East. JOHN D. HUGHEY

***JUDSON COLLEGE.** The administrations of John Ingle Riddle (*q.v.*), 1943–60, Conwell A. Anderson, 1960–65, and James H. Edmondson, 1966–69, have commingled the best of the past with modern scientific educational methods to assure quality education. Judson in 1965 adopted a modified academic calendar permitting graduation under an accelerated three-year program. The B.S. degree was reinstated in 1967. Students select from 29 areas of concentration. New buildings constructed since 1956 were King Science Hall (1959), Riddle Gymnasium (1960), Robert Bowling Memorial Library (1963), Julia Tarrant Barron Residence Hall (1963), the Judson Union (1968), and a new residence (1969). Most of the campus buildings were built after 1952. Judson is a "sister college" to Duksung Woman's College, Seoul, Korea. The college has entered into Inter-institutional cooperation with Marion Institute and the University of Alabama. CALVIN C. TURPIN

JUNIOR MUSICIAN. A music quarterly for Junior choirs published by the Church Music Department of the Baptist Sunday School Board, beginning with the fourth quarter, 1963, and concluding with the third quarter, 1970. It was replaced in Oct., 1970, by a new quarterly, *Young Musicians.* W. HINES SIMS

K

***KANSAS ASSOCIATIONS.**

I. New Associations. CENTRAL. Effective Oct. 1, 1964, six churches from the Wheatland Association and three from the Cheyenne Association formed the Central Association. In 1969, 12 churches and one mission reported 67 baptisms, 1,591 members, $129,930 total gifts, $16,528 mission gifts, and $531,474 property value.

EASTERN NEBRASKA. Organized Dec. 1, 1958, with four churches and two missions, all formerly affiliated with the Smoky Hill Association. In 1969, 14 churches and four missions reported 198 baptisms, 3,977 members, $356,794 total gifts, $51,183 mission gifts, and $1,497,697 property value.

SMOKY HILL. Organized July 2, 1956, with four churches which came out of the Wheatland Association, they were joined by two others within six months, including the First Southern Baptist Church, Lincoln, Nebr., Nebraska's first Southern Baptist church. In 1969 eight churches and one mission reported 89 baptisms, 1,476 members, $142,230 total gifts, $15,647 mission gifts, and $728,375 property value.

WESTERN NEBRASKA. The eight churches of this association voted by July 2, 1966, to change affiliation from the Baptist General Convention of Colorado to the Kansas Convention of Southern Baptists, making possible a unification of the ministry of Southern Baptists in Nebraska. Recognition by the Kansas Convention came Nov. 15, 1966. Their complete transfer of ties came Jan. 1, 1967. In 1969 eight churches and one mission reported 40 baptisms, 446 resident members, $69,748 total gifts, $6,160 mission gifts, and $470,800 property value.

II. Changes in Associations. CHEYENNE. Dissolved Sept. 30, 1964, one church joining High Plains and four helping form the new Central Association.

WHEATLAND. Dissolved Sept. 30, 1964, with one church joining Smoky Hill and six helping form the Central Association. The seventh church remained affiliated with the Kansas convention only. N. J. WESTMORELAND

***KANSAS CONVENTION OF SOUTHERN BAPTISTS.**

I. History. Official action to open work in Nebraska under the sponsorship of Kansas Convention of Southern Baptists was taken on

May 11, 1955, by the executive board. The First Southern Baptist Church of Lincoln, Nebr., was constituted on Sept. 11, 1955, and became the first Nebraska church to affiliate with the convention. The Eastern Nebraska Association was organized in 1959, and in 1966 the Western Nebraska Baptist Association joined the Kansas convention, coming from the Colorado Baptist General Convention. Nebraska churches in 1969 numbered 22 with 4,725 members.

Property was purchased for a new state office building on the west side of Wichita in 1959. The official opening of the building was held on May 5, 1963.

The Church Loan Association of Southern Baptists was organized and chartered in Kansas on Nov. 13, 1957, with Gordon Dorian as its first president. H. H. Whatley was called to be executive vice-president Jan. 1, 1958. By 1968, 254 loans had been made to 115 churches and three associations. Bonds of $4,900,000 had been authorized. In Aug., 1968, the Securities Exchange Commission found the Church Loan Association to be insolvent. Selling of bonds was suspended. H. H. Whatley resigned as executive vice-president effective Dec. 31, 1968.

The Kansas convention, as guarantor of one-fourth the loans made through the Church Loan Association, immediately took action to fulfil its obligation. Convention staff was reduced drastically in 1969, with $78,000 annually going from the convention budget to the Church Loan Association. The 197 churches pledged $672,108 to be paid over a three-year period. Other state conventions pledged $474,565 over a five-year period.

II. Program of Work. *Executive Board and Executive Committee.*—Since 1955 the size of the executive board of the Kansas convention has been increased to 36 members plus the convention president, vice-president, recording secretary, assistant recording secretary, and historical secretary. Twelve members of the board retire annually, with 12 being elected each year to a three-year term. At least three of the 12 members elected are other than pastors. The board meets four times during the year.

From the executive board are elected eight members who serve on the executive committee along with the convention president, vice-president, and recording secretary. The members are elected at the annual convention meeting, four members being elected each year for a two-year term. The executive committee usually meets monthly between the quarterly executive board meetings. It serves with the executive director of the convention as a nominating committee for the selection of paid employees other than office help. It also serves as the budget committee for the convention.

The Kansas Southern Baptist Foundation, with assets of $24,261 on Dec. 31, 1969, is under the direction of a nine-man board of directors.

N. J. Westmoreland, executive secretary-treasurer of the convention since its organization, Mar. 19, 1946, resigned effective Sept. 30, 1969. The position of executive secretary-treasurer of the convention was combined with that of executive vice-president of the Church Loan Association to form a new position of executive director. James Curtis (Pat) McDaniel was elected to fill that position effective Mar. 1, 1970.

Baptist Digest.—The official publication of the Kansas convention was placed under the control of the executive board of the convention. Hoyt S. Gibson served as editor from Mar. 22, 1954, to May 15, 1957. Joe Novak was editor from June 15, 1957, to Nov. 4, 1959. In 1959 the editorship was made a responsibility of the assistant secretary-treasurer. F. Paul Allison served from Nov., 1959, until Jan. 31, 1966, when he assumed the direction of the Missions Department. N. J. Westmoreland was editor from 1966 until his resignation in 1969. Since Nov., 1968, Mrs. H. V. (Marjorie Moore) Moratto has served as assistant editor.

Educational Ministry.—In 1956 the Department of Religious Education was divided into two departments: Sunday School/Church Music and Training Union/Student Work. M. Ray Gilliland, who had previously served as secretary of the Religious Education Department, became secretary of Training Union/Student Work and served until Dec. 31, 1968. Hilary Brophy served the Sunday School/Church Music Department from its beginning until 1960. The department has been led successively by Howard Halsell, 1960–62, Ray Conner, 1963–64, and Harold L. Inman since 1964. In 1969 the two departments were restructured into one Department of Religious Education with Harold Inman as secretary.

Woman's Missionary Union.—The WMU was led by Miss Ida O. Polk, 1955–56; Miss Eva Berry, Jan. to June, 1957; and Mrs. Collins (Viola W.) Webb, since July, 1957.

Department of Evangelism.—The following men have served as secretary of the Department of Evangelism: Jack Stanton, 1952–56, John Havlik, 1956–61, J. Frank Davis, 1962–63, and Garth L. Pybas, 1965–68. The Brotherhood Department was merged with this department in 1957. In 1969 the combined departments were placed in the charge of the executive secretary-treasurer of the Kansas convention.

Department of Missions.—W. A. Burkey, first secretary of the Department of Missions, resigned June 30, 1957. In 1957 the department was combined with the departments of stewardship and promotion to create the office of assistant executive secretary-treasurer. F. Paul Allison came to this position in Feb., 1958. In 1960 the missions became a separate department with Meeler Markham as secretary until the end of 1965. Samuel Russell was associate executive secretary-treasurer and secretary of missions, 1965–66. F. Paul Allison again directed the work of the department, 1966–67. Galen F. Irby served in this capacity, 1968–69.

In 1969 the Kansas convention reported 197 churches, 52,436 members, and an enrolment of

KANSAS STATISTICAL SUMMARY

Year	Associa- tions	Churches	Church Member- ship	Baptisms	S. S. Enrol- ment	V.B.S. Enrol- ment	T. U. Enrol- ment	W.M.U. Enrol- ment	Brother- hood En- rolment	Music Enrol- ment	Mission Gifts	Total Gifts	Value Church Property
1955	11	111	17,828	2,170	19,009	9,379	8,153	3,444	1,364		$129,845	$ 980,930	$ 2,835,299
1956	11	120	20,629	2,073	21,609	10,978	9,177	3,735	1,511		153,164	1,199,543	3,616,994
1957	12	127	23,240	1,884	23,899	11,428	10,401	4,546	1,898	1,195	174,361	1,263,069	4,286,109
1958	12	132	25,148	2,045	24,765	12,216	11,573	4,886	2,168	1,776	207,163	1,473,887	5,051,850
1959	13	141	26,729	2,473	28,228	13,606	12,906	5,432	2,876	1,862	233,847	1,671,726	6,773,468
1960	13	153	30,424	2,462	30,307	14,834	14,369	6,209	2,951	1,752	260,041	1,928,398	7,713,443
1961	13	158	33,141	2,521	32,034	15,811	15,206	6,612	3,368	2,223	290,021	2,169,094	8,833,923
1962	13	164	35,936	2,410	33,697	16,177	15,925	6,670	3,347	2,451	329,494	2,393,129	10,698,392
1963	13	170	38,719	2,480	35,123	17,127	16,413	7,298	3,215	2,718	339,546	2,541,492	11,654,163
1964	12	171	41,122	2,389	37,233	19,280	17,092	7,486	3,006	3,696	349,765	2,780,268	12,557,859
1965	12	179	45,222	2,484	39,111	19,030	16,663	7,672	2,436	4,051	397,841	3,365,381	15,838,894
1966	12	182	46,917	2,302	39,425	19,940	16,953	7,598	2,507	4,202	441,638	3,437,796	16,158,446
1967	13	197	50,115	2,907	40,514	22,299	17,870	7,914	2,777	4,544	448,848	3,649,027	18,116,734
1968	13	197	52,334	2,600	40,848	16,599	19,543	7,724	2,364	4,495	502,403	4,143,092	19,460,786

MRS. PATRICIA GOELLER

40,482 in Sunday School, 17,643 in Training Union, 6,844 in WMU, and 2,319 in Brotherhood. Church property was valued at $19,695,-306. Total receipts were $4,505,491, and the churches reported giving $594,566 to missions.

MRS. H. V. MORATTO

KEEGAN, GILBERT KEARNIE (b. Bunkie, La., Jan. 31, 1907; d. St. Louis, Mo., Sept. 13, 1960). Pastor, denominational leader, and national director of Southern Baptist student work. Educated at Northwestern State College (B.A., 1927), Natchitoches, La., and Southwestern Baptist Theological Seminary (Th.M., 1933), he received the D.D. from Howard Payne College, Brownwood, Tex., in 1945. He married Marian Morgan, daughter of missionary parents to Brazil, on May 12, 1933. They had one child, Kathleen, born Sept. 24, 1939.

Keegan served the following Baptist churches as pastor: First, Natchitoches, La., 1932–35; Emmanuel, Alexandria, La., 1937–41; First, Longview, Tex., 1941–45; and Temple, Los Angeles, Calif., 1945–50. Between his ministry in Natchitoches and Alexandria, he served as educational secretary (Sunday School, Training Union, and BSU) for the Louisiana Baptist Convention, 1935–37.

Following Frank H. Leavell's (*q.v.*, Vol. II) death, Keegan became the second national director of Southern Baptist student work. He served as secretary of the Student Department of the Sunday School Board, SBC, from 1950 until his untimely death while en route to Hawaii to dedicate a new Baptist student center.

Keegan thrilled thousands with his solo voice. He also loved to write—both prose and poetry as well as hymns. He compiled his most select *Baptist Student* editorials into a small volume entitled *Your Next Big Step* (1960), designed for students entering college.

Keegan held membership on the SBC Executive Committee, the Baptist World Alliance executive committee, and served as chairman of the administrative committee of the BWA's Youth Department. He was eager that non-Christian students, including those from other countries, receive the warmth and witness of Christian friends. He led students and those working with them professionally to relate Student Summer Missions to the Home and Foreign Mission Boards of the SBC. He also initiated a movement among Baptist faculty members in the various colleges and universities. While president of the Southwestern Seminary Alumni Association, he conceived the idea of a campaign to raise $750,000 toward the erection of the Truett Memorial Library and Auditorium and personally directed it toward and beyond that goal. Upon his death, the Keegan Memorial Scholarship Fund was deposited with the Southern Baptist Foundation by friends and his wife to be used at Southwestern Seminary primarily to assist students preparing to do student work.

DAVID K. ALEXANDER

KELLY, LLOYD CASWELL (b. Mount Sterling, Ala., Apr. 13, 1874; d. Madison, Ind., Dec. 10, 1955). Son of Sarah Jane (Felts) and Solomon S. Kelly, he attended the Baptist Academy at Healing Springs, Ala., Mississippi College, Howard College (now Samford University), Georgetown College (A.B., 1902), and the Southern Baptist Theological Seminary, 1903–04.

He was pastor of the 21st Ave. Baptist Church, Birmingham, Ala., where he was ordained in 1899. Other pastorates were Flemingsburg, Sharpsburg, and Mt. Pisgah in Fleming County, Ky., 1902–04. He started the *Kentucky Issue,* which became the organ of the Kentucky Anti-Saloon League. In 1907 he married Nancy Brent Newland. Pastor at Orlinda, Tenn., 1907–14, he returned to Kentucky in 1914 to the First Baptist Church, Campbellsville. He served the First Baptist Church, Pineville, 1920–42. Here he started a summer assembly which developed into Clear Creek Mountain Preachers School in 1926 (now Clear Creek Baptist School). After retirement in 1954 he lived at Campbellsville and died at his daugher's home in Madison, Ind. LEO T. CRISMON

***KENTUCKY ASSOCIATIONS.**

I. New Associations. ANDERSON. Formerly known as Baptist (1827–1956) Association. In 1968, 13 churches reported 84 baptisms, 3,688 members, $159,334 total receipts, $21,942 total missions, and $977,000 property value. Churches located mainly in Anderson County.

FULTON COUNTY. Organized on Oct. 18, 1960, at Crutchfield Church, by messengers from 13 churches, dismissed from West Kentucky (1893) Association. In 1968, 13 churches reported 84 baptisms, 3,491 members, $190,214 total gifts, $33,296 mission gifts, and $860,000 property value.

GREEN VALLEY. Organized on Oct. 22, 1958, at Immanuel Baptist Temple, Henderson, by messengers from 22 churches of the West Kentuckiana (1948) Association, located in Henderson and Webster counties. In 1968, 25 churches reported 258 baptisms, 9,139 members, $681,669 total gifts, $102,084 mission gifts, and $3,586,000 property value.

NORTHERN KENTUCKY. Organized on Aug. 31, 1967, at Covington, First Baptist Church, by the union of North Bend (1803) and Campbell County (1827) Associations, and by messengers from 59 churches located in Boone, Kenton, and Campbell counties. In 1968, 61 churches reported 994 baptisms, 29,697 members, $371,886 mission gifts, $2,358,219 total gifts, and $12,243,000 property value.

PIKE. Organized on Sept. 11, 1958, by messengers from 11 churches, dismissed from Enterprise (1876) Association at Road Fork Baptist Church. In 1968, 17 churches reported 191 baptisms, 5,207 members, $308,465 total receipts, $43,963 total missions, and $1,575,000 property value.

TAYLOR COUNTY. Organized on Aug. 19, 1957, at Campbellsville Church, by messengers from 15 churches, dismissed from Russell Creek (1804) Association. In 1968, 17 churches reported 65 baptisms, 5,867 members, $393,489 total receipts, $76,667 mission gifts, and $2,558,000 property value.

TWIN LAKES. Organized on Nov. 19, 1962, at Leitchfield, First Church, by messengers from three churches, located in Grayson County, as the result of a division in Goshen (1817) Association. In 1968, four churches reported 38 baptisms, 1,367 members, $93,756 total receipts, $18,892 total missions, and $421,000 property value.

II. Changes in Associations. BAPTIST. See Anderson Association.

*CAMPBELL COUNTY. See Northern Kentucky Association.

GOOSE CREEK. Voluntarily disbanded in 1958.

GREEN RIVER. Withdrew voluntarily from affiliation with Kentucky Baptist Convention, in 1961, after nominal cooperation. Now independent.

GREENVILLE. Now noncooperative, with feeble existence. Missionary churches organized Red River (1955) Association.

NORTH BEND. See Northern Kentucky Association.

SOUTH CONCORD. Noncooperative since 1967.

WEST KENTUCKIANA. Dissolved at formation of Green Valley Association in Henderson and Webster counties (Kentucky), and Southwestern Indiana Association, in Posey, Vanderburgh, and Warrick (Indiana) counties in 1958.

WENDELL H. RONE, SR.

KENTUCKY BAPTIST BOARD OF CHILD CARE. Established by an act of the General Association of Baptists in Kentucky (now Kentucky Baptist Convention) in 1953, it united what had been the Children's Commission of the general association and the boards of trustees of Spring Meadows and the Kentucky Baptist Children's Home (now Glen Dale). The board was incorporated in 1954. Quarterly meetings are held. Members of the 20-member board are elected by the convention for limited terms, assuring a rotating membership. The purpose of the board is to provide and promote a unified program of care and services for dependent children for whom Baptists in Kentucky are responsible. Presently the program is one of group care in three children's homes, and related social services. C. FORD DEUSNER

KENTUCKY BAPTIST CONVENTION (cf. Kentucky, General Association of Baptists in, Vol. I).

I. Change of Name. The General Association of Baptists in Kentucky changed its name to Kentucky Baptist Convention at the annual session, Nov. 14, 1961. The title of moderator was changed to president, and general secretary-treasurer to executive secretary-treasurer. The convention empowered and directed the moderator and clerk "to execute proper Articles of

Amendment, and to certify the action of this body in so amending said Charter to the Secretary of State of the Commonwealth of Kentucky. . . ." The Negro Baptist state body had been called the General Association of Colored Baptists in Kentucky, but a year following the change of name among white Baptists, the General Association dropped the word "Colored" in its name, thus assuming the full name of the white convention prior to 1961.

II. New Departments of Work. *Department of Evangelism.*—Activated by the executive board of the convention Nov. 10, 1964, it was one of the departments given approval by the general association at the 1959 session. Prior to 1959 evangelism and missions were in the same department. It was felt that more emphasis should be placed on evangelism by making it a department. Thomas Hicks Shelton became secretary of evangelism on Sept. 1, 1965. He has led in a vigorous program of evangelism for the churches and associations. Fullest cooperation was given to the Crusade of the Americas by the department, as well as by the executive board and staff. Kentucky cosponsored the Toledo-Piqua, Ohio Crusade of the Americas in 1969. In 1970 a new project of youth evangelism was started.

Department of Interracial Cooperation.—The executive board of the convention authorized setting up a Department of Interracial Cooperation with a full-time secretary on Nov. 15, 1966, to be supported cooperatively by the convention and the Home Mission Board's Department of Work with National Baptists. On Mar. 1, 1967, Herman Ihley (*q.v.*) began work as department secretary. Previously work with National Baptists had been under the direct missions department, but the urgency of the social crisis and the favorable attitude of both white and Negro Baptists led to a separate department. In 1966 the executive board created a Baptist joint advisory committee composed of its denominational cooperation committee and a similar committee of the General Association of Baptists in Kentucky. This committee proposed creation of a department to the program committee which recommended it to the board.

Significant progress was made in building bridges of understanding and promoting interaction between persons, churches, and associations and the two state groups. The churches felt new freedom because of convention action and encouragement. Exchange of pulpits, choirs, and leaders in all phases of work increased. Most churches recognized an "open door policy" for membership, but there has been to date no widespread membership integration. A new development came in "dual alignment," whereby by 1969, 12 Negro churches and one white church have become affiliated with both state bodies: at the annual convention in 1967, three churches—Washington Street, Paducah; Corinthian, Frankfort; and New Hope, Ashland; at the 1968 convention, five churches—Ebenezer, Louisville; New Hope, Louisville; Mt. Zion, Bowling Green; Friendship, Wheelwright; and Mt. Olive, Jenkins; at the 1969 convention, four churches—Greater Norris Chapel, Henderson; First Perryville, Fourth Street, Owensboro; Good Shepherd, Louisville, became dually aligned with the convention. They also affiliate in the associations.

At the annual meeting of the general association, Aug. 13, 1969, meeting at the New Vine Baptist Church, Fort Spring, the Cecilia Baptist Church, Cecilia, Ky., became dually aligned with the general association—the first white Baptist church in the Southern Baptist Convention to have a dual affiliation.

Joint activities between the white and black conventions include: a joint session of the two state bodies, Nov. 17, 1967; annual youth nights since 1967; and a joint evangelistic conference in 1969. More than 100 black churches participated in the Crusade of the Americas by having revivals during the spring of 1969. A growing acceptance between the races is a heartening result.

Initial work is also done in relation to Jewish people. The department secretary has channel responsibilities with a ministry for aging and the Christian life committee.

Church Administration Services.—While not a full department, church administration services is an outgrowth of church survey and development ministry, a subprogram in the Department of Direct Missions. With the growth of the Church Administration Department of the Sunday School Board, SBC, the need was felt for more emphasis on assistance to all churches and church officers, particularly deacons. On Sept. 1, 1967, G. R. Pendergraph, director of the church development ministry, was named consultant for church administration services, and transferred from the Direct Missions Department to the administrative office. His work was enlarged to include the current major programs of church administration.

Stewardship Promotion Department.—The executive secretary-treasurer is responsible for the promotion of the Cooperative Program and general stewardship. However, in 1955 William Hayden Curl was a general worker under the general secretary, entitled director of missionary training and stewardship revivals. Adolph M. Vollmer handled promotion. On Oct. 1, 1957, Thomas Bluford Chaney became director of the Forward Program of Church Finance in the state, and then associate secretary of the Stewardship Promotion Department until Dec. 31, 1961. Robert J. Hastings became the first secretary of the department, Oct. 15, 1960, and set up a vigorous program: stewardship development for churches and associations, Cooperative Program promotion, and public relations. He resigned Sept. 1, 1965, and was succeeded by Michael Lee Speer, Dec. 15, 1965, who continued this work until June 30, 1967, when he became director of stewardship development for the Stewardship Commission, SBC. On Dec. 1, 1967, Jesse C. Stricker became secretary. He has shown imagination and vigor in promotion and public relations, including building up a radio network to 25 stations carrying a weekly broadcast called "Kentucky Newscope."

Kentucky Baptist Foundation Department.—The convention approved in its 1959 session that "the Kentucky Baptist Foundation shall be a department of the Executive Board of the General Association of Baptists in Kentucky with a full-time secretary. . . . that all general policies of the . . . Foundation shall be approved by the state Executive Board. . . . funds shall come from the . . . Cooperative Program. . . ."

Church Music Department.—The convention approved a full-time program of church music with a full-time secretary on Nov. 15, 1959. Eugene Francis Quinn had been serving part-time since Sept. 10, 1956, while attending the Southern Baptist Theological Seminary. He was employed full-time in May, 1959. Music ministry enrolment has shown remarkable growth—from 28,584 in 1961 to 44,273 in 1969. Use of music camps at Cedarmore, statewide festivals, associational clinics, and promotion of vast numbers of choirs for the annual youth nights of the convention (since 1962) account for much of the progress.

III. Development and Growth. William Cooke Boone (*q.v.*) was general secretary and treasurer from 1946 until his retirement, Oct. 1, 1961. Much progress was made during his term of service, including a new Kentucky Baptist Building completed in 1957 at 10701 Shelbyville Road, Middletown, Ky.; the Booz, Allen, and Hamilton Survey completed in 1958; the broad recommendations of the committee to study the survey to the convention in 1959 laid the foundations for progress in the sixties; approval of a Christian education statewide campaign for capital needs; and placing a Baptist church in every county seat.

He was succeeded by Harold Glen Sanders. It was his responsibility to carry out the sweeping changes of 1959 and the Christian education advance campaign approved in 1961 and launched in 1963. He was made responsible for the Christian education program since there was no longer a department. His primary responsibility being the Cooperative Program, receipts grew from $1,681,980 in 1955 to $3,675,875 in 1969. The 1970–71 goal was $4,100,000.

Reflecting something of the expanding economy of the nation and the growth of the denomination, Kentucky Baptists had a continuous growth in most areas until a peak was reached in 1964, particularly in the church organizational enrolments. Total gifts received in the churches increased from $18,124,907 to $39,648,212; value of church property went from $61,277,902 in 1955 to $189,203,318 in 1969. Convention capital worth went from $15,487,772 to $61,466,477—in spite of losing Magoffin Institute, Bethel, and Kentucky Southern colleges. Church membership in Kentucky increased from 577,575 to 666,836; the number of churches decreased from 2,278 to 2,192 as a result of the migration from the mines and fields to the cities, leaving isolated churches to die while new churches are being born where the people are.

Church Organizations.—Enrolment growth of Sunday School, Training Union, Brotherhood, and WMU reached a peak about 1964 and declined; but church music enrolment in the state has grown from 28,584 in 1961 to 44,273 in 1969.

Correlation and Coordination.—The outstanding characteristic of the growth and development in the convention is the factor of correlation, coordination, and cooperation. The staff of the executive board, led by the executive secretary, has achieved marked success in teamwork, multidepartment statewide projects such as the annual associational officers' briefing each fall starting in 1967, youth assemblies and annual youth night since 1962, and the annual denominational emphasis planning. In cooperation with the Inter-Agency Council, SBC, state strategy was a program of SBC planning with state conventions and associations for the churches. The church phase was called church programing, and *Plan for Church Advance Manuals I, II, III* were used by many. Coordinated promotion planning, the successor to state strategy, is simpler, and has been highly successful since 1968. Again the state, association, and SBC leaders plan and promote jointly for each of the churches. Organizationally, coordination is represented by associational and church councils growing in number. It was outstanding in the "Shaping the 70's Conferences" for the Oct. 1, 1970, changes in grouping, grading, and curriculum in all organizations of the convention.

Christian Education.—Since 1955 one new college has begun in 1962 and closed in 1969—Kentucky Southern College in Louisville. Closed are Magoffin Institute, Mountain Valley, in 1962; and Bethel College, Hopkinsville, in 1964. Encouraged by increased funds from the convention, the Christian education advance campaign, development and alumni programs, and increased enrolments, the remaining three colleges and two schools have made significant progress but face inflation costs with difficulty. They are Georgetown, Cumberland, and Campbellsville colleges, Oneida Institute, and Clear Creek Baptist School. This work is under the executive secretary-treasurer and Christian education committee. It is no longer a department. Total plant funds of all colleges and schools in 1969 were $20,673,551; total worth $28,461,459.

Benevolent Institutions.—The board of child care continues its operation of homes at Spring Meadows, Glen Dale, and Morehead and has added a program of foster homes, adoptions, and ministry to unwed mothers. C. Ford Deusner has been general superintendent since Jan., 1963, succeeding Sam Ed Bradley (*q.v.*). In 1969 plant funds were $3,626,089; total worth $5,496,853.

Kentucky Baptist Hospitals.—The governing

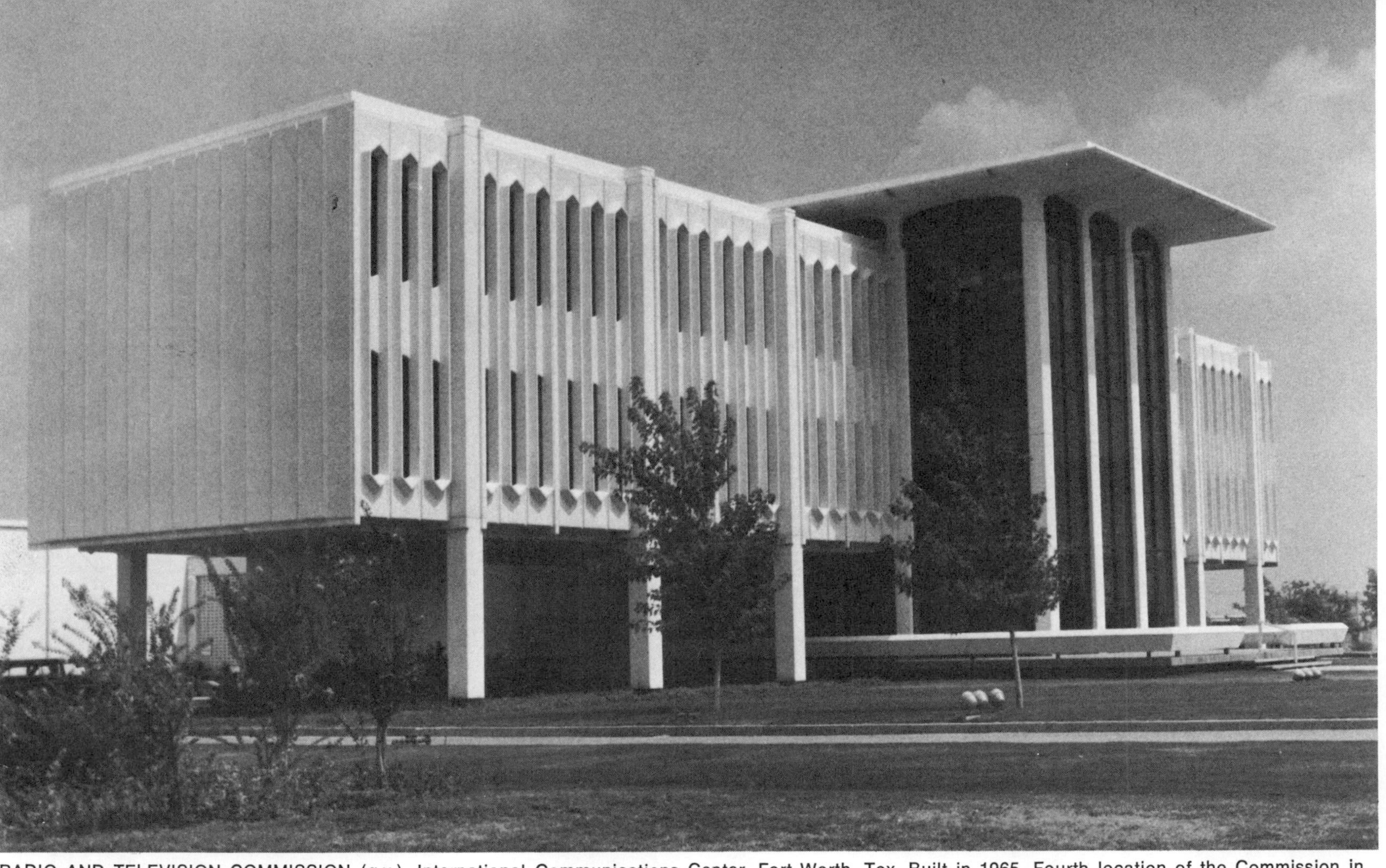

RADIO AND TELEVISION COMMISSION (*q.v.*). International Communications Center, Fort Worth, Tex. Built in 1965. Fourth location of the Commission in its 32-year history. Building contains 42,000 sq. ft. of floor space.

CEDARMORE KENTUCKY BAPTIST ASSEMBLY (*q.v.*). *Top:* Boone Lodge, 1964. All-purpose conference center. Cost $600,000. *Center:* Ferguson-Jaegle Conference Center built in 1969 at cost of $180,000.

STUDENT CENTER, MOREHEAD, 1970. Near campus of Morehead State University, Morehead, Ky.

group was changed by approval of the 1968 convention to "Baptist Hospitals, Inc.," with Hubert Lee Dobbs, president, having served in a similar capacity since 1951. Present bed capacity is Louisville 417, Paducah 214, and Lexington 235. The convention also approved an expansion program beginning in 1970 for all the hospitals and a new complex in the St. Mathews area of Louisville. Plant funds in 1969 were $12,500,000, with a total worth of $20,500,000.

Business Department.—Since 1956 the volume of work in the office of the office manager and accountant increased greatly. In Nov., 1963, the convention changed the name of the position to business manager. The responsibility now includes accounting, office management, purchasing, payroll, and all business activities of the staff of the executive board. Garnett B. Morton has held this post since 1952, during which time the accounting employees have grown from 4 to 14. Property of the executive board exceeds $3,000,000, including the Kentucky Baptist Building, Cedarmore Assembly, *Western Recorder,* and seven student centers, including the new center at Morehead (1970) now under construction, to cost in excess of $376,000.

Brotherhood Department.—Organized in 1954 Lucien E. Coleman, Sr., was secretary until 1958 when Forrest Ray Sawyer succeeded him. Originally a ministry to men, in 1954 WMU began the transition of transferring boys' work to the Brotherhood in 1957. The program in Kentucky, as in the SBC, was revised in 1958, 1960, and 1970. Enrolment of men has declined since 1964 but the boys enrolment took an upswing in 1969. The programs are (1) mission education and (2) mission activity.

Direct Missions Department.—Achel Buford Colvin succeeded Eldred M. Taylor as secretary of the department, Aug. 1, 1958. At the annual state convention, Nov. 18, 1959, the report of the "committee of 17" came as a recommendation of the executive board, outlining a new direct missions program including (1) increasing support of missionaries by the associations, (2) combining two or more associations into districts with a missionary, and (3) enlargement of the eight-day rural church program. Reasonable progress was made in these directions, and the task was adapted to the population trend to the cities and the growing emphasis on Christian social concern. Robert C. Jones succeeded J. Edward Cunningham as director of the mountain mission program which also received vigorous attention. Work is cooperatively done with the HMB, SBC, in Christian social ministries language missions, rural-urban missions, and in-service guidance at Clear Creek Baptist School, Campbellsville, and Cumberland colleges. The "three regional missionaries" were discontinued. Several programs were transferred to other departments: evangelism became a department in 1965, interracial cooperation became a department in 1967, church enlargement survey was enlarged to church administration services and transferred to the office of the executive secretary in 1967, and schools of missions were transferred to the Brotherhood Department and the name changed to "World Missions Conferences" in 1967. In 1965 through the investment of an anonymous donor, the communities missions program was launched in five counties where the missionary visited five communities each week in direct ministry to people. The donor's investment phased out in 1970 but this work continues. In 1970 there were the following missionaries at work: three metropolitan, 13 district, 33 associational, nine county, 22 local, five community, and 20 special workers.

Training Union Department.—James H. Whaley, Sr., has been secretary since 1953. In 1956 two male associates, and in 1958 Mickey Joyce Martin, were added to the staff, the latter for elementary work. The basic program follows the SBC program. Collateral or channel programs in the convention to which this department relates are: vocational guidance (1961), church audiovisual education (1966), church recreation (1966), church administration (1966–67), and family life (1967).

Annuity Department.—Baynard Francis Fox was director of Kentucky retirement plans, and special representative of the Annuity Board in Kentucky and Tennessee, resigning May, 1964, for a position with the Annuity Board in Dallas, Tex. On Aug. 1, 1964, Arthur Wycliffe Walker became secretary of the department. The annuity program has been upgraded and enlarged several times since 1956. Churches are encouraged to pay the full dues of pastors and staff and to pay 10 per cent on the entire salary and house allowance. The executive board began this plan for employees in 1969.

Baptist Student Union Department.—The secretary, James Chester Durham has served since 1941. In 1956, eight campus ministers served eight campuses; in 1970, 15 served 23 campuses, with BSU work on five other campuses. The term "BSU Director" was changed to "Campus Minister." There are three associate department secretaries—one general associate, Emery E. Smith, while Otto V. Spangler began work with five western campuses in 1967, and Quentin Lockwood, Jr., began work with five eastern campuses in 1969. New property was purchased in Lexington and Morehead, but the only new student center is at Morehead, to be completed in 1970 at a cost of approximately $326,000. Refurnishing of some existing centers was done. The great change during the decade 1960–70, was the commuting student and the community college system. The student ministry to a majority of students must be accomplished from Monday through Friday each week. This takes the form of study groups, action groups, daily devotional, and fellowship periods.

Sunday School Department.—Roy Everett Boatwright has served as secretary since 1952. While the enrolment, following national trends, reached a peak of 429,697 in 1959 and then declined, Vacation Bible School enrolment con-

KENTUCKY STATISTICAL SUMMARY

Year	Associa-tions	Churches	Church Member-ship	Baptisms	S. S. Enrol-ment	V.B.S. Enrol-ment	T. U. Enrol-ment	W.M.U. Enrol-ment	Brother-hood En-rolment	Music Enrol-ment	Mission Gifts	Total Gifts	Value Church Property
1955	81	2,278	577,575	25,571	419,715	159,094	104,759	66,238	16,670		$3,286,739	$18,124,907	$ 61,277,902
1956	81	2,244	589,807	22,337	423,438	162,670	108,031	65,827	21,199		3,535,376	19,494,557	73,374,356
1957	82	2,278	604,482	24,299	387,698	167,301	112,817	67,904	16,183		3,711,444	22,916,371	85,550,736
1958	83	2,279	615,001	22,847	422,384	182,180	117,262	72,235	18,230		3,886,541	22,731,794	99,989,317
1959	82	2,249	613,430	25,068	429,408	162,703	117,887	72,939	18,655		4,050,355	23,193,454	100,951,671
1960	83	2,225	617,507	21,253	425,138	159,713	116,387	73,027	15,730		4,213,110	24,652,442	110,575,872
1961	82	2,184	620,414	20,901	424,419	163,434	118,623	71,745	14,088	28,584	4,108,482	24,333,962	114,112,867
1962	82	2,168	618,085	20,492	419,679	165,241	119,448	70,489	12,955	28,232	4,605,483	26,197,490	128,678,200
1963	83	2,193	635,476	19,120	418,752	157,943	117,237	67,812	13,700	36,599	4,670,115	27,115,878	133,866,532
1964	81	2,164	650,825	18,398	419,207	165,016	117,135	70,055	12,724	39,969	4,879,724	28,723,965	143,942,740
1965	82	2,210	643,641	19,190	412,208	166,369	109,949	69,053	10,636	38,297	5,180,027	31,470,864	148,162,334
1966	82	2,222	649,391	17,908	401,942	177,755	104,389	67,159	17,338	39,078	5,396,799	31,506,531	166,187,587
1967	81	2,207	651,945	19,153	397,008	160,856	101,594	65,120	17,402	43,559	5,708,876	33,429,882	167,848,492
1968	80	2,209	658,389	18,200	392,908	156,618	105,565	64,143	17,204	43,794	6,086,352	36,941,148	177,066,000

HAROLD G. SANDERS

tinued to grow from 159,094 in 1955 to 189,062 in 1969. Channel programs of the SBC also include weekday religious education, kindergarten, libraries, and church architecture. Great emphasis was given to leadership training, stewardship, enlargement, working with the associational organizations through clinics, workshops and conferences at Cedarmore Assembly, literature, and consultations.

Youth Night.—Struck by the few laymen and the absence of young people at the annual meetings, the new executive secretary-treasurer, Harold G. Sanders, proposed an annual youth rally in Kentucky. The time was right for a youth emphasis during the decade of dissent—the sixties. Beginning on the last night of the annual convention, the first annual youth night at the Sports Arena in Owensboro more than filled the 8,000-seat center. Since 1967 youth nights have been jointly sponsored by the Negro and white Baptist state bodies. Attendance ranged from 8,000 in Owensboro to 28,000 in Louisville. Evangelism and music were featured. These rallies stimulated youth work in churches and associations throughout the state.

HAROLD GLEN SANDERS

***KENTUCKY BAPTIST FOUNDATION.** James C. Austin succeeded A. M. Vollmer, the first executive secretary, in 1964. Austin served until Nov., 1967. Grady L. Randolph became executive secretary on Mar. 1, 1969. The assets of the foundation in 1969 were about $5,000,000.

GRADY L. RANDOLPH

KENTUCKY BAPTIST HISTORICAL COMMISSION. An agency created in 1966, made up of nine members elected by the Kentucky Baptist Convention, plus the curator of the commission's collection and of the Kentucky Baptist Historical Society's collection and the Kentucky member of the Southern Baptist Historical Commission for the purpose of collecting, preserving, and publishing Kentucky Baptist historical materials. The commission handles the funds made available from the Kentucky Baptist Convention for this purpose. The Kentucky Baptist Historical Society remains a body made up of popular membership for the above purpose also.

LEO T. CRISMON

***KENTUCKY BAPTIST HOSPITAL.** Located in Louisville, Ky., the hospital completed phase one of its construction program which added a lobby, gift shop, coffee shop, business office, and two new elevators plus other remodeling in 1965. A part of phase two, with a seven-story addition enlarging the emergency suite and adding 100 patient beds with other improvements, was completed in 1967. Total beds increased from 345 in 1954 to 414 in 1969. In 1967 the hospital purchased a 52-acre tract in the St. Matthews area for another hospital building and for other related facilities. A fully accredited three-year school of nursing is maintained. A school for X-ray and laboratory technology is also available. Since 1965 Homer D. Coggins has been the administrator, now called executive vice-president, in the relationship with Baptist Hospitals, Inc. H. L. DOBBS

KENTUCKY SOUTHERN COLLEGE. A liberal arts college begun in 1962 under the Long Run Baptist Association, later sponsored by the Kentucky Baptist Convention (1963–67), and released on request of its trustees to operate as an independent Baptist college. On Jan. 1, 1969, it was merged into the University of Louisville.

In 1955 Long Run Association appointed a committee to raise funds to begin a college branch of Georgetown College, but in 1959 it was decided by the association and by the convention that it become a distinct college. It was located at 9001 Shelbyville Road on a 232-acre tract provided through the Leroy Highbaugh family. Funds were raised by the association for a Baptist college of academic excellence destined, when accredited and financially stable, to enter the convention's family of colleges.

On Mar. 7, 1960, Rollin Scofield Burhans became president. Later that year the first building, a president's home, was provided by the Carlisle Avenue Baptist Church, Louisville, Arthur W. Walker, pastor. A generous offer of V. V. Cook, Sr., promising $2 for each $1 raised in the association, netted $1,800,000. Classes opened in the fall of 1962 on the campus of Southern Baptist Theological Seminary, then moved to the new campus in the fall of 1963. Boarding students moved onto the campus in 1964. The first graduating class was in 1964. The Student Union building was completed in 1967, part of a master plan.

In 1961 the Kentucky convention voted a statewide capital funds Christian education advance campaign and invited the new college into its family and into participation in the campaign. After much consultation, the college trustees asked Long Run Association to transfer ownership to the convention. This was approved by the executive board, Aug. 27, 1962. The convention's executive board approved it, subject to convention action, on Nov. 13, 1962. It was approved with favorable terms, including continuity of trustees, encouragement for accreditation, a junior college portion of the Cooperative Program, and 20 per cent of the funds to be raised in the Christian education advance campaign.

Under good leadership, the college had a bright beginning. Growth in student body, development of highly trained faculty, and construction of 11 additional buildings by 1967 were the goals. However, it was living on borrowed money. Inflation set in. Capital needs consumed some operating funds. The next round of fund drives slowed down, and the state's campaign realized one-third of the $9,000,000 in cash and pledges. However, the other $6,000,000 in 1966 was budgeted with a $300,000 annual allocation for all participants "remaining in the fold"—the college to receive about $77,000 annually. Financial problems plagued the college.

On Mar. 10, 1967, the trustees requested release from the convention and $1,800,000 in cash, to seek funds from government and other sources. The executive board on that date reluctantly granted release, $500,000 in cash by July, and a five-year participation in the capital funds allocation.

Still no solution came, due to large debts, inability to attract income, and decline of enrolment. On Oct. 27, 1967, the trustees voted to merge with the University of Louisville. However, a valiant student movement to raise funds with the slogan "Save Our School" was encouraged by a substantial pledge of Leroy Highbaugh. The University of Louisville withdrew for the time their offer to merge. This gave the college only a temporary reprieve and the trustees began to seek an honorable way out through merger with several institutions, including Western Kentucky University, Georgetown, and finally, with the University of Louisville. On Jan. 1, 1969, the university took over and the merger whereby the university assumed all debts and received all assets (above $7,000,000) was completed by late summer of 1969. HAROLD GLEN SANDERS

KERR, ROBERT SAMUEL (b. Ada, Okla., Sept. 11, 1896; d. Washington, D. C., Jan. 1, 1963). Attorney, statesman, prominent Baptist layman. Educated at Oklahoma Baptist University (1911–12), East Central College (1909–11; 1912–15), and the University of Oklahoma (1915–16), he was admitted to Oklahoma Bar in 1922. He was a Mason, a deacon, Sunday School teacher, and president of the Baptist General Convention of Oklahoma, 1944. Entrance into political life began when he became governor of Oklahoma in 1943. In 1949 he was elected to the United States Senate, a post he held until his death.

He was Oklahoma Baptist University's greatest benefactor up to his time. His gifts to the school totaled almost $1,000,000. In addition to his gifts to the University, Kerr was generous in giving to church and other denominational causes with his total contributions approximating 30 per cent of his net income. He gave equally of his time and talents as a speaker, advisor, committeeman, and board member of Baptist organizations at all levels, including the Southern Baptist Convention. A public memorial marks the place of his burial near Ada, Okla. J. M. GASKIN

KERSEY, RUTH MAY (b. Hanover County, Va., Mar. 21, 1889; d. Richmond, Va., Nov. 8, 1958). Missionary to Nigeria, 1920–55. Educated at Woman's College, Richmond, Va., and WMU Training School (B.M.T., 1916), she enrolled for nurses' training after hearing an appeal made by a medical missionary to Nigeria. She graduated from Retreat for the Sick, Richmond, in 1920, and was appointed to Nigeria, arriving in

Ogbomosho in 1921. She served as a nurse in Ogbomosho hospital and founded the Home for Motherless Children (later named Kersey Home), Ogbomosho, in 1925. She gave most of her missionary life to service of African children. She retired in 1955 due to illness.

I. N. PATTERSON

***KIAMICHI BAPTIST ASSEMBLY.** Since 1955, the number of church cabins has increased to 70, and assembly-owned property, which consists of an administration building, chapel, swimming pool, water plant, and caretaker's home, has increased in value to $150,000. The assembly is managed by an elected executive committee consisting of the president, vice-president, secretary, treasurer, and 10 other committee members. The officers are the legal trustees and conduct all business with the consent of the executive committee.

Churches in Atoka, Frisco, LeFlore, Pittsburg, and Sans Bois associations cooperate in financial support and operation of the assembly. Its 1969 budget of $13,156 was met with funds from area church and associational budgets, $1,200 from the state convention, and registrations fees.

Two summer encampments are held annually, one for juniors and another for older youth. Attendance increased from 763 in 1954, to 1,055 in 1969. The peak registration was 1,117 in 1963.

Presidents during the years 1954–69, were Forest A. Upchurch, Wayne Britton, Herman Highfill, Jesse Marvin Gaskin, Robert S. Jackson, Kenneth Lay, and Sewell Farrell. Ernest Smallwood began serving as business manager in 1957. James Miller became president in 1969.

The assembly began a new ministry to the TB hospitals in the area when William Smith was made chaplain May 15, 1958. The role of the assembly was to collect money and supervise this work in a liaison capacity. ROBERT S. JACKSON

KIMBROUGH, BRADLEY THOMAS (b. Ashland, Miss., Oct. 30, 1880; d. Memphis, Tenn., June 23, 1960). Son of Judge Bradley Thomas and Sarah Burton (McDonald) Kimbrough, he graduated from Oxford, Miss., High School, 1895; University of Mississippi (B.A., 1899); and did three years of graduate study in University of Berlin, Germany. From Southern Baptist Theological Seminary he received a Th.M. in 1922 and Th.D. in 1924. He taught in Mississippi and Texas before coming to Louisville, Ky., where he taught in Louisville Male High School, DuPont Manual High School, and Alex. G. Barrett Junior High School, all in the Louisville City School system. He was principal of the Louisville Baptist High School, operated by the Eighteenth St. Baptist Church, 1947–54, and at East Baptist Church, 1954–55. Pastorates which he held in Louisville were Audubon, Eastern Parkway, and Lee's Lane. He published *Jubilee in '53: the Sesquicentennial History of the Long Run Association of Baptists* (1953), and *The History of the Walnut Street Baptist Church, Louisville, Ky.* (1949).

On June 19, 1913, he married Edith Jewell Lonnon who survived him at death. They had two sons, Bradley Thomas, Jr., and George.

LEO T. CRISMON

***KIND WORDS SERIES.** Although the periodical called *Kind Words* passed out of existence in 1929, the Sunday School Board's leisure-reading periodicals for children and youth continued to be designated as The Kind Words Series until Oct., 1970. With the board's launching of its new set of periodicals in Oct., 1970, The Kind Words Series as such came to an end.

HOWARD P. COLSON

KING, EDWIN DAVID (b. Green County, Ga., Apr. 12, 1792; d. Marion, Ala., Jan. 11, 1862). Army officer, planter, educator, and church leader. An officer in the War of 1812 and with General Andrew Jackson in the battle of New Orleans, King moved to Perry County, Ala., in 1816. He led in establishing the town of Marion, and Siloam Baptist Church. A large planter in the black belt, he was one of first trustees of the University of Alabama. At a trustee meeting he met Milo P. Jewett (*q.v.*) and persuaded him to go to Marion to establish a school for young women. Thus originated Judson College, which opened Jan. 1, 1839. King also led in the selection and purchase of the first site for Howard College, which opened in Marion, Jan. 3, 1842. He was chairman of Judson College trustees, 24 years, and Howard College trustees, 20 years. He was a representative of Alabama Baptists at the 1845 meeting in Augusta, Ga., that founded the Southern Baptist Convention. Largely through King's influence the Home Mission Board, SBC, was first located at Marion, Ala., where it remained until 1882.

A. HAMILTON REID AND FANNA K. BEE

KIRK, JACOB EMORY (b. Rural Retreat, Va., Dec. 2, 1882; d. Oklahoma City, Okla., Sept. 23, 1962). Educated in Virginia public schools, Oklahoma Baptist College, and Ottawa University (1914), he married Mary Amelia Young, Aug. 31, 1908. After her death in May 14, 1952, he married Mary Virginia Lee, July, 1953. Pastorates he served included Weleetka (1914–19), Holdenville (1919–49), and Agnew Avenue, Oklahoma City, Okla. (1949–53). Kirk served on numerous boards and committees of the Oklahoma convention and preached the annual sermon in 1953. J. M. GASKIN

KITCHEN, THURMAN DELNA (b. Scotland Neck, N. C., Oct. 17, 1885; d. Wake Forest, N. C., Aug. 28, 1955). Physician and college president. Son of William Hodge and Maria (Arrington) Kitchin, he received the B.A. from Wake Forest College in 1905, studied at the University of North Carolina for one year, and received the M.D. degree from Jefferson Medical College in 1908. He practiced medicine at Lumberton, 1908–10, and Scotland Neck, 1910–17. His brother, W. W., served as governor of North

Carolina, with his father and another brother serving in the United States Congress.

Kitchin joined the faculty of the Wake Forest College School of Medicine in 1917 as professor of physiology and pharmacology. He became dean of the medical school in 1919, and president of the college in 1930. He served as dean until 1936, and as president until his retirement in 1950. His administration brought tremendous changes to the college.

In 1908 Kitchin married Reba Clark of Scotland Neck. Their sons are Truman D., Jr., Irwin Clark, and William Walton Kitchin.

Kitchin was president of the North Carolina Medical Association, 1928–29, and was active in numerous medical and educational organizations. He was a member of Phi Beta Kappa and Omicron Delta Kappa. He was author of *Lectures on Pharmacology* (1929), *The Doctor and Citizenship* (1934), and *Doctors in Other Fields* (1938). He is buried in Scotland Neck.

ELIZABETH BRANTLEY

KITTIWAKE ASSEMBLY. See GULFSHORE and KITTIWAKE ASSEMBLIES.

KLECKNER, WILLIAM ALBERT (b. near Logansport, Ind., May 22, 1875; d. Gary, Ind., Jan. 2, 1956). Pastor, district missionary, teacher, and author. He married E. Blanche McMahan, Aug. 2, 1900. They had one son, Robert. Kleckner received the M.A. from Missouri University (1932), and the honorary D.D. from Hannibal-LaGrange College, 1950. He served as acting president of Hannibal-LaGrange College, 1940–41, and as head of the college's English department, 1944–53. Author of several poems, he also wrote the novels *A Lily of Samaria* (1927) and *Jezebel* (1928).

FLORENCE GROVES

KNIGHT, RYLAND (b. Shelbyville, Ky., Feb. 20, 1876; d. Atlanta, Ga., July 9, 1955). Pastor, denominational servant. He received degrees from Princeton University (A.B., 1896); Southern Baptist Theological Seminary (Th.M., 1899, Th.D., 1900); University of Richmond (D.D., 1910). His father was a Kentucky Baptist minister, Aaron Brightwell Knight, and his mother was Josephine (Ryland) Knight, daughter of Robert Ryland (*q.v.*, Vol. II) of Virginia. In 1910 Knight married Julia Brook Ryland. Following her death in 1923, he married Bess Acre in 1925.

His pastorates were: Dover, Shelby County, Ky.; First, Ashland, Ky.; Calvary, Richmond, Va.; First, Clarksville, Tenn.; Immanuel, Nashville, Tenn.; Delmar, St. Louis, Mo.; Second, Atlanta, Ga.; Second Ponce de Leon, Atlanta, Ga.; First, Pulaski, Va. He was president of the executive board, Tennessee Baptist Convention, 1920–25. Knight served the following SBC boards: FMB, 1905–12, 1935–45; SSB, 1918–25; HMB, 1931–34. He is buried in West View Cemetery, Atlanta, Ga.

JOHN S. MOORE

KOINONIA FARM. See JORDAN, CLARENCE LEONARD.

***KOREA, MISSION IN SOUTH.** By the end of the sixties, a decade of significant growth, the 240 churches cooperating with the Korean Baptist Convention reported over 9,000 members. Missionary staff rose to 65. In addition to evangelism and church development, special ministries were undertaken among Korean women, students, and servicemen. Korean Baptists participated in Asia-wide Sunday School and stewardship campaigns and gave special emphasis to use of mass media. The Pusan hospital moved to its new location in 1968.

JAMES D. BELOTE

L

LACKEY, ROBERT WORTHINGTON (b. Cameron, I. T., now Okla., Aug. 29, 1885; d. Fresno, Calif., Nov. 30, 1966). The seventh of 11 children born to Henry H., a Cherokee Indian, and Elena (Gentry) Lackey, he was converted at 12 and was baptized into Mt. Home Missionary Baptist Church near Hartshorne, I. T. Ordained at 18, he served churches in Bowers, Blackwell, Drumright, Wilburton, and Oklahoma City, Okla., and First Southern Baptist Church, Bakersfield and Kerman, Calif. He married Alma Victoria Hawkins, Feb. 6, 1906.

Lackey attended Oklahoma Baptist College (now Oklahoma Baptist University), was active in the Democratic party, and held various appointive positions in state and federal government. In 1940 he moved to California where he took the initiative in organizing the Southern Baptist General Convention of California, which he served as executive secretary for four years. He also edited *The California Southern Baptist* and later served as missionary of the California convention and the Home Mission Board, SBC.

Lackey took strong positions doctrinally and on civic righteousness, and opposed the Ku Klux Klan from the pulpit and wherever the issue arose. Once an opponent attacked him on a crowded downtown street, but Lackey severely mauled him. Sympathetic bystanders volunteered to pay his fine, but he smiled and said, "No, thank you, gentlemen, that is a chore that I reserve for myself." FLOYD LOONEY

LAMBDIN, JERRY ELMER (b. Grainger County, Tenn., Dec. 4, 1889; d. Nashville, Tenn., Jan. 24, 1960). Christian educator and leader of the Training Union movement. A consuming conviction that every church member needs training was the strongest motivating force in his life. In response to this conviction, he served as president of the BYPU in the Broadway Baptist Church, Knoxville, Tenn.; president of the Knox County, Tenn., BYPU Federation, (1913–17; president of the BYPU Convention of Tennessee, 1916–17; BYPU secretary of Alabama, 1917–25 (except for a period of service in the Field Artillery during World War I); general field secretary and associate editor in the Baptist Sunday School Board's BYPU Department, 1925–29; and secretary of the latter department, 1929–59 (the name was changed to Training Union Department in 1934).

His formal education began in a one-room school near Rutledge, Tenn. He graduated with honors from the University of Tennessee, and did graduate work at Southern Baptist Theological Seminary, George Peabody College, and Columbia University.

In 1919 he married Ina Smith, who not only became a devoted helpmate for 40 years but, also, a valuable colleague in Training Union work.

Under Lambdin's leadership, the church member training program in Southern Baptist churches grew from an enrolment of 500,000 in 1929 to more than 2,500,000 in 1959. From an organization almost exclusively for young people, he guided its expansion into a fully graded church training program with provisions for all age groups. Other innovations he introduced included Youth Week, Christian Home Week, associational Training Union work, "M" Night (Mobilization Night), and a special design for Training Union enlargement campaigns accompanied by leadership training. He guided the growth of the Convention-wide Training Union assemblies at Ridgecrest and Glorieta from the first assembly at each place to massive assemblies in 1959 which registered more than 10,000 people. Under his leadership the number of Training Union periodicals increased from six to twenty-two and employees in the Training Union Department increased in number from three to more than fifty. His writings included *The Baptist Training Union Manual* (1942), *Building a Church Training Program* (1946), and multitudinous tracts and articles in denominational publications. His strong passion for Training Union work quickened interest in church membership training in Baptist churches around the world.

"Jerry Lambdin's great ambition for the Training Union," summarized one biographer, "was to make it progressive, growing with the needs of churches, but true to the Bible and the great doctrines of Baptists. To this purpose he devoted every ounce of his strength, time, and energy." RAYMOND M. RIGDON

LANE, JOHN BENSON (b. New Bern, Craven County, N. C., Sept. 11, 1901; d. Columbia, S. C., Nov. 28, 1969). Educational and denominational worker. Son of Frederick and Laura (Wallace) Lane, he was licensed to the ministry in 1922 and graduated from New Orleans Baptist Theological Seminary, 1924. He served the following Baptist churches as educational director: First, Blytheville, Ark., 1924–29; First, Pine Bluff, Ark., 1930–31; and First, Spartanburg, S. C., 1936–37. Lane also served as associate in the Sunday School Department of the North Carolina Baptist State Convention, 1937–44, and as director, Baptist Training Union (Church Training) Department, South Carolina Baptist Convention, 1944–68, which grew from 638 churches with 33,000 enrolled to 1,426 churches and 140,000 enlisted. He suggested the organization of the South Carolina Religious Education Association and helped organize the Southeastern Religious Education Association. He married Lillian Bryant of New Bern, N. C., Dec. 24, 1922. DANIEL W. CLOER

LANGUAGE MISSIONS, HOME MISSION BOARD PROGRAM OF. Southern Baptists' ministry among the people in the United States and Puerto Rico who are characterized by their connection with a language culture other than English. Through the Department of Language Missions, the Home Mission Board is responsible for the appointment of missionaries to serve among these groups and for providing leadership in all areas of Southern Baptist life, in the task of winning these people to Christ.

In 1959 a restructuring of the board's work made major elements, formerly administered through the Department of Direct Missions, a part of a new Department of Language Groups Ministries. In 1964 the name was changed to the Department of Language Missions. The program has two main thrusts: (1) to lead in the establishing and growth of language churches and missions; (2) to lead English-speaking churches to minister to persons of language-culture backgrounds through a ministry that identifies with the language and culture background of the people.

In 1969 the department participated in mission work in 29 state conventions with work in 41 states, the District of Columbia, and Puerto Rico. The department also administers work in Cuba and Panama. In 1969 approximately 1,200 persons served in a mission relationship to the board. A large portion of these are serving as pastors of language congregations, with the board and state conventions jointly supplementing the salary of the pastors.

More than 1,200 Southern Baptist churches

and missions are identified with the various language groups. These include Spanish, French, Chinese, Japanese, Italian, Russian, Korean, Portuguese, Czechoslovakian, Filipino, Ukrainian, Polish, and more than 40 different American Indian tribes. Work with the deaf and ministry to internationals is directed by this department.

In 1963 Spanish language instruction was initiated, in cooperation with the Mexican Baptist Bible Institute in San Antonio, Tex., for missionary candidates serving in Spanish-speaking work. About 170 scholarships awarded annually assist young people in college and seminary who are planning to enter some type of language missions work.

A program of refugee relief was initiated in 1962 in response to the plight of Cuban refugees in the United States. By 1969 more than 5,500 persons had been assisted in resettlement. WMU literature in Spanish is provided by this department for Spanish-speaking congregations in the United States.

Loyd Corder, secretary of the Department of Direct Missions, became secretary of the new department in 1959. In 1966 he was succeeded by his associate since 1960, Gerald B. Palmer. In 1966 Elias Golonka, the field worker in the department since 1963, became assistant secretary with responsibility for leadership in Northeastern United States. Oscar Romo came in 1965 with responsibilities for the Southwest. L. D. Wood, who served in Panama from 1960, came in 1966 with responsibilities for the Southeast and the Caribbean area. Irvin Dawson began service in 1966 as assistant secretary with responsibilities for the Northwest.

See also Chinese, Home Missions To, Vol. I; Indians, Home Missions To, Vol. I; Japanese, Home Missions To, Vol. I; Italians, Home Missions To, Vol. I; French, Home Missions To, Vol. I; Russians, Home Missions To, Vol. II; Deaf, Missions To, Vol. I. GERALD B. PALMER

LANHAM, EDITH CAMPBELL CRANE (b. Baltimore, Md., Dec. 17, 1876; d. Spartanburg, S. C., Sept. 27, 1933). Second corresponding secretary, Woman's Missionary Union, SBC. The daughter of Clara Merryman and Henry Ryland Crane, Edith was educated in Misses Adams School and Bryn Mawr School, Baltimore, and Bryn Mawr College, near Philadelphia. Her sisters were Laura Merryman (Mrs. George H. Whitfield), Claris I. (editor of *Our Mission Fields,* 1912–14), and Helen Bond (student religious worker).

Edith was elected corresponding secretary of WMU, Sept. 1, 1907. Under her leadership, significant developments in WMU were: organization of Young Woman's Auxiliary and Order of Royal Ambassadors; foundations laid for organization of Girls' Auxiliary; development of departments of personal service and mission study; and promotion of organized efforts in enlistment. She served as editor of *Our Mission Fields* from Oct., 1911, to Jan., 1912. In 1911 she represented WMU on the planning committee for the first women's meeting in connection with the Baptist World Alliance, which meeting resulted in the organization of the women's committee of the BWA. She was elected recording secretary of the new committee. Due to illness, she resigned her position with WMU, Jan., 1912.

On Dec. 27, 1912, Edith Crane married Samuel Ticker Lanham, a lawyer from Spartanburg, S. C. They had two daughters: Margaret Merryman and Louisa Tucker (Mrs. C. R. Spell). Mrs. Lanham is buried in the churchyard of Tabernacle Methodist Church, Spartanburg, S. C.

JOSEPHINE NORWOOD

LATIMER, LEON MOBLEY (b. Anderson County, S. C., Oct. 2, 1886; d. Greenville, S. C., Aug. 16, 1968). Pastor and denominational leader. Son of William Clement and Susan Josephine (Mobley) Latimer, he was baptized at the Rutledge Baptist Church, Rutledge, Ga., in 1903. He was educated at Mercer University (A.B., 1908), Southern Baptist Theological Seminary (1908–09), and Rochester Theological Seminary (B.D., 1911). Mercer University conferred on him a D.D. degree in 1931 and Atlanta Law School conferred the LL.D. in 1952. He received the Algernon Sydney Sullivan Award from Furman University and was elected honorary alumnus of Furman University in 1953.

Latimer served as moderator of Flint River Association in Georgia (1925), trustee of Southern Seminary (1925–47), member of Home Mission Board (1928–30), vice-president of Texas Baptist Convention (1932–34), president of Southern Seminary Alumni Association (1939–40), a member of the general board in Alabama, Texas, and South Carolina, and president of South Carolina Baptist Convention (1951).

While pastor of First Baptist Church, (1934–52 and emeritus 1952–68) Greenville, S. C., he exerted great influence on Furman University and its students. His other pastorates included: First, Salem, Ohio (1911–13); First, Sylacauga, Ala. (1913–16); Parker Memorial, Anniston, Ala. (1916–21); First, Griffin, Ga. (1921–30); and First, Austin, Tex. (1930–34).

On May 24, 1911, he married Mary Greer of Lafayette, Ala. They had two daughters: Loulie (Mrs. Ollin J. Owens) and Mary Sue (Mrs. James P. Wesberry). After the death of his first wife he married Emma Lenora Cooper of Laurens, S. C., July 17, 1947. DANIEL W. CLOER

LATOURETTE, KENNETH SCOTT (b. Oregon City, Ore., Aug. 9, 1894; d. Oregon City, Ore., Dec. 26, 1968). American historian of missions. His grandfather was one of the early settlers of Oregon. Latourette was educated in McMinnville College (later Linfield College), Ore., and at Yale University. While at McMinnville he joined the Student Volunteer Movement for Christian Missions, and throughout his life took an active part in that organization. After completing doctoral studies at Yale, he spent two years (1910–12) as a teacher at Yale-in-

China at Changsha. Illness forced his return to America. He then taught in Reed College, Ore., and Denison University, Ohio, before assuming the professorship of missions at Yale University in 1921, where he continued to labor until his retirement in 1953.

His major interest was in the education of successive generations of students, especially in matters related to the world mission of the church, and in writing on East Asian history and Christian missions. He was one of the pioneers among American scholars in the study of East Asia. His first widely known books were *The Development of China* (1917) and *The Development of Japan* (1918). These were folowed by *The History of Christian Missions in China* (1929), a work which has remained unrivalled in its field; and *The Chinese: Their History and Culture* (1934), a two-volume standard work. From this emphasis on China his studies soon expanded to a global coverage. The work for which he is most famous and which has become the major work on the history of missions is his seven-volume study of *The History of The Expansion of Christianity* (1937–45). In this he covered six continents, 20 centuries, and all branches of the church. Some of his other books are *History of Christianity* (1953), a five-volume *Christianity in a Revolutionary Age,* and *A History of Christianity in the Nineteenth and Twentieth Centuries* (1958–62).

In addition to his writing and teaching, Latourette played an active role in the central councils of the missionary movement. He was a member of the board of the American Baptist Foreign Missionary Society for over 20 years, president of the American Baptist Convention for one term, and an ordained Baptist preacher. He was actively involved in the International Missionary Council, the International YMCA, the Yale-in-China board, and was president of the Far Eastern Association and of the Japan International Christian University Foundation. He was long active in the World Council of Churches and played a part in drafting its constitution. He served as president of the American Society of Church History and of the American Historical Association. He was a bachelor. While visiting his sister in Oregon City, Ore., he was struck by a car and died.

CHARLES FORMAN

LATTER DAY LUMINARY. See Missionary Magazines, Baptist (Vol. II).

LAWRENCE, JOHN BENJAMIN (b. Florence, Rankin County, Miss., July 10, 1871; d. Atlanta, Ga., Sept. 5, 1968). Pastor, educator, home missions executive, editor, and author. He was educated at Mississippi College (A.B., 1899; M.A., 1902). Lawrence received the D.D. from Louisiana College (1910) and LL.D. from Oklahoma Baptist University (1926). He married Helen Alford, Nov. 15, 1900. They had six children: John Hewitt, Meriam Hoy, Katherine Alford, Elizabeth M., John B., Jr., and Helen Rebecca. After the death of his wife, he married Helen Huston in 1949.

Lawrence was ordained in 1900 and served the following Baptist churches as pastor: Greenwood, Miss., 1900–03; Brownsville and Humboldt, Tenn., 1903–07; Coliseum Place, New Orleans, La., 1907–10; First, New Orleans, 1910–13; and First, Shawnee, Okla., 1921–26. He served his denomination in the following capacities: executive secretary, Louisiana Baptist Convention and editor of the *Baptist Chronicle,* 1908–09; corresponding secretary of the Mississippi Baptist Convention, suprintendent of Mississippi Baptist Education Commission, and editor of the *Baptist Record,* 1913–21; president of Oklahoma Baptist University, 1922–26; executive secretary of the Missouri Baptist Convention, 1926–29; executive secretary-treasurer of the Home Mission Board, 1929–54; vice-president of the Southern Baptist Convention, 1916–17; a member of the Public Relations Commission, SBC; and a trustee of Oklahoma Baptist University. He also was a trustee of the State Industrial and Training School of Mississippi, a Mason, an Odd Fellow, and a Shriner.

During his tenures as executive secretary in Mississippi and president of Oklahoma Baptist University, Lawrence's business acumen assisted in the economic stability of those two groups. During the denomination's 75 Million Campaign, he led Mississippi to be the first state convention to underwrite its goal. As executive secretary in Missouri during a Convention-wide stewardship emphasis, he led in the establishment of stewardship and Brotherhood departments.

Lawrence's active ministry culminated in 24½ years as executive secretary-treasurer of the HMB, a position he assumed when the agency was near collapse from an indebtedness of $2,500,000, due in part to the defalcation of $900,000 by Treasurer C. S. Carnes (*q.v.,* Vol. I). For most of those years, he also edited *Home Missions;* and for eight years was radio speaker for the "Good News Hour," produced by the HMB. During his first 14 years, he led in repaying the staggering debt and rebuilding the board's integrity. On May 12, 1943, the board became free of debt for the first time in over a quarter of a century.

For his almost 11 remaining years at the helm of the mission board, Lawrence led in a period of enlargement and expansion, particularly in the areas of evangelism, chaplaincy, and direct missions. Significant events during Lawrence's period of service included the termination of operation of El Paso Sanatorium and the Mountain School program, the beginning of Sellers Home and Adoption Center, modern city missions program, Convention-wide promotion of schools of missions, chaplaincy ministry, publication of *Home Missions,* cooperative work with Negroes, rural church program, western missions involvement, student summer missions, the Church Extension Loan Fund for "pioneer" areas, juvenile rehabilitation, correspondence Bible course, work with migrants, Roman Catholic Information Service, Tentmakers program, the organization of Department of Cooperative Missions and reestablishment of the Department of Evangelism, and purchasing the first office building. The expansion under Lawrence provided the thrust which would later place Southern Baptist churches in each state of the United States, in addition to work in Cuba, Panama, the Canal Zone, and Puerto Rico.

Lawrence retired at the beginning of 1954 at age 82, but he continued his active involvement and concern for the denomination, writing and publishing three books in the next six years. He is the author of 23 books: *Power for Service* (1909), *The Biology of the Cross* (1913), co-author of *Church Organization and Methods* (1917), *State Mission Manual for Mississippi* (1917), *Paul's Bible School of Baptism* (1922), *Outline Studies in the Book of Revelation* (1922), *Outline Studies of the Bible* (1925), *Stewardship Applied in Church Finance* (1928), *Missions in the Bible* (1931), *The Bible a Missionary Book* (1935), *Taking Christ Seriously* (1935), *Missions and the Divine Plan for Support* (1936), *et al., Preaching the Doctrine of Grace* (1939), *Stewardship Applied in Missions* (1940), *Home Missions in the New World* (1943), *Peril of Bread* (1943), *The Religion of Power* (1944), *The Holy Spirit in Missions* (1946), *Cooperating Southern Baptists* (1948), *Kindling for Revival Fires* (1950), *The Holy Spirit in Evangelism* (1954), *A History of the Home Mission Board* (1958), and *A New Heaven and a New Earth* (1960).

COURTS REDFORD

*LAWS AFFECTING BAPTISTS.

Maryland. *Constitution.*—The Declaration of Rights of the State of Maryland in Articles 36, 37, and 38 deals specifically with religious bodies. Article 36 originally stated, "That as it is the duty of every man to worship God in such manner as he thinks most acceptable to him. . . ." However, this first sentence has been the subject of many court actions and is no longer deemed tenable. The article still insures an individual's religious freedom and goes on to assert that every man might worship God in such manner as he deems proper. The court decisions in recent years also asserted that the fact a person does not believe in God should not bar him from participation in legal activities such as jury service. Those same courts determined that it is no longer necessary to declare a belief in God and make oath upon the Bible for the purpose of testifying in any court proceedings. The present (1970) oath merely requires a witness to make oath that he will tell the truth under penalty of perjury. Article 37 stated that no religious test is to be required as a qualification for any state office other than a declaration of belief in the existence of God. This, too, has been altered by court decision so that today no such declaration is necessary. Article 38 designates that it is proper for ministers and religious institutions to receive gifts from individuals by Will and that, since 1948, any gift or devise contained in the Will of any person can be received by the minister or denomination without the necessity of any consent by the legislature of the state.

Incorporation.—A religious body in Maryland does have the right to incorporate. The right of incorporation can be exercised by a majority vote of the congregation of any church. The congregation must elect not less than four nor more than 25 persons to act as trustees for the congregation to manage the estate and property of the church. The trustees so elected shall hold in the name of the corporation any of the assets of the congregation and may conduct the business of the corporate body. The powers granted to the trustees applies only to the management of property and no authority is given over matters of doctrine or discipline. It is necessary that the church in its corporate charter advise the state of its plan specifying the time and manner of the election of the trustees and the perpetuation of their succession. Any change in the manner of election of trustees must be reported to the proper state agency. Since the power of any Baptist church rests with its membership, it has been the practice in Maryland that all corporate action of the trustees must be confirmed by way of a resolution of the congregation directing the trustees or a specific officer of the religious body to act on behalf of the congregation. The church must pay the recording fee for incorporation but is exempt from the original and annual franchise tax. It is possible for a Baptist church to function in Maryland without incorporation. However, the title to any properties of such a body must be held in the names of individual trustees, thus creating a far more difficult situation with respect to the ownership and transfer of real property and other assets.

Taxation.—Religious bodies in Maryland are exempt from real estate taxes for houses and buildings and the furniture contained therein where used exclusively for public worship. Parsonages used in connection therewith and the grounds apertinent to such houses are also exempt from real and personal property taxes. However, religious bodies are not exempted from water use taxes, sanitary and sewer charges, or paving and sidewalk assessments. Any property held or used for investment or rented by a religious society or church, shall not be exempt from taxation unless said rent or the interest or income from such investment shall be used exclusively for religious or benevolent purposes or in the payment of interest on church indebtedness. Churches and religious bodies are not required to pay inheritance taxes in Maryland on all gifts received from a deceased person. There is no income tax on a church where no part of the net earnings inure to the benefit of any individual member of said religious body. Churches in Maryland are also exempt from any sales tax when tangible personal property is purchased for use in carrying on the work of the religious body.

Marriage.—Marriages in Maryland are no longer required to be performed exclusively by a religious ceremony. Civil ceremonies are valid and are recognized. However, any minister of the gospel or official of a religious order may join persons in marriage. It is important to note that the marriage ceremony must be performed in the county in which the license was issued or, if in Baltimore City, the license must be issued from the Court of Common Pleas. The minister must affirm that the place of marriage is in the same jurisdiction as the license.

Ministers.—Ministers of the gospel of an established church of any denomination are not compelled in Maryland to testify in relation to any communications made to him in confidence by one seeking his spiritual advice or consolation. A minister cannot serve as a state Senator or Delegate. ALAN H. STOCKSDALE

Virginia. There have been some changes in the laws affecting churches in Virginia since 1956.

Quantity of land a church may own.—The quantity of land church trustees may take or hold outside of a city or town and within the same county has been increased from 75 acres to 250 acres. The council of a city or town now, by ordinance, authorize church trustees to take and hold within the city or town 20 acres instead of 10 acres, as formerly. Added to permissible uses are a church manse, parsonage, or rectory.

Value of personal property a church may own.—The personal estate which a church may take or hold at any one time has been increased from a total value of $2,000,000 to $5,000,000.

Service of process on out-of-state churches.—If a church is located outside of the state and transacts business within the state, process may be served on any trustee or officer in the city or county where he may be found, or on the clerk of the State Corporation Commission, who shall be deemed to have been appointed an agent of the church by virtue of the transaction of business in the state. This provision treats churches as other unincorporated associations.

Liability for breach of contract.—Virginia's adoption of the Uniform Commercial Code resulted in some difference in the provision relating to personal liability of trusteees, boards, or others who sign contracts on behalf of the church in so far as negotiable instruments are concerned. The statute provides that (1) an authorized representative who signs his own name to an instrument is personally obligated if the instrument neither names the person represented nor shows that the representative signed in a representative capacity, and that (2) except as otherwise established between the immediate parties, he is personally obligated if the instrument names the person represented but does not show that the representative signed in a representative capacity, or if the instrument does not name the person represented but does show that the representative signed in a representative capacity, and that (3), except as otherwise established, the name of an organization preceded or followed by the name and office of an authorized individual is a signature made in a representative capacity.

Liability for injuries caused by defective premises.—A church may be subject to liability for injuries to persons caused by defective premises. However, a recent case has held that a church, as a charitable institution, enjoys immunity from liability to persons who are beneficiaries of the church's bounty. This would appear to include persons attending worship services or visiting the church to view its architectural features or objects of artistic interest.

Miscellaneous provisions affecting churches.—The miscellaneous provisions affecting churches as enumerated in the second paragraph on page 780 of Volume II have been changed or removed by statute.

Marriage and ministerial privileges.—The provision declaring that the minister shall be guilty of a misdemeanor for failure to return to the clerk of the court the licenses and certificates of the clerk and his own certificates of the time and place of the marriage within five days of the date of the ceremony, has been eliminated. However, for failure to do so, the bond will still be forfeited. The provision forbidding performance of marriage ceremonies between white and colored persons has been repealed.

JACK S. SHACKLETON

LEADERSHIP. Whether the leader is appointed by the organization or elected by the group, his role may be thought of as that of a reconciler between the needs and goals of persons in the organization and the needs and goals (both normative and situational) of the organization. His basic strategy should be the creation of an organizational environment in which persons perceive the most attractive opportunities for fulfilling organizational needs and goals.

The integration of personal and organizational goals means that a person would be encouraged to develop the full range of his creativity and competency in ways which would result in both personal fulfilment and increased organizational effectiveness. It is in the best interests of both the organization and the individual to create such an organizational environment. Individuals profit by the fulfilment of their higher level (social, esteem, and self-actualization) needs, and the organization profits by obtaining the full potential of a person's motivational energies.

The performance of a need-reconciling function tacitly assumes that influence can be exerted in both directions; that is, both organization and personal goals may be modified as a result of the influence of the other party. Research has shown that a leader's effectiveness in exerting influence "downward" in an organization is correlated with ability to exert influence "upward." If influence is to go effectively in either direction, therefore, it must flow in both directions. This can happen only in an environment characterized by mutual trust, mutual support, and open communications. It should be anticipated that so long as neither party (individual persons and the organization) violated the trust of the other, then influence would not only be multidirectional, but also everincreasing as both parties progressively opened themselves up to the influence of the other.

Identification.—The most powerful means of influence available to any person, organization, or cause is identification. If a person completely identifies himself with a group or a cause, he accepts the goals and values of that group as his own. He consciously directs his efforts toward achieving those organizational goals, and he gains intrinsic satisfaction through their achievement.

A group responds to a leader to the extent they perceive him to offer the best available way of achieving the goals with which they are identified. Leadership, therefore, is a function of identification by the group, not just a function of the inherent qualities of the leader. When significant identification exists, all the other forms of influence which a leader may have at his disposal, e.g., legitimate authority and persuasion, become both more powerful and less necessary.

Influence through service.—The leadership behavior necessary to facilitate identification is service. The leader expresses this service both to individuals and the organization most adequately through creating an organizational environment in which persons may best fulfil their deeper motivational needs and goals by actively working toward the achievement of organizational goals. His influence is directly related to the degree to which this is accomplished.

The leader's servicing of needs should be genuine and not manipulatory. Manipulation may be defined as those influences which give the illusion, but not the fact, of serving needs. Open, admitted coercion is more desirable than manipulation on both ethical and practical grounds. Ethically, manipulation involves creating human relationships which are lacking in integrity. From a practical viewpoint, manipulation is dangerous because of the likelihood of its being recognized for exactly what it is—deceit. The mistrust which results among those who suspect they are being manipulated produces strong negative reactions and provokes ingenious efforts to defeat the leader's purposes.

Commitment.—The most signficant and valuable consequence of identification is that people will direct their own efforts toward achieving the goals with which they identify. They will voluntarily expend more energy and exercise greater care in accomplishing such goals than could ever be elicited from them with other inducements. This is commitment.

Commitment results from identification with goals which fulfil the higher-level motivational needs for belonging, esteem, and self-actualization. Intrinsic satisfactions are received from accomplishments associated with the goals with which one has become identified.

Jesus and servant-leadership.—The image of the servant is consistently and persistently portrayed by Jesus. Servant-leadership may be regarded as normative for Christian leadership. The behavioral sciences have in recent years revealed more about the nature of human behavior and how it is influenced, and it is now possible to see that servant-leadership is not only a lofty sentiment but also the means by which the leader can be most effective. The Christian servant-leader, serving as a reconciler between the needs of the church and the needs of persons, is able to serve the best interests of either one or the other only to the extent that he is able to serve the best interests of both.

Identification with Christ and with God's People.—The role of church leaders is to enable a church to identify itself as the people of God who are seeking to identify with what God is doing in the world. There are both individual and corporate levels of identification—individually identifying with Christ, and corporately identifying with God's people and with God's action in the world.

The view of the pastor as the enabler-of-identification rejects the attempt to find a master or integrative role among the usual "offices" of the ministry. The pastor is not viewed primarily as preacher, or teacher, or pastor-director, or pastoral counselor. All of these constitute different means by which the pastor facilitates identification.

The pastor's principal strategy for enabling identification is to create a climate in which individual Christians can best express their Christian faith and commitment by actively directing their efforts toward advancing the goals of the church. This strategy of integration does not mean simply to perpetuate and enhance the traditional, closed-system church. It means that a Christian should be able to express his commitment and identity "in Christ" most fully through actively expending his efforts toward achieving the church's goal of identifying itself with God's work in the world.

Bibliography: Chris Argyris, *Integrating the Individual and the Organization* (1964). J. C. Bradley, "A Transactional Theory of Church Administration" (Unpublished Ed. D. dissertation, Southern Baptist Theological Seminary, 1969). Daniel E. Griffiths, *Behavioral Science and Educational Administration* (1964). Daniel Katz and Robert L. Kahn, *The Social Psychology of Organization* (1966). Douglas McGregor, *Leadership and Motivation* (1966). Abraham H. Maslow, *Motivation and Personality* (1954).

See also Church Administration, Vol. I.

J. C. Bradley

LEAVELL, MARTHA BOONE (b. Clarksville, Tenn., June 24, 1894; d. Nashville, Tenn., Nov. 4, 1960). Daughter of Arthur Upshaw Boone (*q.v.*, Vol. I) and Eddie Belle (Cooke) Boone, she received the B.A. from Shorter College, Rome, Ga. She married Frank H. Leavell (*q.v.*, Vol. II) in 1917; they had three children: Eddie Belle (Mrs. John P. Newport), Mary Martha, and Frank Hartwell. Mrs. Leavell was a team member in Religious Focus Weeks on Baptist college campuses, and wrote *Building a Christian Home* (1936) and *The Eternal King* (1942). She was employed by the Sunday School Board as a part-time field worker for the Home Education Department, 1950–59.

HOWARD P. COLSON

LEAVELL, ROLAND QUINCHE (b. Oxford, Miss., Dec. 21, 1891; d. Chattanooga, Tenn., Jan. 15, 1963). Pastor, evangelist, educator, world traveler, and author. Son of George Washington (*q.v.*, Vol. II) and Corra Alice (Berry) Leavell, he was the eighth of nine sons. His father, an ex-Confederate soldier and a businessman, was a consecrated Baptist layman. His mother, a very devout Christian, had a profound influence upon Leavell. On June 26, 1923, Leavell married Lilian Forbes Yarborough. They had three children: Mary Delia (Mrs. H. W. Bowman), Lilian Landrum (Mrs. W. M. Fountain, Jr.), and Dorothea Yarborough (Mrs. C. A. Hudson).

Leavell taught mathematics in the Oxford, Miss., high school, 1911–13. He received both the B.A. and the M.A. degrees from the University of Mississippi in 1914, and the Th.M. (1917) and the Th.D. (1925) degrees from the Southern Baptist Theological Seminary. For two years, 1917–19, he served as secretary to the Overseas Young Men's Christian Association and was stationed in France.

Having been ordained by Oxford First Baptist Church in 1913, Leavell served as minister of the following First Baptist churches: Oxford, Miss., 1919–23; Picayune, Miss., 1925–27; Gainesville, Ga., 1927–36; and Tampa, Fla., 1942–46. In 1927 he was a member of the Foreign Mission Board, SBC, from Mississippi. In 1929–30 he was vice-president of the Georgia Baptist Convention, and from 1929 to 1936 he served as a member of the Home Mission Board, SBC, from Georgia.

Leavell's relationship to the HMB proved an immediate preparation for his extensive leadership of Southern Baptists in evangelism and missions. He served as superintendent of evangelism, HMB, 1937–42. In this position he gave impetus to the cooperative efforts of the churches in the development of evangelistic methods and in the promotion of simultaneous evangelistic crusades. A member of the committee on evangelism of the Baptist World Alliance, he served first as secretary, 1939–55, and afterward as chairman, 1955–60, of the committee.

Leavell served as president of the New Orleans Baptist Theological Seminary from July 1, 1946, to May 1, 1958, when he was named president emeritus following a serious illness that forced his retirement. Under his leadership the 75-acre Gentilly campus site was purchased in 1947, and the seminary relocated in the newly developed facilities in 1953. Both the faculty and the student body were greatly enlarged. Extensive revisions were made in the curricula and the awards, and the major departments were reorganized as the School of Theology, the School of Religious Education, and the School of Church Music. Full accreditation was achieved for the School of Theology and the School of Religious Education in the respective national professional accrediting associations.

In 1920 Leavell toured mission fields in China and Japan; in 1934 and 1955, in the Near East; and in 1934, 1937, 1947, 1949, and 1955 in Europe. He considered his participation in the Foreign Mission Board's preaching mission to Japan in 1951 a most profound influence on his life and work. He was visiting lecturer to four South American theological seminaries in 1953. In 1959–60 he was vice-president of the Mississippi Baptist Convention, and he served as first vice-president of the SBC, 1961–62.

Following his formal retirement Leavell resided in Jackson, Miss. With improved health, he pursued a vigorous schedule of preaching and writing. In a period of less than four years he authored five published books. Leavell contributed numerous articles to state Baptist papers and missions journals. His fifteen published books include the following titles: *An Unashamed Workman: Landrum Pinson Leavell* (1932); *Winning Others to Christ* (1936); *A Handbook for the Southwide Baptist Revival of 1939* (1939); *Helping Others to Become Christians* (1939); *Preaching the Doctrines of Grace* (ed.), (1939); *Saving America to Save the World* (1940); *The Romance of Evangelism* (1942); *Christianity Our Citadel* (1943); *Evangelism, Christ's Imperative Commission* (1951); *Corra Berry Leavell, A Christian Mother* (1952); *The Sheer Joy of Living* (1961); *Studies in Matthew: The King and the Kingdom* (1962); *Prophetic Preaching Then and Now* (1963); *The Apostle Paul, Christ's Supreme Trophy* (1963); and *The Christian's Business: Being a Witness* (1964). The last three volumes were published after his death.

Leavell's death in 1963 came while he was conducting a series of studies in the Gospel of Matthew at the First Baptist Church of Chattanooga, Tenn. In that year his commentary on Matthew was used by Southern Baptist churches in the annual January Bible Study Week. Funeral services were held in the memorial chapel bearing his name on the campus of New Orleans Baptist Theological Seminary, with burial in the Leavell family plot at Oxford, Miss.

J. HARDEE KENNEDY

***LEBANON, MISSION IN.** The missionary staff grew to 26 by late 1969. Some were engaged in international projects—a seminary, publications, and broadcasting for the Arab world. Others worked in the Beirut school, in a reading room and book store, and with a correspondence course. One had an itinerant ministry in countries where no missionaries resided. Lebanese Baptists numbered 450 in 1969. Conflict in the Middle East created attitudes which hindered evangelistic and missionary work, but there was religious liberty in Lebanon. JOHN D. HUGHEY

LEE, ERNEST EUGENE (b. Ripley, Tenn., Sept. 26, 1876; d. Covington, Ga., Dec. 21, 1962). He attended Emory College, Oxford, Ga. He married Ava Bomar of Chapel Hill, Ga., in 1903. A salesman and insurance manager from 1896 to 1906, he later served as B.Y.P.U. secretary of Indian Territory (1902–04) and Texas (1906–08), and as B.Y.P.U. and Training Union field secretary for the Sunday School Board, 1908–46. Lee wrote the *Junior B.Y.P.U. Manual* (1913) and the *Intermediate B.Y.P.U. Manual* (1915). Characterized by enthusiasm and friendliness, Lee was popular with young people, who nicknamed him "Hot Dog" Lee. During his later years he wrote a regular column in *The Baptist Training Union Magazine* called "Me and My Experiences."
HOWARD P. COLSON

LEE, INMAN EDWARD (b. Franklin County, Ill., Dec. 23, 1887; d. Carbondale, Ill., June 29, 1969). Pastor and denominational leader. Son of Robert W., a Baptist minister, and Josephine (Phillips) Lee, he attended Ewing College, Shurtleff College (B.A., 1911), and Central Baptist Theological Seminary, Kansas City, Mo. (B.D., 1915). He married Beatrice Flannigan, Dec. 25, 1911. They had two children, Helen Louise Lee Heinen and Edward Lee.

His Illinois pastorates included the First Baptist churches of Pinckneyville, 1916–20, Herrin, 1920–28, Harrisburg, 1928–36, and DuQuoin, 1939–53. Upon terminating his ministry at Harrisburg, he served Illinois Baptists as Sunday School and Training Union secretary, and editor of the *Illinois Baptist,* 1937–39. He served on the state board of directors for 31 years, and three different times as chairman (1923–26, 1940–46, and 1951–52). He was elected president of the Illinois Baptist State Association, 1935–36. He represented Illinois Baptists to the Southern Baptist Convention, serving on the Home Mission Board for eight years, the Foreign Mission Board for nine years, the Sunday School Board for eight years, and the Executive Committee, 1948–53. Lee retired in July, 1953. The churches where he served as pastor designated their 1969 state mission offerings as the "I. E. Lee Memorial" for a new church at Rock Island. He is buried in the Sunset Memorial Park, DuQuoin, Ill. MYRON D. DILLOW

***LIBERIA, MISSION IN.** At the invitation of the Liberia Baptist Missionary and Educational Convention, the Foreign Mission Board began sending missionaries to Liberia in 1960, thus resuming a relationship suspended in 1875. Ricks Institute, Baptist boarding school, was strengthened, a Bible school opened, and an encampment developed. Missionary assistance was given to Bassa-speaking groups within the Liberia Baptist Native Direct Conference. In 1969 missionaries numbered 36 and 210 churches reported 21,902 members. H. CORNELL GOERNER

***LIBRARY, CHURCH.** The church library of the seventies is seen as a media center of instructional materials, both printed and audiovisual. The Program of Audiovisual Education of the Sunday School Board was assigned to the Church Library Department in Oct., 1966. Florida Waite served as secretary of that department from 1943 to 1957. Wayne E. Todd became secretary in 1959.

In 1962, a revised plan for the local church library organization was suggested. Rather than dividing library work between two groups—a library staff and a library committee—it was suggested that there be only one group, to be known as church library staff. Position titles recommended in 1968 are: director of library services, director of printed materials education, director of technical processes, director of circulation, and director of promotion. Plans suggested for the seventies include a literature librarian and a music librarian. The total number of church libraries registered with the department in Sept., 1969, was 18,301.

In Dec., 1956, 18 leaders of the Convention met in Nashville to study the work of the associational church library organization. It was determined that the purpose of this associational organization should be to start new libraries and to encourage and strengthen existing ones. In 1960 there were 12 associational and four state organizations. By Sept., 1969, there were 374 associations with at least one person carrying library promotion and education responsibilities, and 10 state organizations.

The objective of the Program of Church Library Service, as approved by the Convention in 1965, is to offer guidance and assistance in establishing, strengthening, and extending the library ministry in churches and among other groups such as associations, homes, institutional homes, assemblies, student centers, and hospitals.

Many materials have been developed to assist church library workers. These include a church library services magazine, study course books, flipcharts, posters, and an achievement guide.

The Sunday School Board—with assistance from other Convention agencies—offers free library materials to each Southern Baptist church or mission beginning a library for the first time. These materials include books, audiovisuals, and vertical file items. In 1969 this plan was expanded to include Spanish Baptist churches and missions through a gift of selected Spanish and English materials. WAYNE E. TODD

LIBYA, MISSION IN. Southern Baptists sent Harold and Dorothy (Amos) Blankenship, missionary associates, to Tripoli in 1965 to work with the First Baptist Church. With 35 charter members, the church was organized in 1962 by a group of Americans employed by oil companies and American military personnel at Wheelus Air Base. An Air Force sergeant, the late Vonley C. Day, was its first pastor. The English-language church, which welcomes into its fellowship people of all nationalities and races, reported 348 members at the end of 1969. Libya is not open to direct Christian mission work.

HAROLD L. BLANKENSHIP

LIFE AND HEALTH BENEFITS DEPARTMENT. Established by the Annuity Board, SBC, on May 1, 1964, to provide individual and group life and health insurance for employees of Southern Baptist churches, conventions, agencies, and institutions. Three insurance plans were established.

Life Benefit Plan: An individual reducing term minimum cost insurance plan. Offers level coverage in amounts from $10,000 to $30,000 as determined by salary for death prior to age 45, with annual reducing amounts thereafter. Coverage terminates at retirement with a small paid up benefit for 10 years minimum participation. Inaugurating the program Oct. 1, 1964, on 5,558 lives, the Annuity Board underwrote the plan until 1966, when it transferred the risk to Group Life and Health Insurance Company of Dallas to afford greater safety and to meet certain legal requirements. Ownership and administration was retained by the Annuity Board. With the transfer slight modifications were made in amounts of coverage and rates at later ages. On June 30, 1969, a total of 11,524 persons were insured for $185.3 million. Death claims on 131 lives total $1,478,085 for the period Oct. 1, 1964, to June 30, 1969.

Group Life Insurance Program: A group term life insurance program inaugurated July 1, 1967, to provide custom designed group plans for church or denominational employers of 10 or more persons. This program was underwritten by Northwestern National Life Insurance Company for the Annuity Board. On June 30, 1969, total coverage was $19.1 million in 40 groups composed of 3,521 persons.

Health Benefit Plan: A convention-wide group plan of hospital-surgical-major medical insurance offered to individuals or groups (except hospital employees). This plan, designed according to Annuity Board specifications, is underwritten by Blue Cross-Blue Shield. Benefit structure provides full cost of semi-private room with unlimited ancillary services after a $25 deductible, a $300 maximum surgical schedule, 80–20 per cent co-insurance major medical after a $100 deductible with a $5,000 one year—$10,000 lifetime maximum per person. Coverage is provided without health requirements. Preexisting conditions are covered immediately. Flat national rates prevail. Coverage may be continued after retirement. Inaugurated Oct. 1, 1965, with 5,969 members the plan covered 15,499 as of June 30, 1969.

On July 1, 1969, the Division of Insurance Services operated by the Home Mission Board was transferred to the Life and Health Benefits Department. At the time the department name was changed to Department of Insurance Services.

BAYNARD F. FOX

LIFE BENEFIT PLAN. See LIFE and HEALTH BENEFITS DEPARTMENT.

LINCOLN, ABRAHAM (grandfather of President Lincoln) (b. Va., 1738; d. Jefferson County, Ky., May, 1786). He came from Rockingham County, Va., and entered land on Long Run Creek, Jefferson County, Ky., on May 20, 1780. In Virginia he was a member of a prominent family and belonged to Linville Creek Baptist Church. "There is every reason to believe that this pioneer brought his religion along with him and that the Linville Creek Baptist Church had a new birth on Long Run." He was killed by an Indian on Long Run Creek in May, 1786. He was the father of Thomas Lincoln (1778–1851), who also was born in Virginia. Thomas Lincoln was the father of Abraham Lincoln (1809–65), President of the United States.

LEO T. CRISMON

LINGUISTIC PHILOSOPHY. Linguistic philosophy approaches reality through a logical analysis of language. It designates primarily two philosophical movements: (1) logical atomism and (2) logical positivism. Logical atomism, as represented by Bertrand Russell, held the basis of all language to be "atomic facts" which could be verified only by sense evidence. Thus, to verify the statement "That is green," I utter the word "green" and point to a "green" color. While such "atomic propositions" could be built up into more complex statements which Russell called "molecular statements," nevertheless, there are *no* molecular facts but only atomic ones. This meant that language had merely a univocal or *singular* logic: its function was to denote "atomic facts" such as colors, physical objects, or chemical and psychological processes. It also meant that language's correspondence with actual facts is to be settled by empirical methods and techniques.

Linguistic positivists such as Moritz Schlick and Rudolph Carnap also held the logic of language to be singular: language is simply a way to represent our sense impressions of physical objects encountered in history, and it is to be verified only by appeal to sense-experience. The sole task of philosophy is the pursuit of linguistic meaning, and *whatever meaning language has depends on its method of sense-verification.* Alfred J. Ayer's statement that "the meaning of a proposition is its method of verification" came to be called the "Verification Principle," and in its second or modified form ("a statement has meaning if there are no possible ways of falsifying it") is regarded as the touchstone of logical positivism. Since *metaphysical* language refers constantly to realities which are regarded as transcending finite man's sense experience (e.g., God, the soul, and immortality), linguistic positivists proclaimed all such language to be "meaningless" or at the most "purely emotive."

Theologians, in their attempt to meet the challenge which the verification principle posed to theological language, have often accepted the unspoken premise of both logical atomists and Logical Positivists—namely, that language has only a *"univocal* function" or a "singular logic," rather than an *"equivocal* function" or a "manifold logic." Thus, e.g., William Hordern says that the function of theological language is to point to a "Convictor" who has "convicted" the believer using the language and that, therefore, verification involves checking the speaker's depth of conviction; R. B. Braithwaite says that theological language has only one purpose: to express the speaker's intention to *act* in a certain ethical way (and hence the verification or justification of the language is to be found in the *action* indicated rather than in the *content* of what is said); and Paul van Buren says that since we cannot any longer experience the being designated by the word "God" in this "God-is-dead" or "secular" world, we simply must give up all "God-talk"!

All these responses to linguistic philosophy go astray by resting in the thought of the "earlier" Ludwig Wittgenstein (which was akin to that of the logical positivists) and forgetting the thought of the "later" Wittgenstein (which was more like that of the functional analysts). The "later" Wittgenstein and all functional analysts hold that language is like a carpenter's tool box, containing *many* tools each having *diverse* or *manifold* functions. Taking this hint, some theologically-inclined functional analysts have held a *manifold* logic to be involved in theological or religious language and have therefore suggested that there are *many* possible ways of verification. Three contemporary exemplifications of such Christian Functional Analysts are Dallas M. High, Frederick Ferré, and Robert Jenson.

BIBLIOGRAPHY: R. B. Braithwaite, *An Empiricist's View of the Nature of Religious Belief* (1955). Frederick Ferré, *Language, Logic and God* (1961). Dallas M. High, *Language, Persons, and Belief* (1967). Robert Jenson, *The Knowledge of Things Hoped For: The Sense of Theological Discourse* (1969). Bertrand Russell, *Logic and Knowledge Essays, 1901–50* (1956). Paul Van Buren, *The Secular Meaning of the Gospel* (1963). ELLIS W. HOLLON, JR.

LITES, WILLIAM JACOB (b. Fort Jessup, La., Nov. 25, 1892; d. Albuquerque, N. Mex., Apr. 7, 1967). Minister of education and Sunday School secretary. One of 13 children born to Thomas Jefferson and Martha Lee (Atherton) Lites, he was a rural evangelist for American Sunday School Union, traveling throughout Louisiana organizing Sunday Schools, preaching, teaching, and leading "singing schools." Lites was educated at Baylor University (A.B., 1924) and the Baptist Bible Institute, now New Orleans Baptist Theological Seminary. During World War I he served in the medical corps. He served as minister of education in First Baptist Church, Galveston, Tex., 1924–27. He became associate secretary of the state Sunday School Department of Texas in 1927. In 1945 Lites joined the staff of the Baptist Convention of New Mexico as Sunday School secretary. He held this position until his retirement in 1961. After retirement, he was associated with A. B. Culbertson Company in church financing. HERBERT E. BERGSTROM

LITTLETON, HOMER RICHERSON (b. Martin, Ga., Mar. 20, 1904; d. Toccoa, Ga., Apr. 18, 1964). Missionary to Nigeria (1940–47) and Gold Coast (1947–64). Educated at Mercer University (1931), he was pastor of Georgia churches, 1931–40. He married Ossie Price, May 28, 1932. In Nigeria he taught in the Iwo Baptist college, 1940–43, and acted as principal of the Iwo industrial institute, 1945–47. Pioneer missionary in the Gold Coast (Ghana), he lived in Kumasi and during his latter years was chairman of the Ghana Mission. GEORGE W. SADLER

LLOYD, BENJAMIN (b. Hancock County, Ga., Oct. 6, 1804; d. Butler County, Ala., Jan. 14, 1860). Minister of the Primitive Baptist church and hymnologist. Reared in west Georgia, he was baptized into the Mount Pisgah Baptist Church, Bibb County, Ga., in 1822. Married to Naomi Ann Cox, Feb. 22, 1832, he was also ordained that year. A leader in the formation of the Liberty Association (East Alabama) in 1836, he withdrew two years later to assume a major role in creating the Beulah Association of the Primitive Baptist churches. He published *Primitive Hymns* (1841), a hymnal of lasting service, its most recent edition being in 1967. Serving pastorates in Chambers, Coosa, and Butler counties, Ala., he was active in the Wetumpka Association and, at the time of his death, moderator of the Ebenezer Association of the Primitive Baptist churches.

BIBLIOGRAPHY: Oliver C. Weaver, "A Pioneer Primitive Baptist in Alabama," *Alabama Review*, Apr. 1968. OLIVER C. WEAVER

LONG RUN BAPTIST, THE. The official publication of the Long Run Association of Baptists. It was begun at Louisville, Ky., Jan., 1950, and it continues to the present (1970). Editors have been H. Floyd Folsom, 1950–52; Ben F. Mitchell, Feb., 1953—Jan., 1967; G. Allen West, began in July, 1967. An earlier paper, *The Long Runner*, was published 1941–42; then a page in the *Western Recorder*, with the heading "The Long Runner" was used, 1943–46, while J. Perry Carter was superintendent. LEO T. CRISMON

LORD, FRED TOWNLEY (b. Burnley, Lancashire, Eng., Oct. 27, 1893; d. Greenville, S. C., Feb. 9, 1962) . Minister, editor, university professor, and leader of world Baptists. Son of Jonathan and Ann (Townley) Lord, he was educated at Rawdon Baptist College, Leeds (1910) , the University of Manchester (B.A., 1913) , and the University of London (B.D., D.D.) . He received honorary degrees from William Jewell College (D.Litt.) , Eastern Baptist Seminary, Philadelphia (D.D.) , East Texas Baptist College, Marshall (LL.D.) , Carson Newman College (LL.D.) , Mercer University (LL.D.) , University of Richmond (LL.D.) , and Furman University (D.D.) .

Lord married Sarah Alice Entwisle, June 16, 1917. They had two children: Marcus Townley and Monica (Mrs. R. S. George) . Ordained in 1916, Lord served as pastor of the following English Baptist churches: Turret Green Church, Ipswich, 1916–20; Acton Church, 1920–26; Queen's Road Church, Coventry, 1926–30; and Bloomsbury Central Church, London, 1930–58. In 1918 Lord lectured on social history and citizenship with the Army Service Schools of the British Expeditionary Forces. He served as editor of *The Baptist Times,* London, 1941–56. From 1958 until his death Lord was visiting lecturer and professor of Religion at Furman University.

Among the many offices held by Lord, the following are particularly noteworthy; national president of the British Sunday School Union; chairman of the board of the Carey-Kingsgate Press; chairman of the scholarship committee of the Baptist Union; member of the Religion Advisory Committee of the British Broadcasting Corporation; president of the Baptist Union of Great Britain and Ireland; and president of the Baptist World Alliance, 1950–55.

Besides numerous articles in many periodicals, Lord was author of the following published works: *Man and His Character* (1926) ; *The Master and His Man* (1928) ; *The Man in the Dark Room* (1927) ; *The Unity of Soul and Body* (1929) ; *The Acts of the Apostles* (1930) ; *Christ on the Road* (1932) ; *Light Your Beacons* (1933) ; *Christ in the Modern Scene* (1936) ; *Great Women of the Bible* (1939) ; *Great Women in Christian History* (1940) ; *Conquest of Death* (1940) ; *A History of the Baptist Missionary Society* (1941) ; *The Faith That Sings* (1951) ; *The Treasure of the Gospel* (1952) ; *You Can Master Life* (1955) ; and *Baptist World Fellowship, A History of the Baptist World Alliance* (1955) .

Lord combined in his personality the finest qualities of dedication, insight, gentility, scholarship, and good humor to give an example of the best in Christian leadership among Baptists. Whether spoken or written, his words reflected his winsome personality and were remarkably effective. In performing the tasks of his manifold ministries, Lord often worked with those who were high in the councils of government during and after the crisis years of World War II. Whether conferring in such circles or dealing with the humblest parishioner or student, Lord manifested an enlightened concern and ability which caused him to be highly regarded by those who knew him. JOE M. KING

***LORD'S SUPPER.** In contrast to baptism, discussions on the Lord's Supper were much less intense and widespread in the Christian world in the period 1955–70. However, there were some significant efforts at interfaith understanding growing out of the ecumenical movement, and some Baptist scholars reexamined their positions with reference to the Supper. Also the Roman Catholic Church, through Vatican II, made considerable concession to contemporary human needs.

Several British Baptist pastors are moving in the direction of a more sacramental view of the Supper. Representative of this group are Neville Clark and Stephen Winward. Clark writes: "Our examination of the New Testament teaching reveals that at every point baptism and the eucharist drive us back for their true understanding to other more central and pervasive doctrines, to christology, ecclesiology, and eschatology." He asserts that the sacraments are given to the church to be the channels of her life and power. "Liberal theology was wrong. The Church did not create the sacraments; rather are the sacraments perpetually creative of the Church."

Winward declares that although Christ's sacrifice on the cross was a "once-for-all" act for our salvation, the "remembrance" and the "recalling" of the sacrifice are more than a mere recollection or a memorial service. He states: "In the eucharist, Christ is present, and the saving event is contemporary and operative. For where Christ is present, there also is his immortal sacrifice. . . . The eucharist is a sacrifice because *the* sacrifice is present. . . . We do not offer him, but he offers us, the participants by grace in the effects of his one sacrifice."

John E. Skoglund, American Baptist, agrees with Calvin that "Christian worship, rightly understood, consists in the union of Word and Table; and that when one of these basic elements is excluded or underplayed, worship is impoverished." However, while he is most anxious for the liturgical renewal, he is working for it within the Baptist tradition and theology. He decries the adoption of "high church" forms and ritual just because they look or sound "nice."

Franklin M. Segler, Southern Baptist, calls for the observance of the Lord's Supper as a central part of a worship service and not merely as an addendum. It must always be interpreted in relation to the person of Christ. He asserts: "In the New Testament the primary emphasis is given to the experience and relationship of the believer to his Lord and not to the administrator or to the method of the administration of the ordinances."

After paying due respect to the differing

points of view of Southern Baptists, Segler declares: "There is a place for the denomination, but to place any given denomination above the body of all believers is presumption and idolatry."

Although her basic theological doctrines relating to the eucharist remain virtually unchanged, the Roman Catholic Church has brought the service much closer to the people for their benefit and for the prosperity of the Church. Outstanding changes include the use of the language of the people instead of Latin, moving the altar toward the people and using it more like a table with the priest behind it facing the congregation, and the giving of both elements to the people instead of reserving the cup for the clergy only.

BIBLIOGRAPHY: Neville Clark, *An Approach to the Theology of the Sacraments* (1956). Franklin M. Segler, *Christian Worship: Its Theology and Practice* (1967). John E. Skoglund, *Worship in the Free Churches* (1965). Stephen E. Winward, *The Reformation of Our Worship* (1965). JOHN T. WAYLAND

LORD'S SUPPER, CLOSE COMMUNION (cf. Lord's Supper, Requisites to, Vol. II). The practice of both close communion and open communion goes back to near the beginnings of English Baptist history. In the open communionist view, it was believed that the local church partook of the Supper as a part of that fellowship of believers whose circumference extended to the bounds of the worldwide body of Christ. Communion belonged to the church universal, and was to be celebrated by all those who had had the experience of faith in Christ. In the early 19th century, Robert Hall, Jr., stated clearly the main position of the open communionists: "that no man, or set of men, are entitled to prescribe as an indispensable condition of communion, what the New Testament has not enjoined as a condition of salvation."

On the other hand, the close communionists thought that the requirements for admission to the Lord's Supper were exactly those of local church membership, i.e., faith and believer's baptism by immersion. The close communion stand has often been called, therefore, a stand for "close baptism," since close communion Baptists have traditionally excluded from the Supper persons who have not been baptized by immersion on a profession of faith.

It can be seen that the close communion position has focused upon the qualifications of the individual believer. In principle, for example, a Methodist who has been baptized by immersion on a profession of faith would be eligible to partake of the Supper in a Baptist church, if he were invited to do so by the church.

When the Landmark Movement arose near the middle of the 19th century, the Landmarkers became primarily concerned with the question of the authority of the administrator. Administration of the Supper, they affirmed, was in the hands of the local Baptist church. Any celebration apart from the jurisdiction of a local Baptist church was invalid. Moreover, since the Landmarkers rejected the immersions of non-Baptists, the latter were ineligible to partake of the Supper, on the grounds that, by Landmark standards, they had not been baptized.

Moreover, many Landmarkers have believed traditionally in strict local church communion. This practice restricts the celebration of the Supper to the membership of the local church under whose auspices the ordinance is observed. It makes ineligible for participating in the Supper not only non-Baptist Christians who happen to be present, but also visiting Baptists.

In 1960 the Research and Statistics Department of the Sunday School Board, SBC, conducted a survey of 361 Baptist churches in representative areas of the Southern Baptist Convention, for the purpose of determining practices with respect to the Lord's Supper. According to this survey, 18.3 per cent of these churches confined participation in the Supper to their own members; 8.6 per cent invited only Baptists to partake; 12.2 per cent invited all Christians present to partake; and 40.4 per cent made "no reference as to who may partake."

The survey revealed that a sizable contingent of Southern Baptist churches were still observing strict local church communion during the middle decades of this century. An appreciably smaller number were adhering to the traditional close communionist position. Almost half of the churches surveyed had gone over to what might be described as a covert open communionism which allowed non-Baptist Christians who were present in Baptist communion services to participate in the Supper without either invitation or rebuff. On the other hand, about one tenth of the churches appeared to be explicitly open-communionist.

Although the open communion question is not necessarily involved with that of "alien" immersions, the two questions are frequently grouped together by Southern Baptists in their discussion of the ordinances. JAMES E. TULL

***LOTT CAREY BAPTIST FOREIGN MISSION CONVENTION.** In 1970 the convention supported 144 missionaries in Guyana, Haiti, India, Liberia, and Nigeria. The headquarters are located at 1501–11th Street, N.W., Washington, D. C. 20001. The president in 1970 was M. L. Wilson, New York City, with a budget of $294,817.29. WENDELL C. SOMERVILLE

LOUISIANA, HURRICANE DISASTERS. During the years 1957–69 three natural disasters —all hurricanes—crippled Louisiana Baptist work in coastal areas, damaging or destroying many churches and missions.

Hurricane Audrey (1957).—The worst killer storm in Louisiana history, it swept a 20-foot tidal wave over the Cameron and Creole areas.

An estimated 400 lives were lost and approximately 50,000 cattle perished. The force of the hurricane waters swept away gravestones and washed bodies from graves in some areas.

Mrs. Glenn Allen Tupper, retired minister's wife, was drowned. Wallace Primeaux, pastor of Oak Grove, and W. Z. Lewis, pastor of Cameron, and their families barely escaped. Oak Grove Church lost 11 members and its building.

The Louisiana Baptist Convention named three pastors, James Middleton of Shreveport's First Baptist Church, W. L. Sewell of Bossier City's First Church, and George A. Ritchey of Mansfield's First Church, to serve as hurricane disaster committeemen. A convention hurricane disaster emergency fund was set up, with a minimum goal of $100,000 named. Louisiana Baptist churches contributed $127,970 to the emergency fund.

Hurricane Betsy (1965).—While not as destructive of life as Audrey, it claimed the distinction of being the most costly storm in recorded history. Damage to housing and other properties exceeded $1,000,000,000.

Storm-pushed waters backed up the Mississippi River and inundated Plaquemine and St. Bernard parishes and several large residential sections of New Orleans. At New Orleans within one hour, the river rose 3.5 feet, later rising to a height of 12.4 feet. Over 300,000 Louisianians evacuated or changed their place of residence. Flood waters reached cities and towns up to 70 miles inland.

Betsy destroyed or severely damaged 23 Baptist churches and six pastors' homes. A hurricane committee was named including Robert L. Lee, executive secretary, Louisiana convention; Mercer Irwin, executive secretary of New Orleans Association; Harold Gallaspy, associate executive secretary of New Orleans Association; Carl Conrad, secretary of Direct Missions, state convention; and moderators of storm-damaged associations. The convention set a goal of $585,000 to be raised to repair and restore properties, replace equipment, supplement and pay pastors' salaries, and to provide funds for miscellaneous relief. A total of $180,240 was received through the Baptist Building business office for this relief.

Hurricane Camille (1969).—With winds estimated up to 160 m.p.h., it flooded Plaquemine peninsula and did great damage from Triumph to Venice. Churches in Venice and Triumph were completely lost. Venice also lost a pastor's home. Buras-Triumph and Riverview churches lost pastors' homes and both church buildings were severely damaged. New mission chapel at Empire remained intact, but the interior was gutted.

The denominational cooperation committee of the state convention, in regular session, extended an official appeal to all churches for relief of churches and workers sustaining loss in the storm. George Ritchey of Mansfield headed the committee, which estimated damages to churches at $250,000. The business office of Baptist Building reported gifts of $74,639 to the hurricane Camille disaster fund.

JOHN W. GREEN

*LOUISIANA ASSOCIATIONS.

I. New Associations. CHAPPAPEELA. Organized Oct. 12, 1965, at Spring Creek Baptist Church, Spring Creek. It came from Tangipahoa Association and is located in Tangipahoa Parish. Its first annual meeting was held Oct. 10, 11, and 13, 1966, in Hammond and Ponchatoula. In 1969, 17 churches and missions reported 227 baptisms, 5,948 members, $373,495 total gifts, $60,973 mission gifts, and property value of $1,795,000.

GULF COAST. Organized Oct. 11, 1960, at First Baptist Church, Morgan City. It came from Adolphe Stagg Association and is located in St. Mary, Lafourche, and Assumption Parishes. Its first annual meeting was held Oct. 16–17, 1961, at First Baptist Church in Patterson. In 1969, 16 churches and missions reported 176 baptisms, 4,123 members, $383,492 total gifts, $53,866 mission gifts, property value of $1,910,168, and a total church debt of $716,952.

LATANGI. Organized Jan. 7, 1956, at Antioch Baptist Church. It came from Amite River Association and is located in Livingston and Tangipahoa Parishes. Its first annual session was held Oct. 5–6, 1956, at New Beulah Church. In 1969, 20 churches and missions reported 178 baptisms, 4,293 members, $190,569 total gifts, $17,446 mission gifts, and $995,123 property value.

NORTHWEST. Formed Oct. 1, 1969, after two years of planning, by the dissolution of three associations (Bossier, Caddo, and North Caddo) and a district organization. It is located in Bossier and Caddo Parishes. An executive secretary who formerly served as superintendent of missions for the three associations now serves the new one. In 1969, 87 churches of the three associations reported combined totals of 2,040 baptisms, 62,810 members, $5,765,499 total gifts, $1,023,912 mission gifts, and property value of $28,556,290.

II. Changes in Associations. BOSSIER. Located in northwest Louisiana it was in existence for 46 years, and was one of three associations comprising the former District VI, with an executive secretary (superintendent of missions) serving all three. In 1969, 23 churches reported 498 baptisms, 11,808 members, $872,489 total gifts, $123,842 mission gifts, $4,072,750 total church property value, and $1,076,938 church debt. It was dissolved in Oct., 1969, to become part of the newly organized Northwest Association composed of this association, Caddo, and North Caddo associations.

CADDO. Located in the southern half of Caddo Parish in northwest Louisiana and including the city of Shreveport, it was in existence for 77 years. It was one of three associations in the former District VI, with an executive secretary (superintendent of missions) serving all three. In 1969, 47 churches reported 1,422 baptisms, 45,795 members, $4,645,998 total gifts, $853,130 mission gifts, $23,384,840 total church property value, and $5,307,949 church debt. It was dissolved in Oct., 1969, to merge with Bossier and North Caddo associations to form the new Northwest Association.

North Caddo. Located in the northern part of Caddo Parish in northwestern Louisiana it was in existence for 22 years, one of three associations comprising the former District VI, with an executive secretary (superintendent of missions) serving all three. In 1969, 17 churches reported 120 baptisms, 5,207 members, $247,012 total gifts, $37,940 mission gifts, $1,098,700 total church property value, and $231,089 church debt. The association was dissolved in Oct., 1969, along with Bossier and Caddo associations to organize the new Northwest Association.

M. H. FIELDS

***LOUISIANA BAPTIST CHILDREN'S HOME.** D. C. Black was succeeded as superintendent in 1962 by Wade B. East. The governing board elected by the Louisiana Baptist Convention consists of 15 trustees.

Two additional cottages were erected in 1956, making nine for institutional care of children. Through a designated gift by Miss Lallage Feazel, an administration building was erected in 1964. Capital assets in 1969 were $1,512,985, with no capital indebtedness.

The report of 1969 showed 153 children at the home for institutional care. In 1964 a foster care ministry was begun. From 450 to 500 children are assisted annually besides those in institutional care.

Cooperative program allocation for 1970 was $197,000, which provides half of the operating budget. Other income was from endowment of approximately $101,000, individual gifts, wills, memorials, farm operations, and the annual fall food roundup.

CHARLES S. MCILVEENE

***LOUISIANA BAPTIST CONVENTION.**

I. History. After an intensive management study in 1958 the following priorities for convention programs were approved: support for church and mission programs, Christian education for developing leadership in the churches and missions, and institutions offering Christian services for special human needs.

The Sesquicentennial.—The first Baptist church in Louisiana, the Half Moon Bluff Baptist Church, was organized on October 12, 1812, near what is now Franklinton, Louisiana. Recognition of the sesquicentennial of Baptist work in Louisiana was made at the 1962 convention. Special recognition was given to the Calvary Baptist Church, Bayou Chicot, as the oldest Baptist church in Louisiana and to the Mississippi Baptist Association from which Baptist work in Louisiana began. A special memorial service was held at the original site of the Half Moon Bluff Baptist Church. A replica of the original building had been erected by a committee of laymen on the Louisiana State Fair Grounds and moved to the original building site for the occasion.

Baptist Building.—In 1956 the convention approved the recommendation of the executive board of the Louisiana Baptist Convention to build a new Baptist Building in Alexandria. Bids were opened during the 1958 convention. The building was dedicated in 1960 in a formal service during the convention. Containing 59,000 square feet of space, the building houses all the departments of work of the convention's executive board in addition to providing space for the Baptist Book Store, the Baptist Foundation, and the *Baptist Message*. An additional half acre of land was purchased in 1965 to make a total land area of about four and one-half acres.

Convention Reorganization.—A comprehensive management study of the Louisiana Baptist Convention was undertaken in 1957 by the firm of Booz, Allen, and Hamilton. The report was adopted at the 1958 convention.

Resulting from this study a new constitution and bylaws were presented to the convention in 1958. They were adopted in 1959. At this time the executive board was reorganized in accordance with the new constitution. It is composed of one member from each association with an additional member for each 10,000 church members. Maximum membership from any association was five until it was changed to seven in 1968. Its work is organized under the operating, program, and denominational cooperation committees and their appropriate subcommittees. Further refining of management procedures was accomplished by the adoption of a business and financial plan in 1965.

The student work of the convention was reorganized in 1965. At that time all of the student work was brought under the jurisdiction of the Student Department with all salaries of local student directors to be paid solely by the executive board.

A public relations department was added in 1968. John W. Green was elected director.

A Louisiana Baptist History Committee was added to the list of standing committees of the convention in 1961. A historical society had been active for some time. In addition to the task of collecting and preserving the history of the Louisiana Baptists, this committee was assigned the responsibility for writing a new history of Baptists in Louisiana. In 1967 responsibility was given to this committee to aid in the establishment of a library and archives on the third floor of the Baptist Building; it was named the Mae Lee Room in honor of the late wife of the executive secretary, Robert L. Lee. A historical atlas of Baptists in Louisiana is (1970) in process of completion.

The district missions program of the state came under study and reorganization. As adopted in 1961 the program provided for each area to choose between field secretaries to be paid by the executive board of the convention, associational missionaries who receive a salary supplement from the executive board, or no field worker. Provision was also made for special workers employed by the state board as needed.

Christian Education.—Founded in 1917 the Acadia Baptist Academy is a state approved boarding high school owned and operated by the Louisiana Baptist Convention. After an intensive study by a joint committee of the academy board of trustees and the executive board in 1956 the convention approved leaving the academy at its present location and building for an increased student body. This decision was reiterated in 1967.

Louisiana College, founded in 1906, is the only institution of higher learning owned and operated by the Louisiana Baptist Convention. During the period under consideration the convention authorized an increase in the size of the board of trustees and put this board on a rotating basis.

The Louisiana Baptist Convention Crusade for Louisiana College was launched in 1964 in a three stage program to raise $2,000,000 to build a science center and auditorium-religious education building. Pledges and gifts exceeded the goal. The science center was occupied in 1969.

Religious instruction for students attending state-supported colleges and universities came under the consideration of Louisiana Baptists. First appointed in 1953, a committee to study possibilities of providing credit instruction in religion at the state-supported colleges and universities functioned until 1958. This committee sought state approval to establish Chairs of Bible on the campuses. In 1967 a new committee was appointed. This committee recommended in 1968 to the convention and to the Louisiana College board the plan of extension credit through Louisiana College. A pilot project was projected for the 1969–70 session on the Baton Rouge campus of Louisiana State University.

Institutional Changes.—At the 1957 convention approval was given to the establishment of a home for the aged on a 116 acre tract of land given by the First Baptist Church, Arcadia, in Arcadia, La. Trustees were elected at the 1958 convention. The Arcadia Baptist Home for the Aged began operation in that year.

The hospital ministry of Louisiana Baptists underwent some changes in the period 1956–69. A comprehensive set of hospital policies was adopted in 1966.

The Willis-Knighton Memorial Hospital in Shreveport was offered to the Louisiana Baptist Convention for operation in 1959. The next year the convention declined the offer after study by the hospital subcommittee of the executive board's program committee.

Not only was one hospital rejected but two were released. The lease agreement with the town of Homer was terminated for the lease and operation of the Homer Memorial Hospital in Homer, La., in 1967. In 1969 the Baton Rouge General Hospital, Baton Rouge, La., which had been owned and operated by the convention since 1944, was released to an independent board of trustees.

The *Baptist Message,* founded in 1886 and published by the executive board since 1919, was made a separate agency with its own board of trustees in 1963. Previously it had bought a printing press and had established a printing plant in the old Baptist Building. Its format was changed to a magazine format in 1962.

Mission Work in Louisiana.—Because of its location and its heavy concentration of people with French ancestry and Roman Catholic religious background, Louisiana has long been considered a mission area.

Concentrated in New Orleans, several Southern Baptist Convention institutions are located in Louisiana. The New Orleans Baptist Theological Seminary and the Southern Baptist Hospital are both in New Orleans. In addition the Home Mission Board operates the Baptist Friendship House, the Baptist Rescue Mission, Carver Center, Sellers Baby Home and Adoption Center, Rachel Sims Mission, and until 1969 the Good Samaritan Home, all in New Orleans.

In 1960 the French mission work of the Home Mission Board was merged with the work of the Missions Department, now called the Direct Missions Department, of the Louisiana Baptist Convention. The state Missions Department served as administrator. The final year the HMB participated in salary supplements for "career missions pastors" was 1968. This is now (1970) all borne by Louisiana Baptists. The HMB does continue to share in Louisiana Baptists' work with Negro Baptists.

A pilot project in missions to recreational areas was begun in the summer of 1969 in a joint project. A HMB student summer missionary worked in this project.

In 1966 a special committee was appointed by the president of the convention to study the program of evangelism. This report was adopted in 1968 along with a job description for the secretary of evangelism. Leonard Sanderson became secretary of evangelism that year. In the same year an invitation was accepted from the Korean Baptist Convention and Foreign Mission Board for a Korean evangelistic crusade for 1970.

Devastating hurricanes hit the Louisiana coast in 1957 (Audrey), 1965 (Betsy), and 1969 (Camille). Each time extensive damage was done to Baptist churches and property in areas considered mission areas. Each time Louisiana Baptists rallied with hurricane relief funds to aid the stricken churches.

Financial aid, evangelistic help, and prayer support were given to aid the Utah-Idaho Baptist Convention in 1964.

The period of 1956–69 was a time of solidification, reorganization, and advance in every phase of work of the Louisana Baptist Convention. A time of maturity and growth had been reached. JAMES E. CARTER

II. Program of Work. *Executive Board.*—A convention reorganization was effected beginning in 1959 following a management study of the convention.

Top: LOUISIANA BAPTIST CONVENTION (*q.v.*) BAPTIST BUILDING, Alexandria, La. Occupied in 1960. Property value $1,829,498. *Center:* LOUISIANA COLLEGE (*q.v.*). Located in Pineville, La. Science-Math Building, occupied Sept., 1969, is one of 19 buildings.. *Bottom:* ARCADIA BAPTIST HOME (*q.v.*), Arcadia, Louisiana. A home for the aging. Houses 55 residents.

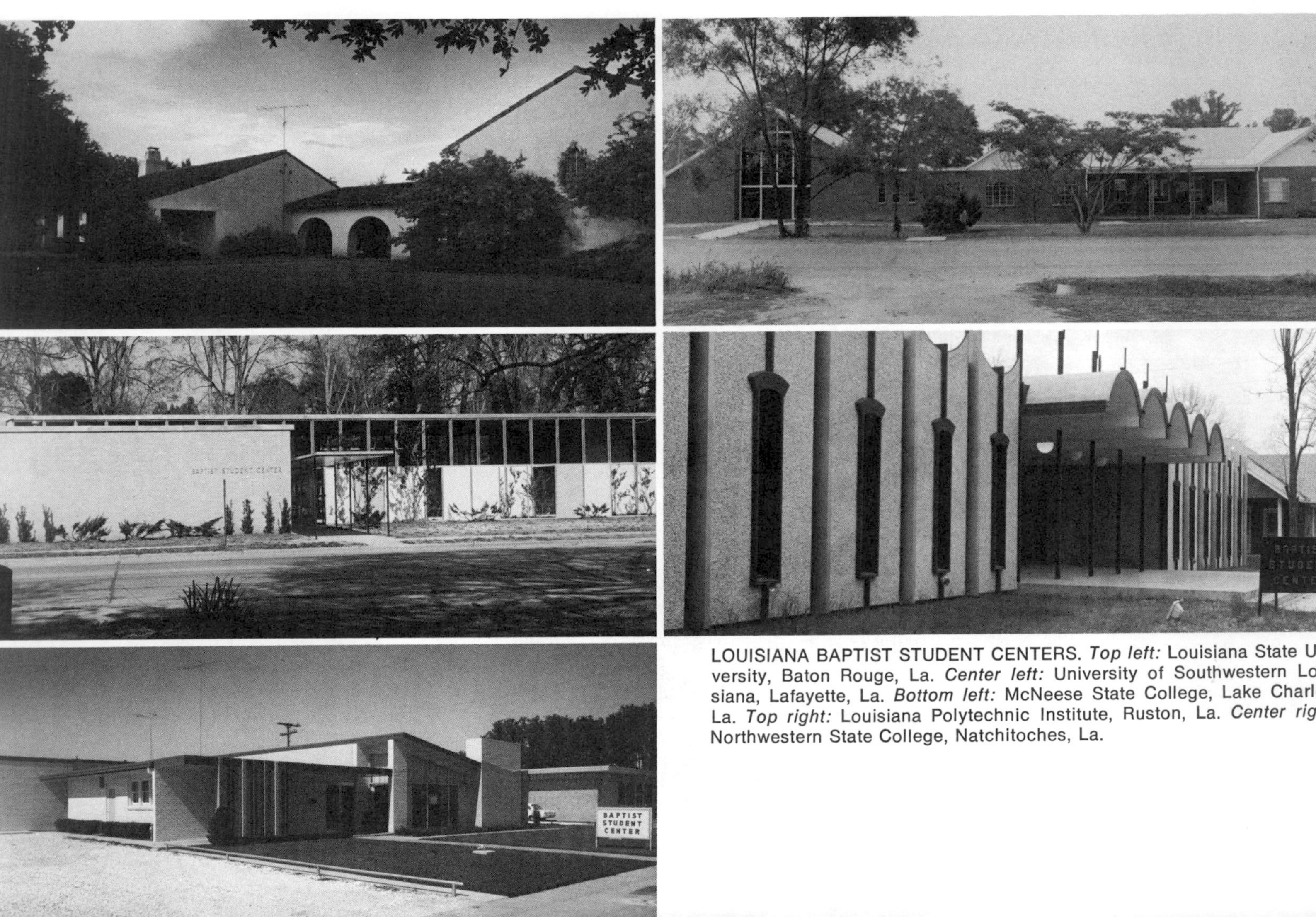

LOUISIANA BAPTIST STUDENT CENTERS. *Top left:* Louisiana State University, Baton Rouge, La. *Center left:* University of Southwestern Louisiana, Lafayette, La. *Bottom left:* McNeese State College, Lake Charles, La. *Top right:* Louisiana Polytechnic Institute, Ruston, La. *Center right:* Northwestern State College, Natchitoches, La.

Missions.—Fred B. Moseley served as secretary of promotion and missions, 1956–58, and W. L. Stagg, Jr., 1960–63. Carl E. Conrad has served from 1964, having been an associate in the department.

The missions budget was $250,000 in 1969. The convention entered a joint plan with the Home Mission Board, SBC, in 1960 and has gradually assumed the more than $40,000 contributed by the HMB.

The direct missions program has consisted of pastoral missions, French radio broadcasting, a Good Will Center, mission schools, and hospital chaplaincy work, with 65 missionary families in 1969. The department provides salaries and fringe benefits for missionaries according to an upgraded scale adopted in 1961, and makes mission land grants and building loans. Since 1956 more than $970,000 has been loaned to mission situations, more than $303,960 given on land purchase, and more than $1,500,000 paid on salary supplements.

The Department of Work with National Baptists for the past 10 years has maintained an average of 16 extension centers with an average enrolment of 314. Twelve people are employed on a part-time basis working with National Baptists, with a full-time missionary in Angola Prison. These workers taught an average of 27 study courses, conducted an average of 93 Bible schools, held three youth encampments, and assisted in student work at Southern University, Grambling College, and Dillard University. Few National Baptists in Louisiana have not been directly or indirectly touched by the department's work.

Educational Ministry.—Sunday School statistics for 1968 indicate growth: 1,291 schools and 114 mission schools, with enrolment of 289,270. There were 1,091 Vacation Bible Schools enrolling 142,266. There were 101 kindergartens, seven day care and week care schools, and 493 church libraries. Awards earned in 575 churches totaled 27,290. The department gives guidance in planning buildings to help implement the programs.

The Church Training and Administrative Services Department has as its director Charles M. Lowry, who succeeded Jimmy Crowe in 1967. Associates in the department were Mrs. A. L. Russell (1957), Norman E. Hodges (1959–65), Mrs. Elmer Bilbray (1959–62), James R. Jones (1966–), J. D. Scott (1967–), and Helen May (1969–). In 1967 the name of the department was changed from Training Union to Church Training and Administrative Services. The department now carries responsibility for the programs of church training, church administration, church recreation, vocational guidance, audiovisuals, and family ministry.

Brotherhood Secretary Grady E. Welch came to the department in 1961 upon the resignation of Fred Forester. John Winters is the present (1970) associate. The department's main emphasis is the involvement of men and boys in mission action. The department sponsors camps, basketball tournaments, and track and field meets, state Royal Ambassador Congress, and state Brotherhood conventions.

In 1964 the Missions Promotion Department divided and became the Stewardship Department and Direct Missions Department. W. L. Stagg, Jr., became secretary of the Stewardship Department in 1964 and retired in 1968. Grady E. Welch then became stewardship secretary. The main emphasis of the department is the promotion of the stewardship program and Cooperative Program giving in the churches.

Since 1956 three men have served as secretary of the Department of Evangelism: R. O. Cawker, Jaroy Weber, and John Havlik. Following a 1966 comprehensive study of convention evangelism needs. Leonard Sanderson was elected evangelism director with executive status, working with all departments rather than as secretary of a department. The department's ministry includes special campaigns outside the state, as in current (1970) plans for a crusade in South Korea in June, 1970. A special committee is studying evangelism needs in the state to plan an evangelistic thrust in 1971–72.

The Church Music Department assists churches in establishing, strengthening, and expanding their music programs through training schools, clinics, and conferences. The department plans associational and state festivals (choral and instrumental) for juniors and youth. L. C. Alexander retired as state music secretary, Feb. 1, 1966, and Carroll Lowe was named his successor on that date.

The Student Department under the leadership of Udell Smith reported over 21,000 Baptist students in Louisiana in 1969. Since 1956 new student centers have been constructed at Nicholls State College, Thibodaux, and at Louisiana State University, New Orleans. New centers replaced former inadequate buildings at Northwestern at Natchitoches and Northeast State at Monroe. Currently (1970) there are 27 Baptist Student Unions, 13 campus directors, and two associates in the Student Department.

Hospitals.—The Louisiana Baptist Convention's policy against acceptance of federal funds, the increasing availability of such funds and the increasing cost of medical faculties and equipment combined to place the hospitals of Louisiana Baptists at a financial disadvantage. Resulting from this situation, in 1967 the Louisiana Baptist Convention honored the request of the town of Homer and released the Homer Memorial Hospital to the town of Homer. At the 1969 annual meeting of the Louisiana Baptist Convention in Baton Rouge the convention responded favorably to the request of the board of trustees of the Baton Rouge General Hospital and released it from convention ownership and control, thereby making it an independent agency in the hands of the current trustees.

Louisiana Baptist Convention now owns and controls only two hospitals, Alexandria Baptist Hospital and Beauregard Memorial Hospital. In 1969 Alexandria hospital had 207 beds, with assets of $5,094,650. Beauregard hospital had 91

LOUISIANA STATISTICAL SUMMARY

Year	Associa-tions	Churches	Church Member-ship	Baptisms	S. S. Enrol-ment	V.B.S. Enrol-ment	T. U. Enrol-ment	W.M.U. Enrol-ment	Brother-hood En-rolment	Music Enrol-ment	Mission Gifts	Total Gifts	Value Church Property
1955	50	1,167	346,402	16,172	251,270	92,308	122,050	48,536	19,288		$2,510,812	$17,095,576	$ 55,982,946
1956	51	1,195	357,306	14,279	260,517	113,318	123,938	47,319	20,324		2,647,921	16,204,083	63,031,803
1957	51	1,215	365,515	14,257	267,851	106,760	124,306	49,967	14,728		5,248,933	18,047,474	74,399,502
1958	51	1,239	380,681	16,388	274,403	116,393	129,805	50,625	26,019	27,981	3,453,976	19,276,268	81,565,395
1959	51	1,254	388,953	17,512	281,778	108,382	134,426	52,062	25,412	27,616	3,612,787	20,648,016	90,041,472
1960	51	1,258	401,314	16,000	288,857	118,844	135,360	52,880	21,815	25,490	3,708,794	21,498,212	93,946,852
1961	52	1,268	409,959	16,986	288,123	119,193	137,068	53,924	20,811	27,833	4,032,061	22,174,786	104,877,698
1962	52	1,279	420,045	15,366	288,834	118,985	136,281	51,254	18,884	30,904	4,070,627	23,431,897	99,773,291
1963	52	1,286	426,385	13,856	290,261	121,828	136,368	51,505	19,611	34,991	4,114,292	24,294,833	127,360,440
1964	52	1,299	430,557	14,042	289,754	120,839	134,258	51,091	18,932	34,146	4,358,053	25,461,595	135,174,018
1965	52	1,298	439,813	14,170	291,499	125,786	133,210	50,170	18,974	37,840	4,733,889	28,370,608	144,768,242
1966	53	1,302	448,982	14,196	289,871	123,294	129,623	49,008	15,542	39,763	5,194,740	29,954,904	152,161,216
1967	53	1,298	456,474	15,713	289,452	124,025	125,582	48,267	16,700	43,395	5,704,370	31,903,378	161,371,809
1968	53	1,303	463,360	15,857	287,894	122,388	141,859	46,961	16,405	44,006	5,767,813	35,131,084	173,678,236

BERNIECE CAMP

beds, assets near $1,000,000, and was complimented by Westwood Manor Nursing Home.

M. E. MERCER AND RAY P. RUST

LOUISIANA BAPTIST ENCAMPMENTS AND ASSEMBLIES (cf. Louisiana Baptist Encampment, Vol. II) . In 1970 the Louisiana Baptist Convention did not own or operate an encampment. But there were several other encampments in Louisiana owned and operated by districts, associations, or churches.

MANDEVILLE ENCAMPMENT, located at Mandeville, La., is operated by Districts XI, XII, and XIII.

DRY CREEK BAPTIST ASSEMBLY, formerly Southwest Louisiana Baptist Encampment, is located at Dry Creek, La. Assembly directors maintain a full summer schedule of assemblies as well as special meetings throughout the year. This assembly is owned and operated by an elected board of trustees from five associations: Carey, Beauregard, Luther Rice, Mt. Olive, and Vernon.

CLARA SPRINGS ENCAMPMENT, located near Pleasant Hill, La., is owned and operated by a board of trustees from District VIII. The facilities were donated in 1953.

ACADIAN ASSEMBLY, which began in 1948, is held annually on the campus of the Acadia Baptist Academy near Eunice, La.

SLIGO BAPTIST ASSEMBLY is owned and operated by the Northwest Louisiana Baptist Association. It is located near Shreveport, and maintains a full summer schedule as well as special occasions throughout the year.

FRIENDSHIP ENCAMPMENT is owned and operated by the Jackson Baptist Association as a summer assembly. The facilities were formerly the Friendship School. In the same parish, the First Baptist Church of Jonesboro owns and operates an encampment known as Camp Davis, near Minden. District V owns and operates Camp Harris as a summer assembly and for special purposes throughout the year. Camp Stallion, near Baton Rouge, is leased and operated by the Judson Baptist Association. Camp "Tall Timbers," located 15 miles south of Alexandria, La., on highway U. S. 165, is owned and operated by the Louisiana Woman's Missionary Union and is under the direct supervision of the WMU state executive-secretary. "Tall Timbers" is a modern assembly for year-round use. It was completed in 1963 and involved an investment of $500,000.

J. D. SCOTT

***LOUISIANA BAPTIST FOUNDATION.** In 1958 following a convention-wide management study, the responsibility for promotion of endowment and capital giving was transferred from the Louisiana Baptist Foundation to the executive board. The major responsibility of the foundation continued to be fund management. However, in 1963 the foundation was again assigned the promotion of endowment and capital giving for the convention. Two years later, when budget funds were made available, Glenn

E. Bryant was employed to direct this new program. From 1965 through 1969, 118 wills were written or were in process of being completed, wherein $1,600,000 was designated in bequests to Baptist causes.

In Dec., 1969, the foundation produced a 28½ minute videotape in high-band color entitled, "What Happens to What You Leave?" The program was shown over the major TV stations in Louisiana with a potential viewing audience of 3,500,000 families, or 11,000,000 persons, throughout the Arkansas-Louisiana-Texas area.

Assets of the foundation increased from $1,534,735 in 1954 to $3,341,000 in 1969. Income disbursements for the same period came to $2,084,702. Total income from investments paid to all causes and beneficiaries, from the inception of the foundation in 1944 through 1969, amounted to $2,437,024.

The investment policy of the foundation includes a diversified portfolio, with about 57 per cent invested in quality and growth common stocks. About 93 per cent of the operating budget for the foundation is received through the Cooperative Program. For the year 1969, it was $54,500. Herschel C. Pettus has served as executive director since 1948. H. C. PETTUS

LOUISIANA BAPTISTS AND THE CHURCH-STATE ISSUE. Because of the historic Baptist commitment to religious liberty and their position as a minority in much of the state, Louisiana Baptists maintained an active interest in the relationship between church and state. Practically every year in the period of 1956–69 the Louisiana Baptist Convention approved a resolution dealing with the subject. The public affairs committee of the convention made detailed reports to the convention on the issues of the year.

Government participation in education and medical care caused increased interest by 1965. At the 1965 convention a special committee was appointed "to study our theological position on religious liberty and report back to the Louisiana Baptist Convention meeting next year a statement on religious liberty and guidelines for the institutions and agencies of the Louisiana Baptist Convention." Composed of pastors, lawyers, and educators the committee's report was accepted in 1966. Rather than dealing with the particular kinds of government aid then available, guidelines were drafted to give direction for future actions. Care was taken that in any form of cooperation with the government the basic integrity of the institution should be maintained by clearly defined procedures without the institution becoming dependent on government funds. Trustees were given freedom to make decisions. No funds relating to the teaching of religion would be received. Direct grants were prohibited.

The issue of the use of public funds for private and sectarian schools was prominent in this period. Citizens for Educational Freedom formed an active Louisiana organization and pressed their case before the Louisiana legislature.

In addition to resolutions opposing the goal of this group, the convention approved the recommendation of the public affairs committee in 1968 "That our Executive Secretary be authorized to make contact with the leaders of other groups opposing the plans of Citizens for Educational Freedom and to join forces with theirs in an effort to inform our legislators on our position relative to state aid for private and parochial schools."

The *Baptist Message* carried on an active campaign to inform the Baptist people of the state of the developments in this issue.

Perry R. Sanders, president of the convention in 1968, appeared before the Louisiana legislature to articulate Baptist thinking on this issue. At the 1969 convention special commendation was given to Sanders for his activities relative to this problem. JAMES E. CARTER

***LOUISIANA COLLEGE.** During the period 1956–69 an expansion program made major physical changes to the campus of Louisiana Baptists' only college. Six new buildings were constructed; two major additions made to Cottingham Hall, dormitory for women, with a third addition nearing completion; one addition to Tudor Hall, dormitory for men; and complete renovation of the cafeteria and the building used by the department of education. The new buildings include a home for the Wildcat Band (1957); Weathersby Fine Arts building (1961), including offices, classrooms, and a small auditorium for the departments of art, music, and speech; H. O. West Physical Education building (1964), including gymnasium facilities seating 4,800 spectators; a maintenance building (1966); 20 apartments for married students (1967); and a science center (1969), including offices, laboratories, classrooms, and observatory for the departments of biology, chemistry, mathematics and physics. The 1970 value of capital assets was $7,615,701.

The Louisiana Baptist Convention launched a three year capital fund drive in 1966 with a goal of $2,000,000 to erect a science building and an auditorium. The science center was completed debt free in 1969. Construction on the auditorium was planned for 1970.

In the spring of 1969, after studious appraisals, the trustees voted to discontinue intercollegiate football. This action, together with the establishment in Rapides Parish of a branch of Louisiana State University, had an as yet unmeasured effect on enrolment of the college.

Cumulative graduates numbered 4,300 in 1969. Cumulative enrolment was 1,276 for the 1968–69 session, with 60 faculty members. The governing board of the institution numbers 33 trustees. The 1969–70 operating budget was $1,636,620.33. Cooperative Program allocation for 1970 was $608,600, with an endowment of $2,680,000. CHARLES S. MCILVEENE

***LOVE.** Christian love is the spontaneous, creative, caring love that is expressive of God's nature and extended to undeserving men in Jesus Christ. Christians are called to exercise toward their fellowmen the same love which God has shown them in Christ. Christian love is defined in terms of the life and death of Christ. First Corinthians 13 is the classic statement concerning love and, in a genuine sense, is Jesus interpreted in terms of love.

Men who accept God's love in Christ are empowered by the Holy Spirit to live thankfully and obediently toward God in response to his love and are enabled by the Holy Spirit to love their fellowmen (Gal. 5:22; John 15:12; I John 4:7–12). God's love evokes men's faith and men's faith evokes love.

The Greeks had several different words meaning love. The word for love most often used in the New Testament is *agapē* (a-gä-pā). Another Greek word for love is *eros,* which is used to express love of deep desire, passionate aspiration, and sensuous longing. It emphasizes the worth of the object and the desire to possess it. Often *eros* has a sexual connotation. *Storgē* is a word for love that expresses the kind of affection members of a family have for one another. Neither *eros* nor *storgē* is ever used in the New Testament. An additional word meaning love is found in the New Testament. It is *philia,* and describes different kinds of love (cf. John 11:3,16; Matt. 10:37; John 21:15–17). The adjective *philos,* which means loving or devoted, is used 29 times in the New Testament and forms of the verb *philein* are used more than 30 times.

On the other hand, the word *agapē* is used almost 120 times in the New Testament and the verb *agapan* is used 130 times. The noun and verb are also widely used in the *Septuagint,* the Greek version of the Old Testament made prior to 130 B.C., and used by the early church. On the other hand, the word *agapē* was not widely used by the Greeks themselves; they preferred to use other words for love.

Clearly the word *agapē* was chosen by the writers of the documents in the New Testament to express their understanding of love. *Agapē* is used in the *Septuagint* to express different kinds of love (cf. Jer. 2:2; Deut. 4:37; Hosea 11:1; Gen. 22:2; Hosea 3:1). When Jesus quotes the commandments to love God and neighbor (Deut. 6:4; Lev. 19:18) he was referring to passages in the *Septuagint* that use the verb *agapan.* The Gospels also refer to teachings of Jesus which contain the word *agapē* (Matt. 5:43–45).

Since the word *agapē* was not widely used by the Greeks, and since the other Greek words for love had connotations of a distinctive sort, Christians were able to fill *agapē* with Christian meaning. In fact, it is employed to express various kinds of love in the New Testament (cf. John 17:26; Rom. 8:37; I Cor. 2:9; II Thess. 2:16; Matt. 5:43–48).

The meaning of love in the New Testament, expressed by the word *agapē,* is not a mere continuation of what is found in the Old Testament. Love is redefined in terms of Jesus himself. It is the reality found in Jesus and in God's relationship to him (Mark 1:11; Matt. 12:18). It involves man's mind, emotion, and will, understood in the light of God's love revealed in Christ (cf. Matt. 5:43–48). Love must be understood in the light of the life and death of Christ as Romans 5:6–10 and John 3:35–36 clearly indicate. In a classic way I John demonstrates that God's love, which men know in Jesus Christ, is the kind of love they are called to show to the neighbor—a spontaneous, creative, caring love. Theologians, among them Augustine, A. Nygren, and Paul Tillich, differ in the ways they assess the relationship between *agapē* and *eros.*

BIBLIOGRAPHY: Anders Nygren, *Agapē and Eros,* translated by Phillip S. Watson (1953). Ceslaus Spicq, *Agapē in the New Testament* (1965).

RAYMOND BRYAN BROWN

LOWER CRITICISM. A term used to designate the study involved in establishing the original text of the biblical writings.

See TEXTUAL CRITICISM.

RAYMOND BRYAN BROWN

LOWREY, LAWRENCE TYNDALE (b. Blue Mountain, Miss., Aug. 14, 1888; d. Blue Mountain, Miss., May 23, 1966). Educator, author, and college president. Son of Booth and Patti Elizabeth (Lowry) Lowrey; graduated from Mississippi Heights Academy in 1905; received the B.S. and A.M. degrees from Mississippi College in 1909 and 1913. Lowrey attended Columbia University, earning the A.M. and Ph.D. degrees in 1914 and 1918. Lowrey was awarded LL.D. degrees from Baylor University (1957), Mississippi College (1959), and Union University (1960). He married Elizabeth Veene Cockroft, Sept. 2, 1919. Two children were born, Robert Booth and Jean. His first wife died in 1950. On Mar. 28, 1952, he married Mrs. Ernestine Higdon Eastland.

During his career as an educator he served as principal of the Fair River High School in Mississippi, 1909–11; vice-president of Hillman College, 1911–13; fellow in American History at Columbia University, 1915–16; instructor in history at Smith College, 1916–18; associate professor and professor of history at the University of Southern California, 1919–25; and president of Blue Mountain College, 1925–60. Lowrey's esteem among his peers was evidenced by his service as president of the Mississippi Association of Colleges, 1927–28, and president of the Mississippi Foundation of Independent Colleges, 1956–60. He served his denomination as president of the Mississippi Baptist State Convention, 1938–40; member of the Southern Baptist Education Commission, 1928–40; trustee of Tri-State Baptist Hospital, 1937–49, 1950–53; and trustee of Southeastern Baptist Theological Seminary, 1951–1961. Author of *Northern Opin-*

ion of Approaching Secession (1918), Lowrey was also co-author of *A Syllabus of American Constitutional History.*

In addition to his educational and denominational service, Lowrey was a civic-minded patriot. He served as a lieutenant in the United States Army, 1918, a member of the Federal Alien Enemy Hearing Board, 1941–45, and governor of Rotary International District 140, 1944–45. EARL KELLY

LUTHER RICE COLLEGE. An independent Baptist coeducational senior liberal arts college owned and operated in Alexandria, Va., by the Luther Rice College Corporation. Classes were first conducted in 1967 in Franconia Baptist Church. Thirty-two acres of adjoining land were purchased for a campus. C. L. Bishop is president. C. L. BISHOP

LUTHER RICE SEMINARY. An independent Baptist institution, chartered and opened for classes in 1962. Central Baptist Church, Jacksonville, Fla., provided facilities for the young seminary through 1969. Central's pastor, Robert Gee Witty, initiator of the idea for the seminary, became its president in 1968. Other presidents were Clyde Jones, Pat Wimberly, and Burton Humphreys. The S.T.B., B.D., Th.M., Th.D., and Ed.D. degrees are offered. More than 1,000 students studied at the institution, 1962–69.

C. EARL COOPER AND JAMES E. MCREYNOLDS

LYNN (OR LINN), BENJAMIN (b. Chester County, Pa., 1750; d. Huntsville, Ala., Dec., 1814). Indian scout and explorer. Having lived with the Indians in the old Northwest, he could fight them bitterly in war, but could also live amicably with them in peace. He was at Kaskaskia on the Mississippi in 1777, and at Vincennes on the Wabash in 1779, and at Old Chillicothe on the Big Miami in Ohio in 1780. He was married in the fort at Harrodsburg on July 9, 1777, to Hannah Sovereigns (Severns), who taught him to read. Influenced by her family and also by associates in hunting and exploring, he entered a new career at the age of 30, that of a Baptist preacher. About 1785 he moved from Louisville to the area now in Nelson County, where he founded and/or served three Baptist churches: South Fork, Level Wood, and Pottingers Creek. Around 1792 he moved to Green County. While there, at the close of the Great Revival, 1800–02, he left the Baptist denomination to become a follower of Barton W. Stone. He moved to Madison County, Ala., about 1810.

LEO T. CRISMON

M

MACKIE, GEORGE CARLYLE (b. Yadkinville, N. C., Nov. 12, 1902; d. Wake Forest, N. C., Jan. 8, 1969). Physician and professor. Son of Milas Wilson and Martha Lee (Myers) Mackie, he made profession of faith while a student at Wake Forest College and was baptized by W. R. Cullom (*q.v.*). He held a B.A. (1924) and a B.S. (1926) degree from Wake Forest College, and an M.D. degree from the University of Pennsylvania (1928). He interned at the Philadelphia General Hospital. Returning to Wake Forest Medical School in 1930, he served as Professor of Physiology and Pharmacology until 1941 when the school moved to Winston-Salem, N. C. In 1934 he married Kathleen Gilmer Robinson of Merion, Pa. They had two sons: James Wilson and G. C., Jr. He served as college physician from 1941 to 1956, when Wake Forest College moved to Winston-Salem, N. C. He chose to remain in Wake Forest to continue private practice and to serve as physician to Southeastern Baptist Theological Seminary which had opened in the fall of 1951. A life-member of the American College of Physicians, he was chosen "General Practitioner of 1961" by the members of the North Carolina State Medical Society. In 1968 buildings at Wake Forest University and at Southeastern Baptist Theological Seminary were named in his honor. After dying at his desk after a busy day, he was buried in the Seminary Cemetery in Wake Forest, N. C. JAMES H. BLACKMORE

MACON, LEON MEERTIEF (b. Whatley, Clarke County, Ala., Oct. 25, 1908; d. Birmingham, Ala., Nov. 15, 1965). Pastor, editor, author, and denominational leader. Son of James William and Martha (Kelly) Macon, he was ordained July 27, 1932, at Dauphin Way Baptist Church, Mobile, Ala. He was a graduate of Howard College (A.B., 1933, also D.D., 1949) and Southern Baptist Theological Seminary (Th.M., 1938). On Sept. 12, 1934, he married Emily May Bodden of Mobile, Ala. He served as pastor of First Baptist churches in Bay Minette, 1935–37; Athens, 1938–42; Atmore, 1942–44; and Bessemer, Ala., 1946–50; and in West Point, Miss., 1944–46. Macon served as a member of the Alabama Baptist executive board, 1936–37, 1938–43; Radio and Television Commission, SBC, 1948–53; Historical Commission, SBC, 1954–60; Southern Baptist Encyclopedia executive committee and state chairman, 1953–57. He was editor and business manager of *The Alabama Baptist,* 1950–65, and was president of the Alabama Baptist State Convention, 1962–64. He was author of *Salvation in a Scientific Age, The Seven Sayings on the Cross,* and *You Choose a Cross* (published posthumously 1966). He was buried in Elmwood Cemetery, Birmingham, Ala. EMILY BODDEN (MRS. LEON) MACON

MADDRY, CHARLES EDWARD (b. Chapel Hill, N. C., Apr. 10, 1876; d. Chapel Hill, N. C., Sept. 17, 1962). Sixth executive (corresponding) secretary, Foreign Mission Board, 1933–44, and secretary emeritus, 1945–62. He received a Ph.B. from the University of North Carolina, and attended Southern Baptist Theological Seminary and University of Texas. Honorary degrees were conferred on him by the University of North Carolina, Baylor University, Wake Forest College, and Stetson University. In 1906 he married Emma Parker. He was pastor of churches in North Carolina, Kentucky, and Texas for 20 years and served North Carolina Baptists in executive positions several years.

When he became secretary, in the midst of the depression, the board was more than $1,000,000 in debt and had no more borrowing power. In 1944, for the first time since its creation in 1845, the board was able to report no indebtedness. Maddry led the board through most of the difficult days of World War II and prepared the way for postwar advance. When he retired the board had 504 missionaries under appointment.

Other achievements of his administration were the establishment of a pension plan for missionaries (1933); publication of *The Commission,* missionary journal (begun in 1938), which he edited for five years; election of regional secretaries to help direct overseas work; establishment of the department for missionary personnel (1943) and tightening requirements for missionary appointment; distribution of more than $1,000,000 of relief funds in famine-stricken areas of the world; and opening mission work in Hawaii and Colombia.

Maddry wrote *Day Dawn in Yoruba Land* (1939), *Christian Ownership* (1940), *Christ's Expendables* (1949), *Charles E. Maddry, an Autobiography* (1955), and an unpublished history of the FMB.

Maddry wrote a high record of administrative ability, tender compassion for all mankind, and a remarkable spiritual challenge which many will never forget. BAKER J. CAUTHEN

***MAGOFFIN BAPTIST INSTITUTE, (Mountain Valley, Ky.).** This mountain elementary school closed its doors on Aug. 31, 1961. Its properties, assets, and an annual grant from the Thompson Foundation in Washington, D. C., were turned over by the trustees of the Kentucky Baptist Convention to Oneida Baptist Institute, Oneida, Ky. The last chairman of the trustees was E. Gaines Davis, Jr., attorney from Frankfort, who is process agent for Magoffin whose charter is renewed from year to year. For several years the buildings were used for the Magoffin Baptist Assembly, sponsored by Three Forks and adjoining Baptist associations. The last presidents were Thomas H. Frances (1954), Gordon Duncan (1955), James E. Brown (1956–59), and Frank C. Campbell (1960).
HAROLD GLEN SANDERS

MAINE, SOUTHERN BAPTISTS IN. See MARYLAND, BAPTIST CONVENTION OF.

MALAWI, MISSION IN. Two Southern Baptist missionary couples who had formerly served in Southern Rhodesia moved to Blantyre in July, 1959. Known then as Nyasaland, the former British protectorate became the independent nation of Malawi in 1964, and missionaries formed the Malawi Mission, separate from Rhodesia. William and Blanche (Clement) Wester remained in Blantyre, while LeRoy and Jean (Flowers) Albright moved to Lilongwe, 200 miles north. Blantyre became the mission's administrative center, and a modern headquarters building was dedicated in 1969. A Bible school was founded at Lilongwe in 1965 and a publication center, producing materials in the Chichewa language, was established.

Mission stations were opened at Salima (1966), on the shore of Lake Malawi, and at Nkhota-Kota (1969), 75 miles north. The Baptist Lakeshore Medical Service, based at Salima, was begun early in 1970. Using a motorboat, an African medical team accompanied by evangelistic workers reached villages along the lake otherwise all but inaccessible during much of the year. Zomba, in Palomba Valley, became a mission station and an agriculture specialist arrived in 1970 to strengthen the community development program and evangelistic outreach. At the beginning of 1970 the mission was composed of 19 missionaries who worked with 60 African pastors serving 90 churches, with approximately 5,000 members. H. CORNELL GOERNER

MALAYSIA-SINGAPORE, MISSION IN (cf. Malaya, Mission in, Vol. II). Political changes in this area influenced mission work. The mission's name was changed in 1967 from Malaya to Malaysia-Singapore Mission. Missionaries entered Sabah in 1964; permission to enter Sarawak was granted in 1969. Student work and an encampment program coupled wth religious education promotion are strengthening the total Baptist witness. The maturing of the convention and the development of cooperative ventures with the mission are recent events of long-range significance. In Dec., 1969, 51 missionaries were serving in 13 stations. R. KEITH PARKS

***MARGARET FUND.** In 1961 the administration of Margaret Fund Scholarships was

transferred to the Home Mission Board and the Foreign Mission Board. Woman's Missionary Union continues to award special scholarships provided by the interest on trust funds.
BETTY BROWN

***MARRIAGE AND FAMILY.** See PASTORAL CARE.

***MARS HILL COLLEGE.** Mars Hill is a four-year liberal arts college located at Mars Hill, N. C., west of Asheville. Its reorganization from junior college status was approved by the North Carolina Baptist State Convention in 1960, and the first bachelor's degrees were awarded to 146 graduates in 1964. In 1961 Mars Hill was the first Baptist college in the state to admit an American Negro as a full-time undergraduate student. Also in 1961 the college named its new auditorium and fine arts building for Robert Lee Moore (*q.v.*, Vol. II), president, 1897–1938.

Fred Blake Bentley succeeded Hoyt Blackwell as president in 1966. Under Blackwell, campus facilities were expanded and modernized, and the transition was made to senior college status. Under Bentley the college launched a 10-year development program, "Emphasis on Excellence," to enrich curriculum, upgrade faculty, and improve facilities. In addition the college began to re-think its concept of liberal arts education. Responding to problems facing nearby urban and rural communities and to the search by students for learning and living experiences, the college initiated an academic program to integrate classroom teaching with service-learning for the benefit of both students and communities. The program received national recognition and has been used as a model by other colleges in the South.

In 1967 the Southern Association of Colleges and Schools fully accredited Mars Hill as a senior college. Earlier the college's music department was accepted in the senior college division of the National Association of Schools of Music. Although tied intimately with the southern Appalachian region, Mars Hill is not strictly a local institution. In the fall of 1969, the college began its 114th year with over 1,250 full-time students from 26 states, the District of Columbia, and three foreign countries.
JACK WILLIS

MARTIN, JOHN SANTFORD (b. Hamptonville, Yadkin County, N. C., May 20, 1886; d. Winston-Salem, N. C., Apr. 14, 1957). Newspaper editor. Son of Asbury and Victoria (Brown) Martin, he received the B.A. from Wake Forest College in 1909. He studied in the Wake Forest School of Law in 1910. While he was looking for a place to practice law, he was offered and accepted a job as reporter on the *Winston-Salem Journal.* He was editor of the *Journal,* 1912–52, and also was editor of the *Twin City Sentinel* after 1927, when the two newspapers merged. From 1952 until his retirement in 1954, he was editor of the *Sunday Journal and Sentinel* editorial page.

Martin was private secretary to Gov. T. W. Bickett, 1917–20, and was author of *The Letters and Papers of Thomas Walter Bickett* (1921). He taught Sunday School classes at the First Baptist Church of Winston-Salem for 25 years and was a deacon. He served on the general board of the Baptist state convention and was a member of the convention's educational council and the board of directors of the *Biblical Recorder.* He was a trustee for North Carolina Baptist Hospital, 1947–51. Martin was a member of the State Department of Conservation, 1926–43, and was chairman, 1941–43. He was chairman of the State Board of Education, 1954–56. He was awarded honorary degrees from Western Carolina College and Wake Forest. Martin married Ava Michael Poole on Oct. 2, 1910. Their children are J. S., Jr., and Mrs. Edwina (Martin) Crowther.
ELIZABETH BRANTLEY

MARTIN, MAURICE HARDESTY (b. Grandbury, Hood County, Tex., Aug. 12, 1902; d. Riverside, Calif., Jan. 1, 1969). The daughter of John Pettigrew Hardesty, a pioneer Texas Baptist preacher, Maurice Hardesty was converted at age 10 and retained an active membership in some Baptist church until her death. She graduated from Hardin Simmons University (B.A., 1936), and from the University of Southern California (M.S. in Ed., 1959). Additional studies included the California College of Arts and Crafts, University of Colorado, and art instruction from E. C. Eisonlohr, Dallas, Tex., and Grant Beach School in Los Angeles. She married Willie E. Martin in 1930. She taught public school in Texas prior to serving on the faculties of Hardin Simmons University and California Baptist College. At the latter school she organized and taught in the art department, and was director of the women's dormitory in the early years of the institution. Later, she became college hostess and continued to fill that position even after retirement. She held active membership in numerous professional organizations.
CECIL M. HYATT

MARTIN, WILLIAM PLUNKETT (b. near Stonewall, Appomatox County, Va., July 9, 1893; d. New Orleans, La., June 17, 1961). Evangelistic singer, church musician and seminary professor. He was one of five children born to Ethelbert and Agnes Martin. An important early influence was his pastor, George Braxton Taylor. From 1903 through 1913 Martin lived with the Taylor family in Lynchburg, where he received his first musical training and experience. He studied at Moody Bible Institute (1913–15), graduating from its music course. As an evangelistic singer with the Home Mission Board (1916–22), Martin was one of the denomination's first full-time church musicians. Martin and James W. Jelks compiled for the board the songbook *Songs of Redemption* (1920). He married Ruby Stanley of Lafayette, Ala., on

June 29, 1921. Their children are W. P., Jr., and Stanley. Martin was music director of First Baptist Church, Shreveport, La., 1922–23, and director of music and education of St. Charles Avenue Baptist Church, New Orleans, 1923–27. Martin was again an evangelistic singer with the board, 1927–28, and with evangelist William Carey Barker, 1928–35. Martin was then assistant to the pastors (in music and education) of First Baptist Church, LaGrange, Ga., 1935–37, and Barton Heights (now Northminister) Baptist Church, Richmond, Va., 1937–42. The remainder of Martin's life was spent on the music faculty of New Orleans Baptist Theological Seminary. He succeeded E. O. Sellers (*q.v.*, Vol. II) as head of the music department in 1945, and led in its expansion to the School of Church Music. Martin taught at the seminary until his death in 1961. He was buried at Lafayette, Ala. The seminary's Martin Music Library is named in his memory. HARRY ESKEW

***MARY HARDIN-BAYLOR COLLEGE.** Six buildings have been constructed and three remodeled on the college campus since 1955. Leonard L. Holloway succeeded Arthur K. Tyson as president in 1966. In 1968 a baccalaureate degree was conferred upon the first male, William G. Tanner became the 19th president, and a baccalaureate nursing degree program with Scott and White Hospital was established. The academic program continues to progress. Gifts, endowment, and enrolment have consistently increased annually; however, the enrolment has shown a slight decrease since 1968 due to the opening of a junior college in the county.
WILLIAM G. TANNER

MARYLAND, BAPTIST CONVENTION OF (cf. Maryland Baptist Union Association, Vol. II.)

I. Era of Expansion. The following statistics are one indication of the expansion of Maryland Baptists during the period, 1956–70. In 1956 there were 141 churches and 25 missions, with a membership of 43,562. By 1969 these figures had increased to 436 churches and 25 missions reporting a membership of 93,897. In 1956 total gifts received for all purposes in the churches totaled $2,742,279; in 1969, the total was $9,425,769. Cooperative Program gifts in 1956 were $296,576; in 1969, $853,774. In 1956 there were seven district (local) associations within the convention (under association); in 1969 there were 20.

Turning Point.—The year of 1957 stands as the unmistakable turning point in the life and thrust of Southern Baptists in Maryland. Prompted by the growth of the previous 20 years, Maryland Baptist life had the resources and impetus to launch the greatest era of expansion in the history of Baptists in the state. Three major things characterize 1957: the general prosperity of the nation which Maryland shared, the election of Roy D. Gresham as executive secretary of the convention's state mission board, and the entrance of Southern Baptists into the Northeast.

The growth of Baptists immediately prior to 1957 and the prosperity of the Baptist constituency both demanded and provided the basis of the expansion of the state convention. Roy D. Gresham, a native of South Carolina and the successful pastor for 12 years of the Middle River Baptist Church in suburban Baltimore, was elected executive secretary to assume office Jan. 1, 1958. He actually came to the office in Nov., 1957, to acquaint himself with the details of convention operation before the retirement of C. C. Thomas (*q.v.*) executive secretary since Apr., 1949.

Another historic event in 1957 was the establishment of the Manhattan Baptist Chapel in New York City. The chapel was sponsored by the College Avenue Baptist Church, Annapolis, Md., and was a step that would eventually lead to an 11-state convention for Maryland Baptists.

Significant Changes.—At the time of organization (1836) of the statewide Baptist body in Maryland, the use of "association" was in vogue. Hence the name, Maryland Baptist Union Association. As the correlation of programs, agencies, and institutions progressed, Maryland Baptists changed the name of the state organization to The Baptist Convention of Maryland. The name change was part of an overall study of the constitution by a special committee chaired by E. E. Garland, pastor of First Baptist Church, Baltimore. The first reading of the constitutional changes was in 1959, with final approval given in 1960.

Offices of staff members of the state mission board and those of related organizations were in the Baptist Building at 23rd and St. Paul Streets, Baltimore. A new Baptist Building was begun in Apr., 1964, on five acres of land on York Road in Lutherville, a Baltimore suburb. Dedication services were held July 17, 1965, with Porter Routh, executive secretary of the Southern Baptist Convention's Executive Committee, as guest speaker. Value of the land and building is more than $500,000. The four-floor structure provides office space for all departments, The Maryland Baptist Foundation, the Children's Aid Society, and *The Maryland Baptist*. The Baptist Book Store occupies most of the first floor of the Baptist Building.

In 1957 the first full-time editor was elected for *The Maryland Baptist*. Gainer E. Bryan, Jr. came in November to edit the state Baptist paper which had previously been a monthly, 16-page magazine edited by the executive secretary. Within the next seven years, the paper advanced to a weekly with column inches equal to any state Baptist paper in the Southern Baptist Convention.

The Baptist Home of Maryland (for the aged), founded in 1915 through the interest of Willoughby M. McCormick, became an agency of the convention in 1965. Previously the home had been managed by trustees who were not elected by the convention. The home moved to its present location in northwest Baltimore County with the purchase of an estate once the home of General Douglas MacArthur. A wing, named for the founder, was completed in 1970 and doubled the capacity of the home. Approximately 55 guests are cared for in the facility.

II. Organizational Expansion. Rapid growth and geographical expansion in the 1957–69 era was paralleled by an expansion of program organizations and their attendant personnel.

In 1957 the staff of the state mission board included C. C. Thomas, general secretary; L. J. Newton, secretary of the Department of Religious Education; Allen J. Beck, treasurer of the board and secretary of Brotherhood and Royal Ambassador Department; and Miss Josephine C. Norwood, executive secretary of Woman's Missionary Union.

Other staff members were Jimmy J. Hartfield and Miss Betty Jeane Weeks, assistants in the Department of Religious Education; Miss Erleen Gaskin, youth secretary in the WMU; and appropriate office secretarial help.

Training Union.—The first step in the expansion of board ministries was the creation of a department of Training Union and Baptist Student Union. Jimmy J. Hartfield was elected secretary. The new department began functioning in Jan., 1958. This step enabled the Department of Sunday School, and Church Building to come into existence, eliminating the previous Department of Religious Education.

The Maryland Baptist Assembly at Hood College, Frederick, each July is promoted primarily by the Sunday School Department. Approximately 800 persons attend the one-week event which features worship, studies in church organizational programs, Bible conferences, pastors' conferences, and youth work.

Brotherhood-Stewardship.—In 1960 a Brotherhood-Stewardship Department was created, Allen J. Beck became secretary, yielding his role as treasurer to Gilbert E. South, new business manager, who served within the administration department. South later also became executive secretary of the Baptist Foundation of Maryland, created by the convention in 1957.

Missions-Stewardship.—J. N. Evans was elected secretary of the Missions-Stewardship Department in 1960, the first year for Maryland Baptists to have such a department. Evans served until June, 1965, when he became director of metropolitan missions for the Home Mission Board, SBC. E. Milford Howell, a Texas pastor and former missionary to Nigeria for 21 years, became the department secretary in Nov., 1966.

Church Music.—The promotion of church music was assigned to the Brotherhood Department in 1961. John E. Saunders was elected secretary in Sept., 1961. James C. Allcock, Jr., became associate secretary in charge of church music in Apr., 1966. In 1969 church music was made a full department.

Student Work.—By action of the 1965 convention, student work became a full department in 1966, with Keith H. Harris becoming secretary in Feb., 1966. Ministry to students on campus was enlarged, including assumption of the responsibility for Baptist student ministry at the University of Maryland which was previously done by the District of Columbia Baptist Convention.

Woman's Missionary Union.—During this period, WMU expanded with the addition of staff members and the development of Camp Wo-Me-To. Though technically an auxiliary to the convention with its own executive board, WMU now functions more like a department of the state mission board with finances handled through the central office, salaries and staff members approved by the board, and the staff functioning as a department in staff meetings and general events.

Staff Changes.—In 1960 L. J. Newton resigned to accept a position with the Baptist Sunday School Board, SBC. He was succeeded by John M. Tubbs who served as Sunday School and church building secretary until Oct., 1969, when he became director of the Education Division of the Baptist Convention of New York. Charles R. Barnes, pastor of the Severna Park Baptist Church, was elected to the post in 1970.

Jimmy J. Hartfield, Training Union secretary, was appointed by the Foreign Mission Board, SBC, to serve in Mexico. He was succeeded on June 1, 1960, by Sam A. High, pastor of the Loch Raven Baptist Church, Baltimore.

Miss Marjorie Perkins became consultant for children's work in the Sunday School and Training Union departments in 1963. She had been on the staff of the First Baptist Church, Decatur, Ga.

Evangelism promotion is a part of the administration department, Roy D. Gresham, secretary. In 1965 Fred E. White was elected consultant in evangelism and Sunday School enlargement. In 1970 Gilbert E. South was promoted to administrative assistant with the rank of department head.

Other expansion in this period included the creation of Central Services, Raymond Hoffman, superintendent. All supplies and printing, except *The Maryland Baptist,* are handled through this office with 1,350,000 printing impressions made annually.

The staff of the state mission board in 1970 numbered 31 in the Baptist Building at Lutherville.

III. Difficulties and achievements. Despite the rapid growth and apparent success of the era, it was not without its difficulties and failures. Most notable of these was the effort to establish a Baptist college in Maryland.

Maryland Baptist College.—Maryland Baptists had never owned or operated a college, although they had shared somewhat in the founding of Columbia College (now George Washington University) by Luther Rice at the beginning of the 19th century.

In the fifties there developed the idea of a Baptist university in the nation's capital. Promotion of this idea resulted in the formation of a committee of 30, composed of 10 members from each of three state conventions—Virginia, D. C., and Maryland.

When Virginia and the District of Columbia conventions decided they neither needed nor could finance a college in the Washington area, Maryland Baptists continued to discuss the feasibility of a Baptist college somewhere in geographical Maryland.

The idea of a Maryland Baptist college became controversial, debated at two points: the need for a college to train leadership to continue growth; and the inability of a small state convention to properly finance a school of respectable academic quality.

At the 1962 annual meeting of the convention in Frederick, the report of the committee on higher education reviewed all the study that had preceded the formulation of the recommendations. The following recommendations were presented:

1. That the Baptist Convention of Maryland establish a junior college when sufficient funds are available. Such condition to be determined by this body at an annual meeting.

2. That a continuing committee be appointed to: (1) publicize the prospective college; (2) investigate and encourage financial support; (3) search for and recommend a suitable location; (4) take such steps as may be needed to bring the college into existence.

3. That the committee be required to make annual reports to the Baptist Convention of Maryland.

4. That the state mission board be requested to provide a reasonable amount for the expenses of the committee.

Lengthy debate in the morning session delayed passage of the motion until the afternoon session. An effort to make the action unanimous failed when opposition to such a motion was expressed.

Promotion of the college and the soliciting of funds from the constituency was assigned to a nine-member, "initial" board of trustees elected by the convention in subsequent sessions. John R. Cummins, Baltimore, was employed as Development Director and a horse farm of 140 acres was purchased for a campus at Walkersville, near Frederick. Renovation and remodeling of the manor house for a president's home and barns for utility, office, and assembly space began in 1965.

Conwell A. Anderson, president of Judson College in Alabama, was elected president of the Maryland Baptist College in Aug., 1965. In a dispute with the trustees over whether the college would be a two-year or four-year school, Anderson resigned and left the state by Nov., 1965.

In Aug., 1966, ground was broken for the construction of a chapel, the first building on the campus, to be named in honor of Samuel A. Rosenstock who had given the college an estate note in the amount of $150,000.

Eugene Kratz, a staff member of the Texas Baptist Christian Education Commission, was elected president of the school and assumed office in Sept., 1966. In 1967 the board of trustees, now expanded to more than 20 members with Melvin Lea, a Frederick surgeon, as chairman, presented to the state mission board an analysis of the situation and proposals for developing the college.

The document outlined campus and curriculum development, faculty and administration expansion, student costs and proposals for financing the entire project. A request was made for approval of a $5,000,000 capital funds campaign, $2,500,000 immediately, and $2,500,000 in deferred gifts. The convention was requested to contribute 10 per cent ($250,000) of the initial amount. In a special session in July, 1967, the state mission board deemed the proposals not financially feasible.

In the Nov., 1967 session of the convention, the decision was made to terminate the project. Indebtedness at that time was more than $660,000.

After consideration of several alternatives, the convention voted in special session, Sept., 1968, to sell the campus with all buildings, including the completed chapel, for $500,000 net. Final disposition of the property and the settlement of all obligations for the college came in 1969. Maryland Baptists entered the new decade with no college, nor debt on the venture, but generally agreed the decade of the 1960's was not the age to start a new college.

D. C.-Maryland Relations.—The population growth of metropolitan Washington, D. C., created problems as well as opportunities for Baptists. After its beginning as an association in the latter part of the 19th century and later becoming a small state convention, the District of Columbia Baptist Convention began reaching beyond the D. C. lines in the first quarter of the 20th century.

Virginia Baptists' leadership drew a hard line at the Potomac River, insisting that churches in Northern Virginia be a part of that state convention even if they were an integral part of metropolitan Washington.

Maryland Baptists' leadership was not as firm and, as a result, churches like the First Baptist churches of Silver Spring, Wheaton, and Bethesda, Md., were affiliated with the D. C. convention.

District churches sponsored missions in the new and growing suburbs of Maryland. Changing communities in the District caused several larger congregations to relocate in Maryland. By 1965, 38 of the 61 D. C. churches were in geographical Maryland. The percentage of D. C. church members residing in Maryland was even higher than the percentage of D. C. congregations in the state. Tensions began to develop between churches of the two conventions whose fields overlapped. There was no agreement whereby a relocating D. C. church respected the location of an existing Maryland church.

Neither was there a plan for placing new missions.

In an effort to resolve the tensions, representatives from the two conventions began meeting to discuss a solution to the matter. Albert McClellan, program-planning secretary for the Executive Committee, SBC, was asked to analyze the situation with a written report to be presented to the group discussing the relationships.

McClellan pointed out the need for a unified strategy in greater Washington, and the problems of the overlapping conventions. He outlined options to resolve the conflict, one of which was the merger of the two conventions.

Resistance to merger came at two points: the dual alignment of the D. C. convention with the American Baptist Convention and the SBC, which the Maryland convention, affiliated only with the SBC, would not accept, and the insistence of some D. C. pastors to retain both dual alignment and their identity in the nation's capital.

McClellan concluded merger was not feasible in 1966, but perhaps by 1970. During this period, a joint committee was established by both conventions sending elected members for discussions each six months. Ways of cooperation were discussed and some programs—evangelism conferences, education and music camps, and student ministries—were initiated.

By 1970 leadership in the Maryland convention concluded that merger would be a liability for their convention and dismissed the idea as feasible. Also by this time, the D. C. convention had begun declining in members and the number of churches. Financial problems emerged. The joint committee of the two conventions continued to meet.

New Conventions.—The establishment of the Manhattan Baptist Chapel in New York City in 1957 began a penetration of the Northeast by Southern Baptists that enlarged the Maryland convention to include all or part of 11 states—Maryland, Delaware, New Jersey, Pennsylvania, New York, Connecticut, Massachusetts, Rhode Island, New Hampshire, Vermont, and Maine.

The Baptist Convention of New York was the first new convention to be formed out of the Maryland convention. In Sept., 1969, at Central Baptist Church, Syracuse, approximately 100 churches and missions, with more than 10,000 members in New York, northern New Jersey, and southwest Connecticut, formed the 31st state convention in the SBC. Paul S. James was elected executive secretary and John M. Tubbs was elected director of the education division. Offices are located in Syracuse.

SBC churches in Pennsylvania and southern New Jersey formed a fellowship, looking toward convention constitution in Oct., 1970, with operations beginning Jan. 1, 1971.

Joseph Waltz, superintendent of missions for the Pittsburgh area, was elected executive secretary in June, 1970. Churches in western Pennsylvania, as was the case in western New York,

MARYLAND STATISTICAL SUMMARY

Year	Associations	Churches	Church Membership	Baptisms	S. S. Enrolment	V.B.S. Enrolment	T. U. Enrolment	W.M.U. Enrolment	Brotherhood Enrolment	Music Enrolment	Mission Gifts	Total Gifts	Value Church Property
1955	7	133	41,165	3,239	43,222	17,962	9,629	7,591	2,015		$ 348,642	$2,233,540	$ 2,835,299
1956	7	136	43,749	2,894	46,353	18,375	11,139	8,405	2,450		411,423	2,657,437	12,203,706
1957	7	141	47,226	3,203	48,353	19,667	12,106	9,013	3,182	3,409	447,605	2,957,422	14,242,014
1958	7	149	50,010	3,051	49,164	21,885	12,885	9,623	4,025	3,453	499,009	3,060,527	15,447,722
1959	7	158	53,831	3,600	51,926	22,122	14,358	10,698	4,156	4,288	525,700	3,359,579	17,826,126
1960	8	172	56,512	3,163	55,417	22,724	15,506	10,583	4,228	4,137	594,478	3,740,953	18,951,320
1961	8	191	60,468	3,525	57,664	24,786	17,164	10,711	4,667	5,083	616,011	4,148,134	22,121,799
1962	8	203	63,798	3,580	59,305	26,751	17,627	12,052	4,806	5,337	710,350	4,654,738	23,571,463
1963	11	221	67,161	3,493	63,697	27,901	18,922	13,005	4,967	6,006	756,713	4,935,156	26,479,610
1964	15	244	73,768	4,419	68,505	37,268	19,940	13,109	4,954	6,614	853,288	5,641,079	28,808,414
1965	15	257	77,345	4,367	69,664	32,822	19,262	13,502	4,179	6,195	1,009,445	6,335,201	30,880,839
1966	14	263	79,256	4,152	69,897	35,406	19,222	13,994	4,195	7,218	1,111,675	6,654,096	33,777,196
1967	14	275	84,011	4,658	72,332	39,081	20,351	14,038	4,174	8,141	1,178,106	7,226,719	37,434,392
1968	18	299	90,626	5,197	76,198	37,207	24,449	14,000	4,630	8,268	1,258,185	8,645,387	37,921,745

MRS. PATRICIA GOELLER

were affiliated with the Baptist State Convention of Ohio.

New England Southern Baptist churches formed a general association in Oct., 1967, with three district associations—Upper New England, Massachusetts, and Southern New England. Elmer Sizemore is the executive minister for the general association which has offices in Worcester, Mass.

Delaware is expected to remain in the Maryland convention for some time. The entire state is an association, perhaps something unique among Baptists in America. John Tollison is area missionary, with offices in Dover, the capital.

Summary.—The period 1957–70 was one of growth and expansion unequaled in the history of Maryland Baptists. The college crisis did not leave lasting damage. The pioneer work of the Northeast gave a refreshing challenge to the one and one-third century-old Maryland convention. The population growth of the state, particularly in the suburbs and new cities like Columbia, will give Maryland Baptists an adequate challenge for the decade of the seventies.

R. G. PUCKETT

MARYLAND, BAPTIST FOUNDATION OF. The trust agency of the Baptist Convention of Maryland and of the institutions owned and operated by the convention. The foundation is charged with the responsibility of procuring and servicing trust funds in accordance with the designation of the donors. Offices are located in the Baptist Building, 1313 York Road, Lutherville, Md. The first executive secretary, Gilbert E. South, also serves as the administrative assistant of the convention's state mission board. Total assets as of Dec. 31, 1968 (book value) amounted to $398,907 with the approximate market value of $850,000. Numerous scholarship funds and memorial funds have been created since the foundation's beginning in 1959. The Endowment Fund of the Baptist Convention of Maryland was turned over to the foundation to be held in trust and to collect and disburse income under a written agreement. This is presently the largest of its trust accounts. The WMU of Maryland also has placed its funds in trust with the foundation. The foundation encourages Christian estate planning through the writing of wills, creating of "living trusts," and annuities. Its services include assistance in the planning of estates, writing wills, and in acting as executor and administrator of estates.

See also MARYLAND ENDOWMENT FUND, VOL. II.

GILBERT E. SOUTH

***MARYLAND, BAPTIST HOME OF (FOR AGED).** The home was moved in 1964 from Baltimore to Owings Mills, Md., just north of Baltimore. This new facility was bought for $270,000 and was converted at a cost of approximately $200,000. The original capacity of this new home was 28 residents, plus an infirmary with 10 beds. A new wing was added to the home in 1969–70 to accommodate an additional 24 guests making a total capacity of 52. Other buildings on the 24-acre property provide for the resident director, the caretakers, and resident maids, nurses, etc. The Baptist home, formerly an independently owned institution, became an agency of the Baptist Convention of Maryland in 1965. The convention now elects the trustees of the home and approximately 11 per cent of the income of the home is provided by the state mission board from the Cooperative Program. In 1964 the home initiated a new plan whereby two types of guests are admitted. "Plan A" guests are paying guests, admitted for a stipulated monthly fee; "Plan B" guests pay an entrance fee, plus other assets, but make no monthly payments. Endowment funds of the home are approximately $775,000 and the property value is approximately $900,000.

ROBERT WOODWARD

***MARYLAND ASSOCIATIONS.**

I. New Associations. ARUNDEL. Organized in 1968 at College Avenue Baptist Church, Annapolis, Md., composed of 18 churches and one chapel, formerly part of Severn Association. Roland C. Smith was first moderator. In 1969, 19 churches reported 405 baptisms, 6,200 members, $642,004 total gifts, $86,500 mission gifts, $2,997,363 property value, and $797,349 church debt.

CENTRAL. Organized Nov., 1963, at First Baptist, Upperco, Md., with nine churches, formerly part of Susquehanna Association. George W. Townsend was the first moderator. In 1969, 12 churches reported 89 baptisms, 1,828 members, $137,463 total gifts, $20,646 mission gifts, $450,000 property value, and $183,737 church debt.

DELAWARE. Organized Oct., 1967, at First Southern Baptist Church, Dover, Del., composed of six churches and two chapels with 2,297 members. The churches had been members of the Eastern or Susquehanna associations. Charles W. Adams was first moderator. In 1969 six churches and two chapels reported 67 baptisms, 2,473 members, $238,184 total gifts, $38,063 mission gifts, $982,000 property value, and $428,493 church debt.

DELAWARE VALLEY. Organized in Oct., 1962, at Haines Road Baptist Church, Levittown, Pa., composed of three churches and three chapels, with 460 members. Richard C. Bracken was first moderator. In 1969, 15 churches and seven missions reported 279 baptisms, 2,798 members, $367,229 total gifts, $52,886 mission gifts, $1,144,156 property value, and $772,613 church debt.

KEYSTONE. Organized Nov., 1962, at Valley Baptist Church, Middletown, Pa., with four churches and 371 members. Kenneth A. Estep was the first moderator. In 1969, 14 churches and eight missions reported 253 baptisms, 2,150 members, $275,018 total gifts, $29,134 mission gifts, $981,000 property value, and $537,328 church debt.

MASSACHUSETTS. Organized in Oct., 1967, at Brunswick, Me., with eight churches and one chapel, with 1,015 members. Merwyn Borders was the first moderator. In 1969 eight churches and five missions reported 91 baptisms, 1,410 members, $122,654 total gifts, $15,834 mission gifts, $360,000 property value, and $210,617 church debt.

POTOMAC. Organized in 1963 at Nanjemoy, Md. Composed of seven churches, two missions, and 2,359 members. They had been members of the Southern District Association. Parker S. Hooper was the first moderator. In 1969, 11 churches and two missions reported 153 baptisms, 3,027 members, $253,870 total gifts, $60,097 mission gifts, $897,500 property value, and $236,477 church debt.

PRINCE GEORGES. Name changed in 1969 from Severn, of which the churches forming the Arundel Association in 1968 had also been a part. In 1969, 17 churches and six missions reported 377 baptisms, 7,962 members, $900,891 total gifts, $122,926 mission gifts, $4,352,700 property value, and $1,770,666 church debt.

SUSQUEHANNA. The name was changed from Northern in 1961. In 1969, 22 churches and one mission reported 323 baptisms, 7,709 members, $612,565 total gifts, $95,285 mission gifts, $2,679,000 property value, and $775,798 church debt.

SOUTHERN NEW ENGLAND. Organized Oct., 1967, at Brunswick, Me., composed of 11 churches and six missions, 1,136 members in Connecticut and Rhode Island, formerly affiliated with the New England Association. The first moderator was Jim Schneider. In 1969, 11 churches and nine missions reported 231 baptisms, 1,871 members, $211,383 total gifts, $32,213 mission gifts, $471,500 property value, and $224,635 church debt.

UPPER NEW ENGLAND. Organized at Brunswick, Me., in Oct., 1967, with five churches, one mission, 699 members, formerly a part of the New England Association. The territory includes Maine, New Hampshire, and Vermont. The first moderator was W. Edwin Jackson. In 1969 six churches and two missions reported 44 baptisms, 654 members, $83,376 total gifts, $13,872 mission gifts, $291,800 property value, and $137,871 church debt.

II. Changes in Associations. NEW ENGLAND. Organized in 1962 at Emmanuel Baptist Church, Springfield, Mass., composed of eight churches and 13 missions, 1,141 members. The first moderator was Owen Sherrill. This organization provided the members for the Massachusetts, the Southern New England, and the Upper New England associations when they organized in Oct., 1967.

NORTHEASTERN. Organized in Oct., 1960, at Manhattan Baptist Church, New York, N. Y., with four churches, 11 chapels, 1,060 members. The first moderator was Paul S. James. Other associations replaced it in 1962.

NORTHERN DISTRICT. Name changed to Susquehanna in 1961.

SENECA. Name changed to Montgomery in 1961.

SEVERN. Organized in Oct., 1963, at Severna Park, composed of 29 churches, three missions, 9,539 members, formerly a part of the Southern District Association. Roland C. Smith was the first moderator. The Arundel Association was formed from Severn in 1968, and the name was changed to Prince Georges in 1969.

SOUTHERN DISTRICT. Became extinct when Potomac and Severn were formed in 1963.

CLINE L. VICE

***MARYLAND BAPTIST, THE.** Official news organ of the Baptist Convention of Maryland. It is published weekly as an 8 or 12-page tabloid. First Maryland Baptist paper was *The True Union,* founded 1849. Present name first appeared in 1865. It was published under various names and with some intermittence until 1934 when the present name was reinstated. All staff members were voluntary, including the near 40-year tenure of Francis A. Davis (*q.v.*), editor. Gainer E. Bryan, Jr., a native of Georgia, graduate of Mercer University and the Southern Baptist Theological Seminary, became the first full-time, salaried editor in Nov., 1957. The paper was then a 16-page, monthly magazine. Published semimonthly as an 8 or 12-page magazine 1958–60, it advanced to 16 pages in 1961. In Jan., 1962, weekly publication of eight pages was begun. An eight-page tabloid (equal to 16-page magazine) was started in 1964. Periodic 12-page issues now supplement the regular eight-page editions. Bryan resigned in Apr., 1966. R. G. Puckett, associate editor of *The Western Recorder* and the first editor of *The Ohio Baptist Messenger* (1958–61), became editor in Aug., 1966. Puckett, a native of Kentucky, is a graduate of Western Kentucky University and The Southern Baptist Theological Seminary. Offices of the paper are in the Baptist Building, 1313 York Road, Lutherville, Md. Southern Baptists in the Northeast began receiving the paper in 1957. Circulation on Jan. 1, 1970, 17,600. Church budget subscriptions are $1.50 per year; individual, $2.00. In recent years the paper has been nationally recognized for its high journalistic standards, comprehensive news coverage, and controversial editorial positions.

R. G. PUCKETT

MASON, GEORGE JEFFERSON (b. Isla, Hemphill County, Tex., May 29, 1881; d. Dallas, Tex., Mar. 23, 1963). Denominational leader. Converted at age 14 at New Hope Baptist Church, Sabine County, Tex., he graduated from Baylor University in 1908. In 1919 he married Janie Bodine at St. Augustine, Tex. Mason served as superintendent of schools at Hamilton and Vernon, Tex., and as associate editor, *Vernon Record.* In 1920 he began 11 years service with the executive board of the Baptist General Convention of Texas. Elected as first executive secretary, Baptist Foundation of Texas, May, 1931, he served in that capacity until retirement June, 1951. Under his leadership the foundation grew from $2,000,000 to over $17,000,000. He was a deacon of the Cliff Temple Baptist Church, Dallas, Tex. He received LL.D. degrees from Baylor University, Howard Payne College and Bishop College.

J. C. CANTRELL

MASS MEDIA. The mass media are the resultant of forces set in motion when groups of men first huddled together against the cold and danger of primitive times. The tool of language came before history, and the tool we know as the alphabet came in the very dawn of history. Sometime between the beginning of language and the invention of the alphabet, man developed highly ingenious ways of storing knowledge and transmitting information. Smoke signals and drum beats were the first broadcasts, and the first libraries were collections of cut stone tablets.

Since then mass media has come of age and an explosion in the media has occurred in the last century. There has been mass circulation of printed materials for less than two centuries, radio for only about 40 years and television just since 1941. In 1970 approximately 94 per cent of the homes of America received broadcasts through nearly 100,000,000 television receivers. Mass circulation newspapers and newsmagazines combine with broadcasting to provide the United States with the most complete system of mass communications the world has yet to see. Unavoidably, the mushrooming expansion of these relatively new communication media has created some grave moral problems.

As is the case with broadcasting, the press has its continuing problems which concern Christian citizens—misleading advertising, onesided presentations of controversial issues, the sordid and sensational extremes of "yellow journalism," and civil rights violation through what is called "trial by newspaper."

Obviously, all the effects of mass media upon persons are not necessarily "evil," but it is an undeniable fact that mass media have affected the behavior patterns of the American public to an extent that it is both appalling and promising.

Mass media in its so-called "amoral" stance have developed a curious morality whereby, like the Pied Piper of old, America's young follow enthusiastically. Mass communications have helped develop an indifference and a noninvolvement to the problems of our day. Mass media cannot be blamed for all of man's faults or weaknesses, but the role mass media now play in structuring human behavior should not be underestimated.

The Christian Life Commission, SBC, conducted two major conferences on the subject of authentic morality and the mass media during 1967; published a study pamphlet on "Issues and Answers: Mass Media"; originated the publication of the book, *Morality and the Mass Media,* by Kyle Haselden; and has continued to emphasize the critical moral problems confronting modern man as related to mass media.

FLOYD A. CRAIG

MASSACHUSETTS, SOUTHERN BAPTISTS IN. See MARYLAND, BAPTIST CONVENTION OF.

MASSEE, JASPER CORTEMUS (b. Marshallville, Macon County, Ga., Nov. 22, 1871; d. Atlanta, Ga., Mar. 27, 1965). Son of Drewry Washington and Susan Elizabeth (Bryan) Massee, he was educated at Mercer University (A.B., 1892), where he decided to enter the ministry, and Southern Baptist Theological Seminary (1896). He held honorary degrees from Carson-Newman College and Mercer. His Baptist pastorates included First, Orlando, Fla.; Tabernacle, Raleigh, N. C.; First, Chattanooga, Tenn.; Baptist Temple, Brooklyn, N. Y.; and Tremont Temple, Boston, Mass.

In Raleigh, Massee's stand on race brought him into conflict with Josephus Daniels, local editor and later Secretary of the Navy. From 1920–26, he was spokesman for the Fundamentalists in the Northern Baptist Convention. "The Laodicean Lament," his address in 1926, brought a measure of reconciliation between opposing groups in the convention.

Massee was author of 23 books and numerous articles. Retiring from Tremont Temple in 1929, he preached in Bible conferences nationwide. From 1938–41, he was guest professor at Eastern Baptist Seminary.

In 1893 he married Mrs. Sallie Steward, who died in 1895. They had one son, Richard D. On June 30, 1896, he married Mary Ola Oliver. They had four children: Joseph C., Logan J., Marjorie, and William C. After Mary's death in 1932, he married Edna Blair, Aug. 25, 1935.

BIBLIOGRAPHY: Russell, C. Allyn, "J. C. Massee, Unique Fundamentalist." *Foundations,* Oct.–Dec., 1969.

R. QUINN PUGH

"MASTERCONTROL." See RADIO AND TELEVISION COMMISSION, THE.

MASTERS, FRANK MARIRO (b. Franklin County, Tex., July 28, 1870; d. Mayfield, Ky., Apr. 4, 1959). Son of Mary Ellen Penn and Basil Earl Masters, he was educated at Calhoun College, Kinston, Tex. (A.B., 1892), and Southern Baptist Theological Seminary (Th.M., 1897). He received a D.D. degree from Oklahoma Baptist University in 1922. He was ordained at the Kingston, Tex., Baptist Church in 1894. He was a school principal in Texas, 1892–94 and served Baptist churches in Kentucky, Texas, and Oklahoma, 1898–1914. He was president of Oklahoma Baptist University, 1915–20; field secretary and state missions secretary for the Arkansas Baptist Convention, 1920–28; and president of Bethel College, Russellville, Ky., 1931–33. He taught at the West

MIDWESTERN BAPTIST THEOLOGICAL SEMINARY (*q.v.*), Kansas City, Mo. Founded in 1957. *Top:* Library (*left*), auditorium (*center*), and administrative offices (*right*). *Center left:* Apartments and residence hall. *Center right:* Spire and reflection pool. *Bottom left:* Classroom building. *Bottom right:* Residence hall.

Top to bottom: MARYLAND BAPTIST CONVENTION (*q.v.*) BUILDING, Lutherville. Erected in 1965 at a cost of $500,000. UNIVERSITY BAPTIST CHURCH. Located in Baltimore, Md., near Johns Hopkins University. OAK GROVE BAPTIST CHURCH, near Bel Air, Md. Sanctuary occupied in 1965. BAPTIST HOME OF MARYLAND (*q.v.*), Rainbow Hall. Located northwest of Baltimore.

Kentucky Bible Institute, Clinton, Ky., and the Baptist Bible Institute, Mayfield, Ky., 1950–59. The author of many manuscripts related to Baptist history, he is best known by *A History of Baptists in Kentucky* (1953).

On June 9, 1898, he married Lillie W. Randolph. They had five children: Catharine (Mrs. J. Roy Rosser), E. Randolph, C. Karfoot, Frank M., Jr., and Julian P. Masters. LEO T. CRISMON

MAXWELL, JOHN CHAPPELL (b. near Starkville, Miss., Nov. 10, 1837; d. Greenwood, S. C., Aug. 12, 1899). Physician, statesman, and philanthropist. Shortly after his birth, his family returned to their native South Carolina. Educated at Furman Institution (Winnsboro, S. C.), Erskine College (1856), and the School of Medicine, the University of Pennsylvania (1859), he served in the Confederate Army as Regimental Surgeon. After the war he returned to Greenwood County, S. C., and practiced medicine. His first wife, whom he married on May 17, 1866, was Anne Benjamin Richardson. They had one child. After her death he married her sister, Sara S. Richardson, Oct. 27, 1868. They moved to Greenwood where he practiced medicine for the remainder of his life. They had four children. Only one of his five children lived beyond the early years. This child, Constance ("Connie") Pope Maxwell, died of scarlet fever, Apr. 28, 1883, at age of eight. To perpetuate her memory, the Maxwells joined with the Baptists of South Carolina in establishing the Connie Maxwell Orphanage (now Connie Maxwell Children's Home). The Maxwells left much of their estate to the orphanage. Maxwell served as president of its board of trustees, 1891–98, and was physician to the children and staff.

Maxwell was elected to the South Carolina Senate in the "Red Shirt Campaign" of 1876 which ended Reconstruction in South Carolina. He served in the senate until 1886, retiring voluntarily. He, his second wife, and Connie are all buried in the campus of the children's home. JOHN C. MURDOCK

McCABE, JAMES PLEASANT, JR. (b. Bedford County, Va., Nov. 11, 1876; d. Martinsville, Va., Oct. 15, 1956). Pastor, civic leader, denominational servant. He was educated at the University of Richmond (M.A., 1902); University of Chicago (B.D., 1906); Southern Baptist Theological Seminary (Th.D., 1907). In 1914 he was married to Sue Martin who died in 1945. He married Mrs. Nell Mullins Dodson in 1948.

McCabe was pastor of Big Island and Hunting Creek Baptist churches, Bedford County, Va., 1903–04; First Baptist Church, Martinsville, Va., 1907–47. He led in the organization of 18 churches in the Martinsville area. His influence was felt in the business, industrial, and economic life of the community.

He served as president of the Charles B. Keesee Educational Fund, Inc.; vice-president, Baptist General Association of Virginia; member, Baptist General Board of Virginia. Also he was a trustee of Averett College, Hargrave Military Academy, Virginia Baptist Children's Home, Virginia Baptist Hospital, University of Richmond, and Southern Baptist Theological Seminary. He was buried in Martinsville, Va. CHEVIS F. HORNE

McCALL, DRUIE ANSELM (Scotchie) (b. Star, Rankin County, Miss., Aug. 8, 1895; d. Chicago, Ill., June 16, 1959). First in Mississippi to hold title, executive secretary, McCall succeeded R. B. Gunter (*q.v.*) in 1939 as corresponding secretary of the Mississippi Baptist Convention Board. The son of J. M. McCall, he attended Mississippi College, but graduated from the University of Mississippi (B.S., 1917), and received his teacher's license. First Church, Oxford, ordained him to the gospel ministry (1916). He married Margie Parks of Winona, Miss., Feb. 12, 1917. At the university he played both football and basketball and was captain of the basketball team. While in the Southern Baptist Theological Seminary, he served as pastor of the Highland Park Church, Louisville, Ky.; returned to Mississippi as pastor of the Lynn Baptist Church, which church led the state in per capita gifts to missions for four years. During his ministry at the Griffin Memorial Church, Jackson (1925–34), a new building was erected.

Called from the pastorate of First Church, Philadelphia, Miss. (1934–39), he became corresponding secretary of the convention board. During his administration, the work of the state convention board was strengthened, the Brotherhood, Music, and BSU departments were added, all state denominational indebtedness was paid off (1945), and a Baptist building, in front of the State Capitol was purchased (1945). Controversy during the last years of his service as executive secretary and treasurer led to his resignation Feb. 28, 1950. He then became pastor of the Tabernacle Baptist Church, Chicago. He authored one book, *The Language of Heaven*. McCall was buried in Jackson, Miss. C. B. HAMLET, III

McCALL, ROY CARL (b. Transylvania County, N. C., Sept. 28, 1900; d. Easley, S. C., Oct. 1, 1964). Industrialist and philanthropist, son of S. E. and Lucy (Gillespie) McCall, he was educated at Rosman High School, Rosman, N. C. He married Belle Roper, Pickens County, S. C., on Nov. 6, 1921. They had three children: Roy C., Jr., Gilbert B., and Jo Ann (Mrs. John C. Cobb). McCall served as a deacon, teacher, and leader of the First Baptist Church, Easley, S. C. He was chairman of the trustee board, Royal Ambassador Camp, South Carolina Baptist Convention, and president of South Carolina Brotherhood Convention, 1962. He and his wife gave a 121-acre tract of land in upper Pickens County, S. C., to be used as a RA camp. This camp site was named McCall Royal Ambassador Camp in 1965.

McCall was founder and president of the Easley Rotary Club, president of the South Carolina Chamber of Commerce, and a National Councillor for this organization. He was also a member of the National Association of Manufacturers, having served on the regional advisory committee and the federal subsidies committee. Among the firms he directed were the following: president, McCall Manufacturing Company, vice-president, Greer Manufacuring Company, owner of McCall Cotton Merchants at Easley, president, Home Building and Loan Association, director, Carolina National Bank, director, Southern Bank and Trust Company, vice-president and treasurer, Fibers Associates, Inc., vice-president, Keowee Mills, and vice-president, Starcross, Inc., and McCall Brothers and Company. In 1962 McCall made a world mission tour, visiting many mission points of Southern Baptist work.

He was more than generous with his money and time for civic, church, and denominational causes. For his contribution to Easley in its total life, he received the first award for Easley's "Citizen of the Year" in 1951. He is buried in Greenlawn Cemetery, Easley, S. C.

DAVID G. ANDERSON

McCONNELL, FERNANDO COELLO, JR. (b. Gainesville, Ga., Mar. 22, 1890; d. Anderson, S. C., May 25, 1958). Pastor, denominational worker. Son of Fernando Coello and Emma (England) McConnell, he was educated at William Jewell College, Liberty, Mo., 1907–11; Baylor University, Waco, Tex., 1911–13; Southern Baptist Theological Seminary, Louisville, Ky., Th.M., 1923; and Stetson University, DeLand, Fla., D.D., 1923. He was pastor of the First Baptist churches of Tifton, Ga., 1923–27; Murfreesboro, Tenn., 1927–30; Jacksonville, Fla., 1930–40; and Anderson, S. C., 1940–55. McConnell served as trustee of Tennessee College, Murfreesboro, Tenn.; president, Florida Baptist Building Corporation; member of Executive Committee, SBC; and vice-president, Florida Baptist Convention. He married Choc Belle Murray on Sept. 10, 1914; they had three children: Martha Howe, Mary Murray, and Fernando Coello III. DANIEL CLOER

McCOY, LEE HAROLD (b. Guthrie, Logan County, Okla., Feb. 14, 1915; d. Fort Worth, Tex., July 5, 1965). Minister of education and seminary professor. Son of Edward and Dora Bell (Corn) McCoy, he received the B.S. from Oklahoma Baptist University, 1941, and M.R.E. and D.R.E. from Southwestern Baptist Theological Seminary (1948 and 1957). Converted at 19, he joined University Baptist Church, Shawnee, Okla., which ordained him as deacon in 1937. He married Virginia Ann (Cook) McCoy, Aug. 23, 1938. They had one daughter, Nancy Ann (Mrs. Donald Carl Enas).

He was an officer in the United States Naval Reserve in World War II. Before and after the war he was Minister of Education in First Baptist Church, Charlottesville, Va. In 1947 he went to First Baptist Church, Shawnee, Okla., and while there was ordained as Minister of Education, 1948. After serving Olivet Baptist Church, Oklahoma City, and First Baptist Church, Abilene, Tex., he joined the faculty of Southwestern Seminary, 1954–65. He was president of Oklahoma State BSU Convention, 1936–37; Oklahoma Baptist Religious Education Association, 1948–49; and Southwestern Baptist Religious Education Association, 1957–58. He wrote *Understanding Baptist Polity* (1964) and numerous articles. McCoy was buried in Laurel Land Cemetery, Fort Worth, Tex.

JAMES D. WILLIAMS

McGINTY, CLAUDIUS LAMAR (b. Norwood, Warren County, Ga., Feb. 9, 1885; d. Forsyth, Ga., Dec. 10, 1958). Educated at Mercer University (B.S., 1904; A.B., 1912) and the Southern Baptist Theological Seminary (Th.B., 1911; Th.M., 1912; Th.D., 1913), he also received the D.D. degree from Stetson University. Ordained at Broadway Baptist Church, Louisville, Ky., in 1911, he married Annie Ruby Herndon, Sept. 8, 1909. They had one daughter, Marian Lamar (Mrs. Carey T. Vinzant). He taught school in Georgia, 1904–09. His Baptist pastorates include: Millville and Glens Creek, Ky., 1911–13; Fifth Avenue, Rome, Ga., 1913–15; First, Cartersville, Ga., 1915–19; Hampton, Ga., 1919–26; Millville, Ky., 1928–30; Fisherville, Ky., 1930–34; and Buechel, Ky., 1934–37. Dean of Christianity departments and professor of Old Testament and systematic theology, Mercer, he was professor of Bible in WMU Training School, 1926–37.

McGinty returned to Georgia in 1937 as director of endowment for Bessie Tift College and was president of the college, 1938–47. After retirement (1947), he became a book consultant in Atlanta, returning to Forsyth in 1955. He was a member of the Georgia Baptist Board of Missions, 1918–19. He wrote *From Babylon to Bethlehem: A Survey of Inter-biblical History* (1929), *A Guide to the Study of the New Testament* (1935), *Sermon Outlines from the Four Gospels* (1961), *Sermon Outlines for Holy Living* (1960), and *A Book of Dedications* (1955). MARION MCGINTY VINZANT

McINTOSH, MARTHA E. See BELL, MARTHA E. MCINTOSH.

McINTOSH, WILLIAM HILLARY (b. Fair Hope Plantation, McIntosh County, Ga., Apr. 4, 1811; d. Macon, Ga., Apr. 22, 1890). Home missions executive, pastor, missionary, and denominational leader. Son of William Jackson and Maria (Hillary) McIntosh, he was educated at Furman Theological Institution, S. C. He was ordained by the South Newport Baptist Church, McIntosh County, Ga., Mar., 1836. He married five times, with eight children born to these unions. He was survived by his last wife, Maria Ellen McIntosh, and three children. His pastorates include Darien, Ga., 1840–49; Eufaula,

Ala., 1849–54; Marion, Ala., 1855–71; Macon, Ga., 1872–75; and Cedartown, Ga., 1885–86.

Active in denominational life, McIntosh was the seventh corresponding secretary of the Home Mission Board, SBC, 1875–82, which agency he had served as president, 1857–71. Serving cautiously and conservatively in trying times, his secretaryship terminated when the board was moved to Atlanta and was reorganized. He delivered the Southern Baptist Convention annual sermon in 1861, was president of the Alabama state convention in 1863, and was honored with the D.D. degree by both Baylor University and Columbian College in 1868.

In 1848 he was appointed as one of the Domestic (now Home) Mission Board's first two missionaries "to the colored people." After serving as the board's corresponding secretary, he spent most of his closing years in missionary service as theological instructor to Negroes in Georgia. He is buried in Laurel Grove Cemetery, Savannah, Ga. ARTHUR B. RUTLEDGE

McMILLAN, EDNA SUSAN (b. Attala County, Miss., July 9, 1870; d. Tulsa, Okla., Dec. 19, 1966). Born of Methodist parents as Edna Susan Brown, she graduated with honors from Huntsville Female College, Huntsville, Ala., 1890. She married a Baptist, George McMillan, with whom she went to what is now Muskogee, Okla., in 1902. While in Muskogee she became a Baptist, and moved to Bristow, Okla., in 1907. She was president of Woman's Missionary Union of Oklahoma, 1927–38; chairman, WMU advisory board in Oklahoma, 1939–48; and was honored when WMU of Oklahoma named its annual state missions offering for her in 1939. She is buried at Bristow, Okla. J. M. GASKIN

McMURRY, MILDRED FRANKLIN DODSON (b. Franklin, Ky., Nov. 18, 1897; d. Birmingham, Ala., Jan. 2, 1965). Woman's Missionary Union leader, writer, and speaker. Daughter of a Baptist minister, Franklin Pierce Dodson, and Delilah (Mays) Dodson, she received an A.B. degree from Tennessee College for Women in 1920, and did postgraduate work at the University of Chicago in 1924. She taught English and Spanish until she married William McMurry, a Baptist minister, on June 4, 1925. They had one daughter, Billie Bridge (Mrs. A. Stoddard Emmons). Active in WMU in Tennessee, Mississippi, West Virginia, and Kentucky churches where her husband held pastorates, she held numerous offices in associational, district, and state WMU. She served as state WMU mission study chairman in Tennessee, 1928–41 (excepting 1935). She was vice-president of West Virginia Baptist Convention, 1945–46. Following her husband's death in 1950, she joined the WMU, SBC, staff in 1951 and moved to Birmingham. She served first as mission study director, then was made secretary of the Department of Missionary Fundamentals in 1954, and Promotion Division Director in 1957. This position she held until her retirement in Nov., 1962. That same month Oklahoma Baptist University conferred on her the Doctor of Letters degree, and the North American Baptist Women's Union elected her its president.

Mrs. McMurry was the author of *Constraining Love* (1939), *Educating Youth in Missions* (1960), and *Spiritual Life Development* (1964). She wrote missionary programs for *The Window of YWA* (Mar., 1936–July, 1939), and numerous features for *Royal Service* and *Tell*. Widely sought as a speaker, she visited Israel in 1961 as a guest of the state of Israel. In 1963 she was elected a member of the Baptist World Alliance Executive Committee. She is buried in Springfield, Tenn. DORIS DEVAULT

McNEELY, LYDIA WAYNE WALKER (b. Comyn, Commanche County, Tex., Sept. 27, 1897; d. Ft. Worth, Tex., Apr. 16, 1957). Professor of piano, Southwestern Baptist Theological Seminary, 1920–57. She graduated from the public schools of Proctor, Tex., where the family moved shortly after her birth. In Jan., 1920, she came to Southwestern Seminary as a student-teacher of piano. The following Apr. 27, she married Edwin McNeely of the faculty of the seminary's School of Church Music. One daughter, Marilyn (Mrs. James Dunn) now (1969) lives in Dallas, Tex. Academic degrees include B.S.M., Southwestern Seminary; M.M., Cincinnati Conservatory; further studies were pursued at Texas Christian University, University of Cincinnati, Chicago Musical College, and Chautauqua Musical College. Mrs. McNeely studied piano privately with William Beller, M. Boguslawski, Ernest Hutcheson, Edwin Hughes, and Silvio Scionti. She was buried in Laural Land Cemetery, Ft. Worth, Tex. ROBERT DOUGLASS

McWILLIAMS, CORA FRANCES COWGILL (b. Caldwell County, Mo., Sept. 4, 1876; d. St. Joseph, Mo., July 30, 1969). She served as state mission study director, WMU Training School trustee, Margaret Fund trustee, president of Missouri Woman's Missionary Union, 1934–41, and vice-president of the Convention-wide WMU for seven years. The second woman to be a member on the Foreign Mission Board, she served for seven years. Mrs. McWilliams was state chairman and Convention-wide chairman when WMU, SBC, celebrated the Golden Jubilee in 1938. For 15 years she was a member of the executive board of the Missouri Baptist General Association. The daughter of James and Ellen Cowgill, she was educated in the public schools of Hamilton and Cowgill. At age 16 she enrolled in Liberty Female College. In Sept., 1895, she married George McWilliams. She is buried in Elmwood Cemetery, Kansas City, Mo. MARY O. BIDSTRUP

MEADHAVEN NURSING HOME. SEE MONTGOMERY BAPTIST HOSPITAL.

MEDEARIS, FRANK C. (b. Knoxville, Tenn., July 3, 1881; d. Winfield, Kans., June 20, 1964). One of 11 children, he moved to Missouri in 1910, where he was a farmer until several years after entering the ministry and while he served several churches. His pastorates included Missouri churches: Pepsin, Bethany, Avilla, Saginaw, Duenweg, and Temple of Carthage. He also served First Baptist, Burden, Kans. (1915–22; 1933–42), and Northwest Baptist, Miami, Okla. In 1919 he led the Burden Church to withdraw from the Northern Baptist Convention in protest of its participation in the Inter-Church World Movement and to join the Perry Baptist Association of Oklahoma, the Baptist General Convention of Oklahoma, and the Southern Baptist Convention.

While serving the Spring River Association as missionary (1923–33; 1942–46), he was able to minister constructively to five Kansas churches that cooperated with Southern Baptists and Missouri Baptists, all located near the Missouri border. They were: Wirtonia; Macedonia; First, Baxter Springs; First, Arma; and First, Lawton. Thus, his ministry prepared six churches to survive, grow, and participate in the development of the Kansas Convention of Southern Baptists after 1946. He said that more than once he dreamed that someday there would be a convention of Southern Baptists in Kansas. His work figured vitally in subsequent growth of Southern Baptists in Kansas.

His first wife and mother of his six children, was Mary Headley, who preceded him in death by more than 12 years. His second wife, Lucy Miller, survived him. Tom Medearis, a brother, served as executive secretary of Missouri Baptists for many years. N. J. WESTMORELAND

***MEDICAL MISSIONS.** In recent years there has been significant growth in medical mission work. From one overseas hospital in 1948, Southern Baptists now operate a total of 21. A total of 47,586 inpatients and 631,977 outpatients were treated through these hospitals and clinics in 1968.

In 1961 the Foreign Mission Board elected Franklin T. Fowler to fill the new position of medical consultant. The same year the Medical Volunteer Program was created. Under this program eligible Baptist physicians and dentists are invited to spend a period of time working with missionaries on the field. They pay their own expenses and stay from three weeks to four months. The Special Project Nurse program was begun in 1963 to meet emergency nursing needs. Under this program a nurse is sent to a field to work in an existing institution for a period of two years. In 1965 the Special Project-Physicians and Dentists was begun. Under this project physicians or dentists are sent for one year to serve in a functioning medical work. In 1968 the Medical Receptorship Program was inaugurated. This involves Baptist third year medical students who spend a minimum of eight weeks during the summer working with medical missionaries on the field.

In the last several years much thought has been given to a clarification of the aim of medical missions. It is contained in the program statement of the Foreign Mission Board: "To provide medical assistance to people in foreign countries as an expression of Christian love and as a means of witness in order that they may be brought to God through Jesus Christ." This expression proves concern not only for man's physical being, but also for his eternal health as it helps communicate to him God's total love through Jesus Christ. The concept of medical missions can be expressed by a triangle. One side is that of *service,* which may be preventive or curative. The second side is that of *teaching* and *training*. The base of the triangle is that of *witnessing*. The concern is for the total man, his present, his future, and his eternal health.

The trends in medical missions, or health missions as it properly should be called, are diverse. Curative medicine is a very important part of the health mission. However, more and more emphasis is being given to the teaching and training aspect. Preventive medicine is rapidly becoming an important part of health missions. Through ambulatory clinics, infant maternity clinics, community health approaches, vaccination projects, health education programs, family planning, etc., the concept of preventing suffering and fostering health is becoming more important. Health missions is becoming a team approach. The team is composed of the physician with his various specialities, the dentist, the nurse, the hospital administrator, the laboratory technologist, the physiotherapist, the hospital chaplain, the dietician, etc. But all are really a part of the greater team, the mission, as together with their national brethren they endeavor to preach the gospel and witness unto the Saviour of all mankind.

FRANKLIN T. FOWLER

MEIN, JOHN (b. Newcastle upon Tyne, England, Feb. 16, 1883; d. Jacksonville, Fla., July 29, 1962). Author, educator, and missionary. Educated at Moody Bible Institute (1909) and Southern Baptist Theological Seminary (1912), he received D.D. degree from Georgetown College. Appointed in 1914, he served in Brazil until 1953, then in the Bahamas until 1956, organizing Bahamas Baptist Bible Institute, Nassau. In Brazil he founded the Baptist academy in Alagoas and directed several schools, including North Brazil Baptist Theological Seminary, Recife. He married Elizabeth Margaret Fehsenfeld in 1912. Their son David is a missionary in Brazil. After Elizabeth's death in 1946, John married Mildred Cox. CHARLES W. DICKSON

MELTON, SPARKS WHITE (b. Wilmington, Fluvanna County, Va., Mar. 3, 1870; d. Norfolk, Va., Apr. 1, 1957). Minister, pulpiteer. Son of physician John T. and Anne White Melton, he attended business school, Richmond College (three years), and Crozer Theological Seminary. Lyles Baptist Church ordained him on Apr. 19, 1892. He married Laura Virginia Nelson on Apr. 28, 1895. They had one child, James Carroll Melton. Following seminary studies Melton had three pastorates: Franklin Square Church, Baltimore, Md., 1895–1900; First Church, Augusta, Ga., 1900–08; and Freemason Street Church, Norfolk, Va., 1908–52. In Norfolk he was a prime exponent of ministry to the inner city and became known as "Norfolk's Pastor." His preaching gifts were widely recognized. He preached the Centennial Sermon for the University of Richmond and delivered at "Monticello" the address for the national celebration of the 150th anniversary of the Declaration of Independence. One book of sermonic meditations, *Will He Find Faith?* (1934), came from his pen. He served as president of the Baptist General Association of Virginia, 1931–34. Both Mercer University and the University of Richmond awarded him honorary degrees. He was buried in Fluvanna County, Va. WILLIAM L. LUMPKIN

MELTON, WILLIAM WALTER (b. Navarro, Tex., Jan. 19, 1879; d. Waco, Tex., Oct. 6, 1967). A west Texas cowboy who did not have formal education until he was 22, when he entered Decatur Baptist College. In 1910 he entered Southwestern Baptist Seminary. He earned his B.A. degree from Baylor University in 1919 at the age of 40. Baylor later gave him a D.D. He married Orah Shipp on Sept. 14, 1905, in Newport, Tex., and they had six children. He served as pastor of Seventh and James Baptist Church, Waco, Tex., for 29 years, then as pastor of Columbus Avenue Baptist Church, Waco, Tex., from 1945 until retirement in 1957. In 1941 he was elected executive secretary of the executive board of the Baptist General Convention of Texas. He wrote the following books: *Stories From Life, The Making of a Preacher, The Waste of Sin* (1922), *Sifted But Saved* (1925), *The Fellowship of Angels* (1932), *The Splendor of His Glory* (1936).

JOE WELDON BAILEY

MEMORIAL BAPTIST HOSPITAL, HOUSTON (cf. Memorial Hospital, Houston, Vol. II). In 1969 the hospital had a 954-bed capacity. This institution pioneered in a unique satellite hospital system with the addition of three general hospitals in suburban Houston between 1962 and 1965. The hospital is accredited by the Joint Commission for Accreditation of Hospitals and for nursing education by the National League for Nursing; and is approved by the Council on Medical Education and Hospitals of the American Medical Association. A five-floor addition to the central unit was constructed in 1965 at a cost of $6,000,000. An adjacent undeveloped block was purchased in 1967 for future needs. In 1969 the capital assets of the hospital were valued at $25,154,165, and indebtedness totaled $13,130,633. For the fiscal year ending June 30, 1969, 44,450 patients were admitted; 7,051 charity patients were treated at a cost of $633,052 and 402 professions of faith were made. The total expenditures were $20,973,299, with $145,735 received from the Baptist Cooperative Program. JOE F. LUCK

***MEMORIAL HOSPITAL, BAPTIST, GADSDEN.** In 1963 this Alabama hospital was enlarged to accommodate 225 beds, and an expansion program underway (1970) will bring the total to 325. The hospital is financed entirely within its own income and from special gifts. There are 400 employees with an annual payroll of $2,500,000. J. Cecil Hamiter was appointed administrator in 1957, and became president in 1969. Charles W. Roe became assistant administrator in 1963, and vice-president in 1969.

GEORGE W. RIDDLE

MEMORIAL HOSPITAL, BAPTIST, KANSAS CITY, MO. In 1944 the Kansas City Baptist Association formed a hospital committee, and in 1948 acquired 23½ acres at the present site. Two sub-floors of the building were completed in 1953. The Missouri Baptist General Association agreed in 1956 to take responsibility for building and operating the hospital through a board of trustees.

As of Jan. 16, 1960, only two floors in the nine-story building were complete. The first patients were admitted on Jan. 20, and by October five floors and 167 beds were in use. A construction program in 1963 brought the bed complement to 315. A nine-story wing was added in 1966, increasing the bed capacity to 385 and providing additional space for several departments.

This acute general hospital has designated areas for maternity, pediatrics, medicine, surgery, ophthalmology, orthopedics, urology, group nursing, surgical intensive care, cardiac intensive care, self-care, and emergency service. Professional education in eight paramedical fields is accredited in the hospital: Licensed Practical Nursing, Associate Degree Nursing, Baccalaureate Degree Nursing, Clinical Pastoral Education, Inhalation Therapy, Medical Technology, Radiologic Technology, and Surgical Technology.

The medical staff of 450 along with some 950 employees had cared for 270,000 patients by 1969. Two volunteer organizations, the Baptist Memorial Hospital Auxiliary of over 900 members and the Honorary Board of Governors with 450 members, have helped financially and through volunteer service. Hamilton V. Reid has served as executive director since 1960.

RICHARD DAYRINGER

***MEMORIAL HOSPITAL, BAPTIST, MEMPHIS.** Expansion since 1959 brought the bed capacity to 1,513 in 1969. The hospital plant, together with auxiliary services and land value, brings the institution to an approximate asset value of $65,000,000.

Approximately 50 per cent of its patient days

apply to patients who come from outside of Memphis and Shelby County. In 1969 the annual admission of patients was at the rate of 50,000 and total patient days at the rate of 475,000. Outpatient visits of all kinds were at the annual rate of approximately 320,000. The medical staff of the hospital includes some 650 physicians, most of whom are medical specialists. The hospital offers medical education programs including internships and medical residencies in internal medicine, general surgery, neurosurgery, pediatrics, obstetrics-gynecology, radiology, orthopedics, and pathology. Also, the hospital provides some phases of the clinical experiences for students from the University of Tennessee College of Medicine. The hospital conducts the following formally approved education programs: professional nursing, practical nursing, medical technology, X-ray technology, medical records library science, certified laboratory assistants. A major emphasis of the hospital's program has been service to those unable to pay. This service amounts to $1,750,000 per annum.

The 1969 budget of the hospital was $35,000,000. For income, the hospital relies principally upon charges to private patients and payments from contracting agencies. Supplemental income from subsidiary operations germane to the hospital's overall purposes is another source of income. The hospital employs some 3,250 persons on a full-time basis and 300 on a part-time basis. The hospital is licensed by the state of Tennessee, is fully accredited by the Joint Commission on Accreditation of Hospitals, is an underwriting member of the area Blue Cross Plan, and is approved for Medicare and Medicaid participation. FRANK S. GRONER

***MEMORIAL HOSPITAL, BAPTIST, OKLAHOMA CITY.** Out of an original dream by Andrew Potter (*q.v.*, Vol. II), a survey committee was appointed by the board of directors of the Baptist General Convention of Oklahoma in 1951 to study Oklahoma City's hospital needs. The convention in 1952 approved a recommendation to build a 250-bed hospital, designed for future expansion, and that a school of nursing be provided for 150 students.

In 1955 a 70-acre site in northwest Oklahoma City was selected, ground was broken May 17, 1956, and a building contract was let Feb. 27, 1957. The $4,600,000 facility admitted its first patient, Apr. 15, 1959. John M. Hendricks was the first administrator. A $4,000,000 expansion program began in 1963, which was completed in 1965.

The final class in the hospital's own school of nursing was graduated in 1970, but thereafter the nurses' training program begun in 1968 by affiliation with Central State College, Edmond, Okla., was continued.

In 1969 the hospital's capacity was 376 adults and 55 bassinets, with 88 per cent occupancy. Property value was over $12,000,000, with a debt over $5,000,000. There were 815 full-time employees, and a gross income of about $9,000,000. During its first decade of operation the hospital admitted over 15,000 patients for 121,033 patient days of service. James L. Henry has been administrator since 1960. J. M. GASKIN

***MEMORIAL HOSPITAL, BAPTIST, SAN ANTONIO.** Currently a 679-bed, 100 bassinet general hospital, Baptist Memorial is expanding by adding two satellites, the 168-bed Northeast Baptist Hospital in Nov., 1970, and the 168-bed Southeast Baptist Hospital in Nov., 1971. Each will be a completely organized and staffed hospital answering medical needs of two important areas of San Antonio which had been without adequate facilities in the past, but which will operate under the same board of trustees and administration. With the completion of three major additions and renovation of existing properties since 1952, the hospital is valued in excess of $14,750,000 and employs 1,800 personnel. It served over 30,000 admitted patients in fiscal year 1968. A fully accredited teaching hospital, Baptist Memorial operates a School of Nursing, and conducts schools in medical technology, X-ray technology, and surgical technology. DAVID GARRETT

***MERCER UNIVERSITY.** George Boyce Connell (*q.v.*), who succeeded Spright Dowell (*q.v.*) as president in 1953, died in 1959. Major campus improvements during the Connell administration were construction of a classroom building named for Professor Otis Dewey Knight, and a student center named for Connell after his death. The Southern School of Pharmacy in Atlanta became an adjunct of Mercer in 1959. New sources of revenue were sought and the convention entered a matching program for capital funds in 1955. Rufus Carrollton Harris, a Mercer graduate and former dean of its Law School, became president in 1960, having retired from the presidency of Tulane University.

In the sixties, three major problems confronted the university: the question of racial integration, expanding the campus in a crowded area of Macon, and finding new sources of revenue to meet demands of ever-increasing costs. Black students began enrolling in 1963. The second question remained unsolved at the end of the decade. The third caused concern within the Georgia Baptist Convention when the trustees sought federal aid. The convention was divided on the question. Some held that government grants and loans below commercial interest rates violated the traditional interpretation of the principle of separation of church and state. The convention in 1969 session acknowledged the legal right of the trustees to administer the institution under the charter issued by the state of Georgia.

President Harris early formulated plans for upgrading the college in academic standards, endowment, and physical growth. More buildings were constructed, including the Eugene W.

Stetson Memorial Library and the Hugh M. Willet Science Center. Faculty salaries and the operating budget were raised through income from higher tuition payments and other sources. Current operating expenses increased from $1,700,000 in 1960–61 to $5,700,000 in 1969–70, endowment rose from $6,000,000 to $11,500,000, physical assets increased from $6,000,000 to $13,700,000, faculty grew from 80 to 110, and average compensation rose from $6,017 to $11,557. Forty-one per cent of the faculty held the doctorate. The student body grew by 50.7 per cent between 1954 and 1969—from 1,297 to 1,955 in the three units: Liberal Arts, Law, and Pharmacy. Libraries of the three units contained more than 150,000 volumes. Stetson Library grew from 76,510 volumes in 1957 to 108,482 in 1967–68. SPENCER KING

***MEREDITH COLLEGE.** In Sept., 1966, E. Bruce Heilman succeeded Carlyle Campbell as president. The student body, representing 18 states and two foreign countries, has grown from 681 in 1956, to 903 in 1968–69. The enrolment for the fall semester of 1969–70 was 1,000. The faculty and administration numbered 84 in 1968–69, including 14 part-time faculty members, and the number for the fall semester of 1969–70 is 87. A total of 5,776 students have graduated from the institution, 2,129 of them since 1956.

From 1956–69, two residence halls, two buildings for classrooms and laboratories, an infirmary, a home economics residence, and a library were erected, and a physical education building was under construction in 1970. Heilman initiated a $5,000,000 capital fund campaign to which more than $3,126,000 in gifts and pledges were contributed in 1968–69.

The college had an endowment of $1,206,342 in 1969–70. In 1968–69, the North Carolina Baptist State Convention appropriated to Meredith $241,863.60. The budget for 1969–70 was $2,321,130.

The academic program was liberalized, allowing students more freedom of choice in courses the first two years than was possible in preceding years, while keeping a broad foundation for specialization. A plan of cooperation with the five other colleges in Raleigh, including North Carolina State University, widens curriculum offerings at Meredith. E. BRUCE HEILMAN

METROPOLITAN MISSIONS, HOME MISSION BOARD PROGRAM OF (cf. City Missions, Vol. I). Begun in May, 1845, when attention was called to the need and challenge of missions in the cities, especially in New Orleans. With the growth of urban areas, city missions received increasing attention. In 1959 the HMB's Department of City Missions, with Fred B. Moseley as secretary, became part of the Division of Missions, charged with providing leadership in mission centers, rescue missions, juvenile rehabilitation, and Jewish work. Roman Catholic information service was added later. A "Big Cities Program" (1957–61) channeled financial aid to selected cities to assist with salaries of pastors and to provide loans for building sites.

In 1962 when Moseley became executive secretary of the Washington-Oregon convention, he was succeeded by Harold C. Bennett as department secretary. He, in turn, was succeeded by J. N. Evans in 1966 when Bennett went to serve on the staff of the Texas convention.

On Jan. 1, 1964, the department was renamed the Department of Metropolitan Missions and was assigned the task of serving all metropolitan associations in the Southern Baptist Convention, except those in the newer areas. The department's services were thus extended to any Convention-related church or association located in a Standard Metropolitan Statistical Area (an area having over 50,000 population). Ministries heretofore attached to the department were reassigned to other programs, freeing the department to develop metropolitan mission strategy and to plan programs for strengthening and enlarging a Christian witness in the cities. By 1970 staff members assisting Evans in this work were Russell F. Bennett, Jr., and George A. Torney.

The stated objective is to assist churches, associations, and state conventions in analyzing needs and developing strategy for ministry in the cities. Through study and research, by means of conferences and writing, through conducting experimental mission programs, and by serving as an information center on urban life and ministry, basic principles, techniques, and programs are discovered and shared with those who serve in metropolitan America. The selecting and orienting of superintendents of missions and mission pastors and providing help for their support when it is requested and available, are responsibilities of the department which serves as a channel through which other board programs may be coordinated and related to the associations. A close cooperative relationship is maintained with state mission leaders and other convention agencies which serve metropolitan churches and associations.

The program received Convention approval in 1966 as one of the board's 12 programs of work. J. N. EVANS

MEXICAN BAPTIST BIBLE INSTITUTE. Established in 1947 by the San Antonio Baptist Association to provide training for Spanish-speaking pastors and Christian workers. For 15 years it was owned and operated by the association in cooperation with the Baptist General Convention of Texas. In Nov., 1962, the Baptist General Convention of Texas voted to sponsor the school, and since Jan., 1965, has assumed full responsibility for its operating budget. The Institute is a four-year theological institution offering basically the same subjects as those offered by a seminary. The trustees are named by the executive board of the Baptist General Convention of Texas. CHARLES P. MCLAUGHLIN

MEXICAN BAPTIST CHILDREN'S HOME OF TEXAS (cf. Mexican Baptist Orphans Home, Vol. II). Since Jan. 1, 1960, the home has been included in the Cooperative Program and is one of the four child care institutions under the Human Welfare Commission of the Baptist General Convention of Texas. At the end of 1957, 12 cottages for children were completed with each having the capacity for 12 children and private quarters for the houseparents. In 1964 a new $85,000 Gregory Chapel and Annex was constructed in honor of the first administrator. Total assets in 1969 were $1,398,785. The Home is licensed by the State Department of Public Welfare. J. Ivey Miller succeeded E. G. Gregory as administrator on Jan. 1, 1960.

J. IVEY MILLER

***MEXICO, MISSION IN.** With 69 missionaries stationed in 13 centers in 1969, the mission serves the entire republic. New ministries initiated since 1956 include university student work, book stores in Mexico City, Guadalajara, and Torreon, and agricultural missions in Oaxaca. The Baptist hospital in Guadalajara, Jalisco, increased its capacity to 89 beds. Enrolment at the Mexican Baptist Theological Seminary grew to 63 resident and 180 extension students. The Iguala student home was discontinued.

JAMES D. CRANE

MEYER, LELAND WINFIELD (b. East New Market, Md., May 5, 1892; d. Georgetown, Ky., Mar. 15, 1963). Educated at Western Maryland College (A.B., 1914) and Columbia University (A.M., 1920; Ph.D., 1931), he married Emma DeWitt Vories Aug. 10, 1922. He was principal of the Hurlock, Md., High School, 1914–17, and taught at the University of Iowa, 1920–21; Franklin College, Franklin, Ind., 1921–22; and Georgetown College, Georgetown, Ky., 1922–32, as professor of history and political science. Meyer resigned from the Georgetown faculty in 1938 after an extended illness. He wrote *Georgetown College, Its Background and A Chapter in Its Early History* (1929, reprinted in 1967) and *Life and Times of Colonel Richard M. Johnson* (1932). Meyer's Georgetown history was written from a wealth of original material which was subsequently lost in the fire destroying the college library in Apr., 1930.

Meyer played professional baseball for two seasons before World War I. In 1926 he was chosen a member of the European Conference of American Professors of International Relations for study at Geneva and the Hague and was a guest of the Carnegie Endowment for International Peace. He was among the honorees at a state dinner given by Holland's Queen Wilhelmina.

He was a popular teacher at Georgetown. In 1930 the senior class dedicated the college annual to Meyer as one "whose genial character, genuine scholarship, classroom inspiration, and high ideals have endeared him to the hearts of every one of us."

KENNETH FENDLEY

***MIAMI BAPTIST HOSPITAL (Okla.).** The capacity at Miami Baptist Hospital in 1969 was 92 beds and 15 bassinets. Property value, including buildings and equipment, was $988,455 with no debt. There were 170 employees. Occupancy was reported at 77 per cent.

J. M. GASKIN

MICHAELS, JOHN WALTER (b. Petersburg, Va., Dec. 19, 1852; d. Fort Smith, Ark., Sept. 29, 1942). First missionary to the deaf. Having lost his hearing as a boy, Michaels attended the Virginia School for Deaf and Blind at Staunton and Gallaudet College in Washington, D. C., from which he received two honorary degrees, B.P. and D.D. He served in the field of education for the deaf in Virginia and Arkansas, under appointment by the Arkansas mission board for a number of years. Appointed by the Home Mission Board in 1906, he pioneered in Baptist work with the deaf in the southern states and as far west as Arizona. He wrote *A Handbook of the Sign Language of the Deaf* (1923).

IRVIN DAWSON

MICHIGAN, BAPTIST STATE CONVENTION OF.

I. Beginnings. The first Baptist church in the state was organized in 1822 by a handful of pioneers in what is now Pontiac. The first Southern Baptist church was organized in Jackson, Mich.

Southern Baptist organized work dates back to 1951, when Motor Cities Association of Southern Baptist Churches in Michigan was organized with six churches: New Hope Baptist and Antioch Baptist of Detroit; First Baptist of St. Clair Shores; and First Southern Missionary Baptist of Roseville. Two other churches, Manoah Baptist and East Side Baptist (both of Detroit), supported the association without formally affiliating with it. This new association elected Olin Sisk as interim missionary and Coy Sims as the first moderator. Other pastors instrumental in initiating the organization of the association were Edgar Roberts, Thomas Sivil, H. T. Starkey, Malcolm Sledd, and Emmett Pryor. In 1952 the association elected Fred Hubbs, a Baylor University student, as the first missionary. That same year Eder Memorial and Samaritan Missionary churches affiliated with the association.

In Jan., 1953, the Home Mission Board, SBC, joined the Arkansas Baptist State Convention in support of the mission work in Michigan. The association was aided greatly by the Arkansas convention and its leaders in each department of work. Arkansas' continuing interest in Michigan's mission outreach is evidenced by the fact that many Arkansas churches are supporting Michigan's project 500 missions. The support comes in forms of prayer, finances, and personnel.

In 1955 one other missionary, W. E. Walker, was appointed to serve with Hubbs. He served until 1956, at which time he assumed work in Tennessee. Truett Smith of Texas came in

1955 to serve as mission pastor and seminary extension director.

In 1956 Michigan Southern Baptists began state fellowship meetings, looking forward to the organization of a state convention. Alfred Mullins, pastor of Pontiac's Columbia Avenue Baptist Church, served as the first president of the fellowship. Vernon Bellue of Hebron Baptist Church served as the second and last president. Kenneth Day was added to the associational staff as a missionary in 1957.

II. Convention Organized. The Baptist State Convention of Michigan was organized in Nov., 1957, with 52 churches. H. T. Starkey was elected as the first convention president. Elected as first vice-president and second vice-president were Manion Boyd and Edgar Roberts, respectively. Fred D. Hubbs was elected executive secretary of the convention, and Kenneth Day became state director of missions. Truett Smith was asked to direct the seminary extension and edit the *Michigan Baptist Messenger*. Joe Watson was elected director of religious education in 1958.

Men serving as convention presidents since 1959 are as follows: Marion Boyd, 1959–60; Ray Babb, 1961–62; Hubert Keefer, 1963–64; E. Clay Polk, 1965–67; Max Cadenhead, 1968–69; and James Jones, 1969–70.

Under the leadership of Fred Hubbs, Michigan Southern Baptists have often attempted and done the impossible. Though it had barely been organized and could hardly pay salaries in 1958, the convention bought Bambi Lake, a state encampment, for $44,000. An acquaintance gave Hubbs $7,000 of the $14,000 needed for the down payment on the day of the deadline.

The state office occupied a store building on Grand River in Detroit from 1957 to 1963. In 1963, the convention purchased Priscilla Inn for $60,000. Valued at $500,000 in 1970, this building served not only as a state office but also as a home for single women. As an indication of Southern Baptist growth in Michigan, in 1966 the convention listed 145 churches and 52 missions.

III. Program of Work. The convention's constitution provides for an executive board consisting of 27 members excluding the four convention officers. This board is responsible for administering the business affairs of the convention between annual meetings. The executive committee of the convention is made up of the convention officers and the chairmen of the four standing committees. The first vice-president serves as chairman of the executive committee.

The program of work of the convention is divided into four divisions: administration, missions, religious education, and special ministries. Fred Hubbs is director of the Administration Division, which is charged with giving direction to the business of the convention. Serving as assistant to Hubbs in this division is Fred Trachsel. The division includes the department of publication which is responsible for the publication of the *Michigan Baptist Advocate*. Editor Hubbs is assisted by Mrs. LaVerne Watson. Circulation was 3,935 in 1969.

The Missions Division, which has the responsibility for mission expansion and evangelism, has been directed by Robert Wilson since July, 1962. Prior to this date he served four years as a superintendent of missions. The Missions Division is divided into four departments: evangelism, language missions, interracial work, and Christian social ministries.

W. B. Oakley, secretary of the department of evangelism, has been employed by the convention since Jan., 1963, serving many of those years in stewardship and Brotherhood as well as evangelism. Eugene Bragg, secretary of the department of language missions, began his employment in July, 1963. W. T. Moore has served as secretary of the department of interracial work since Sept., 1966. Max Cadenhead has served as secretary of the Christian social ministries department since Feb., 1969.

When the convention was organized, the state was divided into three areas which were served by three superintendents of missions. In 1970 nine superintendents of missions were serving in nine areas and 13 associations: Jay Dannelley, Dale Cross, Eldon Hale, Claude Roy, Allan Pollack, Vernon Wickliffe, Loren Ames, Willard Martin, and Marion Boyd. The Missions Division is closely related to the Home Mission Board in all of its work. The two agencies have a cooperative agreement through which the HMB channels thousands of mission dollars into Michigan.

Joe Watson has served as the director of the Religious Education Division since 1958. He was the only man in this division until Feb., 1963, when Stanley Howell became secretary of the department of Training Union and student work. Howell resigned to begin work with the Baptist Sunday School Board in 1964. In Aug., 1964, Harold E. Crane, Jr., became secretary of the department of Training Union, music, and student work. Crane had served as music director of Merriman Road Baptist Church, 1955–59, before attending Southwestern Baptist Theological Seminary.

Miss Frances Brown has been serving as director of Woman's Missionary Union since 1958. In 1968 WMU became a department in the Religious Education Division, with Miss Brown as departmental secretary.

Jack Elliott, after having served part-time in the department of Brotherhood for several years, became secretary of the department of Brotherhood and student work, Jan., 1970.

Fred Hubbs serves as director of the Special Ministries Division. This division is charged with the operation of Priscilla Hall which serves as a residence for some 90 single women. Among these residents are students, working women, retirees, and rehabilitation patients. This division is also responsible for the operation of Bambi Lake, the convention's encampment, which is used not only for GA and RA campers, but also for numerous other activities during the entire year. Leon Fuller has served as camp manager since 1958. This division also maintains the facilities of the Baptist Center. The program of work of the center is carried on by the Missions Division. The Special Ministries Division also oversees the operation of the Michigan Baptist Institute. The institute serves as a training center for preachers and lay people who desire further training for Christian service. It is staffed by state personnel and volunteer pastors.

In 1969, 170 churches reported 2,075 baptisms, 34,193 total members, 26,702 in Sunday School, and 10,225 in Training Union. EUGENE BRAGG

Sunday School.—Sunday School work in Michigan has been closely linked with the successes and failures of outreach, soul-winning, and church growth from the infancy of the organized work. In 1952 Michigan Sunday Schools had an enrolment of 1,603.

Early in the organized work, Howard Bryan was asked to serve as associational superintendent. Three years later, enrolment had reached 6,000, with the state divided into five zones. In 1958 Joe Watson, native of Whitesboro, Tex., became the convention's first director of religious education, with the responsibility of overseeing Sunday School, Training Union, music, student, and Brotherhood secretaries, as well as church administration consultants. By 1959 enrolment was 12,689, and in 1960 Sunday School recorded its largest gain of any year. In 1959–60 Michigan led the SBC in percentage of Sunday School growth.

Watson has continued as Sunday School secretary, in addition to director of the Religious Education Division. Michigan entered the 70's with 27,000 enrolled in 200 churches and church-type missions. JOE WATSON

Training Union.—In 1956 there were 37 churches in one association, the Motor Cities Association, affiliated with the Arkansas Baptist Convention. Activities that year in Training Union were centered in 30 churches represented at "M" Night, with a total of 460 present, zone rally meetings, and a general conference meeting. Study course promotion resulted in 614 awards being earned in 11 of the 37 churches. The enrolment in 1956 was 2,849. A. R. Milton served as the associational (statewide) director.

In 1957, 45 out of 46 churches had a Training Union, with an enrolment of 3,361. Study course awards increased to 937 for the first nine months. A special clinic held in June of that year gave special emphasis to the training of children's workers in Training Union. Milton served as the last Motor Cities associational director. The state convention gave new direction to the work of Training Union.

Joe Watson, elected director of religious education for the new convention in 1958, reported 4,867 enrolled in 53 churches and 1,000 attending "M" Night. An associational Youth Night was conducted. Many goals were set in relation to Training Union study course awards using a vigorous associational Training Union plan and promotion. Stanley Howell became state Training Union secretary in 1963. In that year enrolment reached 8,575 in 121 churches and 28 church-type missions.

An associational Training Union enlargement campaign was held in 50 churches in 1964. An Honor Church program was instituted to give recognition to churches which promoted all phases of the Training Union program. Howell left Michigan to join the Baptist Sunday School Board, and in July Harold E. Crane, Jr., of Shreveport, La., succeeded him. "M" Night attendance totaled 1,794 persons. One of the highlights of the year was the state Youth Festival, enrolling 250 persons from 35 churches. By 1969 there were 168 churches and 79 missions in the state convention reporting a Training Union enrolment of 10,225.

Music.—In 1956 the music program of Michigan Baptists reported 35 choirs with an enrolment of 445. Bill Compere was the associational music director. The following year Compere left Michigan and was succeeded by Joe Watson. Watson was the first music secretary in the new state convention.

In 1964 Harold E. Crane, Jr., succeeded Watson. Eighty-three choirs reported an enrolment of 2,005 in 10 associations. Music festivals, held in seven areas reported a total attendance of 505. In 1969 evangelism-music clinics were held in five associations with emphasis upon the use of music in revivals. The music program of the state convention is involved in every other program in arranging for congregational, choral, or instrumental leadership for all calendar projects. HAROLD E. CRANE, JR.

Brotherhood.—From the beginning the Motor Cities Baptist Association recognized the importance of involving laymen in effective service to Christ through the church and denomination. Bill Nail, pastor of Providence Baptist Church, Flint, was the first associational Brotherhood president, serving through 1955. He was succeeded by Harold E. Crane, Jr., minister of music and education at Merriman Road Baptist Church, Garden City. In 1956 the convention's decision to transfer responsibility for Royal Ambassadors to the Brotherhood gave new impetus to the work. Of 37 churches that year, 25 reported Brotherhood organizations with 485 men enrolled and 16 RA chapters with 180 boys enrolled.

Joe Watson assumed responsibility for Brotherhood in Mar., 1968, as the secretary of religious education. The first two weeks of Michigan RA camp were held that same year, registering 90 boys. In 1959 Brotherhood responsibility was transferred to Truett Smith, secretary of Christian education. He led in organizing the first state Brotherhood convention in 1960, with 100 men in attendance. The first Brotherhood retreat registered 36 men, and the first Brotherhood leadership conference registered 68.

With the resignation of Smith in 1961, the promotion of Brotherhood was moved to the Missions Division. One of the highlights of 1962 was a registration of 173 boys in the three weeks of RA camp. In Jan., 1963, Brotherhood responsibility was shifted to the new secretary of evangelism, stewardship, and Brotherhood, W. B. Oakley. The peak year for the work under his leadership was 1966, with 739 RAs in 41 chapters. In 1967 the first state RA Congress was conducted with a total attendance of 240.

Reorganization of the convention in 1968 sent the departments of evangelism, stewardship, and Brotherhood in three different directions. Brotherhood rejoined the other church program organizations in the Religious Education Division, with Jack H. Elliott, a native of Eudora, Ark., in charge.

During this period, RA enrolments continued to climb, while those of Baptist Men's units were fluctuating. A total of 78 churches reported Brotherhood units in 1969, with 821 men and 889 RAs enrolled. Mission action workshops and state Brotherhood workshops became regular training events. On Jan. 1, 1970, Elliott became a full member of the staff in the position of secretary for Brotherhood and student work.

Student Work.—In 1968 Joe Watson helped organize the first Baptist Student Union in Michigan at Michigan State University in East Lansing. The following year, work was also begun at the University of Michigan in Ann Arbor. The first BSU retreat, held in 1960, registered 34. The first BSU convention was held jointly with Ohio in 1961 and included 16 students from Michigan. In 1962 Michigan held its own BSU convention, with 63 in attendance. By this time, work had been started for Flint Junior College and Wayne State University.

As associate in the Kentucky Training Union department, Stanley Howell was added to the religious education staff in 1963. Student work was one of the departments of work assigned to him. Baptist Student Unions were organized at Eastern Michigan University and Western Michigan University during his 16 months of service, bringing the total number of campuses with BSU work to six. He was succeeded by Harold E. Crane, Jr., in 1964. The high point of student work under Crane was 1965, when the BSU retreat was attended by 68 and the BSU convention by 95. Work was still being done by volunteer directors on the six campuses, and new organizations were soon to be begun at Northern Michigan University, Oakland University, and Ferris State College. The total number of student members was 137 in 1968. Progress was not constant in all locations, and a high turnover of students and volunteer directors led to periodic inactivity at most campuses. In addition, the convention-wide study of student work produced several years of uncertainty and flagging enthusiasm.

MICHIGAN STATISTICAL SUMMARY

Year	Associations	Churches	Church Membership	Baptisms	S. S. Enrolment	V.B.S. Enrolment	T. U. Enrolment	W.M.U. Enrolment	Brotherhood Enrolment	Music Enrolment	Mission Gifts	Total Gifts	Value Church Property
1957	5	53	8,397	1,207	8,614	2,297	3,647	1,491	796	813	$ 63,778	$ 586,220	$ 1,836,625
1958	5	63	10,840	1,482	10,557	4,211	4,991	1,939	1,184	965	86,717	699,163	2,675,450
1959	5	74	12,980	1,487	12,875	6,229	5,886	2,288	1,538	1,172	107,227	883,177	3,318,359
1960	7	92	15,353	1,423	16,209	7,658	7,013	3,065	1,804	1,335	129,126	1,003,148	4,167,380
1961	7	99	19,003	1,625	17,962	8,606	7,639	3,530	1,982	1,474	129,778	1,118,762	5,018,861
1962	9	114	21,362	1,486	20,488	9,392	8,226	3,786	1,833	1,522	165,297	1,360,588	5,848,532
1963	10	121	22,837	1,460	21,726	10,138	8,413	3,981	2,104	1,803	191,044	1,477,160	6,683,335
1964	10	131	25,087	1,915	25,678	11,162	9,582	4,171	2,305	2,315	241,781	1,829,781	8,183,359
1965	10	141	25,589	1,798	25,782	12,208	9,448	4,282	1,782	2,520	307,971	2,222,405	9,159,231
1966	12	148	28,362	1,894	26,390	12,919	9,395	4,418	1,750	2,579	318,624	2,333,905	11,022,486
1967	12	156	30,603	2,265	27,649	15,676	9,685	4,697	1,781	2,633	340,060	2,499,153	12,145,686
1968	12	168	32,560	2,031	27,736	14,647	10,598	4,837	1,642	3,013	391,784	2,924,344	13,435,786
1969	12	168	34,198	2,075	26,702	17,363	10,225	4,193	1,600	2,755	399,548	2,967,695	14,461,546

ROBERT WILSON

On Jan. 1, 1970, Jack H. Elliott, formerly of Arkansas and Texas, became full-time secretary of student work and Brotherhood. New Baptist Student Unions were soon organized at the University of Detroit, Monroe County Community College, and Macomb County Community College. In addition, efforts to revive all inactive campus units were set in motion, reaching toward the goal of 12 local organizations by the end of 1970. JACK ELLIOTT

Woman's Missionary Union.—When the Motor Cities Baptist Association was organized in 1951, Mrs. George Thomas was elected to serve as the first WMU president. At the end of the first year there was WMU work in seven churches with a total enrolment of 125 women and 100 young people. In 1954 Mrs. Marvin Byrn was elected president and served three years. In 1957 there were 39 societies, with a membership of 1,130, 7 YWA organizations, 37 GA organizations, and 19 Sunbeam Bands.

The WMU became a department of the state convention in 1957. At the organizational meeting, Mrs. James R. Culley was elected as the first state WMU president. On Nov. 1, 1958, Miss Frances Brown, a native of Cobden, Ill., was employed by the convention to serve as state secretary, a position she still (1970) holds. The total number of organizations in 1958 was 47 Woman's Missionary Societies, 18 Young Woman's Auxiliaries, 44 Girls' Auxiliary organizations, and 34 Sunbeam Bands. The total enrolment was 2,037. In 1970 there were 105 Woman's Missionary Societies, 21 Young Woman's Auxiliaries, 149 Girls' Auxiliary organizations, and 144 Sunbeam Bands, with a total enrolment of 4,193.

Girls' Auxiliary camps began in 1958, directed by Joe Watson. There were two weeks of camps, one of which was combined with Royal Ambassadors. There was a total attendance of 79 girls and workers. In 1969, three weeks of camps were held, with a total attendance of 231. A YWA retreat has been held annually at the camp near Roscommon since Feb., 1959. FRANCES BROWN

MICHIGAN ASSOCIATIONS.

I. Extant. BAY AREA. Organized Oct. 20, 1962, with four churches and one mission, coming out of the Genesee Baptist Association. In 1969 seven churches reported 11 baptisms, 569 members, $59,664 total gifts, and $3,806 mission gifts.

CENTRAL. Organized Oct. 8, 1960, with eight churches coming from the Western Association. In 1969, 11 churches reported 110 baptisms, 2,442 members, $204,160 total gifts, and $16,176 mission gifts.

GENESEE. Organized Oct. 3, 1957, as one of the five associations organized from Motor Cities Association. On Oct. 20, 1962, four churches and one mission from Genesee organized the Bay Area Association. On Nov. 3, 1962, the Upper Peninsula Association was organized with four churches. In 1969, 19 churches reported 319 baptisms, with 4,522 members, $418,317 total gifts, and $39,602 mission gifts.

GREATER DETROIT. Organized in 1957 as one of the original five associations when state convention was organized. In 1969, 32 churches reported 464 baptisms, with 9,283 members, $747,583 total gifts, and $66,268 mission gifts.

HURON. Organized in 1957 this association held its first meeting at Merriman Road Baptist Church, Garden City, Oct. 11, 1958, with 15 churches reporting. It was one of the original five associations formed when the state convention was organized. When associational lines were adjusted in 1963, some churches joined Detroit Association. In 1969, 13 churches reported 183 baptisms, 2,757 members, $227,502 total gifts, and $21,887 mission gifts.

LENDALE. Organized in 1969 with four churches from the Southeastern Baptist Association, located in Lenawee and Hillsdale counties.

MACOMB. Organized Oct. 19, 1964, by churches from Clinton Association. The first annual meeting was held at First Baptist Church, St. Clair Shores, on Oct. 14–15, 1965, with 12 churches. In 1969, 14 churches reported 164 baptisms, 3,125 members, $335,383 total gifts, and $40,328 mission gifts.

OAKLAND. Organized Oct. 19, 1964, by churches from Clinton Association. The first annual meeting was held Oct. 11–12, 1965, with 13 churches represented. In 1969, 14 churches reported 171 baptisms, 3,267 members, $377,150 total gifts, and $57,922 mission gifts.

SOUTH CENTRAL. Organized Oct. 16, 1965, by five churches from the Western Baptist Association. In 1969 nine churches reported 194 baptisms, 1,445 members, $134,545 total gifts, and $8,721 mission gifts.

SOUTHEASTERN. First annual meeting was held Oct. 6–7, 1961, at Monroe Missionary Baptist Church, Monroe, Mich., with 16 churches. Four churches withdrew in 1969 and formed the Lendale Baptist Association. In 1969, 21 churches reported 205 baptisms, with 4,276 members, $262,572 total gifts, and $18,738 mission gifts.

SOUTHWESTERN. Organized Oct. 16, 1965, by three churches and four missions from the Western Association. In 1969 four churches reported 65 baptisms, 600 members, $50,587 total gifts, and $2,445 mission gifts.

UPPER PENINSULA. Organized Nov. 3, 1962, with seven churches. In 1969 seven churches reported 905 members, with 93 baptisms, $67,146 total gifts, and $5,399 mission gifts.

WOODLAND. Organized Oct. 19, 1963, out of the Western Association in Grand Rapids and Muskegon area. In 1969, 10 churches reported 77 baptisms, 858 members, $62,487 total gifts, and $5,213 mission gifts.

II. Extinct. CLINTON. Organized in 1957 this was one of the five original associations formed when the state convention was organized. On Oct. 19, 1964, two new associations were organized from Clinton Association: Oakland and Macomb.

MONROE ASSOCIATION. Organized in 1960 it changed the name to Southeastern Baptist Association in 1961.

MOTOR CITIES. Organized in 1951 with six churches. In 1953 the Home Mission Board joined the Arkansas Baptist State Convention in support of mission work in Michigan. When the first organized work started as the Motor Cities Association of Southern Baptist Churches in Michigan, six churches officially organized the association with two others giving support. They were the New Hope Baptist Church of Detroit, the Antioch Baptist Church of Detroit, the First Baptist Church of St. Clair Shores, the First Southern Missionary Baptist Church of Pontiac, the Mt. Pleasant Baptist Church of Flint, and the Bethel Baptist Church of Roseville. At the last annual meeting in the Motor Cities Association on Oct. 1, 1957, held with the Bethel Baptist Church of Roseville, there were a total of 49 churches. The churches then met on Oct. 31 with the Fairview Baptist Church in Detroit and constituted the Baptist State Convention of Michigan. At this meeting the churches affiliated with the new state convention and also organized themselves into five associations: Detroit, Clinton, Huron River Valley, Genesee, and Western.

WESTERN. Organized in 1957 it was one of the original five associations when the state convention was organized. In 1960 eight churches withdrew to organize Woodland and Central associations. On Oct. 16, 1965, the association divided into Southwestern Association with three churches and four missions, and South Central Association with five churches. ROBERT WILSON

MID-CONTINENT BAPTIST BIBLE COLLEGE (cf. West Kentucky Baptist Bible Institute, Vol. II). A four-year Bible college growing out of the West Kentucky Baptist Bible Institute originally located in Clinton, Ky., and now relocated in Mayfield, Ky. The three-year institute program, however, is still maintained to provide training for older students and those with previous limited training.

President O. C. Markham succeeded W. A. Sloan, the last president of Baptist Bible Institute at Clinton. The college is governed by a board of trustees, two members of which are elected by each of the following Southern Baptist associations: Graves, Blood River, West Union, West Kentucky, Fulton County, Ohio River, Caldwell, Little River, and Union (Illinois). Operating on the trimester plan, the college enrolled 125 in 1969. O. C. MARKHAM

***MID-MISSIONS.** As of Jan. 1, 1970, Baptist Mid-Missions had a total of 867 missionaries under appointment to 29 areas overseas and 21 types of ministry in North America. A total of 787 of these are active. The largest number, 213, are assigned to the continent of Africa, while the largest single country is Brazil with 110. The largest number under appointment in North America are to the Jews. Special projects include airplane ministry, Bible institutes and seminaries, hospitals and medical centers, publication work, and schools for missionaries' children. Major emphasis is given to evangelism and church planting. HELEN E. FALLS

MIDWESTERN BAPTIST RELIGIOUS EDUCATION AND MUSIC ASSOCIATION. A group of interested Missouri Baptist religious educators formed the Midwestern Baptist Religious Education and Music Association (MWBREAM). They held their first annual workshop May 8–10, 1969, at Midwestern Baptist Theological Seminary, Kansas City, Mo.

This is the latest addition to existing regional religious education fellowships. The membership of the Baptist Religious Education and Music Association of Missouri first discussed forming the MWBREAM. The major objectives are: (1) continuing professional development for local church and denominational educators, and (2) fellowship among Baptist educators in the midwestern region.

The workshop was conducted by the following program personalities: Robert J. Havighurst, professor of developmental psychology of the University of Chicago; A. V. Washburn and James Hatley of the Sunday School Board, SBC; Clifford Ingle, Philip Briggs, Doran McCarty; Everett Reneer, and DeWitt Matthews of the Midwestern Seminary faculty; Don Brown of William Jewell College music faculty; and J. W. Fisher of the Missouri Baptist Convention's Department of Baptist Men.

The following persons were elected as the initial officers: Harvey Wright, president; Phil Stanberry, program vice-president—education; James Fuller, program vice-president—music; and Florence Hoff, secretary-treasurer.
PHIL STANBERRY

MIDWESTERN BAPTIST THEOLOGICAL SEMINARY. A coeducational institution of the Southern Baptist Convention, authorized on May 29, 1957, opened in Sept., 1958, located in Kansas City, Mo.

Background.—Midwestern was an outgrowth of Southern Baptists' rapid growth, numerically, and geographically, during and after World War II. Between 1845 and 1945 the Convention founded no theological institution but took over three institutions founded by affiliated individuals and groups: The Southern Baptist Theological Seminary (1859), Southwestern Baptist Theological Seminary (1908), and New Orleans Baptist Theological Seminary (1917).

The number of Baptist college students committed to church vocations grew from 3,300 in 1946 to 5,800 in 1953. The Convention decided in 1949 to establish "two new seminaries, one in the West, and one in the East, . . . as soon as suitable sites can be had and adequate plans be made for financing the same without injury or impairment to our existing seminaries." In taking over Golden Gate Baptist Theological Seminary and starting Southeastern Baptist Theological Seminary in 1950, the Convention implied that seminaries should be located within reasonable distances of churches to provide them with pastors and to afford pastoral work for students. Also in 1950, it decided not to operate Bible institutes, a policy which it reaffirmed in 1955.

Creation.—In 1953 the Convention set up a special committee, under the chairmanship of Louie D. Newton, of Georgia, to study its "total program of theological, religious, and missionary education, as it involves financial support." There were three major steps in the committee's work over a period of four years: (1) its 1953–55 study of ministerial students (4,379 in seminaries and 6,500 in Baptist colleges in 1955) which suggested a faster growing need in the West than in the East, (2) its 1956 dealings with Central Baptist Theological Seminary, Kansas City, Kan., and (3) its 1956–57 effort to select a city for a new seminary.

As a result of Southern Baptists' expansion into "western and pioneer" areas, the Convention affirmed in 1944, 1949, and 1951 that its territory was unlimited. In some areas tension developed in relations with other Baptists, especially Northern (American after 1950) Baptists. In the Midwest, Central Seminary (founded in 1902), served both American and Southern Baptist churches. When Southern Baptists began to consider a sixth seminary, Central Seminary's officials invited Newton's committee to come to its campus in Feb., 1956, to discuss "on what grounds the Southern Baptist Convention would give financial aid" to Central Seminary, two thirds of whose students and several of whose trustees and teachers were Southern Baptists. The committee explained to Central Seminary's officials "the plan by which Southern Baptists own and operate our seminaries," a plan calling for the Convention to elect trustees of institutions which it finances. On May 8, 1956, the American Board of Education and Publication recommended that "Central Seminary align itself definitely and positively with the American Baptist Convention" and that "the entire membership of the Board of Directors be composed of members of American Baptist churches." Several Southern Baptist trustees and professors resigned, and some students suspended their schooling. On May 31, 1956, the committee reported to the Convention that, between February and May, "the need for theological training for Southern Baptists in the Mid-west has become more acute." It had investigated a proposed site near Topeka but decided that "it was not suitable for seminary purposes." On the committee's recommendation the Convention amended its bylaws, effective in 1958, to prevent allocating funds "for any agency or institution for which the Convention does not elect trustees or directors." It also decided to establish a new seminary, consistent with "the policy . . . that beginning now it [Convention] will not undertake joint ownership, support, and administration of any new theological institution with any other Baptist body."

During the next year the committee grappled with "the basic philosophy in creating a new seminary"—whether it should be a missionary or pioneer nucleus "around which to build a great Baptist constituency" or a service-institution "in an area where there are already churches, colleges, and large numbers of pastors and ministerial students from which to draw enrolment and support." It tried to combine these basic philosophies. It gathered data on each state's population and rate of change, number of Southern Baptist churches and members, balance between urban and rural Southern Baptist churches, churches with over 300 members, and anticipated growth between 1955 and 1965. It counted Southern Baptist churches in the "territory" and within 250 miles of each seminary, and within 250 miles of each city under consideration for the new seminary. Within 250 miles of Chicago, Denver, and Seattle were 516, 81, and 80 churches, respectively. Within 250 miles of Jacksonville were 2,753 churches; Florida's population was growing more rapidly than Southern Baptist membership, one of the few areas where this was so. Within 250 miles of Kansas City were 2,242 churches; the number of Missouri churches had declined, but church membership had recently gained by 25 per cent, and "pioneer" states were to the west and north.

On the committee's recommendation on May 29, 1957, the Convention voted to locate the new seminary in Kansas City, Mo., to elect a board of trustees, and to provide it with operating and capital funds. It defeated efforts to locate it in Chicago and Denver. It instructed the board to secure a charter like Golden Gate Seminary's and Southeastern Seminary's, to open the seminary when funds are available, and "to qualify for accreditation at the earliest possible date."

Trustees.—The original board consisted of 29 trustees—10 "local" trustees "from the State of Missouri" and 19 state trustees from states (including the District of Columbia) with cooperating conventions entitled to representation. In 1960 the Convention authorized the seminary to change its charter, to add one trustee and to provide that "local" trustees be within 300 miles of Kansas City. Kansas gained representation in 1961, but local trustees continued to come "from the State of Missouri." In 1969 the board was enlarged from 30 to 35 members to give representation to Colorado, Indiana, Michigan, Ohio, and Washington-Oregon.

Trustees met shortly after the 1957 Convention and elected officers: H. I. Hester of Missouri (president), W. Barry Garrett of Arizona (first vice-president), John Watson of California (second vice-president), W. Ross Edwards of Missouri (recording secretary), and Joe Hurst of Missouri (treasurer). Among the board's earliest actions were naming the new institution Midwestern Baptist Theological Seminary, authorizing negotiations on a site, setting up a committee to prepare legal documents, and naming a committee, under the chairmanship of Robert E.

Humphreys (*q.v.*) of Kentucky, to nominate a president. Shortly thereafter the board employed L. R. Elliott (*q.v.*), retired librarian of Southwestern Seminary, to begin a library.

In Oct., 1957, the board adopted the Convention's confession of 1925 as the seminary's doctrinal standard and elected Millard J. Berquist as president. In Dec., 1957, the board received title to 99.4 acres for the school's campus. It planned toward the school's opening in Sept., 1958.

Those who have served as president of the board are: Hester (1957–61), Conrad Willard of Missouri (1961–62), Malcolm Knight of Florida (1962–65), Robert W. Jackson of Georgia (1965–67), Earl O. Harding of Missouri (1967–69), and Norman H. McCrummen of Alabama (1969–70).

Administration.—Midwestern Seminary's first president was M. J. Berquist, native of Kansas City, and graduate of William Jewell College (B.A., 1932) and Southern Seminary (Th.M., 1935; Ph.D., 1942). He served as pastor of churches in Missouri, Ohio, and Florida before accepting Midwestern Seminary's presidency. He had served on the boards of Southern Seminary and the Radio and Television Commission and as president of the Florida Baptist Convention.

Hester became Midwestern Seminary's vice-president in 1961, coming from the positions of vice-president and professor of William Jewell College. John W. Goodwin (1964–68) and Robert D. Meade (1968–) served as assistant to the president. Eugene Bryant (1958–66) and Kenneth Kerr (1966–) served as business manager. V. Lavell Seats has served as acting registrar and dean of students since 1958.

Instructional Program.—Midwestern Seminary opened to students in 1958. Its original degree was the post-collegiate, three-year Bachelor of Divinity, changed in 1967 to Master of Divinity. It has offered a shorter diploma in theology to a limited number of persons above 30 years of age who lack college degrees. In 1965 it inaugurated the two-year Master of Religious Education and the one-year Master of Theology beyond the B.D.

Accreditation.—In keeping with the Convention's 1957 directive, the seminary adopted accredited standards for its program from the beginning. After graduating its first class in 1961, a prerequisite for applying, the seminary sought and secured associate membership in the American Association of Theological Schools (AATS) in 1961. Encouraged by AATS officials, the seminary planned for full accreditation before the normal five-year waiting period ended. However, due to controversy, the seminary delayed its formal application until mid-1963. In mid-1964, on the basis of its investigation, the AATS conferred full membership with two notations—respecting restraints on faculty members' academic freedom and the seminary's four-day schedule of classes. The AATS removed the former notation in June, 1966; the latter, in Dec., 1966. Since then its accreditation by AATS has been unrestricted.

Midwestern Seminary is also seeking to enlarge its accreditation. In 1968–69 it developed plans to seek accreditation in the North Central Association of Colleges and Secondary Schools; in 1969–70 it conducted an intensive self-study which constitutes the basis of its application.

Faculty.—Midwestern Seminary enlarged its faculty as it expanded its curriculum and added degrees. In 1958–59 the faculty consisted of the president, librarian, and four teachers to offer first-year courses. In the next two years the seminary added second- and third-year courses and enlarged its faculty to meet the need. Since the school's first four years, adding of new faculty members was due to adding of degrees or to vacancies created by resignations.

Through 1969, 23 persons have served on Midwestern Seminary's faculty. Three have resigned, and one was dismissed. In the order of their election, they are Berquist (1957–), Ralph H. Elliott in Old Testament (1958–62), Joseph T. McClain in New Testament (1958–61), V. Lavell Seats in missions and evangelism (1958–), William H. Morton in biblical archaeology (1958–), Keith C. Wills as librarian (1958–66), G. Hugh Wamble in church history (1959–), J. Morris Ashcraft in theology (1959–), George D. Thomason in New Testament (1959–), Roy L. Honeycutt, Jr., in Old Testament (1959–), Clifford Ingle in religious education and church administration (1959–), C. DeWitt Matthews in preaching (1959–), M. Pierce Matheney in Old Testament (1960–), John C. Howell in ethics (1960–), Alan Gragg in philosophy and theology (1961–66), Heber F. Peacock in New Testament (1961–63), Everett Reneer in psychology and pastoral care (1962–), Philip H. Briggs in religious education and church administration (1965–), K. David Weekes as librarian (1966–), Doran McCarty in philosophy and theology (1967–), Kenneth R. Wolfe in New Testament (1968–), and B. A. Sizemore, Jr., in Old Testament (1968–). Each has basic college, seminary, and graduate degrees. Since 1965 the seminary's sabbatical program has enabled faculty members to undertake graduate or research work away from the seminary each seventh year.

Controversy.—During its early years Midwestern Seminary was the focal point of Southern Baptists' controversy over the Bible. It began in 1959 with certain students, critical of biblical teaching, who, under the banner of "Conservative Party," tried but failed to elect officers to the student organization. With the encouragement of some regional ministers, they agitated against certain teachers for a year or so. In 1960 several trustees met with criticized professors and expressed support, after which criticism subsided.

Criticism flared anew in mid-1961 with Broadman Press's publication of Elliott's, *The Message of Genesis*. Leadership in the controversy came from ministers in the Midwest, many of whom had been connected with Central Seminary before its split. By the fall, controversy had spread beyond the Midwest, with Elliott's book receiving passionate criticism. A special committee of Midwestern Seminary's trustees conducted a hearing, including both Elliott and critics, and recommended supporting him, a recommendation which the full board approved on Dec. 28, 1961. In late Jan., 1962, the Sunday School Board defended its publication of the book in light of "the historic Baptist principle of the freedom of the individual to interpret the Bible for himself, to hold a particular theory of inspiration of the Bible which seems most reasonable to him, and to develop his beliefs in accordance with his theory."

Controversy intensified—against Midwestern Seminary's trustees for supporting Elliott, against the Sunday School Board for publishing his book, against "liberalism" in general, against Elliott and Midwestern Seminary in particular. In May, 1962, one editor, noting that only 3,304 copies of Elliott's book had been sold, suggested that "great numbers must either be borrowing the book or they must be letting other people do their thinking," the latter of which he viewed as unfair.

The 1962 Convention, meeting in June in San Francisco and dominated by controversy, adopted two resolutions: (1) affirming faith "in the *entire* Bible as the authoritative, authentic, infallible Word of God" and (2) opposing theological views which undermine the Bible's "historical accuracy and doctrinal integrity" and requesting "trustees and administrative officers of our institutions and agencies" to remedy situations which threaten "our historic position." A messenger made, but later withdrew, a motion instructing the Sunday School Board to cease publishing Elliott's book. Another made a similar motion, but the Convention voted it down. In July, 1962, the Sunday School Board upheld an administrative decision not to reprint Elliott's book.

When Midwestern Seminary's trustees met in special session in Sept., 1962, some favored dismissing Elliott immediately, but most favored trying to resolve the problem. One-third of Midwestern Seminary's trustees were new, having been elected in 1962 to fill vacancies caused by removal from one state to another or by failure to renominate some trustees eligible for another term. During the next month a special committee conferred with Elliott and the administration. All parties agreed on nine principles relating to biblical teaching, including the historical-critical method. Trustees and administration wanted Elliott to say that he would not seek another publisher. Elliott held that such a statement would leave the impression that he was retracting what he had written, an impression he was unwilling to permit. When the full board met on Oct. 25, 1962, it, on the committee's recommendation, approved the nine principles and dismissed Elliott for insubordination.

Elliott's dismissal did not immediately end the controversy. It affected many involved in Midwestern Seminary's life—trustees, administration, students, alumni, and friends—and relationships between them. Before his dismissal Elliott was the specific focus, but discussion also raised suspicion of theological education.

In Mar., 1963, Midwestern Seminary's trustees, taking no action against any other professor, adopted a tenure statement. Midwestern Seminary continued to come under attack, including an official action of a state convention's executive body. Friends rallied to the seminary's defense. In May, 1963, the Convention, meeting in Kansas City, repeatedly obstructed efforts of critics to censure Midwestern Seminary; it applauded speeches by the president of Midwestern Seminary's board and a Kansas City layman. Overt opposition ceased, but suspicion remained for several years.

Enrolment.—Midwestern Seminary's cumulative enrolment has fluctuated during its first 12 years: 151 in 1958–59, 296 in 1959–60, 342 in 1960–61, 304 in 1961–62, 282 in 1962–63, 206 in 1963–64, 184 in 1964–65, 195 in 1965–66, 227 in 1966–67, 262 in 1967–68, 261 in 1968–69, and 257 in 1969–70. Fluctuation is due to several factors: (1) inflated enrolments during the seminary's early years due to transferees from Central Seminary and older ministers of the area who began their education when a seminary was located near them; (2) graduating of large classes in 1961 and 1962; and (3) controversy which led some students to withdraw before and others after a professor's dismissal. Midwestern Seminary's lowest enrolment occurred in 1964–65, after which it rose to a stable plateau in the late sixties.

Students.—Midwestern Seminary's student organization, begun in 1959, directs student affairs and represents students in dealing with administration and faculty.

Alumni.—Between 1961 and 1969 Midwestern Seminary conferred degrees or diplomas on 432 persons, 17 of whom received two degrees each. The first class, 1961, formed the seminary's alumni association, whose presidents have been Clyde Riddle, Robert Muncy, Hubert Byrd, Elwyn Hays, Cloyce Davis, James Kautz, Gary Farley, Eugene Vickrey, and Frank Kirkland, each serving a year. About one graduate out of seven serves under formal appointment as foreign or home missionary or as military chaplain, and some serve in "pioneer" work. Most, however, serve churches in the Midwest.

Campus.—Midwestern Seminary's campus consists of 207 acres: 99 acres acquired in 1957 and 117 acres in 1960, minus nine acres sold in 1960 to two churches adjacent to the campus. A major highway slices eight acres from the rest of the campus.

The campus is located in Clay County, Mo., about six miles directly north of downtown Kansas City. Campus acreage is part of an estate developed during Missouri's pioneer days by the Vivion family and held continually by heirs. The owner had numerous offers to sell for three or four times what the seminary paid but did not want her estate to be cut up into small lots for suburban development. Until World War II farms dominated the area, but suburban growth accelerated thereafter, especially in the fifties. During the sixties suburban Kansas City expanded beyond the campus. Major developments underway in 1970 point to further growth which will make the seminary a mid-town institution. The seminary is adjacent to Interstate 29 northward from Kansas City, about two miles from the place where it merges with Interstate 35. Two U. S. highways pass by the campus. The campus is convenient to numerous industries and businesses.

Buildings.—Using facilities belonging to Calvary Baptist Church in 1958–59, the seminary moved in Sept., 1959, to its first permanent facilities. In 1970 the buildings included: administration, library, temporary chapel, faculty-classroom buildings (all entered in 1959), classroom-student center building (entered in 1961 and adapted in 1969 to house a cafeteria), maintenance building (1963), residence hall (opened in 1963 and modified in 1969 to provide 40 units accommodating 80 persons), an apartment complex (48 units completed in 1965 and 20 units to be available in 1970), and the president's home and surrounding buildings (donated for this purpose and entered by the president in 1967). Major buildings are of contemporary design and blend well with the campus's rolling terrain; exteriors consist of weathered sandstone, blue tile, and glass.

Campus and buildings were fully financed with capital needs funds from the Convention, with one exception. Matching funds—from capital needs funds and loan funds to be repaid from rentals—finance the apartment complex.

G. HUGH WAMBLE

MILLER, ROSCOE C. (b. Hodgenville, Ky., Apr. 25, 1871; d. Oklahoma City, Okla., Oct. 5, 1944). Minister and denominational leader. Educated in Kentucky public schools and William Jewel College, he received an honorary D.D. from Oklahoma Baptist University in 1936. Pastorates included Wichita Falls, Tex., Joplin, Mo., and Hugo, Mangum, and Durant, Okla. He was president of the Baptist General Convention of Oklahoma, 1922–23. During his Durant pastorate (1927–40), he served with distinction on the state board during some acute crises. He is buried at Durant.

J. M. GASKIN

***MINISTERIAL RELIEF AND RETIREMENT, OKLAHOMA.** On Jan. 1, 1957, Oklahoma had 322 churches with 395 employees in the Annuity Board programs. On Oct. 1, 1969, there were 702 churches with 886 employees enrolled in Plan A of the Southern Baptist Protection Program. Employees of 13 Oklahoma Baptist institutions were enrolled, most of them in Plan B. A total of 3,170 memberships were held in all six SBC plans for Oklahoma in 1969. Roscoe C. Miller, Jr., was employed by the SBC Annuity Board and the Oklahoma convention, Feb. 1, 1957. He has served as state annuity secretary since that time.

ROSCOE C. MILLER, JR.

MINISTRIES OF THE CHURCHES, NEW. See CHURCHES, NEW MINISTRIES OF THE.

***MINISTER'S RELIEF FUND, VIRGINIA BAPTIST.** In 1968 the total assets were $122,053.42. From 1958 to 1968 the Fund assisted an average of 13 beneficiaries in amounts ranging from $100 to $500. The rising cost of medical care brought more requests for aid in this area. Further financial assistance has been made available to more needy ministers' widows.

CHARLES H. RYLAND

MISSION EDUCATION PROMOTION CONFERENCE (cf. Missionary Education Council, Vol. II). The Missionary Education Council had its final session, Oct. 31, 1966. The Southern Baptist Convention approval of program assignments for the Woman's Missionary Union and Brotherhood included their working together in missionary education. The Foreign and Home Mission Boards were instructed to continue the cooperative relationship with WMU and Brotherhood in the promotion of missionary education. A Mission Study Coordination Conference was set up to continue the work of the missionary education council which included selection of annual themes for the graded mission study of the FMB and HMB, promotional plans, specifications for books, suggested authors, reviewing outlines and manuscripts of the mission books. The membership of this group came from WMU, Brotherhood, FMB, and HMB.

Mission Education Promotion Conference later became the official name of this new group (MEPC). A coordinating group with two members each from WMU and Brotherhood, and one each from FMB and HMB was assigned to give overall directions to the MEPC and approval to the editorial and promotion committees.

WMU and Brotherhood requested the privilege of doing the mission teacher's guides which the two mission boards granted. The mission boards continue to produce the mission books as they have from the beginning.

HELEN E. FALLS

MISSION FRIENDS. Since Oct., 1970, the missions organization for preschool children (birth through age five, or school entrance) in Woman's Missionary Union's graded program of missionary education. In ways appropriate to the age group, the organization leads preschool children to participate in the basic WMU tasks. Materials and plans for leaders are provided in *Start.*

BETTY BROWN

***MISSIONARY EDUCATION COUNCIL.** See MISSION EDUCATION PROMOTION CONFERENCE.

MISSIONARY PERSONNEL, HOME MISSION BOARD DEPARTMENT OF. On Aug. 14, 1958, the Home Mission Board committee to study its organization and work recommended the organization of a personnel department. The recommendation was approved, and the new department was assigned the responsibility of helping to select all personnel except those nominated and elected by the board: screen all applicants, approve those qualifying for appointment, keep a file on volunteers, provide guidance as needed for candidates, and orient new personnel.

Glendon McCullough was elected secretary of the department which was activated Mar. 1, 1959. After studying personnel needs, reasons for short tenure, and after consulting with state convention leadership, the department recommended basic qualifications for missionary appointment. These were adopted in Dec., 1959, and were strengthened by the board in 1968. The first orientation session for new missionaries and the first public commissioning service were held during Home Missions Week, Glorieta, Aug., 1960.

In 1966 the department published a looseleaf missionary manual reflecting current philosophies, procedures, and regulations, which are kept up to date for all missionaries.

Two department associates, Cecil D. Etheredge (beginning July 1, 1965) and P. Edward Rickenbaker (beginning Apr. 15, 1967) work with candidates for missionary appointment, visit each seminary twice annually, and work with the leadership of state conventions in a specified geographical area. Edward E. Seabough (beginning July 1, 1968) works with all persons below seminary level considering missionary service and is responsible for recruiting US-2 candidates. GLENDON MCCULLOUGH

***MISSIONS.** *The teaching of missions.*—When Midwestern Baptist Theological Seminary was established in 1957, a professor of missions and evangelism was included in the first faculty. All six seminaries do not presently (1970) have two full-time professors of missions, but most have a missionary to serve as visiting professor while on furlough.

When Carver School of Missions and Social Work became a part of Southern Baptist Theological Seminary in 1957, the courses in social work were added to the curriculum in the seminary, where a full curriculum in missions was offered already.

The history of missions.—An Assembly of the International Missionary Council was held at Accra, Ghana, in Dec., 1957. At the Third Assembly of the World Council of Churches held at New Delhi in Nov., 1961, it was voted to incorporate the work of the International Missionary Council in the Division on World Missions and Evangelism of the World Council. Work will continue through the Christian Councils affiliated with the WCC.

With the rapid growth of independence in Africa during the decade of the sixties, Christianity grew proportionately, especially in the countries south of the Sahara. Many new countries were entered. For example, in 1960 Southern Baptists had missionaries in eight countries on the Continent, and that number had grown to 16 by 1969.

Following is an estimate of the number of adherents of non-Christian religions in 1966:

Buddhists	167,094,000
Confucianists	357,855,000
Hindus	408,991,000
Judaism	13,000,000
Muṣlims	465,237,000
Shintoists	67,762,000
Taoists	52,331,000
Zoroastrians	150,000
Others, including primitive and no religion	758,801,000

Adherents of Christian religions in 1966:

	Protestant	Orthodox and Eastern	Roman Catholic
Africa	21,608,509	17,500,000	29,100,000
Asia	18,545,389	1,450,000	53,200,000
Europe, including USSR	179,415,167	99,000,000	237,500,000
North and Central America	80,801,000	3,585,000	118,550,000
South America	10,311,500		143,000,000
Oceania	9,649,073	90,770	3,700,000
Totals	320,326,638	121,625,770	585,050,000

In 1970 there were approximately 46,000 Protestant and 64,700 Roman Catholic missionaries at work. Almost every nation, tribe, and language group had been influenced by missionaries. But at the beginning of the seventies Christianity faces in many areas increasingly indifferent and even hostile forces. Secularization appears particularly evident in Europe and North America. Resident missionaries are barred by government restrictions from about one-third of the world's land area and population. In some lands Christians face active persecution. In others, large groups are resistant to the Christian message. HELEN E. FALLS

***MISSIONS, SCHOOLS OF.** See WORLD MISSIONS CONFERENCES.

MISSIONS COMMITTEE, CHURCH AND ASSOCIATION. An administrative service committee which, according to guidelines approved by the coordinating committee of the Inter-Agency Council in Jan., 1970, makes studies, recommends plans, and administers work assigned to it by a church or an association. It coordinates its work with program organizations through the church and/or associational council. The committee works according to church and associational policy and procedure with appropriate committees in procuring finances, facilities, and personnel. It also establishes and maintains communications with other religious groups, public officials, and institutions and services related to its interest. FRED B. MOSELEY

***MISSISSIPPI ASSOCIATIONS.**

I. New Associations. ADAMS. Organized by 11 churches which withdrew from the Union Association, Sept. 24, 1956, to organize along county lines. In 1968, 14 churches reported 5,824 members and $2,156,200 property value.

QUITMAN. Organized along county lines, Oct. 12, 1961, by 10 churches from the Riverside Association. In 1968, 11 churches reported 3,511 members and $907,250 property value.

HINDS-MADISON. Formed by the merger of the two associations in Oct., 1968, then reporting 65 churches, 52,277 members, and $23,475,616 property value.

II. Changes in Associations. HINDS. Was merged into Hinds-Madison Association in 1968.

MADISON. Was merged into the Hinds-Madison Association in 1968. R. A. MCLEMORE

***MISSISSIPPI BAPTIST CONVENTION.**

I. History. In 1955 the convention included 75 associations, 1,734 churches, and a membership of 430,134. In 1968 there were 77 associations, 1,886 churches, and 526,350 members. The receipts from the Cooperative Program increased from $1,810,770 to $3,666,334, or slightly more than 100 per cent. The total value of church property increased from $73,873,835 in 1957 to $160,704,726 in 1968.

Chester L. Quarles (*q.v.*) was executive secretary-treasurer of the board from Apr. 1, 1950, until his death, July 6, 1968. The duties of this office were divided and A. L. Nelson was named treasurer in 1968 and W. Douglas Hudgins, who had been pastor of the First Baptist Church of Jackson and had served as interim secretary of the board, became executive secretary on Feb. 3, 1969. The following have served as presidents of the convention since 1957: S. R. Woodson, Columbus, 1957–59; M. F. Rayburn, Meridian, 1959–61; W. Douglas Hudgins, Jackson, 1961–63; Russell Bush, Columbia, 1963–67; Earl Kelly, Holly Springs, 1963;–67; and Claude Townsend, Florence, 1967–69.

The board introduced two new activities into its program, the Gulf Shore Assembly, and the Christian Action Commission.

The Mississippi Baptist Convention Building was completed in Apr., 1968. As early as 1955, the board began to make plans for a building to meet its needs. Construction was begun in July 1966, on a four-story building located on the corner of Mississippi and President streets, Jackson. The site is across the street from the First Baptist Church and near the State Capitol.
R. A. MCLEMORE

II. Program of Work of Mississippi Baptists. *Administration.*—The administrative body of the Mississippi Baptist Convention is the Mississippi Baptist Convention Board, composed of 100 members, one from each of the 76 cooperating district associations in the state, plus 24 "at-large" members who are elected from the more populous associations. The 76 members are nominated in each case by the association and elected by the convention. The 24 members are nominated by the convention's committee on nominations and elected by the convention.

The convention grants to the board the authority to supervise the general work of the convention and promote certain phases of its program of state missions. The home of the board is the Mississippi Baptist Convention Building in Jackson, a four-story structure completed and occupied in 1968 at a cost of $1,100,000.

The executive secretary (1969) of the board is W. Douglas Hudgins. The treasurer and business manager is A. L. Nelson.

The board elects a nine-man executive committee which is empowered to carry on the work of the convention as directed by the convention board. The committee is also trustee of all convention funds.

Missions.—The work of state missions is carried out by the board as well as other institutions, boards, agencies, and commissions maintained by the convention. The Cooperative Program (mission) budget of the convention for 1968–69 was $4,200,000.

The board promotes state missions primarily through the nine departments and two assembly facilities at Pass Christian on the Gulf Coast, Gulfshore Assembly, and Camp Kittiwake. (Camp Kittiwake was completely demolished and Gulfshore Assembly was practically destroyed by hurricane Camille that struck the Mississippi Gulf Coast, Aug. 17, 1969).

The nine departments maintained by the board are the following, including staff personnel and budget for 1969: Evangelism, secretary and office secretary, $34,714; Stewardship, director, two associates, and two office secretaries, $67,704; Brotherhood, director, associate, and two secretaries, $51,447; Church Music, director and two office secretaries, $57,260; Cooperative Missions, director, three associates, and four office secretaries, $76,192; Student Work (including BSU campus work), director and office secretary, $103,973; Sunday School, director, four associates, and two office secretaries, $82,551: Training Union, director, three associates, and two office secretaries, $84,072; Work with National Baptists (including Mississippi Baptist Seminary), director and office secretary, $70,529.

The Department of Work with National Baptists cooperates in promoting the Mississippi Baptist Seminary (for Negroes).

The Baptist Record.—This official journal of the convention and the board is under supervision of the board, which annually elects all its regular personnel. The budget for 1969 was $222,576.

Other work sponsored by the board includes church building aid, pastoral aid, tracts, State Sanitorium evangelism, religious education association, work with language groups, and associational missions.

Woman's Missionary Union.—WMU is auxiliary to the state convention and has offices in the Baptist Building. It maintains a comprehensive program of mission promotion through the WMU Department, supervised by a director, four associates, and four office secretaries. It also owns and operates Camp Garaywa near Clinton.

Colleges.—The convention owns and maintains four colleges, each operated by a separate board of trustees, as follows:

Mississippi College (1968–69) has a property valuation of $8,458,245, an endowment of $2,030,156, a budget of $2,694,789, and a total enrolment of 3,124. Blue Mountain College has a property valuation of $1,856,534, an endowment of $1,209,179, a budget of $599,785, and a total enrolment of 679. William Carey College has a property valuation of $3,982,731, an endowment of $562,765, a budget of $1,200,000, and a total enrolment of 1,143. Clarke Memorial College, the only junior college of the four, has a property valuation of $1,492,088, an endowment of $478,678, a budget of $366,481, and a total enrolment of 314.

Other agencies.—The convention also maintains several other boards, institutions, agencies, and commissions, each operated by a separate board of trustees, as follows:

Board of Ministerial Education, Baptist Foundation, Mississippi Baptist Hospital, Baptist Children's Village, Christian Action Commission, Education Commission, and Historical Commission.

The convention cooperates with the Annuity Board of the SBC. The Annuity Board secretary for the state has an office in the Baptist Building.

The convention cooperates with the American Bible Society in its work.

The Baptist Memorial Hospital, Memphis, Tenn., is jointly owned by the Arkansas, Tennessee, and Mississippi Baptist conventions and is operated by a board of 27 trustees, nine of whom are elected by each body.

The Gilfoy School of Nursing at Mississippi

MISSISSIPPI STATISTICAL SUMMARY

Year	Associations	Churches	Total Membership	Baptisms	S. S. Enrolment	V.B.S. Enrolment	T. U. Enrolment	W.M.U. Enrolment	Brotherhood Enrolment	Music Enrolment	Mission Gifts	Total Gifts	Value Church Property
1955	75	1,734	430,134	16,766	287,392	128,294	128,177	55,802	16,850		$2,395,183	$14,682,311	$ 59,980,055
1956	75	1,751	436,732	15,739	289,570	125,307	128,292	55,718	17,496		2,802,940	16,230,555	67,396,395
1957	76	1,770	443,100	15,728	293,773	130,044	131,280	55,911	19,134	27,168	2,942,585	17,096,048	73,873,835
1958	76	1,784	450,723	17,195	298,817	136,906	135,434	60,404	22,955	30,753	3,158,981	17,881,697	81,361,954
1959	76	1,796	460,921	18,557	307,315	139,658	139,619	62,905	24,510	35,833	3,373,202	19,536,460	88,244,897
1960	76	1,806	468,739	16,288	311,582	160,125	140,153	62,733	25,434	33,375	3,637,233	20,750,299	94,785,258
1961	76	1,820	476,395	16,575	318,044	141,464	144,874	62,875	25,622	35,627	3,762,717	21,932,967	101,817,563
1962	77	1,828	483,689	15,824	320,517	147,224	146,408	61,945	25,267	39,553	4,003,806	23,497,253	109,412,010
1963	77	1,826	490,804	15,416	323,535	150,822	145,907	62,865	25,032	43,343	4,187,544	24,339,498	116,928,323
1964	77	1,839	497,354	15,768	323,725	147,799	144,900	64,497	24,767	48,114	4,392,310	25,740,466	125,193,120
1965	77	1,856	504,456	15,372	322,534	155,653	140,514	61,194	19,109	45,014	4,715,389	27,984,566	131,433,249
1966	77	1,866	510,497	15,904	322,649	154,440	140,324	61,613	18,723	49,037	5,219,171	30,238,462	142,097,313
1967	77	1,877	518,260	16,345	321,590	150,902	140,259	61,353	18,053	56,891	5,615,241	32,103,650	152,952,665
1968	77	1,886	526,350	15,784	320,303	144,200	146,748	59,687	18,585	60,316	6,038,745	36,159,337	160,704,726

JOE ABRAMS

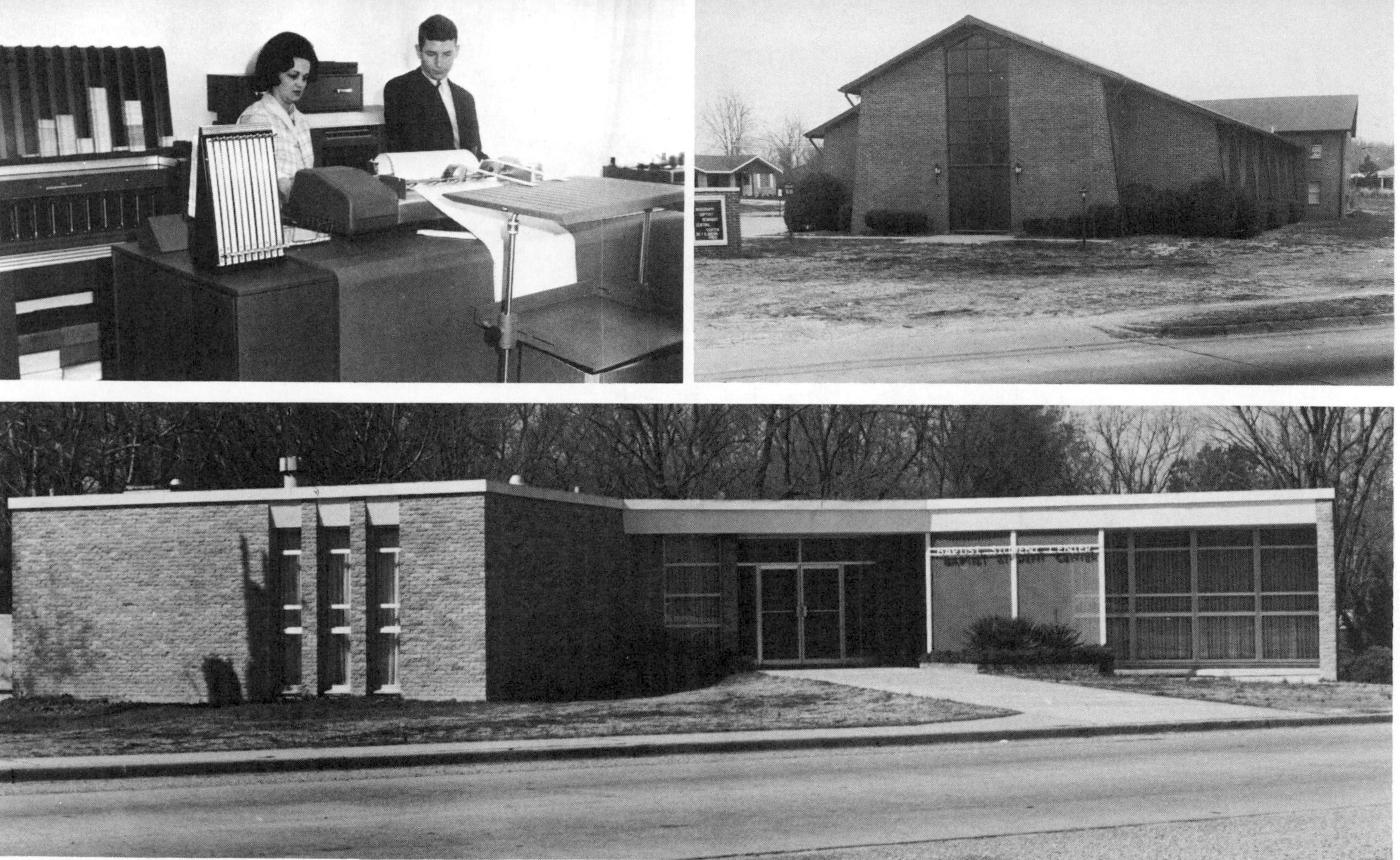

Top left: BAPTIST BUILDING, Jackson, Miss., computer center. *Top right:* MISSISSIPPI BAPTIST SEMINARY (*q.v.*). Headquarters and central center of the seminary system, Jackson. *Bottom:* BAPTIST STUDENT CENTER, at Mississippi State University, Starkville.

MISSISSIPPI BAPTIST CONVENTION (*q.v.*) BUILDING, Jackson, Miss. Architect's drawing of building erected in 1968 at a cost of $1,100,000.

Baptist Hospital is currently being phased out, and is being replaced by the Mississippi College School of Nursing which opened in Sept., 1969. The new school will offer a B.S. in nursing with class work to be done at the college and clinical work at the hospital. JOE ABRAMS

***MISSISSIPPI BAPTIST FOUNDATION.** An agency organized by the Mississippi Baptist Convention in 1943. Harry L. Spencer was the executive secretary from Sept. 1, 1950, until his retirement Dec. 31, 1967. He was succeeded by Carey E. Cox. During Spencer's administration the assets increased from $636,061.63 to $2,715,347.28. In June, 1969, they were $3,404,030.10. The operating budget is provided by the Cooperative Program. The nine-member board traditionally consists of two ministers and seven laymen. CAREY E. COX

MISSISSIPPI BAPTIST HISTORICAL COMMISSION. Created Nov. 14, 1956, by the Mississippi Baptist Convention to carry on the work of the Mississippi Baptist Historical Society, the commission is composed of nine members elected to three-year rotating terms. This agency promotes the historical interests of the convention. One project has been the microfilming of church records. Publications include: "Mississippi Baptist Historical Commisson," "Leaves of Gold from Our Baptist Heritage," and "Highlights of Mississippi Baptist History."

Jesse Laney Boyd (*q.v.*) was secretary of the commission until his death, June 24, 1967. Reed Dicken served as interim secretary. R. A. McLemore became secretary on July 1, 1968.

See also MISSISSIPPI BAPTIST HISTORICAL SOCIETY, VOL. II. R. A. MCLEMORE

***MISSISSIPPI BAPTIST HOSPITAL.** The addition of a sixth and seventh floor to the Simmons addition in 1962 brought the total bed capacity to 400. In 1964 the Gilfoy School of Nursing building was erected. An administrative wing was added to the hospital in 1965. Other improvements have included installation of a vital cobalt unit for the treatment of cancer (1965), the building of a laundry, the addition of a cafeteria, a new emergency room, and a variety of renovations and modernizations. In 1970 a 100-bed Progressive Care Unit was opened.

In 1970 plans were under way to begin in 1971 the construction of a 600-bed, $25,000,000 totally-new hospital across the street from the present location, with the present facility scheduled ultimately to become an extended-care facility of approximately 300 beds, making a total medical complex of 1,000 beds. A fund drive for $2,000,000 was two-thirds complete by mid-June, 1970.

The hospital is fully accredited by the Joint Commission on Accreditation and has approved training programs for interns plus schools of radiologic technology, medical technology, inhalation therapy, and practical nursing, with the Gilfoy School of Nursing scheduled to phase out in 1971 to be replaced by the Mississippi College School of Nursing.

Land, buildings, equipment, and other assets are valued at $9,555,000. Patient income in 1969 was $7,000,000, while Cooperative Program gifts totaled $107,000 and designated gifts $11,000. The value of charity work in 1969 was $165,000. MIKE WILKINSON

***MISSISSIPPI BAPTIST SEMINARY.** A system of 35 centers, strategically located throughout the state, which has been described as "a seminary on wheels to multiply the power of the Lord." Founded in 1942, the seminary's primary aim is to train the masses at the grass roots in Christian leadership and Bible study for social action unto better human relations. With an interracial board of trustees and faculty the seminary is open to all qualified people. It is jointly sponsored and financed by the Mississippi Baptist Convention Board, the Home Mission Board, and local National and Southern Baptist churches. The enrolment in 1969 was 2,180, including 383 ministers, 638 women, 311 laymen, 372 young people, and 476 children. The Th.B. and B.R.E. degrees, diplomas in Junior College and English Bible, and certificates in Christian Training are offered. The seminary has had three presidents: Herbert L. Lang, 1943–56; William A. Keel, 1956–59; and William P. Davis, 1959– . WILLIAM P. DAVIS

MISSISSIPPI, CHRISTIAN ACTION COMMISSION OF. An agency organized by the Mississippi Baptist Convention in 1964. Since 1958, the convention board had maintained a Temperance Department, headed by C. M. Day. Prior to this, the convention contributed to the "United Dry's," an interfaith organization to combat efforts to weaken the prohibition laws.

The commission was initiated by a long-range study committee, who felt that the churches were concerned beyond the "temperance movement." Therefore, the 12-member group was commissioned to achieve these objectives: A. To emphasize the biblical teachings that relate to the following areas of work: (1) alcohol and drug abuse, (2) church-state relationships, (3) Christian citizenship, (4) Christian home life, (5) pornography, (6) human relationships, (7) other moral and social problems as the need arises; and B. To provide such aids, materials and services as will assist the churches to be correctly informed of facts, trends, and conditions related to the areas of work assigned.

When feasible, the commission works with existing convention agencies, institutions, and departments of Baptist life. The work is supported by Cooperative Program allocations.

The commission forms policy statements, not to speak for the convention, but to give the position of the commission on the issues, with possible solutions in dealing with them. The approach is educational rather than promotional. However, interpretative conferences are conducted dealing with the various programs.

J. Clark Hensley became the first executive director in July, 1966. J. CLARK HENSLEY

***MISSISSIPPI COLLEGE.** The college had a 47 per cent increase in enrolment between 1957 and 1968. Of the 10,333 degrees granted, 4,777 were given during this period. The enrolment in the graduate school increased from 83 to 329. The curriculum was expanded by the addition of the Bachelor of Music Education degree, the Master of Arts degree, and the Master of Business Administration. The library holdings increased to 110,000 volumes and seven major buildings were added to the plant. The campus was doubled in size to include 280 acres. There were 79 full-time professors in 1968, 34 per cent of whom held the terminal degree and average faculty salaries were "C" on the American Association of University Professors scale. The total assets of the college increased from $4,491,000 to $12,025,000.

Dotson McGinnis Nelson (*q.v.*) retired as president in 1957, after a 25-year administration and was succeeded by Richard Aubrey McLemore, former dean and acting president of Mississippi Southern College (University of Southern Mississippi). On McLemore's retirement in 1968, William Lewis Nobles, former dean of the Graduate School, University of Mississippi, became president. R. A. MCLEMORE

MISSOURI, CHAIRS OF BIBLE IN. The Missouri Baptist Convention maintains four chairs of Bible located at the University of Missouri, Columbia, Central Missouri State College, Warrensburg, Southwest Missouri State College, Springfield, and Southeast Missouri State College, Cape Girardeau. Teachers in these schools are as follows: Columbia, Fred Neiger, Warrensburg, Curtis Hutcherson, Springfield, Charles Johnson, and Cape Girardeau, Thomas Messer. Southwest Missouri State College announced recently that they would establish a department of religion. The other state colleges may also establish departments of religion. (See also articles under names of above mentioned institutions in Vols. I and II).

CLIFFORD INGLE

MISSOURI, CHRISTIAN LIFE COMMISSION OF. The commission was established by the convention in 1960 to succeed the Temperance and Christian Life Committee. Adel J. Moncrief was elected chairman, with Ernest Waite, vice-chairman, K. P. Wilkinson, secretary, and Alvin G. Hause, O. R. Shields, Thomas S. Field, J. L. Wilson, J. J. Russell, and Owen Sherrill, commission members. The purpose of the commission is "to encourage the churches . . . to challenge their membership to the ideal of maximum Christian living." The family, human rights, economics, moral concepts, and citizenship are five areas of the commission's work. In 1964 the commission was designated as the convention's link to the Baptist Joint Committee on Public Affairs. The 1966–67 reports to the convention were listed from the Christian Life Commission and Public Affairs Committee. PAUL M. LAMBERT

***MISSOURI BAPTIST CHILDREN'S HOME.** The home is licensed by the state of Missouri to serve infants and school age children who are in need of homes. Main offices and campus are in Bridgeton, Mo. Three group homes are located in a rural setting near Gray Summit, Mo. An office is maintained in Kansas City, Mo., staffed by two case workers. The home maintains a staff of more than 50 and serves on the average of 150 boys and girls on campus and in group homes. An additional 250 are served in foster and preadoptive homes.

The home maintains a department of social work with a director of social work, a supervisor of social work, and a staff of 6 to 10 social workers in a statewide program of service to children. All children of school age who live on campus or in group homes attend public schools. Upon graduation from high school, those students wishing to continue their education, and who are qualified, may choose the Missouri Baptist college of their choice. The home provides such students with board, room, and books for two years. The college provides the tuition.

The current annual budget of the home is over $369,000. Support is provided by the Cooperative Program of the convention, an annual Thanksgiving Offering, birthday offerings, gifts from individuals, bequests, and endowment income. Edgar Blake is director of the home.

G. ELMO PURVIS

MISSOURI BAPTIST COLLEGE (cf. Hannibal-LaGrange College, Vol. I). A two-campus liberal arts college with separate facilities and faculties at Hannibal and St. Louis, Mo. The college is a consolidation in 1967 of the former Hannibal-LaGrange College and the Missouri Baptist College of St. Louis, chartered in 1963.

The Hannibal-LaGrange College continued to grow from the enrolment of 336 in 1956 to 798 at the time of consolidation. In 1957 its charter was revised conveying ownership and control to the Missouri Baptist Convention. It was accredited by the North Central Association of Colleges and Secondary Schools in 1958, and in 1960 launched a 10-year expansion program.

Baptists in the St. Louis area expressed interest in founding a college by beginning classes in 1957 in the activities building of Tower Grove Baptist Church. Rufus W. Crozier was the dean of what was styled St. Louis Baptist College, with an enrolment of 54. Academic responsibility for the classes was assumed by Hannibal-LaGrange College and the work continued under the official title of the Hannibal-LaGrange Extension Center with Crozier as director.

With interest growing, the St. Louis Baptist Association requested the Missouri Baptist Convention to establish a college in the area and to enter a campaign for $1,500,000 for that purpose.

The convention acted favorably toward the proposal by authorizing the campaign and ordering the executive board to negotiate for a site. A corporation was formed with the name Missouri Baptist College of St. Louis to hold title and develop the property.

The pledging of the amount needed by the churches of the Cuivre, Franklin County, Jefferson, and St. Louis Baptist Associations permitted the purchase of a site in western St. Louis County. Three buildings were planned and were under construction in 1967.

Meanwhile, a study of the trustees indicated some advantages to consolidation of the Baptist educational efforts in eastern Missouri. Recommended by the boards of Hannibal-LaGrange College and of Missouri Baptist College of St. Louis, the consolidation was approved by the Missouri Baptist Convention in Oct., 1966, and effected by a new charter on June 7, 1967. L. A. Foster, who had been president of Hannibal-La-Grange for 17 years, became president of the consolidated institution.

The college was operated thereafter by a board of trustees of 27 elected by the Missouri Baptist Convention, nine of whom were to reside in Marion County and adjacent counties, nine in St. Louis and adjacent counties, and nine in other Missouri counties.

In the spring of 1967 the North Central Association of Colleges and Secondary Schools granted a transfer of accreditation to the new college thereby permitting both campuses to operate on this approved basis.

The St. Louis campus began operation on the new site on Sept. 16, 1968, with an enrolment of 189 students. At the same time the extension center was phased out. Three buildings were completed, a library, an administration building, and a gymnasium. The plan for the St. Louis campus was for a continuation of the two-year curriculum until the fall of 1971, when the addition of a third and fourth year is projected.

The Hannibal-LaGrange campus enrolled 504 students in the fall of 1968. The campus was expanded by the addition of a women's dormitory and a library-science complex.

CARL GOODSON

MISSOURI BAPTIST CONVENTION (cf. Missouri Baptist General Association, Vol. II).

I. Convention Structure. A series of revisions in the structure of the convention began in 1956. Convention nominating procedures were changed that year when the convention authorized an annual nominating committee of 25 representative persons, appointed at least 90 days before the annual meeting. The committee nominates members of the executive board, trustees of the Missouri Baptist Foundation, and board members of the institutions, commissions, and agencies of the convention.

In 1958 the convention changed its name from Missouri Baptist General Association to Missouri Baptist Convention. Earl O. Harding is (1970) executive secretary.

Until 1956, the recording secretary and the statistical secretary were the same. In 1956 the work of the statistical secretary and responsibility for the compilation and publication of the convention annual were transferred to the new office of Promotion and Publicity.

Growing emphasis upon Christian social action led to the establishment of the Missouri Baptist Christian Life Commission in 1959 as a state counterpart to the Southern Baptist Christian Life Commission.

The business structure of the convention was revised in 1960 when it was changed from a *pro forma* type of organization to a not-for-profit organization. A major part of the change was the addition of new offices and departments. The office of Promotion and Publicity was created in 1956 to handle general promotion, publicity, special events and projects, convention arrangements, and other public relations programs. In 1967 its name was changed to Office of Communications.

In 1956 the department of Stewardship and Missions was divided into two offices: (1) Stewardship and Church Finance and (2) Missions. The office of Stewardship and Church Finance turned mainly to the promotion of church financial programs and general stewardship principles and practices. The office of Missions carried out a program of liaison with associational missionaries, surveys of churches and associations, establishment of new churches and chapels, and schools of missions. Later, both offices became divisions of work. The Stewardship Promotion Division took on promotion of two additional phases of work—the Cooperative World Missions Program and the Southern Baptist Annuity Program. The Missions Division included four departments—Work with Baptist Men, Work with National Baptists, Special Ministries, and Woman's Missionary Union, in addition to Associational Administration. In 1967 further refinement of the division type of organization placed both Stewardship and Church Finance and Missions in the Program Emphasis Division as departments, with the regular church organizational departments transferred to the Church Channel Division. Late in 1969, another revision took place in which Stewardship and Church Finance became a division again and Missions became the Department of Associational Administration.

The convention's effort to help churches secure building funds took the form in 1956 of the Business Trust Fund which was incorporated in 1957 as the Missouri Baptist Building Fund. The building fund secured investments and made loans to qualified churches. In 1962 it was changed from a corporation with its own board of trustees to a department of the convention's work, and in 1968 became a department of the new Bond and Loan Service Division.

Another convention commission was created in 1962 when a study of the relationship between the long standing Missouri Baptist Historical Society and the Missouri Baptist Convention produced the concept of the Missouri Baptist Historical Commission as a more effective agency for procurement and preservation of Missouri Baptist historical materials.

When the question arose in 1964 as to whether a wider distribution of membership and a better representation of churches and associations on the convention's executive board were needed, the convention authorized a study. A year later, the committee of nine reported that there was already a fair geographical distribution of board membership and a consistent effort to hold duplication of membership on boards to a minimum. Two recommendations from the study were adopted: that no person should serve on more than two boards of Missouri Baptist related institutions, commissions or agencies, including the executive board, and that the convention have two vice-presidents instead of one.

II. Program Organization. From 1954 to 1969, organization of the convention's state offices and its program of work underwent an evolution from an organization of separate departments, sometimes loosely related, to a division type coordinating all areas of convention activity in a team effort toward central objectives.

In 1958 a department of Work with the Deaf began with other special ministries added later and the name changed to the department of Special Ministries. In 1965 the name of the Brotherhood Department was changed to Work with Baptist Men. In 1968 the Training Union Department became the Department of Church Training.

Two new divisions were added in 1967—Program Emphasis and Church Channel. The Program Emphasis Division was given responsibility for program planning and structure and the Church Channel Division was made responsible for implementing the planned programs in the churches. The Program Emphasis Division included the departments of Associational Administration, Evangelism, Stewardship, Survey, and Work with National Baptists. The Church Channel Division included the departments of Work with Baptist Men, Church Music, Church Training, Student Work, Sunday School, and WMU.

In 1969 the departments of Evangelism and Stewardship returned to division status, and the office of Program Analysis was set up to analyze convention programs of work for decision and assignment by the administration, replacing the Program Emphasis Division.

In its present form, the division plan of organization includes eight divisions—Bond and Loan Service, Publishing (Missouri Baptist Press), Editorial (*Word and Way*), Church Channel, Evangelism, Stewardship, Higher Education, and Social Service. The last two divisions are yet to be activated. Two offices, Communications and Program Analysis, are part of the administration. Directly responsible to the executive secretary are Windermere Baptist Assembly, Research and Statistics, Purchasing-Construction-Maintenance, Associational Administration, Survey, and Work with National Baptists.

III. Policy Changes and Determinations. A series of changes in the charters of institutions affiliated with the Missouri Baptist Convention began in 1956. The purpose was to assure ownership and control of these institutions by the convention. By 1964 all institutions able to do so legally had amended their charters to this end.

The method of nominating convention officers and trustees of institutions and agencies was changed in 1956 by amending the convention bylaws to set up a nominating committee of 25 representative members 90 days before each annual meeting. The convention made further change in this method in 1961 by approving nomination of convention officers from the convention floor.

Because of a lack of cooperation and sympathy with the purposes of the convention, the convention in 1956 requested that churches of Old Path Association be omitted from the list of convention churches after the 1956 convention annual.

In 1961 the question of federal grants to institutions brought a reaffirmation of the convention policy that no Missouri Baptist institution could accept government grants or financial assistance from questionable sources.

Another policy determination occurred in 1962 when the convention voted to restrict fellowship with double aligned churches to those having membership in the convention before 1962. In 1969 the convention authorized a study "to see if there are ways that any local church . . . may have affiliation with other Baptist Conventions without sacrificing membership in the Missouri Baptist Convention."

After prolonged study of its relationship with the Missouri Baptist Hospital in St. Louis, the convention in 1966 granted the request of the hospital that its independent status be recognized, along with the fraternal relationship existing between the hospital and the convention.

IV. Institutional Development. In a 12-year period through 1969, the convention was engaged in a near constant development of its institutions, a three-phase program operating simultaneously.

Educational Institutions.—This development occurred in two sectors—colleges and student centers. In 1957 the convention began giving monthly financial assistance to an extension of

Hannibal-LaGrange College in St. Louis. In 1959 consideration was given to the possibility of a new Baptist College in the St. Louis area. Such a school was authorized in 1960, with a statewide financial campaign for this and three other Missouri Baptist colleges. The partially successful campaign provided funds for initial projects in the St. Louis situation as well as the three established colleges. Organization of the St. Louis college was approved in 1962, and two years later the convention became co-guarantor with St. Louis area churches of a $1,250,000 bond issue for the first buildings. During the next two years, consolidation of Hannibal-LaGrange College (Hannibal) and Missouri Baptist College (St. Louis) was explored and approved. The two schools merged under the name of Missouri Baptist College, and broke ground in 1967 in west St. Louis County for the St. Louis campus. The proposed four-year college became operative in 1968.

Meanwhile, the three established Missouri Baptist colleges were expanding. Southwest Baptist College, Bolivar, became a four-year school in 1964, and in the next five years expanded its facilities. Hannibal-LaGrange erected four buildings. William Jewell College, Liberty, added a new library and more housing.

In a 10-year period beginning in 1956, new student center buildings were erected adjacent to state school campuses in Springfield, Rolla, Jefferson City, Kirksville, Maryville, and St. Joseph. Chairs of Bible were established at some of these centers: Jefferson City in 1956, Kirksville in 1957, and Rolla in 1960, making seven with the four already established at Columbia, Springfield, Warrensburg, and Cape Girardeau. The name of the Chairs of Bible was changed to Religion and Philosophy Centers in 1965.

Benevolent Institutions.—Since 1955, Missouri Baptists' three benevolent institutions underwent extensive development. In 1956 the convention assumed ownership of the partially constructed Baptist Memorial Hospital in Kansas City, approved changes in the hospital charter assuring convention control, and instituted a bond issue to finance completion of the hospital building. The Home for Aged Baptists, Ironton, began a three-phase expansion program in 1962. The Missouri Baptist Children's Home, Bridgeton, in 1966 and 1967, expanded its resources for an advanced child-care program involving 400 children annually, by selling and leasing some of its valuable property.

Windermere Baptist Assembly.—Late in 1955, the convention initiated a study of its needs for a statewide assembly, and authorized negotiations for property in the Lake of the Ozarks area in 1956. The Windermere property at Roach, Mo., was purchased in 1957 for $171,000. The original 20 buildings increased to 55 by 1969, and the value of the year around assembly facilities reached $2,000,000.

V. Financial Program. The convention's financial program is fourfold—the Cooperative World Missions Program, Capital Needs, Bond and Loan Services, and Special Offerings.

Cooperative World Missions Program.—This is the basic program for support of the convention's missionary, educational, and benevolent causes. A long-range plan for increasing Cooperative Program funds from $1,700,000 to $3,000,000 was adopted in 1956. The plan sparked a series of annual increases that ranged from $100,000 to more than $300,000, until in 1969 the annual Cooperative Program receipts were $3,800,000. Intensive promotion establishing the Cooperative Program as a percentage item in every church budget annually, and increasing that percentage each year, was promoted.

Capital Needs.—The capital needs of both the convention and the churches began to receive major attention in 1956. A capital needs goal of $5,000,000, including $2,900,000 for educational institutions, was adopted and the Business Trust Fund, forerunner of the Missouri Baptist Building Fund, was set up.

Fund raising for capital needs of the educational institutions first took the form of using excess Cooperative Program funds. This method proved to be slow, and the convention turned to a statewide multi-million dollar campaign conducted by a national fund raising organization in 1961. The campaign was only partially successful but provided funds for initial phases of development at all Missouri Baptist colleges. Bond issues were also used for capital needs, the first one in 1957 for building Baptist Memorial Hospital and expanding Windermere Baptist Assembly. Other bond issues occurred in 1962, 1965, and 1967.

Bond and Loan Service.—Efforts after 1956 to assist churches in securing funds for building purposes followed two lines, the Missouri Baptist Building Fund and the Convention Guaranteed Bond Program. The building fund raised money by offering investments at rates of interest varying according to the term of investment and lending these funds to churches at a rate of interest sufficient to defray operational costs. The bond program began in 1964 and by the end of 1969 Missouri Baptist churches had issued $5,700,000 in Broadway bonds guaranteed by the convention through a guaranty fund provided by a percentage of all bond issues.

Special Offerings.—Three special statewide offerings for state, home, and foreign missions have been approved by the convention for many years. Only one of them—state missions—had an official annual convention-approved goal until 1967 when the convention began establishing and approving annual goals for all three offerings. A director of special mission offerings was employed late in 1969 to provide statewide promotion of all three special offerings.

VI. Special Activities. Since 1956 Missouri Baptists have engaged in a cooperative mission program in Iowa where there was only one established Southern Baptist church until that

MISSOURI STATISTICAL SUMMARY

Year	Associa-tions	Churches	Church Member-ship	Baptisms	S. S. Enrol-ment	V.B.S. Enrol-ment	T. U. Enrol-ment	W.M.U. Enrol-ment	Brother-hood En-rolment	Music Enrol-ment	Mission Gifts	Total Gifts	Value Church Property
1955	83	1,755	405,023	21,697	323,857	133,555	92,235	67,594	21,774		$2,993,254	$18,162,968	$ 56,215,618
1956	83	1,741	409,091	17,526	333,139	130,507	95,894	68,428	17,873		3,499,217	18,257,674	62,535,467
1957	82	1,745	415,044	18,738	332,657	135,986	97,476	69,467	24,766		3,589,315	18,651,653	69,938,271
1958	82	1,763	428,198	19,688	339,475	139,066	99,297	70,976	25,151		4,068,679	19,589,413	75,720,363
1959	82	1,764	439,619	21,135	346,063	138,804	106,284	72,748	25,293		4,105,332	21,285,165	84,537,563
1960	82	1,771	443,148	17,488	345,335	140,943	104,985	72,905	25,178		4,237,438	22,293,105	91,198,515
1961	82	1,782	456,268	18,603	352,284	145,922	107,773	75,481	25,344		4,329,255	23,205,335	101,409,174
1962	82	1,802	466,941	18,033	351,732	150,931	107,948	73,717	24,487		4,764,493	24,494,886	107,112,260
1963	82	1,809	473,346	16,142	350,462	150,966	106,279	74,203	24,380		4,914,920	25,648,886	114,400,589
1964	82	1,823	477,917	16,664	353,791	154,291	105,866	76,458	23,179		5,200,294	27,067,728	122,278,393
1965	83	1,845	485,982	15,865	352,807	159,337	104,383	75,360	22,147		5,246,008	28,594,334	135,846,098
1966	83	1,842	494,593	15,530	352,141	151,954	103,454	73,876	20,964	33,784	5,640,065	30,680,557	134,270,224
1967	83	1,854	500,968	16,268	347,891	160,078	104,796	73,201	20,349	34,862	6,104,468	33,628,321	134,117,513
1968	83	1,820	503,145	16,370	347,700	153,363	115,448	71,124	19,616	42,267	6,283,832	35,190,361	154,403,936

LLOYD COLLINS

time. In cooperation with the Southern Baptist Home Mission Board and individual Missouri churches, the convention invested large sums of money in establishing and developing churches and chapels in Iowa, until by 1970 there was a Southern Baptist Church in nearly every major population center in the state.

Two related activities receive support from the convention. For several years the Christian Civic Foundation of Missouri and Americans United for Separation of Church and State, a national organization, received support through church budgets, a practice encouraged by the convention. In 1958 these organizations became part of the annual state mission offering and have since received convention as well as church support.

The convention was more active in the decade 1960–70 in public issues than at any time in its history. Its firm stand on separation of church and state, strong support of public schools, clear position on racial crisis, and active participation in legislative matters are examples.

VII. Expansion of Convention Headquarters. When convention offices moved in 1949 from Kansas City to Jefferson City, a new Baptist Building was erected and expected to be adequate for many years. Ten years later, larger quarters were needed. In 1964 a new Baptist Building was authorized on a new 17-acre site, and financing was approved in 1966. Meanwhile, favorable developments in downtown Jefferson City turned attention to another site and on Dec. 1, 1969, the convention purchased the seven-story Missouri Hotel and began immediately to remodel the building for the convention's state offices. LLOYD COLLINS

MISSOURI BAPTIST CONVENTION, ANNUITY BOARD WORK OF. State convention promotion of Annuity Board work started in Missouri in 1957. The Missouri and Oklahoma conventions and the Annuity Board jointly employed R. C. Miller as annuity secretary for the two states. In 1959 J. E. Rains was employed by the Missouri convention as full-time annuity secretary. He was succeeded by James Smith in 1963. J. W. Fisher has served in this position since Sept., 1963. J. W. FISHER

MISSOURI BAPTIST CREDIT UNION. Organized in the Baptist Building, Jefferson City, Mo., on Apr. 29, 1963, the Credit Union is chartered by the state of Missouri for the participation of all employees of the Missouri Baptist Convention, cooperating churches, associations, institutions, and immediate families of such employees. Walter Herrington was president of the board of directors of the Credit Union in 1970. GEORGE HIXSON

***MISSOURI BAPTIST FOUNDATION.** Charter amended Aug. 28, 1957, to allow the foundation to administer trust funds for other than Baptist causes for reasons approved by the trustees of the foundation. Thomas W. Nelson became executive secretary-treasurer in Nov., 1962. Trust funds totaling $5,100,000 were being administered as of Sept. 30, 1969. The Earl O. Harding Scholarship Trust was established in 1970 for the purpose of providing scholarships to Baptist colleges. THOMAS W. NELSON

MISSOURI BAPTIST HISTORICAL COMMISSION (cf. Missouri Baptist Historical Society, Vol. II). H. I. Hester reported to the Missouri Baptist Convention in 1960 that there had been discussions to set up a Missouri Baptist Historical Commission to replace the Historical Society. In 1961 the society recommended to the convention that two members of the executive committee of the convention be appointed to help the society bring appropriate recommendations which, if approved, would establish the commission. Willard Bright and James Smith were appointed. The society presented four recommendations to the convention in 1962.

(1) That a Missouri Baptist Historical Commission be created to collect, preserve, catalogue, and make available such books, pamphlets, periodicals, manuscripts, pictures, autographs, records and other matters as will aid in the preservation of the history of Baptists in general and of Missouri Baptists in particular.

(2) That the Commission shall consist of nine (9) members who shall be nominated and elected by the Missouri Baptist Convention. Their term of service shall be for three years. No members shall be elected to serve for more than two consecutive terms. The terms shall be adjusted so that one third of the members shall be eligible for election each year.

(3) That the archives of the Commission shall remain in the Library of William Jewell College and shall be under the supervision of the college librarian.

(4) That the Commission, after organization, shall survey the financial needs for operation and shall submit to the Finance Committee of the Missouri Baptist Convention a request for such funds.

The convention thereby created the commission and the society dissolved.

When William Jewell College built a new library building, the convention provided special funds for new and spacious archives in the new library. Miss Opal Carlin served as librarian of William Jewell College and assisted the commission by acting as director of the archives. After many years of service, she died in 1965. The librarian of William Jewell College is now automatically the director of the archives. H. I. Hester has been appointed by the commission as custodian of the archives. The commission employs Miss Mabel Thomason to catalog archive materials.

The Commission began an aggressive program in 1968 to send a representative to speak to the annual associational meetings in Missouri. In 1969 the commission had a representative before 50 of the 83 associations. The commission produced slides, scripts, and pamphlets to educate Baptists about the work of the commission and to assist in collecting historical data. The society had published five volumes of *Missouri Baptist Biography*. The last was published in 1925. The commission voted in 1969 to publish volume six. The date set for publication was the summer of 1970, with H. I. Hester as the editor.

DORAN C. MC CARTY

***MISSOURI BAPTIST HOSPITAL.** The hospital moved into its new $8,000,000, 320-bed facility in west St. Louis County in late 1965. This was one of the first hospitals in the Midwest planned, constructed, and equipped along Progressive Patient Care lines. The hospital currently ministers to 900 patients per month. The Missouri Baptist Convention recognized in 1966, at the hospital's request, its independent status, and "the fraternal relationship which exists between the Hospital and the Convention." A program of spiritual ministry and training in pastoral care is conducted through the chaplain's office, and a program of nurses training is carried out in cooperation with Missouri Baptist College. ROBERT E. SMITH

MISSOURI BAPTIST PRESS. See MISSOURI BAPTIST CONVENTION.

MISSOURI BAPTISTS, BOND AND LOAN SERVICE DIVISION OF. The purpose of the division is to aid churches and institutions in arranging suitable financing for building projects. It is primarily a service of counseling, programming, and guidance. Churches needing up to $25,000 are assisted through the building fund. This fund also receives monies for deposits and pays an interest rate in keeping with the current market. Churches needing above $25,000 issue their own bonds which are guaranteed by the Missouri Baptist Guaranty Fund. In 1969 Arthur H. Stainback was director of the division, and Harry Cameron was secretary of the building fund. A. H. STAINBACK

***MISSOURI HOME FOR AGED BAPTISTS.** Located in Ironton, Mo., the home receives strong support from Missouri Baptists which enables the home to continue and expand its ministry. The completion of two new wings in 1962 and 1968, and a new administration building in 1965, increased the capacity from 100 to 176. An outpatient service is provided which assists about 30 additional persons who stay in other nursing homes. John H. Burney was honored in 1968, on his 15th anniversary as superintendent. W. R. RIGGS

MIXON, FORREST ORION (b. Early Branch, S. C., Apr. 16, 1900; d. Murfreesboro, N. C., Oct. 28, 1956). Pastor and college president. Son of William P. and Sallie Shuman Mixon, he was educated at Furman University (B.A., 1926), and Southern Baptist Theological Seminary (Th.M., 1929; Ph.D., 1932). He received the honorary D.D. from Furman University in 1947. He served several pastorates in

South Carolina, Kentucky, Georgia, and North Carolina from 1926–51. In 1929 Mixon married Daisy Lou Major of Belton, S. C. Their children are Forrest Orion, Jr., and Carole Lynn (Mixon) Hale.

Mixon was president of the Baptist State Convention of North Carolina, 1949–50, and assumed the presidency of Chowan College, Murfreesboro, N. C. in 1951, where he served until his death. Under Mixon's leadership, the college's enrolment increased from 131 to 251. One major emphasis was the development of a competent and mature faculty. Under his administration, the college was accredited by the Southern Association of Colleges and Secondary Schools, Dec. 19, 1956.

Mixon also served as a member of the general board of the North Carolina Baptist Convention, and as a trustee of the Southern Baptist Theological Seminary. He is buried in Raleigh, N. C. PHIL ROYCE

MIZE, WILLIAM GOEBEL (b. Trigg County, Ky., Feb. 12, 1900; d. Jackson, Miss., Feb. 21, 1969). He was the son of Joseph Young and Nannie Campbell Mize who moved to Silver Creek, Miss., in 1914. He graduated from Brookhaven High School and received the B.B.A. from the University of Mississippi. Mize married Clara Amelia Ray of Durant on June 20, 1923. They had four children: W. G., Jr., Jerry Lawrence, Nancy Ray, and Ruby.

Mize was for 12 years manager of the Baptist Book Store, Jackson; two years educational director of the First Baptist Church, Brookhaven; business manager of the Baptist orphanage in 1935; and from 1936 until his retirement in Oct., 1960, superintendent. His administration was characterized by the payment of an accumulated debt, the construction of a modern plant, and the introduction of modern concepts in child care. Mize served as president of the Southeastern Conference of Orphanage Executives and Workers, 1949–50; president of the Child Care Executives of SBC, 1950–51; vice-president of Mississippi Baptist Convention, 1946; deacon First church, Jackson, for 37 years; and member of Board of Education for Jackson Public Schools, 1960–65. WHEELER C. CATHEY

MOBILE COLLEGE. Founded in 1961 as a four-year, coeducational liberal arts college by the Alabama Baptist State Convention which elects its trustees and provides financial support, the college awards both the B.A. and B.S. degrees. Located 12 miles north of downtown Mobile, Ala., the campus is composed of 400 acres. The Mobile community, under the leadership of T. T. Martin, contributed more than $1,500,000 at the time of the founding of the institution and has continued its generous support. It is the only private, four-year college to be founded in Alabama in more than 50 years and was accredited by Southern Association of Colleges and Schools in 1968. William K. Weaver, Jr., the founding president, was appointed Apr. 1, 1961. J. L. Bedsole, who served as first chairman, board of trustees, was awarded the first honorary degree in 1968. The charter class of 181 students was admitted in Sept., 1963. Sixty-six were graduated in May, 1967, as members of the first graduating class. The fall, 1969, enrolment was 426. Original faculty was composed of 12 persons, with 27 serving in 1969. Total investments in plant in 1969 amounted to $3,150,000, and included five buildings. The motto of the College is "The fear of the Lord is the beginning of wisdom." Seeking to provide a personalized education in a crowded world, it ranks among the top of Southern Baptist Colleges in percentage of students who are Baptists and in the percentage of its student body preparing for the ministry. WILLIAM K. WEAVER, JR.

MONTANA, BAPTISTS IN. See NORTHERN PLAINS BAPTIST CONVENTION, and COLORADO, BAPTIST GENERAL CONVENTION OF.

MONTGOMERY BAPTIST HOSPITAL. Founded by Montgomery Baptist Association, Aug. 15, 1955, it is owned by the association, incorporated under the laws of Alabama, and operated by a board of directors appointed by the association. The hospital opened on July 29, 1963, with a bed capacity of 195. It is a member of American Hospital, American Protestant Hospital, and Southern Baptist Hospital Associations, and other regional and local related organizations. It is accredited by the Joint Commission on Accreditation of Hospitals, and approved for training of interns, nurses, and medical technologists.

Meadhaven, a 43-bed nursing home, is owned and operated by the hospital. The establishment of the home was made possible by a gift of $500,000 from Mr. and Mrs. Arthur M. Mead, Montgomery, Ala. W. Taylor Morrow serves as administrator of both institutions. FRANK TRIPP

MOORE, HIGHT C (b. Globe, Caldwell County, N. C., Jan. 28, 1871; d. Ridgecrest, N. C., May 24, 1957). He married Laura Miller Peterson. They had one son, Joseph P. Educated at Wake Forest College (B.A., 1890) and Rochester Baptist Theological Seminary, he served the following North Carolina Baptist churches as pastor: Moorehead City, 1890–93; Brown Memorial, Winston-Salem, 1893–94; First, Monroe, 1894–98; First, New Bern, 1898–1903; and First, Chapel Hill, 1903–04. He served as assistant recording secretary, Baptist State Convention of North Carolina, 1898–1907, and also as statistical secretary, 1905–07. Moore was Sunday School secretary of the North Carolina convention three years, 1904–07. During 1907–08, he served as a field secretary of the Sunday School Board, SBC. He was editor of *The Biblical Recorder,* the state Baptist paper of North Carolina, 1908–17. Junior secretary of the Southern Baptist Convention, 1914–19, he served as senior secretary, 1920–46.

The climax of Moore's ministry was in the

position of editorial secretary of the Sunday School Board. He served as co-editorial secretary and managing editor, 1917–27, and then editorial secretary, 1927–43. In this position he was responsible for guiding the editorial policy and interpreting the editorial ministry of the board, all the while serving as editor of *The Teacher* and other publications, while also giving general supervision to the board's editorial activity. From 1924–43, he served on the International Sunday School Lesson Committee.

The third major area of Moore's ministry was in the field of writing. During early pastoral days, he published *Seaside Sermons,* also *Select Poetry of North Carolina.* He was the author of nine books, chiefly related to the training of Sunday School teachers. For 35 years (1918–52), he wrote *Points for Emphasis,* an annual Sunday School lesson commentary. During retirement, three more volumes came from his pen. For nearly 15 years (1929–43), he gave a weekly broadcast of the International Sunday School Lesson over radio station WSM in Nashville. He also aided Bernard W. Spillman (*q.v.,* Vol. II) in the founding of Ridgecrest Baptist Assembly in 1907. When Moore retired at the end of 1943, he established his home at Ridgecrest.

Moore's counsel was sought in matters of denomination-wide importance, and his influence through his writing exercised a crucial influence in all Southern Baptist churches.

CLIFTON J. ALLEN

MOORES, JESSE ALVIN (b. Henderson, Tex., Sept. 27, 1923; d. Dallas, Tex., May 3, 1968). Director, Electronic Data Processing Department, Annuity Board, SBC, he was first employed by the board in 1953 as bookkeeper. He was the son of Jesse N. and Lillian (Dickerson) Moores. Converted at age 11, he later graduated from Dallas Technical High School and attended Southwestern Louisiana Institute two years. Then he served in the United States Army Air Force, 1942–45. He married Maryanne Butler, Mar. 22, 1944. They had three sons: Jesse Lee, Thomas Page, and Michael Alan.

JOHN D. BLOSKAS

MORGAN, JAMES PERRY (b. Dunn, N. C., Dec. 14, 1910; d. Raleigh, N. C., Oct. 6, 1966). Minister of education, and Training Union secretary for the Baptist State Convention of North Carolina. Morgan's father, Perry, was secretary of the Sunday School and Training Union departments of the Baptist State Convention before serving as manager of Ridgecrest Baptist Assembly. Morgan graduated from Wake Forest College, cum laude, in 1934, and did graduate work there and at Duke University.

From 1934 until 1950, except for service with the Air Force, 1942–46, he was minister of education at First Baptist Church, Durham, N. C. In 1951 he was elected Training Union secretary for the Baptist State Convention and continued in that position until his death. He regularly contributed articles to Sunday School Board publications, especially the *Training Union Magazine,* and was widely known throughout the Southern Baptist Convention. He married Maxine Slaughter on Mar. 22, 1942. They had two daughters, Susan and Elizabeth Morgan.

TOBY DRUIN

MORGAN, WILLIAM CLAUDE (b. Perry County, Miss., Aug. 29, 1902; d. Jackson, Miss., Mar. 13, 1964). Second employed secretary, Church Music Department, Mississippi Baptist Convention Board, from Nov. 1, 1950, until his death. Converted under preaching of C. A. Wroten, Morgan was baptized at the Moorhead, Miss., church. He graduated from Mississippi College in 1926 and from Southwestern Baptist Theological Seminary in 1931. Earning a Bachelor of Music degree from Chicago's Vandercook College of Music in 1938, he passed an examination requiring the playing of 27 different instruments. His specialties were in piano, organ, and trombone. He married Kate Durham Polk, July 10, 1926, by whom he had one daughter, Joy Durham.

For 12 years Morgan taught music, in Mississippi high schools and at Copiah-Lincoln Junior College. He received lifetime teaching certificates in piano, orchestra, band and public school music. After service at Crystal Springs and Vicksburg, Miss., churches as minister of education and music, he became associate in the Training Union Department, Mississippi Baptist Convention Board, Jackson, Mar. 1, 1947. When Luther A. Harrison, the board's first music secretary, drowned a week later, Morgan added music promotion to his duties. In 1950 the board elected him music secretary.

ANN WASHBURN MCWILLIAMS

MOROCCO, MISSION IN. Southern Baptist work in Morocco was begun in 1967 by Merrel and Arlene (Jensen) Callaway, stationed in Oujda until their transfer to Yemen in 1968. A year later, the only missionaries under assignment to Morocco were Joseph and Nancy (Walker) Newton, stationed in Rabat. There were no Christian churches composed of Moroccan believers. Europeans residing in Morocco make up the few Roman Catholic and Protestant churches. In 1969 the only Moroccan Baptist, Admad Marzuk Benali, was a student at the Arab Baptist Seminary in Beirut, preparing to return and work among his own people.

JOSEPH A. NEWTON

MORRIS, CLYDE CALHOUN (b. Dillon, Miss., Oct. 29, 1855; d. Ada, Okla., Oct. 24, 1956). Minister and denominational leader. From Union University he received an A.B. in 1915. He was ordained at Jackson, Tenn., in 1911. Pastor of First Baptist, Ada, 1918–49, he also served on the boards of the Baptist Foundation of Oklahoma and Oklahoma Baptist University; was president of the state convention, 1933–36; and founded radio stations KADA, Ada, in 1934, and KWSH, Wewoka, and television station KTEN, Ada, in 1946. The last 15 years of his Ada pastorate he had a daily Bible study period on station KADA. He was named to the first Radio Commission of the Southern Baptist Convention. When doctrinal controversies raged in the twenties, Morris was a leader among Oklahoma forces for Fundamentalism. J. M. GASKIN

MOSS, CASIMIR (b. Caldwell Parish, La., Sept. 26, 1874; d. Winnfield, La., Oct. 10, 1961). Son of Thomas A. Moss and Eva (Meredith) Moss, he was educated in Louisiana public schools and graduated from Tulane University law school, New Orleans, in 1901. On Mar. 17, 1897, he married Ophelia Eleanor Wallace and they had two children: Mrs. Ophelia Storey and Casimir D.

Moss was superintendent of Winn Parish Schools, 1900–08. An attorney at law, he served as judge of 5th and 8th Judicial Districts of Louisiana, 1912–34, and 1935 until retirement in 1954.

He was an outstanding Christian layman, serving as president of Louisiana Baptist Convention (1917–18), president of the Louisiana Baptist Brotherhood, trustee of Louisiana Baptist Children's Home at Monroe, trustee of Baptist Hospital at Alexandria, and vice-president of the Southern Baptist Convention (1918).

For many years he was a member of the First Baptist Church, Winnfield, and led in the organization and building of Laurel Heights Church there, where he was a deacon at the time of his death. He served extensively as a lay preacher. JOHN G. ALLEY

MOUNT BAKER BAPTIST ASSEMBLY. A summer assembly facility near Glacier, Wash., close to the Canadian border, operated by Southern Baptists of the Northwest. It consists of about 100 acres formerly used as a Civilian Conservation Corps Camp in the thirties. It was purchased in Nov., 1952, by authority of the Oregon-Washington Convention, at a cost of $12,500. Lots were leased to recover part of the sum, and old buildings were used for over 10 years. Improvements were made and dozens of privately owned cottages were erected. The distance of the facility from most of the Baptist constituency, and its availability for summer use only, caused the committee in charge to recommend in 1966 that the assembly be sold and that an assembly facility be located elsewhere. The convention referred the matter to its executive board. As of 1969, no practical solution had been found to the problem. A caretaker lives on the grounds, and some groups other than Baptists rent the facility in the summer. It is in a beautiful Cascade Mountain setting, about 20 miles from Mount Baker. ROY L. JOHNSON

MUIRHEAD, HARVEY HAROLD (b. Eagle Springs, Tex., Dec. 19, 1879; d. Dallas, Tex., Nov. 2, 1957). Missionary to Brazil. Graduate of Baylor University (A.B. and D.D.) and Southwestern Baptist Theological Seminary (Th.M., Th.D.), Muirhead married Alyne Guynes, June 20, 1905. Appointed to Brazil in 1907, he served as president of American Baptist College and North Brazil Seminary in Recife, and later headed Baptist college and South Brazil Seminary in Rio. He served as the Foreign Mission Board's field secretary, 1938–40, and president of Mexican Baptist Theological Seminary, El Paso, Tex., 1941–43. He retired in 1947. GENE H. WISE

MURRELL, JESSE FRANK (b. New Boston, Tex., Oct. 26, 1888; d. Hugo, Okla., Feb. 24, 1962). Minister, hospital administrator, and denominational leader. Educated at East Texas Normal College (1909), and Southwestern Baptist Theological Seminary (1920–22), he received the D.D. from Howard Payne College in 1933. He married Bonnie Beatrice Bell in 1914.

Following four years in public school work, he served as pastor of the following Texas churches: Rosen Heights, Forth Worth, 1920–23; First, Gainesville, 1923–28; First, Greenville, 1928–30; and First, Denison, 1930–42. He served First Church, Hugo, Okla., 1942–48. He was administrator of Miami Baptist Hospital, Miami, Okla., 1948–52, and Oklahoma Baptist Hospital, Muskogee, Okla., 1952–55. Upon retirement in 1955 he moved to Hugo, Okla. There he led a campaign for funds to build the Hugo Golden Age Home, and was its first administrator (1955–62). The hospital wing of the home is named for him. Murrell is buried at Hugo, Okla. J. M. GASKIN

***MUSIC, BAPTIST.** Significant historical development has occurred in the music life of Southern Baptist in the more than dozen years covered in this volume. Generally, the organized effort of music activities in Southern Baptist churches dates primarily from the forties, though some evidence may be found earlier. However, accurate records of enrolment for the total constituency have been kept only since 1957. The following information is the total enrolment of music programs for the Southern Baptist Convention as reported on the annual individual church letters:

Year	Enrolment	Year	Enrolment
1957	553,021	1964	923,871
1958	622,694	1965	872,186
1959	682,477	1966	945,004
1960	646,696	1967	1,019,130
1961	715,104	1968	1,038,290
1962	791,477	1969	1,062,494
1963	859,608		

In 1964 the Church Music Department of the Sunday School Board sponsored the National Conference of Southern Baptist Musicians at Louisville, Ky., Feb. 11–13. The three-day conference featured 12 choral and instrumental groups from Southern Baptist colleges and seminaries. There were 3,575 registrants. Talmage W. Dean was commissioned to compose on oratorio, "Behold, the Glory of the Lamb," which was premiered at the conference.

The acceptance of *Baptist Hymnal* (1956) by Southern Baptist churches as the most widely used hymnal in Southern Baptist history is evidenced by the fact that from Mar., 1956, through Jan., 1970, 5,659,390 copies were distributed.

To encourage and strengthen congregational singing among new congregations, the Sunday School Board offered 25 copies without cost to each new church and mission beginning in 1960. In response to this offer, 84,525 hymnals were given free to 3,381 new churches and missions through 1969.

Baptist Hymnal is the first Baptist compilation in America to have a companion or handbook which provides background information regarding the hymns, tunes, authors, composers, and sources. This handbook, *Hymns of Our Faith,* by William J. Reynolds, was published in 1964. A historical introduction deals with Baptist hymnody in America and provides a listing of hymn collections published in America by or for Baptists.

An increase in the activity and involvement of youth choirs was strongly evident in the past decade. Baptist youth choirs participated in touring trips, singing in churches, schools, shopping centers, etc. Mission tours became popular with youth choirs spending a week or several days in a mission area engaged in Vacation Bible Schools, door-to-door witnessing, taking a religious census, as well as singing together.

Good News, a Christian folk musical, which appeared in 1967, marked a new trend in the music of youth choirs. Musicals, given in schools, theaters, store buildings, and shopping malls, became a new means of sharing the gospel in the "marketplace," beyond the walls of the church house.

Increasingly popular with youth choirs is music that reflects the tempo, the sound, the beat, and the pulse of contemporary experience, with appropriate borrowing from a mixture of the present sounds of rock, pop, folk, gospel, blues, and jazz, in greater or lesser proportions. Added to these is the growing interest in the use of electronic music and aleatory music in the church.

In 1960 the Church Music Department initiated a series of hymn writing competitions designed to encourage and stimulate creative hymn writing among Southern Baptists. In each competition several hundred entries were received. The winning texts and authors were as follows:

1960: "O Lord of Life, Thy Calm We Seek," Mary E. Hall; "Christ in Thee My Heart Rejoices," Sybil L. Armes.

1962: "Praise the Lord, the King of Glory," Delma B. Reno; "We Praise Thee with Our Minds, O Lord," Hugh T. McElrath; "O Lord, My Lips Can Never Speak," Betty B. Moody; "How Gracious Are Thy Mercies, Lord," Sybil L. Armes.

1964: "Walk Ye in Him," Roy H. Corley; "I See the Christ Among the Crowd," Mary E. Hall; "Come, All Christians, Be Committed," Mrs. Clarence Lloyd; "Faith for the Service," Mrs. L. H. Figh, Jr.; "Give to Your God This Fast of Christian Service," Mrs. Ferman F. Stamp; "Lord, Light My Soul with Holy Flame," Robert E. Brickhouse; "Lord, We Give Ourselves unto Thee," James T. Bolding; "O Gracious Lord, Accept Our Praise," Erwin C. Johnson.

1966: "In This Age of Noise and Turmoil," Beth Rice Luttrell; "Increase in Knowledge of Thy God," Betty P. Barrett.

1968: "Where's the Promise of the City," G. Temp Sparkman; "O Son of Man, Who Walked Man's Way," William N. McElrath; "Lord, Lead Thy Church," Kate W. Woolley; "To Those of Strength and Joy and Peace," Felix O. Cox, Jr.; "Lord of Loving, Lord of Healing," Diane O. Jordan; "Our Voices Sing Great Hymns of Praise," Virginia J. Swick; "We Lift Our Hearts in Songs of Praise," Lilian Y. Leavell.

1970: "Arise Now, Fellow Christians," Diane O. Jordan; "Free to Be Me," Kate W. Woolley.

Beginning in 1967, the Church Music Department began conducting annual Church Music Seminars in the Church Program Training Center, Nashville, Tenn. These seminars provided concentrated study in specific music oriented subject areas.

In 1969–70 emphasis was placed on *Shaping-the-70's* field service, interpreting the program and products for the coming decade. This emphasis, planned cooperatively by agencies of the SBC, provided direct music training to every constituent church.

See also Hymnals, Baptist; Music Education, Baptist. WILLIAM J. REYNOLDS

MUSIC, CHRISTIAN HOME. A nonprofit music ministry conducted by the Radio and Television Commission of the Southern Baptist Convention. Founded in 1957 in response to audience demand for records of music heard on broadcasts produced by the commission, Christian Home Music (CHM) is an adjunct of the commission's department of program music, directed by Miss Joe Ann Shelton. Its purpose is threefold: to promote the growth of the commission's radio and television audiences, to fulfil the desire of these audiences for recorded inspirational music, and to raise funds for the commission. The project initially received a $4,000 annual operating budget, with all income above expenses placed in the operating fund of the agency. Christian Home Music has cleared funds for the commission each year, never contributing less than $1,500 to the support of the commission in any year. To keep pace with the improving quality of production in the commercial record industry, CHM in 1967 engaged a professional recording engineer. In 1968 it produced its first compatible stereophonic recordings. CHM now produces from 10 to 12 long-playing record albums each year. The commission makes its records available free to radio-TV stations and to pastors who have need of such music for radio-TV programs. EDWARD SHIPMAN

***MUSIC EDUCATION, BAPTIST.**

IN INSTITUTIONS. Twenty-two junior colleges and 38 senior colleges are in operation in 1970. The curriculums of these Southern Baptist colleges reflect concern for higher quality musical performance standards and the training of church musicians and public school music teachers.

There has been a marked increase of interest by Baptist colleges in higher standards of musical instruction as encouraged by the National Association of Schools of Music. By 1970, 18 of the 38 senior colleges were accredited by NASM. Due to educational costs relatively few Southern Baptist colleges offer graduate music degrees. By 1970 there were approximately 750 college students in Southern Baptist colleges preparing to be church musicians.

The four Southern Baptist seminaries offering degrees in church music had approximately 400 music majors enrolled in 1969–70. The demand from the churches for seminary music graduates far exceeds the supply. Three of the four degree granting seminaries are accredited by the National Association of Schools of Music, the Southern Association of Schools and Colleges, and the American Association of Theological Schools. The seminaries have been able to maintain their emphasis upon music as a ministry while still meeting national musical accreditation standards. The majority of the seminary music students are enrolled for the two-year graduate Master of Church Music degree which is based upon a college music major. Three of the seminaries have students enrolled for the Doctor of Musical Arts and Doctor of Education music degrees. A diploma course consisting of two to three years of seminary instruction, but without college prerequisites, is available for those qualified to undertake study.

Four major areas of expansion and concern exist, namely: (1) the enlistment of more musically gifted youth to dedicate their life to a spiritual ministry through music, (2) increased financial support to train these young people in our colleges and seminaries, (3) a meaningful incorporation of both keyboard and orchestra instrumental music into our worship services, and (4) increased emphasis upon the use of church materials which will have meaning and communicate spiritually with our church congregations. FORREST H. HEEREN

IN BAPTIST CHURCHES. Following the 1944 instructions of the Southern Baptist Convention to the Sunday School Board to "set going a constructive educational program of church music among Southern Baptists," the board expanded its music department. A comprehensive program of music education, publication, and promotion was established and experienced phenomenal growth under the secretaryship of Walter Hines Sims, who succeeded B. B. McKinney (*q.v.*, Vol. II) in 1952. Publication of *Baptist Hymnal* in 1956, with Sims as editor, gave a solid base for the program.

In 1959 the SBC instructed all agencies to define their programs. The program statement for church music is "to assist churches, associations, and state conventions in establishing, conducting, enlarging, and improving the music program in the churches." The program includes research, program design, publishing, field services, and cooperative relationships with other programs. Program growth resulted in an expanded design in 1969.

Tasks of the music program in the churches are stated as (1) teach music, (2) train persons to lead, sing, and play music, (3) provide music in the church and community, and (4) provide and interpret information regarding the work of the church and the denomination. Churches implement the tasks through graded choral and instrumental groups, music study groups, and music activity groups.

Dated curriculum material giving guidance for music in worship, witness, ministry, outreach, education, and cooperative mission actions is provided. Eight new graded music periodicals began publication in Oct., 1970: administration, *The Church Musician* and *The Music Leader;* adults, *Choral Overtones* and *Choral Tones;* youth, *Opus One* and *Opus Two;* and children, *Young Musicians* and *Music Makers.* Recordings of music in the periodicals are available for learning and demonstration.

The program is responsible for Broadman Music, Broadman Records, and Convention Press music and publications which cover a broad spectrum from simple gospel hymn and folk music to larger choral works and music dramas for use in the churches. The program at the Sunday School Board consults with the churches on their program and supplies counsel, materials, music, promotion and guidance in achieving their music education objectives.

W. HINES SIMS

IN CONVENTIONS AND ASSEMBLIES. By 1970, 31 state conventions employed music secretaries who were giving emphasis to the continuing development of music education and performance programs in the churches within their geographical boundaries. The rapid growth of church music during the past two decades created within these state conventions the need for new and innovative approaches to music program leader training.

A significant approach was the enlistment and training by the state music secretary of special workers to further extend and amplify his ministry and service to churches and their music leaders. These special workers were enlisted and trained on the basis of function, *i.e.:* choral-vocal, instrumental, age-division, or general administration methods and materials, associational music work, etc. They were then assigned specific, continuing leader training tasks.

Other approaches conducted by state conventions during this period include: (1) retreats for the full-time minister of music or the volunteer, part-time music director; (2) age-division and/or general administration workshops, conferences, and clinics; (3) instrumental and choral reading clinics; and (4) cooperative leader training events sponsored by two or more church program organizations, *i.e.*, kindergarten or elementary workshops.

A youth music workshop was added to the annual summer assembly schedule in 1968 by the Church Music Department of the Sunday School Board. This experience provided for talented youth opportunities for both spiritual and musical growth.

Ridgecrest and Glorieta Church Music Leadership conferences in 1969 involved more than 9,000 persons enrolled in leader-member training activities, giving further evidence of the dynamic interest in church music. RAY CONNER

MUSIC FOR PRIMARIES. A music quarterly for Primary choirs published by the Church Music Department of the Baptist Sunday School Board, beginning with the fourth quarter, 1966, and concluding with the third quarter, 1970. It was replaced in Oct., 1970, by a new quarterly, *Music Makers.* W. HINES SIMS

MUSIC IN MISSIONS. The use of music in mission outreach is not a new phenomenon: the injunctions of Paul to sing are recorded in his letters to his own mission fields. William Carey sang a Bengali hymn at the baptism of Krishna in Serampore in 1800, and composed a hymn on the occasion of the translation of the New Testament into Bengali. The tradition of the Bagby family in Brazil is replete with the use of music as a basic tool, and pioneer Brazilian missionary Solomon Ginsberg wrote many original hymns in Portuguese to proclaim the gospel. "Music in missions" is as old as missions itself, just as music and Christianity have been closely identified throughout history.

In 1951 the Southern Baptist Foreign Mission Board appointed Mr. and Mrs. Donald Orr the first missionary specialists in music. They served as teachers in the International Baptist Seminary in Cali, Colombia, extended their ministry to the churches, and worked among national pastors, convincing them of the power of music in evangelism. The second music missionaries, the William Ichters, were appointed for promotional work in Brazil in 1956, and embarked upon a remarkably successful career. Judson Blair, appointed for general evangelism in Argentina, became in effect a music missionary early in the 1950's; Edward Nelson was appointed for Chile in 1957, and Boyd Sutton for Brazil in 1959. Music in missions received considerable encouragement and publicity during this period in *The Church Musician.*

During the sixties, the number of music missionaries increased almost fivefold. Additional music missionaries under appointment of the FMB in 1970 included: Phillip M. Anderson, Philippines; Kent W. Balyeat, Argentina; Bwain Boothe, Thailand; Roger W. Cole, South Brazil; June Cooper, Japan; Thomas W. Graham, Japan; Clint Kimbrough, South Brazil; Milton Lites, Taiwan; John McGuckin, Argentina; L. G. McKinney, Hong Kong; Wayne Maddox, Okinawa; Joseph W. Mefford, Spain; Darrell Mock (missionary associate), Japan; William R. O'Brien, Indonesia; James T. Owens, Mexico; Lawrence Rice, Venezuela; Michael Simoneaux, Japan; J. Frederick Spann, North Brazil; James D. Watts, Italy; J. Conrad Willmon, Lebanon; Gene O. Wilson, South Brazil; and Ralph Yoars, Hong Kong. More than 200 additional missionaries are engaged in part-time music work.

The music missionary is normally appointed to one of two basic assignments, music promotion or teaching, but his actual activities are quite varied. Some have developed "pilot church" programs to demonstrate the possibilities of music. Other activities may include music camps, music journalism, music publication, and the use of music programs in mass communications.

A music missionary must acquire highly specialized techniques. In addition to the musical terminology of a new language, he must often learn a new system of notation. Sometimes he will learn to play strange or different instruments. Frequently he works with people who have never seen printed music, or with a style of singing that reflects a different culture. Many hymn-translations assume a Western theological background, and the missionary must learn to scrutinize the language of hymns in relation to a given culture. In tonal languages, a hymn may require a different melody for each stanza. Nevertheless, the balance-sheet reflects enormous success on the part of missionary musicians in the face of radical adjustments.

The sixties also saw a new impetus in the use of indigenous music. William O'Brien attained dramatic results with the use of Indonesian folksongs. In cooperation with the leading choreographer of modern Javanese and Balinese ballet, he explored the use of the ballet to express the Christian gospel. J. Conrad Willmon spearheaded the publication of an Arabic hymnal for the Middle East that included many indigenous tunes. In the Orient, a hymnal committee, with L. G. McKinney as chairman, completed a hymnal in Mandarin which included approximately 100 indigenous Chinese hymns—words and music.

The FMB has expanded the scope of its efforts in music. Concert tours by Christian artists have been of great benefit in mission areas. These concerts sometimes function as a wedge in transcultural communication to attract people normally hostile to Christian preaching; often they are evangelistic in nature. Musical performances were an integral part of the Japan New Life Crusade (1963), the Philippine Crusade (1968), and the Crusade of the Americas (1969). The FMB regularly appoints music workers in its Journeyman program, and the orientation of new missionaries usually includes a week of emphasis in music missions. Claude H. Rhea, Jr., served as Consultant in Church Music for the board, 1967–69.

An extensive program of research in the techniques of music in missions was begun in 1965 at Southwestern Baptist Theological Seminary. This resulted in the first course in the subject in a theological seminary in 1967. The Church Music Department of the Sunday School Board regularly includes classes in music missions during Church Music Leadership Conferences at Ridgecrest and Glorieta assemblies each summer.

A summary of world missionary opinion concerning the functions of music in missions includes the following: music allows the reticent and timid an expression of their faith in Christ; it has broken the barrier against women's participation in some cultures; it is valuable in enlisting children and youth; it is a useful medium for teaching theological concepts; it is especially effective in evangelistic crusades; and it has functional use in almost any sphere of mission effort. Missionary Bud Bickers (Malawi) states, "Music is vital as it is the one common expression readily understood and felt by all the people, regardless of language or education. It is a major key in developing new work."

THOMAS W. HUNT

MYERS, LEWIS ALEXANDER (b. Pinola, Miss., Mar. 19, 1893; d. Hot Springs, Ark., May 9, 1966). Editor, teacher, pastor, and author. Converted at a very early age (four years), he was baptized and leading prayer meetings at eight years of age, out-spelling his schoolmates at 10, and contributing an occasional article to the denominational paper at 12. He was educated at Mississippi College (A.B., 1915), University of Mississippi (LL.B., 1921), and Southwestern Baptist Theological Seminary (B.E., 1925; M.R.E., 1927). He served as editor of the Simpson County (Mississippi) *News,* 1920–23; *Southwestern Evangel,* 1925–30; *Arkansas Baptist,* 1937–43; *Word and Way,* 1945; and *Baptist New Mexican,* 1947–60. Myers taught in the School of Religious Education at Southwestern Seminary and was director of public relations of the same institution. Pastor in Tennessee and associate pastor of First Baptist Church in New Orleans, he was also a member of the Social Service Commission, Education Commission, and constitution revision committee of the Southern Baptist Convention. President of New Mexico Religious Liberty Association, he was a member of the Governor's Committee on Clean Literature (New Mexico). He served for four years in the Mississippi legislature and in both World Wars. He was a member of the Southern Baptist Encyclopedia Committee. He wrote *History of New Mexico Baptists* (1965).

HERBERT E. BERGSTROM

N

NATIONAL BAPTIST CONVENTION, USA, INC., FOREIGN MISSION BOARD. In 1967 this board listed six countries in Africa and one in Central America as their mission fields. However, there were missionaries under appointment to only Liberia and Malawi, the earliest fields entered. There were national workers in the others—Ghana, Lesotho, Nicaragua, Sierra Leone, and South Africa. Some institutional work was done in five of these countries. Sixteen missionaries were supported with an overseas work budget of $153,012 in 1967. In addition, $26,000 was spent in North America.

HELEN E. FALLS

NATIONAL BAPTISTS, HOME MISSION BOARD PROGRAM OF WORK WITH. The Southern Baptist Convention's relation to Negroes expressed through its Home Mission Board, continued to expand and to change in the name, nature, and organization of this work during 1956–69. The words "colored" and "Negro" have been used with individuals and groups of African ancestry. In 1959 the board changed the name of this work from the Department of Negro Work to the Department of Work with National Baptists.

The work included religious instruction, training ministers, extension classes, student work, evangelism, and general missionary work. This approach was usually direct, spotty, and to or for the Negro. Beginning in 1959, cooperative agreements with state conventions placed the work in the mainstream of state mission work and brought it into cooperative relations between state conventions and the board. "With" began to replace "help," "to," and "for." In this same year the board's organizational structure was changed, placing Work with National Baptists in the Division of Missions. In 1966 the Convention adopted the board's program statement which included this work as one of its 12 programs.

Expansion was reflected in budget and person-

MISSOURI BAPTIST BUILDING, Jefferson City, Mo. Converted downtown hotel building occupied in early spring, 1971, erected at cost of $2,000,000.

Top left: MISSOURI BAPTIST CHILDREN'S HOME (*q.v.*), Bridgeton, Mo. *Top right:* HOME FOR AGED BAPTISTS (*q.v.*), Ironton, Mo. Located in Arcadia Valley, Missouri Ozark Mountains, 100 miles south of St. Louis. *Center:* BAPTIST MEMORIAL HOSPITAL (*q.v.*), Kansas City, Mo. Began operations Jan., 1960. Valued at $9,000,000 with 375 beds. *Bottom:* WINDERMERE BAPTIST ASSEMBLY (*q.v.*), Roach, Mo. Located on Missouri's Lake of Ozarks, near Camdenton.

nel. In 1956 the budget was $135,000; in 1969, $508,000. Scholarship assistance to National Baptist students amounted to $3,925 in 1957; in 1969 this aid had increased to $30,000. A loan fund was set up in 1959 to aid National Baptist churches. Funds made available in 1960 helped establish a Chair of Bible, construct BSU buildings and educational centers, and provide state assembly grounds for National Baptists.

There have been growth and change in personnel. In 1956 one staff person and 58 missionaries were working in 16 states and the District of Columbia. In 1968 three staff persons and 98 missionaries were working in 27 states and the District of Columbia. Guy Bellamy, secretary of the department since 1949, retired in 1964 and was succeeded by Victor T. Glass, associate secretary since 1957. W. R. Grigg and Emmanuel McCall joined the staff as associates in 1966 and 1968 respectively. VICTOR T. GLASS

NAYLOR, GEORGE RUFUS (b. Coffman County, Tex., Sept. 6, 1869; d. Okla., Nov. 15, 1954). Minister and pioneer rural missionary in Oklahoma. He attended Celina Academy, Collin County, Tex., 1893–95. Ordained in Cook County, Tex., in 1898, he became pastor at Waggoner, I. T., in 1901. Following other Oklahoma pastorates, he was general field man for the Oklahoma state convention and the Home Mission Board, 1920–30. One year during this period he recorded 497 sermons, 265 people baptized, and over $30,000 raised for the missions enterprise. J. M. GASKIN

NEGRO BAPTISTS. See, also, ALABAMA NEGRO BAPTISTS.

NEGRO BAPTISTS IN TEXAS, WORK WITH. Under the auspices of the Home Mission Board a ministry to National Baptists was initiated. The Baptist General Convention of Texas staff increasingly was aware of the challenge and in cooperation with the HMB various ministries to Negro groups and individuals evolved. Because of the response of Texas Baptist and National Baptist leaders, as well as convention agencies, a formalized program and necessary personnel developed. This interest and activity precipitated the following convention action in 1968:

> The State Missions Commission should be encouraged to change the name of the "Program of Work with National Baptists" to read "The Program of Negro Missions"; and that the program objective be changed to read as follows: "The objective of the Program of Negro Missions is to assist churches and associations in their efforts to minister to Negroes."

The program is assigned to the Direct Missions Department and is directed by the secretary of the department. DARWIN FARMER

NEGROES. See NATIONAL BAPTISTS, HOME MISSION BOARD PROGRAM OF WORK WITH.

NELSON, DOTSON McGINNIS (b. Tallahatchie County, Miss., Dec. 18, 1880; d. Clinton, Miss., Oct. 26, 1962). A graduate of the Charleston, Miss., high school, Nelson entered Mississippi College and graduated there in 1907 as second honor man in his class, distinguishing himself as a debater and orator. Later in life he was frequently called "the silver-tongued orator of Mississippi." After teaching in the public schools of the state, he entered the University of Chicago for the study of law. Admitted to the state bar in 1910, he began the practice of law in Brookhaven, Miss., but left law practice to become assistant professor of chemistry at Mississippi College in 1911, transferring later to the department of physics. In 1914 he married Mary White of Brandon, Miss. They had two children: Dotson M., Jr., and Mary White. During World War I he served in the United States Army.

Because of the financial crisis facing the Baptist colleges of the state, Nelson was given a leave of absence from the college in 1921 to serve as executive secretary of the Mississippi Baptist Education Commission. He led in raising more than $1,000,000 for the Baptist colleges of his state. Nelson earned both Master's and Doctor's degrees in physics from Indiana University.

Following his work with the Education Commission, Nelson returned to the college in 1925 as professor of physics and head of that department. He was elected to the presidency of the college and began his service on June 1, 1932. Although the college was deeply in debt and without commercial credit, he managed its business affairs so ably that his first year ended without a deficit and continued that way throughout his 25 years as president. In 1942 he led the trustees to purchase Hillman College and thus made Mississippi College coeducational. Under his leadership the college experienced steady and sound growth in students, faculty, endowment, and physical facilities. The administration-classroom building on the campus bears his name, and one of the three new residence halls for women erected during his presidency bears the name of his wife.

HOWARD E. SPELL

NEW ENGLAND, SOUTHERN BAPTISTS IN. See MARYLAND, BAPTIST CONVENTION OF.

NEW HAMPSHIRE, SOUTHERN BAPTISTS IN. See MARYLAND, BAPTIST CONVENTION OF.

NEW JERSEY, SOUTHERN BAPTISTS IN. See MARYLAND, BAPTIST CONVENTION OF and NEW YORK, BAPTIST CONVENTION OF.

***NEW MEXICO, BAPTIST CONVENTION OF.** Among the most significant changes in the convention was the election of a new executive secretary. After serving as executive secretary for 30 years, Harry P. Stagg resigned, effective Jan. 31, 1968. He was succeeded by R. Y. Brad-

MRS. EUNICE HOYLAND

NEW MEXICO STATISTICAL SUMMARY

Year	Associations	Churches	Church Membership	Baptisms	S. S. Enrolment	V.B.S. Enrolment	T. U. Enrolment	W.M.U. Enrolment	Brotherhood Enrolment	Music Enrolment	Mission Gifts	Total Gifts	Value Church Property
1955	14	223	64,307	4,350	54,701	24,106	21,819	8,900	4,178		$ 582,053	$3,037,507	$10,646,103
1956	14	219	65,359	3,824	56,390	27,085	22,615	9,309	4,606		628,115	3,225,975	11,768,952
1957	15	234	69,008	3,991	58,119	26,927	23,835	9,338	3,601		648,364	3,547,399	12,785,305
1958	16	226	73,705	4,312	61,539	26,897	24,777	10,528	3,770		807,791	3,838,194	14,983,583
1959	18	248	76,161	4,285	61,327	27,301	25,346	11,028	3,384	4,183	761,229	4,050,814	16,724,288
1960	18	263	78,719	4,006	63,173	29,994	26,009	11,449	3,319	4,397	820,629	4,626,281	18,202,097
1961	18	247	81,036	4,268	62,693	30,897	25,824	11,299	3,340	4,633	848,283	4,637,829	20,124,546
1962	18	251	84,097	4,235	62,272	30,149	25,568	11,542	3,022	5,156	663,399	4,881,192	21,201,576
1963	17	246	86,310	3,611	62,283	31,004	25,600	11,470	3,403	6,236	869,621	5,165,166	23,151,728
1964	17	250	87,751	3,565	60,926	30,074	25,213	11,385	2,684	6,851	899,739	4,994,476	24,947,412
1965	17	247	90,088	3,612	60,106	29,717	23,987	11,012	2,803	6,912	912,392	5,208,661	25,464,138
1966	17	254	90,402	3,256	57,227	27,743	23,238	10,219	4,184	6,915	925,321	4,763,754	26,376,328
1967	16	252	89,588	3,615	56,034	28,088	22,175	9,899	4,043	7,316	989,232	5,491,612	28,315,150
1968	16	253	91,633	3,067	54,294	27,447	21,473	9,590	4,067	7,246	1,058,012	5,783,849	28,554,143

ford, pastor of First Baptist Church, Sante Fe. During the Stagg period, the membership increased 600 per cent, staff members increased nearly 700 per cent, convention worth increased over 1,000 per cent, and Cooperative Program receipts increased over 4,000 per cent.

Other resignations during this period included Eva Inlow (1961), who resigned as executive secretary of Woman's Missionary Union after serving 26 years; Bernice Elliott (1961), who resigned as New Mexico WMU youth director after serving 17½ years; W. J. Lites (*q.v.*), resigned in 1961 as Sunday School secretary after serving 17 years; Truett Sheriff (1967), as director of the Student Department after serving 11 years; Alton Green (1967), as secretary of evangelism, after serving eight years; and Horace Burns (1966), as editor of the *Baptist New Mexican* after serving seven years.

Circulation of the *Baptist New Mexican* reached an all-time high during the period 1956–70, as 96 per cent of the Baptist families in the state were subscribers of this publication. This percentage exceeded any other state publication in the Southern Baptist Convention.

The convention acquired property near Cloudcroft for a Royal Ambassador camp in Jan., 1963, and made several improvements on this property.

The funds in the New Mexico Baptist Foundation has grown significantly. W. C. Ribble was elected as executive secretary-treasurer of the foundation, Sept. 1, 1959, and under his leadership the foundation grew in influence and funds. This fund exceeded $1,000,000, much of which was loaned to Baptist churches in New Mexico for their building programs. This money is loaned through the New Mexico Baptist Church Loan Cooperation.

Mr. and Mrs. Walker C. Hubbard were recognized during the meeting of the state convention in Clovis, Nov., 1966, upon the completion of 30 years as superintendent and matron of the Baptist Children's Home, Portales. They continue to serve in these capacities.

In Nov., 1962, the convention commemorated its 50th anniversary in conjunction with its annual meeting in Roswell. Several Convention-wide leaders were on hand to aid in this historic meeting.

It was with regret that the executive board voted to close the Parkview Medical Center, effective June 30, 1963. This center, which first opened its doors in 1952 with such a great promise, had experienced much difficulty in obtaining and retaining competent medical help to operate the center. The financial investment had also exceeded the expectations of the convention, and the center had been without a physician for periods of time including one long period of time, 1958–60.

HERBERT E. BERGSTROM

*NEW MEXICO ASSOCIATIONS.

I. New Associations. MOUNTAIN VALLEY. Formed in 1962 when Lincoln and Otero associations disbanded. In 1969, 19 churches reported 224 baptisms, 4,896 members, $306,524 total gifts, and $55,929 mission gifts.

North Pecos Valley. Organized in 1956 out of Pecos Valley Association. In 1969, 23 churches reported 268 baptisms, 10,662 members, $546,398 total gifts, and $81,142 mission gifts.

Santa Fe. Formerly Atomic, the name was changed in 1955. In 1969, 12 churches reported 92 baptisms, 2,866 members, $297,455 total gifts, and $49,263 mission gifts.

South Pecos Valley. Formed in 1956 out of Pecos Valley Association. In 1969, 12 churches reported 133 baptisms, 5,135 members, $309,664 total gifts, and $55,987 mission gifts.

Western. Organized in 1958. In 1969, 8 churches reported 96 baptisms, 2,120 members, $217,337 total gifts, and $17,091 mission gifts.

II. Changes in Associations. Atomic. Disbanded in 1955 to form the Santa Fe Association.

Lee. Organized in 1958, it disbanded in 1966.

Lincoln. In 1955 Lincoln became Lincoln-Otero. In 1957 Lincoln again became a separate association and Otero became an association. In 1962 the Lincoln and Otero associations disbanded and formed the Mountain Valley Association.

Pecos Valley. Disbanded in 1956. Churches affiliated with the North Pecos Valley and South Pecos Valley associations.

HERBERT E. BERGSTROM

NEW MEXICO BAPTIST STUDENT WORK (cf. New Mexcio Bible Chairs, Vol. II). Three new student centers were constructed in New Mexico, 1957–70: Western New Mexico University, Silver City (1957); New Mexico State University, Las Cruces (1960); and New Mexico Highlands University, Las Vegas (1964). The center at the University of New Mexico, Albuquerque, was removed by the city of Albuquerque for street improvement. Property adjacent to the old center was purchased in 1964 to relocate the center.

In 1970 there were five full-time campus ministers (Baptist Student Union Directors) located at Eastern New Mexico University, University of New Mexico, New Mexico State University, Western New Mexico University, and New Mexico Highlands University. These men also serve as teachers in the Chairs of Bible. The chair at Eastern New Mexico University is accredited by the school in Portales; the others are accredited by Hardin-Simmons University in Abilene, Tex.

All campuses experienced changes in personnel, as well as the secretary of the department of student work. In 1970 there were three men holding Th.D. degrees, one with a Th.M., one with two M.A.'s and a B.D., and one with a B.D. degree. In addition to their teaching responsibilities, which must be maintained at an acceptable academic level, these men supervise the student organizations (BSU, International Student ministry, and Baptist Faculty fellowships) and spend many hours counseling students.

BRYCE SANDLIN

***NEW ORLEANS BAPTIST THEOLOGICAL SEMINARY.** The decade and a half from 1955 to 1970 produced a multiplicity of changes both in the external environment and internal structure of the New Orleans Baptist Theological Seminary. Not only did the surrounding metropolitan area expand rapidly from about 750,000 to considerably over 1,000,000 residents, but adjacent areas which had ready access to the city by means of more adequate transportation arteries experienced similar growth. Government facilities involved in space research, strategic industrial developments, a branch of the state university enrolling over 10,000 students, and numerous cultural attractions contributed to the number and character of the growth. Many of the newer residents migrated from areas representing Southern Baptist strength. This factor, coupled with an aggressive Baptist witness through the churches of the New Orleans Association and other agencies such as the Seminary, Hospital, or Home Mission Board ministries supported by the Southern Baptist Convention produced substantial Baptist progress in the city. About 20 additional churches emerged and membership increased from less than 25,000 to about 42,000.

Personnel changes.—The seminary, likewise, experienced change. President Roland Q. Leavell (*q.v.*) guided the institution until May 1, 1958, when his request for retirement was approved following a serious illness. Named president-emeritus by the trustees, Leavell completed an active administration that involved moving to a new campus, organizing the academic program into distinct schools, gaining additional accreditation, and providing for a rapidly expanding faculty and student body.

For about a year between the illness of Leavell and the arrival of a new president, professor J. Washington Watts served as acting president. Having taught at the institution since 1931 and served in a similar capacity between previous administrations, Watts knew from personal experience both the problems and opportunities facing the school. His annual report to the SBC (1958) reflected the abounding optimism which characterized the seminary and the denomination during the late fifties. At that time the seminary reported 39 faculty members and a previous year's enrolment of 1,087. The acting president noted that construction of a seminary chapel would begin immediately. Five goals for the next decade anticipated additional funds for endowment and buildings, increases in student enrolment, faculty personnel, and library holdings, and adoption of a three-semester academic session.

Under the able leadership of Watts, the seminary proceeded with projects already in progress and initiated others that appeared feasible. This insured a relatively smooth transition when the trustees elected H. Leo Eddleman as the school's fifth president. Widely known among Southern Baptists, Eddleman accepted the New Orleans challenge, thereby terminating almost five years as president of Georgetown College, Georgetown, Ky. Former experience included the pastorate of Parkland Avenue Baptist Church, Louisville, Ky., a professorship in Old Testament and Hebrew at Southern Baptist Theological Seminary, and a term of missionary service in Palestine. The president-elect assumed his duties on Feb. 1, 1959, and was officially inaugurated on Feb. 26, 1959, in ceremonies involving participation by three past presidents. Provided with new leadership and undergirded by a national resurgence of interest in religion, the seminary faced the future with confidence.

President Eddleman reported to the Convention in May, 1959, that he found at New Orleans "an efficient working organization and the effective teaching staff highly productive for Southern Baptists." Noting the virtual completion of the chapel and a dormitory for men, he outlined future goals similar to those previously mentioned. "The world's problems are basically theological," he observed, "and Southern Baptists are wise to maintain and expand Bible-centered seminaries for training the leaders of both today and tomorrow." Eddleman participated in this task at New Orleans for 11 years before submitting his resignation, with Feb. 28, 1970, as the effective date. The trustees named James D. Mosteller as acting president during the interim period.

Faculty personnel who signed the *Articles of Religious Belief* on attaining faculty status from Sept., 1957, to Dec., 1969, included the following: Robert R. Soileau, Thomas L. Tedford, Joan Stockstill, Harold L. Rutledge, H. Leo Eddleman, Vernon Latrelle Stanfield, George Collins Herndon, Clifford E. Tucker, William A. Mueller, William H. Souther, Claude L. Howe, Jr., George W. Harrison, Donald W. Minton, A. Ray Baker, Kenneth R. Hartley, Samuel J. Mikolaski, Malcolm W. Tolbert, William L. Hooper, William W. Adams, Leonard L. Holloway, James D. Belote, Harry Eskew, Clark Pinnock, Clyde R. Walker, Hermon V. Warford, Jr., James A. Brooks, Eugene N. Patterson, Mrs. Mildred E. Souther, James D. Mosteller, Randall Veazey, Joe H. Cothen, George L. Kelm, and Paul W. Gericke. In 1969, 22 of these individuals remained at New Orleans, comprising over half of the regular faculty strength of the seminary.

Student enrolment fluctuated slightly throughout the 15 years under consideration, generally suggesting trends toward expansion during the earlier years followed by tendencies evidencing a leveling process. Declining religious interests in the colleges, local conditions including two serious hurricanes and a campus rehabilitation program, and upgraded academic requirements seemingly affected the enrolment at points. Average cumulative enrolment during the 1959–69 decade totaled 938 students, fluctuating from 1,004 students in 1960–61, to 861 in 1965–66.

Academic adjustments.—Another area characterized by change, especially during the sixties, was the academic program of the seminary. From 1956 to 1958, students without college degrees enrolled in the School of Christian Training, where they received separate instruction and appropriate diplomas from a faculty directed by Thomas J. Delaughter. After that time such students enrolled on a limited basis in the other three schools and attended regular seminary classes.

The School of Theology received its first dean on Aug. 1, 1959, with the appointment of faculty member J. Hardee Kennedy to that position. Kennedy guided the school through a crucial decade before resuming classroom responsibilities on a full-time basis. James D. Mosteller was appointed as his successor beginning June 1, 1969.

Former directors of the other two schools were designated also as deans in 1959, which produced a uniform structure with three schools under separate deans that remained unaltered from that time. John M. Price, Jr., continued to lead the School of Religious Education. W. Plunkett Martin (*q.v.*) was succeeded, however, by Claude Rhea (1960–63), and William L. Hooper was appointed dean of the School of Church Music after the latter resigned.

Early in 1963 President Eddleman conferred with the faculty about the possibility of the seminary gaining accreditation in the Southern Association of Colleges and Schools. An intensive institutional self-study followed that provided the additional accreditation on Dec. 1, 1965. The National Association of Schools of Music approved the School of Church Music for membership on Nov. 21, 1966. The entire seminary retained its previous membership in the American Association of Theological Schools following the periodic self-study and visitation in 1969. Academic adjustments instituted often resulted from positive suggestions produced by these and related studies.

The seminary adopted a revised statement of purpose in 1965. Each school examined its subsidiary purposes and evaluated its program in light of the institutional statement. The revision cited below appears in each annual *Bulletin*.

> The primary purpose of New Orleans Baptist Theological Seminary is to provide quality instruction at the graduate level in theology, religious education, and church music. The curricula and activities are designed to aid in developing spiritually mature leaders who are intellectually informed, vocationally skilled, and compassionately committed for Evangelical-Christian ministries in the modern world. The aim of the Seminary is to inspire missionary and benevolent activities, incite research and writing, and provide numerous consultative and advisory services, thereby fulfilling its responsibility as an academic community, a denominational agency, and a fellowship of faith.
>
> The program of instruction is to be biblical in orientation and relevant in application. Confessional commitments of the seminary are centered in Jesus Christ as Savior of believers and Lord of life, through

his death and resurrection, and in the Bible as the inspired Word of God.

The Seminary provides six graduate degree programs and diploma courses for students without college prerequisites. Each school offers the Master's degree as the first professional degree. The School of Theology revised its curriculum structure in 1966 and adopted the Master of Theology instead of the Bachelor of Divinity as the standard theological degree following a three year course of study. The other two schools sought to strengthen and extend their graduate offerings. The Master of Religious Education and Church Music degrees require two years for completion, but both schools have instituted a third year of study leading to the Specialist in Education degree. The Doctor of Education degree has also been awarded since 1967 by these schools for qualified candidates. The latter degree replaced a previously existing program in the School of Religious Education, but it represents an entirely new area of offerings in the School of Church Music. The School of Theology retained previous terminology for its highest advanced degree, but procedures and requirements involved in the program were analyzed and adjusted from time to time.

The stated purpose of providing quality education at the graduate level motivated not only the curriculum changes noted but a consistent concentration upon expanding the library resources of the seminary. Aided financially by the Sealantic fund, additional seminary appropriations, and designated gifts the library acquired over 50,000 books and bound periodicals within a decade, increasing the total holdings by 1968 to 108,000 volumes. The Robert G. Lee Reading Room in the library building contains the large personal collection of this popular pastor and evangelist, while the Martin Music Library housed in the E. O. Sellers (*q.v.*, Vol. II) building contains a valuable specialized collection of over 6,000 books and 7,000 other musical pieces. Additional trained personnel were added to the library staff, and plans were projected for another library building that would provide more adequate facilities for utilization and expansion.

The establishment of two additional lectureships provided participants an opportunity for sharing insights in specialized areas. The J. Thomas Gurney Evangelism lectures originated in 1960 as an annual series, while the Carver-Barnes Lectures delivered initially in 1962 rotate among the Southern Baptist seminaries. The first series considers varied aspects of evangelism, and the second focuses attention upon distinctive Baptist emphases.

Physical resources.—The annual operating budget of the seminary expanded substantially during the period, deriving funds primarily from the Cooperative Program of the Convention but also from student fees, endowment investments, designated gifts, and auxiliary enterprises. The Board of Development created by the trustees in 1961 served in implementing seminary projects, concentrating especially upon raising funds for a new library building. Concurrently the Women's Auxiliary provided contributions for student scholarships. The seminary foundation accepted as a major responsibility the securing and managing of endowment funds, which were augmented by several special appeals including an Anniversary Campaign conducted by a professional organization.

Additional buildings constructed on the campus enlarged available seminary services and increased student and faculty housing. The Roland Q. Leavell Chapel was dedicated and a gymnasium completed in 1959. Almost a decade later the Baptist Book Store relocated into spacious new facilities, providing vacated space for campus printing operations. Seminary personnel benefitted also from a trailer park (1961) and a commissary (1968) conveniently accessible. Hamilton Hall (1959), a dormitory for men, and Willingham Manor (1961), an apartment complex, provided comfortable student housing as did the three-storied apartment building erected (1966) for larger families. Several faculty residences were constructed as needs arose, for most faculty members resided on the campus throughout the period under consideration.

A major campus rehabilitation program required much attention after 1963. Following a series of surveys and recommendations by prominent architectural firms, the SBC in 1964 allocated $1,600,000 distributed over a three year period for the project. Specifications included installing a drainage system throughout the campus, utilizing waterproofing techniques on certain buildings, replacing sidewalks and water services, and repairing several buildings, streets, and parking areas. Although delayed at times by adverse weather conditions and other factors, the program progressed toward completion and terminated before the end of the decade.

The 75-acre campus at 3939 Gentilly Boulevard favorably impresses both local personnel and visitors because of its beautiful and functional qualities as a theological institution. Individuals involved in numerous ways with the affairs of the seminary possess a genuine sense of gratitude for the role that all Southern Baptists have played in founding and supporting the "School of Providence and Prayer."

Additional ministries.—The most significant contributions of the seminary continued to be reflected in the activities of its capable and loyal alumni, who served in many responsible positions around the world. The majority of these fulfilled pastoral, educational, or musical functions within local churches, though a growing number taught in educational institutions or ministered in other ways. A report in 1969 indicated that one out of every 11 degree graduates of the institution had been appointed to foreign mission service. Among the 382 graduates or former students appointed for such service in 58 areas of the world, 279 were still serving in that capacity.

A creative faculty likewise contributed regularly toward an enlarged educational outreach through books, articles, and personal contacts, as well as by sponsoring special occasions on the campus. An annual Pastors Conference stressing Bible study, worship, and discussion of contemporary issues became an established feature after the first in 1962. Specialized workshops for religious education or music personnel almost always appeared on the calendar of events, as did additional emphases such as conferences for evangelists or laymen.

The seminary celebrated its 50th anniversary Oct. 3–6, 1967, looking carefully at the past and anticipating the future. William A. Mueller was commissioned to write the seminary history, and an *Anniversary Bulletin* containing the significant addresses of the week received wide circulation. The latter publication suggested that the institution needed a theological journal, and possibility became reality in Oct., 1969, with the launching of *The Theological Educator* by the administration and faculty. Ample evidence indicated at the close of the decade that the New Orleans Seminary responsibly fulfilled the role cited in its statement of purpose as an academic community, a denominational agency, and a fellowship of faith.

BIBLIOGRAPHY: Mueller, William A., *The School of Providence and Prayer: A History of the New Orleans Baptist Theological Seminary* (1969).

CLAUDE L. HOWE, JR.

NEW YORK, BAPTIST CONVENTION OF. I. Southern Baptist Beginnings in New York. Nearly a complete decade was required to develop strength for organizing the Baptist Convention of New York in the fall of 1969. The Northeastern Baptist Association, affiliated with the Baptist Convention of Maryland, was organized in Apr., 1960, by five churches. These were the Delaware Valley Church in Levittown, Pa.; the Madison Baptist Church in Madison, N. J.; the Manhattan Baptist Church in New York City; the Park Church in Irvington, N. J.; and the Screven Memorial Church in Portsmouth, N. H. These churches at the time of forming the association sponsored six chapels. A planning meeting was held in Portsmouth, N. H., on Feb. 22, 1960, looking toward the organizing of an association. On Apr. 29, in New York City, the association was formed.

On Aug. 29 and 30, 1960, the Northeastern Regional Fellowship met at Manhattan Baptist Church in sessions sponsored by the Maryland and Ohio conventions. The Northeastern region included the states of Maine, New Hampshire, Vermont, Massachusetts, Rhode Island, Connecticut, New York, Pennsylvania, New Jersey, and Delaware. The purpose of the meeting was to develop a spirit of unity among the members of the new churches and chapels over this wide area.

A second meeting of the Northeastern Association was held in Wrightstown, N. J., Oct. 19 and 20, 1962, and the second meeting of the Northeastern Regional Fellowship was held May 20 and 21, 1963, at the First Southern Baptist Church in Syracuse, N. Y. Present for this meeting were 120 interested persons, and a committee was appointed which brought the recommendations to the body that the Regional Fellowship meet one year hence, that regional officers be elected by nomination from the floor, and that special committees be established looking toward the possible formation of a regional convention.

The next meeting of the Regional Fellowship was in Levittown, Pa., May 1, 1964, when it was determined that the geographical area was too large and that smaller fellowship units would be desired. In Sept., 1965, the New York-Northern New Jersey Area Fellowship met in Rome, N. Y. A Regional Fellowship Meeting was held in Tonawanda, N. Y., in Sept., 1966, and at an historic meeting in Boston, Sept. 22 and 23, 1967, it was determined that the churches in the six New England States would work together in some sort of organizational pattern and that the churches in New York State, Northern New Jersey, and Southwestern Connecticut would look toward forming their own convention. The New England churches have since formed the Baptist General Association of New England and divided their work into three associations.

Largely attended meetings of the representatives of New York, northern New Jersey, and southwestern Connecticut churches were held in Endicott, N. Y., in the spring of 1968 and at Brooklyn, N. Y., in the fall of 1968. David Morgan, Brooklyn pastor, served as the first president of the Baptist Fellowship of New York. In the September meeting at the Brooklyn Church, Paul James, who had served as the first president of the Northeastern Regional Fellowship and first moderator of the Metropolitan New York Baptist Association, was elected to succeed David Morgan. When James resigned this office to become executive secretary of the new convention, he was succeeded by Hartmon Sullivan of Niagara Falls.

II. Convention Organized. On Sept. 29, 1969, 333 people met in Central Baptist Church, Syracuse, to constitute the Baptist Convention of New York as the 31st Baptist state convention to be affiliated with the Southern Baptist Convention. This convention was organized with 70 churches, 27 chapels, and 10,494 members. The theme of the constituting convention was "Born to Serve." The new Convention elected Paul S. James as executive secretary-treasurer of the new convention and John M. Tubbs as director of the division of education. It also adopted a budget of $422,060 for 1970 when the convention actually began its full operations Jan. 1. Of this budget, 15 per cent was for Southern Baptist world mission causes. The convention elected Kenneth Lyle of Westbury, N. Y., president and established its headquarters in a modern office building in downtown Syracuse.

III. Chronology of Churches in the New York Area. Manhattan Baptist Church was the first Southern Baptist Church organized in New York

City. Organized on Jan. 10, 1958, it was formerly a chapel of College Avenue Church, Annapolis, Md. From 1958 until May 12, 1962, all new Southern Baptist churches organized in the area were chapels of Manhattan Church. Other Southern Baptist churches that were organized between 1958–69 in the New York area are as follows:

In 1960: Screven Memorial, Portsmouth, N. H. (Feb. 22) ; Delaware Valley, Levittown, Pa. (Mar. 20) ; and Madison, Madison, N. J. (May 1) .

In 1961: Farmingdale, Farmingdale, N. Y. (Jan. 1) ; Champlain Valley, Plattsburg, N. Y. (Mar. 17) ; Emmanuel, Springfield, Mass. (Mar. 18) ; Hartford, Hartford, Conn. (Aug. 26) ; Ridgecrest, Newburgh, N. Y. (Sept. 1) ; Pleasant Valley, New London, Conn. (Nov. 17) ; and First, Brooklyn, N. Y. (Dec. 15) .

In 1962: Suburban, Pompton Lakes, N. J. (Mar. 11) ; Vassar Road, Poughkeepsie, N. Y. (May 12) , formerly chapel of Manhattan and Ridgecrest churches; and Bergen, Westwood, N. J. (Sept. 9) , formerly chapel of Manhattan Church.

In 1963: Raritan Valley, Edison, N. J. (Mar. 10) , formerly chapel of Madison Church; Greenwich, Greenwich, Conn. (Apr. 27) , formerly chapel of Manhattan Church; Emmanuel, Riverhead, N. Y. (July 14) , formerly chapel of Farmingdale Church; and Central Nassau, East Meadow, N. Y. (Sept. 30) , formerly chapel of Farmingdale Church.

In 1964: Highland Avenue, Jamaica, N. Y. (June 8) , formerly chapel of Manhattan Church; First Spanish of Manhattan, New York City (July 26) , formerly chapel of Manhattan Church; and Monmouth, Eatontown, N. J. (Sept. 17) , formerly chapel of Raritan Valley Church.

In 1965: Evangel, Bronx, N. Y. (July 9) , formerly chapel of First Church, Brooklyn; and Nazareth, West New York, N. J. (Sept. 26) , formerly chapel of Bergen Church.

In 1966: North Shore, Kings Park, N. Y. (Jan. 8) , formerly chapel of Farmingdale Church; French, Brooklyn, N. Y. (June 19) , formerly chapel of First Church, Brooklyn; and Bronx, New York City (Nov. 6) , formerly chapel of First Church, Brooklyn.

In 1967: Terrill Road, Scotch Plains, N. J. (Apr. 9) , formerly chapel of Madison Church; First Spanish, Passaic, N. J. (June 10) , formerly chapel of Nazareth Church; Central Spanish, Paterson, N. J. (July 29) , formerly chapel of Bergen Church; Westchester, Hartsdale, N. Y. (Nov. 19) , formerly chapel of Greenwich Church; and Wilton, Wilton, Conn. (Dec. 10) , formerly chapel of Greenwich Church.

In 1968: Grace, Lake Grove, N. Y. (Jan. 21) , formerly chapel of Emmanuel Church; Park Slope, Brooklyn, N. Y. (Apr. 7) , formerly chapel of Highland Avenue Church; First Spanish, Hoboken, N. J. (Apr. 14) , formerly chapel of Nazareth Church; Richboro, Staten Island, N. Y. (May 26) , formerly chapel of Manhattan Church; Patmos, New York City (June 28) , formerly chapel of First Church, Brooklyn; Calvary, Medford Station, N. Y. (July 14) , formerly chapel of Emmanuel Church; Calvary Spanish, Brooklyn, N. Y. (Aug. 11) , formerly chapel of First Church, Brooklyn; and Southside, Kingston, N. Y. (Sept. 21) , formerly chapel of Ridgecrest and Vassar Road churches.

In 1969: Ebenezer Spanish, Elmhurst, N. Y. (Mar. 15) , formerly chapel of Highland Avenue Church; Bethlehem Spanish, Elizabeth, N. J. (Mar. 30) , formerly chapel of Nazareth Church; Emmanuel Spanish, Newark, N. J. (Sept. 13) , formerly chapel of Bethlehem and Nazareth churches; Twin County, Kendall Park, N. J. (Sept. 20) , formerly chapel of Westchester Church; Calvary, Matawan, N. J. (Sept. 21) , formerly chapel of Monmouth Church; Somerset Hills, Bernardsville, N. J. (Sept. 21) , formerly chapel of Madison Church; Hope, Roxbury, N. J. (Sept. 23) , formerly chapel of Madison Church; and Hackensack Spanish, Hackensack, N. J. (Sept. 24) , formerly chapel of Nazareth Church.

In addition to those above, other churches, children and grandchildren of these, have been organized in the New England and Delaware Valley areas. The following churches in the Metropolitan New York Baptist Association were organized separately from the above: First Polish, Brooklyn, N. Y., 1932, and Zion Temple, Richmond Hill, N. Y., 1961. PAUL S. JAMES

NEW YORK, BAPTIST STUDENT WORK IN. Efforts toward the establishment of a student ministry within the present Baptist Convention of New York began when Baptist students at Princeton University, Princeton Seminary, and Westminster Choir College formed a large fellowship there in the late forties. Although it was led largely by Southern Baptist students and sought Southern Baptist help, denominational agencies at the time felt that they could not assist the group. This fellowship did stir interest in a student ministry in the Northeast, but unfortunately the group had virtually ceased to exist before that interest bore fruit.

In the spring of 1959, Jimmy Hartfield, state student worker for the Baptist Convention of Maryland, surveyed several schools in New York City but because it was so late in the school year did not attempt to begin a student ministry. In the fall Gene Maston, formerly a student worker in Louisiana and the leader in establishing student work in Chicago, came to Columbia University as a graduate student. He had already been interested in the Princeton group and agreed to work with students in New York on a volunteer basis. In Nov., 1959, he and his wife entertained the students who were members of the Manhattan Baptist Church in their home, and from this occasion there came the first Baptist Student Union in the Northeast in Feb., 1960. It was composed of both graduate and undergraduate students from a number of schools in the city and met monthly for discussions and fellowship. Through the cooperation of the academy chaplain and the efforts of one cadet, Odus Elliott, a second BSU was established at the United States Military Academy at West Point in Feb., 1961.

In May, 1961, the Maryland convention in cooperation with the Northeastern Baptist Association and with funds from the Sunday School Board appointed Maston to serve as full-time director of student work in the New York City area. That fall his work was enlarged to include all the northeastern states, and through this enlarged ministry, student work was begun at Harvard University, Massachusetts Institute of Technology, the United States Coast Guard Academy, and Yale University over the next few years.

In New York, largely through the work of two students, Bethlyn Bates and Ronnie Parelman, a BSU was organized at Vassar College in Mar., 1962, and the following fall the New York City group divided to form both an undergraduate and a graduate group. In Mar., 1965, students from the University of Syracuse in the Central Baptist Church of Syracuse, led by Lomita Hudnall, formed yet another BSU. In all these ministries a number of students who were not Southern Baptists or were not Christians were active participants.

After several years of negotiations between representatives of the Maryland convention, the Metropolitan New York Association, and the Sunday School and Home Mission boards, a second full-time worker was secured. In July, 1966, Caby Byrne came to direct student work at West Point as well as the United States Merchant Marine Academy on Long Island and the Coast Guard Academy. In the fall of 1967 Margaret Eakin found work in New York City and moved there in order to serve as a volunteer worker with international students at Columbia University. The following fall Albert and Betty Jo Bell came as US-2 workers to direct the student work in Syracuse. After Gene Maston resigned as regional director in the summer of 1968, his responsibilities were divided, and Ray Gilliland, formerly state student worker in Kansas, came in Feb., 1969, to direct Baptist student work in New York City. With the establishment of the Baptist Convention of New York in the fall of 1969, John Tubbs, along with other responsibilities, became the first director of state student work for the new convention.

GENE MASTON

NEW YORK, METROPOLITAN, BAPTIST ASSOCIATION. One of three associations formed from the Northeastern Baptist Association, the Metropolitan New York Baptist Association held its organizational meeting Oct. 20, 1962, at First Baptist Church, Wrightstown, N. J., after the final session of the Northeastern Association. Paul James, the first moderator, presided at this meeting of 40 messengers representing 1,285 members of eight churches: Bergen, Madison, and Suburban of New Jersey; Farmingdale, First (Brooklyn), Manhattan, Ridgecrest, and Vassar Road of New York. The associational office, originally located in the Manhattan Church building, was moved to its present location, 330 West 58th Street, New York City, in 1966. From this office, the area of the association extends approximately 100 miles in all directions, covering 31 counties where 20,000,000 people live in New York, New Jersey, and Connecticut.

In 1963, James was appointed Metropolitan New York area director by the Home Mission Board, SBC. He served the association in this capacity until he became executive secretary-treasurer of the New York Baptist Convention in 1969.

By 1969, the association had grown to 42 churches. The 1968 reports showed 5,919 church members in 34 churches, 5,418 enrolled in Sunday School, 1,770 in Training Union, 1,282 in WMU, 544 in Brotherhood, and 928 in Music Ministries. During the first six years, 2,003 persons were baptized.

The association was affiliated with the Baptist Convention of Maryland from its organization in 1962 until the end of 1969 when it became part of the Baptist Convention of New York.

Associational ministries include work with American and international students in several institutions; camps for Juniors and Young People each summer; retreats, rallies, and music programs for youth; a retreat for ministers each winter; and financial assistance for missions and pastors where it is needed. Other ministries include church-type chapels (missions), missions in high rise apartment buildings in New York City, educational work in Harlem, a Christian youth hostel in New York City, youth centers, and migrant work among Spanish-speaking people and Negroes in the Hudson Valley and on Long Island. Many churches and missions in the association conduct services in either French, Japanese, Polish, Portuguese, or Spanish.

Southern Baptists have supported the work of the association through the HMB and through individual churches. The Nashville Baptist Association adopted Metropolitan New York as sister association in 1963 and has assisted in many ways including cash gifts to churches, arranging for loans and bond sales, and sending individuals and busloads of people for evangelistic work and Vacation Bible Schools. Other churches throughout the Convention have also provided similar assistance to churches and missions in the association. This support has contributed much to the growth of this "pioneer" mission work.

Ken Lyle became superintendent of missions of the Metropolitan Baptist Association in Jan., 1970.

HARRY WATSON

NEW YORK, N. Y., MANHATTAN BAPTIST CHURCH. Manhattan Baptist Church had its beginning in the fall of 1956 when James Aaron came with his family to New York City as a graduate student at New York University.

Finding no church which satisfied them, the Aaron family sought out other Southern Baptists who might share their feelings. On Feb. 3, 1957, they and John Moore met with Ray Roberts, executive secretary of the Southern Baptist convention of Ohio, to discuss the establishment of a Southern Baptist work in New York City. In the following weeks they found other interested Southern Baptists, and on May 7, 1957, began Sunday morning worship services at the McBurney YMCA on West 23rd St. They soon secured Huber Drumwright, then studying at Princeton Seminary, to preach for them. The College Avenue Baptist Church at Annapolis, Md., much closer than any of the Ohio churches, adopted the group as its mission on July 21, 1957, and thus began the long involvement of Maryland Baptists in Southern Baptist work in the Northeast.

In August the fellowship group called Paul James, pastor of the Baptist Tabernacle in Atlanta, Ga., to be their pastor, and at the same time the Home Mission Board appointed him as the director of all board work in the Northeast. He began his dual responsibilities the first Sunday of Nov., 1957.

At the Hotel New Yorker, on Jan. 10, 1958, the mission was constituted into the Manhattan Baptist Church with 99 charter members. Two months later the church moved to a new meeting place at the New York Center, a Seventh Day Adventist church on West 46th St. During its first year as a church the membership doubled, and in Mar., 1959, the church moved once again, this time to a church facility in an apartment building at 311 West 57th St., which had a worshipful Gothic auditorium and considerable office and educational space. Substantial financial help from the HMB made possible the rental of this building for the next 10 years.

Meanwhile the church began to establish missions, and on Feb. 22, 1960, Screven Memorial Church at Portsmouth, N. H., was the first of these to become a church. Since that time 15 other missions sponsored wholly by the church and two sponsored jointly with other churches have become churches. While some of these were quite distant from the church, nine were in New York City or nearby, and to each of these the church gave leaders and members from among its own active membership. Each of these missions has played a key role in the development of Southern Baptists throughout the Northeast. The four oldest churches in the New England General Association were missions of the church, as was the first Southern Baptist work in the Philadelphia area, out of which grew the Delaware Valley Baptist Association and eventually part of the Pennsylvania state convention. Two of the first churches in the language ministry in New York were missions of the church along with two churches in upstate New York, and almost every church in the Metropolitan New York Baptist Association was either a mission of Manhattan Church or is directly descended from it.

Because the work was expanding James resigned as pastor, effective Dec. 15, 1963, to devote full time to his other job as director of work in the Metropolitan association. During the next 18 months two interim pastors, both studying at Princeton Seminary, led the church: Peter Rhea Jones, and James W. Cox. In May, 1965, Maurice Fain came as pastor from the Napoleon Avenue Baptist Church, New Orleans, La., and remained until July 31, 1967. During that time the church began a ministry to the deaf, and under the leadership of Buryl Red continued development of its widely regarded music ministry.

Since Fain's resignation the church has had two interim pastors, Denton Lotz and William M. Pinson, both visiting scholars at Union Seminary. During this period a music and drama group has made films and recordings to be used in both evangelistic outreach and missionary education. The church has begun a ministry to foreign speaking people with a Bible class and translation of the worship services into Japanese and with plans for a similar ministry in other languages. It has augmented its work among the deaf by employing a part-time minister to the deaf. Members of the church choir have assisted in making recordings for music periodicals published by the Church Music Department of the Sunday School Board, SBC, since 1964. Because rent on the old building was more than doubled, the church moved again in Feb., 1969, this time to rented quarters in the Church Center for the United Nations at 44th St., and First Ave. As in the past the church continues to draw a highly diverse membership. In turn it has sent over 2,400 of its members not only to establish missions in the Northeast but to places of lay and professional religious leadership throughout the world. GENE MASTON

NEW YORK, RELIGIOUS EDUCATION IN THE BAPTIST CONVENTION OF. Religious education has played a vital role in the development of Southern Baptist churches in the Northeast. The new churches are built around Bible study. The typical congregation began as a home fellowship Bible study group. A fully graded Sunday School is organized when the mission chapel begins Sunday worship services. Often interested families are located during mission Vacation Bible Schools in unchurched communities, and a church grows out of the nucleus thus gathered.

While Sunday School has traditionally been the evangelistic arm of the church, in the Northeast persons are often enlisted in Sunday School following their initial involvement in worship services and church membership.

Congregations quickly recognize the need for a church training program. Some chapels have begun with Training Union and Sunday evening worship services, while members continued to attend morning services at the sponsoring church until a sizeable membership was gathered. A few churches have experimented with a Sunday morning schedule of Bible study, church training, and missions education, followed by the morning worship service.

Organizations of Baptist men have developed more slowly than Sunday School and Training Union. The churches cooperate in area and associational Brotherhood rallies, which sometimes involve men of other Baptist groups. Royal Ambassador programs for boys are thriving in many churches. The Brotherhood Commission, SBC, has coordinated the sending of hundreds of men from across the nation to help establish new work in the Northeast. These men, usually coming at their own expense, have participated in community religious surveys, witnessing visitation, and evangelistic services. Sometimes the men have come to help a young church erect a building.

The associations are planning a coordinated approach to religious education, with interprogram scheduling and leadership training wherever possible. John M. Tubbs was employed in 1969 as the first director of the education division of the Baptist Convention of New York.

DE LANE MARLIN RYALS

NEW YORK, SOUTHERN BAPTISTS IN UPSTATE. Southern Baptists began to meet the spiritual needs of New York State in 1954 when an Alabama pastor, R. Z. (Zig) Boroughs, resigned his church and came to minister to some of his nonresident members living in Niagara Falls. In June, 1955, the 54 members constituted the LaSalle Baptist Church.

In June, 1957, two years after the constitution of the LaSalle Baptist Church in Niagara Falls, three members of that church went to Syracuse to meet with a group to organize a Southern Baptist mission. The mission grew out of the efforts of laymen led by W. C. Ferguson, a General Electric engineer of Tucson, Ariz. Paul Becker, a native Syracusan, felt led to resign his church in South Carolina and become pastor of the new mission in Syracuse in Oct., 1957. The mission was constituted into a church in November with 30 charter members. In less than one year, enrolment was more than 100 in Sunday School. A feeling of great encouragement rested upon the church when the property at 347 Cortland Avenue was purchased from the Christian and Missionary Alliance. Later, this property was sold, and the present property near downtown Syracuse was acquired. Central Baptist Church has been the mother and sponsoring church of seven missions. One of these is the church at Rome, which, under the leadership of J. T. Davis of Louisiana, has sponsored five chapels which are now churches.

In Aug., 1957, Paul Nevels, missionary in Ohio, assisted the LaSalle Church in beginning a mission in a YMCA building in Buffalo. Constituted Sept. 12, 1958, the Erie Baptist Church met for four years in a YMCA building before purchasing suburban property and changing the name to Amherst Baptist Church. Walter C. Heilig began his ministry with Erie Church in Jan., 1958.

The Home Mission Board and the State Convention of Baptists in Ohio jointly asked Arthur L. Walker to serve as area missionary for Western New York and Northwestern Pennsylvania. At the time of his arrival in May, 1958, there were four churches and one mission, affiliated with the Cuyahoga Association in Ohio.

Frontier Association was organized on Sept. 23, 1958, in the LaSalle Church with five churches and two missions. In 1959, the five churches and two missions reported 103 baptisms, 586 members, $51,929 total gifts, $4,749 mission gifts, and $130,000 property value.

The Rochester Baptist Church began in 1959 with a Florida couple whose name was sent to the area missionary by their pastor. Under the pastoral leadership of William H. Raper, this church has given liberally of its leadership and resources to begin other churches in the Rochester area.

By 1961, there were eight churches and 15 missions in Frontier Association. On Sept. 29, 1961, in the Syracuse Church, three of these churches and their nine missions formed the *Central Association*. This association has been served by John Tollison and J. Eldon Jones as superintendents of missions.

Following the resignation of Arthur Walker, Charles E. Magruder began serving as superintendent of missions for Western New York in Jan., 1962.

A Polish congregation had closed its doors and in Dec., 1963, the Home Mission Board, SBC, purchased the 62 year old building in the inner city of Buffalo. Michael Odlyzko, having recently arrived from Poland, began serving this congregation in Mar., 1964. The board also appointed Byron Lutz in Jan., 1968, to serve as English pastor with the responsibility to develop weekday ministries in the Fillmore Baptist Church.

The Peace Bridge Chapel, beginning in Sept., 1967, to serve the west side of Buffalo, was sponsored by Grand Island under the leadership of Stanley Bullis, a retired army colonel.

By 1968, the nine churches and nine missions in the Frontier Association reported 172 baptisms, 1,317 members, $167,160 total gifts, $17,820 mission gifts, $526,200 property value, and $254,174 church debt.

In 1969, Calkins Road, Fredonia, and Fillmore churches were constituted. The three churches and two missions in the Rochester area organized a new association in Oct., 1969. With the two churches in Pennsylvania affiliating with the Greater Pittsburgh Association, the 11 churches and nine missions in western New York in 1969 had 1,103 members.

Central Association divided in 1968 to form three associations: *Adirondack, Central,* and *Southern Tier*. In 1969, these showed the following statistics: Adirondack, four churches, two chapels, and 668 members; Central, eight churches, one chapel, and 1,132 members; and

Southern Tier, four churches, three chapels, and 587 members. EVA B. MAGRUDER

NEW YORK ASSOCIATIONS. See New York, Metropolitan Baptist Association. New York, Southern Baptists in Upstate.

***NEW ZEALAND BAPTIST MISSIONARY SOCIETY.** The society is the missionary arm of the Baptist Union of New Zealand. Constitutionally, they are different organizations but work as one body. Present missionary work is done in Tripura State in India and the districts of Chandpur and Brahmanbaria in East Pakistan. Because of restrictions concerning new personnel entering India, there are only 12 missionaries in Tripura. The work is fully integrated with the national church in which there are presently 4,381 members. There were 429 baptisms in 1969. The national church is autonomous but not yet self-supporting.

Institutional work is still subsidized from New Zealand. This includes a theological school in which 18 men are enrolled in a two-year course and St. Paul's School with 215 students. In addition, there are 70 village schools. There is a 40-bed hospital with five dispensaries. One national and one New Zealand doctor are assigned to this work.

In East Pakistan New Zealand Baptists work in cooperation with other Baptist missionary societies in neighboring areas—British, Australian, and Southern Baptists. There is a primary school at Brahmanbaria in which 300 are enrolled. It is entirely staffed by national workers, all of whom are Christian. Bible teaching cannot be compulsory but every effort is made to convey the Christian message to all pupils. The major work in the Chandpur field is the production of literature. The society produces most of that used by the 55,000,000 people in East Pakistan. There are 86 members of churches related to the New Zealand Baptist Missionary Society here. Thirteen New Zealand missionaries work in this field. The society is negotiating with other Baptist societies to cooperate in supporting missionaries. One couple has already been appointed to the Congo in association with the American Baptist Foreign Mission Society. The possibilities of short-term appointments for young people are being explored. HUGH NEES

NEWTON, WILLIAM CAREY (b. Kerr, N. C., Oct. 6, 1873; d. Richmond, Va., Dec. 24, 1966). Missionary to China (1902–39). Newton was educated at Wake Forest College (B.A., 1895; D.D., 1925) and Rochester Theological Seminary (Th.B., 1898). He spent his early years in Nigeria, where his parents and older sister were missionaries, and where all three died of African fever. Although Newton desired to return to Africa, the Foreign Mission Board deemed it unwise and appointed him and his wife, the former Mary Woodcock, to China. There he was pastor of churches in four cities and served as professor in North China (Bush Memorial) Baptist Theological Seminary, Hwanghsien. EUGENE L. HILL

NICHOLSON, DAVID BASCOM (b. Clinton, N. C., Feb. 17, 1886; d. Athens, Ga., Jan. 15, 1962). State secretary of student work. Graduating from Mercer University in 1910, Nicholson returned to study law. He began the practice of law in 1912. That same year he married Dixie Jay. They had three children: David B., Jr., Dixie Jay (Mrs. Robert Franklin), and Laurie (Mrs. D. W. Johnston). In 1912 Nicholson became a pastor. He also served as dean at Brewton-Parker Institute. For a while he served as a general missionary for Georgia Baptists, working with Frank Leavell (*q.v.*, Vol. II), Georgia BYPU secretary. In 1925 he became secretary of Georgia's Department of Student Work. When elected, he was instructed to organize a campus ministry program at the University of Georgia and share findings with other schools in the state. In 1951 there were 21 Baptist Student Unions served by Nicholson and six associates. AUBREY L. HAWKINS

NICOL MUSEUM OF BIBLICAL ARCHAEOLOGY, THE. A gift of $25,000 by the Murray P. Nicol family of Anchorage, Ky., enabled the creation of the Nicol Museum in the fall of 1959 at the Southern Baptist Theological Seminary. The museum was "dedicated to the task of displaying archaeological and linguistic artifacts that are representative of the historical environment in which both Old and New Testaments were conceived," in the words of the donors upon the occasion of the gift.

Replicas of classical artifacts, such as the Rosetta Stone, the Obelisk of Shalmaneser III, the Siloam Inscription, the Lachish Panel, and the Moabite Stone were obtained from originals in the British Museum and are on display. More significantly, the Nicol Museum exhibits genuine artifacts from excavations at Jericho, Jerusalem, Shechem, Bethel, and 'Ai, in which seminary faculty members and graduate students have participated. It is, therefore, an extension of the classroom from the point of view of teaching at Southern Seminary, and a means of participating at the frontiers of biblical research in Palestine from the point of view of graduate studies. JOSEPH A. CALLAWAY

***NIGERIA, MISSION IN.** The mission expanded its activities as it moved into the second century of work. In cooperation with the Nigerian Baptist Convention, an ambitious program of expansion was launched in 1958. Achievement of political independence in 1960 caused a new emphasis upon transfer of responsibility from the mission to trained Nigerians. The mission staff reached a high of 247 in 1967. By the end of 1969, it had declined to 218, partly because of difficulties in securing entrance permits for new missionaries. Missionaries cooperate with 658 national pastors serving 492 churches with 78,171 members.

H. CORNELL GOERNER

NONEVANGELICALS, HOME MISSION BOARD PROGRAM OF WORK RELATED TO. Established Jan., 1966, by the Home Mission Board, with Joseph R. Estes as secretary. Its objective of working with and assisting "churches, associations, and state conventions in witnessing to people of non-Christian world religions and to all other nonevangelicals" is implemented through research, writing, and programing in the area of Southern Baptists' encounter with the Jews and Judaism, Catholicism, members of the sects, and members of the non-Christian world religions. Sects include Mormons, Jehovah's Witnesses, Christian Scientists, and other such groups. World religions include Islam, Hinduism, Buddhism, Confucianism, Shinto, and other non-Christian groups in the United States.

The work related to Jews and Catholics, previously located in several departments, was assigned to this new department. William B. Mitchell and William E. Burke, respectively directors of these two areas, were assistant secretaries. M. Thomas Starkes (1967–) came as assistant secretary with a main responsibility in research.

Four area missionary-directors supervise and promote the work over multistate sections of the country. Glenn A. Igleheart and William R. McLin were added in this capacity in 1968. In 1969 A. Jase Jones, and in 1970 Lloyd N. Whyte were appointed.

The department provides printed materials which inform Southern Baptists of the faith and life of nonevangelical religious groups in the United States; recommends to churches, associations, and conventions specific activities designed to cultivate relations with adherents of these religions; conducts leadership conferences on local and regional bases; and initiates dialogue with the leadership of these other religions. Assistance in bearing witness to faith in Christ is offered Southern Baptists through all these means.

JOSEPH R. ESTES

NORDENHAUG, JOSEF (b. Oslo, Norway, Aug. 2, 1903; d. Arlington, Va., Sept. 18, 1969). Editor, educator, preacher, theologian, and denominational executive. He attended the public schools of Oslo and the University of Oslo, 1921–27, earning his Master of Science degree in the fields of chemistry, geophysics, and astronomy. Earlier he had learned cabinet making from his father who operated a furniture store.

Nordenhaug responded at the age of 25 to the call to enter the ministry, and went to the United States in 1928 for study at the Southern Baptist Theological Seminary, where he earned Th.M. and Ph.D. degrees majoring in New Testament Greek. He chose the Louisville seminary because he had come to know its president E. Y. Mullins, on Mullins' visit to Norway as president of the Baptist World Alliance.

Nordenhaug returned to Norway in the fall of 1932 and served as assistant pastor of the First Baptist Church of Oslo until he moved to the United States in 1933 to become pastor of the Irene Cole Memorial Baptist Church in Prestonburg, Ky. He was pastor of the Baptist Church, Vinton, Va., 1936–41, and of the Rivermont Avenue Church, Lynchburg, Va., 1941–48. In July, 1948, he became editor of *The Commission,* the world mission journal published by the Foreign Mission Board, SBC.

Nordenhaug was president of the international Baptist Seminary in Ruschlikon, Switzerland, 1950–60, developing the newly-born institution into an agency for increased cooperation and fraternal understanding among Baptist unions in Europe. During his presidency he served as European representative of the FMB, SBC, in matters of relief and rehabilitation, and was instrumental in bringing extensive aid for construction of chapels and youth camps and theological schools in Austria, France, Germany, Holland, Hungary, Norway, and Switzerland. He also served as chairman of the Baptist Relief Committee for Hungary after the Hungarian uprising in 1956.

He was elected general secretary of the Baptist World Alliance at the World Congress in Rio de Janeiro, in 1960. Beginning work in Nov., 1960, Nordenhaug gave enthusiastic and effective leadership to a promotional program.

His administrative leadership developed the Alliance into a more democratic organization. Bylaw changes adopted in 1965, authorized member conventions and unions to name their own representatives to the BWA Executive Committee, whereas the committee previously had been elected by the Quinquennial Congresses.

Nordenhaug married Helen Bacon Rampp of Louisville, Ky., in 1934. They had two children, Theodore and Karin (Mrs. Paul Ciholas).

C. E. BRYANT

***NORMAN COLLEGE.** In 1956 the college was accredited by the Southern Association of Colleges and Schools. The college won first national award presented by Freedoms Foundation, Valley Forge, Pa., for best campus program furthering the American way of life. The college initiated the Wall-Clark farm enterprise in 1956. In 1958 a home for the president was completed, and the Norman-Vereen College of Nursing was organized. The convention assumed ownership and control of the college from 16 Baptist associations in southwest Georgia in 1960. In 1962 the college organized a precollege division for high school graduates with grades too low for college enrolment. A honors program, an independent study program structured to meet the needs of particularly superior students, and an enrichment program for high achievers were developed and established in 1967. The following buildings were completed and dedicated in the years 1960–69: the Warren T. Baker Memorial Chapel and Auditorium complex, 1960, a new cafeteria and student center, 1961, an international Friendship Garden, 1963, the Dick Gresham Gymnasium, 1965, and two air-conditioned and carpeted dormitories, Fender Hall for women and Norman Hall for men, 1969. Other additions or remodeled buildings include: the installation of a new pipe organ in Baker Auditorium, 1964, remodeled and re-equipped the biology and physics laboratories and classrooms, 1965, converted Clark Hall into faculty office building and conference rooms, 1966, renovated and refurnished the library, 1967, and established a learning center to help students work independently in acquiring learning skills, 1968.

In 1967 the college established the Upward Bound Program. A campus minister and director of religious activities was appointed in 1967. Thomas Renfro succeeded Guy N. Atkinson as president in 1968. SARAH MASHBURN

***NORTH AMERICAN BAPTIST ASSOCIATION.** See BAPTIST MISSIONARY ASSOCIATION OF AMERICA.

NORTH AMERICAN BAPTIST FELLOWSHIP. Because the several Baptist conventions, conferences, and associations in North America had come to know each other better in the Baptist Jubilee Advance (1959–64), a desire arose to continue the cooperative relationship.

On Mar. 14, 1963, the Jubilee central committee formally suggested that the Baptist World Alliance (BWA) establish a North American Baptist Fellowship "in order to conserve the gains and values which have resulted from the Baptist Jubilee Advance and to increase opportunities for fellowship and for sharing mutual concerns."

The BWA administrative committee approved the concept in principle and appointed a committee, with Frank H. Woyke of the North American Baptist General Conference as chairman, to study means for implementation of the idea. A statement of bylaws was drafted and approved by the BWA Executive Committee at its meeting in Hamburg, Germany, Aug. 19, 1964. It provided that the fellowship would come into being "when as many as five North American members of the Baptist World Alliance signify willingness to belong to the Fellowship."

Josef Nordenhaug, General Secretary of BWA, announced in Mar., 1966, that six eligible bodies had voted to participate. They were the American Baptist Convention, Baptist Federation of Canada, National Baptist Convention of Mexico, Progressive National Baptist Convention, Inc., Seventh Day Baptist General Conference, and Southern Baptist Convention.

Representatives of the participating bodies met in Washington on Mar. 28 for an organizational meeting of the fellowship. V. Carney Hargroves of Philadelphia, representing the American Baptist Convention, was elected chairman, and Jennings Randolph of West Virginia, representing the Seventh Day Baptists, was named co-chairman.

Shortly after the meeting, Hargroves released a statement signed by presidents of the member groups declaring:

"Baptists in North America have a great deal in common and can work together for a common good. Wherever they are located they have similar forms of polity, of belief, of practice. Such differences as occur, which are often those of emphasis, can and should serve as challenges rather than as means for division. . . . We need to know each other better, we need to emphasize our common concerns, we need to plan special projects together. We need to walk together in keeping with the directives of Jesus Christ."

The general committee meets annually in November for general discussion and sharing of ideas. Hargroves initiated a plan for separate special interest group discussions, with the groups then sharing their combined thoughts.

After two years of leadership, the committee in 1968 elected Duke K. McCall of Louisville, Ky., representing the SBC, as chairman, and L. Venchael Booth of Cincinnati, Ohio, representing the Progressive Convention, as co-chairman.

Frank H. Woyke was elected associate secretary of the BWA in July, 1968, giving one-third of his time to the work of the fellowship.

A directory of leaders in the member conventions has been published, so that any leader in one group can find his counterpart in another group.

BYLAWS

Article I. NAME.

The name of the organization shall be the North American Baptist Fellowship, a Committee of the Baptist World Alliance.

Article II. PURPOSE.

The purpose of the organization shall be:

A. To continue the gains and values growing out of the Baptist Jubilee Advance program (1959–64).

B. To make possible opportunities for fellowship and the sharing of mutual concerns.

C. To cooperate with all departments of the BWA.

It shall have no authority over any Baptist church nor undertake any work for which the member bodies are responsible.

Article III. MEMBERSHIP.

Baptist bodies of North America holding membership in the Baptist World Alliance shall be eligible for membership in the North American Baptist Fellowship.

Article IV. ORGANIZATION.

A. The office of the Fellowship shall be the Washington office of the BWA.

B. There shall be a General Committee of the Fellowship. It shall consist of—

1. Three representatives named by each body plus one representative for every million members or major fraction thereof.
2. One representative appointed by any depart-

ment of the North American Baptist Fellowship.
3. The President and the General Secretary of the BWA.
4. Three North American members of the BWA Executive Committee named by the General Secretary.
5. The officers of the Fellowship.

C. Departments may be established by the Fellowship as needs arise, in keeping with BWA policy.

D. The officers shall be—
Chairman and *Vice Chairman* to be elected by the General Committee annually from its members.
Secretary who shall be a secretary of the Baptist World Alliance designated by the General Secretary of the BWA.
Treasurer who shall be the Western Treasurer of the BWA.

Article V. MEETINGS.
The General Committee shall meet annually to carry out the above purposes.
The General Committee may arrange occasional continental fellowship meetings.

Article VI. FINANCES.
The work of the N.A.B.F. shall be financed within the framework of the Baptist World Alliance budget by funds contributed by the North American member bodies, organizations and individuals.

Article VII. AMENDMENTS.
Amendments to the Bylaws of the N.A.B.F. shall be by two-thirds majority vote of the Executive of the BWA upon recommendation of at least two-thirds of the members of the General Committee.

C. E. BRYANT

NORTH AMERICAN BAPTIST WOMEN'S UNION. One of six continental unions of the Women's Department of the Baptist World Alliance. At the meeting of the BWA in Cleveland, Ohio, in 1950, women from 15 nations met together to discuss continental organizations. It was suggested that Mrs. Edgar Bates, Ontario, Canada, call together a group of women for the purpose of organizing a North American Baptist Women's Union.

Mrs. Bates called this meeting to order in Washington, D. C., Apr. 27, 1951. Those present were: Mrs. George R. Martin and Blanche Sydnor White (proxy for Alma Hunt), Southern Baptist Convention; Mrs. Frank Wigginton, American Baptist Convention; Nannie Burroughs, National Baptist Convention of USA, Inc.; and Mrs. C. W. Dengate and Mrs. Bates, Baptist Federation of Canada. After discussion, the group voted to begin the NABWU with Mrs. Bates as chairman and Mrs. Wigginton as secretary-treasurer.

The first continental general assembly was held in the First Baptist Church, Columbus, Ohio, Nov. 2–4, 1953. More than 800 registered delegates attended. The seven women's groups represented were: United Baptist Women's Missionary Union of the Maritime (now Atlantic) Provinces; Women's Missionary Auxiliary of the Baptist Union of Western Canada; Baptist Women's Missionary Society of Ontario and Quebec; Women's Auxiliary to the National Baptist Convention, USA, Inc.; Woman's Auxiliary of the National Baptist Convention of America; National Council of American Baptist Women; and Woman's Missionary Union, SBC.

At the BWA in London, England, 1955, representatives from the North American groups met together, as did representatives from other continents. At the close of the London meeting, Mrs. Maurice B. Hodge, Portland, Ore., was elected president of the NABWU; Mrs. W. C. Smalley, Edmonton, Canada, secretary; and Mrs. R. L. Mathis, Waco, Tex., treasurer.

The continental general assembly is held every five years, about midway between the sessions of the BWA. The second NABWU assembly was held in Toronto, Canada, Nov. 5–7, 1957, at the Yorkminster Baptist Church. More than 800 attended. The officers were reelected.

At the third assembly in St. Louis, Mo., Nov. 13–15, 1962, there were approximately 600 in attendance. Mrs. William McMurry, Birmingham, Ala., was elected president. Following Mrs. McMurry's death in Jan., 1965, Alma Hunt, executive secretary, WMU, SBC, was elected acting president. The fourth general assembly was held at the Sheraton Park Hotel, Washington, D. C., Nov. 16–18, 1967. Miss Hunt presided during the sessions. Mrs. I. Judson Levy, Nova Scotia, was elected president.

In addition to the seven national groups listed already, seven groups were added to the membership: Woman's Auxiliary, Lott Carey Baptist Foreign Mission Convention; Woman's Missionary Union of the North American Baptist General Conference; Women's Work, Baptist General Conference; Jamaica Baptist Women's Federation, Jamaica Baptist Union; Women's Society of the Seventh Day Baptist General Conference; Women's Auxiliary, Progressive National Baptist Convention, Inc.; and General Baptist Women's Mission Board, Inc., General Association of General Baptists.

The purpose of the NABWU is: (1) to provide Baptist women of North America with information concerning the BWA; (2) to promote a closer relationship between Baptist women of North America and Baptist women in other parts of the world; and (3) to suggest opportunities for broadening the avenues open to Baptist women for service.

The executive committee of the union is composed of the officers of the union, the president of each cooperating constituent women's organization, the national executive secretaries of the aforesaid member bodies, the North American women members of the executive committee of the BWA, and five members-at-large.

A bulletin, *The Tie,* begun in the spring of 1961, is published twice a year and distributed free.

At the first assembly of the NABWU in Columbus, 1953, it was voted to promote a Day of Prayer to be held on the first Friday in December. By vote of all continental unions, this was changed to the first Monday in November, effective in 1963. The Day of Prayer is a unifying

BAPTIST CONVENTION OF NEW YORK (*q.v.*). Powelson Building, Syracuse, N. Y., contains offices of convention on two floors.

SOUTH CAROLINA BAPTIST CONVENTION (*q.v.*). Baptist Building located at Columbia, S. C.

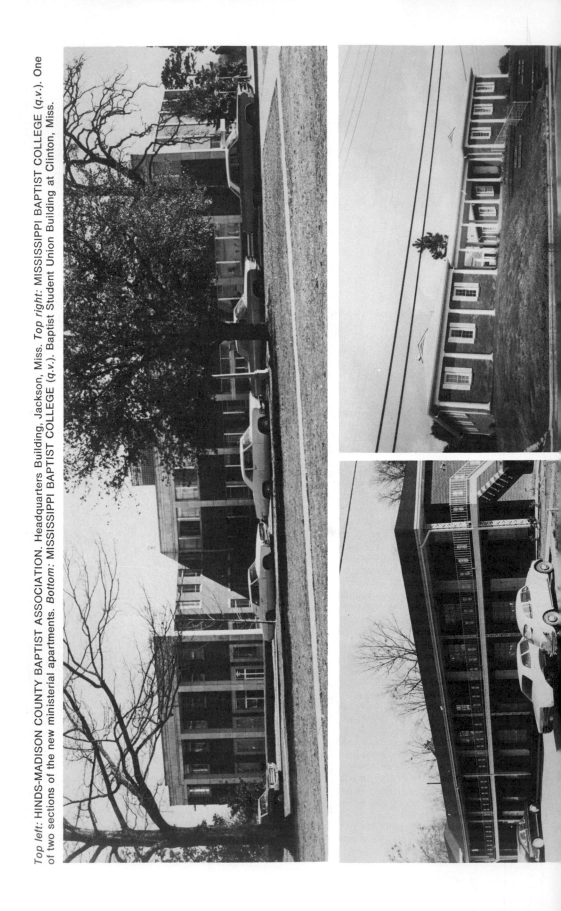

Top left: HINDS-MADISON COUNTY BAPTIST ASSOCIATION. Headquarters Building, Jackson, Miss. *Top right:* MISSISSIPPI BAPTIST COLLEGE (*q.v.*). One of two sections of the new ministerial apartments. *Bottom:* MISSISSIPPI BAPTIST COLLEGE (*q.v.*). Baptist Student Union Building at Clinton, Miss.

force in the life of Baptist women around the world. The continental unions are financed through the Baptist Women's Day of Prayer offering. One half of the offering given by NABWU is used for NABWU work; the other half goes to the Women's Department of the BWA, portions of it designated for continental women's unions and BWA relief work.

Program material for the Day of Prayer is planned each year by a designated continental union. It is printed in English, then sent to continental groups for necessary translation.

DORIS DEVAULT

***NORTH CAROLINA, BAPTIST STATE CONVENTION OF.** The period between 1957 and 1968 was one of prosperity and growth for the Baptist State Convention of North Carolina. Statistics show that the biggest gains were in the area of finances. Gifts to missions and to local churches more than doubled. Church membership increased substantially, but the number of new churches coming into the convention was relatively small. Moreover, this period in the history of the convention represented an era of expanding programs and services, reflecting both the fervor and insight of Baptist leadership.

In the period from 1956 to 1969, the number of churches increased from 3,238 to 3,454, while membership grew from 829,109 to 1,005,833. Mission gifts increased from $5,841,678 to $11,482,229. Total church giving moved from $37,508,394 to $79,068,000. Sunday School enrolment increased from 736,000 to 746,178. Training Union enrolment decreased from 177,359 to 163,364. Woman's Missionary Union increased from 153,437 to 160,355. Brotherhood increased from 42,499 to 45,855.

M. A. Huggins retired as secretary of the convention in 1959, after 29 years of service. Huggins was succeeded by Douglas M. Branch (*q.v.*), who served as secretary-treasurer from 1959 until the time of his death in 1963. Claude F. Gaddy, formerly executive secretary of the Council on Christian Higher Education, served as interim secretary from Feb., 1963, to Dec. 31, 1963. He was succeeded by W. Perry Crouch on Jan. 1, 1964.

Committee of 25.—The event which had the most far-reaching effect on the convention during this period was the adoption of the report of the committee of 25 on May 5, 1959. This committee was charged with studying the business management, organizations, and programs of the convention. It was also asked to study and make recommendations concerning the colleges and social service agencies. Professional consultants were used for the first time.

The two significant contributions of the committee of 25 were the correlation of all Baptist work under one administrative program, and the adoption of an orderly plan to meet the educational and service needs of a rapidly growing convention. The divisions of work were outlined and stronger ties were established between the general board and the institutions.

In addition to this, it should be noted that the report of the committee resulted in some significant changes in the composition of the general board, established guidelines for the election of a general secretary-treasurer, changed the financial plan of the convention from a percentage to a performance budget, restructured the convention committees, made significant recommendations concerning the social service ministeries, established new policies concerning the colleges, and suggested significant changes in the constitution and bylaws of the Baptist state convention.

Separation of Church and State.—The committee of 25 also made landmark recommendations concerning convention policy on the separation of church and state. These guidelines, particularly as they related to federal, state, or local tax monies, have been frequently referred to and were reaffirmed by the Baptist state convention in its annual session in Fayetteville, N. C., in 1969. The decade since 1956 in the state convention was marked by considerable controversy over the use of public monies by Baptist institutions.

The committee of 25 outlined the following divisions of work: business management, stewardship promotion, missions, church programs, Christian higher education, and social services. The committee report was amended from the floor to create division status for the Department of Evangelism.

With the adoption of the recommendations of the committee of 25 in 1959, in a special session in Greensboro, N. C., each division was assigned specific duties and responsibilities. In 1968 the convention authorized a new division of Church Life and Public Affairs.

Six of these divisions now have full-time directors and a full-time director is to be employed for the Christian Life and Public Affairs Division by July 1, 1970.

Division of Business Management.—The convention instructed this division to account for all monies received, record all gifts from the churches, keep permanent records, make an annual accounting to the convention through certified audits, upon authorization make distribution of Cooperative Program funds, and assist the general secretary-treasurer in preparing budgets and all other financial matters.

Division of Stewardship Promotion.—Earle Bradley (*q.v.*) was named the first division director in 1945, and served until his death in 1962. He was succeeded by O. J. Hagler. The division was assigned the responsibility of promoting the total program of North Carolina Baptists as it related to the financial needs and to the cultivation and growth of Christian stewardship. This included responsibility for promoting the Cooperative Program and the special state mission offering in September, and for developing and promoting programs designed to assist the local church in increasing its sense of stewardship. Four departments were established for carrying out the work of the division: Stewardship Development, Stewardship Promotion, Program Services, and Annuity. In 1969 the Department of Program Services was renamed the Department of Communications.

Division of Missions.—E. Lowell Spivey was named the first director and served until his retirement in 1966. He was succeeded by Howard Ford. This division was assigned the responsibility to help new churches, provide aid for lots for new church buildings, provide pastoral aid in needy situations and help with salaries of superintendents of missions in the various associations, and promote schools of missions, pastors conferences, seminary extension work, and other aids for pastors and churches. In addition to this, the Division of Missions was asked to develop special work among the deaf, the Indians, and those in the military areas. Interracial work was promoted constantly, and new work was launched in urban centers with families in distress, alcoholics, juvenile problems, and other social problems. New work was started with migrants and in resort areas. The work of the division was assigned to the division director and in six separate departments of the division: City and Metropolitan Missions, Town and Country and Seminary Extension, Interracial Ministry, Ministry to the Deaf, Fruitland Bible Institute, and Chaplaincy Ministry.

In 1965 a committee of the general board recommended that Fruitland Bible Institute, established in 1946, be upgraded into a full nine-month school for preachers. A new administration building and library were constructed, all of the property reconditioned, and the enrolment limited to 150 a quarter. This school is operated entirely as a part of the Division of Missions.

The convention purchased the childhood home of George W. Truett (*q.v.,* Vol. II) near Hayesville, N. C., in 1936 and renovated and refurnished it. The home is now open to the public. The Division of Missions was also asked to work with the churches in region 10 in developing and maintaining the Truett Camp for young people.

Division of Church Programs.—Following the work of the committee of 25, one of the divisions established was the Division of Church Programs. For several years the general secretary served as acting director. In 1966 Nathan Brooks, Jr., was named the first full-time director. Beginning with five basic departments outlined by the committee of 25, the work was expanded to embrace 10 departments and 19 separate programs. The departments are as follows: Sunday School, Church Training, Brotherhood, Student Work, Church Music, Church Building Planning, Camps and Retreats, the North Carolina Baptist Assembly, Statistics and Survey, and Fruitland Conference Center. In addition, WMU coordinates and correlates its work with the departments in the division.

In 1949 the convention purchased from the Federal Government 248 acres and buildings on a site known as Fort Caswell. These properties were remodeled into a modern summer assembly and in 1968 a commodious auditorium with a capacity of 1,000 was added. A 10 weeks' summer assembly program was conducted each year and the property rented to church and associational groups during the other nine months of the year. About 10,000 people use these facilities each year.

In Jan., 1962, the Brotherhood led in securing 1,047 acres of mountainous land near Asheboro, N. C., and has constructed camp facilities for boys there. A permanent dining room was built, as well as facilities for leaders and buildings for about 150 boys per week during summer months. A policy was also adopted to allow churches and associations to use these facilities for retreats. A conference center was established for leadership training at Fruitland during the summer months.

Baptist Student Centers have also enjoyed a period of growth during this era. To date, the following centers have been constructed: Appalachian Regional University at Boone, N. C.; Western North Carolina Regional University at Cullowhee, N. C.; University of North Carolina at Greensboro; Duke University at Raleigh, N. C.; and East Carolina University at Greenville, N. C.

Woman's Missionary Union.—WMU is an auxiliary to the state convention of North Carolina, but works very closely with the Division of Church Programs. In 1957, after fostering Royal Ambassadors for 49 years, WMU turned the leadership of boys over to the Brotherhood. The entire structure of WMU was changed in 1968 to conform to the plans suggested by WMU, Southern Baptist Convention. In 1968 they reported 2,435 societies for women, 941 YWA organizations, 3,460 Girls' Auxiliaries, and 3,216 Sunbeam Bands, with a combined membership of 168,608. Sara Ann Hobbs became executive secretary of WMU on Oct. 1, 1968, succeeding Miriam Robinson, who resigned to accept a teaching position in Belmont College in Nashville, Tenn.

Camp Mundo Vista, a camp for girls, was built by the WMU and dedicated in June, 1969. This camp is capable of serving 200 girls a week. There are 30 separate buildings.

Division of Evangelism.—J. C. Canipe for many years served as secretary of the Department of Evangelism. In 1959 the Division of Evangelism was created, and Julian S. Hopkins was named the first director. Upon his retirement in 1969, he was succeeded by William C. Lamb. The division was assigned the responsibility for promoting evangelism in North Carolina through all the work of the general board, evangelistic clinics, special associational meetings, through printed literature, conferences, and the annual Evangelistic Conference. A full-time associate was added to this division in 1961.

Division of Social Services.—The committee of 25 established a Council of Christian Social Services composed of a committee of the general board and administrators of the three social service institutions: The North Carolina Baptist Hospital, The North Carolina Baptist Children's Homes, and the Homes for the Aging, Inc. The general secretary has served as director of the council. At least once per year the council meets to review the work of the three social service institutions and make their report to the general board.

At the close of the sixties, the Baptist Hospital and the Bowman Gray School of Medicine at Wake Forest University had formed a medical center with a worldwide reputation. This included: a school of nursing, a paramedical school, and a school of pastoral care, all conducted under the directors of the board of trustees of the hospital.

More than $32,000,000 was spent on the expansion program. In addition to Cooperative Program funds, the hospital received large amounts through the annual Mother's Day offering.

From 1956 to 1970 the Children's Homes also expanded their facilities and services. In addition to the homes at Kinston and Thomasville, homes were established at Pembroke, Chapel Hill, and Waynesville. Social service work and statewide foster home programs were expanded. In 1970 a home was established in Asheville for unwed mothers. The social service agencies received substantial support through the Cooperative Program and the annual Thanksgiving Offering.

The Homes for the Aging also increased their ministry by three new homes located at Hamilton, Albemarle, and Yanceyville. This program also received financial assistance both through the Cooperative Program and through an annual special offering.

Division of Higher Education.—Claude F. Gaddy served as executive secretary of the Council on Christian Higher Education (called division after 1959) from 1946 to his retirement in 1961. His successor, Harold Cole, resigned after a brief tenure. Ben C. Fisher served as director of the division from 1962 to 1970. The council was established in 1946 as a means of correlating the programs of the various colleges, developing uniform accounting procedures, and providing better communication between the colleges and the churches in the convention. The council has changed little in structure. After 1957 the council assumed broader responsibilities in promoting the cause of Baptist higher education in North Carolina.

Since 1956 Wake Forest College has had university status; Campbell and Mars Hill colleges moved from two-year to four-year institutions; and in the fall of 1969 Gardner-Webb College added a junior year, anticipating the graduation of the first senior class in 1971. Since 1957 the Baptist colleges of North Carolina have experienced their largest growth. Enrolment moved from 6,648 students in 1957 to more than 12,000 in 1968. Baptist colleges' current expenditures jumped from $6,000,000 in 1957 to an estimated $32,000,000 by the end of 1969. During this same period North Carolina Baptist colleges added to their plant value approximately $50,000,000.

Study Committees.—During the period from 1956 to 1968, the Baptist State Convention appointed several special committees with the assigned task of studying certain problems and making specific recommendations to the convention. In addition to the committee of 25, the convention also appointed the committee of 9, the committee of 17, the committee on advance program for the colleges and student work, the committee of 28, and the committee of 20. The major concern of all of these committees was the financing of Baptist higher education and the relationship of the colleges to the Baptist State Convention.

Race Relations.—Although the period between 1956 and 1969 was one of marked improvement in race relations, as the state convention entered the seventies few of the 3,450 missionary Baptist churches had any black people in their memberships. However, there were significant indications of changing attitudes.

In 1955 the convention passed a resolution asking all of its institutions to open their doors to minority groups. In 1960 the convention reaffirmed its position. During this period Wake Forest University admitted black graduate students and admitted black students to summer school. Mars Hill was the first college to admit Negro students to regular classes. The Christian Life Committee of the convention again in 1961 urged Baptist institutions to open their doors to people of all races. This was approved by the convention. By 1969 all Baptist colleges, the Baptist Hospital, and the Children's Homes had opened their doors to minority groups.

Prior to the establishment of a Department of Interracial Cooperation in 1957, there was little or no contact with the black Baptist churches. However, when this department became operative, a new and constructive relationship developed.

In 1964 in Greensboro, the Baptist State Convention of North Carolina and the General Baptist State Convention held a joint meeting, the first such meeting to be held in the Southern Baptist Convention. In 1969 a record number of black and white churches observed Race Relations Sunday. During this year, all records were broken in the amount of literature distributed upon request by the Department of Interracial Cooperation.

As early as 1947, the North Carolina Baptist Student Union Convention was completely interracial. In 1950 a black student was elected to the state officers' council. In 1963 a black student was elected as a representative to the general board. In 1969, at the fall convention meeting in Durham, the Baptist Student Union's constitution was revised to provide three non-white members from minority groups to serve on the executive committee of the State Baptist Student Union Council.

The good neighbor council was established by

NORTH CAROLINA STATISTICAL SUMMARY

Year	Associa-tions	Churches	Church Member-ship	Baptisms	S. S. Enrol-ment	V.B.S. Enrol-ment	T. U. Enrol-ment	W.M.U. Enrol-ment	Brother-hood En-rolment	Music Enrol-ment	Mission Gifts	Total Gifts	Value Church Property
1955	73	3,191	807,667	35,607	724,463	264,074	169,579	147,800	36,001		$ 5,270,147	$33,751,927	
1956	75	3,238	829,109	32,468	736,635	275,479	177,359	153,437	42,449		5,841,678	37,508,394	$151,027,923
1957	75	3,266	846,263	33,798	749,530	270,443	184,582	159,949	49,640		6,171,043	39,317,242	165,730,576
1958	75	3,307	871,272	34,836	757,149	288,360	187,611	166,137	54,053		6,570,660	41,458,447	177,970,338
1959	78	3,336	893,679	36,660	772,353	285,114	191,656	169,091	53,867		6,905,541	44,121,134	194,431,762
1960	79	3,369	913,176	30,337	772,420	288,130	189,849	169,931	51,607		7,211,431	46,788,109	210,627,483
1961	80	3,389	932,415	32,485	784,435	292,214	191,424	170,374	53,628		7,465,315	53,264,212	225,287,959
1962	80	3,396	940,955	30,881	783,231	294,118	188,813	169,399	52,958		8,239,667	56,151,675	239,839,934
1963	80	3,399	948,842	27,289	776,227	299,084	186,818	169,917	50,282		8,574,428	56,973,374	258,385,726
1964	80	3,423	962,813	29,725	781,116	299,593	183,035	170,172	48,470		8,976,754	60,137,136	276,180,282
1965	80	3,436	974,954	27,649	776,998	296,350	174,451	170,325	47,449		9,648,669	66,576,530	288,296,526
1966	80	3,442	984,844	27,815	765,432	289,369	165,463	164,719	45,785	102,628	10,373,667	69,700,598	303,175,844
1967	80	3,441	995,749	29,089	757,681	295,461	162,346	164,074	45,404	102,875	10,818,359	72,890,045	329,626,793
1968	80	3,454	1,005,833	28,522	746,178	295,397	163,364	160,355	45,855	103,899	11,482,229	79,068,271	347,618,452

TED W. WILLIAMS

former Governor Terry Sanford, Jan. 18, 1963, and by the close of Governor Dan Moore's administration in 1967, it had become a statutory agency of state government. The purpose of the council was to improve race relations. Baptist pastors and laymen played an important part in establishing and developing the work of this council.

During the sixties, black students played a significant role in the civil rights movement. A & T College students in Greensboro began on Feb. 1, 1960, the nonviolent protest "sit-ins," which later swept the nation. Shaw University (Baptist) students were instrumental in desegregating restaurants, theaters, and public recreational facilities in Raleigh.

In 1969 the Supreme Court issued an order for immediate compliance with the Civil Rights Act, particularly as it was related to secondary education. The most controversial part of this issue was the matter of busing children from one district to another in order to achieve racial balance. Following the Supreme Court's order for the immediate desegregation of public schools, racial tensions again increased in North Carolina.

The sixties saw the emergence of both black and white extremist groups. "Christian Academies" and private schools sprang up rapidly, particularly in the east. As the decade closed, both black and white extremists' organizations seemed to be losing their thrust, but the reaction to intensified public school integration was creating new tensions.

In summary, it may be said that the period of the sixties was a time of racial progress in the Baptist State Convention of North Carolina. However, most of this progress came at the leadership, convention, and institutional level. During the sixties the convention passed numerous resolutions calling for an end to segregation. Pastors and laymen urged brotherhood and tolerance. Nevertheless, as the convention prepared to enter the seventies, racial prejudice and deep-rooted intolerance continued to be widespread in the local churches, both rural and urban.

Convention Presidents.—Between 1955 and 1969 the following have served as president of the convention: J. C. Canipe, Hendersonville; A. L. Parker, Friendly Avenue Baptist Church, Greensboro; C. B. Deane, Rockingham attorney; Nane Starnes, West Asheville Baptist Church; Howard J. Ford, Winter Park Baptist Church, Wilmington; Carl E. Bates, First Baptist Church, Charlotte; Claud B. Bowen, First Baptist Church, Greensboro; and John Lawrence, Forest Hills Baptist Church, Raleigh.

BEN C. FISHER

NORTH CAROLINA, COUNCIL ON CHRISTIAN LIFE AND PUBLIC AFFAIRS OF THE BAPTIST STATE CONVENTION OF. One of the seven major program divisions of the convention. The council was established by the convention in 1968, on recommendation of a special study committee appointed in 1967. The initial proposal that a Christian Life Commission be created was made in 1964 by the Christian Life committee.

The council began to function in early 1969 under the leadership of its chairman, Ed Brandon, a layman from Raleigh. Twenty persons serve on the council, four of whom are ex officio members. Eight members are from the general board. The other eight members serve four-year terms. W. Perry Crouch, general secretary-treasurer of the convention, was acting director of the council in 1970.

The council is charged with responsibility in family life, human relations, moral issues, economic life and daily work, citizenship, public affairs, and related fields. Its work is promotional, informational, consultative, and advisory in relation to the areas of assigned responsibility. The council cooperates with the Christian Life Commission, SBC, and with the Baptist Joint Committee on Public Affairs in areas of mutual interest. The council works with the Christian Action League of North Carolina in efforts to deal with alcohol problems. The council is also authorized to cooperate with other North Carolina organizations in rendering indirect services to associations and churches. THOMAS A. BLAND

***NORTH CAROLINA ASSOCIATIONS.**

I. New Associations. CENTRAL. Formed in 1958 from the Piedmont Association, with 30 churches in and around High Point in Guilford, Randolph, and Forsyth counties. In 1969, 33 churches reported 562 baptisms, 15,655 members, $1,568,227 total gifts, $227,446 mission gifts, $5,919,499 property value, and $756,130 church debt.

CHEOAH. Organized in 1958 with 20 churches from Tennessee River Association. Cheoah centers in and around Robbinsville in Graham County. In 1969, 20 churches reported 84 baptisms, 3,688 members, $101,192 total gifts, $11,513 mission gifts, $565,000 property value, and $127,756 church debt.

CULLOM. Organized in 1958 with 30 churches from Tar River Association. Cullom centers in and around Henderson in Warren, Halifax, Mecklenburg (Va.), and Vance counties. In 1969, 29 churches reported 161 baptisms, 8,555 members, $493,450 total gifts, $86,292 mission gifts, $2,956,850 property value, and $150,797 church debt.

NEW RIVER. Formed in 1960 with 23 churches from Atlantic, Eastern, and Wilmington associations. New River centers in and around Jacksonville in Onslow, Duplin, Pender, and Jones counties. In 1969, 29 churches reported 389 baptisms, 9,639 members, $578,492 total gifts, $63,154 mission gifts, $2,479,597 property value, and $341,067 church debt.

NORTH ROANOKE. Formed in 1955 from the old Roanoke Association. North Roanoke organized with 49 churches in and around Rocky Mount and Roanoke Rapids in Nash, Edgecombe, Halifax, and Northampton counties. In 1969, 60 churches reported 703 baptisms, 22,030 members, $1,508,882 total gifts, $233,503 mission gifts, $7,158,043 property value, and $801,114 church debt.

POLK. Formed in 1969 with 16 churches from Green River, Carolina, and Sandy Run associations. Polk centers in and around Columbus in Polk County. In 1969 these churches reported 93 baptisms, 3,400 members, $193,291 total gifts, $18,323 mission gifts, $647,400 property value, and $52,421 church debt.

ROCKY FACE. Formed in 1949 with several churches from Alexander Association. Rocky Face is located in Alexander and Iredell counties. In 1969, 16 churches reported 84 baptisms, 3,116 members, $163,076 total gifts, $24,707 mission gifts, $701,000 property value, and $105,094 church debt.

SANDHILLS. In 1959 the South Sandy Creek Association changed its name to Sandhills. In 1969, 26 churches reported 298 baptisms, 5,677 members, $374,259 total gifts, and $61,423 mission gifts.

SOUTH ROANOKE. Formed in 1955 from the old Roanoke Association. South Roanoke organized with 46 churches in and around Wilson, Greenville, Tarboro, Washington, and Williamson in Wilson, Greene, and Pitt counties. In 1969, 51 churches reported 419 baptisms, 16,310 members, $1,222,937 total gifts, $176,832 mission gifts, $6,341,270 property value, and $904,142 church debt.

THERON RANKIN. Formed in 1955 from South Fork Association with two churches from South Mountain Association. Theron Rankin organized with 27 churches in and around Hickory in Catawba and Burke counties. In 1969, 36 churches reported 562 baptisms, 15,483 members, $1,519,231 total gifts, $259,362 mission gifts, $8,374,895 property value, and $1,456,945 church debt.

TRUETT. Formed in 1970 with 74 churches by a union of West Liberty and Western North Carolina associations. Truett centers in and around Murphy in Cherokee and Clay counties. In 1969 these churches reported 217 baptisms, 11,720 members, $325,493 total gifts, $55,733 mission gifts, $1,195,973 property value, and $26,210 Church debt.

II. Changes in Associations. SOUTH SANDY CREEK. Organized on Oct. 24, 1949, at the First Baptist Church of Carthage by 19 churches, 17 of which had requested dismissal from Sandy Creek Association because it comprised "a large and scattered territory." In 1959 South Sandy Creek changed its name to Sandhills Association.

WEST LIBERTY. On Aug. 4, 1970, West Liberty merged with Western North Carolina Association to form Truett Association.

WESTERN NORTH CAROLINA. On Aug. 4, 1970, Western North Carolina merged with West Liberty to form Truett Association.

TED W. WILLIAMS

***NORTH CAROLINA BAPTIST FOUNDATION.** A corporation created under the laws of the state of North Carolina in Nov., 1920, and as such is authorized to "receive, own, hold, administer, and distribute any kind of property —real, personal, or mixed." Since 1956 the assets of the corporation have grown from one quarter of a million dollars to more than one million dollars in 1969. In 1962 C. Gordon Maddrey became the first full-time executive secretary of the foundation. Under Maddrey's administration, the assets of the foundation have advanced from $253,191 on June 30, 1962, to $1,042,963 on June 30, 1969. As a charitable corporation, the foundation has no stockholders but receives and administers any kind of property and gifts to be used for the promotion of the missionary Baptist cause in general or any specified object of the missionary Baptist denomination.

The foundation is managed by a board of 15 directors, elected by and accountable to the state convention. Their term is for a five-year period and three are elected each year. The foundation has been charged with the responsibility of procuring, safeguarding, and investing endowment and other trust funds, and disbursing these funds according to the wishes of the donors. BEN C. FISHER

NORTH CAROLINA BAPTIST HOMES, INC., THE. This agency, with William A. Poole as superintendent, operates five homes for aging people, along with an extended care nursing unit, all of which serve 200 people. Resthaven and the Hayes Home are located in Winston-Salem. The nursing unit, with a capacity for 56 patients, adjoins the Hayes Home. The other homes are located in Albemarle, Hamilton, and Yanceyville. This ministry to the aging is one of Christian nurture and love. It offers full life care to persons 65 years and above. It is supported by North Carolina Baptists through two vital sources, a special offering and the Cooperative Program. The homes have 20 trustees who are elected by the State Baptist Convention of North Carolina and who are responsible to the convention. WILLIAM A. POOLE

***NORTH CAROLINA BAPTIST HOSPITALS, INC.** This institution has expanded its facilities and is now (1970) engaged in an extensive development program. Since 1954 it has added an 80-bed Progressive Care (minimal care) unit, a 124 unit apartment residence for nursing students and other students and hospital personnel, and has more than doubled its land properties. With the completion of the current program it will have 691 patient beds and 48 bassinets, a paramedical school building for a coordinated program of the schools of nursing and other allied health programs, a new power plant to serve the entire Medical Center, and a School of Pastoral Care building. The property value of the hospital will be above $41,500,000. In 1969–70 approximately 700 students were enrolled in the various schools and training programs with the capacity to be increased by more than 50 per cent upon completion of the expansion program in 1972.

The 1969–70 budget of the hospital was $12,100,000. In 1968 there were 18,682 admissions to the hospital for 154,349 days of care. There were 95,295 visits to the service clinics from 95 of the 100 counties of the state, 13 other states, and one foreign country. There were 68,652 visits to the private clinics. The charity work not reimbursed by welfare and health agencies amounted to $1,130,000. Income from the Cooperative Program was $219,388 and income from the Mother's Day Offerings for charity work was $321,327. The hospital is racially integrated in all areas. W. K. MCGEE

NORTH DAKOTA, BAPTISTS IN. See NORTHERN PLAINS BAPTIST CONVENTION, and COLORADO, BAPTIST GENERAL CONVENTION OF.

***NORTH GREENVILLE JUNIOR COLLEGE.** Growth in enrolment, increase in financial support by the South Carolina Baptist Convention, and expansion of the curriculum and the physical plant mark the years 1956–70. The college erected Donnan Administration Building, including offices, classrooms, and library (1955), Turner Auditorium (1958), a women's dormitory (1961), and Crain Science Hall (1962). In 1957 the institution was granted full accreditation by the Southern Association of Schools and Colleges. Murphree Claude Donnan, president of the school since 1928, retired in August, 1962, but continued to serve the college as director of development until Jan., 1964.

Thomas Lawton Neely, pastor of Holly Springs Church and former missionary to South America, succeeded him. Neely had served as administrative assistant to the president, 1958–62. Under his leadership the expansion program was continued. Buildings added included a second wing of a women's dormitory, Foster Student Center (1966), Tuttle Clinic, a health center and medical facility (1967), and a men's dormitory (1970).

Between 1956 and 1970 enrolment practically doubled, ranging close to 500. The number of graduates each year (1960–70) ranged between 100 and 150. During the first half of the sixties the largest percentage of students enrolled were preparing for the ministry or other religious vocations. After 1965 the largest number were preparing for some phase of teaching. Two significant attainments reached in 1969 were the completion of the self-study required by the Southern Association for reaccreditation, and the enlargement of the board of trustees to 25 members. In 1969 property, buildings, and equipment were valued at $2,525,307. H. J. HOWARD

NORTH PACIFIC COAST, BAPTIST CONVENTION OF (1878–86). The one general organization of Baptists of the Northwest from 1878 to 1886. Most Northwest Baptists lived in Oregon in the 19th century. On July 4, 1868, at

Brownsville, Ore., they organized the General Baptist Association of Oregon. It became the Oregon Baptist State Convention in 1870, and the Baptist Convention of Oregon and Washington Territory in 1871. This body gradually ceased to function, but was reorganized as the Baptist Missionary and Educational Society at Albany, Ore., June 25, 1877. The name was changed to Baptist Convention of the North Pacific Coast on Oct. 31, 1878, at Oregon City. Its field of operation consisted of Oregon, Washington, and Idaho Territories, and British Columbia. It was officially disbanded in 1886, chiefly because some Baptists of Oregon (largely from the South) believed better missionary work could be done by separate conventions in the vast area. ROY L. JOHNSON

NORTH PACIFIC COAST, BAPTIST CONVENTION OF (1893–1900). Name adopted in 1893 by a group of Baptists of the Northwest who organized the East Oregon Baptist Convention in Aug., 1892, at Heppner, Ore., to seek affiliation with the Southern Baptist Convention and to separate from Baptists of the Northwest who accepted "alien immersion" and practiced "open communion." Consisting largely of Southern Baptists who migrated from the South, this group made petition to the SBC in 1893. It was referred to a committee which reported unfavorably at the SBC annual meeting in 1894. The Northwest group continued their petitions for five or six years, but finally concluded that further efforts were useless and dissolved their convention in June, 1900. The descendents of some of these same Baptists were leaders of the convention in Oregon-Washington that did attain SBC recognition and approval in 1949—56 years after the first petition for affiliation was presented. ROY L. JOHNSON

NORTHEAST, SOUTHERN BAPTISTS IN. See MARYLAND, BAPTIST CONVENTION OF, NEW YORK, BAPTIST CONVENTION OF, and OHIO, STATE CONVENTION OF BAPTISTS IN.

NORTHERN PLAINS BAPTIST ASSOCIATIONS.

I. Extant. EAST RIVER (South Dakota). Organized Nov. 2, 1964, by messengers from four churches east of the Missouri River which withdrew from South Dakota Association of Southern Baptists.

FRONTIER (Wyoming). Organized Jan. 6, 1958, in order to provide for a more effective program on an associational basis, by messengers from five churches which had previously been in the Old Faithful Association.

GLACIER (Montana). Organized Aug. 20, 1966, at Townsend, Mont., by messengers from six churches which had been affiliated with the Treasure State Association.

GREEN RIVER (Wyoming). Organized May 11, 1964, by messengers from churches in the southwest part of the state, which had formerly been in Old Faithful Association.

HI-LINE (Montana). Organized Sept. 20, 1959, by messengers from three churches formerly in the Montana Southern Baptist Association, plus Calvary Baptist Church, Glasgow.

NORTH DAKOTA WESTERN and NORTH DAKOTA EASTERN. Created in Sept., 1962, when North Dakota Southern Baptist Association was divided into two associations designated North Dakota Western and North Dakota Eastern.

OLD FAITHFUL (Wyoming). Organized at Billings, Mont., Sept. 24, 1953, by messengers from seven churches in Wyoming which, by mutual consent with messengers from churches in Montana and the church in Williston, N.D., dissolved the Wyoming-Montana Southern Baptist Association for the purpose of organizing two new associations, Old Faithful and Montana-North Dakota Southern Baptist Association.

TREASURE STATE (Montana). Formerly the Southwest Montana Southern Baptist Association which had been organized June 27, 1958, at Deer Lodge, Mont., by messengers from churches which had withdrawn from the Montana Western Association.

TRIANGLE (Montana). Formerly Montana Western Baptist Association. Name changed to Triangle during the 1958 annual meeting of the original association.

WEST RIVER (South Dakota). Organized Nov. 15, 1956, by messengers from four churches in Old Faithful Southern Baptist Association in Wyoming which withdrew from the Wyoming Association to form West River. With the establishment of missions in eastern South Dakota, the association changed its name to South Dakota Association of Southern Baptists, Sept., 1963. When East River Association was formed Nov. 2, 1964, the area west of the Missouri River again adopted the name West River.

YELLOWSTONE (Montana). Formerly Montana Eastern Southern Baptist Association. New name adopted at its annual meeting Sept. 8, 1961, at Trinity Baptist Church, Billings, Mont.

YELLOWSTONE (Wyoming). Organized in 1961 by messengers from six churches which had previously been in Old Faithful Association.

II. Extinct. MONTANA EASTERN SOUTHERN BAPTIST ASSOCIATION. Organized Nov. 12, 1957, by churches which remained in the Montana Association when Montana Western Association was organized. Changed name to Yellowstone Association of Southern Baptists (Montana), Sept. 8, 1961.

MONTANA-NORTH DAKOTA SOUTHERN BAPTIST ASSOCIATION. Organized at Billings, Mont., Sept. 24, 1953, by messengers from five churches in Montana and one in North Dakota, which by mutual consent with messengers from Wyoming, dissolved the Wyoming-Montana Southern Baptist Association for the purpose of organizing two new associations. Montana-North Dakota Southern Baptist Association dissolved Dec. 14, 1954, when the North Dakota churches withdrew to form North Dakota Southern Baptist Association and the Montana churches the Montana Southern Baptist Association.

MONTANA SOUTHERN BAPTIST ASSOCIATION. Name adopted by churches left in Montana after the organization of the North Dakota Southern Baptist Association was formed, Dec. 14, 1954.

MONTANA WESTERN SOUTHERN BAPTIST ASSOCIATION. Organized Nov. 12, 1957, by messengers from five churches in Western Montana which withdrew from the Montana Southern Baptist Association. Name changed to Triangle Association in 1958.

NORTH DAKOTA SOUTHERN BAPTIST ASSOCIATION. Organized Dec. 14, 1954, at Williston, N. D., by messengers from five churches in North Dakota which withdrew from the Montana-North Dakota Southern Baptist Association. Dissolved in Sept., 1962, when North Dakota Western and North Dakota Eastern associations were formed.

SOUTH DAKOTA ASSOCIATION OF SOUTHERN BAPTISTS. The name adopted in Sept., 1963, by the association which had formerly been organized as West River Association of Southern Baptists. It ceased to exist when on Nov. 2, 1964, the name West River was again adopted for the area west of the Missouri River and the area east of the river adopted the name East River.

WYOMING-MONTANA SOUTHERN BAPTIST ASSOCIATION. Organized Feb. 17, 1953, at Casper, Wyo., by messengers from churches in Wyoming, Montana, and North Dakota. In Sept., 1953, the churches in Wyoming withdrew to form the Old Faithful Association. The churches in Montana, and the church at Williston, N. D., formed the Montana Association.

NICY MURPHY and O. L. BAYLESS

NORTHERN PLAINS BAPTIST CONVENTION.

I. Southern Baptist Beginnings. Prior to the summer of 1951 not one Southern Baptist church existed in the states of Wyoming, Montana, North Dakota, and South Dakota, the area now included in the Northern Plains Baptist Convention. People in these states with Southern Baptist beliefs or backgrounds had affiliated with churches of other denominations or had become inactive.

In the late forties and early fifties an increased population of Southern Baptists in this area was occasioned principally by the establishment of military installations, expansion of the oil industry, and the construction of missile bases. Unable to find the kind of churches to which they had been accustomed (the closest Southern Baptist church was in Salt Lake City, Utah, nearly 400 miles away), families began meeting together for fellowship and Bible study. They were concerned not only for the spiritual welfare of their families, but for the residents whose spiritual needs were not being met by the existing churches.

Development by States—Wyoming.—The first service within the four-state area conducted by Southern Baptists for the purpose of organizing a church-related work was June 24, 1951, in Casper, Wyo. A small group, made up primarily of families connected with the oil industry, met in the Mountain States Power Company building for Bible study. Two weeks later, O. R. (Benny) Delmar of Tollison, Ariz., met with this group and conducted worship services. Following the evening service a business meeting was called and the group voted to organize a Southern Baptist church the following Sunday. On July 15, 1951, in the City-County Building, the First Southern Baptist Church of Casper was constituted. Delmar was called as pastor, and the church affiliated with the Baptist General Convention of Arizona.

This new church sponsored missions in Wheatland, Cheyenne, and Cody, and by the end of 1952 a Southern Baptist church had been constituted in each of these cities. Churches in Newcastle, Sheridan, and Worland were formed in 1953 and the following year five more came into being: Mt. View, Casper; Orchard Valley (now Emmanuel), Cheyenne; Grace Southern (now Bethel), Rawlins; and First Southern (now Hillcrest), Riverton.

Highland, Cody, sponsored a mission in Greybull which became the Grace Baptist Church in 1954. First Southern, Cheyenne, started work in Laramie in Mar., 1956, and this became a church (now Trinity) the next year. First Southern, Casper, sponsored the Westwood Baptist Mission in Casper. This mission became the Boyd Avenue Baptist Church. It, in turn, gave leadership in organizing a mission in Gillette which became the First Southern Baptist Church in Aug., 1963.

Thus the work spread. A mission spirit seemed to characterize the churches in Wyoming. Many churches, though small in membership and weak financially, reached out into other needy areas to establish missions and churches.

In the fall of 1952, Delmar was elected area missionary for Wyoming and Montana. Later, North Dakota was added. He served in this capacity until May 1, 1955, when Robert L. Smith was assigned to Wyoming as area missionary. Delmar kept Montana and North Dakota.

Montana.—The First Southern Baptist Church of Casper continued its outreach, even to Billings, Mont., 300 miles away. The W. C. King family, members of the Casper church, moved to Billings. About the same time the Alvie McCaslin family whom Delmar had known in Texas, moved from that state to a ranch 72 miles west of Billings. Through Delmar the two families became acquainted and made plans to begin a mission.

In Sept., 1952, an announcement was placed in the local newspaper that a Southern Baptist mission would be organized at a meeting Sept. 15 in the Seventh Day Adventist church building. Eighteen members began the new mission.

Glen Braswell, pastor of the First Baptist Church of Merkel, Tex., and Delmar had been juniors together in the First Baptist Church of

Seminole, Okla., and later, roommates at Oklahoma Baptist University. Delmar invited Braswell to preach in a revival for the mission in October. After the last morning service of the revival, the mission called Braswell to be its pastor. Then on Dec. 7, the mission became the First Southern Baptist Church (now Emmanuel), with 32 charter members and Braswell as the pastor. A building purchased from the Trinity Lutheran Church housed the congregation.

During the summer of 1953, the new church in Billings sponsored missions in Glendive, Poplar, Wolf Point, and Great Falls, and before the year's end these had become churches. First Southern, Great Falls, started a mission at Shelby in Apr., 1954. This mission soon became a church. A family which had been members of First Southern, Billings, moved to Forsythe and became the nucleus of a mission work there. From this beginning a church was organized, June 13, 1955. In July, 1955, missions were organized at Baker and Butte. These soon became chuches.

In Mar., 1957, W. A. Wiggins, who had been pastor of the First Southern Baptist Church of Cheyenne, Wyo., since 1952, was approved by the Home Mission Board and the Colorado Baptist Convention as the Colorado convention's first pastoral missionary. He and his family moved to Missoula and led in constituting the Trinity Baptist Church. This church sponsored missions in Deer Lodge, Hamilton, Bozeman, and Kalispell, which later became churches.

Next, work was started in Helena, the capital city. Two student summer missionaries, one of whom was Joe Thomas Odle, son of Joe Odle, editor of the Mississippi Baptist state paper, took a religious survey and were instrumental in starting a mission. It was organized into a church (now Calvary) on June 15, 1958, under the leadership of Albert Casteel, a pastoral missionary. This church sponsored missions in Townsend, Helena Valley, and Three Forks, which became churches. In similar ways the work spread to other cities, and churches were constituted.

Superintendents of missions have included Delmar, 1952–60; A. Wilson Parker, 1960–63; Joe Smith, 1963–66; and Leroy Smith, 1967– .

North Dakota.—Families connected with the oil industry were reponsible for beginning Southern Baptist work in North Dakota. Moving to the area around Williston in the early fifties, they found no churches which conformed to their beliefs and method of worship and witness. Delmar, who in the fall of 1952 had become area missionary for Wyoming, Montana, and North Dakota under the direction of the Arizona convention, was asked by these families for assistance in starting a Southern Baptist witness in Williston.

On Mar. 8, 1953, he and nine others met together in a Seventh Day Adventist church building for a Bible study. Twenty were present for the worship service in which Delmar preached. The following Sunday this group organized the First Southern Baptist Church of Williston, with 12 charter members. Missions of the Williston church at Ray and Watford City were next constituted into churches. After ten years, the transfer of oil people left the churches at Williston and Ray so weak that they became inactive. (Only recently has the work been reactivated, under the leadership of the pastor at Watford City.)

In June, 1954, a mission sponsored by the First Baptist Church of Glendive, Mont., was started in Dickinson, N. D., in the basement of the community building. It was constituted into a church on Aug. 29, 1954, with 24 charter members.

In the fall of 1954 a small group of Southern Baptists in Bismarck secured the Gold Room in the basement of the Patterson Hotel in which to hold services. They continued to meet for two months and then on Dec. 10, the First Southern Baptist Church (now Capitol Heights) was constituted, with eight charter members. Six months later Glenn Field, a pastor in Georgia, was called as the pastor. This church sponsored a mission in nearby Mandan, an oil refinery town. This became the Baptist Temple in 1959.

Military families connected with the Minot Air Force Base were responsible for beginning Southern Baptist work in Minot in 1960.

Southern Baptist work in Eastern North Dakota began with the coming of W. J. Hughes to Grand Forks as a pastoral missionary in 1958. The First Southern Baptist Church (now Faith), constituted June 14, 1959, has led in the establishment of the Calvary Baptist Church of Emerado (1961), near the gate of the Grand Forks Air Force Base; Finley Baptist Church of Finley (1964); the First Baptist Church of Devils Lake (1964); and two across the state border, in Minnesota: Hallock Baptist Church, Hallock, and the First Baptist Chapel of East Grand Forks. Calvary, Emerado, began a mission in Larimore, which became a church in 1964.

In Fargo, the largest city in the state, Southern Baptist work was started by a pastoral missionary, Ruel Cook. The Temple Baptist Church of that city was constituted, Aug. 17, 1958.

Area missionaries who have served in North Dakota include Delmar (see section on Wyoming), Roy Owen, who came in Nov., 1956, and served both North and South Dakota until Nov., 1961; and John H. Allen, who served both states until the coming of Albert S. Lamm in Sept., 1962. Lamm served in North Dakota only, making it possible for Allen to devote full time to South Dakota.

South Dakota.—Southern Baptist work in South Dakota had its beginning in Rapid City early in 1953. A group of Southern Baptists invited L. A. Watson, general missionary for the Baptist General Convention of Arizona, to meet with them for counsel. On Mar. 25, 1953, the First Southern Baptist Church (now Calvary) was constituted in the home of Sgt. Clydal Donaho, with 22 members. In July, 1953, L. H.

Roseman was called as pastor. He served for more than 10 years. All the churches in South Dakota have been directly or indirectly influenced by the outreach of this first church.

Within a few months after the church was constituted it helped start missions in Lemmon and Sturgis. The First Baptist Church of Sturgis was constituted, Feb. 13, 1955, with 17 members. The Mission Baptist Church of Lemmon, organized in July, 1954, was dissolved in May, 1962. In 1955 the Rapid City church extended help to Pierre, the capital city, 180 miles to the east. This work developed into the Capitol Heights Baptist Church in Mar., 1955. This church in turn sponsored work at Mitchell which resulted in the organization of the Calvary Baptist Church in 1961. It also began a mission at Eagle Butte on the Cheyenne River Indian Reservation.

In Jan., 1958, a mission Sunday School sponsored by First Southern, Rapid City, was started at Box Elder, a small community near Ellsworth Air Force Base. In May of that year the mission was constituted into Temple Baptist Church, with 54 charter members. This new church sponsored a mission in the north part of Rapid City. This resulted in the constitution of the Knollwood Baptist Church in 1960.

In Jan., 1958, Aberdeen was approved as a pastoral mission field and Dave Goodman was named as pastoral missionary. On Nov. 19, 1961, the church organized, taking the name South Side Baptist Church. This church (now inactive) began a mission at Webster.

It was not until June, 1963, that Southern Baptist work was started in Sioux Falls, the largest city in the state. On Jan. 23, 1964, the mission started there was constituted into the Sioux Valley Baptist Church.

Other churches in South Dakota included the Huron Baptist Church of Huron (1965) and the First Baptist Church of Webster (1967).

Superintendents of missions who served in South Dakota included Robert L. Smith, whose area also included Wyoming (1955–57); Roy Owen (1957–61); and John Allen (1962–67).

All of the Southern Baptist churches in Wyoming, Montana, North Dakota, and South Dakota affiliated first with the Arizona convention since it was the closest state convention. On Nov. 21–23, 1955, when the Colorado Baptist General Convention came into being, they affiliated with it. All the departments of work in the Colorado convention bore the same relationship and felt the same responsibility for the work in the states to the north as they did to the work in Colorado.

Twelve years passed, during which time groundwork was laid by the Colorado convention for the forming of a new state convention to be composed of churches in the four-state area. A steering committee made up of an elected representative from each of the 13 associations in the area had selected Rapid City, S. D., as the site for the convention offices. A subcommittee of the steering committee had prepared a suggested budget and another had drawn up a proposed provisional constitution and bylaws. LEROY SMITH, A. WILSON PARKER, J. T. BURDINE, JR., JOHN P. BAKER, and NICY MURPHY

II. Organization and Developments. The Northern Plains Baptist Convention, 30th among the state conventions of the Southern Baptist Convention, was organized Nov. 7–9, 1967, in a meeting held in the Calvary Baptist Church of Rapid City, S. D. This body was made up of messengers from 75 Southern Baptist churches in the states of Wyoming, Montana, North Dakota, and South Dakota. Each of these churches had, by a vote of its members, declared its desire to become a part of the new convention.

Lewis Adkison, immediate past president of the Colorado convention, presided. E. J. Speegle was elected president; David Bunch, first vice-president; Marshall Strother, second vice-president; Ralph Ehren, recording secretary; and Troy Corzine, assistant recording secretary.

In the meeting of the executive board, which was interspersed with the sessions of the organizational meeting, John P. Baker was elected executive secretary-treasurer. For the previous five years he had served as director of the departments of missions and stewardship for the Colorado convention. Prior to that he had held pastorates in Texas and Colorado.

Robert M. (Bob) Lawrence, who had been serving for a year as director of religious education in the four-state area under the direction of the Baptist Sunday School Board and the Colorado convention, was asked to continue in this capacity. Lawrence had served churches in the Colorado convention in the religious education and music fields for nine years prior to this.

The board also voted to retain Leroy Smith as superintendent of missions in Montana. Smith had been serving in this capacity for a year under the Colorado convention. Prior to his coming to Colorado in 1956, he had served the Arizona convention for eight years as secretary of evangelism. In Colorado he had served as secretary of stewardship and missions and associate to the executive secretary, superintendent of city missions in Denver, and later as a pastor in Denver.

Also retained were R. L. Mefford, Eugene Branch, A. L. Davis, C. Ballard White, and Harold Heiney, missionaries to the Indians; Ross Harmonson, David Bunch, and W. J. Hughes, pastoral missionaries; and Carrol Smith, professor of Chair of Bible and director of Baptist Student work on the campus of the University of Wyoming, Laramie.

The board, in its meeting on Dec. 7–8, 1967, elected Miss Nicy Murphy as executive secretary of Woman's Missionary Union. She had served in a similar capacity for 11 years in the Colorado convention.

The board employed three superintendents of missions: J. T. Burdine, a pastor in Alaska, for the state of North Dakota; O. R. Delmar for

Wyoming; and A. Wilson Parker, who had formerly served as a pastor and as area missionary in Montana and as a pastor in McCook, Nebr., for South Dakota.

In Mar., 1968, the administration secured June Upchurch for bookkeeper and office secretary to the executive secretary. Other part-time office secretaries were secured for the other departments.

A former residence in downtown Rapid City was purchased and renovated to provide office space. Office furniture was a gift of the Mississippi Baptist Convention.

To facilitate and coordinate their activities better, the churches are grouped voluntarily into associations. These number 13: five in Montana, four in Wyoming, and two each in the Dakotas.

When the convention held its first annual meeting, Nov. 5–7, 1968, in Worland, Wyo., the formation of one new church was reported, the Emmanuel Baptist Church of Havre, Mont. Since South Side, Aberdeen, S. D., had disbanded temporarily, the count remained at 75.

Five new churches were constituted during the calendar year of 1969. Four of these were in South Dakota. They included North Sioux Baptist Church, Sioux Falls; First Baptist Church (Indian), Eagle Butte; Sioux Baptist Chapel (Indian), Rapid City; and Knollwood Baptist Church, Rapid City, which had reverted to mission status in Dec., 1968. The First Baptist Church in Kemmerer, Wyo., was constituted in November.

The second annual meeting was held in Billings, Mont., Nov. 4–6, 1969. W. J. Hughes, pastor of the Faith Baptist Church, Grand Forks, N. D., was elected president.

Records at the close of 1969 showed a total of 79 churches, distributed by states as follows: Wyoming, 23; Montana, 32; North Dakota, 11; and South Dakota, 13. Twenty-six church-type missions and 23 fellowship and Bible study groups were also in operation. Church membership totaled 11,551.

Sunday School enrolment numbered 9,429; Training Union, 4,114; WMU, 1,770; and Brotherhood, 492. Vacation Bible Schools totaled 117, including 42 mission schools. Enrolment was 7,788.

Total contributions reported by the churches amounted to $1,094,417, with $72,134 going through the Cooperative Program.

The convention contributed 12 per cent of all undesignated funds to the Cooperative Program for world missions causes. Gifts to special mission causes included $12,483 to the Lottie Moon Christmas Offering for foreign missions; $7,996 to the Annie Armstrong Easter Offering for home missions; and $5,000 to the state mission offering. NICY MURPHY

III. Program of Work of the Northern Plains Baptist Convention. The general convention is made up of messengers elected by churches cooperating with and contributing to its work. It meets annually.

The officers of the convention are president, first vice-president, second vice-president, recording secretary, and assistant recording secretary. They are elected annually by the convention.

The convention elects an executive board to represent its total interests and program. It is empowered to act for the convention between annual meetings except that it cannot impose its own will upon the convention by contradicting or rescinding any action of the convention taken at its regular meeting. The board is also authorized to employ all convention personnel except office secretaries. Although the staff is small in number, most of the usual departments found in any state convention are promoted.

The executive secretary-treasurer, in addition to his administrative duties, promotes the departments of evangelism, stewardship, missions, and Brotherhood.

The director of religious education promotes Sunday School, church training, Baptist Student Union, and church music. He is also a consultant in church architecture.

WMU is promoted by an executive secretary who directs all the age-level activities.

Evangelism.—The Department of Evangelism promotes evangelism in the local churches through clinics and conferences, distribution of literature, a state evangelism conference, and promotion of revival meetings. In 1968–69 the Crusade of the Americas was given strong emphasis.

Stewardship.—Through the Stewardship Department individuals and churches are made aware of their stewardship responsibilities. Clinics are held and literature is distributed. Churches are encouraged to give through the Cooperative Program on a percentage basis.

Missions.—A superintendent of missions serves each of the states in the convention, giving encouragement to the churches and coordinating the work of the associations and states.

Language work with the Indians is in six locations, three in Montana, two in South Dakota, and one in North Dakota.

The Missions Department also disburses salary supplements to around 30 churches and missions.

Brotherhood.—The Brotherhood is promoted through an annual state meeting, associational and local clinics and conferences, and distribution of materials. State Brotherhood officers were elected at the 1969 annual meeting. Chester Johnson was elected president.

Sunday School.—In helping Sunday Schools accomplish the tasks assigned to them by the church, the state convention through the director of religious education, distributes leadership materials, directs clinics, institutes, workshops, and area conferences. Vacation Bible Schools receive strong promotion. VBS clinics for the training of workers are held each year.

Training Union.—Four state Training Union conventions were held in 1969 in which Junior memory drill, Intermediate sword drill, and Young People's better speakers' tournaments were held. Training Union "M" Night is also given strong promotion.

Baptist Student Union.—Baptist student activities are conducted on four campuses. The work is promoted through conventions, retreats, and workshops. In 1969 the number of students reached through this ministry numbered 92.

Church Music.—Two associations conducted choral workshops in 1969, Old Faithful and Montana Yellowstone.

Church Architecture.—Informational materials and services of the Church Architecture Department are free to all churches upon request.

Woman's Missionary Union.—WMU was organized in Nov., 1967, at the time of the organization of the convention. Mrs. Ray Gilliland was elected president. It promotes missionary education and participation for all age levels. The weeks of prayer and offerings for home, foreign, and state missions are promoted annually. Clinics and conferences, distribution of promotional materials, an annual state meeting, and two state council meetings are some of the means through which the work is promoted.

Chair of Bible.—In the fall of 1966 a Chair of Bible was started on the campus of the University of Wyoming by the Colorado Baptist General Convention. Since the university is in the area of the Northern Plains convention, this ministry was retained. Carrol Smith served as the professor until his resignation in the summer of 1969.

Finances and Sources of Income. Article VIII, Sections 1, 2, and 3 of the constitution of the Northern Plains convention state the financial policy. They declare the Cooperative Program to be the chief means through which the convention shall support its missionary endeavors. They further state: "All funds of this convention shall be raised by voluntary contributions providing this does not prevent acquiring funds or property by bequest, or use of any income from property that may be bequeathed to or purchased by the agencies thereof." They stipulate that "All designated offerings and special gifts accepted by this convention shall be applied strictly according to the expressed will and direction of the contributor."

In addition to Cooperative Program contributions received from the churches, the convention receives financial help from several other sources. The largest source is the Home Mission Board, SBC, which, on the basis of a cooperative agreement with the state convention, contributes a major share of the total mission budget. Other SBC agencies which contribute financially are the Sunday School Board, the Brotherhood Commission, and WMU.

Some state conventions have made notable contributions, Mississippi leading in amount and consistency. Many individuals and churches have also given generously.

Additional funds are received through an annual State Missions Offering which is given by the churches in connection with a season of prayer observance. JOHN P. BAKER

Publications.—The convention's news is published every two weeks on a page in the *Rocky Mountain Baptist,* official organ of the Colorado Baptist General Convention, O. L. Bayless, editor. The news is compiled and edited in the offices of the Northern Plains Convention. John P. Baker served as editor the first year. Miss Nicy Murphy then became editor. NICY MURPHY

NORTHWEST BAPTIST ASSOCIATION. See OREGON-WASHINGTON, BAPTIST ASSOCIATIONS OF.

NORTHWEST BAPTIST CONVENTION. See OREGON-WASHINGTON, BAPTIST GENERAL CONVENTION OF.

NORTHWEST BAPTIST CONVENTION (1888–97). The name adopted by a body of Baptists representing churches of western Washington (Territory) and British Columbia, constituted June 16, 1888, at Tacoma, Wash. Twenty of the 39 churches, with 1,145 members, were represented. Its stated purpose was to cooperate with the American Baptist Home Mission Society in evangelizing Washington Territory, British Columbia, and Alaska; plant and aid churches in the area; and direct educational work among Baptists. When British Columbia Baptists organized their own convention in July, 1897, the Northwest Baptist Convention soon changed its name to Western Washington Convention. Although Baptists from the South were scattered among the churches, this body never was affiliated in any way with Southern Baptists as such.
ROY L. JOHNSON

NORTHWEST BAPTIST FOUNDATION. An organization of Southern Baptists in the Northwestern United States, with offices in Portland, Ore., to acquire and administer funds for loans to churches and assist Baptist institutions, agencies, and churches in accordance with the wishes of donors of funds. Directors of the foundation are elected by the Baptist General Convention of Oregon-Washington which authorized organization of such an agency in 1954 and approved its charter in 1955. Special gifts from William Fleming of Texas, Mr. and Mrs. Homer A. Hyde of Texas, and others increased the foundation's funds to more than $322,000 in 1969, including student loan funds and special funds administered for associations. Harry G. Bonner became the first full-time executive secretary of the foundation in Nov., 1967. It is incorporated as a nonprofit corporation under Oregon law. ROY L. JOHNSON

***NORTHWESTERN ASSEMBLY.** In 1969 property value was $50,000, consisting of 40 acres of land, seven buildings, and a swimming pool. The assembly is incorporated, and owned by Northwestern Baptist Association. Debt was only $600. J. M. GASKIN

NORWEGIAN BAPTIST CONGO MISSION (cf. Norwegian Baptist Foreign Mission Society, Vol. II). In the Bas-Uélé province of the Congo, mission field of the Norwegian Baptist Union, Baptist churches were experiencing steady growth and membership totaled 9,778 in 1956. There were 1,072 baptisms in that year, with 3,782 in preparation for baptism. Despite serious dissension in regard to such practices as speaking in tongues, prophecy, visions, and public confession—which resulted in the breakaway of a large number of evangelists and churches in the following year—overall growth continued in those churches related to the mission.

In 1959 the Baptist church union of Bas-Uélé was given independence, with church buildings and other property being turned over to it by the mission. Leadership responsibility was assumed by Congolese and missionaries served increasingly in an advisory capacity. The union received legal recognition in 1964 as l'Eglise Baptiste du Bas-Uélé.

Following political independence of the Congo in 1960, there were several years of disorders, rebellion, and widespread violence. In Bas-Uélé the most serious disturbances began in 1964; mission stations were pillaged, schools closed, medical work destroyed. Some church leaders and many members were killed. Large parts of the population fled into the forests or across the border. Those missionaries who had not managed to evacuate were held hostage for up to six months, until their release in 1965. Throughout three difficult years church services and evangelistic work continued, and to some extent local primary schools also.

In 1967 five missionaries returned, carried out extensive relief activities, and began the reconstruction of mission and church buildings. Eight more missionaries arrived the following year. They resumed medical work, setting up three clinics and two dispensaries, and opened two secondary schools.

There were 21 Norwegian Baptist missionaries in Bas-Uélé in 1969. Congolese pastors numbered eight at last report, evangelists 159. There were 5,438 pupils in primary schools, 80 students in secondary schools, and 10 in the pastors' school in Bondo. Church membership totaled 16,219. Norwegian Baptists, with 61 churches and a membership of 6,500 in their own country, devoted 566,246 kroner ($79,306) to their Congo mission work in 1969.

JOHN ALLEN MOORE

O

OAK HILL ACADEMY. This school was founded in 1877 near Mouth of Wilson, Grayson County, Virginia, to serve children of the New River Association of Virginia and North Carolina without the advantage of adequate public schools. In 1921 the Baptist General Association of Virginia assumed responsibility for the academy. Since the development of good state-supported schools in the area, Oak Hill has offered its services to students with special needs, home problems, poor adjustment in the local school, older people preparing for church-related vocations, and high-school students from other lands.

Under the presidency of Joseph C. Hough (1958–66) a strong program of renovation and upgrading was carried out with increased support from the denomination. His successor, Robert B. Isner, has continued this development. In 1968 there were 214 students enrolled in classes at the high school level, and 22 of them were graduated. Accreditation has been granted by the Virginia Department of Education and by the United States Government for teaching of foreign students.

CARRINGTON PAULETTE

OATES, JOHN ALEXANDER (b. Sampson County, N. C., June 2, 1870; d. Fayetteville, N. C., Feb. 12, 1958). Lawyer and Baptist leader. Son of John Alexander and Mary Ashford Oates, he entered Wake Forest College in 1888, interrupted his studies to teach in Sampson County schools, and received the B.A. from Wake Forest in 1895. He studied law at the college in 1910, and practiced law in Fayetteville, 1910–50. He became the first judge of the Cumberland County Recorder's Court in 1913. About 1892 he became managing editor, owner, and publisher of *The North Carolina Baptist,* a Baptist journal which, under Oates's leadership, merged with the *Biblical Recorder* in 1908. In 1908 he organized the State Anti-Saloon League.

Oates was elected to the state senate in 1917. He was president of the Wake Forest College board of trustees (1913–14 and 1941–48), and served on the board for 40 years. He was president of the Baptist State Convention, 1915–17. He was a deacon of the Fayetteville First Baptist Church, and was superintendent of the Sunday School for 40 years. In 1953 he published *The Story of Fayetteville and the Upper Cape Fear.*

Oates married Emma E. Dodd on May 20, 1897. After her death, Feb. 28, 1928, he married Isabelle Charters Crowder, June 17, 1931. Their children are John Alexander and Mary Ashford Oates. ELIZABETH BRANTLEY

*OHIO, STATE CONVENTION OF BAPTISTS IN.

I. History. Continuous growth in all areas of its organization and work has been experienced by the State Convention of Baptists in Ohio since its organization on Jan. 8, 1954. Under the leadership of Ray E. Roberts, executive secretary-treasurer, the convention's progress was marked by two major emphases: evangelism and missionary expansion through establishing new churches and missions.

Growth since 1955.—Near the end of 1955, the 75 churches and 27 missions of the convention's six associations reported a membership of 12,957. Baptisms were reported at 1,779. A five-year program adopted in 1955 called for 200 churches and 10 associations by the end of 1960, with 34,000 members. Attainment by the end of 1960 showed 216 churches and 97 missions in 11 associations, with 35,807 members. The next five years (by the end of 1965) saw the number of associations double to 22, the number of congregations increase to 338 churches and 130 missions and the membership grow to 63,457.

By the end of 1968, the convention was composed of 400 churches and 147 missions with a membership of 82,164. The average annual gain in membership, 1954–68, was 5,176 with the greatest gain in one year, 6,620, registered in 1967, the year of the Dayton New Life Crusade. Each year, except one, has shown an increase in baptisms, from 608 in 1954 to 6,589 in 1968, an average of 4,267 per year.

In May, 1961, the Southern Baptist Convention meeting in St. Louis granted Ohio representation on SBC boards and agencies, though the required 25,000 members had been surpassed by mid-1959.

Expansion in new areas.—Expansion of Southern Baptist work throughout Ohio and into the neighboring states to the east followed a natural course through development of an area missions program. In early 1955, five associations were served by three area missionaries: Darty F. Stowe in southern Ohio, George R. Gaddie in central Ohio, and Ottis E. Denney in northern Ohio. In Feb., 1955, Gaddie moved from Dayton to Toledo, and the following August the Maumee Valley Association was organized with five churches and one mission. Maumee Valley encompassed 22 counties, with the missionary serving from Toledo. On Jan. 20, 1961, the Lakeland Association was formed by six churches and a mission in the Sandusky and Fremont areas. This area of Northwest Ohio was served successively by Denney (1954–55), Gaddie (1955–56), J. Kenneth Allaby (1956–59), James M. Palmer (1959–64), and James O. Coldiron (1964–). In 1969 the two associations reported 24 churches, 13 missions, and 4,307 members.

Following Gaddie's move from Dayton to Toledo in 1955, Darty Stowe served the entire southern half of the state until Jan., 1956, when he moved to Columbus to assume the dual role of missionary in the Columbus area and state missions director. In October, William H. Slagle succeeded Stowe in southwest Ohio, serving Central, Greater Cincinnati, and Southwestern associations until June, 1957, when Richard Carlton came to serve Greater Cincinnati Association. Ultimately, another missionary was placed in Hamilton to serve Southwestern Association, allowing Slagle to develop a city missions program in Dayton. Thus, Greater Dayton (formerly Central) Association was served by area missionaries Gaddie (1954–55), Stowe (1955–56), Slagle (1956–61), and W. Paul Payne (1962–69). In 1968 Greater Dayton reported 63 churches, 13 missions, and 21,063 members.

Greater Cincinnati Association, in 1954, covered more than 17 southern counties. With the organization of Scioto Valley and Greater Miami Valley (now Southwestern) associations in early 1955, the Greater Cincinnati area was narrowed to six counties. In Nov., 1962, Southern Hills was formed by 12 churches and five missions of Greater Cincinnati. The two associations have been served by area missionaries Stowe (1954–56), Slagle (1956–57), Carlton (1957–66), and Orville Griffin (1967–). Greater Cincinnati reported 48 churches and eight missions in 1969 with 12,594 members. Southern Hills had 15 churches and four missions with 1,308 members.

Southwestern Association, covering two counties, was served by missionaries Stowe (1955–56), Slagle (1956–59), and O. D. Denney (1959–62), with the latter giving his full time to the one association. In Sept., 1961, five Southwestern churches and a mission in the Middletown area joined with one Greater Dayton church and one Cincinnati church in organizing the Miami Valley Association. The succeeding missionaries served both associations: Ronald Griffin (1963–64) and Laurin H. Gardner (1965–). The two associations, covering the Hamilton-Middletown area, reported in 1969 a total of 50 churches and 12 missions with 11,849 members.

With the formation of the Maumee Valley Association in 1955, the territory served by Erie Association was narrowed to 23 Ohio counties. The area included the cities of Cleveland, Youngstown, Akron, Canton, and Mansfield, and already calls were coming for help in establishing new work in New York and Pennsylvania.

Erie reported 14 churches and five missions in the fall of 1955. The following April, Denney resigned to accept an Akron church, and Paul Nevels left a church near Hamilton to become the area missionary. Bolivar Drive Baptist Church in Bradford, Pa., united with Erie in Sept., 1954, and on June 24 of the next year LaSalle Baptist Church in Niagara Falls was constituted as the first Southern Baptist church in New York State. The coming of these two churches marked the beginning of concerted efforts to penetrate New York and Pennsylvania from Ohio. On Sept. 7, 1957, 10 churches and 10 missions of Erie Association, including those in New York, Pennsylvania, and one in West Virginia, organized the Cuyahoga Association. Since that time, Erie has given churches to form two other associations: Summit (organized Jan. 9, 1960, with seven churches and two missions) in the Akron area, and Buckeye Central (organized Oct. 19, 1964, with seven churches and three missions) in the area of Mansfield. Erie remains to serve a large area between Akron and Mansfield. In July, 1960, O. R. Delmar came as missionary for the Akron-Mansfield area, leaving Nevels to serve Cuyahoga Association. Thus, the area of Erie, Summit and Buckeye Central associations was served by Denney (1954–56), Nevels (1956–60), Delmar (1960–61), and Marvin Palmer (1962–).

Paul Nevels continued to answer the calls of churches in New York and Northwestern Pennsylvania until May 1, 1958, when Arthur L. Walker moved from an Ohio pastorate to Buffalo, N. Y., to become the area missionary. On Sept. 23, 1958, Frontier Association was constituted with five churches and two missions. Three years later Frontier had expanded until it included churches from Erie, Pa., to Syracuse and Utica, N. Y., and from the upper Adirondacks to Endicott and Elmira in the Southern Tier. On Sept. 29, 1961, three churches and nine missions formed the Central New York Association. Walker continued to serve this area as missionary until Nov., 1961, when he resigned to become state missions director in Ohio. Charles Magruder moved from Athens, Ohio, the following January and served the two associations until the end of 1963, at which time Central Association transferred affiliation to the Baptist Convention of Maryland. Ohio joined with Maryland in sponsoring the new Baptist Convention of New York, which was organized in Syracuse, Sept. 25–26, 1969, to become operative Jan. 1, 1970. On Oct. 24, 1969, three Frontier churches and two missions in the Rochester area formed the Greater Rochester Association. These two associations had a combined membership of 1,100 in 12 churches and 7 missions, with Magruder as area missionary.

Though Maryland was ultimately to give sponsorship to the work in New York City and along the Atlantic Coast, it was Ohio's executive secretary who first responded to a call from New York City. Roberts met with two families on the mezzanine of the Penn-Sheraton Hotel in Feb., 1957, and again on May 5 at the first meeting of the mission that was to become Manhattan Baptist Church. Twenty-seven people met at the 23rd Street YMCA for this meeting. Charles Jolly, a longtime friend of Roberts, led his church at Annapolis, Md., to sponsor the new work.

Since its own beginning in 1957, Cuyahoga Association has given birth to two other bodies: Northern Ohio (organized in Lorain County on Sept. 16, 1961 with nine churches and one mission), and Steel Valley (organized in the Youngstown area on Oct. 1, 1965). The area of the three associations was served successively by Denney (1954–56), Nevels (1956–63), and William H. Slagle (1963–65). Steel Valley received its own missionary in Dec., 1965, when Ross L. Hughes was transferred from Columbus. After that time, Cuyahoga and Northern Ohio were served by H. Raymond Langlois (1965–67) and John E. Witte (1967–). In 1969, Cuyahoga reported 3,148 members in 19 churches and 10 missions. Northern Ohio had 11 churches and 8 missions with 2,838 members, and Steel Valley listed 12 churches and 14 missions with 1,538 members.

Scioto Valley Association was organized on Jan. 28, 1955, with eight churches and seven missions. The area to be served included Columbus and all of the hill country of Southeast Ohio. Darty Stowe served this area (1954–56) from Cincinnati. John I. Snedden became the resident missionary on Jan. 1, 1957, and served until Feb., 1958, when he became area missionary for West Virginia. On Oct. 12, 1957, seven Columbus area churches with their eight missions organized the Capital City Association. Five West Virginia churches and one mission affiliated with Scioto Valley organized Pioneer Association on Oct. 31, 1958. On Nov. 11, 1960, seven churches and nine missions in both Ohio and West Virginia formed the Upper Ohio Valley Association. Muskingum Valley Association in the area of Zanesville and Cambridge was organized Mar. 2, 1963, by three churches from Capital City and one church and one mission from Scioto Valley. Robert E. Hall became the missionary for the area of Scioto Valley, Muskingum Valley, and Upper Ohio Valley on May 1, 1958, and still (1970) serves there. In 1969 Scioto Valley reported 10 churches and 2 missions with 1,496 members, while Muskingum Valley numbered 978 members in nine churches and six missions.

John Snedden continued to serve all of West Virginia, leading in setting up a state missions committee and later a state association composed of churches affiliated with Ohio, Kentucky, and Virginia. Greater Huntington Association, with four churches and four missions, grew out of the Pioneer Association on Sept. 11, 1961. The West Virginia work affiliated with Ohio numbered 22 churches and 11 missions with a membership of 4,104 in 1969.

In Aug., 1958, a mission was started in Pittsburgh, Pa., sponsored by the Evangel Baptist

Church, Weirton, W. Va. In Oct., 1959, Joseph Waltz became the pastor of the Pittsburgh church and director of Southern Baptist expansion efforts in western Pennsylvania. Resigning the church in Jan., 1964, Waltz served as area missionary and led in developing the Greater Pittsburgh Association. Organized out of Upper Ohio Valley Association on Sept. 13, 1963, with four churches and five missions, in 1969 it had a fellowship of 2,177 members in 17 churches and 12 missions.

Southern Baptist work in the capital city of Columbus began in 1953 with two missions that started about the same time. The first to constitute was Whitehall Baptist Church on Oct. 1, 1953, and it was followed by Southside Baptist Church on the following Jan. 3. On Oct. 12, 1957, the Capital City Association was organized with seven churches and eight missions from the Scioto Valley fellowship. Ross L. Hughes became area missionary for Capital City Association in Feb., 1960, thus relieving Darty Stowe to give full attention to direction of the state missions program. After Hughes's transfer to Steel Valley in Dec., 1965, the association was served by Glen W. Ray (1966–68) and Charles Brashear (1969–). Capital City reported in 1968 a membership of 9,240 in 48 churches and 13 missions.

West Central Association was organized on Jan. 4, 1964, with seven churches and five missions, some from Maumee Valley and some from Greater Dayton associations. Reporting 12 churches and 4 missions in 1969 with 1,795 members, this association was served by Paul Nevels (1963–65) after his transfer from Cleveland, and by Cary Harden (1966–) who came from a Cleveland pastorate.

ARTHUR L. WALKER

II. Program of Work. The State Convention of Baptists in Ohio has experienced considerable growth since its meager beginning in 1954. In that year, the state convention staff consisted of an executive secretary-treasurer, office secretary, secretary of religious education, whose wife served as his associate, and three pioneer missionaries. In 1970 the program of work was as follows:

Administration.—The administrative body of the convention is the state executive board, composed of 54 members representing the various areas served by the convention. These members are nominated and elected by the convention at their annual meeting. Members are elected for three-year terms, one-third of whom are elected at each annual meeting of the convention. Persons become eligible for reelection after one year. Paid workers of the convention's departments of work are ineligible for board membership.

The convention grants to the board the authority to function in its cooperative work and handle its affairs between the annual meetings. The board appoints all missionaries and other employees and has the responsibility of fixing all salaries of all workers employed and to determine the fields of work for each.

The officers of the convention are the president, two vice-presidents, recording secretary, assistant recording secretary, executive secretary-treasurer, and a historical secretary. These officers are elected annually by the convention and duly installed at the closing session of the convention meeting. These officers also serve as officers of the state executive board. In the first meeting of the board after the annual state convention, the president has the responsibility of appointing committees including an administrative committee, a finance committee, and a committee for each of the various departments or phases of the work of the convention.

The Cooperative Program budget, including all allocations to all convention boards, agencies, and causes is recommended by the board to the convention for adoption.

In 1970 one man served as the convention's executive secretary-treasurer. As executive secretary-treasurer, he is chief executive, administrative and promotional agent of the convention and the board. As treasurer, he is in charge of all properties and funds of the convention, under supervision of the board, keeps a record of receipts and disbursements, and makes a written report annually to the board and convention.

Ray E. Roberts was elected executive secretary-treasurer when the convention was organized in 1954 and continues to serve in that position (1970). Darty F. Stowe served as associate executive secretary-treasurer. He first came to work with the convention in 1954. He assists with the administrative details of the convention and is responsible for annuity, Baptist Foundation, church loans, bond underwriting, and scholarships.

Ohio Baptist Messenger.—This paper is the official journal of the convention and is under supervision of the Ohio Baptist Messenger committee of the board and operates as any other department of the convention. The *Messenger* is published weekly, its purpose being to publish religious news and Baptist doctrines and promote the work of the convention. In 1970 L. H. Moore served as editor, having come to the position in Jan., 1967. Its circulation was almost 10,000 in 1969.

Annuity.—The objective of the Annuity Department is to assist pastors, church, and denominational employees and the churches in interpreting, enrolling, and participating in the different plans of protection provided through the Annuity Board of the Southern Baptist Convention. Darty F. Stowe served as director for this department in 1970.

Brotherhood Department.—The objective of the state Brotherhood department is to assist the associations and churches in developing a program of missionary education and mission activity for Baptist men and Baptist boys. William H. Slagle became director of the department in 1967 and plans, promotes, and directs camps and state meetings relating to men and boys' work.

Sunday School and Church Building Department.—This department offers the churches in the convention help through church and associational leadership training schools, state assemblies, and regional conventions as well as furnishing other information and free literature. The department is also responsible for providing consultation services to churches on new church buildings and remodeling or rearranging older buildings to accommodate the church programs. Other programs directed by this department include church library services, church kindergartens, Vacation Bible School, and Week-day Bible study. The director of the department in 1970 was Charles E. Raley, who assumed the position in July, 1965.

Church Training and Music Department.—This department offers the churches in the convention help through special church and associational enlargement training clinics, regional conventions, and summer assemblies. It provides free literature and other helps with regard to church training. Music promotion is also a responsibility of this department, and opportunities for musical growth are provided through music festivals and church and associational music clinics. The department also helps with music for other events such as state conventions and state evangelistic conferences. Gilbert Wilder served as director of this department in 1970, having assumed the responsibility in Jan., 1970.

Baptist Student Union—This department works with college students on the college campuses located in the territory of the state convention. It aims at organizing BSU organizations and providing a spiritual ministry for college students. In 1970 the department was composed of Grady Evans, who served as director for the department in addition to being the field worker for southwestern Ohio. Other field workers were Louis McNabb, serving central Ohio, and Ronnie Hawkins, serving southeastern Ohio. Formerly a part of the Training Union Department, BSU became a separate department in Jan., 1970.

Woman's Missionary Union Department.—This department offers the churches in the convention help with the work of WMU, which includes Young Women's Auxiliary, Girls' Auxiliary, and Sunbeams. Assistance is given to the churches through special church and associational clinics, state conferences, summer assemblies, free literature, and other helps. The department also promotes the state missions offerings, Annie Armstrong Easter Offering for home missions, and the Lottie Moon Christmas Offering for foreign missions. Mrs. A. L. Kirkwood became director of this department in Oct., 1961. Miss Jeanette Henderson, youth director (1970), came to her position in June, 1964.

Evangelism and Stewardship Department.—This department gives encouragement to the evangelistic programs of the churches by promoting revivals, providing the annual state evangelistic conference, associational evangelism clinics, and also promotes stewardship through conferences, tracts, and audio-visual materials. W. Leonard Stigler, director of the department in 1970, began his service in 1959.

Missions Department.—This department directs the work of the area and associational missions, the starting of new missions, schools of missions and special ministries such as Christian social ministry, mission centers, Baptist family services, migrant missions, work with National Baptists, and language missions. The department correlates the overall mission program of the state convention with the work of the Home Mission Board, SBC. Arthur L. Walker has served as director of the department since Oct., 1961.

In 1970 Nelson Russell served as an associate in the department in charge of Christian Social Ministries. Other personnel included 11 area superintendents of missions, six language pastors, two associate missionaries, one youth and family service director, four Baptist center directors, and two US-2 missionaries.

State Baptist Assembly.—The Seneca Lake Baptist Assembly, Senecaville, Ohio, is owned and operated by the convention. The assembly consists of over 200 acres of choice land overlooking Seneca Lake. Facilities include an auditorium with conference rooms, family-style dining facilities, a manager's home, and accommodations for sleeping approximately 300 guests in both private and dormitory-type facilities. Assemblies for all age groups are provided throughout the summer. Arlie Carter became manager of the assembly in Nov., 1967.

Baptist Foundation.—The foundation seeks to serve any Baptist cause fostered by or having the official sanction of the state convention or the SBC in the furtherance and development of charitable, educational, and religious activities under the supervision of the state convention and the SBC. It seeks to encourage and motivate the making of gifts, bequests, devises, donations, and benefactions by deed, will, gift, annuity, contract, or otherwise, for the advancement, promotion, extension, and maintenance of the various charitable, educational, and religious causes fostered by the convention. The foundation was officially launched in Nov., 1968. In 1970 Willard Dobbs was president of the board and Darty F. Stowe was executive director.

DARTY F. STOWE

Buildings.—The Baptist Building, housing offices of the staff of the convention, is located at 1680 East Broad Street, Columbus, Ohio. In July, 1957, at a called meeting of the executive board of the convention, there was a unanimous vote to purchase the house and lot at this address for the sum of $42,000. Offices were then moved from rented quarters at 30 South Fourth Street and on Oct. 8, 1957, the facility was dedicated. In 1960 the structure was completely renovated at a cost of $50,000, changing the

OHIO STATISTICAL SUMMARY

Year	Associa-tions	Churches	Church Member-ship	Baptisms	S. S. Enrol-ment	V.B.S. Enrol-ment	T. U. Enrol-ment	W.M.U. Enrol-ment	Brother-hood En-rolment	Music Enrol-ment	Mission Gifts	Total Gifts	Value Church Property
1955	6	75	12,957	1,779	15,843	7,086	4,116	1,495	362		$ 73,849	$ 792,932	$ 650,800
1956	6	94	14,926	1,861	18,492	7,551	5,689	1,834	765		101,751	1,046,239	3,331,771
1957	6	132	18,458	2,289	24,045	11,213	7,024	2,712	1,094		141,695	1,241,095	4,161,958
1958	8	150	23,389	3,281	29,699	13,946	9,503	3,849	1,264		154,158	1,410,011	5,751,930
1959	10	191	29,492	3,841	32,184	16,730	11,817	3,894	2,765		203,844	1,907,373	7,152,388
1960	11	225	35,807	4,035	41,966	19,050	14,850	6,137	2,510		269,941	2,470,983	9,310,631
1961	14	265	41,376	4,918	48,169	23,362	17,221	6,342	2,919	2,370	304,053	2,785,069	12,939,241
1962	17	272	47,364	5,117	53,662	28,503	19,769	7,851	3,107	2,866	365,332	3,397,229	
1963	19	291	51,861	5,194	57,991	31,493	20,876	8,444	3,854	3,838	505,214	3,831,491	
1964	20	309	57,505	5,839	57,505	36,266	21,623	8,343	3,756	4,587	486,887	4,417,736	10,147,546
1965	21	326	63,457	5,892	69,793	39,868	23,038	10,751	3,782	5,050	631,825	5,507,279	23,345,980
1966	22	354	69,389	6,088	69,339	40,865	24,564	11,608	5,478	6,466	717,162	5,813,407	26,476,232
1967	22	381	76,009	6,670	77,597	38,522	26,912	11,975	4,106	7,727	830,971	6,586,907	29,287,655
1968	22	391	82,164	6,589	79,145	47,332	29,914	12,505	4,395	7,929	937,694	7,647,875	32,136,000

L. H. MOORE

front from a dwelling appearance to an office building appearance. The building contains 10,000 square feet of floor space.

In Apr., 1964, the contract was signed for the construction of a Baptist Book Store center building to be built at a cost of $104,975 on property adjacent to the Baptist Building. In Dec., 1964, the Baptist Book Store was moved from rented quarters in downtown Columbus to the new facility at 1667 East Broad Street, leased from the state convention. The two floors occupied by the book store contain 6,500 square feet of floor space. The building was dedicated on Jan. 7, 1965. BERT E. WILLIAMS

*OHIO ASSOCIATIONS.

I. New Associations. BUCKEYE CENTRAL. Organized Oct. 19, 1964, by seven churches and three missions which had been affiliated with Erie Baptist Association. Its territory includes all or parts of Morrow, Richland, Ashland, and Crawford counties. In 1968 six churches and two missions reported 77 baptisms, 876 members, and $64,245 total gifts.

CAPITAL CITY. Organized Oct. 12, 1957, at the Whitehall Baptist Church in Columbus by seven churches and eight missions from Central Baptist Association. Its territory includes all or parts of Franklin, Pickaway, Delaware, and Licking counties. In 1968, 47 churches and 14 missions reported 1,031 baptisms, 9,240 members, and $943,512 total gifts.

CUYAHOGA. Organized Sept. 7, 1957, at the First Southern Baptist Church, Cleveland, Ohio, with 10 churches. Its territory included all or parts of Ashtabula, Trumbull, Cuyahoga, Lake, and Mahoning counties. In 1968, 13 churches reported 225 baptisms, 2,070 members, and $322,680 total gifts.

FRONTIER. Organized Sept. 23, 1958, at LaSalle Baptist Church, Niagara Falls, N. Y., by five churches and two missions. Its territory covers Erie, Niagara, and Monroe counties. In 1968 nine churches and nine missions reported 152 baptisms, 1,246 members, $140,567 total gifts.

GREATER DAYTON. Organized Feb. 25, 1954, as the Central Baptist Association with 14 churches. In 1961 the association changed its name to the Greater Dayton Baptist Association. The association covers all or parts of Montgomery, Green, Clark, Darke, Miami, Preble, and Warren counties. In 1968, 63 churches and 13 missions reported 1,396 baptisms, 21,063 members and $2,262,912 total gifts.

GREATER HUNTINGTON, WEST VA. Organized Sept. 11, 1961, with four churches and four mission congregations at the Westmoreland Baptist Church in Huntington. Its territory includes Wayne and Cabell counties. In 1968 seven churches and three missions reported 151 baptisms, 2,237 members, and $143,897 total gifts.

GREATER PITTSBURGH, PA. Organized Sept. 13, 1963, with four churches and five missions from the Upper Ohio Valley Baptist Association at the Pittsburgh Baptist Church in Pittsburgh,

Pa. In 1968, 13 churches and 14 missions reported 143 baptisms, 1,882 members, and $374,031 total gifts.

LAKELAND. Organized Jan. 20, 1961, at the Fremont Baptist Church, Fremont, Ohio, with six churches and one mission. Its territory includes all or parts of Sandusky, Huron, Ottawa, and Erie counties. In 1968 nine churches and two missions reported 70 baptisms, 951 members, and $80,235 total gifts.

MIAMI VALLEY. Organized on Sept. 11, 1961, at the Central Baptist Church in Middletown, Ohio, with seven churches and one mission. Its territory includes all or parts of Butler, Montgomery, Warren, Preble, and Hamilton counties. In 1968, 15 churches and 3 missions reported 269 baptisms, 3003 members, and $215,323 total gifts.

MUSKINGUM VALLEY. Organized Mar. 2, 1963, by four churches and one mission which had affiliated with Scioto Valley and Capital City associations. The churches were in Coshocton, Guernsey, and Muskingum counties. In 1968 eight churches and six missions reported 70 baptisms, 801 members, and $79,055 total gifts.

NORTHERN OHIO. Organized Sept. 16, 1961, as the North Central Baptist Association with nine churches and one mission at the Lorain Baptist Church in Lorain, Ohio. In 1962 the name was changed to Northern Ohio Baptist Association. In 1968, 11 churches and 4 missions reported 389 baptisms, 2,910 members, and $273,281 total gifts.

PIONEER. Organized Oct. 31, 1958, with five churches in the Witcher Baptist Church, Belle, W. Va. The association covers all or parts of Webster, Kanawha, Mercer, and Putnam counties, W. Va. In 1968 eight churches and one mission reported 99 baptisms, 1,325 members, and $107,523 total gifts.

SOUTHERN HILLS. Organized Nov. 9–10, 1962, at the Northside Baptist Church, Bethel, Ohio, by 12 churches and 5 missions from the Greater Cincinnati Association. Churches were located in Clinton, Clermont, Brown, and Warren counties. In 1968, 15 churches and 1 mission reported 101 baptims, 1,296 members, and $107,901 total gifts.

SOUTHWESTERN. Organized Mar. 11, 1955, as the Greater Miami Association with 13 churches. The territory served included parts or all of Butler, Warren, and Hamilton counties. The association changed its name in 1957 to the Southwestern Baptist Association. In 1968, 36 churches and 4 missions reported 435 baptisms, 8,154 members, and $606,643 total gifts.

STEEL VALLEY. Organized Oct. 1, 1965, at the Austin Village Baptist Church in Warren, Ohio, with eight churches and six missions from Mahoning, Columbiana, Ashtabula, Trumble, Portage, Cuyahoga, and Lake counties. In 1968, 11 churches and 12 missions reported 220 baptisms, 1,254 members, and $197,436 total gifts.

SUMMIT. Organized Jan. 9, 1960, with seven churches and two missions at the Immanuel Baptist Church, Barberton, Ohio. Its territory includes all or parts of Summit, Portage, Stark, and Medina counties. In 1968, 14 churches and 4 missions reported 202 baptisms, 1,693 members, and $174,373 total gifts.

UPPER OHIO VALLEY. Organized Nov. 11, 1960, at the Temple Baptist Church, Moundsville, W. Va., with nine churches from the Scioto Baptist Association. The association covered all or parts of Harrison, Monongalia, Monroe, Wood, Washington, and Marshall counties, W. Va. In 1968 four churches and four missions reported 76 baptisms, 993 members, and $82,357 total gifts.

WEST CENTRAL. Organized Jan. 4, 1964, with seven churches and five missions from the Maumee Valley and Greater Dayton Baptist associations at the Woodlawn Baptist Church, Lima, Ohio. Territory includes Allen, Van Wert, Hancock, Shelby, and Miami counties. In 1968, 14 churches and 3 missions reported 159 baptisms, 1,647 members, and $137,468 total gifts.

II. Changes in Associations. CENTRAL. In its 1961 meeting at the North Dayton Baptist Church, Dayton, Ohio, the association voted to change its name to the Greater Dayton Baptist Association.

GREATER MIAMI VALLEY. In Sept., 1957, the association changed its name to the Southwestern Baptist Association. S. FELTON CARTER

OHIO BAPTIST MESSENGER. An eight-page newsmagazine, published weekly by the State Convention of Baptists in Ohio, it appeared first as a mimeographed associational newsletter edited by Ray E. Roberts, on Aug. 18, 1952. A Nov., 1952, issue appeared in printed form as the journal of the White Water Baptist Association. This publication continued monthly as the news organ of that association until the formation of the State Convention of Baptists in Ohio on Jan. 8, 1954. With the formation of the new convention, *The Ohio Baptist Messenger* became the official journal of that body and was continued as a monthly publication with editorial duties shared by Ray E. Roberts, executive secretary, and George W. Fletcher, educational secretary.

In May, 1958, R. G. Puckett became editor and remained in that position until Sept., 1961. During these years the paper became a 12-page, semimonthly publication. Upon Puckett's resignation, George W. Fletcher became acting editor until Apr. 1, 1962, when Lynn M. Davis, Jr., was elected editor. Davis served until Aug. 1966. The paper had become under his editorship an eight-page weekly publication. L. H. Moore, editor of *The Illinois Baptist,* 1957–67, was elected editor in Nov., 1966, and assumed his post on Jan. 1, 1967. In 1969 circulation of the paper was 9,724. The management of the paper is vested in the Ohio Baptist Messenger committee of the state convention's executive board. The 1969 budget for its operation totaled $50,519.40. Two hundred-seventy-five of the 408 churches in the state send the paper to their members through the budget plan.

L. H. MOORE

OKINAWA, MISSION IN. Southern Baptists entered Okinawa on Feb. 26, 1960, when Alvin E. "Bud" and Doris (Scalf) Spencer transferred from Japan. The newly organized Central Baptist Church, started by Baptist servicemen and their dependents called Spencer as pastor. Okinawa, largest in the Ryukyu chain of islands extending between Taiwan and Japan, is approximately 70 miles long. At the height of American control of the islands, there were up to 100,000 American troops, dependents, civilians, and commercial entrants living there.

Another missionary couple, William and Mary (Gulley) Medling, moved from Japan to Okinawa in 1965. Besides serving English-language churches, they have made a strong contribution to work in the Japanese-language churches. Early in 1970 four Southern Baptist missionary couples were working on Okinawa. Most of the work was concentrated in three active English-language churches—Central, Koza, and Naha Lakeshore—which were the main support for the 13 missions and 13 churches in the Okinawa Baptist Association that use the Japanese language. ALVIN E. SPENCER, JR.

***OKLAHOMA, BAPTIST GENERAL CONVENTION OF.** The work of this convention is supervised by an executive committee and 12 other committees of a 60-member board of directors. The chief administrator is the executive secretary-treasurer. Since 1951 this position has been filled by Thomas Bert Lackey. The convention's work is administered by the following departments:

Child Care.—On Sept. 7, 1956, the board of directors established the department of child care with H. Truman Maxey as executive director. He was succeeded upon retirement by Lowell Milburn, Dec. 31, 1969. The department directs the work of Baptist Children's Home and Boys Ranch Town, with a combined total budget in 1969 of $495,000. Largest source of income was the Cooperative Program, providing $105,000, with endowment income providing $74,000, followed by $59,000 from the annual Thanksgiving Offering, plus numerous lesser sources.

Missions.—On Jan. 1, 1960, the department of missions began a cooperative ministry with the Home Mission Board, SBC, in associational missions, and with language and National Baptist groups. Sam W. Scantlan was secretary of the department until his retirement Dec. 31, 1966, when he was succeeded by J. T. Roberts.

National Baptist work was directed by J. T. Roberts from 1960 until Jan. 1, 1967, when he was succeeded by Henry Chenualt, who resigned Sept. 1, 1968. On Nov. 1, 1968, John W. Brill assumed this position.

Laddie Adams succeeded Bailey O. Sewell (*q.v.*) as director of Language Missions, Aug. 15, 1966. Robert Haskins took over this work Jan. 16, 1970, after Adams left the work for a pastorate.

The department of missions was reorganized in Jan., 1970, with the secretary in charge of associational work, world missions conferences, rural and urban missions, metropolitan work, new missions and churches, special ministries, the statewide Bible conference, and special missions emphases. John W. Brill was associate in charge of National Baptist Work and Christian social ministries. Robert W. Haskins was the other associate in charge of language missions, work with nonevangelicals, seminary extension work, and chaplaincy services.

J. T. ROBERTS and JOHN BRILL

Woman's Missionary Union.—WMU in Oklahoma functions as a department of the state convention, although it exists as an auxiliary with its own officers and executive board composed of the officers and three members at large. The annual meetings are held just prior to the state convention sessions.

The executive secretary supervises the work and serves as a medium of contact between the convention and the local women's organizations. Margaret Hutchinson (*q.v.*) served as secretary, 1948–63, when she was succeeded by Abbie Louise Green, a native of Tennessee who had previously served as young people's secretary for Oklahoma WMU, 1949–56.

In 1969, WMU received $75,469 from the Cooperative Program in Oklahoma. The 1968 reports show 39,079 members in 3,036 organizations. ABBIE LOUISE GREEN

Evangelism.—During the years 1955–69, the simultaneous evangelistic crusades played a vital role in Oklahoma evangelism. In 1955 there were 1,038 churches which participated in these campaigns.

A downward trend in evangelism began in 1958 when 175 churches reported no baptisms. The 727 churches reporting two or more revivals accounted for 85.6 per cent of the baptisms that year. The next year there was a statewide liquor fight which was credited with dividing Baptists' attention and hindering efforts in evangelism.

In 1958 Thomas Paul Haskins retired as state evangelist, and Jack C. Carroll became associate in the department of evangelism and brotherhood. Carroll left the department for a post with the Baptist Foundation Jan. 1, 1960, and was succeeded by Robert R. Chambers (*q.v.*), Feb. 1, 1960. After 15 months, Chambers died following a short illness, and July 1, 1961, Eugene Stockwell came as an associate with special emphasis on Brotherhood work. In 1968 Stockwell returned to a pastorate, and the same year the work was divided with Brotherhood becoming a separate department. John Allen Pennington continued as secretary of evangelism until his retirement in 1969.

In 1969, Jerold R. McBride became secretary of evangelism bringing a renewed emphasis on lay witnessing. McBride works with each of the 37 associations and their respective chairmen of evangelism to encourage witnessing and evangelistic outreach. The program is implemented by an annual evangelism conference, associational conferences and rallies, lay witnessing clinics,

Top: OKLAHOMA BAPTIST CHILDREN'S HOME (*q.v.*), Oklahoma City. Phillips' Building is the infirmary and music building. *Center:* BOYS RANCH TOWN (*q.v.*), Jimmy Johnson memorial at entrance. R. C. Howard, Sr., memorial cottage in background. *Bottom:* OKLAHOMA CITY BAPTIST GOLDEN AGE HOMES (*q.v.*), entrance to Lackey Manor.

Top: BAPTIST MEMORIAL HOSPITAL, Oklahoma City, Okla. (*q.v.*). Hospital and Doctors' Medical Building. *Center and bottom:* OKLAHOMA BAPTIST UNIVERSITY (*q.v.*), Shawnee, Okla. Raley Chapel and Student Union Building.

and special publications. JEROLD R. MCBRIDE

Stewardship and Finance.—The period 1955–69 was marked by growth in Cooperative Program giving in Oklahoma from $1,828,703 to $2,364,360. Total church gifts went from $14,859,270 to $21,226,327. The Forward Program of Church Finance accounted for most of the increases.

In 1963 a 12-year plan for mission advance was adopted asking the churches to increase their annual receipts by five per cent and their Cooperative Program percentage by one per cent each year. By 1967 the churches had increased their total income by $9,000,000, and Cooperative Program gifts by nearly $1,000,000. Mounting needs of BSU work and Oklahoma Baptist University caused the first special session in the history of the convention to convene at Shawnee, May 19, 1967, to consider a revision of the 12-year plan and to adopt a program of advance for five years. A basic budget was to be adopted annually providing a 57–43 per cent division of funds between state and SBC causes. Beyond the basic budget, money received would be divided 75–25 per cent between Oklahoma Baptist University and BSU work. Following its adoption, this plan was given to the state in 10 district rallies, and at the end of 1969 the results were seen in $749,716.53 in advance funds in addition to regular budget allocations. Total Cooperative Program gifts in 1969 were $3,590,636.99. In 1969 there were 356 churches giving through the Cooperative Program on a weekly basis.

In 1961 Joe L. Ingram became assistant executive secretary for the convention, and since that time has led in stewardship promotion. In 1967 he created a promotional plan called "Tither's Enrolment Day." That year 732 churches reported 73,760 tithers. The next year 816 churches ordered TED materials and reported 87,460 tithers. JOE L. INGRAM

Religious Education.—Sunday School and Training Union are included in the work of the Religious Education department. On Jan. 1, 1966, J. Lyle Garlow became secretary, succeeding E. W. Westmoreland who served from 1942 until his retirement, Dec. 31, 1965. Workers in the department include Alga Motychak, director of preschool and children's work since Apr., 1957; Hugh Willoby, who became director of youth work in Jan., 1963, at the retirement of Sophia Duerksen; and Bill C. Haggard, director of Training Union work since 1965. The 70/70 Launch Plan used throughout the SBC to begin the seventies was developed in Oklahoma. The Religious Education department develops the annual programs for Falls Creek Assembly.

LYLE GARLOW and BILL HAGGARD

Public Relations.—Prior to the resignation of Arthur Davenport as public relations director in 1958, this office held department status. His successors, including Richard T. McCartney, 1958–62, Floyd Craig, 1962–67, and Joan Harvison, 1967–69, have worked under the supervision of the convention's executive office. The public relations office tells the story of Baptist work in

OKLAHOMA STATISTICAL SUMMARY

Year	Associations	Churches	Church Membership	Baptisms	S. S. Enrolment	V.B.S. Enrolment	T. U. Enrolment	W.M.U. Enrolment	Brotherhood Enrolment	Music Enrolment	Mission Gifts	Total Gifts	Value Church Property
1955	44	1,263	413,984	22,702	305,909	113,507	119,342	47,254	20,735		$2,786,726	$14,859,270	$ 55,089,675
1956	42	1,267	426,315	20,554	312,948	117,068	121,649	48,659	21,617		3,254,429	17,338,693	63,914,141
1957	45	1,251	433,658	19,564	313,898	119,520	124,046	50,503	23,896		3,364,828	17,836,994	69,951,230
1958	45	1,285	442,377	19,408	318,321	120,217	126,437	52,244	25,918		3,597,574	19,324,515	74,889,067
1959	44	1,293	452,783	18,748	324,786	121,522	129,594	55,277	26,769		3,220,052	20,518,798	82,266,060
1960	41	1,307	461,508	18,229	326,518	123,276	130,937	54,116	25,282		3,119,346	21,226,327	89,531,507
1961	41	1,322	472,176	18,810	332,082	127,777	133,511	56,328	25,824		3,495,744	22,057,478	95,529,461
1962	41	1,328	482,727	17,837	332,145	127,106	131,408	54,051	25,133	33,154	3,382,264	23,385,947	101,972,141
1963	41	1,335	493,381	16,766	334,655	129,233	132,967	56,588	25,564	34,772	3,458,936	23,963,766	108,281
1964	41	1,340	502,183	16,207	336,008	126,212	130,005	56,986	24,879	37,460	3,691,956	24,611,126	115,412,054
1965	41	1,357	510,808	16,193	333,675	136,504	124,351	55,139	17,904	35,411	4,579,817	26,353,636	119,899,092
1966	41	1,364	512,712	16,700	330,943	141,819	121,263	53,546	17,895	38,556	4,075,586	27,117,050	123,442,121
1967	41	1,362	529,079	17,900	328,166	136,179	119,866	52,138	17,129	40,187	4,546,726	28,683,660	132,731,510
1968	41	1,366	535,616	17,937	326,578	128,520	127,733	49,040	16,006	40,737	5,500,377	32,435,386	138,473,336

J. M. GASKIN

Oklahoma via all types of news media. It produces "Oklahoma Newsbreak" which is heard weekly over 15 Oklahoma radio stations.

JOE L. INGRAM

Church Music.—Gene Bartlett became secretary of the church music department Jan. 1, 1954, and Mary June Tabor became associate the same date. Two annual choir festivals are held: for youth choirs beginning in 1953, with 25,215 attending through 1969; for junior choirs beginning in 1955, with 30,247 attending through 1969. The youth music workshop began in 1956, and in 1960 the Singing Churchmen were organized. In 1969 there were 75 full-time ministers of music or combination men in Oklahoma.

Student Work.—In 1958, Baptist student work was assigned to the department of religious education with Clyde Clayton as director. On June 1, 1968, a separate department was formed for student work with Clayton as secretary. In 1969 there were 25 BSU organizations in Oklahoma, with 13 full-time and 12 part-time directors. Property value is over $1,000,000. There are about 250,000 Baptist and Baptist preference students in Oklahoma colleges where there are BSU's.

Brotherhood.—Beginning in 1948 Brotherhood work was included in a department with evangelism. In 1957, Royal Ambassador work was transferred from joint sponsorship to this department with Bob Banks as secretary. The convention's board voted, May 7, 1968, to form a separate department for Brotherhood and RA work, with Bob Banks as secretary and Henry Chenault became associate.

In 1960 Brotherhood reached its peak with work in 961 churches, but in 1969 it had dropped to 446. RA work peaked in 1965, with 1,087 chapters in 546 churches. It dropped in 1969 to 874 chapters in 475 churches.

The RA Congress had its largest attendance in 1966 with 3,000 attending. The Baptist Men's Meeting in recent years had about 1,000 in attendance, with a record of 1,314 in 1963.

J. M. GASKIN

***OKLAHOMA ASSOCIATIONS.**

I. New Associations. BECKHAM MILLS. Organized July 10, 1956, at Sayre by 15 churches with 5,019 members from Beckham Association, and nine churches with 1,697 members from Mills Association. First annual session in 1957, total reported gifts were $215,913.

ROGERS. Organized at Memorial Heights Church, Claremore, Oct. 11, 1956, out of Tulsa-Rogers Association. First annual session in 1957 reported 20 churches with 5,145 members and property valued at $598,000.

SANS BOIS. Organized Sept. 30, 1960, when 26 messengers from six churches in Haskell County and 29 messengers from seven Latimer County churches met at Kinta, Okla. In 1969, 25 churches reported 4,859 members, $22,043 total gifts, $38,891 mission gifts, and $725,525 property value.

SOUTHWEST. Organized in 1959 out of Jackson-Greer and Harmon associations with 25 churches and a membership of 8,915. In 1969 there were 31 churches with 13,259 members in Harmon, Greer, and Jackson counties.

TULSA. Organized out of Tulsa-Rogers Association in a meeting at Immanuel Church, Tulsa, Oct. 9–10, 1956. Messengers from 68 churches in Tulsa County represented 41,232 members in the organizational meeting. In 1969, 91 churches reported 2,230 baptisms, 61,552 members, and $598,824 total gifts.

II. Changes in Associations. *GREAT PLAINS INDIAN. Disbanded Sept. 16, 1961, its seven churches with 463 members affiliated with Anglo associations in their respective areas. They have continued their ethnic connection by membership in the Great Plains Indian Baptist Fellowship.

GREER COUNTY. Organized Sept. 11, 1890, at Fairview Church, Martha, Tex. (now Okla.), with six churches and 141 members. It cooperated with Texas Baptists until 1900. By 1906 there were 53 churches. It was the parent body of the Jackson-Greer Association (now extinct), and of the present Southwest Association.

HASKELL. Met for its 48th and final session with the First Baptist Church, Stigler, Okla., Sept. 29–30, 1960. Messengers voted to merge with Latimer Association to form the new Sans Bois Association.

LATIMER. Met for its 22th annual session, Sept. 22–23, 1960, with the Gowen Church, with 63 messengers present from 14 churches. They voted to merge with Haskell county churches to form the San Bois Association.

TULSA-ROGERS. Held its last meeting Oct. 9–10, 1956, when it granted the petition of churches in Rogers County to form a separate body. Distribution of assets included granting $10,000 for a missionary's home and $2,500 for a contingency fund to the Rogers County group. At the time of division the parent body had 86 churches with a total membership of 45,058.

J. M. GASKIN

OKLAHOMA BAPTIST CHILDREN'S HOME (cf. Oklahoma Baptist Orphans' Home, Vol. II). Located at Oklahoma City, the Oklahoma Baptist Children's Home reported 130 boys and girls in residence in 1970. Property consists of 15 buildings on 40 acres of land, valued at $1,750,000, with no debt. James V. Browning, superintendent since Sept. 1, 1954, directs the work of 35 full-time employees.

J. M. GASKIN

OKLAHOMA BAPTIST CHRONICLE, THE. The official organ of the Oklahoma Baptist Historical Society. The first number of the semiannual publication was issued in the spring, 1958. It is published by the Messenger Press, 1141 N. Robinson, Oklahoma City. Jesse Marvin Gaskin, historical secretary for the Baptist General Convention of Oklahoma since 1953, has been editor since publication began.

J. M. GASKIN

***OKLAHOMA BAPTIST FOUNDATION.** Operating on a $126,178 annual budget provided by the state convention in 1969, the foundation reported $10,000,000 in assets and an annual investment income of about $500,000. The church building loan trust fund showed 156 loans in force in 1969, for a total of more than $54,000,000. An office was opened in Tulsa, Feb. 1, 1965, where a staff member spends one week each month. In 1966 the state convention voted to amend the bylaws of the foundation to provide for four-year rotating terms for directors. Thomas E. Carter succeeded Horace Lee Janes as assistant secretary, Sept. 1, 1962, and when Auguie Henry retired, Dec. 31, 1967, Carter succeeded him as executive secretary.

THOMAS E. CARTER

OKLAHOMA BAPTIST HISTORICAL SOCIETY. Organized at Oklahoma City, Okla., Nov. 14, 1956, this society adopted a constitution of eight articles. First president was Jesse Marvin Gaskin, historical secretary of the Baptist General Convention of Oklahoma since 1953. The society is auxiliary to the nine-member Historical Commission which is elected by the state convention. There were 141 charter members, of whom six were life members, and Norman W. Cox (*q.v.*) was made an honorary life member. There were 131 members in 1969, with 22 having life memberships. Annual memberships cost $2, and life membership is $25. All members receive *The Oklahoma Baptist Chronicle* without charge. J. M. GASKIN

***OKLAHOMA BAPTIST HOSPITAL (Muskogee, Okla.).** Closed Sept. 15, 1962, due to growing financial difficulties, antiquated equipment, and the competition of a new municipal hospital in Muskogee. The state convention reported a $192,000 deficit on the hospital at the time it closed. J. M. GASKIN

***OKLAHOMA BAPTIST UNIVERSITY** (Shawnee, Okla.). The 27-year administration of John Wesley Raley (*q.v.*) continued until 1961, during which the Kerr Memorial Dormitory and the main unit of the John Wesley Raley Chapel were completed and dedicated in 1962.

James Ralph Scales, executive vice-president since 1953, was the third layman to be elected president. His tenure (1961–65) was marked by a strong emphasis on academic growth and activity, and was a time of consolidation in the building program of the postwar years. Chief among these developments were the strengthening of the faculty, expansion of library and language facilities, and the renovation of several major buildings. Upon Scales's resignation in 1965, Vice-President Evans Taylor Moseley became acting president. Since Grady Coulter Cothen became president July 1, 1966, there has been a marked growth in three important areas: undergirding of financial support, significant academic advance, and resumption of a major building program. Action by the state convention in 1967 allocating funds to the university sharply increased the school's income for the 1968–69 academic year to $670,982, an increase of $223,712 over that of fiscal 1966–67. In the same year the university received the largest single gift in its history, two trust funds totaling approximately $5,000,000 from the estate of the late Mrs. Louise M. Prichard of Oklahoma City. Gifts from other sources brought the endowment to more than $3,800,000 as of Jan. 1, 1970. The university budget for 1969–70 was $2,690,000.

In 1968 the university had a 13 per cent increase in enrolment. This level was maintained in the fall of 1969 with a total of 1,642, and a cumulative enrolment of 1,980 for 1968–69. In 1969 there were 5,360 living alumni and 17,000 former students on record with the Bison Alumni Association. The faculty in 1969 consisted of 118 members, 93 of whom were full-time and 24 holding doctoral degrees. After three years of intensive study a new curriculum was voted in 1969, with its implementation projected for the 1970–71 session. The university library of 81,095 volumes had a circulation of 28,000 in 1968–69. In May, 1969, ground was broken for a $1,400,000 student center to be completed in 1970. Financed by special subscription, the gifts and pledges for capital funds totaled $1,008,000 by Dec. 31, 1969.

E. W. THORNTON

OKLAHOMA CITY GOLDEN AGE HOMES (Oklahoma City, Okla.). A movement began in 1958 which culminated in the founding of the Baptist Golden Age Homes complex and groundbreaking at the present site on Sept. 21, 1963. Lackey Manor, a 109-bed nursing home named for Thomas Bert Lackey, and 20 apartment units are valued at about $1,500,000. The complex is located on 35 acres of land deeded in 1963 to Baptist Laymen's Corp., which still holds title to the property but management is under the administration of Baptist Memorial Hospital. J. M. GASKIN

***OKLAHOMA SCHOOL OF RELIGION.** The Oklahoma Baptist State Convention, a National Baptist body in Oklahoma, voted, Oct. 24, 1963, to close the Oklahoma School of Religion. In its place a chair of Bible and a BSU program were initiated adjacent to Langston University, a predominantly Negro state school. This program began with the 1963–64 school year, largely due to the effects of growing integration in public education. Negro Baptists diverted some of the funds formerly used for this school to provide scholarships at Oklahoma Baptist University. The former school facilities were destroyed by fire on Sept. 14, 1965, with a $50,000 loss, of which about $19,000 was covered by insurance. J. M. GASKIN

OLIVE, EUGENE IRVING (b. Wake County, N. C., Dec. 7, 1890; d. Winston-Salem, N. C., Mar. 6, 1968). Minister, college chaplain, and college official. Son of William J. and Mary Bland Olive, he attended Buie's Creek Academy, received the B.A. from Wake Forest College in 1910, and the Th.M. from Southern Baptist Theological Seminary in 1918. Olive also studied at the University of North Carolina. He was a public-school teacher and principal in Cumberland County, N. C., 1910–15, and at the same time served as pastor for several rural churches. Later he held pastorates in Dunn, 1918–21, Mount Airy, 1921–24, Chapel Hill, 1924–35, and North Wilkesboro, 1935–40.

Olive joined the Wake Forest College staff in 1940 as pastor of Wake Forest Baptist Church and chaplain for the college. He became the college's director of public relations and alumni activities in 1947, and was director of alumni activities from 1955 until retirement in 1961. He also was editor of the Wake Forest magazine. After retiring, he was active in a program planning retirement for ministers.

Olive married Iva Lanier Pearson on June 29, 1926. They had one daughter, Emily Carolina (Mrs. W. C. Rankin). Olive and his wife were the first members of the Wake Forest staff to move to Winston-Salem (1952). Before moving he arranged for the sale of the old campus as the new home of Southeastern Baptist Theological Seminary. He was acting editor of the *Biblical Recorder,* 1941–42, a trustee of Wake Forest College, 1934–40, and the author of a number of publications of the American Baptist Publication Society and Southern Baptist Sunday School Board. ELIZABETH BRANTLEY

***ONEIDA INSTITUTE.** A Baptist high school in Oneida, Ky., which dropped the eighth grade in 1958, now (1970) has 185 students all on a work-study basis. In 1962 President J. Chester Sparks retired and David C. Jackson, principal and coach, became president. Oneida has a faculty of 12 and a staff of 13 members. A college preparatory school, it also teaches vocational subjects. It operates a farm, a natural gas business, and cable TV for the community. It has 6,000 acres of land. In 1962 the Kentucky Baptist Convention turned over to Oneida the total assets of Magoffin Institute when it closed. Marvin Hall, the administration and classroom building, burned in 1964. In 1969, three new buildings were dedicated: Marvin-Wheeler Hall, Carnahan Hall, and the Student Center. The gym was completed, with classrooms and the library, in 1965 and named the J. Chester Sparks Health Building. In 1969 the budget was $220,000 and the total assets valued at $2,100,000. The legal name is Oneida Baptist Institute. HAROLD GLEN SANDERS

OREGON, BAPTIST GENERAL CONVENTION OF. Organized Apr. 13, 1948, in Portland, this body changed its name to Baptist General Convention of Oregon-Washington after acceptance for affiliation with the Southern Baptist Convention. In its annual meeting in Nov., 1969, the general convention changed its name to Northwest Baptist Convention, to be effective in Nov., 1970, provided such change did not conflict with other officially registered names.

See also OREGON-WASHINGTON, BAPTIST GENERAL CONVENTION OF, VOL. II. ROY L. JOHNSON

*** OREGON-WASHINGTON, BAPTIST GENERAL CONVENTION OF.** The convention voted in Nov., 1969, to change its name to Northwest Baptist Convention effective Nov. 3, 1970. Presidents of the convention have been John R. Canning (*q.v.*), Leslie F. Minnis, Herman E. Wooten, Buren L. Higdon, Jack W. McKay (first Canadian to serve as president), Harry G. Bonner, and Carrol E. Bolin. The following men have served as executive secretaries: Robert E. Milam, first executive secretary, 1956–61; Roland P. Hood, interim secretary until Jan., 1962, and secretary, 1966–68; Fred B. Moseley, 1962–65; and William Eugene Grubbs, Dec., 1968– .

In 1969 the convention operation consisted of the administrative office; business office; Church Services Division (Sunday School, Church Training, Brotherhood-evangelism, women's work, music, student work, etc.); stewardship promotion (assigned to executive secretary of Northwest Baptist Foundation); Cooperative Missions Division (directing all the missionaries in various fields and types of ministry in the Northwest); the *Pacific Coast Baptist;* Bailie Memorial Boys' Ranch (administered by a board elected by and responsible to the convention or its executive board); and committees of the convention's executive board (executive, administrative, program, finance, and institutions, agencies, and facilities). There are also standing committees, some named by the board and some elected by the convention. The convention offices have been located in Portland, Ore., since its organization in 1948.

Between 1955 and 1969 the number of churches doubled, and membership tripled. Church property values increased from $2,871,137 to more than $16,000,000. Total gifts in 1955 were $806,870, and they increased to more than four times that sum in 1969. Total mission gifts likewise were about four times as much in 1969 as the 1955 figure of $101,752. The annual budget of the convention increased about 10 per cent or more per year. The budget approved for 1970 was $528,607, with $201,317 to come from Southern Baptist boards and the remainder to come from churches of the Northwest. The steady growth in numbers and gifts indicates in part the effect of Southern Baptist contributions to Baptist work in the Northwest.

During the administration of Fred B. Moseley, the convention debts on its office building and Mt. Baker Assembly were consolidated in a new bond issue of $75,000, which also financed part of the cost of the first cottage at Bailie Memorial Boys' Ranch and provided funds for a chapel at the Mt. Baker Assembly. A gift of land in Texas by Mr. and Mrs. Homer A. Hyde of Friona, Tex., provided over $160,000 in additional assets for the Northwest Baptist Foundation to be administered as loans to churches. The Canadian Southern Baptist Conference was organized to assist the churches of Canada that were affiliated with the Oregon-Washington convention. Moseley resigned as executive secretary to return to the staff of the Baptist Home Mission Board in Atlanta, Ga.

The convention voted in 1965 at Madras, Ore., to consider purchasing a fraternity house adjacent to the University of Washington in Seattle to become a Baptist Student Center. Previously owned properties of the convention there had been sold. The matter was referred to the convention's executive board which completed details of the transaction and opened the facility for use, after needed remodeling. It houses about 40 men, but serves meals to about twice that number of young people, as well as provides operational space for Baptist student activities, Bible teaching, etc. The convention employed the first full-time director of Baptist student work for the university in 1969. Student work on various campuses of the Northwest, including Canada, is under the general direction of the director of student work in the convention office at Portland. Finance for part of the student ministry is provided by the Student Department of the Sunday School Board, SBC, in Nashville, Tenn.

During the administration of Roland P. Hood, further reorganization of the staff was completed, and an administrative plan book was published to give guidance to board members and employees in their various tasks and relations. Statistical reports indicated continued growth in number of churches and members. Hood retired at the end of Nov., 1968, after 20 years of service with the convention, first as the only general missionary in the Northwest employed by the California convention before the Oregon-Washington convention received recognition by the Southern Baptist Convention, and later as director of missions and stewardship, and then as executive secretary.

William Eugene Grubbs, a native of Alabama and former missionary to the Philippines and superintendent of evangelism in California, became executive secretary on Dec. 1, 1968.

ROY L. JOHNSON

OREGON-WASHINGTON (NORTHWEST-BAPTIST CONVENTION) STATISTICAL SUMMARY

Year	Associations	Churches	Church Membership	Baptisms	S. S. Enrolment	V.B.S. Enrolment	T. U. Enrolment	W.M.U. Enrolment	Brotherhood Enrolment	Music Enrolment	Mission Gifts	Total Gifts	Value Church Property
1955	12	109	13,245	1,843	17,748	9,557	7,421	1,987	827		$101,752	$ 806,870	$ 2,871,137
1956	14	120	14,663	1,718	20,092	10,944	7,863	2,801	1,073		116,719	944,439	3,180,677
1957	15	133	16,714	1,554	21,809	10,206	8,855	3,216	1,141		142,945	1,097,953	3,927,160
1958	17	146	19,305	2,043	23,872	12,084	9,964	4,131	1,470		156,264	1,276,218	4,588,400
1959	18	149	21,699	2,006	25,172	12,989	10,922	4,618	1,511		188,517	1,457,775	5,243,411
1960	19	156	23,281	1,828	25,971	13,557	11,312	4,556	1,507		198,787	1,490,315	6,207,898
1961	20	168	24,733	1,815	27,501	14,564	12,485	4,521	1,497		209,870	1,601,689	7,163,685
1962	20	173	26,409	1,933	28,459	15,514	12,734	4,616	1,526		240,649	1,713,804	8,282,194
1963	21	179	27,896	1,771	29,081	16,049	12,588	4,681	1,372		271,545	1,824,948	9,799,120
1964	21	185	29,805	2,274	30,721	17,153	13,439	5,148	1,282		300,040	2,068,012	10,843,161
1965	21	188	30,935	2,153	31,107	18,031	13,401	5,234	1,199		320,873	2,477,580	12,033,282
1966	21	193	33,329	2,092	33,329	17,151	14,032	5,303	1,354		368,921	2,415,457	13,156,800
1967	21	197	35,384	2,051	32,542	20,211	14,833	5,661	1,163	3,023	396,002	2,761,137	14,523,683
1968	22	205	37,652	2,158	33,107	19,976	15,672	5,497	1,465	3,212	428,937	3,208,154	15,075,206

ROY L. JOHNSON

*OREGON-WASHINGTON ASSOCIATIONS.

I. Extant Associations. CAPILANO ASSOCIATION. Organized in 1956 by Baptists in British Columbia, Canada, who were affiliated with Southern Baptists in the Oregon-Washington Convention. In 1969 the association included nine churches and missions.

CASCADE ASSOCIATION. Organized in 1955 by some of the churches in Oregon formerly affiliated with Upper Williamette Association. In 1969 the association included nine churches and missions.

CENTRAL ASSOCIATION. Organized in 1955 by some of the churches in Oregon formerly affiliated with Upper Williamette Association. The association included eight churches and missions in 1969.

COAST ASSOCIATION. Organized in 1956 by churches in Oregon formerly affiliated with Myrtlewood Association, but its first statistics were listed in 1957. In 1969 the association included five churches and missions.

COLUMBIA BASIN ASSOCIATION. Organized 1950 by some of the churches in Oregon and Washington formerly affiliated with Washington State Association. In 1969 the association included 20 churches and missions.

COULEE ASSOCIATION. Organized in 1955 by churches in north central Washington formerly affiliated with Inland Empire Association, and named for the Coulee Dam in its area. In 1969 the association included 11 churches and missions.

DOUGLAS ASSOCIATION. Organized in 1961 by churches formerly affiliated with Siskiyou and Cascade Associations in central west Oregon. First statistics were published in 1962. In 1969 the association included three churches and missions.

EVERGREEN ASSOCIATION. Organized in 1950 as one of three associations in Washington. It included churches of northwest Washington, with those on the Olympic peninsula. It became in time a metropolitan association for the Seattle area. In 1969 the association included 43 churches and missions.

INLAND EMPIRE ASSOCIATION. Organized in 1954 by churches in the Spokane area of northeast Washigton, and includes churches in the north part of Idaho. Once there were churches of Canada affiliated with it. In 1969 the association included 19 churches and missions.

INTERSTATE ASSOCIATION. Organized in the fall of 1958 as a result of planned mission program by churches of the Portland-Vancouver area, and the name was chosen because of the two-state area included, Oregon-Washington. Although primarily a metropolitan body, it has churches affiliated as far as 100 miles from Portland. In 1969 the association included 39 churches and missions.

JUNIPER ASSOCIATION. Organized in 1957 by churches across the Cascade mountains from Portland, Ore., which desired an association of their own rather than try to affiliate with the proposed new Interstate Association which was to be primarily metropolitan. In 1969 the association included six churches and missions.

KLAMATH ASSOCIATION. Organized in 1951 by churches in Oregon Baptist Association when the latter divided into became four associations. It was named for the area which took its name from the Klamath Indians of the region. In 1969 the association included seven churches and missions.

LEWIS-CLARK ASSOCIATION. Organized in Sept., 1959, in the Lewiston, Idaho–Clarkston, Wash., area. This area bears the "marks" of the Lewis-Clark expedition of 1804–07. In 1969 the association included six churches and missions.

MIDWEST ASSOCIATION. Organized in Nov., 1957, by representatives of three churches of Edmonton, Canada. These churches were formerly affiliated with Inland Empire Association. In 1969 the association included 10 churches and missions.

MOUNT BAKER ASSOCIATION. Organized Oct. 7, 1951, at Hamilton, Wash. It became international in 1954 when Kingcrest and Kings Road churches of Vancouver, Canada, were added to its roll. The association took its name from famous Mt. Baker which is in its area. In 1969 the association included nine churches and missions.

MOUNT RAINIER ASSOCIATION. Named for famous Mt. Ranier, this body was organized Jan. 9, 1968, at Highland Hill Church in Tacoma, Wash., as a result of plans made at the annual meeting of Olympic Association in Oct., 1967. The purpose was to make the Olympia-Tacoma area into a metropolitan association. In 1969 the association included 12 churches and missions.

MYRTLEWOOD ASSOCIATION. Organized by representatives of three churches at North Bend, Ore., May 21, 1952. First named Southwest Oregon Baptist Association, this body changed its name to Myrtlewood in 1955. In 1969 the association included five churches and missions.

OLYMPIC ASSOCIATION. Organized by representatives of three churches at Bremerton, Wash., in Feb., 1953, the first annual meeting was in Sept., 1953. In 1969 the association included 11 churches and missions.

PLATEAU ASSOCIATION. Organized Dec. 2, 1960, at Ridgecrest Church, Kamloops, British Columbia. Its churches stretched from Penticton to Prince George in 1969—a distance of 500 miles. George Irvin, native of Kentucky, was the leader in the outreach in this area from his church in Kamloops. In 1969 the association included five churches and missions.

SISKIYOU ASSOCIATION. Organized Apr. 29, 1951, one of four bodies supplanting the former Oregon State Association. The new body took the name of the mountains in its area. Organizational meeting was in Temple Baptist Church (later First Southern) in Medford, Ore. In 1969 the association included seven churches and missions.

SOUTHWEST WASHINGTON ASSOCIATION. Organized in 1950 as one of three bodies replacing the Washington State Association. First annual meeting was at First Baptist Church, Longview, Wash., Oct., 1951. In 1969 the association included 11 churches and missions.

YAKIMA VALLEY ASSOCIATION. Constituted in 1959 by churches in the Yakima Valley, Wash., area, formerly affiliated with Columbia Basin Association. In 1969 the association included 10 churches and missions.

II. Extinct Associations. MULTNOMAH ASSOCIATION. Organized in the Northwest Oregon area around Portland in 1951. It was disbanded in 1958 so most of its churches could become part of the Interstate Baptist Association to begin a city mission (later metropolitan) program of work in the Portland-Vancouver area.

Northwest Baptist Association. Organized Apr. 25, 1947, at Trinity Baptist Church, Springfield, Ore., by representatives from seven churches in Oregon and Washington, whose members expressed a desire to affiliate with Southern Baptists in California, since that was the nearest state convention of Southern Baptists. Three other churches were represented at the first annual meeting of the association at Longview, Wash., Oct. 20–22, 1947. The first moderator was R. E. Milam of Portland, Ore. The association accepted ownership of the *Pacific Coast Baptist,* which had been published regularly since 1931. Included in the work sponsored by the body were assistance to Golden Gate Baptist Seminary, mission work in Alaska, and a missionary on the field in the Northwest. There were 1,704 members and 171 baptisms reported by the 10 churches in 1947. A summer assembly was also conducted on rented property. The association was disbanded when representatives from its 15 churches organized the Baptist General Convention of Oregon, Apr. 13, 1948, at Portland. These same representatives then formed two associations—one for Oregon and one for Washington.

Oregon Baptist Association. Organized by representatives of eight churches in Apr., 1948. It was merged into four associations in 1951: Klamath, Siskiyou, Multnomah, and Upper Williamette associations.

Southwest Oregon. Organized in 1952, but changed its name to Myrtlewood Association in 1955.

Upper Williamette Association. Organized in 1951 as one of four associations in Oregon, it was divided into Central and Cascade associations in 1955.

Washington Baptist Association. Organized Apr. 13, 1948, involving seven churches. In the fall of 1950 it was deemed best to divide into three associations in Washington, and the "Washington" name was dropped when the following associations came into being: Evergreen Association, in the Seattle and northwest Washington area; Southwest Washington Association; and Columbia Basin Association, in the eastern Washington area. ROY L. JOHNSON

OSBORNE, MARK RAYBURN, SR. (b. Penrose, N. C., Mar. 3, 1889; d. Columbia, S. C., Feb. 1, 1966) . Pastor and state convention officer. Son of Henry and Loula (Young) Osborne of Transylvania County, N. C., he attended Asheville Farm School, Fruitland Institute, and graduated from Furman University in 1917. Furman awarded him a D.D. degree in 1954. Converted at age 14, he joined Enon and later Little River Baptist Church. He served with the Home Mission Board, SBC, during World War I, and later as associate pastor and secretary-treasurer of First Baptist Church, Greenville, S. C. He then served the following churches: Ebenezer, S. C., Lake Swamp, S. C., Ebenezer and Edisto in Orangeburg Association, and as interim in various churches beginning with his retirement in 1955. He was president of the state pastors' conference in 1948 and vice-president of the South Carolina Baptist Convention in 1955. Known for his humor and musical talent, he was in demand as an after dinner speaker and song leader. In 1917 Osborne married Dora Elizabeth Bishop of Cedar Mountain, N. C. They had three children: Mark, Jr., Millard H., and Alice Louise.

DANIEL W. CLOER

OUACHITA BAPTIST UNIVERSITY (cf. Ouachita Baptist College, Vol. II) . During the period 1956–69, marked changes were made in six basic areas: academic organization, administrative restructure, faculty, student body, finances, and physical plant.

Academic organization.—The board of trustees authorized a Division of Graduate Studies under a director, and with programs leading toward a M.A. in Religion and in American Civilization in three areas: American Culture and History, American Language and Literature, and American Society and Thought. The faculty established the four curricula, published the first "Graduate Catalogue Issue 1959" in August, and began classes Sept. 14, with 20 enrolled. Doyle Leon Lumpkin, first graduate, earned the M.A. in Religion. Those four programs were discontinued by the graduate council and are being phased out. The board authorized a program leading toward a M.M.E. degree, which was begun Sept. 4, 1961. President Phelps was notified that a preliminary accreditation was granted on the five programs by the North Central Association of Colleges and Secondary Schools (NCA) . The M.M.E. became M.A. in Music with programs in four areas—applied music, church music, music education, and theory-composition. The National Council for Accreditation of Teacher Education (NCATE) gave advance approval on programs leading toward M.S.E. in elementary and in secondary education.

Among other developments, the board authorized a reorganization into a University of three schools—School of Arts and Sciences, School of Nursing (Little Rock) , and the Graduate School, each under a dean. The School of Nursing was discontinued, although 55 enrolled in its first class. The Graduate School with its 10 programs received full accreditation. The board authorized the elevation of the department of music into a School of Music under a dean. That faculty reorganized and developed programs of studies by Sept. 6, including graduate programs. All three schools revised and refined their curricula to furnish the student with an instructional aid for his living in the 20th century.

Administrative restructure.—The restructure began with the election of Ben M. Elrod as vice-president for development. Later the executive committee of the board of trustees elevated James Orr and Henry Lindsey to vice-president for finance and academics, respectively. The committee elected Joseph T. McClain vice-president for administration. It had previously named Marvin Green acting president while Phelps was on leave, 1968–69. After Phelps resigned on Mar. 31, effective May 31, 1969, Lindsey was named acting president for June 2–Aug. 15, at which latter date, the board named Donald M. Seward, head of the mathematics department, interim president until the arrival on Feb. 1, 1970, of Daniel R. Grant, who had been previously elected president.

Faculty.—The faculty increased from 50 in 1956 (including 15 professors, 14 of whom held earned doctorates, 11 associate professors, 17 assistant professors—all of the latter two groups had work above the M.A. level—and 7 instructors) to 117 in 1969 (including 29 professors and 31 associate professors, of which two groups 31 held earned doctorates, 31 assistant professors, 18 instructors, and 8 teaching fellows). The faculty retirement policy was expanded to cover all full-time employees of the University. The first written "Faculty Tenure Policy" appeared in the first Faculty Handbook, and has been revised year by year. The president appointed a committee, composed of the heads of the seven academic divisions, the dean of academic affairs, the dean of graduate studies, and the business manager, and instructed them to develop a "Faculty Salary Scale Policy." The board approved an administratively revised policy—maximum increase of 20 per cent—which became effective on the contracts for 1966–67.

Student body.—A honors committee, appointed Oct. 7, 1963, presented a program that the faculty approved. Thirty-seven enrolled in the fall semester of 1964, and five more for the second semester. Based upon the fall enrolment of regular students in each case, the student body increased from 674 in 1956 to an all-time high of 1,647 in 1966, but dropped to 1,320 in 1969. Graduate enrolment increased from 20 in 1959, to 64 in 1969. The number of undergraduate degrees granted annually increased from 117 in 1956, to an all-time high of 316 in 1968. Graduate degrees granted (1961–69) totaled 78, including 45 M.A., 24 M.S.E., and 9 M.M.E. degrees. Integration began at Ouachita when Mr. and Mrs. Michael Mohapi Makosholo of Gatooma, Rhodesia, registered, Jan. 25, 1962. He was the first black man to graduate from the University. The WMU of Central Baptist Association (Arkansas) made monthly contributions to the expenses of the Makosholos. Samuel Abolade Afolabi of Ikirun, Nigeria, was the first black man to earn a graduate degree at the University. Eighty-two Negro students enrolled in the spring of 1969. Students in physical education and music have won national recognition. The Tiger basketball team ranked third in the NAIA (1965), and Leon Clements was elected All-American. He played on the Goodwill Basketball Team, sponsored by the State Department of the United States in South American countries during the summer of 1965. The Tigerettes were ranked by AAU fourth, fifth, and sixth twice. Patsy Hill and Myrna De Berry were All-American (1969–70); De Berry was captain of the United States Women's Goodwill Team, endorsed by the AAU and State Department of the United States for a playing tour of South American countries in the summer of 1969. Three other Tigerettes were on the team—Patricia Ramsey, Linda Gamble, and Carol Bollinger. In NAIA tennis, the team of Jean Michael Pellizza and Jorge A. Saucedo ranked third (1967); and both men were All-Americans. From the School of Music, Deborah Mashburne, a junior, is studying (1969) at the Mozarteum, Salzburg, Austria, on a Rotary International scholarship won in national competition.

Finances.—The convention put Ouachita in its budget of 1956 for $175,000 for operations and $50,000 for capital needs. That combined quota was 16.14 per cent of the Cooperative Program Budget. The College received that fiscal year $230,710.39 from receipts of the Cooperative Program. In 1969 the convention put the University in its budget for $384,070 for operations and $140,126 for capital needs. That combined quota was 19.67 per cent of the Cooperative Program Budget of the convention. At the end of the fiscal year 1969 (May 31), the University had received $479,126.45 from the Cooperative Program. The endowment and its earnings for the year amounted to $694,684.07 and $28,505.30 respectively in 1956, but rose to $1,957,759.01 and $98,695.45 in 1969. The total incomes at the end of the fiscal year in each case were $694,684.07 in 1956, and $3,004,354.71 in 1969. The total amounts of expenditures were $638,914.48 in 1956, and $2,777,989.26 in 1969. The total amounts for faculty salaries were $166,835.89, and $691,443.30 in 1956 and 1969, respectively.

Physical plant.—From 1956 to 1969, the physical plant increased from 19 to 31 permanent buildings. The cost of new construction for academic and housing facilities totaled $4,296,147.42. Additions and annexes to existing buildings for other services cost $479,204.30, and the cost of new properties acquired was $124,530. The total value of all physical assets rose from $1,847,082.23 to $7,470,841.56. Indebtedness on the physical assets at the end of fiscal year 1969 was $3,560,826.24.

GEORGE T. BLACKMON

P

PACIFIC COAST BAPTIST. The official newspaper of Southern Baptists in the Pacific Northwest. Leonard B. Sigle of Oklahoma, then pastor in Klamath Falls, Ore., was founder and first editor. First issue was June 4, 1931, under name of *The Regular Baptist*. The second issue appeared under date of June 27, 1931, named *Pacific Coast Baptist,* Vol. I, No. 1. The paper was an organ for Middle Oregon Association, the Interstate Baptist Mission, the Northwest Baptist Association, and then passed into the hands of the newly organized Baptist General Convention of Oregon in 1948. Sigle was not editor all the time, but was connected with it as the chief owner and thus largely determined which organization of Baptists it would represent. C. Ervin Boyle, current editor (1969), began his service in 1951. Circulation of the semimonthly paper in 1969 was nearly 6,000.

See also OREGON-WASHINGTON, BAPTIST GENERAL CONVENTION OF, VOL. II. C. E. BOYLE

PAKISTAN, MISSION IN. The Pakistan Mission traces its beginning to the arrival of Troy and Marjorie (Trippeer) Bennett in East Pakistan, Feb. 7, 1957. Contributions to this beginning had been made by Baptist families serving in Dacca and through prayers of Southern Baptists for an opportunity to commence missionary endeavor among the masses of India-Pakistan. Efforts initiated by the Australian Baptist Missionary Society to transfer a portion of its responsibility to another mission body led to exploratory investigations by Winston Crawley, then Foreign Mission Board secretary for the Orient. Upon arrival of the Bennetts, Australian Baptists introduced them to leaders of the East Pakistan Baptist Union, the convention with which affiliation would be established the following year. This union, representing 15 churches and approximately 375 members, now would cooperate with Baptist missions of Australia, New Zealand, and the United States.

Centers of missionary endeavor were continued in Faridpur, Comilla, and Dacca. In 1957 both Faridpur and Comilla had active church congregations with primary schools. An industrial school emphasizing vocational training was also located at Faridpur. Dacca became the center for language study, mission office, book store, publications, reading rooms, and community service centers (in the suburban localities of Mirpur and Tongi). Easter, 1963, marked the organization of Immanuel Baptist Church of Dacca, first church to result directly from the witness of Southern Baptists in East Pakistan. During most of the church's existence through 1969, W. Trueman Moore served as pastor. In Jan., 1965, James and Betty (Cecil) McKinley moved to Feni to open a new area of work. From this center a number of library-preaching points have appeared in the Naokhali District. During 1969, significant developments were seen in areas of literature production, planning for radio broadcasting, agricultural evangelism, community health-social services, nonresidential theological study, and the first province-wide evangelistic campaign in East Pakistan.

CHARLES A. BECKETT

PALM BEACH ATLANTIC COLLEGE. A coeducational institution offering liberal arts studies with emphasis on oceanography. The college was charted by the state of Florida in 1968 and opened with a freshman class that September. It is located at the First Baptist Church, West Palm Beach, Fla. Plans call for a permanent campus in Palm Beach Gardens on a 200-acre tract donated by John D. MacArthur. The college is owned and operated by the Palm-Lake Baptist Association which elects the 24-member board of trustees, all of whom are Baptists from the association.

The college was begun as a result of Florida Baptist Convention action in 1962 and 1963 endorsing the proposal for a junior college. In 1964 the convention accepted Palm-Lake Baptist Association's offer and requested the association to raise $1,500,000 toward founding the college. Trustees were elected and a charter was prepared. Midway through the campaign, the funds were offered to Evangelist Billy Graham who was considering building a college. When Graham dropped his plans, Palm-Lake Association decided on Mar. 15, 1968, to open the college that fall, elected trustees and named the institution Palm Beach Atlantic. The new trustees named Jess Moody, pastor of the First Baptist Church, West Palm Beach, president, and selected retired Union University President, Warren Jones, Sr., to design the curriculum. In November, upon their own request, the original board of trustees was released by the convention.

The college opened in 1968 with 125 students. When a sophomore class was added in 1969, the enrolment increased to 200 students. The first graduating class was scheduled for 1972. Courses are offered in the liberal arts leading toward bachelor of science and bachelor of arts degrees.

The college seeks to instil in all students the dignity of work and a vital concern in Christian service to others. Students are required to work five hours per week in the "Workshop" program for community service to people in need: e.g., working with blind children, mentally retarded, the aged, migrants, and painting homes in the slum areas. JESS MOODY

PANAMA AND CANAL ZONE, MISSIONS IN (cf. Panama and Canal Zone, Baptists In, Vol. II). In 1956, 19 Baptist churches and 26 missions were in Panama and the Canal Zone. By 1970 these had grown to 40 churches and 80 missions, with about 6,000 Baptists out of a total population of 1,300,000. The churches cooperate through associations organized along ethnic lines. The Bocas and Central associations are primarily composed of churches serving persons of West Indian background; the Panama, Interior, and Chiriqui Associations of Spanish-speaking Panamanians; the San Blas Association of churches on the islands of the San Blas Archipelago; and the Canal Zone Association of churches whose memberships are largely United States citizens.

These churches cooperate with the Panama Baptist Convention, organized in 1959 and gradually assuming responsibilities for work carried by the Home Mission Board. The board, through its Department of Language Missions, works in a cooperative relationship with the convention. R. G. Van Royen served as superintendent of the work, 1953–60, followed by L. D. Wood, 1960–65. Joe Carl Johnson became superintendent in 1966. In 1970, 18 missionaries from the United States served in Panama.

The board provides assistance to the Panama work, primarily through fraternal aid to the churches, and joins the convention in financial support of Cresta Del Mar assembly at Santa Clara and the Panama Theological Seminary in Arraijan which enrolled 15 students in 1969. The Marvel Iglesias Medical Clinic, established in 1965 on the island of Aligandi, serves the San Blas Islands. Daniel Gruver was appointed as the first medical missionary. GERALD B. PALMER

PARADISE VALLEY BAPTIST RANCH. See ARIZONA SOUTHERN BAPTIST CONVENTION.

***PARAGUAY, MISSION IN.** The Asuncion hospital was the first Baptist hospital established in South America. A new pediatric ward was inaugurated in 1964. Separate quarters for the school of nursing were dedicated in 1961. The hospital has ministered to physical need, torn down prejudices, and contributed to the prestige of evangelical work. Its chaplaincy program is designed to help the sick, hospital personnel, and churches in a variety of ways.

FRANK K. MEANS

PARLIAMENTARY AUTHORITY AND RULES OF ORDER. The Southern Baptist Convention operates under a constitution which includes bylaws, a business and financial plan, and a Convention procedure.

The constitution may be amended by a vote of two-thirds of the members present, providing (1) no amendment may be considered after the second day of the Convention, and (2) that an amendment shall be approved by two successive annual sessions of the Convention. The bylaws of the constitution may be altered by a two-thirds majority vote at any time except on the last day of the Convention.

Since 1965 the parliamentary authority of the Convention has been the latest revised edition of *Robert's Rules of Order.* From 1900–65, the Convention used Kerfoot's *Parliamentary Law.* Prior to 1900 Mell's *Manual of Parliamentary Practice* was used.

The purpose of parliamentary law is to assist the Convention in accomplishing in the very best possible manner the work for which it was constituted. Basic is the right of the majority to decide while at the same time protecting the right of the minority to be heard.

To facilitate proper action on all matters, and to enable all messengers to know when certain items will be discussed, the Convention amended its bylaws in 1957 by instructing the Committee on Order of Business to "provide periods of time during the early days of the Convention for the introduction of all matters requiring a vote not scheduled on the agenda, and, when introduced (unless the Convention then gives its unanimous consent for its immediate consideration) shall fix times for the consideration of the same." Parliamentary authority and rules of order are to be used as a guide. The Convention is to be conducted at all times by rules of Christian conduct. LEE PORTER

***PASTORAL CARE.** Pastoral care refers to the ministry to persons, sometimes designated as shepherding or the care of souls. This ministry includes a pastoral relationship in the various experiences of life. Pastoral ministry is offered to the family, small groups in intimate associations, and to individuals. It is a redemptive ministry which seeks to aid persons in their relationship to God and to other persons, in their personal growth as Christians, and in handling their problems in the crises of life.

The care of souls is primarily a ministry in the preparation for living. It includes such areas as guidance for children and youth, counsel in courtship and preparation for marriage, comfort and support in the crises of illness and death, marriage counseling, alcohol and drug addiction, and sexual aberrations.

Methods of pastoral care include pastoral preaching, group counseling, individual counseling, the ministry of visitation, and conducting weddings and funerals.

Training in pastoral care is provided on many levels in our denomination. Various agencies of the Southern Baptist Convention provide programs and literature. The Sunday School Board through *Home Life,* vocational guidance, sensitivity training in personnel, *Church Administration,* and other divisions, implements this ministry to persons. The Home Mission Board provides training through the chaplaincy programs: military, institutional, and industrial. Broadly speaking, the HMB implements pastoral care in action through social work and other special ministries. Action groups and other ministries of Woman's Missionary Union and the Brotherhood also provide guidance and literature. In the preparation for overseas missions the Foreign Mission Board provides special conferences for training in interpersonal relations.

The local churches of the SBC are centers for "equipping the saints" for their ministry to persons in the world. According to New Testament teachings all Christians are mutually ministers to one another and to all persons in need outside the church. Many churches have staff members designated to serve as ministers in the care of the souls, along with the pastor whose primary duties include shepherding. Members of the church in other occupations—medicine, psychology, psychiatry, legal professions, public education, social work, etc.—with their particular skills are often enlisted in this ministry.

Southern Baptist seminaries are continually developing a program of training for church leaders in pastoral care. Each of the seminaries has a department responsible for this area of training. These departments are designated by various titles: psychology of religion and pastoral care, pastoral care, psychology and counseling, psychology of religion, and pastoral ministry.

All of the seminaries provide general courses in pastoral care, courses in clinical pastoral education, and graduate seminars. Each seminary provides 12 or more courses in this area of training. In recent years some of the seminaries have graduated students with Th.M. and Th.D. degrees in pastoral care. A list of the theses written in this field are on file with the Historical Commission in Nashville.

Clinical Pastoral Education.—Perhaps the greatest advances in seminary education have been made in clinical pastoral education. The clinical approach to teaching pastoral theology takes theology into specific clinical settings such as hospitals, jails, and child-care institutions. More recently such social agencies as Family Service Organizations, Visiting Nurses' Associations, etc., are being used. The student uses the case method of inquiry into the issues of life and death, sin and salvation, and despair and hope in suffering people of all ages and situations in life. This study is done under careful supervision of a trained supervisor.

Collaboration with people of other professions than the ministry itself is essential to the method. Instruction involves mutual evaluation and support alongside one's fellow students. This approach to the study of pastoral theology is in effect at all six of the Southern Baptist theological seminaries. All of these schools have one or more staff members who give much of their time to the clinical teaching and learning of pastoral theology.

One of the first pioneers in this field was Gaines S. Dobbins at the seminary in Louisville. He brought the founder of this movement, Anton Boisen, to the campus as a visiting lecturer. Boisen was an intrepid explorer of man's suffering and of ways of teaching theological students to understand "the living human documents" of people's own lives.

Dobbins also brought Seward Hiltner, the first executive secretary of the Council for Clinical Training, to the campus. They worked together in the establishment of the first supervised clinical program under the leadership of Dobbins and Chaplain Ralph Bonacker, of Norton Memorial Infirmary in Louisville. This program was established in 1944. It was followed by programs at the Baptist Hospital in Louisville under the joint supervision of Dobbins and Chaplain Wayne E. Oates of Baptist Hospital. The next program was established at the Kentucky State Hospital at Danville, Ky., with the joint supervision of Dobbins and Oates also, inasmuch as the program at Baptist Hospital had been taken over by Chaplain James Lyn Elder after Oates went to Kentucky State Hospital for the purpose of establishing a program in the mental hospital.

The North Carolina Baptist Hospital called Richard Young as chaplain, and in 1947 established the program which now is the School of Pastoral Care. Dobbins and Oates served as consultants and enlisted the students for the first program at North Carolina Baptist Hospital. When Southeastern Baptist Theological Seminary was established, this program was taken over by this school, and a joint program with the School of Pastoral Care has been in action since the beginning of the school.

At Southwestern Baptist Theological Seminary foundations for a program of clinical pastoral education were begun in 1955. The council of administrators at Texas Medical Center, Houston, Tex., inaugurated a movement to form the Institute of Religion in the center in 1954. A theological seminary committee comprised of representatives from five seminaries in Texas—Southwestern Baptist Seminary, Fort Worth, Perkins School of Theology of Southern Methodist University, Dallas, Austin Presbyterian Theological Seminary, Austin, Episcopal Theological Seminary of the Southwest, Austin, and Bright Divinity School of Texas Christian University, Fort Worth—was asked to assist in a survey to establish guidelines and to propose a program of training for clinical pastoral education at the Institute of Religion. Jesse Northcutt and Franklin Segler served on this committee.

From that time Southwestern Seminary has affiliated with the Institute of Religion in providing clinical training for its students.

Southwestern Seminary assisted in developing programs of clinical training in local centers at Fort Worth and Dallas. C. W. Brister assisted in these developments. Approved institutions in these communities, Harris Memorial Hospital, All Saints Episcopal Hospital, and United States Public Health Service Hospital, of Fort Worth, Parkland Hospital, Dallas, Baylor Hospital, Dallas, and the Dallas Pastoral Care Center, under the direction of Kenneth Pepper, cooperated in providing orientation in pastoral care for Southwestern Seminary students, and it is hoped that they will soon be an approved center for clinical pastoral education.

Southwestern Seminary allows credit for clinical training taken in any center approved by the Association for Clinical Pastoral Education. A number of students have taken the Th.M. degree with a major in clinical pastoral education and one has taken the Th.D. degree. Several graduates are now serving as supervisors in clinical pastoral education in hospitals and other institutions.

Courses for clinical training are provided both in the School of Theology and in the School of Religious Education. Professors certified for clinical pastoral education include: C. W. Brister, Franklin Segler, and John W. Drakeford, with Gerald E. Marsh working toward certification.

At New Orleans Baptist Theological Seminary, the program of clinical pastoral education has been led by John Price and his associates in conjunction with Southern Baptist Hospital under the joint leadership of Price and Myron Madden, chaplain at the hospital. The social work emphasis was developed in relation to the Tulane School of Social Work, and extensive clinical facilities as far away as Mandeville State Hospital were supervised by Price and his associates.

The program of clinical pastoral education at Golden Gate Baptist Theological Seminary has been conducted under the leadership of James Lyn Elder in conjunction with the cluster of clinical pastoral education facilities in the Bay area. The Institute of Pastoral Care and the Council for Clinical Training have collaborated with the Seminary in providing joint programs.

Midwestern Baptist Theological Seminary has a department in psychology of religion and pastoral care under the guidance of Everett V. Reneer. Clinical training is provided in Baptist Memorial Hospital, Kansas City, under the supervision of Richard Dayringer, and in other approved centers across the nation.

In the late fifties a plan to unify all the clinical pastoral education groups in the country was initiated. However, the plan got no further than a mutual agreement on minimum standards for the supervision of clinical pastoral education. As a result, the various hospitals and schools where clinical pastoral education was being offered by Southern Baptists joined together and formed the Southern Baptist Association for Clinical Pastoral Education. This group met in conjunction with the regular meeting of the Southern Baptist Conference on Counseling and Guidance until 1966. At this time, they voted to dissolve their own independent organization and to become a part of the newly formed Association of Clinical Pastoral Education. Since 1967 this national group has embraced all the constituency of the Southern Baptist group which no longer maintains a separate identity. The function of the national association is several-fold: fellowship, certification of supervisors according to common standards, accreditation of hospital and other institutional centers where training is being offered, and mutual assistance in the placement of persons who are clinically trained.

However, Southern Baptists have maintained a considerable amount of autonomy because all the programs are under the auspices of either Baptist hospitals or Baptist seminaries or both. Likewise, the professors and chaplains in these institutions have a common history in the previous association of Southern Baptists. Regional homogeneity provides the strongest bond of autonomy in the various regions of the national organization. In maintaining regional organizations, the national group has maintained the strengths of the previously regionally focused groups.

Pastoral Care in Community Relations.—Pastoral care includes a corrective mode of ministry. It aims at relieving or removing those factors that hinder spiritual growth. As a corrective ministry, pastoral care works with other service agencies in the community. It seeks out and uses the "helping professions" and their practitioners. This is done in the spirit of cooperation, not competition. The concept of "the healing team" is an established one. Pastors have long collaborated with physicians, nurses, and social workers in serving persons' needs.

The whole person is thus served, not merely a part of him. Body, soul, and spirit are not seen as separate components but as aspects of total personality. Service is directed to this total, "spiritual" self.

The whole referral ministry rests upon religious workers' willingness to acknowledge their limitations. Second, this service requires knowledge of community resources. And this information must be more than superficial. Personal acquaintance with helping programs and personnel is essential to effective referral. Since there are important differences between various healing programs and between practitioners in the same area, nothing less than detailed, personal information about available services and personnel will suffice for those engaged in pastoral care.

Third, pastoral care, in its use of community resources, skilfully presents the matter to those it serves. Persons with problems do not feel that they are being "brushed off." Rather, they are assured that they are being given the best help possible. Ministers make clear that cooperative service is being rendered them. Appointments are then made and support is given while treatment goes on.

In this collaborating with community agencies, pastoral care implies, if it does not explicitly state, that all helping programs and persons are at a basic level involved in ministry. By communicating this understanding to helping professionals, an evangelism to the "up and out"—well-trained and effective non-Christians —is practiced.

There is no limit to the number of community resources with which pastoral care may collaborate. Hospitals, clinics (both public and private), and service agencies of all kinds are potential healing partners.

In addition, counselors and therapists in private practice may be involved in pastoral care. Wherever healing service is being given, in fact, and wherever there are persons receptive to the "healing team" idea, collaboration between pastoral care and community resources may go on.

Our Ministry to the Aging.—Baptists have always had a Christian concern for the aging members of families, churches, communities, and beyond. However, few specialized programs of ministry to the aging were begun before the turn of the century. One of the first formal emphases by Southern Baptists was in the establishment of various Baptist homes for the aging across the Convention. Such states as Missouri pioneered in this work. Kentucky, Maryland, Virginia, Texas, Georgia, North Carolina, District of Columbia, Oklahoma, Florida, and several other conventions have also established such homes. In addition, groups of Baptists more recently have established church-related corporations supporting and fostering retirement homes. Baptist hospitals have served those with special physical problems related to aging. Monumental among these ministries has been the Baptist Geriatric Hospital at San Angelo, Tex.

All six Southern Baptist seminaries provide one or more courses in some ministry to adults. Such course content may be from the perspective of pastoral care, religious education, educational principles, or psychology. One of the seminaries has an entire semester's course on later adulthood.

All boards, agencies, and commissions have provided some structured programs and ministries for the aging. Although most of this work has not been correlated, it has been significant and has provided foundations for some more organized concerns of the present time. A need for correlation of this ministry was evidenced by the recommendations of the conference on "An Expanding Recreation Ministry to Older Adults," held in Nashville, Tenn., Jan., 1960. Part of the recommendations were:

> That the Sunday School Board propose to the Inter-Agency Council that consideration be given to definite terminology in this field and further consideration be given the terms, "older adults" or "aging adults" as possibilities. It is suggested that such a decision might be deferred until after the White House conference in 1961. (This is the working terminology and not an attempt to name an age group in the organization.)
>
> This group is convinced that no agency, department, or commission should have total responsibility for ministering to older adults but that each agency discharge its responsibility to this age group as they do with all other age groups.

In other recommendations of this conference, there were suggestions that the Baptist Book Stores also cooperate in this emphasis on a ministry to the aging. In the years following this recommendation such action was taken by most agencies, commissions, and boards, and provision is now made for this age group.

Other conferences like the Nashville meeting have been held in recent years, such as the conference, "Problems on the Aging," held at Louisiana College, Pineville, La., Apr., 1960.

The most expanding ministry in the decade, 1960–70, has been that of the local churches. Pastors and other vocational staff members shepherd and guide aging adults through pastoral care. Such a counseling ministry provides the individual attention needed. Many experimental programs for "senior citizens" and "golden age groups" have been launched in hundreds of Baptist churches affiliated with the Convention.

The increase in the number of Christian family emphases in churches brought about a consciousness of the needs of this group. Special conferences at the two Southern Baptist assemblies and state assemblies, as well as leadership materials in various board publications must have helped.

Literature on Pastoral Care by Southern Baptist Authors.—Following is a bibliography of writings in pastoral care by Southern Baptist authors since 1956:

Bassett, William, *Counseling the Childless Couple* (1963); Bell, Donald, *The Family in Dialogue* (1968); *How to Get Along with People in the Church* (1960); Brister, C. W., *Pastoral Care in the Church* (1964); *People Who Care* (1967); Drakeford, John W., *Counseling for Church Leaders* (1961); *Farewell to the Lonely Crowd* (1968); *Great Sex Swindle* (1965); *Home: Laboratory for Life* (1965); *Psychology in Search of a Soul* (1964); Knowles, Joseph, *Group Counseling* (1964); Madden, Myron, *The Power of the Blessing* (1969); Oates, Wayne E., *Alcohol: In and Out of the Church* (1966); *Christ and Selfhood* (1961); *On Becoming Children of God* (1968); *Pastoral Counseling and Social Problems* (1962); *Protestant Pastoral Counseling* (1962); *Religious Dimensions of Personality* (1957); *The Christian Pastor* (revised and enlarged edition, 1964); *The Holy Spirit in Five Worlds* (1968); *The Revelation of God in Human Suffering* (1959); *What Psychology Says About Religion* (1959); with Frank Stagg and Glenn Hinson, *Glossalalia* (1967); Oates, Wayne E., and Andrew Lester, *Pastoral Care in Crucial Human Situations* (1969); Segler, Franklin M., *The Broadman Minister's Manual* (1968); *Christian Worship: Its Theology and Practice* (1967); *The Christian Layman* (1964); *A Theology of Church and Ministry* (1960); *Your Emotions and*

Your Faith (1970); Young, Richard K., and Albert M. Meiburg, *Spiritual Therapy* (1960).

FRANKLIN M. SEGLER, A. DONALD BELL, JAMES LYN ELDER, WAYNE E. OATES.

PASTORAL PSYCHOLOGY. See PASTORAL CARE.

***PEACE AND SOUTHERN BAPTISTS.** Concern for world peace on the part of Southern Baptists is evidenced by formal action being taken in support of peace at annual Conventions held in 1958, 1959, 1960, 1963, 1967, 1969, and 1970. Most of these resolutions were of a general nature, reaffirming a quest for peace with justice in the world, supporting the President and the United States Government in the pursuit of peace, and asserting the deep conviction that the only hope for lasting peace is in Jesus Christ, the Prince of peace.

In 1958 a Special Committee on World Peace was appointed by the president of the Southern Baptist Convention. In its report, presented to the Convention in 1959, Southern Baptists were urged to support world peace through increased world missions and prayer, the promotion of international understanding and goodwill, the support of our government in achieving international agreement on disarmament, and the prayerful support of the United Nations.

The Christian Life Commission has sponsored a Southern Baptist observer at the United Nations for extended periods since 1960. The commission has also held leadership seminars at the United Nations for Southern Baptists in 1960, 1962, and 1963 and a conference on "Christianity and World Issues" in New York in 1966.

In 1967 the Convention received a strong detailed statement on world peace as part of the annual report of the Christian Life Commission. The statement was amended to preclude any suggestion of "the withdrawal of United States forces from Vietnam apart from an honorable and a just peace."

In 1970 the Convention resolved to "give full support to the Commander-in-Chief of our nation in those efforts to bring about a just and honorable peace and to accelerate efforts to bring home at the earliest possible time our combat forces in Vietnam."

The Christian Life Commission by virtue of its program assignment from the Convention has taken the lead in communicating biblical truth regarding world peace. In 1963 special summer conferences were held at Glorieta and Ridgecrest on "The Things That Make for Peace."

The Public Affairs Committee contributes to the emphasis on peace through information and conferences in the related areas of military and international affairs. Other boards and agencies produce curriculum and general literature in the area of world peace.

ELMER S. WEST, JR.

PEACHTREE-ON-PEACHTREE INN. A ministry of the Georgia Baptist Convention to the elderly. A gift to the convention by Fred Beazley and the Beazley Foundation of Norfolk, Va., 1966. It was formerly Peachtree-on-Peachtree Hotel in Atlanta. Located at 176 Peachtree Street, NW, in the heart of downtown Atlanta, it was accepted by the convention in Nov., 1966. The Inn received its charter of incorporation on Nov. 22, 1966, through efforts led by the convention's Executive Secretary-Treasurer Searcy S. Garrison. Complete renovation of the building was effected during 1967–68. The Inn was opened for residents in Jan., 1967, and the first resident, Homer S. Yeats, came almost immediately.

William L. Rainwater was the first administrator. W. A. Parker, Sr., was elected president of the board of trustees. Cecil T. Underwood was elected administrator in Nov., 1967. The Inn operates under a board of 15 trustees elected by the convention.

The main purpose for which this corporation is formed "shall be to . . . give proper care, maintenance and recreation to elderly men and women who otherwise could not afford adequate facilities and provide for their physical, mental and spiritual welfare and to do any and all things which might be necessary to accomplish the stated objectives."

The Inn is a resident home; there are no nursing facilities. When nursing care is needed it is necessary for the resident to leave the Inn and go into a nursing home or hospital with the hope of returning to the Inn upon recovery.

CECIL T. UNDERWOOD

PENDLETON BAPTIST LIBRARY, J. M. This library was established in Carthage, Tenn., on Jan. 10, 1959, by R. D. Brooks to make available materials on Baptists in the United States to ministers and Sunday School teachers. The library is particularly designed for rural ministers who may not be able to afford a formal education. Named in honor of the 19th century Landmark Baptist, James Madison Pendleton (*q.v.*, Vol. II), the library has on exhibit a writing table which belonged to Pendleton when he taught New Testament at Union University in Murfreesboro, Tenn. In 1970 a permanent structure for the library was being planned on Carmack Avenue in Carthage.

R. D. BROOKS and TERRY L. JONES

PENLAND, GEORGE HARVEY (b. Hayesville, Clay County, N.C., Jan. 3, 1888; d. Dallas, Tex., Oct. 24, 1958). Attorney, businessman, lay leader. He attended Grayson College and Baylor University. He married Helen Edmond in 1912 at Waco, Tex., where he practiced law, 1912–29. He led a successful campaign in 1928 to keep Baylor at Waco. Moving to Dallas, he served as general solicitor for Missouri-Kansas-Texas Railroad; director, Southwestern Drug Corporation, Reynolds-Penland Company, and Republic National Bank; trustee of Wadley Research Institute. A nephew of George W. Truett (*q.v.*, Vol. II), Penland was a member of First Baptist Church, Dallas, 1930–58. For many years he was a member and chairman of Baylor Hospital's Board of Trustees. Penland is buried in Waco, Tex. J. C. CANTRELL

PENNELL, THOMAS CYRUS (b. Mack's Creek, Camden County, Mo., Feb. 2, 1893; d. Shreveport, La., May 31, 1959). Son of Larkin Granville and Rachel (Russell) Pennell, he was educated at Southwest Baptist College (B.A., 1922), Bolivar, Mo. He was converted at age 16, ordained in 1914, and served half-time churches while in college. Other pastorates were Ash Grove and Mountain Grove, Mo., and Ingleside Baptist Church, Shreveport, La., 1929–59.

He married Alice Wharton Noland, Oct. 2, 1930, and they had three children: Elsie (Mrs. Carl E. Johnson), Mary (Mrs. William E. Smith), and Thomas C., Jr. Pennell served on the Louisiana Baptist Convention executive board for 17 years, three years as president; moderator of Caddo Baptist Association, 1957–59; and president of Louisiana Baptist Convention, 1958. He conducted many revivals, spoke to numerous youth groups, and wrote articles for state and convention-wide publications. Louisiana College awarded him an honorary D.D. degree in 1958.

While Pennell was at Ingleside Church 32 young men entered the ministry, several to serve in foreign missions. Also during this pastorate he led in the organization of three other churches: Sunset Acres, Emmanuel, and Parkhurst. JOHN G. ALLEY

PENNSYLVANIA, SOUTHERN BAPTISTS IN. See MARYLAND, BAPTIST CONVENTION OF, and OHIO, STATE CONVENTION OF BAPTISTS IN.

PENNSYLVANIA–SOUTH JERSEY, BAPTIST CONVENTION OF. Southern Baptist work in the Pennsylvania–South Jersey area began in 1957 as Southern Baptist families came together in their homes to study the Bible. The first church was constituted in 1958. The early churches in the western part of Pennsylvania began cooperating with Southern Baptists through the State Convention of Baptists in Ohio. Those in the eastern part of Pennsylvania and in the southern part of New Jersey cooperated through the Baptist Convention of Maryland, and became a part of the Northeastern Baptist Association and the Northeastern Baptist Fellowship.

In 1963 the Northeastern Baptist Fellowship voted to look toward the establishment of three state conventions in the northeast. The churches of Pennsylvania and the southern part of New Jersey formed the Pennsylvania–South Jersey Baptist Fellowship. They held annual meetings until Oct. 3–4, 1969, when a constitution and bylaws were adopted, and the date of Oct. 2–3, 1970, was set for the constitution of the Baptist Convention of Pennsylvania–South Jersey in Harrisburg, Pa. The new convention, with approximately 90 churches and chapels and 10,000 members working in three associations, became the 32nd state convention to be affiliated with the Southern Baptist Convention.

GEORGE WOODROW BULLARD

***PERRY MEMORIAL HOSPITAL (Perry, Okla.).** In 1969, 46 employees operated this 28-bed hospital with 55 per cent occupancy. Property value was $240,241. J. M. GASKIN

***PERU, MISSION IN.** The mission adopted a long-range strategy calling for the successive occupation of Peru's chief cities. Efforts have been made to reach university students. Three book stores provide churches with indispensable materials. Radio and television played prominent roles in opening Baptist work in Piura. A theological institute, located first in Lima but later in Trujillo, helps discover and train future leaders. An encampment was established near Lima, at Santa Eulalia. FRANK K. MEANS

PETITPAS, PETER BERT (b. Nova Scotia, Canada, Aug. 1, 1887; d. Lake Arthur, La., Sept. 29, 1966). One of seven children born to Roman Catholic parents, he was educated in a Catholic convent where he studied for the priesthood. He quit school and moved to Washington state where he was converted to the Baptist faith at age 21 in a service led by a Salvation Army worker. At his conversion his family turned against him, though his mother later became a Baptist.

He came to Louisiana at the urging of a man from Crowley, and a friend sent him to Austin (Tex.) Institute, where he received some Bible training. He was ordained in Beaumont, Tex., in 1920, and married Diana Miller there in 1923. He was a general missionary in Texas, then returned to Louisiana. In 1934 he married Edith Deville of Ville Platte, La. He preached for 50 years, serving as pastor at Oak Grove, Lake Arthur, Jennings, Kaplan, Miller French community, Nunez, and Church Point, La. He was missionary and evangelist, holding many tent revivals. Most of his work was in south Louisiana among the French people, starting mission work, or strengthening that which had already been begun. JOHN G. ALLEY

PETROFF, ERNEST ALEXSANDER (b. Sliven, Bulgaria, Mar. 17, 1887; d. Orlando, Fla., Apr. 17, 1965). Son of General Peter Stoycheff and Ernestine Mavradieva Petroff, he received his early education from the parish priest of Sliven. He attended Samokove College in Bulgaria and later earned the B.A. degree from Clinton College in Kentucky. At 17, he went to America, where new job opportunities eventually led him to Chicago and to other parts of Illinois. At Alta Pass, Ill., when 20 years old, he was converted and later joined a Baptist church. Within a year he entered the ministry and was aided by pastor C. W. Culp to return to school. Petroff spent most of his 59-year ministry in evangelism. He was associated with Thomas Theodore Martin (*q.v.*, Vol. II) and the Blue Mountain Evangelistic Force of Blue Mountain, Miss., and with the Southern Baptist Home Mission Board (1913–16). He preached in many revivals in Oklahoma and Arkansas and in Northern (American) Baptist churches in Kansas. A unique result in Kansas was his influence on churches and people who later became important factors in the development of the Kansas Convention of Southern Baptists. Petroff gave the last 20 years of his ministry to the following Baptist pastorates: First, Danville, Ky., 1938–42; Deadrick Avenue, Knoxville, Tenn., 1942–47; and West Side, Hamilton, Ohio, 1947–58. The State Convention of Baptists in Ohio was organized in his church building, and he was its moderator at the time of his resignation from the latter pastorate. He also helped organize the Greater Miami Valley Baptist Association of Ohio and was its first moderator.

On Oct. 15, 1913, he married Lola Griffith. After her death he married Ida Mable Fields, Sept. 14, 1935. At the time of his death from a heart attack, he was serving as interim pastor of a Baptist church in Orlando, Fla.

N. J. WESTMORELAND

PETTIGREW, WILLIAM ROBERT (b. Humbolt, Tenn., June 30, 1900; d. Louisville, Ky., Dec. 12, 1965). He was educated at Union University, Jackson, Tenn. (A.B., 1922), and Southern Baptist Theological Seminary (Th.M., 1927). Ordained at Humbolt, Tenn., on Sept. 30, 1919, his pastorates included Hazelwood Church, Louisville, 1924–27; First, Springfield, Tenn., 1927–36; Citadel Square, Charleston, S. C., 1936–46; and Walnut Street, Louisville, Ky., 1946–65.

Union University conferred on him the D.D. in 1946. C. R. Daley wrote of him in the *Western Recorder:* "Of those who have served the Lord among Baptists in this generation, none was greater than Dr. W. R. Pettigrew." Pettigrew himself wrote, "I had a rather cataclysmic and revolutionary experience, which revealed to me that I was not prepared for Sunday simply because I had two well worked out sermon outlines; that I could only be really ready for the services when I had during the previous week won at least one soul to Christ, and had that one dedicated to the Christian duty of making his confession public by uniting with the church in one of the services on Sunday. Since that date there have been only three Sundays when I was in my pulpit, that there has not been at least one who united with the church."

Pettigrew married Mary Moody Yancey, Sept. 4, 1920. They had two daughters: Mary Elizabeth (Mrs. Joe Madison King) and Ruth (Mrs. Lawrence Dillard). LEO T. CRISMON

***PHILIPPINES, MISSION IN.** Evangelistic responsiveness, local leadership, and continued expansion are marks of this work. Student work has been given strong emphasis in five centers. Agricultural missions was inaugurated in May, 1964. Cohesion has been found in the erection of a Baptist building. *Philippine Baptist House* on television was begun with a "live" Filipino cast. In Nov., 1968, an evangelistic crusade sponsored by the 11,458 Baptists resulted in 6,117 professions of faith. In 1969 there were 96 missionaries in 19 locations on Luzon, Cebu, and Mindanao.

R. KEITH PARKS

PHILLIPS, WILLIAM PRESSLEY (b. Lampasas, Tex., Sept. 17, 1882; d. Tyler, Tex., Oct. 23, 1958). Son of Daniel W. and Nellie (Mellon) Phillips, he was educated in Lampasas public schools and Southern Baptist Theological Seminary. He married Lucille Mellon in 1912. His denominational service began in 1913 as Sunday School field secretary for Kentucky Baptists. He served briefly as one of the first paid Sunday School superintendents (educational director) at First Baptist Church, Tyler, Tex.

In 1916 Phillips became state Sunday School secretary for Texas. Particularly effective was his promotion of the work of Convention Bible classes.

He succeeded Harry L. Strickland (*q.v.*, Vol. II) as secretary of the Organized Class Department of the Sunday School Board, SBC, in 1925. The name of this department was changed immediately to Young People's and Adult Department, which signified the beginning of a major contribution in departmentalization for Young People and Adults in the churches. Two of his books, *The Adult Department of the Sunday School* (1935) and *Adults in the Sunday School* (1947), formed the basis for the great advance in Adult work. Phillips served as head of the department of Young People's and Adult Sunday School work until 1943, and he continued as superintendent of Adult work until his retirement in 1953. His leadership in bringing Southern Baptist churches to a major emphasis on Adults through multiple departments and classes and age grading resulted in the enlistment and teaching of multitudes of adults.

A. V. WASHBURN

PIKE, JOHN CALVIN (b. Polk County, Mo., Jan. 25, 1863; d. Springfield, Mo., Dec. 21, 1957). A graduate of Southwest Baptist College and Central Missouri State College, Pike taught in public schools (at Hamilton, Mo., J. C. Penney was one of his students), Pierce City College, and Southwest Baptist College where he served as professor of psychology, president, and dean. The Southwest college named an auditorium and gym in his honor (Pike Auditorium). He married Mary S. Smith, 1887. They had one daughter, Caroline. DORAN C. MCCARTY

***PINE CREST CHILDREN'S HOME.** Mrs. Virginia Fields, resident director since Jan., 1957, was given the title of superintendent, effective Aug. 1, 1959. From that date Pine Crest became practically independent of its sponsoring institution, Spring Meadows. This was sealed by the Articles of Incorporation, which were filed with the state on Jan. 7, 1966. On Oct. 1, 1965, Mrs. Fields retired. W. Robert Elliott succeeded her. Under his superintendency Pine Crest's first full-time social worker was employed. Construction of a new residence for the superintendent was completed in the summer of 1966. On July 1, 1969, this home had 46 children under care. C. FORD DEUSNER

PIONEER MISSIONS, HOME MISSION BOARD PROGRAM OF. Pioneer missions, historically considered as those areas to which Southern Baptists extended work from older areas, has been a concern of Southern Baptists almost since the organization of the Southern Baptist Convention in 1845 when the Board of Domestic Missions sent missionaries to the expanding west. In 1883 the Convention approved a recommendation that "the Home Mission Board make speedy and special efforts to meet the demands for preaching the gospel in western territories and for this region that a district secretary and general evangelist be appointed by the Home Mission Board."

Pioneer missions today has the objective "to work with and assist churches and associations and state conventions in surveying mission opportunities, analyzing trends, developing growth studies, discovering new cooperative ventures, and coordinating Home Mission Board interests in the newer and weaker areas of the Convention."

Some special areas of concern are simultaneous evangelistic projects, chaplaincy ministries, church loans, establishment of churches, associational administration, field guidance ministry, language missions, work with National Baptists, Christian social ministries, and work related to nonevangelicals.

Pioneer missions as emphasized by the Department of Pioneer Missions, HMB, includes the following areas: Alaska, Connecticut, Delaware, Hawaii, Idaho, Iowa, Maine, Massachusetts, Minnesota, Montana, Nebraska, Nevada, New Hampshire, New Jersey, New York, North Dakota, Pennsylvania, Puerto Rico, Rhode Island, South Dakota, Utah, Vermont, Wisconsin, and Wyoming. When the South Burlington, Vt., Baptist church was constituted, July 6, 1963, Southern Baptists then had one or more churches in every state of the Union.

This happened in less than a half century, triggered by large shifts of population induced by opportunities offered in industry, business, and education, plus military assignments causing an estimated 1,300,000 Baptists to leave the southern states between 1940 and 1950. Additional large numbers moved during subsequent years.

In 1959 the Convention instructed the board to "continue emphasis on work in areas where there is no state convention or where the state convention is not well established." This the board sought to do principally through the Department of Pioneer Missions (created in 1959), but also through other departments and programs. When state conventions reach the 25,000 mark in membership, and thus qualify for representation on the boards and agencies of the Convention, the board provides basic assistance through the Metropolitan and Rural-Urban Missions Departments rather than through the Pioneer Missions Department.

Although Southern Baptists made an effort to establish churches in California in the 1850's this work was discontinued in the 1860's. By 1940 there were 13 Southern Baptist churches in California; in 1942 these had expanded to 33 recognized by the Convention as the Southern Baptist State Convention in California. In 1944 the Convention reaffirmed the fact that it was free of territorial limitations within the United States. Almost a century earlier the Convention had included such a provision in its constitution.

Responding to persistent calls coming from the west, the board's involvement in western mission work began in 1944 with the establishment of city missions programs in San Diego, Los Angeles, and San Francisco, Calif., and in Albuquerque, N. Mex., and Phoenix, Ariz. Fred A. McCaulley was appointed by the board as field worker for the western states in 1946.

Between 1940 and 1948 five state conventions were formed in the west and midwest. Churches also began developing in the north central portion of the United States, largely resulting from migration of southerners to those areas. Work east of the Mississippi was called "pioneer," and A. B. Cash was appointed to lead in this area in 1954. From 1954 to 1955 Geo. W. Cummins served as superintendent of the board's ministries to western states. In 1959 both western and pioneer missions were assigned to the newly created Department of Pioneer Missions with Cash as department secretary.

Work in the northeastern states began in 1951. By 1963, one or more churches had been established in each of the states from Delaware to Maine. In Sept., 1957, the board elected Paul S. James as pastor of the congregation then meeting in Manhattan. In early 1958 this group was constituted as the Manhattan Baptist Church, and from this church work has spread to other parts of New York state, New Jersey, and throughout the New England states. Work opened in western Pennsylvania in 1959, with the appointment of Joseph Waltz as director of mission work there. In 1960 Elmer Sizemore was appointed to serve as director of Southern Baptist work in New England.

A. B. Cash retired as secretary of the department in 1967 and was succeeded by M. Wendell Belew. Two staff associates were added, Francis J. Redford and Quentin Lockwood, who provide field services in the eastern and western sections of the nation respectively.

See also PIONEER MISSIONS, VOL. I.

M. WENDELL BELEW

PITT, WILLIAM HENRY, SR. (b. Memphis, Tenn., Mar. 13, 1917; d. Baton Rouge, La., Dec. 5, 1969). Businessman, minister, associational missionary, state stewardship secretary, and staff member Stewardship Commission, SBC. The son of Thomas Luther and Joy Beatrice (Scoggins) Pitt, he graduated from Union University (B.A., 1957) and Southern Baptist Theological Seminary (B.D., 1960). He married Olivia Talbert, Memphis, Tenn., Oct. 4, 1936. They had three children: William H., Jr., Phillip Ronald, and David Talbert.

Pitt was a salesman for wholesale businesses in Memphis and New Orleans, 1935–50. Bartlett Baptist Church, Memphis, Tenn., ordained him as a deacon in 1947 and as a minister in 1950. He served as associational missionary, Gibson County Association (Tenn.), 1954–59; pastor in Tennessee, 1950–54, and Kentucky, 1959–60; secretary of the Stewardship Department, Tennessee Baptist Convention, 1960–69; and Tennessee representative on the Stewardship Commission, SBC, 1961–68.

Pitt was director of endowment and capital giving service of the Stewardship Commission, May–Dec., 1969. Under his leadership the "Together We Build" program of capital fund raising for churches was developed to further effectiveness. Representing the commission, he furnished leadership for the Kansas Convention of Southern Baptists in their successful effort to raise $725,000 in their churches, which was the basis for financing of $1,600,000 deficit in church bond operations.

His death from a heart attack terminated his brief service with the commission.

MERRILL D. MOORE

***PLACE OF MEETING, SOUTHERN BAPTIST CONVENTION.** Since 1963 the Executive Committee of the SBC has had the responsibility of recommending to the Convention the place and date of the annual meeting of the Convention. Paragraph 9, (5) (d), of the Convention Bylaws reads: "The Executive Committee is specifically authorized, instructed and commissioned to perform the following functions: To recommend to the Convention a time and place and to have oversight of the arrangements for the meetings of the Convention, with authority to change both the time and place of the meetings in accordance with the provisions of Article XI, Section 3, of the Constitution." The Convention Procedure specifies "Convention Site: No city shall be considered a meeting place for the Southern Baptist Convention in which there is a considerable distance between the available hotels and the Convention Hall."

ALBERT MCCLELLAN

PLYLER, JOHN LANEY (b. Travelers Rest, S. C., Jan. 12, 1894; d. Greenville, S. C., Apr. 5, 1966). Lawyer, judge, and educator. Son of John Robert and Mary Thompson (Earle) Plyler, he was the third of five children. His father was an educator and Baptist minister. Plyler graduated *magna cum laude* from Furman University (B.A., 1913). He served for three years as teacher and coach at Greenville High School, where he produced a state championship basketball team.

Plyler served in World War I as a volunteer and rose to the rank of second lieutenant. After the war he earned an LL.B from Harvard University, and began the practice of law in Greenville in 1921, as a member of the firm of Haynsworth and Haynsworth. In 1924 he became a partner in the firm of Mann and Plyler. From 1922 to 1932 he was a member of the Furman University Law School faculty and was dean of this school, 1928–32. In 1935 Plyler was chosen judge of the Greenville County Court, and was reelected for a second term shortly before accepting the presidency of Furman University on Jan. 1, 1939.

During his 25-year tenure as president of Furman, Plyler ably led the institution in a manifold program of expansion and strengthening. A larger and stronger faculty, expanded library and research facilities, and an increasingly alert and more challenging student body came as a result of Plyler's efforts. His greatest contribution was made in planning and promoting the moving of Furman University to a new campus of 1,100 acres, five miles north of Greenville. Ground was broken in Oct., 1953, and the move and consolidation from two old campuses was completed by 1961.

During the Plyler administration, Furman was admitted to the American Association of University Women, granted an R.O.T.C. unit, and elected to the Southern University Conference. By the fall of 1944 the Plyler administration had lifted from Furman the burden of debt inherited from the depression. During World War II Plyler assumed the duties of treasurer at Furman in addition to the presidency.

Plyler received the honorary LL.D. from Erskine College (1939) and from Wofford College (1953). Furman University awarded him the Litt.D. degree in 1954. He was president of the South Carolina Association of Colleges in 1951–52, and president of the Southern University Conference in 1959–60. As a member of an 11-man national committee of college presidents named in 1951, he helped to work out recommendations on college football which were widely adopted. Plyler was a member of the commission on colleges and universities of the Southern Association of Colleges and Secondary Schools, and a member of the executive committee of this association. Plyler served as president of the South Carolina Baptist Convention, 1947–48. As an active member of the First Baptist Church of Greenville he served in numerous positions, including deacon. He was a member of the Newcomen Society of North America and of the New York Southern Society.

On June 11, 1932, Plyler married Beatrice Elizabeth Dennis of Moncks Corner, S. C. They had three sons: John L., Jr., James Dennis, and Rembert Keith.

JOE M. KING

POINDEXTER, WILLIAM ROBERT (b. Milan, Tenn., Sept. 29, 1886; d. Charleston, S. C., Jan. 17, 1968). Son of William Hillary and Mary (Mills) Poindexter, he received his education at Laneview College, Milan, Tenn., and Union University (B.A.), Jackson, Tenn. He married Carrie Elizabeth Lowry, Memphis, Tenn., on Dec. 16, 1921. They had two children: Merle (Mrs. J. Alvin Gilreath) and Robert Lowry Poindexter.

Poindexter served as pastor of the following Baptist churches: Raleigh, Shelby Co., Tenn.; Egypt, Shelby Co., Tenn.; First, Dayton, Tenn.; First, Lawrenceburg, Tenn.; First, Scotsborough, Tenn.; Woodlawn, Birmingham, Ala.; Union Avenue, Memphis, Tenn.; Whitehaven, Shelby Co., Tenn.; First, Easley, S. C.; First, Williamston, S. C.; Colonial Heights, Columbia, S. C.; and Mount Pleasant, Charleston, S. C. He is buried in Woodlawn Memorial Gardens, Greenville, S. C. DAVID G. ANDERSON

POLLUTION. The pollution of the air, soil, and water is a result of man's mismanagement of the world that God created. The Psalmist's proclamation that "the earth is the Lord's" is a truth that is echoed throughout the Scriptures. In order to have a proper relation to nature, therefore, one must first have a relation to the God who acts in history. Indeed, environmental pollution is so serious that a depth of motivation which comes from a relationship to God is required to bring a lasting solution.

Southern Baptists are giving increasing attention to pollution problems. Denominational curriculum materials contain explorations of the many aspects of the ecological crisis from a biblical perspective. The Christian Life Commission, SBC, has developed resources which offer specific plans of study and action for church groups and for individual Christians.

At the 1970 session of the Southern Baptist Convention in Denver, messengers adopted this resolution on the environment:

WHEREAS, human beings have for a long while recognized their need for food, clothing, and shelter, and

WHEREAS, God has created man to be a creature also who needs clean air, pure water, and an environment which contributes to his general health, and

WHEREAS, man has created a crisis by polluting the air, poisoning the streams, and ravaging the soil,

THEREFORE, BE IT RESOLVED, by the messengers of the Southern Baptist Convention meeting at Denver, June 1970, that we call upon churches to help remedy this environmental mismanagement by practicing and proclaiming a positive awareness that "the earth is the Lord's" and

BE IT FURTHER RESOLVED, that we urge Christians everywhere to practice stewardship of environment and to work with government, industry and others to correct the ravaging of the earth, and

BE IT FURTHER RESOLVED, that we request the Christian Life Commission to take the lead in working with other agencies of the Convention to encourage effective education and action to meet the environmental crisis. HARRY N. HOLLIS, JR.

POLSTON, FRANCIS OREN (b. Lockwood, Mo., Aug. 20, 1893; d. Portales, N. Mex., Oct. 23, 1966). School principal, postmaster, pastor, and missionary. After graduating from State Teachers College of Springfield, Mo. (A.B., 1917), he moved to New Mexico where he was principal of the Rock Lake School in Roosevelt County for nine years. He then became postmaster in Melrose, N. Mex., for nine years. He married Mattie D. Monroe in 1917. They had four children. Licensed to preach by the First Baptist Church of Melrose, he entered Southwestern Baptist Theological Seminary in 1933. While at Southwestern Seminary, he was pastor at Garner, Tex. Called as district missionary of Plains, Portales, and Tucumcari associations in 1934, he served in this position for 25 years. From 1959 until his death, he was missionary of the Portales Association. Polston traveled well over 1,000,000 miles as missionary, conducting Bible Schools, revivals, etc. He was an effective personal worker and baptized many converts. He was president of New Mexico Training Union Convention in 1931 and preached the annual sermon for the convention in 1961. HERBERT E. BERGSTROM

POND, WILLIE YATES, SR. (b. Albermarle, N. C., Dec. 8, 1880; d. Corpus Christi, Tex., Dec. 24, 1967). Pastor and denominational leader. Pond married Helen Ferguson, Dec. 24, 1905, and they had three children: W. Y. Pond, Jr., Mrs. B. G. Anderson, and Mrs. P. E. Vinson. Graduating from Baylor University in 1919, he served as pastor of the First Baptist churches in the following Texas towns: Winnsboro, Coleman, Hillsboro, and Breckenridge. Pond was superintendent of the Department of Evangelism, in Texas, 1925–32, and was active in evangelistic work for 25 additional years. Significant evangelistic movements during his tenure included: statewide evangelistic conference in Fort Worth, 1927; "Texas for Christ" movement, 1935; and Crusade of Evangelism, 1945, observing the 100th Anniversary of the Southern Baptist Convention. C. WADE FREEMAN

PONDEROSA SOUTHERN BAPTIST ASSEMBLY. Colorado Baptist General Convention assembly near Monument, Colo. Development began with purchase of the 1,433 acre H. H. Hoopingarner ranch in 1960, and subsequent building of facilities. The first assembly, a pioneer week, was held Aug. 1–5, 1960. The facilities were dedicated "to the glory of God," June 20, 1964. The tract of land has been reduced to approximately 700 acres by numerous subdivisions. The receipts from the sale of lots were used in improvements and debt reduction. The facilities are used throughout the summer months by convention agencies in promotion of their programs. The assembly is operated by an assembly committee of the convention executive board. Joe Cherry is employed as resident supervisor of building and grounds. O. L. BAYLESS

PORNOGRAPHY. Consistent opposition to pornography has been expressed by Southern

Baptists throughout the years. This opposition grows out of the conviction that pornography distorts God's gift of sexuality, demeans the family, undermines morality, debases male and female, and warps character.

Southern Baptists have responded to the pornography problem in many ways. (1) Strong Convention resolutions have been passed calling for evangelistic, legislative, and economic efforts to counter the effects of pornography. In 1969, for example, messengers to the Southern Baptist Convention meeting in New Orleans voted unanimously to "urgently request the Christian Life Commission to unite, organize, and mobilize to correct and overcome the abuses of pornography now being perpetrated against citizenry, young and old, in our nation, in line with the program assignment of the Christian Life Commission." (2) Special conferences have been conducted by the commission to prepare Southern Baptists to oppose pornography. In 1957 a conference on "Traffic in Obscene Literature" was held at Glorieta Baptist Assembly. In 1967 conferences on "Morality and the Mass Media" were conducted at Ridgecrest and Glorieta Baptist Assemblies. (3) Resource materials, such as pamphlets, journal articles, and reprints, have been distributed by the commission. (4) Denominational curriculum materials have dealt with this problem in relation to its effect on youth and adults. (5) The commission is conducting a continuing education and action program to oppose pornography.

HARRY N. HOLLIS, JR.

PORTUGAL, MISSION IN. Z. C. Taylor, Southern Baptist missionary and executive secretary of the newly organized Foreign Mission Board of Brazilian Baptists, journeyed to Portugal in 1908 to serve as moderator at the organization of the country's first Baptist church. The small group who comprised that first church were fruit of the witness of Joseph Jones, English businessman who resided in Porto. For 50 years Brazilian Baptists counted Portugal their primary mission field.

At the request of both the Portuguese and Brazilian Baptist Conventions for Southern Baptists to join in the evangelization of Portugal, the Foreign Mission Board asked veteran missionaries to Brazil, A. R. and Mabel (Henderson) Crabtree, to examine firsthand the needs and make recommendations. From that year of 1959 when the Portuguese Baptist Convention numbered 20 churches with less than 1,000 members, the work has grown to 36 churches with slightly more than 2,000 members. These churches were served in 1969 by 20 national and 3 missionary pastors.

The Portuguese Baptist Convention maintains mission work in Angola and Mozambique on the African continent, active evangelism program including occasional simultaneous crusades, weekly radio ministry, book store in Lisbon, summer encampment program for all ages, scholarship ministry to aid young Christians in securing an adequate education, and seminary to provide theological training for those preparing for the ministry. Growth by baptisms averaged 7.5 per cent per year during the sixties.

See also PORTUGAL, BAPTIST UNION of, VOL. II.

GRAYSON C. TENNISON

POTEAT, HUBERT McNEILL (b. Wake Forest, N. C., Dec. 12, 1886; d. Wake Forest, Jan. 29, 1958). Educator, author, and musician. Son of William Louis Poteat (*q.v.*, Vol. II), he was educated at Wake Forest College (B.A., 1906; M.A., 1908) and Columbia University (Ph.D., 1912). In 1912 he became professor of Latin languages and literature at Wake Forest where he taught until his retirement in 1956. He taught Latin at Columbia University summer sessions, 1924–42.

Poteat, who was considered a foremost authority on Cicero and Pliny, was the author of several books and numerous articles on classical subjects. He also wrote the book *Practical Hymnology* (1921). Poteat played numerous organ recitals. For 40 years he was organist and choir director at Wake Forest Baptist Church. He was Imperial Potentate of the Shrine of North America, 1950–51, president of the North Carolina Literary and Historical Association, 1944, president of the Classical Association of the Middle West and South, 1937–38, and vice-president of the American Classical League, 1948–50. He held honorary degrees from the University of North Carolina and Lehigh University. He was a member of Omicron Delta Kappa and Phi Beta Kappa. He married Essie Moore Morgan on June 26, 1912. Their sons were H. M., Jr., and William M. Poteat. ELIZABETH BRANTLEY

POVERTY. The problem of poverty in the affluent American society is a complex one. A measure of poverty commonly used since 1964 is a family income under $3,000. In 1969 poverty was a way of life for an estimated 25,000,000 Americans.

Those classified as living in poverty oftentimes are the very old and the very young. The old are often sick, immobile, and lonely. They tend to live out their lives in neighborhoods that have deteriorated. The very young oftentimes live in depressed areas where vandalism, sexual offenses, and narcotic traffic are frequently allowed to go unchecked. Oftentimes where police force is used, it becomes oppressive in nature.

Racial discrimination abounds in poverty areas where the poor are often nonwhite minorities. These persons work at the lowest-paying jobs and usually suffer a higher unemployment rate than do whites. These poor are usually unskilled and uneducated and are often poorly motivated to better themselves because of the cultural effects of poverty. Many of the poor suffer some mental or physical disability.

Scores of Southern Baptists have rendered effective service in the war against poverty, among whom are William H. Crook who served as director of VISTA (Volunteers in Service to America); Ross Coggins, who served as director of VISTA for the Southeast regional office of the Office of Economic Opportunity; and Ralph A. Phelps, Jr., who was director of the Southeast regional office of OEO.

The Christian Life Commission has produced a pamphlet on "Poverty" which is part of the "Issues and Answers" series. The material and cover photograph received wide distribution through various religious papers. A resource paper and other materials on the subject are available from the Christian Life Commission.

The Christian Life Commission's 1968 conference in Washington, D. C., on "Christian Action in a Disordered Society" and the 1969 conference in Chicago on "The Church's Mission in the National Crisis" both dealt directly with poverty and problems related to it. William H. Crook's address on the subject from the 1968 conference and Jesse Jackson's address from the 1969 conference were both carried on the National Broadcasting Company's "Faith in Action" radio network.

Local Baptist churches support work with the poor through mission action groups and special activities involving young people.

W. L. HOWSE III

POWELL, WILLIAM FRANCIS (b. Auburn, N. C., July 10, 1877; d. Nashville, Tenn., June 5, 1959). Distinguished pastor and denominational leader. Son of E. C. and Sara (Young) Powell, he was converted at the age of 12 in a revival meeting at Mt. Moriah Church below Raleigh. After graduating from Wake Forest College, he was principal of Fruitland Institute, a Baptist school in Hendersonville, N. C., 1900–03. He completed seminary training at Southern Baptist Theological Seminary. Powell received an honorary D.D. from Carson-Newman College (1916) and Wake Forest College (1920), and the LL.D. from Union University (1934). He married Winnie Patton of Morganton, N. C., Dec. 18, 1906. They had three daughters: Sarah (Mrs. Corbin Chapman), Margaret (Mrs. D. V. Johnson, Jr.), and Frances (Mrs. T. M. Melden, Jr.). His pastorates were: First, Morganton, N. C., 1906; Calvary, Roanoke, Va., 1907–13; First, Chattanooga, Tenn., 1913–17; First, Asheville, N. C., 1917–21; First, Nashville, Tenn., 1921–55. He served as president of The Baptist Sunday School Board of the Southern Baptist Convention, 1921–54. He is buried in Woodlawn Cemetery, Nashville, Tenn.

FRANKLIN PASCAL

POWERLINE. See RADIO AND TELEVISION COMMISSION, THE.

PRATT, EUGENE TALMADGE (b. Parsons, Kans., Aug. 8, 1911; d. Jefferson City, Mo., Apr. 18, 1965). He married Fama Ann Boyd of Texas in 1935. They had four children. Pratt graduated from William Jewell College (B.A., 1934), Southwestern Baptist Theological Seminary (Th.M., 1938), and Southern Baptist Theological Seminary (Th.D., 1948). He served as pastor of churches in Missouri, Kentucky, Texas, and Illinois. He also served as superintendent of missions, Chillicothe, Mo., division, 1938–42; director of evangelism, Missouri Baptist Convention, 1957–62; associate professor of evangelism, Southwestern Seminary, 1962–65; and director of evangelism, Missouri Convention, Jan., 1965, until his death.

H. H. MCGINTY

***PREACHING, HISTORY OF.** After World War II, the effort to rebuild earth's shattered countryside and heal the battered human spirit largely bypassed preaching's importance. Subsequently, disillusionment with man's inability or unwillingness to implement Christianity's social ideals in a transitional era caused multitudes to conclude that the world could make its own adjustments without preaching's help. Further, the Korean and Vietnam conflicts accentuated the discontent with preaching's inability to influence any national military or political action. One prominent minister's call for a moratorium on all preaching rallied many critics, both clerical and secular.

Consequently, for the last 25 years, belief in the imperativeness of preaching for the redemption of modern man and his society has been weakened greatly. The preacher's role in shaping culture has dwindled so steadily that many young men have retreated from the ministry as a vocation. Meanwhile, the cry from the streets has been for involvement in "healing humanity's hurt," not for flowery rhetoric that contents itself with being heard but ignored.

In addition, the plush economic affluence of the last 15 years has provided many modern men with material means to greatly change their life style. Yet youths on campuses and in city parks and streets have marched, chanted, screamed, and destroyed life and property to focus attention on their impatience for immediate social action instead of talk about someday changing America's indolent contentment with the status quo. Inflamed minority groups have also added to the deep embitterment of modern life.

What has preaching said amid the social turmoil? Most of it has been guardedly quiet on controversial issues. A few pastors have voiced prophetic biblical insights on the meaning of the current unrest, but in some instances such men have lost their pulpits and thus their audiences. Thus modern preaching generally has stayed with the "safe" themes about preparing men for a future world, avoiding whenever possible the faith's explosive sociological implications for the here and now. As a result, the "idealistic secularist" has often assumed the leadership for current change while preaching's image as the inspirational source for revolutionary transformation of man's existence has continued to diminish in influence and credibility.

Belatedly, the pulpit's traditional evangelistic note on behalf of individual salvation has been blended in some denominations with the call for social responsibility. But this combination has not always produced harmony in thought and action.

So, midway of the 20th century, as man's cultural pattern radically changes, Christian preaching struggles to be true to its ancient redemptive purpose by broadening its impact so as to affect noticeably the transformation of the total man and his society. Whether preaching will experience a resurgence in its importance to the process, and whether the preacher's role will assume larger proportions, await the revelation of the ensuing years.

BIBLIOGRAPHY: D. J. Randolph, *The Renewal of Preaching* (1969). John Killinger, *The Centrality of Preaching in the Total Task of the Ministry* (1969). C. DE WITT MATTHEWS

PREACHING, NEW METHODS OF. An agelong characteristic of Baptist worship has been its focus on the man in the pulpit with an open Bible out of which he proclaims God's purposes. Baptists, therefore, will continue to keep the sermon central in worship. Further, Baptists not only think that a pastor should preach effectively, but they strongly believe that preaching is God's way of insuring the continuity of the church.

Currently, increasing experimentation is being done in preaching methods. The dialogue sermon, for instance, has risen in popularity, but it disappoints if carelessly done. Sometimes it produces only confusion. Often it just pools collective ignorance. Ideally, it is a serious effort to get congregations involved in the preaching process.

"Feedback" sessions after the sermon may reveal the preacher's lack of clarity and allow the congregation's real interests to rise to the surface. The talk-backs may occur at a weeknight time, or at the Sunday evening worship when the morning sermon is analyzed and applied. Some ministers have enlisted selected members to assist in sermon preparation, but most of them are too self-conscious to try this departure. Such sermonic sharing efforts can supplement the traditional sermon format, not displace it. So, variety in preaching's methodology is being tried by some younger ministers in a few Baptist churches.

Other methods employed include the monologue, the drama, the song-sermon, poetic recitation, and antiphonal preaching, using verse choirs and specialized readers to respond to the preacher's questions or assertions. These have brought to "the creative moment of delivery" added congregational interest in the sermon's "listenability." However, the necessity of training others to participate sharply limits such efforts.

Generally, Southern Baptists are slow to adopt new preaching processes. A historically traditional people, they tend to cling to the time-honored authoritarian sermon as God's chosen method of proclamation.

However varied or stereotyped Southern Baptist preaching becomes, most Baptists would agree with Emil Brunner that "Where there is true preaching, where, in obedience of faith, the Word is proclaimed, there, in spite of all appearances to the contrary, the most important thing that ever happens on this earth takes place." C. DE WITT MATTHEWS

***PREACHING, SOUTHERN BAPTIST.** The significance of preaching continues to be central in the thought of most Southern Baptist preachers. Inherent in a pastor's call to the ministry is the primary function of preaching. Administration, counseling, and promoting are pressing matters that demand much time; but the pastor does not think of these activities as primal in his call to the ministry.

The sermon in a Southern Baptist church traditionally has been the central part of the Baptist worship service. Although some changes are evident, it remains true that the sermon is of paramount importance. Southern Baptist preachers desire their full time, at least 30 minutes, in the pulpit; and the congregation expects to hear a "sermon with substance," that is, a sermon of some length. However, in the second half of the 20th century, a trend has developed calling for shorter, more concise sermons.

The Sunday evening worship hour has always been a preaching service of importance to Baptists. When other churches of the community cease to have evening preaching, most Southern Baptist churches continue. Although the evening time of preaching is not as popular as it once was, the Sunday evening service is attended by those most faithful to the church. In most churches those who attend are the older adults who have developed their lives in an active corporate worship environment, the middle-aged who have found, in preaching, encouragement and succour for themselves and their children, and the young people and children who are either required by parental encouragement and example or by heartfelt need to find a closeness to God that comes through public worship and preaching.

The midweek prayer service through the years has been an integral part of the church life of Southern Baptists. In the past this has been a time of preaching. Even now if the pastor feels so led, he will deliver a sermon to his congregation at the prayer service. In more recent years the midweek prayer service has sometimes been devoted to a service of prayer or a period of devotions.

Revival meetings have provided concentrated periods of preaching. There are those who say that the time of revivals is past. They point to preachers who no longer schedule revivals in their churches and decline any invitation to preach in a protracted meeting of revival. In many instances the emphasis has changed from proclamation to entertainment. Promotional gimmicks and musical come-ons often allow time for only a tacked-on sermon. More emphasis is sometimes given to attendance than to the spiritual aspects of the meeting. Two-week revival meetings with preaching in the morning and evening of each day have generally given way to one-week preaching meetings with only evening services, and these, in turn, are giving way to half-week preaching meetings or week-end revivals.

Revival meetings are not as well attended as they once were. The pressing schedules of modern living, travel distances in urban churches, and materialism of the day hinder both church members and the unchurched. However, many revival meetings are conducted annually with substantial gains in church membership. Even when the number of converts is small, many churches find revival preaching a vital source of spiritual renewal for the church members.

Individual Southern Baptist ministers of some renown of the last 10 years include evangelist Billy Graham. His evangelistic preaching and organizational ability have been effective on a worldwide scale. His ministry has been characterized by its simplicity, depth of caring, and a personal sense of the guidance of the Holy Spirit. Herschel Hobbs, pastor of First Baptist Church, Oklahoma City, is widely known because he has been the Baptist voice most used by the Radio and Television Commission, SBC. His messages have been explanatory of Baptist doctrine and expository of biblical passages. State Baptist papers have printed his thoughts and sermons. Theodore Adams of First Baptist Church, Richmond, Va., has had national coverage in some newsmagazines. He represents a large segment of Baptist preaching that is characterized by depth of concern and love for his people. Another well-known preacher of the sixties was Roy McClain, of First Baptist Church, Atlanta, Ga. During the past decade he was recognized as one of the 10 best preachers in America by at least one national newsmagazine.

There is no indication at this time that Baptist preaching will succumb to the desire of some of the Baptist constituency for a more completely liturgical service. Baptist preaching is attuned to the times. Within the last decade some subjects hitherto considered improper in the pulpit have been accepted and even welcomed. Preaching recently has concerned itself with matters of race, poverty, sex, housing, war and peace, and other related subjects. Some preachers have become strong advocates of a much greater emphasis on social action. Others have felt that the emphasis on missions and evangelism is adequate. Still other ministers feel that the present times of turbulence and change demand the greater emphasis of a both/and proclamation, both social action and missions and evangelism.

The Vietnam conflict has brought anew to the mind of the Christian minister the perplexing ethical question of war. The idea of necessary or just wars has plagued the thinking and preaching of ministers. Preachers have searched their own souls seeking the Christian stand on war. The Southern Baptist pulpit has not been reckless in its pronouncements on race. Neither has it surrendered to the demands of prejudice. On occasion there has been courageous and bold preaching on the issues of race. The "age of Aquarius" has spotlighted the problems of drug use and abuse, and the preaching of the gospel has, as always, spotlighted the love, security, and significance found in the presence of God in Christ. Preaching in the last decade remained constant and pointed the way out of a life of tension into the peace that comes from a genuine relationship with the Lord of life.

Preaching has changed in location, as well as in manner, in the last decade. One Southern Baptist minister has received much publicity for his ministry in the French Quarter of New Orleans. Another has received wide recognition for his preaching ministry among the "hippies" on the West Coast. His dress and manner has allowed him to preach a conservative Baptist theology to a mass of young and old people who are in need of assurance and help. Many churches sponsor preaching ministries in shopping centers, drive-in theaters, lakeside resorts—wherever the people are. Southern Baptist preaching is geared to reach into every strata of society with the good news of God in Christ.

See also SERMONS, BAPTIST; PREACHING, HISTORY OF; PREACHING, NEW METHODS OF.

HADDON EUGENE COTEY

PRICE, HENRY CLAY (b. Wesson, Copiah County, Miss., May 22, 1903; d. Portland, Ore. Aug. 8, 1963). A graduate of Mississippi College and New Orleans Baptist Theological Seminary, he married Dorothy Marie Wittenmyer of Bartlesville, Okla. Two sons were Henry Dodds and John Douglas. Converted at DeQuincy, La., Price was ordained in 1925 at Clinton, Miss. Early pastorates were in Mississippi and Louisiana. He was school superintendent and teacher one year in Fernwood, Miss., and superintendent and Bible teacher at Acadia Baptist Academy, Eunice, La., three years, before becoming pastor of First Southern Baptist Church, Portland, Ore., in 1948. There he served until death. He was the second president of the Oregon-Washington Baptist Convention, and served on its board and on many committees. He is buried in Lincoln Memorial Park, Portland.

ROY L. JOHNSON

PROBE. A monthly mission magazine for Royal Ambassadors 12–17 years of age, published by the Brotherhood Commission since Oct., 1970. This program magazine replaced *Ambassador Life*. DARRELL C. RICHARDSON

PROBE (LEADERSHIP EDITION). A special edition of *Probe* for Royal Ambassador leaders published by the Brotherhood Commission since Oct., 1970. Through an insert, "Pioneer Plans," it provides program plans to be used by counselors and officers in weekly R.A. chapter meetings. This publication replaced *Ambassador Leader*. DARRELL C. RICHARDSON

PROGRAM PLANNING, SOUTHERN BAPTIST CONVENTION. In 1958 the Convention authorized the Executive Committee (1) to develop a reporting format that would present information on the programs, promotional plans, achievements, and costs of all the causes sponsored by the agencies; (2) to develop and maintain an organizational manual describing the functions and relationships of all SBC programs; and (3) to reorganize its staff and committee structure in order to accomplish this work.

It was soon discovered that a distinction was necessary between "correlation" and "coordination." Correlation is the process of bringing programs into complementary relationship with each other and is an Executive Committee responsibility. Coordination is the detailed day to day working together of the Inter-Agency Council. The Executive Committee proceeded to secure basic relationships of programs to each other. Early study showed five kinds of SBC agency programs: (1) basic educational or channeling programs, such as Sunday School and Training Union; (2) profit-producing programs, such as literature sales; (3) service programs, such as church library and church recreation; (4) emphases programs such as Public Affairs and Christian Life; and (5) representative programs such as seminaries and foreign mission programs.

Study showed that many existing programs were unclear and overlapping, and that some operated without Convention mandate. From 1959 through 1966 the Executive Committee sponsored program studies and conferences that led to the systematic description of programs and the elimination of much overlapping and many duplications. All of the program statements were approved by 1966. They include 95 programs and three services under the auspices of the 20 agencies, the Executive Committee, and the Woman's Missionary Union, and are printed in "The Organization Manual of the Southern Baptist Convention" which has the force of Convention bylaw. These statements do not completely eliminate all overlapping, but provide descriptions which enable the agencies to manage certain necessary overlapping.

The coordination of programs takes place in the Inter-Agency Council, especially in its coordinating committee. Here the relationships of established programs are discussed and working agreements are developed. Problems of coordination which cannot be solved by this group are referred to the Executive Committee by the related agencies.

Another aspect of program planning is Convention long-range emphasis planning. This is conducted by the Executive Committee, utilizing the organized relationships of the Inter-Agency Council. The first development of this plan was for the years 1964–69. It centered on the theme, "The Church Fulfilling Its Mission." The second was for the period of 1969–73 with the theme, "Living the Spirit of Christ." The third theme was for 1973–79 with the theme, "Sharing Christ." All the agencies and the state conventions participate in emphases planning.

The detailed program planning for the 95 programs is the responsibility of the program leaders working under the direction of the agencies to which the programs are assigned. Program budgeting and program evaluation are also part of program planning and are the responsibilities of the Executive Committee. Program budgeting is the relationship of work done by the programs to financial resources. Program evaluation is the perennial review of programs to determine the efficiency with which the work assigned is accomplished.

ALBERT MC CLELLAN

PROGRAMING FOR THE CHURCHES, 1959–69.

SOUTHERN BAPTIST CONVENTION ACTIONS, 1923–59. Southern Baptist churches sought for nearly 50 years to achieve the correlation and coordination of their programs. The greatest progress came during the decade of the sixties. The new program suggestions and materials, which became available Oct. 1, 1970, can be understood best by an overview of the chain of developments from 1923 through 1969. In 1959 the SBC meeting in Louisville, Ky., climaxed 36 years of effort to correlate and coordinate its church programs by adopting a recommendation of its Committee to Study Total SBC Program to the effect that one of the functions of the Executive Committee should be "to maintain an official organization manual defining the responsibilities of each agency of the Convention for conducting specific programs and for performing other functions. The manual shall cite the action of the Convention that assigned the programs and other functions to the agency. The Executive Committee shall present to the Convention recommendations required to clarify the responsibilities of the agencies for programs and other functions, to eliminate overlapping assignments of responsibility, and to authorize the assignment of new responsibilities for programs or functions to agencies." This statement was added to the Bylaws of the SBC in 1960.

The Convention defined a program as "a basic continuing activity of primary importance in achieving the objective (s) of an organization." Each agency was instructed to define its programs, to budget them, and to report on them annually.

The action of the Convention in 1959 has proved to be a major turning point in Southern Baptist life. It is doubtful whether the Convention at any time in its history has taken an action more far reaching than this.

The 1959 SBC action was not a single action appearing as the only one of its kind. Rather it was the culminating event in a long series of actions. To understand the significance of this action one must understand the circumstances facing the Convention and its agencies during the first five decades of this century.

The official minutes of the SBC are a historical record of the earnest spiritual search by Southern Baptist church leaders for a solution to SBC program unification, correlation, and coordination. The following excerpts are representative of numerous other actions.

The SBC in 1923 elected the following people to serve as a committee on correlating and defining the work of various departments of Convention activities: F. S. Groner (*q.v.*, Vol. I), Texas, chairman; J. E. Dillard (*q.v.*, Vol. I), W. E. Atkinson (*q.v.*, Vol. I), John E. Briggs (*q.v.*), C. W. Duke, J. P. Nichols, I. E. Lee (*q.v.*), C. M. Thompson (*q.v.*, Vol. II), Ben Johnson, O. C. S. Wallace (*q.v.*, Vol. II), N. T. Tull, David H. Harris, T. F. Havey, C. E. Maddry (*q.v.*), A. N. Hall (*q.v.*), T. C. Skinner, E. C. Dargan (*q.v.*, Vol. I), and E. B. Jackson. The committee made a detailed report to the Convention in 1924. No changes in the organizational structure of the Convention were recommended.

N. T. Tull, of the above committee, however, presented a minority report which called for a reorganization of the Convention's work under four boards in order to eliminate overlapping and to achieve coordination and correlation of Convention programs.

Following considerable debate of these differing reports and recommendations, the Convention voted to refer the whole matter of correlation and definition of Convention activities to a committee of one from each state to report in 1925.

In 1925 the Convention approved the recommendations of its Committee on Correlation of Convention activities: "That the Foreign Mission Board, the Home Mission Board, the Inter-Board Commission . . . (student work), the Sunday School Board, the Relief and Annuity Board and the Laymen's Work be continued as at present," except that the HMB was instructed by the Convention in separate action to reestablish a department of evangelism. Another recommendation provided that the maintenance and appointment of the Sunday School Lesson Committee of the Convention hereafter be under the supervision of the Sunday School Board.

In 1926 the Convention authorized the Sunday School Board to establish a Department of Church Administration, with the publication of a monthly journal "devoted to the general subject of the administrative side of church life."

The SBC Committee on Business Efficiency called attention to the need for a detailed survey of all the affairs and activities of the Convention and its agencies. It stated that such a study would enable the Convention to reevaluate all of its work to eliminate overlapping and duplication, and to redefine and limit the work of its agencies. On recommendation of this committee, the Convention in 1927 instructed its Executive Committee to make a complete survey of the work of the Convention and its agencies.

The survey should give concerning each agency: (1) the general type of work being done by the agency; (2) departments of work; (3) policies governing the work; (4) methods employed; (5) business management; (6) financial condition; and (7) make recommendations concerning any changes needed to be made.

The survey should (1) point out any overlapping and duplication of work being done by two or more agencies; (2) recommend a redefining of the work and limits of the work to be done by each agency; (3) recommend the reassignment of work to the agencies—assigning to each agency the work included within its redefined limits; (4) recommend whether any new work should be undertaken either by an existent agency or by a new agency to be created; and (5) recommend whether any work now being done by agencies should be discontinued.

The Convention in 1937 approved the following resolution offered by George W. Sadler (Missouri):

Whereas, The multiplication of organizations is tending to mechanize our denomination life, and

Whereas, There is much overlapping and lost energy as a result of this excessive organization; be it

Resolved, That the Southern Baptist Convention now in session appoint a committee whose duty it shall be to survey the situation with a view to coordinating and correlating the numerous units of our denominational work.

The Convention in 1938 approved the following recommendations of the Committee on Coordination and Correlation:

1. We further recommend that representatives of the boards and auxiliaries of the Southern Baptist Convention responsible for the work of the Sunday School, the BTU, and WMU, and the Brotherhood, meet as soon as possible, and thereafter at least once a year, for conference and cooperation looking to effectual coordination and correlation of programs, calendar activities, mission study, *Bible readings,* training courses, financial plans and objectives, evangelistic and personal service activities, socials, associational meetings, *standards,* requirements, and the like. We suggest that this Committee be properly related to the present Committee on Calendar of Denominational Activities.

2. We recommend that the agencies which set up standards and programs take a sympathetic attitude toward pastors and churches who may feel that their local situation does not permit their having all the things necessary to meet the standards.

Continued in 1939 by the Convention for further "study, counsel, and report," the Committee on Coordination and Correlation in 1940 stated that its policy from the beginning had been:

1. To place responsibility for setting up correlated standards and programs upon the denominational agencies [WMU, Mission Boards, Brotherhood, and Sunday School Board].

2. To place responsibility for coordination and

correlation of (1) organizational leadership and (2) expressional activities upon the pastors and churches with the recommendation that this be done by the formation of a pastor's cabinet or *church council.*

The SBC approved the recommendation of the committee: That representatives of denominational agencies be requested to continue their conferences, holding at least one meeting a year; and commended the idea of inviting all denominational agencies to participate in the meetings, plus pastors with experience in the area of coordination.

The SBC Committee on Church Organizations reported in 1948 that it had "sought to study the situation, to discover the needs, to present the results to the several agencies for their consideration, and to lead in discussion of possible ways and means of better coordination and correlation and greater organizational efficiency." The SBC in 1948 approved the following recommendations which, according to the committee, indicated directions toward which discussion and action shall move but are not mandatory as to details:

That, by voluntary agreement of representatives of the several Convention agencies at the joint meeting in Memphis, January 27–28, 1948, definite conference or conferences be held during the coming year with a view to further consideration of these programs and others of like nature; that the recommendations made above, if adopted by the Convention, be considered and so far as possible carried out in consultation and conference with the Committee on Church Organizations and representatives of agencies and auxiliaries; that the report of results be made to the 1949 meeting of the Convention; that the Committee continue its study of needs not covered in this report, and that the Executive Committee be authorized to provide for expenses of the Committee in the same amount as heretofore.

On Sept. 23, 1948, representatives of the FMB, HMB, Sunday School Board, the WMU, and the Brotherhood formally organized the *Inter-Agency Council* "to help correlate and coordinate the educational activities in our churches, both on the denominational and local church levels."

In 1950 the Committee on Church Organizations reported that the Inter-Agency Council pledged itself to "regular meetings, to discussion and clearing of joint problems, to cooperative concern for the churches in devising and projecting plans and materials, continuous coordination of organizational programs and correlation of emphases and events suggested for the churches." On recommendation of this committee the Convention in 1950 discharged the Committee on Church Organizations and assigned its work to the Inter-Agency Council. No report from the Inter-Agency Council appears in the SBC *Annuals* for the years 1952–57, since the council was instructed not to make such reports.

In 1958 the SBC Committee to Study Total Southern Baptist Convention Program stated that it found the lack of correlation of effort to be a more general and serious problem than duplication of effort among the agencies. The committee indicated that members of the council "should endeavor to consider and reflect local church and state convention views and needs."

On recommendation of the Committee on Total Program, the Convention authorized the Inter-Agency Council "to serve as the organization through which the various agencies of the Convention should correlate their work. The functions of the Inter-Agency Council should be to:

(1) Consider program problems of importance to Convention agencies and plan ways to overcome them through cooperative effort.
(2) Consider the need for cooperation in establishing and carrying on new programs authorized by the Convention and plan the ways in which that cooperation should be achieved.
(3) Consider the need for cooperation to overcome problems, eliminate duplication of effort, or otherwise improve the effectiveness of existing programs and plan ways in which that cooperation should be achieved.
(4) Recommend to Convention agencies the measures that they should take to correlate their programs with those of other agencies and to strengthen their programs so they can contribute more effectively to the total Convention effort.
(5) Develop specific plans for conducting programs cooperatively.
(6) Prepare a *proposed denominational calendar* for consideration by the Convention's Committee on Denominational Calendar.

One can conclude from the multitudinous actions of the Convention that at least three needs have been a primary concern continuously since 1922.

Need to better define denominational programs.—The need to define programs, both of the church and of the Convention, was a necessary prerequisite of correlation. Correlation could be identified and established. The public cry was for correlation but the subtle demand was for identification of program distinctives.

Need for correlation and coordination of denominational programing and long-range planning.—Paramount in the minds of church leaders was the need for correlation. Although this need was felt in the life and activity of the churches, the churches constantly called upon the SBC agencies to do something. Evidently, they were unable to discern the lack of a disciplined approach in the programing and long-range planning activity of SBC agencies. But they were able to perceive that without correlation and coordination there was fragmentation of the *church,* duplication and overlapping of activity, organization, and leadership, and an overall loss of energy.

Need for knowledge and skills in programing and long-range planning.—The need for simple, workable principles and procedures for directing programing and long-range planning was essential. They were to become the content to be taught and followed. They were to be the basis for developing disciplined, competent technicians. Without such, the problems of programing and long-range planning could not be solved.

EFFORTS OF THE SUNDAY SCHOOL BOARD TO ESTABLISH A FOUNDATION AND GUIDELINES FOR CHURCH PROGRAMING. For some time preceding the 1959 SBC meeting, the Sunday School Board, under the leadership of James L. Sullivan, had been seeking an answer to the problems of the churches and the Convention as they related to the board. The reorganization of the board and the definition of organizational responsibility completed in 1954 laid the foundation for the solution to the long-time problem. The reorganization prepared the board to act swiftly following the Convention action in 1959.

For two or three years the staff of the Education Division, under the direction of W. L. Howse, had searched for a means which would enable its personnel to correlate and coordinate their programs. This need was felt by the employees of other Convention agencies who sensed the seriousness of the problems faced by the churches. The action of the Convention in 1959 spurred these efforts and, in fact, made the discovery of a framework for programing imperative.

WORK OF TASK FORCE III. It soon became apparent that the programs assigned to the Sunday School Board by the Convention could not be defined until the tasks of these programs in the churches were known. It was logical, then, to assume that the first step was to work with the churches to discover with them the scope of their programs. In further discussions, however, it became apparent to Education Division personnel that another step was needed before approaching the churches. This was to make an intensive study of the New Testament in order to discover the nature, purpose, and functions of New Testament churches.

When this decision was made, Task Force III was created to conduct this study. The title resulted from the fact that it was the third task force established to do special work on programing assignments. It was constituted in 1961 with W. O. Thomason, assistant to the director of the Education Division, as chairman. Members of Task Force III were chosen from six departments in the division as follows: David K. Alexander and Nell Magee, Student; Ellis Bush, Family Life; Eugene Chamberlain, Melva Cook, Crawford Howell, and Roger Skelton, Sunday School; Doris Monroe and Maines Rawls, Training Union; Idus Owensby and L. J. Newton, Jr., Church Administration; and Clifford Holcomb, Church Music. Members were released from many of their regular responsibilities so as to devote at least one half of their time to this intensive study.

While Task Force III members were studying the New Testament, the Research and Statistics Department of the Sunday School Board was asked to obtain a sample of Southern Baptist churches so that members could involve these churches in an intensive study of New Testament teachings on the nature, purpose, and function of churches. Twenty-one churches were chosen by the department for this study. The churches were located from New Jersey to the state of Washington and from Texas to Colorado. Many types and sizes of churches were chosen.

When Task Force III completed its intensive study of the New Testament, members then went by twos to the 21 churches. Study groups were constituted in each church, and members of the task force visited these churches on numerous occasions to continue their studies with members of the study groups.

It was from these studies that the first statement of church functions was developed. The functions agreed upon by task force members and the participating churches were: to worship, to proclaim, to educate, and to minister.

STUDY OF SOUTHERN BAPTIST CONVENTION ASSIGNMENTS TO THE SUNDAY SCHOOL BOARD SINCE 1845. The study by Task Force III was paralleled by an intensive study of the Convention's assignments to the Sunday School Board from 1845. The present Sunday School Board was not established until 1891. However, soon after the SBC was organized, it began to take actions which had a direct bearing on programs now assigned to the Sunday School Board. For that reason, it was necessary to study carefully all actions of the Convention with regard to its assignments of programs.

DEVELOPMENT OF LONG-RANGE PLANNING AND PROGRAMING. The Church Administration Department began developing a long-range planning service for churches in 1961. This study was directed by skilled professional consultants and was participated in by representatives of most SBC agencies. The functions and tasks later written into *A Church Organized and Functioning* were included in the materials prepared for use by the churches in long-range planning. The first-draft materials were studied carefully by approximately 1,000 persons in at least 50 pilot church situations. Subsequent versions and study have provided three types of programing and long-range planning assistance to churches: church development, church programing, and church long-range planning services.

APPROVAL OF PROGRAM STATEMENTS BY SOUTHERN BAPTIST CONVENTION. The leaders of the Sunday School, Training Union, church music, and church administration programs at the Sunday School Board, along with other board program leaders, developed program statements which the board approved and presented to the program committee of the SBC in 1962. These program statements included the statement of tasks of the corresponding programs in the churches. The basic philosophy underlying these statements was that a church is an organism and that it organizes itself to conduct its basic continuing activities of primary importance. The original program statements were revised and the delineation of church programs were deleted because they were not needed as integral parts of the Convention's program statements. But, basic concepts remained unchanged. Sunday School Board program statements were approved by the SBC at Atlantic City in 1964.

Development of Church Programs and Tasks. When the Convention program statements were being developed, progress was made in reaching agreement on statements of church programs and tasks. Tasks of the congregation, pastor, staff members, deacons, church officers, committees, and church organizations were defined in terms of the nature, purpose, and functions of a church. These were approved by the Coordinating Committee of the Inter-agency Council.

The materials gathered by Task Force III, information gleaned from a study of the Convention's assignments to programs at the Sunday School Board, the findings of the Long-Range Planning Service of the Church Administration Department, and the statements of church programs and tasks provided the main resources from which the book *A Church Organized and Functioning* was written.

When the first edition of 40,000 copies was published in 1963, a questionnaire was inserted in each book for purposes of feedback. Many helpful suggestions which came from the questionnaires were incorporated in the revision of the book in 1966. Additional revisions were made and the book was published in 1969 as *A Dynamic Church: Spirit and Structure for the Seventies.*

Principles of Programing. A series of principles for churches to use in programing its basic tasks were developed:

1. The church is the basic unit of all programing.
2. Church organization exists to carry out church tasks.
3. All tasks of the church program organizations should be programed and planned in relationship to other organizations.
4. A church program organization's relationship to a church's priority tasks determines its position in the church's plan of organization.
5. A church needs a strategy for properly relating assistance which it receives from the association, the state convention and the SBC. For this reason, these Baptist bodies should work together in developing this strategy.

Early Efforts in Programing and Long-Range Planning. Following up in their basic work, the personnel of the Education Division established their first *planned* approach to programing and long-range planning. The division's long-range goal was established: to make available by Oct. 1, 1970, program suggestions and materials for use by churches in developing and conducting a unified, correlated, and coordinated program. The activity called for to support the goal was *a kind of* correlated programing. Several projects were formed. Project 600, a vestige of this early effort, is still used by the Convention to plan the *channeling* of information from other agencies for inclusion in Sunday School Board periodicals and field services. This early effort broke down through a lack of experience, assignment, supervision, and technical skill.

In response to the above problem, the use of the planning process, Program Evaluation and Review Technique (PERT), was instituted. The coordination and assignment of work was improved by the use of the method.

Church Program Development Group. Following Convention action in 1959, representatives of the church program organizations at the Sunday School Board met frequently with representatives of the WMU and the Brotherhood Commission. In the fall of 1964 the representatives decided to form a voluntary organization and meet monthly to work on mutual problems. This organization became known as the Church Program Development Group (CPDG). Special teams of personnel from the agencies with assignments in research, program design, and editorial and field services began to meet together monthly also. Conferences of age group, associational, and general administration personnel began to meet periodically to share information and evaluate various plans proposed by members. All of these groups were referred to generally as the At-Home Week organization.

Members of the Church Program Development Group were also members of the Church Program and Services Subcommittee of the Coordinating Committee of the IAC. This dual membership created additional responsibilities, meetings, and activities.

In 1969 the Church Program Development Group was merged with the Church Program and Services Subcommittee under the aegis of the Coordinating Committee. The members of the subcommittee in 1969 were: Bob Boyd, William P. Clemmons, Byron Clendinning, Howard Foshee, Elmer Gray, W. A. Harrell, Philip B. Harris, Lloyd Householder, W. L. Howse, Edward Rollins, Charles Roselle, W. Hines Sims, W. O. Thomason, Wayne Todd, A. V. Washburn, Norman Godfrey, June Whitlow, Loyd Corder, John Havlik, Fred Moseley, Jesse Fletcher, W. L. Howse III, and James Lackey. The research, program design, editorial, and field services teams were also combined with the work groups of the Coordinating Committee. The age group, administration, and associational conferences were enlarged but did not become a part of the structure of the Coordinating Committee.

Program Base Designs and the Church Dated Plan. While the agencies had spent much time and energy in clarifying their work and establishing better correlation, the work in the churches was still of great concern. When *A Church Organized and Functioning* was introduced in 1963, work was already underway to further detail the work a church needs to do to carry out its mission. When tasks were grouped by SBC organizations for use in developing materials for churches, older leadership materials became obsolete. The massive design work needed before new program suggestions and products could be introduced in Oct., 1970, was undertaken. This work was divided into two major phases, the development of the Program Base Designs and the development of the Dated Plan.

Base designs were developed for all church programs and services. The base designs gave a statement of why the program existed, what its work was, and how and why it performed its work. The essential elements of base designs included statements on Biblical foundations, philosophy, needs, basic intentions, program structure, relationships, organization, human resources, physical resources, financial resources, and planning administration controls. Designs were completed starting in 1968 for a church, the Bible teaching, church training, church music, WMU, Brotherhood, church recreation, church library, family ministry, vocational guidance, and pastoral ministries programs. These and other basic documents form the Data-Dex collection housed in Dargan-Carver Library, Sunday School Board. The documents are available on loan from the library.

The base designs serve as a foundation on which dated plans can be built. The dated plan is the sum total of all program suggestions and related curriculum materials to be offered by the denomination to the churches for a particular time period. The dated plan tells what and how materials and products will be available to churches to assist in their work. The dated plan is developed primarily from the basic approaches in the program structure element in base designs. The needs of persons and central issues faced by churches are also essential ingredients. The dated plan includes activities from the education, worship, missions, outreach, and ministry strategic plans. The dated plan process required the service of a computer because of the large quantity of information used and the evaluation needed. The dated plan process was used first for the 1970–71 year.

PROGRAMS AND MATERIALS FOR THE SEVENTIES.

1. *Grouping and Grading.*—An organizational plan for all Church Program Organizations was developed which is flexible enough to be used by various types and sizes of churches. The four major divisions of the plan—Adult-Youth-Children-Preschool—provides a framework for meeting the needs of the smallest to the largest church. School age children and youth are grouped according to age or grade. It was approved in Dec., 1966, for use by churches Oct. 1, 1970.

2. *Six Church Literature Series.*—Six church literature series were developed to meet the educational needs of different churches, provide various approaches to education in the churches, and to prepare and engage more people in the church's life and work. The six series include:

Convention Uniform.—Improved Bible centered, life-orientated curriculum for adults and youth using International Lesson outlines in Sunday School; and traditional content of the Training Union curriculum for adults in *Source* with traditional methods and design.

Life and Work.—Improved Bible-centered, church-oriented, action-inducing curriculum for adults and youth. Using Life and Work outlines in Sunday School, Training Union, church music, WMU, and Brotherhood, with both traditional and recently proven methods, and increased use of contemporary design.

Forefront.—An innovative Bible-based curriculum for adults strongly oriented to contemporary issues using innovative methods and designs.

Foundation.—An improved curriculum for children and preschoolers in Sunday School, Training Union, church music, WMU, and Brotherhood to be used with either Convention Uniform or Life and Work. Bible centered and vitally suited to needs of growing children.

Support.—Supplements and enriches the other series through leadership, leisure reading, and devotional publications.

Program Helps.—Undated merchandise materials which are essential to establishing, carrying out, and improving programs or services.

3. *New Church Study Course.*—Two new study courses began Jan. 1, 1970. The Christian Development Course offers study and credit for adult and youth church members. Study units will be available in the course for children and preschoolers. The Christian Leadership Course will provide courses in general and specialized leadership training. A series of leadership diplomas will be offered based on credit for completion of courses.

STATE SHAPING THE 70'S CONFERENCES. Conferences were held in all state conventions to train key leaders from all associations to interpret the changes to come in the 70's with special emphasis upon new materials to be available Oct. 1, 1970. These key leaders returned to their associations and conducted conferences for church personnel. Thirty special seminars were conducted to train church staff members to be able to better use the materials available in Oct., 1970. The field services in 1969–70 were the most intensive of any period in history. W. L. HOWSE

PROJECT 500. A two-year effort under the Home Mission Board's leadership as part of the Southern Baptist Convention's 1968–69 emphasis on "Evangelism and World Missions." Its objective was to involve the denomination in establishing 500 new churches or church-type missions in carefully-defined strategic locations throughout areas of the nation formally entered by Southern Baptists since 1940. It involved a special appeal for funds through the Annie Armstrong Offering and a special effort by mission leaders in giving assistance in these locations as part of a continuing program of establishing new churches and church-type missions.

At the end of 1969, a total of 211 new churches and missions had been established.

FRED B. MOSELEY

***PROMOTION, SOUTHERN BAPTIST METHODS OF.** From 1956–70, the most significant change was a shift from the charismatic one leader approach to a coordinated team approach. There are exceptions to this, but generally this was the direction. This shift altered procedures for some of the agencies. The following developments characterized Southern Baptist promotion in 1970:

1. Promotional programs affecting the churches are generally developed in two ways: Some agencies form a close working relationship with state program leaders and develop programs that are jointly supported by both groups. Others develop programs which are then presented to state program leaders for correction and promotion. Both methods are considered consistent with Southern Baptist polity.

2. State program leaders are depended upon to promote Southern Baptist Convention programs. Most SBC programs promoted in the states are regarded not merely as SBC programs, but as a program also of the state conventions.

3. Associations are increasingly recognized as important units for communication and training. Both SBC and state program leaders invite the counsel of associational superintendents of missions in planning programs for the churches.

4. Effort has been made to consolidate SBC and state promotion plans into a single emphasis promotion plan. The first effort was under the theme, "The Church Fulfilling Its Mission," 1965–69, the second, "Living the Spirit of Christ," 1969–73, and the third, "Sharing Christ," 1973–79. Once adopted by the Convention, the plans are binding on the agencies but not the churches.

5. Coordinated Promotion Planning attempts to consolidate SBC and state support of the emphasis plans outlined above. The program leader whose programs directly touch the churches regularly meet together to coordinate their work. These plans in turn are communicated to the state program leaders. An effort is made to secure concerted effort of all SBC, state, and associational personnel behind a single plan developed in the states on the basis of SBC planning. Two notable efforts were the Shaping of the 70's Conference in 1969–70 and the Leadership Readiness Conference in 1970–71.

6. The Inter-Agency Council and its coordinating committee have a vital part in SBC promotion. Many of the plans developed by the group named above are developed and carried out by the Inter-Agency Council or its coordinating committee. The coordinating committee meets four times yearly to make sure programs are working together as they touch the churches.

7. The coordinating committee has developed axioms of promotion which generally guide them in their work. These axioms provide that effective promotion should:

grow out of clearly identifiable needs and opportunities faced by Southern Baptists; be shaped by worthy goals and contribute to reaching them; be made the assignment and responsiblity of one competent person; require that the promoter be sold on his product; have the full support of management and multiprograms; be easily identified with the trademark of its promoter; have a clearly identified target audience; be person or church centered and emphasize benefits to the user; be expressed in simple, uncomplicated, and easily understood terms; products and programs should be as complexity-free as possible; be made more effective by products and programs that measure up to the claims of the promotion; be developed around a timely, exciting, compelling, and significant idea; have a positive appeal; be repetitive; be designed to have personal, face-to-face contact; be designed to secure a response; take advantage of new and advanced communication media; use devices that are imaginative and attention-getting; be enthusiastic; change its emphasis frequently so as to avoid loss of interest and support; utilize action words and phrases.

ALBERT MCCLELLAN

PROVENCE, HERBERT WINSTON (b. Greenville, S. C., Nov. 2, 1873; d. Greenville, S. C., Sept. 14, 1957). Son of Samuel Moore and Indie (Watkins) Provence, he married Mary Hall, Nov. 16, 1898. They had two children, Herbert Hall and Ruth. Ordained in 1892 by the New Bridge Baptist Church, Highland Springs, Va., he was educated at Bethel College, Russellville, Ky.; Richmond College, Richmond, Va. (M.A., 1894); and Southern Baptist Theological Seminary (Th.M., 1897; Th.D., 1898). Provence served as pastor of Baptist churches in Montgomery, 1898–1902, and Ensley, 1902–04, both in Alabama. He was on the Alabama state mission board and the state vice-president for Foreign Mission Board, SBC. While serving as a missionary in Shanghai, China, 1904–11, he was secretary-treasurer of the Shanghai Mission and first president of the China Baptist Conference, representing all British and American Baptist missions in China. Active in building the University of Shanghai, he was also a member of the board of trustees (treasurer) and building committee. Provence was pastor in Clinton, Miss., 1912–13, then professor of Bible and philosophy at Mississippi College, 1913–14. He then moved to Furman University, Greenville, S. C., where he taught, 1914–31, first as chairman of the department of English and later as chairman of the department of religion. While at Furman Provence served as part-time pastor with the Concord (1916) and Crossroads Baptist churches in the Saluda Association; Shady Grove Baptist Church, Belton, S. C., 1918–20; and the Standing Springs, Unity, and Berea (1927) Baptist churches in the Greenville Association. In 1931 he became president of Greenville Womans' College, Greenville, S. C., and worked toward the coordination of the college with Furman University, which was accomplished in 1933. After retiring from educational work in 1933, he joined his son in the printing business. He was pastor of White Oak Baptist Church, Greenville, S. C., 1940–42.

Provence was joint author of *Life of Christ* in Chinese. He wrote a Sunday School feature ("The Heart of the Lesson") in the Greenville *Piedmont* for a number of years and lessons for Sunday School quarterlies. J. A. SOUTHERN

PRUITT, THOMAS PITTS (b. Ashland, Wis., May 19, 1893; d. Hickory, N. C., Nov. 16, 1958). Lawyer and Baptist layman. The son of a minister, John Bunyan Pruitt, and Sabra (Pitts) Pruitt, he attended Wake Forest College, 1910–13. He received his LL.B. degree from the University of Florida Law School in 1914 and practiced law briefly in Florida before moving to North Carolina. He practiced law in Catawba County for 43 years and served as president and as a member of the Law Examiners. Pruitt devoted much of his time to First Baptist Church, Hickory, where he was a deacon. Pruitt served as Sunday School superintendent for 29 years. He served as a trustee of North Carolina Baptist Children's Homes (25 years), Wake Forest College, and Meredith College. He served on the Executive Committee of the Southern Baptist Convention, and at the time of his death had been chairman of the committee of 25 for the state convention. Pruitt married Adelyn McComb on Dec. 31, 1918. They were the parents of three daughters. TOBY DRUIN

***PUBLIC AFFAIRS COMMITTEE, BAPTIST JOINT.** Composed of the 15-member Public Affairs Committee of the Southern Baptist Convention and similar committees from seven other Baptist bodies in North America, the Baptist Joint Committee on Public Affairs (BJCPA), is the only joint programing agency of Baptists in North America. By action of the SBC the Public Affairs Committee works directly with the joint committee and has no other staff except that employed by the BJCPA.

In 1961 the SBC approved a program statement to implement the work of this committee with the SBC. The fourfold program is summarized as follows:

1. A Program of Public Affairs Study and Research. Through this program the BJCPA "studies carefully the field of church-state relations, developing interpretations and comments as this field can be seen in the contexts of the current scene in the National Capital and basic Baptist concepts."

2. A Program of Church-State Public Relations. This program is authorized to represent Baptist viewpoints to non-Baptist groups, such as government at all levels, nongovernmental organizations, and other religious bodies.

3. A Program of Public Affairs Information. Under this activity the BJCPA maintains a working news service in the nation's capital. It sends a constant flow of information to Baptists through the denominational publication and news channels and through other special services.

4. A Program of Correlation of Baptist Influence in the Field of Church-State Relations. The organizational nature of the BJCPA poses two special problems in promotion of its basic concern of religious liberty. In almost every state of the United States two or more of the sponsoring bodies are at work. In some states there are as many as five. The problems are (1) to secure action within any one of these groups and (2) to get the several groups to plan a common strategy. The correlation program is an attempt to solve these problems. An effective instrument in the correlation program is the committee's monthly bulletin, *Report from the Capital.*

By 1971 the BJCPA had progressed through two chapters or stages of its development. The first was the administration of Joseph Martin Dawson, the first executive director of the BJCPA. Upon Dawson's retirement in 1953, the BJCPA reevaluated its methods in the light of its experience in approaching public affairs issues on a joint basis. New approaches and development of the work of the BJCPA began under the leadership of C. Emanuel Carlson, who succeeded Dawson in 1954.

A Time for Change.—By 1953, when the time came to elect a new executive director, the Public Affairs Committee had begun to analyze the methods to be used for the application of Baptist insights to public affairs. The basic need was to find ways of analyzing the issues and of educating the people. The issue of freedom had become as broad and as deep as the issue of man.

The fields of public education, public welfare, public health, and others, were all responding to the people's demand for more and better services from government. Thus the issues of church-state relations were both domestic and foreign, and persistently confronted all religions with the basic questions about the values that they represented. A new and strong emphasis on the dignity of man under God was needed as the foundation for all institutional policies in both church and state.

Aims in the New Approach.—To lead in the formulation of the new program the committee sought out the services of an educator who was broadly trained in the social sciences and in education but who was also deeply involved in the educational work of the churches.

The new executive director undertook to plan public affairs emphases with the following objectives:

1. To enhance obedience to the lordship of Christ, both in the person and in the church group, by deepening and broadening Baptist concern for the independence of churches from government authorities and from political emphases that seek to make the churches the captives of their environment;

2. To give expression to the compassionate gospel of Christ so that, through having seen

the love of God actively at work in the children of God, people might understand and believe in God's redeeming love;

3. To disseminate enough objective factual information through Baptist channels so that people may thoughtfully choose the social values that they should support through the democratic political process, with the same stewardship under God that they had learned in the church;

4. To create materials, channels, and opportunities for Baptist leaders and people to talk deliberately about public issues and the meaning of freedom under God with other fellow Christians who had other backgrounds but who also accepted the truth that God has come in Christ; and

5. To build an appreciation of Baptists in the minds of public leaders by letting those leaders see that Baptists care for people and are interested in the common good in all communities, states, and nations.

The Readiness for Response.—The response to this call to a far-reaching involvement with Christ in the needs of people and in the organized life of communities and societies could not come hastily. However, the response of leaders to various program developments came quickly.

As the Washington office's "Information Service" undertook to provide objective and verified accounts of developments and trends in the nation's capital, Baptist Press named the director of the Information Services as its regional editor. Thus, a new fast channel was opened for the flow of information from the capital. Hundreds of reports that had been personally verified thereby became available each year to the editors of Baptist state papers and to other channels.

Report from the Capital, the mimeographed monthly newsletter, grew in content and format and became a specialized piece on public affairs for church program leaders. With responsible materials available, the several Sunday School Board channels increased their roles in nurturing mature and constructive Christian influence in national and community life.

For in-depth study of particular issues and topics, an annual religious liberty conference was developed using small group workshop methods. With a collection of research papers in hand, more than a thousand Baptist convention leaders have contributed three days or more to an intensive sharing of their insights and convictions as they have attempted to clarify and state the meaning of the Baptist movement for modern public issues.

Gradually, the Washington office and staff became an important resource for denominational leaders and agencies that needed to react to, or evaluate movements, reports, press inquiries, etc., as contemporary opinion makers.

As the quality of this work was observed by public officials, by the public press, and by denominational leaders of other traditions, the Baptist insights on religious liberty and proper church-state relationships became a contemporary worldwide resource for new plans and positions. In a variety of consulting and observing roles the staff shared in the formation of numerous denominational reports, in interdenominational positions, and in general public opinions.

With reference to numerous national, state, and local issues, political planning and drafting committees, as well as community dialogue groups, began to request the help of Baptist expertise in keeping peace and goodwill while resolving problems that involve religious conflicts or tensions.

The modern relaxation of religious defensiveness and the resulting maturity of religious conversations between various faiths and their several segments was the result of many forces and was aided by many groups. However, the Baptist contribution was led in a significant way by the BJCPA, in which the SBC works through its Public Affairs Committee.

Some Specific Issues.—From 1956 to 1970, the Public Affairs Committee of the SBC, in cooperation with comparable other Baptist committees and the Washington staff, led in applying the principles of freedom to numerous public issues. Illustrations of these can be listed briefly as follows: authority of school boards to prescribe or require prayer or devotions; power of military leaders to prescribe worship and require attendance; tax exemption for houses of worship as a judicial issue; tax support for religious elementary and secondary schools; college dormitory loans from government credit agencies; loans to college students from public funds; use of Peace Corps personnel in religious schools in foreign nations; exports of surplus food to feed needy populations; government food surpluses given to church youth camps; federal and state hospital grants for religiously owned hospitals; religious tests for public office and for candidates; and government rehabilitation contracts with church-related agencies.

The Public Affairs Committee has become the agency of the SBC that leads in at least these five functions: (1) analyzing contemporary public trends and developments in the light of biblical insights; (2) providing the opportunity for Christians to find the strength of a mutual stewardship of influence with reference to modern public issues; (3) representing Baptist opinions recorded by Baptist conventions and agencies; (4) enumerating and interpreting present-day meanings of traditional Baptist principles; and (5) monitoring government hearings, reports, actions, judicial decisions, etc., regarding which Baptists generally need fast and authentic knowledge.

The Public Affairs Committtee has become the SBC's major provision for a concerted attempt to participate in historic decisions in the public arena. It appears that the new developing program is thereby pointing the way to a

SOUTHERN BAPTIST HOSPITAL (*q.v.*), New Orleans, La. Chartered Sept. 5, 1924, by the Hospital Commission, SBC.

BAPTIST MEMORIAL HOSPITAL (*q.v.*), Jacksonville, Fla. Established in 1953.

SOUTHERN BAPTIST CONVENTION (*q.v.*) OBSERVES 125th ANNIVERSARY. A total of 13,692 messengers were registered at the 125th anniversary session of the SBC meeting in Denver, Colorado, June 1–4, 1970.

new and clearer Christian witness in the context of modern public needs.

W. BARRY GARRETT

PUBLIC RELATIONS. The public relations profession began taking form between the two World Wars. By the forties it was becoming a prominent part of the American scene and in the fifties it entered Southern Baptist life. The most frequently quoted definition is stated as follows: "Public relations is the management function which evaluates public attitudes, identifies the policies and procedures of an individual or an organization with the public interest, and executes a program of action to earn public understanding and acceptance." Public relations is an orchestration of wide variety of skills to win favorable attitudes and direct support. It draws heavily on journalism, social science, psychology, research, communication, advertising, marketing, promotion, publishing, audiovisuals, broadcasting, art, public speaking, and other specialized skills to achieve attitude and opinion change. Public relations is a planned effort at persuasion aimed at single individuals although mass media may be utilized.

In Baptist life, as elsewhere, the public relations functions were often performed in isolation from each other long before the term entered the dictionaries. But it was not until it began approaching professional status around 1950 that Baptist agencies and organizations began hiring individuals with this specific title. The Baptist Public Relations Association was formed in 1954 with a dozen charter members. By 1970 the organization had about 200 members with another 150 Southern Baptist workers who were eligible for membership. In a major reorganization of the structure of the Southern Baptist Convention in the period from 1956 to 1959, the SBC Executive Committee created the first Convention-wide public relations position. W. C. Fields, who had been editor of the *Baptist Record* in Mississippi, was elected public relations secretary for the Executive Committee in 1959. A Public Relations Advisory Committee of 15 persons was authorized by Convention action to counsel the Executive Committee staff and its public relations service. By 1970 the Baptist Public Relations Association was one of the strongest and most active denominational public relations organizations to be found anywhere in the world. Its members are active in the Religious Public Relations Council, an international body drawing qualified professionals from all religious faiths. Baptist public relations personnel were likewise active in the Public Relations Society of America. Some of the Baptist public relations personnel were among the 1,800 persons who had been "accredited" by PRSA.

In 1965 the SBC Executive Committee adopted a recommendation from its Public Relations Committee that the following goals be adopted from the denomination in communication and public relations. Goals relating to the internal life of the SBC are: (1) Full opportunity for the free flow of information in all directions. (2) Basic data to the constituency for enlightened opinion and as a frame of reference for intelligent action. (3) Dependable denominational sources of information and interpretation, having a high degree of credibility. (4) Skilled personnel with adequate organization and equipment, to help keep Baptist life relevant to a rapidly changing social order. (5) Effectiveness in conveying aims and motivations as well as the details of action programs. (6) A sense of belonging, a consciousness of participation by Baptists generally in their denomination life.

External goals for corporate communication by Southern Baptists, as adopted by the Executive Committee are: (1) Public understanding of who Baptists are, what they are doing, and why. (2) Acceptance by the mass media of Baptists as honest, straightforward Christians working seriously at their task. (3) General confidence in the altruism and fairmindedness of Baptist policies. (4) The name "Baptist" automatically associated with reasonableness and intelligence as well as dedication. (5) A working relationship with all communications media based on professional competence and mutual respect. (6) Clear lines of communication with all outside media. (7) A reputation for all Baptist general bodies, agencies and corporate entities as being good influences in government; in the social, economic, and cultural life of the country as well as in religious affairs. A central point of reference in the practice of effective public relations and communications among Baptists was noted in the Executive Committee action: "to keep Christian goals clearly before our own Baptist people and Christian values before the public."

W. C. FIELDS

PUERTO RICO, MISSIONS IN. Southern Baptists began mission efforts in 1964, determining that the Commonwealth should be treated as any other area of the nation. To avoid duplication, conferences were held with American Baptists, active since 1902.

Milton S. Leach, superintendent of missions since 1964 (previously director of Spanish work in Miami), directs three regional missionaries: Albert Casteel, E. McKinney Adams, and Donald T. Moore, who serve consultant roles, train pastors and lay leaders, and start missions.

Ramey Air Force Base personnel in Aguadilla created the first congregation in the mid-1950's, and in 1963 consideration was given to affiliating this church and two others with the Florida Baptist Convention. Instead, the Puerto Rico Baptist Association, relating directly to the denomination, was organized July 31, 1965, with five churches and five missions. By 1970 there were four English-speaking churches, five Spanish-speaking churches, and about 20 missions.

Outreach includes Spanish Baptist Hour

broadcasts, a semireligious magazine, and a correspondence Bible course. The Borinquen Church, Aguadilla, sponsors a Bible institute in which men attend classes and pastor missions concurrently. Similar institutes are planned for other regions to provide native pastors.

See also PUERTO RICO BAPTIST CONVENTION, Vol. II. DALLAS M. LEE

Q

QUARLES, CHESTER LEW (b. Wiggins, Miss., May 18, 1908; d. Cuzco, Peru, July 6, 1968). Minister, denominational worker, and denominational executive. Son of Hugh A. and Grace Herrington Quarles, he was stricken with polio as a child and carried a withered arm for the rest of his life. He professed faith in Christ at 13, and was baptized in the First Baptist Church, Troy, Ala. At 16 he decided to enter the ministry. Quarles earned an A.B. at Howard College in Birmingham, where he participated in numerous extracurricular activities. During student days at Southern Baptist Theological Seminary, he served as an educational worker and youth director for Broadway Baptist Church in Louisville. After graduation (Th.M., 1933) Quarles accepted the pastorate of the Baptist Church at Newton, Ala., which included working with three small rural churches nearby. In 1935 he accepted a position as state Training Union and Student Work secretary for Alabama, a position he held for five years. He married Virginia Cooper of Tylertown, Miss., in 1936. They had three children: Mary Virginia, Chester Leland, and Grace Elaine.

He was associate Convention-wide Training Union secretary, directing associational work, 1940–42. Quarles served as pastor of the First Baptist Church, Leland, Miss., from 1942 to 1947, when he became pastor of First Baptist Church, Sylacauga, Ala. In Mar., 1950, the Mississippi Baptist Convention board chose him as its executive secretary, a position he held until his death. Shortly after his becoming secretary the responsibility of treasurer was added to his position. During his tenure, the board greatly expanded its ministry. The Cooperative Program receipts increased from $802,918 in 1950, to $3,670,491 in 1968. Two state assemblies, Kittiwake and Gulfshore, were purchased and developed, and the new Baptist Building in Jackson was planned and erected.

He received the following honorary degrees: D.D., Mississippi College, 1952, and D.H., Mississippi Baptist Seminary, 1966. Quarles participated in several overseas preaching missions, and conducted many tours to Europe, the Holy Land, and South America. Among the many denominational posts Quarles served are the following: first vice-president, SBC, 1958, president of the SBC Executive Secretaries Association, 1955, president of the Alabama Baptist executive board, 1949–50, president of the Alumni Association, Southern Baptist Theological Seminary, and member of the Foreign Mission Board, SBC.

Quarles died during a mission trip to South America. His body was returned to Jackson, Miss., and was buried in Lakewood Memorial Park. JOE T. ODLE

QUEEN, JAMES FLOYD (b. Mableton, Cobb County, Ga., Sept. 28, 1886; d. Little Rock, Ark., Oct. 6, 1962). Minister and educator. Son of James L. and Annie Marie (Moss) Queen, he married Idelia Hartsfield, 1907. They had four children: Arle Emil, Lowell Wilbur, James Ivan, and Virginia. He married Mrs. A. P. (Irene) Blaylock in 1944. Queen was educated at Ouachita College (A.B., 1917; D.D., 1950). Baptized into Emmet Baptist Church (Ark.), 1904, he was ordained by Wellsville Baptist Church, Arkadelphia, Ark., 1910. He served the following Arkansas Baptist churches as minister: Ozan, Howard County, 1912–13; Emmet, Hempstead County, 1914–15; First, Stephens, 1917–18; First, De Queen, 1923–34; First, Prescott, 1934–37; and Park Place Church, Hot Springs, 1937–45. He also served as pastor in Oklahoma: Paul's Valley Church, 1919–20, and Comanche First Church, 1920–23. He was chaplain of the Arkansas Baptist Hospital, Little Rock, 1945–57. Queen taught at Southern Baptist College, Walnut Ridge, Ark., 1957–62. He was vice-president of the Arkansas Baptist State Convention, 1942.

GEORGE T. BLACKMON

R

***RACE RELATIONS.** Changes in race relations in the United States occupied a prominent place in the thoughts and actions of most citizens during the sixties. Congress passed civil rights' laws which, along with additional rulings of the Supreme Court, broke down almost every legal barrier to full freedom of choice and action for Negroes in such fields as education, employment, housing, public accommodation, and intermarriage.

These laws slowly brought about profound changes in society. Integration in schools, transportation, and public accommodations became an accepted fact in broad areas of the nation. However, there was evidence toward the end of the sixties that black people, as well as Indians, Mexican-Americans, and other ethnic groups, were still far from being fully accepted into the social fabric of national life.

The dominant leader in the Civil Rights' Movement was a Baptist minister, Martin Luther King, Jr., whose tragic assassination on the evening of Apr. 4, 1968, shocked the nation and the world.

The emphasis on nonviolence had been weakening prior to King's death. Since 1968 a much more militant approach to civil rights has emerged. "Black Power," a slogan made popular in 1966, has come to epitomize the spirit of a vast segment of black people in America, particularly the young. Many whites have a limited understanding of Black Power, hearing it only as a battle cry of black militants. They associate it with looting, burning, and violence. Actually, it is developing into a broad philosophy of Negro identity in at least three areas: (1) pride in being black; (2) recovery of racial rootage in African heritage; and (3) emphasis upon Negro self-determination, including the development of Negro-owned enterprises and political control of Negro communities.

Along with the growing concept of Black Power is an emphasis on "black separatism." The Christian church is divided on the validity of this emphasis. There are a number of black caucuses or black consortia in the larger integrated church bodies. However, many Christian leaders, black and white, cling to the conviction that reconciliation in Jesus Christ leaves no place for separatism.

While Southern Baptists have continued to adopt strong resolutions in the area of Christian race relations, notably in "A Statement Concerning the Crisis in Our Nation," adopted in 1968, most of the churches have moved slowly, if at all, to open their doors to people of all colors and races. Nevertheless, an encouraging number of churches are indicating a change of attitude on race.

A study made by the Home Mission Board, SBC, in 1968 indicated 510 churches with black members plus 3,724 churches which had officially indicated a willingness to receive Negro members. In addition to action by local churches receiving black members, district associations and state conventions have received at least 100 black churches into their fellowships. Also, the reverse has been true in that some white churches have been dually aligned with Negro Baptist conventions at the state and national level. In the Southern Baptist Convention in 1970 there were at least four predominantly white or all-white congregations who had Negro pastors.

Changes have taken place in higher education. All Southern Baptist seminaries and nearly all Baptist colleges and universities have black students. Many of these institutions are developing curricula in black studies.

Numerous conferences, seminars, and workshops have been held in the field of race relations at all levels of Southern Baptist life. The Christian Life Commission sponsored conferences at Ridgecrest and Glorieta Baptist assemblies in Aug., 1964, on "Christianity and Race Relations" and, in general, has provided leadership for Southern Baptists as they seek to grapple with the problems of race.

The commission has produced a number of tracts, articles, and study papers on the subject. The Sunday School Board, through its curriculum materials and especially in a resource unit, *We Hold These Truths,* has provided helpful information on this complex issue.

The HMB has an extensive program through its Department of Work with National Baptists. The HMB and the Christian Life Commission jointly have sponsored Race Relations Sunday each year since 1965. The observance of this emphasis has grown to such an extent that it included more than 7,500 churches in 1970.

One of the more significant movements is the development of "companion churches," where a white Baptist church and a black Baptist church cooperate in joint endeavors such as Bible study, mission action projects, tutoring programs, combined worship services, fellowship meetings, and discussion groups. All of these relationships take place on a volunteer basis without the loss of identity by either church body. Many feel this to be one of the most helpful ways to affirm our common commitment to Christ as his disciples. ELMER S. WEST, JR.

RACHEL SIMS MISSION. Established in New Orleans in 1919 by the Home Mission Board, it provides a weekday ministry for people of the Irish Channel section. Activities designed to meet the needs of people include Bible study, recreation, music, camping, distribution of food and clothing, family counseling, tutorial assistance, and job placement. Career missionaries, student interns, seminary students, and volunteer workers from local churches constitute the staff. CHARLES MCCULLIN

RADFORD, OSBORNE KILLEBREW (b. Hopkinsville, Ky., Mar. 2, 1901; d. Jacksonville, Fla., Apr. 28, 1960). Businessman, assembly manager, educational director, denominational servant. Graduate (B.A.) of University of Kentucky, he married Minnie Bell, May 7, 1927. Following a period in the insurance business, he became business manager of the Clear Creek Baptist Assembly, Clear Creek, Ky. He served as educational director of First Church, Pineville, Ky., First Church, Hopkinsville, Ky., and First Church, Winter Haven, Fla. In 1926 he was named associate to W. W. Willian in the Sunday School and Training Union Department of the Florida Baptist Convention and in 1938 was appointed state secretary of the convention's Training Union Department. He led in the development of church training in Florida Baptist churches. Radford instituted four District Training Union Conventions in 1946 and expanded them to eight in 1955.

CECIL B. CARROLL

RADICAL THEOLOGY. "Radical Theology," sometimes called "the death-of-God theology," is the first theological movement to have (1) interpreted the traditional *kenosis* or "self-emptying" of God *absolutely* or *radically,* and to have (2) combined this radical interpretation of *kenosis* with an *eschatological* interpretation of history. To Thomas J. J. Altizer and William Hamilton, the two main promulgators of Radical Theology, contemporary Christians can live authentic Christian lives only when they ". . . recognize that the death of God is an historical event" and that "God has died in our time, in our history, in our existence"—and, having made this recognition, then live redemptively by finding Christ in the face of the neighbor.

The radical theologian insists that "in the time of the death of God, we have a place to be. It is not before the altar; it is in the world, in the city, with both the needy neighbor and the enemy." What seems to give the radical theologian this "secular" orientation is probably his reliance on three particular thinkers: Paul Tillich, Friedrick Nietzsche, and Georg Hegel. Tillich insisted that any religious symbol (such as the name "God") has died if it no longer conveys to man the "immediate awareness of the unconditioned," and, hence, he predicted the *linquistic* death of God. Nietzsche's postulation of radical naturalism entailed the affirmation of oneself (i.e., of one's will-to-power) as the basis of morality instead of the old, idealistically-defined God; he said: "Dead are all the gods! What gods there are danceth in me!" Thus, Nietzsche predicted the *ethical* death of God. Finally, Hegel foreshadowed the *ontological* death of God by incorporating the principle of contradiction or negativity in his understanding of the Absolute Spirit. Altizer says of Hegel's definition of Spirit as the "pure process of becoming its other" the following: "Negativity is the power and the process of the self-realization or the self-mediation of the Hegelian Absolute, Subject or Spirit. Accordingly, Spirit is the kenotic or emptying process of negativity; as such it is the true actuality (*Wirklichkeit*) of the world, for Spirit is the inherently negative or the negativity found in Being *per se*."

Here, then, are three of the main sources for Radical Theology, and these sources tell us much about its content. *First,* Radical Theology takes its stand *absolutely* or *radically within the contemporary atheistic culture* indicated by Nietzsche and, in our time, Tillich. That is, it assumes that the hallmark of "secular" man "come of age" is that he no longer hears any revelation from God and can therefore no longer appeal to God as a problem-solver or wish-fulfiller. William Hamilton insists that the "neo-orthodox reconstruction of the Christian doctrine of revelation seems to have broken down for some." The neo-orthodox theologian would say that while we cannot know God, He has nevertheless made himself known to us. *Now,* however, the situation is: "As before, we cannot know, but now it seems that he does not make himself known, even as enemy." Thinking, perhaps, of the black Sunday School children blown to bits by a bomb in Birmingham, Ala., Hamilton says: "We are not talking about the absence of the experience of God, but about the experience of the absence of God."

Second, Radical Theology takes the *kenosis* or *self-emptying of God* in the Incarnation *radically* or *utterly seriously.* Reacting dramatically against the traditional interpretation of God as *actus purus*—an interpretation which has always opened the traditional view of the Incarnation to the charge of Deism (e.g., if God is *pure* act without *any* admixture of potentiality, as Thomas says, how, on this basis, could the Incarnation really *mean* anything to Him—i.e., how could the Incarnation, the self-emptying and the taking of humanity back into the bosom of God, be *real?*) —the radical theologian understands *kenosis* as involving dialectically "a pure or radical negation, a self-negation of Spirit in which Spirit kenotically becomes its own other, existing as the actual opposite of its own original or initial identity." This self-negation of Spirit makes possible its real historical movement, a movement in which Spirit evolves to its absolute form only by progressively negating its own expressions, that is, only by "dying" after it has "lived." A significant passage of Altizer's is the following:

> Even when the theologians have re-discovered the *agapē* or total self-giving of God, they have confined it to the movement of the Incarnation, and thus have dualistically isolated God's love from the primordial nature and existence of God Himself. So long as God is known in his primordial form as an eternal and unchanging Being, he can never be known in his incarnate form as self-giving or self-negating Being. The radical Christian refuses to speak of God's existence . . . because he knows that God has negated and transcended himself in the Incarnation, and thereby has fully and finally ceased to exist in his original or primordial forms. To know that God *is* Jesus, is to know that God himself has become flesh: no longer does God exist as transcendent Spirit or sovereign Lord, now God *is* love.

Thus, the radical theologian, learning from Hegel, teaches that God *is* Jesus, and by this he means that the Incarnation is a total and all-consuming act: as Spirit becomes the Word that empties the Speaker of himself, the whole reality of Spirit becomes incarnate in its opposite. God, therefore, "dies," and in this way the radical Christian feels that only he really witnesses to the full reality of Jesus or the Incarnate Word (because he alone responds to the totally kenotic movement of God) . Altizer (and probably Hamilton also) is convinced that ". . . apart from what Hegel called the process of absolute negativity, there lies no way of apprehending the ontological reality of the Incarnation," and unless the Incarnation is known as effecting an *absolute negation* of the primordial or essential Being of God, there can be no knowledge that God *is* love.

Third, Radical Theology interprets *history radically* or *utterly seriously*. The radical theologian is convinced that, despite the fact that Jesus' own Gospel was deeply rooted and grounded in an eschatological framework, Christian theology has *never* actually been able to assimilate this fact, and, correspondingly, has always held on to the past with a "fanatical conservatism." Theology should remember that eschatological faith *cannot* come to *our* time in the original (primordial) form, and "it must move into the future by negating the past." The Incarnate Word must be understood as continuing in a genuinely forward-moving process of self-negation and hence self-transformation. We, too, like the Incarnate, self-negating Word, must pass through the "darkness of the death of God," so that the "epiphany of Christ" can occur.

Thus, in contrast to Oriental mysticism—which emphasizes a negative historical movement which is essentially a *backward* movement to the primordial Totality (to *Nirvana* or the *Brahman-Atman*) —*Christian* faith is understood by the radical theologian to involve a negation which is at one and the same time *forward* (dialectical) and *eschatological*. Attacking the "spiritualization" of eschatology by the ancient and medieval church fathers, who through the use of Hellenistic concepts postulated a mystical and sacramental redemption which portrayed Jesus as the supreme *logos spermatikos* or Divine Word (the ancient "Logos-Christology") , Radical Theology bravely interprets redemption *eschatologically* instead of sacramentally. Jesus is interpreted as a "charismatic" type of redeemer, who is possessed of the charismatic gift and power of healing and exorcism, and who demands a personal decision from every hearer concerning the inbreaking of the kingdom of God. But his powers are not the powers of a *mere* miracle-working rabbi, nor even of a *mere* prophet; in Jesus they are *the operations of the power of the dawning Kingdom of God which brings in the new eschaton.* Altizer and Hamilton, *contra* both the 19th century liberals, and R. Bultmann as well, are convinced that

> . . . all efforts to abandon, spiritualize, or demythologize the eschatology of Jesus and the primitive church must be recognized as perilous, since they invariably lead to a transformation or negation of both the person and the message of Jesus himself. Nothing could more forcefully demonstrate the intimate relation between the person and message of Jesus, between Jesus the prophet-Messiah and Jesus the Word. Christologies that are noneschatological lose not only the Jewish-Biblical roots of Christianity but abandon the historical Jesus as well. The Christian way is an eschatological way; when it ceases to be such, it loses all contact with the original proclamation of Jesus.

If (1) history is authentic and not illusory, and if (2) "God is a forward-moving process of kenotic metamorphosis," and if (3) redemption is eschatological, then it is obvious that it follows *both* that (1) revelation cannot be finished and complete *and* that (2) the Incarnation and the Crucifixion cannot be understood as isolated or once-and-for-all events.

Fourth and last, Radical Theology takes *radically* or *utterly seriously both Christ and the humanity He came to "enflesh"* and to save. Drawing on William Blake's tremendously-moving (but ambiguous and mystical) vision of Christ as the "Universal Humanity" (sec Blake's poem, "The Marriage of Heaven and Hell") , the radical theologian challenges us to cease using a God-oriented theology as an escape from reality or as a buttress for the status quo, and to embrace instead a neighbor-oriented theology which courageously affirms with the secular city that "God is dead" but that we *wager our lives* that His Incarnate Word is being resurrected anew in the face of the needy neighbor. The radical theologian importunes us earnestly: "Dare we bet upon a totally incarnate Christ, whose contemporary presence negates his previous epiphanies . . .?" When the Christian bets or "wagers" that God is dead, he is betting upon the real and actual presence of the fully incarnate Christ. Thus, a "Christian wager" upon the death of God is a wager upon the presence of the living Christ, a bet that Christ is now at least potentially present in a new and total form—namely, on the savage streets of the secular city and in the face of the godless but needy neighbor.

BIBLIOGRAPHY: Altizer, Thomas J. J. and William Hamilton, *Radical Theology and the Death of God* (1966). ————————, *The Gospel of Christian Atheism* (1966). Cooper, John Charles, *The Roots of Radical Theology* (1967). ELLIS W. HOLLON, JR.

RADIO AND TELEVISION, MISSIONARY USE OF. Radio and television are vital tools available for use in all forms of mission endeavor. These electronic media cross state, national, and international boundaries and are equally useful in domestic and foreign missions.

For example, in 1958, the Baptist General Convention of Texas, through its state mission offering, began sponsorship of *La Hora Bautista* (*The Baptist Hour*), on station KGBT in Harlingen, Texas. The purpose was to minister to the Spanish-speaking people of the Rio Grande Valley in south Texas. That purpose was accomplished, but the radio waves did not stop at the border. They continued on south, crossing through Mexico and other Central American countries. Thus, what began as a state mission project, became a mission tool serving state, home, and foreign interests.

Radio and television waves cross all barriers, and reach people where they are—at home, in a car, in the hospital, etc. Radio and television can reach individuals beyond the personal or institutional Christian witness. They can go into the high-rise apartment in urban areas, into the hovel of the tenant farmer, or through the Iron and Bamboo Curtains with equal ease.

Each week broadcasts in Russian and Chinese beam to Russia and mainland China from stations in Ecuador, the Philippines, and Korea. The purpose is to proclaim Christ to non-Christians and to encourage Christians to remain true to their faith.

While these media alone can be used to spread the gospel, the most effective use of them is made when they are reinforced by other forms of Christian witness. Perhaps the greatest contribution that radio and television have made to Southern Baptist advance in the United States in the past decade is in the so-called "pioneer areas" of the North, East, and West. One of the basic problems in the establishment of churches and missions in these areas has been the uncertainty in the minds of many people as to who "Southern Baptists" are. Many view them as holding extreme religious and political views. The production of quality radio and television programs, used on local stations as well as the national networks, has helped Southern Baptists to overcome this stigma. Thus, radio and television are playing a part in providing the necessary atmosphere and climate into which the seeds of personal witness may be sown.

The world has been termed a "global village," ever shrinking because of new means of transportation and communication. The mass media are not ends in themselves—they are but means to an end. The message is not new—but there are new ways of telling it. Southern Baptists are using radio and television in ever increasing efforts to reach the world. JERRY PILLOW

***RADIO AND TELEVISION COMMISSION, THE.** Permission for the commission to move from its Atlanta, Ga., location at 1585 Ponce De Leon Ave., SE, to Fort Worth, Tex. was granted at the Southern Baptist Convention, St. Louis, Mo., in June, 1954. The move was effected in June, 1955, and a new Southern Baptist Radio-TV Center was opened at 6248 Camp Bowie Blvd., in a rented building in the Ridglea shopping center.

The plan to purchase property and build a functional communications center from which to serve the radio and television needs and opportunities of the denomination was 10 full years in becoming reality. The move to the new 42,000-square-foot International Communications Center at 6350 West Freeway was made in July, 1965. The property, building, and equipment represent an investment of approximately $1,000,000. Leaders and messengers of the Southern Baptist Convention meeting in Dallas took part in dedication ceremonies in June.

In 1969 the Capital Needs Committee of the Executive Committee, SBC, allocated funds for a sound stage to be erected behind the present headquarters building. Construction was delayed pending allocation of funds for equipment and personnel. As the denomination's income rose and as the leadership recognized the place of radio and television in the spreading of the gospel, the commission received additional funds. In 1955 the Cooperative Program allotted $197,000 to the work of the commission, and it received $136,373.82 by mail and through miscellaneous income. By contrast, in 1969, the commission's Cooperative Program allotment was $1,208,750, with an additional $254,628 received by mail and in miscellaneous income.

Although the commission produced only *The Baptist Hour* for radio when it began operations in Texas, the following spring saw the launching of *This Is the Answer* on television. Other programs produced in 1955–56 included *Moral Side of the News,* religious news, and *Chapel Upstairs,* devotional, each 15 minutes long.

La Hora Bautista was begun in 1958. Leobardo Estrada was the speaker for this modified worship program in Spanish for more than a decade. Programs in Spanish ultimately increased to five, and devotional type programs in Portuguese, Italian, Navajo, Japanese, Chinese, Russian, and Polish were begun as the Home Mission Board ascertained needs among minority language groups.

By 1959 *The Baptist Hour* was carried by an average of 455 stations, or half of the total stations carrying the five weekly radio programs produced and distributed by the commission at this point. The previous year the commission had installed Herschel H. Hobbs, pastor of the First Baptist Church, Oklahoma City, as regular preacher on the program. In Apr., 1959, the commission inaugurated a new concept in religious programming in the "magazine" format of *MasterControl.**

The following year brought continuing changes in the programming philosophy of the commission and a move to diversified production and distribution of radio programming. The purpose of diversification was to help a station reach a larger portion of its multifaceted audience, and thus to reach larger numbers with the gospel. By Jan., 1961, the number of programs being sent out each week had reached 1,100.

In 1962 the commission located and began the purchase of a four-and-one-half-acre site for the new commission headquarters. Network opportunities increased to eight different programs that year, and circulation of *The Beam,* monthly publication of the commission, rose to 28,000.

The agency reported in 1964 that the Convention's Executive Committee had made it possible for the denomination to be ranked as the third force in the free world in total broadcasts and hours of broadcasting. *Radio Free Europe* and the *Voice of America* were first and second. *U.S. News and World Report* for Aug. 31, 1965, cited the VOA as broadcasting 90 hours a week into South America. During the same period, the commission broadcast 80 hours in the southern hemisphere.

The number of broadcast outlets using Southern Baptist programs increased in 1964 by 25.82 per cent, to 1,720. At the same time, the commission received a 9.56 per cent budget increase through the Cooperative Program.

The 30th anniversary of the agency since its inception as a radio committee for the denomination was observed in the fall of 1968. At the same time, Paul M. Stevens was honored for 15 years of service as the director. The commercial value of the time given to the denomination through the commission in 1968 was estimated at $3,500,000.

Professional consultation on the use of radio and television by other Southern Baptist agencies, state conventions, and local Baptist churches offered by the commission's technical assistance department resulted in increased denominational relationships. A total of 250 military and institutional chaplains received aid from the department in 1968.

One of the most successful ventures in the life of the commission was the production of *JOT,* a 4½-minute animated cartoon series which caught the imagination and heart of children wherever it was shown. In its first two years on the air, on a restricted 40 stations, *JOT* drew half a million cards and letters from children.

The commission reached deeper into the potential audience for its programming in 1969, and took hold of a larger segment than ever before. Through the launching of new radio and television programs, the commission originated a broadcast somewhere in the world on the average of every three minutes during the year, for a total of 152,022 separate broadcasts.

Commission programs produced in the name of the denomination increased to 44 during the year, and the total number of programs aired weekly to 2,500, an all-time high. New stations were added at the rate of about one a day, accounted for primarily by *PowerLine,* a half-hour radio program for teen-agers, with a format of "top 40" music, interspersed with comments on the lyrics to achieve a presentation of the gospel in contemporary teen-age terms. Another new radio program in 1969 was *Country Crossroads,* featuring a magazine format and based on country and Western music and its well-known performers.

The Answer series was scheduled to have its name and style phased out in 1970, to make way for a shift in emphasis, from drama to live and filmed documentaries, in a series called *The Human Dimension.*

The general reorganization of the commission in 1969 included the establishment of an advertising agency concept begun under the name of *TimeRite, Inc.,* for the general benefit of the entire denomination. Three *TimeRite* representatives were operating out of offices in Wilmington, N. C., Dallas, Tex., and Fresno, Calif., to service the radio and television needs of local churches, associations, state conventions, and other agencies of the Southern Baptist Convention.

Ten hours of broadcast time were given by the nation's three large radio-TV networks during the year, at an average value of $70,000 per hour. A one-hour film special, *Ecce Homo,* produced jointly with the National Broadcasting Company's religious television unit at the British Museum, was awarded a gold first place medal by the Television Academy of Arts and Sciences in 1969. Southern Baptists continued to gain about one hour of time a year from the networks.

Also organized during the year were *The Centurymen,* 100-voice male singing group composed of ministers of music from Southern Baptist churches in 21 states. The purpose of the choir was to provide music for the commission's broadcast programming and to represent the denomination internationally. *The Centurymen's* premier performance was on NBC-TV, Dec. 28, 1969.

The Baptist Hour closed its 29th year of regular broadcasting on 454 stations. Herschel H. Hobbs began his 12th consecutive year as the program's preacher. CLARENCE DUNCAN

RAGLAND, GEORGE (b. Richland Va., Aug. 4, 1876; d. Lexington, Ky., May 19, 1957). The son of Alice and John F. Ragland, he was baptized by J. B. Hutson, pastor of the Pine Street Baptist Church, Richmond, Va. He was educated at Richmond College (A.B., 1896) and at Johns Hopkins University (Ph.D., 1921). The early part of Ragland's career was spent in teaching, as professor of Greek at Baylor University, 1901–10, and as professor of Ancient Languages, Georgetown College, 1910–22. On Nov. 22, 1922, he was ordained and spent the rest of his life as pastor of the First Baptist Church, Lexington, Ky. Remembered as "a vehement contender for his convictions," he edited *The Sling and Stone,* a monthly promotional publication, from 1926 until his death, and was active in many phases of denominational work. On Aug. 20, 1902, he married Elizabeth Margaret Rawlings of Spottsylvania, Va.

LEO T. CRISMON

RALEY, JOHN WESLEY (b. Rosebud, Tex., Aug. 15, 1902; d. Shawnee, Okla., May 19, 1968). Minister, educator, and denominational statesman. He received an A.B. degree from Baylor University, 1923; Th.M. degree from Southwestern Baptist Theological Seminary, 1927, and Th.D. from Eastern Baptist Seminary, Philadelphia, 1933. Baylor awarded him the honorary D.D. degree in 1949. Following a short career as public-school teacher, he became a minister. Pastorates included Smithville, Tex. (where he married Helen Thames in 1929), and Bartlesville, Okla. He became president of Oklahoma Baptist University in June, 1934; became chancellor in 1961, and president emeritus in 1965. His administration as OBU president was marked by stability, organic growth, and material development. Honors included membership in *Who's Who in America* from 1936 until his death, and induction into the Oklahoma Hall of Fame in 1958. He is buried in Rest Haven Cemetery, Shawnee.

J. M. GASKIN

RATLIFF, WILLIAM THOMAS (b. Raymond, Miss., Sept. 16, 1835; d. Raymond, Miss., Jan. 12, 1918). He married Mary Olive Cook of Edwards, June 18, 1856, to which union was born 10 children. Ratliff was educated at Mississippi College. He enlisted in the Confederate army and became captain of an artillery company. After the war, he served successively as Probate Clerk, Chancery Clerk, Sheriff, and County Administrator of Hinds County. An ardent advocate of prohibition, he served as president of the Anti-Saloon League. He was a member of the Vicksburg Military Park Commission and a member and president of the board of trustees of the Department of Archives and History.

A devoted Baptist, Ratliff was a deacon for 43 years and active in associational and state work, serving as president of the state convention in 1906. He was named to the board of trustees of Mississippi College in 1872, and the next year was elected president of the board. He held this office for 45 years, working with four college presidents. Ratliff was a generous financial supporter of the college but the presidents testified "the money he has given is as nothing compared with the value of his wise counsel." Ratliff Hall, a dormitory for men, was named in his honor.

BIBLIOGRAPHY: *The Baptist,* June 7, 1900, p. 6; "Ratliff Papers," Library of Mississippi College.

R. A. MCLEMORE

RAY, BURTON JUSTICE (b. Raleigh, N. C., Jan. 2, 1883; d. Franklin, Va., Aug. 17, 1965). Baptist layman and denominational leader. He was the son of John E. and Finis (Carter) Ray. His father was the first executive secretary of the Baptist State Convention of North Carolina. Ray was educated at Wake Forest College (A.B., 1903; M.A., 1904) and Cornell University (Ph.D., 1909). In 1915 he married Sallie Shepherd Camp and was the father of Robert C. and John E. Ray, III. Trained as a chemical engineer, he was employed by, and became secretary-treasurer of the Camp Manufacturing Company, Franklin, Va.

He was a deacon, Sunday School teacher, and treasurer of the Franklin Baptist Church; moderator of the Blackwater Association, 1933–35; president, Baptist General Association of Virginia, 1941; president of the board, Virginia Baptist Children's Home, 1934–42; member, Board of Missions and Education, 1943–49. He rendered outstanding service on the finance committee of the Board of Missions and Education and was instrumental in the establishment of the Relief and Annuity program for Virginia Baptist ministers.

IRA D. HUDGINS

RAY, JAMES MELVIN (b. San Saba, Tex., Nov. 11, 1907; d. Tucson, Ariz., May 12, 1966). Pastor and chaplain. Ray married Ann Smithey in 1933. They had three children: James Robert, Mrs. Marsha Ray Turbyfill, and Michele Ray. He earned the A.B. degree from Baylor University in 1941. As a chaplain in World War II he was awarded the following: Bronze star with Oak Leaf Cluster; Presidential Citation; Croix de Guerre with Palm; American Campaign Ribbon; ETO Ribbon with five battle stars; World War II Victory Ribbon; and the French Fourragere. He was a lieutenant colonel in the retired reserve with 17 years of recognized time. Ray held several pastorates in Texas before moving to New Mexico in 1948. While pastor of the First Baptist Church of Carlsbad, N. Mex., 1948–58, he served in the following capacities: Executive Committee, SBC, for two terms; Relief and Annuity Board, SBC, for one term; president of New Mexico Baptist Pastors' Conference; president of New Mexico State Mission Board for two terms; and served on "Morals and Decency Committee" of New Mexico under two governors. He was pastor of Olivet Baptist Church in Honolulu, Hawaii, 1958–60. In Hawaii he served as secretary of the Baptist Foundation of Hawaii and as president of the board of trustees of the Hawaiian Baptist Academy. In Arizona he was pastor of the Boulevard and Wetmore Baptist churches, and served as a member of the executive board of the Arizona convention.

HERBERT E. BERGSTROM

RAY, REX (b. Whitewright, Tex., Nov. 11, 1885; d. Dallas, Tex., Jan. 31, 1958). Southern

Baptist missionary to China and Korea. He received an A.B. degree from Baylor University, Waco, Tex., in 1917. Appointed a missionary to China in 1919, he did evangelistic and educational work in the city of Wuchow and surrounding areas until 1944. In 1920 he married Janet Gilman in Canton, China, and they had five children. Following two years in America, he served as superintendent of the Tai Kam Baptist leper colony until Communist rule forced him to leave. Transferred to Korea in 1951, he did evangelistic and relief work until his retirement in 1955. A son, Daniel B. Ray, is (1970) a missionary in Taejon, Korea.

L. JACK GRAY

***RECREATION, CHURCH.** The leisure revolution which started after World War II moved into full swing during the 1960's. Church recreation came to be one of the most rapidly expanding areas of Southern Baptist church life. The Church Recreation Department was established at the Sunday School Board at the request of the Southern Baptist Convention. Demands for its services increased rapidly from the beginning. Church action during this period sheds some light on this demand. Over 8,000 churches annually report the existence of an elected recreation staff in their program organizations.

Well over $500,000,000 are invested in the recreation facilities of Southern Baptist churches. This is exclusive of camps and assembly grounds owned by churches, associations, state conventions, and SBC bodies. Paid church staff positions with identified recreation responsibilities are common. Each state convention has a staff member with at least a part of his responsibility related to the recreation ministry.

Recreation used as a means of outreach, mission action, enlistment, and education is common. Church recreation speaks directly to the life-style of the leisure-oriented world in which churches today find themselves. Its adaptability to the creative and innovative makes recreation an ideal ally of the endeavors of the church of the leisure society.

While recreational opportunities are most commonly planned for youth, every age group, especially senior adults, receive an increasing ministry through this medium. Recreation can help any type of church to grow in Christian fellowship and understanding. At the same time it can give a church of any stage of development a way of adjusting to its environment, reaching out to its constituency, and communicating its message. Through the use of recreation, churches find a means to accomplish immediate and pragmatic organizational goals. At the same time, churches find in recreation a means by which they can speak to the leisure-related problems of their constituency and community.

ROBERT M. BOYD

REDACTION CRITICISM. A research methodology used primarily in the study of the Synoptic Gospels. Developed by Günter Bornkamm, Hans Conzelmann, Willi Marxsen, and others in the middle fifties, redaction criticism has been widely discussed and utilized in America since about 1967–68. Works on the subject have been available generally in English since 1969.

Redaction criticism seeks to understand the gospels as complete literary works and not as collections of pericopes as in form criticism. The emphasis of this discipline is not upon the community as the causal factor in gospel writing, but upon the writer of the gospel himself, the evangelist, who is considered to be an author in the fullest sense of the term and who articulates his own theological ideas and concepts by means of the gospel he writes.

Therefore, as distinct from form criticism which focuses upon the oral or preliterary period, redaction criticism looks to the actual process of writing the Gospels as a basis for theological evaluation. By means of comparative study the redaction critic seeks to discover variations and similarities in the written materials of the individual Gospels and thereby to determine the use which each author makes of his sources and, hopefully, the theological motivation behind that utilization. Redaction criticism is not antithetical to form criticism but is an extension of form critical insights into the literary process.

BIBLIOGRAPHY: Willi Marxsen, *Mark the Evangelist,* translated by Roy A. Harrisville (1969). Norman Perrin, *What Is Redaction Criticism?* (1969).

DONALD E. COOK

REDDING, JOSEPH (b. Germantown, Fauquier County, Va., 1750; d. Scott County, Ky., Dec., 1815). Converted and baptized by William Marshall in 1771, being 21 years of age with a wife and two children, he began to preach immediately in the surrounding country. John Taylor (*q.v.,* Vol. II) was associated with Redding (sometimes spelled Reding) in this early ministry. In 1772 he moved to South Carolina, but was discontented there, and moved back to his former home in Fauquier County, Va. Because of a disagreement in doctrine with William Marshall, he moved to Hampshire County, nearer the frontier. In the fall of 1779, with a company of emigrants, principally members of churches which he had built up, he took a boat at Redstone (now Brownsville, Pa.) and descended the Monongahela River to Pittsburgh, then down the Ohio. They were delayed because of wrecking the boat and arrived at Bear Grass (Louisville) in Mar. or Apr., 1780. He soon returned to Hampshire County, Va., because of the Indian War in Kentucky. After a sojourn in South Carolina, 1784–89, he returned to Kentucky and became an active preacher in Elkhorn Association. He was pastor of the Great Crossings Church from about 1793 to Apr., 1810, then at Dry Run until the end of his life. He, with Dry Run Church, went into Licking Association in Aug., 1810. LEO T. CRISMON

REDNOUR, AUSTIN GILBERT (b. Steeleville, Ill., Apr. 1, 1901; d. Carbondale, Ill., Aug. 17, 1968). Pastor, associational superintendent of missions, and pioneer missionary in northern Illinois. Son of H. C. and Maude (Williamson) Rednour, he was one of the first students to attend the Southern Illinois College of Bible, located at Southern Illinois University, Carbondale, but received no degree. He married Marjorie Gregory in 1923, who preceded him in death. They had three children: Bill, Wayne, and Eva Mae (Sawyer). In 1956 he married Jane Keith Scarborough. His two stepchildren were Curtiss Scarborough and Marilyn Scarborough Parks.

All of his pastorates were in Illinois, including Baptist churches at Jamestown, Fairview, Willisville, Dutch Ridge, Steeleville, Ellis Grove, Carbondale, and Royalton. His first pastorate was at Jamestown in 1933. He was superintendent of missions in four Illinois associations: Nine Mile (1942–45), Williamson (1945–48), Saline (1948–50), and East Central (1956–63). Many believed his greatest contribution was in 1950–52 as a pioneer missionary for the Illinois Baptist State Association. In this position, he helped develop some of the earliest Southern Baptist work in the Chicago, Ill., and Gary, Ind., areas. He is buried at Steeleville, Ill.

ROBERT J. HASTINGS

REIFF, EVAN ALLARD (b. Bartlesville, Okla., Dec. 4, 1907; d. Abilene, Tex., Mar. 11, 1962). Pastor and educator. Son of Fred Leighton and Sarah L. Reiff, he married Velma Bennett on June 5, 1934. They had three children: Evangeline (Mrs. Nathan Newman), George Frederick, and John David. Reiff received the B.A. from Oklahoma Baptist University, Shawnee, Okla., 1930; and the M.A. (1931) and Ph.D. (1937) from Iowa State University. He taught at Oklahoma Baptist University, 1935–36; Ottawa University, Ottawa, Kans., 1936–43; and Eastern Baptist Theological Seminary, Philadelphia, Pa., 1946–50. He was pastor of First Baptist Church, Atchison, Kans., 1942–46. Reiff served as president of Sioux Falls College, Sioux Falls, S. Dak., 1950–53, and of Hardin-Simmons University, Abilene, Tex., 1953–1962. During his presidency Hardin-Simmons University strengthened the academic program, enlarged the endowment, and increased the financial and physical assets of the school.

CHARLES R. RICHARDSON

***RELIEF AND ANNUITY BOARD.** See Annuity Board.

***RELIGIOUS EDUCATION.**

I. Aims. Religious education, hardly identifiable as an individual or separate discipline prior to the 20th century, is rapidly claiming respect and gaining a sense of purpose and objective.

Of signal consequence is the fact that religious education is serious about being a "practical theology." Aware that its doctrine of God, its Christology, its anthropology, its doctrines of revelation, church, the Scriptures, and salvation must be the basic formative factors in all that is undertaken in its name, religious education can now be seen doing its homework conscientiously for the first time. D. Campbell Wyckoff, in *Theory and Design of Christian Education Curriculum,* indicates that Christian education in America has come through a missionary phase, an educational phase, and is now (1970) in a theological phase. The steps taken by Southern Baptist leaders in this direction are evidence that a theological ground for religious education is being sought. In the local church greater attention to biblical, historical, and systematic theology seems to be developing.

The aim in contemporary religious education to state clearly and define precisely the objectives of religious education also deserves attention. Each denomination has addressed itself to the task of declaring its own objectives. Local churches have joined in the trend. By asking the question, "What are we trying to do through religious education?" religious educators have been able better to center upon outcomes, processes, and criteria for evaluation.

The aim to know and understand the religious and spiritual development levels of the learner is gaining in importance. Growing out of a concern for knowing and meeting individual needs, this aim brings into play the aptitude factor and strives to design materials and organize groups according to religious needs and aptitudes. New plans for grouping and grading are being incorporated in many church programs on the basis of public-school patterns, while at the same time some churches are studying carefully the nongraded system of groupings that is being tried on at least a pilot basis in some of the more progressive public institutions.

Another aim of religious education is to deal seriously with the learning-teaching process. The teacher and the teaching situation are being reevaluated. The role of the minister as educator and the function of the educator as minister are being more clearly defined. Both are being challenged more often to do actual teaching in the local church. What Gordon E. Jackson of Pittsburgh Theological Seminary has to say about the pastor should be applied to the minister of education as well:

> The burden of teaching in the average congregation must fall on the pastor. . . . Therefore, the pastor should be carrying a major load of the teaching of the congregation. Is it too much to expect that his teaching load will be as high as eight to ten classes a week? Obviously, some reorientation of ministry would be necessary. Here each pastor has to make the fitting response before God as to what is crucial in his ministry. . . . It may be a class during the church school hour; another on Sunday evening in lieu of a second preaching service; a mid-week evening class; a class or two with children or youth after school; two or three classes in the early afternoons for women who may be freer

at such time or for retired people; an early morning class for business men; now and then an *ad hoc* class or two arising out of a situation in the church, such as planning for a new building. . . . A pastor can even teach his people how to do careful exegesis, actually whetting the appetites of some to do work in Hebrew and Greek!

Competence of lay teachers and leaders is also an emphasis within the scope of this aim. Pastors and ministers of education are being singled out for the role of leadership trainers. In-service procedures and laboratory workshop techniques are being used in many churches. Assigned subject specialization and faculties of teachers are being suggested.

Most evident of all, and perhaps most important of all, is the aim to make religious education relevant. To be caught up in the all-encompassing function of the church—reconciliation of man to God and of man to man—and to bring this function into full implementation, is the underlying aim of all other aims. The words, "application," "involvement," "service," "mission," and "ministry" are all related to the aim for relevance. From grass roots to executive levels, eagerness to be "doers" of religious education and "not hearers only" grows greater throughout the true church.

ROBERT E. POERSCHKE

II. Curriculum. From 1950 to 1970 practically every evangelical denomination in the United States had a major revision of its curriculum for religious education. This trend began in 1941 at the Atlantic City conference of the Presbyterian Church in the U. S. A. That conference and subsequent conferences resulted in the publication in 1948 of *Christian Faith and Life: A Program for Church and Home.* The Protestant Episcopal Church introduced its new Seabury Curriculum the following year. Other denominational groups also issued new curricula. Books were published setting forth the educational theory and theological foundations underlying the curriculum.

The major publication during the sixties related to curriculum in religious education was *The Church's Educational Ministry: A Curriculum Plan.* This was the report of the Cooperative Curriculum Project in which 16 different denominational groups, including Southern Baptists, participated. The project addressed itself to the basic question, "What kind of curriculum is needed by our churches today in the task of Christian education?" The study embraced a wide spectrum of subjects related to biblical, theological, and educational issues underlying the process of curriculum design.

In its design the project sought to achieve a synthesis of two competing approaches to curriculum in Christian education—subject matter, information or Bible-centered, and learner-centered. This integration of approaches has been "described as the dynamic encounter of the gospel with the persistent life issues of the learner in his whole field of relationships." The design was developed for the use of curriculum planners at the national denominational level and set forth suggested definitions of (1) the objective of Christian education, (2) the scope of the curriculum for Christian education, (3) the context of the curriculum, (4) the learning tasks in Christian education, and (5) the organizing principle of the curriculum. An abridged report for use by curriculum planners on the local church level was published under the title *A Design for Teaching-Learning.*

Southern Baptists have been among the more recent of the curriculum revisers with the release of the Life and Work Curriculum in 1967. This curriculum sought to coordinate the programs of Sunday School, Training Union, Brotherhood, and Woman's Missionary Society and to offer alternatives to existing curriculum for youth and adults in the first two organizations listed.

A new 70 Onward Curriculum was introduced in Oct., 1970, including several alternate series. This was the first time Southern Baptists had fully coordinated curriculum materials for all age groups designed jointly by Woman's Missionary Union, the Brotherhood Commission, and the Sunday School Board.

ROBERT A. PROCTOR, JR.

III. Methodologies. In recent years, many advances have been made in the field of instructional methodology. Indicated here are some of those which seem to be most noteworthy, particularly with regard to their relevance to church-learning activities.

Programmed Instruction.—Programmed instruction has been accepted both for what it can and for what it cannot do. Its main contribution seems to have been in focusing attention on the importance of stating learning goals in specific terms. In this sense it has influenced most other areas of education today. Southern Baptists have produced some programmed materials in the form of special study units and helps for officers in organizations.

Team Teaching.—Recently many churches have initiated team teaching efforts. Unfortunately most of these efforts might be more accurately described by the term "turn teaching." Churches which have used this approach generally have made the traditional "assembly period" into a large group instruction period in which basic Bible teaching has been conducted. Small group follow-up sessions have then been directed by group leaders or teachers who have built upon the foundation laid in the large group. It would be a mistake to say that churches have incorporated flexible grouping as practiced in public schools in connection with team teaching, for there has been little or no individually prescribed instruction upon which flexible grouping might be based.

Closed Circuit Television.—As late as 1970 churches generally made little use of closed circuit television due to the lack of adequate equipment. Churches which developed facilities for closed circuit television found their efforts limited because few libraries of educationally valid videotapes exist.

Cassette Tapes.—Perhaps no other innovative technique offers more promise to churches than the use of cassette tapes designed to elicit learner response. Because of the economy and the greater flexibility afforded by this approach, cassette tapes have preempted to a large degree the dial access audio systems which many colleges adopted in the late sixties. Churches, however, face the same obstacles here as in the use of videotapes. Libraries of educationally valid tapes for use in religious education are nonexistent. The development of teaching guides to accompany the tapes and the use in the tapes of variations of programmed instruction are needed.

Learning Goals and Objectives.—Some progress has been made in the analysis of possibilities of the use of behavioral objectives in religious education. But a great many religious educators have resisted this concept. The resistance it seems has been due largely to a misunderstanding of behavioral objectives, especially as they relate to the effective domain (attitudes and values). Several Southern Baptist agencies have built such instructional objectives into their curriculum materials where feasible. At the present time religious educators need to study carefully the problem of levels of generality in statements of goals and objectives.

BIBLIOGRAPHY: H. P. Colson and R. M. Rigdon, *Understanding Your Church's Curriculum* (1969). W. L. Howse and W. O. Thomason, *A Dynamic Church* (1969). D. R. Hunter, *Christian Education as Engagement* (1963). D. C. Wyckoff, *Theory and Design of Christian Education Curriculum* (1961).
LEROY FORD

***RELIGIOUS HERALD, THE.** With W. E. Cullers as manager, *The Religious Herald* has maintained a circulation of approximately 35,000 subscribers. In Feb., 1968, the trustees sponsored a dinner in honor of the editor, Reuben E. Alley, Sr., who completed 30 years of service with the publication in Sept., 1967. Alley retired as editor on May 31, 1970, and Julian H. Pentecost assumed editorial responsibilities on June 1, 1970. REUBEN E. ALLEY, SR.

***RELIGIOUS LIBERTY.** The economic stability of agencies and particularly institutions such as colleges, hospitals, and homes for children and the aged was threatened in the late fifties and the sixties. This precipitated a struggle for denominational integrity during the rapidly expanding affluence occasioned by a burgeoning productivity and accompanying inflationary pressures.

The purist view of "absolute separation of church and state" was confronted by efforts of denominational leaders and institutional heads who sought to maintain stability in the face of rising costs and increasing enrolments. Governments at all levels were hard pressed to render services to people on a basis of equality and equity. Government programs expanded many times over to fulfil goals and legislation to provide educational, medical, and welfare services to people without regard to race, creed, or origin. Many denominational institutions, long since serving entire communities and states (with some recruiting from the entire nation), found themselves facing the need to restudy and evaluate their purposes, clientele, and functions.

Public funds were becoming increasingly available to persons within institutions of all kinds. Many public programs were available to institutions themselves as the government sought to utilize existing institutions as well as to begin new ones. Contracts for services purchased became a bridge of cooperation between state and federal governments and private institutions. Other major national programs made it possible to erect additional buildings through grants as well as low-interest loans.

Baptists found themselves facing several hard questions in the sixties which related to the principle of religious liberty. Some of the questions were: Should we accept public funds in the form of grants to erect buildings to expand our institutions? Can we properly apply for and use public funds which are available as loans at an interest rate lower than the prevailing commercial rate? Can we deny a student or professor the right to a public grant or loan because he is enrolled or teaching in a private institution? Should we cooperate with government programs at public expense for services rendered by a private institution on a contract basis?

These questions confronted Baptists with a real crisis in the late sixties. The Southern Baptist Convention, under the leadership of its Education Commission, conducted a two-year study, 1965–67, titled "Baptist Education Study Task" (BEST). It involved more than 8,000 persons in study groups, writing, and seminars and climaxed in two three-day conferences in Nashville one year apart. The findings began to document the answer to one basic question, "What is the difference between 'religious liberty' and 'separation of church and state'?"

The study and dialogue approach allowed very little time for polemics and authoritarian viewpoints to sweep people along without thoughtful examination of all the facts and principles involved.

Religious Liberty and Separation of Church and State.—Southern Baptists began to distinguish between the biblical principle of religious liberty and the constitutional provision for its recognition in the nation. They were able also to distinguish between the impossibility of absolutism and a realistic view of separation of church and state. "Absolute separation" came through as a cliché which never was viable and in fact had never been practiced by

Baptists. To be sure, religious freedom was practiced in America, but it was regulated by law. A man could not continue long to practice religion with snakes when people died of snakebite as a result. Nor could a man openly practice bigamy as a religious right. Building codes, traffic regulations, health laws—all restrict churches and church members in their religious practices.

In the late sixties it became clearer than ever before to most responsible Baptist leaders that their institutions were, of necessity, related to public policy in the area of their specialty in terms of their functions. In other words, they were not exclusively "church" as long as they served the public with a function other than religion.

Southern Baptist representatives participated with representatives of other Baptist bodies in annual religious liberty conferences, 1957–68, in Washington, D. C. These conferences contributed significantly to a positive understanding of religious freedom and a viable view of separation of church and state in the 20th century. These consultations dealt with such subjects as the biblical basis of religious liberty, church-state relations in the field of education, the churches and American tax policies, church-state aspects of the churches' involvement in human need, and other topics.

The findings from these conferences became advisory material to the Baptist Joint Committee on Public Affairs. The committee made additional studies and published policy statements on several vital issues. Advisory information was also transmitted to the several Baptist groups comprising the committee through their committee representatives. Various Baptist conventions used such findings and information in adopting positions and actions in annual sessions.

Vatican Council II.—The Roman Catholic Declaration on Religious Freedom approved by Vatican Council II in 1965 represents a turning point for religious freedom. It correlates the tenets of the Roman Church with major Protestant groups. It thus presents a united front by the religious communities of the world on religious liberty.

Two things are evident in this development which are of great significance to Baptists. First is the candor of its basis for freedom within the church. The declaration updated the Roman view that only the Church has rights. It moved to a position which allowed for the premise that people have rights. This dimension is one which makes other religious groups vulnerable to debate on internal freedom in the years ahead. Second, the resolve to exercise full religious liberty by the Catholic fathers does not of itself bring it to pass.

SBC Positions on Religious Freedom and Public Policy.—The SBC, meeting in Detroit in May, 1966, approved the following resolution concerning religious liberty:

In the historic Baptist concern for religious liberty the separation of the state from the church has been and continues to be an important policy.

In view of the renewed efforts to change the effect of the First Amendment, this Convention reaffirms the resolution adopted in 1964 with reference to the adequacy of the First Amendment as the legal basis for implementing our concern. We continue to oppose any and all attempts to modify this guarantee against establishments of religions and against interference with the free exercise of religion.

The importance of the policy of separation of church and state is increased rather than diminished by the overlappings of public concerns with church concerns, and by the numerous complexities associated with public provisions for health, welfare, and education.

In view of the increasing complexity of public programs of fiscal support, we commend the state conventions and the institutional trustees that have undertaken careful analyses of institutional policies with a view to the safeguarding of our historic concern for these principles. We likewise commend the Education Commission for launching a broadly representative study of contemporary denominational programs and needs in higher education.

We urge all who plan or operate religious activities to refrain from seeking public funds for the advancement of sectarian causes. We also urge all public agencies that support educational, health or welfare activities of any kind to safeguard against the use of public funds for the support of, or the advancement of sectarian causes, purposes, or projects.

Southern Baptists spoke to numerous public affairs issues during this period: Social Security, Hill-Burton Act, war and peace, tax aid for churches, religious liberty and the First Amendment, the church-state relations, civil disorder, human freedom, and many others.

Religious Liberty Controversies.—The Southern Baptist Convention and many state conventions spent much time during the period 1954–69 dealing with public affairs issues. Responses of Southern Baptists to two of the major issues of the period, for example, reflect concern for cherished Baptist insights into the Scriptures relating to full religious freedom.

1. Religious Tests for Public Office. The 1960 presidential election brought the nation to another major religious debate. Protestant fears of a Catholic in the White House created a debate on religious tests for public office. Most Southern Baptist spokesmen, resolutions, and published articles at the time viewed the prospect with alarm. The Baptist Joint Committee on Public Affairs was among the few in Baptist ranks that stood for "no religious tests for public office" in the early days of the outbreak of oratory and penmanship.

John F. Kennedy repeatedly asserted his devotion to the policy of separation of church and state, his opposition to an ambassador to the Vatican, and his objection to federal aid to parochial schools. He declared that no one in the Roman Catholic Church spoke for him. Yet the religious issue stubbornly and heatedly persisted. Perhaps the three most significant reasons were the nature of the Catholic faith, certain activities on the part of Kennedy himself, and the political maneuvering of all the politicians.

In May, 1960, the SBC adopted a resolution which supported the constitutional guarantee that a man's personal faith should not be a test of his qualification for public office.

2. Religious Liberty and Public Devotions. Three Supreme Court cases in the sixties resulted in a clarification of the place of religion in the public schools. These were the New York Regents' prayer case (*Engel* v. *Vitale,* 1962), Bible reading in Pennsylvania (*Abington School District* v. *Schempp,* 1963), and Bible reading and the Lord's Prayer in Maryland (*Murray* v. *Curlett,* 1963).

The opinion of the Supreme Court in the New York Regents' prayer case is the underlying philosophy in the decisions in the Pennsylvania and Maryland Bible reading and Lord's Prayer cases. The Court concluded: "Government in this country, be it state or federal, is without power to prescribe by law any particular form of prayer which is to be used as an official prayer in carrying on any program of governmentally sponsored religious activity" (*Engel* v. *Vitale*).

In the New York Regents' prayer case on June 25, 1962, the Supreme Court found that the recitation of prayer is a religious exercise and not merely social heritage. It was declared unconstitutional as a violation of the establishment clause of the First Amendment "because that prayer was composed by government officials as a part of a governmental program to further religious beliefs."

Conclusions which readily can be drawn from a careful study of the decisions are (1) the court did not express hostility to religion; (2) the court did not establish a religion of secularism; (3) the court did not put God out of schools or out of public life in America; (4) the court did not eliminate all religious expressions from public life.

The furor which spread across the nation in the wake of these court decisions found Baptists reluctantly but appropriately seeing the decisions as upholding their biblical insights into religious liberty. They were reluctant to give up cultural privileges in areas where they were in a large majority but could see the validity of the decisions in keeping with their own views of conscience and freedom. These cases were a classic example of the highest court in the land upholding the First Amendment as an adequate safeguard to religious liberty in the nation.

See also Supreme Court of the United States and the First Amendment's Religion Clauses, Vol. III.

JAMES M. SAPP

RELIGIOUS SCENE, NEW DIMENSIONS OF THE UNITED STATES. Martin E. Marty has suggested that the last two decades with reference to the American religious situation fall into three rather clear divisions: "religious revival" in the 1950's, "religious renewal" until about 1965, followed by "religious revolution." Perhaps these designations are too formal and dramatic but they nevertheless suggest "the dimension of change" in recent American religion. The late sixties involved what has been called "retrenchment" in religion and marked—perhaps specifically, perhaps not—a return to "religious revival" with Billy Graham, a Southern Baptist, as its focus. What lies beyond the era of the "Middle American" ushered in by the Nixon administration (1968) is problematical, but the "revolutionary" tides in religion and politics were still quite evident in 1970.

Rapidity of change in the sixties was matched in importance by the extension of the scope of religion. The historian must consider not only the velocity of change but also the increasingly larger stage on which the change occurred. Thus both the accelerating pace of change and an enlarged definition of what it is "really like" to be religious require scrutiny. The current trend is away from stressing religion as localized in certain western institutions to a broad consideration of religious possibilities.

Efforts of the Roman Catholic Church (RCC) and Protestantism in the sixties to adjust to the rapid changes in and the enlarged scope of religion were not notably successful. The effort of Roman Catholicism to update itself, which has actuated a commendable openness toward other traditions, sacred and secular, has been unsuccessful nevertheless at crucial points. The picture presented by the RCC in the current scene is somewhat confused. The hopes of Vatican II, some quite utopian, have been scaled down considerably in the face of the reality of an institution under pressure imposed by an authoritarian past. For example, Pope Paul VI took a hard line against birth control in his Encyclical *Humanae Vitae* (1968). Added to this was his opposition to the softening of clerical celibacy. Despite his view that celibacy offered a challenge which would attract young men into the clergy, 4,000 priests left the RCC in the United States in 1969. And despite his reaffirmation of the Church's ban on artificial birth control, a recent survey shows that 64 per cent of RC wives in America are using the pill and other contraceptives.

Conventional ecclesiastical and theological forms are no longer plausible to a growing number of Roman Catholics, clerical and lay. For example, a Catholic sociologist speaks of "traditional dogma" as "problematical," questions the "relevancy of the old liturgy," and declares the "need for social relevance." Papal teaching has elicited widening confusion among the laity and many Catholic theologians. Speaking of "the revolt in Catholicism," Marty says: "Disunity and not unity, divergence and not convergence characterized life in the church body once pictured as the most unified and most potent as a symbol for larger Christian and human unity."

In Protestantism, the theologians of secularity

began with needed efforts to relate theology to the secular temper of the sixties and some of them ended in esoteric speculation about "the death of God." Others wrestled responsibly to make the Christian faith meaningful to modern man. But theology, whether of the "death of God" variety or aimed at "the secular city," was too pallid and sophisticated to appeal to activist youth who wanted "a part of the action" in order to change the world. And so the religious "action" began to turn to unexpected places like Arthur Blessit's night club on Sunset Strip in Los Angeles, called "His Place," where he appeals to his young congregation in argot clearly understood: "Jesus is just the best trip, man. You don't have to drop acid to get high—all you have to do is to pray and you go all the way to heaven."

Young people are interested not in death—of God or anything else—but life, free in quality and wide-ranging in scope. For the most part they are dropouts of middle class culture. Some occupy a no-man's-land between the values of their parents, which they find uninteresting and uninspiring, and the "hippie" culture of their peers. They are intensely religious in implicit and nontraditional ways, ranging from postdrug fundamentalism to an inspiring dedication to humanity in the Peace Corps. This non-institutional religion appeals particularly to young people, though it is not confined to them. Some of it goes beyond specifically Christian perspectives and takes the form of curiosity concerning spiritualism and extrasensory perception. The occult, sometimes involving witchcraft and black magic, has a surprising appeal. There is some experimentation with drug-induced "religious" experience (LSD, mescaline, etc.).

The current religious situation is characterized by a polarity between adherents of conventional institutional religion (Christianity and Judaism mainly) and avant-garde churchmen who though working within historically rooted religious traditions are involved in experimentation, sometimes radical, in strategy and theology. There is also a growing interest in other "totalistic religions," which William G. McLoughlin has described as "Marxism for the friend of the masses, Pentecostalism for the Biblical literalist, Zen Buddhism for the avant-garde, ritual or mysticism for the highbrow, third-party politics for the activist, affluent heathenism or professional absorption for the middle class."

Huston Smith's study, "Secularization and the Sacred: The Contemporary Scene," contains a brilliant exposition of the "origins and locales of new religiousness," which he pinpoints as eastern mysticism, science and the study of consciousness, and the so-called mind-expanding drugs. "When, in this year of our Lord 1967," wrote Smith, "57 per cent of the American public said 'religion is losing its influence,' they should have said (if given the opportunity to be precise), 'institutional religion is losing its influence in certain areas of life where its presence used to be more evident.'" Then, he added, "But institutionalized religion isn't all of religion, and the fact that the sacred is withdrawing from certain spheres doesn't mean it isn't moving to others."

Maybe Rabbi Stephen Riskin is right when he says that the 20th century is finally "giving the soul its due. We have passed the age of rationalism and are understanding that we relate to a Higher Being." *Time* magazine commented: "In every faith and in every believer, there is once again a burgeoning awareness of God."

BIBLIOGRAPHY: D. R. Cutler, ed., *The Religious Situation: 1968* (1968); *The Religious Situation: 1969* (1969); J. J. Gustafson, ed., *The Sixties: Radical Change in American Religion* (1970).

PENROSE ST. AMANT

***REPRESENTATION, SOUTHERN BAPTIST CONVENTION BASIS OF.** The basis of member representation to the Southern Baptist Convention has remained unchanged since 1957 except that in 1966 the Constitution was amended to provide that "Each messenger shall be a member of the church by which he is appointed." In 1970 the SBC Executive Committee provided that SBC program leaders, not elected as messengers by their churches, could speak without vote on matters pertaining to their programs. ALBERT MCCLELLAN

RESEARCH. See STUDY AND RESEARCH.

***REVIEW AND EXPOSITOR.** The faculty of Southern Baptist Theological Seminary operates the journal through a board of six professors and a staff of five. These eleven professors constitute the editorial board. Each board member normally serves for three years, so rotated as to provide for two new members each year. The staff consists of the editor-in-chief, managing editor, business manager, book review editor, and recording secretary. The president of the seminary serves as editor-in-chief. Other staff officers are elected by the faculty club for five-year terms of service.

Each issue of *Review and Expositor* consists of scholarly articles and book reviews. Until 1959 the articles were largely volunteer and independent of one another as to theme. Since Jan., 1959, each issue is built upon a selected theme, and articles for the most part are prepared by assignment. Themes explored are basically ones relating to biblical and theological study and the nature and ministry of the church. As set forth by President E. Y. Mullins (*q.v.*, Vol. II) in the initial issue in Apr., 1904, each writer bears responsibility for his article, maximum freedom being allowed to the writer. In addition to the usual six or seven articles built around a selected theme, the journal frequently publishes faculty or Founders' Day addresses.

FRANK STAGG

RHODE ISLAND, SOUTHERN BAPTISTS IN. See MARYLAND, BAPTIST CONVENTION OF.

RHODESIA, MISSION IN (cf. Southern Rhodesia, Mission in, Vol. II). Continuing work dating to 1950, the mission opened an encampment in 1957. Two years later, work was extended to Nyasaland (Malawi) and Northern Rhodesia (Zambia), but separate missions were later formed. Advance in the sixties included establishing a publishing house at Gwelo and enlarging Sanyati hospital (1961), forming a convention (1963), and opening recording and photographic studios at Salisbury (1968). In 1969, 56 missionaries were serving in 10 stations, cooperating with 4,049 Baptists in 45 churches.

H. CORNELL GOERNER

RIDDLE, JOHN INGLE (b. Huntsville, Ala., June 27, 1890; d. Huntsville, Ala., May 11, 1968). Educator. Son of James Matthew and Ann (Bradford) Riddle, he married Vera Esslinger, May 29, 1918. Riddle was educated at Butler High School, Huntsville, University of Alabama (A.B.), and Columbia University (M.A., Ph.D.). He was principal of Cullman County High School, 1917–18, education director of Camp Sheridan, 1918–19, principal of Etowah County High School, 1920–25, superintendent of schools, Tuskegee, Ala., 1925–28, assistant state supervisor of secondary education 1929–32, teacher at Alabama College, Montevallo, Ala., 1933–42, and president of Judson College, Marion, Ala., 1943–60. He retired to Huntsville, Ala. He was author of *The Six Year Rural High Schools* (1937) and writer of Sunday School lessons and articles for church and school publications. He was a member of the Southern Baptist Education Commission, the rural school survey commission, president of Alabama Association of Secondary School Principals and Association of Colleges for Women, a Mason, and a member of Pi Gamma Mu and Phi Delta Kappa.

MRS. A. HAMILTON REID

***RIDGECREST BAPTIST ASSEMBLY.** Since 1956 the Sunday School Board has invested more than $500,000 annually in capital improvements at this assembly. The outstanding project was the replacement of historic Pritchell Hall with a new 105-bedroom unit which serves as a focal point for the entire assembly grounds. In addition to the bedrooms, Pritchell Hall contains the administrative offices, reservation office, gift shop, several conference rooms, and two large lobby areas for guests.

Other housing facilities built since 1956 include Whiteoak Lodge, Woodland Lodge, three Mount View units, boys and girls staff dormitories, and Springdale family units. Crystal Springs Annex was built as conference space and a new warehouse and maintenance buildings were completed.

In 1966–67 Rhododendron Hall was replaced by a new modern unit including 49 bedrooms, several multi-purpose classrooms, a 450-seat auditorium, and a 450-seat dining hall with a new kitchen.

On Nov. 1, 1967, Kenneth McAnear succeeded Willard K. Weeks who had served as manager since Nov. 1, 1950. In 1968 Holly Hall was constructed containing 64 bedrooms. The following year a 32-unit Royal Gorge Apartment complex was completed and a campground for tent and trailer camping was opened.

Beginning with the winter of 1967, Ridgecrest became a year-round assembly. Many special denominational, state, and church conferences and retreats are held throughout the winter months.

Camp Crestridge for Girls, started in 1955, continues to develop at a rapid rate under the direction of Arvine Bell. Several new buildings were constructed, with the chapel building serving as a camp focal point.

Monroe Ashley was named director of Camp Ridgecrest for Boys in Feb., 1969. Several new buildings were completed since 1956. Leadership of the camp has been under the direction of 15 managers since 1929, namely: Frank E. Burkhalter, Charles W. Burts, John W. Hughston, Jr., J. D. Franks, Jr., Darrell C. Richardson, Richard C. Burts, Jr., J. W. Hill, Perry Morgan, Nat J. Brittain, James R. Howlett, George W. Pickering, Harry McCall, Jr., Wayne Chastain, Kenneth Bryant, Darrell C. Richardson, and Monroe Ashley.

Approximately 38,000 guests registered at Ridgecrest in 1969 for worship, fellowship, conference, and leadership training.

HUBERT B. SMOTHERS and H. E. INGRAHAM

RIDGEWAY, ELMER (b. Kenton, Tenn., June 18, 1887; d. Oklahoma City, Okla., Sept. 7, 1968). Minister and denominational leader. Educated at Union University (A.B.) and Southwestern Baptist Theological Seminary, he also received a D.D. from Howard Payne College. During his first pastorate at Davis, Okla., he married Frances Dodson in 1910. He served pastorates at Sallisaw, Stillwater, Cordell, Duncan, Blackwell, and Frederick, in Oklahoma; and at Gadsden, Ala., and San Angelo, Tex. In 1934 he became pastor of Immanuel Church, Oklahoma City, and while there (1940) he led a statewide debt-retirement campaign for the Baptist General Cnvention of Oklahoma. He was Brotherhood and institutional secretary for the Oklahoma convention, 1943–46, and state evangelist, 1946–48. In 1948 he became pastor at Crown Heights, Oklahoma City, where he served until his retirement in 1952.

J. M. GASKIN

RIGELL, WILLIAM RICHARD (b. Slocomb, Geneva County, Ala., Nov. 4, 1887; d. Johnson City, Tenn., Apr. 1, 1963). Educated at a Baptist academy at Newton, Ala., Howard College, University of Chicago (M.A., Ph.B.), Union Theological Seminary, Rigell later received the D.D. from Howard College. He married Ethel Gillespie of Birmingham in 1919. They had two children, W. R., Jr., and Martha Elizabeth. He was a YMCA worker with the army, 1916–18. Rigell was pastor of the following First churches in Alabama: Prattville, 1916–18, Sheffield, 1919–21, and Gadsden, 1921–30. He was pastor of the Central Baptist Church, Johnson City, Tenn., 1930–53. He was an instructor in religion at East Tennessee State College until his retirement in 1962. Rigell served on the executive boards of the Alabama Tennessee Baptist conventions, and on the Foreign and Home Mission boards. He was a trustee of Howard, Carson-Newman, and Virginia Intermont colleges. Rigell wrote *Investments in Christian Living* (1930), and *Prophetic Preaching* (1936).

JAMES A. CANADAY

RILEY, BENJAMIN FRANKLIN (b. Monroe County, Ala., July 16, 1849; d. Birmingham, Ala., Dec. 14, 1925). Minister, educator, and historian. Son of Enoch and Sophronia (Autrey) Riley, he attended Erskine College (B.A., 1871), Southern Baptist Theological Seminary for one year, Crozer Theological Seminary (Pennsylvania), 1874–76. He received the following honorary degrees: the D.D. from the University of Alabama (1885), Erskine College (1887), and Baylor College (1903); the LL.D. from Simmons College, Texas (1907); and F.S.Sc. from the Society of Science, Letters and Art, London, England (1898). He was ordained as a Baptist minister in 1872. Riley married Emma Shaw on June 21, 1876. They had four boys and four girls. He served as pastor of the Baptist churches of Carlowville, Snow Hill, and Livingston (all in Ala.) during 1876; the Baptist churches of Albany, Ga., 1877–78; Opelika, Ala., 1879–82; and First Church, Houston, Tex., 1900–07. Riley was president of Howard College in Birmingham, Ala., 1888–93. He served as professor of English and Oratory at the University of Georgia, 1893–1900. While at the university, he preached locally, toured Europe and the United States, and wrote. In 1907 Riley accepted the full-time job of president of the Anti-Saloon League of Texas. In June, 1909, Riley moved to Birmingham, Ala., as organizer and head (to 1913) of the newly formed Southern Negro Anti-Saloon Federation. In retirement he wrote, lectured, and preached regularly. In 1909 he was vice-president of the Southern Baptist Convention. Among the many books which Riley wrote are *History of the Baptists of Alabama* (1895), *A History of the Baptists in the Southern States East of the Mississippi* (1898), *History of the Baptists of Texas* (1907), *The White Man's Burden* (1910), *The Life and Times of Booker T. Washington* (1916), *The Baptists in the Building of the Nation* (1922), and *A Memorial History of the Baptists of Alabama* (1923). Riley is buried in Elmwood Cemetery, Birmingham.

TERRY L. JONES

RISK, DAVID FRANKLIN (b. Long Beach, Calif., Apr. 19, 1888; d. St. Louis, Mo., Jan. 21, 1962). Converted at Weston, Mo., he graduated from William Jewell in 1911. Risk served as pastor of the following Baptist churches in Missouri: Weston, Pleasant Hill, Lamar, Salisbury, Clinton, and Water Tower in St. Louis. He was elected moderator of the St. Louis Baptist Association and of the Missouri Baptist General Association, 1956–57. He served on the boards of Hannibal-LaGrange College, Missouri Baptist Children's Home, and Sunday School Board, SBC. Risk married Clara Van Hoy, 1913, and they had one son, Edwin, and four daughters: Ellen Herbst, Shirley Clark, Clare Nelson, and Martha Jean Votaw.

DORAN C. MCCARTY

ROBINSON, HENRY WHEELER (b. Northampton, Eng., Feb. 7, 1872; d. Oxford, Eng., May 12, 1945). British Old Testament scholar. Robinson became a member of College Street Baptist Church, Northampton, on profession of faith, Mar. 28, 1888. He was educated at Regent's Park College, London, the University of Edinburgh (M.A., 1895), Oxford University (B.A., 1898), and he studied briefly in Marburg University and Strassburg University.

After his marriage to Alice Laura Ashford in 1900, Robinson was pastor successively of the Baptist Church in Pitlockry in Perthshire, 1900–03, and of St. Michael's Baptist Church, Coventry, 1903–06. While professor of church history and philosophy of religion in Rawdon Baptist College, Leeds, 1906–20, he gained wide recognition through the three books he wrote. A serious illness in 1913 made a profound impression on him which is reflected, in part, in a trilogy republished together in 1955 under the title, *The Cross in the Old Testament.*

Elected principal of Regent's Park College, London, in 1920, he led in relocating it fully in 1938 as a school attached to Oxford University. During his years at Oxford, Robinson taught Old Testament, a field in which he possessed exceptional gifts. He retired as principal of Regent's Park in 1942.

Robinson was a committed Baptist. He served as president of the Baptist Historical Society, 1921–45, and was the author of *Baptist Principles Before the Rise of Baptist Churches* (1911) and *The Life and Faith of the Baptists* (1927). An extensive bibliography of Robinson's scholarly work appears in a festschrift, *Studies in History and Religion* (1942), edited by Ernest A. Payne. A memoir, *Henry Wheeler Robinson,* written by Payne, appeared in 1946. Highlights of Robinson's scholarly work are his emphasis on Christian experience, a study of Hebrew psychology, an effort to understand suffering, and the relations of time and eternity.

RAYMOND BRYAN BROWN

ROBINSON, JOSEPH RAYMOND (b. Baltimore, Md., Feb. 3, 1902; d. Wake Forest, N. C., June 3, 1955). Pastor, seminary instructor, and business manager. Son of Joseph S. and Minnie Wigginton Robinson, he was a graduate of Hargrave Military Academy (Chatham, Va.), University of Richmond (A.B., 1931), Union Theological Seminary in Richmond (B.D., 1934), and Southern Baptist Theological Seminary (Th.M., 1948). He married Katherine Wilmoth of Chase City, Va., June 27, 1931. They had one son, Joseph Carrol. Ordained in 1936 at the Second Baptist Church of Richmond, Va., he held three pastorates in Virginia: Maysville Field in Buckingham County, Liberty of Newport News, and Buckroe, Hampton. Also, he served as pastor of the First Church of Brodhead, Ky. In 1951, he was elected bursar of Southeastern Baptist Theological Seminary where he "rendered yeoman service in helping to organize the young seminary." In addition to his duties as business manager, he taught a class in homiletics (1951–52), assisted S. L. Stealey (*q.v.*) in church history (1952–53), and worked with setting up the library. He died of a heart attack at his desk on June 3, 1955, and is buried in the Seminary Cemetery at Wake Forest, N. C.

JAMES H. BLACKMORE

ROBINSON, THEODORE HENRY (b. Edinbridge, Kent, England, Aug. 9, 1881; d. Ealing, England, June 26, 1964). British Old Testament scholar. The son of W. V. and Emily Jane (Page) Robinson, he was educated at St. John's College, Cambridge, Regent's Park College, and the University of Goettingen. He received the D.D., Litt.D., and Th.D. degrees. Robinson married Marie Helen Joseph in 1906. They had one daughter.

Robinson served as professor of Hebrew and Syriac, Serampore College, Bengal, India, 1908–15. He was appointed lecturer in Semitic Languages, University College, Cardiff, in 1915. He remained there until he retired in 1944, having been given the title of professor in 1927. While at University College, he also served as tutor in South Wales Baptist College, Cardiff.

Robinson was one of the founders of the Society for Old Testament Study, served as president in 1928 and 1946, and was honorary secretary, 1917–46. He was the first convener of the Old Testament panel of the New English Bible. His international stature as an Old Testament scholar was recognized in 1950, when a festschrift, entitled *Studies in Old Testament Prophecy* was published in his honor, containing articles written by an international group of scholars.

A bibliography of Robinson's works through 1946 is included in his festschrift. He is especially well known for *An Introduction to the Books of the Old Testament* (1934) (with W. O. E. Oesterley), *The Decline and Fall of the Hebrew Kingdoms* (1926), *Israel in the Eighth and Seventh Centuries,* and *An Outline Introduction to the History of Religions* (1926). He was the author of commentaries on Matthew and Hebrews in the Moffatt series. He also contributed 78 articles to the *Encyclopedia Britannica,* 14th edition (1929). Robinson's piety is especially evident in his book *St. Mark's Life of Jesus.*

RAYMOND BRYAN BROWN

ROCKY MOUNTAIN BAPTIST. A monthly bulletin under this name began publication in Nov., 1952, by the Southern Baptist Association of Colorado, S. W. Driggers, editor. The association publication ceased Dec., 1955. Colorado Baptist General Convention began publication of *Rocky Mountain Baptist,* as official publication, Mar., 1956. Willis J. Ray, executive secretary of the convention, edited the paper until Dec., 1959, when J. Kelly Simmons, editor of the *Baptist Beacon* of Arizona, was elected editor. In Jan., 1960, the paper became a weekly publication. Simmons resigned May 19, 1961, to become editor of the *California Southern Baptist,* and Ray again assumed editorship. In June, 1962, O. L. Bayless, secretary of evangelism for the Colorado convention, assumed duties as editor. Bayless served in dual capacity until Jan. 1, 1965, when he became full-time editor. He changed the format from a magazine to a tabloid newspaper. The paper is financed by subscriptions, advertising, and the Cooperative Program. In 1969 the circulation was 10,300. O. L. BAYLESS

RODEN, MARGARET FROST (b. Lexington, Ky., June 13, 1881; d. Louisville, Ky., Sept. 17, 1961). Daughter of J. M. Frost (*q.v.*, Vol. I), she was educated at Ward's Seminary and Vanderbilt University, Nashville, Tenn. She was a capable speaker and did general elementary field work and writing for the Sunday School Board on a free-lance basis from 1910 until she married George E. Roden in 1941.

HOWARD P. COLSON

RODGERS, JOHN BETHEL (b. Polk County, Fla., Dec. 4, 1881; d. Miami, Fla., Apr. 26, 1968). Pastor and denominational leader. Rodgers married Zula Fincher, Apr. 2, 1911. They had four children: John B., Jr., Evelyn, Martha Joyce, and Betty. Licensed to the ministry by First Church (now Central), Miami, he was ordained in 1907 by First Church, DeLand. He was a student at Stetson University in 1904 and attended Southern Baptist Theological Seminary in 1916. The following year he began mission work in Miami Baptist Association extending from West Palm Beach to Key West. He was the prime organizer of several Miami area churches, including First, South Miami (Larkin); and First, Perrine. He assisted in organizing several other area churches: Stanton Memorial; Allapattah; First, Hialeah; Seventy-Ninth Street (West Little River); Emmanuel (Faith); First, North Miami; First, Hollywood; First, Dania; Northwood, West Palm Beach; and churches in Lake Worth, Pahokee, Belle Glade, and South Bay. Rodgers was the first director of mission work for the Florida Baptist State Board of Missions.

He was pastor of churches in Oviedo, Green Cove Springs, Mayo, Alachua, Milton, Bowling Green, and Panama City; he also served Lemon City (now First Church), Miami, and Queens Park Church (now Lakeview), Miami. Rodgers has been described as "the greatest single Baptist servant in Southeast Florida in the earlier part of Twentieth Century." He is buried in the Dade Memorial Cemetery, Dade County, Fla. HANKINS F. PARKER

ROGERS, JAMES STERLING, SR. (b. Mayfield, Graves Co., Ky., Mar. 3, 1871; d. Conway, Ark., Apr. 24, 1963). Minister, executive, educator. Son of James Thomas and Martha Ann (Sawyer) Rogers, he married Sallie Curry, Dec. 23, 1893. Their children were Velna Lee (Mrs. Ed. S. Campbell), 1897, James Sterling, Jr., 1905, Martha Jean (Mrs. Frank Nunnally), 1912, Mary Louise (Mrs. V. H. Gregson), 1921. He married Virgie Speaker in 1951 and Mrs. Clem Wiley in 1955. As a teen-ager Rogers moved to Paragould, Green Co., Ark., in 1885. Denied an education in early years, he graduated from grammar school, Paragould, 1895, H. S. Thompson's Classical Institute, Paragould, 1898; Ouachita Baptist College (A.B., 1901); Southern Baptist Theological Seminary (Th.M., 1904); Southwestern Baptist Theological Seminary (Th.D., 1914). He also attended Clinton (Ky.) College, University of Chicago, and Moody Bible Institute (Chicago). Ouachita College awarded him a D.D. degree in 1912. Converted and baptized into Oak Grove Baptist Church (Ky.) in 1881, he was ordained by Rock Hill Baptist Church, Paragould, in 1891. Arkansas pastorates included Clarendon, 1904; Searcy, 1904–07; Ohio Street, Pine Bluff. Rogers was professor of Bible, Ouachita College, 1911–12, 1914–15, and professor of New Testament, Southwestern Baptist Seminary, 1919–21; executive secretary of Arkansas Baptist State Convention 1908–11, 1915–19, 1921–29; president of Central Baptist College, 1929–41; president of Arkansas Baptist State Convention, 1941–42; author *The History of Arkansas Baptists* (1948).

GEORGE T. BLACKMON

ROSSELL, WILLIAM HARVEY (b. Beverly, Burlington City, N. J., Nov. 8, 1914; d. Fort Hamilton, N. Y., Aug. 12, 1964). Army chaplain, seminary professor, and author. His parents were William Redding and Mary Beyer Rossell. He received the B.A. degree from Elizabethtown College in 1939. He earned the following degrees from Eastern Baptist Theological Seminary: Th.B., 1937; B.D., 1941; Th.M., 1947. In 1949 he completed a Ph.D. degree in Hebrew and Cognate languages at Dropsie College. Rossell was commissioned as an Army chaplain in Sept., 1942. He served with distinction in the Pacific Theatre for two years attaining the rank of Major, winning the Purple Heart and two battle stars. Rossell served as professor of Biblical Philology at Central Baptist Theological Seminary in Kansas City, Kans., 1949–54; and as professor of Old Testament at Southwestern Baptist Theological Seminary, Ft. Worth, Tex., 1954–64. He wrote, *A Handbook of Aramaic Magical Texts* (1953), *A Glossary of Ruth* (1954), and *Handbook of Ruth* (1957). Rossell married Marguerite Hoover in 1943. They had two sons: John Edward and David William. Rossell was buried at Mt. Holly, N. J.

RALPH L. SMITH

ROUNDS, JAMES BURLEY (b. Drumbo, Ontario, Canada, Mar. 9, 1876; d. Oklahoma City, Okla., July 21, 1965). Minister, missionary, and denominational statesman. He received a two-year graduate degree in theology from Southern Baptist Theological Seminary in 1897 and a D.D. from Oklahoma Baptist University in 1922. Ordained to the ministry at Caney, Kans., in 1899 his pastorates included Dewey, Okla., and Trinity, Oklahoma City. He was missionary to the Indians, 1901–11; state BYPU secretary in Oklahoma, 1912–19; assistant corresponding (executive) secretary for the Baptist General Convention of Oklahoma, 1919–22, and corresponding secretary, 1922–23. In 1917 he helped found Falls Creek Baptist Assembly, Davis, Okla. Rounds directed Indian Missions work for the Home Mission Board, 1943–51. Books written include *The Revelation* and *The Ten Commandments for Today.* J. M. GASKIN

ROUSE, IRVING ELDRIDGE (b. Pearl River County, Miss., Sept. 16, 1894; d. Tallahassee, Fla., Aug. 29, 1959). Son of a farmer, George Irving Rouse, and Harrett Corine Newman, he was educated at Pearl River County Agricultural High School, Poplarville, and Mississippi College, graduating in 1920. While in the United States Navy (July 6, 1917–Dec. 24, 1918), he attended Harvard. He taught and coached athletics at Agricultural High School, Lafayette County, Oxford, Miss. (1920–21); was principal of Mississippi Industrial and Training School, Columbia (1922); was dean of Hazard Junior College, Hazard, Ky. (1929–31). He married Sarah Allman, Aug. 27, 1929. While a pastor in Louisville, Ky. (1931–41), he earned his Ph.D. from the Southern Baptist Theological Seminary. From the pastorate of the Fifth Avenue Baptist Church, Hattiesburg (1941–46), he was elected president of Mississippi Woman's College, Hattiesburg, Oct. 14, 1946. Under his energetic leadership the school was reopened in 1947 as a senior college for women. The Mississippi Baptist Convention made it a co-educational senior college in 1953. It was renamed William Carey College and a men's dormitory was built. He offered his resignation Apr. 25, 1956, effective July 1, 1956. The new library building was dedicated in 1958 as the Rouse Library. Rouse was buried in Louisville, Miss.

C. B. HAMLET, III

ROUTH, EUGENE COKE (b. Plum, Fayette County, Tex., Nov. 26, 1874; d. Dallas, Tex., May 12, 1966). Son of Joseph Edward and Mary Ellen (Stramler) Routh, he was educated at the University of Texas (B.A., 1897). He received the D.D. from Baylor University in 1918. He married Mary Mildred Wroe on Dec. 20, 1897. They had six children: Mary Lucile (Mrs. Clinton E. Burnett), Ross Holland, Alice

Elizabeth (Mrs. J. C. Pool), Porter Wroe, Eugene Copass, and Leila Katherine (Mrs. W. W. Arnett). After the death of his first wife, he married Mary Alice Routh on July 7, 1926.

Ordained a minister in May, 1901, he served as associational missionary of Lampass (1901–03) and San Marcos (1903) associations, both in Texas. After serving as pastor of Lockhart Baptist Church, Lockhart, Tex., 1903–07, Routh served as editor of the following Baptist publications: *The South Texas Baptist* (San Antonio), 1907–12, the Texas *Baptist Standard,* 1912–28, the Oklahoma *Baptist Messenger,* 1928–43, and the Foreign Mission Board, SBC, publication *The Commission,* 1943–48. Among the 11 books he wrote, the following are most notable: *The Story of Oklahoma Baptists* (1932), *The Word Overcoming the World* (1941), and *Adventures in Christian Journalism* (1951). Routh spent the last few years of his life at the Buckner Baptist Trew Home in Dallas, Tex. TERRY L. JONES

ROWLEY, HAROLD HENRY (b. Leicester, England, Mar. 24, 1890; d. Cheltenham, Oct. 4, 1969). British Baptist Old Testament scholar, missionary to China. Son of Richard and Emma Rowley, he was educated at Wyggeston School, Leicester; Bristol Baptist College and Bristol University (M.A.); Mansfield College and St. Catherine's Society, Oxford (B. Litt.); and the University of London (D.D.). In 1918 he married Gladys B. Shaw; they were parents of one son and three daughters.

He served as minister of the United Church (Baptist-Congregational), Wells, Somerset, 1917–22; missionary of the Baptist Missionary Society in China, 1922–30 (and associate professor of Old Testament literature, Shantung Christian University, 1924–29); assistant lecturer in Semitic languages, University College of South Wales and Monmouthshire, Cardiff, 1930–34; professor of Semitic languages, University College of North Wales, Bangor, 1935–45 (also lecturer in the history of religions, 1940–45; vice-principal, 1940–45; dean, Bangor School of Theology, 1936–45); and professor of Semitic languages and literature, 1945–49, professor of Hebrew language and literature, 1949–59, dean of the Faculty of Theology, 1953–56, and emeritus, 1959–69, of the University of Manchester.

Rowley served as examiner in Hebrew and Semitic languages and other related disciplines for various British and continental universities during periods between 1936 and 1963. He was awarded honorary doctorates by the universities of Durham, Wales, Oxford, Edinburgh, Manchester, Uppsala, Zürich, Marburg, McMaster, and Strasbourg. He was a Fellow of the British Academy (and recipient of its Burkitt Medal in 1951), member of the Norwegian Academy of Science and Letters, foreign member of the Royal Flemish Academy, member of the Royal Society of Letters of Lund, honorary member of the Society of Biblical Literature (U. S. A.), and honorary fellow of the School of Oriental and African Studies, London.

Rowley served as joint secretary of the Society for Old Testament Study, 1946–60 (and president in 1950), as president of the Baptist Union of Great Britain and Ireland, 1957–58, and as chairman of the Baptist Missionary Society, 1961–62. He delivered the Schweich Lectures (1948), the Julius Brown Gay Lectures at Southern Baptist Theological Seminary (1953), the Jordan Bequest Lectures (1954), and the Edward Cadbury Lectures (1965). His writings include the following: *Aspects of Reunion* (1923); *The Aramaic of the Old Testament* (1929); *Darius the Mede and the Four World Empires in the Book of Daniel* (1939); *The Relevance of the Bible* (1942); *Submission in Suffering: A Comparative Study of Eastern Thought* (1944); *The Missionary Message of the Old Testament* (1945); *The Re-discovery of the Old Testament* (1946); *European Scholars and Publications Chiefly Relating to the Old Testament During the War Years* (1946); *The Authority of the Bible* (1949); *The Biblical Doctrine of Election* (1950); *The Growth of the Old Testament* (1950); *From Joseph to Joshua: Biblical Traditions in the Light of Archaeology* (1950); (ed.) *Studies in Old Testament Prophecy: Presented to Theodore H. Robinson on His Sixty-Fifth Birthday* (1950); *Submission in Suffering and Other Essays in Eastern Thought* (1951); (ed.) *The Old Testament and Modern Study* (1951); *The Servant of the Lord and Other Essays on the Old Testament* (1952); *The Zadokite Fragments and the Dead Sea Scrolls* (1952); *The Unity of the Bible* (1953); *The Dead Sea Scrolls and Their Significance* (1955); *The Faith of Israel* (1956); *Prophecy and Religion in Ancient China and Israel* (1956); *Jewish Apocalyptic and the Dead Sea Scrolls* (1957); *The Dead Sea Scrolls and the New Testament* (1957); (ed.) *Eleven Years of Bible Bibliography* (1957); *The Dead Sea Scrolls from Qumran* (1958); *The Changing Pattern of Old Testament Studies* (1959); *The Teach Yourself Bible Atlas* (1960); (O. T. ed.) *Peake's Commentary on the Bible* (rev. ed., 1962); *Men of God; Studies in Old Testament History and Prophecy* (1963); *From Moses to Qumran* (1963); (co-ed.) [*Hastings'*] *Dictionary of the Bible* (rev. ed., 1963); (ed.) *A Companion to the Bible* (rev. ed., 1963); *Worship in Ancient Israel* (1967); *The Origin and Significance of the Apocrypha* (1967); *Dictionary of Bible Themes* (1968); and *Dictionary of Bible Personal Names* (1968). Rowley was editor of *The Journal of Semitic Studies* from 1956 to 1960. A *Festschrift* was presented to Rowley on his 65th birthday: *Wisdom in Israel and in the Ancient Near East,* ed. M. Noth and D. Winton Thomas.

JAMES LEO GARRETT, JR. and RAYMOND BRYAN BROWN

***ROYAL SERVICE.** The 50th Anniversary of *Royal Service* was celebrated in 1956 with a year-long observance. The slogan for the year was "Every Woman with Her Own *Royal Service*." The July number was designated the anniversary issue. Forecaster, a promotional section, was added in Oct., 1957. Ethalee Hamric became editor of *Royal Service* in Jan., 1957, when Juliette Mather retired. In Oct., 1969, when Ethalee Hamric accepted responsibility for *Dimension,* Rosanne Osborne became editor of *Royal Service*. Subscriptions in 1956 were 298,076 and in 1968 were 453,263.

DORIS DEVAULT

RURAL-URBAN MISSIONS, HOME MISSION BOARD PROGRAM OF. The Department of Urban-Rural Missions (renamed Rural-Urban Missions in 1966) was created in the HMB's 1963 reorganization. Lewis W. Newman, director of in-service guidance and the board's ministry to rural churches in the Department of Associational Missions, was named secretary.

Assigned to the new department were the board's ministries in mountain missions; in-service guidance; church development; resort missions; and cooperative work with state conventions, associations, and churches located in open country and in centers with populations up to 50,000.

C. Wilson Brumley became department secretary Jan. 1, 1966. John B. McBride, elected assistant July 1, 1966, and Roy W. Owen, elected assistant Jan. 1, 1968, respectively give direction to mountain and resort missions work and leadership to in-service guidance and rural and small-city areas.

Increased leisure time and the proliferation of resort communities received attention through research, conferences, and pilot projects. Awareness conferences, projects using college students in the summer, use of US-2 missionaries, and direct financial assistance became procedures to assist churches, associations, and state conventions in ministering to leisure/resort communities.

Mountain missions conferences and church-centered missions programs have been emphasized in Appalachia. In 1967 the board began working cooperatively with other denominations in the Commission on Religion in Appalachia, emphasizing consultation; research, study, and education; coordination; and projects.

The board's in-service guidance ministry participates in providing field guidance, denominational information and history, and curriculum materials to assist students serving rural churches. Working with state mission boards, the board by 1970 was in consultation with five seminaries, three Bible schools, and 16 colleges and universities.

Rural and small cities received attention through two Convention-wide rural church conferences in 1959 and 1966. Declining rural communities, rural-urban fringe, in-service training for rural ministers, poverty, and ministering to leisure/resort communities were focal points of study, research, and planning during the sixties. Assistance is given through church pastoral aid and consultation in establishing churches in conventions organized since 1940.

See also RURAL MISSIONS, Vol. II.

C. WILSON BRUMLEY

RUSSELL, SAMUEL DREW (b. Nocona, Tex., May 27, 1917; d. Wichita, Kans., Jan. 4, 1967). Son of Jessee A. and Myrtle (Williams) Russell, he lived most of his life in Oklahoma and Texas where his father was a well-known pastor of Baptist churches. He was graduated from Wayland Baptist Junior College and Oklahoma Baptist University (1939), and did graduate work at Baylor University and Southwestern Baptist Theological Seminary. While serving in his first pastorate at Omega, Okla., 1938, he was ordained by the First Baptist Church, Watonga, Okla. Following his graduation from college, he served a two-year pastorate at Cranfils Gap, Tex., where he met and married Council Fanette Jones. They had one daughter, Montie Ann. Russell served 10 years as superintendent of missions for the Union Baptist Association, Oklahoma. He then served as pastor of the Kentucky Avenue Baptist Church, Oklahoma City, for four years and of the First Baptist Church, Anadarko, Okla., for three years. He then served the churches of the Wichita, Kans. area, and as executive secretary of the Sedgwick County Baptist Association, Dec., 1, 1958, to Feb. 28, 1966, a tenure that saw the doubling of most phases of the work. His leadership was marked by a strong evangelistic emphasis and wise counsel in church administration and religious education. He served as associate executive secretary-treasurer of the Kansas Convention, supervising the Department of Missions from Mar. 1, 1966, until his death in a train-car accident.

N. J. WESTMORELAND

***RUSSIA, BAPTISTS OF.** See ALL-SOVIET COUNCIL OF EVANGELICAL CHRISTIANS-BAPTISTS AND COUNCIL OF CHURCHES OF THE EVANGELICAL CHRISTIANS AND BAPTISTS.

RYLAND, GARNETT. (b. King and Queen County, Va., Dec. 17, 1870; d. Richmond, Va., Feb. 2, 1962). College professor and Baptist historian. Scion of noted Virginia families, his parents were Charles H. (*q.v.*, Vol. II) and Alice Marion (Garnett) Ryland. Educated at Richmond College (A.M., 1892) and Johns Hopkins (Ph.D., Chemistry, 1898), he taught at Brownsville Female College, Tenn., 1893–94; Beaumont College, Ky., 1894–95. He held professorships at the University of Maine, 1898–1901; Converse College, S.C., 1901–03; Georgetown College, Ky., 1903–17; University of Richmond, Va., 1917–45 and professor emeritus, 1945–62.

Ryland was a member of Phi Beta Kappa and Phi Kappa Phi; fellow, A.A.A.S.; fellow, Chemical Society (London); Councilor, A.C.S.; president, Virginia Academy of Science; chairman, Virginia Commission on Interracial Cooperation;

trustee, Virginia Union University.

He was author of *The Baptists of Virginia, 1699–1926* (Richmond, 1955), and numerous historical and scientific papers. He was secretary–treasurer and librarian of the Virginia Baptist Historical Society; deacon, Westhampton Baptist Church, Richmond; moderator, Dover Baptist Association (1929–30); member, Virginia Baptist General Board (1933–43).

On Dec. 21, 1909, he married Lewella Payne, Scott County, Ky. His children are: Mary (Mrs. Donald R. Fessler); Charles H.; Alice (Mrs. Robert E. Giles); R. Payne; Hannah (Mrs. Julian D. Sanger). He received honorary Sc.D. from Georgetown College and University of Richmond. He was buried at the Upper King and Queen Baptist Church, King and Queen County, Va. WOODFORD B. HACKLEY

S

SACRED HARP. A shaped note tunebook compiled by B. F. White (*q.v.*, Vol. II) and E. J. King of Hamilton, Ga., printed in Philadelphia in 1844. In its 264 pages were included newly composed tunes, but more significantly appeared those sacred folk tunes which were a common heritage of folks in the South. Many of these tunes had become "attached" to the hymns in the "words only" collections of such Baptist compilers as Andrew Broaddus (*q.v.*, Vol. I), William Dossey, Staunton S. Burdett, and Jesse Mercer (*q.v.*, Vol. II).

This tunebook and others of its kind by Southern compilers preserved a heritage of such sturdy folk tunes as "Bellevue" ("How firm a foundation"), "Amazing Grace" ("Amazing grace, how sweet the sound"), "Pisgah" ("When I can read my title clear"), "Holy Manna" ("Brethren, we have met to worship"), "Promised Land" ("On Jordan's stormy banks I stand"), and "Arise" ("Come, ye sinners, poor and needy").

The enduring character of this tunebook is evidenced by the fact that *Sacred Harp* singings may be found each week throughout the year somewhere in the areas of Alabama, Georgia, Florida, Tennessee, Mississippi, and Texas. According to the 1969–70 *Directory of Annual Sacred Harp Singings* the following singings were scheduled for 1970: 212 one-day singings (usually Sunday), 32 two-day singings (usually Saturday and Sunday), two three-day singings (Friday, Saturday, Sunday), 39 Friday night singings, 63 Saturday night singings, and 28 Sunday night singings. This total of 376 singings involving 412 days during 1970 indicates a strong interest in this tradition. Three editions of this tunebook are currently used in the above singings—the Cooper, the White, and the Denson. By far the most widely used is the Denson edition, the latest revision having been made in 1966.

BIBLIOGRAPHY: G. P. Jackson, *The Story of The Sacred Harp Singings* (1944); G. P. Jackson, *White Spirituals in the Southern Uplands* (1933). *The Sacred Harp* (facsimile of the third edition with historical introduction) Broadman (1968).

WILLIAM J. REYNOLDS

SAMAVESAM CONVENTION OF TELUGU BAPTIST CHURCHES (cf. Telugu Baptist Convention, South India). The name adopted by the former Telugu Baptist Convention of South India upon its reorganization in Jan., 1962. With the American Baptist Foreign Mission Societies and the Baptist Union of Sweden channeling their gifts through this responsible field organization, there have been continuous numerical growth and expansion in all phases of the work. A general council and numerous boards and committees meet regularly to assume the increasing responsibilities, including mission property, which are being transferred to the Indian leadership. The Telugu Baptist women and youth are also organized in their conventions. In 1967, 553 churches reported 4,886 baptisms, 193,318 members, and 460 pastors organized into 27 field associations of the Samavesam. Eight of the churches are in Madras, two in Mysore State, the remainder in Andhra.

Three hospitals, with nurse's training and several clinics, provide medical care, while a seminary and teacher training schools, as well as grade and high schools, several with vocational training, serve to train Telugu leadership for the churches.

The construction of new church buildings and chapels is proceeding constantly. From the Chapel Aid Fund 34 new buildings were aided in construction during 1965–66. The World Mission Campaign of the American Baptist Convention has provided funds for buildings and equipment for schools and other institutions.

In Jan., 1966, the adoption of the constitution of the new Baptist Council on Cooperation in World Mission united the Samavesam with the (mother) American Baptist Foreign Missionary

Society and the other overseas areas in support of the Baptist World Mission. The convention is a participating member in the East Asia Christian Conference, the World Council of Churches, the Baptist World Alliance, and the Baptist Council of Cooperation in World Mission.

One of the most significant developments in the South India mission was the decision of the Samavesam to move its B.D. and G.Th. programs of theological education from the Ramapatnam campus to the Andhra Christian Theological College in Rajahmundry. Plans are under way to transfer the interdenominational institution to the American Baptist Mission property in Hanamkonda as a new site for the merged seminaries.

On the Ramapatnam campus the rural pastors' course (vernacular) has been revised and strengthened, with 60 students enrolled during 1969–70, including 12 from the Canadian Baptist seminary in Kakinada. An intern program has been initiated for the third-year students. The total number of students in all phases of theological education is 142.

JAMES D. MOSTELLER

SAMFORD UNIVERSITY (cf. Howard College, Vol. I). Samford University is situated in the Shades Valley area of suburban Birmingham, Ala. It was moved from the East Lake section of Birmingham to the new, but incomplete, campus in 1957. Leslie S. Wright succeeded Harwell G. Davis as president in 1958. Completion of the master plan is expected by 1980.

In 1961 the Cumberland School of Law, brought from Lebanon, Tenn., became a part of then Howard College. In 1965 graduate study leading to master's degrees in several fields was reinstituted. On Nov. 9, 1965, the Alabama Baptist State Convention meeting in Montgomery voted that the name and status of Howard College be changed to Samford University. This was in honor of benefactor Frank P. Samford, whose family had long been identified with Baptist causes in Alabama. It was in recognition of the school's strong and diverse educational program. Following renaming, the University administrative structure was reorganized. By the fall of 1970, reporting to the president were vice-presidents for academic affairs, financial affairs, and student activities. The academic program was grouped in six schools, each headed by a dean. These were the Cumberland School of Law, the Howard College of Arts and Sciences, the Schools of Business, Education, Music, Pharmacy, and Graduate Studies. In 1969–70 Samford adopted a new calendar which provided for an experimental interterm in January.

Enrolment in Sept., 1969, totaled 2,676, of whom 232 were enrolled for graduate study and 383 for law. There were 134 full-time faculty members. In July, 1970, the library had 240,000 volumes, 1,129 maps, more than 300,000 manuscripts, and received 1,210 periodicals. These included the official depository collection of the Alabama Baptist Historical Society.

LEE N. ALLEN

***SAN MARCOS BAPTIST ACADEMY.** The academy has total assets of $5,000,000 and a permanent endowment of $350,000. William Crook, pastor of the First Baptist Church of Nacogdoches, Tex., became the president in 1961. During his administration a boys' dormitory, an academic building, a bell tower, recreational areas, and a book store were added to the campus. Jack E. Byrom, pastor of the First Baptist Church of San Marcos, assumed the presidency in 1965. Under his guidance the institution built a new president's home, an outdoor theater, a junior boys' dormitory, and a library. Plans are being made for a student chapel and recreation center. The present enrolment is 520.

MRS. RAMSEY YELVINGTON

SANDERS, ROBERT LEE (b. Oconee County, S. C., Apr. 7, 1882; d. Hot Springs, Ark., Nov. 25, 1964). Son of John Baylis and Sarah (Jenkins) Sanders, he married Rena Dozier Wood on Nov. 28, 1906. They had one son, Robert Lee, Jr. He was educated at Patrick Military Academy, Anderson, S. C.; George Peabody College, Nashville, Tenn.; and the University of Nashville Medical College, receiving the M.D. degree in 1906. After four years as a fellow in surgery, Mayo Clinic, he entered the practice of surgery in Memphis, Tenn., in 1920, where he remained until death. He organized the Sanders Clinic in 1932.

A general surgeon, he published some 90 scientific papers. Sanders served as senior surgeon, chief of staff, and president of staff of Baptist Memorial Hospital, Memphis, and as professor of surgery of the University of Tennessee College of Medicine. Member of the board of trustees of Southern Medical Association from 1917 till death, he also served as its president. He was affiliated with numerous professional organizations, serving as president of four.

During World War I, Sanders served as a Major in charge of the surgical service. He was an active member of the First Baptist Church, Memphis. He received the LL.D. from Union University, Jackson, Tenn., and Erskine College, South Carolina. He was awarded the Cancer Award in 1951 by the American Cancer Society, and received the Honor Award (1953) from the Mississippi Valley Medical Association for distinguished service in the teaching and practice of clinical surgery. He is buried in Memorial Parks Cemetery, Memphis, Tenn.

R. PAUL CAUDILL

SAYRE MEMORIAL HOSPITAL (Sayre, Okla.). The last of Oklahoma Baptists' leased hospitals was acquired in 1961 when citizens of Sayre, Okla., asked the Baptist General Convention of Oklahoma to operate their new hospital. The convention assumed operation of the 30-

bed facility, Feb. 15, 1961. In 1969 property value was $1,045,179, with no debt. Capacity had increased to 65 beds, with an 86 per cent daily occupancy. There were 68 employees.

J. M. GASKIN

SEARS, A. D. (b. Fairfax County, Va., Jan. 1, 1804; d. Clarksville, Tenn., June 15, 1891). He came from Virginia to Kentucky in 1823 and settled in Bourbon County. In 1828 he married Ann B. Bowie. After studying the writings of Andrew Fuller (*q.v.*, Vol. I) and the New Testament, he decided to join the Baptists, whom he had earlier despised. On July 19, 1838, he and his wife were baptized by Ryland T. Dillard (*q.v.*, Vol. I) into the fellowship of the David's Fork Church. In Feb., 1840, he was ordained by that church. He preached at Georgetown and Forks of Elkhorn (not being pastor at either place), and held meetings in several other churches. After conducting a meeting at the First Baptist Church, Louisville, he was called as pastor, serving until July, 1849. For a year he was general agent of the General Association of Baptists in Kentucky. In July, 1850, he accepted the pastorate of the First Baptist Church of Hopkinsville, remaining until 1860. When the Civil War began, he went south. In 1864 he attempted to return to Kentucky, but he was hindered by military authorities. In Jan., 1866, he accepted the pastorate of the church at Clarksville, Tenn., where he remained until his death.

LEO T. CRISMON

SECOND VATICAN COUNCIL. Called by Pope John XXIII in 1959, Vatican II met in four sessions (1962–65) with the purpose of bringing the Roman Catholic Church up to date. Twenty-first in Rome's listing of ecumenical councils, the council adopted the themes of inner renewal of the Church and reunion with the "separated brethren." The attendance of council fathers in St. Peter's basilica in Vatican City varied from 2,000 to 2,500 and included cardinals, bishops, abbots, and heads of orders. Non-Catholic observers were also present by invitation for all sessions.

Sixteen documents were promulgated. The *Constitution on the Church* defines the Church as the People of God composed of various groups including laity, restores the diaconate as a "permanent grade of the hierarchy," and concludes with a summary of Marian teaching. The *Constitution on Divine Revelation* strongly emphasizes the Scriptures but nevertheless declares: "Both sacred tradition and sacred scripture are to be accepted and venerated with the same sense of loyalty and reverence." The *Constitution on the Sacred Liturgy* authorizes changes such as increased use of the vernacular in church ceremonies and the communion of bread and wine for laymen in certain cases. The lengthy *Constitution on the Church in the Modern World* is addressed to the "whole of humanity" and deals with problems in contemporary society.

The *Decree on the Bishops* asserts the notion of collegiality, i.e. the bishops have a shared teaching and ruling responsibility to be exercised in union with the pope. The *Decree on Ecumenism* is unique in Roman Catholic history. Its friendly tone recognizes separated bodies of Christians as *churches* and notes that in past disputes and schisms "the fault has sometimes been on both sides." Bishops are urged to promote ecumenical activity and encourage dialogue with other churches, and Catholics are to show their concern for their separated brethren.

The *Declaration on Non-Christian Religions* denounces anti-semitism and rejects the charge of the Jews' collective guilt for Christ's death. The *Declaration on Religious Freedom* survived a bitter and hard-fought battle in the Council to be adopted 1,997 to 224. It explicitly declares the right of the individual to his own religious beliefs and locates its basis to be in "the dignity of the human person" and "the revealed word of God." "Faith is of its very nature a free act," and all coercion "should be excluded."

Out of the council also came some reorganization of the Roman Curia as well as the establishment of the Synod of Bishops. However, some pressing concerns in the Church were not dealt with, such as clerical celibacy and birth control. Finally, in Vatican II there was to be seen a new concern for the laity and the importance of biblical studies. It demonstrated a genuine diversity of views on many issues together with a new openness to consider and implement new ideas. The spirit of friendliness manifested in the council and the Church's newly embraced position on religious freedom augur well for improved relations and dialogue between Protestants and Catholics in the future.

BIBLIOGRAPHY: W. M. Abbott, ed., *The Documents of Vatican II* (1966). R. M. Brown, *Observer in Rome: A Protestant Report on the V. C.* (1964). W. M. Patterson, "A Baptist Historian Views Vatican II," *Baptist History and Heritage* (July, 1966).

W. MORGAN PATTERSON

SEDBERRY, LELAND STANFORD (b. Buena Vista, Carroll County, Tenn., June 30, 1891; d. Nashville, Tenn., Oct. 12, 1970). Minister, denominational leader. Educated at McTyeire Preparatory School, Vanderbilt University, University of Chicago, and Southern Baptist Theological Seminary (Th.M., 1923), he served as pastor of the following Tennessee Baptist churches: Chapel Hill; First churches of Cornersville, Duncanville, Mars Hill, Lewisburg, Gallatin, Brownsville, Murfreesboro, and Lascassas; and Lockeland, Nashville. Sedberry served as executive secretary and treasurer of the Southern Baptist Commission on the American Baptist Theological Seminary in Nashville, 1949–61. After retirement he served as interim pastor in several churches in Nashville, Franklin, and Huntsville. He was on the board of trustees of Cumberland College, Lebanon, and Tennessee College for Women at Murfreesboro.

President of board of directors of Tennessee Baptist Children's Home, Nashville Baptist Pastors' Conference, Middle Tennessee Baptist Pastors' Association, and a member of Tennessee Baptist Convention's executive board, he was an active member of First Baptist Church, Nashville, at the time of his death. In 1928 he married Ruth Banks. They had three children: Leland S., Jr., Jane Lassiter (Mrs. Terry Jones), and Ann Banks (Mrs. Jerry Ratcliff). MELBA LITTLE RAY

SEEVER, HAROLD WILLIAM (b. Cincinnati, Ohio, Feb. 29, 1912; d. Mobile, Ala., Sept. 27, 1966). Pastor and denominational leader. Educated at Westover Hills High School, Cincinnati, Georgetown College (A.B., 1934), and Southern Baptist Theological Seminary (Th.M., 1937), he received the D.D. from Georgetown College, 1949. Baptized in Ohio in 1920, he was ordained at Crittenden, Ky., May 8, 1932. Seever married Ahleida Mae Brunk, Mar. 31, 1934. They had one daughter, Ahleida Joan. He served rural Kentucky churches while in college and seminary. His full-time Baptist pastorates were First Church, Williamstown, Ky., 1936–39; Bainbridge Street, Richmond, Va., 1939–43; First, Florence, S. C., 1943–49; and Dauphin Way, Mobile, Ala., 1949–66. He was president of the Alabama Baptist State Convention, 1957–58, a member of the Executive Committee, Southern Baptist Convention, 1958–65, and its chairman, 1963–65. He was buried in Mobile.

HUGH C. BAILEY

SELLERS BAPTIST HOME AND ADOPTION CENTER. Established by the Home Mission Board in New Orleans in 1937, it is the only Southern Baptist Convention agency-sponsored institution giving professional service to unwed mothers and planning the adoption of their babies. The adoption program, begun in 1948, assures the placement of babies in homes of persons qualified to be parents. The staff includes a director, chaplain, registered nurses, and social workers. The charitable cooperation of physicians and the Southern Baptist Hospital provides medical care for both mothers and babies. Counseling ministries and religious services "provide disturbed young women with spiritual resources." CHARLES MCCULLIN

SEMINARY EXTENSION DEPARTMENT. A channel through which the six Southern Baptist seminaries conduct cooperatively a major portion of their off-campus training. On July 1, 1963, the home office of the department was moved from Jackson, Miss., to Nashville, Tenn. It is located in the Southern Baptist Convention Building, 460 James Robertson Parkway.

The work of the department is financed by allocations from the six seminaries supplemented by income from nominal tuition fees. The annual allocation from the six seminaries is $90,000, which is subscribed equally by the six seminaries.

The curriculum includes more than 40 courses in the biblical, theological, historical, and practical areas. Three basic certificates, each requiring 16 courses, are offered. The courses of study leading to these certificates are in pastoral training, religious education, and Christian life development. An Advanced Certificate may be earned by taking 12 additional courses, with two courses from each of the four areas. All Seminary Extension courses are on a college level. Several colleges grant degree credit for Seminary Extension courses taken. Five of the six seminaries accept credit for Seminary Extension courses in their diploma programs for students who do not have college degrees.

Seminary Extension courses are offered both in extension centers and by correspondence. During the fall and spring sessions of 1968–69, 218 centers operated with 4,149 individual students enrolled in 5,517 courses. In the school of correspondence, 1,307 individual students were enrolled; course enrolments were 1,859. A grand total of 5,456 students enrolled for 7,376 Seminary Extension courses. These students represent 44 states and 8 foreign countries. Fifty-two certificates were granted. The most rapid growth in recent years has come in the area of correspondence work. The number of students enrolled increased 165 per cent from Aug. 1, 1963, through July 31, 1969. The rate of increase during the last year of this period was 56 per cent in comparison with an eight per cent overall increase for all types of correspondence courses offered in America.

Although the department was established originally to serve ministers unable to secure seminary training, the student body has expanded to include many seminary alumni doing refresher work and laymen and women. In 1968–69, 74.37 per cent of the students were laymen and women.

Lee Gallman, first director of the department served from May 1, 1951, until Nov. 1, 1960. Ralph A. Herring served from Aug. 1, 1961, through Dec. 31, 1968. Raymond M. Rigdon became director on May 1, 1969. G. Ray Worley served as interim director for brief periods immediately prior to and following Herring's term of office.

The department publishes a monthly bulletin, entitled *Extension News,* which carries information on Seminary Extension work and other matters of interest in adult education. Four department associates promote and service the work in major regions of the United States. Present associates and the dates they began work with the department are: G. Ray Worley (1959), Paul Jakes (1960), John M. Ross (1963), and Cline W. Borders (1963). Former associates and their dates of service are Ray K. Hodge (1955–58), W. A. Whitten (1955–63), Albert Fauth (1957–62), Frank Koger (1959–62), and Gene Wallace (1959–60).

RAYMOND M. RIGDON

SENECA LAKE BAPTIST ASSEMBLY. Owned and operated by the State Convention of Baptists in Ohio, it began with the authorization of the leasing of 153 acres of land adjacent to Seneca Lake in southeastern Ohio, by the executive board of the convention in Jan., 1954. Subsequent purchase of this 153 acres later in 1954, and acquisition of small tracts in the years following brought the assembly properties to a total of 203 acres.

First assemblies were held in the summer of 1954, and the young people attending were housed in tents and in a rented dwelling adjacent to the area. Assembly leaders conducted services in an open-sided tabernacle already on the property. Dormitory units were built in 1957, 1959, and 1960. A water system was installed in 1959. In 1960 a combination dining hall-chapel was constructed. A $25,000 swimming pool was added to the facilities in 1965. In 1967 four cottage-type dormitories were erected and, in 1968, the Buckeye Lodge with accomodations for single occupancy was opened. A tabernacle with an auditorium of 800 seating capacity, a first floor with conference rooms, fellowship halls, recreation areas, book store, and other facilities was begun in 1968 and completed in 1969. Assembly property was valued at $400,000 in the convention's 1969 financial statement.

The first camp or assembly manager was John Ashcraft, who also served as part-time Brotherhood secretary and supervised the camp program, 1955–58. In 1958 Leonard Ferguson, a seminary student serving for the summer months in Ohio, acted as the summer manager and stayed on in this capacity until 1960, when he became associate Brotherhood secretary and camp manager. He served until 1964 and was succeeded in that year by Hubert Six, Jr., another seminary student who served in the summer as camp manager, 1965–66. In 1967 Nolan Ford became the first full-time assembly manager but served only the one assembly season. In Nov., 1967, Arlie Carter, an Ohio pastor, was elected camp manager and assumed the position in the fall of 1968, and serves now (1969) as the assembly manager.

Attendance at the assembly programs has increased from 156 persons in the two-week camping season of 1954, to a record 2,216 persons in a full summer program in 1968. In addition to the camps for Royal Ambassadors, Girls' Auxiliaries, WMU, and laymen, many local church groups and statewide conferences use the assembly facilities throughout the year.

LEONARD FERGUSON

SENEGAL, MISSION IN. Farrell and Elizabeth (Barnett) Runyan, previously missionaries to Nigeria, became residents of Dakar, capital of Senegal, in Sept., 1969. As the first Southern Baptist missionaries in Senegal, they concentrated on the thriving seaport city with over 600,000 people, in which there were two small evangelical churches. Attention was directed to university students and the educated middle class, using the French language. Plans included possible development of religious services and social activities among the dominant Wolof people in the midst of a strong Muslim culture. Earlier, Conservative Baptists had established a mission station at Thies. H. CORNELL GOERNER

SEPARATE BAPTISTS IN CHRIST, CURRENT (cf. Separate Baptists, Current, Vol. II). This Baptist group is organized into the following district associations: South Kentucky with 33 churches; Nolynn (Kentucky) with 15 churches; Mt. Olive in Tennessee with five churches; Central Indiana with 17 churches; Northern Indiana with eight churches; and the Ambraw Association in Illinois with nine churches. In 1970 Separate Baptists had 87 churches with about 7,500 members.

Besides meeting annually in district associations, Separate Baptists also assemble annually in a general association. They have no central headquarters but maintain a home and foreign mission board, which operates with a very limited income, and a ministers' conference. Separate Baptists also support Sunday Schools and youth camps but no colleges or seminaries. Some of their churches use the Sunday School literature of the General Baptists, an Arminian body. Separate Baptists correspond with the Christian Unity Baptist Association, a small independent association which is located primarily in western North Carolina, but do not cooperate with interdenominational bodies or with the Baptist World Alliance.

ALBERT W. WARDIN, JR.

***SERMONS, BAPTIST.** In order to understand the sermons of 1958–70, one must understand that the total scope of sermonic work includes the use of the Bible, with correct hermeneutical principles, with a balanced theological perspective, with an adequate understanding of the audience, and with creative uses of written and oral rhetoric.

Moreover, the true nature of sermons must be understood. About 600 years ago, during the scholastic age, creative homileticians described sermons as being expository, textual, and topical. By "expository" it was meant that the sermon presented an explanation of a text; "textual" meant that the text furnished the major divisions of the sermon, while the subdivisions of the sermon could come from any source; "topical" meant that the topic or title, rather than the text, furnished the content and structure for the sermon. Since these terms possess multiple meanings in current popular usage, no one can tell just what they mean now. They are confusing and contradictory categories for classifying sermons.

A new approach in identifying the true nature of sermons can be found in *A Quest for Reformation in Preaching*. This volume identifies sermons as to authority, purpose, and form. These three categories are all inclusive and comprehensive for the classification of sermons: of authority, because it is the basic question in religion; of purpose, because without purpose one cannot really preach; and of form, because without form one cannot communicate anything. These categories relate to sermons as follows:

1. Sermons as to authority mean that the messages can be tested as to their relationship to the meaning of the Scripture text. Exhaustive examinations of published sermons reveal five categories of sermons as to authority: (1) the direct biblical sermon uses the text according to its true and natural meaning; (2) the indirect biblical sermon uses the text with some slight deviation from its meaning; (3) the casual biblical sermon uses the text with a free and loose relationship; (4) the corrupted biblical sermon uses the text with some type of corruption of its meaning; and (5) the combination biblical sermon uses the text in some combination of the first four.

2. Sermons as to purpose mean that messages can be tested as to purpose or objective of the text and sermon. There are six major objectives or purposes found in Scripture and sermons: (1) the evangelistic purpose (that lost men be saved); (2) the doctrinal purpose (that Christians learn God's truth); (3) the ethical purpose (that Christians have proper relationships with others); (4) the devotional purpose (that Christians love and worship God); (5) the actional or consecrative purpose (that Christians serve God with their time, talent, and personality); and (6) the supportive purpose (that Christians secure God's grace and strength as needed for all needs).

3. Sermons as to form mean that messages can be tested as to structure: the homily sermon (or informal sermon) treats texts or titles or both informally; and the rhetorical sermon treats texts and titles with introductions, body points, conclusions, and invitations. Various degrees of organization are used.

Southern Baptists, and other Baptists, have produced many outstanding preachers during the 20th century. Representative preachers, primarily Southern Baptists, of the period 1958–70 may be classified under five major categories: Baptist statesmen, pastor-preachers, educators and denominational leaders, evangelists, and civil rights leaders.

Baptist Statesmen.—H. H. Hobbs, one of the most prolific ministers ever produced by Southern Baptists, has been pastor of the First Baptist Church of Oklahoma City, Okla., since 1949. Numerous books, sermon pamphlets by the Radio and Television Commission (Hobbs has been the Baptist Hour preacher for years), and many volumes of sermons have come from his pen. Hobbs is a biblical preacher with strong direct biblical authority. His sermons cover virtually the entire range of purpose. In form, Hobbs has been largely an organized rhetorical preacher. Hobbs will be remembered in Baptist history for statesmanlike qualities as well as for his sermons and other writings.

William Franklin (Billy) Graham, world famous evangelist and Baptist statesman, preaches casual biblical sermons more than direct biblical sermons apparently because of his desire for relevant material which will communicate with modern audiences. The view that relevance can be secured by casual biblical sermons more easily than by direct biblical sermons is held by many preachers. This view, however, is incorrect.

Graham makes use of books, newspaper articles, radio, television, movies, and huge crowds in outdoor stadiums to reach people by the millions. Graham is a superior preacher, despite his modest claims to the contrary. He does, however, use two questionable homiletical procedures: (1) he often criticizes theological education in general and homiletical training in particular; and (2) he uses Scripture from 10 to 15 places in one sermon. Only a master preacher, as is Graham, can utilize so much Scripture from multiple sources in one sermon.

Other able Baptist statesmen preaching effective sermons during 1958–70 have been Theodore Lionel Adams, Vernon Carney Hargroves, W. R. White, and Edward Pruden.

Pastor-Preachers.—Wallie Amos (W. A.) Criswell, pastor of the First Baptist Church, Dallas, Tex., since 1945, has led the church to become the largest Baptist church in the world, with an average Sunday School attendance of more than 5,000. Along with Hobbs and Graham, Criswell preaches often and publishes much. Primarily, Criswell is a direct biblical preacher. He disturbs some of his hearers and readers with his hermeneutical principles, ethical pronouncements, and strong statements about science. However, after he became president of the Southern Baptist Convention in 1968, he began to modify his ethical statements on race. He will be remembered for his church, sermons, controversies, and warm spiritual preaching.

James David (J. D.) Grey, pastor of the First Baptist Church, New Orleans, La., will be remembered for his strong oratorical ability, sparkling humor, and Convention service and leadership. Grey has left few written sermons, but his messages seem to be casual biblical sermons as to authority and primarily consecrative as to purpose. His sermons are rhetorical as over against homily in form.

Among those who will be remembered for their direct biblical sermons are H. Franklin Paschall, Robert Jackson (Jackie) Robinson, Hillyer Hawthorne Straton, Carl Bates, Lavon Brown, Charles Trentham, and Perry Webb.

More casual biblical sermons (similar to the old topical sermon) have been preached in recent years than any other type. This type of sermon can be valid and helpful if it is creative, appealing, and purposeful. Among those who have so preached have been Wayne Dehoney, H. Guy Moore, August McCurdy Hintz, Leonard Carlyle Marney, Eric William Hayden,

Robert Green (R. G.) Lee, Clarence William Cranford, J. P. Allen, John Claypool, J. H. Jackson, S. M. Lockridge, Roy Angell, Roy McClain, Walter Moore, K. Owen White, Ralph Langley, James Flamming, Alan Redpath, and Peter McLeod.

Educators and Denominational Leaders.—Professors, administrators, and other denominational leaders generally have allowed their pulpit skills to atrophy while attending to other responsibilities, but a number of them are strong preachers.

H. Gordon Clinard, for example, the Billy Graham professor of evangelism at Southern Baptist Theological Seminary, compares favorably with Harry Emerson Fosdick in style, while avoiding Fosdick's problems with the Bible and theology. Clinard uses the basic correct sermon forms as to authority—direct, indirect, combination, and casual—and keeps a strong accent on direct biblical sermons. In treating purpose, he uses all the basic objectives in a well-orbed ministry. Although one of the ablest preachers of this era, he is reluctant to publish his sermons.

Jesse J. Northcutt, dean of the School of Theology of Southwestern Baptist Theological Seminary, is another strong biblical preacher. Northcutt, while not producing sermons with the brilliant style qualities of Clinard, probably surpasses him as a preacher of direct biblical sermons. Northcutt's chapel messages for young ministers (delivered at Southwestern Seminary) offer a model for consecrative preaching.

Wayne Ward, talented professor of theology at Southern Baptist Seminary, preaches direct biblical sermons, strong convention messages, and warm evangelistic messages. In 1961 his sermon on "The Gospel of Jesus Christ" (also published in *More Southern Baptist Sermons*) was selected to be used by *Christianity Today* as an example of outstanding Southern Baptist sermons. This sermon is a direct biblical sermon using a few passages of Scripture with evangelistic purpose. The form is rhetorical with three major points and no subdivisions.

This sermon by Ward, along with Fosdick's sermon on "Handling Life's Second Best" and S. M. Lockridge's "The Mission of the Church," constitute three of the most inspiring sermons in print by Baptists during the second half of the 20th century.

Other educators and denominational leaders who have preached strong direct biblical sermons during the period 1958–70 have been Ray Summers, Robert E. Naylor, Duke McCall, Earl Guinn, Curtis Vaughan, William Tolar, Huber Drumwright, Frank Stagg, Clyde Francisco, Fred Fisher, and Jack MacGorman.

Other educators and denominational leaders have preached quality messages while frequently mixing the casual biblical sermons with direct biblical messages. These men include Vernon L. Stanfield, Winston Pearce, C. DeWitt Matthews, James Cox, Wayne E. Oates, John Boyle, John Killinger, John Newport, Clyde Fant, James Sidlow Baxter, Kenneth Chafin, Paul Stevens, Baker James Cauthen, and James L. Sullivan.

Civil Rights Leaders.—Sermons by civil rights leaders show a heavy, although natural, accent on ethical purpose. They have tended to use indirect, casual, and combination biblical sermons much more than direct biblical sermon. Among these able sermonizers have been Foy Valentine, Jimmy Allen, William (Bill) Lawson, Jesse Jackson, Clarence Jordon, Martin Luther King, Jr., Benjamin E. Mays, and others. The greatest name in the list is Martin Luther King, Jr., who will be remembered more for his courageous and inspirational leadership on many levels than for just his sermons.

Evangelists.—These men often preach gospel sermons at the expense of other objectives for preaching. Although there is only one authentic source for gospel messages, the Bible, these men far too often ignore direct biblical sermons and preach casual biblical sermons. Some evangelists also use questionable techniques in publicizing themselves and in extending sermon invitations. The more able evangelists try to avoid these faults. Among those who have succeeded in varying degrees are Angel Martinez, John Bisagno, Vance Havner, Bill Glass, C. E. Autrey, and Charles Forbes Taylor.

Baptist sermons and preaching for the period 1958–70 present distinct qualities:

Weakness. (1) Most Baptist sermons have been average, fair, and poor. (2) Many sermons have been corrupt as to biblical authority. (3) A serious neglect of study for sermons has been practiced by all too many ministers. (4) Many preachers have neglected careful sermonic workmanship. (5) A serious confusion of roles has beset ministers. (6) The use of high pressure procedures and strange "gimmicks" in sermonic work increased. (7) The shameful practice of gross plagiarism by many otherwise honorable ministers continued.

Areas of strength. (1) Many energetic ministers have been active during this period. (2) A large percentage of these men have had quality professional training. (3) Sermons revealed a wide diversity as to purpose. (4) Strong men have preached direct biblical sermons. (5) Ministers as a whole have demonstrated a high level of sincerity and spiritual dedication. (6) The number of ethical sermons has increased sharply. (7) Ministers, through their sermons, have revealed a keen awareness of national and world conditions. (8) The ministry has revealed itself to be more diverse than ever in its areas of service. (9) Laymen have been increasingly active in preaching.

Bibliography: H. C. Brown, Jr., *The Cutting Edge: Critical Questions for Contemporary Christians*, 2 Vols (1969); *More Southern Baptist Preaching* (1964); *Southern Baptist Preaching* (1959); *A Quest for Reformation in Preaching* (1968). Wallie Amos Criswell, *Expository Sermons on Revelation* (1962). William Franklin Graham, *The Challenge: Sermons from Madison Square Garden* (1969).

SOUTHEASTERN BAPTIST THEOLOGICAL SEMINARY (*q.v.*). *Top left:* Binkley Chapel, Wake Forest, N. C. Symbol of Southeastern Seminary to its 2,213 alumni. *Top right:* Stealey Hall provides offices for administration and faculty. *Bottom left:* New student center on old campus. *Bottom right:* Denny Hall houses the seminary library.

SHADES MOUNTAIN BAPTIST CHURCH, Birmingham, Ala. Organized 1901. Sanctuary seats 1,450; dedicated in 1963.

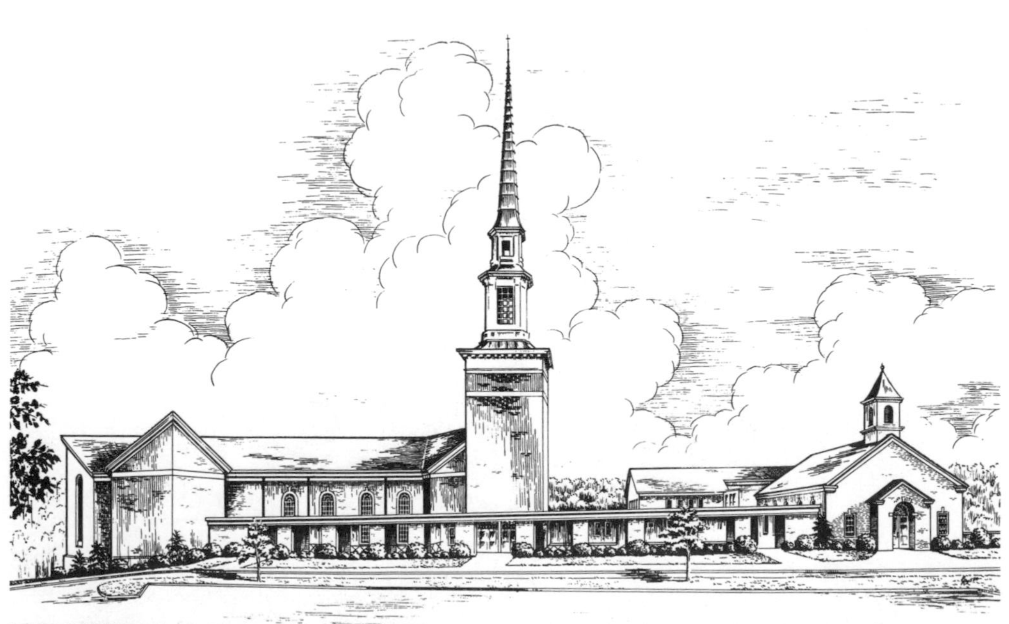

MOUNTAIN BROOK BAPTIST CHURCH, Birmingham, Ala., founded in 1944. Buildings completed in 1967, valued at $2,400,000.

H. H. Hobbs, *Christ in You* (1961). Martin Luther King, Jr., *Strength to Love* (1963). J. Winston Pearce, *Seven First Words of Jesus* (1966). Perry Webb, *He Made the Stars Also* (1968).

See also PREACHING, SOUTHERN BAPTIST.

H. C. BROWN, JR.

***SEVENTH DAY BAPTISTS.** Their distinctives are worship on the Biblical Sabbath, while abstaining from gainful work, and a marked individualism. They "cherish liberty of thought as an essential condition for the guidance of the Holy Spirit" as affirmed in their *Statement of Belief,* 1937. The conference is a constituent member of the Federal Council of Churches (National Council of the Churches of Christ in the U. S. A.) and of the World Council of Churches.

Denominational structure is decentralized through the Seventh Day Baptist Missionary Society (home and foreign work), the American Sabbath Tract Society (publications, Sabbath promotion), the Seventh Day Baptist Board of Christian Education (Bible study, youth programs, etc.), the Women's Society, the Seventh Day Baptist Memorial Fund (pensions, students grants, etc.), and the Seventh Day Baptist Historical Society. Local churches support missions and benevolences through the General Conference "Our World Mission" (OWM). Giving to local and denominational OWM purposes in 1968 totaled $459,412. In 1968 membership in 65 churches in the United States and 60 mission churches totaled 12,564. Fraternal conferences in Brazil, Germany, Guyana, S. A., Holland, Jamaica, W. I., Malawi, East Africa, Mexico, and New Zealand are associated with the U. S. A. conference in the Seventh Day Baptist World Federation (SDBWF) organized in 1964.

The leading periodical of Seventh Day Baptists is *The Sabbath Recorder,* a weekly which was 125 years old in 1969.

Annual sessions of the General Conference provide policy decisions and a major program emphasis besides national and international fellowship. The general secretary's offices at the Seventh Day Baptist Building, Plainfield, N. J., coordinate the ongoing work of the conference in consultation with the commission (including the conference president elected annually) which has interim responsibility for stewardship and budget promotion, service to local churches, public and interchurch relations. Alton L. Wheeler is general secretary of the conference.

The Center for Ministerial Education is located at the Seventh Day Baptist Building, and through its dean and the Council on Ministerial Education advises theological students enrolled in various seminaries, makes grants-in-aid to them, and provides training in denominational beliefs, history, and polity. The center supplants the Alfred University School of Theology, formerly sponsored by the denomination but closed in 1963.

BIBLIOGRAPHY: Davis C. Woolley, ed., *Baptist Advance* (1964). *Seventh Day Baptist Yearbook.*

ALBERT N. ROGERS

SEWELL, BAILEY OTIS (b. Oakley, Tenn., Nov. 13, 1905; d. Oklahoma City, Okla., June 4, 1966). Minister and missionary. Educated at Oklahoma Baptist University (A.B., 1936), he served Oklahoma pastorates in Shawnee, Calvary Baptist Church (1936–40); Portland Ave., Oklahoma City (1940–49); and superintendent of missions in Comanche-Cotton Association of Oklahoma (1949–54). He was director of Indian mission work for the Baptist General Convention of Oklahoma from 1954 until his death.

J. M. GASKIN

SEX EDUCATION. In response to a society that often misunderstands and misuses sex, an increasing number of Southern Baptist churches are providing special programs for youth and adults. The programs are based upon a biblical understanding of sexuality which emphasizes the goodness of sexuality as an aspect of God's creation, the power of sex and sexual temptation and thus the need for controls, and the possibility of the wholesome expression of sexuality through the gracious empowering of God's redemptive Spirit.

Messengers to the Southern Baptist Convention, meeting in New Orleans in 1969, passed the denomination's first resolution on sex education. This resolution encouraged individuals, groups, and churches to make fuller use of the limited family life and sex education materials available in the denomination. It also requested "the Christian Life Commission of the Southern Baptist Convention to take the lead in encouraging all agencies and curriculum planners of our Convention to give increasing attention to basic and special resource materials on family life and sex education for Southern Baptist families and churches, in accordance with program assignments of respective Convention agencies."

Working with the Sunday School Board and other Convention agencies, the Christian Life Commission has a continuing program of guidance and resources to help Southern Baptist homes and churches provide responsible sex education.

HARRY N. HOLLIS, JR.

SHERMAN, SAMUEL STERLING (b. Vermont, Nov. 24, 1815; d. Chicago, Ill., Nov. 22, 1914). Educator. Sherman was educated in Vermont schools and at Middlebury College (A.B., 1838). The LL.D. degree was bestowed on him in 1876 by William Jewell College, and in 1888 by his alma mater. He taught Latin and Greek at the University of Alabama, 1839–41. In Jan., 1842, he became president of Howard College. On Aug. 19, 1845, he married Eliza Dewey of Philadelphia, and they had seven children. In June, 1851, he resigned as president of Howard College to operate his privately owned school, Brownwood, near La Grange, Ga. He also served as president of Judson College, 1855–59. Returning north, he became a member of the Board of Education and State Board of Normal Schools in Wisconsin. He was both president and trustee of Milwaukee Female College. FANNA K. BEE

SHIRLEY, JAMES THOMAS (b. Union Springs, Ala., Nov. 30, 1913; d. Fort Worth, Tex., Dec. 25, 1964). Son of James T., Sr., and Willie Bell (McLarty) Shirley, he graduated from Howard Payne College (A.B., 1939), Brownwood, Tex., and studied at Southwestern Baptist Theological Seminary (1939–41), Fort Worth. He served as superintendent of missions in Madison County, Tenn., pastor of First Baptist, St. Johns, 1943–61, and Glenstone Church, Springfield, Mo., 1961–64. Shirley served as chairman of the executive board of the Missouri Baptist Convention and as a trustee of Hannibal-LaGrange College. He was a member of the Executive Committee and the Radio and Television Commission of the SBC. He was twice president of the Missouri Baptist Convention, 1959–60. Shirley married Willie Lou Bell, Dec. 25, 1938. They had five children: Karl, David, Anne (Mrs. John Bailey), Sylvia, and Becky. ROBERT E. SMITH

SHOCCO SPRINGS ASSEMBLY. Located in Talladega, Ala., it was purchased in 1947 by the executive board of the Alabama Baptist State Convention. Major additions to the assembly include Royal Ambassador and Girls' Auxiliary camps in 1965, 460 acres of land, and several major buildings. The first all-year building, Shocco Inn, was occupied in 1967. Other buildings were renovated to make possible the accommodation of 500 guests in the summer and 300 in the winter. Waymon C. Reese was director from Mar. 1, 1956, to Jan. 31, 1970. George Ricker became director on Feb. 1, 1970.

See also ALABAMA BAPTIST ENCAMPMENTS, Vol. I. GEORGE RICKER

SHORT, JAMES AUBREY (b. Butlerville, Ark., Apr. 12, 1909; d. Anchorage, Alaska, May 30, 1964). Evangelist and pastor. Converted at age 14, he joined the church when he was 17. In the fall of 1929 he entered Jonesboro College, a Baptist college in Jonesboro, Ark., where he graduated from high school and junior college. In the summer of 1931 he decided to enter the ministry. In Feb., 1932, the Ward Baptist Church called him as pastor. Short was ordained by the Walnut Street Baptist Church, Jonesboro, Ark., on May 18, 1932. In the summer of 1932 he led his first tent revival, with 64 conversions. In a second revival that summer, 46 were converted. He entered Ouachita College in the fall of 1932 and the following spring married Mary Lucy Fulmer of Oxford, Miss., whom he had met in Jonesboro College. In 1934 Short became pastor of the Baptist Church in Lovington, N. Mex. He resigned in Aug., 1936, to attend Hardin-Simmons University, Abilene, Tex. While attending Hardin-Simmons he was pastor of two half-time churches. In the fall of 1938 he enrolled in Southwestern Baptist Theological Seminary. From May 1939 to Dec. 1942 he was pastor in Rochester, Tex. This proved to be one of the most fruitful periods of his ministry with over 900 decisions in a three-year period. He was pastor of the Birchman Avenue Baptist Church, Fort Worth, 1942–47, and of the First Baptist Church, San Benito, Tex., 1947–52. He served for three years as superintendent of evangelism for the Louisiana Baptist Convention before returning to the San Benito church in 1955.

In the fall of 1959 he became pastor of the Hamilton Acres Baptist Church, Fairbanks, Alaska. In Aug., 1962, he accepted the pastorate of the Faith Baptist Church, Anchorage, Alaska. Short served as moderator of three associations, district chairman of evangelism, and member of board of trustees of Valley Baptist Academy, Valley Baptist Hospital, and Decatur College. He was president of the Alaska Baptist Convention at the time he met his death in an airplane accident. MRS. MARY L. SHORT

***SHORTER COLLEGE.** Under the leadership of two presidents, George A. Christenberry (1953–58) and Randall H. Minor (1958–), the college has grown in enrolment, property value, and endowment. Since 1955 average yearly enrolment has been 738, with 939 total in 1968–69. In 1957 dormitory housing on campus was first provided for male students, who now comprise almost half of the student body. More recently, Negro students have been enrolled, and foreign students continue to be present.

All the older buildings have been renovated. Three new structures have been completed: the Walter Pope Binns Student Center, dedicated by the Callaway Foundation, Inc.; Freshman Hall, a women's dormitory; and the Library-Administration Building. The Mildred Arnall Peniston Library honors a Shorter alumna. Greystone Dormitory in downtown Rome houses all male boarding students. A home adjoining the campus has been acquired as a residence for the president. Property value increased to $4,867,-425. Endowment totaled $1,498,188, much of this provided by the Georgia Baptist Convention, which again assumed formal control of the college in 1957 by electing the trustees. Total budget for 1969–70 was $1,328,000. The Bachelor of Science in medical technology degree was added, in cooperation with Floyd Hospital, Rome, Ga. Facing the centennial year in 1973, officials were planning an appropriate celebration. In addition, a long-range development program was initiated to provide an auditorium, a library building, and further endowment. ROBERT GARDNER

SIMMONS, BRYAN (b. Franklin County, Miss., Dec. 18, 1876; d. Laurel, Miss., Nov. 13, 1969). Born the eleventh of 12 children, he attended school in Natchez, Miss., and graduated from Mississippi College (1898) and Southern Baptist Theological Seminary. He married Linda Osborn. In Jan., 1900, he was ordained to the ministry. Simmons promoted the 75 Million Campaign, Baptist Orphanage, and Baptist Hospital fund drives, collecting $25,000 for the first unit of the present Baptist Hospital building, and served as the third superintendent of the hospital. Simmons was president of Clarke Memorial College, 1916–18, and served two terms as president of the Mississippi Baptist Convention, 1932–33. He preached the centennial convention sermon in Natchez, 1936. He supported the attempt to move the orphanage from Jackson to Newton in two special sessions of the convention in 1930. Among his many pastorates in Mississippi were Gallman, Flora, Brandon, Pickens, and West Laurel. After retirement he wrote in the Ellisville weekly newspaper a column, "Musings of a Minister," which were compiled in a booklet. He is buried in Ellisville, Miss. C. B. HAMLET, III

SIMMONS, JOSEPH KELLY (b. Westminister, Tex., June 11, 1904; d. Fresno, Calif., Feb. 1, 1963). Son of Robert and Virginia Lee (Roland) Simmons, he was educated at Baylor University (B.A., 1930) and Southwestern Baptist Theological Seminary. He was a reporter for the Sherman *Democrat* while attending junior college. He married Ruby McCreary in Feb., 1927. After her death, June, 1949, he married Edna Jones McCreary, May 31, 1954. He was a chaplain with the United States Army in World War II. Simmons served as pastor in the Texas cities of San Gabriel, Thorndale, Carrizo Springs, Kingsville, Gilmer, and Waco. He served as missionary of the Arizona convention, in Idaho and Arizona. He became editor of the Arizona *Baptist Beacon* in 1958, the *Rocky Mountain Baptist,* Apr. 1, 1960, and *The California Southern Baptist,* May, 1961, holding this last post until his death. J. TERRY YOUNG

SIMMS, ROBERT NIRWANA (b. Guyandotte, W. Va., May 14, 1876; d. Raleigh, N. C., Oct. 6, 1963). Lawyer, civic leader, and Baptist layman. Son of Albert Meredith and Mary Frances (Steward) Simms, he received the B.A. and completed legal instruction at Wake Forest College in 1897. He was licensed and began practicing law the same year in Raleigh. Simms was attorney for several railroads. He was a member of the North Carolina General Assembly, 1901–02, and was named a presidential elector in 1904. Simms was a deacon at Tabernacle Baptist Church in Raleigh from 1900 until his death, and organized and taught the Simms Baraca Class for more than 60 years. He was president of the Baptist State Convention of North Carolina, 1938–40. From 1902–46 he was a trustee of Meredith College, and he was on the first board of directors of Southeastern Baptist Theological Seminary, 1950–52. Simms was active in civic life and served as president of the Raleigh Chamber of Commerce. He was a Master Mason. Simms married Virginia Adelaide Egerton in 1908. They had six children: R. N., Jr.; Mrs. A. L. Haskins, Jr.; John M.; Albert E.; Steward B.; and William G. Simms. TOBY DRUIN

SIMPSON, JAMES HENRY (b. Poplar Springs, Laurens County, S. C., Dec. 5, 1890; d. Greenville, S. C., Jan. 24, 1965). Teacher, businessman, and minister. Son of James W. and Ella Elizabeth (Beeks) Simpson, he was educated at Furman University (B.A., 1914) and Southern Baptist Theological Seminary (Th.G., 1925). He received the honorary D.D. from Furman, 1956. He was teacher at North Greenville Baptist Academy (now North Greenville Junior College), Tigerville, S. C., 1914–15; registrar, Furman University, 1916–17; business manager, Furman, 1917–20; and teacher, Greenville City High School, 1920–23. Licensed by Pendleton Street Baptist Church, Greenville, S. C., in Jan., 1921, and ordained Mar. 5, 1922, he was pastor of the following South Carolina Baptist churches: Rocky Creek and White Oak, Greenville, 1922–23; Central, Darlington, 1925–29; First, Johnston, 1929; First, Woodruff, 1930–40; Grace, Sumter, 1941–52; and Ridge Spring, Ridge Spring, 1953–56. Simpson was moderator of Spartan Baptist Association, 1933–35, and of Santee Baptist Association, 1943–47. Under the South Carolina Baptist State Convention, he was assistant recording secretary, 1929–38; recording and statistical secretary, 1939–54; trustee, South Carolina Baptist Foundation, 1949–52; member of the general board, serving on these committees: executive, missions, finance, and capital needs; and president of the convention, Nov., 1955, to Nov., 1956. He was South Carolina State Member, Home Mission Board, SBC, 1949–55. Simpson married Margaret Amelia Anderson of Abbeville, S. C., Aug. 30, 1916. They had two children: James Henry, Jr., and Mildred Lourean Simpson. Simpson was stricken while conducting devotions at the Men's Bible Class, Pendleton Street Baptist Church, Greenville, and was dead on arrival at the hospital. He is buried in the Woodlawn Memorial Park, Greenville, S. C. JEAN MARTIN FLYNN

SIMPSON, LEONARD KIRKLIN (b. Poplar Springs, Laurens County, S. C., Nov. 27, 1885; d. Greenville, S. C., Nov. 16, 1963). Son of James W. and Ella Elizabeth (Beeks) Simpson, he was reared on the farm. Simpson was educated at Furman University (B.A., 1910) and Southern Baptist Theological Seminary (Th.B., 1921; Th.M., 1922). Furman conferred on him an honorary D.D. in 1945. Simpson was assistant teacher at North Greenville High School (now North Greenville Junior College), Tigerville, S. C., 1910–12, and principal, 1913–19. Called by Mush Creek Baptist Church in the North Greenville Baptist Association, he was ordained in 1912. He was pastor of Camp Creek, Lima, Locust Hill, Fairview, and Milford Baptist churches in the North Greenville association. He was pastor of North Baptist Church, North, S. C., 1922–27; First Baptist Church, Simpsonville, S. C., 1927–40; and McCormick Baptist Church, McCormick, S. C., 1941–56. Simpson was moderator of the Greenville Baptist Association, 1934–40, and of the Abbeville Baptist Association, 1945–55. He was a trustee of Greenville Woman's College, Greenville, S. C., 1932–38, and Furman University, 1943–55. He was president of the South Carolina Baptist State Convention from Nov., 1952, to Nov., 1953. Simpson married Cora Martin Long of Cheraw, S. C., June 2, 1914. They had no children. He is buried in the Poplar Springs Baptist Church cemetery.

JEAN MARTIN FLYNN

SIMS, ANNIS IONE HOPE (b. Lockhart, Union County, S. C., June 7, 1893; d. Columbia, S. C., Dec. 2, 1959). Daughter of William David and Mattie (Hannah) Hope, she was reared at Lockhart, where her father was a physician. She attended Union Seminary, Union, S. C., and taught two years in Lockhart. She and Charles Furman Sims (*q.v.*) were married June 25, 1918. They had six children: Margaret Hope (Mrs. S. L. McCleskey), Ruth, Martha (Mrs. Richard Carpenter), Sara, Annis (Mrs. J. W. Beach), and Charles F. Sims, Jr. She is buried in the Washington Baptist Church cemetery, Greenville County, S. C.

JEAN MARTIN FLYNN

SIMS, CHARLES FURMAN (b. the Ware Place, Greenville County, S. C., Feb. 20, 1893; d. Greenville, S. C., Dec. 11, 1961). Son of Abner B. and Emma (Sullivan) Sims, he was educated at Furman University (B.A., 1915), and Southern Baptist Theological Seminary (Th.M., 1920; Th.D., 1927). Furman conferred on him an honorary D.D. in 1950. From 1915 to 1917 he was principal of the public school at Lockhart, S. C., where he met Annis Ione Hope whom he married June 25, 1918. They had six children. Ordained by Washington Baptist Church in 1915, Sims was pastor of Long Run Baptist Church near Louisville, Ky., while he was a seminary student. In 1920–21 he was a fellow in the department of Homiletics and sociology, Southern Seminary. He was pastor of the First Baptist Church, Liberty, S. C. (1921–27), and of the First Baptist Church, Greenwood, S. C. (1928–42). Sims was enlistment secretary, South Carolina Baptist Convention, 1943–50, and general secretary-treasurer, general board, South Carolina Baptist Convention, 1950–61. He was slated to retire from the latter office Dec. 31, 1961. At the time of his death, he had been president of the Baptist State Convention 24 days. He is buried in the Washington Baptist Church cemetery near the Ware Place.

See also SIMS, ANNIS IONE HOPE, Vol. III.

JEAN MARTIN FLYNN

SIPES, LEONLESS MARCELLOUS (b. Mineral Springs, Howard County, Ark., Sept. 12, 1884; d. Little Rock, Ark., Nov. 20, 1964). Pastor, educator, and author. Son of William M. and Henrietta (Green) Sipes, he married Sallie Moore, June 30, 1910. They had four children: Leon M., William Burke, Margaret (Mrs. J. C. Hensley), and Frank Moore. Converted and baptized into Columbus Baptist Church, Columbus, Ark., in 1900, he was ordained in 1904. Educated at Ouachita Baptist College (A.B., 1911), and Southwestern Baptist Theological Seminary (Th.M., 1916), he received the D.D. from Ouachita in 1924. His Arkansas pastorates were: Tillar, College Hill (Texarkana); Lewisville; Conway First, 1916–21; Little Rock First, 1921–29; Pulaski Heights, Little Rock, 1932–41; and Bellvue, Little Rock, 1954–56. He was pastor emeritus of the Pulaski Heights Church, 1956–64. His Texas pastorates were: First, Mansfield and Seminary Hill Church, Ft. Worth. Sipes served as vice-president and professor of Central Baptist College, Conway, Ark., 1929–31, and professor of pastoral efficiency, 1941–53, and associate to the president, 1941–45, at Central Baptist Theological Seminary, Kansas City, Kans. He was editor of the *Baptist Advance* (Arkansas), 1931–33. He was co-author with H. E. Dana (*q.v.*, Vol. I) of *A Manual of Ecclesiology* (1944). He authored *The Palm Tree Christian* (1956). Sipes was president of the Arkansas Baptist State Convention, 1937–38, and preached the annual sermon, 1926. He also served as president of the Kansas Baptist State Convention, 1946–47.

GEORGE T. BLACKMON

SLING AND STONE. See RAGLAND, GEORGE.

SMITHERMAN, JAMES EMORY, SR. (b. Liberty Hill, Bienville Parish, La., Jan. 2, 1882; d. Shreveport, La., May 17, 1967). His father was engaged in farming, milling, ginning, and banking. He attended Louisiana Polytech (1901–04), taught during summers (1901–03), was assistant principal of schools in Ruston, La. (1904–05), principal of schools at DeRidder, La. (1905–07), and graduated from Louisiana State University, Baton Rouge, in 1909.

In 1910 he married Ina Hill Thompson, who died in 1946. They had four sons: James E., Jr., Gustavus Scott, Robert Emerson, and Eugene Alston Smitherman. Smitherman was a lawyer with oil and investment interests. He was an active Baptist, and his church, the YMCA, and LSU were his dominant interests.

He joined First Baptist Church in Shreveport in 1914, serving as deacon for over 40 years, culminating his work as chairman of the building committee for the new church structure on the old Dodd College site. He had an abiding interest in the Louisiana Baptist Children's Home, Monroe, where he provided Smitherman Cottage in 1925, still in use.

He was one of the founders and builders of the Shreveport YMCA and an active member for over 40 years, serving as president for 10 years, and was president emeritus at the time of his death.

He served on the board of supervisors at LSU, 1940–58, serving as chairman for two successive terms. He was responsible for the building of many campus buildings in Baton Rouge. He had no published works, but was acknowledged to be gifted with clarity of expression and the ability to say much in few words.

JOHN G. ALLEY

SOLOMON, EDWARD DAVIS (b. Coldwater, Miss., Dec. 26, 1875; d. Jacksonville, Fla., Sept. 13, 1957). Pastor, evangelist, denominational executive, and editor. Graduate of Mississippi College (A.B., 1898), student at Southern Baptist Theological Seminary (1898–1900), he studied at Baylor University and Spurgeon's College, London, England. Stetson University, DeLand, Fla., awarded him the D.D. in 1943. Solomon married Josie Crawford, Nov. 12, 1907. They had three children: Edward C., William H., and Crawford. Ordained in 1898, he served as pastor successively of First Church, Kaufman, Tex.; First Church, McComb, Miss.; Main Street Church, Hattiesburg, Miss.; Fifteenth Avenue Church, Meridian, Miss.; and St. Charles Avenue Church, New Orleans, La., 1919–23. He also served as corresponding secretary, Louisiana Baptist Convention, 1924–30; editor, *Florida Baptist Witness,* 1931–49; vice-president, Mississippi Baptist Convention, 1912; and vice-president Southern Baptist Convention, 1941–42. Solomon conducted evangelistic meetings in 12 Southern states, built three churches, and was prominent in founding Mississippi Woman's College, Hattiesburg, Miss., and Southern Baptist Hospital, New Orleans. Solomon also was a chaplain in the Spanish-American War and World War I. He was a trustee of Southern Baptist Hospital, New Orleans; Baptist Hospital, Alexandria, La.; and Leland University, Baker, La. He was active in the establishment of Baptist Memorial Hospital, Jacksonville, Fla. As a member of the SBC future program commission, he helped to originate the Cooperative Program in 1925. One of the earliest proponents of the church budget subscription plan for the Baptist state paper, he secured during his Louisiana secretaryship the first state Baptist convention's official approval and active promotion of the plan among the churches. W. G. STRACENER

SOPHIA SUTTON ASSEMBLY. A Mississippi Baptist encampment located about eight miles northwest of Prentiss, Miss., on Highway 42. Founded in 1954 when Sophia Sutton Begley deeded to the trustees of Mississippi Baptist Seminary, then under the leadership of William A. Keel, 119 acres of land "to multiply the power of the Lord," the encampment now comprises 239 acres. It has been developed under the leadership of William P. Davis, Keel's successor, and S. L. Richmond, director of the assembly. During 1968, more than 25,000 people received some type of Christian witness, 796 professed faith in Christ, and 216 dedicated their lives to Christian vocations while attending conferences.

Assembly facilities include a spacious auditorium, amphitheater, swimming pool, three dormitories, dining room and kitchen, three buildings for conferences, classrooms, library, administrative offices, student activities, clinic, trade shop, and children's activities, three athletic fields, and many well-marked nature trails.

WILLIAM P. DAVIS

SOURCE CRITICISM. Source criticism is most often understood as an investigation of the sources used by Matthew, Mark, and Luke. The first three Gospels are often referred to as "Synoptic" Gospels because they contain a great deal of similar material. They "look at" Jesus in ways that are similar. The Gospel of John is different in many ways from the other three and is not considered one of the Synoptic Gospels.

Source criticism undertakes to analyze and clarify the literary relationships of the first three Gospels. Therefore, it is a form of "higher criticism," and is basic to form criticism and redaction criticism. The similarities and dissimilarities of the gospels, involving content, order, language, and style, lead scholars to undertake to explain the literary relationships.

Many scholars believe that the best solution to the problems is to hold that there are two basic sources of the Synoptic Gospels, the Gospel of Mark and Q. The material that is common to Matthew and Luke and absent from Mark is called "Q," from the German word *Quelle,* "source." It is not certain whether the form of Q was written or oral.

Some scholars believe that most of the material found in Matthew only comes from a source, written or oral, which they designate "M." They refer most of the material found only in Luke to a source called "L." There are, therefore, four possible sources of the Synoptic Gospels: Mark, Q, M, and L. Roman Catholic scholars traditionally hold to the priority of the Gospel of Matthew. F. C. Grant's book, *The Gospels: Their Origin and Their Growth* (1957), gives a clear treatment of the search for multiple sources in the Gospels.

While the precise term, "source criticism," is applied most often to analysis of the Synoptic Gospels, some scholars believe that the author of the Fourth Gospel utilizes sources also. And for more than 200 years scholars have detected what they believe are sources in books of the Old Testament. This is especially true of the Pentateuch (and particularly in the books of Genesis and Exodus), in which many scholars find evidence of documents, some of which they designate J, E, D, P. The study of sources in books of the Old Testament may be followed in Otto Eissfeldt's, *The Introduction to the Old Testament* (1965).

See also DOCUMENTARY HYPOTHESIS, Vol. III.

RAYMOND BRYAN BROWN

***SOUTH CAROLINA ASSOCIATIONS.**

New Associations. ALLENDALE–HAMPTON. Organized in 1958 with 24 churches from the Savannah River Association, and is located in the southern part of the state. In 1969, 29 churches reported 104 baptisms, 7,002 members, $482,439 total gifts, $71,353 mission gifts, and $2,513,200 property value.

GREER. Organized in 1959 with 23 churches from the North Spartan (3), North Greenville (11), Spartan (6), and Greenville (3) associations, and is located in the northwestern part of the state. In 1969, 28 churches reported 375 baptisms, 15,386 members, $1,466,048 total gifts, $311,531 mission gifts, and $6,365,928 property value.

PALMETTO. Organized in 1965 with 19 churches from the Greenville (5), Saluda (9), and Piedmont (5) associations, and is located in the western part of the state. In 1969, 21 churches reported 206 baptisms, 8,252 members, $625,753 total gifts, $96,063 mission gifts, and $2,758,150 property value.

SPARTANBURG. Organized in 1960 with 17 churches from the North Spartan (9) and Spartan (8) associations, and is located in the northern part of the state. In 1969, 16 churches reported 214 baptisms, 9,824 members, $1,027,-238 total gifts, $150,151 mission gifts, and $5,351,031 property value.

WILLIAMSBURG. Organized in 1960 with 18 churches from the Southeast Association, and is located in the eastern part of the state. In 1969, 19 churches reported 134 baptisms, 4,900 members, $488,986 total gifts, $79,145 mission gifts, and $2,629,000 property value.

DANIEL W. CLOER

SOUTH CAROLINA BAPTIST CONVENTION (cf. South Carolina, State Convention of the Baptist Denomination in, Vol. II). *The General Board.*—In 1959 the convention changed its name to South Carolina Baptist Convention. The general board was renamed the General Board of South Carolina Baptist Convention. In 1965 the convention enlarged the membership of the general board by authorizing the election of one member from the area of each association with membership of up to 15,000; two members from the area of each association with membership from 15,000 to 25,000; and three members from the area of each association with membership of more than 25,000.

In 1960 the convention approved plans for the erection of the present Baptist Building, 907 Richland Street, Columbia. That same year the convention approved recommendations of a study committee to create new services and departments and enlarge the promotional staff of the general board.

Staff.—The business manager serves as chief accountant, purchasing agent, and building superintendent. The office of public relations handles general publicity, compiles and prints the convention annual, coordinates department programs through an annual calendar of activities, and compiles statistics. The office of program services supplies and distributes tracts, audiovisuals, and other materials; furnishes editorial services for departments; and prints departmental and convention materials.

The convention continued, as at present, the existing departments: Sunday School, Church Training, Music, Brotherhood, and Woman's Missionary Union. The following new departments were created:

Missions.—The missions department promotes mission emphasis weeks in the churches; ad-

SOUTH CAROLINA STATISTICAL SUMMARY

Year	Associations	Churches	Church Membership	Baptisms	S. S. Enrolment	V.B.S. Enrolment	T. U. Enrolment	W.M.U. Enrolment	Brotherhood Enrolment	Music Enrolment	Mission Gifts	Total Gifts	Value Church Property
1955	39	1410	446,757	18,833	392,227	148,328	128,798	92,102	15,651		$3,984,960	$21,029,408	$ 78,963,300
1956	39	1427	456,432	18,563	397,733	146,611	131,660	103,810	16,599		3,923,225	21,531,974	87,291,822
1957	39	1441	468,076	18,429	405,683	139,042	136,296	107,372	18,268	34,382	4,570,131	24,130,295	99,627,134
1958	39	1460	478,611	17,968	408,750	160,083	138,444	113,218	19,360	39,299	4,334,912	22,803,160	107,763,903
1959	40	1479	429,614	20,364	417,491	154,053	142,784	115,207	20,847	41,739	4,537,231	24,706,796	116,570,538
1960	41	1495	503,191	17,628	419,283	159,275	143,676	115,617	20,929	39,125	4,751,726	26,543,108	123,813,032
1961	43	1501	512,418	17,742	424,750	159,592	145,863	117,006	21,201	42,868	4,954,720	27,361,601	133,588,955
1962	43	1516	520,524	17,397	428,768	167,243	151,435	116,932	20,628	47,475	5,249,484	29,844,840	143,696,313
1963	43	1531	527,780	16,205	426,117	169,513	147,452	116,203	28,650	51,039	5,568,250	31,059,012	153,282,947
1964	43	1551	535,431	17,836	428,743	177,317	146,283	117,056	20,949	54,606	6,351,569	32,466,651	158,570,606
1965	43	1554	544,978	16,338	431,432	170,789	144,638	120,567	19,413	53,178	6,262,696	36,365,253	175,118,148
1966	44	1566	555,888	16,333	426,856	168,948	140,497	118,159	19,955	57,246	7,090,196	39,367,368	192,207,032
1967	44	1572	565,497	16,689	424,159	177,608	140,557	117,492	20,740	63,632	7,259,976	41,941,646	205,020,469
1968	44	1580	574,495	16,075	423,051	180,306	147,644	115,130	19,651	64,460	7,800,745	47,910,499	219,468,890

DANIEL W. CLOER

vises missions committee in respect to financial aid to mission pastors and churches; promotes creation of missions and churches; promotes a cooperative ministry with National Baptists, migrants, and other mission projects not assigned to other departments; and serves as director of associational superintendents of missions.

Evangelism.—This department aids pastors and churches in finding the best-known methods and techniques in creative evangelism; coordinates the efforts of the departments of the general board in evangelism emphases; promotes campus evangelism; promotes simultaneous revival campaigns through associational and state conferences on evangelism.

The implementation of these changes and enlarged general board staff resulted in the election of directors in all of these areas and programs of work during 1962–65.

In 1954 the convention elected a committee to explore the feasibility of a written history of South Carolina Baptists and to search for a qualified historian for this task. In 1956 a contract was signed with Joe M. King of Furman University to write the history. The convention assigned this project to the South Carolina Baptist Historical Society for supervision and implementation. In 1964 *A History of South Carolina Baptists* was published. The entire publication of 4,500 copies was disposed of during 1964–65 through sales and distribution to libraries, institutions, and agencies of the Southern Baptist Convention and state conventions.

During 1969 the convention celebrated the 50th anniversary of the founding of the general board. Highlights of this celebration included recognition of missions and churches established; successful promotion of 75 Million Campaign; adoption of the Cooperative Program in 1925; and expansion of the educational and benevolent institutions and agencies of the convention through increased financial support through the current and capital appropriations.

The South Carolina convention appointed in 1967 a committee to present annually plans and programs for the celebration of the 150th anniversary of the convention in 1971. The celebration of this anniversary included, among other activities: a history of the convention; writing contests in history and music; anniversary observances in churches and associations to include histories of each church and association; and anniversary sessions in 1971 at First Baptist Church, Columbia, where the convention was organized, and at the Columbia Coliseum for sessions of pageantry and drama.

HORACE G. HAMMETT

***SOUTH CAROLINA BAPTIST HOSPITAL.** The hospital program of South Carolina Baptists is divided into the Columbia and Easley divisions. A total of 334,655 patients have been served since the Baptist Hospital was first opened. Hospital assets are valued at $12,871,721 with 410 beds and 48 bassinets. In 1969, 16,926 patients and 2,155 infants were served with a total of $555,636 given in free service. Educational programs operated by the hospital include a school for practical nurses, X-ray technicians, laboratory technicians, surgical technicians, and pastoral care. The hospital also has an affiliation with the University of South Carolina for their associate and Bachelor degrees nursing programs.

The Easley division (known as the Easley Baptist Hospital and adopted by South Carolina Baptist Convention in 1955) began upon the joint suggestion of Ellison S. McKissick, Roy C. McCall, and Julien D. Wyatt in 1947, and opened for patients July 1, 1958, with 73 beds. A new wing was built in 1969, bringing the total bed capacity to 98. WILLIAM BOYCE

SOUTH CAROLINA BAPTISTS AND RACE RELATIONS. In 1935 the social service committee of the South Carolina Baptist Convention urged that (1) pastors lead in developing "Christian attitudes" and "Christian respect for Negroes," (2) white and black churches cooperate for helpful race relations, and (3) the convention seek to establish cooperative relationship with the Negro Baptist convention so that they could work "together in building up the cause of Christ among all peoples of both races." During the decades of 1950–70, there were developments consistent with these ideals. First, there was no opposition by the convention or any of its agencies to the school desegregation decision (1954) nor was there any support for prosegregation endeavors. Second, continued support for religious education has been given to the black colleges by the convention and WMU (in cooperation with the Home Mission Board, SBC), and through Vacation Bible Schools sponsored for or with Negro churches. Third, an agreement was made for the white convention to employ a "worker with National Baptists" with an advisory committee representing both the white and black state Baptist conventions.

Fourth, the four state Baptist colleges all desegregated their student bodies after 1963. Fifth, the policies of other convention agencies are progressing toward nondiscrimination in services. Sixth, through special studies and its annual reports, the Christian life and public affairs committee of the convention has repeatedly supported Christian principles in race relations.

Seventh, pastors and churches have, in the main, resisted the establishment of segregated community schools in their facilities (though a few have been set up by churches or held in church facilities). Eighth, some pastors are refusing to accept a call from a church that excludes black members, and others insist on making clear their position in favor of an inclusive church membership policy before being considered by a pulpit committee. A 10 per cent survey of pastors in Jan., 1970, indicated that two-thirds of respondents believed that a

New Testament church should allow black members, though 60 per cent thought their congregations would not accept them.

HOWARD H. MCCLAIN

SOUTH DAKOTA, BAPTISTS IN. See NORTHERN PLAINS BAPTIST CONVENTION, and COLORADO, BAPTIST GENERAL CONVENTION OF.

***SOUTH TEXAS CHILDREN'S HOME.** The main campus now consists of 14 cottages and over 12 service buildings. A group home was opened in Aug., 1969, near Goliad on a 700-acre tract of land left by Mrs. Fanny Marshall, Victoria, Tex. A college residence was opened in Aug., 1969, near Bee County College in Beeville, Tex. A social service department directs foster home and mother's aid programs and is qualified to handle adoptions. The various facilities and programs of the home provide for 225 children. The home is supported by the Cooperative Program and gifts from churches and individuals. With property valued at $1,600,000 the home operated in 1969 on a budget of $325,000.

J. MELBURN SIBLEY, JR.

SOUTH WEST AFRICA, MISSION IN. On invitation of Windhoek Baptist Church and with full approval of Baptist Union of South Africa, the Foreign Mission Board, SBC, sent Charlton and Betty (Huckaby) Whitson to South West Africa in July, 1968. Whitson was called to pastor the English-language congregation, organized four years earlier. The church doubled its membership during the first year of Whitson's ministry, to a total of 56 members in 1969. A small Baptist group at Walvis Bay, 250 miles away, was considered a mission of the Windhoek church and was visited by Whitson one weekend each month.

H. CORNELL GOERNER

***SOUTHEAST TEXAS, BAPTIST HOSPITAL OF (Beaumont).** In 1958 the hospital added two five-story wings to its building, increasing its capacity to 273 beds and 50 bassinets. The institution added an auditorium, medical library, and another student nurse dormitory in 1962, a Radiological Cobalt center in 1964, and new engineering and purchasing buildings in July, 1969. On Sept. 7, 1969, it opened a new women-children hospital, containing over 50,000 sq. ft. of floor space and 100 beds. Owned and operated by the Baptist General Convention of Texas, the hospital has assets totaling $7,442,701.43.

GUY H. DALRYMPLE

***SOUTHEASTERN BAPTIST THEOLOGICAL SEMINARY.** The seventh academic session (1957–58) began with an enrolment of 714 and three new teachers: R. C. Briggs as professor of New Testament; John W. Eddins, Jr., as instructor in theology; and H. H. Oliver as special instructor in New Testament. The first scholarly issue of the seminary bulletin, *The Outlook,* was released in October. The office of dean was established by the board of trustees, and Olin T. Binkley was named to fill that post. In the spring, the seminary was host to its first student missions conference, the library (totaling 28,800 cataloged volumes) was moved into its new building, and the renovation of the chapel was completed. In June, 1958, the seminary received full accreditation from the American Association of Theological Schools. In addition to the regular summer school, 173 persons attended the second one-week summer conference, July 7–11.

In the fall of 1958 work was begun on the Ruby Reid Child Care Center, which was made possible by a bequest from Miss Reid of Wake Forest, N. C., gifts from the Baptist Sunday School Board, and a grant from the Z. Smith Reynolds Foundation. In 1959 the seminary gave Groves Stadium, a part of the properties purchased from Wake Forest College, to the Wake County Board of Education. With the participation of outstanding sociologists and other specialists from the North Carolina State College in Raleigh (N. C.), an interdisciplinary course on the rural community was initiated.

Twenty-five new duplex apartments were filled quickly for the fall term in 1959. J. B. Weatherspoon came as a visiting professor. Others who joined the faculty that fall were: Emily K. Lansdell as professor of missions; John I Durham as instructor in Old Testament; George H. Shriver, Jr., as instructor in church history; H. Max Smith as artist-in-residence; and James Sistrunk as assistant librarian. The fall enrolment was 734. A new pipe organ, the gift of Walter M. Williams (*q.v.*), and his wife, was dedicated on Oct. 1, 1959. An endowment fund of $10,000 for student aid was received from the estate of H. E. Miller, Sr. An extension course for chaplains at Fort Bragg was started during that academic year.

During the tenth session (1960–61) the first of the Carver-Barnes Memorial Lectures, given in honor of W. O. Carver (*q.v.,* Vol. I) and W. W. Barnes (*q.v.*), were delivered by Theron D. Price. Max Gray Rogers became an instructor in Old Testament. A housing shortage for single women was relieved by the purchase of Jo Williams' Guest House, just across the street from the campus. The final installment of the $1,600,000 pledged to Wake Forest College for the campus was paid on Jan. 1, 1961. In the annual meeting of the board of trustees, the administrative building was renamed Stealey Hall in honor of the seminary's first president, and Emery B. Denny was chosen as the board's president to succeed W. Perry Crouch who had served in that capacity since 1952. Truman S. Smith was elected director of student affairs.

R. Eugene Owens joined the faculty as assistant professor of preaching, and John W. Shepard, Jr., became a visiting professor in the fall of 1961. In cooperation with the State Missions Department of the Baptist State Convention of North Carolina, Southeastern Seminary began sponsoring the work of a Japanese student-pastor with the Japanese wives of servicemen living in North Carolina near military bases. In their annual meeting on Feb. 15, 1962, the trustees voted to rename the Music-Religion Building in honor of Scott B. Appleby, who had contributed liberally to the student aid fund. The seminary bulletin (Jan.–Feb., 1962) reported the following significant actions:

The Board of Trustees unanimously adopted a joint report made by the Committee on Instruction and the Executive Committee. This report dealt with problems of doctrine and teaching methods.

Although certain members of the faculty will be required to re-examine their instruction methods and doctrinal presuppositions in the perspective of the school's Abstract of Principles, no formal charge was made against any member of the instructional staff.

Enrolment dropped to 595 in September, 1962. I. N. Patterson and Benjamin Ray Lawton taught as visiting professors. In their meeting in Feb., 1963, the trustees elected Olin T. Binkley as president of the seminary to succeed Sydnor L. Stealey (*q.v.*) who was retiring July 31. J. Glenn Blackburn was chosen as the board's new president. Regular conferences, such as the religious education-church music workshop, student missions conference, chaplains' day, were held in the spring.

Prior to the opening of school in 1963, George R. Beasley-Murray led the faculty's annual retreat; then on Aug. 29–30, he delivered the convocation lectures. John I Durham was made acting academic dean, and James H. Blackmore was elected director of public relations. Lyman C. Franklin became manager of the cafeteria. On Oct. 17, Olin T. Binkley was installed as the seminary's second president. In his inaugural address, he cited four requirements for the advancement of theological education: (1) systematic and thorough study by qualified students under the guidance of able and dedicated teachers; (2) the need of financial resources and the reflection of the educational aims of a school in its annual budget as well as in its long-range plans; (3) the sincere worship of the living God; and (4) an indefectible loyalty to Jesus Christ and his way of life. The center of this school, he declared, is "the mind of God as disclosed in Jesus Christ, and every process of thought on this campus is related to that center." He pledged to administer the seminary's generous policy of faculty tenure with integrity and without wavering but warned "that this policy of tenure gives no sanction or protection whatsoever to the betrayal of trust or to disloyalty to Jesus Christ as He is presented to us in the New Testament."

At the annual meeting of the board of trustees in Feb., 1964, Raymond B. Brown was elected professor of New Testament, and Claud B. Bowen was chosen by the board as its new president. Later in the spring W. Christian Sizemore was appointed assistant cataloging librarian. On June 11, the seminary was singularly honored when its president, Olin T. Binkley, was elected president of the American Association of Theological Schools. Edward A. McDowell, Jr., and M. Ray McKay retired from the faculty on July 31.

In 1964 Martha W. Janes became Health Center nurse, and David Mein served as a visiting professor. The administrative staff was strengthened by the addition of Wilbur N. Todd as business manager and Fred T. Badders as director of student activities. A statement on "a complex issue," which was described as having troubled the seminary since 1960, was released by the board of trustees on Feb. 18, 1965. The theological dimensions of this difficulty were identified as being related to "the predominance of one point of view in the interpretation of the New Testament." The trustees stated that at the request of President Stealey a committee on instruction of the board had been elected and that this committee has interviewed members of the faculty, May 15–17, 1961. Upon the recommendation of this committee, the board (on Feb. 15, 1962) had "authorized procedures aimed at clarification of issues through consultation, including a process of inquiry and counsel with some members of the faculty" and had "agreed that the committee on instruction should complete this assignment by February 18, 1965."

The 1965 statement reported that "no formal charge of deviation" from the Abstract of Principles had been made against any member of the instructional staff and expressed profound gratitude for "the devotion and faithful work of able and dedicated teachers who comprise the faculty" and "unqualified confidence" in the personal integrity and professional competence of the seminary's president. They declared that from the beginning of this inquiry, the principle of responsible academic freedom had been observed with utmost care and concluded their statement with these paragraphs:

The requirement regarding the theological covenant outlined in the Abstract of Principles and signed by each member of the faculty is fully compatible with the document on academic freedom and tenure which was adopted as an advisory norm by the American Association of Theological Schools in 1960 and which explicitly states that a theological institution may expect its faculty to subscribe to a confessional or doctrinal standard.

This is a Southern Baptist seminary, established and maintained by the Southern Baptist Convention, and it is the responsibility of the trustees to formulate policies in harmony with the nature and purpose of the school. The faculty and students are encouraged to participate in creative theological inquiry and to make effective use of the resources of this school which is thorough in scholarship, sound in Christian theology, and vitally related to the churches.

In conjunction with the Carver-Barnes lectures, the first of the annual pastors' seminars was held Mar. 9–12. G. Henton Davies was guest-professor for the summer school.

The 15th academic year (1965–66) opened with Donald E. Cook's joining the faculty as assistant professor of New Testament and Henlee H. Barnett's giving the convocation lectures. Donald D. Moore was appointed director of student activities and resident counselor. A. C. Reid and David Mein taught as visiting professors; Beth C. McLeod directed the Ruby Reid Child Care Center. On Feb. 16, 1966, the new dormitory for women was dedicated. Raymond Bryan Brown was chosen academic dean, and John I Durham became administrative associate to the president. Robert E. Poerschke joined the faculty as associate professor of religious education. The George T. Noel III Memorial Scholarship Fund was established by his family and friends. Additional duplex apartments were constructed during the summer, making a total of 88 duplex apartments built by the seminary.

H. Eugene McLeod was elected librarian and assistant professor of bibliography. Upon the recommendation of the faculty and in accord with a recommendation of the American Association of Theological Schools, the trustees (Feb. 16, 1967) voted to change the name of the seminary's basic degree from *Bachelor of Divinity* to *Master of Divinity*. (The new nomenclature became effective with the fall semester of 1967.) As in previous years, Neal Peyton conducted classes in dactylology (sign-language for the deaf) on the campus. Other courses in specialized ministries included seminars on mental health at Dorothea Dix Hospital in Raleigh, N. C., which were conducted by William R. Steininger, lecturer in pastoral care. At its meeting on June 1, 1967, the Alumni Association voted to sponsor an annual giving program. In cooperation with the Home Mission Board and the District of Columbia, the seminary conducted a four-week seminar of urban studies (June 12–July 9) in Washington, D. C. Edwin C. Osburn retired as librarian and associate professor of bibliography on July 31.

Archie L. Nations and Ellis W. Hollon, Jr., joined the faculty in the fall of 1967 as associate professor of New Testament and associate professor of philosophy of religion, respectively. The seminary began offering a two-year sequence of study leading to the Master of Religious Education degree, in addition to its three-year program of Master of Divinity with Religious Education. Significant changes were made in the curriculum leading to the Master of Divinity degree: the number of hours in the core curriculum was reduced, and three new interdisciplinary courses were introduced. An honors program was instituted. Special conferences that year included a dialogue with a team of top program leaders in the SBC and a conference on witnessing to the nonevangelicals. The new student center was named Mackie Hall in honor of George C. Mackie (*q.v.*) and his wife of Wake Forest, N. C. He was seminary physician from the opening of the seminary in 1951. He and Mrs. Mackie had made generous gifts of time and money for the beautification of the seminary campus. The following bequests and gifts were accepted by the board of trustees: the Laura D. Powers Endowment Fund for Student Aid, the James I. Miller Endowment for Student Loan Fund, the James I. Miller Library Endowment Fund, the Chaffin-Dickey Memorial Loan Fund, and the Lillie Norket Student Loan Fund. The receipts from the first annual alumni giving program totaled $8,869.72.

Theodore F. Adams, I. N. Patterson, and Walter Ross strengthened the instructional staff as visiting professors for the 1968–69 term. Walter Sanders served as lecturer in pastoral care. A Monday afternoon class for continuing theological education on "The Church and Contemporary Issues" featured such leaders as Brooks Hays and Thomas Cronin. Enrolment that fall totaled 582. The new health center was opened, and Elizabeth Ann Smith joined the library's staff as catalog librarian. On Feb. 13, 1969, the board of trustees voted to name the seminary chapel in honor of Olin T. Binkley, the seminary's second president, and the library building for Emery B. Denny, former Chief Justice of the Supreme Court of North Carolina and long-time friend of the seminary. Gifts from friends in Richmond, Va., made possible the purchase of a videotape recording machine for the preaching classes. The annual alumni meeting in New Orleans on June 12 reached a record attendance of 762. David Fite, missionary-alumnus who had been imprisoned in Cuba for forty-two months, was given a grateful welcome. The Urban Studies Seminar was conducted June 16–July 11, in the Research Triangle area of North Carolina. The seminary became the recipient of a $50,000 bequest from the estate of Annie C. Womble. Receipts from the second alumni giving program totaled $13,480.75.

On Oct. 8, 1969, John W. Carlton entered upon his duties as professor of preaching by signing the Abstract of Principles. James R. Moseley became the seminary physician. For its 19th term, the seminary had 570 students enrolled in all its programs leading to degrees and certificates. Its faculty consisted of 24 professors, with additions of two visiting professors and four instructors. Library holdings totaled 184,890 separate items. From its beginning through 1969 Southeastern Seminary granted 1,918 Master of Divinity or Bachelor of Divinity degrees; 166 Master of Theology degrees; two Master of Religious Education degrees; and 262 Certificates in Theology—a total of 2,348 degrees and certificates to 2,213 individuals. These men and women, found throughout the nation and in many parts of the world, are "the earnest" of the seminary's stewardship to our fellow Baptists and to the Lord Jesus Christ whose servants we are. JAMES H. BLACKMORE

See also STUDENT ACTIVITIES, SOUTHEASTERN BAPTIST THEOLOGICAL SEMINARY.

SOUTHERN BAPTIST BUSINESS OFFICERS, CONFERENCE OF. An annual meeting of business officers of local, state and Convention-wide institutions and agencies. Beginning Feb. 21, 1963, as Baptist Educational Institution Business Officers, the group changed the name of their meeting in 1964 to Conference of Southern Baptist College Business Officers and in 1965 to Conference of Southern Baptist Business Officers. The latter reflected the broadening base of participation which soon included representatives of hospitals, homes for the aging, and child-care institutions. In 1970 the conference was enlarged to include business officers of local churches and denominational agencies, boards, commissions, state papers, and foundations.

The annual conferences, hosted by the Annuity Board, SBC, in Dallas, have provided a balance in programing between general sessions, with speakers and panel presentations, and divisional or individual workshop sessions, with one or more specialized and technical discussions.

The following men have served as chairmen of the conferences: H. L. Mitchusson, Texas, 1963 and 1964; H. Evan Zeiger, Alabama, 1965; Troy Womack, Texas, 1966; H. Graves Edmondson, Florida, 1967; William G. Kersh, Oklahoma, 1968; R. Leigh Pegues, Alabama, 1969; Flynn T. Harrell, South Carolina, 1970; and F. T. Bowman, North Carolina, 1971.

FLYNN T. HARRELL

***SOUTHERN BAPTIST COLLEGE.** In 1968 the college was admitted to full standing and ownership in the life of Arkansas Baptist State Convention. The college is controlled by a board of trustees appointed by the convention. In 1969 the assets of the college were valued at over $4,000,000. The state convention provided $85,000 of the total budget of $1,000,000 in 1968–69.

The enrolment of 1,222 students in the 1968–69 academic year was the highest in the history of the college. During the same year the Community of Science Complex was completed and put in use. The building has a total floor space of over 16,000 square feet. Hubert Ethridge Williams has served as president of the college since 1941.

TERRY L. JONES

SOUTHERN BAPTIST COLLEGES AND SCHOOLS, THE ASSOCIATION OF (cf. Southern Association of Baptist Colleges and Schools, Vol. II). The association continues to function along the lines originally established. On June 14, 1966, in the interest of clarity the name was changed to The Association of Southern Baptist Colleges and Schools. Much of the work of the association is planned by a joint administrative committee.

In 1962 the annual meeting of the association was held at Wake Forest University and has since met on four other campuses in addition to Nashville. In these sessions the presidents and deans deal with the urgent problems faced by church colleges today. The association participated fully in the Baptist Education Study Task (BEST), 1965–67.

In 1967 the association and the Education Commission voted to publish a short history of Southern Baptists in higher education. This book, *Southern Baptists in Christian Education,* was written by H. I. Hester and was produced by the Graphic Arts Department of Chowan College. It was released in 1968.

Officers are elected annually with the exception of the secretary-treasurer who has served continuously since the organization of the association.

H. I. HESTER

***SOUTHERN BAPTIST CONVENTION, THE.** The Southern Baptist Convention entered the 1956–70 era by accepting President C. C. Warren's challenge at the Convention in Kansas City to double the number of preaching stations by 1964—the anniversary of 150 years of organized Baptist work on a national level in North America. Setting a goal of 30,000 more preaching points, the Convention launched the 30,000 Movement. Also in 1956, the messengers set aside 1959–64 for the Baptist Jubilee Advance, five years of special evangelism emphases climaxing with the Third Jubilee Celebration. In 1964 the SBC and the American Baptist Convention held simultaneous annual meetings in Atlantic City, N. J. At the conclusion other North American Baptist bodies joined with these conventions in celebrating the Third Jubilee.

In order to continue the spirit of cooperation and fellowship developed by the participating Baptist bodies during the years of Jubilee planning, a North American Baptist Fellowship was proposed. The SBC rejected the proposal in 1964, but a year later voted to take part in the North American Baptist Fellowship as long as such participation was not construed as a step toward organic unity and the fellowship was a part of the Baptist World Alliance.

In 1965 the Convention approved a cooperative venture to involve Baptists in North, Central, and South America in fellowship and joint evangelistic efforts. Called the Crusade of the Americas, it climaxed with a hemisphere-wide evangelistic effort in 1969.

A far-reaching action taken in 1956 was the naming of a committee to make a study of "our total Southern Baptist program." Douglas M. Branch, North Carolina, was chairman. Growing out of this committee's recommendations was the concept of program budgeting and a greater effort to correlate programs, curriculae, and meetings of the various SBC agencies affecting the local churches. The Inter-Agency Council was enlarged and strengthened to provide the structure through which the Convention agencies could work to correlate their program efforts. Between 1960 and 1967 the Convention adopted a program statement for each agency, describing the work assigned to it. Agency programs were designed to prevent unnecessary overlapping of work, to lessen tensions between agencies, and to make possible a more objective study of budget needs.

The Total Study Committee also recommended that the Executive Committee and smaller agencies of the SBC secure housing facilities separate from the Sunday School Board. The SBC Building was constructed in Nashville with money furnished by the Baptist Sunday School Board and occupied in 1963 by the Executive Committee, Baptist Foundation, Stewardship Commission, Education Commission, and Christian Life Commission. The Seminary Extension Department offices were moved there the same year from Jackson, Miss.

In 1957 a sixth seminary was authorized and located in Kansas City, Mo. Named Midwestern Baptist Theological Seminary, it was limited in scope of work to a school of theology. Millard J. Berquist was named president.

Another agency was formed at the Louisville Convention in 1959 when the Stewardship Commission was established. Stewardship promotion responsibilities formerly borne by the Executive Committee were transferred to the new agency which named Merrill D. Moore as executive director. An amendment to transfer the stewardship responsibilities to the Sunday School Board was narrowly defeated.

Ownership and control of Carver School of Missions and Social Work, Louisville, Ky., was transferred from Woman's Missionary Union to the SBC. It remained a separate institution with Nathan Brooks as president until 1963 when, by Convention action, it was merged with adjacent Southern Baptist Theological Seminary.

The Convention gave first approval in 1970 (votes of two consecutive Conventions required) to releasing the hospitals at New Orleans, La., and Jacksonville, Fla., from Convention ownership so they could be more flexible in securing financial support.

In 1956 effort was made to change the name of the Sunday School Board to the Board of Education and Publication of the Southern Baptist Convention. The idea was abandoned the next year due to lack of support. In 1960 the Relief and Annuity Board was renamed the Annuity Board in recognition that relief was no longer a sizable portion of its work.

Efforts to drop the word "Southern" from "Southern Baptist Convention" developed as the Convention work moved into all 50 states. In 1956 messengers refused to consider changing the name. In 1965 they asked the Executive Committee to study the matter, but in 1969 the committee reported surveys showed "no gathering of preference around any change of name at the moment."

Territorial restrictions limiting the SBC to the United States came into question as Southern Baptist work spilled over into Canada from the Northwest and developed in Europe near pockets of United States military personnel and their families. In 1957 a Committee on Canadian Baptist Cooperation was formed to deal with tensions. The committee's plan for giving help to Canadian Baptists through the Sunday School Board and Home Mission Board, while at the same time recognizing the autonomy and strength of the Canadian Baptist group, was approved in 1958. In the same Convention an amendment was proposed which would allow churches in Canada to be a part of the SBC. In 1962 a proposed constitutional amendment to eliminate territorial restrictions of the SBC to the United States and its territories was sidetracked to the Executive Committee for study by a margin of 2,696 votes to 2,042. The following year the sponsor of the amendment had the Convention agree to withdraw it from consideration, and no further action was taken.

Membership in the Convention continued to grow, from 8,708,823 in 1956 to 11,489,613 members in 1969. Six state conventions reached the 25,000 members required for representation on the SBC Executive Committee, boards, and agencies: Kansas and Ohio (1961), Indiana (1962), Colorado and Oregon-Washington (1963), and Michigan (1965). In 1958, upon Convention instruction, the Foreign Mission Board began transferring its work in Hawaii to the Hawaii Baptist Convention.

In 1959 the Home Mission Board was asked to develop a plan for closer cooperation in mission work with the state conventions, placing its emphasis on work in areas where there was no state convention or where the state convention was not well established. State conventions were encouraged to assume full financial and administrative responsibility for all mission work in their areas as rapidly as feasible.

HMB surveys in New York City in 1957 resulted in Paul James being sent in 1958 as pastor-director of Southern Baptist work in the Northeast. Southern Baptist churches soon were found as far north as Caribou, Me. By 1963 there were Southern Baptist churches in all 50 states, Vermont the last state to be entered.

State conventions formed, but lacking 25,000 members for full SBC representation by 1970, included Utah-Idaho Southern Baptist Convention (1964), Northern Plains Baptist Convention (1968), Baptist Convention of New York (1969), and West Virginia Convention of Southern Baptists (1970).

Expansion in the Northeast, as well as in other "pioneer" areas, did not prevent a slackening in the growth rate of the Convention. In 1960 there was alarm over a decline in seminary enrolment, a decline that continued until 1962. Some of the church organizations, including Sunday School, began to show a decline in membership in 1965. Church membership figures continued to climb, but at a slower pace.

In 1967 there was much discussion over the fact that states with small Southern Baptist membership had a larger proportionate representation on boards of trustees and commissions of the SBC than did states with large memberships. But the attempt to reduce the proportion of membership from smaller state conventions failed.

In 1958 a bylaw change required all Convention committees, boards, and commissions to begin including both laymen and ordained persons, with no category contributing more than two thirds. In 1961 another move for more lay participation was made when the Committee on Boards, Commissions, and Standing Committees was doubled in size to include two members from each state, one a layman. In 1963 the first woman vice-president, Mrs. R. L. Mathis, was elected. And in 1968 the Convention asked that opportunities be provided for broader participation by young people in the decision-making processes of Southern Baptists at all levels.

At most annual meetings from 1956 to 1970, messengers reaffirmed the conviction that the Cooperative Program was the best channel for financially supporting the cooperative world mission efforts of the churches. In 1956 the principles of cooperation between the state conventions and the SBC affecting the Cooperative Program, as agreed upon in 1934 and 1951, were reaffirmed with the following additions:

"We further recognize the right of any state which chooses not to deduct any items before division between State and Southern Baptist Convention objects and to adjust their percentages accordingly—it being clearly understood that any state dividing on a straight percentage distribution is in complete harmony with the principles of this understanding.

"That we look with favor as an ideal upon a single percentage distribution between State and Convention-wide causes of Cooperative Program funds."

Cooperative Program receipts for SBC causes grew from $14,260,302 in 1957 to $27,433,440 in 1969. Prior to 1965, receipts above the basic Cooperative Program goal were divided 75 per cent to the Foreign Mission Board and 25 per cent to the Home Mission Board. In 1965 the division was changed to two thirds for the Foreign Mission Board and one third for the Home Mission Board.

In 1969 the HMB and several state conventions assisted the Kansas Convention of Southern Baptists when that convention and its church loan agency were declared insolvent because of a $1,600,000 deficit in the church bond and loan program.

Doctrinal disputes centered around two publications during the period 1956–70. When the Convention met in San Francisco in 1962, controversy centered on *The Message of Genesis,* written by Ralph H. Elliott, a professor at Midwestern Baptist Theological Seminary. A motion asking the Sunday School Board to discontinue publishing the book was defeated, but all SBC agencies and institutions were requested to take necessary steps to insure that "faith in the historical accuracy and doctrinal integrity of the Bible" was not threatened. Elliott was dismissed by the seminary trustees when he would not voluntarily withhold his book from a second printing and offered it to

HISTORICAL TABLE OF THE SOUTHERN BAPTIST CONVENTION, 1957–70

Date	Place of Meeting	Registration	Presidents	Secretaries	Preachers
1957	Chicago, Illinois	9,109	C. C. Warren, N. C.	James W. Merritt, Ga.; Joe W. Burton, Tenn.	Herschel H. Hobbs, Oklahoma
1958	Houston, Texas	11,966	Brooks Hays, Arkansas	James W. Merritt, Ga.; Joe W. Burton, Tenn.	Robert E. Naylor, Texas
1959	Louisville, Kentucky	12,326	Brooks Hays, Arkansas	James W. Merritt, Ga.; Joe W. Burton, Tenn.	R. Paul Caudill, Tenn.
1960	Miami Beach, Florida	13,612	Ramsey Pollard, Tennessee	James W. Merritt, Ga.; Joe W. Burton, Tenn.	Ralph A. Herring, N. C.
1961	St. Louis, Missouri	11,140	Ramsey Pollard, Tennessee	James W. Merritt, Ga.; Joe W. Burton, Tenn.	A. B. Van Arsdale, Ala.
1962	San Francisco, California	9,396	Herschel H. Hobbs, Oklahoma	James W. Merritt, Ga.; Joe W. Burton, Tenn.	H. Franklin Paschall, Tenn.
1963	Kansas City, Missouri	12,971	Herschel H. Hobbs, Oklahoma	James W. Merritt, Ga.; Joe W. Burton, Tenn.	Carl Bates, N. C.
1964	Atlantic City, New Jersey	13,136	K. Owen White, Texas	James W. Merritt, Ga.; Joe W. Burton, Tenn.	Enoch C. Brown, S. C.
1965	Dallas, Texas	16,053	W. Wayne Dehoney, Tennessee	Joe W. Burton, Tenn.; W. Fred Kendall, Tenn.	John H. Haldeman, Florida
1966	Detroit, Michigan	10,414	W. Wayne Dehoney, Tennessee	Clifton J. Allen, Tenn.; W. Fred Kendall, Tenn.	Ray E. Roberts, Ohio
1967	Miami Beach, Florida	14,794	H. Franklin Paschall, Tennessee	Clifton J. Allen, Tenn.; W. Fred Kendall, Tenn.	Landrum P. Leavell, H. Texas
1968	Houston Texas	15,071	H. Franklin Paschall, Tennessee	Clifton J. Allen, Tenn.; W. Fred Kendall, Tenn.	W. Douglas Hudgins, Mississippi
1969	New Orleans, Louisiana	16,678	W. A. Criswell, Texas	Clifton J. Allen, Tenn., W. Fred Kendall, Tenn.	Scott L. Tatum, Louisiana
1970	Denver, Colorado	13,692	W. A. Criswell, Texas	Clifton J. Allen, Tenn., W. Fred Kendall, Tenn.	Grady C. Cothen, Oklahoma

another publisher when the Sunday School Board decided not to reprint.

The most far-reaching action growing out of the controversy was the establishment of a special committee composed of men then serving as presidents of the various state conventions, and SBC President H. H. Hobbs, to prepare a statement of Baptist faith and message. The report of the Committee on Baptist Faith and Message was adopted in 1963 at Kansas City without change. In 1969 messengers defeated a motion that would have required writers for SBC publications and seminary faculty members to sign an additional doctrinal statement and reaffirm the 1963 statement as the guideline for Convention agencies in carrying out their work.

Another book occupied the attention of messengers at Denver, Colo., in 1970. By a vote of 5,394 to 2,170, the Convention asked the Sunday School Board to withdraw Volume I of *Broadman Bible Commentary* from further distribution and rewrite it with "due consideration of the conservative viewpoint." Additional motions which would have made the Executive Committee the doctrinal "watchdog" for the Convention and would have required all who teach at the seminaries or write for the Sunday School Board to adhere to a closely defined viewpoint of the Bible were ruled out of order. Again, the "Baptist Faith and Message" of 1963 was reaffirmed.

Another focal point of Convention action during these years was the Christian Life Commission, primarily because of the diversity of views on the part of messengers regarding the problem of racism. In 1958 at Houston, an attempt to strike the section of the commission's report dealing with racial problems and to curtail its budget was defeated. The next year, when a resolution was presented asking that the 1954 Convention's favorable action regarding the Supreme Court's school segregation order be rescinded, it was ruled that one annual session could not rescind action taken by a previous annual session.

In 1964 in Atlantic City, the commission received a setback. A substitute statement on race relations was adopted as part of the Christian Life Commission's report. At the same time references to capital punishment as being contrary to the spirit and teaching of Christ and a call to abolish capital punishment was deleted.

In 1965 an attempt to censor the commission by deleting a $18,500 budget increase was defeated by a substantial majority, and in 1967 a motion to abolish the commission lost.

When the Convention met at Houston in 1968, riots, tensions, and trouble tore at the heart of many cities in the United States following the assassination of Martin Luther King. Messengers voted (approximately 73 per cent in favor) for "A Statement Concerning the Crisis in the Nation," presented by the Executive Committee. It was a stronger statement on racism than had ever been adopted before. To implement the concern expressed, the HMB was instructed to take the lead in working with the denomination's agencies in facing problems related to the national crisis. The same year the first Negro missionary was appointed by the FMB.

At Denver in 1970, several unsuccessful attempts were made to censor the leadership of the Christian Life Commission because of a Christian Morality Seminar the commission conducted earlier in the year at Atlanta, Ga. But strong opposition was voiced because representatives of nonbiblical views of sex and ethics were allowed on the program to debate with Southern Baptist theologians and because a black political leader spoke at the seminar.

The race issue loomed big throughout the period 1956–70 in the United States. In 1958 Brooks Hays, representative to Congress from Little Rock, Ark., and president of the SBC, was reelected to a second term. He was overwhelmingly supported by actions at several state conventions even though he suffered political defeat in his home district as a result of his moderate views on race.

"Kneel-ins" and other attempts to attend Southern Baptist churches by black persons brought mixed reactions. Some churches welcomed them, many did not. Gradually the issue switched from church attendance to church membership for Negroes. First Baptist Church, Oklahoma City, in 1962, while Pastor H. H. Hobbs was serving as SBC president, voted not to accept a 15-year-old Negro as a member on the grounds "his motives for membership were wrong." But by 1965 the church did receive Negro members.

Also in 1965, First Baptist Church, Richmond, Va., accepted two Nigerian students into full membership after considerable debate and attempted legal action by some members to forestall the move. In Mississippi, Southern Baptist churches collected money to rebuild Negro houses of worship burned by racists. And by then most Baptist schools had signed the Civil Rights Compliance Act.

By 1970 a change in the attitude of Southern Baptists as a whole toward the race question had taken place. A growing number of churches were receiving Negro members, but much evidence of racism in individuals and churches remained.

Federal aid to Baptist institutions, like the race issue, was a continuing problem. In 1959 Texas Baptists rejected a hospital offered them in Texarkana, because it had been built partly with federal funds. In 1962 Southern Baptists joined with others to insure the defeat of a bill in Congress that would have granted public aid to sectarian colleges.

All sentiment was not against accepting federal grants and loans for schools and other institutions, particularly among college administrators who felt the pinch of rapidly rising costs. And after Congress in 1965 passed the College Aid Bill and the Elementary and Sec-

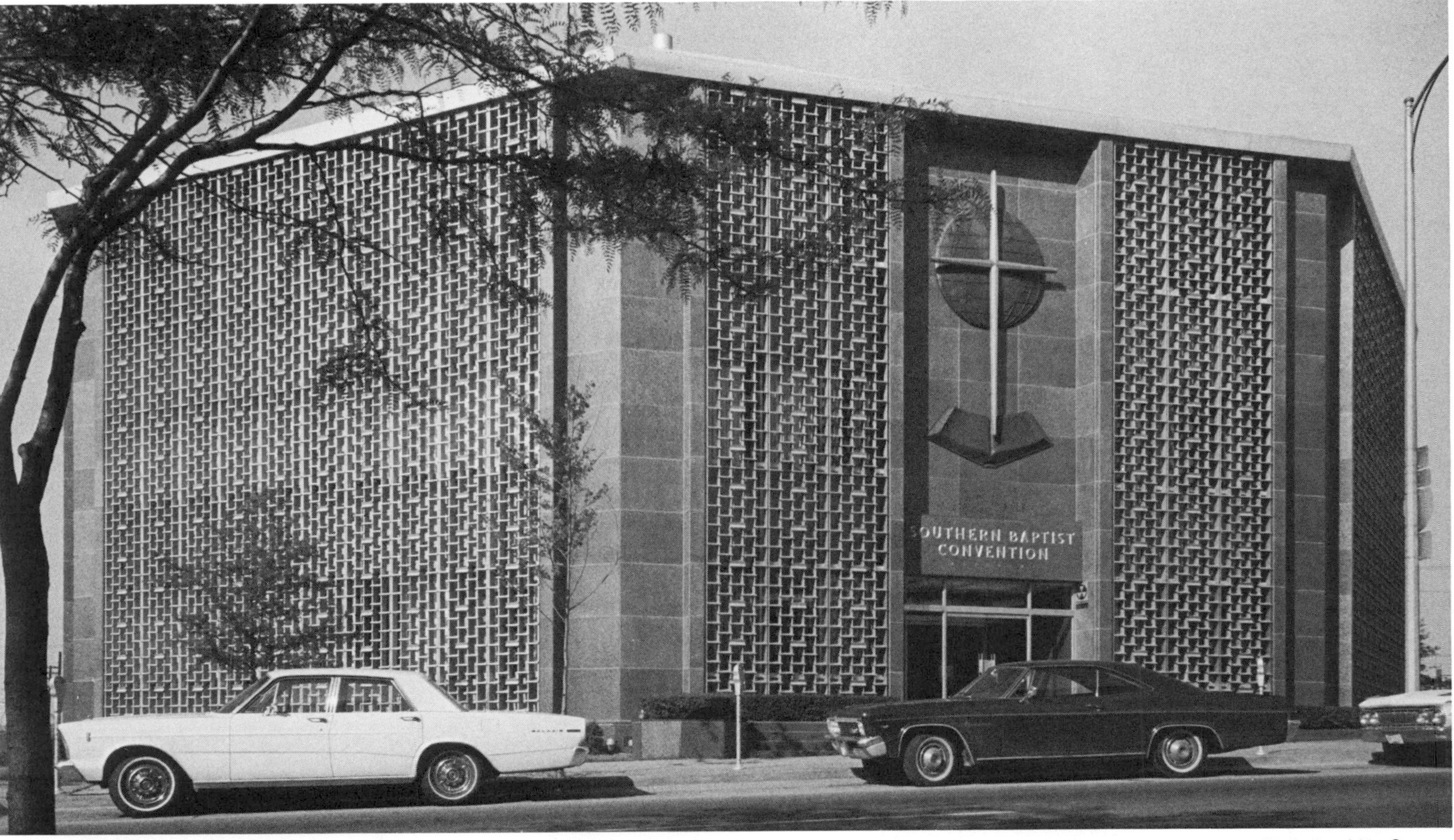

SOUTHERN BAPTIST CONVENTION (*q.v.*) BUILDING, Nashville, Tenn. Erected in 1963, it houses the offices of the Executive Committee, Christian Life Commission, Education Commission, Southern Baptist Foundation, Stewardship Commission, and Seminary Extension Department.

BROOKS HAYS
1958–1959

RAMSEY POLLARD
1960–1961

HERSCHEL H. HOBBS
1962–1963

K. OWEN WHITE
1964

W. WAYNE DEHONEY
1965–1966

H. FRANKLIN PASCHALL
1967–1968

W. A. CRISWELL
1969–1970

PRESIDENTS
of the
SOUTHERN BAPTIST CONVENTION
1958–1970

NUMBER OF SOUTHERN BAPTIST CHURCHES REPORTING MAJOR ITEMS—1969

SBC and State Conventions	Total No. Active Churches	NUMBER REPORTING:									
		Baptisms	Additions by Letter	Sunday School	VBS	TU Ongoing	WMU	Brother-hood	Music Ministry	Total Gifts	Mission Gifts	Church Property
SBC	**33,943**	**28,323**	**28,714**	**33,358**	26,282	**24,084**	**22,935**	**14,191**	**18,074**	**32,482**	**32,478**	**31,897**
Open Country	14,229	10,491	10,542	13,782		8,017	6,891	3,618	4,723	13,132	13,229	13,023
Village	4,550	3,538	3,658	4,488		2,839	2,838	1,295	1,748	4,407	4,434	4,302
Town	3,698	3,359	3,459	3,684		2,991	3,176	1,812	2,491	3,658	3,646	3,597
City	11,466	10,935	11,055	11,404		10,237	10,030	7,466	9,112	11,285	11,169	10,975
Alabama	**2,910**	**2,413**	**2,422**	**2,852**	**2,273**	**2,248**	**1,762**	**1,099**	**1,299**	**2,734**	**2,785**	**2,703**
Open Country	1,630	1,249	1,236	1,580		1,099	707	363	423	1,476	1,521	1,467
Village	351	276	283	345		263	226	110	134	340	346	333
Town	264	243	249	263		245	232	143	180	260	262	257
City	665	645	654	664		641	597	483	562	658	656	646
Alaska	**36**	**33**	**34**	**34**	**30**	**30**	**29**	**15**	**23**	**34**	**34**	**34**
Open Country	5	4	4	4		3	4		2	4	3	4
Village	1	1	1	1			1	1	1	1	1	1
Town	6	5	5	5		5	4	3	2	5	6	6
City	24	23	24	24		22	20	11	18	24	24	23
Arizona	**227**	**210**	**213**	**223**	**186**	**181**	**169**	**98**	**131**	**224**	**219**	**218**
Open Country	13	9	10	13		8	7	2	1	13	11	11
Village	23	21	21	22		12	11	3	9	23	23	23
Town	34	28	29	33		19	18	7	11	33	33	32
City	157	152	153	155		142	133	86	110	155	152	152
Arkansas	**1,180**	**935**	**1,003**	**1,162**	**867**	**940**	**623**	**336**	**458**	**1,131**	**1,145**	**1,103**
Open Country	467	305	346	454		318	124	53	73	432	439	417
Village	270	207	224	266		198	117	42	55	258	265	255
Town	154	147	151	154		144	123	52	94	154	154	151
City	289	276	282	288		280	259	189	236	287	287	280
California	**848**	**735**	**766**	**834**	**724**	**701**	**608**	**381**	**527**	**828**	**812**	**777**
Open Country	28	21	22	26		18	13	10	13	26	25	26
Village	26	18	20	26		12	10	2	7	26	24	21
Town	94	72	80	93		64	52	21	34	92	91	87
City	700	624	644	689		607	533	348	473	684	672	643
Colorado	**121**	**110**	**110**	**121**	**105**	**102**	**99**	**65**	**74**	**120**	**120**	**116**
Open Country	4	2	3	4		2	2	1		4	4	4
Village	9	7	6	9		6	5	3	2	9	9	8
Town	24	19	19	24		18	17	7	10	24	24	22
City	84	82	82	84		76	75	54	62	83	83	82
Dist. of Columbia	**59**	**56**	**55**	**55**	**43**	**42**	**55**	**26**	**54**	*	*	*
City	59	56	55	55		42	55	26	54	*	*	*
Florida	**1,438**	**1,265**	**1,330**	**1,421**	**1,054**	**1,228**	**1,047**	**740**	**993**	**1,414**	**1,387**	**1,372**
Open Country	387	293	329	377		297	196	130	180	377	360	360
Village	149	115	125	144		109	83	46	69	144	139	145
Town	166	149	160	165		137	133	73	112	163	162	159
City	736	708	716	735		685	635	491	632	730	726	768
Georgia	**2,967**	**2,429**	**2,478**	**2,883**	**2,197**	**2,074**	**2,026**	**1,409**	**1,432**	**2,812**	**2,767**	**2,820**
Open Country	1,497	1,123	1,138	1,429		897	791	477	461	1,373	1,354	1,413
Village	350	242	255	342		206	241	111	105	338	329	322
Town	277	254	263	276		238	248	176	197	272	270	271
City	843	816	822	836		733	746	645	669	829	814	814
Hawaii	**29**	**28**	**29**	**29**	**23**	**25**	**27**	**15**	**19**	**29**	**29**	**29**
Town	4	4	4	4		3	3	1		4	4	4
City	25	24	25	25		22	24	14	19	25	25	25

* Not reported

NUMBER OF SOUTHERN BAPTIST CHURCHES REPORTING MAJOR ITEMS—1969

SBC and State Conventions	Total No. Active Churches	NUMBER REPORTING: Baptisms	Additions by Letter	Sunday School	VBS	TU Ongoing	WMU	Brotherhood	Music Ministry	Total Gifts	Mission Gifts	Church Property
Illinois	**881**	**695**	**696**	**869**	**592**	**511**	**562**	**307**	**375**	**849**	**862**	**818**
Open Country	239	136	141	233		75	83	31	47	223	233	214
Village	153	108	109	152		60	80	32	42	147	149	138
Town	140	121	119	140		86	107	50	71	139	139	135
City	349	330	327	344		290	292	194	215	340	341	331
Indiana	**217**	**192**	**193**	**217**	**184**	**141**	**155**	**86**	**113**	**214**	**209**	**198**
Open Country	17	14	13	18		12	11	4	6	17	17	15
Village	14	13	12	14		6	6	3	5	14	14	10
Town	28	19	19	27		10	15	8	6	26	25	22
City	158	146	149	158		113	123	71	96	157	153	151
Kansas	**197**	**178**	**181**	**196**	**168**	**182**	**163**	**98**	**128**	**195**	**195**	**187**
Open Country	9	5	3	9		6	7	2	3	9	9	6
Village	12	9	10	12		12	6	3	4	12	12	12
Town	38	34	35	38		31	30	12	18	38	38	37
City	138	130	133	137		133	120	81	103	136	136	132
Kentucky	**2,140**	**1,712**	**1,689**	**2,078**	**1,434**	**1,109**	**1,184**	**617**	**785**	**1,982**	**2,005**	**1,987**
Open Country	1,155	831	804	1,101		437	437	187	204	1,025	1,039	1,042
Village	375	300	298	369		198	219	87	119	352	364	351
Town	198	179	186	198		131	166	89	125	195	196	195
City	412	402	401	410		343	362	254	337	410	406	399
Louisiana	**1,301**	**1,113**	**1,184**	**1,289**	**966**	**1,102**	**857**	**501**	**700**	**1,270**	**1,254**	**1,258**
Open Country	615	472	526	606		468	283	134	200	591	583	585
Village	167	146	151	166		133	113	61	84	164	163	163
Town	138	128	135	138		132	115	70	96	136	134	135
City	381	367	372	379		369	346	236	320	379	374	375
Maryland	**319**	**289**	**293**	**316**	**259**	**233**	**278**	**174**	**243**	**311**	**312**	**283**
Open Country	36	27	28	35		23	28	13	21	34	34	33
Village	19	18	18	19		11	16	14	12	18	19	19
Town	38	34	35	38		27	35	22	28	37	37	35
City	226	210	217	224		172	199	125	182	222	222	196
Michigan	**157**	**145**	**142**	**154**	**127**	**106**	**114**	**67**	**84**	**152**	**143**	**137**
Open Country	11	10	9	11		7	8	5	7	11	11	8
Village	4	4	4	4		1	2	1	1	4	3	3
Town	13	9	10	11		6	8	3	3	12	10	11
City	129	122	119	128		92	96	58	73	125	119	115
Mississippi	**1,864**	**1,511**	**1,574**	**1,807**	**1,321**	**1,477**	**1,071**	**664**	**1,094**	**1,790**	**1,759**	**1,779**
Open Country	1,093	817	851	1,042		779	453	227	506	1,030	1,004	1,022
Village	267	218	230	262		214	158	72	144	260	258	258
Town	157	137	152	156		146	146	94	129	155	154	156
City	347	339	341	347		338	314	271	315	345	343	343
Missouri	**1,794**	**1,432**	**1,409**	**1,768**	**1,436**	**1,196**	**1,311**	**771**	**906**	**1,747**	**1,766**	**1,692**
Open Country	714	467	452	695		345	370	185	195	679	691	646
Village	407	311	302	400		239	289	131	147	398	405	389
Town	237	229	224	237		201	232	144	182	237	237	234
City	436	425	431	436		411	420	311	382	433	433	423
New Mexico	**240**	**206**	**216**	**239**	**204**	**195**	**180**	**139**	**136**	**235**	**233**	**233**
Open Country	29	17	20	29		14	10	11	8	26	27	27
Village	49	36	41	48		29	26	20	10	48	47	48
Town	29	27	28	29		24	24	14	14	29	28	29
City	133	126	127	133		128	120	94	104	132	131	129

NUMBER OF SOUTHERN BAPTIST CHURCHES REPORTING MAJOR ITEMS—1969

SBC and State Conventions	Total No. Active Churches	NUMBER REPORTING:									
		Baptisms	Additions by Letter	Sunday School	VBS	TU Ongoing	WMU	Brother-hood	Music Ministry	Total Gifts	Mission Gifts	Church Property
North Carolina	**3,393**	**2,834**	**2,763**	**3,364**	2,872	**1,843**	**2,420**	**1,423**	**2,084**	**3,216**	**3,270**	**3,163**
Open Country	1,960	1,548	1,464	1,936		837	1,158	579	926	1,811	1,862	1,783
Village	371	298	293	368		185	287	147	234	353	361	346
Town	330	302	305	329		229	303	180	284	327	328	323
City	732	686	701	731		592	672	517	640	725	719	711
Northern Plains	**76**	**66**	**69**	**76**	72	**51**	**60**	**32**	**35**	**75**	**75**	**75**
Open Country	1			1								1
Village	2	1		2		1				2	2	2
Town	12	8	11	12		3	6	1	3	12	12	12
City	61	57	58	61		47	54	31	32	61	61	60
Ohio	**397**	**363**	**363**	**388**	306	**292**	**294**	**182**	**243**	**389**	**381**	**357**
Open Country	23	15	15	19		11	11	8	8	19	19	17
Village	16	13	12	16		9	11	8	5	16	16	15
Town	51	44	46	50		34	36	14	29	51	50	47
City	307	291	290	303		238	236	152	201	303	296	278
Oklahoma	**1,352**	**1,114**	**1,110**	**1,301**	1,016	**1,058**	**855**	**510**	**605**	**1,287**	**1,290**	**1,236**
Open Country	423	269	253	373		235	141	71	71	369	371	350
Village	263	204	216	261		180	119	50	54	258	261	244
Town	212	205	204	213		202	192	97	138	209	210	205
City	454	436	437	454		441	403	292	342	451	448	437
Oregon-Washington	**214**	**192**	**196**	**212**	172	**180**	**160**	**63**	**132**	**212**	**208**	**206**
Open Country	6	2	5	6		5	3		3	6	6	4
Village	9	9	7	9		4	3		1	9	9	8
Town	35	28	32	35		28	29	8	15	35	33	3
City	164	153	152	162		143	125	55	113	162	160	160
South Carolina	**1,586**	**1,368**	**1,385**	**1,572**	1,365	**1,298**	**1,411**	**1,033**	**1,209**	**1,557**	**1,549**	**1,564**
Open Country	817	660	661	805		599	674	446	517	792	788	804
Village	146	116	115	146		117	136	87	111	145	145	146
Town	171	156	164	171		155	166	115	155	171	169	168
City	452	436	445	450		427	435	385	426	449	447	446
Tennessee	**2,666**	**2,218**	**2,183**	**2,609**	2,029	**1,790**	**1,513**	**893**	**1,123**	**2,450**	**2,452**	**2,452**
Open Country	1,463	1,131	1,070	1,419		761	565	275	337	1,270	1,295	1,291
Village	283	232	229	280		204	173	68	107	273	268	268
Town	212	188	194	209		184	173	91	128	210	207	205
City	708	667	690	701		641	602	459	551	697	682	688
Texas	**3,851**	**3,268**	**3,459**	**3,819**	2,929	**2,976**	**2,635**	**1,775**	**2,087**	**3,779**	**3,770**	**3,686**
Open Country	935	596	724	918		536	310	184	188	893	901	862
Village	629	482	540	620		361	332	129	184	613	619	599
Town	483	454	465	483		404	422	237	309	481	481	475
City	1,804	1,736	1,730	1,798		1,675	1,571	1,225	1,406	1,792	1,769	1,750
Utah-Idaho	**63**	**55**	**53**	**63**	44	**45**	**45**	**21**	**30**	**63**	**62**	**58**
Village	2	2	1	2		2	2	1		2	2	2
Town	15	9	10	15		8	11	5	4	15	14	13
City	46	44	42	46		35	32	15	26	46	46	43
Virginia	**1,420**	**1,158**	**1,111**	**1,407**	1,280	**728**	**1,222**	**651**	**952**	**1,383**	**1,385**	**1,356**
Open Country	652	468	415	639		225	495	220	323	622	622	611
Village	183	131	135	183		67	166	63	102	180	181	173
Town	138	127	125	138		77	130	75	114	136	138	137
City	447	432	436	447		359	431	293	413	445	444	435
Miscellaneous					4							

COOPERATIVE PROGRAM FUNDS FOR OPERATING BUDGETS OF SBC AGENCIES, 1959-69

	1959	*1960*	*1961*	*1962*	*1963*	*1964*	*1965*	*1966*	*1967*	*1968*	*1969*
*Foreign Mission Board	$ 5,890,000	$ 7,090,000	$ 7,910,417	$ 8,452,410	$ 9,019,303	$10,921,081	$11,123,505	$11,829,531	$12,426,836	$13,018,000	$13,836,619
Home Mission Board	1,630,000	2,080,000	2,074,071	2,277,156	2,342,498	3,227,345	3,759,103	4,117,766	4,347,468	4,600,000	4,984,000
Annuity Board	325,000	325,000	325,000	250,000	250,000	250,000	250,000	250,000	250,000	225,000	125,000
Southern Seminary	536,700	557,491	580,881	546,404	582,000	606,348	648,387	719,952	804,394	965,228	1,148,000
Southwestern Seminary	562,700	698,458	780,224	805,348	825,000	851,921	900,099	963,766	1,027,495	1,184,381	1,387,000
New Orleans Seminary	462,700	515,013	525,782	541,367	561,000	591,735	638,173	658,518	682,054	755,921	875,000
Golden Gate Seminary	288,700	291,200	318,449	336,691	332,000	359,400	386,085	401,569	421,819	481,003	525,000
Southeastern Seminary	416,700	464,912	496,652	481,149	492,000	510,472	527,603	537,633	548,848	613,203	693,000
Midwestern Seminary	192,500	262,926	298,012	301,041	308,000	330,124	357,653	351,562	348,390	403,264	475,000
Total Seminaries	2,460,000	2,790,000	3,000,000	3,012,000	3,100,000	3,250,000	3,458,000	3,633,000	3,833,000	4,403,000	5,103,000
**Radio and TV Commission	335,000	400,000	475,000	480,000	502,000	550,000	800,000	900,000	977,000	1,085,000	1,250,000
American Seminary	70,000	80,000	88,000	88,000	88,000	88,000	88,000	88,000	90,600	90,600	95,000
Carver School	140,000	150,000	160,000	160,000	40,000						
Southern Baptist Hospitals	25,000	25,000	25,000	25,000	35,000	35,000	35,000	35,000	36,000	36,000	36,000
Brotherhood Commission	120,000	120,000	179,500	179,500	179,500	185,000	185,000	205,000	226,100	235,000	260,000
Public Affairs Committee	28,000	33,000	60,000	60,000	65,000	70,000	82,500	98,000	104,000	111,400	111,400
Southern Baptist Foundation	30,000	31,400	38,500	40,500	45,500	52,000	54,000	60,000	61,800	67,000	80,000
Education Commission	41,000	48,000	60,000	62,000	67,000	74,500	76,500	88,000	94,000	110,000	125,000
Historical Commission	33,000	38,000	42,500	44,500	46,500	50,500	78,000	83,000	90,500	95,000	102,000
Christian Life Commission	23,000	31,500	35,000	37,000	49,000	56,500	71,500	90,000	100,000	125,000	170,000
Stewardship Commission						65,000	65,000	83,000	83,000	83,000	83,000
Convention Budget	180,000	200,000	200,000	200,000	200,000	200,000	200,000	200,000	200,000	200,000	200,000
Totals	$11,330,000	$13,441,900	$14,672,988	$15,368,066	$16,029,301	$19,074,926	$20,326,108	$21,760,297	$22,920,304	$24,484,000	$26,561,019

* Capital funds included as operating.
** Does not include $1,000,000 of capital funds 1959–1963 to be used as revolving fund for films.

JOHN H. WILLIAMS

SOUTHERN BAPTIST REPORTS—1957–69

Year	Membership	Baptisms	SS Enrolment	VBS Enrolment	TU Enrolment	WMU Enrolment	Brotherhood Enrolment	Church Property	Mission Gifts	Total All Gifts	Churches
1957	8,966,255	389,716	6,972,350	2,777,104	2,414,584	1,324,295	511,521	1,662,512,890	70,015,299	397,550,347	31,297
1958	9,206,758	407,892	7,096,175	2,908,157	2,503,920	1,395,974	582,497	1,825,474,318	74,750,699	419,619,438	31,498
1959	9,485,276	429,063	7,276,502	2,910,258	2,608,110	1,456,192	617,263	2,009,254,164	77,753,190	453,338,720	31,906
1960	9,731,591	386,469	7,382,550	3,004,730	2,664,730	1,484,589	619,105	2,204,351,556	81,924,906	480,608,972	32,251
1961	9,978,488	403,315	7,506,846	3,088,721	2,724,369	1,496,634	628,087	2,385,175,418	84,434,006	501,301,714	32,598
1962	10,193,052	381,510	7,570,455	3,176,559	2,747,581	1,489,352	628,063	2,567,836,860	91,433,845	540,811,457	32,892
1963	10,395,940	355,325	7,610,727	3,176,307	2,748,553	[1]1,512,840	634,651	2,751,429,716	96,077,109	556,042,694	33,126
1964	10,601,515	374,418	7,671,165	[2]3,216,238	2,722,029	[1]1,509,484	603,696	2,954,380,965	100,164,740	591,587,981	33,388
1965	10,772,712	361,634	7,659,638	3,394,953	2,610,187	[1]1,469,739	483,219	3,080,663,120	106,743,944	637,958,846	[3]33,797
1966	10,949,493	360,959	7,603,685	3,388,924	2,552,073	[1]1,459,828	463,553	3,273,868,971	115,197,437	669,779,972	[3]33,949
1967	11,142,726	378,937	7,579,203	3,439,325	[4]2,560,384	[1]1,444,428	457,770	3,495,020,717	120,454,869	711,775,365	[3]34,147
1968	11,332,229	373,025	7,545,513	3,227,705	[5]2,725,097	[1]1,407,673	448,738	3,656,597,050	128,023,731	761,877,082	[3]34,295
1969	11,489,613	368,225	7,418,067	3,648,255	[5]2,648,388	[1]1,291,221	430,339	3,900,472,691	133,224,335	809,608,812	[3]34,335

[1] Figures include statistics from the churches as well as college and hospital YWAs. [2] Reported incorrectly in 1965 Southern Baptist Handbook
[3] Nonreporting churches are included. "Nonreporting" refers to those still affiliated with the Convention, but who have not submitted a report for three or more years.
[4] Includes, for the first time, two new phases of the church's training ministry: new church member orientation and leader training.
[5] Includes cumulative new member orientation, church leader training, and member training projects as well as the traditional Sunday evening enrolment.

ondary Education Act, with provisions for aiding sectarian schools, more and more state conventions began to restudy the church-state implications. The following year four state conventions took action denying approval of federal grants or loans to their institutions. Four other conventions gave approval. Several hospitals were released from state convention ties and thus were free to accept federal grants.

In 1966 Baptist Education Study Task (BEST), a two-year comprehensive study of Baptist higher education, was begun with particular emphasis on finances and the problem of federal aid. Conclusion of the study brought no final solution to the problem, only an emphasis on the freedom of the trustees of each school to decide what to do. During 1956–70 opposition to accepting any kind of federal loans or grants decreased considerably. But wide differences of opinion over what constituted a violation of church-state relations remained.

In 1967 speeches at the annual meeting in Miami Beach, and in related meetings, revealed an increased interest in ministering to human needs on the part of churches and individual Christians. The "crises statement" in Houston the next year further evidenced this concern. Other Baptists reacted, and conflicting viewpoints clashed in a "social action *versus* evangelism" controversy. Those favoring more social action said Southern Baptists' interest in other people could not begin and end on whether they were saved. Those fearing social action said it was a step toward a social gospel and an emphasis on good works to the neglect of leading men to a life-changing experience through faith in Jesus Christ. By 1969 many voices were heard calling for a balance between evangelism and social action.

Attendance at the annual meetings continued to grow, with 16,866 messengers registered at New Orleans in 1969. Internal moves were made to stabilize the operation of the Convention. In 1960 the president was instructed to confer with the vice-presidents before naming the Committee on Committees and Resolutions Committee. In 1961 the Committee on Order of Business was made a permanent committee with rotating membership, and the Committee on Committees was enlarged to include two members from each state Convention.

In 1960 messengers voted to require action by two consecutive Conventions to discontinue an agency. And in 1963 it was voted to require action by two consecutive Conventions for a change in the constitution. In 1968 the terms of office for board members of agencies were lengthened from three to four years except where charters had other provisions. Board members were still eligible to serve two consecutive terms.

Charges of voting irregularities at the 1964 Convention led to more careful supervision of vote tabulation by the registration secretary and the establishment of a Credentials Committee. In 1965 computer cards were used for the first time as ballots for a quick vote count.

The SBC celebrated its first 125 years at the 1970 meeting in Denver, Colo. But even as the messengers took a look at their past they were looking at the decade ahead as they adopted programing objectives and emphases for each year through 1979—in keeping with the underlying objective of the Convention "to lead men to God through Jesus Christ, the living Lord."

See also BUDGET OF THE CONVENTION; DEBT AND SOUTHERN BAPTISTS; EXECUTIVE COMMITTEE OF THE SBC; PROGRAM PLANNING, SBC; PROMOTION, SOUTHERN BAPTIST METHODS OF; REPRESENTATION, SBC BASIS OF. LEONARD E. HILL

SOUTHERN BAPTIST CONVENTION, PLACE OF MEETING. See PLACE OF MEETING, SOUTHERN BAPTIST CONVENTION.

SOUTHERN BAPTIST CONVENTION PROGRAM PLANNING. See PROGRAM PLANNING, SOUTHERN BAPTIST CONVENTION.

SOUTHERN BAPTIST EDUCATOR, THE. This 16-page news magazine carries articles of lasting interest on Christian higher education and news from the 73 Baptist campuses. The subscription is $1.50 a year and the circulation (1970) is about 7,000. For several years the Association of Southern Baptist Colleges and Schools has provided some supporting funds for the publication from the annual dues of the schools. This support is repaid in subscriptions for the faculties and trustees of the schools.

RABUN L. BRANTLEY

***SOUTHERN BAPTIST FOUNDATION.** *Financial Data.*—Trust fund assets increased from $1,873,069 at the end of 1955 to $11,020,708 on Sept. 30, 1969, as Southern Baptist individuals and agencies recognized and utilized the services of the foundation. Annual distributable earnings rose from $56,437 to $529,729 during this period, with wise investments resulting in the average rate of return increasing from 4.79 per cent to 5.99 per cent. In 1967 the Convention approved a change of fiscal year to Sept. 30 for the foundation. It operates on a modest budget received from the Convention Cooperative Program receipts. No part of any gift or its earnings is used to defray operating costs.

This period was marked by changes as well as development in the life of the foundation. Fluctuation in economic trends necessitated adjustment of its investment policy from 70 per cent in bonds and mortgages and 30 per cent in common equities to a complete reversal of 30 per cent in fixed income securities with not over 70 per cent of its cash invested in common stocks. The alteration in policy was gradual and taken in four steps as actions of the financial markets warranted change.

Professional investment counseling has been provided without cost to the foundation through the generosity of one of its directors. This enables the foundation to keep abreast with latest techniques and realize full benefits in the market places. Investments are conservative because the foundation considers all funds as a trust. Safety of principal comes before liberal returns or desire for rapid growth. Every facet of investing is carefully scrutinized. Baptists may be assured of continued growth under prudent management of all funds.

Charter Change.—A change in the charter of the foundation relating to its board of directors was necessary. Its executive committee was enlarged to not fewer than nine nor more than 15 members. It is constituted by some of the most astute Christian businessmen of the Convention, who are well versed in investments. They have been successful in their own affairs, and are dedicated to the investment of all funds entrusted to the foundation.

Program of Work Adjusted.—Modification of the foundation's program of work became necessary. The foundation was relieved of the responsibility for developing and promoting giving for the benefit of SBC agencies in 1959, resulting from objection on the part of state foundations, and on recommendation by the committee to study the total Southern Baptist program. The years that followed this action have been marked by a spirit of cooperative and unified effort of all state foundations and Southern Baptist Foundation, with a realization that combined effort will perpetuate wealth for Christian development throughout the Convention.

Objective and Work Programs Assigned.—The objective of the foundation was established by the Convention, along with its programs of work. The foundation supports the Convention in its objective of the propagation of the gospel by receiving gifts as the agent of the Convention in any form, such as legacies, trusts, deeds, and gift annuities, either designated or undesignated, for any missionary, educational, or benevolent cause. It conducts on behalf of Convention agencies, or any other Baptist body or institution which might use its office, a dependable and prudent investment service, consistent with the highest ideals of Christian stewardship. It offers consultative service in the general field of estate planning by advising any person desirous of leaving a portion of one's estate to a Baptist cause or causes.

Organization and Personnel.—J. W. Storer retired as executive secretary-treasurer on July 31, 1967, after more than 10 years of service. Trust funds more than tripled during this period, and the foundation's image in Southern Baptist life was reinforced by his persistent, dignified endeavor. On Aug. 1, 1967, Kendall Berry, a businessman of Blytheville, Ark., came as the first layman to serve the foundation as its executive secretary-treasurer. New innovations are being put into effect, which are resulting in increased earnings for Baptist causes, and unlimited services to individuals desiring to perpetuate their stewardship.

The foundation has only five employees. Mrs.

E. W. Bess, Jr., administrative assistant, has completed 20 years of service, having been with the foundation almost since its inception. The foundation moved to its present quarters, located in the Southern Baptist Convention Building, 460 James Robertson Parkway, Nashville, Tenn., in Feb., 1963. KENDALL BERRY

***SOUTHERN BAPTIST HOSPITAL.** Raymond C. Wilson served as administrator of this SBC hospital in New Orelans from 1953 until 1969 when the board of directors restructured management positions. They promoted Wilson to the newly created position of executive director. The board appointed three additional men to new administrative positions: J. D. Stoudenmier, fiscal affairs administrator; Edward H. Clarkson, health care administrator; Fred H. Willie, property services administrator. The new alignment of duties permitted a concentration of administrative talent in areas of related activity.

Southern Baptist Hospital operates five programs of educational opportunities: the department of pastoral care, school of medical technology, school of radiology, surgical technician training program, and an intern and resident training program.

In 1969 Mather School of Nursing, a diploma program sponsored by Southern Baptist Hospital, merged educational facilities with those of William Carey College, Hattiesburg, Mississippi, to offer a baccalaureate program of nursing.

Between 1960 and 1969 an expansion program resulted in the following additions: a service facility including a 423-car garage with rooftop helicopter landing pad for emergencies; a new laundry and enlarged power plant; a 54-family apartment building for hospital staff in answer to an urgent need for housing interns and residents; eight-story additions North and South Wings of the hospital; renovation of the hospital interior.

In 1965 Southern Baptist Hospital purchased 14 acres of land in Algiers (New Orleans), La. at a cost of $600,000 to provide a site for a future satellite or branch hospital. In 1966 the purchase of Taylor House, a 70-bed extended care unit was authorized providing facilities at costs considerably below costs to care for the patient in a general hospital. Completion of the expansion program enlarged the bed capacity of Southern Baptist Hospital to 670 and the value of the physical plant to $20,000,000 in 1969.

In 1968 the hospital treated 19,229 inpatients and 21,067 outpatients and recorded 3,857 births. The institution contributed medical services valued at $239,457 for persons unable to pay. The hospital received $16,500 from the Convention's Cooperative Program and $888 from other denominational gifts. The operating expenses for 1968 were $9,544,921. Southern Baptist Hospital services are provided for Foreign Mission Board personnel and Sellers Baptist Home and Adoption Center.

CHARLES E. BLACKMON

SOUTHERN BAPTIST HOSPITALS, INC. (cf. Southern Baptist Hospital Commission, Vol. II). The hospital ministry of Southern Baptists, as conducted for the Southern Baptist Convention by the board of directors of Southern Baptist Hospitals, Inc., operates in accordance with the following statement of Baptist hospital functions:

> A Baptist hospital exists to bring men into a saving relationship with God through faith in Jesus Christ by means of direct personal witness as occasion presents, and by a positive Christian interpretation of the experiences of disease, disability and death. . . . Functions as an instrument of God's grace in enriching and prolonging human life within the scope of Divine Providence. . . . Enlists and teaches those called to the healing arts, encourages their maximum development in talent and skill and provides the setting within which these may be performed as ministries of the highest order. . . . Makes available the full resources of the hospital to those people least able to pay in such ways as to preserve human dignity and worth.

This objective is developed by two hospitals, Southern Baptist Hospital in New Orleans, La., and Baptist Memorial Hospital in Jacksonville, Fla., through four programs: (1) A high quality accredited program of general hospital care in an atmosphere reflective of Christian ideals and Baptist integrity. (2) A program of educational opportunities for young people specializing in health care or seeking professional competence in clinical pastoral education. (3) A program of hospital care to persons with special needs and the medically indigent within budget limitations. (4) A program of consultative services to other Baptist hospitals in securing an overall Convention emphasis in Baptist hospital work. In 1941 the charter was amended changing the name from "Hospital Commission of the Southern Baptist Convention" to "Southern Baptist Hospital."

The Bethesda Foundation was established in 1965 as a nonprofit organization to support charitable and educational programs of the hospitals. Included are medical, nursing, and paramedical educational programs; hospital and medical services for the indigent; and provision for future capital needs of the hospitals, including equipment and buildings.

In 1967 a charter change was made whereby state members of the Executive Committee were chosen from any members of the cooperating state conventions rather than specifically designated states. The Convention also accepted recommendations for a change in the charter whereby the corporate name was changed from Southern Baptist Hospital to Southern Baptist Hospitals, Inc. The statement of objectives and purposes broadened to include operation of "other health care facilities including teaching and training facilities for health care personnel" and the power "to organize and operate subsidiaries."

Executive secretary-treasurers of the board of directors in recent years have been: Frank

Tripp, 1947–59, T. Sloan Guy, 1959–66, and Hardy M. Harrell, since 1966. Charles E. Blackmon has served as assistant executive secretary-treasurer of the board and as director of the Bethesda Foundation since 1965.

CHARLES E. BLACKMON

SOUTHERN BAPTIST PASTORS' CONFERENCE. The conference began meeting in 1935 at the call of Monroe Elmon Dodd (*q.v.*, Vol. I), then president of the Southern Baptist Convention. The announcement of the first meeting stated that the purpose would be the consideration of vital matters in connection with the work of the minister, particularly evangelism. The conference continued to meet immediately prior to the annual session of the Convention.

Dodd arranged the program and served as chairman until succeeded by Herschel H. Hobbs in 1950. Hobbs also was requested to preside at the 1949 meeting due to Dodd's illness. Originally the chairman and a director of music were the only officers. Later a vice-chairman and secretary-treasurer were elected. Since 1955 the chairman, now known as president, has been restricted to a one-year term. The programs have been developed to deal with spiritual, missionary, evangelistic, doctrinal, and practical problems of the pastor. By stated purpose, debates, resolutions, and promotion of special interests have been avoided.

ARTHUR L. WALKER, JR.

SOUTHERN BAPTIST PERIODICAL INDEX. A comprehensive author and subject index to 36 Southern Baptist periodicals. The Historical Commission, SBC, has published the index annually since 1965 in cooperation with 18 other Convention agencies.

LYNN E. MAY, JR.

SOUTHERN BAPTIST PROGRAM, COMMITTEE TO STUDY TOTAL. Committee authorized by the Southern Baptist Convention on May 30, 1956, on recommendation of the Convention's Executive Committee. Douglas M. Branch (*q.v.*), North Carolina, a member of the Executive Committee, was appointed chairman. There were 22 other members: B. Locke Davis, Alabama; W. Barry Garrett, Arizona; Brooks Hays, Arkansas; R. C. Miller, California; Robert S. Cooper, District of Columbia; Cecil Carroll, Florida; Monroe F. Swilley, Jr., Georgia; Archie E. Brown, Illinois; E. N. Wilkinson, Kentucky; R. Houston Smith, Louisiana; J. Winston Pearce, Maryland; W. Douglas Hudgins, Mississippi; Grant Davis, Missouri; L. D. Ball, New Mexico; Bryce L. Twitty (*q.v.*), Oklahoma; Mrs. Horace G. Hammett, South Carolina; Maxey Jarman, Tennessee; Carr P. Collins, Texas; Garis T. Long, Virginia; M. H. Mabry, Florida; Kendall Berry, Arkansas; and J. I. Alford, Georgia.

The committee became known as the "Survey" Committee, and was often referred to as the "Branch" Committee. The purpose approved by the Convention was "to study the functions of the agencies and boards of the Southern Baptist Convention, and their relationships with the churches; with the state conventions, and with other agencies and boards of the Convention, with a view of finding the most effective way of promoting the Kingdom through the Southern Baptist Convention." The committee employed the firm, Booz, Allen, and Hamilton of Chicago, as consultants. H. Lawrence Wilsey of this firm worked closely with the committee until its final report in 1959.

At the 1957 SBC the committee reported finding two things: (1) that "Southern Baptists constitute one of the major spiritual forces in America today," and (2) "we must awaken our people to the tremendous responsibility we have in winning America and the world to Jesus Christ." The committee also said that it was being guided by the purpose of the Convention as stated in the preamble of the constitution, the Convention's commitment not to exercise authority over any other Baptist body, the belief that all Baptist groups aim toward "the extension, and establishment of the Kingdom of God on earth," and by its belief that the Convention can do its best work by not duplicating the work of other Baptist bodies. It also said that it felt that each SBC agency is "morally bound to serve the best interests of the total Southern Baptist Convention program."

The committee made its first substantive report to the Convention at Houston in 1958. It brought 38 recommendations, of which 22 were approved and 16 were referred back to the committee. The ones approved are as follows: required the Executive Committee to develop a more adequate reporting format to provide information on promotion plans, accomplishments, and costs of Cooperative Program items; made clear that the Executive Committee is not to approve Convention agency budgets; opened the way for an Executive Committee public relations program and a separate headquarters building for the Eexecutive Committee; reorganized the Executive Committee staff; recognized the WMU as an auxiliary which should be continued; established the Inter-Agency Council as an official body for the correlation of agency programs; required the Sunday School Board (1) to furnish full information about gifts to state conventions, (2) to refrain from making gifts to SBC agencies, and (3) to contribute funds to the SBC operating budget; established a separate Stewardship Commission; made minor changes in the nature of special and standing committees; provided that all SBC boards and committees include both ordained and lay persons as members, with not more than two-thirds of the members of any group being drawn from either category; instructed the Foreign Mission Board to terminate mission work in the state of Hawaii; requested the Relief and Annuity Board to keep its procedures up to date; affirmed the principle of state ownership of Baptist hospitals, commended the hospitals for financing themselves out of earnings, and declared the Convention would establish no more hospitals; asked that more effective use be made of existing seminaries; requested the agencies to keep under constant review their programs, organizational structures, personnel, administration, and administrative services.

One year later (1959) at Louisville, Ky., the committee made its final report. It proposed 22 recommendations, of which all were adopted except one. The recommendation which was rejected would have authorized the seminaries to charge tuition. The ones adopted are as follows: authorized the Home Mission Board to continue as a separate agency and that it (1) increase its emphasis in the weaker state convention areas, (2) continue and accelerate board and state cooperation in mission work, endeavoring to establish "a single mission program," (3) where feasible to turn administrative responsibility for direct mission work to the states, (4) when possible to turn financial responsibility for mission work to the states, (5) provide for gradual control of work in Cuba and Panama to local conventions, (6) continue to sponsor church loans, and (7) strengthen its internal organization; asked all SBC agencies to utilize the services of the Baptist Sunday School Board; defined commission status for any agency as being that which "does not sponsor institutional programs or programs of great complexity or magnitude"; asked the commissions to correlate their work with the work of other agencies; confirmed the establishment of a Stewardship Commission; authorized continuation of the Carver School of Missions and Social Work; restricted the SBC Foundation to the care of such money as came to it, limiting it from promotion of giving; specified the membership of the Inter-Agency Council; required the membership of the Public Affairs Committee to be included in the Convention by-laws; asked the Executive Committee to maintain an organization manual; recognized the Radio and Television Commission as the sole SBC producer of films for television use. ALBERT MC CLELLAN

SOUTHERN BAPTIST PROTECTION PROGRAM (cf. Southern Baptist Protection Plan, Vol. II). Inaugurated Jan. 1, 1968, the program replaces all previously offered plans of the Annuity Board, SBC, and is composed of three parts: Plan A, Plan B, and Plan C. A member can determine the benefits he has in Plan A by finding the numeral designation which is applicable to him. That numeral is listed under each benefit to which the member is entitled.

Plan A-10 is the plan currently open to new members, and includes all ministers who have joined since January 1, 1968.

Plan A-11 replaced Southern Baptist Protection Plan and Baptist Employees Protection Plan;

Plan A-12 replaced Ministers Retirement Plan, Widows Supplemental Annuity Plan, and Ministers Security Plan;

Plan A-13 replaced Baptist Board Employees Retirement Plan, Institutional Employees Retirement Plan, Widows Supplemental Annuity Plan, and Baptist Board Employees Security Plan;

Plan A-14 replaced North Carolina Ministers Retirement Plan, Widows Supplemental Annuity Plan and Endorsement;

Plan A-22 replaced Ministers Retirement Plan;

Plan A-23 replaced Baptist Board Employee Retirement Plan and Institutional Employees Retirement Plan;

Plan A-24 replaced North Carolina Ministers Retirement Plan;

Plan A-25 Replaced Baptist Employees Retirement Plan.

Age Benefit

Plan A-10, A-11, and A-25 have an age benefit equal to 1½ per cent of salary for each year of participation in the plan. Example: A member joins Plan A at age 25, retires at age 65, having maximum contributions during this period; his benefit would be 40 times $60.00, or $2,400 per year.

Plan A-12, A-13, A-14, A-22, A-23, and A-24 have an age benefit equal to 50 per cent of average salary over 25 years prior to attaining age 65.

Disability Benefit

Plan A-10, A-11, A-12, A-13, and A-14 provide a maximum disability benefit equal to potential age benefit.

Plan A-22, A-23, A-24, and A-25, provide a maximum disability benefit equal to potential age benefit with a maximum of $1,200 per year.

Widow Benefit

Plan A-10, A-11, A-12, A-13, and A-14 have a maximum widow benefit which is 40 per cent of members age or potential age benefit. (In no case under A-12, A-13, A-14 will widow benefit be less than provided by Widows Supplemental Annuity Plan or Ministers Security Plan.)

Plan A-24 has a maximum widow benefit which is 50 per cent of age benefit (payable only after member is age 65).

Minor Dependent Child Benefit

Plan A-10, A-11, A-12, A-13, and A-14 provide a minor dependent child benefit equal to a maximum 15 per cent of members age or potential age benefit (maximum 60 per cent of member's benefit).

Educational Benefit

Plan A-10, A-11, A-12, A-13, and A-14 provide an educational benefit for first four years of college immediately following high school equal to 40 per cent of age or potential age benefit (maximum, $600 per year per child).

Minimum Payment

Plan A-10, A-11, A-12, A-13, and A-14 assure a minimum payment equal to twice the age or potential age benefit.

Plan A-11, A-12, A-13, A-14, A-22, A-23, A-24, and A-25 assure a minimum payment equal to the member's accumulated credits (specified dues plus interest).

Cost of A Plans

The cost of Plan A-10, A-11, A-12, A-13, and A-14 is 10 per cent of member's salary paid by the church or employer (maximum $33.34 per month) with half that amount added by state convention.

Plan A-22 cost is 6 per cent of member's salary paid by church (limit $20 per month) with half that amount added by state convention.

Plan A-23 and A-25 cost is 8 per cent of member's salary paid by employer (limit $26.67 per month).

Plan A-24 cost is 8 per cent of member's salary paid by church (limit $26.66 per month) with half that amount added by state convention.

Plan B replaced Age Security Plan. It is a money accumulation plan with no minimum or maximum contributions. It may be a member's basic plan or supplemental to Plan A. It provides an age, disability and death benefit based on the accumulations.

Plan C replaced Variable Benefit Fund. It is supplemental to Plan A or Plan B. Funds are invested in selected common stocks. Each dollar invested buys units (similar to a mutual fund), the value of which is determined by market price of stocks held as of the last day of the previous month. The number of units and the value of the unit at the time of retirement determines the age or disability benefit. In the event of death before entering upon a benefit, the beneficiary may elect the type of benefit to be paid on the basis of the value of the member's accumulated units.

See also ANNUITY BOARD.

MRS. MABLE H. MC CARTNEY

***SOUTHERN BAPTIST THEOLOGICAL SEMINARY.** In the fifties and sixties Southern Seminary engaged in a struggle to keep pace with the demands of theological education of Christian ministers for changing churches in a changing world. Whereas formerly the role of ministers was conceived of mainly in terms of pastoral care and missions or evangelism, the shift from a largely rural to a largely urban society in the South during and following World War II complicated the task of the churches. It created the necessity of diversified ministries and consequently of diversified theological education.

In response to this need Southern Seminary initiated in 1948 a School of Church Music and in 1952 a School of Religious Education, both offering specialized curricula designed to fulfil directly the desires of the churches for ministers of music, education, children's work, youth work, student work, recreation, visual education, library work, secretarial work, and other specialized tasks. The School of Theology shifted reluctantly from its heavy emphasis on the traditional theological subjects—Bible, church history, homiletics, and theology—to introduce new areas of study and to make changes in its curricula. Developing an area begun by Gaines S. Dobbins, in the early fifties Wayne E. Oates demonstrated the value of studies in pastoral care and clinical training for pastors and chaplains. A limited program of field education also developed, but in 1956 the faculty of the School of Theology tabled a motion to procure a full-time director of field work.

At the same time the growth of student enrolment, which reached a peak in 1951, the creation of two new schools, and the addition of new faculty made administrative changes necessary. Until the presidency of Ellis A. Fuller (*q.v.*, Vol. I), 1946–51, the seminary's president served as an active professor and chairman of the faculty. A number of special duties devolved upon him, but neither the size of the student body nor of the faculty required him to devote full time to administration. When Duke K. McCall assumed the presidency in 1951, he could no longer function as a full-time teacher and administrator as well. Gradually he introduced changes in an administrative structure which still had essentially the same shape with which the seminary began in an effort to distribute his load and to ensure a more effective operation of the School of Theology. After serving several years as chairman of the faculty of the School of Theology, with the faculty's concurrence, in May, 1956, he named an acting dean with a view to appointing a permanent dean subsequently.

A complicated combination of academic and administrative changes generated unrest in the faculty of the School of Theology and prepared the conditions for a major rift in the academic year 1957–58. Both faculty and administration evidently had a single goal, to develop a program of education which would equip ministers to serve competently in the complex church setting of the time; but they envisioned different ways to achieve it. Some members of the School of Theology faculty believed it could be reached best by building the seminary's academic program, and they betrayed some evident misgivings regarding the academic character of certain practical studies which were being introduced into the curriculum. The strength of this thinking manifested itself in a major change in the B.D. curriculum in Sept., 1956, when required courses in Old Testament, New Testament, and theology were enlarged from five to eight hours and in church history from five to six, and a course in speech reduced from four to two. Additions were made to the faculty of the first four departments in order to compensate for the increased hourly load. On the other hand, a number of faculty members resisted the expansion of the Department of Psychology of Religion. When this department was continued in the School of Theology in 1953 and was not shifted to the newly organized School of Religious Education, the School of Theology faculty stipulated that it would have one professor and one instructor. As a consequence of its popularity, a second full-time faculty member was added in 1956. As the growth of a program of clinical pastoral education made mandatory the replacement of the second full-time professor who resigned in 1957, some members of other departments balked. When a prospective candidate for the position was brought for an interview in 1957, they expressed hostility to the addition and his proposed rank. Nevertheless, the addition was made.

At the same time other faculty members of all three schools believed the goal could be achieved best by more immediate attention to practical education. This conviction was intimately bound up with a high level of sensitivity to the needs, demands, and criticisms of the constituency of the Southern Baptist Convention. The curriculum of the School of Religious Education catered directly to these needs, a fact which created resentment on the part of those who stressed academic training in theology. Several professors in the School of Theology also oriented their teaching toward the practical needs of the churches and taught their subjects with deference to the denominational situation.

The president of the seminary, whose administrative role placed him in a position which was answerable to the three faculties, to the trustees of the seminary, to the denomination, and to the American Association of Theological Schools (A.A.T.S.), which accredits the institution, confronted a mediatorial task which exposed him to conflicting pressures. As one trained in theology himself, on the one hand, he sympathized with the then sizeable portion of his theology faculty who stressed thorough academic training in theology. He displayed his sympathies in encouraging the addition of thoroughly qualified faculty in various departments and in attempting to reward those who engaged in solid academic pursuits. Promotions no longer occurred automatically but on the basis of demonstrated competence with a heavy emphasis on teaching and writing proficiency. He edited a symposium of scholarly papers for a book entitled *What Is the Church?* which represented the *avant garde* of Southern Baptist thought on ecclesiology. Enlisting research help from members of his faculty, he undertook to write *Broadman Comments* for 1958 and to prepare a "definitive history" of Southern Seminary in connection with its hundredth anniversary, later written by William A. Mueller. He encouraged participation of the faculty in academic and ecumenical meetings. Among non-Southern Baptists he gained an image of an academic leader in theological education.

As a longtime denomination leader, third president of the Baptist Bible Institute (1943–45) —now New Orleans Baptist Theological Seminary—and former executive secretary of the Executive Committee of the SBC (1945–48), he possessed a keener sensitivity than many faculty members to the gap which separated the seminary from the churches. As an educational institution preparing ministers for the generation ahead, a seminary is as it were a "think tank." Nevertheless, it seeks necessarily to serve the present generation of the churches as well. So the president also shared the views of those who advocated a practical training for the churches in their current state. He encouraged innovated programs in church music, religious education, communications, clinical training, and so on. He represented to the denomination the image of the seminary as a serving agency. He sought to cultivate closer relationships between the seminary and other denominational agencies—most of which defined their roles in terms of denominational service.

The perhaps mandatory but painful ambiguity of the president's office appears to have produced several misunderstandings. A sizeable part of the faculty of the School of Theology began to air their grievances in informal meetings during 1957–58. Among other things they criticized delay of promotions for some faculty members as compared with rapidity of promotions for others, the apparent arbitrariness in adding new faculty, the representation of the seminary to the denomination, certain actions of the president in evident disregard of their expressed views, and the failure to appoint a permanent dean. When the president did announce the man he preferred as dean, he bypassed the professor preferred by a large segment of the faculty. Distressed by this major faction, some members of the faculty expressed alarm about the morale of the faculty and stated that it had lost confidence in the administration of the president.

Before the April meeting of the trustee committee on the School of Theology, a rumor began to circulate that the president was seeking, with the assistance of selected trustees, to fire two or three of the professors who had voiced the strongest opposition. The result was that 13 professors formed a power bloc and refused to negotiate except as a bloc. In special conferences with the trustees they remained adamant in their position and were interpreted by the trustees eventually to have refused to accept anything less than the removal of the president. After lengthy investigation the trustees voted 42 to 7 in favor of affirming their confidence in the president. Since members of the bloc declined to negotiate individually, the trustees proceeded to discharge all of them at once. One of the 13 subsequently altered his position and negotiated separately for a return, but the others remained resolute in their decision.

The firing *en masse* of 13 faculty members brought the matter to the attention of the A.A.T.S. This accrediting body sent a committee to investigate the vexed situation. The committee recommended that a decision with regard to the possible "removal of accreditation" of the seminary be deferred for one year, that "adequate steps" be taken concerning financial provisions for the dismissed professors, and that the commission on accrediting require an inspection of the seminary in the fall of 1959. This inspection was carried out by a second committee. After examining the records and interviewing administration, faculty, trustees, and students, the committee recommended that the A.A.T.S. issue certain specific notations, *inter alia,* concerning faculty-student ratio, the supervision of students in the graduate program, and the adequacy of library facilities. They urged an extension of the financial provisions of the 12 men discharged, the establishment of adequate safeguards regarding tenure of faculty members, improvement in faculty salaries, and a stronger sabbatical leave program.

Provision for the inspection and the response to it by Southern Seminary was handled by a faculty-trustee committee, which Penrose St. Amant, who assumed the deanship of the School of Theology June 1, 1959, served as chairman. Three official reports were made to the A.A.T.S. and in Dec., 1961, all notations were removed and Southern Seminary, whose accreditation remained intact through the entire process, resumed a normal relationship to the association.

Since 1958 Southern Seminary has undergone a continuous evolution from the background of the incident described above and in response to the constantly changing needs of the churches. There was considerable fumbling and groping for the right way to prepare ministers and to define the purpose of theological education. By 1970 the preparation was seen more distinctly in terms of comprehensive and specialized theological and professional education. Comprehensive education would embrace (1) the learning of certain essential data about the Bible, church history, theology, and other subjects; (2) the development of basic skills (e.g.) in languages; and (3) personal and spiritual development. Specialized education would entail the immense number of church-related ministries now engaged in by the churches and their agencies. The faculties awakened slowly to the need for deliberate planning to achieve these objectives.

In this era all three schools revised their degree programs and curricula. Whereas in 1956 the School of Theology offered the B.D., Th.M., and Th.D. as its basic theological degrees, by 1970 it had added an S.T.D., designed especially to prepare men for the pastoral ministry on an advanced level, and an M.A., offered in conjunction with the University of Louisville Department of History. The designation M.Div. also replaced the B.D. and holders of the B.D. were offered the opportunity to receive the M.Div. through summer study at the Seminary. Whereas in 1956 the School of Church Music offered M.S.M. and D.S.M. degrees, by 1970 it had substituted a Doctor of Musical Arts for the latter and offered combined degrees in music and religious education or in music and theology. Whereas in 1956 the School of Religious Education offered an M.R.E. and D.R.E. as its basic degrees, by 1970 it had replaced the D.R.E. with a Doctor of Education (Ed.D.) and added the degree of Graduate Specialist in Religious Education and, as a result of the merging of the Carver School of Missions and Social Work in 1963 with the seminary, special degrees in social work and missions.

The development of new degree programs represented externally some of the changes which the curricula of the three schools were undergoing. In 1965 the curriculum committee of the School of Theology, for example, initiated a thorough study of its curriculum. A survey of student and alumni revealed a strong concern among students to have a freer hand in planning their own courses of study and among alumni to have greater opportunity for specialized study. As a result of the study, the faculty of the School of Theology left to each of its four divisions—biblical, historical, theological, and practical—the decision regarding what it would require of students pursuing the basic theological degree within an allotted number of hours. The result was a diversified curriculum which allowed each student considerable freedom to elect his courses. In an effort to coordinate theoretical and practical knowledge both the School of Theology and the School of Religious Education developed supervised field education. New areas of study developed. In 1966 the seminary inaugurated the Billy Graham Chair of Evangelism. In 1969 it created a Department of Church and Community.

The 1965 curriculum survey also launched a study of pedagogical methods and materials. Various faculty members began to experiment with team teaching, audiovisuals, guided research, etc. Pursuant to this interest, the combined faculties in 1968 formed an education committee to study and make recommendations regarding the improvement of teaching. This committee proposed that each professor be allowed to determine whether he would require class attendance, thus permitting each to innovate more readily. The curriculum and education committees in 1969–70 jointly studied and recommended procedures whereby students could propose courses and, with faculty consultation, arrange for their conduct.

This period saw the development of concern about the personal formation of the Christian minister. In 1957 the seminary employed a dean of students and subsequently a dean of women. An effort was made to increase the amount of individual guidance and counsel offered by various faculty members. The Department of Psychology of Religion supplied specialized guidance through individual or group counseling. The traditional daily worship services and prayer groups were supplemented by retreats. By student request the seminary employed a chaplain in 1969. For the first time, in 1969 the faculty members offered a team-taught course on the minister's devotional life.

As the degree changes indicate, the graduate programs of all three schools underwent modifications. The School of Theology replaced its formerly elective curriculum with a seminar system. In accordance with A.A.T.S. recommendations, the number of graduate students supervised by one professor was limited to five. In 1962 the dean of the School of Theology appointed a director of graduate studies with the responsibility of improving the procedures of the graduate program.

The entire educational program of the seminary was enhanced by endowment of lectureships and scholarships. The C. Edwin Gheens family of Louisville made generous grants which enabled the seminary to invite distinguished lecturers in several areas of specialization each year. The McCall family established the Lizette Kimbrough McCall Foundation to promote world evangelism through lectures, sermons, and other special exercises. As a result of the merger of the Carver School with the seminary, the seminary was enabled to offer Luther Rice and Adoniram Judson scholarships for prospective missionaries and other scholarships in social work or missions. The woman's committee of the seminary also endowed one or more scholarships for women in their first year.

The extensive loss of faculty in 1958 necessitated a major rebuilding in the School of Theology. With faculty concurrence in 1959 the president recommended to the trustees the election of Penrose St. Amant, professor of church history at New Orleans Baptist Theological Seminary, as dean of the School of Theology and as David T. Porter Professor of Church History. Under St. Amant's leadership additions were made to vacant chairs in various departments. A third professor was added also to the Department of Psychology of Religion and of Christian Ethics. Full faculty participation in the choice of faculty additions was established as a policy. Both the School of Church Music and the School of Religious Education increased the size of their faculties. The faculty-building program involved also the improvement of an already existing program of sabbatical leaves. The trustees made provision for regular sabbaticals at full salary. The deans arranged for younger faculty members to take their leaves early in their careers, thus providing an opportunity for fuller development of academic and teaching skills. Sabbaticants who were not recipients for scholarships from other sources received sabbatical supplements which would enable them to pursue their projects in a place of their choice.

Meantime, the trustees and administration sought to raise faculty (and staff) salaries to the median level of salaries in A.A.T.S. member schools. Unfortunately, the cost of theological education rose significantly during the years under study. In 1956–57 the trustees had hired the consultant firm of Booz, Allen, and Hamilton to study the seminary's structure and to make recommendations for its more efficient operation. With considerable pressure to raise salaries for faculty and staff they again hired the same firm in 1965–66. After a thorough study Booz, Allen, and Hamilton proposed a revised system of promotions and remunerations. By the older system a professor almost automatically moved up within rank year by year, though promotions from rank to rank were subject to the recommendation of the appropriate dean in the light of the judgments of the full professors. The new system extended the scale within each rank and seemed to make a full professorship more difficult to attain. Though theoretically it provided for rapid promotion of those who functioned effectively, in practice it retarded anticipated promotions and caused embarrassment to some. In 1968–69 the faculties called for a restudy of the system.

To encourage academic and church endeavors, the trustees provided funds for participation in professional society conferences and for attendance at the annual meeting of the Southern Baptist Convention. With encouragement of the deans faculty members published a creditable number of books and articles both of a scholarly and of a popular nature. They fulfilled requests of the churches, the agencies, and the denomination for specialized counsel and assistance. A continuing theological education program for pastors, conducted by the seminary's faculty, was instituted, involving three or four conferences per year lasting four days each. A similar off-campus program was also launched.

The growth of the seminary's educational program, faculty, and student body necessitated the expansion of the administrative staff. Whereas in 1956 the business affairs of the seminary were directed by the president with the assistance of a superintendent of grounds and buildings, treasurer, dean of students and director of admissions, director of public relations, and registrar, in 1968 a director of administration and business manager, Badgett Dillard, was appointed to coordinate these functions. Several new administrative positions were added in the interim to share the administrative load —an office services supervisor, a director of alumni affairs, a director of student housing and personnel, an executive director of the Southern Seminary Foundation, a director of college relations, and an executive assistant to the president.

After 1958 the general academic structure of the seminary retained essentially the same configuration. There were three schools, each headed by its own dean. The School of Theology continued in four divisions—biblical, practical, historical, and theological—until 1969, when the latter two were combined into the historical-theological division. One change in the configuration occurred when the merger of the Carver School of Missions and Social Work with the seminary placed upon the latter the educational functions formerly discharged by the Carver School. A Department of Social Work was attached to the School of Religious Education and degree programs in social work and religious education designed. Special degrees were also offered in conjunction with the Kent School of Social Work of the University of

Louisville. Representing an attractive career area for many young Christians, the department grew rapidly.

The impending retirement of Hugh Peterson, after 35 years as dean of administration and director of admissions, provided an occasion for the faculty, administration, and trustees to consider the feasibility of a general restructuring of the academic administration. The business administration had been coordinated under a director of administration and business manager, thus relieving the president of direct responsibility for it, but the coordination of the academic administration through the deans of the three schools still fell directly upon the president. One possible solution was a merger of the schools. For the School of Church Music this was not feasible in view of its highly specialized curriculum. The School of Religious Education confronted similar difficulties, inasmuch as it offered a regular two-year degree program, whereas the School of Theology offered a regular three-year one. The president, therefore, initially proposed to coordinate the academic programs of the schools by means of an academic vice-president or dean of the seminary. The proposal met with mixed responses from the school faculties. After lengthy consultation with faculty and administration the president projected his plan to the executive committee of the board of trustees in Jan., 1969. The committee deferred action pending a thorough study of the academic administration.

Meanwhile, after 10 years (1959–69), Penrose St. Amant tendered his resignation as dean of the School of Theology, desiring to resume full-time teaching duties in church history. His resignation offered the administration and faculty a second opportunity to weigh the pros and cons of restructuring. Faculty sentiment seemed to oppose a major change. After soliciting faculty responses individually the president recommended for trustee action the election of William E. Hull as dean of the School of Theology and, upon Dean Peterson's retirement, Allen W. Graves, dean of the School of Religious Education, as dean of administration. Ernest Loessner was elected acting dean of the School of Religious Education in 1969, and dean in 1970. The dean of students assumed the job of director of admissions formerly connected with the office of dean of administration. The duties of the dean of administration were redefined and related more fully to the role of liaison between the three schools, between the seminary and its accrediting agencies, and between the seminary and other institutions. The president now had a coordinator of academic affairs as well as a coordinator of business affairs. His own energies could focus upon the liaison between the seminary and the denomination and upon its general development as an educational institution.

In accordance with the general trend of the sixties in higher education, students were invited to share more directly in the administration of the seminary. For many years students assumed responsibility for special missions emphases, operated a student government, and played some part in campus discipline. Now they were invited by the faculty to participate in committees of all three schools. The president of the student body began to work more closely with the administration and staff in handling student complaints and requests.

As the seminary's program grew, enrolment increased, and the demands of theological education changed, old buildings were remodeled and new ones built. Mullins Hall, the men's dormitory, underwent a complete renovation, beginning in 1963. After the closing of the Carver School in 1963, the buildings were partially occupied by the School of Church Music. The specialized needs of this school, however, persuaded the trustees to authorize the erection of a new edifice adjacent to Alumni Chapel. The building, erected in 1969–70, was named in honor of V. V. Cooke, a Louisville trustee and benefactor of the seminary. Another significant addition was the James P. Boyce (*q.v.*, Vol. I) Library, erected in the centennial year 1958–59. Library holdings continued to grow. Besides books, periodicals, scores, and printed materials they began increasingly to include audiovisual materials. Property once used as the president's home was sold in 1962 to the Louisville Presbyterian Theological Seminary for the development of a new campus.

The ever growing demand of the churches for specialized types of ministerial training during the sixties forced Southern Seminary to seek closer affiliation with other institutions in the Louisville area. The clinical training programs produced special ties with Louisville General Hospital and Central State Hospital, plus a number of other institutions. The field education program entailed the development of working relationships, among other things, with churches, schools, charitable agencies, clinics, and missions. The social work education program necessarily led to the establishing of ties with the Kent School of Social Work, orphanages, homes for the elderly, correctional institutions, and the like. A concern to offer students the widest possible educational advantages within the limit of its resources induced the seminary to enter into two inter-institutional affiliations. The first of these, called TEAM, was composed of five theological schools in the Louisville area—Asbury Theological Seminary, Lexington Theological Seminary, Louisville Presbyterian Theological Seminary, St. Meinrad's Archabbey, and Southern. TEAM held one faculty colloquy in 1969. It scheduled for Jan., 1971, an Interterm, a one-month school term in which students might take advantage of curriculum offerings on other campuses and professors might offer joint seminars or courses. The second, called Kentuckiana Metroversity, involved eight Louisville area educational institutions. By virtue of this affiliation students from each of the participating schools could use the facilities of the other schools without additional cost.

Top: SOUTHWEST BAPTIST COLLEGE (*q.v.*), Bolivar, Mo. A representative building on the new Shoffner Campus. *Center left:* MISSOURI BAPTIST COLLEGE (*q.v.*), St. Louis campus. *Center right:* MISSOURI BAPTIST COLLEGE (*q.v.*), Hannibal, Mo. Administration Building, Hannibal-Lagrange Campus. *Bottom:* WILLIAM JEWELL COLLEGE (*q.v.*), Liberty, Mo. New $1,500,000 library (1965).

SOUTHERN BAPTIST THEOLOGICAL SEMINARY (*q.v.*), Louisville, Ky. *Top:* The James P. Boyce Centennial Library contains two archaeological museums, the Billy Graham collection, a music library, conference facilities, and an outstanding collection of theological materials. *Bottom:* THE BILLY GRAHAM COLLECTION (*q.v.*). A room containing memorabilia from the famous Baptist evangelist's career, located at Southern Baptist Theological Seminary, Louisville, Ky.

For many years Southern Seminary was accredited by the American Association of Theological Schools. The development of diversified programs and affiliations with schools not directly involved in theological education warranted a search for further accreditation. When the Southern Association of Colleges and Schools began to offer accreditation to special-purpose institutions, the seminary applied to it and received accreditation in 1967. In addition, the School of Church Music became an associate member of the National Association of Schools of Music in 1966.

In 1970 the seminary was facing the future with some optimism but also with evident concern. The trustees, administration, and faculty were asking inevitable questions about the escalation of the cost of theological education, about new techniques in education, about the purpose of a theological seminary, about the role of students in the educational process, about the possibility of programmed learning, about the striking of a balance between comprehensive and specialized theological education, about the relationship between structures and persons, about the improvement of the physical plant, about salaries and benefits for employees, about relationships with the denomination, etc. Some observers were remarking that the day of special theological schools had passed and that theological education would become the responsibility of the colleges and universities. For Southern Seminary much depended upon the decision of Southern Baptists, whether they would support theological education of ministers for the churches in the manner required by the times.

Faculty members in order of election since 1956 were:

Hammar, Russell A. (1920–), 1957–60
Bushnell, William Carman (1921–), 1957–65
Hinson, Grady Maurice (1930–), 1957–
Ferguson, Roy Pylant (1932–), 1957–58
Howington, Nolan Patrick (1917–), 1957–67
Thurman, William Peyton (1913–), 1957–
Southard, Samuel, Jr. (1925–), 1957–66
Hull, William Edward (1930–), 1958–
Sims, John Norman (1928–), 1958–67
Hutchens, Elizabeth Glenn (1924–), 1958–
Callaway, Joseph Atlee (1920–), 1958–
Ellis, Edward Earle (1926–), 1958–60
Russell, Charles Allyn (1920–), 1958–59
Vardaman, Ephraim Jeremiah (1927–), 1959–
Summers, Ray (1910–), 1959–64
St. Amant, Clyde Penrose (1915–), 1959–
Culpepper, Hugo Hurlston (1913–), 1959–64, 1970–
Kelley, Page Hutto (1922–), 1959–
Garrett, James Leo (1925–), 1959–
Bennett, George Willis (1919–), 1959–
Cox, James William (1923–), 1959–
Patterson, W. Morgan (1925–), 1959–
Brown, Raymond Bryan (1923–), 1960–64
Haworth, David Swan, Jr. (1906–), 1960–
Tate, Marvin Embry, Jr. (1925–), 1960–
Barefoot, Hyran Euvene (1928–), 1960–62
Williams, Donald Leigh (1934–), 1961–
Mueller, David Livingstone (1929–), 1961–
Deering, Ronald Franklin (1929–), 1961–
Kliewer, Peter Archie (1922–), 1961–66
Cromer, William Rush, Jr. (1923–), 1961–
Carlton, John W. (1920–), 1962–69
Songer, Harold Stanley (1928–), 1962–
Hinson, Edward Glenn (1931–), 1962–
Holloway, Leonard (1923–), 1963–65
Wilkey, Jay Weldon (1934–), 1963–
Delamarter, Walter R. (1924–), 1963–
Stagg, Frank (1911–), 1964–
Chafin, Kenneth (1926–), 1965–70
Hicks, Wade Bryant (1925–), 1965–
McIntosh, Ellen Marie (1920–), 1965–68
Good, James West (1934–), 1965–
Langrave, John Phillip (1935–), 1965–
Hustad, Donald Paul (1918–), 1966–
Coleman, Lucien Edwin (1931–), 1966–
Lin, Richard R. (1925–), 1967–
Jones, Peter Rhea (1937–), 1968–
Boyle, John Howard (1926–), 1969–
Polhill, John Bowen (1939–), 1969–
Davis, Cora Anne (1937–), 1970–

BIBLIOGRAPHY: William Mueller, *A History of the S. B. T. S.* (1959). GLENN HINSON

SOUTHERN BAPTISTS, GROWTH OF. See GROWTH OF SOUTHERN BAPTISTS.

SOUTHERN SEMINARY FOUNDATION. Southern Seminary Foundation was incorporated under the laws of Kentucky in 1961, to establish a foundation to promote all the branches of knowledge and research in the field of Christian education; to establish and administer endowment, scholarship, and other funds for the use and benefit of the Southern Baptist Theological Seminary and the students who may seek an education at that institution; and to encourage, foster, promote, and implement the continuous education and activity of the alumni, and their academic and financial interest in the seminary. In addition to being involved in the planning and implementing of ways and means to achieve future goals, the foundation, through its staff, provides counsel to donors who wish to benefit the seminary through deferred gifts, bequests, and other forms of charitable giving. In 1964, Paul G. Kirkland was named executive director, and in 1970, James L. Powell, Jr., became the assistant director. PAUL G. KIRKLAND

***SOUTHWEST BAPTIST ASSEMBLY.** Property value in 1969 was $112,000, with a debt of $7,500. The annual budget is provided jointly by Southwest, Concord-Kiowa, Beckham-Mills, and Tillman associations, and from the state convention. A resident manager cares for the 23 buildings. In 1969 registration totaled 613.

J. M. GASKIN

***SOUTHWEST BAPTIST COLLEGE.** In the spring of 1956, the college had its largest graduating class with 125 sophomores receiving diplomas. On Apr. 5, 1957, the college received full accreditation as a junior college from the North Central Association of Colleges and Secondary Schools.

John W. Dowdy served as president of the college until May, 1961. J. E. Rains served as interim president until Robert E. Craig became president. Under the leadership of Craig, 1961–67, the college sought accreditation as a four-year institution. Third-year classes began in 1965 and fourth-year classes in 1966. Simultaneously, the college began a major development program to provide facilities for an increasing number of students. In 1962 a dormitory for 222 men was erected and dedicated to Titus Beasley, a history professor at the college for more than 30 years. The college acquired the new Shoffner campus of 102 acres and constructed a field house (1963), fine arts building (1963), Leslie Hall (women's dorm, 1963), and a new men's dorm (1966). Construction of the field house helped to offer a strong athletic program after a fire in Mar., 1962, destroyed Pike Auditorium.

There was a record enrolment of 1,386 in the 1968 session. There were 375 enrolled in summer school, 11 international students, with a total of 31 states and 17 denominations represented on campus. Approximately 82 per cent of the 1968–69 enrolment indicated Baptist preference.

In 1969 there were 35 buildings on the two campuses (Shoffner and Stufflebam), with 123 acres. Thirteen buildings were added between 1962 and 1969. The newest buildings on the Shoffner campus are the Felix Goodson College Union Building and the Estep Library. The former cost $500,000. It houses a six-lane bowling alley, book store, post office, student organizational and work rooms, and locker space for commuting students. The dining, TV, and music areas afford the college students opportunity to relax in front of an open fireplace in the carpeted lounge. The Union Building houses a Little Theatre with a seating capacity of 250, and a small chapel open to students for prayer services and private meditation. The college completed the Estep Library ($450,000) in the fall of 1969. It has space for 100,000 volumes, faculty study rooms, private reading carrels, reading space for approximately 475 students, and lecture rooms.

Along with the growth of enrolment and buildings, there has been academic growth. The number of people holding faculty rank has increased from 27 in 1956 to 75 in 1969. There are 15 departments offering a major and 19 offering a minor. The college grants the B.A. degree. The college is accredited by the North Central Association, the University of Missouri, and the Missouri State Department of Education. From 1967 to 1970 the college conferred 526 B.A. degrees. Since 1956 the college has added the following administrative departments: Development Office, Student Financial Aids Office, Placement Office, Alumni Office, and College Relations Office.

When Craig resigned in 1967, Courts Redford (former president) became interim president. James L. Sells was inaugurated as president, Oct. 22, 1968.

The total assets of the college, including land, buildings, and equipment amount to $3,961,632. The support of the college on a percentage basis in 1968–69 was: gifts, 2.16 per cent; Missouri Baptist Convention, 9.17 per cent; student fees, 52.34 per cent; and auxiliary enterprises and all other, 36.33 per cent. The total budget for 1968–69 was $2,180,000. LINDA SHEEHY

***SOUTHWEST BAPTIST HOSPITAL (Mangum, Okla.).** In 1965 the citizens of Mangum, Okla., voted to build a new municipal hospital to be financed by a bond issue and matching federal funds. May 25, 1965, the board of directors of the Baptist General Convention of Oklahoma voted to sell the Southwest Baptist Hospital to Mangum for $25,000, which was the convention's original investment in the institution. Mangum operated it as a city hospital while the new facility was under construction.

J. M. GASKIN

***SOUTHWESTERN BAPTIST THEOLOGICAL SEMINARY.** The story of Southwestern Baptist Theological Seminary since 1956 may be divided into well-defined periods: the J. Howard Williams period, 1956–58, and the Robert E. Naylor period, 1958–).

I. The J. Howard Williams Period. John Howard Williams (*q.v.*) became president of the seminary in 1953. Having previously served as executive secretary of the Baptist General Convention of Texas, he had been a pastor in Texas and Oklahoma. His vigorous leadership at the seminary was characterized by a challenge and a program to raise "ten million dollars for expansion and endowment to enable Southwestern to meet new responsibilities and opportunities throughout the world."

A Jubilee Expansion Campaign preoccupied President Williams' time during this period. A campaign committee was named early in 1956. The success of that campaign is described in President Williams' own words in a special Golden Jubilee edition of the official seminary publication, *Southwestern News,* in Jan., 1958:

> In 1953 the trustees approved the launching of a ten million-dollar expansion program for new buildings and equipment and additional endowment. That program is proceeding remarkably well. Funds from the Southern Baptist Convention through the Cooperative Program, given and promised, have been the biggest factor in the success of this movement. Hundreds of friends have added their gifts and we are well on our way towards success. We have received in cash and commitments something over five million dollars. The campus has been improved, trees set out, topsoil scattered and grass planted. Fort Worth and Barnard Halls have been re-conditioned. Two magnificent wings have been added to Memorial Building; a trailor court with twenty-six units was built and twenty-six more are to be added soon.

Forty-two acres of land have been acquired and paid for and now twelve apartment buildings are nearing completion. These will house ninety-six families in quarters with one and two bedrooms. Four apartments have been provided for missionaries home on furlough. These are fully equipped even to silverware and linens, and two other apartments are now under construction. Some fifteen or twenty pieces of additional property facing the campus have been purchased during this time, and $714,551.76 have been added to the endowment.

President Williams died on Sunday, Apr. 20, 1958, following a severe heart attack. Funeral services were held on Apr. 22 on the seminary campus.

II. The Robert E. Naylor Period. On Sept. 1, 1958, Robert Ernest Naylor became the fifth president of the seminary. He had been pastor of the Fort Worth Travis Avenue Baptist Church and chairman of the seminary board of trustees.

Purpose.—The objectives for the seminary are set forth in two documents: the charter and the program statement for seminaries of the Southern Baptist Convention. A simplified statement of purpose was adopted in 1968 and says: "The primary purpose of the Southwestern Baptist Theological Seminary is to provide graduate education for men and women preparing for Christian ministry."

Students.—Students come to the Fort Worth campus from every continent of the world and every state of the Union. Over one third of all students enrolled in Southern Baptist seminaries are in Southwestern. Annual enrolment has averaged over 2,000 for 20 years. The 1968–69 enrolment was the largest in over 10 years. Over 5,000 degrees and diplomas have been granted during President Naylor's administration, over 250 having received doctoral degrees from the three schools.

Faculty and Administration.—The faculty grew from 55 full-time members in 1958 to 76 in the fall of 1969, with immediate plans for the addition of 15 to 20 more. Two additions to the administrative staff were John Earl Seelig, assistant to the president, 1960, and Major General Robert Preston Taylor, director of institutional resources, 1966. An average of six professors are on sabbatic leave each year participating in research and study, writing projects, serving as guest professors, and traveling. Southwestern professors are prolific writers, and produce an average of a dozen books a year, contribute liberally to periodicals, books, journals, and encyclopedias. They write music of all kinds.

Curriculum.—The seminary has been characterized by a flexible curriculum. In the School of Theology a major change was made in the nomenclature for the first theological degree from bachelor of divinity (B.D.) to master of divinity (M.Div.). In 1960 the doctor of theology program was reorganized on the basis of area studies including core areas, interrelated disciplines, and electives. In 1961 a program was begun to permit graduate work to be done in connection with the Institute of Religion at Houston, Tex., and other qualified institutions.

The individual curriculum has become the main focal point in the School of Religious Education. Many new courses have been added, including programed instruction and principles of research, church and denominational polity, church staff relations, church business administration, literacy, radio and television, curricula writing, group therapy, human relations, and others. The D.R.E. degree was replaced by the Ed.D. in 1967.

The School of Church Music has shifted from historical and theoretical emphases to the areas of methods, materials, and performance skills. The doctor of church music degree was instituted in 1961 and changed to the doctor of musical arts in 1968. Southwestern was the first seminary to receive full membership in the National Association of Schools of Music.

The ministry of music and the music education departments were combined. Ensemble activities have been moved from church music education to conducting; hymnology and music in the Christian church have been moved from history to the ministry of music departments. The core of courses in the ministry of music department designated for nonmusicians is emerging as a cohesive unit. Areas offered are hymnology, church music literature, practice of church music, philosophy of church music, fundamentals of music, and congregational song leading.

Fleming Library.—The seminary libraries have experienced growth in resources and services since 1958. Holdings increased from 144,402 in 1958 to over 400,000 in 1969. Fleming Library is now the second largest theological library in the United States. The renovation of Cowden Hall permitted the music library to move into large, modern quarters in 1961, making it one of the first separately housed church music school libraries.

Financial Assets.—Receipts from the Southern Baptist Convention Cooperative Program show a steady growth from $529,730 in 1957–58, to $1,302,575 in 1968–69. Total receipts during the period exceed $10,000,000 for operating expenses and $3,000,000 for capital needs.

Total assets of the seminary have increased from $11,727,556.37 in 1958, to $19,788,926.51 in 1969, for a 69 per cent increase. Endowment funds increased 94 per cent during the period, from $3,384,038.06 to $6,551,731.12.

Construction and Improvements.—Twelve new buildings—the Robert E. Naylor Student Center, the Walsh Medical Center, and 10 apartment buildings in the J. Howard Williams Memorial Student Village—have been constructed since 1958.

The $1,273,000 student center was occupied Mar. 1, 1965. The center, a three-level structure, situated in the heart of the campus, has become the hub of seminary community life. It houses all dining facilities, game rooms, banquet and meeting rooms, parlors and lounges, reception areas, the post office, book store, commuters' room, offices, and a refreshment center. The building was named the Robert E. Naylor Student Center by the board of trustees in Feb., 1968, highlighting activities commemorating the seminary's 60th year and Naylor's tenth year as president. The celebration used the theme: "Sixty and Ten."

The Walsh Medical Center was dedicated on Aug. 25, 1969. Named for the F. Howard Walsh family of Fort Worth, the $205,000 medical facility contains 6,000 square feet of space and houses medical and dental facilities for faculty and students and their families. F. Howard Walsh, major contributor to the building, has served as trustee for the seminary since 1963, and is a director of the Southern Baptist Foundation. He also served as a member of the seminary advisory council. W. Gordon Maddox, director of the medical center, came out of retirement in 1963 to be the first resident seminary physician.

Major additions were made in student housing. Expansion of the student village took priority with $1,522,021 being spent on the facilities since 1958. Ten buildings with 80 apartments were constructed. Seven of the buildings have been named: Amarillo, Earl O'Keefe, Ruth and Luther Adams, Howard Trigg, Fleming-Massey, Mary and Homer Jackson, and Adeline and George McQueen Buildings. Total replacement value of the student village exceeds $2,500,000.

Another major step for student housing took place when the B. H. Carroll Park Apartments were secured. This park, located five blocks from the main campus, contains 21 acres of land and 184 living units. All units have been renovated with central air conditioning. Many other perimeter properties have been bought for housing, so that the seminary owns about 600 units for married students.

Three major buildings on the main campus received major and complete renovation during the period: Cowden Hall—$480,696, Barnard Hall—$326,534, and Fort Worth Hall—$489,068. Cowden Hall houses the School of Church Music. Barnard Hall is the residence hall for single women, and Fort Worth Hall, for single men.

Price Hall, the School of Religious Education building, received a new roof and will undergo complete renovation in the immediate future. The ground floor in Memorial Building was converted to use by the School of Theology.

Alumni.—In 1969 there were 26,413 students and former students of Southwestern Baptist Theological Seminary. They serve on every continent of the world, many in strategic leadership positions, many in difficult, obscure places. The majority of graduates serve church staffs as pastors, ministers of education, ministers of music, age group workers, and related ministries. Others serve as missionaries, teachers, evangelists, and denomination workers.

A Convention-wide alumni organization has been functioning for many years. Those who have served as president of the group since 1958 include J. C. Segler, Enoch C. Brown, Homer G. Lindsay, Sr., Rheubin L. South, Hugh Bumpas, James S. Riley, Joseph B. Flowers, Warren C. Hultgren, and Gerald Martin.

In addition there are 30 state alumni associations, two of these having been organized in the fall of 1969, one in New York and one in the Northern Plains area.

Board of Trustees.—The seminary is administered by a board of trustees elected by the SBC. Since 1958 the following have served as chairman: William Fleming (*q.v.*), 1958–63; J. H. Steger, 1963–65, Fort Worth physician; William Shamburger, 1965–67, pastor, First Baptist Church, Tyler, Tex.; and James E. Coggin, 1967–69, pastor, Travis Avenue Baptist Church, Fort Worth, Tex.

Development Foundation.—A Development Foundation was organized in 1960 to serve the seminary in purchasing perimeter properties. J. T. Luther, Fort Worth businessman, is chairman of the foundation. Other members of the board of directors include James E. Coggin, H. B. Fuqua, Jenkins Garrett, Donald J. Singletary, Earle N. Parker, and F. Howard Walsh.

Advisory Council.—The seminary Advisory Council is a group of laymen who serve as an advisory body in planning, promoting, and building the seminary in its total impact. They interpret the program of the seminary and its ministry through every available means, create good will for the seminary, and challenge this good will into active support. They seek to provide methods, plans, and finances for continuing scholarship, buildings, and endowment for the seminary. Tom Joseph, lawyer-banker from Round Rock, Tex., is the chairman of the council.

JOHN EARL SEELIG

***SOUTHWESTERN JOURNAL OF THEOLOGY, THE.** A publication of scholarly and practical interest published by the faculty of the School of Theology, Southwestern Baptist Theological Seminary, Fort Worth, Tex. The first series, which began in 1917, was discontinued in 1931. The second series began in Oct., 1958, with James Leo Garrett as editor. Garrett served as managing editor through Apr., 1959, when H. Gordon Clinard assumed editorship and served through Apr., 1963, followed by William R. Estep, 1963–67. William L. Hendricks has served from 1967 to the present (1969). Robert E. Naylor, president of the seminary, has served as editor-in-chief since the beginning of the second series.

The format has generally been thematic, with the fall issue devoted to the portion of Scripture used in Southern Baptist churches for January Bible Study. Bible study issues are: Oct., 1958, Gospel of Mark; Oct., 1960, I Corinthians; Oct., 1961, Jeremiah; Oct., 1962, Gospel of Matthew; Oct., 1963, Epistle to the Ephesians; Oct., 1964, Deuteronomy; Oct., 1965, Gospel of John; Oct., 1966, Amos; Oct., 1967, Gospel of Luke; Oct.,

1968, Isaiah; and Oct., 1969, Epistle of James. The spring issue has dealt with contemporary issues and interests in Southern Baptist life, e.g., Apr., 1964, historical view of Baptists; Apr., 1965, Christianity and moral issues; Apr., 1966, proclamation and witnessing; Apr., 1967, ministering in a technological age; Apr., 1968, Christianity and the arts; and Apr., 1969, Baptist perspectives of ordination. In addition to topical articles, each issue of the *Journal* has a section of book reviews of the most current and useful religious publications. Since the Oct., 1958, issue 1,923 reviews have appeared.

In Apr., 1961, the editorial board of the *Journal* broadened its purpose to include the disciplines of music and religious education. A representative of each of these fields serves on the editorial board.

Circulation of the *Journal* has grown steadily to a current figure of 2,200. It is made available to a broader readership through journal abstract services in both this country and abroad. Abstracts of *Journal* articles appear in *Religious and Theological Abstracts* and *Internationale Zeitschriftenschau fur Bibelwissenschaft und Grenzgebiete.* WILLIAM L. HENDRICKS

***SPAIN, MISSION IN.** Since 1948 Southern Baptists have helped Spanish Baptists acquire many new church buildings, purchase seminary property, operate the seminary, open a book store, begin radio broadcasts, publish books and periodicals, and extend considerably their evangelistic outreach. During the 21 years following 1948, the number of missionaries increased from 4 to 31, and church membership climbed from 1,510 to 5,500. JOHN D. HUGHEY

***SPANISH BAPTIST PUBLISHING HOUSE.** See BAPTIST SPANISH PUBLISHING HOUSE.

SPECIAL MISSION MINISTRIES, HOME MISSION BOARD DEPARTMENT OF. This department, in the Division of Missions of the HMB, was authorized in 1965. E. Warren Woolf was elected department secretary effective Jan. 1, 1966. The ministries assigned to the department had been administered through an office established in 1961 with Beverly Hammack as secretary. Miss Hammack served as an assistant in the new department until her resignation in 1967. She was succeeded by R. Donald Hammonds. E. Emery Smith joined the staff early in 1970. The ministries of the department are:

**Student Summer Missions.*—Begun by the board in 1942 when 11 students were appointed, this number increased to 922 by summer, 1969. While meeting needs on mission fields, these college and seminary students discover their interest and aptitudes for mission service. Serving 10 weeks, they assist in strengthening the ministry of churches in pioneer areas; establishing new missions; carrying out creative ministries in metropolitan and resort areas; with migrants; and in church building construction.

Christian Service Corps.—Approved in 1964, it has the objective of involving adult lay people in mission actions. Volunteers work on either a short-term (two to ten weeks) or a long-term (moving to the mission field indefinitely) basis. College students who take summer jobs in places where they assist in a mission task were included in 1970.

US-2 Ministry.—Begun in 1965, it offers college graduates the opportunity to serve two years in specific mission assignments through various board departments. Those assigned to this department are engaged, by agreement with the Sunday School Board, in ministry to college and university students on campuses in pioneer areas. E. WARREN WOOLF

***SPRING MEADOWS CHILDREN'S HOME.** The home became a multiple service child care agency in 1957, with the inauguration of social services under the direction of Claud Turpin. In 1959 Superintendent Sam Ed Bradley (*q.v.*) was promoted to the office of general superintendent by the Kentucky Baptist Board of Child Care. In this position he became responsible for the administration and promotion of the total child care program of Kentucky Baptists. In 1959 J. D. Herndon succeeded Bradley at Spring Meadows, becoming its seventh superintendent. Former superintendents were: Miss Mary Hollingsworth, 1869–1905; Miss Mary Abercrombie, 1905–11; Miss Mattie Priest, 1912–19; O. M. Huey, 1919–38; A. M. Vollmer, 1940–46; Sam Ed Bradley, 1947–59. Spring Meadows observed its centennial in June, 1969. A historical pageant was presented on the home's campus on June 21. On June 22, the children, staff members, board members, and friends of Spring Meadows were honored guests at a memorial worship service held at the Walnut Street Baptist Church in Louisville. Wayne Dehoney, pastor, delivered the memorial sermon.

J. D. HERNDON

SPURGEON LIBRARY. The personal library of Charles Haddon Spurgeon (*q.v.*, Vol. II) is housed in the Memorial Library at William Jewell College, Liberty, Mo. A full-scale replica of Spurgeon's study adjoining the Spurgeon Room holds part of the 5,103 volumes acquired by purchase from the Spurgeon family for $3,500 in 1905. Rare and unique Puritan literature forms the heart of the collection which includes works by noted and little-known Puritan clerics and laymen: Prynne, Hale, Hooker, Milton, Henry Smith, Browne, Fuller, Crashaw, Quaries, etc. Rare bibles ("breeches bible"), commentaries, Spurgeon's sermons, and about 2,000 items of history, science, and literature are included. Noteworthy are 18th and 19th-century magazines and accounts by traveling missionaries and scientists. Several hundred works predate 1700 and additional volumes are reprints of earlier authors. WILLIAM W. CUTHBERTSON

STALLWORTH, IDA ROCHESTER FORD MITCHELL (b. Bolivar, Mo., May 14, 1880; d.

Cuba, Ala., Jan. 16, 1969). A WMU leader for 70 years, she was converted under the preaching of her father, Benjamin J. Mitchell. In Dec., 1897, she moved to Cuba, Ala., as the bride of Fletcher B. Stallworth. After his death from tuberculosis (1915), she attended the Normal School at Livingston and the University of Alabama. In 1919 her only child, 17-year-old William, was killed in a train accident. The next fall, Mrs. Stallworth entered the WMU Training School in Louisville. She served as executive secretary of the Alabama WMU, 1923–28, and 1933–40. From 1940 to 1943, she was state president and a vice-president of the WMU of the Southern Baptist Convention. Her service on the Alabama WMU executive board continued until 1958. She was buried in Cuba, Ala.

HERMIONE DANNELLY JACKSON

STANFIELD, MAX CARMAN (b. Gooding, Idaho, Mar. 9, 1915; d. Oklahoma City, Okla., July 19, 1963). Minister, denominational leader, and ardent temperance worker. He graduated from Oklahoma Baptist University in 1935, Southwestern Baptist Theological Seminary (Th.M., 1938), and Central Baptist Seminary (1950, Th.D.). He married Virginia Mae Denning, Aug. 20, 1936. They had two children. He was state missionary, 1942–43, and served several state pastorates, including Putnam City Church, Oklahoma City, from 1947 until his death. A leader of the United Dry Association of Oklahoma, he was secretary, 1950–57, and president in 1958. He was president of the Baptist General Convention of Oklahoma, 1955–56, and served on the Oklahoma Baptist University board of trustees, the state board of directors, and the Home Mission Board, SBC.

J. M. GASKIN

STARKE, VESTER FLOYD (b. Nashville, Tenn., July 16, 1905; d. Chattanooga, Tenn., Apr. 10, 1950). Son of George Law and Dokie (Floyd) Starke, he was educated at Watertown High School, Carson-Newman College (B.A.), and Southern Baptist Theological Seminary (Th.M.). He married Olive Perle Groom, Sept. 4, 1928. They had three children: George Law, Marlyn, and Karen Joy. Starke was ordained July 4, 1926. He held pastorates at Greenbrier, Carthage, Elizabethton-First, Old Hickory-First, and Brainerd-Chattanooga, Tenn. Starke served on the executive board of the Tennessee Baptist Convention, chairman of Tennessee Baptist Convention camp committee, trustee of Carson-Newman College and East Tennessee Baptist Hospital, member of the evangelistic committee of the Southern Baptist Convention, and member of the Annuity Board, 1948–50. He was active in community and civic work. He is buried in Woodlawn Cemetery, Nashville.

W. L. BAKER

START. Since Oct., 1970, the quarterly periodical for leaders and teachers of Mission Friends. Published by Woman's Missionary Union, the magazine contains basic resources for conducting Mission Friends meetings and activities, features of interest to Mission Friends leaders and teachers, and Pacesetter, the leadership section. Helen M. Allan is editor. BETTY BROWN

STEALEY, SYDNOR LORENZO (b. Martinsburg, W. Va., Mar. 7, 1897; d. Raleigh, N. C., July 24, 1969). Pastor, professor, seminary president, and author. Son of a Baptist minister, Clarence Perry Stealey (*q.v.*, Vol. II), and Anna Jamieson (Sydnor) Stealey, he graduated from Oklahoma Baptist University (B.A., 1920) and Southern Baptist Theological Seminary (Th.M., 1927; Ph.D., 1932), where he was fellow to Edgar Young Mullins (*q.v.*, Vol. II). He received four honorary degrees: D.D., Oklahoma Baptist University, 1943; D.D., Wake Forest College, 1953; D.D., Furman University, 1954; and LL.D., William Jewell College, 1959. On Oct. 16, 1920, he married Jessie Wheeler of Wynnewood, Okla. They had two children, Louise (Mrs. Frank Vance) and Sydnor L., Jr. He served as 2nd Lieutenant in the United States Army during World War I, and was principal of a high school in Ringling, Okla., 1920–22. He was ordained in 1922, and served as teacher at William Jewell College, 1922–24, and as pastor of Baptist churches in Missouri and Kentucky, 1925–32. Other pastorates followed: First Church, Bloomington, Ind., 1932–34; Bainbridge Street Church, Richmond, Va., 1934–38; and First Church, Raleigh, N. C., 1938–42. He was professor of church history at Southern Baptist Theological Seminary, 1942–51. In Feb., 1951, he was elected the first president of Southeastern Baptist Theological Seminary, which opened that fall on the Wake Forest College campus with 85 students and four faculty members. He guided the institution through its formative years and saw it win full accreditation by the American Association of Theological Schools in June, 1958. He served on the executive committees of the Baptist state conventions in Indiana and North Carolina and was a member of the Southern Baptist Convention's executive committee, 1938–43. He contributed articles to various encyclopedias and Baptist periodicals. He edited *A Baptist Treasury* (1958), a source book on Baptist history. In 1961 the administration building at Southeastern Seminary was named Stealey Hall in his honor. Stealey retired July 31, 1963. He is buried in the Seminary Cemetery at Wake Forest, N. C. JAMES H. BLACKMORE

***STETSON UNIVERSITY.** As Stetson moved to the end of the fifties, it faced economic difficulties following a decline in student enrolment. Because of increased support from the convention throughout the decade, however, the university was able not only to move toward a sound basis of operations, but through other gifts and loans was able to construct several new buildings. They included three men's dormitories, named Smith, Carson, and Gordis Halls, a new food facility, named the Carlton

Union, and a new library at the College of Law in St. Petersburg.

In 1957, following tension in the state convention of 1956 over the question of control of Stetson, a new agreement was made whereby new trustees of Stetson would be elected by a joint Convention-Stetson trustee committee.

In 1958 the university opened an extension department to serve Florida Baptist churches. Within a year nine extension centers were in operation. Also in 1958 the university celebrated its 75th anniversary with a convocation and the launching of a fund-raising campaign. The university also renovated the old post office building to house the recently acquired Gillespie collection of rare minerals.

In 1961 new tensions developed in the state convention over Stetson's charter, but by 1962 the conflict was resolved by an agreement that a voluntary system of rotating trustees would be developed. In 1963 the convention approved a special fund-raising drive to match a $1,500,000 grant by the Ford Foundation to Stetson. The drive was successful and the grant received.

Between 1961 and 1970 nine new buildings were constructed on the campus. They included five small dormitories, the DuPont-Ball Library Building, Davis Hall, which houses the School of Business, Sage Hill, which is the new science center, and Presser Hall, which houses the School of Music.

Stetson began the new decade of the sixties with an enrolment of 2,101 in 1961. Although enrolment dropped to 1,796 in 1962, by 1969 it had reached an all-time high of 2,921. In 1969 the university had a faculty and administrative staff of 122, a library containing 180,375 volumes, an annual budget of $5,675,750, and property, including endowment, valued at $21,097,485.

In the fall of 1965 the university began a new academic calendar by revising the general education program and creating a five-week winter term between the fall and spring terms. The purpose of the new calendar was to allow for more flexibility and experimentation in the academic program.

In 1966 new tensions arose between Stetson and the convention over the acceptance of a Federal grant by Stetson for constructing the new science building. The convention appropriation for Stetson was cut in half. The next year, however, the amount was increased, and Stetson trustees agreed to accept no more Federal grants for construction.

In 1967 a new air-conditioned men's dormitory was completed at the DeLand campus and construction begun on a million dollar classroom-administration building at the College of Law in St. Petersburg.

Also in 1967 J. Ollie Edmunds resigned as president of Stetson after 20 years in that post. The trustees named him chancellor of the university and elected Paul F. Geren (*q.v.*) as the new president.

In 1968–69 the university established and dedicated the Lula Terry Sparkman House for a new missionary-in-residence program. Two missionary families, the Cecil Northcutt family and the William Hickman family have occupied the home. Also the international dimension of the university was enlarged with acceleration in the number of study-abroad programs both in the summer and in the winter term.

In the spring of 1969 Geren resigned his position as president to be effective June 23. But June 22, 1969, he died in an automobile accident near London, Ky. Immediately the trustees designated the vice-president for financial affairs, John E. Johns, to act as chief executive officer. In Apr., 1970, the trustees elected Johns as the new president. E. EARL JOINER

STEWARDSHIP COMMISSION OF THE SOUTHERN BAPTIST CONVENTION. Created by the Convention in actions 1958–60, this agency was assigned responsibility for leadership in three programs: Cooperative Program promotion, stewardship development, and endowment and capital giving promotion.

I. History. The Apostle Paul taught stewardship to the early Christians. He promoted an offering for the poor saints at Jerusalem and supervised its collection and distribution. Luther Rice called on Baptists in early 19th century America to give support to missions (particularly the mission of Adoniram Judson in Burma) and to education (particularly to Columbian College in Washington, D. C.). In the first decade of the 20th century little was done in the Southern Baptist Convention in stewardship promotion beyond the public pleas for support of the Foreign and Home Mission Boards, and the experimental and relatively expensive work of field agents in raising funds for mission support.

The post World War I period and the 75 Million Campaign saw intensive efforts throughout the Convention and the states related to it, to communicate the message of support of missionary, educational, and benevolent causes, and the message of Christian liberality in giving. The work of Lee R. Scarborough (*q.v.*, Vol. II) and Frank E. Burkhalter (*q.v.*) and later of C. E. Burts (*q.v.*, Vol. I) and Walter M. Gilmore (*q.v.*, Vol. I) was effective. In 1925 this promotion work was done through a Conservation (later Cooperative Program) Commission. In 1929 it was committed to the young Executive Committee of the Convention, in 1931 to a newly created and short-lived Promotion Committee, and again in 1933 to the Convention's Executive Committee.

In 1933 Frank Tripp became leader of the Hundred Thousand Club, and in 1936 James Edgar Dillard (*q.v.*, Vol. I) was called to the Executive Committee as its first director of promotion. Walter Gilmore in 1932 became director of publicity and in 1947 was succeeded by Cyril E. Bryant. In 1948 Merrill D. Moore became director of promotion and associate secretary and in 1949 Albert McClellan was named director of publicity (later director of publications).

In 1959 the Committee to Study the Total Southern Baptist Program, Douglas M. Branch (*q.v.*), chairman, made one of its recommendations:

"A Stewardship Commission should be established to assume responsibility for the stewardship promotion program now conducted by the Executive Committee. . . . When the Stewardship Commission is established all stewardship promotion work now conducted by the Executive Committee should be transferred to the Commission."

This recommendation secured first approval at the 1958 Convention in Houston and second approval at Louisville in 1959. Commissioners were named by the 1960 Convention at Miami. They organized by naming Harold G. Sanders of Florida as chairman. Merrill D. Moore, director of promotion for the Executive Committee, was chosen executive director-treasurer. The commission became fully operative, Jan. 1, 1961.

II. Objectives. The objectives of the commission are:

To support the Southern Baptist Convention objective of bringing men to God through Jesus Christ by (1) Leading in the development of church members as good stewards of possessions. The nurture and growth of Christians in the standards of accountability to God for use of possessions as taught in the Bible should be the basic or primary objective of any program sponsored by the Commission. (2) Assisting the Southern Baptist Convention and the general bodies in the raising of funds necessary for financing the Convention's programs. This should include the Convention's primary mission plan, the Cooperative Program, and endowment and capital giving.

III. Programs. The two stewardship programs then carried by the Executive Committee were committed to the new commission, namely the programs of Cooperative Program promotion and stewardship development. In addition the agency was given a third program, endowment and capital giving promotion. These were defined by the commission in the first program statement developed for one of its agencies. Within a few years such a program statement was developed for each Convention agency. The Stewardship Commission's programs are defined as follows:

(1) The Program of Stewardship Development which seeks to make clear the meaning of stewardship in the lives of the members and to raise the level of giving to standards consistent with the highest ideals of biblical stewardship. Areas considered as parts of this program in addition to 'tithes and offerings,' are church finance, church budgets, the every-member canvass, the conservation of gains in giving, and related fields.

(2) The Program of Cooperative Program Promotion which seeks to make the members aware of the Cooperative Program as the vital central plan for support of mission, educational, and benevolent undertakings of the state conventions and the Southern Baptist Convention. In cooperation with the states and the Executive Committee, it seeks at all times to raise and maintain a high level of giving by the churches through the Cooperative Program.

(3) The Program of Endowment and Capital Giving which seeks: (a) To coordinate the efforts of the state conventions and the Southern Baptist Convention agencies in the raising of money from individuals through wills, living trusts, annuities, and outright gifts. This is understood to be primarily a responsibility of coordination and general promotion and does not provide that the Commission or its staff shall be responsible for direct contact with individual donors. (b) To assist churches, upon request, in securing funds for capital needs.

IV. Relationships. The commission is related in its work to several bodies, agencies, offices, programs, and program leaders.

To State Executive Secretaries.—The Convention has agreed that "stewardship promotion in the several states is the primary responsibility of the state conventions." While the Convention and its agencies have the right to direct access to the churches, in the interest of efficiency and to prevent overlapping of effort, the work of promotion is done in each state primarily by the state conventions, with the assistance of the SBC, its agencies and program leaders.

The state executive secretaries have primary responsibility for all programs of the state conventions, including the program of Cooperative Program promotion and stewardship development. Hence one of the primary relationships of the Stewardship Commission is that with the state executive secretaries.

State Stewardship Secretaries.—The multiplication of responsibilities and burdens of the state executive secretaries led to the naming in the fifties of a state stewardship secretary in each state who could carry this responsibility, in some cases as a department head on the staff organization and in others, as assistant or associate executive secretary. These men in most cases give full time to this work, but in some of the smaller states this responsibility is assigned along with other responsibilities, such as superintendent of missions, etc. The commission works with them directly through semiannual conferences conducted by the commission; work groups on each of the three program areas, personnel for which are named by the commission; and through annual meetings and activities of their own professional association of stewardship secretaries.

Editors of State Papers.—The most direct approach to most Baptists in a given state is through the state paper. Editors of these papers are key leadership personnel in promotion of stewardship, the Cooperative Program, and capital giving. The commission and the state stewardship leadership work closely with these editors.

Southern Baptist Convention Agencies.—The commission works closely with program leaders of each of the Convention agencies directly and through the Inter-Agency Council of the Convention. It works particularly closely (1) with the Sunday School Board's program leaders in

Sunday School, church training, church administration, administrative services, church library, audio-visual, church music, and editors of all publications of the board; (2) with the Foreign Mission Board, its administration and division of promotion; (3) with the Home Mission Board, its administration and division of promotion, and editors of its publications; (4) with the Executive Committee of the Convention, in its responsibility for the well-being of the Cooperative Program; and (5) with the seminaries in their training of future pastors and other leaders in the Convention.

V. Methods of Work. The commission does most of its work through and in cooperation with other program leaders and other persons.

The Baptist Program.—This monthly periodical published by the Executive Committee, SBC, is the primary channel of publication for the commission for reaching pastors.

Cooperative Planning.—Plans for promotion of the Cooperative Program and for stewardship development and for materials for use with such plans are made cooperatively through the work of a work group named annually for each of the areas, and through semiannual meetings of the stewardship secretaries, which are usually held in Nashville. These materials are made to assist in achieving program goals which are mutually agreed upon. Some are purchased by the states through the use of state promotion funds derived from Cooperative Program sources.

Channeling.—The commission has no monthly or quarterly periodical publications. It relies therefore on materials which it develops and channels through each of the state papers and through the publications and curriculum material of other Convention agencies.

Procedures in Stewardship Development.—The commission offers complete packages of procedures and necessary materials for a church to use in developing its members in Christian stewardship and in raising the budget of the church. In 1955 *et seq* the predecessor office of Stewardship Promotion in the Executive Committee, SBC, took initiative and gave leadership in the development of the Forward Program of Christian Stewardship. A *guidebook* describes the necessary actions for a church's stewardship emphasis and budget subscription. The necessary organization is set forth, and duties of each responsible person described. Special actions are indicated for each officer, on a calendarized schedule, a fellowship dinner, training for canvassers, and canvass plans are set forth. Thousands of churches have used the Forward Program with remarkable success.

Growth in Christian Stewardship is a similar set of procedures with essential materials available, for use of smaller churches.

Procedures and materials for Christian family money management and stewardship development in the family are available.

Suggestions for Tithers Enrolment Week and a Weekend Stewardship Revival are available.

A set of procedures for use by Baptist associations is available which gives assistance to an association in building its own budget and in leading churches in the association to higher levels of stewardship development for their members. It is called Stewardship Development Guide for Baptist Associations. Materials directed to youth in stewardship have been developed.

Assistance to Baptist Foundations and Others.—The commission, through plans developed and materials prepared and distributed, seeks to help create an atmosphere within which foundation executives, development officers, and others have greater success in securing capital gifts for Baptist causes from outright gifts, living trusts, testamentary trusts, and bequests. The commission also provides other assistance to such executives. Among these is an annual Foundation and Development Officers Institute where outstanding leaders share information and skills.

Professional Assistance in Capital Funds Campaigns.—The commission provides professional-level assistance to churches, institutions, and conventions in capital fund campaigns, on a cost-recovery basis. It has served one state convention in raising $1,600,000 in an emergency. It is continually serving churches in capital fund-raising campaigns for building programs, using its own *Together We Build* approach, plan, and materials.

SBC Stewardship Services.—Through its SBC Stewardship Services, an auxiliary enterprise of publication, materials for each of these procedures are available to the churches. The commission also distributes to the offices of the state conventions materials which have been cooperatively developed for use particularly in Cooperative Program promotion.

VI. Principles. The commission operates on certain distinct assumptions.

1. Stewardship is a biblical doctrine and an important part of the life and practice of a Christian.

2. Stewardship is primarily a spiritual concept. Its practice involves spiritual commitment. It is not man's plan for raising money, but God's plan for rearing his children. Its primary motivations are spiritual, not material.

3. A church is responsible for teaching stewardship to its members and leading them in its practice, just as it has a similar responsibility in connection with each other biblical doctrine.

4. In addition to generalized teaching of stewardship, a church should also provide at least annually a project which seeks to enlist every member in the practice of Christian stewardship. The use of proven procedures and materials is of great value.

5. Mission support waits on concern for persons and stewardship conviction.

6. The commission has responsibility for giving assistance to each state convention and the churches related to each convention. The commission works primarily with and through the staffs of the state conventions. This agency seeks

to help get the best job done. That means its best work is done in helping others do their work better.

7. Baptists have, because of their biblical convictions and the use of effective materials, made significant progress in stewardship development and mission support. We have, however, scarcely touched the hem of the garment.

MERRILL D. MOORE

STEWART, WILLIE JEAN (b. Clanton, Ala., Oct. 3, 1887; d. Nashville, Tenn., Dec. 1, 1963). Sunday School lesson editor. She was educated at the University of Alabama, Columbia University, Normal College, Birmingham, Ala., and WMU Training School. In 1924, after a number of years of teaching and doing religious work in Birmingham and Pratt City, Ala., she joined the staff of the Sunday School Board. She edited the series of graded lessons for the elementary grades which began in Oct., 1930. Later she was editor of *Storytime* (weekly paper for younger children) and *The Sentinel* (weekly paper for Juniors). She retired in 1953.

HOWARD P. COLSON

STIGLER, HUEY WALTON (b. Gleason, Tenn., Feb. 3, 1883; d. Clinton, Okla., Oct. 21, 1969). Minister and denominational leader, Stigler was educated at Hall Moody (1908–11) and Union University (A.B., 1922). He received the D.D. from Oklahoma Baptist University, 1934. Ordained at Martin, Tenn., Sept. 15, 1909, he was pastor at Ridgley, Tenn., 1908–19. Oklahoma pastorates included Marlow, 1925–27; Frederick, 1928–38; and Clinton, 1938–56. Member of the convention board in Oklahoma a total of 27 years, he was chaplain at Oklahoma Baptist Hospital, Muskogee, 1957–62, and Sayre Hospital, 1962–67.

He married Eula Maye Donnel, July 10, 1910. She died Aug. 22, 1922. His second marriage was on Dec. 23, 1924, to Lula Ruth Pitts, Custer City, Okla.

J. M. GASKIN

STIGLER, NOLAN MERTON (b. Gleason, Tenn., Jan. 19, 1891; d. Shawnee, Okla., Feb. 2, 1962). Minister and educator, his pastorates included First Baptist, Martin, Tenn. (1933–38), and Blackwell, Okla. (1939–48). He married Lattie Rochelle at Bradford, Tenn., in 1914. Educated at Hall-Moody Institute and Union University (A.B., 1919; A.M., 1926; and D.D., 1933), he was ordained Aug. 17, 1915. Stigler was dean of Jonesboro College, Ark., 1924–28, and served on many convention boards and committees in Tennessee and Oklahoma. As a member of the Oklahoma Baptist University faculty he headed that school's extension Bible classes, 1951–61. He is buried at Bradford, Tenn.

J. M. GASKIN

***STILLWATER MUNICIPAL HOSPITAL (Stillwater, Okla.).** Operated by the Baptist General Convention of Oklahoma from 1952 to 1970 when the convention terminated its lease to clear the way for the city of Stillwater to erect new facilities. During these 22 years the hospital cared for over 55,000 patients.

J. M. GASKIN

STORER, JAMES WILSON (b. Burlington, Kans., Dec. 1, 1884; d. Nashville, Tenn., Apr. 12, 1970). Pastor, executive secretary of the Southern Baptist Foundation, and president of the Southern Baptist Convention. Son of Lewis B. and Lydia (Burnette) Storer, he was educated at William Jewell College (B.S., 1912), Liberty, Mo. He received honorary doctorates from William Jewell, Union University (Jackson, Tenn.), and Oklahoma Baptist University. On Dec. 31, 1912, he married Nora Isobel Wilbanks. They had no children.

Storer served as pastor of Baptist churches in Richmond, Va.; Greenwood, Miss.; Pauls Valley, Okla.; and Paris and Ripley, Tenn. He was pastor of the First Baptist Church, Tulsa, Okla., 1931–56. He was president of the Baptist General Convention of Oklahoma, 1939–41, and vice-president of the Tennessee Baptist Convention. He served as president of the board of trustees for Oklahoma Baptist University, 1941–56.

Storer served as president of the SBC, 1953–54, and chairman of the SBC Executive Committee. He was chairman of the Committee on Theological Education of the SBC which recommended sites for two of the denomination's six seminaries. He lectured at all six seminaries.

While executive secretary-treasurer of the Southern Baptist Foundation, 1956–67, Storer saw the corpus of the foundation increase from about $3,000,000 to almost $9,000,000. Upon his retirement from the foundation in 1967, the SBC Executive Committee paid tribute to him in a special feature honoring him as both denominational leader and "Baptist wit."

Active in numerous civic and historical organizations, Storer was a 32nd degree Mason. He wrote *Truth Enters Lowly Doors* (1937), *By-Ways to Highways* (1938), *Major Messages of the Minor Prophets* (1940), *These Historic Scriptures* (1952), and *The Preacher: His Belief and Behavior* (1953).

KENDALL BERRY

***STUDENT ACTIVITIES, NEW ORLEANS BAPTIST THEOLOGICAL SEMINARY.** Student life at the New Orleans Baptist Theological Seminary in the 15 years prior to 1970 was characterized by a wide range of activities. The field mission program continued to be a practical outlet for the energies and service ambitions of students. During the period reports indicated an average of 30,000 contacts and 1,669 baptisms per year. Students also participated in three missionary days each year. Their participation centered primarily in state club meetings held prior to the general assembly. The clubs are student organizations, and the programs generally featured missionaries and mission volunteers from the student body. These groups also fostered social activities patterned to increase the fellowship among students and student families from like geographical areas. Further contribution was made to spiritual life on the campus by Spiritual Emphasis Week. Sponsored by the student council, this activity annually presented outside speakers, but students were utilized in all other areas of responsibility.

Additional involvement of student families came through the campus Woman's Missionary Union. Encouraged by wives of faculty members and by faculty women, the student wives served in a number of circles. In most years there were active youth organizations for the campus children. Students in Carey Hall, the dormitory for single women, participated actively in the Young Woman's Auxiliary. As an outreach of all these organizations, members of the seminary family participated in volunteer work at several mission centers sponsored in the area by the Home Mission Board.

Student leaders were continually active in a variety of community services. In 1965 members of the student body joined the faculty in rendering aid over an extended period of time to victims of hurricane Betsy. Similar aid was given for a shorter period of time in 1969 to individuals in Louisiana and Mississippi who were displaced by hurricane Camille. The spirit of community service was also evidenced in repeated campaigns to organize blood donors for the benefit of members of the seminary family and of other needy individuals.

In the last several years of the period students became involved in frequent dialogue with students from the only other seminary in the area, Notre Dame Seminary. Such dialogue included group discussions of important issues and took place on each campus. Relationships were further enhanced by inter-campus participation in such sports as basketball, volleyball, touch football, and Ping-Pong. All of these sports were already a continuing part of the extra-curricular activities sponsored by the student council for members of the student body.

In keeping with the trend of the times, most of the students and many of their wives were employed during this period. Theological students served churches in the general area, with some of them cummuting by plane to churches more than five hundred miles distant. Others served in a wide variety of positions in churches and in related agencies. Students in music and religious education also found appropriate employment in churches or worked in volunteer positions. Students who could not find employment in churches worked in a wide range of secular positions ranging from part-time jobs to regular jobs. Wives of the students were employed in an equally wide range of religious and secular positions.

GEORGE C. HERNDON

***STUDENT ACTIVITIES, SOUTHEASTERN BAPTIST THEOLOGICAL SEMINARY.** Experience, under proper supervision and with adequate discipline, is a vital learning process for students at Southeastern Seminary. To supplement the basic courses of theological education, the seminary requires Master of Divinity degree candidates to take a course in field education and to engage in two projects which are evaluated by persons in charge of the projects and by the director of field education, Garland A. Hendricks, or his assistant, Ted Janes. Although the seminary cannot guarantee a position to any student, the directors of field education office endeavor to present opportunities of service or employment to every student seeking their assistance. The fact that 70 per cent of all students enrolled at Southeastern Seminary find remunerative employment in approximately 500 churches within a 300-mile radius of the school speaks well of their efforts. Other students minister in hospitals, prisons, shopping-centers, rest-homes, camping grounds, schools, churches, colleges, and other institutions or areas of special need. During the summer, some students serve as pastor-assistants, retreat-chaplains, evangelists, youth-directors, chaplain-interns at hospitals, missionary ministers, and special city-workers.

Instead of the traditional student government, Southeastern Seminary has a Student Coordinating Council, composed of elected students who assist the administration in coordinating various student activities and in promoting the general welfare of all students. The areas of their concern are reflected in the names of the council's committees: devotional, athletic, drama, ethics, extension, music, social, and welfare. Students also serve on most of the faculty committees. This student involvement strengthens and enriches the educational process.

As Binkley Chapel is the center of the campus, so worship is the center of the seminary life. Under the leadership of students, professors, and prominent visitors, devotional services are held daily at ten o'clock. On special days, missionary speakers, scholars, and other Christian leaders broaden the vision and deepen the commitment of students and others.

Opportunities of fellowship and recreation are offered in numerous clubs, choral groups, drama troupes, a vigorous intramural athletic program, golf-course, tennis courts, and a large modern gymnasium. Concerts, plays, art-galleries, and other cultural privileges in Raleigh, Durham, and Chapel Hill are many and varied.

While they are not a part of the regular curriculum of study at Southeastern Seminary, these student activities contribute to the fulfillment of the seminary's motto: "that the man of God may be complete, thoroughly furnished for every good work" (II Tim. 3:17).

JAMES H. BLACKMORE

***STUDENT ACTIVITIES, SOUTHWESTERN BAPTIST THEOLOGICAL SEMINARY.** A significant development in religious activities of students at Southwestern Baptist Theological

Seminary during the decade, 1959–69, was the establishment of a field work requirement as a part of the Master of Divinity curriculum. Beginning in the fall semester of 1961, the requirement was made that all Master of Divinity students must enrol during their second year of study in a supervised field work program. Two semester hours of credit are granted for this work. It requires the student to be engaged in a place of service in a church where he is responsible for the spiritual development of a group of people. A faculty member in the Pastoral Ministry department supervises the field work activities of the students. A field work requirement has been a part of the Religious Education curriculum for many years.

The Pioneer Penetration evangelistic program carried out in the spring of each year is another significant student activities development. This program first began in 1959 as a student-promoted endeavor with about 20 students conducting revival services in struggling churches in Ohio. These students paid their own expenses. With the counsel and help of the evangelism department of the seminary, contacts were made with missionaries in Ohio, and a program was developed to conduct student-led revivals in churches in that state each spring. The program was later enlarged to include churches in Indiana, Michigan, and Illinois. Since 1965, the Pioneer Penetration program has been underwritten by the Panhandle Baptist Foundation which provides the funds to pay the basic expenses of the students who conduct the revival services. In April of 1968 and 1969, about 70 men conducted revival services in over 60 churches located in 12 different states in the northwestern, midwestern, and northeastern sections of the country.

The completion of the Robert E. Naylor Student Center building in Mar., 1965, opened up wider opportunities for student activities in social and cultural areas. The seminary added a director of student activities as a full-time member of its staff. The activities utilizing the facilities of the student center include social affairs of various kinds, banquets, musical and dramatic entertainments, art exhibits, and other activities which help the students and faculty members in their social and cultural development.

The summer mission program of the seminary was enlarged in the summer of 1969 to include mission work in several northeastern states as well as the work in the Bahama Islands. Ten students were sent to New York, New Jersey, Pennsylvania, and Ohio to work in the ghetto areas with children and teen-agers, to do Vacation Bible School work, to help establish new missions, and to work with churches in areas of special need.

The activities of students in Southwestern Seminary have primarily majored in areas which give expression to the purpose of their training. New opportunities for such expression are continually being sought.

FELIX M. GRESHAM

***STUDENT SUMMER MISSIONS.** See SPECIAL MISSION MINISTRIES, HOME MISSION BOARD DEPARTMENT OF.

STUDY AND RESEARCH IN THE SBC.

I. Background. For years programs of the Southern Baptist Convention invested limited resources in research. Studies have been made by the Research and Statistics Department of the Sunday School Board, the Department of Survey and Special Studies at the Home Mission Board, and the Historical Commission. Graduate students at Southern Baptist seminaries and colleges have conducted studies in many areas. A few outside groups or *ad hoc* committees have completed research projects for the Convention or certain agencies of the Convention.

In 1959 the Southern Baptist Convention asked each agency to define its responsibilities for conducting specific programs and for performing other functions. The development of statements has done more than any other action to bring to the attention of program leaders and the Convention as a whole the need for research. Research is designed to furnish information to decision-makers about problems which they are trying to solve. Research may also be used as a tool to discover existing and potential problem areas. Consequently, many program structures include a section on research. The following statement is typical of research activity within many programs:

The Program on Sunday School Promotion.
Study and Research.

1. Discover the needs of various types and sizes of churches, associations, and state conventions.
2. Gather basic information and data needed in designing programs and curricula for suggested use by churches, associations, and state conventions.
3. Discover principles, methods, and procedures of education, administration, and promotion.
4. Study trends and developments in education, administration, and promotion.
5. Evaluate and test existing and proposed programs for use by churches, associations, and state conventions.

Research in the Convention is defined as a critical inquiry which has for its purpose the examination of methods, conditions, conclusions, institutions, programs for the testing of theoretically formulated hypotheses.

There are two distinct levels of research: (1) basic research and (2) operational research. Basic research is directed toward discoveries which could contribute to man's total "store of knowledge." The research project, "The Motivation of Church Leaders," is an example of basic research.

Operational research is less far-reaching in scope and is directed toward the solving of an immediate problem of a program. Most research now under way in the Convention is operational. The research project, "The Programs of a Small Church," is an example of operational research.

There are a number of basic methods which can be used in conducting research to seek various types of information. Any one or a combination of these methods may be used to investigate a single problem. The methods are:

Historical research.—This method of research is concerned with the careful analysis of history to insure proper interpretation of past events.

Descriptive explanatory research.—A comprehensive examination and measurement, descriptive and/or explanatory in nature, of existing conditions in a particular area. Descriptive research is concerned with a detailed picture of current conditions or relationships. Explanatory research is designed to provide insight and answers concerning the "why" and "how" of observed conditions or relationships.

Developmental and change research.— A long-term or longitudinal investigation is made of individuals, churches, or institutions to discover origin, direction, trend, rate, pattern, and limit of change in significant factors.

Clinical and case research.—An examination which focuses on subjective investigation of individuals and/or groups. Interpretation and diagnosis are based on the observation and intuition of the observer(s). This method uses special subjective techniques to collect data.

Experimental research.—An empirical investigation in which control is retained over the variables involved and the conditions under which the variables are observed. This method of research may be used to discover which method, procedure, or sequence of action is best for reaching the goal of the program leader.

Study in the SBC is defined as a careful, orderly use of methods to study problems encountered in relation to programs of the Convention. While study is related to research, it is not limited by the rigid controls of research. Results from study can be used to augment research or to substitute for it when research is unavailable or when time is too limited. It can also be used in areas where the skill and techniques of research have not been developed to the level that valid research can be accomplished.

The two types of study are described below.

Integrative review of research.—These studies are based on completed research. They include abstracts of completed research, a synthesis of the findings from relevant research, and conclusions and implications.

Integrative review of opinions.—These studies are based on the opinions of authorities or scholars in the field, occasionally with references to completed research.

The elements considered in planning, conducting, and evaluating study and research are:

1. *Problem.*—This element gives the background and reason for the study or research. It will indicate who has the problem and why the problem is worth investigating.

2. *Purpose.*—A specific statement of why the particular study or research is being undertaken. In some research a hypothesis (es) is given.

3. *Limitations.*—The scope of the investigation is indicated. The limitations indicate what will and will not be investigated.

4. *Problem Analysis.*—The basic questions to be answered by the study or research are listed.

5. *Methodology.*—The number and type of subjects, the method of securing information, the treatment of the information once it is secured, and the type of reports needed are described.

6. *Organization.*—The way the personnel will be structured to carry out the work.

7. *Personnel.*—The people needed to carry out the study or research as listed. The training needed by persons who will conduct the research is specified.

8. *Schedule.*—The dates when the events in the project will be completed.

9. *Budget.*—The detailed cost of personnel and the direct expenses which will be needed to conduct the study or research are listed.

10. *Administrative Controls.*—The means for controlling the study or research in order to complete the work on schedule are explained.

JAMES H. DANIEL

II. Selected Responsibilities in Research.

RESEARCH AND STATISTICS DEPARTMENT. Beginning in 1921, the year after its organization, the department has regularly reported to the Convention concerning surveys and studies of Baptist life. Sociological inquiry and survey methods were widely utilized in such research, mostly socio-cultural, conducted during the period 1920–50.

Department research activity and capability began expanding measurably in the mid-1950's. A program of research and statistical analysis, as adopted by the Convention, is an assignment of the department. One research subprogram statement is: "(1) Consult with groups such as personnel of Convention or state convention agencies on research needs or proposed projects, and (2) Plan, conduct, and report on projects that are requested by Convention or state convention agencies or other groups, within budget limitations and as agreed upon."

In carrying out its assignment, the department serves as a central, operational research group in working with other programs of the Sunday School Board and provides a complete consulting and conducting research service to other agency and Convention groups. Its activities and capabilities are concentrated in three types of research described above in section I on Background: *descriptive and explanatory, developmental and change,* and *experimental.*

Projects in the following classifications are regularly conducted, either for others or at the initiation of the department: attitude or opinion research; marketing research; publication readership; materials or program evaluative research; and measurement of knowledge and understanding.

Some recent projects are: evaluation of new member orientation materials and program; factors relating to church "dropouts"; profile of Sunday School Board customers; readership of the *Baptist Program;* assessment of program of the Christian Life Commission; evaluation of program of work with students; marketing study of children's books; profile of Southern Baptist pastors; and compensation of selected church staff members.

The department's professional staff has various disciplines represented in academic preparation and experience: sociology, statistics, religious education, marketing research, psychology, political science, education, and mathematics.

Emphasis is placed on the use of current, professionally respected methodology in conducting all research activities. A departmental program of methodological seminars is in operation, involving internal and outside leadership. Innovation is systematically encouraged. Association is maintained with other religious research organizations and the research community at large. MARTIN B. BRADLEY

BAPTIST JOINT COMMITTEE ON PUBLIC AFFAIRS. In 1961 the Southern Baptist Convention approved the program statement for the Committee on Public Affairs. One of the four programs approved was "The Program of Public Affairs Study and Research." This program directs the Committee "to conduct, promote, counsel, and advise with leaders of the cooperating conventions in study and research concerning the meaning of Baptist heritage and practice with respect to contemporary public policy and to provide them with continuing research facilities and opportunities from the vantage point of the nation's capital."

In keeping with this responsibility the committee has structured its research program on three different levels:

(1) *Analysis and Interpretation.*—A major portion of the agency's research is done at this level, utilizing both the traditional and the empirical research methods. At the request of the committee the staff has conducted in-depth research in a number of areas of religious liberty and church-state relations in order to better understand the bases of Baptist beliefs and to examine both the scriptural and political aspects of these beliefs. They have also requested that research be done on contemporary problems of public policy with an analysis made of the possible alternative responses. These serve to guide the committee as it takes positions on policy issues. Research of this type is sometimes printed up in staff reports or other pamphlets which are available to conventions and churches. The results of unpublished research are also available on request. This research often leads to testimony before legislative and administrative committees to advise them in shaping public policy. The committee staff is also engaged in legal research in public and constitutional law. Such research may lead to the submission of an *amicus curiae* brief to state to the courts the committee's position on the issues in a case.

In addition, the SBC has, from time to time, directed the agency to do research and writing on public policy questions which concern the nation and, therefore, the denomination. A request to research the political, economic, and social impact of the deployment of an anti-ballistic missile system is illustrative of the denomination's concerns.

(2) *Promotion of research.*—The committee staff encourages and solicits research on church-state relations on the part of pastors, professors, editors, students, *et al.* At times only topics are suggested. At other times general outlines or research designs are provided. The results are either published by the committee or they are kept as reference for the staff in other research.

(3) *Cooperation in research.*—The committee staff cooperates with other agencies in planning and executing research projects. In addition, the staff recommends to the conventions and the agencies those research projects which those groups are uniquely qualified to undertake.

Research by those with intensive research training is viewed by the committee as the only sound basis for action in public affairs.

JOHN W. BAKER

DEPARTMENT OF SURVEY AND SPECIAL STUDIES. The Home Mission Board, since its beginning in 1845, has been actively involved in study and research. In the early years of home missions, the work was performed by the executive secretary and his limited staff. Later the Department of Enlistment and Cooperation engaged in surveys and studies during its organizational life. Study and research were performed during the depression years, under the direction of the mission study office. From 1943 to 1953, Courts Redford, the assistant executive secretary, gave direction to study and research for home missions. The rural church program, working with Redford, developed the church community survey and performed studies throughout the rural South from 1944 to 1958. In 1958, when the HMB adopted its new organizational structure, a department of survey and special studies was formed with the assigned task of study and research.

The department functions as a service ministry in the general administration of the Board, and provides services in survey, study, and research for all of the programs of home missions. Although the department does not perform all the study and research for these programs, it acts as a coordinator for the research related to home missions. The department develops survey techniques; directs large area religious surveys; and trains mission personnel, pastors, and other leaders in the field of survey. Manuals are designed describing methodology and organization for self study in determining the potential for the many mission and evangelism projects. Also, through the use of these survey methods and trained personnel, primary data are gathered for churches in metropolitan areas, associations, and other church groups for determining needs in mission strategy planning and for use in study and research.

The department performs both basic and operational research in relation to the programs of the HMB. The methodology used could be classified primarily as descriptive/explanatory, developmental and change, and experimental. In connection with the study and research projects, documents of the findings are published and distributed to related personnel for use in evaluating past performance and planning strategy for the future.

These published documents relate to home mission program work in state conventions, associations, metropolitan areas as well as special projects. The department performs studies within the Board which are used in making administrative decisions. It also maintains a close working relationship to other religious research groups in the nation.

Leonard G. Irwin is secretary of the department and Tommy R. Coy, Donald F. Mabry, Orrin D. Morris, and William A. Powell, Sr., serve as associate secretaries. LEONARD G. IRWIN

EDUCATION COMMISSION, SBC. The Education Commission is constantly engaged in some type of research, mainly in the assembling, preparing, and circulating of facts and figures concerning higher education in the United States, and particularly higher education as sponsored by Southern Baptists. The needs of the schools for the latest information is vital to their own planning and very existence. Knowing what other colleges are doing and the reasons why they are doing it is helpful to Baptist college administrators and faculty.

The commission undertakes to have available information on budget and accounting problems, the latest facts on school calendars, testing procedures and results, admission policies, fund-raising information, accreditation standards, and other matters.

Upon request of a college or a state convention, the commission staff engages in surveys and studies relating to the Christian education field in a state, or assists with a solution for a college's individual problem. In several instances during the 1960's the commission staff assisted local groups in determining whether a new college in a location was feasible.

The commission has offered consultative services to college administrators on specific problems, such as new buildings and campus development.

The commission undertakes to keep abreast of the educational standards in operation in all the regions where Baptists have schools. It furnishes assistance in personnel and information to colleges that are working toward accreditation or when their 10-year evaluative studies are in progress.

The commission has participated in several dissertation studies conducted by graduate students. In this way the student is helped and the central information files of the commission are enriched. RABUN L. BRANTLEY

EDUCATION DIVISION, SUNDAY SCHOOL BOARD. In 1962 the programs in the Education Division of the Sunday School Board recognized study and research as a subprogram. The Education Division Office serves as the administration office of the division. The Education Division includes the Sunday School, Church Training, Church Music, Church Administration, Student, Church Library, Church Recreation, and Church Architecture Departments.

The division director with the department manager and his supervisors are responsible for planning and conducting study and research activity. The Education Division Office research consultant assists in overall coordination of study and research activity of the division to eliminate duplication and to serve as liaison with outside groups in study and research related matters. The Sunday School Department and Church Training Department research and program design consultants assist in planning, conducting, evaluating, and implementing study and research in these departments. By 1969 the Church Music, Church Administration, Church Recreation, and Church Library Departments had employed research and program design consultants to assist in study and research activity.

The Education Division conducts its study and research activity using the personnel in the division and outside assistance when needed.

Since the Research and Statistics Department of the Service Division already had a close relationship to the subprograms of study and research in the Education Division, the Education Division did not develop a technical survey research data collection and analysis unit. Instead, it continues to utilize the facilities of the Research and Statistics Department for this specialized service.

Major study and research projects which have been conducted include:

RP-003 Leadership in Southern Baptist Churches
RP-056 Grouping and Grading
RP-073 Practices and Problems Relating to the Church Study Course
RP-012 Church Music Ministries Information
RP-055 The Constituency of Southern Baptist Churches
RP-059 Motivation of Church Workers
RP-105 Church Programs in the Small Church
RP-001 The Ability of Children to Grasp Biblical and Theological Concepts
RP-104 Evaluation of Field Services
SP-030 The Learning Process
SP-013 The Theory of Communications
SP-021 A Church Fulfilling Its Mission Through Worship
SP-023 A Church Fulfilling Its Mission Through Proclamation and Witness
SP-024 A Church Fulfilling Its Mission Through Education
SP-027 A Church Fulfilling Its Mission Through Ministry

SP-062 A Church Fulfilling Its Mission Through Evangelism and World Missions
RP-013 A Study of Commuting Students
RP-060 Student Constituency Analysis
RP-085 Evaluation of Life and Work Curriculum

JAMES H. DANIEL

HISTORICAL COMMISSION, SBC. The Historical Commission conducts a subprograam of study and research as a basic part of its assigned "Program of Utilization of Historical Materials in Serving the History of Interests of Southern Baptists." From its beginning the commission has assisted SBC agencies, state conventions and their agencies, associations, churches, and individuals in historical matters. To assist the executive secretary in expanding this service, the commission added a research director to its staff in 1956.

A vast wealth of Baptist historical resource materials has been procured and preserved by the Historical Commission in Dargan-Carver Library, a Baptist research center in Nashville, Tenn. The commission staff evaluates the relative worth of these resources, utilizes the materials in historical research projects, and helps others doing research in Baptist history to make maximum use of these resources.

Upon request the commission conducts specific research projects and studies to provide historical information about Baptists in general and Southern Baptists in particular. The staff also employs historical research to solve problems in Baptist history, to provide a historical base for denominational program evaluation and development, and to serve particular history needs of Baptist agencies and organizations. Between 1959 and 1965, for example, the commission conducted a comprehensive research project for the Southern Baptist Convention Program Committee. At the committee's request a resumé of significant events in the history of each SBC agency was prepared. These studies were utilized in developing and coordinating agency program statements in keeping with Convention assignment. By request of the SBC Inter-Agency Council in 1967, a 230-page integrative study on the work of the Baptist association for use in program design was compiled. Of necessity the commission staff is highly discretionary in what projects it undertakes, assigning priorities to the ones that will be of maximum benefit.

Research assistance is given to leaders of Baptist organizations and agencies who request historical information regarding some facet of Baptist life and work. The commission gives special assistance to Baptist editors in need of verification of historical events, dates, et cetera. The staff also maintains a limited historical information service for writers, research personnel, and others in need of specific information. Staff members provide research assistance and counsel for churches, agencies, institutions, and other Baptist organizations that are writing their history.

Because of its involvement in historical research, the commission is represented on the Study and Research Work Group of the Coordinating Committee of the Inter-Agency Council.

LYNN E. MAY, JR.

III. *Statistics and Records. In comparison with other denominations, Southern Baptists have traditionally placed great value on the accumulation and use of statistics concerning their activity. Since 1920, direction of this effort has centered in the Research and Statistics Department (formerly called Department of Survey, Statistics, and Information) of the Sunday School Board. Department secretaries, often cast in the role of "denominational statistician," have been: Eugene Perry Alldredge, 1920; Porter W. Routh, 1945; Jacob Pinckney Edmunds, 1951; and Martin B. Bradley, 1963.

IBM equipment was utilized for processing denominational statistics beginning in the late forties. More advanced data processing equipment, including a computer, has been employed extensively in the sixties. Such processing allows timely and detailed analysis of data from individual reports of Convention churches. Many current operations would be unthinkable without existing computerization.

Tabulations of selected statistics are made annually on a county basis. Also, separate summaries by size and location of church are produced and analyzed each year.

Special studies of statistical material are accomplished both upon initiation of the Research and Statistics Department and upon request of other programs or Convention agencies. Such studies as those involving statistical trends for a state convention, joint analysis of U. S. census and Convention data, analysis of baptisms, and the relationship of church debt to total receipts are accomplished.

Statistical data is provided to Convention leaders and agencies and is disseminated to Southern Baptists at large. Baptist Press serves as a channel for various releases. *The Quarterly Review,* edited by the Research and Statistics Department, is a primary medium. The July–August–September issue has for many years been The Southern Baptist Handbook. Another issue generally contains a listing of abbreviated statistical records for approximately 1,500 churches.

Reports from nearly all Convention churches are submitted on a Uniform Church Letter. This Letter was first used in the mid-twenties and was strategic as a means of encouraging comparability and completeness of reports. Since 1965 the Letter has been a four-part carbon form, with copies for the church, association, state convention, and SBC.

The Research and Statistics Department designs and prints the Uniform Church Letter annually, utilizing wide counsel of associational clerks, pastors, state convention personnel, agency program leaders, and the coordinating committee of the Convention's Inter-Agency Council.

MARTIN B. BRADLEY

SUMNER, MARTIN TYLER (b. Milton, Mass., Sept. 6, 1815; d. Verbena, Ala., Aug. 22, 1883). Home missions executive, denominational leader, and pastor. Son of Arthur Sumner, he graduated from Brown University in 1832. He received the D.D. from Richmond College (now University of Richmond) in 1866. He married Georgiana S. Hubbell of Vermont, Oct. 9, 1839, who predeceased him, Feb. 6, 1880. Six children survived the parents.

Moving to Richmond, Va., c. 1840, he was ordained by Second Baptist Church, Mar. 14, 1842. He served as pastor of churches in Dover Association, Va., for over 15 years, also teaching school during the first 10 years and working as agent for American Tract Society, 1854–57. Sumner was on the first board of managers of the Foreign Mission Board, SBC, serving 1845–50; and was also that board's first recording secretary.

On Jan. 1, 1858, he became financial secretary of the Domestic (now Home) Mission Board, SBC, and four years later became the board's sixth corresponding secretary. Serving from Jan., 1862, to Sept. 25, 1875, Sumner led in the denomination's first chaplaincy ministries. His secretaryship was marked by vigorous efforts to launch a strong home missions program despite the difficulties of the reconstruction period. In 1875 he became president of Judson Female College (Alabama) for one year, then agent for Southern Baptist Theological Seminary and later for the American Baptist Publication Society. He returned to the pastorate in Athens, Ala., in 1880, serving until shortly before his death. ARTHUR B. RUTLEDGE

***SUNBEAM ACTIVITIES.** During the period 1955–70, annual circulation of *Sunbeam Activities* increased from 27,238 to 312,228. Editors who served during the period were Juliette Mather, 1955–57; Elsie Rives, 1957–60; Abbie Louise Green, 1960–62; Betty Thomas, 1963; Mrs. Lee N. Allen (née Catherine Bryant), 1964–67; Mary Anne Forehand, 1967–69; and Mrs. Jesse Tucker (née Iva Jewel Burton), 1970. Publication of *Sunbeam Activities* ceased with the July-August-Sept., 1970 issue, and unfulfilled subscriptions were transferred to the new magazines *Start, Aware,* and *Discovery*.

BETTY BROWN

***SUNBEAM BAND.** In 1957 Sunbeam Band was divided into Nursery, Beginner, and Primary Sunbeam Bands. Increased emphasis was placed on leadership training and the use of graded units of study, which led to substantial gains in membership. Sunbeam leaders were advised in 1958 to grade Sunbeam children further by providing separate activities for eight-year-old Primaries. In 1959–60, summer day camping for eight-year-olds was introduced, special associational leadership workshops were promoted, and anniversary goals were set. The 75th Anniversary of the organization was observed in 1961. Part of the observance was the publication of Helen Monsell's *The Story of Cousin George,* based on the life of George Braxton Taylor (*q.v.*), founder of the Sunbeam Band. In Oct., 1959, the name "World Friends" was given to the eight-year-old Primaries, and special materials for use with this age group were introduced.

Providing leadership at the Convention level from 1955–70 were: Margaret Bruce, secretary, department of youth, 1955–57; Elsie Rives, Sunbeam Band secretary, 1955–57, director of Sunbeam Band Department, 1957–59, editorial-promotion associate, 1959–60; Abbie Louise Green, Sunbeam Band director, 1959–63; Betty Thomas, editorial-promotion associate, 1961–63; Mary Hines, Sunbeam Band Director, 1963–70; Mrs. Lee N. Allen (nee Catherine Bryant), editorial associate, 1963–67; Mary Anne Forehand, editor of Sunbeam Band materials, 1967–69; and Mrs. Jesse Tucker (nee Iva Jewel Burton), editor of Sunbeam Band materials, 1970.

In Oct., 1970, when the change in grouping-grading was effected, Sunbeam Band was replaced by new organizations. Nursery and Beginner children became members of Mission Friends, and Primary children became members of Girls in Action and Royal Ambassadors.

BETTY BROWN

***SUNDAY SCHOOL.** Major trends in Southern Baptist Sunday School work since 1956 may be characterized by aroused concern and cautious optimism. Considerable writing in various religious publications and some in the secular press would eliminate Sunday School as a major factor of influence in today's life. However, evidence challenges this view with regard to Southern Baptists. The comparative Sunday School strength of Southern Baptists probably became more apparent during the fifties than in any other similar period. While other major denominations recorded slowing enrolment gains or the beginning of a declining enrolment, Southern Baptist Sunday Schools continued to grow. The vigorous promotional leadership of J. N. Barnette (*q.v.*) and his colleagues of the Sunday School Board was a significant factor in this growth.

The annual net gain in Sunday School enrolment in 1954 reached a peak of more than 597,000. In 1956 the report to the Southern Baptist Convention showed a Sunday School enrolment gain of 3,233,000 for the preceding 12-year period, 1946–57. Growth continued at a slower rate until 1964, when enrolment reached 7,671,165.

The slowing trends that had struck other major denominations a decade earlier became a reality for Southern Baptists when, in 1965, an 11,000 loss in Sunday School enrolment was reported. The next three years showed a continuing slight decline, with a total loss of approximately 125,000 or a total enrolment of 7,545,513 in 1968.

The decade of the 60's was a period of transition for Southern Baptist Sunday Schools. It was recognized that massive changes in the environment in which churches work would require adjustment in structure and curriculum. However, Southern Baptist Sunday School leaders believed that the basic principles which proved effective for the preceding 50 years were still valid. Therefore, the Sunday School program during the 60's experienced restatement and the updating of organizational structure and curriculum.

In 1959 the SBC instructed denominational agencies to define their programs. Sunday School leaders, along with leaders of other church program organizations, recognized the necessity of correlation and the centrality of the church in all programing. This resulted in the identification of church functions. Later it was reflected in changes in basic program design.

The tasks of the Sunday School have been stated as follows: teaching the biblical revelation; reaching unenlisted persons for Bible study; leading them to commitment to Christ and involvement in the life and work of the church; leading church members to worship, to apply the teaching of Christ in everyday living, to witness and minister to church members and prospects, to guide members in their progressive development toward Christian maturity; and providing for members information regarding the work of the church and denomination.

Organizational proposals for the seventies reflect the concept that the Sunday School organization is responsible for providing a comprehensive Bible teaching program for the church. No less emphasis is placed upon the Bible teaching work of the Sunday School in the church building on Sunday, but strong emphasis is given to "extension activities" which include additional approaches involving persons in Bible study outside the church building.

A New Grouping-Grading Plan was inaugurated providing a framework for establishing departments, classes, and units within four divisions: Preschool (birth through five—or to the beginning of school); Children (ages 6–11—or grades 1–6); Youth (ages 12–17—or completion of high school); Adult (completion of high school—or 18 and above). New terminology in organizational structure is indicated in several instances. In addition to those called for in the New Grouping-Grading Plan, the following changes were made in organizational terms:

Cradle Roll work was expanded into the work of the family ministry leader in the Adult departments as related to parents; and outreach visitors in Preschool departments as to enrolment of babies.

Extension Department became Homebound Department.

Young People Away Department became Adults Away.

Superintendents became directors.

There were also changes in the terminology for other general and age-group officers.

During the sixties some major improvements in Southern Baptist curriculum plans were developed. New Graded lesson courses were prepared for Beginners, Primaries, Juniors, and Intermediates. Also, the Life and Work Series for Young People and Adults was introduced. For the seventies the Closely Graded Series was dropped. In addition to the Convention Uniform Series and the Life and Work Series, three other series are offered by the SSB—Forefront, Foundation, and Support Series. The hopeful aspect of Sunday School in this period is underscored by the anticipated use of these major improvements. Also, many Sunday Schools are now growing and prospering. A survey by *Christian Life* magazine in 1969 listed the largest 50 Sunday Schools in point of attendance. These ranged from 5,762 to 1,404. Twenty-two of these Sunday Schools were Southern Baptist.

BIBLIOGRAPHY: Howard P. Colson and Melva Cook, *The Sunday School at Work,* 1969–70 (1969).

A. V. WASHBURN

***SUNDAY SCHOOL BOARD, THE.** Outstanding features of the board's life and service during the period 1957–70 included the fuller definition of its purpose, the careful delineation of its programs, the coordination of its ministries, significant advancement along several fronts, the facing of some unprecedented problems, and the development of new plans for the 70's characterized by greater flexibility in the programs recommended to the churches.

In 1960 the board was doing its work through 18 major programs. By 1965 the board was conducting 25 programs officially approved by the Southern Baptist Convention.

I. Significant Advance. NEW PROPERTY AND BUILDINGS. The board's enlarging opportunities called for the expansion of its physical facilities. In 1959 the Operations Building in Nashville was completed. Two of its major uses are the storage and shipment of church literature, books, and supplies. In 1960 the north wing of the Administration Building was remodeled. A remodeling of the Frost Building was completed in 1962, and of the west wing of the Administration Building in 1964. Corresponding improvements in physical facilities at the assemblies include new Pritchell Hall at Ridgecrest (1964) and Holcomb Auditorium at Glorieta (1966).

The Van Ness Auditorium, housed on the first floor of the board's Administration Building, was constructed when the former chapel became inadequate to accommodate all of the board employees, as well as various denominational meetings held at the board. The new auditorium, completed Dec. 1, 1968, seats 1,050 persons.

THE BAPTIST JUBILEE ADVANCE. The board took seriously its part in the Convention-wide effort to establish 30,000 new missions and preaching stations between 1959 and 1964. The Sunday School Department took the lead, working diligently with the 30,000 Committee. When this movement was merged into the Baptist Jubilee Advance, this program received major emphasis. Although the goal of the 30,000 Movement came far short of realization, it did produce significant expansion of Southern Baptist outreach and was an outstanding means of establishing work in new areas.

New Programs of Work. A Church Administration Department was set up on July 1, 1958, with Howard B. Foshee as secretary. The board had not had such a department since 1936. Also in 1958, at Convention request, the board established a program for study and leadership relative to church-related vocations. In 1962 the Church Recreation Service was given departmental status.

In 1956 the Convention authorized a committee to study, with professional help, the total program of the Convention through its agencies. Several parts of its reports in 1958 and 1959 dealt with the Sunday School Board. The board was commended for efficient operation. Agencies of the Convention were asked to continue utilizing the board as the Convention's publishing agency to the fullest feasible extent. There were also provisions relating to book store operations and the appropriation of board funds to assist the state conventions and the SBC. The board was forbidden to transfer funds to other Convention agencies or committees.

Coordination of Ministries. In previous years efforts had been made to coordinate the work of Convention agencies to eliminate overlapping and inefficiency. Under the leadership of James L. Sullivan as executive secretary-treasurer of the board, significant progress was made toward unifying the work within the board, achieving closer cooperation with other agencies of the Convention, and developing a new program which magnifies total planning in the local churches.

Within the board, coordination was aided by the definition of objectives and programs so as to discover areas of overlapping. The development of the Church Study Course for Teaching and Training, launched Oct. 1, 1959, is an illustration of such unification.

Through extensive inter-agency consultation, the board was able to correlate its work with other boards and agencies. As a result, improvement in the harmony of all Southern Baptist educational programs was achieved.

Probably the most outstanding example of inter-agency correlation previous to 1970 was the development of the Life and Work Curriculum. This alternate curriculum for Adults and Young People was jointly planned by the Sunday School, Training Union, and Church Music departments of the board together with WMU and the Brotherhood Commission. The Sunday School phase of the curriculum majored on teaching the Bible as the basis of the balance of the plan. Study materials for each of the other areas of work were correlated with the Sunday School materials and with one another. This new correlated curriculum became available for use in the Oct.–Dec. quarter of 1966. Use of Life and Work materials was interpreted on the field by an extensive program to acquaint the constituency with the curriculum.

Organizational Changes. In 1961 the board changed some of its structure. The old Business Division was replaced by the Publishing Division with Herman L. King as director. Included in this division are the departments of Wholesale Merchandise Control, Wholesale Advertising, Wholesale Sales, Church Literature, and Procurement. Also, the old Merchandise and Sales Division became the Book Store Division with Keith C. Von Hagen as its director. In addition, the Office of Management Services was created to plan and direct administrative and managerial support services to the board units. Ben R. Murphy was the first director of this office; he was succeeded by Wayne H. Chastain in 1967.

In 1962 the Office of Denominational Relations was created to deal with public relations matters. The name was changed to Office of Public Relations in 1967. Gomer R. Lesch is the director. Also in 1962, the Office of Personnel was made an adjunct to the Executive Office. The director is Leonard E. Wedel. The same year, the title of J. M. Crowe was changed from administrative assistant to associate executive secretary-treasurer.

Effective Mar. 1, 1965, the Church Architecture, Church Library, and Church Recreation departments were transferred from the Service Division to the Education Division; and the Art Department was moved to the Publishing Division. As a result, the Service Division came to consist of the Dargan-Carver Library, the Research and Statistics Department, and Glorieta and Ridgecrest Baptist assemblies.

Effective Oct. 1, 1965, the Broadman Books Department and the Broadman Films Department were transferred from the Education Division to the Publishing Division. On the same date the Program of Family Ministry was transferred to the Training Union Department, and *Home Life* magazine was lodged in the Sunday School Department.

Improved Operation. During the sixties, procedures were developed for processing merchandise orders by modern accounting methods. Economies were brought about that compensated for expenses involved in adding personnel and equipment. The board was able to bring about some savings that helped stave off effects of the nationwide business recession of early 1961.

In 1966 the board's management processes were further unified by means of a goal-oriented approach. By this means the administrative staff, through group decision-making, establishes boardwide goals that are designed to accomplish the board's overall objective. After such goals are established, strategic actions are developed to accomplish the goals. Management periodically reviews progress toward the goals and takes actions that seem indicated.

The board began using computers for business purposes in 1961. By 1970 their use had broadened and increased to the point that large amounts of data are stored for the purpose of evaluating and improving the action plans that make up the board's dated plan for its programs, including curriculum plans which are implemented in the various quarterlies and other periodicals.

II. Areas of Service. Beginning in 1960, the work of the board has been reported, according to Convention instructions, under the heading of programs rather than under departmental headings. This format will be followed in the following account.

THE WORK OF PUBLISHING. The board's five programs of publishing provide the major materials needed by the churches in their educational ministries.

Church Literature.—From time to time the board has issued new periodicals planned to strengthen the total educational ministry of the churches. In Oct., 1960, *Church Recreation* and *The Church Library Magazine* were introduced with highly gratifying circulations.

A new set of Primary Closely Graded Sunday School lessons was completed in 1961. A similar set of Junior Closely Graded lessons was completed in 1962. A year later came the new Beginner Closely Graded Series and the new Intermediate Cycle Graded Series. All of these series of lessons continued in use until Oct., 1970.

In the fall of 1963, *Sunday School Lessons Simplified* replaced *Sunday School Lessons for the Deaf,* and *Training Union Quarterly for the Deaf* became *Training Union Quarterly Simplified.* These publications are designed to meet the needs of all adults with limited reading vocabularies. Also in the fall of 1963, *The Junior Musician* (quarterly) made its appearance.

In the Training Union area, a mutliple series of curriculum materials became effective in 1963, as follows: The Southern Baptist Membership Training Series, The Southern Baptist Special Training Series, and The Southern Baptist Training Union Leadership Series.

In 1964 an erroneous listing of some books in the July–September issue of *Baptist Young People's Quarterly* caused the board great embarrassment and required much time and expense in correspondence and speaking engagements in the effort to apologize for and explain the error. The error, however, resulted in a strengthening of editorial procedures to prevent future errors of this kind.

The Life and Work Curriculum was described earlier under the heading of "Coordination of Ministries." About 56 per cent of the Adult and Young People's Sunday School circulation and about 63 per cent of the Training Union circulation for the fall quarter of 1966 were Life and Work materials.

The circulation figures for 1969 provide a glimpse into the continuing ministry of the board's church literature publishing program. The circulation of periodicals and graded lessons totaled 14,179,171. The total circulation of church bulletins for the year was 1,436,200 copies; of special study materials, 1,713,337; and of supplementary materials, 130,967.

Broadman Books.—The objective of this publishing program is to "edit, produce, and distribute books of Christian content and purpose for all ages and which are representative of Southern Baptist life and thought . . . in such classifications as Bible study, Christian biography and fiction, devotional experiences, inspiration, evangelism, doctrine, stewardship, missions, ethics, Christian history, and family life."

The two-volume *Encyclopedia of Southern Baptists* was among the many books published in 1958. In Oct., 1963, one of Broadman Press's largest publishing ventures was released—*The Bible Story Book* by Bethann Van Ness. It consists of 762 pages, 298 stories, 40 full-page, full-color Bible illustrations, and 90 spot illustrations.

Broadman Readers Plan began operation in Jan., 1964. It provides 12 books each year in the areas of personal, family, church, and denominational life. Persons who enrol in the plan receive three books each quarter. They may keep the books and remit $1.00 per book, or they may return the books for credit. In 1970 there were approximately 14,500 subscribers.

The following statistics are typical of the work of the Broadman Books Department. In 1969 the department received 846 manuscripts for appraisal and published 54 books. The total number of copies printed was 547,801. There were 126 reprints—610,829 copies. Authors' royalties totaled $96,582.

Possibly the most ambitious publishing venture of the board in its entire history was *The Broadman Bible Commentary,* a 12-volume set of books covering the entire Bible. Volumes 1 (Genesis and Exodus) and 8 (Matthew and Mark) appeared in Oct., 1969. Volumes 2 (Leviticus through Ruth) and 9 (Luke and John) appeared in May, 1970. The remaining volumes are scheduled to appear at six-month intervals until all 12 are out. All of the authors are Baptist scholars, most of them being Southern Baptists. Many hold professorships in the seminaries maintained by the Convention. The editor of the entire commentary is Clifton J. Allen, retired editorial secretary of the board.

At the 1970 Convention the board was requested to withdraw Volume 1 and have it rewritten "with due consideration of the conservative viewpoint." At its Aug., 1970, semiannual meeting the board voted to comply with this request.

Broadman Films.—In 1950 the board instistuted a program for production and distribution of audiovisual materials under the name Broadman Films. In 1959 an agreement was reached with the Radio and Television Commission relative to the production and distribution of films. The objective of the program is (1) to produce and distribute films and filmstrips to assist churches in their program and circulation needs, to assist SBC agencies and state conventions in their work, and to meet the need for general religious films; and (2) to provide a channel of distribution for nontelevision use of television films produced by the Radio and Television Commission.

Typical of the work of the Broadman Films Department is the release in 1968 of nine films and 36 filmstrips and slide sets. In 1969 five films and 24 filmstrips and slide sets were produced.

The Ministers Tape Plan was launched, Jan. 1, 1970. The plan offers cassette tapes for ministers' in-service training and personal study.

Broadman Music.—The wide influence of the Church Music Department is illustrated by the fact that *The Church Musician* by 1965 had reached a circulation of over 83,000. By 1969 there were five music periodicals: *The Church Musician* with a circulation of 70,307; *The Youth Musician,* 67,334; *The Junior Musician,* 81,332; *The Children's Music Leader,* 22,195; and *Music for Primaries,* 54,269—making a total circulation of over 295,000.

New titles of church music in octavo form are regularly produced, as well as cantatas, oratorios, gospel songs, hymns, and other musical forms for meeting the needs of the churches. Also an extensive ministry in the recording field has developed. This service has been enlarged each year. Churches can secure choral music for their choirs and at the same time obtain records of this music by expert choirs, thus enabling any church to take advantage of the best in interpretation and techniques.

Music publishing releases during 1969 included 13 recordings, 11 musical books, 10 hymns and hymn arrangements, and 80 choral octavos.

Broadman Supplies.—The objective of this program is "to design, produce and distribute a variety of church supplies, equipment, and educational aids which will contribute to the efficiency of the churches and to individual spiritual development." Such items include record systems for the various church organizations, clerks, and treasurers; a variety of certificates; absentee, prospect, and birthday cards; maps, bulletin boards, and registry boards; booklets on the duties of church officers and committees; Lord's Supper supplies, offering plates, offering envelopes, and various types of robes; and novelties, pins, and pennants.

Convention Press.—The objective of Convention Press is "to edit, produce, and distribute through Baptist Book Stores books, booklets, and pamphlets which are curricular in content and prepared especially for Southern Baptist use." When the Church Study Course for Teaching and Training, a merger of the Sunday School, Training Union, and Church Music courses, was launched on Dec. 1, 1959, it contained 192 titles, all of them publications of Convention Press. Vacation Bible School textbooks and pupils' books are also published under this name, as are foreign mission books and *Baptist Hymnal.* By Jan. 30, 1970, this hymnal had attained a sale of 5,659,390 copies.

One of the major Convention Press books each year is the one published for guidance in January Bible Study, one of the most popular features of Southern Baptist life. In 1970 the circulation of the book surpassed 392,000.

Book Store Ministry.—In 1970 the board was operating 46 regular book stores, 8 seminary and college stores, and 2 summer stores (at Ridgecrest and Glorieta). Baptist Book Stores have been characterized as "service stations" for the denominational program. A few of them are operated at a loss, but they are continued as a service to the denomination.

RIDGECREST AND GLORIETA. On July 24, 1957, Ridgecrest celebrated its 50th anniversary with a special program. That summer there were 31,246 registered guests. At Glorieta there were 12,057. In 1969 Ridgecrest had a total of 36,325 registered guests, and Glorieta had 27,131.

E. A. Herron retired as manager of Glorieta, Oct. 31, 1966, after 15 years of service and was succeeded by Mark Short, Jr. Willard Weeks retired as manager of Ridgecrest, Oct. 31, 1967, after 17 years of service and was succeeded by Kenneth R. McAnear.

FIELD SERVICES. *Sunday School Promotion.*—J. N. Barnette (*q.v.*) retired as secretary of the Sunday School Department, Jan. 1, 1958, after 30 years of service. He had headed the department since 1943. He was succeeded by A. V. Washburn, who continues as secretary of the department.

The major purpose of this program is the promotion of a growing enrolment and development of Sunday School leadership. In 1958 Lawson Hatfield came to the department as superintendent of new work in a special effort to increase the number of branch Sunday Schools and missions. This was part of the 30,000 Movement. During 1959 Southern Baptist Sunday School enrolment reached 7,276,502, the largest Sunday School enrolment of any denomination.

The design of programs for recommendation to churches has always been an important part of field services. In 1962 the board defined the task of the Sunday School as follows: (1) teach the biblical revelation, (2) reach all prospects for the church, (3) lead all church members to witness daily, (4) lead all church members to worship daily, (5) provide opportunities for the personal ministries of the church, (6) provide organizational leadership for special projects of the church, and (7) provide and interpret information regarding the work of the church and denomination.

In 1964 plans were completed for promoting the Adult Thrust, which was the first step in an effort to achieve an enrolment of 10,000,000 in Southern Baptist Sunday Schools by 1970. Total Sunday School enrolment at the end of 1964 reached 7,671,165. This was 60,438 more than at the end of 1963. But the rate of enrolment gains was beginning to decline, and the momentum of the Adult Thrust was not sufficient to reverse the trend. In fact, by Sept. 30,

1969, Sunday School enrolment had decreased to 7,418,067, a loss of 127,446 as compared with the preceding year.

Vacation Bible School Promotion.—No phase of the Southern Baptist educational program has been more faithfully or vigorously promoted than Vacation Bible School. The success of this movement may be partially judged by the following statistics. In 1953 there were 21,741 schools with a total enrolment of 2,059,163. In 1969, 28,176 schools enrolled 3,648,255.

Weekday Bible Study Promotion.—This program was developed as a part of Sunday School promotion until 1964, after which it was identified as a separate program, although located in the Sunday School Department. Weekday Bible Study includes formally scheduled opportunities for concentrated teaching of the Bible and other curriculum areas to pupils of public-school ages in study classes and other weekday programs. It includes, also, special teaching opportunities for children in kindergarten, child care programs, and nursery schools.

Training Union Promotion.—J. E. Lambdin (*q.v.*) retired as secretary of the Training Union Department at the end of 1959. His wife, who had served as an editor in that department, retired at the same time. In December a Convention-wide Southern Baptist Training Union Convention was held in Atlanta, Ga., honoring Lambdin on the occasion of his retirement and welcoming the new secretary, Philip B. Harris. During the tenure of Harris, the very active field program has continued; but a complete new program design has been effected.

In the 1950's many churches began conducting classes for new members, using the book *Your Life and Your Church* by James L. Sullivan. The circulation of this book has exceeded 1,200,000. Growing out of this emphasis, the position of director of new church member training was created as a part of the local church Training Union staff. In this connection a new program of New Member Orientation was developed under the leadership of Earl Waldrup and released to the churches, beginning in Oct., 1961.

It came to be the feeling of a number of Training Union leaders that, along with new program plans, a new name would help this organization. With the assistance of a group of professional consultants and the approval of the elected board, the name "Quest" was chosen but was judged to be inappropriate by the Convention in New Orleans in June, 1969.

Church Music Promotion.—Beginning in 1960, there was a definite deepening and broadening of this program. During the next five years, every phase of it was subjected to intensive evaluation. In 1965, in collaboration with the state and associational music workers, the basic design for a new associational music program was worked out. The field work of the Church Music Department reached large proportions. Between 50,000 and 100,000 people each year participated in conferences, clinics, music festivals, music camps, and other kinds of meetings.

One of the goals of the department was "to assist churches to achieve by September 30, 1966, a Music Ministry enrolment of 1,010,000 through establishing, enlarging, improving, and reporting their music programs." By 1968 the program had surpassed this goal and reported an enrolment of 1,038,298. W. Hines Sims continued as head of this department until his retirement Aug. 31, 1970.

Church Administration Service.—In order to offer church leaders the best kind of suggestions, this department has engaged in a number of research projects. These include studies of church organization, a church membership records system, plans for a comprehensive church program, characteristics and capacities of adult leaders in the churches, the work of the minister of education, and the organization and work of the church council.

The project to aid churches in conducting long-range planning of their total programs involved cooperation between several of the agencies of the Convention. In 1965 the department issued the first *Church Program Guidebook.* It also promoted vigorously the church council plan for local churches. The 1969 report indicated that there were then church councils in 11,658 churches. Provision of program design, materials, and leadership training for improving the work of deacons and of administrative services in the churches is also an important part of this department's work.

Audiovisual Education Service.—The name of the Audio-Visual Aids Department was changed to Broadman Films Department in 1962. The next year the program was unified by transferring the audiovisual education consultants of the Sunday School and Training Union departments to the Broadman Films Department. The Program of Audio-Visual Education Service was established on Mar. 15, 1963, and assigned to that department. A program design for church audiovisual education was developed and an annual resource guide produced and distributed to the churches. Plans were set up for a Convention-wide program of enlistment and training, including the promotion of this service in states, associations, and churches through workshops, clinics, and other kinds of conferences.

Student Work.—The objective of this program is "to assist churches, campus Baptist organizations, associations, and state conventions in establishing, conducting, enlarging, and improving their programs for college and university students and faculty members including internationals." Between 1960 and 1965, the Student Department had designed several new programs intended to meet the changing conditions of student life. The field services of the program continued the extensive use of Focus Weeks; campus evangelism on non-Baptist campuses; extensive promotion of the work through state conventions, retreats, clinics, and similar meetings; and the organization of Baptist faculty fellowships and new BSU organizations, with particular emphasis in the pioneer areas. Following the death of G. Kearnie Keegan (*q.v.*), David K. Alexander became director of the department. He was succeeded by Charles Roselle in 1969.

Family Ministry.—In Feb., 1963, nearly 500 selected persons gathered in Nashville for the Southern Baptist Conference on Family Life. Conferences also were held with various other agencies of the Convention to explore ways of relating the family ministry to the programs of those departments. In 1964 program designs were formulated for structuring this ministry, and emphasis on family life has been given at a number of the weeks at Ridgecrest and Glorieta. Byron A. Clendinning supervises the Family Ministry Section, which is a part of the Church Training Department.

Vocational Guidance.—In 1958 the board employed John M. Tubbs as church-related vocations counselor. A central file was developed on volunteers for church-related vocations, and a series of pamphlets on such vocations was prepared and circulated. Lloyd Householder succeeded Tubbs in 1960 and served in this capacity until 1967. In 1961 the Convention voted to enlarge the program to include the area of all vocations as related to Christian youth. In Dec., 1963, the first vocational guidance clinic was held in Nashville. A design for the implementation of vocational guidance by churches was completed in 1967. In 1970 it was reported that the program was maintaining a file containing the names of some 18,000 church-related vocations volunteers. Correspondence with these young people and others interested in vocational choice averages about 100 letters a month. William P. Clemmons is the present (1970) director of the program.

Church Architecture Consultation.—For many years this department has been receiving from 7,500 to 9,500 requests for assistance annually. During 1967, 228 requests were received from churches in 27 foreign countries. In 1969, 398 church committees and architects visited the department offices in Nashville for consultation regarding building projects. Building conferences were held in 28 states, involving 582 churches. A total of 923 architects were engaged in consultation by department personnel both in Nashville and on the field. This number includes architects who attended the special architectural conference in Nashville in Mar., 1969.

The department answers the many requests that come to it by consulting with architects, studying sketches and drawings, assisting in the preparation of blueprints and specifications, providing general information concerning materials, acoustics, furnishings, decorations, lighting, heating, air-conditioning, and similar items. Members of the staff visit churches whenever possible to aid in these matters. An increasing area of service has been the assistance given to state Baptist projects such as office buildings, encampments, homes for the aged, Baptist colleges, as well as aid for building needs on mission fields. W. A. Harrell heads the department.

Church Library Service.—Under the leadership of Wayne E. Todd, who succeeded Florida Waite in 1959, this department has made steady progress. The program has goals for the extension of library ministry in the establishment of new libraries; the establishment of associational organizations; the establishment of state library organizations; and the enlistment of church libraries in the Broadman Readers Plan. In addition to the use of church libraries for the collection of good books, the department has taken on the further responsibility of promoting the use of audiovisuals. Also, the concept of the library as a curriculum resource center has been developed and promoted. The 1968 report showed 16,022 libraries registered with the department. By 1970 this number had grown to 18,391.

Church Recreation Service.—In 1962 Robert M. Boyd succeeded Mrs. Agnes Durant Pylant as secretary of this department. Its objective is "to create in the churches, associations, and state conventions an awareness and understanding of the needs for and the opportunities in Christian recreation and to provide leadership training to help the churches meet these needs and utilize these opportunities." Each year the number of churches and individuals assisted in this area has increased. In 1968, 6,951 churches reported recreation committees. This number grew to 7,588 in 1969.

Research and Statistical Analysis.—The old name, Survey, Statistics, and Information Department was changed in 1958 to Research and Statistics Department. Under the leadership of Martin B. Bradley, the department functions in four basic areas: (1) compiling denominational statistics, (2) interpreting denominational statistics, (3) special research projects, and (4) master mailing list maintenance. In the area of special research, the department has engaged in projects in a wide area of interest both to the board and to the denomination at large.

Bible and Tract Distribution.—The objective of this program is "to distribute Bibles to the armed forces, provide financial assistance to the American Bible Society for Bible distribution, and to make available to the churches evangelistic, doctrinal, and other general tracts." In 1965 a revision was made as to the pattern of tract distribution. This provides that state conventions may obtain tracts on an agreed formula and become the sole distribution channel to churches and associations, except for those tracts listed in board periodicals, which are supplied directly to the churches by the board. In 1969 the board distributed a total of more than 7,750,000 tracts. In addition, 400,000 copies of "The Baptist Faith and Message" were distributed.

Besides the tract ministry, *The Braille Baptist* has continued to be supplied free of charge to several hundred blind people. In 1961 the board began publishing a new monthly magazine called *Intermediate Braille Baptist* which is supplied without charge to blind youth.

For a number of years the board has made an annual contribution of $5,000 to the American Bible Society to help provide Bibles for the armed forces.

DENOMINATIONAL COOPERATION AND ASSISTANCE. This phase of the board's ministry involves two relationships: one with state convention boards and the other with the SBC.

Cooperative Education and Promotion Work with State Boards.—The objective of this program is to provide funds out of the net earnings of the board to assist Baptist state conventions in the promotion of their work, especially in the areas of education and church architecture. The following figures indicate the extent of this kind of assistance:

1958	$624,891
1963	874,732
1965	921,000
1966	933,962
1967	964,000
1968	898,326
1969	923,000

Southern Baptist Convention Support.—In 1958 the Convention gave specific instructions to the board concerning appropriations for Convention support. These instructions were amended in 1959 to the effect that the board should share with the Convention one-third as much as was shared with the state boards in cooperative work. This sum totaled $259,749 in that year. In addition, between 1962 and 1964 the board provided a total of $1,200,000 for construction of the SBC Building on James Robertson Parkway in Nashville. This structure houses all of the Convention agencies located in Nashville, except the Sunday School Board and the Historical Commission. In 1965 a total of $299,-059 was transferred to the Convention under the regular formula, and in addition the board provided space for other Convention agencies at a cost of $41,677. In 1966 the amount given to the Convention was $373,400. In 1967 it was $1,410,000, a million of which was earmarked for seminary endowments. The appropriation to the Convention in 1968 was $409,837; in 1969, $394,930.

MATTERS RELATING TO MULTIPLE PROGRAMS. *Art Services.*—The following summary appeared in the board's 1965 report: "The Art Department serves practically every program of the Board. It designs covers for all periodicals, provides inside layout and design for many periodicals and all books, designs book jackets, provides artwork for catalogs and space advertising, offers photography services, designs Baptist Bulletin Service covers, and renders many miscellaneous art services." In preparation for the 70's, the Art Department was considerably enlarged. By 1970 it had a total of 35 professional artists on its staff, plus two photographers. Herman F. Burns, who had served the board 41 years, retired as director of the Art Department, June 30, 1970.

Church Program Training Center.—This facility at Nashville was opened in Oct., 1966. The center offers comprehensive, intensive, short-term training opportunities to persons desiring to learn the latest developments and innovations in specific areas of work. Seminars, workshops, and individual guided study are offered. In 1969, 31 seminars and workshops were conducted with a total attendance of 531.

Coordinated Promotion Planning.—In Dec., 1963, the board presented to the state executive secretaries a plan of cooperation with state conventions. This was first called State Strategy Planning. It involved a procedure in which joint planning and goal setting for promotion and field services would be done by representatives of the Sunday School Board and other Convention agencies working together with any given state convention. Three years later, the name of the plan was changed to Cooperative Denominational Planning and still later to Coordinated Promotion Planning. In 1969 the plan involved 29 of the state conventions. These 29 conventions scheduled planning meetings in which detailed plans for the year 1970–71 were made. In 1967 the board appointed Keener Pharr, who had served since 1959 as director of field services for the Sunday School Department, to guide this work. George L. Euting succeeded him in 1969.

Personnel.—Some idea of the extent of the board's operation may be gained from the fact that in 1970 it had a total of 1,483 regular employees. Of these 911 were in Nashville, 535 in the book stores, 27 at Ridgecrest, and 10 at Glorieta. In addition, some 300 to 400 part-time employees are used for special needs such as the heavy shipping periods when literature orders are being filled for the churches.

In addition to personnel already mentioned, the following professional workers retired between 1957 and 1970 (figures indicate year of retirement, position at retirement, and total number of years of service at the Board): Robbie Trent, 1959 (S S children's editor, 30), Robert L. Middleton, 1962 (director, Business Division, 37), William Hall Preston, 1964 (student worker, 37), Noble Van Ness, 1965 (director, Operations Department, 43), Harold E. Ingraham, 1966 (director, Service Division, 44), Mrs. Novella Preston, 1966 (editor, Church Music Department, 42), Mrs. Lillian Moore Rice, 1966 (children's book editor, 22), Sibley C. Burnett, 1967 (VBS promotion, S S Department, 29), Donald F. Ackland, 1968 (adult editor, S S Department, 19), J. P. Edmunds, 1968 (S S Board representative, Office of Denominational Relations, 37), Clifton J. Allen, 1969 (editorial secretary, 31).

III. Unprecedented Problems. During the period under survey, the general religious situation of the country, plus the social, political, and economic changes created for the Sunday School Board some unprecedented problems.

Slowdown of Enrolment Gains. The 1963 report of the board to the Convention stated that the rate of growth of the church program organizations "has not been sufficiently large to be satisfactory because we have not reached enough people for Bible study and membership training. . . . A failure to reach people inevitably affects everything we do." The 1965 report stated, "The slowdown in growth in Sunday School, Training Union, Music Ministry, and VBS enrolment has caused great concern to the Board." And the 1966 report said, "The record for 1965 reveals a continued slowdown in increase in the enrolments in the church program organizations. . . . The Board is trying to develop and promote plans which churches, associations, and state conventions can use to reverse this trend." But the trend was not reversed. In fact, the 1970 report showed that the 1969 Training Union enrolment "ongoing and cumulative" was 2,648,388, a loss of 76,709 from the previous year's record. Sunday School enrolment was 7,418,067, a loss of 127,446 from the previous year.

Decrease in Circulation of Church Literature. The decrease began to show in 1963. That year the circulation of Sunday School publications dropped 1.2 per cent and of Training Union publications 2.8 per cent. In 1965 the circulation of Sunday School curriculum pieces did show a slight increase of .2 per cent, but the corresponding figure for Training Union was a 3.2 per cent decrease. Not all the trend of periodical circulation since 1963 has been downward. In 1966, for example, the circulation of Sunday School quarterlies increased .4 per cent; of Training Union, 3.5 per cent; and of general quarterlies 3.4 per cent. The 1970 report indicated a 1.2 per cent increase of Sunday School quarterlies but an 11.4 per cent decrease of graded items, and a 6.7 per cent decrease of Training Union quarterlies.

During 1970 a study was made to determine the cause of losses in circulation. The first phase of the study indicated that between 95.5 and 98.5 per cent of Southern Baptist churches were using literature from the Sunday School Board. Most of those not using the board's literature were very small churches which did not account for a very large circulation.

Tax Problems. The board has regularly paid taxes on property which it leased or rented to other firms. But in 1960 the city assessor placed all the Nashville property of the board on the tax books for that year. The board protested the assessment. The case was heard by the city and state boards of tax equalization, and the latter ruled that the property in question was tax exempt. The city appealed the ruling to the Tennessee Supreme Court, which on Sept. 7, 1962, held that the board's parking areas and cafeteria were taxable.

In 1969 the Metropolitan tax assessor of Nashville and Davidson County placed an assessment against all Davidson County properties of the Sunday School Board. The state tax equalization board expressed the legal opinion that (1) property used for printing operations was subject to tax; (2) property used for publication of nonreligious materials was subject to tax; and (3) property used for administration activity not related to religious purpose was subject to tax. It also classified Broadman Press as a secular publisher (which it is not). It did hold, however, that the board's church literature area of work was nontaxable. It did not comment on the service programs. The board appealed the decision of the equalization board.

The Metropolitan Government of Nashville and Davidson County also appealed the decision of the Tennessee equalization board and even challenged the state constitution's legality in making institutions like the Sunday School Board tax free in any area of work, apparently with the view of carrying the case to the United States Supreme Court. As late as October 1, 1970, the question had not been settled.

In 1969 a tax assessment of $10,000,000 was also placed against Glorieta Baptist Assembly which is operated by the board in New Mexico. In Sept., 1970, the court ruled that all property at Glorieta was tax exempt, except the filling station, washeteria, and gift shop.

IV. New Plans for the 70's. A simplified plan of organization for all the church programs, a New Grouping-Grading Plan, and a new curriculum plan for all church program organizations were developed. A major activity during late 1969 and early 1970 was a strong promotional effort involving a series of "Shaping the 70's Conferences" held across the nation, in which WMU and the Brotherhood Commission also participated.

New Program Designs for Church Organizations. For several years the Sunday School, Church Training, and Church Music departments have been designing simplified and flexible plans for recommendation to the respective church program organizations for use in the 70's. These were introduced in the Shaping the 70's Conferences. Along with the new plans, some significant new terminology was also introduced.

New Grouping-Grading Plan. After much study and research, the decision was reached jointly with WMU and the Brotherhood Commission to introduce a New Grouping-Grading Plan for the churches, beginning in Oct., 1970. The new plan abolished the old names, except Adult, and classified the age divisions as Preschool (birth through 5 years), Children (6–11), Youth (12–17), and Adult (18 and up). The plan also relates the ages to the usual grading followed by public schools and provides flexibility to meet the needs of churches of varying sizes.

New Periodicals and Periodical Series. In harmony with the New Grouping-Grading Plan, the board in Oct., 1970, introduced a number of new periodicals in its church literature offerings and dropped a number of the old ones. A plan was developed for arranging all church literature in seven series. Each series has its unique purpose, characteristics, and target group. The series are: Convention Uniform Series, Life and Work Series, Forefront Series, Foundation Series, Support Series, Program Help Series, and Campus Ministry Series.

V. Organizational Leadership, Oct. 1, 1970. THE ADMINISTRATIVE STAFF. James L. Sullivan, executive secretary-treasurer; J. M. Crowe, associate executive secretary-treasurer; Howard P. Colson, editorial secretary; Gomer Lesch, director, Office of Public Relations; Leonard E. Wedel, director, Office of Personnel; Wayne H. Chastain, director, Office of Management Services; W. L. Howse, director, Education Division; (vacant), director, Service Division; Herman L. King, director, Publishing Division; Keith C. Von Hagen, director, Book Store Division.

THE EXECUTIVE MANAGEMENT GROUP. All of the above administrative staff members and the following:

Office of Management Services.—Charles E. Lee, assistant to the director; Don Early, manager, Administrative Services Staff; David P. Turner, manager, Budget and Accounting Staff; Hilton M. Austin, manager, Property Management Staff; Robert M. Turner, manager, Systems Staff.

Education Division.—W. O. Thomason, assistant to the director; Howard B. Foshee, secretary, Church Administration Department; W. A. Harrell, secretary, Church Architecture Department; Wayne E. Todd, secretary, Church Library Department; (vacant), secretary, Church Music Department; Robert M. Boyd, secretary, Church Recreation Department; Charles Roselle, secretary, Student Department; Edward Rollins, manager, Student Department; A. V. Washburn, secretary, Sunday School Department; Charles Livingstone, manager, Sunday School Department; Philip B. Harris, secretary, Church Training Department; Lloyd Householder, manager, Church Training Department.

Service Division.—Helen Conger, librarian, Dargan-Carver Library; Mark Short, Jr., manager, Glorieta Baptist Assembly; Martin B. Bradley, secretary, Research and Statistics Department; Ken McAnear, manager, Ridgecrest Baptist Assembly.

Publishing Division.—H. S. Simpson, assistant to the director; (vacant), managing art director, Art Department; Crawford Howell, manager, Broadman Consumer Sales Department; Ras B. Robinson, manager, Broadman Products Department; Steven R. Lawrence, manager, Broadman Trade Advertising Department; Jimmy D. Edwards, manager, Broadman Trade Sales Department; James W. Clark, manager, Church Literature Department; Dessel Aderholt, manager, Marketing Services Department; John O. Jackson, manager, Procurement Department.

Book Store Division.—Bill Graham, manager, Campus Stores Department; Jay O. Turner, manager, Central Stores Department; William J. Brown, manager, Eastern Stores Department; E. Odell Crowe, manager, Retail Advertising and Sales Promotion Department; V. L. McGlocklin, manager, Western Stores Department.

VI. Periodicals Launched, 1958–69. *Adult Bible Teaching Guide* (1966–70), quarterly; succeeded by *Adult Bible Teacher. Adults Training for Action* (1966–70), quarterly; succeeded by *Source* and *Skill* and *Now. Adult Training Guide* (1966–70), quarterly; succeeded by *Source for Leaders* and *Skill for Leaders* and *Now for Leaders. Adventure* (1962–), weekly; formerly *The Sentinel. Baptist Married Young People* (1956–66), quarterly. *Baptist Young Adults* (1956–66), quarterly. *Beginner Bible Stories* (1964–70), quarterly; formerly *Beginner Bible Story. The Beginner Leader* (1956–70), quarterly; succeeded by *Guide C for Preschool Teachers. Bible Lesson Digest* (1964–), quarterly set of leaflets. *Bible Study for Adults* (1966–70), quarterly; succeeded by *Adult Bible Study. Bible Study for Married Young People* (1966–70), quarterly; succeeded by *Young Adult Bible Study. Bible Study for Young Adults* (1966–70), quarterly; succeeded by *Young Adult Bible Study. Bible Study for Young People* (1966–70), quarterl,, succeeded by *Young Adult Bible Study. Bible Study Leaflet* (1967–), quarterly set of leaflets. *Bible Study for Senior Adults* (1966–70), quarterly; succeeded by *Senior Adult Bible Study. The Children's Music Leader* (1966–70), quarterly; succeeded by *The Music Leader. Church Administration* (1958–), monthly. *The Church Library Magazine* (1959–70), quarterly; succeeded by *Media: Library Services Journal. Church Nursery Guide* (1956–70), quarterly; succeeded by *Guide A for Preschool Teachers* and *Guide B for Preschool Teachers. Church Recreation* (1959–), quarterly. *Invitation to Bible Study* (1969–), quarterly leaflet. *The Junior Musician* (1963–70), quarterly; succeeded by *Young Musicians. La Fe Bautista* (1963–), quarterly. *Life and Work Pocket Commentary* (1966–70), quarterly; succeeded by *Bible Pocket Commentary. Living With Children* (1956–70), quarterly. *Music for Primaries* (1966–70), quarterly; succeeded by *Music Makers. Primary Parent Leaflet* (1960–70), quarterly. *Sunday School Lessons for the Deaf* (1957–63), quarterly; succeeded by *Sunday School Lessons Simplified* (1963–), quarterly. *Sunday School Senior Adults* (1964–), quarterly. *Training Adults* (1966–70), quarterly; succeeded by *Source for Leaders* and *Skill for Leaders* and *Now for Leaders. Training Union Quarterly Simplified* (1962–70), quarterly; succeeded by *Source Digest. Training Young People* (1966–70), quarterly; succeeded by *Source for Leaders* and *Skill for Leaders* and *Now for Leaders. Young People's Bible Teaching Guide* (1966–70), quarterly; succeeded by *Adult Bible Teacher. Young People's Training Guide* (1966–70), quarterly; succeeded by *Source* and *Skill* and *Now. Young People Training for Action* (1966–70), quarterly; succeeded by *Source* and *Skill* and *Now*. *Your Invitation* (1969–), quarterly leaflet. *The Youth Musician* (1966–70), quarterly; succeeded by *Opus One* and *Opus Two*.

VII. Periodicals Launched or Current, Oct., 1970. CONVENTION UNIFORM SERIES (for Youth and Adults). Sunday School quarterlies: *Sunday School Youth A. Sunday School Youth B. The Youth Teacher. Sunday School Young Adults. Sunday School Adults. Sunday School Senior Adults. The Adult Teacher. Sunday School Lessons Simplified. On the Wing. Bible Lesson Digest* (set of leaflets). Training Union quarterlies: *Source. Source for Leaders. Source Digest. La Fe Bautista.*

LIFE AND WORK SERIES (for Youth and Adults). Sunday School quarterlies: *Youth in Discovery. Youth in Discovery: Teacher. Youth in Search. Youth in Search: Teacher. Youth in Action. Youth in Action: Teacher. Young Adult Bible Study. Adult Bible Study. Senior Adult Bible Study. Adult Bible Teacher. Simplified Bible Study. Bible Study Pocket Commentary. Bible Study Leaflet.* Training Union quarterlies: *Alive. Alive for Leaders. Becoming. Becoming for Leaders. Care. Care for Leaders. Skill. Skill for Leaders.* Church Music quarterlies: *Opus One. Opus Two. Choral Tones. Choral Overtones.*

FOREFRONT SERIES (for Adults). Sunday School quarterlies: *Context. The Collegiate Teacher. Advanced Bible Study.* Training Union quarterlies: *Now. Now for Leaders.*

FOUNDATION SERIES (for Preschoolers and Children). Interprogram quarterlies: *Guide A for Preschool Teachers. Guide B for Preschool Teachers. Living. Growing.* Sunday School quarterlies: *Preschool Bible Teacher C. Bible Learners. Bible Learners: Teacher. Bible Discoverers. Bible Discoverers: Teacher. Bible Searchers. Bible Searchers: Teacher.* Training Union quarterlies: *Guide C for Preschool Teachers. Exploring A. Exploring A for Leaders. Exploring B. Exploring B for Leaders. Exploring C. Exploring C for Leaders.* Church Music quarterlies: *The Music Leader. Music Makers. Young Musicians.*

SUPPORT SERIES. For Sunday School: *Outreach, Bible Teaching Program Monthly. Preschool Leadership,* quarterly. *Children's Leadership,* quarterly. *Youth Leadership,* quarterly. *Adult Leadership,* monthly. *Your Invitation,* quarterly leaflet. *Invitation to Bible Study,* quarterly leaflet. *Open Windows,* quarterly. *Bible Reader's Guide,* quarterly. For Training Union: *Church Training,* monthly. For Church Music: *The Church Musician,* monthly. Interprogram periodicals: *Look and Listen,* weekly. *More,* weekly. *Adventure,* weekly. *Event,* monthly. *People,* monthly. *Home Life,* monthly.

SUPPLEMENTARY PERIODICALS. *The Student,* monthly. *Collage,* quarterly. *Church Administration,* monthly. *The Deacon,* quarterly. *Search,* quarterly. *Proclaim,* quarterly. *Church Recreation,* quarterly. *Media: Library Services Journal,* quarterly. *The Quarterly Review.*

BIBLIOGRAPHY: R. A. Baker, *The Story of the S S Board* (1966). HOWARD P. COLSON

SUNDAY SCHOOL EXTENSION ACTIVITIES. In the organization recommended by the Sunday School Board, beginning Oct. 1, 1970, the extension director of a Sunday School is responsible for all of the extension activities. He may enlist teachers or directors for each activitiy as needed.

Sunday School extension activities give additional Bible study opportunities to those involved in the Sunday morning departments and classes, and provide an avenue for reaching for Bible study persons not involved in the Sunday morning departments and classes. These activities include eight types.

(1) Vacation Bible School—an age-graded school conducted during vacation time, with not less than 12 and preferably 30 or more hours devoted to study and action in Bible and related content areas.

(2) Weekday Bible Study—an age-graded Bible course (36 sessions), with emphasis on content, which meets at some time other than Sunday.

(3) Bible Conference—a series of studies on any portion or portions of the Bible. They support rather than duplicate the Sunday School lesson course.

(4) Fellowship Bible Classes—Bible study groups (usually short-term) meeting in homes to involve unreached persons in Bible study and lead to membership in the Sunday School and the church.

(5) Bible Study Course—Bible study based on the resources and requirements of the New Church Study Course. Such approaches as special weeks of study (such as January Bible Study), individual home study, study in retreat or camp setting, preview studies, or Bible Survey plan are used.

(6) Family Bible Study—a distinctive course of study for use in the home.

(7) New Sunday School—a Sunday School started in an area where a church is needed, with the intent of its becoming a church. (Sunday Schools started in areas where a church is not anticipated are regarded by program leaders of the Southern Baptist Convention as the responsibility of the mission organizations).

(8) Correspondence Bible Courses—Bible courses sponsored by a local church for individual study based on a distinctive curriculum and requiring written work with systematic reviews and evaluations by the instructor. They are not a part of the New Church Study Course.

MELVA COOK

SUPREME COURT OF THE UNITED STATES AND THE FIRST AMENDMENT'S RELIGION CLAUSES. The First Amendment, added to the United States Constitution in 1791, reads:

> Congress shall make no law respecting an establishment of religion, or prohibiting the free exercise

thereof; or abridging the freedom of speech, or of the press; or the right of the people peaceably to assemble, and to petition the Government for a redress of grievances.

Each of its clauses may relate to the practice of religion, but here attention will center on the opening clauses which specifically mention it.

For over a century the amendment was said to limit only the Federal Government's power. But between the years 1925 and 1947 the substance of all its clauses were incorporated one at a time into the due process clause of the Fourteenth Amendment by judicial decision. That clause restricts state power. This incorporation reached the "free exercise" clause in *Cantwell* v. *Connecticut* (1940) and the "antiestablishment" clause in *Everson* v. *Board of Education* (1947). Since then the vast majority of First Amendment court cases on these clauses has been occasioned by some exercise of state power.

Different schools of interpretation have developed respecting the meaning of the amendment. Some commentators say that its protections are absolute, interpreting the words "no law" literally. For example, they argue that governments cannot abridge freedom of press by any obscenity laws. Other legal commentators, however, say that First Amendment rights are relative. They argue that all rights must be balanced against the legitimate exercise of government power. Since the latter view has generally prevailed, the legal meaning of these rights cannot be found by analyzing the words of the amendment alone. Rather, it is best found by studying the law as it developed in actual cases.

The most authoritative legal opinions concerning such cases are written by the United States Supreme Court when it reviews cases which originated in lower federal or state courts. These opinions are published annually in the *United States Reports*. Parties dissatisfied by the lower courts' decisions initiate the review process. The high court has considerable discretion over which pleas for review it will honor. Therefore, the body of law produced by the Supreme Court on any broad topic is not necessarily comprehensive respecting that topic.

The precise number of Supreme Court decisions on the religion clauses is elusive. Sometimes the Court will discuss religious issues at length in an opinion, but the actual turning point of the decision will relate to some other constitutional clause. For example, in deciding that children can receive state-required education in schools operated by religious groups, the Court based its decision on the property rights of the schools' owners. Yet, the issue of free religion was important in the opinion, and that part of the opinion still serves as precedent for disputes on the "free exercise" clause. (See *Pierce* v. *Society of Sisters* [1925]).

With this information in mind, it can be said that the Supreme Court has handled some 50 cases in which there was significant discussion of issues raised by the free-exercise and antiestablishment clauses. Of the 50, the far greater part centered on the issue of the free exercise of religion rather than on its establishment. However, since the two clauses are interrelated, many cases decided on either clause inevitably raise the other.

Since decisions of the Supreme Court are so important to an understanding of the First Amendment's religion clauses, a representative sample of them will be summarized here. From these much can be learned, both about the kinds of controversies raised under these clauses and about the views of the highest court on their meaning.

Some Free Exercise Cases.—The first case that centered on the free exercise of religion was *Reynolds* v. *United States* (1878). Congress had legislated against polygamy in the territories. Reynolds, a member of the Mormon church in the territory of Utah, practiced polygamy. Charged with violating the law, he claimed that polygamy, being an expression of his religious belief, was protected by the First Amendment. The Supreme Court in rejecting his contention said that there was a legal distinction between freedom to believe something and freedom to act on that belief. The former was absolute. The latter could be limited when individual actions inspired by religion were subversive of good public order. Also, the Court argued that when the First Amendment and similar state declarations were adopted, no one supposed that laws against polygamy were being repealed. Thus, the free exercise clause could not mean that such laws were improper. This decision is representative of most that limit religious freedom in support of some generally accepted social standard.

In *Jacobson* v. *Massachusetts* (1905), the Court rejected a claim of the free exercise of religion when it approved compulsory vaccination against smallpox. And while it upheld as a proper exercise of congressional power a law providing for military draft exemption for religious conscientious objectors and ministers (*Arver* v. *United States* [1918]), it denied that there was a constitutional right to be freed from the duty to bear arms on grounds of religious conviction (*United States* v. *Macintosh* [1931]).

From these cases in which Federal Governmental power was upheld against free exercise claims, we turn to a sample of cases in which the power of the several states was limited by similar claims.

When in *Cantwell* v. *Connecticut* (1940) the Court held that the protection of the First Amendment limited state power affecting religious expression, it also decided that the use of language sharply critical of other faiths must be protected. The protection was required even if, in the view of a policeman, the language so excited some people that a breach of the peace was threatened. Further, the Court said that a law which required the permission of a city official before a religious group could solicit funds door to door violated the free exercise clause.

Dramatically overturning in time of war its own earlier decision, the Supreme Court asserted in *West Virginia State Board* v. *Barnette* (1943) that no schoolchild could be required to repeat the flag salute if his religion forbade him to do so.

Marsh v. *Alabama* (1946) concerned the right to distribute religious literature in a company-owned town. The Court protected the religious right against what amounted to an antitrespass law.

Niemotko v. *Maryland* (1951) and *Fowler* v. *Rhode Island* (1953) both protected the rights of unpopular religious groups to use public parks for religious meetings when other religious groups enjoyed such privileges.

The fact that this sample of cases restrictive of state power all involved members of the Jehovah's Witnesses is noteworthy. Commonly, the frontiers of legal freedoms have been expanded by unpopular groups rather than by socially accepted groups.

A few free exercise cases during this period did not involve the Witnesses. For example, *Torcaso* v. *Watkins* (1961) struck down a Maryland law requiring an oath averring belief in God for those applying to become notaries public on grounds of both of the First Amendment's religious clauses. The freedom of church bodies to settle their own doctrinal disputes without interference from civil courts was affirmed in 1969 in *Presbyterian Church in the United States* v. *Mary Elizabeth Blue Hull Memorial Presbyterian Church.* The defendants had received title to church properties from the highest court of Georgia on grounds that they held to the original doctrines of the Presbyterian church. The Supreme Court said that issues of religious doctrine could not be handled by any civil authorities.

Occasionally, a decision has gone in favor of the power of the states. A license can be required of religious groups parading on public streets (*Cox* v. *New Hampshire* [1941]). Child care laws can regulate the work of children selling religious literature (*Prince* v. *Massachusetts* [1944]).

In these free-exercise cases the much publicized prayer decisions have not been included because these arose under the antiestablishment clause. Also, the 1965 draft law cases have not been included because in them the Court dealt only with the meaning of the statute respecting conscientious objectors, not with the First Amendment.

Some Establishment of Religious Cases.— Not until 1947 did the Supreme Court settle a case squarely on grounds of the establishment clause. The case, *Everson* v. *Board of Education,* asked if reimbursement payments by a school district to parents for the bus rides of children attending parochial schools were an unconstitutional establishment of religion. In deciding by a 5 to 4 vote that the payments were allowable, the Court made a distinction—often called the child benefit test—between aid to the person and aid to the religious institution. The former was said to be proper. The latter was not.

Objection to the child benefit test was voiced by some who argued that under it the state could aid religious institutions indirectly in many ways. Still the Court continues to use it. In *Board of Education* v. *Allen* (1968), it served the Court in a decision which approved a New York state program making textbook loans to pupils in all schools.

In part, because of the objection just noted, the Court's majority included in its *Everson* opinion a much-quoted paragraph which can be interpreted as sharply restrictive of even very indirect aid to religious institutions. That paragraph included this statement: the establishment clause means "at least this. . . . No tax . . . large or small can be levied to support any religious activities or institutions, whatever they may be called, or whatever form they may adopt to teach or practice religion." Since some churches regard all their activities as expressions of religion, these words seemed to threaten government aid to church-related hospitals, medical schools, and other welfare agencies. But the threat did not in fact stop government programs aiding many such agencies.

The exact words of the controversial paragraph were repeated when in 1948 the Court rejected as an establishment of religion the teaching of elective courses on religion within the public schools during school hours by teachers chosen by churches and approved by the school board (*McCollum* v. *Board of Education*). But in 1952 the Court approved the practice of released-time religious education where classes were taught off school grounds by teachers not approved by any public official (*Zorach* v. *Clauson*).

Controversy concerning the establishment clause was heightened when three decisions called the "prayer cases" were handed down in 1962 and 1963 (*Engel* v. *Vitale, Abington School District* v. *Schempp,* and *Murray* v. *Curlett*). Together, they found the Court forbidding, as an improper establishment of religion, school directed devotional exercises including the special exercise of reading Bible verses and the classroom repetition of a state-written prayer and the Lord's Prayer. Knowing these decisions would create strong protest, the opinions included assertions that religion and the Bible could be studied in regular courses, and that any school promotion of the "religion of secularism" was improper. Thus, the thrust of these opinions was aimed only at special religious exercises practiced at the behest of school authority.

Critics of these opinions feared that the Court was limiting religious influence in the society. Supporters of these opinions argued that if the state could not properly finance religion, it also could not promote it by use of state-employed teachers. A few critics claimed that the decision was a limitation on freedom of religion. Defenders of these decisions rejoined that no free exercise of religion was threatened. Only state power to impose religious exercises was restricted.

Studies have estimated that before these decisions about half of the nation's school systems had some sort of regular religious exercises, however brief. Since the decisions at least a few school systems have refused to obey the Court's mandate. Several post-*Schempp* efforts to amend the Constitution to permit state-promoted religious exercises have failed.

At the core of the *Schempp* decision the judges stated another test for the meaning of the establishment clause that may be read to modify the much-quoted paragraph in the *Everson* opinion. The test was this: to avoid the limits of the antiestablishment clause, state actions affecting religion must have "a secular legislative purpose and a primary effect which neither advances or inhibits religion." Earlier the Court had used essentially the same test in upholding Sunday blue laws by arguing that such laws are now the product of secular rather than religious purposes (*McGowan* v. *Maryland* [1961]).

One Supreme Court decision treated the propriety of a state law which attempted to promote a religious doctrine. Finding in *Epperson* v. *Arkansas* (1968) that a law which prohibited the teaching of the theory of evolution was inspired by a "particular religious doctrine" concerning the origin of man, the Court declared it to be an unconstitutional establishment of religion. The Court refused to decide on the plaintiff's plea that the law also improperly abridged freedom of expression.

A Comparative Statement.—While interpretations of the Supreme Court's work on the First Amendment's religious clauses vary, scholars who view practices of foreign states generally agree that persons in the United States have a comparatively broad freedom of religion. They also agree that church and state are compartively widely separated by law in the United States.

See also Religious Liberty, Vol. III.

WALFRED H. PETERSON

SURVEY AND SPECIAL STUDIES, DEPARTMENT OF. This department had its official beginning in 1958 when the Home Mission Board adopted a new organizational structure providing for a department of survey and special studies in the Division of Missions. While the board had conducted surveys and studies from its inception in 1845, there had never been a department with this single assigned task. In 1963 the department was shifted from the missions division to Administration.

The department objective is "to make available the collection, compilation, and interpretation of data in helping mission leaders to visualize plans, conduct and evaluate their work." The department, in carrying out its objective develops survey techniques; directs large-area religious surveys; and trains mission personnel, pastors, and other leaders in the field of survey. It conducts studies and research related to strategy planning for home mission programs and publishes reports related to the findings. The department maintains a close working relationship with other religious research organizations within the denomination and with other denominations.

Billy T. Hargrove, formerly in the Department of Cooperative Missions was elected the first secretary. In 1960 Leonard G. Irwin was elected associate secretary, coming from a pastorate in Florida. Upon the resignation of Hargrove, who went to an Arizona pastorate in 1962, Irwin was elected secretary. Expansion of the department staff since then has added William A. Powell, Sr., Orrin D. Morris, Donald F. Mabry, and Tommy R. Coy as associate secretaries.

See also Study and Research in the SBC.

LEONARD G. IRWIN

T

TAIWAN (FORMOSA), MISSION IN (cf. Formosa, Mission in, Vol. I). The first of several island-wide evangelistic crusades was held during 1957. By the end of the sixties, the number of preaching centers had reached 100—44 churches and 56 mission chapels—with approximately 10,000 members. Strong centers of student work were developed in Taipei, Taichung, and Tainan. A radio-TV studio building was completed in Taipei in 1968; and Baptist Book Stores made possible distribution of Christian literature in nine strategic centers. In 1969, 69 missionaries were under appointment to Taiwan.

JAMES D. BELOTE

TAYLOR, GEORGE BRAXTON (b. Stanton, Va., Apr. 25, 1860; d. Roanoke, Va., Mar. 9, 1942). Pastor, educator, author, founder of the Sunbeam Band. Son of George Boardman Taylor (*q.v.*, Vol. II) and Susan Spottswood (Braxton) Taylor, he was a direct descendant of Carter Braxton, one of the signers of the Declaration of Independence. His father was appointed missionary to Italy in 1873, and the younger Taylor preached his first sermon there. He received his B.A. from Richmond College in 1881, graduated from the Southern Baptist Theological Seminary in 1886, and received his D.D. from Mercer University in 1894. He also studied at the University of Virginia and the University of Rome.

In 1886 he accepted his first pastorate, the Fairmount Baptist Church in Nelson County, Va. There, on Nov. 14, 1886, he and Mrs. Anna Elsom (*q.v.*) organized the Sunbeam Missionary Society for children, destined to become worldwide in scope as the Sunbeam Band.

For many years "Cousin George," as he called himself to the children, prepared program and promotional materials for the Sunbeams. The materials were published first through *The Religious Herald,* a weekly newspaper; later, beginning in June, 1887, a "Sunbeam Corner" was included in the *Foreign Mission Journal.*

In addition to holding pastorates in Virginia, North Carolina, and Georgia, Taylor was professor of English Bible at Hollins College, 1903–28, and resident chaplain there, 1903–33. He was a trustee of the University of Richmond, Southern Baptist Theological Seminary, and Virginia Baptist Orphanage; and a member of Phi Delta Theta and Phi Beta Kappa fraternities. Books he wrote include *The Life and Letters of Rev. George Boardman Taylor, D.D.* (1908), four volumes of *Lives of Virginia Baptist Ministers* (1912), and *Southern Baptists in Sunny Italy* (1929).

He married Jessie Cabell, of Nelson County, in 1888; she died in Aug., 1893. They had one son, George Cabell Taylor, who died at age 30.

DORIS DE VAULT

TAYLOR, OURY WILBURN (b. Lynn Grove, Calloway County, Ky., Sept. 11, 1885; d. Nashville, Tenn., July 8, 1958). Pastor, editor, author, and denominational leader. Son of John and Susan Elizabeth (Ford) Taylor, he was educated at Hall-Moody Institute, Martin, Tenn., and Union University, Jackson, Tenn. (A.B., 1919). He was awarded the D.D. degree by Union University, 1933. On Sept. 11, 1917, he married Virgie B. Glover. They had two sons, Wilburn Lincoln and Charles Byron.

Ordained in 1906, he served several rural churches before becoming pastor of First Baptist Church, Trenton, Tenn., in 1914. Later he served at Franklin (1917–18) and Bolivar (1918–20), Tenn., and at Sturgis, Ky. (1920–26). While serving as pastor at Halls, Tenn., in 1933, he was elected editor of the *Baptist and Reflector* of Tennessee. He held this position until his retirement in 1950. He served on the Southern Baptist Historical Commission, 1952–57.

Following his retirement he was asked to write a history of Tennessee Baptists. His first volume, *Early Tennessee Baptists* (1957), dealt with the period from 1769 to 1832. He was working on his second volume at the time of his death. He is buried in Woodlawn Memorial Park, Nashville, Tenn.

EURA RICH LANNOM

TEAGUE, ELDRED BURDER (b. Newberry District, S. C., Jan. 20, 1820; d. Tuscaloosa County, Ala., Nov. 24, 1902). Educator and minister. Eldest son of farmer John Williams and Mary (Davis) Teague, he married Sophie Nelson Blount, June 15, 1843. After her death he married Louise Emeline Philpot, June, 1861. He attended the University of Alabama, 1836–40, and received a master's degree, 1843. After beginning a teaching career, he was ordained in 1844. He served pastorates in Alabama and La Grange, Ga., for 20 years. Teague was president of East Alabama Female College, Tuskegee, 1865–69, and pastor at Selma, Ala., 1869–76. He then retired from the active ministry and returned to his 680-acre farm in Shelby County, Ala. During the next 20 years he served many small and part-time churches in central Alabama. In 1885 he introduced the resolution at the state convention which resulted in the removal of Howard College to East Lake (Birmingham). Adjacent Ruhama Baptist Church, then meeting once a month, called Teague and voted to meet weekly. He served 1886–88. Because of failing health he completely retired from the ministry in 1896, thereafter living with his children. He is buried at Columbiana, Ala.

LEE N. ALLEN

TEASDALE, THOMAS COX (b. Sussex Co., N. J., Dec. 2, 1808; d. Columbus, Miss., Apr. 4, 1891). Pastor, evangelist, denominational leader. Grandson of a Baptist preacher who had emigrated from England, he studied at the Literary and Theological Seminary, Hamilton, N. Y., and received an honorary D.D. from Union College, Schenectedy, N. Y., 1852. He married Delia Lottridge of Hoosic Falls, N. Y., Nov. 16, 1831.

Teasdale served as pastor in East Bennington, Vt., 1830–32; evangelist in Philadelphia, Pa., and vicinity, 1832–36; and pastor successively at Newton, N. J., 1836–40; First Baptist Church, New Haven, Conn., 1840–45; Grant Street Baptist Church, Pittsburgh, Pa., 1845–50; First Baptist Church, Springfield, Ill., 1850–52; E Street Baptist Church, Washington, D. C., 1852–58; and First Baptist Church, Columbus, Miss., 1858–69.

On Sept. 15, 1869, he was elected corresponding secretary of the first Sunday School Board of the Southern Baptist Convention, then located in Memphis, Tenn. For a time the work flourished under his leadership, but he inherited many problems and was especially beset by the financial collapse of 1872. On Sept. 15, 1872 he resigned, and the board was unable to find a replacement. In 1873 the Convention abolished this first Sunday School Board, transferring its work to the Domestic and Indian Mission Board.

From 1874 to 1881 Teasdale was professor of rhetoric and elocution in the University of Tennessee. He also served as acting pastor in Knoxville. Throughout his ministry he held frequent revival meetings in many parts of the country, usually with outstanding success. From 1885 until his death he resided in Columbus, Miss.

BIBLIOGRAPHY: L. S. Foster, *Mississippi Baptist Preachers* (1895); Thomas C. Teasdale, *Reminiscences and Incidents of a Long Life* (1891).

HOWARD P. COLSON

***TELL, A MISSIONS MAGAZINE FOR GIRLS.** On Jan. 31, 1957, Juliette Mather, *Tell*'s editor since its inception, retired. Dorothy Weeks, associate editor, succeeded her and served until 1968. Oneta Gentry became editor in 1969. During the period 1955–68, *Tell*'s circulation increased from 99,180 to 312,228. In Nov., 1959 a leadership edition was begun with the addition of the leadership insert Plan-it. Publication of *Tell* ceased with the Sept., 1970 issue. New age groupings for girls necessitated new magazines: *Accent* for girls 12–17, and *Accent,* Leader Edition for leaders; *Discovery* for girls 6–11, and *Aware* for their leaders. BETTY BROWN

***TELUGU BAPTIST CONVENTION, SOUTH INDIA.** See SAMAVESAM CONVENTION OF TELUGU BAPTIST CHURCHES.

***TENNESSEE ASSOCIATIONS.**

I. New Associations. ALPHA. Organized Sept. 4, 1960, at First Baptist Church, Centerville, by messengers from nine churches located in Lewis, Perry, and Hickman counties and affiliated previously with Maury Association. The name *Alpha* was developed from the slogan: "*A*dvancing *L*ewis, *P*erry, *H*ickman *A*rea." The association has a written constitution and articles of faith and employs a superintendent of missions. In 1969, 10 churches and two missions reported 43 baptisms, 1,352 members, $102,355 total gifts, $17,740 missions gifts, $413,500 property value, and $78,129 church debt.

CENTRAL. Organized Sept. 7, 1958, at Gath Baptist Church, McMinnville, by messengers from 12 churches located principally in Warren County and affiliated previously with Duck River, Salem, or Union associations. The association has a written constitution, subscribes to "The Baptist Faith and Message" statement of the Southern Baptist Convention of 1925, and employs a superintendent of missions. In 1969, 15 churches and one mission reported 109 baptisms, 3,618 members, $205,941 total gifts, $24,508 missions gifts, $1,068,000 property value, and $169,209 church debt.

CLINCH. Organized Oct. 26, 1966, at First Baptist Church, Sneedville, by messengers from two churches located in Hancock County and affiliated previously with Mulberry Gap Association, for the purpose of providing opportunity for closer cooperation with the Tennessee Baptist Convention and the Southern Baptist Convention. Meetings have been held annually since organization, and in 1969 the two churches reported five baptisms, 372 members, $17,395 total gifts, $1,784 missions gifts, $110,000 property value, and $16,000 church debt.

COPPER BASIN. Organized Nov. 15, 1960, at Mine City Baptist Church, Ducktown, by messengers from 14 churches located in the southeastern area of Polk County and affiliated previously with Polk County Association. It has a written constitution but no articles of faith and employs a superintendent of missions. In 1969, 14 churches reported 27 baptisms, 2,580 members, $99,834 total gifts, $13,928 missions gifts, $346,000 property value, and $60,935 church debt.

HARDIN COUNTY. Organized Sept. 17, 1967, at First Baptist Church, Savannah, by messengers from 10 churches located principally in Hardin County and with one exception affiliated previously with Indian Creek Association. It has a written constitution and articles of faith. In 1969, nine churches reported 34 baptisms, 1,824 members, $103,363 total gifts, $10,502 missions gifts, $506,000 property value, and $107,141 church debt.

HAYWOOD COUNTY. Organized Oct. 17, 1967, at Holly Grove Baptist Church by messengers from 10 churches located in Haywood County and affiliated previously with Big Hatchie Association. It has a written constitution and subscribes to "The Baptist Faith and Message" statement of the Southern Baptist Convention of 1925. In 1969, 11 churches reported 102 baptisms, 3,553 members, $268,945 total gifts, $38,623 missions gifts, $1,192,621 property value, and $191,336 church debt.

II. Changes in associations. CUMBERLAND PLATEAU. Formerly Cumberland County Baptist Association, the name was changed to "The Cumberland Plateau Baptist Association" by action of the association in session at Oak Hill church, Crossville, on Oct. 28, 1969. Its new constitution, adopted in the same action, defines its articles of faith as "those adopted by the Southern Baptist Convention assembled in Memphis, Tenn., May 14, 1925, revised May 9, 1963." This association is not to be confused with the noncooperating body known as the Cumberland Plateau Association of Baptists.

WEST UNION. Ceased reporting to the convention after 1963, and subsequently was dropped from the list of extant cooperating associations. Its churches in the main identify themselves as "United Baptist Churches of Christ."

LESLIE BAUMGARTNER

***TENNESSEE BAPTIST CHILDREN'S HOMES, INC.** Approximately 500 homeless and orphaned children are given care annually on four campuses and their related services. These campuses are composed of 868 acres and 46 buildings and valued at $2,370,000. The budget for 1969–70 was $687,300, and the per capita cost of care was approximately $1,370. This ministry is supported through the Cooperative Program and an annual Mother's Day Offering in the churches, supplemented by personal gifts, bequests, and memorials. The central office is located in the Tennessee Baptist Convention building at Brentwood, and the statewide program is administered by an executive director-treasurer. Twenty-seven men and women serve on the board of trustees, representing the three grand divisions of the state.

The children attend public schools and churches off the campuses. This ministry of benevolence and missions is a multi-service program, including group care, foster homes, adoptions, family assistance, work with unwed mothers and mothers' aid. The cottage concept of operation was adopted and begun by the board in 1969. The first was constructed on the Chattanooga campus at a cost of $75,000 and provides for 10 children and houseparents.

JAMES M. GREGG

***TENNESSEE BAPTIST CONVENTION.** In annual session, Nov. 13, 1957, at First Baptist Church, Nashville, the convention approved a recommendation of its allocation committee that the executive secretary-treasurer appoint a survey committee to work closely with him "in making a full and complete analytical survey of all our institutions, agencies and State Mission Programs." The convention authorized the survey committee to obtain additional and specialized help in making the survey. The executive secretary was authorized to administer the details of the survey.

Survey and reorganization.—On Dec. 3, 1957, in the annual meeting of the executive board of the Tennessee Baptist Convention, a survey committee was appointed consisting of 12 members, four from each of the three grand divisions of the state. The committee on Jan. 14, 1958, decided to recommend the employment of the management consultant firm of Booz, Allen, and Hamilton to give the professional counsel needed. At a called meeting of the administrative committee of the executive board, Feb. 18, 1958, the recommendation was made and the administrative committee voted to employ the management consultant firm "to conduct a planning and administrative survey of the Tennessee Baptist Convention."

Representatives of the firm interviewed more than 100 individuals for approximately one hour each concerning the programs and work of the convention. About 2,500 questionnaires were sent to pastors, lay moderators, and state missionaries. Audits, reports, bylaws, objectives, and programs for all the agencies, institutions, and state mission programs were analyzed and studied. The consultant firm made its report to the survey committee which contained three volumes. The survey committee made a progress report to the Tennessee convention in its annual session in Bellevue Baptist Church, Memphis, Nov. 12, 1958, and requested another year to make its final report. The committee studied the recommendations and findings of the management consultant firm. The report was revised and adapted to the needs of the convention according to the evaluation and study of the committee. The final report was made to the convention meeting in Gatlinburg, Nov. 9, 1959.

Changes adopted called for reorganization of administrative processes to carry out the programs of the convention. The general objective of the convention was defined to be: "To bring men to God through Jesus Christ." Two means of reaching this objective were given. First, by evangelism—winning men to God; and second, by education—developing spiritually those who are won. A specific objective was adopted: "To assist Baptists and Baptist churches in Tennessee to carry out the Great Commission." Four program objectives were adopted. They were: first, to strengthen the work of Tennessee Baptist churches and associations; second, to promote the objectives of the Southern Baptist Convention; third, to educate for Christian leadership; and fourth, to render Christian benevolent service. Program support and operating objectives were adopted which defined means for reaching these objectives.

Complete reorganization of the executive board was recommended. Its membership was increased from 54 directors to 75. Twenty-five members were to be elected from each of the three grand divisions of the state and it was to be objective in representing all of the interests and programs of the Tennessee convention. Members were to serve for a three-year term. After two terms they rotate off the board one year before reelection. The president of the Tennessee Baptist Convention and the state Woman's Missionary Union president were to serve as ex-officio members of the executive board.

The work of the executive board was redefined so that it would be carried out through seven standing committees—administrative, Christian services, denominational cooperation, education, public affairs and Christian life, state missions, and Tennessee Baptist program committee. Each member of the executive board serves on at least one of the committees. Committees have from 12 to 16 members. The administrative committee is made up of six members of the executive board, six chairmen of the other operating committees, the president of the convention, and the president and vice-president of the executive board. Each committee's work is carefully defined and is assigned certain responsibilities and areas of the work assigned to the executive board by the convention. An operational manual defines methods and processes by which they operate.

The standing committees of the Tennessee convention were completely reorganized.

Twenty-two reporting and operating committees were abolished. The education, historical, and hospital commissions were dissolved and their functions assigned elsewhere. Seven standing committees were established to carry out the work of the convention as assigned. The committee on arrangements plans the program for the annual session of the convention and recommends the order of business. The committee selects the place and recommends the time and the preacher of the annual convention sermon. The committee on credentials registers the messengers for the annual session, makes decisions concerning the seating of messengers, and administers all votes by ballot. The committee on boards nominates all members for the executive board, the institutions, and agencies. The committee on committees nominates all convention committees. The committee on resolutions has assigned to it all resolutions presented to the convention. The committee on audits meets annually to review all audits of the executive board, institutions, and agencies. The committee sees that the executive board carries out the mandates of the convention concerning auditing. The committee on the journal edits the journal of the proceedings of the convention sessions as submitted by the recording secretary.

The budgeting process and methods of financing the needs of the Tennessee Baptist Convention and its agencies and institutions underwent major changes. The distribution of Cooperative Program funds was figured on a percentage basis after certain preferred items had been deducted. The new method was set up on a single percentage division between the state convention and the SBC with no preferred items. Budgets for all state programs were to be made on the basis of budget requests and priority needs rather than on a percentage basis. Institutions and agencies, as well as state missions programs and convention administration budget requests, were to be submitted to the office of the executive secretary-treasurer by a fixed date early in the summer. Formats were provided for this purpose. These budget requests were reviewed by the executive board committees assigned to these areas of work. The education committee reviewed the budget requests of the three colleges and the academy. The Christian services committee reviewed the requests of the hospitals and the children's homes. The state missions committee reviewed the budget requests of all state missions departments. The administrative committee reviewed the budget requests of the administrative, general convention, *Baptist and Reflector,* and Tennessee Baptist Foundation. After these reviews, which would either modify the requests or approve them, they were passed on to the Tennessee Baptist program committee. This committee is assigned the responsibility of carefully studying the anticipated income for the coming year, recommending a total budget to the executive board for its approval, and recommendation to the Tennessee Baptist Convention for adoption as the budget for the coming year. The budget was to be printed in the state paper in summary form at least two weeks before the annual session of the convention.

The *Baptist and Reflector,* the state paper, had been administered by the Tennessee Baptist Press Corporation. The corporation was dissolved and its board of directors discontinued. The administration of the business affairs of the publishing of the paper was assigned to the administrative committee of the executive board. Full editorial freedom was assured the editor and guidelines were set up to assure this in the administrative process. A circulation manager was recommended and added to the staff.

New departments of work within the state programs.—Three new departments have been added to the state work. Two of these resulted from expansion of services recommended by the survey. The first added was that of the stewardship department. A department secretary was employed and the department began operation on Sept. 5, 1960. This department was assigned the work of promoting the giving to world missions through the Cooperative Program, developing a program of stewardship education, providing counselling service to churches and associations for the improvement of their stewardship programs, and the promotion of the Forward Program of Church Finance.

The program services department was an expanded service recommended by the survey. It was set up to serve all the departments, to process incoming and outgoing mail, provide printing services on offset presses, automatic typewriters, and to administer tract service through display and filling orders from churches.

The protection plans department replaced the retirement plans service which had been under the direction of the executive secretary. A department secretary was employed in cooperation with the Annuity Board of the SBC. The department promotes all retirement and insurance programs administered by the Annuity Board. The department began service on Aug. 1, 1966.

There have been increases in the staffs of other departments. Growth of the work and the need for more services made this necessary. Four departments added a man assistant to the department secretary. They are—church training, Sunday School, church music, and student department. WMU added other staff members. Secretaries and nonprofessional workers were added as needed. A news writer was added to the office of the assistant to the executive secretary who is in charge of news releases.

Expansion and growth of Baptist student work.—The increase in enrolment in state universities and colleges and the adding of the community college system brought the necessity of expansion in the work of the Baptist Student Union. The number of Baptist students enrolled in the state universities and colleges outnumbers Baptist students in the Baptist colleges owned and operated by the Tennessee Baptist Conven-

TENNESSEE BAPTIST CONVENTION (*q.v.*) BUILDING, Brentwood, Tenn. Erected in 1970, valued at $1,563,000. Houses 16 departments and agencies.

WOMAN'S MISSIONARY UNION (*q.v.*) BUILDING, Birmingham, Ala. Purchased in Jan., 1951, for $475,000. In 1960 the top two stories were added.

tion. Student centers were built adjacent to these campuses and student directors administer the programs in the centers. New buildings were erected at Cookeville, Johnson City, Martin, Clarksville, Harrogate, and two in Memphis. The student center at Vanderbilt University in Nashville was relocated and a new building erected. The student center at the University of Tennessee in Knoxville was relocated and enlarged. The building at the University of Chattanooga was remodeled. A dwelling house was purchased at Murfreesboro and serves temporarily as a center until a building can be erected. A building is under construction at the Community College in Columbia. A site was purchased in Cleveland and a building will be erected adjacent to the Community College.

Joint work with the Home Mission Board.—After the expansion of Southern Baptist work into pioneer areas, the HMB found it necessary to restudy its work in the older states in order to have more money for the rapidly expanding work in the new areas. The HMB began working out joint agreements with state conventions in 1960. The Tennessee convention entered into a joint agreement in cooperative planning of the work in the state. The work is reviewed at the beginning of each year in the areas of joint work which were agreed upon. The HMB shares in the budget at the rate of 30 per cent and the Tennessee convention assumes the other 70 per cent. The state missions department administers the work according to terms in the agreement. The joint agreement was approved by the Tennessee convention in annual session, Nov. 16, 1960, when the convention met in the First Baptist Church in Nashville. The effective date was set for Jan. 1, 1961. This work includes work with National Baptists, mission centers, juvenile rehabilitation, and with the deaf.

First Volume of Tennessee Baptist history published.—The executive board of the Tennessee convention employed O. W. Taylor, retired editor of the *Baptist and Reflector,* to write the early history of Tennessee Baptists. After extensive research into the early history, Taylor completed the first volume in July, 1957. It was published and distributed at the annual session of the convention in Nov., 1957.

Special study of Christian education.—The education committee of the convention's executive board, with the presidents of the Tennessee Baptist colleges, made a study of the work of Tennessee Baptists in Christian education. The purpose was to propose a definition and to make a study of the philosophy, objectives, and aims of the Tennessee Baptist programs of Christian education. On Apr. 4, 1963, Norman W. Cox (*q.v.*), Mobile, Ala., was employed as research editor in this study. Cox had retired as pastor and more recently as the executive secretary-treasurer of the Historical Commission, SBC. Writers were obtained to prepare articles for the state Baptist paper covering almost every phase of Christian education. From the material in these articles, a booklet was published giving

TENNESSEE STATISTICAL SUMMARY

Year	Associations	Churches	Church Membership	Baptisms	S. S. Enrolment	V.B.S. Enrolment	T. U. Enrolment	W.M.U. Enrolment	Brotherhood Enrolment	Music Enrolment	Mission Gifts	Total Gifts	Value Church Property
1955	64	2,644	687,393	30,143	510,682	190,706	160,113	82,441	25,015		$4,066,468	$23,676,997	$ 87,432,035
1956	64	2,595	679,053	27,923	505,727	198,802	162,515	81,841	33,960		4,702,246	25,048,056	104,663,459
1957	64	2,700	706,508	30,044	527,090	202,283	173,140	84,978	30,504		4,503,424	26,848,936	120,990,165
1958	65	2,616	729,338	30,895	532,048	216,590	180,979	90,216	35,776		4,683,537	28,747,454	133,621,369
1959	65	2,658	735,266	32,172	535,665	208,961	184,648	91,812	31,364		4,964,621	30,546,246	141,623,233
1960	65	2,672	758,829	28,727	542,420	210,529	192,140	91,753	32,698		5,213,890	32,532,246	154,039,656
1961	67	2,683	776,715	30,456	550,645	205,218	195,540	91,930	32,166	45,436	5,344,234	33,851,693	165,807,930
1962	67	2,720	792,589	28,417	554,179	208,588	197,444	90,782	31,769	51,011	5,705,518	36,737,993	179,660,813
1963	67	2,724	801,960	25,869	522,396	208,835	196,040	91,339	32,889	57,466	6,044,969	37,510,538	189,772,347
1964	67	2,648	819,069	27,514	554,862	210,792	200,461	95,220	33,493	66,431	6,426,817	40,628,786	210,956,866
1965	67	2,671	830,954	27,651	552,174	211,245	194,982	92,722	28,173	65,270	7,048,429	44,466,794	213,236,345
1966	66	2,680	842,890	25,790	548,274	204,869	189,972	91,719	29,080	67,716	7,738,491	46,824,784	222,511,227
1967	67	2,678	855,440	27,876	547,615	212,534	191,246	89,998	28,652	70,371	8,262,776	50,583,544	239,068,697
1968	69	2,683	866,545	26,462	540,342	209,249	197,001	86,749	27,158	72,458	8,898,660	55,998,397	317,417,000

WALLACE E. ANDEROSN

the summary and conclusions drawn from research and study.

New Executive Board Office Building.—At the regular midyear meeting of the executive board, May 18, 1965, a long-range planning committee was appointed to study plans for relocating and erecting a new office building for the Tennessee convention. Fidelity Hall at Belmont College, which had been used as an office building since 1951, was no longer adequate and Belmont College needed additional facilities. On June 7, 1966, the executive board gave the committee authority to proceed with plans for a new building. On Sept. 27, 1966, the committee recommended that the executive board purchase property at 1907–1919 Belmont Boulevard, Nashville, as a site for the building.

On May 11, 1967, the long-range planning committee voted to employ Earl Swensson Architects, Inc., to design the building. Preliminary plans were presented for a building permit. An appeal was required to the Board of Zoning Appeals of the Metropolitan Government of Nashville for a zoning variance for parking facilities on the site. The variance was denied by the zoning board. On Sept. 26, 1967, the committee recommended that the executive board purchase a new location on Franklin Road, Brentwood, consisting of six and one half acres of land. The executive board approved the purchase and the Belmont Boulevard property was sold to Belmont College. On Nov. 13, 1967, the long-range planning committee was renamed executive board building committee and given authority to proceed with building plans at the new location.

The architect's final plans were approved on Jan. 24, 1968. Contract documents were submitted for bids. J. A. Jones Company was the low bidder. Ground was broken on May 17, 1968, and construction began immediately. The contract called for construction to be completed in 365 days and the project was completed about June 1, 1969.

As the building was nearing completion, the cornerstone was laid with appropriate ceremonies administered by the building committee on May 10, 1969. On July 30, 31, and Aug. 1, the offices were moved. The building was officially opened with a chapel service on Aug. 4, 1969. Formal dedication services were held in the chapel on Nov. 12, 1969, during the annual session of the Tennessee Convention in Nashville.

Fidelity Hall was sold to Belmont College with the office furniture for the college to use in its expanding program. The new office building at Brentwood is the first office building the convention has erected in its 96-year history.

Growth of churches and associations.—Growth has been steady through the years. In 1956 reports from the churches showed a total membership of 679,053 in 2,595 churches. In 1968 reports indicated a membership of 866,545 in 2,683 churches. The West Union association quit reporting and was dropped in 1964. Six associations have organized since 1956—Alpha, Central, Clinch, Copper Basin, Hardin, and Haywood. Sixty-nine associations are cooperating with the Tennessee convention. New associations were formed by regrouping some of the churches in older associations and are designed to carry better programs in a more concentrated area.

Growth in stewardship is revealed in the following: the Cooperative Program budget for 1957 was $2,800,000, while the budget for 1970 was $5,675,000. Total receipts in the churches in 1956 were $25,048,056, and for 1969 it was $58,797,580. Total receipts in the treasurer's office of Cooperative Program gifts in 1956 were $2,606,065.99, and for 1969, the total was $5,383,426.26. Designated gifts have increased. In 1956 designated receipts totalled $593,305.47, while in 1969 receipts totalled $2,022,410.80.

W. FRED KENDALL

***TENNESSEE BAPTIST FOUNDATION.** Jonas L. Stewart succeeded Henry J. Huey (*q.v.*) as executive secretary in July, 1968. Huey died while still in office in Feb., 1968. The assets on Oct. 31, 1969 were $4,337,267.96. Income paid out during the fiscal year 1968–69 was $213,731.73, including $61,977.93 to the Cooperative Program. Operational expense for the foundation is provided from Cooperative Program funds. The budget in 1969 calls for expenditure of $39,676. JONAS STEWART

***TENNESSEE BAPTIST HISTORICAL SOCIETY.** Prior to 1967, no formal organization of a Tennessee Baptist historical society existed. On Mar. 18, 1967, the East Tennessee Chapter of the Tennessee Baptist Historical Society was organized at Morristown. Paul Cates, Jefferson City, was elected president; Roy G. Lillard, Benton, vice-president; and Mrs. Perry Walker, Morristown, secretary-treasurer.

A Middle Tennessee Chapter was organized on Mar. 30, 1967, at Belmont College. The chapter elected John D. Freeman, president; Carl Daw, vice-president; and Mrs. Joseph Kyzar, secretary-treasurer.

On June 26, 1969, the West Tennessee Chapter was organized at Union University. Officers elected were: Henry West, president; Robert L. Newman, vice-president; and David Irby, secretary-treasurer.

The officers of the three chapters met at Brentwood on Aug. 15, 1969, and adopted bylaws and a constitution which established an administrative council of the Tennessee Baptist Historical Society, composed of the presidents, vice-presidents, secretary-treasurers, past presidents of each chapter, and a representative of the Tennessee Baptist Convention.

Carl Daw, Murfreesboro, was elected to serve as chairman of the administrative council and David J. Irby, Jackson, as vice-chairman; Roy Lillard, Cleveland, was elected as secretary-treasurer. Gene Kerr is the appointed representative of the Tennessee Baptist Convention.

The constitution sets forth that the objects of

the society shall be to promote interest in Baptist history and to assist in locating and preserving historical materials of special interest to Baptists. The society shall strive to present to the public information about historical records, materials, and sites of interest, and promote the preserving of current records.

The society is not considered a subsidiary unit of the Tennessee convention. Its purpose is to promote and preserve history of interest to Tennessee Baptists. The relationship should be one of mutual cooperation and support by Tennessee Baptist Convention. GENE KERR

TENNESSEE TEMPLE SCHOOLS. Four independent Baptist institutions sponsored by the Highland Park Baptist Church of Chattanooga, Tenn., which is not affiliated with, and is antagonistic toward, the Southern Baptist Convention. The church's pastor, Lee Roberson, began Tennessee Temple Bible School in 1946. Temple Baptist Theological Seminary, opened in 1948, offers degrees in divinity and religious education. Tennessee Temple College, organized in 1950, offers a B.A. degree. In 1968 over 1,600 students were enrolled in these three schools. An elementary school was begun in 1951. These schools, housed in over 50 buildings adjacent to the Highland Park Church, adhere to a premillennial interpretation of the Bible.
ALBERT W. WARDIN, JR.

TERRELL, ROBERT FRANCIS (b. Essex County, Va., Sept. 27, 1885; d. Starr, S. C., Apr. 7, 1957). Son of John M. and Mary (Swann) Terrell, he was educated at the University of Virginia (B.S.), Colgate-Rochester Seminary (B.D., M.A.), and a teacher's degree from the College of William and Mary. After teaching two years in Virginia, he was principal of Spartan Academy, Groce (Lyman), S. C., 1921–22. He was pastor of two churches in the Spartan Association: Bellview, 1922–26, and Antioch, 1924–26. He was circulation manager of the *Baptist Courier,* 1926–34, and 1941–57. He held a similar position with the *Biblical Recorder* in North Carolina, 1935–40. Terrell died while conducting morning services at Starr Baptist Church, Starr, S. C. He finished his sermon and announced the closing hymn "When I Survey the Wondrous Cross." After two stanzas, he requested the congregation to sing the third stanza, read the words aloud, and fell during the singing. He is buried in Woodlawn Memorial Park, Greenville, S. C. JEAN MARTIN FLYNN

TERRY, DANA (b. Evergreen, La., Oct. 24, 1877; d. Lake Charles, La., Aug. 9, 1959). Son of Adolphus John, a Baptist minister, and Rachel Elizabeth (Brunson) Terry, he was educated at Louisiana State Normal College, Richmond College (B.A., 1907), and Southern Baptist Theological Seminary (Th.M., 1910). He was ordained in 1907 by Bayou Rouge Baptist Church in Avoyelles Parish, La. He married May Hayden of Louisville, Ky., Oct. 25, 1910, and Mrs. Georgia Cordill, Oct. 27, 1941.

His pastorates were First churches of Brinkley and Hot Springs, Ark., Natchitoches, Kentwood, and Winnsboro, La., and the Eastdale Church in Lake Charles, La., the latter after he was past 70, having been retired for seven years. While at Natchitoches he baptized a junior boy named G. Kearnie Keegan (*q.v.*), who years later was to direct the SBC program of student work in Nashville.

Terry served as moderator in Natchitoches, Tangipahoa, Deer Creek, and Carey associations, and president of the board of trustees of Louisiana Baptist Children's Home, Monroe, on whose board he served for 30 years.

He founded Lake Charles branch of Union Seminary, which conferred on him the D.D. in appreciation of his service. He taught for a time at Southwest Louisiana Baptist Bible Institute.
JOHN G. ALLEY

***TEXAS, BAPTIST GENERAL CONVENTION OF.**

I. History of Convention. The history of the Baptist General Convention of Texas between 1954 and the present (1969) has been characterized by vigorous leadership, organizational restructuring, and a continuing growth.

Vigorous leadership.—Presidents of the convention during this period have been James N. Morgan (1953–54), J. Ralph Grant (1955–56), E. H. Westmoreland (1957–58), M. B. Carroll (1959–60), James H. Landes (1961–62), K. Owen White (1963), Abner V. McCall (1964–65), J. Carroll Chadwick (1966–67), and Gordon Clinard (1968–69). Roy L. Johnson, one of the recording secretaries since 1943, moved to another state and was replaced by Cecil G. Goff (1959–69), while D. B. South continued as senior recording secretary, a post he has filled since 1927. Two veterans continue their service: R. A. Springer as treasurer of the executive board, and J. Earl Mead as secretary of the corporation. The executive secretaries have been Forrest C. Feezor (1953–60), and Thomas A. Patterson (1961–). Eula Mae Henderson has been executive secretary-treasurer of Woman's Missionary Union during the period. Regular goals, looking toward purposeful achievement, were set, generally for a five-year period at a time.

Organizational restructuring.—In 1959 after two years of intensive study by a 25-member survey committee using the services of a professional management firm, a radical updating of the organizational structure was made. It provided basically four program thrusts (state missions, education, human welfare, and Christian life), supported by the executive and financial administrative staff and unified by a structured cross-program correlation through a program coordinating committee. In 1963 in order to eliminate overlapping and imbalance, an area plan was introduced. This replaced the geographical districts with areas, into which the associations grouped themselves in smaller units than had been possible under the district organization. Each area included from one to four associations to be served by a missionary. The ideal proposed that each area (except in the case of large cities) would consist of from 50 to 100 churches with a total resident membership of from 12,000 to 28,000.

Continuing growth.—Although there have been slight numerical losses in some of the auxiliary organizations among Texas Baptists since 1954, church membership grew from 1,363,685 in 3,569 churches in 1954 to 1,841,841 members in 3,920 churches in 1968. Total receipts rose from $61,203,915 in 1954 to $130,449,742 in 1968. Mission gifts increased from $10,956,358 in 1954 to $23,407,168 in 1968.

ROBERT A. BAKER

II. Program of Work. The Baptist General Convention of Texas consists of messengers from cooperating Southern Baptist churches in the state. Each church is entitled to a minimum of two messengers with no church having more than 25. The basic objective of the convention is "bringing men into a right relationship with God through Jesus Christ." The convention meets each fall to hear reports and inspirational messages and to conduct BGCT business such as electing members of the executive board, institutional boards, and officers for the BGCT, and approving an annual world missions Cooperative Program budget. The budget includes missions, education, and benevolence and in 1970 amounted to $14,500,000. In addition, there are three mission offerings promoted each year. The development departments of the various agencies seek to promote capital giving and endowment.

Responsibilities for many phases of Texas Baptist work are delegated to boards, which employ personnel and appoint committees or commissions to carry out assignments. The executive board is composed of 180 elected members and 12 ex officio members. The ex officio members are the convention officers and the presidents of the subsidiary and auxiliary conventions. Offices for the various phases of BGCT work are in Dallas, Tex.

A new plan of organization for the BGCT and its executive board was approved in 1959. Most phases of promotional and church-related work for the BGCT are functions of the executive board, exceptions being the *Baptist Standard,* the Baptist Foundation, and the Woman's Missionary Union. (See articles under their titles.) Sixty of the 180 elected board members are elected each year for a term of three years. No person is eligible to serve more than two successive elective terms and one third must be lay workers. All areas of the state must be represented. The board meets quarterly and has one special session just before the convention. The board has four commissions, two committees, a general administrative staff, a public relations department, and a church loan service.

The program coordinating committee reviews all recommendations from the commissions and committees. It commends, evaluates, and correlates various programs and services and brings to the executive board and the BGCT proposals for the Cooperative Program budget.

The business administration and audit committee evaluates the treasurer's work and employs the convention auditors. It establishes criteria for audits and qualifications for auditors to be employed by convention agencies, and reviews the audits.

In 1969 the structure, administrators, and functions of conventions program of work were as follows:

The executive secretary, T. A. Patterson, executes, promotes, and coordinates plans and policies of the convention and the executive board. The treasurer, R. A. Springer, receives and disburses all Cooperative Program mission funds, serves as secretary of the executive board and personnel officer. Jay L. Skaggs is assistant treasurer and controller, and Cecil G. Goff is statistician.

The Public Relations Department, Billy Keith, director, works through all information media to keep Baptists and the general public informed on Texas Baptist activities.

The Christian Life Commission, James L. Dunn, secretary, interprets practical Christianity in the areas of family life, public morals, race relations, Christian citizenship, economic life, and religious liberty. Associates are Phil Strickland and Charles Petty.

The Human Welfare Commission, James Basden, secretary, works with nine hospitals, four children's homes, and two homes for the aged in program development, budget coordination, and promotion.

The Christian Education Commission, Woodson Armes, secretary, works with 10 schools in curriculum development, accreditation, and budget coordination, and with Baptist Student Union programs.

The Student Division, W. F. Howard, director, seeks to meet the spiritual needs of students attending colleges and universities. It sponsors extensive BSU work and Bible chairs at both Baptist and state-supported schools.

The State Missions Commission, Charles McLaughlin, secretary, through programs of promotion and direct support seeks to facilitate and supplement the work of the churches in pursuing the overall denominational objectives, allocating Cooperative Program funds within the limitations of the budget. The commission has four divisions and 10 departments. Eugene Greer is program planning associate, Harry Hamblen is area missions coordinator, and Elmin Howell is river ministry coordinator.

The Church Services Division, Hooper Dilday, director, functions to help churches to discover, enlist, win, and develop people through three departments. It also provides services in church library, church administration, precollege and noncollege youth work, camps, and vocational guidance.

The Sunday School Department, James Frost, secretary, assists the churches in reaching more people, winning more people, and teaching the Bible more effectively.

The Church Training Department, Ed Laux, secretary, assists the churches in training members and leaders to perform the functions of the church.

The Church Music Department, V. F. Forderhase, secretary, helps the churches in the functional use of music in worship, proclamation, education, and ministry.

The Missions Division, Charles Lee Williamson, director, helps churches extend their mission outreach through four departments.

The Church Building and Pioneer Missions Department, Taylor Pendley, secretary, assists churches in all phases of planning appropriate buildings, and assists in selected pioneer states in church and missions growth.

The Texas Baptist Men (Brotherhood), W. L. Smith, secretary, assists churches in enlisting, developing, and utilizing men and boys in missions.

The Direct Missions Department, Darwin Farmer, secretary, assists in the programs of research, special studies, church extension, rural-urban missions, Christian social missions, work with Negroes and nonevangelicals.

The Language Missions Department, Dallas P. Lee, secretary, assists churches and associations in their programs with language-culture groups.

The Stewardship Division, Cecil Ray, director, promotes Cooperative Program and stewardship through three departments.

The Development Department, Robert Longshore, secretary, provides assistance to Baptist causes and institutions in securing funds for operation, endowment, and capital expansion.

The Church Stewardship Department, Douglas Brown, secretary, helps generate biblical stewardship in churches, assists in establishing sound financial programs, and provides family money management materials.

The Estate Stewardship Department, W. F. Vanderburg, secretary, assists churches with stewardship programs and individual financial planning in the area of wills, trusts, etc.

The Evangelism Division, C. Wade Freeman, director, promotes evangelism through personal, church-directed, and mass evangelism. Its ultimate objective is to help create motivation and to organize a witnessing program.

The WMU has a cooperative relationship through the State Missions Commission.

The Church Loan Association, Don Singletary, president, makes loans for construction to Baptist churches in Texas and the Church Loan Corporation makes loans to Baptist churches outside of Texas.

The BGCT in cooperation with the Annuity Board of the SBC makes available a retirement

TEXAS STATISTICAL SUMMARY

Year	Associations	Churches	Church Membership	Baptisms	S. S. Enrolment	V.B.S. Enrolment	T. U. Enrolment	W.M.U. Enrolment	Brotherhood Enrolment	Music Enrolment	Mission Gifts	Total Gifts	Value Church Property
1955	121	3,641	1,425,930	69,696	1,054,822	417,226	428,845	167,554	86,439		$12,334,380	$ 66,478,742	$260,422,367
1956	122	3,717	1,475,127	65,930	1,095,497	428,098	451,824	168,672	89,853		13,702,916	72,861,301	287,822,049
1957	124	3,758	1,511,857	62,283	1,111,421	432,043	462,068	179,136	97,816		14,791,179	76,863,469	310,619,881
1958	125	3,793	1,548,101	64,225	1,128,519	439,097	467,418	184,599	105,788		15,432,003	80,596,389	338,295,101
1959	125	3,819	1,590,703	64,817	1,147,666	435,666	477,733	197,620	107,605	82,831	15,699,042	86,329,281	372,200,071
1960	125	3,845	1,625,980	59,777	1,162,927	430,155	484,167	201,444	107,205	96,538	16,311,930	88,770,091	400,082,725
1961	123	3,889	1,660,449	60,541	1,171,321	450,601	482,300	201,729	105,659	106,226	16,592,891	91,746,841	426,662,198
1962	123	3,901	1,688,251	57,638	1,172,949	460,679	477,671	196,620	104,959	117,125	18,145,199	98,109,727	449,303,069
1963	123	3,891	1,715,742	54,587	1,173,707	456,326	466,184	198,075	101,370	124,745	19,415,670	98,178,726	475,732,928
1964	123	3,900	1,745,474	56,564	1,181,725	452,443	455,443	193,738	98,706	136,737	19,160,233	101,786,719	498,256,918
1965	120	3,927	1,765,876	53,908	1,169,519	504,149	435,092	186,401	74,917	138,800	20,261,706	108,311,181	512,888,243
1966	122	3,920	1,788,184	53,538	1,152,486	519,258	420,076	184,807	70,636	144,750	20,906,597	111,990,070	535,484,540
1967	121	3,932	1,811,240	55,495	1,143,687	506,262	417,796	180,922	66,484	155,178	21,683,686	117,322,683	558,951,117
1968	121	3,920	1,841,841	54,719	1,137,900	464,164	430,101	176,861	63,822	156,583	23,407,168	130,449,742	578,419,598

CECIL G. GOFF

program for church and denominational workers. R. A. SPRINGER

TEXAS, CHAPLAINCY PROGRAMS. See CHAPLAINCY PROGRAMS IN NON-BAPTIST INSTITUTIONS (Texas).

TEXAS BAPTIST CAMPS. There were 23 Baptist encampments operating in Texas in 1969. During the summer of 1968, 120,100 people attended, with 4,036 making a profession of faith in Christ, and with 1,811 giving their lives to a church-related vocation. These camps are owned and operated by local area boards, selected by associations. Each of the encampments plans its own programs and each has a full-time resident manager. In 1964 these camps requested that a closer relationship with the Baptist General Convention of Texas be developed, and the state convention assigned this relationship to the Church Services Division. The programs of these encampments are planned to meet the needs of youth and church leaders. The programs include Bible study, doctrinal study, evangelism, music, recreation, and conferences to train church leaders.

R. HOOPER DILDAY

***TEXAS BAPTIST CHILDREN'S HOME.** The campus now includes a total of 20 buildings, all constructed of Austin stone. Owned by the Baptist General Convention of Texas, the home, with 10 cottages, has capacity for 100 children. An additional 100 children are served through a foster home and adoption program, plus casework services in their own homes. All preschool-age children are cared for in foster homes. Some children remain in care until the completion of high school. The home then individually plans with them for college, special training, or employment. Financial support is provided through the Cooperative Program and by gifts of churches and interested individuals.

CHARLES I. WRIGHT

***TEXAS BAPTIST FOUNDATION.** Commissioned by the Baptist General Convention of Texas to receive gifts and bequests as endowment to provide a continuing source of income to Texas and Southern Baptist causes, the foundation is entirely self-supporting and does not receive any funds from the Cooperative Program for operating expenses. Administration is vested in 12 prominent Baptist laymen, each elected for a three-year term by the convention. Property and funds are held in trust for designated causes. Income earned from investments is distributed according to specific directions of the donor. The book value of the foundation's assets in 1969 exceeded $86,000,000. J. C. Cantrell has been executive secretary since 1954.

J. C. CANTRELL

TEXAS BAPTIST MEMORIALS GERIATRIC CENTER. Founded by Mrs. Elsie Gayer at San Angelo, Tex., in 1951 as a hospital for tubercular patients. In 1957 the Baptist General Convention of Texas assumed the ownership and operation of the institution. The program, originally for tubercular patients only, was expanded to include geriatrics and subsequently a division for mentally and emotionally disturbed patients. The purpose of the institution is to care for the whole person of the geriatric and the retarded. In 1967–68 new bylaws were adopted to unify the entire program, and H. E. Bruce was named the first executive director in Sept., 1968. Alton Pearson succeeded him in 1969.

The facilities have grown from 14 patient rooms to about 245 beds. Also added were a chapel and nursing home in 1959, an administration building in 1962, and the Elsie Gayer Memorial Building and a large hotel from the Moody Foundation in 1963. H. E. BRUCE

TEXAS BAPTIST MEN. Organized Mar. 1, 1968, it replaced the Brotherhood organization in Texas as the result of a study by a joint pastor-laymen committee of 100. Texas Baptist Men is an affiliate of the Baptist General Convention of Texas. W. L. "Wimpy" Smith was executive secretary in 1969. Roy Akers, first president, was reelected for second term in Oct., 1968. This laymen's group is the state organization for promoting Brotherhood work in churches and associations. Its executive board is composed of 147 men of whom 121 are associational Brotherhood directors. Its major program goals include camps, institutes, schools of missions, prisoner rehabilitation conferences, laymen's crusades, Royal Ambassador rallies, written materials and other training aids, and leading "men and boys to a deeper commitment . . . more meaningful prayer life . . . larger stewardship . . . and to a personal involvement in missions." R. E. DIXON

TEXTUAL CRITICISM. The study of variants in the text of the Bible in an effort to recover the original text of documents that have perished. Since no original biblical manuscripts survive, the biblical text has to be established by the careful study of many different readings that are in existence. For instance, there are 76 Greek papyri, 250 uncial manuscripts, and 2,646 minuscule manuscripts which must be studied in establishing the text of the New Testament. In addition to Greek manuscripts of the New Testament, there are also numerous versions, or translations into other languages, such as Latin, Ethiopic, Coptic, Gothic, and Armenian.

There are approximately 5,000 Greek manuscripts of varying length, age, and importance which are involved in establishing the text of the New Testament. There are 150,000 variant readings in the New Testament alone. In spite of variant readings at many points in both the Old Testament and the New Testament, the field of textual criticism gives confidence that the correct biblical text exists with a high degree of certainty. The methodology employed in establishing the correct text of the New Testament may be studied in J. Harold Greenlee's, *An Introduction to New Testament Textual Criticism,* or in Bruce Metzger's, *The Text of the New Testament.* RAYMOND BRYAN BROWN

***THAILAND, SOUTHERN BAPTIST MISSION IN.** Development continues at a steady rate of growth. Radio and television are utilized. Student work, housed in a strategically located building in Bangkok, enrolled 1,385 students in its activities in 1968. Another student program was begun in Haadyai. The Bangkla hospital with its leprosy clinics serves many and increases opportunity for witness. Encampments and religious education promotion add maturity to the churches' general leadership. In 1969 the 70 missionaries served in 13 stations. R. KEITH PARKS

***THEOLOGIANS, BAPTIST.** *William Owen Carver* (*q.v.,* Vol. I).—Carver, though not strictly a systematic theologian, exerted a considerable theological influence upon Baptists, especially Southern Baptists, during the first two thirds of the 20th century. Probably his distinctive doctrinal contributions were (1) the interpretation of the Bible as the book that was produced by, unfolds, and fosters God's worldwide mission, and (2) the exposition of the Church Universal or the Body of Christ as the total company of the redeemed in Christ, unorganizable and distinguishable from organized churches.

As the book of God's "plan of the ages" the Bible presents missions as "the extensive realization of God's redemptive purpose in Christ by means of human messengers" and as the method of fulfilling God's dealings with the nations, the destiny of mankind, and the Father's eternal promises to the Son. For such missions the individual Christ is the "agent," the churches the conservators, and the world the "beneficiary." The biblical message of missions centers in salvation-reconciliation through the work of Christ (*Missions in the Plan of the Ages*). From the patriarchs to Patmos the Bible contains a missionary message (*The Bible a Missionary Message*). Through his Chosen People, despite their failures, and through his servant Son, God is achieving salvation and its product, righteousness (*God and Man in Missions*). The early Christians appropriated the Old Testament and fulfilled its incompleteness through the New Testament, which, together with the Old Testament, forms the one Bible (*Why They Wrote the New Testament*).

The mission of Christianity is grounded in the mission of the Son of God, Messiah, and Saviour (*The Self-Interpretation of Jesus*). Universal outreach was implicit in the teaching and deeds of Jesus, and the apostolic concept of the unity of humanity has become a tenet of modern humanitarianism (*The Course of Christian Missions*). At the end of the 19th century Carver regarded the individual Christian as the "unit in missionary extension of the Kingdom" and evangelistic, educational, literary, medical, and industrial methods as valid (*Missions and the Kingdom of Heaven,* 1898). The 20th century was to be an era that reaches after Baptist principles and affords the Baptists their greatest opportunity (*Baptist Opportunity*). Carver answered modern objections to missions by pointing to the history of missions and to the nature of Christianity as universal and as bearer of the *summum bonum* and by acknowledging the shift in missionary motivation from patronizing and iconoclastic rescue to loving and adaptable witness (*Missions and Modern Thought*). The doctrine of election must no longer, as it was for a thousand years, be misused so as to relieve Christians of the imperative of world evangelization, for election "is a method of God and not an end" and biblically is more related to service than to salvation (*All the World in All the Word*). Carver severely indicted the Laymen's Inquiry on Foreign Missions for its misunderstanding of the missionary enterprise and as "a surrender of distinctly Christian Missions" in several respects. Carver regarded "the local church" as "the proper center for procuring the support of missions" (*The Furtherance of the Gospel*). Christianity as the coming into the world of God's Son is a unique factor in world order and has as its purpose more than the formation of "Christendom," however expanded. As to the need for a world religion Carver favored "reconception" rather than "radical replacement" or "synthesis" (*Christian Missions in Today's World*).

In 1937 Carver called upon Southern Baptists to be alert to the increasing emphasis on church union and to make their own denomination serve the kingdom of God. He advocated "spiritual unity" but not "church union" of the centralized type. Carver taught the continuing incarnation of Christ in the body of Christ, or the church, and, distinct from this, the "concrete, visible, organized" expression of "spiritual Christianity" in churches. Church organization should be determined by the church's function. The New Testament knows of no organized expression of the universal church. The organized churches are not "saving" institutions but "proclaiming and conserving" agencies. A gigantic merged Protestant church is not the proper goal of the ecumenical movement, but neither should Baptists and other free church groups be so passive about "the ideal of spiritual oneness."

A merged Protestant church would need to avoid "the evils illustrated in the history of the Roman Church," including the power to control secular institutions. The unstructured universal church "can retain its true function as a prophetic presence and voice to all men with its gospel of redemption" (*The Glory of God in the Christian Calling*). The distinctive contribution of Baptists to Christianity is "their insistence on the individual soul in relation to God . . . and in the conception of the entire ecclesiastical autonomy of the church." True church continuity is maintained by the work of the Holy Spirit. Baptists need "more appreciation of the historic community of the Christian faith and life and . . . the sense of community to all believers . . . largely lost in the centuries of . . . struggles for freedom under the persecutions . . . inflicted by Catholics and Protestants. . . ." ("Baptist Churches," *The Nature of the Church*).

Harold Henry Rowley (*q.v.*).—Rowley, a leading biblical, chiefly Old Testament, scholar, frequently wrote about the theological significance of the Bible and treated various theological topics.

The Bible, Rowley sought to show, is to be approached both from the methods of modern scholarship and from spiritual understanding. Though it may be studied scientifically and historically, the Bible is basically a religious book. Rowley rejected passive, infallibilist inspiration, for God's revelation came through responsible persons and supremely in Jesus Christ. Revelation was progressive because of "man's capacity to receive," not because "there was progress in God, or in God's willingness to reveal Himself." Both divine and human, the Bible, Rowley insisted, "*is* the Word of God" and yields in authority only to the Word made flesh (*The Relevance of the Bible*).

Many and varied were the media of revelation in the Old Testament (*The Faith of Israel*). The single "great and ever-memorable fact of Israel's history was the great Exodus." Moses persuaded the Israelites that Yahweh had delivered them from Egypt and chosen them to be his people. Moses likely held to an incipient, but hardly a full-orbed, monotheism (*The Re-Discovery of the Old Testament*), or provided "the seeds of monotheism" (*From Moses to Qumran*). In Israel's sacrificial system Rowley found evidence of various basic meanings of sacrifice: gift, communion, propitiation. Sacrifices were thought to have "potency" but "only when accompanied by genuine penitence and submission." The protest of the pre-Exilic prophets was against sacrifice that was devoid of obedience, and the modern antithesis between the priestly and the prophetic has now rightly been "softened" (*The Unity of the Bible*). Prophecy is to be regarded primarily as forthtelling for God rather than as prediction, and the call and word of Yahweh were quite as important as the early ecstasy (*The Servant of the Lord*). China's sages paralleled Israel's prophets as statesmen and reformers but not as spokesmen for God and critics of the cultus (*Prophecy and Religion in Ancient China and Israel*). Many of the psalms were of cultic origin, but not all (*The Growth of the Old Testament*). Hebrew apocalyptic was "the child of prophecy, yet diverse from prophecy," and pointed to imminent divine intervention in behalf of God's afflicted saints (*The Relevance of Apocalyptic*). The Old Testament ought not to be abandoned by Christianity because of its unique preparation for and frequent citation by the New Testament, but rediscovered in terms of abiding values.

The Apocrypha, significant for the concepts of the law, angels, demons, and life after death, "are deserving of study" (*The Origin and Significance of the Apocrypha*). The Dead Sea Scrolls, with their concepts of the Teacher of Righteousness and two messiahs, "increase our knowledge of the background" for the ministry of Jesus but are often theologically at variance with the New Testament (*The Dead Sea Scrolls and the New Testament*).

The Old and New Testaments do not "duplicate a single message" but "form a single whole." The New Testament blends and modifies Old Testament ideas. The two Testaments, being diverse, have a dynamic unity. It is fitting that the Old Testament be viewed "in terms of that to which it has led as well as of that out of which it arose." Allegorical and typological interpretation should be avoided, but promise and fulfilment and recurring patterns can be discerned.

The God of Israel, whose otherness is balanced by his likeness to man, is the holy, loving one who suffers, redeems, communicates himself by the Spirit, and reigns. He is not to be represented by idols but is faithful to his covenant and is the personal Creator.

Creation in God's image means man's being given a unique "quality of personality" or "spiritual kinship" with God. He has moral freedom, is a social being, and is individually accountable to God. Sin, preeminently "disobedience to the will of God," is universal among men. It is both individual and corporate, both offense against God and man's curse of himself and his fellows. Much, though not all, suffering is "the fruit of sin." Oriental religions as well as Christianity and Judaism recognize both innocent and deserved suffering (*Submission in Suffering*). The book of Job achieves not "an intellectual solution of the problem of suffering" but "the spiritual miracle of the wresting of profit from the suffering through the enrichment of the fellowship of God" (*From Moses to Qumran*).

Rowley, who interpreted the four servant songs (Isa. 42:1–4; 49:1–6; 50:4–9; 52:13 to 53:12) as shifting from the collective meaning (the nation) to the individual meaning (a "future figure" to whom Jesus corresponded), especially in the fourth song, insisted that the concepts of Davidic Messiah, Son of man, and Suffering Servant were not "brought together and fused into one" until united in the mind and teaching of Jesus. Rowley interpreted the death of Jesus as the sacrifice of the Suffering Servant—a view which he thought avoided the extremes of the forensic and moral influence views.

Rowley stressed Yahweh's election of Israel as his holy people through his grace, whether in Abraham or in the time of Moses. This election was for service more than for salvation and had to be renewed by later Israelites; the covenant constituted the response to the gift of election. Israel's election was intended to serve the divine mission to all nations. It was limited to the remnant, extended through proselytes to Judaism, and fulfilled by Christians as heirs who have succeeded both to the mission and to the warnings inherent in election (*The Biblical Doctrine of Election*). Israel's universal mission was classically formulated in Isaiah 40–66 and illustrated by Ruth, the author of Job, and Malachi (*The Missionary Message of the Old Testament*). Israel, through its Psalter, its prayers, its Scriptures, and its sabbath, especially as used and observed in the synagogues, influenced early Christian worship (*Worship in Ancient Israel*).

Christian baptism had its rootage in Jewish lustrations, Jewish proselyte baptism, and the baptism of John the Baptist, but not in circumcision. Responding to the claims of modern pedobaptists, Rowley regarded baptism as a meaningful "symbol," especially "of union with Christ in His death and resurrection." Concerning the "sacrament" (i.e., as "a vow of loyalty") of the Lord's Supper, Rowley rejected both the Tridentine doctrine of the mass as a sacrifice and the reformers' denial of any sacrificial element in the Supper and allowed for sacrificial imagery in addition to the motifs of memorial and thanksgiving (*The Unity of the Bible*).

The Old Testament anticipated as the goal of history for all men the Day of the Lord, the Golden Age, or the kingdom of God. The expectation of Sheol was at times broken by the glimpse of resurrection.

JAMES LEO GARRETT, JR.

THESES IN BAPTIST THEOLOGICAL SEMINARIES, INDEX TO GRADUATE. An author, title, and subject index to theses approved by the six Southern Baptist seminaries and Baptist Theological Seminary of Ruschlikon, Switz. It is published by the Historical Commission, SBC, in cooperation with these institutions. The initial volume, 1894–1962, was issued in 1963. Supplements are published every third year. LYNN E. MAY, JR.

THIBODEAUX, LAWRENCE (b. Branch, Acadia Parish, La., Mar. 3, 1911; d. Laurel, Miss., Aug. 28, 1968). Born of missionary parents he became a French missionary par excellence. Educated in the Pineville and Eunice public schools, and Acadia Academy, he graduated from Eunice high school in 1928. He graduated from Louisiana State University, Baton Rouge, in 1933, and surrendered to the ministry during a revival while a student at LSU.

He married Virginia Eleanor Leblanc of Baton Rouge in 1934 and was ordained later that year. He attended Baptist Bible Institute (now New Orleans Baptist Theological Seminary), 1933–1936 and 1940. He became a missionary to the French people and thus pioneered French missions in south Louisiana. He laid foundations or began work at Grosse, Tete Mission, Erwinville, Fordoche, Bayou Plaquemine, Thibodaux, Belle River Mission, Charpentier Mission, and others. He was pastor in Maringouin, Thibodaux, and Houma. He began French radio broadcasts in 1950 which led to home services and the conversion of an elderly French woman who greatly influenced his work. In 1955 he began the Christ Baptist Church, Houma, of which he was pastor at the time of his death. During most of his years as a missionary he served under the SBC Home Mission Board. The work was difficult and growth was slow, but he was faithful and effective. His funeral was at Christ Church, Houma, and he was buried at Thibodaux. JOHN G. ALLEY

THIRTY THOUSAND MOVEMENT. The organized effort of Southern Baptist churches to establish 30,000 new churches and missions during an eight-year period, 1956–64. It was a part of the Baptist Jubilee Advance program (1959–64), which was designed to celebrate the 150th anniversary of the organization of Baptist work on a national level.

The movement was born when the Southern Baptist Convention, meeting in Kansas City, 1956, accepted the challenge of C. C. Warren, then president of the Convention and pastor of the First Baptist Church, Charlotte, N. C., to "double the number of Southern Baptist preaching places by adding 5,000 new churches and 25,000 missions before the celebration of our third jubilee in 1964."

Arthur B. Rutledge, then director of the Missions Division, Home Mission Board, was elected chairman of the 30,000 Movement Committee. In 1958 Warren left his 14-year pastorate to assume direction of the movement, becoming its first and only director. He was employed jointly by the HMB and the Sunday School Board. These two boards shared equally in the expenses incurred in the general promotion of the effort.

The purpose of the movement became: "To establish 10,000 churches and 20,000 missions by 1964 to reach, teach and win individuals to Christ and train them to live Christian lives." Its slogan, "Every Church with a Mission," was undergirded by the theme song, "To God Be the Glory." A mission was defined as "anywhere one or more members are sent from the local church or churches at regular intervals to preach or teach the Word of God." The movement encompassed the 28 Baptist state conventions, Cuba, the Panama Canal Zone, Foreign Mission Board countries, and areas where Southern Baptist chaplains were stationed.

The HMB, Sunday School Board, Brotherhood Commission, and Woman's Missionary Union cooperated fully in the effort. The Sunday School Board established a new position with the title of "superintendent of new work" to magnify the use of the Sunday School in the movement. The work of the movement committee was implemented through state conventions, district associations, and local churches.

The first mission in the movement, started on June 3, 1956, by the First Baptist Church, Conway, S. C., was the North Conway mission, which was organized into a church, on Dec. 2, 1956. The last church to be constituted was the Monroe Avenue Baptist Church in Bellwood, Ill., on Dec. 31, 1964, Warren's final day to serve as director of the movement.

The final results are significant. The movement committee reported that 24,917 churches and missions had been started between June 1, 1956, and Dec. 31, 1964. A total of 6,682 churches and 18,235 missions had been established. HAROLD CLARK BENNETT

THOMAS, CLIFTON CROMWELL (b. Goochland County, Va., Mar. 29, 1893; d. Richmond, Va., May 20, 1970). Son of Perrie Ezell and Clara Hardaway Thomas, he was educated in the public schools of Virginia, the University of Richmond, the University of Louisville (A.B.), and the Southern Baptist Theological Seminary (Th.M.). He married Elmyra Snead. Thomas was pastor of the following Baptist churches: Temple, Louisville, Ky.; Waverly Place, Roanoke, Va.; First, Newman and Elberton, Ga.; and First, Staunton, Va. He served as general secretary of the Maryland Baptist Union Association, 1949–57. He was assistant pastor of the First Baptist Church, Richmond, Va., from 1958 until his death. He is buried in the cemetery of Goochland Baptist Church.

R. G. PUCKETT

***TIFT COLLEGE.** Growth in the fifties and sixties was reflected in enrolment, building construction and renovation, financial assets, and curriculum offerings. Enrolment for 1969 was 654, including a coordinated program with the Georgia Baptist Hospital in Atlanta. The 1969 graduating class numbered 128. Four new residence halls were built: Monroe, South, Sewell, and West. Upshaw Hall, an older residence, was rebuilt. Other new buildings include Rutland Hall, a cafeteria and modified student center, Tift-Center Guest House, and Vinzant Physical Education Hall, named for Carey Truett Vinzant, retired president who served 1952–69. In 1968 the assets of the college totaled $5,207,124 including an endowment of $1,688,113.

Basically a liberal arts college, the program offers majors in general academic subjects, fine arts, and education. The latest to be added is music education. The teacher training program has twice been approved by the Georgia State Department of Education for periods of five years, the highest recognition accorded by the state. In 1969 Robert W. Jackson succeeded Vinzant as president. EUGENIA W. STONE

TIMERITE, INC. During the planning for the Crusade of the Americas, it became evident that while Southern Baptists were equipped to produce superior materials both for broadcast and print, they possessed no proper channel for the handling of paid advertising and programing. As long as public service or sustaining time was involved, the Radio and Television Commission was prepared. However, if any Southern Baptist entity wished to place paid materials in the media of mass communications, a commercial advertising agency had to be engaged. Therefore, TimeRite, Inc., was organized by the commission to enhance both the ministry of a local group embarking in a broadcast or public relations enterprise, and the placement of commission programing.

TimeRite is a nationally accredited advertising agency, doing business with print and broadcast media across the country. TimeRite was incorporated in Texas, Aug. 23, 1969, with its board of directors drawn from members of the Radio and Television Commission. The agency operates offices on a regional basis in Wilmington, N.C., Dallas, Tex., and Fresno, Calif., serving Southern Baptist churches, associations, state conventions, and their duly authorized institutions.

The TimeRite staff is composed of personnel employed by the Radio and Television Commission, its officers having a wide background in the areas of commercial broadcasting, advertising, and religious broadcasting.

TimeRite approaches media representatives as a professional organization staffed by media professionals who speak directly to the needs and goals of the Southern Baptist group being represented, translating these needs and goals into the terms of the industry. Since TimeRite represents many such groups, it is able to utilize a bargaining power unavailable to the individual church or association seeking to make use of the media. CHARLES RODEN

TINNIN, FINLEY WATSON, SR. (b. Moss Point, Miss., Dec. 8, 1887; d. Shreveport, La., Apr. 21, 1962). Son of John W., a Baptist minister, and Ida (Howell) Tinnin, he was educated at Tulane University, New Orleans, and attended both Southwestern and Southern Baptist seminaries. He received the D.D. from Louisiana College, Pineville.

He married Lizzie Keller McGaffey in 1915, and they had three children: Finley W., Jr., Beverly Vaughn, and Mrs. Elizabeth Trussell.

Tinnin was a chaplain during World War I and served pastorates in Natchez, Miss., Bossier City, Winnfield, Opelousas, and others in Louisiana. His greatest contribution to Baptist work was as editor of the *Baptist Message* of the Louisiana Baptist Convention for 37 years, 1920–57.

Many knew him as a warm friend, a tireless worker, an outstanding denominational leader, and a man dedicated to honesty and the highest ideals of journalism. He never published a book but proofread and assisted many writers.

JOHN G. ALLEY

TIPPETT, TINY WALTER (b. Tippettville, Ga., Oct. 18, 1888; d. Atlanta, Ga., July 29, 1958). State Sunday School secretary and pastor.

Tippett married Lucille VanLandingham, Oct. 25, 1911. They had two children: Malcolm B. and Dorothy L., before her death, June 14, 1914. On June 19, 1922, he married Mary Lang, who died 12 days before his death in 1958. He was educated at Mercer University (A.B.) and the Southern Baptist Theological Seminary. Ordained in 1916, he was pastor of the following Georgia Baptist churches: Tippettville and Lilly, 1916–17; First, Vienna, 1918–27; Byromville, 1919–27; and Prince Avenue, Athens, 1927–35. He led the Vienna church to become the third Sunday School in the Convention to attain the AA1 Standard, a record maintained for seven years. He became Sunday School secretary for the Georgia Baptist Convention, Jan. 1, 1935, retiring on Dec. 31, 1956. He traveled 500,000 miles and gave 6,000 addresses in interest of Sunday School work. His second wife was Young People's leader for the Sunday School Department the 22 years he was secretary. Prior to his Sunday School position, he had been on the Georgia convention's state mission board and was president of the Georgia Baptist Sunday School Convention. JOHN T. TIPPETT

TOGO, MISSION IN. Southern Baptist mission work in Togo began as an outreach of the Ghana Baptist Mission when Clayton Bond, then stationed at Accra, began visiting small groups of Yoruba settlers in and near the city of Lome. On Aug. 8, 1959, the First Baptist Church of Lome was organized, affiliating with the Ghana Baptist Convention. Clayton and Helen (Terry) Bond moved to Lome in 1964, after a period of language study in France. In 1967, the Togo Baptist Association was organized, with only a fraternal relationship to the Baptists of Ghana. That same year Billy and Evelyn (Robinson) Bullington joined the Bonds, and a new mission center was inaugurated in Lome.

In 1968 French-language services were begun and soon eight young men were baptized. Bullington was assisted by Morris Pruit, another new missionary, in courses designed to prepare young men for the ministry. Bible classes in the Ewe language were begun, and plans were projected for opening new mission stations as soon as personnel became available.

H. CORNELL GOERNER

TRINIDAD AND TOBAGO, MISSION IN. Baptist life in Trinidad was begun by freed slaves from the United States, who were promised property in Trinidad in return for fighting on the British side during the War of 1812. The first Baptist church was formed in 1816 and carried on its own work until 1843 when the Baptist Missionary Society of Great Britain sent missionaries. That mission group later withdrew from the Caribbean, thinking churches should be self-supporting, but reentered Trinidad in 1946. Major activity of British Baptists has been in the south where several churches exist. Some churches formerly belonging to British-sponsored work have since organized as Independent Baptists (not to be identified with independent Baptist groups in the United States).

Southern Baptists entered Trinidad in 1962 when Emit and Kathryn (McCluney) Ray transferred from the Bahamas Mission. They established a church in the north. In 1969, six couples were under appointment to Trinidad, where three churches and six mission points reported 379 members. An extensive camp program and theological and lay training ministry are part of the work. The Trinidad mission is responsible for developing work in other English-language eastern Caribbean islands. Two couples living on Antigua assist a national Baptist work in the nearby island of St. Kitts. A radio-television ministry covers the entire Caribbean, and a mission-sponsored radio Bible course has enrolled nearly 1,000 students from the other islands. MRS. DAVID L. MARTIN

***TRI-STATE BAPTIST HOSPITAL.** See MEMORIAL HOSPITAL, BAPTIST, MEMPHIS.

***TRUETT McCONNELL JUNIOR COLLEGE.** In 1964 Warner Earle Fusselle succeeded Joe Hardy Miller as president. The college was accredited by the Southern Association of Colleges and Schools in 1966. In 1969 all faculty members had graduate degrees. Evaluation of the physical facilities was $1,640,256. The following buildings have been added since 1955: a gymnasium, a cafeteria, the president's home, a library, a women's dormitory, a men's dormitory, a faculty apartment building, and a student center building which was completed in 1970. WARNER EARLE FUSSELLE

TRULUCK, JAMES WILLIAM (b. Florence County, S. C., July 19, 1878; d. Florence County, Apr. 2, 1957). A graduate of Furman University, he was teaching school when called to preach. Truluck and Rayford Stroud of Locust Hill, S. C., were married in 1900. Their children were: S. Leo, Ina Mae (Dill), Aline (Jordan), Luby (Hatchell), Serena (Forester), and James W., Jr. Truluck's pastorates were: Elim, 27 years; Scranton, 13 years; Evergreen, 12 years; Sparrow Swamp, 13 years; Hebron; Ariel; St. John; Union; Pamplico; and Beulah. All of these were in Florence County. He and his brother, B. K. Truluck, published a book of sermons entitled *Bill and Ben.* Truluck is buried in the cemetery at Bethel Baptist Church. CLYDE L. FOX

TUCKER, FRED GENTRY (b. Anderson County, S. C., Sept. 3, 1885; d. Louisville, Ky., Aug. 30, 1963). He received his education at Piedmont College, Demorest, Ga., and at Southern Baptist Theological Seminary, 1919–21. He served as pastor of churches in Georgia and South Carolina while in college and became pastor of East Baptist Church, Louisville, in 1921, while still a seminary student. He began working part time as Missionary of Long Run Association in 1935 and in 1937 went to full time with the emphasis developing in institutional work at which he served until his death.

On May 19, 1927, he married Alice Gertrude Johnson of Roanoke, Va. (WMU Training School, 1922). At his death she, four sons, and one daughter survived him.

His death was caused by a car, out of control, striking him as he stood at a bus stop. As he lingered in life, C. R. Daley, editor of the *Western Recorder,* wrote of him, "Fame, fortune, prestige and position never appealed to this man. . . . His example of humility has served as a convicting sermon to many. . . ." A biography of him written by his wife is entitled *Call Him Enoch* (1964). LEO T. CRISMON

***TULAKOGEE BAPTIST ASSEMBLY.** Improvements in 1969 were valued at $300,000, which included 15 buildings. The assembly is incorporated, has a resident manager, and is run by a board of 12 members, with six elected from each of the Tulsa and Muskogee associations. Reports for 1969 included 3,092 campers, a property debt of $60,000, and a budget of $16,036 provided by the supporting associations, the state convention, and campers' fees.

J. M. GASKIN

TURKEY, MISSION IN. Tom Harris, civilian living in Ankara, encouraged the Foreign Mission Board to send missionaries for English-language work. James and Jean (Davis) Leeper, appointed in 1965, first met with a small group, mostly military, in June, 1966. Under a secular government, regulations on religion are restrictive. The group began worshiping in the United States Embassy Snack Bar in July. In Aug., 1966, they organized the Galatian Baptist Chapel, first Baptist church in modern Turkey. Every effort to have a building was rebuffed. Meeting only on Sunday evenings, the church has grown and is self-supporting. JAMES F. LEEPER

TURNAGAIN CHILDREN'S HOME. An institution near Anchorage, Alaska, providing care for orphan and indigent children. Founded in 1949, it has been under the control of the Alaska Baptist Convention since 1957. As early as 1946 leaders of the convention saw the need for a Southern Baptist operated children's home in the Anchorage area. Nothing was done on this project until Mrs. Mildred Lene gave a block of land in Anchorage to the First Baptist Church, the proceeds of the sale of which were to be used to start a Children's Home. B. C. Evans became interested in the project also and gave one hundred acres of his homestead for this purpose. With the help of many individuals a building was erected on the Evans homestead and the home opened in the fall of 1949. For some time Evans supported the home alone. In Nov., 1951, the First Baptist Church, Anchorage, assumed the responsibilities and indebtedness of the home. A few months later the church purchased an additional 47 acres of land from Evans. The church retained title to the property, but a board elected by the Chugach Baptist Association operated the home. The board incorporated the home in 1952. In Jan., 1957, the Alaska Baptist Convention assumed responsibility for operating the home through a board of trustees elected by the convention. The home has a capacity of 14 children. It is located six and one-half miles south of the city of Anchorage on O'Malley Road, a few miles from Turnagain Arm of Cook Inlet, from which the home takes its name. Superintendents of the home have been B. C. Evans, Art Purnell, U. S. Sanders, and Edward Knutsen.

RICHARD A. MILLER

TURNER, RICHARD PERRY, SR. (b. Greenville County, S. C., Aug. 7, 1880; d. Spartanburg, S. C., Dec. 1, 1959). Philanthropist and civic leader. Educated at the Pleasant Hill Community Grammar School near Greer, S. C., he married Annie Moon on Jan. 28, 1926. They had two children: Richard P., Jr., and Sylvia (Turner) Patterson. Concerned with civic affairs, Turner was elected commissioner of the Greer, S. C., Commission of Public Works at its founding in 1935. Aiding worthy but needy students, he was a trustee of the Ellen H. Smith Fund for Ministerial Students, 1950–59. He served as a trustee for North Greenville Junior College, 1932–58, and in 1959 became a life trustee of the institution. The college named Turner Auditorium in his honor. Through the years he was a generous benefactor of the college. Also, he exercised great interest in Connie Maxwell Children's Home, Greenwood, S. C., of which he was a trustee, 1941–42. The First Baptist Church, Greer, S. C., elected him deacon from 1926–50, and, at age 70, he became honorary life deacon. RAYMOND A. MCKINNEY

TWITTY, BRYCE LINTON (b. Terrell, Tex., Oct. 22, 1898; d. Tulsa, Okla., May 15, 1961). Baptist layman, denominational leader, and civic worker. Educated at Southern Methodist University (B.S., 1923; M.A., 1938), he received the Doctorate of Humanities from University of Tulsa, 1960. Twitty reached professional excellence as director of the Hillcrest Medical Center, Tulsa, a post he held at the time of his death. Places of denominational service included president of Baptist Brotherhood of Oklahoma, vice-president of the SBC Brotherhood, board of directors of the Oklahoma Baptist Foundation, and member of the SBC Hospital Commission. He made several trips as a lay preacher to mission fields.

J. M. GASKIN

***TWO-SEED-IN-THE-SPIRIT-PREDESTINARIAN BAPTISTS.** In the early sixties, this group of Baptists still maintained three very small associations—Drake's Creek in Kentucky, Caney Fork in Tennessee, and Richland Creek in Alabama. They now (1970) have no associations, but churches conduct annual three-day meetings. These Baptists have four known, functioning churches with a membership of about 68. Six ordained elders serve the churches.

ALBERT W. WARDIN, JR.

TYLER, WILFRED CHARLES (b. Bogue Chitto, Miss., Sept. 27, 1901; d. Memphis, Tenn., Apr. 7, 1965). College president, pastor, educator, and author. Known to friends as "Luke," he was the son of Luther Lafayette and Florence (Connally) Tyler. He was educated at Mississippi College (B.A., 1922) and Southern Baptist Theological Seminary (Th.M., 1927; Ph.D., 1933). He also studied during the summer of 1922 at the University of Michigan. Mississippi College awarded him the D.D. degree. His long educational career began in Laurel, Miss., where he taught and coached high school athletics, 1922–24. In 1936 Tyler became professor of Bible at Blue Mountain College, and in 1960 became president of the college, a position he held until his death. He served as president of the Mississippi Foundation of Independent Colleges in 1963.

Tyler's pastorates include the College Avenue Baptist Church of Annapolis, Md., 1932–36, and the Cherry Creek Baptist Church in the Pontotoc Association of Mississippi, 1944–54. He married Mary Frances Landrum on Dec. 28, 1932, and they had two children, Luther Landrum and Mary Carol. Tyler and his wife frequently spoke at youth retreats, and they co-authored two books, *The Little World of Home* (1949), and *The Challenge of Christian Parenthood* (1952). For 12 years they were the co-authors of a column in *Home Life* magazine entitled "Let's Read."

EARL KELLY

U

UGANDA, MISSION IN. Hal B. and Patricia (Held) Boone moved to Jinja in 1962, shortly after the former British colony became an independent nation. Boone began a series of mobile medical clinics, which aided in establishing churches in several villages. The Boones were soon joined by Webster and Betty Lou (Wilt) Carroll at Jinja, while Jimmie and Peggy (Ratcliff) Hooten moved to Mbale. Baptist work in Uganda was related to the East Africa Mission, which included also Kenya and Tanzania.

In 1967 the Uganda Baptist Mission was organized as a separate group. Emphasis was placed upon the study of the Luganda language and other dialects used in Uganda. Work began in Kampala, and a Bible school was established in Mbale. In 1969 new stations were opened at Fort Portal and Masindi. By the end of 1969, 109 Baptist churches and preaching points reported 1,889 members.

H. CORNELL GOERNER

UNIFORM SERIES, COMMITTEE ON. An interdenominational committee which selects and organizes Bible material for use in Sunday Schools. It has had a continuous existence since 1872. Southern Baptists have been prominent on it since 1878. Clifton J. Allen, former editorial secretary of the Sunday School Board, SBC, served on the committee 27 years and was chairman, 1960–67. In 1970 the editorial secretary and six other professional employees of the Sunday School Board, SBC, were on the committee which had a membership of 66 persons representing 25 denominations.

The committee plans a general coverage of the Bible material according to six-year cycles, never repeated. Usually one theme covers one quarter of the year and is divided into units and weekly topics for Adult, Youth, and Children's age groups. Beginning with the selection of biblical content, the lessons seek to relate the truths of the Bible to the persistent life concerns of persons. Background Scriptures, focal passages, and memory selections are chosen for each age group. Each cooperating denomination and publisher is free to adapt the material to his own needs and distinctives.

Southern Baptists continue to use Uniform lessons in about 50 per cent of the churches. These lessons are known as Convention Uniform Series.

See also SUNDAY SCHOOL LESSONS, UNIFORM, VOL. II.

WILBUR C. LAMM

***UNION UNIVERSITY.** Buildings completed since 1954 include a gymnasium (1955) and two dormitories for women, Warren F. Jones Hall (1956) and Blythe Hall (1966). The board of trustees voted in 1968 to purchase a new campus site and move the college to a location north of the city. Transition from the old campus to the new is expected by 1972.

For the fall of 1969 the university had a campus enrolment of 778 students, a plant valued at $4,500,000, endowment of $979,286, and an operating budget for the school year 1969–70 of $1,696,604. Union University is fully accredited by the Southern Association of Colleges and Schools and holds membership in the National Association of Schools of Music. Robert E. Craig succeeded Warren F. Jones as president in 1967.

For 144 years Union University and its ancestral institutions have educated thousands of men and women. For 94 years of this period, this institution has operated as a Christian college under Baptist auspices. Its graduates have made contributions in most all areas of life, in both secular and Christian enterprises.

ROBERT E. CRAIG

***UNIVERSITY OF CORPUS CHRISTI.** Since 1955 the university has evolved from a campus of numerous wooden barracks buildings to an installation of nine permanent structures. A tenth, soon to be completed, will house the United States Geological Survey, the first unit in a projected Science Park. Academic growth is reflected in full accreditation by the Southern Association of Colleges and Schools, granted in Dec., 1967. Forty-seven per cent of the faculty have earned doctorates in their fields. Enrolment, showing a steady increase, reached 675 in the fall of 1968, with students drawn from 31 states and six foreign countries. Kenneth A. Maroney is the sixth president.

MARY HAMILTON

***UNIVERSITY OF RICHMOND.** The university continues to make notable progress under its fourth president, George M. Modlin. Rising from humble beginnings at "Dunlora" in Powhatan County in 1830, with one teacher and a few students, it is now the largest privately supported institution of higher learning in Virginia. At the close of the 1968–69 session there were 7,173 students, a faculty of 202 full-time and 94 part-time members, campus property valued at $13,976,740, an endowment of $47,645,750, total assets of $69,214,054, and an annual operating income of $5,589,578. A marked increase in endowment resulted from the benefaction of trustee E. Claiborne Robins, who gave $40,000,000 in June, 1969, and pledged an additional "challenge gift" of $10,000,000 to be matched dollar-for-dollar by gifts from alumni and other sources over a 10-year period.

A seventh college, University College in downtown Richmond, was added in 1962, absorbing the evening classes of the School of Business Administration and providing a two-year day program of liberal arts, undergraduate and graduate evening programs, and an Institute for Business and Community Development. The School of Business was accredited by the American Association of Collegiate Schools of Business in 1965. The university offers 11 different academic degrees: B.A., B.S., B.S. in B.Ad., B.S. in P.Ed., B.Comm., M.A., M.S., M.S. Ed., M.Comm., M.Hu., and J.D. (replacing the LL.B. degree in 1970).

Special programs include: an honors program for superior students with demonstrated capacity for independent study; an advanced placement program for qualified high school students; the summer school abroad program; Tele-College, presenting courses on religion via TV in five Virginia cities; and the School of Christian Education, offering off-campus courses in religion. Other services to Virginia Baptists include the speakers' bureau, lending library, pastors' school, pulpit supply, student mission teams, and services rendered by the university's director for church relations.

The university faculty is widely engaged in professional, religious, community, and public affairs. Faculty research grants, a sabbatical leave program, and other benefits have enhanced the development and well-being of faculty members. The University Center for Psychological Services provides specialized services in vocational testing and counseling. Students have accepted greater responsibility for self-regulation in their social and organizational life.

Additional physical facilities include four memorial dormitories for men, Robins Hall, Dennis Hall, Freeman Hall, and Moore Hall; the School of Business Administration; the Fine Arts Building; and the Crenshaw swimming pool. Another men's dormitory is under construction (1969), and a $4,000,000 athletic center is planned for completion in 1972.

Approval in 1969 of participation in government-funded student aid programs permitted expansion of scholarship opportunities, grants, loans, and part-time employment for needy students. Through the 1968–69 session there have been 15,511 graduates from the various branches of the university.

C. J. GRAY

URBAN MINISTRIES. See GOLDEN GATE BAPTIST SEMINARY, URBAN PROGRAM OF.

URBAN-RURAL MISSIONS. See RURAL-URBAN MISSIONS, HOME MISSION BOARD PROGRAM OF.

URBAN SEMINAR. During the two summers of 1967 and 1968, the District of Columbia Baptist Convention, Southeastern Baptist Theological Seminary, and the Home Mission Board joined together in sponsoring a seminar on urban studies. Each year the seminars were stimulating. In addition to lectures, students were given projects on which they prepared reports. The many resources provided in the city of government were also used.

The curriculum for the seminar was in three major areas: Christian dialogue within the international and interfaith community, an exploration of relevant ways of Christian witness to persons of diverse ethnic and religious identities; the church in the secular city, a study of structures and problems of the secular city including an evaluation of efforts toward renewal of the churches; resources for the church's community ministry, a study of the ways the church may work creatively with government and private agencies for a fulfilment of its ministries.

JAMES O. DUNCAN

***URUGUAY, MISSION IN.** As the staff continued to increase gradually, new centers were opened and the Montevideo theological institute faculty was reinforced. The Crusade of the Americas, well received in Uruguay, excited interest, and churches were strengthened. Uruguay seems poised and ready for significant progress through mass media and student ministries. Relations between Uruguayans and the 22 missionaries are gratifyingly good.

FRANK K. MEANS

US-2 MINISTRY. See SPECIAL MISSION MINISTRIES, HOME MISSION BOARD DEPARTMENT OF.

UTAH-IDAHO ASSOCIATIONS.

I. Extant. BOISE VALLEY. Organized in 1957 by churches formerly associated with the Twin Buttes Association. In 1969, 12 churches reported 101 baptisms, 1,818 members, $14,694 mission gifts, and $123,769 total gifts.

EASTERN IDAHO. Organized in 1957 by churches formerly associated with the Twin Buttes Association. In 1969 six churches reported 60 baptisms, 909 members, $5,703 mission gifts, and $53,459 total gifts.

GIDEON. Organized in 1959 by three churches formerly associated with the Utah Association. In 1969 four churches reported 26 baptisms, 387 members, $3,665 mission gifts, and $29,948 total gifts.

GOLDEN SPIKE. Organized in 1958 by six churches formerly associated with the Salt Lake Association. In 1969, 14 churches reported 54 baptisms, 1,349 members, $15,586 mission gifts, and $121,452 total gifts.

MAGIC VALLEY. Organized in 1957 by churches formerly associated with the Twin Buttes Association. In 1969 seven churches reported 36 baptisms, 626 members, $7,174 mission gifts, and $41,686 total gifts.

MID-STATE. Organized in 1968 by two churches in central Utah. In 1969 two churches reported six baptisms, 244 members, $832 mission gifts, and $11,058 total gifts.

RAINBOW CANYON. Organized in 1967 by churches formerly associated with the Salt Lake Association. In 1969 six churches reported 16 baptisms, 332 members, $3,580 mission gifts, and $29,686 total gifts.

SALT LAKE. Organized in 1955 by nine churches formerly associated with the Utah Association. In 1969, 19 churches reported 128 baptisms, 2,269 members, $24,869 mission gifts, and $203,947 total gifts.

UTAH. The first association in the two-state area, it was organized in 1951 with four churches formerly associated with the Central Association of Phoenix, Ariz. In 1969 four churches reported 10 baptisms, 480 members, $3,348 mission gifts, and $21,089 total gifts.

II. Extinct. TWIN BUTTES. Organized in 1953 by four churches in Idaho formerly associated with the Utah Association. In 1957 this association divided into three associations: Magic Valley, Eastern Idaho, and Boise Valley.

MRS. ANITA LEMKE

UTAH-IDAHO SOUTHERN BAPTIST CONVENTION.

I. Baptist Beginnings. At the close of World War II the discovery of oil and uranium and the production of steel brought a new era into existence in Utah and Idaho. By that time the American population had become highly mobile and Southern Baptists migrated to these states.

The first Southern Baptist church in Utah was the Roosevelt Baptist Church, organized in Roosevelt on July 2, 1944, under the sponsorship of the First Baptist Church, Carrizo Springs, Tex. The Roosevelt Church was instrumental in developing most Southern Baptist work in the two-state area. Southern Baptist churches were organized in Clearfield and Vernal in 1946, Provo in 1948, and Gusher in 1951. Missions at Whiterocks and Fort Duchesne were conducted for the Indians, and out of this work the Ute Baptist Mission was formed. The First Southern Baptist church in Idaho was the Calvary Baptist Church, organized in Idaho Falls in 1951.

II. History of the Convention. Work in the states of Utah and Idaho was started through the efforts of the Arizona Southern Baptist Convention. Little by little, churches and missions came into being.

In 1960 there was an effort on the part of Southern Baptists in these two states to organize a state convention. Messengers were elected from the churches and met at First Southern Baptist Church in Salt Lake City, Utah. Representatives of the Arizona convention, the California convention, and the Home Mission Board were also present. After much discussion concerning the total program of work and the size and number of churches involved, it was decided by a majority that the convention would not be organized at this particular time. A. B. Cash, along with Arthur Rutledge of the HMB, suggested other ways that the states might function for at least five more years without becoming a convention. After the vote was taken, it was decided that a regional missions committee would be organized and would function as an executive board, except that it was to make suggestions to the Arizona convention executive board as to the program of work to be offered. This regional missions committee, working with the Arizona convention and HMB, brought about the beginning of the Utah-Idaho Southern Baptist Convention at the beginning of Jan., 1965.

The convention was organized in Oct., 1964. The executive board was elected and instructed to set up the convention office and employ an executive secretary. Darwin E. Welsh, pastor of

First Southern Baptist Church, Salt Lake City, Utah, was placed in charge of setting up the convention office. It was located in an upper story of his church building. The board elected Charles H. Ashcraft, then pastor of the First Southern Baptist Church, Las Vegas, Nev., and president of the Arizona Southern Baptist Convention, as executive secretary-treasurer of the Utah-Idaho convention. Ashcraft had moderated the convention's organizational meeting. He accepted the position and started his duties on Jan. 1, 1965. At this time, Roland Smith was serving as the religious education secretary. Darwin E. Welsh was elected by the board to serve as the associate executive-secretary and began his work on Mar. 1, 1965. The convention offices were moved to the present (1970) location of 826 South Main, Salt Lake City, in 1966.

The convention was organized with 50 churches. A budget of $149,821 was adopted. There was a 90/10 per cent relationship between the HMB and the Utah-Idaho convention, the HMB furnishing 90 per cent of the mission budget. In 1969 a budget of $251,470 was adopted. In 1970 there is a 95/5 per cent relationship with the HMB.

Eleven new churches were organized by Nov., 1969. At the time of the organization, there were many key people in the churches which added much strength. Since then, few government contracts have been offered to companies in Utah-Idaho. Because of this, many people have left, thereby weakening many churches.

Leaders emphasize that the natives of this area must be reached. Evangelizing them is difficult since the Mormon religion is predominant and its hold on the people is strong. Mormon people are being won to Christ, but the training of these people is a very slow process. In 1969 there were approximately 8,650 members of the Southern Baptist churches in the Utah-Idaho area. Many of them live in the area simply because they have to, not because they want to. There is little desire on the part of most Baptists to live among the Mormons.

The churches are all small, the largest being First Southern Baptist Church in Mountain Home, Idaho, which reaches approximately 342 in Sunday School. This is a very unstable situation since most of the church is made up of people from the Mountain Home Air Force Base. One of the prime means of establishing Southern Baptist work in Utah and Idaho is through Bible Fellowship Classes.

The Trust and Memorial Fund was set up in 1965. This fund was established whereby individuals, churches, or institutions could invest money at the rate of six per cent interest, for the use of interim financing or for purchasing property. This money is loaned upon approval of the trust and memorial committee. When the amount exceeds $1,000, approval must come from the executive board.

The first issue of the *Utah-Idaho Southern Baptist Witness* was published on Jan. 1, 1965. Two issues are published each month with the exception of December when one issue is printed. The executive secretary serves as the editor. The paper is printed in the convention office by offset press.

During 1969 several staff changes took place. Guy Ward, pastor of the First Southern Baptist Church, Salt Lake City, was elected by the executive board to serve as religious education secretary taking the place of Roland Smith who resigned to accept a position with the Sunday School Board, SBC. Darwin E. Welsh was elected by the executive board to take the place of Charles Ashcraft who resigned to become the executive secretary-treasurer of the Arkansas Baptist Convention. Gernice Ward was elected by the board to serve as the convention's first part-time WMU secretary. Prior to this Barbara Embery had served as the WMU president for five years and handled the administrative work for the WMU.

III. Program of Work. The general work of the convention is committed to the executive board. It has the power to act for the convention in the interim between sessions. The executive board consists of 19 members including the convention officers. The convention elects 15 members equitably distributed through the convention territory. Members are elected for three-year rotating terms.

The executive board employs an executive secretary-treasurer for an indefinite term to serve as the official superintendent of all the work of the board. The board appoints all employed personnel, establishes policies, fixes salaries, and determines the departments and fields of work for the accomplishment of the convention's purposes. Since the staff of the Utah-Idaho convention is limited, each staff member must assume several responsibilities. The executive secretary serves as administrator of the convention and the Trust and Memorial Fund, editor, and evangelism secretary. When the office of associate executive secretary-treasurer is vacant, the executive secretary also assumes responsibility for the missions program, Brotherhood, and stewardship. The religious education secretary assumes the responsibility of the total education program of the convention: Sunday School, Church Training, and Church Administration. He also directs the BSU work and handles church architecture.

IV. State Missions. The total program of work is divided into three areas, each under the supervision of one of the following superintendents of missions: Roy Ferguson, Medford Hutson, and Mayo Brown. Seven language missionaries work in Utah-Idaho under appointment of the Home Mission Board.

The Fort Hall Indian Mission in Blackfoot, Idaho, for the Shoshone-Bannock Indians, is under the direction of Earl Jackson. The Indian mission for the students of the Intermountain Indian School in Brigham City, Utah, is under the direction of Bruce Conrad. Calvin Sandlin directs the work at the Ute Indian Mission in Roosevelt, Utah, for the Ute-Ouray Indians.

Two Spanish-speaking missionaries on the field are Pedro Carranza in Salt Lake City and Bill Rutlege in Burley, Idaho. Much of their ministry is aimed toward the migrants and the Spanish-American people who remain in the area. A Spanish Mission in Clearfield, Utah, is led by a Spanish-American layman. The Chinese work began in Salt Lake City in Jan., 1968, under the direction of Yam Yee Lee. Literacy classes and Chinese Vacation Bible Schools have been most successful. In 1970 the Japanese work began under the direction of Elizabeth Watkins, retired missionary who served in Japan for 41 years.

The Concern Center in Salt Lake City was started in 1968 under the direction of Miss Mary Wigger. The center ministers to various age groups and focuses its attention on the total needs of man. The expansion of this work depends on volunteers from the local churches.

The Jack Weeks Chair of Religion, which began in 1969, exists to help students and church workers gain more knowledge of the Bible. Joe H. Music, director, offers classes to pastors, students, and local church leaders. The classes offered are through the Seminary Extension Department. The Chair of Religion is enforced by the P. O. Bocker Memorial Library which now contains 1,475 volumes. The Convention has proposed the establishment of other religion chairs throughout the convention to provide religious education for people who are unable to attend seminary.

The Utah-Idaho convention does not own any property or real estate other than the office equipment and furnishings. Twenty per cent of its undesignated receipts go to world mission causes.

MRS. ANITA LEMKE

V

***VACATION BIBLE SCHOOL.** Southern Baptist Vacation Bible Schools increased to a total of 28,829 in 1968 with an enrolment of 3,227,705. The schools reported 54,833 professions of faith that year. Vacation Bible School, throughout its development, has been the assignment of the Sunday School, both denominationally and in the local church. Today, it reaches its zenith as an extension activity in the church's perennial Bible teaching program. The general administration section of the Sunday School Department of the Sunday School Board is responsible for its promotion, and age-group editors in the department prepare curriculum materials.

Vacation Bible School continues to follow the "learning-by-doing" teaching philosophy which involves pupils in activities relating to and emphasizing biblical truth. Biblical content is interpreted through the use of music, recreation, worship, drama, mission study, and appropriate activity-teaching methods.

The introduction of a new set of curriculum materials annually and the development of a more flexible program made 1970 a transitional year in VBS work. The design calls for 10 three-hour daily sessions. The traditional provision for ages three through 16 years of age has been expanded to include adults.

The necessity for a Bible teaching program adapted to varied local church situations has created a flexibility in VBS work. Faculty training schedules, publicity, organizational structure, daily schedules, and follow-up activities will vary according to the inherent talents, nature, needs, work schedules, and living habits of the individual church constituency. The curriculum materials are practical and adaptable to the needs of individual churches whether large or small.

Vacation Bible School continues to be one of the most effective programs for church outreach. For this reason, mission Bible schools are receiving greater emphasis through the provision of special administrative and curriculum materials.

Follow-up activities, which conserve the results of the school and continue its thrust in the community, are strongly promoted. Churches are encouraged to give additional instruction to those Bible school pupils who made professions of faith, and to visit pupils and parents involved in the school who are not enrolled in the church's ongoing Bible teaching program.

ARTHUR BURCHAM

VALLEY BAPTIST ACADEMY. Established in 1947 by the Lower Rio Grande Baptist Association in cooperation with the Southern Baptist Home Mission Board, Texas Woman's Missionary Union, and the Mexican Baptist Convention. The academy opened on HMB property in Brownsville with a three-man faculty and a student body of 28. In 1948 the institution moved to another Brownsville location and operated there until 1956, when it was moved to Harlingen to occupy buildings formerly utilized by Valley Baptist Hospital. With the move to Harlingen came a shift in sponsorship from the local association to the District 5 Baptist Convention. The school remained under this sponsorship until 1962, when it became an institution of the Baptist General Convention of Texas. Since 1967 the academy has been located on a new 44-acre campus near Harlingen. The school's primary purpose is to provide high school level training for Latin-American young people. JOHN CARTER

***VALLEY BAPTIST HOSPITAL (Harlingen, Tex.).** The Reber Memorial Radiation Clinic was among the first improvements at the new location. John and Louemma Reber, Valley pioneers, donated $125,000 for a cobalt unit and toward the building to house it. The school of nursing, reestablished in 1959, added a $225,000 dormitory and teaching building for training of licensed vocational nurses. In addition provisions have been made for training medical technologists, X-ray technologists, operating room technicians, and medical secretaries. In 1969 the hospital completed a $2,000,000 building which increased its bed capacity to 193 and its property value to $7,000,000. T. H. MORRISON, JR.

VASS, JAMES LELAND (b. Monroe County, Va., 1840; d. Greenville, S. C., July 30, 1906). Minister and denominational leader. After a boyhood spent in Virginia, he graduated from Richmond College, Va., and the Southern Baptist Theological Seminary, Greenville, S. C. After graduation in 1871 he accepted the pastorate of the Baptist Church, Spartanburg, S. C., where he served for 13 years. After brief pastorates at Americus, Ga., and Jackson, Tenn., he accepted a call to Swift Creek Church, Darlington, S. C. When South Carolina Baptists passed a resolution calling for the establishment of a children's home in 1889, Vass was appointed chairman of a committee of seven to suggest a location and plan for the new institution. In 1891 Connie Maxwell Orphanage was chartered, and Vass was elected superintendent. He declined, feeling that he could not leave the pastorate, but at the urging of the trustees, reconsidered and accepted. He raised money and supervised the construction of five permanent buildings at Greenwood, S. C. Differences developed between Vass and certain members of the board of trustees, which led to his voluntary request that he not be re-elected superintendent in 1899. He served until May 31, 1900.

Vass' successor, A. T. Jamison (*q.v.*, Vol. I) said of him:

> The highest encomium of praise that could be passed upon his official administration, perhaps, is that the work he did will stand, and shall not have to be torn away to give place to more mature and approved plans. . . . It is something to say of an agent of the denomination that the money he spent for it was carefully and wisely expended, and that the product of the money will never have to be torn down.

After leaving the orphanage, Vass moved to Belton, S. C. He was pastor of Fork Shoals Church and traveled as representative of the state Baptist convention. He is buried at Greenville, S. C. He married Emma Brown of Virginia. They had three children: Mamie, Lulu, and Leland. JOHN C. MURDOCK

***VENEZUELA, MISSION IN.** In 1958 the Venezuelan Baptist Convention and the mission found themselves hopelessly at odds over policies and procedures. The two organizations decided, reluctantly but mutually, to project their work separately. Providentially, fraternal cooperation was resumed in 1964 and subsequent progress has been very gratifying. Strong English-language churches and student work were organized in or near Maracaibo and in Caracas. A recording studio has strengthened radio and television ministries in Caracas. FRANK K. MEANS

VERMONT, SOUTHERN BAPTISTS IN. See MARYLAND, BAPTIST CONVENTION OF.

VIETNAM, SOUTH, MISSION IN. The Vietnam work began Nov. 1, 1959, with the arrival of the first missionaries, Herman and Dottie (Primeaux) Hayes, in Saigon. Two other couples joined them in 1960 and together projected initial work. In June, 1961, the first decision for Christ was made in the first Vietnamese-language service. First baptismal service was held in Mar., 1962, and first church—Grace, Saigon—organized in Nov., 1962. The mission was united on the central theme of evangelism and church development, the local church being the focal point. The mission, which held its first annual meeting in July, 1961, has worked under war conditions almost from the beginning. Because of war, work has been limited to major cities. However, as Baptists celebrated their tenth anniversary in Vietnam, six churches and 12 chapels reported 1,000 members.

To assist churches, work of a departmental and institutional nature gradually developed: 1962—publications department, to produce literature in Vietnamese; 1963—Baptist Bible Institute, to provide on-the-job training; and 1965—radio-TV ministry, including audiovisuals. Opened near Saigon in Sept., 1967, Vietnam Baptist Theological Seminary will graduate its first class in the spring of 1970.

In addition to work with Vietnamese, the mission participated in an English-language ministry from the beginning. A ministry to the large Chinese community began in 1966, and a missionary couple serves each of these minority language groups. Plans are being made to enlarge the Christian social ministry to refugees and others who suffer because of the war. In 1969, 39 missionaries (career and short-term) served in Saigon, Dalat, Nhatrang, Camranh, Danang, Quinhon, Cantho. Baptists were engaged in evangelistic efforts which they hoped would result in doubling number of Christians and church members by the end of 1970.

HERMAN P. HAYES

VIOLENCE. A broad definition of violence may be said to be any action resulting in the exertion of force, pressure, or influence which directly or indirectly brings injury or abuse to a person or to something of value.

The history of the United States has been the story of the rise and fall of violence in our national life, beginning with the Revolutionary War. At the present (1970) time, violence in this country has risen to an alarmingly high level. Whether one considers assassination, group violence, or individual acts of violence, the decade of the sixties was considerably more violent than the several decades preceding it. The United States is the clear leader among modern, stable democratic nations in its rates of homicide, assault, rape, and robbery and is at least among the highest in incidents of group violence and assassination.

Group violence at the end of the sixties centered in five areas: (1) antiwar and antidraft protest, (2) campus unrest, (3) racial disorder, (4) extremists' tactics, and (5) government action by troops and police. Any assessment of violence could not ignore the Vietnam War, both from the standpoint of the escalation of international violence by the war itself, and as one of the root causes of national violence. The dramatic and dangerous rise in the possession of handguns was an important factor in the rise of individual violence. More than 90,000,000 such guns were privately owned in 1968.

In recent years violence has come to have a broader meaning. Today many citizens are more sensitive to the violence which man unleashes against his environment. Then, too, there are subtle, socially acceptable types of violence which are practiced by many white middle-class citizens. Examples of such violence might be the following: providing second-class schools for certain children, or slaughtering 25,000 people annually in automobile accidents where alcohol was a definite factor, or allowing 25,000,000 poor people to live at a subhuman level in the most affluent country on earth, or giving tacit approval to governmental tapping of the telephones of private citizens, or making it hard for those having the greatest need for money to get a loan, or accepting the fact that food prices are higher in the ghetto than in the suburbs. All of these may be interpreted as forms of violence.

The Southern Baptist Convention has spoken strongly and clearly against the more obvious expressions of violence in our nation. This was done in 1965 and again in 1968, following the assassination of Senator Robert F. Kennedy while the Convention was in session. At that same meeting, the messengers had already adopted "A Statement Concerning the Crisis in Our Nation" which expressed profound convictions regarding the roots of violence often cultivated by poverty, prejudice, injustice, and indifference. There was a brave call for Baptists to make a new commitment to Christ, to uphold the laws of the nation, and to "take courageous actions for justice and peace."

The Christian Life Commission published a tract on violence and a more detailed resource paper on the subject. The Sunday School Board has produced helpful material for study and discussion through its Church Training Department.

ELMER S. WEST, JR.

***VIRGINIA, BAPTIST GENERAL ASSOCIATION OF.**

I. History of the General Association, 1957–69. On Mar. 13, 1962, the new Virginia Baptist Building, on Monument Avenue in Richmond, was opened providing space for the general association's offices. James T. Todd became treasurer of the general association on Jan. 1, 1966, succeeding Kenneth E. Burke. Lucius M. Polhill retired as executive secretary of the general association on Dec. 31, 1967, and was followed by Richard M. Stephenson. In Nov., 1969, the general association voted to restructure a number of its procedures including the organization of the general board and the committees of the general association. The method of allocating operating expenses of Woman's Missionary Union of Virginia was changed from a percentage arrangement to a specific annual request for funds.

In 1969 there were 44 district associations with 1,441 churches and missions, with a membership of 524,261 cooperating with the general association. Contributions in 1969 through the Cooperative Program were $4,484,294, and total mission gifts reached $7,039,364. The total gifts received by churches of Virginia in 1969 amounted to $40,669,616, which was double the amount in 1955. There were 93 mission churches and eight mission centers served by 80 pastors, and 15 district associations employing superintendents of missions.

JOHN S. MOORE

II. Program of Work. *Virginia Baptist General Board.*—In 1960 the name of the Board of Missions and Education was changed to the Virginia Baptist General Board. The board is elected by the general association. Its membership consists of those by virtue of office: the president, first and second vice-presidents, clerk, executive secretary, and treasurer of the Baptist General Association; the president of Woman's Missionary Union, and the Virginia members of the executive committee of the Southern Baptist Convention. Also, each district association proposes one person for nomination to the committee on boards. When the gifts from churches of an association through the Cooperative Program reach $150,000 annually, an additional member is elected, and when such gifts reach $300,000 annually a third member is elected from the district association. In addition, there are eight members at large chosen from eight different associations.

The general board acts in the interim for the general association on such matters as the officers may determine to require action before the next meeting of the general association, and the board reports such action to the next annual session of the body. The board divides itself into four major committees: departments, education, missions and Christian services.

The committee on departments considers and makes recommendations relative to policy and works with the executive secretary in defining and promoting the work of the departments. The committee receives the budgets of the departments and makes recommendations to the budget committee of the general association.

The committee on missions works with the associations and churches in studying areas of need and seeks to assist in the establishment of new churches. The committee receives applications from the associations and churches for support of pastors in mission fields and encourages the churches to become self-supporting. The committee works closely with the committee on urban affairs of the general association with the Extension Board.

The committee on education seeks to coordinate matters involving the Baptist schools and colleges. The committee proposes to the board allocations for Christian ministries at these schools for recommendation to the general association's budget committee. The committee seeks to stimulate support for Christian education.

The committee on Christian services seeks to coordinate plans and make suggestions concerning matters pertaining to the Virginia Baptist Hospital, the Virginia Baptist Homes, the Children's Home, *The Religious Herald,* the foundation, and the historical society.

The executive committee of the board consists of the board's chairman and vice-chairman, the chairman and one other member from each of the four major committees of the board, and the chairman of the budget committee of the general association. The executive secretary serves as ex-officio member.

The board has entire management of the matters committed to its trust and makes by-laws and carrics out plans that seem judicious provided they are in strict accord with the constitution and by-laws and instructions of the general association.

The executive secretary and the treasurer, elected by the general association upon nomination by the board, make reports to the board and its executive committee.

The board promotes a program of missions and education in the local churches and district associations in terms of resource materials and personnel and conducts certain direct mission ministries which are statewide in scope.

To accomplish the above goals the staff of the General Board is organized with three major divisions: church programs, ministries, and services. The church program division is composed of three departments: teaching and training, music, and men. The ministries division directs the work of the departments of missions, campus ministries, and social ministries. The division of services has general management of the Baptist Building, Eagle Eyrie, services department, and retirement planning. In addition to the three

VIRGINIA STATISTICAL SUMMARY

Year	Associations	Churches	Church Membership	Baptisms	S. S. Enrolment	V.B.S. Enrolment	T. U. Enrolment	W.M.U. Enrolment	Brotherhood Enrolment	Music Enrolment	Mission Gifts	Total Gifts	Value Church Property
1955	36	1324	413,801	17,324	345,926	124,958	64,742	114,719	12,689	19,380	$3,356,195	$20,042,328	$ 83,639,477
1956	40	1334	422,881	17,557	400,979	129,512	69,503	115,146	11,965	21,882	3,672,488	21,518,892	90,384,471
1957	40	1340	430,562	16,904	399,170	134,200	71,390	116,649	13,573	24,927	3,858,693	20,254,943	110,881,910
1958	41	1361	445,503	18,398	395,124	134,496	77,277	115,897	13,940	20,252	4,166,203	22,443,757	107,210,402
1959	41	1371	457,659	17,486	406,989	134,236	76,678	106,603	18,886	23,275	4,613,224	28,222,536	117,953,811
1960	41	1383	458,759	18,819	403,430	139,779	76,961	107,377	21,115	28,593	4,616,522	27,906,598	121,760,858
1961	41	1396	467,383	20,152	400,129	145,323	77,244	108,724	23,345	42,006	4,619,810	27,590,660	125,568,005
1962	41	1414	476,526	15,482	408,209	145,550	79,001	108,386	24,445	45,979	5,035,252	27,209,873	142,252,200
1963	42	1419	483,832	14,611	406,693	152,521	79,240	108,708	22,740	38,896	5,249,477	27,957,141	147,233,033
1964	42	1423	492,202	16,489	405,108	149,097	73,559	107,095	21,270	47,500	5,344,521	28,810,831	153,090,553
1965	43	1433	495,276	14,623	413,948	153,266	73,802	104,671	21,554	48,000	5,813,578	32,079,678	167,387,123
1966	44	1442	506,671	14,561	412,126	151,252	68,162	104,127	22,374	47,136	6,194,703	33,461,785	172,722,700
1967	44	1425	514,359	14,969	407,288	146,624	67,458	103,132	21,769	49,124	6,414,955	35,152,394	189,740,560
1968	44	1441	524,261	15,433	405,407	152,886	78,133	102,756	20,861	49,854	6,762,186	39,414,108	198,343,000

PAGE TAYLOR

divisions, there are three offices that are closely related to the office of executive secretary: evangelism, stewardship, and information and research.

Missions in Virginia.—The general board in its mission work stresses the importance of the local church. In every way possible the local church and district association are strengthened by the resources and programs of the board. In recent years the emphasis has been shifting to meet the changing needs of the times. There is increased emphasis on urban work. New ways of presenting the gospel are being sought, and experimental projects are encouraged. The student ministry is being strengthened, and new ways of reaching the college student are being used. The strong educational programs of the past are being updated and made more effective in a new department of teaching and training. A new department of social ministries was established in 1969 to assist pastors and churches in such important areas as drugs, alcohol, sex education, poverty, race relations, and other social problems.

Associational Missions.—Great emphasis is being placed on the development of associational missions. Through the employment of superintendents of missions and the encouragement of local mission planning and projects, the whole state mission program is developing a broader base of concern and operation.

Institutes for Pastors and Laymen.—A number of institutes for pastors and lay persons are planned: a pastoral counseling institute; a family life conference; a school for training of pastors in dealing with the ill at Virginia Baptist Hospital; and two pastors' schools held each year.

Assemblies.—Eagle Eyrie, the Virginia assembly grounds, is used for the promotion of Virginia Baptist work on a year-round basis.

Work with Outside Agencies.—The state mission program includes assistance to various agencies not directly controlled by Virginia Baptists: The American Bible Society; Children's Home of Virginia Baptists, Inc., at Petersburg; Alcohol Education Council, Inc.; and The Chaplain Service of the Churches of Virginia, Inc.

Virginia Baptist Foundation.—The foundation provides a means of strengthening Baptist work through gifts, wills, and legacies.

RICHARD M. STEPHENSON

VIRGINIA, DEPARTMENT OF SOCIAL MINISTRIES. A department of the Virginia Baptist General Board organized in Jan., 1970, by recommendation of a committee of 24 studying the overall work of Virginia Baptists and by approval of the Virginia Baptist General Association. The department serves as an educational resource to churches, associations, and college campuses in confronting social problems and in seeking Christian solutions. This is done by helping Virginia Baptists to become more aware of the moral imperatives of the gospel with regard to such aspects of living as family life, Christian citizenship, human relations, alcoholism and drug abuse, sex education, interdemoninational cooperation, and related areas; and by helping them create the kind of moral and social climate in which meaningful Christian action can take place. The primary program assignment is in the area of Christian social ethics.

Serving within the Division of Ministries of the general board, the department is responsible to the director of the division, the executive secretary of the general board, the committee on departments, and to the general board. This relationship responsibility includes overall goals and plans. It relates to the general association through the Christian life and family life committees of the general association. The department is responsible for maintaining a meaningful and reciprocal relationship with the Christian Life Commission of the Southern Baptist Convention. The commission is considered the basic SBC agency to which the department relates for guidance and resources.

The implementation of program assignments in the area of Christian social ethics is achieved through the Christian Life committee of the general association and associational, local church, and campus Christian life committees. The department assists the committees in keeping fellow Christians aware of social problems, equipping them through educational approaches to deal with the problems, and implementing the solutions through the various community structures.

Social problems are so tremendous in scope that the department has sought means of cooperating with leaders of other denominations who work in the area of social ministries. Persons engaged in this work on a denominational level have formed a Social Concerns Dialogue that meets once monthly in Richmond. This has resulted in an awareness of what others are doing to combat social problems and of sharing what Baptists in Virginia and other places are doing in such confrontation.

GENE WILLIAMS

***VIRGINIA ASSOCIATIONS.**

I. New Associations. FRANKLIN COUNTY. Organized at Rocky Mount Baptist Church, Nov. 26, 1956, with 15 charter members—ten from Blue Ridge, three from Strawberry, and one from Valley. In 1968, 18 churches reported 104 baptisms, 3,478 members, total receipts, $173,264, mission gifts, $21,503, total property value, $817,000.

FREDERICKSBURG. Organized at Fairview Baptist Church, Fredericksburg, Sept. 17, 1957, by ten churches from Goshen Association, six from Hermon, and one from Rappahannock. In 1968, 26 churches reported 297 baptisms, 10,771 members, total receipts, $712,499, mission gifts, $132,034, total property value, $3,464,000.

HENRY COUNTY. Organized May 12, 1957, at First Baptist Church, Martinsville, by 22 churches from Blue Ridge. In 1968, 25 churches, one mission, and one chapel reported 328 baptisms, 10,275 members, total receipts, $916,305, missions gifts, $176,303, total property value, $3,689,000.

HIGHLANDS. Organized June 25, 1957, at Fairlawn Baptist Church, Radford, by 21 churches from Valley and one from Lebanon. In 1968, 24 churches and three missions reported 201 baptisms, 7,380 members, total receipts, $518,000, mission gifts, $60,432, total property value, $3,208,000.

LYNCHBURG. Organized at College Hill Church, Lynchburg, Nov. 1, 1964, by 15 churches from Strawberry and three from Piedmont. In 1968, 20 churches reported 304 baptisms, 10,955 members, total receipts, $894,667, mission gifts, $168,140, total property value, $4,594,000.

MID-TIDEWATER. Organized at Poroporone Church, Shackelfords, June 30, 1959, by 19 churches from Rappahannock and three from Peninsula. In 1968, 25 churches reported 88 baptisms, 5,402 members, total receipts, $408,176, mission gifts, $70,036, total property value, $2,274,000.

MOUNTAIN STATE. Organized Nov. 5, 1965, at Edgemont Church, Bluefield, W. Va., by 15 churches from East River and one from Pioneer Association, Ohio. In 1968, 18 churches reported 184 baptisms, 4,319 members, total receipts, $219,677, mission gifts, $21,737, total property value, $733,000.

SOUTH SIDE. Organized Oct. 26, 1962, at Victoria, by ten churches from Concord and 11 from Appomattox. In 1968, 22 churches reported 168 baptisms, 6,390 members, total receipts, $416,515, mission gifts, $57,430, total property value, $1,980,000.

II. Changes in Associations. ROANOKE VALLEY. Organized as Valley Association in 1841, the association adopted the present name in 1961.

VALLEY. Changed name to Roanoke Valley Association in 1961.

WOODFORD BROADUS HACKLEY

***VIRGINIA BAPTIST CHILDREN'S HOME.** Since 1957 five original buildings have been replaced with new structures, and one new activities building has been added. Twelve cottages house 180 children on the campus with a maximum of 15 children per cottage. House parents are in charge of each cottage. A social service staff of four qualified case workers plus a director of social services work with the children and their families in dealing with problems caused by separation. A total of 350 children receive service through group care, boarding homes, adoption, family aid, and pursuit of higher education.

Total assets of the home in 1969 were estimated at $2,000,000. The operating budget for the fiscal year ending Sept. 30, 1969, was $456,000. The capital outlay between 1959 and 1969 averaged $65,000 per year. Since 1956 R. F. Hough, Jr., has been director of the home.

R. F. HOUGH, JR.

***VIRGINIA BAPTIST FOUNDATION.** The foundation has grown steadily in assets, and as of Dec. 31, 1968, the approximate market value of the agency's investments had risen to $1,707,739.07. The net income from these investments amounted to $65,430.88 in 1968. James R. Bryant continues as executive secretary.

JAMES R. BRYANT

***VIRGINIA BAPTIST HISTORICAL SOCIETY.** In Nov., 1955, the society moved into new quarters generously provided by the WMU of Virginia. Since then the collection has increased to 9,250 books, 820 bound volumes of Virginia associational and Southern Baptist Convention minutes, 774 periodicals, and 261 microfilms (including 26 out-of-state material and 11 foreign). Besides packets of historical material, 1,427 original record books of 302 churches are now on deposit for preservation, and 113 record books of 54 other Baptist organizations. The society has 24 microfilms, 62 volumes of Xerox copies and photostats, and 30 typescripts of similar books. These records (involving 40 missionary associations, six Primitive, one Regular) came from 82 Virginia counties and eight Virginia cities. There are at least 24 archival collections. Since 1962 the society has published annually *The Virginia Baptist Register* (early Virginia Baptist history). The library is open every weekday. WOODFORD B. HACKLEY

***VIRGINIA BAPTIST HOMES.** Since 1956 the Virginia Baptist Home at Culpeper has added new facilities including additional rooms for residents, an office area, an extension to the dining room, and two cottages. The home accommodates 260 residents.

On Nov. 22, 1969, a second home for the aged was opened on a 35-acre tract in Newport News with a capacity of 115 residents and a proposed expansion to provide for 250.

The board of Virginia Baptist Homes employs one general superintendent, F. B. LeSueur, who heads the work at both locations with an administrator at each home. William R. Snead is administrator at Culpeper, and Charles E. Neal is administrator at Newport News. The total assets were $5,460,000 in 1969. The sources of income include funds received from residents, Cooperative Program receipts, special gifts, and income through wills and legacies.

WILLIAM R. SNEAD

***VIRGINIA BAPTIST HOSPITAL.** With completion of the enlargement and renovation of the Mundy Building, 1969–70, the hospital will accommodate 250 patients. There were 7,846 patients admitted and 1,335 babies born at the hospital in 1968. During 1969 the renovated School of Nursing was dedicated; also, a new

EAGLE EYRIE ASSEMBLY (*q.v.*), Lynchburg, Va. Dogwood Hall. The 363-acre Virginia assembly provides facilities for 1,000. In 1969, value $2,500,000.

VIRGINIA BAPTIST HOSPITAL (*q.v.*), Lynchburg, Va. A 250-bed modern hospital with a School of Nursing and a School of Pastoral Care.

VIRGINIA BAPTIST BUILDING, Richmond, Va. Completed in 1962. Provides space for state offices including WMU and *The Religious Herald.*

VIRGINIA BAPTIST HISTORICAL SOCIETY (*q.v.*), University of Richmond, Va. In use since 1955, this facility houses an outstanding Baptist historical collection.

radiology department, outpatient department, and laboratories were completed. Computerized equipment has been installed in the offices. The automated medical department is one of the most modern in the nation. Robert E. Evans, hospital chaplain, opened the School of Pastoral Care in 1967.

In 1968 the Baptist General Association of Virginia contributed $62,294.30. The churches of the state gave $42,000 for indigent medical patients living outside Lynchburg. Total assets were estimated at $7,500,000 in 1969. A 25-member board of trustees governs the hospital. Admission is without regard to race or creed. Charles S. Elliott is administrator.

JOHN S. MOORE

VIRGINIA BAPTIST REGISTER, THE. Published annually in Richmond by the Virginia Baptist Historical Society since Oct., 1962, it is designed primarily to present hitherto unpublished material pertaining to Virginia Baptists, with emphasis on Baptist beginnings in the state, and noteworthy contributions of Virginians to the Baptist denomination. The publication is reasonably documented. Some representative articles are: "Carter's Run: Mother Church"; "The Baptist Struggle in Rockbridge County, 1798–1900"; "To Erect a Seminary of Learning" (Virginia Baptist Seminary); "The Nine Christian Rites in the Early Baptist Churches of Virginia"; "Elder John Alderson, Jr., and the Greenbrier Church"; "Col. Robert Carter, a Baptist"; "Two Bedford Plowboys: a Missionary Tour"; "The Old Dan River Meeting House." The editor is Woodford B. Hackley, University of Richmond, Va.

WOODFORD B. HACKLEY

***VIRGINIA EXTENSION BOARD, INC.** In 1968 the funds available and committed to churches exceeded $750,000. Richard M. Stephenson is (1969) executive secretary of the board.

RICHARD M. STEPHENSON

***VIRGINIA INTERMONT COLLEGE.** Since 1956 the following facilities have been added: a fine arts center containing an educational theater, recital hall, art gallery, music library, music and art rooms; a science hall with facilities for home economics, science, and secretarial studies; a student center with swimming pool; a six-story dormitory; an air-conditioned auditorium with offices and chapel; renovated areas for the division of humanities, modern language laboratories, riding, physical education classes and expanded library facilities.

The two-year high school program was discontinued in 1957. Since 1956 enrolment has doubled, and the faculty has been increased some 28 per cent. Beginning in Sept., 1970, a four-year program leading to the Bachelor of Arts degree was initiated, with the first baccalaureate degrees being awarded in 1972. In 1968 the physical assets were valued at $4,253,597.

R. STUART GRIZZARD

VISITOR, THE. Published monthly at Sayre, Okla., from June, 1940, through Dec., 1950, *The Visitor* was edited by J. Eli Nunn, free-lance printer and Baptist lay leader. Originally issued as the official voice of Beckham Baptist Association, the paper grew as an instrument of promotion for conservative, evangelistic Baptist witness in Oklahoma. It never reached the ambitious goals of its editor, and passed from the scene due to financial conditions and the aging of its founder and publisher.

J. M. GASKIN

VOCATIONAL GUIDANCE, PROGRAM OF. Established by action of the Southern Baptist Convention in 1957, following a year of study by a special committee headed by Allen W. Graves, of Southern Baptist Theological Seminary. The need for such a program had been pointed up by the committee on the 30,000 Movement and by seminary trustees, who foresaw a shortage of church related vocations workers. At the request of the Convention, the Sunday School Board established the program and appointed John M. Tubbs to head the work. Initial efforts included publishing a series of books and tracts on church related vocations, establishing a file of information about volunteers, and some degree of conference work. Lloyd Householder directed the program, 1960–67.

In 1961 the Convention voted to expand the program to emphasize the Christian concerns of all vocational choices, with special emphasis on church vocations. In 1963 the program was moved from the Education Division Office of the Sunday School Board to the Training Union Department, but it continued to consult with all SBC programs. The channeling of vocational guidance materials in all denominational publications came to be fully implemented, and occupational counseling by correspondence reached an average of 300 persons monthly. A design for the implementation of vocational guidance by churches was completed in 1967, making such guidance a basic part of all church organizations. Assistance was also provided to Southern Baptist colleges and seminaries in recruitment of church vocations volunteers.

In 1969 William P. Clemmons assumed leadership of the program and moved to further broaden the base of church and convention work in vocational guidance.

LLOYD HOUSEHOLDER

W

WAKE FOREST UNIVERSITY (cf. Wake Forest College, Vol. II). The name of Wake Forest College was changed to Wake Forest University in 1967 because of the growth and development of the institution. University status was one of many changes that took place during the 17-year administration of President Harold Wayland Tribble which ended with his retirement in 1967. The years following the removal of the college to Winston-Salem, N. C. (1956), saw marked improvement in academic areas and substantial increases in endowment, enrolment, faculty salaries, and scholarship aid. Contributions from various sources during the Tribble administration totaled more than $33,000,000. An honors program for superior students was begun in 1960, and graduate study was resumed in 1961.

James Ralph Scales, former president of Oklahoma Baptist University, succeeded Tribble as president in 1967. Hubert H. Humphrey, then vice-president of the United States, spoke at the Apr., 1968, inauguration. In 1969 the Graduate School was offering work leading to the Master's degree in 12 departments and work for the Master's and Ph.D. degrees at the Bowman Gray School of Medicine. A decision was made in 1969 to establish graduate work in the new Charles H. Babcock School of Business.

Four new buildings and a football stadium were erected between 1960 and 1969. The total number of volumes in the university libraries was increased to 350,000. Scholarship aid had increased to $574,000 in 1969–70, compared to $112,185 in 1956–57. In 1968 the Z. Smith Reynolds Foundation increased its annual grant to the institution from $500,000 to $620,000. The university endowment in 1969 was $22,469,000 (book value), and $40,083,000 (market value). Funds invested in buildings totaled $35,558,000 and equipment value $6,565,000. The school operated on a budget of $18,905,116 in 1969–70, when its enrolment was 3,184.

RUSSELL BRANTLEY

WALKER, CLARENCE O'NEILL (b. Trimble, Tenn., May 29, 1890; d. Lexington, Ky., Aug. 11, 1968). Converted in Ormsby Avenue Baptist Church, Louisville, Ky., he served as a deacon, surrendered to preach, was licensed, and ordained (Nov. 28, 1909) there. He received special training in the preparatory departments of William Jewell College, Liberty, Mo., and of Georgetown College, Georgetown, Ky., 1907–08, and 1908–09. He married Mrs. Glorenna Bush McDaniels on Oct. 14, 1913. After serving churches in central Kentucky, he became pastor of the Ashland Avenue Baptist Church, Lexington, Ky., in Oct., 1916, where he remained until his retirement in Nov., 1966. A vigorous opponent of liberalism and advocate of moral reform, he began publishing the *Ashland Avenue Baptist* in 1922. The Lexington Baptist College was organized (1952) and supported by Walker's church.

LEO T. CRISMON

WALKER, GROVER CLEVELAND (b. York, Sumter County, Ala., Oct. 9, 1890; d. Birmingham, Ala., May 26, 1959). Pastor and denominational leader. Twelfth child of William Henry and Susan Elizabeth (Thorne) Walker, he attended State Teachers College, Livingston, Ala. He was a bookkeeper before his ordination by the York Baptist Church on June 17, 1917. While at Southern Baptist Seminary he served in a student pastorate in Kentucky. Upon completion of his seminary courses in 1919, he returned to Alabama and subsequently served as pastor of Southside Church, Decatur, 1918–21; First Church, Hartselle, 1921–25; Thirty-fifth Avenue Church, Birmingham, 1925–41; and First Church, Trussville, 1941–57. He retired in 1957 and served interim pastorates until his death. He married Ada Lucille Wiseheart of Louisville, Ky., May 7, 1919. Their daughters were Katherine Louise (Mrs. Robert C. Jones) and Martha Sue (Mrs. Eddie R. Greer).

Walker held every elected office in the Birmingham association. He served as secretary-treasurer for the association from 1938 until his death and as recording secretary of the Alabama Convention for the same years.

ARTHUR L. WALKER, JR.

WALKER, JOSEPH (b. Chester County, Pa., Apr. 10, 1804; d. Scottsville, Va., Apr. 7, 1895). Pastor, missionary, denominational executive, and editor. Walker was baptized by James B. Taylor (*q.v.*, Vol. II) in 1831. Later that year in

Norfolk, Va., under the pastorate of R. B. C. Howell (*q.v.,* Vol. I), he became a deacon and was licensed to preach. He attended Virginia Baptist Seminary (later University of Richmond) and served churches at Petersburg and Manchester, Va.

Ordained in June, 1838, at the Baptist General Association of Virginia, he was pastor during the next 12 years of churches in Accomac County, Hampton, Richmond, and Charlottesville, Va.; and Allegheny City, Pa. While in Charlottesville, he helped establish a girls boarding school. In 1850 he became editor of the *Baptist Recorder* and then state missionary agent for the Maryland Union Baptist Association in Baltimore. Encouraged by the Board of Domestic Missions (now Home Mission Board), the Missouri state convention, and J. B. Jeter (*q.v.,* Vol. I), he went to St. Louis and founded the Third Baptist Church in 1850. Between 1853–56, he served as corresponding secretary of the board, during which time the Indian Mission Association was incorporated into the board.

He was editor of the *Christian Index* at Macon, Ga., 1857–59, and then until 1865 served as an army chaplain. Between 1865 and 1880, when he officially retired, Walker again was pastor of churches in Virginia and Missouri. While in retirement, he continued to preach, lecture, and write. His prolific accounts in Baptist newspapers provide excellent sources about Baptist life in the 19th century. A supporter of Landmarkism, he died at age 90 and his funeral was conducted by William E. Hatcher (*q.v.,* Vol. I). A. RONALD TONKS

WALKER, LAURENCE MARVIN (b. Collin County, Tex., Apr. 25, 1901; d. Albuquerque, N. Mex., Aug. 21, 1956). Pastor and public-school teacher. Walker attended public schools in Quay County, N. Mex., where he had moved in 1908. He graduated from Montezuma Baptist College (B.A., 1927) and Southwestern Baptist Theological Seminary (Th.M., 1932). On June 1, 1926, he married Gladys Irwin, in Farmington, N. Mex. Walker was pastor of six churches in Texas and New Mexico. He served his last pastorate, Fruit Avenue Baptist Church, Albuquerque, N. Mex., for 16 years. He also was moderator of Denton (Texas) Association and Central (New Mexico) Association; a member of the board of trustees of Southwestern Baptist Theological Seminary, 1944–49; Executive Committee, SBC, 1950–56; president of the Baptist Convention of New Mexico, 1953 and 1954; and member of New Mexico state mission board for 17 years. He worked with RAs all over the state. Walker preached the annual sermon for Baptist Convention of New Mexico in 1946. He was campaign director for the first Convention-wide Sunday School clinic in Los Angeles in 1955. Under his leadership, Fruit Avenue Baptist Church established three other churches and three missions. HERBERT E. BERGSTROM

WALKER, RAY (b. Jackson, Ala., Apr. 6, 1915; d. Tallassee, Ala., Oct. 7, 1958). Son of Mr. and Mrs. E. E. Walker, he graduated from high school at Magnolia, Ala., May 1, 1936. He attended Howard College, Birmingham, Ala., 1936–38; and Southeastern State College, Durant, Okla., 1942–44. His pastoral labors, begun in Alabama, continued in Oklahoma and were extended to California for about one year, 1944–45. In 1945 he became pastor of the First Baptist Church, Burden, Kans., which was affiliated with the Oklahoma Baptist Convention. While attending that convention's annual session in Oklahoma City, he helped plan the program for the first official, preliminary meeting of Southern Baptists in Kansas at Burden, Nov. 26–27, 1945. Walker was elected president of the Kansas Southern Baptist Fellowship. When the Kansas Convention of Southern Baptist Churches was formed Mar. 19, 1946, at Chetopa, Kans., he was elected president. He held that position until Oct. 15, 1947. Other Kansas Baptist pastorates were: Calvary, Salina, 1947–49; and Bethel, Salina, 1949–51. During his six years in Kansas he led in the establishment of six missions, four of which became churches. He and his wife, Mildred Middleton, had five children: Lynette, Sandra, Donald Ray, Rebecca, and Janalyn. Walker's premature death resulted from a heart ailment suffered during the last 10 years of his life. It forced resignation from his last pastorate in Alabama about six months before his death. N. J. WESTMORELAND

WALL, ZENO (b. Mooresboro, N. C., Aug. 20, 1882; d. Charlotte, N. C., Sept. 12, 1962). Minister. Son of Sidney and Jane (Robinson) Wall, he was a graduate of Mars Hill College and Southern Baptist Theological Seminary. In 1917 he was awarded an honorary D.D. by Mississippi College. Ordained in 1908, Wall served his first pastorate at Marshall, N. C. From 1911–22, he served as pastor of churches in Mississippi at Mt. Olive, Columbia, and Clinton. He returned to North Carolina in 1922 as pastor of First Baptist Church, Goldsboro. On Oct. 1, 1925, he began a 23-year pastorate at First Baptist Church, Shelby. Wall served as president of Gardner-Webb College without pay from 1930–32, was president of the Baptist state convention for four terms, 1933–36, and served more than two years as general superintendent of the Baptist Children's Homes at Thomasville, 1948–50. He was author of three books: *Heartening Messages* (1944), *Verities of the Gospel* (1947), and *A Day for God-Called Men* (1948). He married Ada Kate Ramsey in May, 1911. They had three sons and two daughters.
TOBY DRURIN

WALLACE, BLUMENFELD FRIED (b. Winston County, Miss., May 10, 1884; d. Shreveport, La., June 3, 1964). Son of farmer, lay preacher T. D. Wallace and Laura (Jenkins) Wallace, he attended Clarke Academy, Newton, Miss., and

Mississippi College (A.B., 1906), Clinton. He attended Southern Baptist Theological Seminary, 1908–10. He married Corra Amanda Wylie at Clinton in 1907. They had two children, William B. and Laura Marguerite.

He held pastorates at Sallis, Miss.; Louisville, Ky.; and Bunkle, Pineville, Winnsboro, and Shreveport, La. He served as camp pastor in New Orleans for the Home Mission Board during World War I. He organized Lakeshore and Bethel Baptist churches, Shreveport, serving as pastor of each. He was moderator of Caddo Association, president (1935–36) of Louisiana Baptist Convention and three times vice-president of the convention, and superintendent of Louisiana Baptist Children's Home, 1936–40.

Wallace spent 54 years of his life in Baptist work in Louisiana. He was buried in Forest Park Cemetery in Shreveport, La.

JOHN G. ALLEY

WALLACE, DOUGLAS EUGENE (b. Fort Worth, Tex., Sept. 22, 1923; d. Riverside, Calif., July 9, 1961). Son of A. A. and Ida May (Redding) Wallace, he attended Baylor University (B.A.), Golden Gate Baptist Theological Seminary (Th.M.), and the University of Edinburgh (Ph.D.). Wallace married Lois Ellen Purtyman and had three children. Prior to joining the faculty of California Baptist College, he was a pastor in Arizona. At the college he served as professor of Bible and religious education, and director of seminary extension training.

CECIL M. HYATT

WALLER, GEORGE (b. Spottsylvania County, Va., Sept. 12, 1777; d. Kentucky, July, 1860). Son of William E. Waller (*q.v.*), he moved to Kentucky in 1784, where he had few opportunities for obtaining an education. At the age of 21, he moved with his parents to Shelby County, where he married Polly Ware. They had five sons and four daughters. He made a profession of faith in 1801, was ordained into the ministry the next year, and became pastor of the Buck Creek Church in 1803, when his father returned to Virginia. He served the church 50 years. Traveling all over the state preaching in the interest of missions, "he was a missionary to Louisville before there was a church in that city." He served the Burk's Branch Church for 43 years, the Bethel Church for 32 years, the Harrod's Creek Church, 1831–37, and Walnut Street Church in Louisville, after a division over Campbellism, for three years. With Spencer Clack, Waller was editor of the Bloomfield, Ky., weekly entitled *The Baptist Recorder*. He was elected moderator of the Long Run Baptist Association in 1817, and served in that capacity for 25 years. He was also the first moderator of the General Association of Baptists in Kentucky. Waller is buried in the Buck Creek Cemetery near Finchville. LEO T. CRISMON

WALLER, WILLIAM EDMUND (b. 1740's in Va.?; d. Louisa County, Va., 1820's). The earliest account of Waller's preaching is that he became pastor of County Line Church in his native Spottsylvania County in 1782. He settled in Garrard County, Ky., in 1784. He was a member of the Bryant's Church in Fayette County, 1786–96, where he co-labored with pioneer preachers. In 1798 he made his residence in Shelby County, and organized Buck Creek Church, 1799. He also aided in the formation of the King's Church, which was organized in 1800. In 1803 after the death of his wife, he returned and settled in his native region in Virginia. He married and assumed the pastorate of the Goldmine Church, Goshen Association, in 1807, where he apparently remained until his death at the age of 83. "William Edmund Waller has acquired more fame in modern history from the eminent distinction of his posterity, than from his personal gifts or acquirements." Prominent among his descendents are his sons George, 1777–1860, and Edmund, 1775–1842; grandsons John Lightfoot Waller, 1809–54, Napoleon Bonaparte Waller, 1826–55, and Jonathan Cox Waller, 1812– ?; and his great grandson, William Edmund Waller, Jr., 1845–78. LEO T. CRISMON

WARR, JOHN CAREY (b. Louisville, Ala., Apr. 11, 1913; d. Sandersville, Ga., June 9, 1969). Children's home executive. After graduating from Berry College (B.S., 1937), Rome, Ga., Warr remained there as instructor, director of admissions, and registrar, 1937–46. He married Helen Howell in 1937. They had one daughter, Jacquelyn Kay. He was superintendent of Floyd County schools, 1946–50. Warr served as general manager, Georgia Baptist Children's Home, Inc., with campuses at Baxley, Meansville, and Palmetto, Jan. 1, 1950–June 9, 1969. His administration was highlighted by the addition of the Pine Mountain Campus at Meansville, 1956, the relocation of the Hapeville Campus to Palmetto, 1968, and the overall expansion of social work, enabling the agency to establish multiple service care through the child-care ministry of Georgia Baptists. He was president, Child-Care Executives of the Southern Baptist Convention, 1965–66, and president, Child-Care Executives of Georgia, 1966–67. DAVID H. MC GOWAN

WARREN, LOUIS BACON (b. Atlanta, Ga., Jan. 1, 1876; d. Brunswick, Ga. Dec. 12, 1942). Pastor and home mission leader. Son of E. W. Warren (*q.v.*, Vol. II), he was educated in the public schools of Macon and graduated from Mercer University. He also attended Richmond College, University of Georgia, Southern Baptist Theological Seminary, and the University of Chicago. He received an honorary D.D. degree from Bethel College in Kentucky.

Converted in Apr., 1898, he was ordained in May by the Tattnall Square Baptist Church, Macon, Ga. That same month he enlisted with the American volunteers in the Spanish-American War and was appointed chaplain of the Third Georgia Regiment.

As pastor, he served First Baptist Church, Ocala, Fla.; First Baptist Church, Beaumont, Tex.; First Baptist Church, Owensboro, Ky.; Second Baptist Church, Richmond, Va. Following his Virginia pastorate he became financial secretary of Columbia College, Lake City, Fla., where he served until May, 1913.

Warren became superintendent of the Department of Church Extension for the Home Mission Board in 1913 when the total assets of the department were $76,000. A year earlier a special committee appointed to study the matter of church loans had recommended, "that the Board . . . enter with expedition upon an aggressive campaign to raise a church building loan fund of one million dollars." Warren used two principle methods in his approach to loan fund development: the soliciting of memorials to be recorded in what was known as the Hall of Fame, and the selling of gift annuity bonds. Both approaches proved successful, for in 1922 he reported a paid-in corpus in the loan fund of $1,083,107 and pledges of an additional $575,216. He reported that 1,573 churches had been assisted with the loan funds.

In 1922 he retired because of failing eyesight. He lived in Atlanta after his retirement until 1930 when he built a seaside cottage near Brunswick, Ga. ROBERT H. KILGORE

WASHINGTON, BAPTISTS IN. See OREGON-WASHINGTON, BAPTIST GENERAL CONVENTION OF.

WATSON, STEPHEN LAWTON (b. Marion County, S. C., Aug. 2, 1880; d. Columbia, S. C., Oct. 6, 1966). Missionary to Brazil (1914–50). Watson studied at Wake Forest College, Furman University (B.A., 1909), and Southern Baptist Theological Seminary (Th.M., 1914; Th.D., 1922). As an educator he directed Baptist seminaries in Rio and Recife and school in Belo Horizonte. As an author and editor, he translated, wrote, and edited books in Portuguese for Baptist Publishing House and Bible Press of Brazil, and edited *O Jornal Batista*. Watson also was pastor of local churches and served in executive capacities on denominational boards. He married Annie Miller, June 18, 1914.

EDGAR F. HALLOCK

WATTERS, HENRY EUGENE (b. Graves County, Ky., Sept. 14, 1876; d. Jackson, Tenn., Apr. 15, 1938). Minister and educator. Son of Theodore M. and Josephine (Ransom) Watters, he was educated at Southern Normal University (B.S., 1899) and Union University (A.B., 1903; A.M., 1916). He did graduate work at Brown University, 1905–07; Chicago University, 1933–34; and Southern Baptist Theological Seminary, 1935. He received the honorary D.D. from Hall-Moody Institute, 1906, and the LL.D. from Union University, 1921. For seven years he was principal of public schools in Kentucky and Tennessee. He also taught history at Union University. Watters served as president of these institutions: Hall-Moody Institute, 1905–15; College of Marshall (later East Texas Baptist College), 1916–18; Union University, 1918–31; Georgetown College (Ky.), 1931–34; and Jonesboro Baptist College (Ark.), 1935–37. In addition he was pastor of a number of churches. He married Annette Routon, Aug. 28, 1899. After her death he married Ethel Reed, July 22, 1931. He was the father of four children: Lillian, Evelyn, Everette, and Marden. He wrote *Bible of Super-human Origin* (1908), *Physics Simplified* (1905), *Planning a Life* (1935), and *Youth Makes the Choice* (1938). HOMER WALDROP

WATTS, JOSEPH THOMAS (b. Raleigh, N. C., Mar. 19, 1874; d. Baltimore, Md., Feb. 7, 1957). Minister, denominational leader, and executive. Son of Josiah Turner and Annie Eliza (McIver) Watts, twin brother of Thomas Joseph Watts (*q.v.*, Vol. II). When a young man, Watts was converted from Catholicism. While working for the Illinois Central Railroad he felt called to the ministry, was ordained in 1903, and studied at the Southern Baptist Theological Seminary, 1903–05. Wake Forest College conferred the Doctor of Divinity degree upon him in 1916. Watts held pastorates in Jackson, Miss., Louisville, Ky., and Lexington, N.C. He was the first Sunday School secretary for Kentucky. He served as secretary of education for the Virginia Baptist Board of Missions and Education, 1909–27. He was general secretary of the Maryland Baptist Union Association, 1927–47, and general secretary emeritus, 1947–57. He promoted summer assemblies and teacher training institutes. He led in financial planning for the $75,000,000 Campaign and the Cooperative Program. Watts was vitally interested in every phase of the life and work of the Southern Baptist Convention. His first wife, the former Neva Hawkins, whom he married July 2, 1895, died May 28, 1950. One daughter, Mrs. Elizabeth Trainham, survives (1969). On Sept. 15, 1951, he married the former Emily Rule. Watts was author of *Convention Adult Bible Classes* (1915), *Home and Extension Department of the Sunday School* (1930), *The Growing Christian* (1937), and *The Rise and Progress of Maryland Baptists* (n.d.). The Baylor-Watts Chapel at the Maryland WMU camp, Camp Wo-Me-To, Jarrettsville, Md., was named for him and William H. Baylor (*q.v.*). Watts is buried in the cemetery of the Sater's Baptist Church, the oldest Baptist church in Maryland.

W. CLYDE ATKINS

***WAYLAND BAPTIST COLLEGE.** On July 1, 1963, President A. Hope Owen retired and was succeeded by Roy C. McClung. The college has progressed in every respect. School properties are now valued at $4,587,640 and include 17 permanent buildings on the main campus and 18 other permanent housing units. Temporary buildings are being replaced by permanent structures as the overall expansion and development program of the college continues. Endowment now totals $2,758,935. FLORRIE CONWAY

WEATHERFORD, JOHN (b. Hanover County, Va., c. 1743; d. Pittsylvania County, Va., Feb. 23, 1833). Imprisoned Baptist preacher, Revolutionary soldier. His father, Major Weatherford, moved to Lunenburg (now Charlotte) County, Va., by 1750. John Weatherford became a Baptist around 1762. He began to preach in 1764 and served as an itinerant evangelist until about 1790. Refusing pay for his services he earned his living by farming. Along with other fellow ministers he sought to end the religious establishment in Virginia.

Receiving little education he reached the common man with his simple gospel message. On June 4, 1773, he was arraigned before the Chesterfield County court for preaching without a license. He remained in jail for five months apparently refusing to pledge not to preach for one year in order to gain release. His liberation came through an order secured by Patrick Henry. A number of conversions resulted from his prison preaching.

He married Martha Sublett by whom he had a large family. From 1790 to 1799 he was pastor of Cub Creek Church. Following this he served his last pastorate, Lower Falling Church, until around 1810. He later moved to Pittsylvania County, Va., where he farmed. From 1813 until his death he was a member of County Line Church. Weatherford was buried near Shockoe Church, Pittsylvania County, Va. His fearless preaching and long imprisonment have become legendary. JOHN S. MOORE

WEATHERSBY, HAL MONROE (b. Copiah County, Miss., Sept. 21, 1885; d. Pineville, La., Aug. 15, 1965). Louisiana educator. Son of William Monroe and Hallie (Hennington) Weathersby, he graduated from Mississippi College (B.A., 1905), and the University of Chicago (M.A.). Louisiana College in Pineville conferred upon him the L.D.

He married Matalee Thompson, July 29, 1907, and they had three children: Rose Hunter (Mrs. Murrel Normand), Hal Thompson, and Scott Monroe.

He was dean of Louisiana College, the state's Baptist college in Pineville, for 42 years, where he counselled and guided thousands of young people. He served as president of the Louisiana College Conference, and served one year (1945) as vice-president of the Louisiana Baptist Convention.

Quiet and mild mannered, he was a man of courage and conviction, a scholar, and one who possessed a strong faith.

He had no books published, but authored two chapters in *Messages for Men* (1963) edited by H. C. Brown, Jr. He wrote numerous articles in various denominational publications.

JOHN G. ALLEY

WEATHERSPOON, JESSE BURTON (b. Durham County, N.C., July 21, 1886; d. Raleigh, N.C., Nov. 11, 1964). Pastor, professor, author, lecturer, and Southern Baptist Convention preacher in 1935. Son of William H. and Cynthia (Hopson) Weatherspoon, he was converted and baptized in 1897, and joined the Temple Baptist Church, Durham, N.C., where he was ordained in 1906. He was a graduate of Wake Forest College (B.A., 1906; M.A., 1907) and Southern Baptist Theological Seminary (Th.M., 1910; Th.D., 1911). In 1928 Wake Forest conferred upon him an honorary D.D. His first marriage (Jan. 1, 1913) was to Ada L. Jones of Raleigh, who died in 1957. In 1962 he married Emily K. Lansdell, professor of missions at Southeastern Seminary. He served three pastorates: Oxford Baptist Church, Oxford, N.C., 1911–13; First Baptist Church, Winston-Salem, N.C., 1918–21; Highland Baptist Church, Louisville, Ky., 1922–29, and numerous interim pastorates. He taught in three Southern Baptist seminaries: tutor in Greek at Southern Seminary, 1907–11; professor of Hebrew and Old Testament at Southwestern Seminary, 1913–18; professor of homiletics and sociology, later professor of preaching at Southern Seminary, 1929–58; and as visiting professor of preaching at Southeastern Seminary, 1959–63. In addition to numerous articles in *Review and Expositor* and other religious journals, he wrote Sunday School curriculum materials and published: *The Book We Teach* (1934), a revised edition of *Broadus' Preparation and Delivery of Sermons* (1944), *Sent Forth to Preach* (1954), and *M. Theron Rankin, Apostle of Advance* (1958). He served on many commissions and committees of the SBC, including the Social Service Commission, of which he was chairman, 1944–54. At the annual meeting of the Convention in St. Louis (1954), he brought the Christian Life Commission's recommendation calling for support of the Supreme Court's ruling in regard to segregation in public schools. After discussion, his remarks closed the debate, and the Convention overwhelmingly adopted the commission's recommendation. He delivered the Holland Lectures at Southwestern Baptist Theological Seminary in 1946, and the Hester Lectures on Preaching at Midwestern Baptist Theological Seminary in 1961. He is buried in the Montlawn Memorial Park in Raleigh, N. C..

JAMES H. BLACKMORE

WEBB, WARREN SHELDON (b. LeRoy, N. Y., Nov. 14, 1825; d. Clinton, Miss., Aug. 22, 1910). Pastor, educator, and college president. Youngest of 14 children born to Benoni and Elizabeth (Phillips) Webb, he was educated at Kingsville Academy, Ohio, and Madison (Colgate) University (B.A., 1849; M.A., 1851). Both Howard College and the University of Mississippi awarded him the D.D. degree. J. R. Graves, his Greek teacher, influenced him to go south to teach. Webb's educational career included teaching at Stewart's Academy, Murfreesboro, Tenn., 1849–51; president of Yalobusha Female Institute, Grenada, Miss., 1851–57; superintendent of the Starkville, Miss., school, 1857–59; and president of Mississippi College, 1872–91. J. L. Boyd wrote, "As a college president he controlled his students by the respect they held for him. He was indeed a model president." Webb was ordained in 1851, by the Enon Baptist Church, Murfreesboro, Tenn. His Mississippi pastorates included West Point, 1859–65, Crawfordsville, Okolona, Macon, Deer Creek, Clinton, Brandon, and Line Creek. O. M. Johnson, one of his students, praised Webb in these words: "His dominant talent was to awaken the soul, vitalize the life, to build character. . . . He was the greatest character-builder that the State [*sic*] of Mississippi has ever known." Webb served his denomination as president of the Mississippi Baptist Convention, 1890–92, and as secretary of the board for the Orphans' Home at Lauderdale Springs. Ten children, five sons and five daughters, blessed his marriage to Adelphia Wheeler. EARL KELLY

WEBER, PAUL, SR. (b. Switzerland, Aug. 28, 1884; d. St. Louis, Mo., Nov. 26, 1954) . Missouri pastor and leader. While pastor of the First Baptist Church of Jefferson City, 1920–40, he twice was elected (1936, 1937) moderator of the Missouri Baptist General Association (now Convention) . Weber was superintendent of the St. Louis Baptist Mission Board, 1940–54. Educated at William Jewell College (A.B., 1909; D.D., 1937) and Newton Theological Seminary, he served William Jewell and Missouri Baptist Hospital as a trustee. He was a member of the Home Mission Board and on numerous Baptist state and SBC committees. Weber married Bettie Belle Rose, Jan. 4, 1909, and they had four children: Frank, Paul, Jr., Grace (Mrs. Eugene M. Moore) , and Richard. PAUL WEBER, JR.

WEEKDAY BIBLE STUDY. The definition approved by the Southern Baptist Convention states that Weekday Bible Study "includes formally scheduled opportunities for concentrated teaching of the Bible and other curriculum areas for pupils of public school ages in Weekday Bible Study classes and other programs of Weekday Bible Study. It includes also special teaching opportunities for children in kindergarten, child care programs, and nursery school."

Weekday Bible Study as covered in the Convention statement can be described best by looking at the preschool programs separate from the school-age programs. In 1969 approximately 1,700 churches had weekday nursery schools and/or kindergartens. About 170 of these provided all-day programs for preschool children of working mothers. Enrolled in these daily ministries were approximately 92,000 persons (86,730 pupils and 5,270 teachers) .

Weekday programs for school-age students have developed according to several patterns. The one most often used is a church-centered, free-time (nonpublic school hours) approach to Bible study conducted during the school year. Classes meet at least once a week during some afternoon, on Wednesday evening or on Saturday morning. The setting and approach are more academic than those usually found in Sunday School. A church staff member or some other professionally trained person serves as teacher.

Approximately 86 Southern Baptist churches have Christian day schools providing one or more grades. Thirty of these offer only the first grade. About 50 others have from two to six grades. Only six churches have all grades from kindergarten through high school. These schools are under the sponsorship of the local church and meet in the educational facilities of the church.

In a few communities Southern Baptists have joined with other denominations in providing courses in Bible on a released-time basis. Students are released from the public schools during school hours for an hour or two of Bible study each week.

The Sunday School Board, SBC, has provided a series of Bible-study textbooks to use in various weekday programs for all grades four through high school. They are produced in companion volumes for teacher and student and deal primarily with Bible content and related studies in Christian doctrine and ethics.

See also WEEKDAY RELIGIOUS EDUCATION, Vol. II. JAMES C. BARRY

WEST VIRGINIA ASSOCIATIONS. EASTERN FELLOWSHIP. The first Eastern Fellowship and Crusade Rally were jointly held Sept., 1968, at White Sulphur Baptist Church. At the Eastern Evangelism Clinic meeting at Huntersville Baptist Chapel in 1970, plans were made to constitute into a new association at its next meeting in Sept., 1970. It is now affiliated with the West Virginia state convention.

FRANCIS R. TALLANT

GREATER HUNTINGTON. Organized Sept. 11, 1961, by four churches located in the southwestern part of West Virginia to promote fellowship and further cooperation among the churches, and to disseminate the gospel within its bounds and throughout the world. In 1969 eight churches reported 56 baptisms, 2,408 members, $166,091 total gifts, $18,051 mission gifts, and $1,005,000 property value.

PAUL A. SCAGGS, JR.

MOUNTAIN STATE. Organized Nov. 5, 1965, by 16 churches located in southern West Virginia to assist in developing missions and evangelism in West Virginia. In 1969, 19 churches reported 336 baptisms, 5,886 members, $287,000 total gifts, $24,800 mission gifts, $1,156,000 property value, and $190,000 church debt.

GEORGE BULSON

PIONEER BAPTIST. Organized at Witcher Baptist Church, Belle, W. Va., on Oct. 31, 1958, with five churches and one mission. In 1969 eight churches reported 145 baptisms, 1,388 members, $128,153 total gifts, $13,124 mission gifts, $412,-500 property value, and $133,481 church debt.

OLA COX

UPPER OHIO VALLEY. Organized on Nov. 11, 1960, the constitutional service was held in Temple Baptist Church, Moundsville, with seven West Virginia churches and eight missions. In 1969 seven churches reported 123 baptisms, 1,210 members, $57,287 total gifts, and $25,460 mission gifts.

FLOYD TIDSWORTH, JR.

WEST VIRGINIA CONVENTION OF SOUTHERN BAPTISTS.

I. Baptist Beginnings. Although records are not clear, it seems the first Baptist church in what is now West Virginia was organized about 1743 at Garrardstown in Berkeley County by families who emigrated there from Maryland. That church ceased to function but Baptist influence continued.

As Baptist groups sprang up West of the Alleghenies, these were formed into various organizations. . . . The Western Virginia Association was formed in 1844. . . . In 1850, it voted to divide itself and form . . . the North Western Virginia Association. This . . . group was organized at Clarksburg to aid the General Association of Virginia in preaching the gospel to the feeble and destitute settlements in North Western Virginia.

About 1865, the Baptist General Association of West Virginia was organized with churches which had cooperated with Virginia and Southern Baptists. Records indicate churches at Charles Town, Martinsburg, and Princeton remained with Virginia.

In 1958 there were 33 Southern Baptist churches in West Virginia. Nine of them affiliated with state conventions in Kentucky and Ohio; 24 were in the Virginia General Association.

Early Efforts at Unification, 1958–66.—In 1958 the Home Mission Board employed John I. Snedden as area superintendent of missions in West Virginia. State conventions with churches in West Virginia gave him some financial support. Snedden, assisted by A. B. Cash of the HMB, conducted the first state fellowship meeting in 1958.

The next year West Virginia Pastors' Fellowship was organized to lay the foundation for a state convention. Willard Jenkins, Princeton, was elected president. A missions committee to "devise, develop, and promote a limited program of . . . mission work . . . on a state basis" was elected in 1962 with Alton McEachern, Huntington, chairman. In 1963 the West Virginia Baptist Fellowship was organized with L. B. Huston, Princeton, elected president.

Four district associations with their churches in West Virginia were organized during these years, and Francis R. Tallant was called in 1964 to be religious education director for the state. By 1966 Southern Baptists in the state numbered 54 churches. In that year the Baptist General Association of West Virginia was formed, and Willard Jenkins was elected president.

JOHN I. SNEDDEN

II. History of the General Association. The year 1966 was set for constituting by agency and state leaders in a meeting at Ridgecrest in Aug., 1963. Early in 1966 it became evident that the fellowship would fail to reach two of the guidelines for constituting into a convention at the date set. At the suggestion of the Home Mission Board, the missions committee postponed constituting, and instead set up a prototype state convention organization in order to enlarge better its work. This resulted in a new name—Baptist General Association of West Virginia—a new constitution, and an enlarged budget with 50 per cent of Cooperative Program gifts going to West Virginia work and 50 per cent to the state with which the church was affiliated—Kentucky, Ohio, or Virginia. Of all undesignated gifts, 20 per cent was sent to the Southern Baptist Convention Executive Committee for worldwide causes.

A large residence in a good location in St. Albans was rented to serve as a state office building, and a full-time secretary was employed and asked to serve also as financial secretary. An executive board was elected, as provided for in the new constitution. Through this organization all phases of the work were promoted by means of conventions, clinics, conferences, and other state meetings. The work grew until by the end of the year it was necessary to employ a second full-time secretary and a part-time Woman's Missionary Union director.

The work was divided into three departments: Missions, Religious Education, and WMU. The Missions Department was directed by John I. Snedden. Added to this department was the responsibility of evangelism and men's work. Francis R. Tallant was the director of the Religious Education Department. Besides the regular church programs, this department was responsible for the stewardship promotion and the publishing of the state paper. The director served as editor. Mrs. Elmo Cox served as part-time director of the WMU and assisted in other phases of the state work as a special worker. This organization and program of work did much in the progress and growth toward a state convention in 1970.

State Convention Organized.—At its annual meeting on Oct. 31, 1969, the Baptist General Association voted to constitute itself into a state convention at its next regular meeting. This date was set for Oct. 29–30, 1970, at Witcher Baptist Church, Belle, W. Va. A new spirit was felt by the messengers as they then instructed the executive board to proceed with necessary arrangements for constituting. The necessary plans were made including constitution, budget, and program adjustments for the new convention. The structure and program remained essentially the same because the general association had already been working as a prototype convention. The name West Virginia Convention of Southern Baptists was chosen.

FRANCIS R. TALLANT

III. Program of Work. First of the pioneer areas to develop a "proto-type state convention," the Baptist General Association had churches which participated in four state conventions. It functioned without an executive secretary, looking instead to its executive board and directors of missions-evangelism and religious education for program implementation. It held a convention reserve fund of over $20,000 and disbursed Cooperative Program receipts on an 80 per cent–20 per cent basis.

Executive Board.—Authorized in the constitution of the Baptist General Association of West Virginia to implement its work, the executive board is composed of the general association officers and members elected from the district associations and at large to provide a body of 14 members. The first board met on Dec. 3, 1966, establishing the pattern of quarterly meetings. It is organized into finance, program, missions and evangelism, religious education, and administration committees. The board is instructed to: (1) assist the churches in developing their potential strength, (2) strengthen the district associations, and (3) survey the state to establish new missions and churches.

TOM LANG

Religious Education Department.—In 1964 the missions committee of the West Virginia Fellowship called Francis R. Tallant from a similar position in Kentucky to serve as director of religious education for the state as they looked toward constituting into a state convention. The Sunday School Board, SBC, and the Kentucky and Ohio conventions joined the West Virginia Fellowship in providing salary and promotion expense. The work was under the leadership of the Ohio convention.

This new department was to be responsible for Sunday School, Training Union, music, Baptist Student Union, and church buildings promotion. Soon other responsibilities were added as the state work grew. These included stewardship promotion and publication of the state paper with the department director as editor.

The promotion of these programs was difficult since the churches involved were affiliated with four different states: Ohio, Kentucky, Virginia, and Maryland. It became evident that a program for the state churches was imperative in order to do the most for them. In 1967 the first state Sunday School Convention was conducted with 304 registered. Other state meetings followed this until the state now (1970) holds most of the normal meetings needed.

State Paper.—The first communications media was begun in 1958 by John Snedden as a newsletter sent irregularly to pastors and churches. From 1963–65 Walter Seats, pastor of Altizer Baptist Church in Huntington, served as editor. In 1965 Francis R. Tallant, director of religious education since 1964, was given the responsibility. It became a monthly publication with a circulation of 400 to 500. With the purchase of equipment in 1966, the style was changed to an 11 by 17-inch, eight-page paper by 1970. Its circulation grew to over 2,000, and it was published monthly as a service to the time of constituting into a state convention.

FRANCIS R. TALLANT

Missions and Evangelism Department.—New churches, organization of associations, and development of Southern Baptist work in West Virginia has been the aim of area superintendent of missions, John I. Snedden, since 1958. Election of missions committees, surveys for new work, and churches to sponsor new work have been encouraged. Summer student missionaries have conducted census, mission Vacation Bible Schools, and revivals; and new churches have been started. A net growth of 29 churches and 11 church-type missions occurred during 1958–69. By 1970 there were 50 churches.

L. B. Huston, Princeton, was elected as first state chairman of evangelism, Nov. 4, 1960. The pastors' fellowship meeting in 1962 had an evangelism conference emphasis, and simultaneous revivals were held that fall.

In 1966 a Department of Missions and Evangelism was authorized with John I. Snedden as director. The first statewide evangelism conference was held in 1968 at Westmoreland Baptist Church, Huntington. About 200 were present with over 600 attending the second conference held at Bailey Memorial Baptist Church, Bluefield, in 1969.

In 1962, the first year records were kept, the churches reported 481 baptisms and 7,202 members. By 1969 these had increased to 744 baptisms and 12,641 members.

Baptist Men's Work.—Neighboring states led in Brotherhood work among West Virginia Southern Baptists prior to 1969. That year John I. Snedden was named statewide leader. Eighteen churches had Brotherhood organizations before the year's end. The first Laymen's Witnessing Retreat was held in 1968, with more than 100 men attending.

JOHN I. SNEDDEN

Woman's Missionary Union.—The WMU in West Virginia was started by the executive board of the Baptist General Association of West Virginia. In Dec., 1967, they voted to ask Mrs. Elmo Cox to begin on a voluntary basis to lay the groundwork for the organizing of a state WMU. The women of the state met for the first time at Fairlea, W. Va., on Oct. 4, 1968. Plans were made to strengthen the existing organization in the churches and to assist in starting work in all other churches and missions.

MRS. ELMO COX

***WESTERN BAPTIST HOSPITAL.** From 1953 to 1969 the bed capacity increased from 117 to 214, including a five-bed cardiac care unit and an eight-bed intensive care unit. The hospital is well equipped, the most recent additions being the cobalt unit, the nuclear medicine department, and the electroencephalography department. The hospital operates a school for practical nursing and is affiliated with the Paducah Junior College in a two-year associate degree program for nursing. Since 1965 James V. Dorsett, Jr., has been the administrator, now called executive vice-president in the relationship with the Baptist Hospitals, Inc. (Kentucky).

H. L. DOBBS

WESTERN CONGO BAPTIST CONVENTION (cf. Belgian Congo Mission, Vol. I). The Western Congo Baptist Convention, formerly Belgian Congo Mission, is composed of eight fields. In spite of recent difficulties in the Congo, this work has grown steadily since 1956. One of the major emphases has been on stewardship training, which has resulted in the doubling of pledges by church members. The convention has plans for building a theological school at Kinshasha. Secondary schools suffer from a shortage of teachers. An intensive public health campaign has been waged in the Vanga area.

A formal agreement has been approved outlining the relationship of the convention with the American Baptist Foreign Mission Society in the Congo. When a legal charter has been granted, the properties held by the ABFMS will be turned over to the convention.

Statistics (1969): Missionaries, 100; national workers, 1,933; organized churches, 190; baptisms, 5,779; members, 99,600; seminaries and Bible schools, two; students, 83; schools and colleges, 208; students, 40,700; hospitals and dispensaries, 32; and patients, 131,712.

JAMES D. MOSTELLER

***WESTERN RECORDER.** Chauncey Rakestraw Daley (1918–) became editor of this Kentucky Baptist paper on July 1, 1957. George Raleigh Jewell (1898–) who came to the paper as secretary in 1926 retired in 1963. R. Gene Puckett was assistant editor, June 20, 1963, to July 30, 1966; George W. Knight, Sept. 1, 1967, to Sept. 19, 1968; and Bobby S. Terry, Sept. 26, 1968, to the present (1970). Robert L. Pogue who had been business manager since 1944 retired in July, 1966; George A. Price succeeded him in the same month. A print shop has been operated for many years; its contribution to the total operation was reevaluated in 1968 and the decision was to retain the print shop. New equipment was purchased and installed amounting to over $60,000. The *Western Recorder* depends upon four sources of income: subscriptions, advertising, profits from printing and the Cooperative Program. Circulation stands at about 60,000.

LEO T. CRISMON

WHEELER, THOMAS JEFFERSON (b. Clark County, Ill., Oct. 7, 1870; d. Robinson, Ill., Jan. 30, 1954). Rural preacher. The oldest son of farmer Benjamin F. and Margaret (White) Wheeler, he was converted at the age of 12 and became a charter member of the Mt. Olive Baptist Church in Palestine Association in 1883. He married Rose Ella Ralston on Dec. 31, 1891. They had no children but reared two foster daughters. Although limited to an elementary school education, Wheeler realized the value of formal training and urged young preachers to go to school. He began preaching in 1900 and was ordained by the Mt. Olive Church Apr. 24, 1901. During a ministry of more than 50 years, he was pastor of 17 churches in Palestine, Westfield, and Louisville associations. Most of his ministry was spent in the Palestine Association, where he was clerk for five years, moderator for 23 years, and associational missionary-pastor for 20 years. He was the first pastor of the West Union, Flat Rock, and Oblong churches, and led in the erection of the first buildings at West Union and Flat Rock. His longest pastorate was for 12 years at West Union. An active participant in the formation of the Illinois Baptist State Association, Wheeler served on the board of directors for 25 years. He also served as state evangelist for five years. One of his abiding interests was the collecting of historical materials. For more than 20 years, he was president of the Illinois Baptist State Association's Historical Society. He is author of the *History of Palestine Association of Baptists in Illinois* (1938), and is coauthor with Harmon Etter of the *History of the Illinois Baptist State Association* (1940). He is buried in the Mt. Olive Cemetery, near the church he joined as a charter member, where he preached his first sermon, and where he was pastor for four years.

H. LEE SWOPE

WHITE, (J. L.) JACOB LEE (b. Forsyth County, N. C., Sept. 6, 1862; d. Madison, Fla., Nov. 25, 1948). Pastor and denominational servant. His parents were John and Martha White; his father was a merchant and teacher. He graduated from Wake Forest College (B.A., 1886), which also awarded him a D.D. He received an LL.D. from Stetson University in 1934. He married Dovie Poston of Shelby, N. C., Sept. 22, 1886. They had nine children: Lee McBride, Hubert T., Mabel, W. Royal, J. L., Jr., Charles M., Russell C., Edward P., and Martha (Mrs. R. E. Kunkel). Upon graduating from Wake Forest he was called to First Church, Raleigh, N. C. (then the largest Southern Baptist church in North Carolina). In addition to other pastorates in North Carolina, Tennessee, and Texas, he was pastor of First Church, Macon, Ga., 1895–1906, and First Church, Miami, Fla., 1916–36 (renamed Central in 1936). The Mabel White Memorial Baptist Church of Macon, begun by him as a mission, bears the name of one of his daughters.

He was president of the Florida Baptist Convention, 1924 and 1925; chairman of the board of trustees of Bessie Tift College (now Tift

College), 1895–1905; member of the Foreign Mission Board, SBC, 1918–35; and trustee of Stetson University, 1925–47. He preached the Convention sermon at the 1934 Southern Baptist Convention in Washington, D. C., an event that was especially notable for the fact that his four minister sons sat on the platform with him as he preached. MARTHA WHITE KUNKEL

WHITESIDE, WILLIAM MARION (b. Gastonia, N. C., Dec. 18, 1876; d. Columbia, S. C., Apr. 13, 1963). Educated at Rutherfordton Military Academy and Wake Forest College, he received the honorary Doctor of Humanities from Furman University (1958). Whiteside married Cynthia Ella Wilson of Mills Springs, N. C. They had three sons and three daughters. Upon leaving college he became superintendent of Central Industrial Institute of Columbus, N. C., and served as pastor of four nearby Baptist churches. In 1904 he became pastor of Green Street Baptist Church in Spartanburg, S. C., where he established the Good Samaritan Hospital out of which grew the Spartanburg General Hospital and the present South Carolina Baptist Hospital. The following six years he was efficiency director of the state mission board, serving several churches in industrial areas of South Carolina. On Dec. 18, 1918, he became superintendent-treasurer of the South Carolina Baptist Hospital, where he served until retirement, May 12, 1957. A building at the hospital is named in his honor. During his administration the hospital grew from 80 to 225 beds with assets of $2,151,953. WILLIAM BOYCE

WHITFIELD, BENJAMIN (b. Vilanow, Wayne County, N. C., Jan. 13, 1800; d. Hinds County, Miss., June 13, 1872). The minister-planter most responsible for the acquisition of Mississippi College by the Baptists and its development during the years 1850–72.

Whitfield moved with his family to Clarke County, Ala., where he married his cousin Lucy Eliza Hatch, Aug. 21, 1821. The young couple moved to Society Ridge, Hinds County, Miss., in 1824. To them were born 12 children. He was a very successful businessman, accumulating 20,000 acres and 140 slaves.

He was an organizer in 1824 of the Union Church and its minister. He helped organize the Mississippi Baptist Convention in 1836 and was its president, 1839–43. He was active in all phases of convention life and was instrumental in securing the acceptance of Mississippi College when it was offered to the convention in 1850. Named to the board of trustees, he served as president, except for two short intervals, until his death.

Whitfield helped in securing an endowment of $100,000 and funds for the erection of a chapel in the prewar years. He planned a personal gift of $150,000, but the war wiped out his fortune and the college's endowment. The final week of his life he received the news that the debt accumulated by the college during the war and reconstruction had been paid.

BIBLIOGRAPHY: Emma Morehead W., comp., Theodore Marshall W., ed., *W., Bryan, Smith,* and *Related Families* (1948). R. A. MC LEMORE

WHITTINGHILL, DEXTER GOOCH (b. Hopkins County, Ky., Apr. 7, 1866; d. Mamaroneck, N. Y., May 31, 1956). Missionary in Italy (1900–39). He studied at Madisonville Normal School and Business College (B.S.), Bethel College, and Southern Baptist Theological Seminary (Th.D.). Before going to Italy, he was pastor of churches in Kentucky, Louisiana, and Texas. He was director of the Baptist Theological Seminary in Rome for 38 years and superintendent of Italian Mission approximately 35 years. Twenty volumes in Italian were a partial result of his industry and ability in editorial work. He married Susy Taylor, July 27, 1905. GEORGE W. SADLER

WICKER, JOHN JORDAN (b. Lynchburg, Campbell County, Va., Feb. 12, 1865; d. Richmond, Va., Mar. 17, 1958). Pastor, evangelist, educator. Son of Ambrose and Anne Maria (Reid) Wicker, he studied at Richmond College and Southern Baptist Theological Seminary (Th.G., 1895). He was awarded an honorary D.D. degree by the University of Richmond in 1916. He married Elizabeth Pumphrey in 1892 and had 'the following children: Elizabeth (Mrs. G. H. Mahon, Jr.), John Jordan, Jr., and James Caldwell.

His pastorates were: Mt. Hermon, Caroline County, Va., 1890; Kempsville, Va., 1891; Spurgeon Memorial, Norfolk, Va., 1892–93; Tabernacle, New Albany, Ind., 1894–95; Hampden, Baltimore, Md., 1895–1900; First, Trenton, N.J., 1900–05; Leigh Street, Richmond, Va., 1910–21. He did independent evangelistic work, 1905–10; 1921–30.

From 1930 to 1946 Wicker was president of Fork Union Military Academy, Fork Union, Va. Assuming responsibility for this school which was in financial straits, he ably led it to solvency.

He was a member, Virginia Baptist Board; vice-president, Baptist General Association of Virginia; member, Education Commission, SBC, and FMB, SBC. A contributor to denominational publications and various magazines, he wrote *The March of God* (1943) and *Into Tomorrow* (1946). He was also editor of the *Atlantic Baptist,* 1897–98, and associate editor of *The Commonweal,* 1898–1900. He is buried in Hollywood Cemetery, Richmond, Va. JOHN S. MOORE

WIELAND, PAUL ABBOTT (b. Louisville, Ky., Apr. 6, 1901; d. Trenton, Tenn., Aug. 29, 1959). Wieland was a graduate of Bethel College, Russellville, Ky.; Bible Institute, Fort Wayne, Ind.; and Southern Baptist Theological Seminary, Louisville, Ky. Union University gave him a D.D., 1942. On June 28, 1927, he married Donna Saunders of Rossville, Tenn. They had two daughters. His pastorates included First churches of Ghent, Ky., 1929–34, Bolivar, Tenn., 1934–42, Trenton, Tenn., 1942–57. He served as president of the Trenton Rotary Club and was active in Boy Scout work. He served on the executive committee of the Tennessee Baptist Convention; the Sunday School Board, SBC; the board of trustees of Union University and Baptist Memorial Hospital. He was president of the latter. FRANK S. GRONER

WILDS, AUBER JOHNSON (b. Water Valley, Miss., Jan. 17, 1885; d. Oxford, Miss., May 8, 1969). First full-time Training Union secretary, Mississippi Baptist Convention, Jan. 1, 1918–Jan. 1, 1953. He married Mary Lester Dent of Annieville, Ark., Aug. 2, 1911, and they had two daughters, Lucy Carleton and Mary Dent. The son of a merchant and seamstress, Wilds's education beyond elementary school at Oxford was obtained by personal study. He was a businessman from boyhood: newsboy, Western Union messenger, grocery store clerk, apprentice tailor, and proprietor of a tailor shop. He joined the Oxford Baptist Church at age 12, but was "just a church member" until he had a spiritual awakening 10 years later during the pastorate of Edward Stubblefield. At that time he began work in the BYPU. A neighbor, L. P. Leavell (*q.v.* Vol. II), BYPU secretary of the South, encouraged Wilds to do "special Christian work." In 1917 Wilds sold his business and became BYPU secretary of Mississippi on Jan. 1, 1918. Wilds traveled from Oxford, as there was no BYPU office at Baptist headquarters in Jackson. After the provision of an office years later, he continued to commute to Oxford between office or field responsibilities. Most of his nights in Jackson were spent in his office where he slept on a couch. Wilds wrote a weekly column on Training Union for the *Baptist Record* for more than 30 years. He was president of the Mississippi Baptist Convention in 1947 and 1948. Wilds was buried at Oxford, Miss.

RALPH B. WINDERS

WILKINSON, JAMES CUTHBERT (b. Brooks County, Ga., Oct. 26, 1880; d. Athens, Ga., Dec. 31, 1962). Pastor and educator. Son of William Lee and Mary F. (Bentley) Wilkinson, he was educated at Mercer University (1896–98) and the Southern Baptist Theological Seminary (Th.B., 1900). Mercer University and University of Georgia gave him the D.D. He married Rachel Thompson Baldwin, Oct. 23, 1902. Their two children died in infancy. Ordained by the Bellview Baptist Church, Pittsburgh, Pa., 1900, he was pastor in the following churches: Lakeland, Cherry Creek, Naylor, Eastern Heights, Columbus, 1912–14; Rose Hill, Columbus, 1914–18; First, Milledgeville, 1918–21; and First, Athens, 1921–49. Missionary for the Valdosta Association, he also served as president of the Oaklawn Baptist Academy. He taught at Georgia Military College, Milledgeville. Wilkinson was a member of the Georgia Mission Board, president of the Georgia Baptist Convention, 1944–46; chairman of the executive committee of the Georgia convention; chairman of the convention's education commission; trustee, Mercer University, Shorter College, Tift College; member of the board of directors, *The Christian Index;* member of the SBC Executive Committee; and chairman of the endowment committee, Georgia convention. He was a chaplain of the Grand Knight Templars for 17 years and president of the Athens Rotary Club.

CAREY T. VINZANT

***WILLIAM CAREY COLLEGE.** A fully accredited four-year liberal arts college in Hattiesburg, Miss., which offers four Bachelor degrees and the Master's degree in church music and in music education. The college is divided into three schools—Arts and Sciences, Nursing, and Music. It is affiliated with the Mississippi Baptist Convention and is Christian in its orientation. The campus covers 64 acres of pine-studded land on the south side of Hattiesburg. Nineteen buildings make up the college plant.

In 1956 J. Ralph Noonkester became president. During his administration accreditation by both the Southern Association of Colleges and Schools and the National Association of Schools of Music was obtained and maintained. Twelve major buildings have been added to the plant; the operating budget has grown from $218,000 to $1,500,000; property value has reached $5,500,000, student enrolment has grown from 374 to 881; the faculty has been enlarged and strengthened to include 58 professors, with 25 holding doctorates. J. RALPH NOONKESTER

***WILLIAM JEWELL COLLEGE.** Walter Pope Binns (*q.v.*), president for 19 years, retired in 1962. During his administration, the faculty-staff increased from 35 to 72, and departments from 12 to 17. His administration secured $250,000 endowment for each of six departments and erected buildings valued at $3,000,000. During his administration, the Missouri Baptist Convention increased its financial support from minimal support to $200,000 a year.

Minetry Jones served as interim president until H. Guy Moore assumed the presidency, June 30, 1962. Moore had been pastor of the Broadway Baptist Church, Ft. Worth, Tex. Moore resigned in Aug., 1968. Bobbie G. Olson served as acting president until William Holzapfel succeeded Olson as acting president in June, 1969.

In 1964 the college erected a new library with the capacity to house 250,000 volumes at a cost of $1,198,000. Other recent building projects by the college were: doubling the size of Yates College Union in 1965 at a cost of $900,000, adding a new wing on Semple Hall to house 70 women, and building a new residence hall to house 180 men.

The college added the Bachelor of Science

degree to its curriculum in 1968 in order to permit more specialization by students majoring in the departments of education, physical education, music education, and business administration. In the 1969–70 session, the college enrolment was 875, with a faculty of 71 full-time instructors. The endowment value was $6,000,000. DAVID O. MOORE

WILLIAMS, JOHN HOWARD (b. Dallas, Dallas County, Tex., July 3, 1894; d. Fort Worth, Tex., Apr. 20, 1958). Denominational statesman and seminary president. Williams was the third child in a family of 12 born to Daniel Paul and Emma Julia (Bozeman) Williams. While Williams was very young, the family moved to a farm in the Elam community near Dallas. In 1903 he was converted and baptized at the Pleasant Grove Baptist Church. Forced to drop out of school after the fourth grade due to an eye condition, he did not resume his education until he was called to preach at 16 years of age. He was ordained by the Cole Avenue Baptist Church, Sept. 13, 1914. After attending a vocational night school in Dallas, Williams enrolled at Southern Methodist University, 1915–18, then transferred to Baylor University which conferred on him the A.B. in 1918. He received the Th.M. from Southwestern Baptist Theological Seminary in 1922. Graduate study followed at Southern Baptist Theological Seminary, 1921–23. In 1932 Baylor University conferred upon him an honorary D.D.

Williams married Floy Ettys Kelly, June 23, 1920. They had five children: Martha Genne (Mrs. Frank F. Sandford), Carolyn Lee (Mrs. Joseph T. Mason), John Howard, Kelly Dan, and Floy Kate (Mrs. Marshall D. Woodruff). His education was interrupted by World War I, in which he served as chaplain with the First Army Corps in Europe. Among several pastorates in Kentucky, Oklahoma, and Texas, Williams served First Baptist, Amarillo, 1936–40, and First Baptist, Oklahoma City, 1940–46. Upon two different occasions, he was executive secretary of the Baptist General Convention of Texas, 1931–36 and 1946–53. From 1953 to 1958 Williams was Southwestern Baptist Theological Seminary's fourth president. He served his denomination in other capacities: president of the Baptist General Convention of Texas, 1938–39; president of the board of trustees of Oklahoma Baptist University; president of Texas Alcohol-Narcotics Education, Inc.; and member of the executive committee of the Baptist World Alliance, 1953. Williams was buried in Laurel Land Cemetery, Ft. Worth.

BIBLIOGRAPHY: H. C. Brown, Jr. and Charles P. Johnson (editors) *J. Howard Williams.* San Antonio, Texas: The Naylor Company, 1963.

W. R. ESTEP, JR.

WILLIAMS, SIMON OTHO (b. Golconda, Ill., Sept. 5, 1911; d. Harvey, Ill., Nov. 17, 1962). Pastor, public school teacher, evangelist, and state denominational employee. Son of minister Simon Elijah and Prussia (Barnes) Williams, he received the B.S. from Southern Illinois University in Carbondale, Ill., and attended Southwestern Baptist Theological Seminary, Ft. Worth, Tex. On June 15, 1932, he married Pearl Blanche Partain, who also attended Southwestern Seminary. They had three children: James D., Phyllis June (Mrs. Donald Hansard), and Sandra Sue (Mrs. Ezra Nichols).

Williams taught in the public schools of Pope and Saline counties in Illinois for 15 years. All of his pastorates were in Illinois, and included Baptist churches at Ledford, Ingraham Hill, Gaskins City, Dorrisville, Harrisburg, Zeigler, and Mt. Vernon. He was state evangelism and missions secretary for the Illinois Baptist State Association, 1949–51. From 1951–52, he was state evangelism and Brotherhood secretary for the Illinois Baptist State Association. At the time of his death, he was superintendent of the Baptist Children's Home at Carmi, Ill., an agency of the Illinois Baptist State Association. He served there, 1959–62. He served as assistant clerk and as a vice-president of the Illinois Baptist State Association and was widely used as an evangelist, particularly in Illinois. He is buried in Sunset Hill Cemetery, Harrisburg, Ill.

ROBERT J. HASTINGS

WILLIAMS, WALTER McADOO (b. Liberty, N. C., Mar. 1, 1891; d. Burlington, N. C., May 4, 1959). Son of Joel P. and Flora Anna (Spoon) Williams, he began working at 12 years of age as a sweeper in the Oneida Mills, Graham, N. C., and became one of North Carolina's leading industrialists and outstanding civic and religious leaders. On Jan. 2, 1919, he married Flonie Cooper of Graham, N. C. They had no children. After working for a time as manager of the E. M. Holt Plaid Mills of Burlington, in 1940 he became executive vice-president of Virginia Mills, Inc., at Swepsonville, N. C., where he served until his retirement. His business, civic, and religious interests were far-reaching. At various times he served as trustee of North Carolina Baptist Hospital, and at the time of his death was a trustee of Wake Forest College and Southeastern Baptist Theological Seminary. His magnanimous gifts, which were supported fully by his wife, included the Moller organ in Wait Chapel of Wake Forest University, and the Reuter organ in Binkley Chapel at Southeastern Seminary.

The high school in Burlington was named in his honor. He is buried in Pine Hill Cemetery, Burlington, N. C. JAMES H. BLACKMORE

WILLIAMSON, EDGAR STANLEY (b. Butte, Mont., Dec. 17, 1889; d. Little Rock, Ark., June 20, 1963). Sunday School secretary, Arkansas Baptist State Convention, and State Assembly director, 1937–60. He was graduated from the Bible School of Los Angeles, and attended Eugene Bible University (Oregon), and Southwestern Baptist Theological Seminary, Ft.

Worth, Tex. On Jan. 1, 1920, he married Rowena Ester Armstrong. They had one son, Edgar Stanley II. Ordained by the First Baptist Church, Houston, Tex., Williamson pioneered in serving churches in religious education. Five years prior to his state convention work he was pastor of the First Baptist Church of Paragould, Ark. Williamson enlisted one of the first state music secretaries among Southern Baptists in 1945, developed the district associational representative concept and a student summer field service program to assist rural churches. Ouachita Baptist University, Arkadelphia, Ark., awarded him the D.D. degree (1944). During his 23-year tenure Sunday Schools grew from 683 with 91,542 enrolled to 1,130 with 208,411 enrolled. In 1961 he wrote a guidebook for enlargement. LAWSON HATFIELD

WILLOCK, TOM (b. Topcok, between Nome and Golovin, Alaska, Mar. 15, 1877; d. Salcha River, near Fairbanks, Alaska, July 29, 1961). First Eskimo deacon in a Southern Baptist Church in Alaska. A native Alaskan Eskimo, he was reared by foster parents in sod igloos and tents along Alaska's western coast. At the age of 10 he first heard missionaries speak of Jesus. Denied formal education, he learned to fish, hunt, trap, pan for gold, and drive a dog team. On Thanksgiving Day, 1907, he married Elsie Pannick. Fourteen children were born of this marriage. He lived in several Eskimo villages on the Seward Peninsula and in the Kotzebue Sound area, herding reindeer, working in the gold mines, and hunting and fishing for a living. During World War II he moved to Fairbanks and worked as a carpenter. Converted during a revival conducted by C. Y. Dossey of the Home Mission Board, he served faithfully in the native Mission in Fairbanks, being elected as the first Eskimo deacon in any Southern Baptist Church in 1953. In 1960, at the age of 83, he began to learn to read. Upon learning the word "Jesus", he said, "Let me look at it again, the loveliest name in all the world." He was a constant inspiration to all who knew him. While pulling a fish net from the Salcha River, he was fatally stricken. RICHARD A. MILLER

WILSON, GEORGE S., JR. (b. Webster County, Ky., June 29, 1902, d. Grand Marais, Minn., July 3, 1966). Son of George S. and Virginia (McGill) Wilson, he was educated at Washington and Lee University and Washington and Lee Law School (LL.B., 1925). He married Virginia Queen of Owensboro, Ky., on Oct. 25, 1927. They had one son, George S., III. Wilson was president of the Kentucky Bar Association, 1948–49. He was a trustee of Georgetown College, 1956–66, and of Southern Baptist Theological Seminary, 1960–66. He served on various committees while a trustee at Southern, serving as chairman of the executive committee in 1964. A member of the First Baptist Church of Owensboro, he served as Sunday School superintendent, 1942–56, and deacon, 1936–66. He was a member of several social and professional fraternities. DUKE K. MC CALL

WINDERMERE BAPTIST ASSEMBLY. The Baptist state assembly in Missouri. It is located in a cove on the Niangua arm of the Lake of the Ozarks in Camden County, Mo., and consists of approximately 1,300 acres of land with about three miles of shoreline on the lake. It is owned and operated by the executive board of the Missouri Baptist Convention for the purpose of training and promotion of the missionary, evangelistic, educational, and benevolent work fostered by the convention.

In Sept., 1957, the board purchased Windermere from the Campbell-Taggart Associated Bakeries, which had used it as a vacation spot for its employees. The name Windermere was given to the grounds by one of the owners of the organization because of the resemblance of the area to the Windermere Lakes of England. Mr. and Mrs. Arthur H. Koehler were employed as managers of the assembly on Jan. 1, 1958. During the first summer of operation, two RA camps were held, with 40 boys attending each camp, using the 11 cabins in Spring Valley and Lakeview areas, and the old office building as kitchen, dining hall, and auditorium. The attendance in 1968 was approximately 12,000.

By the summer of 1959, 20 cabins were ready for use in the Cedar Grove area, along with the new auditorium, dining hall, and kitchen. In 1962 a motel was built, and the dining hall and auditorium were enlarged. The auditorium was named the Earl O. Harding Auditorium in July, 1964. The children's building was built in 1963, and the office, snack bar, and manager's residence were completed in 1965. Also, in 1965, 13 cabins were built in the Spring Valley area, and 14 in the Lakeview area for use in GA and RA camps and youth retreats.

Each summer assemblies are conducted by various departments of the convention as follows: GA and RA camps, Family Week, Adult and Youth Music Weeks, YWA. Conference, Sunday School Leadership Week, Church Training and Vocational Guidance Conference, Bible Conference, WMU Week, and Administration Conference, as well as many other conferences and retreats.

In addition to scheduled conferences, almost any time during the year Windermere facilities may be reserved by Baptist families, churches, associations, or other groups, since the auditorium, dining hall, and all cottages are air conditioned for summer and heated for winter. Two types of housing are available, with or without kitchens. Persons staying in housekeeping cottages may take meals in the dining hall. Boating, swimming, fishing, and hiking are part of the recreational program at Windermere.

Windermere is an assembly operated upon Christian principles. People come together for inspiration, fellowship, and to see the beautiful panorama. EARL O. HARDING

***WINDOW OF YWA, THE.** From 1956 to 1968, subscriptions to *The Window of YWA* increased from 34,510 to 70,838. The Idea Notebook, an eight-page promotional insert, was added in Sept., 1956. Laurella Owens became editor in 1957, succeeding Ethalee Hamric who became editor of *Royal Service*. In Oct., 1959, the name of the periodical was shortened to *The Window*. Publication of *The Window* ceased with the Sept., 1970, issue. *Contempo* became the new magazine for Baptist young women. DORIS DEVAULT

WINFIELD, ETHEL (b. Petersburg, Va., Dec. 16, 1887; d. Richmond, Va., Sept. 24, 1969). Assistant to corresponding secretary and secretary of Literature and Supplies Department, WMU, SBC. The oldest of 10 children born to Alexander Jefferson and Mary Watson (Larke) Winfield, Ethel made her profession of faith in Christ and joined a Baptist church when she was 13. She was educated at Southern Female College, Petersburg State Normal School (now Longwood College), Farmville, Va., and the University of Virginia, Charlottesville. She taught in Petersburg public schools before attending the WMU Training School, Louisville, Ky., for two years, graduating in 1916. In Sept., 1916, she became Young People's Secretary of Virginia WMU. Three years later she accepted the position of assistant to the corresponding secretary of WMU, SBC. One of her duties in this position was assisting with the work of the Literature and Supplies Department, which led to her being elected secretary of that department in 1923. From that date until her retirement in 1953, she served in both capacities. She assisted with correspondence, editing, and proofreading. At the same time she managed the rapidly expanding work of the Literature and Supplies Department, keeping watch for helpful materials and writing many leaflets herself. She lived in Birmingham, Ala., from 1921, when the WMU office moved there from Baltimore, until 1968, when she moved to Richmond, Va. She is buried in Petersburg, Va. DORIS DEVAULT

***WINGATE JUNIOR COLLEGE.** Budd E. Smith succeeded C. C. Burris (*q.v.*) as president in 1953. During Smith's administration, in the spring of 1956, Charles A. Cannon pledged a challenge gift of $100,000 to Wingate College trustees. The challenge was met in Jan., 1957, and since that time Cannon has given the college approximately $5,000,000. The support of other donors and of the Cooperative Program of the Baptist state convention has enabled Wingate to add the following facilities: Dickerson Infirmary, Lowery Recreation Center, Cannon Dormitory for Women, Tucker Dormitory for Women, Belk Dormitory for Women, Holbert Dormitory for Men, Bennett Dormitory for Women, Hendricks Dormitory for Men, Bivens-Perry Dormitory for Men, Stewart Hall for Men, Helms Hall for Men, Sanders-Sikes Gymnasium and Physical Education Plant, Austin Memorial Auditorium, Laney Lecture and Recital Hall, Burnside-Dalton Fine Arts Center, Ethel K. Smith Library, Budd E. Smith Science Building, J. Herbert Bridges Business Administration Building (with a computer center), W. T. Harris Dining Hall, Roy L. Holbrook Administration Building, faculty apartments, new president's home, dean's home, and several faculty homes. The holdings in land have increased from 35 acres to 235 acres.

Along with the physical plant expansion the curricula, quality of faculty, and quality of students have improved. In 1969 there were 90 faculty members representing graduate studies in over a hundred graduate schools of America and Europe. The student body has grown from 487 in 1955 to 1,607 in 1969, representing 20 states and 12 foreign countries. The college curricula now include all basic liberal arts preprofessional programs as well as engineering, textiles, and computer science. From 1956 to 1968, several scholarship programs were inaugurated, and the first endowed professorships established. BUDD E. SMITH

WISCONSIN BAPTIST FELLOWSHIP. Composed of three associations in Wisconsin which are sponsored by and affiliated with the Baptist General Convention of Texas. In 1969 the total membership in 40 churches and missions was 4,222. The Wisconsin Fellowship publishes a four-page bulletin monthly. DAVIS C. WOOLLEY

WOLFINBARGER, PETER ABRAHAM (b. Irvine, Ky., Oct. 3, 1927; d. Franklin, Ohio, Feb. 10, 1969). Son of C. N. Wolfinbarger, he became a Christian during a revival at the First Baptist Church, Irvine, in 1945. He married Pauline Flynn, Jan. 3, 1948. They had three sons. He attended the Campbellsville College Extension in Irvine. Wolfinbarger served as missionary in Lee County, Ky., pastor of two Baptist churches in Kentucky: Salem in Estill County and Panola in Madison County. The First Baptist Church, Miamisburg, Ohio, called him as pastor of the Pennyroyal Mission, Oct., 1957. The small mission was meeting in the garage of one of the members. The new mission was constituted into the Pennyroyal Baptist Church. At the time of Wolfinbarger's death the church had approximately 400 members and adequate church buildings. His denominational service consisted of serving as moderator of the Miami Valley Association for two years, and the state executive board. The 1969 Miami Valley Association minutes are dedicated to him. JOSEPH F. HUNT

***WOMAN'S AMERICAN BAPTIST FOREIGN MISSIONARY SOCIETY.** See AMERICAN BAPTIST FOREIGN MISSIONARY BOARDS.

WOMAN'S COMMITTEE OF SOUTHERN SEMINARY, THE. The Woman's Committee of Southern Seminary was founded for the purpose of providing a direct channel for participation of women in the work of the Southern Baptist

Theological Seminary, Louisville, Ky. Interested women join as regular, sustaining, patron, and life members.

In Apr., 1961, President Duke McCall asked Mrs. Ellis A. Fuller, Sr., the wife of the past president, to organize and be executive secretary of this auxiliary group. In Oct., 1961, the charter membership meeting was held. More than 1,500 women have been members since "The Woman's Committee" was organized.

Its objectives are: (1) prayer concern for the seminary family; (2) scholarships: 10 $500 scholarships have been awarded to qualified women students needing financial aid; (3) campus projects: a projects committee discovers and recommends opportunities for special service within the seminary community, such as equipping a women's lounge, establishing a prayer and meditation room, refurnishing consultation rooms for mission board leaders, providing new equipment for furloughing missionary apartments, assisting with establishment of a preschool nursery for wives who wish to take seminary classes, helping with a clothing swap shop for students, working with the student missions committee in securing rooms for college students attending the Student Missions Conference, and expressing personal concern for students in crisis situations. ELIZABETH B. FULLER

WOMAN'S MISSIONARY SOCIETY. Until 1970, the missionary organization for women in Southern Baptist churches. An integral part of WMU history, local missionary societies for women preceded the organization of Woman's Missionary Union. When representatives of these societies met in 1888 to form a general organization, the name first chosen for the union was "Woman's Mission Societies." In 1890 the name of the general organization was changed to "Woman's Missionary Union," and the name "Woman's Missionary Society" was retained as the name of the local church organization for women.

In the WMU headquarters reorganization of 1957, the WMS Department was established as one of the four departments in the Promotion Division. Margaret Bruce, WMU Young People's Secretary since 1948, became the first director of the WMS Department. Ethalee Hamric was elected editor of *Royal Service* and WMS materials. In 1958 Elaine Dickson came to WMU as promotion associate in the WMS Department.

By 1959–60 the WMS Leadership Course for class or individual study had been developed. The first WMS manual was published in 1960. The challenge of more than one WMS in a church was offered as an aid to enlistment and brought into existence alternate plans for the organization of WMS in a church: Plan A, for churches with only one WMS; and Plan B, for churches with more than one WMS. A simplified organization plan for use in small churches was also introduced.

Following the 1965 reorganization of WMU, the WMS director became a part of the Field Services Department; the editor became part of the Editorial Services Department; and the promotion assistant became assistant to the Promotion Divison director.

In 1968 separate officers for WMS and WMU in a church were promoted. That same year an entirely new plan of organization, featuring mission groups rather than circles, was introduced. The 1969 report revealed 23,731 societies with a total of 588,886 members. In Oct., 1970, WMS members became members of Baptist Young Women or Baptist Women. DORIS DEVAULT

***WOMAN'S MISSIONARY UNION.** "Changing" is the most descriptive word that could be applied to WMU for the period 1955–70. Yet, the fundamental purposes of WMU have remained unchanged since its beginning. The changes that came during these years were efforts to keep the WMU program contemporary.

Mrs. George R. Martin completed her presidency in 1956. During her 11 years as president she served on various Southern Baptist committees, completed the reorganization of the Women's Department of the Baptist World Alliance, and led in the organization of continental women's unions.

Mrs. R. L. Mathis, Waco, Tex., was elected president in 1956. That same year WMU adopted recommendations of a firm of management consultants be employed to make an organization study of WMU to determine the most effective way to accomplish WMU purposes. Aims for Advancement were also adopted, replacing Standards of Excellence which had guided WMU organizations in churches since 1911.

Mrs. Mathis inherited with her office the responsibility for completing the transfer of Royal Ambassadors to the Brotherhood Commission and Carver School of Missions and Social Work to the Southern Baptist Convention, both of which were completed in 1957. In that year, also, WMU began promoting the organization of night circles in addition to Business Women's Circles, and participated in World Missions Year. The previous year WMU had clarified its invitation to the entire church to participate in the weeks of prayer and the accompanying offerings.

In Jan., 1957, Juliette Mather, editorial secretary, retired after 35 years in this position and in her former position as young people's secretary. Fulfilling her youthful dream of foreign mission service, she worked in Japan and later in Taiwan.

By Oct., 1957, the recommendations of the management consultants had been studied and modified; the bylaws had been revised; and reorganization of WMU was effected. The new organization called for two divisions under the administration of the executive secretary: a Business Division and a Promotion Division, with a director of each responsible to the executive secretary. La Venia Neal, treasurer since

NEW ORLEANS BAPTIST THEOLOGICAL SEMINARY (*q.v.*). *Top:* J. M. Frost Building of the School of Religious Education is typical of New Orleans architecture with its wrought-iron columns, chimneys, and azalea garden. *Bottom:* Traditional New Orleans wrought-iron gates lead into central area of campus. Roland Q. Leavell Chapel in background.

1953, was elected director of the Business Division.

Included in the Promotion Division were four age-level departments: Woman's Missionary Society, Young Woman's Auxiliary, Girls' Auxiliary, and Sunbeam Band. Mrs. William McMurry (*q.v.*), secretary of the Department of Missionary Fundamentals, was elected director of the Promotion Division.

The reorganization created the new positions of director and promotion associate in each of the four age-group departments and made each department responsible for its own magazine. Professional leadership was expanded in 1958 to include an administrative assistant and a production manager. Mrs. J. H. Godwin, who had been with WMU since 1930, became administrative assistant. Mrs. Clara G. Alston was employed as production manager in 1959, and upon retirement in 1966 was succeeded by Mrs. Ben Bowers.

To provide space for the enlarged organization and additional personnel, two floors were added to the headquarters building purchased in 1951. The work was completed in 1960, giving the building five working floors.

In 1958 the Southern Baptist Convention approved the recommendation of the Committee on Total Program that WMU should be continued as an auxiliary to the SBC, that WMU should continue to perform its present functions, and that the work of WMU should be related to that of SBC agencies through the Inter-Agency Council.

From 1959 to 1962 participation in the Baptist Jubilee Advance and preparation for the observance of WMU's 75th Anniversary gave WMU an added forward thrust. As early as 1957 WMU leaders began planning and setting goals for these two historic events. In support of these goals WMU produced a series of books on WMU aims and developed annual emphases. In addition to related book studies, WMU promoted a soul-winning visitation program in 1958–59; launched a four-year leadership training program in 1959–60; released a stewardship play in 1960–61; and promoted church extension and enlistment in 1961–62.

Also in 1961–62 the 75th Anniversary goals were launched through a Convention-wide promotional conference involving all state WMU leadership, both employed and volunteer. State WMU organizations conducted similar conferences. Lines of communication with associational and local WMU leaders were strengthened by initiating two quarterly bulletins—one for local presidents and the other for associational presidents.

Prayer retreats were introduced into the plans of WMU as preparation for the 75th Anniversary. National retreats for Convention-wide leadership and state leaders, state WMU retreats, and associational retreats were held. The latter included not only women but also members of YWA and GA.

The year 1962–63 marked the 75th Anniversary of WMU and the culmination of the five-year Baptist Jubilee Advance emphasis. The emphasis that year on World Missions gave harmony to WMU's historic emphasis on study, prayer, giving, witnessing, and enlisting persons of all ages in missions.

The five sessions of the Diamond Anniversary Annual Meeting focused attention on the progress of Southern Baptist missions at home and abroad. WMU's historical pageant "Laborers Together with God," by Ted Perry, was presented in the opening session of the SBC.

In 1963 Mrs. William McMurry retired as director of the Promotion Division and was succeeded by Mrs. R. L. Mathis. Mrs. Robert Fling, wife of the pastor of First Baptist Church, Cleburne, Tex., and since 1957 recording secretary of WMU, was elected to succeed Mrs. Mathis as president.

The SBC elected Mrs. Mathis second vice-president in 1963. She was the first woman elected to a Convention office.

When Mrs. Fling assumed office, wide-reaching changes were already in motion. In 1962 the SBC Executive Committee had asked if WMU desired to have its Program Statement prepared, adopted, and incorporated in the SBC Organization Manual along with Convention agencies. In response the WMU Executive Board voted in Jan., 1963, to engage in the programing process. This action necessitated a comprehensive study of WMU's reason for existence, contemporary programs, and relationships to Convention agencies. This study was based on research previously done for Alma Hunt's *History of Woman's Missionary Union* (1964).

Like her predecessor, Mrs. Fling accepted the challange of change, leading WMU through currents of change to higher levels of achievement and closer ties with the denomination. A full partner in the new planning process, WMU had representatives meeting regularly with leaders of other church program organizations to correlate planning. WMU participated in developing task statements for all agencies of the Convention; in developing state strategy materials, through which state and Convention assistance to churches was made available; and in the preparation and promotion of the Life and Work Curriculum materials. Through the Inter-Agency Council, WMU participated in long-range planning for the denomination's 70 Onward emphasis.

In 1965 WMU reorganized its Promotion Division to correspond more nearly to the organization of other Convention agencies with editorial and field services responsibilities. Betty Jo Corum (*q.v.*) joined the staff as director of the newly created Editorial Services Department, and Billie Pate was named director of the new Field Services Department. Elaine Dickson became assistant to the Promotion Division director, also a new position.

The WMU Program Statement was approved by the WMU Executive Board on May 21, 1966, and by the SBC on May 24, 1966. The statement recognizes the place WMU has earned in the churches and in the Convention and reiterates the purpose for which WMU was organized: "to promote Christian missions through the organizations of Woman's Missionary Union in the churches of the Southern Baptist Convention."

To accomplish this objective, the Program Statement assigned to WMU two programs: The Program of WMU Promotion, and The Program of Supporting Services for the Program of WMU Promotion.

The foundational concepts and principles on which the WMU program rests are interpreted in *The Woman's Missionary Union Program of a Church* (1966) by Marie (Mrs. R. L.) Mathis and Elaine Dickson.

Further expansion of the Promotion Division staff was voted in 1967. June Whitlow was added as WMU consultant in church WMU administration and research, and Mrs. Lee N. Allen was transferred to the position of WMU consultant in press relations.

The WMU Executive Board voted in Jan., 1966, to replace the term "community missions" with "mission action," a term to be used by WMU and Brotherhood to connote a broader concept, but including the concepts and activity inherent in community missions. Accordingly, the WMU staff with the help of Home Mission Board personnel began designing mission action guides for areas of specialized mission action.

During 1966 WMU completed design work on new organization plans and materials to be released for use in churches Oct. 1, 1968. The plans reinforced the concept that WMU is one part of a total church program and provided for a simpler and more flexible church WMU organization. Features of the new plans were fewer officers, separate WMU and WMS officers, consistency in terminology, groups formed on the basis of interest to replace circles in WMS, and achievement guides to replace Aims for Advancement for all age-level organizations.

Through 36 state and 905 associational meetings the new plans and materials were interpreted to 75,630 leaders in 1968.

In the summer of 1967 WMU shared with the Brotherhood Commission in planning, promoting, and conducting the first World Missions Conference, an annual event until 1970. During the same period WMU was asked by the Convention's Denominational Emphasis Committee to organize a prayer partner project to support the Crusade of the Americas. Though WMU took the initiative in planning, produced the materials, and did the staff work, details of the project (called Pact) were developed in cooperation with the Home and Foreign Mission Boards. Both boards promoted the project and helped finance it.

A total of 1,120,604 fliers for Pact were printed in English, Spanish, and Portuguese. As a result of the distribution of these fliers, requests for prayer partners were received from 49 states and 24 APO addresses and assignments were made.

In 1968–69 WMU completed plans for recasting the WMU program into the New Grouping-Grading system adopted by the Convention for use beginning in Oct., 1970. Since the grouping-grading plan called for a children's division for ages 6–11, which embraced three years of the Sunbeam Band ages and three years of the Royal Ambassador ages, WMU and Brotherhood worked out plans for the transfer of responsibility for the missionary education of boys six through eight to the Brotherhood Commission.

Approval was given to *Dimension,* a new periodical for WMU officers, and to names for the age-level organizations and periodicals to begin in Oct., 1970, as follows:

DIVISION	ORGANIZATION NAME	PERIODICAL
Adult	Baptist Women	*Royal Service*
	Baptist Young Women	*Contempo*
Youth	Acteens	*Accent* and *Accent,* Leader Edition
Children's	Girls in Action	*Discovery* (for members) *Aware* (for leaders)
Preschool	Mission Friends	*Start* (for leaders)

In 1969 Mrs. R. L. Mathis was once again elected president, succeeding Mrs. R. Fling. Subsequently June Whitlow was promoted to Promotion Division director and Adrianne Bonham was elected WMU consultant in church WMU administration and program design.

In 1970 Mary Hines was promoted to director of Field Services to fill the vacancy created by the resignation of Billie Pate. Adrianne Bonham was elected director of Editorial Services following the death of Betty Jo Corum.

BIBLIOGRAPHY: *History of Woman's Missionary Union,* Alma Hunt (1964). BETTY BROWN

***WOMAN'S MISSIONARY UNION, Auxiliary to the Alabama Baptist Convention.** The first WMU houseparty for leadership training was held at Judson College in June, 1956. A quarterly bulletin, edited by state staff was begun in 1961, as well as an annual *Guide for Associational and District Officers.* In Mar., 1964, the 75th anniversary meeting was held in the Municipal Auditorium, Birmingham. Highlight of this meeting was the release of the history, *Women of Vision,* by Hermione D. (Mrs. Lamar) Jackson. To provide decentralized camping for young people, a WMU camp was built in 1965, consisting of 16 buildings, at the state assembly grounds, Shocco Springs, and adding a staff house in 1966. Continued mission teaching and praying has resulted in increased giving: 1954, Lottie Moon Christmas Offering was $170,863.37, in 1967, $884,297.88; 1955, Annie Armstrong Easter Offering was $79,182.54, in 1968, $320,572.60. In 1968 WMU had 9,380 organizations with 119,013 members. State presidents were: Mrs. Andrew M. Coltharp, 1956–57; Mrs. Albert J. Smith, 1957–63, Mrs. Alex A. Hall, 1963–68; and Mrs. J. W. Triplitt, 1968– . MARY ESSIE STEPHENS

***WOMAN'S MISSIONARY UNION, Auxiliary to the Arizona Southern Baptist Convention.** As the Arizona Southern Baptist Convention spread into adjoining western states organizing churches, so did the work of WMU. In 1955 a new convention was organized in Colorado. At that time Arizona WMU leaders helped to organize the Colorado State WMU organization. Again in 1964 Arizona WMU leaders helped to organize the Idaho-Utah State WMU organization.

Arizona WMU presidents serving since 1955 include: Mrs. Wiley Henton, Mrs. H. E. Martin, and Mrs. R. Q. Kinney. Executive secretaries have been Mrs. Charles Griffin, Miss Almarine Brown, and Miss Mary Jo Stewart, who came to Arizona in Mar., 1969.

Annual camps for Girls' Auxiliary and Royal Ambassadors and house parties for Young Woman's Auxiliary had been established before 1956. (In 1957 the RA work was transferred to the Brotherhood Department.) In the next decade the Arizona WMU plan of work included Sunbeam Band and WMU camps, GA Queens' Courts, prayer retreats, and an increased attendance during WMU week at Glorieta. The first WMU house party was held in 1968 at the Safari Hotel in Scottsdale.

The Ruby Anniversary of Arizona WMU celebrating 40 years of progress, 1928–68, was climaxed with the publication of a new history book, *God's Highway,* by Mrs. G. D. Crow, the third history written and published by WMU. From six organizations in 1928, the work has grown to 730 organizations with a total membership of 7,634 in 1969. This shows an encouraging increase despite the loss of churches with WMU organizations to the new state conventions and the RA chapters which were turned over to the Brotherhood. MRS. G. D. CROW

***WOMAN'S MISSIONARY UNION, Auxiliary to the Baptist Convention of Maryland.** Since 1950, a major project of this state organization has been the development of a camping program. In that year the union purchased a campsite of approximately 150 acres in Harford County with funds given to the union in the estate of Mrs. Eugene Levering, Jr. The WMU named the camp Wo-Me-To (Women and Men of Tomorrow). An average season will include 35 or more church retreats, three RA Camp weeks, five GA weeks, WMU, WMS, YWA, and Sunbeam Band days, two weeks of music camp plus a number of church, RA, associational, or Sunday School picnics. At least 4,000 persons have attended one of the events held each year at the camp for a number of years.

The union has produced four publications since 1958. It published each at a time when the publication would give significant promotion to some phase of the work. In 1959 Blanche Sydnor White wrote *Our Heritage,* history of WMU, 1742–58. The union published *The Story of Camp Wo-Me-To* for the 15th anniversary of the camp. Mrs. Eunice Hayes Ruark and Mrs. J. A. Bearden wrote it. The WMU of Maryland published *Daughter of the Covenant, Edith Campbell Crane, 1876–1933,* by Claris I. Crane, as a part of Maryland's recognition of the 75th anniversary of WMU, SBC. *Far Above Rubies,* written by a group of authors, presents brief biographies of early WMU leaders.

A marker placed on the building at 10 E. Fayette Street, Baltimore states: "First Headquarters Woman's Missionary Union, Auxiliary to Southern Baptist Convention, 1888–1963, was established on this site in 1888 under the leadership of Miss Annie W. Armstrong, first corresponding secretary. Its missionary efforts through prayer and gifts reach around the world. Placed by WMU of Md. (organized in 1871) on March 26, 1963, in recognition of the 75th Anniversary of WMU, SBC." The marker is bronze with the WMU emblem embossed in the left upper corner.

In 1961 the WMU of Maryland began preparation for the celebration of its centennial. They projected plans called "A decade of Dedication" to climax in the 1971–72 observance of the 100th anniversary of the organization of the first woman's work on a state level.

The state mission offering is named for Kathryn Barnes who was the executive secretary from 1921–46. The offering is churchwide in its promotion and includes many mission projects not otherwise supported. One of its features is a scholarship program for young ladies. In addition to granting the scholarships in this offering, the union has the privilege of awarding three endowed memorial scholarships annually beginning in 1970: BWC, Hattie Wilson Norwood, and Captain and Mrs. John T. Willing.

Beginning in 1958, the WMU assisted with the work in the Northeastern states affiliated with Maryland.

See also MARYLAND BAPTIST UNION ASSOCIATION, VOL. II. JOSEPHINE CARROLL NORWOOD

***WOMAN'S MISSIONARY UNION, Auxiliary to the Baptist Convention of New Mexico.** In 1957 the New Mexico WMU under the leadership of Eva R. Inlow, executive secretary, and Bernice Elliott, youth director, was conducting an effective program.

In Mar., 1961, the permanent building program for Inlow Youth Camp was approved by the WMU executive board and board of trustees. Plans were outlined for the new cabins. Promotional plans were made and directed by Miss Inlow and Miss Elliott.

In Aug., 1961, Miss Elliott resigned to become the promotion associate in pioneer areas for WMU and the Home Mission Board of the Southern Baptist Convention. She had served faithfully for more than 17 years as the New Mexico WMU youth director. On Nov. 30, 1961, Eva Inlow, executive secretary, retired after 26 years of faithful service to God and New Mexico WMU. She was succeeded by Vanita M. Baldwin of Florida. In Mar., 1962, Sarah Lett of Florida was elected youth director and served until June, 1966.

From 1962 through 1969 the tasks of New Mexico WMU continued as the program of work: teach missions, lead persons to participate in missions, provide organization and leadership for special mission projects of the churches and missions, and provide and interpret information regarding the work of the church and denomination.

Leadership training was a constant effort of work conducted by the state WMU staff and elected WMU officers. The annual convention was a highlight. The Home and Foreign Mission Graded Series were promoted to precede each of the Weeks of Prayer for home and foreign missions. The observances of the State Season of Prayer, Week of Prayer for Foreign Missions, and Week of Prayer for Home Missions were planned and promoted. Mission action projects were suggested to church WMU organizations.

Missionary education for the children in Sunbeam Band, girls in GA organizations, and young women in YWA organizations across the state were guided by dedicated leaders and directors.

In Mar., 1968, Ruby Hawthorn of Arkansas was elected as youth director. Mrs. Thelma House has served as office secretary since Nov., 1956.

VANITA BALDWIN

WOMAN'S MISSIONARY UNION. Auxiliary to the Baptist Convention of New York. It is interesting to note that WMU work, in the early beginnings of development of Southern Baptist advance in the Northeast, began with the observance of a Week of Prayer for Foreign Missions at the LaSalle Baptist Church, Niagara Falls, N. Y., in Dec., 1954. This church organized the first WMU and Sunbeams on Oct. 19, 1955. The Girls' Auxiliary was started one month later and the groups met for some time in homes since they had no church building.

In 1957 Southern Baptists entered New York City, and WMU was begun within a few weeks. A meeting was held Nov. 19, 1957, in the home of Mrs. Kermit McCarter, Chatham, N. J., for the purpose of organizing the work in the northeastern area. About 12 women came to this meeting, and so great was their enthusiasm they offered to hold several offices each to bring a WMU work into being. Mrs. Dean Styers became the first president. During the Lottie Moon Christmas Offering that December, 12 women with tears of deep emotion brought $305.14, though at that time they were not organized into a church and had no place of worship of their own.

The Week of Prayer for Home Missions Offering the following March was brought to the meeting at the home of Mrs. Bill McIlwain of Morristown, N. J., and amounted to $177.

Since all of the early work in the New England states was sponsored by the Manhattan Church, Mrs. Paul James made long trips to chapels in distant areas to encourage women in their mission organizations. In more than one case the work of the women in missions and chapels led to rapid growth, and these led in reaching out and forming new units. As a result, the first "Area WMU Meeting" composed of Woman's Missionary Societies in northern New Jersey, Manhattan, and Long Island met at the 8th Avenue YWCA in 1957, with 25 present.

It was during the 1968 Week of Prayer for Foreign Missions that Paula Meadows of New Jersey dedicated her life to missionary service, and Chaplain and Mrs. Ted Hagen of Long Island gave themselves for missionary service. The Lottie Moon Christmas Offering goal at that time was $500, but $814 came in, and this ranked eighth in the amounts given in the Maryland Convention which sponsored most of the Northeastern work at that time.

The work upstate was growing under the leadership of Mrs. Arthur Walker of Buffalo. Erie Baptist Church (now Amherst Baptist) women were observing Week of Prayer and organizing new WMU organizations. Work was extended to Syracuse with the organizing of Central Baptist Church in 1957. From this point, WMS organizations were begun in Rome, Potsdam, Endicott, and Elmira. Frontier Association elected Mrs. Henry Johnson as first WMU president on Oct. 17, 1961, and Central Association elected Mrs. John Tollison, Nov. 11, 1961. The GA Houseparty was held at Rome, May 31, 1962, with Mrs. A. L. Kirkwood of Ohio directing.

On Apr. 29, 1960, the Northeast Baptist Association was formed, composed of all churches and chapels in the New York area, northern New Jersey, and the six New England states. Mrs. Paul James was the first WMU president.

That fall, because of the great distances involved in attending the meetings, the Northeastern Baptist Association was divided into smaller associations. The first meeting in New York City was held Oct. 7, 1960, and Mrs. David A. Morgan was the first WMU president. She was followed by Mrs. Kermit McCarter and Mrs. W. W. Boisture. Miss Josephine Norwood and staff of Maryland convention contributed much in leadership and guidance.

The WMU of the Baptist Convention of New York was organized Sept. 25, 1969, in Syracuse, N. Y., with Mrs. Hartmon Sullivan of Niagara Falls elected the president. The first annual meeting was held at Lincoln Avenue Baptist Church, Endicott, N. Y., Apr. 16–17, 1970.

MARY O. KNAPTON

***WOMAN'S MISSIONARY UNION, Auxiliary to Baptist General Association of Virginia.**

Youth.—In 1958 the union expanded its youth organization staff to include a secretary for each division: Sunbeam Bands, Girls' Auxiliary, and Young Woman's Auxiliary. The 1,064 Royal Ambassador chapters with 9,580 members were transferred to the Brotherhood in the same year. The WMU has continued its work with Baptist students by giving financial support to student secretaries in four Baptist schools: Westhampton, Intermont (until 1966), and Averett colleges, and Oak Hill Academy. The union has given scholarship aid to Baptist young women preparing for church-related vocations and missionary service. It also extended aid to youth from American Indian Baptist churches in Virginia and from state mission areas. Thirty scholarships were granted in 1955. Virginia WMU operates three summer camps located at Virginia Beach, Marion, and in Albemarle County. Camp attendance in 1968 was 2,658. Late in 1968 the union decided to purchase property in Mathews County for relocation of the camp formerly at Virginia Beach.

State Missions.—In 1956 Virginia WMU launched work with Spanish-speaking migrants on the Eastern Shore of the state. The union established a Good Will Center in 1959 at Clincho, Dickenson County, where mission Vacation Bible Schools had been conducted previously. Later the work of the center was extended to include weekday activities in Trammel. In 1966 another center was opened at Manassas. The Powell River Association assumed responsibility for direction of the George Braxton Taylor Good Will Center in Lee County in 1968. The Interracial Department sponsored the Department of Christian Leadership and Missions at Virginia Union University, Richmond, Va., through 1967, providing seven missionaries for Liberia, several home missionaries and workers for local Negro Baptist churches, and a camp for Negro girls in Chesterfield County.

General.—In 1956 Mrs. Lester L. Knight of Portsmouth completed 10 years of service as president of the Virginia WMU. She was succeeded by Mrs. O. C. Hancock of Roanoke who served until 1964 when Mrs. E. S. Stratton of Afton was elected. Carrie S. Vaughan became the fifth salaried secretary in 1958 following the resignation of Ellen Douglas Oliver in 1957. The Virginia WMU provided funds for a wing to the Boatwright Memorial Library, University of Richmond, which was dedicated in 1955. This building houses the collection of the Virginia Baptist Historical Society. In 1962 the Union moved its offices to the new Virginia Baptist Building. The number of associational WMU organizations increased from 36 to 44 between 1959 and 1969. The 5,791 societies for women and young people gave $2,242,358 in 1968.

ELLEN DOUGLAS OLIVER

***WOMEN'S MISSIONARY UNION, Auxiliary to Baptist General Convention of Texas.** Increased promotion has been given to the young people's missionary organizations with state leadership for each of the organizations. Amelia Morton served as young people's secretary, 1953–56, and in 1956 she became YWA director following her marriage to J. Ivyloy Bishop. Other YWA directors have been Elaine Dickson, 1957–59; Mary Jane Nethery, 1959–65; and Katharine Bryan 1965– . Robert B. Chapman began work as RA director in 1953. In 1957 the Brotherhood assumed the total promotion of RA work. The GA directors have been Mrs. Tex (Dollie) Culp, 1956–59, and Joy Phillips, 1959–66. Joyce Gill served as Sunbeam Band director, 1957–69.

Eula Mae Henderson, executive secretary-treasurer, 1947– , also served as young people's secretary in 1947. Noemi Cuevas was language missions WMU director, 1965–68.

The following have served as state president: Mrs. Clem (Ethel) Hardy, 1955–61, Mrs. Bert (Leila) Black, 1961–63, four district presidents (Mrs. R. L. Brown, Mrs. H. C. Hunt, Mrs. I. E. Lamberth, and Mrs. Joe T. King) assumed the responsibilities of state president in 1964 following the resignation of Mrs. Black due to health reasons, Mrs. C. J. (Ophelia) Humphrey, 1964–68, and Mrs. H. C. (Inez) Hunt 1968– .

Beginning in 1956 the state mission offering included an allocation for scholarships to Texas Baptist colleges for worthy Latin American students. A similar program for Negro students was initiated in 1966. The Rio Grande Mission Thrust was launched in 1967, and for a three-year period received major emphasis from the Mary Hill Davis Offering as well as the personal involvement of adults and young people.

EULA MAE HENDERSON

WOMAN'S MISSIONARY UNION, AUXILIARY TO THE BAPTIST STATE CONVENTION OF MICHIGAN. See MICHIGAN, BAPTIST STATE CONVENTION OF.

***WOMAN'S MISSIONARY UNION, Auxiliary to the Georgia Baptist Convention.** The executive board, enlarged its staff in 1955 to include three youth directors, adding a WMS director in 1959. Mrs. C. O. Smith, president, 1957–61, succeeded Mrs. John I. Alford, serving during two Georgia anniversary celebrations: the central committee's 80th and WMU's 75th. "Great Was the Company," a pageant by Mrs. Albert Howard, highlighted the 1958 annual meeting, and the 1960 meeting featured *Wrought of God,* the WMU history by Mrs. Frank S. Burney (*q.v.*). Presidents Mrs. Ernest L. Miller, 1961–66, and Mrs. J. J. Clyatt, 1966– , led WMU in transitional years. Janice Singleton, executive secretary-treasurer since 1939, retired Sept. 1, 1963. She was succeeded by Dorothy Pryor, former YWA director, 1955–59, and WMS director since 1959. The Janice Singleton seminary scholarship for potential WMU vocational workers was established in 1967.

In 1964 seminary loan scholarships became gifts; college scholarships were available for C. M. Pearson, National Baptist field worker, was transferred to the convention. Ownership of Camp Glynn, operated by WMU since 1956, was transferred to the convention in 1965. WMU Camp Pinnacle, Clayton, provides 10 weeks of resident camping for girls, a YWA weekend, and two short-term leadership camps each summer. YWA mission tours include YWA conference at Glorieta in alternate years. Basic in teaching missions and mission support is emphasis upon stewardship and the Cooperative Program.

DOROTHY PRYOR

***WOMAN'S MISSIONARY UNION, Auxiliary to the Illinois Baptist State Association.** The progress of the work of Illinois WMU in the period 1956–70 is the result of the solid foundation laid during the 63 years of previous history. In 1955, a total of 408 churches in the state had WMU work. With the increase in the number of churches those having WMU work have increased proportionately, to a 1969 total of 679 with at least one of the organizations.

During the 15-year period adjustments in the constitution of the Illinois Baptist State Association have brought related ones in WMU. In 1959, WMU began receiving all of its funds through the budget of the parent organization, thus eliminating the need of a special WMU fund from the churches to help finance the work.

Since 1955 the number of weeks of state GA camps has grown from two to four, with a weekend retreat added for YWA members. An annual associational officers' conference and prayer retreat added to the calendar in 1959 were conducted with no less than 66 per cent of the associations represented each year.

Personnel changes brought Miss Helen Sinclair to the position of WMU executive secretary in 1955, which place she continues (1970) to fill with the position name changed in 1969 to state WMU director. Miss Dorothy Reed of Arkansas, employed in 1956 as youth director, remained two years with Miss Russell Drinnen of Knoxville, Tenn., coming to the position in 1959. In 1967, Miss Evelyn Tully of Groves, Tex., assumed a portion of the youth work, serving as GA director until 1969. Upon her resignation, Miss Drinnen became assistant WMU director with primary responsibility directed toward youth. Mrs. Helen Williams has served since 1961 as office secretary. State presidents of the period were Mrs. Curtis Martin, Mrs. Paul Hays, Mrs. Theron H. King, and Mrs. James M. Laughlin. In 1970 membership of WMU numbered approximately 23,000. HELEN SINCLAIR

***WOMAN'S MISSIONARY UNION, Auxiliary to the Louisiana Baptist Convention.** On Nov. 17, 1961, the trustees and camp building committee of the WMU executive board opened bids and awarded the contract for the construction of a WMU camp on the property purchased in 1954. Special gifts and an allocation each year in the Georgia Barnette offering for state missions provided money for construction. Buildings include eight cabins, dining hall, staff house, swimming pool, and home for a custodian. Furnishings were bought with receipts from the "Stamp for Camp" plan. Cards, 10 cent stamps and $1 stamps were printed, and WMU members were asked to buy a stamp a month. The camp was dedicated during the 1963 annual meeting of Louisiana WMU. The name chosen was Tall Timbers. Seven Girls' Auxiliary camps and three Royal Ambassador camps were held. In 1966 an activities building and a director-infirmary building were added.

The Hannah Reynolds offering for Christian education provides 25 scholarships at Louisiana College, 25 at Acadia Baptist Academy, nine in seminaries, 11 in seminaries on foreign mission fields, and support for Negro kindergartens in Louisiana.

Reports in 1969 showed 937 Woman's Missionary Societies and 2,699 youth organizations. Mission offerings totaled $907,450.89.

KATHRYN E. CARPENTER

WOOD, JOHN WILBERT (b. Laurens County, S. C., Aug. 27, 1896; d. Anderson, S. C., Apr. 12, 1965). Son of T. T. and Alma (Dodson) Wood, he graduated from Furman University (B.A., 1917), where he played football for four years. He volunteered for service during World War I. He taught in Laurens schools and served as that county's first truant officer.

Wood received training in textiles at Georgia Tech. In 1923 he joined the Riverside-Toxaway Mills and worked up through the firm's ranks to supervisor, superintendent, manager, and general manager of plants in both Carolinas. After the mills were bought by Textron, he remained as vice-president and general manager. In 1947 he was elected president and treasurer of Industrial Cotton Mills, Rock Hill, S. C.

Wood became a member of the Furman Board of Trustees in 1961 and was elected chairman of the board in 1963. He was a charter member of the Furman Advisory Council, past president of the Anderson County Furman Alumni Chapter and chairman of the Greater Furman Fund campaign in Anderson County. He was a member of the South Carolina Insurance Commission, president of the Anderson County Hospital Association, vice-president of the Anderson Chamber of Commerce, vice-president-elect of the Anderson Rotary Club, chairman of the Anderson County Planning and Development Board, and a director of Citizens and Southern National Bank. He served as a chairman of a steering committee for Anderson College's fund-raising campaign.

Wood married Essie Meares. They had two children. GEORGE JOHNSON

WOOLLEY, DAVIS COLLIER (b. Tuscaloosa, Ala., Sept. 22, 1908; d. Nashville, Tenn., Jan. 15, 1971). Pastor, educator, and denominational executive. Son of David Zacchaeus and Mary (Davis) Woolley, he was converted at the age of eight and was ordained to the ministry in 1932 by the First Baptist Church, Columbiana,

Ala. He earned the A.B. in history at Howard College (1930) and the Th.M. (1933) and Th.D. (1945) in New Testament at Southern Baptist Theological Seminary. On June 30, 1942, he married Kate Fristoe Wilkins. They had five children: James D., Katherine, Mary, John T., and Nancy. Student pastorates included three Kentucky churches: Zion, Hendersonville, 1932–35; Mt. Pleasant, Smith Mills, 1933–35; and Waddy, 1942–46. He began his denominational service as student secretary at Auburn University, 1935–40, then served as state secretary of the Training Union and Student departments of the Alabama Baptist State Convention, 1940–42. After serving as pastor of First Baptist Church, Palatka, Fla., 1946–53, he became director of the Howard College Extension Division, Birmingham, Ala., in 1953.

On Sept. 1, 1959, Woolley succeeded Norman W. Cox (*q.v.*) as executive secretary-treasurer of the Historical Commission, SBC. For more than 11 years he provided creative leadership for the commission in developing and expanding its program of recording, procurement, and preservation of Baptist historical materials and its program of utilizing historical materials to serve the history interests of Southern Baptists. He initiated a Baptist Union Catalog, launched the commission's quarterly journal, *Baptist History and Heritage* (1965), began an oral history project, led in the utilization of art to illustrate Baptist history, promoted the indexing of Baptist periodicals and annuals, greatly enlarged the resources of Dargan-Carver Library, and led the Southern Baptist Convention to conduct a meaningful observance of its 125th Anniversary (1970).

Under his administration the commission began publishing an *Index to Graduate Theses in Baptist Theological Seminaries,* the *Southern Baptist Periodical Index,* and updated the *Index to Annuals of the Southern Baptist Convention.* Editor of *Baptist Advance,* the 1964 Baptist Jubilee Advance history, and the author of two books, *Champions of Religious Freedom* (1964) and *Guide for Writing the History of a Church* (1969), he made one of his most significant contributions as managing editor of the ENCYCLOPEDIA OF SOUTHERN BAPTISTS, Volume III, which he led Southern Baptists to launch in 1969. As chairman of the Inter-Agency Council of the SBC, 1961–63, and chairman of this council's Coordinating Committee, 1964–70; he exercised a stabilizing influence on these denominational organizations during a crucial period in their history. LYNN E. MAY, JR.

***WORD AND WAY.** Official journal of the Missouri Baptist Convention since 1945. The convention allocates $40,000 a year to the publishing of the *Word and Way*. H. H. McGinty was editor from 1947 until 1967. During this period the circulation rose from 17,000 to 66,000. W. Ross Edwards served with McGinty for four months and assumed the editorship Nov. 1, 1967, when McGinty retired. Edwards had been pastor of the Swope Park Baptist Church, Kansas City, for 20 years prior to becoming editor.

The staff of the journal consists of an editor, editorial assistant, editorial secretary, accountant, and five mailing clerks. The editor is selected by and is responsible to the executive board of the convention. The paper publishes information about the churches, agencies and programs of the state convention, Southern Baptist Convention, and other groups of interest to Baptists. It has also published information about political issues which have been of interest to Baptists, particularly those issues relating to public morals and the relationship of church and state. *Word and Way* is printed by the Missouri Baptist Press in Jefferson City, Mo. W. ROSS EDWARDS

WORLD COUNCIL OF CHURCHES. Founded in Amsterdam, Holland, in 1948, the WCC brought together in one organization two earlier ecumenical ventures, the "Life and Work" and "Faith and Order" movements. The former sought to have the churches apply the principle of the lordship of Christ to every area of life—social, political, economic; the latter encouraged discussion of doctrinal and ecclesiological issues. In 1961 a third ecumenical stream was integrated into the WCC with the merger of the International Missionary Council.

The constitution of the WCC declares that its basis is "a fellowship of churches which confess the Lord Jesus Christ as God and Saviour according to the Scriptures." Its authority is to "offer counsel and provide opportunity of united action in matters of common interest. It may take action on behalf of constituent churches in such matters as one or more of them may commit to it." The WCC "shall not legislate for the churches."

Since 1948 the WCC has met in Evanston, Ind., U. S. A. (1954), New Delhi, India (1961), and Uppsala, Swed. (1968). Headquarters of the WCC are located in Geneva, Switz., and the general secretary is Eugene Carson Blake. More than 200 church groups in 80 countries hold membership in the WCC.

In 1940 the Southern Baptist Convention took official action declining an invitation to become a charter member of the WCC. That decision has not been altered down to the present (1970).

BIBLIOGRAPHY: D. P. Gaines, *The W. C. C.* (1966). R. Rouse and S. C. Neill, eds., *A History of the Ecumenical Movement, 1517–1948* (rev. 1968). H. E. Fey, ed., *A History of the Ecumenical Movement, 1948–1968* (1970).

See also ECUMENICAL MOVEMENT, THE, VOL. I,
W. MORGAN PATTERSON

***WORLD EVANGELISM, ASSOCIATION OF BAPTISTS FOR.** Following a missionary survey of East Pakistan in 1956, work was opened there. In 1970 there were 46 missionaries assigned to this field. In 1967 missionaries entered New Guinea for the first time with the transfer of an experienced couple from the Philippines. Spain is the most recent addition to the fields, having been entered in 1968. In 1970 the Association of Baptists for World Evangelism had 298 missionaries under appointment. They served in the Philippines, Japan, Hong Kong, East Pakistan, Peru, Colombia, Brazil, New Guinea, Spain, and Chile. In these 10 fields there were approximately 250 organized churches. *The Message,* official organ of this association was made a bimonthly periodical which is mailed free to individuals.

HELEN E. FALLS

WORLD FRIENDS. In Oct., 1959, eight-year-old members of Sunbeam Band were designated a separate age group and were given the name "World Friends." Special materials were introduced for this age group, and a section for World Friends leaders was included in *Sunbeam Activities.* In Oct., 1970, when the New Grouping-Grading Plan became effective, members of World Friends became members of Girls in Action and Royal Ambassadors. BETTY BROWN

WORLD MISSIONS CONFERENCES (cf. Missions, Schools of, Vol. II). Until 1968 these conferences were called schools of missions. In that year the name was changed to world missions conferences. Responsibility for the correlation of the promotion between the Foreign, Home, and state Mission Boards of these conferences in local churches has continued to be in the Department of Missionary Education of the Home Mission Board.

Churches in a given association simultaneously participate in thcsc conferences. In the course of five services (Sunday morning through Wednesday night, or Thursday night through Sunday night) each church will hear five mission speakers—two foreign, two home, and one state.

Since the beginning of this program in 1943, the average total attendance in these conferences has exceeded 1,000,000 per year. Several hundred young persons commit their lives to church-related vocations annually as a result of contact with mission personnel. Lewis W. Martin, secretary of this department from its beginning in 1943 until his retirement Dec. 31, 1965, was succeeded by Kenneth Day, who presently (1970) serves in this capacity. KENNETH DAY

WYATT, VESTER LAFAYETTE (b. Odenville, Ala., Sept. 11, 1893; d. Dothan, Ala., June 19, 1955). Pastor, missionary, and evangelist. Son of James and Angeline Wyatt, he married Martha Morton on Dec. 15, 1915. Wyatt was educated at Etowah County High School, Attalla, Ala.; Howard College, A.B.; Southern Baptist Theological Seminary, Th.M. and Ph.D. He was student pastor of Baptist churches in East Gadsden, Glencoe, Hokes Bluff, Collinsville, Ragland, and 27th Street, all in Alabama. He was also pastor of Paoli and Livonia churches in Indiana, and a church in Middletown, Ky. In 1932 he returned to Alabama as pastor of the East Gadsden church until 1948, when he was employed by the Alabama convention as missionary in the northeastern district of the state. In 1950 he was elected state secretary of evangelism, which place he filled until his death. Wyatt was moderator of Etowah County Baptist Association, vice-president of the Alabama Baptist State Convention, member of the Baptist state executive board, and treasurer of the Etowah County Hospital Association. He is buried in Gadsden, Ala. A. HAMILTON REID

WYOMING, BAPTISTS IN. See NORTHERN PLAINS BAPTIST CONVENTION, and COLORADO, BAPTIST GENERAL CONVENTION OF.

Y

YARBOROUGH, WARREN FORBES (b. Crystal Springs, Miss., Aug. 23, 1897; d. Shawnee, Okla., Feb. 17, 1965). College professor. Son of Warren Furman (*q.v.*) and Mettie (Forbes) Yarborough, he was educated at Howard College (A.B., 1919), now Samford University, and Southwestern Baptist Theological Seminary (M.R.E., 1924; D.R.E., 1932). He married Rubylee James, Aug. 25, 1925. Their children were: James R. and David Forbes. Yarborough served Oklahoma Baptist University, 1925–65, devoting 37 of these years to teaching. An active churchman, counselor, conference leader, writer for religious periodicals, and Baptist Student Union leader, he was also a member of the Education Commission of the Southern Baptist Convention, 1951–59. He revised the textbook, *A Survey of Religious Education* (1959). J. M. GASKIN

YARBOROUGH, WARREN FURMAN (b. Pickens, Holmes County, Miss., Dec. 11, 1868; d. Pickens, Miss., Nov. 20, 1940). Pastor and denominational leader. Son of farmer John and Mary (Toombs) Yarborough, he married Mettie Mae Forbes, Nov. 24, 1896. They had five children: Warren Forbes (*q.v.*), John Marion, Mary D. (Mrs. L. C. Bradley), Lilian Forbes (Mrs. Roland Q. Leavell), and James Furman. Educated at Mississippi College (B.A., 1892) and Southern Baptist Theological Seminary (Th.M., 1896), he received an honorary D.D. from Howard College in 1911. He was pastor of the following Baptist churches: Crystal Springs, Miss., 1896–99; First, Jackson, Miss., 1899–1910; Parker Memorial, Anniston, Ala., 1910–16; First, Hattiesburg, Miss., 1920–26; First, Jasper, Ala., 1927–35; and Pickens, Miss., 1936 until his death. Yarborough served the Alabama Baptist State Convention as executive secretary-treasurer, 1916–20, and state secretary of evangelism, 1926–27. He also served on many boards and committees of state conventions and the Southern Baptist Convention. A. HAMILTON REID

YELVINGTON, JESSE LEONARD (b. Wilson County, Tex., Mar. 27, 1892; d. San Antonio, Tex., Aug. 15, 1966). Pastor and evangelist. Son of Mary Fullerton (LeGette) and Alvaro Yelvington, he married Sarah G. Ramsey in 1911, and they had two children, Ramsey and Harriet Mary (Mrs. Caso March). Yelvington studied law by correspondence and also attended Baylor University Academy. He served as a chaplain in both World Wars. He was pastor of the following Texas churches: West Point Baptist, West Point, 1914–17; First Baptist, Smithville, 1919–25; and Baptist Temple, San Antonio, 1925–38. He was an evangelist for the Texas convention, 1938–43, 1946–57. He also served as a director of the *Baptist Standard*, and as a trustee for Howard Payne College. He wrote *That the World May Believe* (1939), and contributed to *Evangelism in Action Through Christ-centered Messages* (1951).

C. WADE FREEMAN

YEMEN ARAB REPUBLIC, MISSION IN. In late 1963 Yemen's minister of health extended an invitation to the Foreign Mission Board to open medical work in that country, following a visit made by James M. Young, medical missionary to Gaza. Yemen, a Muslim land, was one of very few countries without any mission work by any denomination. In Feb., 1964, John D. Hughey, then newly elected area secretary for Europe and the Middle East, made a survey trip to Yemen with Young and met with officials in the ministry of health. Returning to Richmond, Va., Hughey recommended that Southern Baptists enter this new field and the Youngs be transferred to Yemen.

In Sept., 1964, the Youngs, along with Maria Luisa Hidalgo, a Spanish Baptist nurse, moved to Taiz, principal city in the southern part. They established a small clinic and hospital in temporary quarters until a permanent location could be selected. Jibla, town in a heavily populated mountainous farming district, was chosen and work began on a hospital in early 1967. Dedication ceremony was held in Mar., 1968. In 1969, 10 missionaries were under appointment to Yemen. MRS. JAMES M. YOUNG

***YOUNG WOMAN'S AUXILIARY.** YWA observed its Fiftieth Anniversary in 1956–57, marking the event with eight regional workshops held in the fall of 1956, special anniversary goals, a Convention-wide house party at Carver School of Missions for members of Anne Hasseltine and Grace McBride YWA's, and the presentation at the WMU Annual Session of a pageant depicting YWA history.

In 1961 the Honor Citation for YWA was introduced. Since 1947 YWA members who met certain requirements had been awarded the YWA Citation, now by completing additional requirements, a YWA member could receive an Honor Citation. That same year the YWA for business girls became known as the Career Girls YWA.

In 1965 an alternate, simplified plan of organization was introduced. It featured fewer officers and was designed for use in churches with small number of YWA-age girls.

At the national level, the following persons provided leadership between 1955–70: Margaret Bruce, secretary, department of youth, 1955–57; Doris DeVault, YWA secretary, 1955–57, and director of YWA department, 1957–65; Ethalee Hamric, editor of *The Window of YWA*, 1955–57; Laurella Owens, editor of YWA materials, 1957–70; Billie Pate, promotion associate, 1957–65; Betty Bock, YWA director, 1966–69; Aline Fuselier, YWA director, 1970.

In early 1970, records of YWA showed 8,063 auxiliaries with a total membership of 65,903. In Oct., 1970, members of YWA became members of Acteens or Baptist Young Women.

See also ANN HASSELTINE YWA AND GRACE MCBRIDE YWA. DORIS DEVAULT

YOUTH MUSICIAN. A music quarterly for youth choirs published by the Church Music

Department of the Baptist Sunday School Board, beginning with the fourth quarter, 1966, and concluding with the third quarter, 1970. It was replaced in Oct., 1970, by two quarterlies, *Opus One* and *Opus Two*. W. HINES SIMS

YOUTH WORK, BAPTIST. The development of "youth work" in American churches may be divided into several periods. Prior to the Civil War most American Sunday Schools dismissed or graduated youth at 14, leaving them to develop their own organizations if they wished. Few Sunday Schools or churches sought to provide youth work. Therefore, youth became involved in missionary societies, devotional societies, and, later, led in forming groups such as Christian Endeavor, Epworth League, and the Baptist Young People's Union. Denominationally-conscious churches spent most of the period, 1870–1915, seeking to integrate these groups into local church programs.

The period 1915–45 produced a significant increase in the churches' efforts to provide "youth organizations" under adult leaders who could effectively reach young people. World War II and its aftermath brought a new surge of piety and many youth-led revivals within established churches. Youth seemed content within and challenged by their churches. Perhaps the years 1945–60 are best characterized as those in which attention was given to doing "youth work" without insisting upon particular youth organizations as programing vehicles.

The decade of the sixties brought a strained relationship between many youth and their churches. Some withdrew, blaming the "irrelevance" of the "institutional church." A few sought new opportunities to renew the church from within. Most seemed to accept their churches, often with little commitment or minimal enthusiasm.

To be effective, the churches' future ministry with youth will involve several considerations. First, Christianity must be seen as a unique faith in a context of religious pluralism. A religion which demands a commitment so total that one must "hate" his own family members if they are barriers must also be the balm of reconciliation among men and groups. Second, instead of providing organizations which engage in "youth work," churches and denominations must learn to engage in ministries *with, through,* and *by* youth in comprehensively conceived "youth programs." The objective should be to encourage the creativity which produces authentic youth movements—those that arise from and are sustained by the deeper needs and concerns of youth.

Third, an adult's acceptability as a youth leader must be seen in terms of personal maturity, theological insight, and Christian commitment rather than mere youthfulness and hyperactivity. The best adult leaders should be encouraged to make youth ministry a lifetime pursuit. Fourth, churches must consider cooperative styles of ministry which utilize the strengths of corporate resources available through churches in a given geographical area. Such cooperation is to be desired over the debilitating effects of unbridled competition. Inner-city churches may find that such cooperation is mandatory rather than optional.

Fifth, as C. Ellis Nelson has pointed out, churches that "make it with the 'now' generation" will be those that deal successfully with three issues: (1) the source of religion's authority; (2) the purpose of religion, especially for a growing number of youth who are alarmingly free of guilt feelings and who believe death will be conquered by science; and (3) what makes a person religious?

Finally, churches must encourage youth to join adults in breaking the bonds of isolationism, be they religious, social, economic, geographical, or intellectual. A breakthrough of this kind could mean new challenges for youth who might see their churches as deeply relevant to "the world" into which God sent his Son. The direct experience so prized by the "now generation" might then be found in the churches' youth program.

WILLIAM R. CROMER, JR.

Z

ZAMBIA, MISSION IN. Zambia was still known as Northern Rhodesia when Tom and Mary (Burnett) Small and Zebedee and Evelyn (Krause) Moss moved to Kitwe, a little city on the Copper Belt, in Oct., 1959. At that time, Southern Rhodesia, Northern Rhodesia, and Nyasaland made up the territory of the Central Africa Mission. In 1961, new stations were opened at Lusaka, Mufulira, and Broken Hill (later known as Kabwe) . The Zambia Baptist Mission was organized as a separate body about the time Zambia became an independent nation in 1964.

A modern headquarters building occupied at Lusaka, the capital, in 1966 provided space for a radio recording studio, a publication department, and headquarters for the Bible Way Correspondence Course. New stations were occupied at Chingola and Luanshya, both on the Copper Belt. In 1967, a small seminary was opened at the outskirts of Lusaka. Instruction was in English and Chibemba.

The first mission station in the Eastern Province was established in 1969 at Chipata, when LeRoy and Jean (Flowers) Albright transferred from Malawi. Local work was begun in the Chinyanja language. At the end of 1969, 28 missionaries were at work in Zambia, serving 26 churches with about 1,680 members.

H. CORNELL GOERNER